MANAGEMENT
3rd edition

MANAGEMENT
3rd edition

RICKY W. GRIFFIN

Texas A&M University

HOUGHTON MIFFLIN COMPANY   Boston

Dallas   Geneva, Illinois   Palo Alto   Princeton, New Jersey

For Glenda . . .
It just keeps getting better and better.

COVER PHOTOGRAPH: Skolos, Wedell and Raynor

FIGURE ILLUSTRATIONS: Boston Graphics, Inc.

PART OPENER CREDITS: **Part I:** FUGUE by Charles Sheeler, courtesy of Regis Corporation; Chicago Presidential Towers, Mark Segal/TSW-Click/Chicago. (continued on page 846)

PHOTO CREDITS: **Chapter 1:** p. 8, FORTUNE is a registered trademark of Time Inc. All rights reserved. p. 10, Louie Psihoyos/Matrix; p. 14, Katherine Lambert; p. 18, Gannett; p. 25, Mike Clemmer/Picture Group. **Chapter 2:** p. 37, Barth Falkenberg; p. 44, Frederick W. Taylor Collection, S. C. Williams Library, Stevens Institute of Technology; p. 50, Quaker State Corporation; p. 51, courtesy of AT&T Archives; p. 59, courtesy of Harris Corporation; p. 65, Nina Barnett. **Chapter 3:** p. 81, T. Michael Keza/Nation's Business; p. 88, courtesy of International Business Machines Corporation; p. 92, Chevron Corporation; p. 96, Tim Kelly/Black Star; p. 99, National Steel Corporation; p. 102, Paul Tepley. **Chapter 4:** p. 126, Mason Morfit; p. 133, Bob Bamier/Taylor Corporation; p. 143, David R. Henderson; p. 149, Jonathan Miller. **Chapter 5:** p. 163, Terry O'Neill/Sygma; p. 167, Chuck Nacke/Picture Group; p. 173, Rob Kinmonth; p. 175, Dennis Cox. **Chapter 6:** p. 194, © The Walt Disney Company; p. 197, Henry Groskinsky; p. 199, Alan D. Levenson; p. 207, Andrew Eccles; p. 211, © Neil Selkirk. **Chapter 7:** p. 229, Louie Psihoyos/Matrix; p. 232, Dunkin' Donuts Incorporated, Randolph, MA; p. 240, USAir Group; p. 244, Jules Allen. (continued on page 846)

Printed in the U.S.A.

Library of Congress Catalog Card Number: 89-080938

ISBN: 0-395-43333-9

ABCDEFGHIJ-VH-9543210-89

CONTENTS

Preface   xxi

Acknowledgments   xxv

PART I   **AN INTRODUCTION TO MANAGEMENT**   1

1   **Managing and the Manager's Job**   2

Management and Managers Defined   5

The Management Process   8

    Planning and Decision Making: Determining Courses of
      Action
    Organizing: Coordinating Activities and Resources
    Leading: Motivating and Managing Employees
    Controlling: Monitoring and Evaluating Activities

Kinds of Managers   12

    Levels of Management
    Areas of Management

Critical Roles and Skills   15

    Managerial Roles
    Managerial Skills

Acquiring Management Skills   21

    The Role of Education
    The Role of Experience

The Scope of Management   24

    Management in Profit-seeking Organizations
    Management in Not-for-Profit Organizations

Case 1.1 Management Promotes Efficiency and
Effectiveness at Marriot   30

Case 1.2 Sotheby's: Bringing Management Techniques to
the Art World   32

v

2 The Evolution of Management Thought   34

Why Study History and Theory?   36

Why Theory?
Why History?

The Historical Context of Management   38

Understanding Social Forces
Understanding Economic Forces
Understanding Political Forces

Precursors to Management Theory   40

Management in Antiquity
Early Management Pioneers

The Classical Management Perspective   43

Scientific Management
Classical Organization Theory
Contributions and Limitations of the Classical Management
    Perspective

The Behavioral Management Perspective   48

The Hawthorne Studies
The Human Relations Movement
Organizational Behavior
Contributions and Limitations of the Behavioral Management
    Perspective

The Quantitative Management Perspective   54

Management Science
Operations Management
Contributions and Limitations of the Quantitative Management
    Perspective

Integrating the Major Perspectives   56

The Systems Approach
The Contingency Approach
An Integrating Framework

Contemporary Management Perspectives   63

The Global Imperative
The Concern for Excellence
The Concerns for Quality and Productivity

Case 2.1   UPS Uses Technology in Management   72

Case 2.2   Lloyd's Managerial Evolution   74

3 Organizational Environments and Effectiveness   76

The Nature of Organizational Environments   79

The General Environment   80

The Economic Dimension

The Technological Dimension
The Sociocultural Dimension
The Political-Legal Dimension
The International Dimension

The Task Environment   85

Competitors
Customers
Suppliers
Regulators
Labor
Owners
Partners

The Internal Environment   92

The Board of Directors
Employees

Organization-Environment Relationships   93

How Environments Affect Organizations
How Organizations Respond to Their Environments

Organizational Effectiveness   101

Models of Effectiveness
Managerial Performance

Case 3.1   American Express Manages Its Environment   108

Case 3.2   Environmental Balancing Acts at Guinness   110

ENHANCEMENT MODULE 1   Managerial Career   112

Integrative Case   The Martian Empire   118

PART II   **DECISION MAKING AND PLANNING**   **120**

Managerial Decision Making   122

The Nature of Decision Making   124

Decision Making Defined
Types of Decisions
Decision-making Conditions

Models of the Decision-Making Process   128

The Classical Model
The Administrative Model

Steps in Rational Decision Making   131

Recognizing and Defining the Decision Situation
Identifying Alternatives
Evaluating Alternatives
Selecting an Alternative

Implementing the Chosen Alternative
Following Up and Evaluating the Results

The Behavioral Nature of Decision Making   137

Political Forces in Decision Making
Intuition and Escalation of Commitment

Group Decision Making   140

Forms of Group Decision Making
Advantages of Group Decision Making
Disadvantages of Group Decision Making
Managing Group Decision-making Processes

Quantitative Tools for Decision Making   144

Payoff Matrices
Decision Trees
Other Techniques

Case 4.1   Kellogg: Champion of Breakfast Cereals   154

Case 4.2   Critical Decisions at Porsche   156

5   **Organizational Goals and Planning**   **158**

The Planning Process   161

The Nature of Organizational Goals   162

Purposes of Goals
Kinds of Goals
Responsibilities for Setting Goals

Managing the Goal-Setting Process   167

Managing Multiple Goals
Barriers to Effective Goal Setting
Making Goal Setting Effective

Goals and Organizational Planning   174

Kinds of Organizational Plans
Time Frames for Planning
Responsibilities for Planning

Case 5.1   Borden's Plan for Growth   186

Case 5.2   Fiat Plans for the Long Haul   188

6   **Strategy and Strategic Planning**   **190**

The Nature of Strategic Management   192

The Components of Strategy
The Levels of Strategy
Strategy Formulation and Implementation

Strategy Formulation   196

Strategic Goals
Environmental Analysis
Organizational Analysis
Matching Organizations and Environments

Corporate-Level Strategy   199

Grand Strategy
The Business Portfolio

Business-Level Strategy   204

The Adaptation Model
Porter's Competitive Strategies
Product Life Cycles

Functional Strategies   208

Marketing Strategy
Financial Strategy
Production Strategy
Human Resources Strategy
Research and Development Strategy

Strategy Implementation   212

Structure
Leadership
Information and Control Systems
Human Resources
Technology

Case 6.1   Alcoa: In or Out of Aluminum?   220

Case 6.2   Nissan Motor Company's Strategic Maneuver   222

7 — Tactical and Operational Planning

7 — Tactical and Operational Planning   **224**

The Nature of Tactical and Operational Planning   227

Tactical Planning   228

Developing Tactical Plans
Implementing Tactical Plans

Operational Planning   230

Single-Use Plans
Standing Plans

Contingency Planning   234

Managing the Planning Process   236

Barriers to Effective Planning
Overcoming the Barriers

Using MBO to Implement Plans   241

The Nature and Purpose of MBO
The MBO Process
The Effectiveness of MBO

Case 7.1   Campbell's Plans for Soups and More   250

Case 7.2   France's Thomson Plans Big   252

ENHANCEMENT MODULE 2   Planning Tools   254

ENHANCEMENT MODULE 3   Computers and the Manager   264

Integrative Case   Pepsi Aims to Top Pop Market   268

PART III   **THE ORGANIZING PROCESS**   270

8   Components of Organizational Structure   272

Building Blocks of Organizations   274

Designing Jobs   275

   Job Specialization
   Benefits and Limitations of Specialization
   Alternatives to Specialization

Grouping Jobs   280

   Rationale for Departmentalization
   Common Bases for Departmentalization

Establishing Reporting Relationships   284

   The Chain of Command
   Narrow Versus Wide Spans
   Tall Versus Flat Organizations
   Determining the Appropriate Span

Distributing Authority   289

   The Delegation Process
   Decentralization and Centralization

Coordinating Activities   293

   The Need for Coordination
   Structural Coordination Techniques

Differentiating Between Positions   296

   Differences Between Line and Staff
   Administrative Intensity

Case 8.1   Apple Slices   302

Case 8.2.   IBM in Europe   304

9   Organization Design and Culture   306

The Nature of Organization Design   309

Universal Perspectives on Organization Design 309

The Bureaucratic Model
The Behavioral Model

Situational Influences on Organization Setting 313

Technology
Environment
Size and Organizational Life Cycle

Common Forms of Organization Design 318

The Functional (U-Form) Design
The Conglomerate (H-Form) Design
The Divisional (M-Form) Design
The Matrix Design
Hybrid Designs

Emerging Issues in Organization Design 326

Information-processing Requirements
The Global Organization

Linking Strategy and Organization Design 328

The Simple Structure
The Machine Bureaucracy
The Professional Bureaucracy
The Divisionalized Form
The Adhocracy

Organizational Culture 332

The Importance of Organizational Culture
Determinants of Culture
Managing Organizational Culture

Case 9.1 Organization Design at Philip Morris 340

Case 9.2 ICI's Life Cycle 342

10

Managing Human Resources 344

The Strategic Importance of Human Resource Management 347

The Legal Environment of Human Resource Management 347

Equal Employment Opportunity
Compensation and Benefits
Labor Relations
Health and Safety
Emerging Legal Issues

Job Analysis and Human Resource Planning 352

Job Analysis
Forecasting Human Resource Demand and Supply
Matching Human Resource Supply and Demand

Organization Revitalization   409

    The Need for Revitalization
    Approaches to Revitalization

Training and Development   360

    Assessing Training Needs
    Common Training Methods
    Evaluation of Training

Performance Appraisal and Feedback   364

    Reasons for Appraising Performance
    Common Appraisal Methods
    Providing Feedback

Compensation and Benefits   368

    The Role of Compensation
    Determining Compensation
    Determining Benefits

Labor Relations   373

    How Employees Form Unions
    Collective Bargaining
    Grievances and Discipline
    Future Trends

Case 10.1   Coors and the Unions   384

Case 10.2   Selection at Toyota   386

11   **Organization Change, Development, and
Revitalization**   **388**

The Nature of Organization Change   390

    Forces for Change
    Planned Versus Reactive Change

Managing Organization Change   393

    Steps in the Change Process
    Managing Resistance to Change

Areas of Organization Change   400

    Changing Strategy
    Changing Structure and Design
    Changing Technology
    Changing People

Organization Development   404

    OD Assumptions
    OD Techniques
    The Effectiveness of OD

Recruiting and Selection   355

    Sources for Recruiting
    Common Selection Techniques

Case 11.1   Shake Up at Exxon   414

Case 11.2   Transformation at Daimler-Benz   416

ENHANCEMENT MODULE 4   Participative Management   418

ENHANCEMENT MODULE 5   Managing Creativity and
    Innovation   424

Integrative Case   Johnson and Johnson   430

PART IV

THE LEADING PROCESS   **432**

12

Motivating Employee Job Performance   **434**

The Nature of Motivation   437

    The Importance of Employee Motivation
    Historical Perspectives on Motivation

Content Perspectives on Motivation   439

    The Need Hierarchy
    The Two-Factor Theory
    Other Important Human Needs

Process Perspectives on Motivation   445

    Expectancy Theory
    Equity Theory
    Attribution Theory

Reinforcement Perspectives on Motivation   452

    Kinds of Reinforcement
    Schedules of Reinforcement

Emerging Perspectives on Motivation   456

    Goal-setting Theory
    The Japanese Approach

Motivational Programs   457

    Behavior Modification
    Modified Workweek
    Work Redesign

Organizational Reward Systems   459

    The Effects of Organizational Rewards
    Designing Effective Reward Systems
    New Approaches to Rewarding Employees

Case 12.1   Flexible Steelcase   468

Case 12.2   Hitachi is a Hit with Workers   470

<table>
<tr><td>13</td></tr>
</table>

13 Leadership and Influence Processes

13 Leadership and Influence Processes   472

The Nature of Leadership   474

The Meaning of Leadership
Leadership Versus Management
Power and Leadership

The Search for Leadership Traits   480

Leadership Behaviors   480

The Michigan Studies
The Ohio State Studies
The Managerial Grid

Situational Approaches to Leadership   483

Fiedler's Contingency Theory
The Path-Goal Theory
The Vroom-Yetton-Jago Model
Other Situational Approaches

New Perspectives on Leadership   494

Substitutes for Leadership
Transformational Leadership

Political Behavior in Organizations   496

Common Political Behaviors
Managing Political Behavior

Case 13.1   Armand Hammer, Leader for All Seasons   502

Case 13.2   Samsung on the March   504

14 Interpersonal Processes, Groups, and Conflict

14 Interpersonal Processes, Groups, and Conflict   506

The Interpersonal Nature of Organizations   508

Interpersonal Dynamics
Outcomes of Interpersonal Behaviors

Groups in Organizations   512

Definition of a Group
Types of Groups

Group Formation Processes   515

Why People Join Groups
Stages of Group Development

Characteristics of Mature Groups   519

Role Structures

Behavioral Norms
Cohesiveness
Informal Leadership

Managing Groups in Organizations   528

    Committees
    Work Groups
    The Japanese Approach

Interpersonal and Intergroup Conflict   531

    The Nature of Conflict
    Causes of Conflict
    Managing Conflict

Case 14.1   Groups and Conflicts at the U.S. Olympic
    Committee   540

Case 14.2   International Conflict at First Boston   542

15   Communication in Organizations   544

Communication and the Manager's Job   546

    A Definition of Communication
    The Role of Communication in Management
    The Communication Process

Forms of Interpersonal Communication   550

    Oral Communication
    Written Communication
    Choosing the Right Form

Forms of Group and Organizational Communication   553

    Vertical Communication
    Horizontal Communication
    Communication Networks
    The Grapevine
    Other Forms of Communication

Behavioral Elements of Communication   559

    Perception
    Nonverbal Communication

Managing Organizational Communication   563

    Barriers to Communication
    Improving Communication Effectiveness
    Formal Information Systems

Electronic Communication   568

Case 15.1   Top-Level Communication Problems at Texaco   574

Case 15.2   Communication Key to Unilever's Success   576

Enhancement Module 6   Managing the Individual   578

ENHANCEMENT MODULE 7   Coping with Stress   584

Integrative Case   The Magic of Disney   590

PART V   THE CONTROLLING PROCESS   592

16   The Nature of Control   594

Control in Organizations   597

  The Purpose of Control
  The Importance of Control
  Areas of Control
  Responsibilities for Control
  The Planning-Controlling Link

Steps in the Control Process   602

  Establishing Standards
  Measuring Performance
  Comparing Performance Against Standards
  Evaluation and Action

Forms of Operations Control   607

  Preliminary Control
  Screening Control
  Postaction Control
  Multiple Control Systems

Forms of Organizational Control   609

  Bureaucratic Control
  Clan Control

Strategic Control   612

Managing the Control Process   613

  Developing Effective Control Systems
  Understanding Resistance to Control
  Overcoming Resistance to Control

Choosing a Style of Control   618

Case 16.1   Pan Am's Struggles   624

Case 16.2   Benetton Busting at Its Seams   626

17   Operations Management, Productivity, and
                Quality   628

The Nature of Operations Management   630

  The Importance of Operations

Manufacturing and Production
Service Operations
The Role of Operations in Organizational Strategy

Designing Operations Systems   634

Products and Services
Capacity
Facilities
Technology

Using Operations Systems   639

Operations Management as Control
Purchasing Management
Inventory Management
Quality Control

Managing Productivity   644

The Meaning of Productivity
The Importance of Productivity
Productivity Trends
Improving Productivity

Managing Quality   649

The Meaning of Quality
The Importance of Quality
Approaches to Managing Quality

Case 17.1   Operations Critical to John Deere's Success   656

Case 17.2   Siemans Stresses Productivity and Quality   658

18 Managing Information Systems   660

Information and the Manager   663

The Role of Information in the Manager's Job
Characteristics of Useful Information
Information Management as Control

Building Blocks of Information Systems   666

Determinants of Information System Needs   668

General Determinants
Specific Determinants

Basic Kinds of Information Systems   671

Transaction-processing Systems
Basic Management Information Systems
Decision Support Systems

Managing Information Systems   673

Establishing Information Systems
Integrating Information Systems
Using Information Systems

The Impact of Information Systems on Organizations   677

    Performance Effects
    Organizational Effects
    Behavioral Effects
    Information System Limitations

Recent Advances in Information Management   680

    Telecommunications
    Networks and Expert Systems

Case 18.1   Federal Express Rises to the Challenge   684

Case 18.2   Merrill Lynch: Information International   686

19   **Control Techniques and Methods**   **688**

An Overview of Control Techniques and Methods   690

Budgetary Control   691

    Types of Budgets
    Fixed and Variable Costs in Budgets
    Developing Budgets
    Zero-Base Budgets
    Strengths and Weaknesses of Budgeting

Other Tools of Financial Control   698

    Financial Statements
    Ratio Analysis
    Financial Audits

Using Financial Control Techniques Effectively   703

Operations Control   704

    Areas of Operations Control
    Operations Control Techniques

Human Resource Control   709

    Goals of Human Resource Control
    Human Resource Control Techniques

Marketing Control   712

    Goals of Marketing Control
    Marketing Control Techniques

Case 19.1   Tenneco's Cooking Now   716

Case 19.2   Effecive Control at Swissair   718

ENHANCEMENT MODULE 8   Automation in the Workplace   720

ENHANCEMENT MODULE 9   Managing Decline and
    Cutbacks   726

Integrative Case   Control at Ford   730

PART VI   **SPECIAL CHALLENGES OF MANAGEMENT**   **732**

20   **Entrepreneurship and Small Business**
                       Management   **734**

                       The Nature of Entrepreneurship   736

                       Small Business and the U.S. Economy   738
                           The Impact of Small Business
                           Major Areas of Small Business

                       Small Business Successes and Failures   741
                           Common Causes of Success
                           Common Causes of Failure

                       Starting a Small Business   744
                           Business Plan
                           Ownership and Financing
                           Approaches to Starting a Business

                       Managing the Small Business   749
                           Planning in the Small Business
                           Organizing in the Small Business
                           Leading in the Small Business
                           Controlling in the Small Business

                       Entrepreneurship in Large Businesses   760

                       Case 20.1 Mrs. Fields Has Recipe for Success   764

                       Case 20.2 Exporting at Mentor Graphics   766

21   **Managing in the International Sector**   **768**

                       The Nature of International Business   771
                           The Meaning of International Business
                           Trends in International Business

                       Special Challenges of International Management   774
                           The Economic Environment
                           The Political Environment
                           The Cultural Environment

                       The Structure of the International Economy   784
                           Industrial Market Economies
                           Developing Countries
                           Oil-exporting Countries
                           Eastern Nonmarket Countries

                       The Decision to Go International   788
                           Market Factors
                           Technological Factors
                           Personal Values

Levels of International Involvement   792

    Importing and Exporting
    Licensing
    Joint Ventures
    Direct Investment
    Global Involvement

Case 21.1   Cummins Overcomes International
   Competition   802

Case 21.2   The Globalization of Sony   804

22 — Managing with Ethics and Social Responsibility   806

Individual Ethics in the Workplace   808

    How Ethics Are Formed
    Managerial Ethics
    The Ethical Context of Management
    Managing Ethical Behavior

Ethics, Social Responsibility, and Business   814

    Changing Views of Social Responsibility
    Organizational Constituents
    Areas of Social Responsibility

Managerial Approaches to Social Responsibility   821

    The Social Responsibility Debate
    Approaches to Social Responsibility

The Government and Social Responsibility   826

    Government Regulation of Business
    Business Influence on Government

Managing Social Responsibility   828

    Formal Organizational Activities
    Informal Organizational Activities
    Evaluating Social Performance

Case 22.1   New Emphasis on Ethics at General Dynamics   836

Case 22.2   Toshiba Confronts Social Responsibility   838

ENHANCEMENT MODULE 10   Future Challenges of
   Management   840

Integrative Case   Nestlé World-Class Multinational   844

Name Index   847

Organization and Product Index   856

Subject Index   865

PREFACE

The first edition of *Management* was published in 1984. Since that time, almost a quarter of a million students have used the first or second edition to learn basic management skills, concepts, and practices. Hundreds of colleges and universities around the world continue to use the book. The easy thing to do, then, would have been to prepare a light revision and continue with a "proven" approach to teaching introductory management.

But the world has changed since 1984. The people of the world have created a veritable global village where products, services, people, technology, information, and money flow almost at will across national boundaries that once locked them out. Other changes have centered on controversies of ownership, ethics and social responsibility, employee rights and privileges, technological innovation, and numerous other forces. No manager today can afford to ignore the increased complexity brought about by these changes. During the 1980s, many American firms went through the process of remaking themselves—in partial response to these forces and in partial response to the recognition that they had grown too sluggish. Such firms have emerged as leaner, more efficient, and more responsive companies.

In similar fashion, Houghton Mifflin and I decided to remake this book. We wanted to make it better than it had been in the past and to set new standards of excellence for management textbooks. We left no stone unturned and defined nothing as sacred in our quest for improvement. The challenges were easy to identify: there is so much to management that one could fill several books on the subject; the business world changes so rapidly that what was true yesterday may not be true today; and fitting all the pieces together in an integrated and coherent fashion is more complicated than assembling any jigsaw puzzle.

How did we address the challenges? By carefully analyzing the importance and contribution of every page, paragraph, and sentence, we achieved an effective balance of breadth and depth to provide the introductory student with a general overview of management. We solved the timing problem by using up-to-the-minute examples and references throughout the book. Indeed, most of the examples and citations are taken from the late 1980s, and some were added even as the text went to press. The organizational challenge was addressed by adopting a quasi-modular format. Although written to tell an integrated story, the text retains sufficient flexibility to allow some personalization by the instructor who wants to cover topics in a different sequence.

ORGANIZATION OF THE BOOK

Topical Coverage

Management is organized around the traditional management functions of planning, organizing, leading, and controlling. This framework is generally accepted as the most effective way to describe the management process. Part 1 introduces readers to the basic context in which managers work. The next four parts provide in-depth treatments of each of the four basic functions. Finally, Part 6 describes special challenges of management.

Changes in the Third Edition

The third edition of *Management* is a significant revision of the earlier work. Indeed, there are so many changes that I will only note the most significant ones here. In Part 1, I now cover organizational effectiveness in concert with organizational environments in Chapter 3. Part 2 has been totally revamped by moving the discussion of decision making to Chapter 4. Goals and planning are now discussed in Chapter 5, strategic planning in Chapter 6, and tactical and operational planning in Chapter 7.

In Part 3, components of organization structure have been condensed into a single chapter—Chapter 8. Chapter 9 covers organization design and culture. Staffing, previously covered at the end of the book, has been moved to Chapter 10. Chapter 11 concludes Part 3 with coverage of organization change and related topics.

Part 4 received the least revision and continues to include four chapters devoted to motivation, leadership, groups, and communication. Part 5, in contrast, was substantially revised. Chapter 16 introduces the reader to organizational control. Chapter 17 covers operations management, productivity, and quality. Information systems are covered in Chapter 18. Chapter 19 describes several important control techniques. Part 6 concludes the book by highlighting entrepreneurship and small-business management (Chapter 20), international management (Chapter 21), and ethics and social responsibility (Chapter 22).

Chapters 18 and 22 are completely new. Chapters 8, 14, 17, 20, and 21 have been completely revised. Chapters 3, 4, 5, 6, 7, 9, and 11 received significant revision. The remaining chapters retain their basic outlines from previous editions but have been updated and refined. In addition, all the cases in the third edition are new. The first case at the end of each chapter focuses on a problem or challenge faced by an American organization. The second case at the end of each chapter deals either with a foreign company or with an American company doing business in another country. Each chapter also includes two interesting boxed inserts. "Management in Practice" provides an extended example to amplify a point from the text, and "The Global View" does the same from an international perspective.

In addition, every piece of line art and each table were carefully scrutinized during the revision. Some were retained; some were modified; and many new illustrations were developed. Careful and selective use of photographs also helps bring the material to life. An Integrative Case was added at the end of each part. So, too, were the Enhancement Modules.

Enhancement Modules

One of the most innovative features of the third edition of *Management* is the inclusion of ten Enhancement Modules. These modules enhance the other material by providing focused coverage of special areas of interest such as participative management, stress, and automation. They are distributed throughout the text at the end of each part. However, each was written to stand alone. Thus, an instructor may use them at different points in the text, save them until the end, or not cover them at all.

FEATURES OF THE BOOK

Basic Themes

As in any book, several themes pervade *Management*. One, as noted already, is the international character of the field of management. Examples and cases throughout the book underscore this dimension. Another theme is the need to balance theory and practice. Managers need to have a sound basis for their decisions, but theories that provide that basis must be grounded in reality. Thus, throughout the book I explain the theoretical frameworks that guide managerial activities, and then I provide illustrations and examples of how and when those theories do and do not work. A third theme is that management is a generic activity not necessarily confined to large businesses. Thus, I use examples and discuss management in both small and large businesses as well as in not-for-profit organizations.

Pedagogy

The ultimate purpose of any textbook is to provide students with a resource for learning. The third edition of *Management* was prepared with the student in mind. Each chapter opens with a statement of the learning objectives that the chapter will help students achieve and an outline of the major topics to be covered. Next comes an opening incident—an extended example that sets the tone and draws readers into the material. Each chapter is organized around five to seven major headings, one related to each of the learning objectives. Marginal notes throughout each chapter highlight key terms and definitions. Those that relate to the learning objectives are highlighted with a colored bullet.

The tables and figures were carefully constructed to amplify major points in the text, as were the two boxed features in each chapter. The photographs were chosen to bring the material to life, and I wrote extended captions for each to explain what it illustrates. At the end of the chapter are a summary and a set of three types of discussion questions. The review questions ask students to recall specific information. The analysis questions ask students to integrate and synthesize material. The application questions ask students to take textual material into the real world and use it. The cases also provide additional amplification and application of the material in the text.

Applications

To fully appreciate the role and scope of management in contemporary society, it is important to see examples and illustrations of how concepts apply in the real world. The opening incident, cases, boxed inserts, and photographs all offer applications. In addition to these, I have incorporated literally hundreds of examples directly into the text. Some of them are quite brief; others are detailed. Regardless of length, however, each was used for a purpose—to show how a concept or idea from the text was learned by or used in a real organization.

SUPPLEMENTAL MATERIALS

In addition to this textbook, there are several ancillary items that may be used to promote learning. The *Study Guide*, prepared by Joe G. Thomas, includes a pretest, a list of learning objectives, a posttest, a list of key terms, a completion summary for each chapter, and other learning tools. *Readings in Management*, developed by David Rubinstein, provides other perspectives and views of the field of management. The *Cases in Management*, prepared by Kenneth Thompson and Nick Mathys, may be used for courses with a heavy case orientation. The *Experiential Exercise Book*, developed by Gene Burton, can be used to promote learning through a series of experiential exercises. *Manager: A Simulation* is a computer simulation that gives students practice in managing a business and competing against other businesses.

ACKNOWLEDGMENTS

As any author can attest, far more people are involved in the creation of a book than the person whose name appears on the cover. This book is certainly no exception. I owe an enormous debt to many different people for helping me create this work.

In the early stages of my career, I had the good fortune to work with Skip Szilagyi, Jack Ivancevich, Bob Keller, Art Jago, Mike Matteson, Sara Freedman, Dick Montanari, Ron Ebert, Everett Adam, Jim Patterson, Allen Slusher, Bob Monroe, and Don White. Each has made significant contributions to my intellectual development.

I now have the privilege of working in the wonderful academic climate that exists at Texas A&M University. The rich and varied culture there makes it a pleasure to go to the office every day. Colleagues like Bob Albanese, Dick Daft, Don Hellriegel, Mike Pustay, Mike Hitt, Jay Barney, Bob Hoskisson, and Gareth Jones are invaluable.

Dick Woodman, Stuart Youngblood, David Van Fleet, and Greg Moorhead also deserve special acknowledgment. Each has helped me become a better scholar, but more importantly, each has also helped me become a better human being. Thanks, guys—I appreciate it more than you can know.

An outstanding team of professionals deserves special note for making significant contributions to what I believe is the best package of ancillary materials ever assembled. Tom Keon, Stan Elsea, Fred Williams, David Rubinstein, Joe Thomas, Kenneth Thompson, Nick Mathys, and Gene Burton all accepted my invitation to join the team and accepted my standards for producing the best support materials that could possibly be prepared for students and instructors.

Many reviewers have played a critical role in the evolution of this project. They were asked to take an especially critical and detailed view of everything I did. Acknowledging that any errors of omission, interpretation, or emphasis are my responsibility, I would like to tip my hat to the following reviewers, whose imprint can be found throughout this text:

Ramon J. Aldag
University of Wisconsin

Dr. Raymond E. Alie
Western Michigan University

Jay B. Barney
Texas A&M University

John D. Bigelow
Boise State University

Allen Bluedorn
University of Missouri

Gunther S. Boroschek
University of Massachusetts—Harbor Campus

George R. Carnahan
Northern Michigan University

Thomas G. Christoph
Clemson University

Lou Cisneros
Austin Community College

Charles W. Cole
University of Oregon

Gregory G. Dess
University of South Carolina

Gary N. Dicer
University of Tennessee

Thomas J. Dougherty
University of Missouri

John Drexler, Jr.
Oregon State University

Stan Elsea
Kansas State University

Douglas A. Elvers
University of South Carolina

Ari Ginsberg
New York University, Graduate School of Business

Carl Gooding
Georgia Southern College

George J. Gore
University of Cincinnati

Stanley D. Guzell, Jr.
Youngstown State University

Mark A. Hammer
Washington State University

Paul Harmon
University of Utah

J. G. Hunt
Texas Tech University

John H. Jackson
University of Wyoming

Neil W. Jacobs
University of Denver

Arthur G. Jago
University of Houston

Gopol Joshi
Central Missouri State University

Norman F. Kallaus
University of Iowa

Ben L. Kedia
Memphis State University

Thomas L. Keon
University of Missouri

William R. LaFollete
Ball State University

Dale A. Level, Jr.
University of Arkansas

Myrna P. Mandell, Ph.D.
California State University, Northridge

Barbara J. Marting
University of Southern Indiana

Wayne A. Meinhart
Oklahoma State University

Linda L. Neiler, Ph.D.
University of Miami

Mary Lippitt Nichols
University of Minnesota

Winston Oberg
Michigan State University

E. Leroy Plumlee
Western Washington University

Paul Preston
University of Texas—San Antonio

John M. Purcell
State University of New York—Farmingdale

James C. Quick
University of Texas—Arlington

Ralph Roberts
University of West Florida

Nick Sarantakas
Austin Community College

Gene Schneider
Austin Community College

H. Schollhammer
University of California—Los Angeles

Nicholas Siropolis
Cuyahoga Community College

Robert D. Van Auken
University of Oklahoma

Michael J. Stahl
Clemson University

J. Malcolm Walker
San Jose State University

Charlotte D. Sutton
Auburn University

Fred Williams
North Texas State University

Robert L. Taylor
University of Louisville

Carl P. Zeithaml
University of North Carolina

Mary Thibodeaux
North Texas State University

I would also like to make a few personal acknowledgments. The fine work of Andrew Lloyd Webber, Michael Crawford, John Cougar Mellencamp, Jim Morrison, John Fogerty, Elton John, Phil Collins, Johnny Rivers, and the Nylons helped me make it through many late evenings and early mornings of work on the manuscript that became the book you hold in your hands. And Stephen King, Anne Rice, Clive Barker, Len Deighton, Peter Straub, and Carl Barks provided me with a respite from my writings with their own.

Finally, there is the most important acknowledgment of all—my feelings for and gratitude to my family. My wife, Glenda, and our children, Dustin and Ashley, are the foundation of my professional and personal life. They help me keep work and play in perspective and give meaning to everything I do. It is with all my love that I dedicate this book to them.

I AN INTRODUCTION
TO MANAGEMENT

OUTLINE

Management and Managers Defined

The Management Process
Planning and Decision Making: Determining Courses of Action · Organizing: Coordinating Activities and Resources · Leading: Motivating and Managing Employees · Controlling: Monitoring and Evaluating Activities

Kinds of Managers
Levels of Management · Areas of Management

Critical Roles and Skills
Managerial Roles · Managerial Skills

Acquiring Management Skills
The Role of Education · The Role of Experience

The Scope of Management
Management in Profit-seeking Organizations · Management in Not-for-Profit Organizations

CHAPTER 1

Managing and the Manager's Job

OBJECTIVES

After studying this chapter, you should be able to:

- Define management and managers.
- Identify and briefly explain the four basic management functions.
- Describe different kinds of managers from the standpoints of level and area.
- Identify the primary roles and skills of managers.
- Discuss education and experience as sources of management skills.
- Summarize the scope of management.

OPENING INCIDENT

Who is Donald Petersen? Although not as well known as Lee Iacocca or Donald Trump, Petersen is seen by many as one of America's consummate managers. In the early 1980s, Ford Motor Company lost over $3 billion and seemed destined for decline. When Petersen took the helm, however, things turned around quickly. By 1988, Ford had gained significant market share from General Motors and was earning higher profits than GM and Chrysler combined.

After serving in the Marines during World War II, Petersen got his M.B.A. from Stanford in 1949. He joined Ford soon thereafter, in part because he wanted the security of working for a big company. Over the years, he advanced rapidly from product planning to head of international operations. He became president in 1980.

How did Petersen get Ford back on track? He had a clear vision of the environment facing the U.S. auto industry. He made hard decisions about laying off workers and redesigning products. He saw the importance of planning for the future. He overhauled the company's organization structure by stripping away layers of bureaucracy. He realized the importance of Ford's workers in accomplishing its goals. Finally, Petersen implemented major programs aimed at controlling costs and improving product quality.[1]

*D*onald Petersen is clearly a manager. So, too, are James Kinnear (CEO of Texaco), Joichi Aoi (president of Toshiba), Sir David Wilson (director of the British Museum), Debbie Fields (president of Mrs. Fields' Cookies), Red Auerbach (president of the Boston Celtics), George Bush (president of the United States), John Paul II (pope of the Roman Catholic Church), and Bill Oglevee (owner of Bill's Garden Center in Bryan, Texas). As diverse as they and their organizations are, all of these managers are confronted by many of the same challenges; they strive to achieve many of the same goals; and they apply many of the same concepts of effective management in their work.

For better or worse, our society is strongly influenced by managers and their organizations.[2] Most Americans are born in a hospital (an organization), educated by public schools (all organizations), and buy virtually all of their consumable products and services from businesses (organizations). And much of our behavior is influenced by various government agencies (also organizations). We will define an **organization** as a group of two or more people working together in a structured fashion to attain a set of goals. The goals may include such things as profit (Ford Motor Company), the discovery of knowledge (University of Iowa), national defense (the U.S. Army), the coordination

organization A group of two or more people working together in structured fashion to attain a set of goals of various local charities (the United Way), or social satisfaction (a college sorority). So thoroughly do organizations pervade our society that we could not escape their influence even if we wanted to. Because they play such a significant role in our lives, it is important to understand how organizations operate and how they are managed.

This book is about managers and the work they do. In Chapter 1, we examine the general nature of management, its dimensions, and its challenges. We explain the concepts of management and managers, discuss the management process and present an overview of the entire book, and identify various kinds of managers. We describe the different roles and skills of managers, discuss various ways of acquiring those skills, and examine the scope of management in contemporary organizations. Chapters 2 and 3 deal with management theory and the external environment of management. As a unit, the first three chapters provide an introduction to management. At the end of Part 1, an Enhancement Module provides an extra glimpse into the nature of managerial careers.

MANAGEMENT AND MANAGERS DEFINED

There are probably as many definitions of management as there are books on the subject. Many of the definitions are relatively concise and simplistic. For example, one early writer defined management as "Knowing exactly what you want [people] to do, and then seeing that they do it in the best and cheapest way."[3] As we will see throughout this book, however, management is a complex process—much more complex than that definition leads us to believe. Thus, we need to develop a definition of management that captures the true nature of its complexities and challenges.

Management is perhaps best understood from the viewpoint of systems theory. (Systems theory is described in depth in Chapter 2. At this point, we consider only the components of it that are appropriate for our definition.) Systems theory suggests that organizations utilize four basic kinds of inputs, or resources, from their environments: human, monetary, physical, and information. Human resources include managerial talent and labor. Monetary resources are the financial capital used by the organization to finance both ongoing and long-term operations. Physical resources include raw materials, office and production facilities, and equipment. Information resources are usable data needed to make effective decisions. Examples of resources used in four very different kinds of organizations are given in Table 1.1.

The manager's job involves combining and coordinating these various resources to achieve the organization's goals. A manager at Mobil, for example, uses the talents of executives and drilling platform workers, profits earmarked for reinvestment, existing refineries and office facilities, and sales forecasts to make decisions regarding the amount of oil to be refined and distributed during the next quarter. Similarly, the

Organization	Human Resources	Financial Resources	Physical Resources	Information Resources
Mobil Corp.	Drilling platform workers Corporate executives	Profits Stockholder investments	Refineries Office buildings	Sales forecasts OPEC proclamations
Michigan State University	Faculty Secretarial staff	Alumni contributions Government grants	Computers Campus facilities	Research reports Government publications
City of New York	Police officers Municipal employees	Tax revenue Government grants	Sanitation equipment Municipal buildings	Economic forecasts Crime statistics
Joe's Corner Grocery Store	Grocery clerks Bookkeeper	Profits Owner investment	Building Display shelving	Price lists from suppliers Newspaper ads for competitors

TABLE 1.1

Examples of Resources Used
by Organizations

mayor (manager) of New York City might use current police officers, a government grant (perhaps supplemented with surplus tax revenues), existing police stations, and detailed crime statistics to launch a major crime prevention program in the city.

How do these and other managers go about combining and coordinating the various kinds of resources? They do so by carrying out four basic managerial functions: planning and decision making, organizing, leading, and controlling. Management, then, as illustrated in Figure 1.1, can be defined as follows:

> **Management** is a set of activities, including planning and decision making, organizing, leading, and controlling, directed at an organization's human, financial, physical, and information resources, with the aim of achieving organizational goals in an efficient and effective manner.

■ **management**   A set of activities, including planning and decision making, organizing, teaching, and controlling, directed at an organization's human, financial, physical, and information resources, with the aim of achieving organizational goals in an efficient and effective manner

efficient   Using resources wisely and without unnecessary waste

effective   Doing the right things

The last phrase in our definition is especially important because it highlights the basic purpose of management—to ensure that an organization's goals are attained in an efficient and effective manner. By **efficient**, we mean using resources wisely and without unnecessary waste. For example, a firm like Honda that produces high-quality products at relatively low costs is efficient. By **effective**, we mean doing the right things. Honda also makes cars with the styling and craftsmanship that inspire consumer confidence. A firm could produce

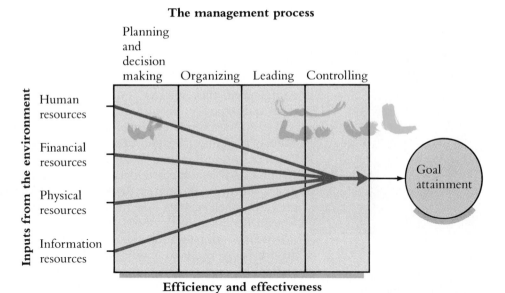

The management process

FIGURE 1.1

A Schematic Diagram of
Management in Organizations

slide rules and buggy whips very efficiently but still not succeed. In general, successful management involves being both efficient and effective.[4]

With this basic understanding of management, defining the term manager becomes relatively simple:

■ **manager**   Someone whose
primary activities are a part of
the management process

> A **manager** is someone whose primary activities are a part of the management process. In particular, a manager is someone who plans and makes decisions, organizes, leads, and controls human, financial, physical, and information resources.

Today's managers face a variety of interesting and challenging situations. And the situation faced by every manager is unique. For example, the average CEO works 60 hours a week, has enormous demands placed on his or her time, and faces increased complexities posed by globalization, domestic competition, government regulation, and shareholder pressure.[5] The task is further complicated by rapid change, unexpected disruptions, and both minor and major crises.

Donald Petersen has spent his entire career at Ford. Although not always happy with the organization, he persevered until he attained a position from which he could do what he thought was best. Carl Icahn, in contrast, makes his living buying and selling other companies. He is distrusted by many who work for him but nevertheless churns out profits from his businesses. A. Bartlett Giametti, commissioner of major league baseball, must deal with players' escalating demands for higher salaries, which threaten the game's financial structure, and drug scandals, which threaten its integrity. It should be clear from just these few examples that the job of manager is unpredictable, fraught with challenges, but also filled with opportunities to make a difference.

THE MANAGEMENT PROCESS

We noted earlier that management involves the four basic functions of planning and decision making, organizing, leading, and controlling. Since these functions compose the framework around which this book is organized, they warrant a detailed introduction. Their basic definitions and interrelationships are shown in Figure 1.2.

Recall the example of Donald Petersen discussed earlier. He saw the value of planning, changed various ways in which Ford was organized, emphasized the human side of things, and took appropriate corrective actions. Each of these activities represents one of the four basic managerial functions illustrated in the figure. "Management in Practice" provides other insights into the managerial functions as carried out by Ronald Perelman of Revlon.

It is important to note, however, that the functions of management do not really occur in a tidy, step-by-step fashion. Managers do not plan on Monday, make decisions on Tuesday, organize on Wednesday, lead on Thursday, and control on Friday. At any given time, a manager is likely to be engaged in several different activities simultaneously. Research has clearly indicated that as many differences as similarities exist in managerial work from one setting to another. The similarities are the phases in the management process; the differences, the emphasis, sequencing, and implications of each phase.[6] Thus, the solid lines in Figure 1.2 indicate how, in theory, the functions of management are performed. The dotted lines, however, represent the true reality of management. In the sections that follow, we explore each of these phases.

Management is applicable to all forms of organizations, not just businesses. For example, in his role as Pope of the Catholic Church, John Paul II is responsible for managing an international organization that is not that much different from a multinational corporation. The Vatican has a huge payroll to meet, must forecast income from contributions and other sources, and deal with an administrative hierarchy. Moreover, it has an elaborate budgetary control system and uses a form of departmentalization very similar to the one used by Exxon. The Pope is advised in administrative areas by a group of 15 cardinals who serve much like a corporation's executive committee. And the Vatican's employees are even unionized!

Planning and Decision Making: Determining Courses of Action

■ **planning** The determination of an organization's goals and deciding how best to achieve them

■ **decision making** Part of the planning process that involves selecting a course of action from a set of alternatives

In its simplest form, **planning** means determining an organization's goals and deciding how best to achieve them. **Decision making**, a part of the planning process, involves selecting a course of action from a set of alternatives. Planning and decision making help maintain managerial effectiveness by serving as guides for future activities. For example, Jack Welch, CEO of General Electric, has established a goal that every business owned by GE will be either number 1 or number 2 in its industry.[7] This goal provides clear managerial guidelines. If a particular business is nowhere near the top of its industry and shows little potential for improvement, GE managers will most likely sell it. On the other hand, a business that is number 3 and gaining on its rivals may receive an extra infusion of resources to gain the number 2 spot. Thus, the goals and plans help managers know how to allocate their time and resources.

Four chapters making up Part 2 of this text are devoted to the planning process. Decision making, though actually a part of all managerial actions, is most closely related to the planning function. Thus,

FIGURE 1.2

The Management Process

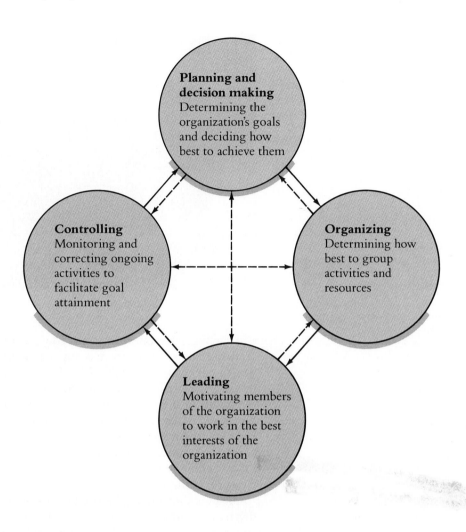

we begin our discussion of planning in Chapter 4 with an in-depth look at managerial decision making. Chapter 5 examines the planning process itself in more detail. Chapters 6 and 7 then focus on two major types of planning done by organizations: strategic planning and tactical planning. Finally, at the end of Part 2, two Enhancement Modules provide additional insights into useful planning and decision-making tools and the role of the computer in managerial planning and decision making.

Organizing: Coordinating Activities and Resources

Once a manager has developed a workable plan, the next phase of management is to organize the people and other resources necessary to carry out the plan. At a basic level, consider the following scenario. You have a $90,000 budget and three subordinates to execute a plan. One approach might involve giving each subordinate a $30,000 budget

James and David Eller are both ranchers and executives. The two brothers own several cattle ranches in Texas. They also own Granada Corporation, a biotechnology firm with annual revenues exceeding $1 billion. Managing Granada clearly requires that they plan, organize, lead, and control. But they also agree that managing their ranches involves many of these same activities. For example, they need to forecast future demand for beef products (planning), organize ranch hands into crews (organizing), motivate the crews to work effectively (leading), and manage costs and inventories (control).

and having each one report to you. A different method might be to establish one subordinate as a supervisor of the other two, who would have budgets of $45,000 each. At GE, Welch has decided that each division head within the company should have a great deal of freedom to run his or her operation as though it were a separate business. Thus, the heads of each of the twenty major businesses that constitute GE have considerable autonomy. Welch has also changed many of the company's bureaucratic rules and procedures. Determining methods for grouping activities and resources is the **organizing** process. Organizing is the subject of Part 3.

■ **organizing** Grouping activities and resources in a logical fashion

Chapter 8 introduces basic elements of organizing, such as job design, departmentalization, authority relationships, span of control, and line and staff roles. Chapter 9 explains how these elements and concepts fit together to form an overall organization structure or design. Processes associated with hiring and assigning people to carry out organizational roles are described in Chapter 10. Finally, organizational change, development, and revitalization—various strategies, approaches, and techniques for changing organizational elements and processes—are the focus of Chapter 11. Two Enhancement Modules at the end of Part 3 focus on related aspects of organizing: participative management and managing creativity and innovation.

Leading: Motivating and Managing Employees

■ **leading** The set of processes used to get members of the organization to work together to further the interests of the organization

Once the organizing process is complete, all management has to do is plug people into the various "slots" and everything will take care of itself, right? Wrong. It is at this point that managers must engage in what some people consider the hardest part of management—leading. **Leading** is the set of processes used to get members of the organization

MANAGEMENT IN PRACTICE

RONALD PERELMAN: MANAGER OR RAIDER?

Ronald Perelman, 44, is the chairman of Revlon, the $2 billion cosmetics giant. Perelman is a skilled manager and a shrewd buyer of companies. The latter ability sometimes confuses outsiders, who wonder whether he is a manager or a raider. He says that he is an "operations guy," a manager, primarily interested in the overall performance of Revlon.

Perelman, with an M.B.A. from the Wharton School of Finance, spent nearly fifteen years buying, selling, and running companies for his father's company in Philadelphia before striking out on his own. He now owns MacAndrews & Forbes Holdings, which in turn owns 49 percent of Compact Video and 100 percent of Technicolor, MacAndrews & Forbes Co. (licorice and other flavorings and extracts) and the Revlon Group (which includes Revlon and Consolidated Cigar). All of this was put together in about ten years—an accomplishment that earned Perelman his reputation as a raider.

Despite his buying behavior, Perelman is clearly a manager who performs the basic functions of management. *Planning:* He is a master planner and strategist, especially in terms of acquisitions. He spent over two years acquiring MacAndrews & Forbes and made five separate tries before buying Revlon. *Organizing:* He links his strategic planning to organizing by assuring that his companies are highly profitable and that each of them maintains only profitable product lines. He does not believe in layers of administration and checking. Decisions at Revlon that used to involve sixty different forms and individuals now involve only one form. *Leading:* Perelman tends to lead by doing and setting examples. He is a cigar-smoking autocrat who tries to have his hand in everything, at least initially. *Controlling:* His concept of control is to focus almost exclusively on financial data; this view is consistent with his basic strategy. For instance, he acquired Cohen-Hatfield, a jewelry store company, and then sold 80 percent of it. Soon he was earning on 20 percent of Cohen-Hatfield's capital the same return that previous managers had gotten from 100 percent, and the sale produced a great deal of cash that he could use for further acquisitions.

REFERENCES: Pat Sloan, "Revlon Shops on Edge," *Advertising Age*, January 11, 1988, pp. 1, 58; Anthony Ramirez, "The Raider Who Runs Revlon," *Fortune*, September 14, 1987, pp. 57–63; Anthony Ramirez, "Revlon's Striving Makeover Man," *Fortune*, January 5, 1987, pp. 54–55; "How Ron Perelman Scared Gillette into Shape," *Business Week*, October 12, 1987, pp. 40–41.

to work together to advance the interests of the organization. For example, at GE, Jack Welch works hard to inspire confidence and trust in other managers, and he expects them to do the same for their subordinates.

The leading function consists of four different activities. Part 4 discusses these activities. The first, motivating employees to expend effort, is discussed in Chapter 12. A second aspect of leading, covered in Chapter 13, is leadership itself. Leadership focuses on what the manager does to encourage organizational performance (rather than on management activities geared to employee needs and expectations). The third part of leading is dealing with interpersonal processes, groups, and conflict. These activities are the subject of Chapter 14. Communication, the fourth significant component of leading, is addressed in Chapter 15. Part 4 concludes with two Enhancement Modules, one dealing with managing individual behavior and the other with coping with stress.

Controlling: Monitoring and Evaluating Activities

■ **controlling** Monitoring organizational progress toward goal attainment

The final phase of the management process is **controlling**. As the organization moves toward its goals, management must monitor its progress. It must make sure the organization is performing in such a way as to arrive at its "destination" at the appointed time. A good analogy is that of a space mission to Mars. NASA does not simply shoot a rocket in the general direction of the planet and then look again in four months to see whether the rocket hit its mark. NASA monitors the spacecraft almost continuously and makes whatever course corrections are needed to keep it on track. Controlling helps ensure the effectiveness and efficiency needed for successful management.

The control function is explored in Part 5. First, Chapter 16 explores the general nature of the control process, including the increasing importance of strategic control. Other important areas of management control—operations management, productivity, and quality—are explored in depth in Chapter 17. Chapter 18 addresses still another critical area of organizational control: the management of information. Finally, Chapter 19 summarizes specific methods and techniques for organizational control. The control discussion concludes with one Enhancement Module discussing automation and another dealing with organizational decline and cutbacks.

These, then, are the four primary functions of management: planning and decision making, organizing, leading, and controlling. Beyond these functions, however, are a variety of special challenges that are of increasing concern and significance to all managers. These special challenges are discussed in Part 6. Chapter 20 discusses the nature of entrepreneurship and small-business management. Chapter 21 describes the special challenge of managing in the international sector. The role of ethics and social responsibility in management is addressed in Chapter 22. Finally, an Enhancement Module identifies other challenges confronting tomorrow's managers.

KINDS OF MANAGERS

Earlier in this chapter we identify as managers several different people from a variety of organizations. Clearly, there are many kinds of managers. One point of differentiation is among organizations, as those earlier examples imply. Another occurs within an organization. Figure 1.3 indicates how managers within an organization can be differentiated by level and area.

■ **levels of managers** Can be differentiated into three basic categories—top, middle, and first-line

Levels of Management

Managers can be differentiated according to their level in the organization. Although large organizations typically have a number of levels

FIGURE 1.3

Kinds of Managers by Level
and Area

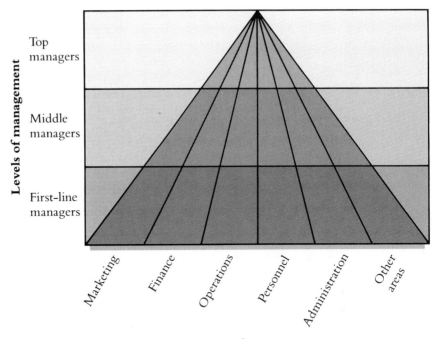

Areas of management

of management, the most common view considers three basic levels:
top, middle, and first-line managers.

Top Managers   Top managers make up the relatively small group of
executives who control the organization. Titles found in this group
include president, vice president, and chief executive officer (CEO).
Thus, Donald Petersen of Ford is a top manager.

Top managers establish the organization's goals, overall strategy, and
operating policies. They also officially represent the organization to the
external environment by meeting with government officials, executives
of other organizations, and so forth. The job of a top manager is likely
to be complex and varied. Top managers make decisions about such
activities as acquiring other companies, investing in research and development, entering or abandoning various markets, and building new
plants and office facilities.[8] They often work long hours and spend
much of their time in meetings and on the telephone.[9]

Middle Managers   Middle management is probably the largest group
of managers in most organizations. Common middle-management titles include plant manager, operations manager, and division head.
Thus, the general manager of a Ford assembly plant in Detroit is a
middle manager.

Middle managers are primarily responsible for implementing the
policies and plans developed by top management and for supervising

Leonade D. Jones is a financial manager for the Washington Post Company. Her first financial management position with the company was as director of financial services. During her stint in that job, she helped achieve dramatic cost reductions and boosted cash flow significantly by improving the operating margin and reducing expenses. Because of her tremendous success, she was then promoted to the position of treasurer, the top financial management position in the firm. She now manages the company's short-term and long-term debt, a $250 million portfolio of liquid assets, and a $500 million pension fund.

■ **areas of managers** Can be differentiated into marketing, financial, operating, human resource, administration, and other areas

and coordinating the activities of lower-level managers.[10] Plant managers, for example, handle inventory management, quality control, equipment failures, and minor union problems. They also coordinate the work of supervisors within the plant. In recent years, many organizations have thinned the ranks of middle managers in order to lower costs and rid themselves of excess bureaucracy. For example, Mobil has eliminated 17 percent of its middle managers since 1982, and Du Pont has made cuts of 15 percent.[11] Still, middle managers are necessary to bridge the upper and lower levels of the organization and to implement the strategies developed at the top. They can also be a significant source of innovation and productivity when given the autonomy to make decisions affecting their operating units.[12]

First-Line Managers   First-line managers supervise and coordinate the activities of operating employees. Common titles for first-line managers are foreman, supervisor, and office manager. A shift foreman within a Ford assembly plant is a first-line manager. These are often the first positions held by employees who enter management from the ranks of operating personnel. In contrast to top and middle managers, first-line managers typically spend a large proportion of their time supervising the work of subordinates.[13]

Areas of Management

Managers at different levels may work in various areas within an organization. In any given firm, there may be marketing, financial, operations, human resource, administrative, and other kinds of managers at all three levels.

Marketing Managers   Marketing managers are those whose primary duties are related to the marketing function—getting whatever the organization produces (be it Ford automobiles, *Newsweek* magazines, or Associated Press news reports) into the hands of consumers and clients. Key areas of concern are product development, promotion, and distribution. Given the importance of marketing for virtually all organizations, the development of managers in this area can be critical. John Akers, CEO of IBM, spent much of his career as a marketing manager.

Financial Managers   Financial managers deal primarily with an organization's financial resources. Their areas of concern include accounting, cash management, and investments. In some businesses, such as banking, financial managers are found in especially large numbers. General Motors' CEO, Roger Smith, started out as a financial manager.

Operations Managers   Operations managers are primarily concerned with establishing the systems that create an organization's products and services. Typical responsibilities include production control, inventory control, quality control, plant layout, and site selection. James Olson, CEO of AT&T, spent much of his career as an operations manager.

Human Resource Managers   Human resource managers are concerned with hiring, maintaining, and discharging employees. They are typically involved in human resource planning, employee recruitment and selection, training and development, designing compensation and benefit systems, formulating performance appraisal systems, and discharging low-performing and problem employees. Until the last several years, human resource managers were not considered to be particularly important in many organizations. Top managers now recognize their value, however, in part because of increased awareness of the contributions of human resources and in part because of the complex legal environment of human resource management. Consequently, although no large companies have CEOs from the ranks of human resource executives, these executives are now making great strides up the organizational ladder.[14]

Administrative Managers   Administrative, or general, managers are not associated with any particular management specialty. Probably the best example of an administrative management position is that of a hospital or clinic administrator. Administrative managers tend to be generalists; they have some basic familiarity with all functional areas of management rather than specialized training in any one area.

Other Kinds of Managers   Many organizations have specialized management positions in addition to those already described. Public relations managers, for example, deal with the public and media for firms such as Philip Morris and Dow Chemical to protect and enhance the image of the organization. Research and development (R&D) managers coordinate the activities of scientists and engineers working on scientific projects in organizations such as Monsanto, NASA, and Merck. Internal consultants are used in organizations such as the Prudential Insurance Company to provide specialized expert advice to operating managers. Many areas of international management are coordinated by specialized managers in organizations like Eli Lilly and Rockwell International. The number, nature, and importance of these specialized managers vary tremendously from one organization to another. As contemporary organizations continue to grow in complexity and size, the number and importance of such managers are also likely to increase.

CRITICAL ROLES AND SKILLS

Certain roles and skills are usually required of all managers, no matter what their specialty or level. The concept of a role, in this sense, is similar to the role an actor plays in a theatrical production. A person does certain things, meets certain needs in the organization, and has certain responsibilities. Management skills are the talents necessary for effective performance. We discuss these roles and skills in the sections that follow.

Managerial Roles

Henry Mintzberg offers a number of interesting insights into the nature of managerial roles.[15] He closely observed the day-to-day activities of a group of CEOs by literally following them around and taking notes on what they did. From his observations, Mintzberg concluded that the formal authority granted to managers by the organization is accompanied by a certain degree of status. This status facilitates interpersonal relationships with superiors, peers, and subordinates. These individuals, in turn, provide managers with the information they need to make decisions. From his analysis, Mintzberg concluded that managers play several different roles and that these roles fall into three basic categories: interpersonal, informational, and decisional (see Table 1.2).

■ **interpersonal roles**
Figurehead, leader, and liaison involve dealing with other people

Interpersonal Roles   There are three **interpersonal roles** inherent in the manager's job. First, the manager is often asked to serve as a *figurehead*—taking visitors to dinner, attending ribbon-cutting ceremonies, and the like. These activities are typically more ceremonial and symbolic than substantive. The manager is also asked to serve as a *leader*—hiring, training, and motivating employees. A manager who formally or informally shows subordinates how to do things and how to perform under pressure is leading. Finally, managers can have a *liaison* role. This role often involves serving as a coordinator or link between people, between groups, or between the organizations. For example, when General Electric sold its small-appliance business to Black & Decker a few years ago, designated managers from each firm had to work together to ensure a smooth transition—that is, they were liaisons for their respective companies.

■ **informational roles**
Monitor, disseminator, and spokesperson involve the processing of information

Informational Roles   The three **informational roles** identified by Mintzberg flow naturally from the interpersonal roles we have just discussed. The process of carrying out the roles of figurehead, leader, and liaison place the manager at a strategic point to gather and disseminate information. The first informational role is that of *monitor*, one who actively seeks information that may be of value. The manager questions subordinates, is receptive to unsolicited information, and attempts to be as well informed as possible. For example, H. Ross Perot learned about and subsequently invested in Steve Jobs's latest venture, the NeXT computer, as a result of a television appearance by Jobs that Perot just happened to watch one evening.

The manager is also a *disseminator* of information, transmitting relevant information back to others in the workplace. When the roles of monitor and disseminator are viewed together, the manager emerges as a vital link in the organization's chain of communication.

TABLE 1.2

Ten Basic Managerial Roles

Category	Role	Sample Activities
Interpersonal	Figurehead	Attending ribbon-cutting ceremony for new plant
	Leader	Encouraging employees to improve productivity
	Liaison	Coordinating activities of two project groups
Informational	Monitor	Scanning industry reports to stay abreast of developments
	Disseminator	Sending memos outlining new organizational initiatives
	Spokesperson	Making a speech to discuss substantive issues
Decisional	Entrepreneur	Developing new ideas for innovation
	Disturbance Handler	Resolving conflict between two subordinates
	Resource Allocator	Reviewing and revising budget requests
	Negotiator	Reaching agreement with a key supplier or labor union

The third informational role focuses on external communication. The role of *spokesperson* involves dealing in a substantive way with people outside the unit or outside the organization. For example, a plant manager at Union Carbide may transmit information to top-level managers so that they will be better informed about the plant's activities. Or the manager may represent the organization before a chamber of commerce or consumer group. Although the roles of spokesperson and figurehead are similar, there is one basic difference between them. When a manager acts as a figurehead, the manager's presence as a symbol of the organization is what is of interest. In the spokesperson role, however, the manager carries information and communicates it to others in a formal sense.

Decisional Roles   The manager's informational roles typically lead to the **decisional roles**. The information acquired by the manager as a result of performing the informational roles has a significant bearing on important decisions that he or she makes. Mintzberg identified four decisional roles.

■ **decisional roles**   Entrepreneur, disturbance handler, resource allocator, and negotiator primarily relate to decisions that must be made

Cathleen Black is publisher of
USA Today. As part of her job,
she must represent the company
in various public functions. This
set of activities is a part of the
figurehead role usually given to a
select group of top managers.
Managers also fill the roles of
leaders and liaisons.

First, the manager has the role of *entrepreneur*, the voluntary initiator
of change. For example, the manager may recognize a problem or spot
an opportunity to be exploited. A manager at 3M developed the idea
for the Post-it Note Pad and then "sold" the idea to others inside the
company. A second decisional role is initiated not by the manager but
by some other individual or group. The manager responds to his or
her role as *disturbance handler* by handling such problems as strikes,
copyright infringements, and energy shortages.

The third decisional role is that of *resource allocator*. In this role the
manager decides who in the unit will be given what resources and who
will have access to the manager's time. For example, a manager typically allocates the funds in the unit's operating budget among the unit's
members and projects. The final decisional role is that of *negotiator*. In
this role the manager enters into negotiations as a representative of the
company. For example, managers may negotiate a union contract, an
agreement with a consultant, or a long-term relationship with a supplier. Negotiations may also be internal to the organization. The manager may, for instance, mediate a dispute between two subordinates or
negotiate a certain level of support from another department.

Mintzberg's research provides us with a number of important insights
into the manager's job. First, simply being aware of the various roles
inherent in the job helps us understand what a manager does. Second,
by observing actual behavior, Mintzberg was able to describe how
managers at the upper levels of an organization allocate their time. He
found, for example, that in a typical day CEOs are likely to spend 59
percent of their time in scheduled meetings, 22 percent doing "desk
work," 10 percent in unscheduled meetings, 6 percent on the telephone,
and the remaining 3 percent on tours of company facilities. (These
proportions, of course, are different for managers at lower levels.)

Finally, the role framework helps us understand why managers do
not move from planning to organizing to leading to controlling in a
neat, systematic fashion. The turbulence of their surroundings demands
a more flexible style. Their schedule is seldom compatible with a logical,
ordered progression of activities. If managers typically spend about 10
percent of their time in unscheduled meetings, it is no wonder that a
successful manager needs to have mastered a variety of skills.

Managerial Skills

All managers need a number of specific skills if they are to succeed.
One classic study of managers identified three important types of managerial skills: technical, interpersonal, and conceptual.[16] Diagnostic and
analytic skills are also prerequisites to managerial success.

■ **technical skills**   Necessary
to accomplish specialized
activities

Technical Skills   **Technical skills** are the skills necessary to accomplish
specialized activities. They are generally associated with the operations
of the organization. For example, David Packard and Bill Hewlett

understand the inner workings of their company, Hewlett-Packard, because they started out as engineers working in a garage. Project engineers, physicians, and accountants all have the technical skills necessary for their respective professions. They each develop basic technical skills by completing recognized programs of study at colleges and universities. Then they gain experience in actual work situations, honing their skills before actually becoming R&D manager, chief of surgery, or partner in a certified public accounting firm. Similarly, the top marketing executive of any large firm probably started as a sales representative or sales manager, whereas the operations vice president was probably a plant manager at one time. Technical skills are especially important for first-line managers. These managers spend much of their time training subordinates and answering questions about work-related problems. They must know how to perform the tasks assigned to those they supervise if they are to be effective managers.

Interpersonal Skills   Managers spend considerable time interacting with people both inside and outside the organization. Recall Mintzberg's description of how top managers spend their time: 69 percent in meetings, 6 percent on the phone, and 3 percent on tours. All these activities involve other people. For obvious reasons, then, the manager

■ **interpersonal skills**   The ability to communicate with, understand, and motivate both individuals and groups

needs **interpersonal skills**: the ability to communicate with, understand, and motivate individuals and groups. It is interesting to note, however, that not all successful managers exhibit good interpersonal skills. Harold Geneen, former chief executive of International Telephone and Telegraph Corporation (ITT), for example, had a reputation for humiliating managers who failed to meet his expectations. Many managers were afraid of Geneen, and many left ITT to seek employment elsewhere. In the long run, harsh treatment tends to increase personnel turnover; moreover, it becomes increasingly difficult to replace those who leave. Other things being equal, a manager who has good interpersonal skills is likely to be more successful than a manager with poor interpersonal skills.

■ **conceptual skills**   The manager's ability to think in the abstract

Conceptual Skills   **Conceptual skills** depend on the manager's ability to think in the abstract. Managers need the mental capacity to understand various cause-and-effect relationships in the organization, to grasp how all the parts of the organization fit together, and to view the organization in a holistic manner. This allows them to think strategically, to see the "big picture," and to make broad-based decisions that serve the overall organization.

A few years ago, Boeing was on the verge of discontinuing its 737 aircraft line because of sliding domestic sales. Then suddenly one manager, Bob Norton, realized that the company needed to take a more global view of the aircraft market. By focusing on the same things that had made the 737 an earlier success in the United States, Boeing was able to reintroduce the aircraft in developing nations. Increased sales there have offset declines at home, and the end result is that the company has been able to maintain a highly profitable product line beyond its normal life expectancy. The conceptual skills of a single manager helped pave the way.[17]

■ **diagnostic and analytic skills**   A manager's ability to visualize the most appropriate response to a situation

Diagnostic and Analytic Skills   Successful managers possess **diagnostic and analytic skills**. A physician diagnoses a patient's illness by analyzing symptoms and determining their probable cause. Similarly, a manager can diagnose and analyze a problem in the organization by studying its symptoms and then developing a solution. For example, a manager at a Texas Instruments plant recently noted that one particular department was suffering from high employee turnover. He analyzed the situation and decided that the turnover was caused by one of three things: dissatisfaction with pay, boring work, or a supervisor with poor interpersonal skills. After interviewing several employees, he concluded that the problem was the supervisor. He reassigned the supervisor to a position that required less interaction with other people, and the turnover problem soon disappeared. The skills to diagnose and analyze enabled him to define his problem, recognize its possible causes, focus on the most direct problem, and then to solve it.

Diagnostic and analytic skills are also useful in favorable situations. The company may find that its sales are increasing at a much higher rate than anticipated. Possible causes might include low price, greater demand than predicted, and high prices charged by a competitor. Diagnostic skills would enable the manager to determine what was causing the sales explosion and how best to take advantage of it.

In summary, then, successful managers are likely to have technical, interpersonal, conceptual, diagnostic, and analytic skills. It is also important to recognize that the importance of these skills varies as one progresses up the organizational ladder. Figure 1.4 indicates the extent to which managers at different levels in an organization need different

FIGURE 1.4

The Importance of Different Management Skills at Different Organizational Levels

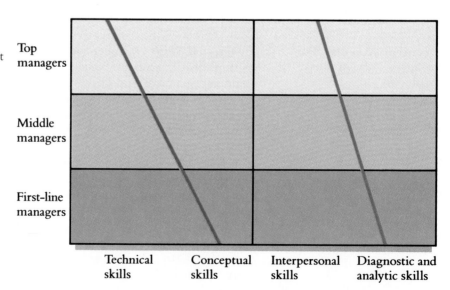

kinds of skills. As one progresses up the organization, fewer and fewer technical skills are needed, because top managers spend little time in actual operating situations and are concerned with broader aspects of the organization. Conceptual skills become proportionately more and more important at higher levels of the organization. Interpersonal skills are important at all levels, but perhaps are slightly less important at the top. Similarly, diagnostic and analytic skills are also important for all managers, but their importance is perhaps a little greater for top managers than for lower-level managers.

ACQUIRING MANAGEMENT SKILLS

How does one acquire the skills necessary to become a successful manager? The most common path, although there are as many variations as there are managers, is the one taken by Donald Petersen of Ford. He combined a formal education with a variety of experiences to develop and refine his management skills. Some managers use their education as a springboard; others rely more on their experience to get the job done.[18] On balance, however, most successful managers use both sources in some proportion to acquire their technical, interpersonal, conceptual, diagnostic, and analytic skills. Figure 1.5 illustrates how this generally happens.

FIGURE 1.5

Sources of Management Skills

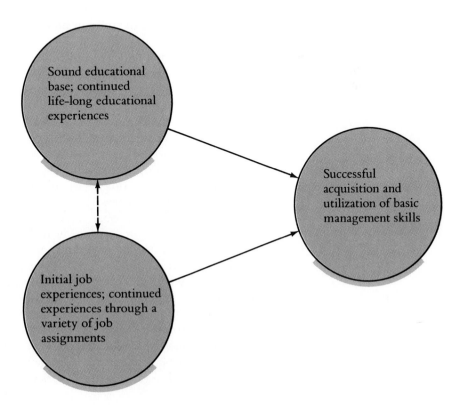

The Role of Education

Many of you reading this book right now are doing so because you are enrolled in a management course at a college or university. You are acquiring management skills in an educational setting. When you complete the course (and this book), you will have a foundation for developing your management skills in more advanced courses.

Enrollments in business schools and colleges have mushroomed in recent years. More and more students are seeking undergraduate degrees in business and management.[19] M.B.A. programs (conferring master's degrees in business administration) have also experienced rapid growth, and they often attract students whose undergraduate majors were in other fields.[20]

Even after obtaining the degree, most prospective managers have not seen the end of their management education. Many middle and top managers periodically return to campus to participate in executive or management development programs (MDPs) ranging in duration from a few days to several weeks. First-line managers also take advantage of extension and continuing education programs offered by institutions of higher education. A recent innovation in extended management education is the Executive M.B.A. program offered by many top business schools. Under this system, middle and top managers with several years of experience complete an accelerated program of study on weekends. Finally, many large companies have in-house training programs for furthering the education of managers.

Formal programs of study in business and management are relatively new. During the first several decades of this century, few successful managers attended college, and those who did usually majored in the humanities or liberal arts. About the closest a person could get to a business degree was to study economics. Even today, some successful executives lack college degrees.

The current trend, however, is clearly toward formal education as a prerequisite to business success. Nonbusiness undergraduates have recently begun to take more and more business courses in an effort to increase their job opportunities. Engineers frequently return to school for M.B.A. degrees. Today, virtually all of this country's top executives have one or more degrees. And the rest of the world is catching up. For example, "The Global View" explains how European business schools have made great strides in recent years.

The primary advantage of education as a source of management skills is that a student can follow a well-developed program of study, becoming familiar with current research and thinking on management. And many college students can devote full-time energy and attention to learning. On the negative side, management education may have to be very general to meet the needs of a wide variety of students, and specific know-how may be hard to obtain. Further, many aspects of the manager's job can be discussed in a book but cannot really be appreciated and understood until they are experienced.

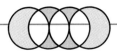

THE GLOBAL VIEW

MANAGEMENT EDUCATION IN EUROPE

Education in business and management is far from new, and the payment of high salaries to business school graduates is not new either. What is new is the rise of business and management education in Europe. European managers, as well as managers from other areas of the world, can now acquire the many different managerial skills from highly respected educational institutions in Europe.

IMI, LBS, IMEDE, IESE, and INSEAD are the recognized leaders among European business schools. IMI, International Management Institute, located in Geneva, Switzerland, is the oldest of these (founded in 1946) and has the most compressed time frame— a nine-month degree program. LBS, the London Business School, is the newest (founded in 1965) and has an American-style degree program. IMEDE, International Management Development Institute, located in Lausanne, Switzerland, was founded in 1957 by Nestlé although it is independent of that company. IESE, the Instituto de Estudios Superiores de la Empresa, in Barcelona, Spain, has religious roots but offers a relaxed atmosphere for its students and has a two-year M.B.A. program much like M.B.A. programs in the United States. INSEAD, the Institut Européen D'Administration des Affaires, in Fontainebleau, France, is the preeminent management education school in Europe. Its graduates frequently take jobs in countries other than their own.

All of these schools require students to undertake some kind of consulting work to increase their analytical and diagnostic skills. The French packaging company Groupe Carnaud reduced inventories and boosted profits by following the advice of a student consulting team. The exhausting pace (usually about 100 hours per week) also helps students develop skills in "working smart" and organizing their time— two of the technical skills needed by managers. Interpersonal skills are sharpened in the melting-pot environment of students from diverse countries and cultures. These skills are strengthened by the use of group assignments rather than individual assignments for most student projects. Conceptual skills are developed through discussions with faculty, with visiting executives, and among students.

REFERENCES: Shawn Tully, "Europe's Best Business Schools," *Fortune*, May 23, 1988, pp. 106–110; G. Bickerstaffe, "Companies and Business Schools Take a New Look at Management Education," *International Management*, October 1983, pp. 66–69; Alistair Mant, "Leadership the Second Coming (The Evolution of Business Leadership in Great Britain)," *Personnel Management*, December 1986, p. 38; David D. Van Fleet and Ella W. Van Fleet, "Education, Business Education, Management Education: A Chronology, 1607–1971," Working Paper Series 2, No. 3, Management History Division, Academy of Management, 1976.

The Role of Experience

This book will help provide you with a solid foundation for enhancing your management skills. However, even if you were to memorize every word in every management book ever written, you could not automatically step into a top-management position and be effective. The reason? Management skills must also be learned through experience. Most managers advanced to their present position from other jobs. By experiencing the day-to-day pressures a manager faces and by meeting a variety of managerial challenges, the individual develops insights that cannot be learned from a book.

For this reason most large companies, and many smaller ones as well, have management training programs developed for their prospective managers. People are hired from college campuses, from other organizations, or from the ranks of the organization's first-line managers and operating employees. These people are systematically assigned to a variety of jobs. Over time, the individual is exposed to most, if not all, of the major aspects of the organization. In this way the manager learns by experience.

The training programs at certain companies, such as Procter & Gamble, General Foods, and General Mills, are so good that some recruiters think of them as a second M.B.A. About half of the people who make it through the General Mills program, for example, use this experience to secure good jobs with other companies.[21]

Even without formal training programs, it is possible for managers to achieve success as they profit from varied experiences. For example, the president of the NBC television network, Robert C. Wright, practiced law and worked in manufacturing, sales, and finance.[22] Of course, natural ability, drive, and self-motivation also play roles in acquiring experience and developing management skills.

Most effective managers learn their skills through a combination of education and experience. As shown earlier in Figure 1.5, some type of college degree, even if it is not in business administration, usually provides a foundation. The individual then participates in an initial job experience and subsequently progresses through a variety of management situations. During the manager's rise in the organization, occasional education "updates," such as management development programs, may supplement on-the-job experience. The next section explores the wide variety of organizations in which modern managers gain the experience they need.

THE SCOPE OF MANAGEMENT

When most people think of managers and management, they think of profit-seeking organizations. Throughout this chapter, we used people like Donald Petersen of Ford and Jack Welch of GE as examples of managers. But we also mentioned examples from sports, religion, and other fields in which management is essential. Indeed, any group of two or more people working together to achieve a goal and having human, material, financial, or informational resources at its disposal requires the practice of management.

Management in Profit-Seeking Organizations

Large Business   Most of what we know about management comes from large profit-seeking organizations, because their survival has long depended on efficiency and effectiveness. Examples of large businesses include industrial firms (Tenneco, British Petroleum, Toyota, Xerox, Unilever, Levi Strauss), commercial banks (Citicorp, Fuji Bank, Wells Fargo, Chase Manhattan), insurance companies (Prudential, State Farm,

Philip Martin is a manager. He is also Chief of the Choctaw Indian Tribe in Mississippi. Under Martin's leadership, the Choctaws have become a major economic force in the state. Businesses ranging from electronics to greeting cards have made the Choctaw Tribe one of the top 20 employers in the state of Mississippi. Managing the extensive businesses of the tribe, like managing a large corporation, requires technical, interpersonal, conceptual, diagnostic, and analytic skills.

Metropolitan), retailers (Sears, Safeway, K mart), transportation companies (Delta Air Lines, Consolidated Freightways, Sohio Pipe Line), utilities (Pacific Gas & Electric, Consolidated Edison), communication companies (CBS, The New York Times Company), and service organizations (Kelly Services, Kinder Care, and Century 21).

Small Businesses   Although many people associate management primarily with large businesses, effective management is also essential for small businesses, which play an important role in the country's economy. In fact, most of this nation's businesses are small. In some respects, effective management is more important in a small business than in a larger one. A large firm such as NCR or Monsanto can afford to lose several thousand dollars on an incorrect decision, whereas a small business may ill afford even a much smaller loss. Small business management is given special attention in Chapter 20.

International Management   In recent years, the importance of international management has increased dramatically. The list of American firms doing business in other countries is staggering. Ford, for example, did almost $8 billion in export trade in 1987.[23] Other major exporters include General Motors, General Electric, Boeing, and Caterpillar Tractor. And even numbers like Ford's are deceptive. For example, the auto maker has large subsidiaries based in many European countries whose sales are not included in the $8 billion. And Boeing had over 40 percent of its total sales in 1987 outside the United States. Moreover, a number of major firms that do business in the United States have their headquarters in other countries. Firms in this category include Shell (the

Netherlands), Fiat (Italy), Nestlé (Switzerland), and Massey-Ferguson (Canada). International management is not, however, confined to profit-seeking organizations. There are several international sports federations (such as Little League Baseball); the federal government has branches (embassies) in most countries; and the Roman Catholic Church is established in most countries too. In some respects, the military was one of the first multinational organizations. International management is covered in depth in Chapter 21.

Management in Not-for-Profit Organizations

Intangible goals such as education, social services, public protection, and recreation are often the primary aim of not-for-profit organizations. Examples include the United Way, the U.S. Postal Service, Girl Scouts of America, the International Olympic Committee, art galleries, museums, and the Public Broadcasting System. Although these and similar organizations may not have to be profitable to attract investors, they must still employ sound management practices if they are to survive and work toward their goals.[24] And they must handle money in an efficient and effective way. For example, if the United Way were to begin to spend large portions of its contributions on administration, contributors would lose confidence in the organization and make their charitable donations elsewhere.

Government Organizations   The management of government organizations and agencies is often regarded as a separate specialty: public administration. Government organizations include the Federal Trade Commission, the Environmental Protection Agency, the National Science Foundation, all branches of the military, state highway departments, federal and state prison systems, and other government units familiar to all of us. Tax dollars support government organizations, so politicians and citizens' groups are acutely sensitive to the need for efficiency and effectiveness.

Educational Organizations   Public and private schools, colleges, and universities all stand to benefit from the efficient use of resources. Taxpayer "revolts" in states such as California and Massachusetts have drastically cut back the tax money available for education, forcing administrators to make tough decisions about allocating the resources that remain.

Healthcare Facilities   Managing healthcare facilities such as clinics, hospitals, and HMOs (health maintenance organizations) is now considered a separate field of management. Here, as in other organizations, scarce resources dictate an efficient and effective approach. In recent years many universities have established healthcare administration programs to train managers as specialists in this field.

Management in Nontraditional Settings   Good management is also required in several nontraditional settings to meet established goals. To one extent or another, management is practiced in religious organizations, terrorist groups, fraternities and sororities, organized crime, street gangs, neighborhood associations, and households. In short, as we noted at the beginning of this chapter, management and managers have a profound influence on all of us.

SUMMARY OF KEY POINTS

Management is a set of activities, including planning and decision making, organizing, leading, and controlling, directed at an organization's human, financial, physical, and information resources, with the aim of achieving organizational goals in an efficient and effective manner. A manager is someone whose primary activities are a part of the management process.

The basic activities within the management process are planning and decision making (determining courses of action), organizing (coordinating activities and resources), leading (motivating and managing employees), and controlling (monitoring and evaluating activities).

Managers can be categorized by level and by area. By level, we can identify top, middle, and first-line managers. Kinds of managers by area include marketing, financial, operations, human resource, administrative, and specialized managers.

Most managers have ten basic roles to play: three interpersonal roles (figurehead, leader, and liaison), three informational roles (monitor, disseminator, and spokesperson), and four decisional roles (entrepreneur, disturbance handler, resource allocator, and negotiator). Effective managers tend to have technical, interpersonal, conceptual, diagnostic, and analytic skills.

Management skills may be acquired through education (formal coursework and continuing education) or experience (training programs and previous jobs). Increasingly, successful managers are drawing on both experience and education as a means of acquiring and developing the skills they need.

Management processes are applicable in a wide variety of settings, including profit-seeking organizations (large and small businesses and international businesses) and not-for-profit organizations (government organizations, educational organizations, healthcare facilities, and nontraditional organizations).

DISCUSSION QUESTIONS

Questions for Review

1. What are the different kinds of managers? How are the different kinds related to one another?

2. Briefly describe the managerial roles identified by Mintzberg. Give an example of each.
3. Identify the different skills of managers. Give an example of each.
4. Briefly describe what is meant by the scope of management.

Questions for Analysis

5. Think about the different managerial roles and skills. Do the skills needed for some roles differ from the skills needed for other roles? Why or why not?
6. Does type of organization affect the roles played by managers within the organization? Why or why not?
7. Do all top executives play the same roles and use the same skills regardless of the size or type of organization in which they work? Why or why not?

Questions for Application

8. Interview a manager from a local organization about how she or he works. Does the interviewee perform each of the functions of management?
9. Go to the library and see how many different managerial skills you can identify in the literature. Can you find ones not in the text? Share your results with the class.
10. Obtain permission and then observe a manager in a local organization at work for a few days. Which functions and skills seem to occupy most of that manager's time? Which occupy the least? How can you account for your findings?

NOTES

1. "A Humble Hero Drives Ford to the Top," *Fortune*, January 4, 1988, pp. 22–24; Alex Taylor III, "Fords for the Future," *Fortune*, January 16, 1989, pp. 36–49.
2. William G. Scott and David K. Hart, *Organizational America* (Boston: Houghton Mifflin, 1979); and Page Smith, *The Rise of Industrial America* (New York: McGraw-Hill, 1984).
3. Frederick W. Taylor, *Shop Management* (New York: Harper & Row, 1903), p. 21.
4. Fred Luthans, "Successful vs. Effective Real Managers," *The Academy of Management Executive*, May 1988, pp. 127–132.
5. Carrie Gottlieb, "And You Thought You Had It Tough," *Fortune*, April 25, 1988, pp. 83–84.
6. William Whitely, "Managerial Work Behavior: An Integration of Results from Two Major Approaches," *Academy of Management Journal*, June 1985, pp. 344–362.
7. "Turning on the Juice," *Fortune*, August 3, 1987, p. 31.
8. See Henry Mintzberg, *The Nature of Managerial Work* (New York: Harper & Row, 1973); Jay A. Conger and John P. Kotter, "General Managers," in Jay W. Lorsch, ed., *Handbook of Organizational Behavior* (Englewood

Cliffs, N.J.: Prentice-Hall, 1987), pp. 392–404; and Whitely, "Managerial Work Behavior."

9. Mintzberg, *The Nature of Managerial Work*. See also Ford S. Worthy, "How CEOs Manage Their Time," *Fortune*, January 18, 1988, pp. 88–97.

10. Rosemary Stewart, "Middle Managers: Their Jobs and Behaviors," in Lorsch, ed., *Handbook of Organizational Behavior*, pp. 385–391.

11. "Caught in the Middle," *Business Week*, September 12, 1988, pp. 80–88.

12. Rosabeth Moss Kanter, "The Middle Manager as Innovator," *Harvard Business Review*, July–August 1982, pp. 95–105.

13. Steven Kerr, Kenneth D. Hill, and Laurie Broedling, "The First-Line Supervisor: Phasing Out or Here to Stay?" *Academy of Management Review*, January 1986, pp. 103–117; Leonard A. Schlesinger and Janice A. Klein, "The First-Line Supervisor: Past, Present, and Future," in Lorsch, ed., *Handbook of Organizational Behavior*, pp. 358–369.

14. Kirkland Ropp, "HR Management for All It's Worth," *Personnel Administrator*, September 1987, pp. 34–40, 120–121.

15. Mintzberg, *The Nature of Managerial Work*.

16. Robert L. Katz, "The Skills of an Effective Administrator," *Harvard Business Review*, September–October 1974, pp. 90–102.

17. Andrew Kupfer, "How to Be a Global Manager," *Fortune*, March 14, 1988, pp. 52–58.

18. See Gib Akin, "Varieties of Managerial Learning," *Organizational Dynamics*, Autumn 1987, pp. 36–48, for additional insights into how managers learn their skills.

19. "Benefit of B.A. Is Greater Than Ever," *The Wall Street Journal*, August 17, 1988, p. 21.

20. "MBAs Are Hotter Than Ever," *Business Week*, March 9, 1987, pp. 46–48.

21. Ann M. Morrison, "The General Mills Brand of Managers," *Fortune*, January 12, 1981, pp. 98–107.

22. Alex Taylor III, "GE's Hard Driver at NBC," *Fortune*, March 16, 1987, pp. 97–104.

23. "The 50 Leading Exporters," *Fortune*, July 18, 1988, pp. 70–71.

24. James L. Perry and Hal G. Rainey, "The Public-Private Distinction in Organization Theory: A Critique and Research Strategy," *Academy of Management Review*, April 1988, pp. 182–201; see also Ran Lachman, "Public and Private Sector Differences: CEOs' Perceptions of Their Role Environments," *Academy of Management Journal*, September 1985, pp. 671–680.

CASE 1.1

Management Promotes Efficiency and Effectiveness at Marriott

The Marriott Corporation started out as a root-beer stand in Washington, D.C., in the hot summer of 1927. When business fell off that winter, the founder, J. Willard Marriott, responded with a plan to convert the root-beer stand into a "Hot Shoppe," which would serve chili con carne and tamales based on recipes from the Mexican embassy. That plan was so successful that he expanded to other locations. Soon there were Hot Shoppes all over the Washington area. In 1937, the firm again responded to its environment by entering the airline catering business with an Eastern Airlines contract. Success there led to further expansion of catering services.

Not until 1957 did Marriott develop plans to link its success in restaurants and catering to hotels. In 1989, the Marriott Corporation was rated the top major hotel chain for business travelers and meeting planners for the fourth year in a row. Marriott's lodging business continues to grow, too.

J. W. Marriott, Jr., the current chairman of Marriott Corporation, is the son of the founder. He is a perfectionist when it comes to cleanliness and attractiveness. Marriott employees must follow a carefully defined, 54-step procedure in making up a room, doing each step in proper sequence. Bill Marriott also believes in keeping in touch with operations and personnel. He travels over 200,000 miles each year to visit all parts of his firm as well as his competitors' businesses.

The Marriott Corporation does over $6 billion in sales. It is organized into three primary areas: lodging, contract services, and restaurants. Lodging accounts for about 40 percent of sales but about half of profits.

Marriott's lodging operation includes nearly 103,000 guest rooms in over 360 hotels and resorts located throughout the United States, Bermuda, Canada, Central America, Europe, and the Middle East. Those units are organized by location and by the type of market served. For instance, the Fairfield Inn group serves the economy or lower end of the market; Courtyard by Marriott serves the middle of the market; and Residence Inn and Marriott Suites serve the high end of the market.

The contract services part of the firm consists of several groups. One is the Marriott Business Food and Services group, with over 1,000 accounts providing employee cafeterias, executive dining rooms, and conference centers. Another is the airline catering service group, Marriott In-Flight Services. The Host International, Inc., group provides airport and nonairport services and shops. The Marriott Health Care Services group serves about 400 healthcare accounts in hospitals, retirement centers, and nursing homes. The Marriott Education Services group serves nearly 600 college and secondary education clients in student and faculty dining facilities, stadiums, and sports arenas.

Restaurant operations include several groups, too. Hot Shoppes currently exists as 16 cafeterias and service restaurants in the Washington, D.C., area. Bob's Big Boy restaurants has over 200 units. About 150 Howard Johnson units are also operated by Marriott. The Roy Rogers chain operates or franchises over 550 restaurants. And Travel Plazas by Marriott operates over 100 restaurants, gift shops, and related facilities on numerous highway systems.

The Marriott Corporation, as a major aspect of its control function, monitors its environment closely. It has been highly effective in responding to and taking advantage of the changing and expanding role of women in business. Marriott is considered to be one of the most effective organizations in the United States in what is known as competitive intelligence or the art of legally spying on competitors. For instance, before launching its Fairfield Inn chain, Marriott sent a team of six employees around the country for six months. The team stayed in every inexpensive hotel chain in existence, gathering information about such things as the quality of room service provided, the brands of soaps and towels used, and the construction and soundproofing of walls. Using that information, Marriott's Fairfield Inn was able to become the number 1 chain in the economy market in its first year of operation.

The Marriott family owns 21 percent of the stock of the firm and seems destined to control the company for some time. Bill Marriott is the CEO; his mother is a vice president and director; and his brother is vice chairman. In addition, his sons and a son-in-law hold managerial positions in the firm, having worked their ways up from menial jobs that helped them learn the business. This home-grown approach to staffing in management enables the firm to respond quickly to opportunities but also can discourage nonfamily members in their quests for top spots in the firm.

Questions

1. What managerial skills are used by managers in the Marriott Corporation? Cite specific examples. Which of the different parts of the management process can you identify? Cite specific examples.
2. Would you like to work for Marriott? Why or why not? Would you like to have Bill Marriott run a company that you owned? Why or why not?
3. How well has Marriott monitored its environment? How essential is that activity to an organization? Why?
4. What is your reaction to the home-grown approach to developing managers? How do you think managers for companies like Marriott should acquire the skills necessary for effectiveness? Why?

REFERENCES: "Rooms at the Inn," *Fortune*, January 2, 1989, p. 62; Brian Dumaine, "Corporate Spies Snoop to Conquer," *Fortune*, November 7, 1988, pp. 68–76; "Hotels Change Pitch to Businesswomen," *The Wall Street Journal*, October 14, 1988, p. B1; "Keeping Business Costs Down Starting 'Cheap' Hotel Trend," *Bryan–College Station Eagle*, October 29, 1988, p. 30; "A Marriott Kid's Place Is in the Company Kitchen," *Business Week*, April 4, 1988, p. 109.

CASE 1.2

Sotheby's: Bringing Management Techniques to the Art World

Sotheby's Holdings Inc. began in England in 1744 and, like other auction houses, was a place where established families that had fallen on hard times could dispose of property to acquire funds. Indeed, that reputation as a place for "used" goods kept the auction business rather small and undistinguished for over two hundred years.

In the 1970s, as collecting became more fashionable and valuable for investment purposes, things began to change. Then in 1983, Detroit real estate entrepreneur A. Alfred Taubman and a group of investors acquired Sotheby's. Since that time, Sotheby's has acquired a new top-management team with backgrounds in business rather than art and an aggressive managerial style based on a team approach to management. In addition, Sotheby's has a new CEO, Michael L. Ainslie, an M.B.A. who was previously president of the National Trust for Historic Preservation.

Ainslie argues that Sotheby's will be able to survive any downturns in the business with its new managerial approach. Although budgeting, cost control, and other managerial techniques were minimal at best in the past, sophisticated budgeting and planning approaches are now being introduced.

Marketing is also being increased. The usual advertising and direct-mail approaches are being continued but are being supplemented by lectures on collections. Another marketing strategy is the befriending of collectors who might sell objects or assign the disposal of property to Sotheby's in their wills. An enlarged staff is being used to solicit business from bank trust departments, estate attorneys, museum curators, and others who control inventories of art.

Still another change in Sotheby's marketing strategy is the handling of catalogs. In the past, catalogs were delayed until it was certain that every item scheduled to be sold at a given auction would be included. As a result, potential buyers sometimes received a catalog only three days before an auction. Now catalogs are sent out much earlier even if a few items are not listed. Further, the number of potential buyers to whom catalogs are sent has been increased, and catalogs are being offered through bookstores.

These changes in marketing were perhaps best evidenced by the successful sale of the estate of the late pop artist Andy Warhol. The catalog was available a month early and sold in bookstores. The sale itself lasted for ten consecutive days, including a Sunday sale for the general public; and Sotheby's chief auctioneer, John L. Marion, considered the best in the business, ran the sale.

Another relatively standard business practice has also been implemented at Sotheby's—paring the product line. Small-ticket items—valued at less than $1,000—usually contribute very little to either revenues or profits; therefore, the manner in which they are handled has been changed. Most small-ticket items are now assigned to Arcade auctions, which are handled by less experienced, less costly employees of Sotheby's.

Ainslie has also reduced overhead costs and the size of the main office staff. He has also begun performance evaluations in an effort to assure that employees consider not just art but also business. Sotheby's financial services division has begun lending money to collectors who put up their art as collateral.

These changes are paying off. For example, sales are up. In 1987 Sotheby's garnered 58 percent of the combined market share of the two dominant auction houses (the other is Christie's). Sotheby's revenues were about $1.4 billion; those of Christie's were $1 billion. Ainslie claimed that Sotheby's won 75 percent of the named collections that were auctioned in 1988. Profits are also up. After overextending itself in the United States, Sotheby's suffered a loss in 1984, but the managerial changes made the company profitable again in 1985. In 1986, net income was $17 million, and 1987 saw that figure approximately triple.

With the art market trend continuing upward and Japanese buyers entering the marketplace, it is expected that these successes will continue. Sotheby's is not resting on its laurels, however. It has announced plans for the first international art auction to be held in the Soviet Union since the Bolshevik Revolution and has begun expanding into both West Germany and Japan.

Questions

1. Which of the different parts of the management process are apparent at Sotheby's? Cite specific examples. What managerial skills are used by the management of Sotheby's? Cite specific examples.
2. What are the pros and cons of applying mangerial techniques to the art world? Are you in favor of doing so? Why or why not?
3. Is Sotheby's expansion into other countries likely to be successful? Why or why not? What other suggestions could you make to assist the firm in the future?

REFERENCES: "What Am I Bid for a Fast-climbing Auction House?," *Business Week*, April 11, 1988, pp. 86–90; Cathleen McGuigan, "The Selling of Andy Warhol," *Newsweek*, April 18, 1988, pp. 60–64; "Sotheby's Art Market Trends," *Forbes*, July 11, 1988, p. 134; Katrine Ames, Maggie Malone, and Donna Foote, "Sold! The Art Auction Boom," *Newsweek*, April 18, 1988, pp. 65–72; "Art Dealers Are Puttin' on the Glitz," *Business Week*, February 27, 1989, p. 83.

OUTLINE

Why Study History and Theory?
Why Theory? · Why History?

The Historical Context of Management
Understanding Social Forces · Understanding Economic Forces · Understanding Political Forces

Precursors to Management Theory
Management in Antiquity · Early Management Pioneers

The Classical Management Perspective
Scientific Management · Classical Organization Theory · Contributions and Limitations of the Classical Management Perspective

The Behavioral Management Perspective
The Hawthorne Studies · The Human Relations Movement · Organizational Behavior · Contributions and Limitations of the Behavioral Management Perspective

The Quantitative Management Perspective
Management Science · Operations Management · Contributions and Limitations of the Quantitative Management Perspective

Integrating the Major Perspectives
The Systems Approach · The Contingency Approach · An Integrating Framework

Contemporary Management Perspectives
The Global Imperative · The Concern for Excellence · The Concerns for Quality and Productivity

CHAPTER 2

The Evolution of Management Thought

OBJECTIVES

After studying this chapter, you should be able to:

- Justify the use of history and theory in management.

- Explain the historical context of management and discuss precursors to modern management theory.

- Summarize and evaluate classical management theory.

- Summarize and evaluate behavioral management theory.

- Summarize and evaluate quantitative management theory.

- Discuss the systems and contingency approaches to management and explain their potential for integrating the other areas of management.

- Identify and describe contemporary management perspectives.

OPENING INCIDENT

Wells Fargo & Company is a business with a sense of history. The company was established in San Francisco in 1852 to provide banking and express services. The Wells Fargo wagon plays a familiar role in many Western movies and is the title of a popular song from *The Music Man*. The express services branch of the company was moved to New York in 1905 and taken over by the government during World War I. After the war, Wells Fargo decided to concentrate solely on the banking business, and today it is the tenth largest banking-services company in the United States.

Wells Fargo has not forgotten its historic past. The company maintains an extensive archival library of its old banking documents and records and has a full-time corporate historian. This interest in history paid off for Wells Fargo. The company was recently sued for $480 million for allegedly stealing an idea from a competitor about credit-card operations. Historical records, however, demonstrated conclusively that Wells Fargo managers had in fact developed the idea in question.[1]

*M*anagers at Wells Fargo clearly recognize the value of history. They even use historical documents to train new managers just joining the company. This practice helps perpetuate the bank's culture and helps prevent managers from repeating the mistakes of the past. Like Wells Fargo, more and more companies are beginning to see the value of remembering their past.[2] Notable other firms that seek to preserve information about their past and their heritage include Polaroid, Consolidated Edison, AT&T, and Navistar.[3]

This chapter provides an overview of the history and evolution of management thought so that you, too, can better appreciate the importance of history in today's business world. We set the stage by establishing the historical context of management. We then discuss the three major schools of management thought: classical, behavioral, and quantitative. Next we describe the systems and contingency approaches to management theory; these approaches help integrate the three schools of thought. Finally, we discuss several contemporary management perspectives that helped to shape managerial practice in the 1980s and promise to have even more impact in the 1990s.

WHY STUDY HISTORY AND THEORY?

Some people question the value of history and theory. Their arguments are usually based on the assumptions that history has no relevance to

Lincoln Electric in Cleveland has been making good use of scientific management for decades. Lincoln's jobs have been meticulously studied and engineered, and employees are paid on a piece-rate pay system. Employees receive yearly merit ratings, and bonuses based on performance. As a direct result of these incentives, Lincoln's employees are more productive than their counterparts in other companies, and Lincoln itself has not had to lay off any of its employees in over 40 years.

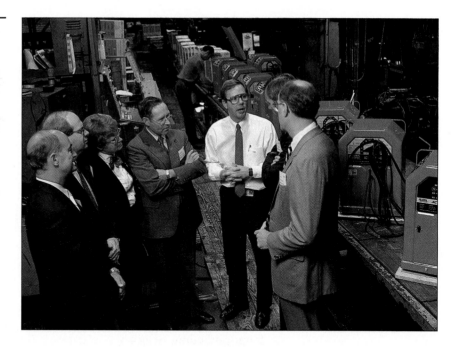

contemporary society and that theory is abstract and of no practical use. This introductory section proposes to demonstrate that knowledge of both theory and history is useful to the practicing manager.

Why Theory?

■ **management theories**
Useful because they help organize information and provide a framework for action

A theory is a conceptual device for organizing knowledge and providing a framework for action. It is a blueprint to help managers build their organizations and a road map to guide them toward their goals. Since management is practiced in the real world, useful **management theories** must always be grounded in reality.[4] It is easy to identify organizations that have explicitly applied different theories of management. Practically any organization that uses assembly lines (such as Bristol-Myers or Weyerhaeuser) is drawing on what we describe later in this chapter as scientific management theory. Numerous organizations, including Kimberly-Clark and Borden, have adopted some aspect of organizational behavior theory to improve employee satisfaction and motivation. And it would be difficult to name a *Fortune* 500 company that does not use one or more techniques from quantitative management theory. Oil companies such as Shell and Texaco, which manage everything from oil fields to gasoline stations while coping with shrinking natural resources, are drawing on systems theory. Universities often use management science models and theories in registration and course scheduling. Firms such as General Foods that establish different management structures for different plants are using contingency theory.

Andrew Grove, CEO of Intel, recognizes the value of theory. He has developed his own operating theory that suggests that organizations need to be agile and responsive. He is working hard to transform Intel into just such a company in accordance with his theory.[5] Many other executives are also using theories either explicitly or implicitly to guide their decisions and actions.

Why History?

As noted in the chapter introduction, awareness and understanding of important historical developments are also important to contemporary managers. Most courses in American history devote substantial amounts of time to business and economic developments in this country, including the Industrial Revolution, the early labor movement, and the Great Depression, and to such captains of American industry as Cornelius Vanderbilt (railroads), John D. Rockefeller (oil), and Andrew Carnegie (steel). The contributions of those and other industrialists left a profound imprint on contemporary culture.[6]

Many managers are also realizing that they can benefit from a greater understanding of history in general. John D. Macomber, former CEO of Celanese, says he learned much about human behavior from *The Adventures of Tom Sawyer*. Ian M. Ross of AT&T Bell Laboratories cites *The Second World War* by Winston Churchill as a major influence on his approach to leadership. Other books often mentioned by managers for their relevance to today's business problems include such classics as Plato's *Republic*, Homer's *Iliad*, and Machiavelli's *The Prince*.[7] Clearly, then, managers believe that they can benefit from a greater understanding of both theory and history.[8]

THE HISTORICAL CONTEXT OF MANAGEMENT

Management thought has been shaped over a period of centuries by three major sets of forces. These forces, as illustrated in Figure 2.1, are social, economic, and political in nature. They continue to affect management theory today.

Understanding Social Forces

social forces The norms and values that characterize the people in a culture

Social forces are the norms and values that characterize the people of any particular culture. Over the years, the changing nature of social forces in the United States has greatly influenced management theory. In the early days of American enterprise, owners generally managed their own companies. As businesses grew, however, professional managers were called in to run them, and organized labor took root. Workers in the larger organizations were often treated with disdain, and bitter strikes polarized management and labor. Vanderbilt proclaimed,

FIGURE 2.1

Forces That Shaped the
Development of Management
Theory

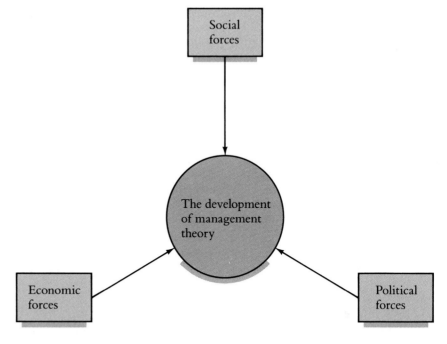

"The public? The public be damned!" Such arrogance would hardly be
tolerated today, but years ago it reflected the power and attitude of
business in our society.

The social contract between workers and the businesses they work
for has changed dramatically over the years. At first, workers were
paid only token wages and worked purely at the whim of their employer. Today's workers, however, have made great strides. Ideas of
liberty and justice in the workplace are becoming increasingly common;
workers are protected by a variety of federal laws; and organizations
themselves are becoming increasingly sensitive to the needs and values
of workers.[9] Changes in these and other social forces have played a
major role in shaping management theories in such areas as motivation,
leadership, and human resource management.

Understanding Economic Forces

economic forces Associated
with economic systems and
general economic conditions
and trends

In similar fashion, **economic forces** have also shaped management
theory. The United States has a market economy based on the principles
of private ownership of property, economic freedom, competitive markets, and a limited role for government. The U.S. market economy
contrasts markedly with planned economies like those in the Soviet
Union and China, where virtually all activities of commerce are heavily
controlled if not owned outright by the government.

Within our economy, the availability of resources, the ease in acquiring those resources, and the kinds of goods and services wanted by

consumers all play a role in dictating what management can do. Moreover, general economic trends and the nature of a firm's competition also greatly affect organizations. The increased competition from other countries in recent years has also played a role. "The Global View" illustrates how the growth of international business has stimulated interest in the historical roots of other economic systems. Within contemporary management theory, economic forces have affected thinking in a variety of areas, including environment analysis, strategic planning, and organization design.

Understanding Political Forces

political forces Governing institutions and general governmental policies and attitudes toward business

The final set of forces that have affected the evolution of management theory are political in nature. **Political forces** associated with governing institutions influence management theory in both general and specific ways. For example, general government policies toward the regulation of business play a significant role in how organizations choose to manage themselves. Management theory regarding companies in highly regulated industries like utilities, for example, varies considerably from parallel theories regarding companies like Sears in less regulated industries such as retailing.

In a more specific case, legal judgments like those handed down against Union Carbide (for its role in the Bhopal, India, catastrophe) and Texaco (for interfering in a previously announced merger between Getty Oil and Pennzoil) have major implications for the management of other organizations. Both general and specific political forces affect management theory in areas like environmental analysis, planning, organization design, employee rights, and control.

PRECURSORS TO MANAGEMENT THEORY

Even though large business firms have been around for only a couple of centuries, management has been practiced for thousands of years. In this section, we describe management in antiquity and then identify important early management pioneers.

Management in Antiquity

The practice of management can be traced back thousands of years. The Egyptians applied the management functions of planning, organizing, and controlling when they constructed the great pyramids. Alexander the Great employed a staff organization to coordinate activities during his military campaigns. The Roman Empire developed a well-defined organizational structure that greatly facilitated communication and control. Management practices and concepts were discussed by Socrates in 400 B.C.; Plato described job specialization in 350 B.C.; and

THE GLOBAL VIEW

THE ROOTS OF MANAGEMENT IN THE FAR EAST

The Far East emerged in the 1980s as a source of managerial ideas. The Five Dragons—Japan, Korea, Taiwan, Hong Kong, and Singapore—are outperforming the United States and Europe according to most economic indicators. "Made in Asia" has come to suggest high-quality, reliable products at low or reasonably low costs. Managers in the West have been working with and studying their counterparts in the Far East to learn the secrets of this success. Many ideas from the Far East have been implemented by organizations in the United States and Europe.

Knowing the origins of the managerial practices of the Far East is useful for understanding the current success of the Five Dragons. Many Japanese businessmen study *A Book of Five Rings* written by a samurai warrior in 1645. The concept of quality circles that surfaced in Japan around 1960 had its origins in the statistical quality-control movement, which began in the United States in the 1920s.

The Far East countries have common cultural roots extending far back in history. Confucian origins have provided a cultural legacy that accounts in part for their business success during the 1980s. Confucius [Kong Fu Ze] was a highly placed civil servant in China around 500 B.C. He became revered for his wisdom, and a group of disciples recorded his every word on scrolls from which they studied and learned. Confucianism has four basic teachings: (1) Unequal relationships between people are normal and required for a stable society. (2) The family is the model for all organizations. (3) Others should be treated in the same manner as one would like to be treated oneself. (4) All people should strive to further their education, work hard, and not spend more than necessary.

Those values, coupled with the emergence of an international marketplace and a political context that fosters economic development, gave rise to the success of the Far East. The blind copying of managerial practices from the Far East without an understanding of the history and culture in which they arose is not likely to be highly successful. Understanding Eastern history and culture, however, may permit Western managers to adopt and adapt Eastern ideas and practices for the betterment of organizations throughout the world.

REFERENCES: David D. Van Fleet and Ricky W. Griffin, "Quality Circles: A Review and Suggested Future Directions," in Cary L. Cooper and Ivan Robertson (Eds.) *1989 International Review of Industrial & Organizational Psychology* (London: Wiley, 1989), pp. 213–233; Geert Hofstede and Michael Harris Bond, "The Confucius Connection: From Cultural Roots to Economic Growth," *Organizational Dynamics*, Summer 1988, pp. 5–21; Miyamoto Musashi, *A Book of Five Rings*, trans. Victor Harris (Woodstock, N.Y.: Overlook Press, 1974).

Alfarabi listed several leadership traits in A.D. 900.[10] Figure 2.2 is a simple time line showing these and other significant management breakthroughs and practices.

Yet, business management was not considered a serious field of study for several centuries. One reason for the lack of attention was that the first discipline devoted to commerce was economics. Economists generally assumed that managerial practice was efficient, and they therefore focused their attention on national economic policies and other nonmanagerial aspects of business. Another reason is that there were very few large organizations until the late 1800s. When family businesses first emerged, their goal was not growth or expansion but survival. If a family could produce and sell enough to sustain itself, nothing else was needed. Finally, even though management was practiced during earliest recorded history, the focus even then was not on efficiency.

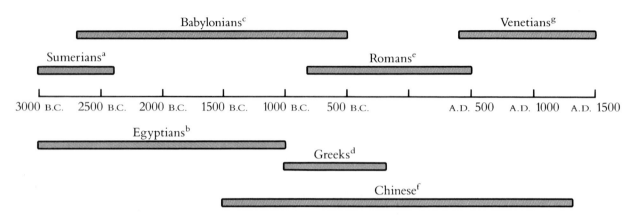

^aUsed written rules and regulations for governance.
^bUsed management practices to construct pyramids.
^cUsed extensive set of laws and policies for governance.
^dUsed different governing systems for cities and state.
^eUsed organization structure for communication and control.
^fUsed extensive organization structure for government agencies and the arts.
^gUsed organization design and planning concepts to control the seas.

FIGURE 2.2

Management in Antiquity

Organizations like the Roman Empire were essentially governmental, with unlimited powers of taxation and little accountability for waste.

Early Management Pioneers

The study of management from a scientific perspective did not begin to develop until the nineteenth century. Two of the earliest pioneers in management theory and research were Robert Owen and Charles Babbage.[11] Robert Owen (1771–1858), a British industrialist and reformer, was one of the first managers to recognize the importance of an organization's human resources. Until his era, factory workers were generally regarded and discussed in much the same terms as machinery and equipment. A factory owner himself, Owen recognized that people deserved more respect and dignity. Accordingly, he incorporated such "radical" innovations as improved working conditions, a higher minimum working age for children, meals for employees, and reduced work hours. He assumed that giving more attention to workers would pay off in increased output. Owen was a pioneer in humane business practice. Although no one followed his lead at the time, his ideas were later developed in behavioral management theory.

Whereas Owen was primarily interested in employee welfare, Charles Babbage (1792–1871), an English mathematician, focused his attention on efficiencies of production. His primary contribution is his book *On the Economy of Machinery and Manufactures*.[12] Babbage placed great faith in division of labor and advocated the application of mathematics to such problems as the efficient use of facilities and materials. In a sense, his work was a forerunner of both classical management theory and quantitative management theory. Nor did he overlook the human element. He understood that a harmonious relationship between management and labor could serve to benefit both, and he favored such devices as profit-sharing plans. In many ways, Babbage was an originator of modern management theory and practice.[13]

In addition to these visionaries, a few other early pioneers deserve mention. Andrew Ure was one of the world's first professors to teach management principles, in the early seventeenth century at Anderson's College in Glasgow. Charles Dupin soon followed suit in France. Daniel McCallum developed several basic principles of management and published one of the first organization charts. In the late nineteenth century, Henry Poor wrote extensively about management inefficiencies in the railroad industry. Poor was the Ralph Nader of his era.[14]

THE CLASSICAL MANAGEMENT PERSPECTIVE

The classical management perspective is a label applied to the beliefs about management that emerged during the early years of this century—ideas that represent the first well-developed framework of management. The emergence of these ideas was a natural outgrowth of both the pioneering earlier works noted above and the evolution of large-scale business and management practices. **Classical management theory** actually includes two different approaches to management: scientific management and classical organization theory.

■ **classical management theory**   Consists of two distinct branches—scientific management and classical organization theory

Scientific Management

Scientific management is concerned with the management of work and workers. It grew from the pioneering research of five people: Frederick W. Taylor (1856–1915), Frank Gilbreth (1868–1924), Lillian Gilbreth (1878–1972), Henry Gantt (1861–1919), and Harrington Emerson (1853–1931). Taylor played the dominant role.[15] As you will see, scientific management has a strong industrial engineering flavor.

■ **scientific management**   The management of work and workers

Frederick W. Taylor   At the beginning of the twentieth century, there was considerable concern about productivity. Business was expanding and capital was readily available, but labor was in short supply. Hence, a primary goal of management was to use existing labor more efficiently. Frederick Taylor was very much interested in developing solutions to the problem of labor inefficiency.

One of Taylor's first jobs was as a foreman at the Midvale Steel Company in Philadelphia, where he developed a strong dislike for waste and inefficiency. At Midvale he observed what he called **soldiering**— a situation in which employees deliberately worked at a slow pace because they feared that if all the work was completed they would be laid off. Managers were unaware of this practice because they had never

soldiering   A situation in which employees deliberately work at a slow pace

Frederick W. Taylor was a pioneer in the field of labor efficiency. He introduced innovations that resulted in higher quality products and improved employee morale. Taylor formulated the basic ideas of scientific management.

analyzed the jobs closely enough to determine how much the employees should be producing.

Taylor observed and timed each element of the steelworkers' jobs. He determined what each worker should be producing, and then he designed the most efficient way of doing each part of the overall task. Next he implemented a piece-rate pay system. Rather than paying all employees the same wage, he began increasing the pay of each worker who met and exceeded the target level of output set for his or her job.[16]

After Taylor left Midvale, he worked for several years as an independent consultant for several companies, including Simonds Rolling Machine Company and Bethlehem Steel. At Simonds he studied and redesigned jobs, introduced rest periods to reduce fatigue, and converted to a differential pay scale. The results were higher quality and quantity of output and improved morale. At Bethlehem Steel, Taylor studied efficient ways of loading and unloading rail cars and applied his conclusions with equally impressive results.

During these experiences, he formulated the basic ideas that were eventually called scientific management. Figure 2.3 illustrates the general steps Taylor suggested. He believed that managers who followed his guidelines would greatly improve the efficiency of their workers.[17]

Taylor's work had a significant impact on American industry. By applying his principles and similar approaches to job specialization, manufacturing organizations came to rely heavily on mass-production techniques. Taylor was not without his detractors, however. Labor argued that scientific management was just a device to get more work from each employee and to reduce the total number of workers needed by a firm. There was a congressional investigation into Taylor's methods, and there is fairly convincing evidence suggesting that Taylor falsified some of his findings and that some of his writing was done by someone else.[18] Nevertheless, Taylor's mark on American society can still be seen today.[19]

The Gilbreths   Frank and Lillian Gilbreth were a husband-wife team of industrial engineers. They were primarily interested in time-and-motion study and job simplification, although Lillian Gilbreth was also concerned with the welfare of the worker. Her doctoral dissertation, dealing with human factors in business, was published in *Industrial Engineering Magazine* in 1912 (the publisher listed her name as L. M. Gilbreth to hide the fact that she was a woman).

One of Frank Gilbreth's most interesting contributions was to the craft of bricklaying. Gilbreth was surprised to find that, even though bricklaying dated back thousands of years, there was no generally accepted technique for doing it. After studying bricklayers at work, he developed procedures for doing the job more efficiently. He specified standard materials and techniques, including the positioning of the bricklayer, the bricks, and the mortar at different levels. He assigned to less expensive laborers the job of carrying bricks to the scaffold and stacking them "best edge up" (something the bricklayers had formerly done themselves). Finally, Gilbreth developed a standard mortar for-

FIGURE 2.3

Steps in Scientific Management

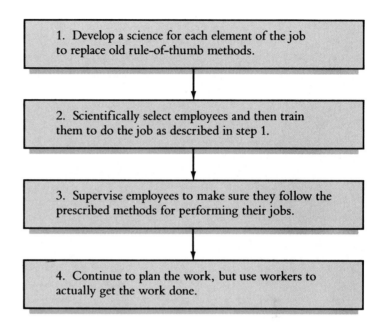

1. Develop a science for each element of the job to replace old rule-of-thumb methods.

2. Scientifically select employees and then train them to do the job as described in step 1.

3. Supervise employees to make sure they follow the prescribed methods for performing their jobs.

4. Continue to plan the work, but use workers to actually get the work done.

mula to ensure consistency. The results of these changes were a reduction in separate physical movements from 18 to 5 and an increase in output of about 200 percent.

Working individually and together, Frank and Lillian Gilbreth developed numerous techniques and strategies for eliminating inefficiency. They applied many of their ideas to their family. Their experiences in raising twelve children are documented in a book and movie called *Cheaper by the Dozen*.

Henry Gantt   Henry Gantt was an associate of Taylor at Midvale, Simonds, and Bethlehem Steel. Later, working alone, he developed two specific techniques for improving worker output. First he developed the Gantt chart. A Gantt chart is essentially a means of scheduling work and can be generated for each worker or for a complex project as a whole. Variations on Gantt charts are still used today. Gantt's second major contribution dealt with pay systems. Under Taylor's differential rate system, a worker's pay was tied entirely to output. Workers who produced a lot made a reasonable wage. If nothing was produced during the day, no wage was earned. Gantt believed that workers were entitled to some minimum wage, and this belief was reflected in his pay system. Workers who produced at the minimum level or below were paid a certain fixed wage. Workers whose productivity exceeded the minimum level were paid a bonus on top of the fixed wage. Gantt extended the system to reward supervisors whose employees exceeded the minimum productivity levels.

Harrington Emerson   Like Taylor, the Gilbreths, and Gantt, Harrington Emerson was one of the first management consultants. He made quite a stir in 1910 when he appeared before the Interstate Commerce Commission to testify about a rate increase requested by the railroads. As an expert witness, Emerson asserted that the railroads could save $1 million a day by practicing scientific management. Emerson was also a strong advocate of specialized management roles within organizations. His argument was based on his observations of the efficiency of military organizations.

Classical Organization Theory

classical organization theory
Focuses on managing the total organization

Whereas scientific management deals with the jobs of individual employees, **classical organization theory** focuses on managing the total organization. Classical organization theory was the precursor of contemporary organization theory. The primary contributors to classical organization theory were Henri Fayol (1841–1925), Lyndall Urwick (1891–1983), Max Weber (1864–1920), and Chester Barnard (1886–1961).

Henri Fayol   Fayol was the Frederick Taylor of classical organization theory: He offered the most definitive statements and made the greatest contributions to this area of management thought. A French industrialist, Fayol was unknown to American managers and scholars until his most significant work, *General and Industrial Management*, was translated into English in 1930.[20] Drawing on over fifty years of his own managerial experience, he attempted to systematize the practice of management to provide guidance and direction to other managers. Part of his thinking was expressed in fourteen principles, or guidelines, for effective management. These are listed in Table 2.1.

Fayol did not intend this list to be exhaustive; the principles simply reflect procedures that he found useful. Other managers before Fayol had probably practiced many of these principles, but Fayol has the distinction of being the first to formalize them. Fayol also was the first to identify the specific managerial functions of planning, organizing, leading, and controlling. He felt that these functions accurately reflect the core of the management process. Most contemporary management books (including this one) still use this framework, and most practicing managers are familiar with this description of their jobs.

Lyndall Urwick   After a career as a British army officer, Lyndall Urwick became a noted management theorist and consultant. He tried to synthesize and integrate scientific management with the work of Fayol and other classical organization theorists. He further advanced modern thinking about the management functions of planning, organizing, and controlling. Like Fayol, he developed a list of general guidelines for improving managerial effectiveness. Urwick is noted not so much for his own contributions as for his synthesis and integration of the work of others.

TABLE 2.1

Fayol's Guidelines for Effective
Management Practice

Division of labor. A high degree of specialization should result in efficiency. Both managerial and technical work are amenable to specialization.

Authority. Authority is needed to carry out managerial responsibilities: the formal authority to command and personal authority deriving from intelligence and experience.

Discipline. People in the organization must respect the rules that govern the organization.

Unity of command. Each subordinate should report to one and only one superior.

Unity of direction. Similar activities in an organization should be grouped together under one manager.

Subordination of individuals to the common good. Interests of individuals should not be placed before the goals of the overall organization.

Remuneration. Compensation should be fair both to employees and to the organization.

Centralization. Power and authority should be concentrated at the upper levels of the organization as much as possible.

Scalar chain. A chain of authority should extend from the top to the bottom of the organization and should be followed at all times.

Order. Human and material resources should be coordinated so that they are in the required place at the required time.

Equity. Managers should be kind and fair when dealing with subordinates.

Stability. High turnover of employees should be avoided.

Initiative. Subordinates should have the freedom to take initiative.

Esprit de corps. Teamwork, team spirit, and a sense of unity and togetherness should be fostered and maintained.

Source: Based on information in Henri Fayol, *Industrial and General Management*, trans. J. A. Coubrough (Geneva: International Management Institute, 1930).

Max Weber   Although Max Weber lived and worked at the same time as Fayol and Taylor, his contributions were not recognized until some years had passed. Weber was a German sociologist, and his most significant work was not translated into English until 1947.[21] Weber's work on bureaucracy laid the foundation for contemporary organization theory, discussed in detail in Chapter 9. The concept of bureaucracy, as we shall see, is based on a rational set of guidelines for structuring organizations in the most efficient manner.

Chester Barnard Chester Barnard, former president of New Jersey Bell Telephone Company, made significant contributions to management in his book *The Functions of the Executive*.[22] In it he proposed a theory about the acceptance of authority. This theory holds that subordinates weigh the legitimacy of a supervisor's directives and then decide whether to accept them. An order is accepted if the subordinate understands it, is able to comply with it, and views it as appropriate given the goals of the organization. The importance of Barnard's work is enhanced by his experience as a top manager.

Contributions and Limitations of the Classical Management Perspective

The contributions and limitations of the classical management perspective are summarized in Table 2.2. Classical management theory is the framework from which later theorists have worked, and many insights derived from it still hold true today. Also, management theorists were the first to focus attention on management as a meaningful field of study. Several aspects of classical management theory will be important when we consider planning (Chapters 4–7), organizing (Chapters 8–11), and controlling (Chapters 16–19).

However, the limitations of classical management theory should not be overlooked. The theory dealt with stable, simple organizations; many organizations today, in contrast, are changing and complex. It proposed universal guidelines that do not fit every organization. Those two drawbacks have been countered by recent developments in quantitative methods, systems theory, and contingency theory. A third limitation of classical management theory is that it slighted the role of the individual in organizations. This role was much more fully developed by the behavioral management perspective.

THE BEHAVIORAL MANAGEMENT PERSPECTIVE

To one degree or another, the developers of classical management theory viewed organizations and jobs from a mechanistic point of view—that is, they thought of organizations as machines and workers as cogs within those machines. Even though most classical management theorists recognized the role of individuals, they focused on controlling and standardizing the behavior of individuals. By contrast, **behavioral management theory** placed much more emphasis on individual attitudes and behaviors and on group processes. It recognized the importance of behavioral processes in the workplace.

Behavioral management theory was stimulated by a number of writers and theoretical movements. One of those movements was industrial psychology, the practice of applying psychological concepts to indus-

behavioral management theory Emphasizes individual attitudes and behaviors and group processes

TABLE 2.2

The Classical Management
Perspective

General Summary	Classical management theory had two primary thrusts. Scientific management focused on employees within organizations and on ways to improve their productivity. Noted pioneers of scientific management were Frederick Taylor, Frank and Lillian Gilbreth, Henry Gantt, and Harrington Emerson. Classical organization theory focused on the total organization and on ways to make it more efficient and effective. Prominent classical organization theorists were Henri Fayol, Lyndall Urwick, Max Weber, and Chester Barnard.
Period of Greatest Interest	1895 to mid-1930s; renewed interest in recent years as a means of cutting costs and increasing productivity.
Contributions	Laid the foundation for later developments in management theory. Identified key management processes, functions, and skills that are still recognized as such today. Focused attention on management as a valid subject of scientific inquiry.
Limitations	More appropriate for stable and simple organizations than for today's dynamic and complex organizations. Often prescribed universal procedures that are not really appropriate in some settings. Even though some writers (such as Lillian Gilbreth and Chester Barnard) were concerned with the human element, many viewed employees as tools rather than resources.

trial settings. Hugo Munsterberg (1863–1916), a noted German psychologist, is recognized as the father of industrial psychology. He established a psychological laboratory at Harvard in 1892, and his pioneering book *Psychology and Industrial Efficiency* was translated into English in 1913.[23] Munsterberg suggested that psychologists could make empirically valuable contributions to managers in the areas of selection and motivation. Industrial psychology is still a major course of study at many colleges and universities.

Another early advocate of the behavioral school of thought was Mary Parker Follett.[24] Follett worked and wrote during the scientific management era, but she anticipated behavioral management theory and appreciated the need to understand the role of behavior in organizations. In particular, she was interested in adult education and vocational guid-

Quaker State Minit-Lube managers recognize the value of their employees, so they place a lot of emphasis on employee attitudes and behaviors. They believe in behavioral management theory, and recognize the importance of behavioral processes in the workplace.

Quaker State sponsors an annual contest to identify the best team of technicians from its stores. The champions were feted at a banquet and their individual accomplishments were recognized by Quaker State when each winner's name and home town was announced over the PA system.

ance. She felt that organizations should become more democratic in accommodating employees and managers.

The Hawthorne Studies

Munsterberg and Follett made significant contributions to the development of behavioral management theory, but the primary catalyst for this movement was a series of studies conducted near Chicago at the Hawthorne plant of Western Electric by Elton Mayo and his associates between 1927 and 1932.[25] (The research was originally supported by General Electric, although the company soon withdrew its sponsorship.) Mayo was a faculty member and consultant at Harvard. The first experiment in what have come to be known as the Hawthorne studies involved manipulating illumination for one group of workers and comparing subsequent productivity in that group with productivity in another group whose illumination was not changed. Surprisingly, when illumination was increased for the experimental group, productivity went up in both groups. Productivity continued to increase in both groups, even when the lighting for the experimental group was decreased. Not until the lighting was reduced to the level of moonlight did productivity begin to decline (and it was at this point that General Electric withdrew).

Another experiment established a piecework incentive pay plan for a group of nine men assembling terminal banks for telephone exchanges. According to classical management theory, every man should try to maximize his pay by producing as many units as possible. Mayo and his associates found otherwise. In particular, they found that the social group informally established an acceptable level of output for its mem-

The Hawthorne studies were a series of early experiments in behavioral management. For example, in one experiment working conditions were manipulated and productivity was monitored. The Hawthorne studies and subsequent experiments led scientists to the conclusion that the human element is very important in the workplace.

bers. Workers who overproduced were branded "rate busters," and underproducers were labeled "chiselers." To be accepted by the group, workers had to produce at the accepted level. As they approached this level, workers slacked off to avoid overproducing.

Other studies (and an interview program involving several thousand workers) led Mayo and his associates to conclude that the human element was much more important in the workplace than previous theorists had realized. In the lighting experiment, for example, the peculiar results were attributed to the fact that both groups of participants received special attention and sympathetic supervision for perhaps the first time. The incentive pay plans did not work because wage incentives were less important than social acceptance in determining output. In short, individual and social processes played a major role in shaping worker attitudes and behavior.[26]

The Human Relations Movement

human relations movement
Argued that workers respond primarily to the social context of the workplace

The **human relations movement** grew from the Hawthorne studies and was a popular approach to management for many years. The human relations view proposed that workers respond primarily to the social context of the workplace, including social conditioning, sentiments, and the interpersonal situation at work. An underlying assumption of the human relations movement was that management concern for the worker would lead to increased satisfaction, which would, in turn, result in improved performance.[27] Two early writers who helped advance the human relations movement were Abraham Maslow and Douglas McGregor.

In 1943, Maslow advanced a theory suggesting that people are motivated by a sequence of needs, including monetary incentives and social acceptance.[28] Maslow's theory of "hierarchical needs" was a primary factor in the increased attention that managers began to give to the work of academic theorists. Maslow's theory is described in detail in Chapter 12.

Whereas Maslow's theory was one of the first in the emerging area of human relations, Douglas McGregor's Theory X and Theory Y perhaps best represent the essence of the human relations movement (see Table 2.3).[29] According to McGregor, Theory X and Theory Y reflect two extreme philosophies that different managers take regarding their workers. **Theory X** is a relatively pessimistic and negative view of workers—it is quite compatible with scientific management. **Theory Y** is more positive and represents the assumptions that human relations advocates make. In McGregor's view, Theory Y was a more appropriate philosophy for managers to adhere to. Both Maslow and McGregor significantly influenced the thinking of many practicing managers.

Theory X   A pessimistic and negative view of workers

Theory Y   Represents the assumptions that human relations advocates make

TABLE 2.3

Theory X and Theory Y

Theory X Assumptions	1. People do not like work and try to avoid it.
	2. People do not like work, so managers have to control, direct, coerce, and theaten employees to get them to work toward organizational goals.
	3. People prefer to be directed, to avoid responsibility, to want security; they have little ambition.
Theory Y Assumptions	1. People do not naturally dislike work; work is a natural part of their lives.
	2. People are internally motivated to reach objectives to which they are committed.
	3. People are committed to goals to the degree that they receive personal rewards when they reach their objectives.
	4. People will both seek and accept responsibility under favorable conditions.
	5. People have the capacity to be innovative in solving organizational problems.
	6. People are bright, but under most organizational conditions their potentials are underutilized.

SOURCE: Douglas McGregor, *The Human Side of Enterprise* (New York: McGraw-Hill, 1960), pp. 33–34, 47–48. Used with permission of the publisher.

Organizational Behavior

Munsterberg, Mayo, Maslow, McGregor, and others have made valuable contributions to management. Contemporary theorists, however, have noted that many assertions of the human relationists were simplistic, inadequate descriptions of work behavior. For example, the assumption that worker satisfaction leads to improved performance has been shown to have little, if any, validity.[30] If anything, satisfaction follows good performance rather than preceding it (these issues are addressed in Chapter 12).

Contemporary behavioral management theory, generally referred to as organizational behavior, acknowledges that behavior is much more complex than the human relationists realized. The field of organizational behavior draws from a broad, interdisciplinary base of psychology, sociology, anthropology, economics, and medicine. Organizational behavior theorists take a holistic view of behavior by considering individual, group, and organization processes.[31]

Organizational behavior is an important element in contemporary management theory. Topics of current interest to people in this field include job satisfaction, stress, motivation, leadership, group dynamics, communication, organizational politics, interpersonal conflict, and the structure and design of organizations. A contingency orientation (discussed more fully later in this chapter) also characterizes the field. Finally, it emphasizes the potential application of research findings. Our discussions of organizing (Chapters 8–11) and leading (Chapters 12–15) are heavily influenced by concepts of organizational behavior.[32]

Contributions and Limitations of the Behavioral Management Perspective

Table 2.4 summarizes the behavioral management perspective and lists its contributions and limitations. The primary contributions relate to ways in which this theory has changed managerial thinking. Managers are now more likely to recognize the importance of behavioral processes and to view employees as valuable resources rather than mere tools. On the other hand, organizational behavior is still very imprecise in its predictions. It is not always accepted or understood by practicing managers, partly because behavioral scholars tend to use technical terms and unfamiliar buzz words. Hence the contributions of the behavioral school have yet to be fully realized.

THE QUANTITATIVE MANAGEMENT PERSPECTIVE

Of the three major schools of management thought, quantitative management theory is the newest. Classical management theory was born

TABLE 2.4

The Behavioral Management
Perspective

General Summary	Behavioral management theory focuses on employee behavior in an organizational context. Stimulated by the birth of industrial psychology, the human relations movement supplanted scientific management as the dominant approach to management in the 1930s and 1940s. Prominent contributors to this movement were Elton Mayo, Abraham Maslow, and Douglas McGregor. Organizational behavior, the contemporary perspective on behavioral management theory, draws from an interdisciplinary base and recognizes the complexities of human behavior in organizational settings.
Period of Greatest Interest	Human relations enjoyed its peak of acceptance from 1931 to the late 1940s. Organizational behavior emerged in the late 1950s and is presently of great interest to researchers and managers.
Contributions	Provided important insights into motivation, group dynamics, and other interpersonal processes in organizations. Focused managerial attention on these same processes. Challenged the view that employees are tools and furthered the belief that employees are valuable resources.
Limitations	The complexity of individual behavior makes prediction of that behavior difficult. Many behavioral concepts have not yet been put to use because some managers are reluctant to adopt them. Contemporary research findings by behavioral scientists are often not communicated to practicing managers in an understandable form.

in the early years of this century, and behavioral management theory began to emerge in the 1920s and 1930s. Quantitative management theory was not fully developed until early in World War II. During that era, managers, government officials, and scientists were brought together in England and the United States to help the military deploy its resources more efficiently and effectively. Led by experts like Professor P. M. S. Blackett, these groups took some of the mathematical approaches to management developed decades earlier by Taylor and Gantt and applied them to logistical problems during the war.[33] Decisions regarding troop, equipment, and submarine deployment were all amenable to mathematical analysis.

quantitative management theory   Applies quantitative techniques to managerial problem solving and decision making situations

After the war, consulting firms like Arthur D. Little, Inc., and industrial firms such as Du Pont and General Electric began to use the same techniques for deploying employees, choosing plant locations, and planning warehouses. Basically, then, **quantitative management theory** applies quantitative techniques to managerial problem solving and decision making. More specifically, quantitative management focuses on decision making, economic effectiveness, formal mathematical models, and the use of electronic computers. In general there are two interrelated branches of the quantitative approach: management science and operations management.

Management Science

Unfortunately, the term management science sounds very much like scientific management, the approach developed by Taylor and others early in this century. But the two have little in common and should not be confused. **Management science** focuses specifically on the development of mathematical models. A mathematical model is a simplified representation of a system, process, or relationship.

management science   Focuses specifically on the development of mathematical models

In its early years, management science focused specifically on models, equations, and similar representations of reality. For example, managers at Detroit Edison used mathematical models to determine how best to route repair crews during blackouts. The Bank of New England used other models to figure out how many tellers needed to be on duty at each location at various times throughout the day.

In recent years, paralleling the advent of the personal computer, management science techniques have become more sophisticated. For example, Hughes Aircraft has constructed very complex and realistic computer simulations to help engineers at General Motors design better instrument panels for automobiles.[34]

Operations Management

operations management   Concerned with helping the organization more efficiently produce its products or services

Operations management is somewhat less mathematical and statistically sophisticated than management science and can be applied more directly to managerial situations. In fact, we can think of **operations management** as a form of applied management science. Operations management techniques are generally concerned with helping the organization produce its products or services more efficiently and can be applied to a wide range of problems.[35]

For example, Rubbermaid and Home Depot use operations management techniques to manage their inventories (inventory management is concerned with specific inventory problems such as balancing carrying costs and ordering costs and determining the optimal order quantity). Linear programming (which involves computing simultaneous solutions to a set of linear equations) helps United Airlines plan its flight schedules, Consolidated Freightways develop its shipping routes, and General Instrument Company plan what instruments to produce at various times.

Other techniques of operations management include network modeling, queuing theory, breakeven analysis, and simulation. All of these techniques and procedures apply directly to operations, but they are also helpful in such areas as finance, marketing, and human resource management. We touch on these techniques in Chapters 4 and 19. The concepts are more fully integrated in the in-depth discussion of operations management in Chapter 17.

Contributions and Limitations of the Quantitative Management Perspective

Like the other management perspectives, quantitative management theory has made significant contributions and has certain limitations. Both are summarized in Table 2.5. Quantitative management theory has provided the manager with an abundance of decision-making tools and techniques and has increased understanding of overall organizational processes. It has been particularly useful in the areas of planning and controlling. On the other hand, mathematical models cannot fully account for individual behaviors and attitudes. Some believe that the time needed to develop competence in quantitative techniques retards the development of other managerial skills. Finally, mathematical models typically require a set of assumptions that may not be realistic.

An important point to keep in mind is that the classical, behavioral, and quantitative approaches to management are not necessarily contradictory or mutually exclusive. Even though some inconsistent assumptions and predictions are made by the three perspectives, they can actually complement each other. Indeed, a complete understanding of management requires an appreciation of the basic tenets of all three schools.

INTEGRATING THE MAJOR PERSPECTIVES

Systems theory and contingency theory are relative newcomers to the field of management. These theories are not yet supported by enough research, practice, and acceptance to qualify as distinct schools of thought, but they can help us integrate the classical, behavioral, and quantitative management theories and can enlarge our understanding of all three.

TABLE 2.5

The Quantitative Management
Perspective

General Summary	Quantitative management theory focuses on applying mathematical models and processes to management situations. Management science specifically deals with the development of mathematical models to aid in decision making and problem solving. Operations management focuses more directly on the application of management science to organizations. Management information systems are systems developed to provide information to managers.
Period of Greatest Interest	1940s to present.
Contributions	The development of sophisticated quantitative techniques to assist in decision making. Application of models has increased our awareness and understanding of complex organizational processes and situations. Has been very useful in the planning and controlling processes.
Limitations	Cannot fully explain or predict the behavior of people in organizations. Mathematical sophistication may come at the expense of other important skills. Models may require unrealistic or unfounded assumptions.

The Systems Approach

■ **system**   An interrelated set of elements functioning as a whole

We briefly introduced systems theory in Chapter 1 in our discussion of the definition of management. A **system** can be defined as an interrelated set of elements functioning as a whole.[36] As shown in Figure 2.4, an organizational system consists of four basic elements: inputs, transformation processes, outputs, and feedback. First, inputs enter the system from the environment. Material, human, financial, and information inputs are the most important for organizations. Next, through technological and managerial processes, the inputs undergo a transformation. Outputs are then produced in the form of a product or service (note that an abstract "product" such as aesthetic pleasure in an art gallery is just as meaningful from a managerial viewpoint as an automobile or a tube of toothpaste), profits or losses (even not-for-profit organizations such as hospitals and universities must operate within their budgets), employee behaviors (relevant to jobs), and information. Finally, the environment reacts to these outputs and provides feedback to the system.

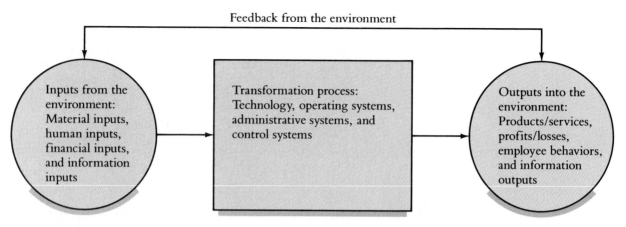

FIGURE 2.4

The Systems View of
Organizations

open systems   Interact with
their environment

closed systems   Do not interact with their environment

subsystem   A system within
another system

synergy   Two subsystems
working together to produce
more than the total of what
they might produce working
alone

Four especially useful ideas that managers can glean from systems
theory are the concepts of open versus closed systems, subsystems and
interdependencies, synergy, and entropy. **Open systems** are systems
that interact with their environment; **closed systems** do not. All organizations are open systems, although the degree of interaction may
vary. A potentially costly mistake that organizations sometimes make
is to assume that they can afford to ignore the environment. The big
U.S. auto companies made this mistake when they chose to ignore the
Japanese import threat for several years. When GM, Ford, and Chrysler
woke and recognized that consumers would indeed buy high-mileage,
high-quality cars even if the nameplate said Nissan or Toyota, it was
almost too late. Managers must be constantly on the lookout for environmental forces that might affect the organization.

Another primary assumption of systems theory is that systems are
made up of elements called subsystems. A **subsystem** is actually a
system within a system. For example, the marketing, production, and
finance functions within Mattel can be thought of as subsystems, but
they are also systems in their own right. Because these subsystems are
interdependent, a change in one subsystem affects other subsystems as
well. If the production department lowers the quality of the toys being
made by Mattel (by buying lower-quality materials, for example), the
effects are felt in finance (improved cash flow in the short run due to
lower costs), marketing (decreased sales in the long run due to customer
dissatisfaction), and perhaps personnel (increased turnover due to workers' loss of pride in work). Organizational subsystems can be managed
with some degree of autonomy, but their interdependence should not
be overlooked.

Synergy is the notion that the whole is greater than the sum of its
parts. Two people, each working alone, may be unable to lift a weight.
Together, however, they may find that lifting the weight is easy. Similarly, organizational units may often be more successful working together than working alone. American Express, for example, has been

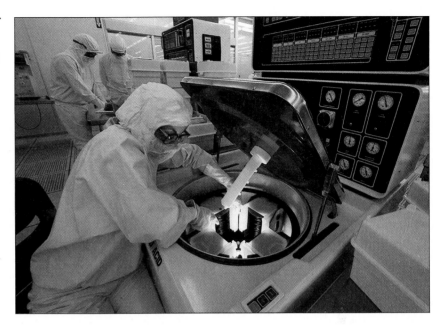

The Harris Semiconductor Sector, a division of Harris Corporation, integrates numerous management theories in its operations. It uses employee work teams trained in quantitative methods to solve a variety of quality-related problems. Employee rewards are a combination of financial incentives and motivational inducements tied to promotion opportunities and skill building. Groups are encouraged to exercise creativity and are given considerable autonomy over how they do their jobs. As a result, Harris has achieved several dramatic breakthroughs in both product quality and product delivery time.

quite successful at cross-selling among its life-insurance, credit-card, stock-brokerage, and financial-planning divisions.[37] Synergy is an important concept for managers because it emphasizes the importance of working together in a cooperative and coordinated fashion.

entropy   A normal process leading to system decline

Entropy is a normal process that leads to system decline. When any system, including an organizational system, does not monitor feedback from the environment and make appropriate adjustments, the system may fail. Witness the problems of Studebaker, W. T. Grant, and Penn Central Railroad. Each of these organizations went bankrupt because it failed to revitalize itself and keep pace with changes in its environment. A primary objective of management, from a systems perspective, is to continually re-energize the organization in order to avoid entropy.

The Contingency Approach

■ **contingency theory**   Suggests that appropriate managerial behavior in a given situation depends on, or is contingent on, a wide variety of elements

The other important recent addition to management theory is the contingency approach. Essentially, **contingency theory** suggests that appropriate managerial behavior in a given situation depends on, or is contingent on, a wide variety of elements.[38] Appropriate behavior cannot always be generalized or extrapolated from other situations. Recall, for example, that Frederick Taylor assumed that all workers would generate the highest possible level of output because doing so would maximize their own personal economic gain. We can imagine some people being motivated primarily by money—but we can just as easily image other people being motivated by the desire for leisure time, status, social acceptance, or any combination of these (as Mayo found at the Hawthorne plant).

A good illustration of the importance of the contingency approach is given in "Management in Practice." In particular, note how Jim Treybig found one style of management to be effective when Tandem Computers was a small company but found it necessary to change his approach when the organization grew into a big company. A few years ago, People Express learned the same lesson—but too late. The firm grew too quickly for its small, laid-back management team and was eventually swallowed by giant Texas Air.[39]

universal approach An at-tempt to identify the one best way to do something

The classical, behavioral, and quantitative perspectives originally tried to find the "one best way" to solve management problems. These approaches, then, were **universal** in orientation. The contingency per-spective holds that universal solutions and principles cannot be applied to social systems such as organizations. Hence, the manager must con-sider as many relevant elements (contingencies) as possible in every new situation. Contingency relationships are considered throughout this book.

An Integrating Framework

We have said that the classical, behavioral, and quantitative schools of management thought are complementary rather than contradictory and that the systems and contingency perspectives can help integrate the three schools. Our framework for relating the various approaches to management is shown in Figure 2.5.

The initial premise of the framework is that the manager, before attempting to apply any concepts or ideas from the three schools of management thought, must recognize the interdependence of units within the organization, the effect of environmental influences, and the need to respond to the unique characteristics of each situation that arises. The ideas of system and subsystem interdependencies and environmen-tal influences foreshadow the importance of a systems perspective, whereas the situational view of management is a prelude to a contin-gency orientation.

With these ideas as basic assumptions, the manager may make use of all the valid tools, techniques, concepts, and theories of the classical, behavioral, and quantitative schools of thought. Armed with classical management theory, organizations can profit from a scientific approach to management. Of course, they should not fall victim to the pitfalls and problems associated with a strict and narrow interpretation of these early ideas. In many contemporary settings, however, the scientific study of jobs and production techniques can enhance efficiency and productivity.

Behavioral management theory is also of use to modern managers. By drawing on the contemporary ideas of organizational behavior, the manager can better appreciate the importance of employee needs and

MANAGEMENT IN PRACTICE

TANDEM COMPUTERS AND CONTINGENCY MANAGEMENT

Tandem Computers was formed in the mid-1970s by Jim Treybig, formerly a manager at Hewlett-Packard. Treybig had innovative ideas about both products and processes. His product was essentially two computers operating in tandem so that if one failed, the other took over and there was no loss of operation. This product had special appeal to banks and airlines, for which a computer failure could prove disastrous. His process was a high-performance, low-control approach to management coupled with stock sharing, company beer parties, and a friendly atmosphere. Initially, both product and process were successful.

For several years everything was terrific. Sales and profits increased, and Tandem was referred to as *the* place to work. Treybig's managerial style was termed the wave of the future. But with growth came problems. The rate of growth of sales and profits declined, and the Securities and Exchange Commission accused the firm of fraud. Working through these issues suggested that the major problem was the low-control part of the management process—it no longer seemed to work.

Trebig instituted a new control system. He kept the high standards and his basic philosophy that everyone should know and understand the goals of the business, but he established a comprehensive system of controls to keep track of what was happening in the firm. He began to hold regular staff meetings and became more directive in his personal style of dealing with others.

The results were impressive. Revenues soared to over a billion dollars during 1987, and profits also rose dramatically. Tandem's average lead time to ship a product is about one week compared to fourteen weeks for the industry as a whole. In satisfaction surveys run in the industry, customers rate Tandem very high. To provide the necessary ingredients for continued success and growth, early in 1988 Tandem acquired Ungermann-Bass, a computer-networking company. This acquisition will enable Tandem's customers to develop low-cost networking services across their operations, and it will increase Tandem's ability to compete with Digital and IBM.

For Tandem Computers, size is an important contingency. What worked well when the firm was small did not continue to work as the firm grew. One managerial style worked well for the small firm, another works well for the larger version of the firm. Treybig's changes were examples of contingency management.

REFERENCES: Kathy Chin Leong, "Deal Fulfills Ungermann Dream," *Computerworld*, Feburary 29, 1988, p. 6; James Daly, "Tandem to Buy Ungermann-Bass," *Computerworld*, February 22, 1988, pp. 85, 90; Jagannath Dubashi, "Instant Gratification," *Financial World*, January 26, 1988, pp. 42–43; Brian O'Reilly, "How Jimmy Treybig Turned Tough," *Fortune*, May 25, 1987, pp. 102–103.

behaviors in the workplace. Motivation, leadership, communication, and group processes are especially important. Quantitative management theory also provides the manager with a set of useful tools and techniques. The development and use of management science models and the application of operations management methods can help managers increase their efficiency and effectiveness.

In choosing and applying any of these ideas, however, the manager must use both a systems and a contingency orientation. Systems theory reminds managers to consider environmental influences. Similarly, managers must recognize the concept of interdependencies—a change in one part of the organizational system may change other parts of the system as well. Finally, the contingency orientation reminds managers

FIGURE 2.5

An Integrative Framework of
Management Theories

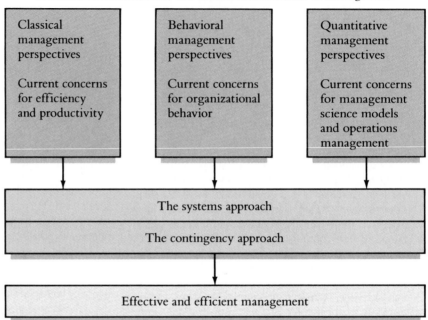

Recognition of system and subsystem interdependencies,
environmental influences, and the situational nature of management

that a tool, technique, concept, or theory that works perfectly in one
setting or situation may not be appropriate in different circumstances.

Consider the new distribution manager of a large wholesaling firm
whose job is to manage one hundred truck drivers and to coordinate
standard truck routes in the most efficient fashion. This new manager,
with little relevant experience, might attempt to increase efficiency and
productivity by employing strict time-and-motion analysis, work specialization, and close supervision (as suggested by scientific management). But doing so may cause decreased satisfaction and morale and
increased turnover (as suggested by organizational behavior). Similarly,
the manager might develop a management science model to use route
driver time more efficiently (from the quantitative school). But this
new system could disrupt existing work groups and social patterns
(from organizational behavior). The manager may create even more
problems by trying to impose programs and practices derived from her
or his previous job. An incentive program welcomed by retail clerks,
for example, might not work for truck drivers.

The manager should soon realize that a broader perspective is needed.
Systems and contingency orientations help provide this breadth. To
solve a problem of declining productivity, the manager might look to
the classical school (perhaps jobs are inefficiently designed or workers
improperly trained), the behavioral school (worker motivation may be
low or group norms may be restricting output), or the quantitative

school (facilities may be improperly laid out or material stockouts may be resulting from poor inventory management). Of course, before implementing any plans for improvement, the manager should try to assess their effect on other areas of the organization.

Now suppose that this manager is involved in planning a new warehouse. He or she will probably consider how to structure the management team and whether to use an incentive system (classical school), what kinds of leaders and work-group arrangements to develop (behavioral school), and how to develop and apply a network model for designing and operating the facility itself (quantitative school).

As a final example, if employee turnover is too high, the manager might consider an incentive system (classical school), plan a motivational enhancement program (behavioral school), or use a mathematical model (quantitative school) to discover that turnover costs may actually be lower than the cost of making any changes at all!

CONTEMPORARY MANAGEMENT PERSPECTIVES

■ **contemporary management perspectives** Include the global imperative, concerns for excellence, and concerns for quality and productivity

In recent years, there has been renewed interest in management theory and practice. This interest is reflected in the increased sales of business books in the mass market and the appeal of charismatic executives like Lee Iacocca. This section summarizes some of these contemporary perspectives.

The Global Imperative

One recent line of new theory development has been spawned by the so-called global imperative. Simply stated, this view holds that we have very quickly become a global village and that managers must adopt a global vision regarding all their activities.[40] Consequently, managerial theories, models, and perspectives must be reformulated to account for a global outlook. Perhaps the most fully developed of such efforts is the Type Z model.

Type Z model An attempt to integrate common business practices from the United States and Japan into one middle-ground framework

The **Type Z** model, as argued by William Ouchi in 1981, is an attempt to integrate common business practices in the United States and Japan into a single middle-ground framework.[41] Ouchi suggests that there are many traditional American firms (which he calls Type A companies) and a similar set of traditional Japanese companies (Type J). He also suggests that a few American firms have achieved great success by adopting a hybrid form of management, which he calls Type Z. Figure 2.6 summarizes the basic characteristics of Type A, J, and Z organizations.

It shows that American and Japanese firms are essentially different along seven important dimensions: (1) length of employment, (2) mode of decision making, (3) location of responsibility, (4) speed of evaluation

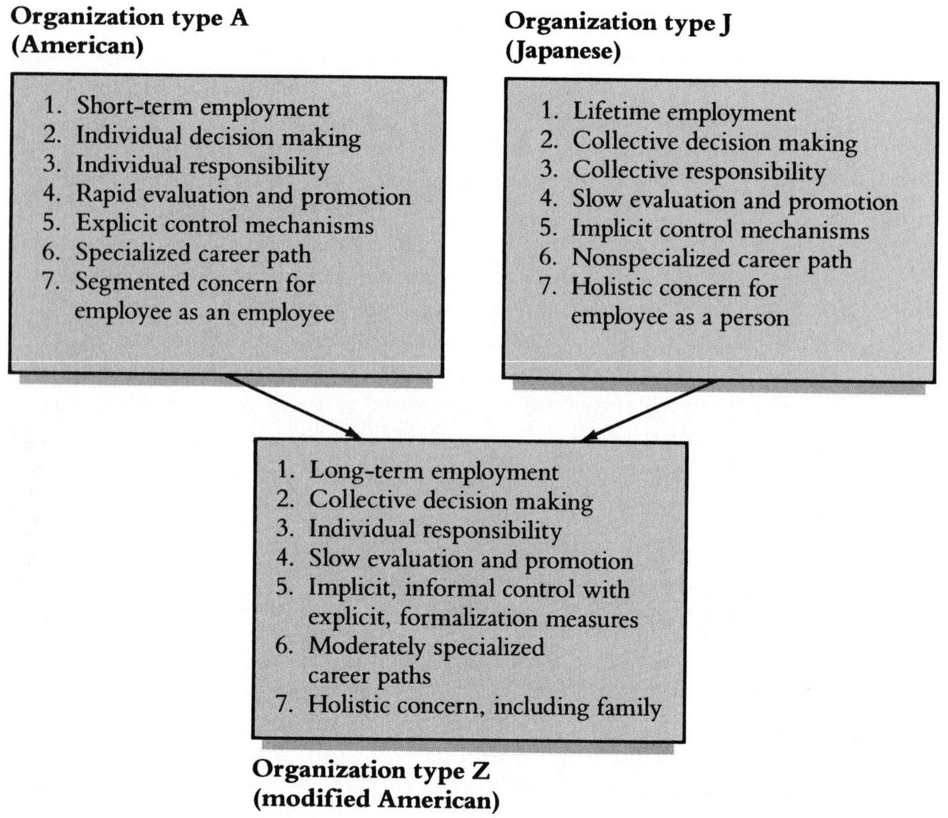

**Organization type A
(American)**

1. Short-term employment
2. Individual decision making
3. Individual responsibility
4. Rapid evaluation and promotion
5. Explicit control mechanisms
6. Specialized career path
7. Segmented concern for
   employee as an employee

**Organization type J
(Japanese)**

1. Lifetime employment
2. Collective decision making
3. Collective responsibility
4. Slow evaluation and promotion
5. Implicit control mechanisms
6. Nonspecialized career path
7. Holistic concern for
   employee as a person

1. Long-term employment
2. Collective decision making
3. Individual responsibility
4. Slow evaluation and promotion
5. Implicit, informal control with
   explicit, formalization measures
6. Moderately specialized
   career paths
7. Holistic concern, including family

**Organization type Z
(modified American)**

SOURCE: Adapted from William Ouchi, *Theory Z,* © 1984, Addison-Wesley Publishing Company,
Inc., Reading, Massachusetts, p. 58 (adapted material). Reprinted with permission.

FIGURE 2.6

Comparison of American,
Japanese, and Hybrid
Organizations

and promotion, (5) mechanisms of control, (6) specialization of career
path, and (7) nature of concern for the employee. For example, some
Japanese firms are characterized by lifetime employment opportunities
and collective decision making, whereas their American counterparts
offer short-term employment and rely on individual decision making.

Ouchi also observes that a few particularly successful American firms
(such as IBM, Hewlett-Packard, Eastman Kodak, and Procter & Gamble) did not follow the typical American Type A model. Instead, they
evolved a hybrid, or Type Z approach that borrows one characteristic
(individual responsibility) from Type A, incorporates three characteristics (collective decision making, slow evaluation and promotion, and
holistic concern) from Type J, and assumes an intermediate stance with
respect to the other three dimensions (for instance, they postulate long-
term employment—as opposed to short-term employment in Type A
and lifetime employment in Type J).

Ouchi's ideas have been well received by practicing managers. His
book was on most best-seller lists for several weeks in 1981, and many
organizations are trying to implement his suggestions. However, con-

Morgan Guaranty, a large New York financial services company, has adopted a true global imperative in its approach to doing business. For example, half of the new recruits that go through its management training program are not United States citizens. Morgan Guaranty believes that the foreign recruits will be useful both in terms of helping U.S. managers better understand foreign cultures and markets and in helping run foreign operations after their training is complete.

troversy has arisen about whether some of Ouchi's research was conducted as scientifically as it should have been.[42] Like many scientific breakthroughs, the Type Z model will quite likely be supplanted by more refined and valid models as we learn more about the international domain of management. Still, it deserves special recognition because it gave early momentum to theory development in the global arena.

The Concern for Excellence

Another popular management perspective is the so-called excellence movement. Originally presented by Thomas J. Peters and Robert H. Waterman, Jr.,[43] this approach suggests that certain "excellent" companies, those with a long-term history of success, do things in a systematic fashion that sets them apart from other firms. The basic set of characteristics that presumably lead to excellence include (1) getting things done on time, (2) staying close to the customer, (3) promoting autonomy and entrepreneurship, (4) maximizing productivity through people, (5) using a hands-on approach to managing, (6) doing what the company knows best, (7) maintaining a simple, lean organizational structure, and (8) promoting both centralization and decentralization simultaneously. Well-known firms presumed to have these characteristics include Digital Equipment, Hewlett-Packard, IBM, Eastman Kodak, Procter & Gamble, Delta Air Lines, Intel, Avon, Maytag, Walt Disney Productions, Dow Chemical, and Du Pont.

The excellence movement has also been a significant catalyst for other theorists and management scholars, although it too has been subjected to criticism.[44] In all likelihood, it will follow the same path as the Type Z model. It has played a major role in developing a new line of thinking about organizations, but it is likely to give way to more fully developed models and ideas.

The Concerns for Quality and Productivity

Another two-pronged area of interest to emerge in recent years has been the concern for quality and productivity. First, as they attempt to understand why Japanese and West German firms have been so successful in this country, American companies have discovered that their foreign counterparts have an edge in quality. As a result, American firms have developed renewed interest in how they can enhance the quality of their products and services.

As a part of this discovery process, American managers have also learned that many of their foreign competitors are producing higher-quality products with fewer resources! Hence, managers have become more and more interested in how to increase the productivity of American workers.[45] In response to these concerns, managers have begun searching for new theories and methods that can help them enhance both quality and productivity. Many of the methods adopted to date represent a synthesis of earlier approaches. For example, Texas Instruments, Westinghouse, and other firms have experimented with so-called quality circles—teams of operating employees who meet regularly to identify and solve quality-related problems in their jobs. The successful use of quality circles requires the manager to understand and implement ideas drawn from each of the major schools of management thought as well as the systems and contingency perspectives.

To put the current enthusiasm for management theory in its proper perspective, we should conclude by commenting on both its pluses and minuses. On the plus side, popular management literature helps bridge the theory-practice gap and brings theorists and managers closer together. It also facilitates the ability of each to learn from the other. Current efforts in theory building are clearly grounded in the reality of organizational life. They represent not pure conjecture but actual organizational practices, problems, and experiences.

On the other hand, there are major drawbacks to some of the ideas presented in popular management theory. One is that the theorists are occasionally too zealous in the presentation of their ideas—that is, they often seem to be prescribing how managers should do things. The problem with prescriptions, unfortunately, is that they implicitly promise results. In the complex world of organizations, however, the promised results may not always emerge. Another major problem with this body of literature is that all too many managers, often with the help of outsiders, jump too quickly onto the latest bandwagon promising instant success.

Much of what the popular literature has to say has some relevance to the practicing manager and may provide interesting and useful insights into how to improve managerial effectiveness. Nevertheless, the manager needs to take the content of these books with a grain of salt. There are few quick fixes for most organizational problems; the manager must draw from a variety of sources and perspectives when deciding how to proceed.

SUMMARY OF KEY POINTS

Theories are important as organizers of knowledge and as road maps for action. Understanding the historical context and precursors of management and organizations provides a sense of heritage and can also help managers avoid repeating the mistakes of others.

Isolated pieces of evidence date interest in management back thousands of years, but a scientific approach to management has emerged only in the last hundred years. Over the course of the development of management thought, three primary perspectives on management emerged. The earliest of these was the classical management perspective. The other two schools of thought are referred to as the behavioral management perspective and the quantitative management perspective.

The classical management perspective had two major branches: scientific management and classical organization theory. Scientific management was concerned with improving efficiency and work methods for individual workers. Classical organization theory was more concerned with how organizations themselves should be structured and arranged for efficient operations. Both branches paid little attention to the role of the worker.

The behavioral management perspective, characterized by a concern for individual and group behavior, emerged primarily as a result of the Hawthorne studies. The human relations movement recognized the importance and potential of behavioral processes in organizations but made many overly simplistic assumptions about those processes. Organizational behavior, a more realistic outgrowth of behavioral management theory, is of interest to many contemporary managers.

The quantitative management perspective and its two components, management science and operations management, attempt to apply quantitative techniques to decision making and problem solving. These areas are also of considerable importance to contemporary managers. Their contributions have been facilitated by the personal computer explosion.

The three schools of management thought should be viewed in a complementary, not a contradictory, light. Each has something of value to offer. The key is understanding how to use them effectively.

Two relatively recent additions to management theory, the systems and contingency perspectives, seem to have great potential both as approaches to management and as frameworks for integrating other schools of thought.

Among contemporary management perspectives, the global imperative and concerns for excellence, quality, and productivity have stimulated much theorizing and experimentation by managers. The approaches developed to this point have both positive and negative characteristics.

DISCUSSION QUESTIONS

Questions for Review

1. Briefly describe each of the major historical approaches to management and identify the most important contributors to each of them.
2. What is a system? What is systems theory? How is systems theory useful to the study of management?
3. Describe contingency theory and outline its usefulness to the study and practice of management.
4. What are some contemporary management perspectives? Which historical approaches seem most closely linked with each of these? Why?

Questions for Analysis

5. What social, political, and economic conditions might have influenced the development of each of the major historical approaches to management? Why?
6. What are the major strengths and limitations or shortcomings of each of the major historical approaches to management? Why?
7. Try to develop an approach to management that encompasses all of the major strengths of each of the major historical approaches to management without also having any of their shortcomings.

Questions for Application

8. Go to the library and locate material on Confucius. Outline his major ideas. Which seem to be applicable to management in the United States today?
9. Identify a local firm that has been in existence for a long time. Interview the current owner about the history of the firm and see if you can gain a better understanding of its current practices by knowing about its past.
10. Read a history of a company in which you are interested. Prepare for the class a brief report that stresses the impact of the firm's history on its current practices.

NOTES

1. "In Wake of Cost Cuts, Many Firms Sweep Their History Out the Door," *The Wall Street Journal*, December 21, 1987, p. 21.
2. Alan M. Kantrow, ed., "Why History Matters to Managers," *Harvard Business Review*, January–February 1986, pp. 81–88.
3. "Profiting from the Past," *Newsweek*, May 10, 1982, pp. 73–74.
4. Jeffrey Pfeffer, "The Theory-Practice Gap: Myth or Reality?" *The Academy of Management Executive*, February 1987, pp. 31–33.
5. "Can Andy Grove Practice What He Preaches?" *Business Week*, March 16, 1987, pp. 68–69 and "Intel to Motorola: Race Ya," *Business Week*, March 13, 1989, p. 42.
6. Daniel Wren, *The Evolution of Management Theory*, 3rd ed. (New York: Wiley, 1987); Daniel Wren, "Management History: Issues and Ideas for Teaching and Research," *Journal of Management*, Summer 1987, pp. 339–350; Page Smith, *The Rise of Industrial America* (New York: McGraw-Hill, 1984).
7. Marilyn Wellemeyer, "Books Bosses Read," *Fortune*, April 27, 1987, pp. 145–148.
8. See also Alan L. Wilkins and Nigel J. Bristow, "For Successful Organization Culture, Honor Your Past," *The Academy of Management Executive*, August 1987, pp. 221–227.
9. William G. Scott, "The Management Governance Theories of Justice and Liberty," *Journal of Management*, June 1988, pp. 277–298.
10. Wren, *The Evolution of Management Theory*.
11. Wren, *The Evolution of Management Theory*.
12. Charles Babbage, *On the Economy of Machinery and Manufactures* (London: Charles Knight, 1832).
13. Wren, *The Evolution of Management Theory*.
14. Wren, *The Evolution of Management Theory*.
15. Wren, *The Evolution of Management Theory*.
16. Wren, *The Evolution of Management Theory*.
17. Frederick W. Taylor, *Principles of Scientific Management* (New York: Harper and Brothers, 1911).
18. Charles D. Wrege and Amedeo G. Perroni, "Taylor's Pig-Tale: A Historical Analysis of Frederick W. Taylor's Pig-Iron Experiment," *Academy of Management Journal*, March 1974, pp. 6–27; Charles D. Wrege and Ann Marie Stoka, "Cooke Creates a Classic: The Story Behind Taylor's Principles of Scientific Management," *Academy of Management Review*, October 1978, pp. 736–749.
19. Edwin A. Locke, "The Ideas of Frederick W. Taylor: An Evaluation," *Academy of Management Review*, January 1982, pp. 14–20. See also Stephen J. Carroll and Dennis J. Gillen, "Are the Classical Management Functions Useful in Describing Managerial Work?" *Academy of Management Review*, January 1987, pp. 38–51; and Wren, "Management History."
20. Henri Fayol, *General and Industrial Management*, trans. J. A. Coubrough (Geneva: International Management Institute, 1930).
21. Max Weber, *Theory of Social and Economic Organizations*, trans. T. Parsons (New York: Free Press, 1947); Richard M. Weis, "Weber on Bureaucracy: Management Consultant or Political Theorist?" *Academy of Management Review*, April 1983, pp. 242–248.
22. Chester Barnard, *The Functions of the Executive* (Cambridge, Mass.: Harvard University Press, 1938).

23. Hugo Munsterberg, *Psychology and Industrial Efficiency* (Boston: Houghton Mifflin, 1913).

24. Wren, *The Evolution of Management Theory*, pp. 256–264.

25. Elton Mayo, *The Human Problems of an Industrial Civilization* (New York: Macmillan, 1933); Fritz J. Roethlisberger and William J. Dickson, *Management and the Worker* (Cambridge, Mass.: Harvard University Press, 1939).

26. For recent interpretations of the Hawthorne studies, see J. A. Seiler, "Architecture at Work," *Harvard Business Review*, September–October 1984, pp. 111–121; Lyle Yorks and David A. Whitsett, "Hawthorne, Topeka, and the Issue of Science Versus Advocacy in Organizational Behavior," *Academy of Management Review*, January 1985, pp. 21–30.

27. Barry M. Staw, "Organizational Psychology and the Pursuit of the Happy/Productive Worker," *California Management Review*, Summer 1986, pp. 40–53.

28. Abraham Maslow, "A Theory of Human Motivation," *Psychological Review*, July 1943, pp. 370–396.

29. Douglas McGregor, *The Human Side of Enterprise* (New York: McGraw-Hill, 1960).

30. Cynthia D. Fisher, "On the Dubious Wisdom of Expecting Job Satisfaction to Correlate with Performance," *Academy of Management Review*, October 1980, pp. 607–612.

31. Paul R. Lawrence, "Historical Development of Organizational Behavior," in Jay W. Lorsch, ed., *Handbook of Organizational Behavior* (Englewood Cliffs, N.J.: Prentice-Hall, 1987), pp. 1–9. See also Larry L. Cummings, "Toward Organizational Behavior," *Academy of Management Review*, January 1978, pp. 90–98.

32. See Gregory Moorhead and Ricky W. Griffin, *Organizational Behavior*, 2nd ed. (Boston: Houghton Mifflin, 1989), for a recent review of current developments in the field of organizational behavior.

33. Wren, *The Evolution of Management Thought*, Chapter 21.

34. "Hughes Steers GM into Gee-Whiz Era," *USA Today*, February 5, 1987, p. 7B.

35. For a recent review of operations management, see Richard B. Chase and Eric L. Prentis, "Operations Management: A Field Rediscovered," *Journal of Management*, Summer 1987, pp. 339–350. See also Everett E. Adam, Jr., and Ronald J. Ebert, *Production and Operations Management: Concepts, Models, and Behavior*, 4th ed. (Englewood Cliffs, N.J.: Prentice-Hall, 1989).

36. For more information on systems theory in general, see Ludwig von Bertalanffy, C. G. Hempel, R. E. Bass, and H. Jonas, "General Systems Theory: A New Approach to Unity of Science," I–VI *Human Biology*, Vol. 23, 1951, pp. 302–361. For systems theory as applied to organizations, see Fremont E. Kast and James E. Rosenzweig, "General Systems Theory: Applications for Organizations and Management," *Academy of Management Journal*, December 1972, pp. 447–465. For a recent update, see Donde P. Ashmos and George P. Huber, "The Systems Paradigm in Organization Theory: Correcting the Record and Suggesting the Future," *Academy of Management Review*, October 1987, pp. 607–621.

37. Monci Jo Williams, "Synergy Works at American Express," *Fortune*, February 16, 1987, pp. 79–80.

38. Fremont E. Kast and James E. Rosenzweig, *Contingency Views of Organization and Management* (Chicago: Science Research Associates, 1973).

39. "Airline's Ills Point Out Weaknesses of Unorthodox Management Style," *The Wall Street Journal*, August 11, 1986, p. 15.

40. See Richard I. Kirkland, Jr., "Entering a New Age of Boundless Competition," *Fortune*, March 14, 1988, pp. 40–48.

41. William Ouchi, *Theory Z—How American Business Can Meet the Japanese Challenge* (Reading, Mass.: Addison-Wesley, 1981). For a recent analysis of Theory Z, see Jeremiah J. Sullivan, "A Critique of Theory Z," *Academy of Management Review*, January 1983, pp. 132–142.

42. William Bowen, "Lessons from Behind the Kimono," *Fortune*, June 15, 1981, pp. 247–250.

43. Thomas J. Peters and Robert H. Waterman, Jr., *In Search of Excellence* (New York: Harper & Row, 1982).

44. Kenneth E. Aupperle, William Acar, and David E. Booth, "An Empirical Critique of *In Search of Excellence*: How Excellent Are the Excellent Companies?" *Journal of Management*, Winter 1986, pp. 499–512; Michael A. Hitt and R. Duane Ireland, "Peters and Waterman Revisited: The Unended Quest for Excellence," *The Academy of Management Executive*, May 1987, pp. 91–98.

45. See Tom Peters, "Restoring American Competitiveness: Looking for New Models of Organizations," *The Academy of Management Executive*, May 1988, pp. 103–109.

CASE 2.1

UPS Uses Technology in Management

Federal Express has lively orange and purple colors; United Parcel Service (UPS) has dull brown. Federal Express is publicly traded; UPS is privately held. Federal Express has an easygoing management with a complaint system; UPS has a tough, engineered management with a union grievance system. Federal Express controls the lion's share of the package-delivery market, but UPS, the second-place firm, is moving to strengthen its position and hopes to overtake Federal Express.

Though second place in terms of market share, UPS has been the most profitable package-delivery company in the United States, and it intends to continue that profitability as it increases revenues and market share. UPS has over 47,000 brown delivery vans and a fleet of over 100 airplanes serving over 850,000 customers. It serves all fifty states, Puerto Rico, Canada, and West Germany.

UPS was formed in 1908 as a messenger service in Seattle, Washington, by James E. Casey. Casey argued that a well-run company must be owned by its managers and managed by its owners. Thus clerks and drivers who become UPS managers share in the narrow ownership of the firm. Indeed, many of those who work their way up through the organization retire as millionaires because of the generous stock-bonus plan. Further, this closely held ownership means that executives do not have to worry about investors from Wall Street when they develop long-range strategies for UPS.

Many of the concepts of scientific management are solidly in place at UPS. Industrial engineers time tasks to establish operating schedules, and every single task has a carefully measured productivity standard determined for it. Whether the task is sorting packages or picking up or delivering them, employees know what is expected of them. They also know that deviations from the standards are not permitted.

Drivers are timed so carefully that their supervisors usually know within six minutes how long the day's pickups and deliveries will take. The loading of delivery vans at the UPS distribution center near Chicago is supposed to proceed at a rate of from 500 to 650 packages each hour. Unloading is supposed to go at about twice that rate. Rewards are linked to predetermined standards, and an employee must do better than usual to earn a reward.

As technology advances, UPS is spending millions to keep its standards tight. To step up its use of technology, UPS bought two small computer companies—one a developer of software, the other a computer design firm with hardware-manufacturing capabilities. Based on the efforts of these two units, field testing of a host of new devices was begun in 1987.

When all of the new instruments are in place, dispatchers will be able to use electronic tracking devices to follow the progress of each vehicle in the field. They will be able to send messages to the drivers through on-board computers. The drivers will have immediate access to computerized routing directions and will be able to record all transactions electronically. Bar graphs on each package will be read by electronic scanners to improve the flow of packages through the distribution centers. Thus, from pickup to delivery, UPS will know where each package is and will be able to report that information to customers.

As its knowledge and experience with computers and the high-tech transfer of information grows, UPS plans to expand its operations into electronic data transfer. By the late 1990s, UPS expects to be a major force in that market. UPS is entering the market gradually and carefully, and management expects that approach to lead to more favorable results.

The strong emphasis on precision has meant that UPS management tends to make all decisions and run the firm centrally. That has caused UPS some image problems. Further, despite low turnover among employees and a historical culture that attracts, develops, and retains talented people, UPS has labor problems.

Although UPS union employees turned down a three-year contract in 1987, the national union ruled that a two-thirds majority was necessary to reject the contract. A militant subgroup within the union charges that the national union and UPS have developed a relationship that is not in the best interests of union members. The subgroup is trying to take over representation of UPS's employees.

UPS clearly has its mission cut out for it. It must develop and utilize technology to compete an overnight delivery with Federal Express. It must counter growing unrest and dissatisfaction among some of its employees. It must overcome competition from other carriers and also from the new technology of facsimile machines.

Questions

1. What characteristics of scientific management can you identify at UPS? Cite specific examples.
2. What characteristics of the classical, behavioral, and quantitative perspectives on management can you identify at UPS? Cite specific examples.
3. Can you identify any characteristics of the systems or contingency approaches to management at UPS? Cite specific examples.
4. In the battle between UPS and Federal Express, which company do you feel will likely be the leader in the industry in about ten years? Why? Carefully support your answer with information about the two firms.

REFERENCES: "Federal Express Faces Challenges to Its Grip on Overnight Delivery," *The Wall Street Journal*, January 8, 1988, pp. 1, 8; Kenneth Labich, "Big Changes at Big Brown," *Fortune*, January 18, 1988, pp. 56–64; Peter Truel, "UPS to Control Its Jet Fleet Ending Management Pact," *The Wall Street Journal*, August 25, 1987, p. 24. "UPS Isn't About to be Left Holding the Parcel," *Business Week*, February 13, 1989, p. 69.

CASE 2.2

Lloyd's Managerial Evolution

Lloyd's of London celebrated its 300th anniversary in 1988. One of the world's best-known business organizations, Lloyd's may also be one of the least understood. It is not a company; it has no shareholders. Lloyd's is a society of underwriters with roots extending back to the sixteenth century.

Marine insurance started in the sixteenth century as ship owners sought to share their risks with others. With the rise of coffee houses in the seventeenth century, business began to be conducted in their quiet surroundings. In 1688 Lloyd's Coffee House opened and promptly became an important center for dealings in marine insurance. In 1769 a group of Lloyd's customers, disgruntled because other types of business were being transacted at Lloyd's Coffee House, formed a new establishment devoted exclusively to marine insurance. When the new location proved to be too small, a special committee was set up to find a larger site. In 1771 the New Lloyd's was established as a place to conduct business, not as a coffee house. It was the precursor of the modern organization known as Lloyd's of London.

Over the years, Lloyd's began to take on specific characteristics. The special committee became a permanent organizational arrangement. It is elected and regulates membership. In 1871 Lloyd's was incorporated by an act of Parliament. Since then, five other acts of Parliament have defined and clarified the nature of Lloyd's. The administration of Lloyd's is through the Council of Lloyd's (much like a board of directors composed of sixteen internal and eight external members) and the Corporation of Lloyd's (much like a central corporate staff organization composed of five groups). Lloyd's agents are located throughout the world. The agents are firms whose job is to send information about shipping and aviation and other news to Lloyd's and to appoint surveyors, who report on damage or loss for claims purposes.

Lloyd's has approximately 30,000 members, or Names, grouped into nearly four hundred syndicates to underwrite each insurance policy. Lloyd's publishes numerous items of marine information for its clientele: *Lloyd's List*, a daily newspaper; *Lloyd's Log*, a public relations magazine; *Lloyd's Shipping Index*, a daily record of about 21,000 merchant vessels; *Lloyd's Shipping Economist*, a monthly, comprehensive analysis of world shipping; and *Lloyd's Loading List*, a guide to cargo-carrying services.

Lloyd's basic strategy is that of a pooling cooperative. By cooperatively pooling resources, Lloyd's can offer larger insurance products for larger risks and coordinate sales to larger buyers and syndicates of buyers. If the risk is going to be great, Lloyd's simply recruits more syndicate partners to absorb that risk. This strategy has obvious strengths, but it also has the disadvantage of inflexibility, since all members must agree to a change.

Resistance to change has created problems for Lloyd's. Some syndicates collapsed as a result of scandals, leaving many Names holding the bag. To the credit of the organization, Lloyd's has been able to weather these storms without protracted legal battles. Nevertheless, such scandals in a major financial institution have resulted in numerous attempts to control and reorganize Lloyd's.

Since 1969 no fewer than three official government reports have been prepared analyzing Lloyd's operations. One criticism that has frequently emerged has been of the pooled cooperative strategy. Nevertheless, the number of Names has risen markedly since the mid-1970s. With the addition of these new Names, Lloyd's has become less of an old-boys club. The new Names come from business, lawyers, physicians, and a few "new rich"—movie stars and professional athletes.

Although Lloyd's basic strategy for doing business has not changed, the manner of enacting that strategy has changed somewhat. The merchant of the past who signed policies in a coffee house as a sideline has been replaced by professional underwriters trained and experienced in the insurance business. Insurance policies no longer must be personally signed by the syndicate underwriter; now there is a central signing office to speed the transaction. Further, computers are everywhere because Lloyd's is no longer just a society of underwriters but also the world center for marine intelligence and publishing.

Some syndicates might make $150,000 in a year for members while others lose $400,000. Because of the nature of claims, profit and loss figures are reported three years late. Despite the late reporting, most members do come out ahead. However, the ultimate risk is the unlimited liability that members incur. Any move to limit member's liability would result in a change of organizational structure because only corporations can have limited liability. Such a move, of course, would require another act of Parliament and would be an even more significant departure from tradition.

Questions

1. How does knowledge about the origins and evolution of Lloyd's help you to understand its present position and problems?
2. Which management perspective(s) is (are) most obvious in the operation of Lloyd's? Cite specific examples.
3. Will Lloyd's have to move to a corporate form of structure and governance? Why or why not?

REFERENCES: "Lloyd's Studies Liability Limit for Its Members," *The Wall Street Journal*, September 9, 1988, p. 12; *Lloyd's of London: A Sketch History* (London: Lloyd's of London, n.d.); Richard P. Nielsen, "Cooperative Strategy in Marketing," *Business Horizons*, July–August 1987, pp. 61–68; William Kay, "More Protection: Is That What Lloyd's Should Provide," *Barron's*, January 26, 1987, pp. 72–73.

OUTLINE

The Nature of Organizational Environments

The General Environment
The Economic Dimension · The Technological Dimension · The Sociocultural Dimension · The Political-Legal Dimension · The International Dimension

The Task Environment
Competitors · Customers · Suppliers · Regulators · Labor · Owners · Partners

The Internal Environment
The Board of Directors · Employees

Organization-Environment Relationships
How Environments Affect Organizations · How Organizations Respond to Their Environments

Organizational Effectiveness
Models of Effectiveness · Managerial Performance

CHAPTER 3

Organizational Environments and Effectiveness

OBJECTIVES

After studying this chapter, you should be able to:

- Discuss the nature of organizational environments.
- Identify the components of the general environment and discuss their impact on organizations.
- Identify the components of the task environment and discuss their impact on organizations.
- Identify the components of the internal environment and discuss their impact on organizations.
- Identify and describe basic kinds of organization–environment relationships.
- Discuss organizational effectiveness.

OPENING INCIDENT

L. S. Shoen created a new industry in 1945 when he launched U-Haul. Having little capital, he financed his business by persuading outside investors to buy trailers for him and then share in the revenues as he rented them to customers. To expand his network, he let rental customers take trailers to cities with no U-Haul franchise and then try to persuade local gas-station operators to open a U-Haul branch. Customers who succeeded paid no fee for using the trailer.

Until the 1970s, U-Haul dominated the industry it had created. Its fleet of 65,000 trucks could be seen everywhere, and profits were skyrocketing. Then the bottom dropped out. The energy crunch forced many independent gas stations (still the heart of U-Haul's rental network) to close. At the same time, Shoen embarked on an ambitious but ill-planned diversification strategy, opening large-scale rental centers offering everything from asphalt mixers to VCRs. The company also allowed its fleet of trucks to fall into disrepair. Soon losses started mounting.

Then came Ryder. After some tough times of its own, the Ryder System got its act together. A fleet of new trucks (many equipped with air conditioning and other amenities), aggressive advertising, a computerized routing, maintenance, and reservation system, and tighter controls allowed Ryder to capture half of U-Haul's market share since 1980. Each firm now controls around 45 percent of the truck rental business. U-Haul is fighting back with its own new trucks, but most observers believe the company can do little to stop Ryder's momentum.[1]

U-Haul held the dominant position in an industry it had created. How did its lead slip away? Why did its managers allow the company to stand still for so long? And why did they make some of the mistakes they made? Managers at U-Haul failed to understand the environment in which they were doing business. It changed, but they did not. Consequently, they fell victim to unexpected changes in that environment while a major competitor was reading the environment much more accurately and seizing its opportunity to leapfrog the venerable moving company.

Clearly, environment is of critical importance to the successes and failures of any organization. If Merck fails to keep pace with scientific research in the pharmaceuticals industry, it will suffer. If Philip Morris ignores consumer perceptions of tobacco, it will suffer. If Toys 'R' Us pays no attention to what its competitors are doing, it too will suffer. Managers need to have a keen understanding of their environment—how it affects them and how they can affect it.

This chapter provides you with insights into the complex relationships that exist between organizations and their environments. First we characterize the nature of organizational environments. We then discuss in detail the forces inherent in three levels of environment: the general, task, and internal environments. We then identify a number of important organization-environment relationships. Finally, we discuss organizational effectiveness, a key indicator of how well an organization is responding to and shaping its environment.

THE NATURE OF ORGANIZATIONAL ENVIRONMENTS

The examples cited above underscore how important it is for managers to understand their environment. The general reason for this importance relates to the consideration of organizations as open systems, discussed in Chapter 2. Recall that as open systems all organizations import resources from the environment and transport outputs back into that environment, and the future actions of the system are influenced by feedback from the environment. Chapter 2 also noted the consequences of a closed-system view—one factor leading to the decline of U-Haul.

external environment
Everything outside an organization that might potentially affect it

The **external environment** is everything outside an organization that might affect it. However, the boundary that separates the organization from the external environment is not always clear and precise. In one sense, for example, stockholders and part-time workers are part of the organization, but in another sense they are part of its environment. The external environment of an organization is composed of two layers: the general environment and the task environment (see Figure 3.1).[2]

■ **general environment**
Those nonspecific dimensions and forces in an organization's surroundings that might affect its activities

An organization's **general environment** consists of the nonspecific dimensions and forces in its surroundings that might affect the organization's activities. These elements are not necessarily associated with other specific organizations. The general environment of most organizations has economic, technological, sociocultural, political-legal, and international dimensions. The **task environment** of an organization consists of specific groups that are likely to influence the organization. The task environment may include competitors, customers, suppliers, regulators, labor, owners, and partners.

■ **task environment** Specific organizations or groups that are likely to affect the organization

■ **internal environment**
The general conditions and forces within an organization

An organization's **internal environment** consists of the general conditions and forces within the organization. Its major components include the board of directors, employees, and the organization's culture.

Not all aspects of the environment are equally important for all organizations. A small, nonunion firm may not need to concern itself too much with unions, for example. A private university with a large endowment (like Harvard) may be less concerned about general economic conditions than might a state university (like the University of Oregon) that is dependent on state funding from tax revenues. Still, organizations need to fully understand which environmental forces are important and how the importance of others might increase.

FIGURE 3.1

The Organization and Its
Environments

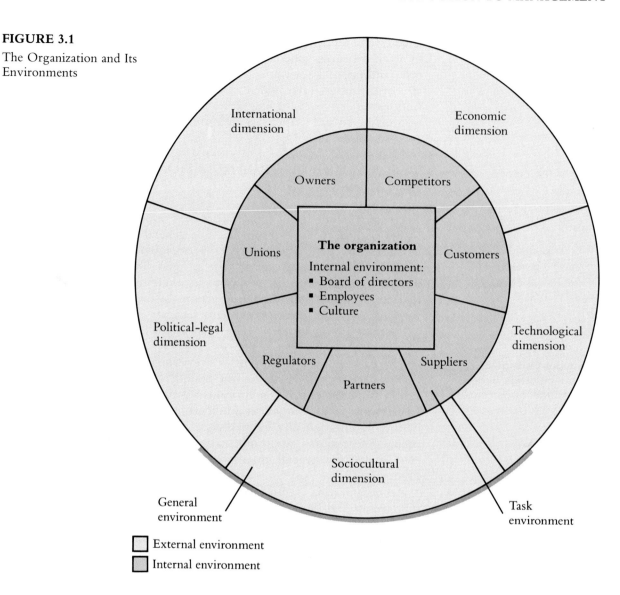

THE GENERAL ENVIRONMENT

The general environment of an organization consists of five dimensions: economic, technological, sociocultural, political-legal, and international. These dimensions are typically not associated with other specific organizations or groups. Instead, they are general forces or processes that interact with each other and also affect the organization as a whole. Each embodies conditions and events that have the potential to influence the organization in significant ways. The general environment of Ford Motor Company is shown in Figure 3.2.

Elements of the general environment often provide business opportunities for astute managers. For example, when travel agent Helena Koenig became a grandmother, she realized that the entire socio-cultural environment in the United States was also changing—there are more and more older people and they are spending more of their money on travel. But since more and more of their children are part of dual-career families, traditional family vacations are getting harder to arrange. So Ms. Koenig developed Grandtravel, a special program that arranges tours for grandparents and their grandchildren. Ticket volume has tripled at her agency since the new program was first introduced.

The Economic Dimension

economic dimension The overall health of the economic system in which the organization operates

The term **economic dimension** refers to the overall health of the economic system in which the organization operates.[3] Economic factors of special importance to business include inflation, interest rates, unemployment, and demand. During times of inflation, for example, a company pays more and more for resources and then must raise its prices to cover the higher costs. When interest rates are high, consumers may be less willing to borrow money and the company itself must pay more when it borrows. When unemployment is high, the company is able to be very selective about whom it hires, but consumer buying may decline. And increased or decreased demand for a firm's products or services will clearly be important. As shown in Figure 3.2, Ford has benefited from low inflation, low interest rates, low unemployment, and booming auto sales but faces a projected sales slowdown because of a glut of automobiles on the market.[4]

The economic dimension is also of vital importance to nonbusiness organizations as well. For example, poor economic conditions affect funding for state universities. Charitable organizations like the Red Cross and the Salvation Army are asked to provide greater assistance during bad times, while their incoming contributions dwindle. Hospitals are affected by the availability of government grants and the number of charitable cases they must treat for free.

The Technological Dimension

technology The set of processes and systems used by organizations to convert resources into products or services

Technology is the set of processes and systems used by organizations to convert resources into products or services. Although technology is

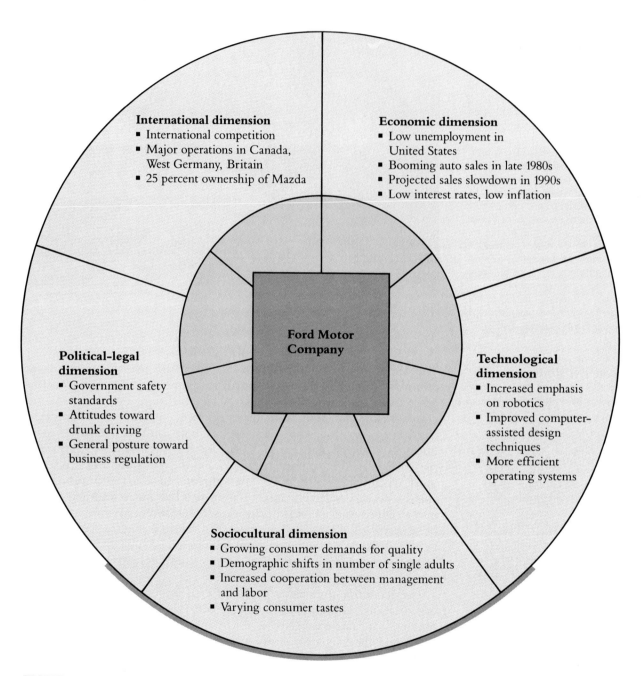

FIGURE 3.2

Ford's General Environment

applied within the organization, the nature and availability of that technology usually comes from the general environment. The rate of technological change in recent years has been spectacular. In just the last four decades we have seen the advent of computers, lasers, integrated circuits, semiconductors, xerography, and other wonders. Presently, computer-assisted manufacturing and design are paving the way for even more significant strides. Computer techniques, for example, allow McDonnell Douglas to simulate the three miles of hydraulic tubing that run through a DC-10. The results include decreased warehouse needs, higher-quality tube fittings, fewer employees, and significant time savings. The U.S. auto industry has historically required five years to take a new car from concept to the showroom. The Japanese can do it in three. Using computer-assisted design, Ford has recently been able to cut its cycle to four years, and some say that by the mid-1990s it will be possible to do it in a year.[5] Another important technological innovation is robots, explored in the Part V Enhancement Module, "Automation in the Workplace."

Management must be concerned with technology and technological innovations to keep pace with its competitors. Failure to support research and development adequately is often cited as a cause of declines in the growth rate of productivity experienced in the United States in the 1970s.[6] Similarly, renewed interest in R&D has played a role in recent increases in productivity. The move to a service-based economy has also affected many organizations. Thus, managers must pay careful attention to the technological dimension of their general environment, monitoring current developments to make informed decisions about investing in new technological breakthroughs.[7]

The Sociocultural Dimension

sociocultural dimension
The customs, mores, values, and demographic characteristics of the society in which the organization functions

The **sociocultural dimension** of the general environment is made up of the customs, mores, values, and demographic characteristics of the society in which the organization functions. Sociocultural processes are important because they determine the products, services, and standards of conduct that the society is likely to value. In the United States, status is important to many people, and some consumers are willing to pay premium prices for Ralph Lauren designer clothes, for example. In certain other countries, such merchandise has no market because consumers put more emphasis on function. Also, consumer tastes change over time. Drinking hard liquor and smoking cigarettes are far less acceptable than they were just a few years ago.

Appropriate standards of business conduct also vary across cultures. In the United States, accepting bribes and bestowing political favors in return are considered immoral. In other countries, the standards are different. Payments to local politicians may be expected in return for a favorable response to common business transactions such as applications for zoning and operating permits. The sociocultural dimension also influences how employees feel about an organization. Japanese workers, for example, often display more commitment and attachment to their organization than American workers do.

The shape of the market, the ethics of political influence, and attitudes in the work force are only a few of the many ways in which culture can affect an organization. Figure 3.2 shows that Ford is clearly affected by things like consumer demands for quality, demographic shifts, and changes in worker-management relations.[8] The important point is that managers should be alert to such effects and to sociocultural variations from place to place.

The Political-Legal Dimension

political-legal dimension
The government regulation of business and the general relationship between business and government

The term **political-legal dimension** refers to government regulation of business and the general relationship between business and government. It is important for three basic reasons: (1) It imposes certain legal constraints on an organization. (2) The extent to which it is pro- or anti-business significantly influences management policy. (3) Its stability is an important element in long-range planning.

First, the legal system partially defines what an organization can and cannot do. Although the United States is basically a free market economy, there is still significant regulation of business activity.[9] Ford, for example, is subject to a growing concern in Washington about automobile safety standards.

Second, pro- or anti-business sentiment in government influences business activity. The acquisition of Eastern Airlines by Texas Air, Continental's parent company, was possible partly because of the pro-business stance of the Reagan administration. If an anti-business attitude had prevailed, the acquisition might have been blocked because of anti-trust regulations.

Finally, political stability has ramifications for long-range planning. No American company wants to set up shop in another country unless the U.S. trade relationship with that country is relatively well defined and stable. Hence, American organizations are much more likely to do business with England, Mexico, and Canada than with Iran and El Salvador. Similar issues are also relevant to assessments of local and state governments. A change in the mayor's or the governor's position can affect many organizations, especially small firms that do business in only one location and are susceptible to deed and zoning restrictions, property and school taxes, and the like.

The International Dimension

international dimension
The extent to which an organization is involved in or is affected by business in other countries

A final component of the general environment for many organizations is the **international dimension**.[10] Multinational firms such as Boeing, IBM, Monsanto, and Exxon clearly affect and are affected by international conditions and markets. Specific issues relevant to Ford are noted in Figure 3.2. For example, Ford employs less than 50 percent of its total work force on American soil. Multinational firms buy, produce, and sell in many different countries. At a more modest level, a growing number of companies are just beginning to export their products and are experimenting with using a foreign agent or a few foreign sales offices. Even firms that do business in only one country may face foreign competition at home, and they may use materials or production equipment imported from abroad. Or a magazine publisher using photographs taken in another country may have to deal with foreign currency exchange rates to pay the photographer.

The international dimension also has implications for not-for-profit organizations. For example, the Peace Corps and the Methodist Church send representatives to underdeveloped countries. Medical breakthroughs achieved in one country spread rapidly to others, and cultural exchanges of all kinds take place between countries. Conditions as diverse as war, immigration, and educational exchange programs all contribute to this process. As a result of advances in transportation and communication technology in the past century, almost no part of the world is cut off from the rest. Virtually every organization is affected by the international dimension. "The Global View" describes how Philips, a European manufacturer, is dealing with the complex international market for home appliances. In Chapter 21 we explore management in the international sector.

THE TASK ENVIRONMENT

Because the impact of the general environment is often ill defined and long-term, most organizations focus more precisely on the task environment. Although it is also quite complex, the task environment provides useful information more readily than does the general environment. The manager can identify environmental factors of specific interest to the organization rather than having to deal with the more abstract dimensions of the general environment.

Figure 3.3 depicts the task environment at Ford Motor Company. As noted earlier, this environment consists of seven dimensions. In Ford's case, competitors include General Motors and Toyota; customers of interest are Ford dealers and Hertz Rent-A-Car as well as individual consumers; suppliers include Goodyear, USX, Eaton, Trinova, and Johnson Controls; and partners include Volkswagen and Nissan. Key regulators of Ford are the Federal Trade Commission and the Environmental Protection Agency; important labor unions include the United Auto Workers; and major owners include the Ford family.

Competitors

competitors Organizations that compete for resources

An organization's **competitors** are other organizations that compete with it for resources. The most obvious resources that competitors vie for are customer dollars. Reebok, Adidas, and Nike are competitors; Whirlpool, Maytag, and Kenmore (Sears) are competitors; and Kroger,

FIGURE 3.3

Ford's Task
Environment

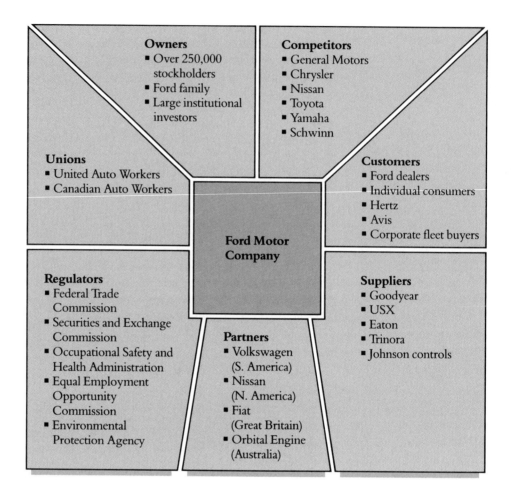

Winn-Dixie, and Circle K are competitors. Competition also occurs between substitute products. Thus, Chrysler competes with Yamaha (motorcycles) and Schwinn (bicycles) for your transportation dollars, and Walt Disney, Club Med, and Carnival Cruise Lines compete for your vacation dollars. Nor is competition limited to business firms. Universities compete with trade schools, the military, other universities, and the job market to attract good students. Art galleries compete with each other to attract the best exhibits.

Organizations may also compete for different kinds of resources besides consumer dollars. Two totally unrelated organizations may compete to acquire a loan from a bank that has only limited funds to lend. In a large city, the police and fire departments may compete for the same tax dollars. Firms compete for quality labor, technological breakthroughs and patents, and scarce raw materials.

Competitive relationships are usually complex. The manager should be alert to the competitive environment and careful not to oversimplify

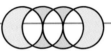

THE GLOBAL VIEW

NV PHILIPS' GLOEILAMPENFABRIEKEN

NV Philips' Gloeilampenfabrieken or simply Philips, as it is more commonly known, is a Dutch consumer electronics firm that has been a dominant manufacturer of electronic products throughout the world for years. Philips' holdings are vast. It owns a controlling interest in North American Philips, which markets products under many brands, including Magnavox, Sylvania, and Norelco. Philips has a major interest in a computer chipmaking facility in Hsinshu, Taiwan. It has subsidiaries scattered widely over the globe, including ones in Chile, Uruguay, and Brazil. Philips also has an arrangement with Sony in Japan for its compact-disk technology.

In the appliance field, although second to Electrolux in Europe, Philips was a distant sixth-place competitor worldwide in 1987 behind Electrolux, General Electric, Matsushita Electric, Whirlpool, and Bosch-Siemens. In 1988 Whirlpool and Philips began discussing a joint venture that would move their combined worldwide sales to third place (and very close to second). The potential is great; the problems, however, are numerous.

In most European countries, there is an appliance maker familiar with the specific country's market peculiarities; thus breaking into Europe is no easy task. The French use high temperatures for cooking and tend to splatter grease onto oven walls. Self-cleaning ovens, then, sell extremely well in France. In Germany, however, cooking is done more slowly and at lower temperatures. There is little splattering of grease, and self-cleaning ovens sell very slowly in Germany. In the past, Philips tried to respond to these national differences with compromise products, which were not profitable. Philips hopes that the deal with Whirlpool will enable it to overcome these problems by using Whirlpool's marketing and production expertise.

The management styles of the two firms are very different, however. As a result, internal adjustment may be necessary in order for the new venture to be successful. Further, Whirlpool had some concerns about the financial condition of Philips, but they were largely allayed when Philips CEO, Cornelis J. van der Klugt, sold several units to better focus the operations of the firm. Klugt also made strong moves to cut employment to further improve Philips' condition.

REFERENCES: Zachary Schiller, Joyce Heard, Karen Wolman and Thane Peterson, "Whirlpool Plots the Invasion of Europe," *Business Week*, September 5, 1988, pp. 70–72; Zachary Schiller and Jonathan Kapstein, "On the Verge of a World War in White Goods," *Business Week*, November 2, 1987, pp. 91–92; Shawn Tully, "A Competitor Who Smells Gunpowder," *Fortune*, August 3, 1987, pp. 43–44; Richard Sharpe, "Philips' New Try," *Management Today*, September 1987, pp. xxv–xxvi.

the information about it that flows into organization. Information about competitors is often quite easily obtained. K mart can monitor J. C. Penney's prices by reading its newspaper advertisements or by sending someone to a store to inspect price tags. Other kinds of information may be more difficult to obtain. Research activities, new-product developments, and future advertising campaigns, for example, are often closely guarded secrets.[11]

customers Individuals or other organizations that pay money to acquire an organization's products or services

Customers

A second dimension of the task environment consists of customers. Typically, the **customer** is the individual or organization that pays

It is essential that organizations recognize who their customers are. At first glance, for example, a computer company might view corporate America as its customer. IBM, however, knows that its customers come from a variety of areas besides business. This elementary school student in Arizona is using IBM's Writing to Read educational program. And she's only one of 300,000 students nationally using IBM software in their education.

suppliers   Organizations that provide resources for other organizations

money to acquire an organization's product or service. In many cases, however, the chain of transaction is more complex. As consumers, for example, we do not buy a bottle of Coke from Coca-Cola. We buy it from Safeway, which bought it from an independent bottler, which bought the syrup and the right to use the name from Coca-Cola.

Customers need not be individuals. Schools, hospitals, government agencies, wholesalers, retailers, and manufacturers are just a few of the many kinds of organizations that may be major customers of other organizations. Common sources of information about customers include market research, surveys, consumer panels, and reports from sales representatives.

Dealing with customers has become increasingly complex in recent years. Many firms have found it necessary to focus their advertising on specific consumer groups or regions. General Foods, for example, has found it necessary to promote its Maxwell House coffee differently in different regions of the country, even though doing so costs two or three times what a single national advertising campaign would cost.[12] Increased pressure from consumer groups about packaging and related issues also complicates the lives of managers.

Suppliers

Suppliers are organizations that provide resources for other organizations. For example, Disney World buys soft-drink syrup from Coca-Cola, monorails from Dae-Woo, food from Sara Lee and Smucker, and paper products from Mead. Suppliers for manufacturers like Corning Glass, Raychem, and Norton include the suppliers of raw materials as well as firms that sell machinery and other production devices. Another kind of supplier provides the capital needed to operate the organization. Banks, stockholders, federal lending agencies, and other investors are all suppliers of capital for businesses. State governments, federal grant agencies, and successful alumni are suppliers of capital for state universities. Other suppliers provide human resources for the organization. Examples include public and private employment agencies like Kelly Services and college placement offices.

Still other suppliers furnish the organization with the information it needs to carry out its mission. Many companies subscribe to periodicals such as *The Wall Street Journal*, *Fortune*, and *Business Week* to help their managers keep abreast of news. Market research firms are used by some companies. And some firms specialize in developing economic forecasts and in keeping managers informed about pending legislation. Most organizations try to avoid depending exclusively on particular suppliers. A firm that buys all of a certain resource from one supplier may be crippled if the supplier goes out of business, is faced with a strike, or raises prices to a prohibitive level. Most organizations try to develop and maintain relationships with a variety of suppliers, although doing so can occasionally be difficult. For example, when Delta Air Lines recently decided to order 100 new jets worth $6 billion, it had only two possible suppliers to turn to—McDonnell Douglas and Boeing.[13]

Regulators

regulators   Units that have the potential to control, regulate, or otherwise influence the organization's policies and practices

Regulators are units in the task environment that have the potential to control, regulate, or influence an organization's policies and practices. There are two important kinds of regulators: government agencies and interest groups.

regulatory agencies   Created by the government to regulate business activities

Government Agencies   **Regulatory agencies** are usually created by the government to protect the public from certain business practices or to protect organizations from one another. Powerful federal regulatory agencies include the Environmental Protection Agency (EPA), the Occupational Safety and Health Administration (OSHA), the Interstate Commerce Commission (ICC), the Securities and Exchange Commission (SEC), the Food and Drug Administration (FDA), the Federal Communications Commission (FCC), and the Equal Employment Opportunity Commission (EEOC). They are typically given official power to conduct investigations, set standards and rates, and levy fines or take other action against firms that violate the laws the agencies were created to enforce.

Many of these agencies play important roles in protecting the rights of individuals. The FDA, for example, helps ensure that the food we eat is free from contaminants, and the EPA tries to keep our environment clean. Most of the agencies have a significant degree of power to carry out their mandates. OSHA, for example, can force a business to stop operating until unsafe working conditions have been corrected. The costs a firm incurs in complying with government regulations may be substantial, but these costs are usually passed on to the customer. Even so, many organizations complain that there is too much regulation at the present time. One study found that 48 major companies spent $2.6 billion in one year—over and above normal environmental protection, employee safety, and similar costs—because of stringent government regulations. On the basis of these findings, the extra costs of government regulations for all businesses have been estimated at more than $100 billion per year.[14] Obviously, the impact of regulatory agencies on organizations is considerable.

Although federal regulators get a lot of publicity, the effect of state and local agencies is also significant. California has more stringent automobile emission requirements than those established by the EPA. And public utility rates are usually set by state agencies.

A good deal of attention is focused on the regulation of business firms, but not-for-profit organizations too must deal with regulatory agencies. Most states, for example, have coordinating boards that regulate the operation of colleges and universities.

interest groups   Formed by
their own individual members
to attempt to influence business

Interest Groups   The other basic form of regulator is the interest
group. Rather than being created by some branch of the government,
an **interest group** is organized by its members to attempt to influence
organizations. Prominent interest groups include the National Organization for Women (NOW), Mothers Against Drunk Drivers (MADD),
the Airline Passengers Association, the League of Women Voters, the
Sierra Club, various consumer groups (such as Ralph Nader's Center
for the Study of Responsive Law and Consumers Union), and industry
self-regulation groups like the National Advertising Review Board and
the Council of Better Business Bureaus. Interest groups lack the official
power of government agencies. They can, however, exert considerable
influence by using the media to call attention to their positions. MADD,
for example, puts considerable pressure on alcoholic-beverage producers (to put warning labels on their products), automobile companies (to make it more difficult for intoxicated people to
start their cars), local governments (to stiffen drinking ordinances), and
bars and restaurants (to limit sales of alcohol to people drinking
too much).

Labor

Organizations must also concern themselves with labor, especially when
it is organized into unions. The National Labor Relations Act of 1935
requires organizations to recognize and bargain with a union if that
union has been legally established by the organization's employees.
Presently, around 23 percent of the American labor force is represented
by unions. Some large firms such as Ford, Exxon, and General Motors
have to deal with a great many unions.

Even when an organization's labor force is not unionized, management should not ignore the role of unions. During the 1970s, Farah
Manufacturing Company, a southwestern clothing company, waged a
bitter legal fight to keep unions out of the company's plants in Texas
and New Mexico. K mart, J. P. Stevens, Honda of America, and Delta
Air Lines have also actively sought to avoid unionization.

Many people think primarily of blue-collar workers as union members, but many government employees, teachers, and other white-collar
workers are also represented by unions. In recent years the activities of
these nontraditional unions have attracted much attention. Recall the
strikes by the major league baseball players and the air traffic controllers
in 1981 and by the National Football League Players Association in
1987.[15]

And even when labor isn't organized, organizations must still be
aware of its importance. For example, experts predict that during the
1990s, the demand for skilled labor will exceed the supply. During that
same decade, U.S.-born white males will become an increasingly small
segment of the labor force. Organizations must take steps now to
modify their jobs to fit the kinds of workers that will be available and
implement training programs to prepare the workers of tomorrow.[16]

Owners

Owners are also becoming a major concern of managers in many businesses. Until recently, stockholders of major corporations were generally happy to sit on the sidelines and let top management run their organizations. Of late, however, more and more of them are taking active roles in influencing the management of companies they hold stock in.[17] This is especially true of owners who hold large blocks of stock. For example, in 1986, Richard Ferris, CEO of United Airlines, decided to embark on an aggressive campaign to develop an integrated travel-services company. In short order, he bought Pan Am's Pacific operation, Hilton International, Westin hotels, and Hertz Rent-A-Car and changed the company's name to Allegis. A Wall Street investment group called the Coniston Partners, who owned around 15 percent of the Allegis stock, decided this was a bad strategy. They pressured the board of directors to fire Ferris and dismantle his short-lived dream.

Another group exerting more and more influence is the managers of large corporate pension funds. These enormous funds control 50 percent of the shares traded on the New York Stock Exchange and 65 percent of Standard & Poor's 500 stocks. AT&T's pension fund, for example, exceeds $35 billion. Since pension funds are growing at twice the rate of U.S. GNP, it follows that their managers will have even more power in the future.[18] And given the increased power wielded by owners (and willingness to use that power), some fear that managers are sacrificing long-term corporate effectiveness for the sake of short-term results. For example, managers at Carnation were afraid to increase advertising costs too much for fear of attracting the attention of institutional investors. As a result, sales declined. After Nestlé took over and loosened the purse strings, sales took off again.[19] Thus, while organizations should never ignore their owners, they are having to be considerably more concerned about them now than in the past.

Partners

partners Two or more organizations working together in a joint venture or similar arrangement

A final dimension of the task environment consists of partners. **Partners** are two or more companies that work together in joint ventures or similar arrangements. As shown in Figure 3.3, Ford has a number of joint ventures, including an arrangement with Volkswagen to make cars in South America and another with Nissan to make vans in the United States. Ford and Mazda also jointly make the Probe automobile. Ventures such as these have been around for a long time, but they became popular in the early 1980s and are now increasing at a rate of around 22 percent per year. IBM used to shun joint ventures but now has 40 active partnerships around the globe.[20]

Such ventures help companies get from other companies the expertise they may lack. Joint ventures also help spread risk. Managers must be careful, however, not to give away sensitive competitive information. For example, when Sperry entered into a joint venture with Hitachi, a

Joint ventures and other forms of organizational partnerships are becoming increasingly common. This drilling barge, called the "Swampmaster," is the result of a joint venture between the national oil company of Nigeria and Chevron, a large U.S. petroleum company. Joint ventures usually allow both companies to be more productive than they could be if they worked alone.

Japanese computer maker, it found that it had to divulge valuable trade secrets in order to make the partnership work.

Joint ventures need not always involve business. Texas A&M University and the University of Texas, for example, often work together to secure government grants. And some churches sponsor joint missionary projects.

THE INTERNAL ENVIRONMENT

As shown in Figure 3.1, organizations also have an internal environment comprised of their board of directors, employees, and organizational culture. As in the external environment, different components of the internal environment are more or less important for different organizations. For example, not every organization has a board of directors. Corporations, of course, are required to have them but nonincorporated businesses and many nonbusiness organizations are not. (Most universities, however, do have a board of regents, and most other large organizations, including hospitals and charities, have a board of trustees that serves essentially the same purpose.) We discuss organizational culture in detail in Chapter 9 but describe the other two dimensions of the internal environment in the following paragraphs.

The Board of Directors

As noted above, a board of directors is required for all corporations. The board is elected by the stockholders and is charged with overseeing the general management of the firm to ensure that it is being run in a way that best serves the stockholders' interests.[21] Some directors are also full-time employees of the firm, usually holding top-management jobs. These directors are called inside directors. Outside directors, in contrast, are elected to the board for a specific purpose—to assist with financial management, legal issues, and so forth. They are not full-time employees of the organization, however. The board plays a major role in helping set corporate strategy and seeing that it is implemented properly. The board also reviews all important decisions made by top management and determines compensation for top managers.

Employees

External labor-force issues, including those associated with unions, are part of the external task environment. Once employees become members of the organization, however, they also become part of its internal environment. When managers and employees embrace the same values and have the same goals, everyone wins. When managers and employees work toward different ends, however, or when conflict and hostility pervade the organization, everyone suffers.[22] Many of the issues that we discuss in Part 4 of the book are aimed at enhancing interpersonal relationships in the organization. Of particular interest to managers today is the changing nature of the American worker. The work force of tomorrow will have more women, more Hispanics, more blacks, and more older people. The worker of tomorrow is also expected to want more job ownership—either partial ownership in the company or at least more say in how the job is performed.

ORGANIZATION-ENVIRONMENT RELATIONSHIPS

The preceding discussion identifies and describes the various dimensions of organizational environments. Because organizations are open systems, they interact with these various dimensions in many different ways. We now turn our attention to these interactions. We first discuss how environments affect organizations and then note a number of ways in which organizations respond to their environments.

How Environments Affect Organizations

Three basic frameworks can be used to describe how environments affect organizations. The first is environmental change and complexity. The other two are competitive forces and environmental turbulence.

Environmental Change and Complexity   One of the first people to recognize the importance of organizational environments was James D.

uncertainty A major force caused by change and complexity that affects many organizational activities

Thompson, an organizational theorist.[23] Thompson suggests that an organization's environment can be viewed along two dimensions: its degree of change and its degree of homogeneity. The degree of change is the extent to which the environment is relatively stable or relatively dynamic. The degree of homogeneity is the extent to which the environment is relatively simple (few elements, little segmentation) or relatively complex (many elements, much segmentation). In Thompson's view, these two dimensions interact to determine the level of **uncertainty** faced by the organization. Uncertainty, in turn, is a driving force that influences many organizational decisions. Figure 3.4 illustrates a simple view of the four levels of uncertainty defined by different levels of homogeneity and change.

The least environmental uncertainty is faced by organizations with stable and simple environments. Although no environment is totally without uncertainty, most franchised food operations (such as McDonald's and Taco Bell) and many container manufacturers (like Ball and Federal Paper Board) have relatively low levels of uncertainty to contend with. McDonald's, for example, focuses on a certain segment of the consumer market, produces a limited product line, has a constant source of suppliers, and faces relatively consistent competition from Burger King and Wendy's.

Organizations with dynamic but simple environments generally face a moderate degree of uncertainty. Examples of organizations functioning in such environments include clothing manufacturers (targeting a certain kind of clothing buyer but sensitive to fashion-induced changes) and record producers (catering to certain kinds of record buyers but alert to changing tastes in music). A clothing manufacturer such as Levi Strauss faces few competitors (Wrangler and Lee), has few suppliers and few regulators, and uses limited distribution channels. However, this relatively simple task environment also changes quite rapidly as

FIGURE 3.4

Environmental Change, Complexity, and Uncertainty

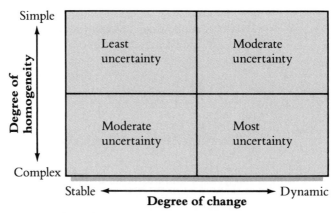

SOURCE: Adapted from J.D. Thompson, *Organizations in Action* (New York: McGraw-Hill, 1967), p. 72. Used with permission of the publisher.

competitors adjust prices and styles, consumer tastes change, and new fabrics become available.

The third combination of factors is one of stability and complexity. Again, a moderate amount of uncertainty results. General Motors, for example, faces these basic conditions. Overall, the organization must deal with a myriad of suppliers, regulators, consumer groups, and competitors. Change, however, occurs quite slowly in the automobile industry. Despite many stylistic changes, cars of today still have four wheels, a steering wheel, an internal combustion engine, and so forth.

Finally, very dynamic and complex environmental conditions yield a high degree of uncertainty. The environment has a large number of elements, and the nature of those elements is constantly changing. Intel, IBM, and other firms in the electronics field face these conditions because of the rapid rate of technological innovation and change in consumer markets that characterize their industry, their suppliers, and their competitors.

Five Competitive Forces   Although Thompson's general classifications are useful and provide some basic insights into organization-environment interactions, in many ways they lack the precision and specificity needed by managers who must deal with their environments on a day-to-day basis. Michael E. Porter, a Harvard professor and expert in strategic management, recently proposed a more refined way to assess environments. In particular, he suggests that organizations view their environments in terms of **five competitive forces**.[24] These are shown in Figure 3.5.

five competitive forces   The threat of new entrants, jockeying among contestants, the threat of substitute products, the power of buyers, and the power of suppliers

The threat of new entrants is the extent to which new competitors can easily enter a particular market or market segment. It takes a relatively small amount of capital to open a dry-cleaning service or a pizza parlor, but it takes a tremendous investment in plant, equipment, materials, and distribution systems to enter the automobile business. Thus, the threat of new entrants is fairly high for a local hamburger joint but fairly low for General Motors and Toyota.

Jockeying among contestants is the nature of the competitive relationship between dominant firms in the industry. In the soft-drink

FIGURE 3.5

Five Competitive Forces

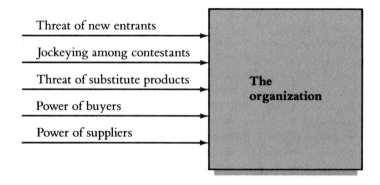

Organizations need to be sensitive to environmental change and complexity. Fitness-conscious consumers have become increasingly concerned about fat in cheese. In response, new companies like First World Cheese have made dramatic inroads into the market by developing cheese and cheese substitutes that are lower in fat, sodium, and cholesterol than cheeses made from whole milk. And the market for such products is growing by 40 percent each year.

industry, Coke and Pepsi often engage in intense price wars, comparative advertising, and new-product introductions. And U.S. auto companies continually try to outmaneuver each other with warranty improvements, rebates, and so forth. Local car-washing establishments, in contrast, seldom engage in such practices.

The threat of substitute products is the extent to which alternative products or services may supplant or diminish the need for existing products or services. The electronic calculator eliminated the need for slide rules. The advent of microcomputers, in turn, has reduced the demand for calculators as well as for typewriters and large mainframe computers. And Nutra-Sweet is a viable substitute product threatening the sugar industry.

The power of buyers is the extent to which buyers of the products or services in an industry have the ability to influence the suppliers. For example, there are relatively few potential buyers for a Boeing 747. Only companies such as American Airlines, United Airlines, and KLM can purchase them; hence, they have considerable influence over the price they are willing to pay, the delivery date for the order, and so forth. On the other hand, Japanese car makers charged premium prices for their cars in the United States during the late 1970s energy crisis because if the first customer wouldn't pay the price, there were two more consumers waiting in line who would.

The power of suppliers is the extent to which suppliers have the ability to influence potential buyers. The local electric company is the only source of electricity in your community. Hence, subject to local or state regulation (or both), it can charge what it wants to for its product, provide service at its convenience, and so forth. Likewise, even though Boeing has few potential customers, those same customers have few suppliers that can sell them a 300-passenger jet. So Boeing too has power. On the other hand, a small vegetable wholesaler has little power in selling to restaurants because if they don't like his or her produce, they can easily find an alternative supplier.

Environmental Turbulence   Although always subject to unexpected changes and upheavals, the five competitive forces can be studied and assessed systematically, and a plan can be developed for dealing with them. At the same time, though, organizations also face the possibility of environmental change or turbulence, occasionally with no warning at all. The most common form of organizational turbulence is a crisis of some sort. Table 3.1 lists a number of crises that different organizations have had to confront in recent years.

The effects of crises like those can be devastating to an organization, especially if managers are unprepared to deal with them. At NASA, for example, the shuttle disaster essentially paralyzed the U.S. space program for almost three years. The cost to Johnson & Johnson of the Tylenol poisonings have been estimated at $750 million in product recalls and changes in packaging and product design.[25] Union Carbide's legal problems arising from Bhopal will not be settled for years.

TABLE 3.1

Examples of Major
Organizational Crises

Date	Organization	Nature of Crisis
1979	Metropolitan Edison	Near meltdown at Three Mile Island nuclear power plant
1982	Johnson & Johnson	Cyanide poisoning of Tylenol capsules results in eight deaths
1984	Union Carbide	Poison gas leak at plant in Bhopal, India, kills 3,000 and injures another 300,000
1985	Jalisco	Bacteria in cheese kills 84
1986	NASA	Space shuttle *Challenger* explodes after takeoff, killing 7 crew members

SOURCE: Based on Ian Mitroff, Paul Shrivastava, and Firdaus E. Udwadia, "Effective Crisis Management," *The Academy of Management Executive*, August 1987, pp. 283–292.

Such crises affect organizations in different ways, and many organizations are developing crisis plans and teams. When a Delta Air Lines plane crashed in 1988 at the Dallas–Fort Worth airport, for example, fire-fighting equipment was at the scene in minutes. Only a few flights were delayed, and none had to be canceled. In 1987, a grocery store in Boston received a threat that someone had poisoned cans of its Campbell's tomato juice. Within six hours, a crisis team from Campbell's removed two truckloads of juice from all 84 stores in the grocery chain. Still, fewer than half of the major companies in the United States have a plan for dealing with major crises.[26]

How Organizations Respond to Their Environments

Given the myriad issues, problems, and opportunities in an organization's environments, how should the organization respond? Obviously, each organization must assess its own unique situation and then react according to the wisdom of its senior management.[27] Figure 3.6 illustrates the six basic ways in which organizations react to their environment. One reaction, social responsibility, is highlighted later in Chapter 22. Notice from the figure that some of these responses are internal to the organization and others have an external focus.

Information Management   One way in which organizations react to the environment is through information management. This is especially important in forming an initial understanding of the environment and in monitoring the environment for future changes. Organizations use

FIGURE 3.6

How Organizations Respond
to Their Environments

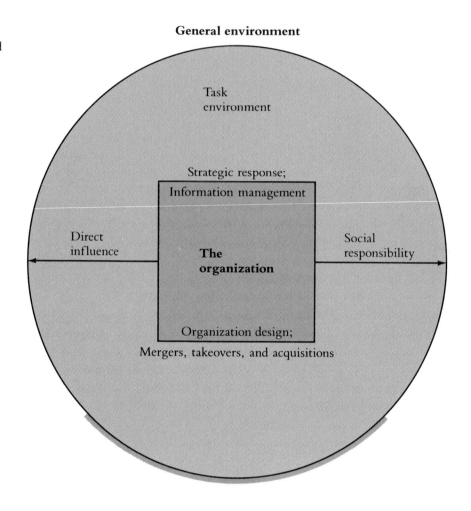

General environment

Task
environment

Strategic response;
Information management

Direct
influence

**The
organization**

Social
responsibility

Organization design;
Mergers, takeovers, and acquisitions

**techniques for information
management** Boundary
spanners, environmental scanning, and management information systems

several techniques for information management. One is defining
boundary spanners. A **boundary spanner** is someone like a sales representative or a purchasing agent who spends much of his or her time
in contact with others outside the organization. Such people are in a
good position to learn what other organizations are doing. All managers
engage in **environmental scanning**, the process of actively monitoring
the environment through observation, reading, and so forth. Within
the organization, Merrill Lynch, Federal Express, Eli Lilly, and many
other firms have also established elaborate **management information
systems** to gather and organize relevant information for managers and
to assist in summarizing that information in the form most pertinent
to each manager's needs (management information systems are covered
more fully in Chapter 18).

Strategic Response   After managers have achieved a basic level of
understanding of their environment, they often formulate a strategic
response. The response may involve doing nothing (for example, if

Irene Harrington is a boundary spanner. She works for National Steel, but she spends much of her time in a Chrysler plant. Her job is to make sure that National's products are meeting Chrysler's needs and specifications as they are delivered and used by the auto maker. National calls this plan its Person-in-Plant Program. Its intent is to build and improve relations with large customers like Chrysler.

they feel they are doing very well with their current approach), altering their strategy a bit, or adopting an entirely new strategy. If the market that a company currently serves is growing rapidly, the firm might decide to invest even more heavily in products and services for that market. Likewise, if a market is shrinking or does not provide reasonable possibilities for growth, the company may decide to cut back. For example, when Tenneco's managers recently decided that oil and gas prices were likely to remain depressed for some time to come, they decided to sell the company's oil and gas business and invest the proceeds in its healthier businesses like Tenneco Automotive.[28] An increasingly common form of strategic response, worthy of separate discussion, involves mergers, takeovers, and acquisitions (we discuss strategy more fully in Chapter 6).

Mergers, Takeovers, and Acquisitions A merger occurs when two or more firms combine to form a new firm. For example, Burroughs and Sperry Corporation recently merged to form Unisys. A takeover occurs when one firm buys another, sometimes against its will (a hostile takeover). Usually, the firm that is taken over ceases to exist and becomes part of the other company. For example, when Texas Air took over People Express, it folded People Express into its existing Continental Airlines operations—painting People Express planes to match Continental's fleet, merging reservations systems, and so forth. Finally, after an acquisition, the acquired firm often continues to operate as a subsidiary of the acquiring company. For example, even though Texas Air also took over Eastern Airlines, Eastern continues to maintain its own planes and handle its own reservations. Companies engage in these kinds of strategies for a variety of reasons. For example, they can ease entry into new markets or expand a firm's presence in a current market.

Organization Design Another organizational response to environmental conditions is through the organization's overall structural design. Research has shown, for example, that a firm that operates in an environment with relatively low levels of uncertainty might choose to use a bureaucratic design with many basic rules, regulations, and standard operating procedures. Alternatively, firms that face a great deal of uncertainty often choose a design with relatively few standard operating procedures, instead allowing managers considerable discretion over how they do things. The former type of design, called a mechanistic organization design, is characterized by formal and rigid rules and relationships. The latter, called an organic design, is considerably more flexible and permits the organization to respond more quickly to environmental change.[29] We learn much more about these and related issues in Chapter 9.

Direct Influence of the Environment Organizations are not necessarily helpless in the face of their environments.[30] Indeed, many organizations are able to directly influence their environment in many different ways. Firms use a variety of techniques for influencing their suppliers. One important strategy is to use a number of different suppliers, thus limiting the firm's dependence on any one. The organization may try to sign long-term contracts with fixed prices as a hedge against inflation. It may also attempt to become a supplier's largest customer to make the supplier more dependent on it. Or it may become its own supplier. Sears, for example, owns many of the firms that produce the goods it sells. Some of these suppliers were purchased by Sears; others were formed for the specific purpose of supplying merchandise to the retailing giant. Du Pont bought Conoco a few years ago partially to ensure a reliable source of petroleum for its chemical operations.

Influencing competitors is obviously more difficult than influencing suppliers. In a sense, though, almost any major activity a firm engages in affects its competitors. When Pioneer lowers the prices of its stereos, Fisher and Sony may be forced to follow suit. When Prudential lowers its life-insurance rates, New York Life and Mutual of Omaha are likely to do the same. For years whenever IBM would do anything, every other firm in the computer industry would follow suit.[31]

Organizations may also influence their customers in a variety of ways. Two common methods are changing the organization's customer base and changing the needs of present customers. The former strategy involves creating new uses for a product, finding entirely new customers, and taking customers away from competitors. Developing new kinds of software, for example, expands the customer base of computer companies. The other approach to influencing customers is to convince them that they need something they did not need before. Automobile manufacturers use this strategy in their advertising to convince people that they need a new car every two or three years.

Organizations also employ a number of strategies for influencing their regulators. Common approaches include lobbying and bargaining. Lobbying involves sending a company or industry representative to Washington in an effort to influence relevant agencies, groups, and committees. For example, the United States Chamber of Commerce lobby, the nation's largest business lobby, has an annual budget approaching $100 million. The automobile companies have been successful on several occasions in bargaining with the Environmental Protection Agency to extend deadlines for compliance with pollution control and mileage standards.[32] Mobil tries to influence public opinion and government action through an ongoing series of ads about the virtues of free enterprise.

Influencing interest groups is more difficult, although some firms attempt to do so. When members of the Moral Majority were strongly criticizing the television networks in the early 1980s, ABC ran a movie that depicted in an unfavorable light an evangelist who was much like that group's leader. The purpose of the movie was to present the public with an alternative perspective on the actions of the Moral Majority and perhaps to reduce the group's influence and power.

Most bargaining sessions between management and unions are also attempts at mutual influence. Management tries to get the union to accept its contract proposals, and unions try to get management to sweeten its offer. When unions are not represented in an organization, management usually attempts to keep them out. When Honda opened its first plant in the United States, it helped establish a plant union to head off efforts by the United Auto Workers to set up a branch of its own union in the plant.

Corporations influence their owners with information contained in annual reports, by meeting with large investors, and by pure persuasion. Partnership agreements are almost always negotiated through contracts. Each party tries to get the best deal it can from the other as the final agreement is hammered out.

In short, organizations have at their disposal a variety of tools and techniques that can be used to influence their environment. The extent to which they use these tools appropriately is a prime determinant of their overall effectiveness.

ORGANIZATIONAL EFFECTIVENESS

We noted in Chapter 1 the distinction between organizational effectiveness and efficiency. Efficiency involves using resources wisely and without waste. Effectiveness is doing the right things. Given the interactions between organizations and their environments, it follows that effectiveness is related to how well an organization understands, reacts to, and influences its environment.[33] U–Haul failed to keep pace with its environment and suffered significant setbacks as a result.

Models of Effectiveness

Unfortunately, there is no clear consensus about what constitutes effectiveness. For example, an organization can make itself look great in the short-term by ignoring R&D, buying cheap materials, ignoring quality control, and skimping on wages. Over time, though, the firm will no doubt falter. On the other hand, taking a longer view and making appropriate investments in R&D and so forth may displease investors who have a short-term outlook. Little wonder, then, that there are many different models of effectiveness.

Systems Resource Approach   The systems resource approach to organizational effectiveness focuses on inputs—that is, on the extent to which the organization can acquire the resources it needs.[34] A manufacturer that can get raw materials during a shortage, a college of engineering that can hire qualified faculty despite competition from industry, and a firm that can borrow at reasonable interest rates are all effective from this perspective. They are acquiring the material, human, financial, and information resources they need to compete successfully in the marketplace. Chrysler was successful from this perspective when, in the late 1970s, it was able to secure large loans and labor cooperation even though it was close to bankruptcy.

Rubbermaid is a good example of a firm that has achieved effectiveness through the goal approach. The company's CEO, Stanley Gault, has set a goal of achieving 30 percent of each year's sales from new products. As a result, literally hundreds of new products have been developed. Rubbermaid's product line includes over 2,000 products, ranging from office supplies to kitchen equipment to toys. Gault's dedication to innovation and his master plan for growth have helped triple sales since 1980.

Goal Approach   The goal approach to effectiveness focuses on the organization's outputs—that is, on the degree of goal attainment achieved by the organization.[35] When a firm establishes a goal of increasing sales next year by 10 percent and then achieves that increase, the goal approach maintains that the organization is effective. GE's overall goal of being either number 1 or number 2 in every industry it enters is used by CEO Jack Welch as an indicator of effectiveness.

Internal Processes Approach   A third approach to organizational effectiveness, the internal processes approach, deals more narrowly with the internal mechanisms of the organization. It focuses on minimizing strain, integrating individuals and the organization, and conducting smooth and efficient operations.[36] An organization that focuses primarily on maintaining employee satisfaction and morale and being efficient subscribes to this view. Whereas the systems resource perspective deals with inputs and the goal approach deals with outputs, the internal functioning approach concentrates on transformation processes. A well-managed firm like IBM is clearly effective from this point of view.

Strategic Constituencies Approach   The strategic constituencies approach to organizational effectiveness focuses on the groups that have a stake in the organization.[37] The strategic constituencies of Ralston Purina, for example, include its suppliers (food producers and container manufacturers), lenders (stockholders and banks), participants (employees and managers), customers, and others who are influenced by the company. In this view, effectiveness is the extent to which the organization satisfies the demands and expectations of all these groups.

Although these four basic models of effectiveness are not necessarily contradictory, they do focus on different things. Yet, as illustrated in "Management in Practice," truly effective organizations like Smucker must balance a variety of factors. Thus, rather than adopting a single approach to effectiveness, organizations need to take a comprehensive approach, like the one illustrated in Figure 3.7.

At the core of this unifying model is the organizational system, with its inputs, transformations, outputs, and feedback. Surrounding this core are the four basic approaches to effectiveness with a fifth link added. The basic argument is that an organization must essentially satisfy the requirements imposed upon it by each of the effectiveness perspectives.

Managerial Performance

managerial performance
The extent to which managers set appropriate goals, develop valid plans and systems for achieving them, and implement those plans efficiently and effectively

Achieving organizational effectiveness is not an easy task. To do so requires that managers perform at a high level.[38] **Managerial performance** is determined by the extent to which a manager (1) sets appropriate goals, (2) develops valid plans and operating systems for achieving those goals, and (3) implements those plans and systems efficiently

MANAGEMENT IN PRACTICE

SMUCKER'S—ITS GOTTA BE GOOD

The J. M. Smucker Company began in 1897 in Orrville, Ohio. It began as a maker of apple butter and cider from apple trees planted by Jonathan Chapman—the Johnny Appleseed of American legend. From these humble beginnings, Smucker's has become one of the most effective organizations in the country. Smucker's is the biggest maker of jams, jellies, and fruit preserves in the United States. With over 600 products and tremendous name recognition, Smucker's has about 36 percent of the market. It is followed by Welch Foods, Inc., which has a 12 percent share, and by Kraft, Inc., with a 9 percent share.

Smucker's financial effectiveness is apparent in many indicators. It is number 1 in market share. It has had steadily increasing sales revenues, earnings, and earnings per share. Smucker's is also effective in its dealings with employees and stockholders. Smucker's is still relatively small; it has only about 1,400 employees. The company is still largely managed by the Smucker family; the CEO is Paul Smucker, and the president, Richard Smucker, is the grandson of the founder, Jerome M. Smucker. The corporate climate is friendly and folksy. New stockholders get personal thank-you notes from the CEO.

Smucker's has achieved this effectiveness through a variety of means. It stays close to employees, growers, and customers. Smucker's managers know each employee by name. If necessary, the company will extend loans to its fruit growers. The company developed for its customers Goober Grape, a mixture of grape jelly and peanut butter in a jar, and it markets guava jelly in Hawaii. Smucker's stresses high quality in all of its products; it exceeds label-mandated minimum amounts of real fruit in its products. Smucker's has also taken step to protect itself from environmental uncertainty by irrigating its fruit crops—a move that paid off in the nearly disastrously dry year of 1988.

Smucker's learns from its mistakes. The company once tried to enter the pickle market but failed and has since concentrated on expansion through its traditional product lines. Those expansions have included fruit ice-cream toppings, bulk fruit fillings for bakeries and yogurt makers, Goober peanut butter, and Knudsen juice, as well as the acquisition in 1988 of the British gourmet preserve-maker Elsenham Quality Foods. Smucker's will continue to strive to expand in the future, too. After all, its market share in 1988 was still smaller than that of Campbell's in soups or Gerber's in baby foods.

REFERENCES: Gary Strauss, "Smucker Has Jelled into Jam Giant," *USA Today*, July 15, 1988, p. 3B; Andrew H. Malcolm, "Of Jams and a Family," *The New York Times Magazine*, November 15, 1987, pp. 87, 109; "JM Smucker Sets Purchase," *The Wall Street Journal*, July 20, 1987, p. 29.

and effectively. A key element of performing at a high level is being aware of one's environment and its meaning for the organization.

SUMMARY OF KEY POINTS

Environmental factors play a major role in determining an organization's success or failure. Organizations have three different environments: general, task, and internal.

The general environment is composed of the nonspecific elements of the organization's surroundings that might affect the activities of the organization. It consists of five dimensions: economic, technological, sociocultural, political–legal, and international. The effects of these dimensions on the organization are broad and gradual.

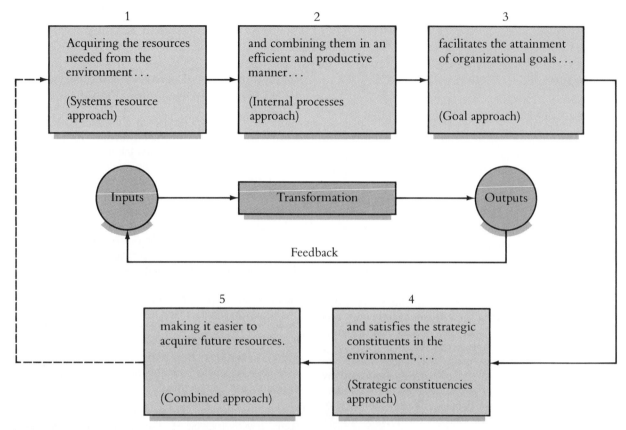

FIGURE 3.7

A Model of Organizational
Effectiveness

The task environment consists of specific dimensions of the organization's surroundings that are very likely to influence the organization. It consists of seven elements: competitors, customers, suppliers, regulators, labor, owners, and partners. Since these dimensions are associated with specific organizations in the environment, their effects are likely to be direct.

The internal environment consists of the organization's board of directors, employees, and its culture.

Organizations and their environments affect each other in several ways. Environmental influence on the organization can occur through uncertainty, competitive forces, or turbulence. Organizations, in turn, use information management, organization design, strategic response, mergers, takeovers, acquisitions, direct influence, and social responsibility to influence their task environments, and they occasionally try to influence broader elements of their general environment as well.

A key indicator of how well an organization deals with its environment is its level of effectiveness. Organizational effectiveness requires that the organization do a good job of procuring resources, managing them properly, achieving its goals, and satisfying its constituencies. Managerial performance plays a key role in attaining effectiveness.

DISCUSSION QUESTIONS

Questions for Review

1. What is meant by the term general environment? Identify and discuss each of the major dimensions of the general environment.
2. What is the task environment of an organization? What are the major dimensions of that environment?
3. What are the major forces that impact upon organization-environment relationships? Describe those impacts.
4. What is organizational effectiveness? How is it studied and assessed?

Questions for Analysis

5. Can you think of dimensions of the task environment that are not discussed in the text? Indicate their linkage to those that are discussed.
6. Through mergers and acquisitions, some organizations come to be part-owners of other firms. How does the nature of partial ownership complicate the organization-environment relationship?
7. How would each dimension of an organization's task environment and internal environment assess the organization's effectiveness? Can an organization be equally effective to each of these different groups? Why or why not?

Questions for Application

8. Go to the library and see how many different ways of assessing organizational effectiveness you can locate. Share your results with the class.
9. Interview a manager from a local organization about his or her organization's environments—general, task, and internal. In the course of the interview, are all of the major dimensions identified? Why or why not?
10. Outline the several environments of your college or university. Be detailed about the dimensions and provide specific examples to illustrate how each dimension impacts on your institution.

NOTES

1. "A New Generation Takes the Wheel at U-Haul," *Business Week*, March 28, 1988, p. 57; "The Family That Hauls Together Brawls Together," *Business Week*, August 29, 1988, pp. 64–66; "U-Haul Hits the Skids," *Newsweek*, September 14, 1987, pp. 54–55; "U-Haul Founders, Children Slug It Out At Meeting," *USA Today*, March 7, 1989, p. 3B.
2. For classic treatments of organizational environments, see James D. Thompson, *Organizations in Action* (New York: McGraw-Hill, 1967); and Richard H. Hall, *Organizations: Structure and Process*, 2nd ed. (Englewood Cliffs, N.J.: Prentice-Hall, 1977). For a general review, see John W. Meyer and W. Richard Scott, eds., *Organizational Environments* (Beverly Hills:

Sage, 1983). For recent perspectives, see Gregory G. Dess and Donald W. Beard, "Dimensions of Organizational Task Environments," *Administrative Science Quarterly*, March 1984, pp. 52–73; and Donald W. Beard and Gregory G. Dess, "Modeling Organizational Species' Interdependence in an Ecological Community: An Input-Output Approach," *Academy of Management Review*, July 1988, pp. 362–373.

3. See Jay B. Barney and William G. Ouchi, eds., *Organizational Economics* (San Francisco: Jossey-Bass, 1986), for an overview of current thinking about linkages between economics and organizations.

4. See "Ford's Record Earnings Dash Hopes," *USA Today*, February 19, 1988, p. 3B.

5. Jeremy Main, "The Winning Organization," *Fortune*, September 26, 1988, pp. 50–60.

6. W. Bruce Chew, "No-Nonsense Guide to Measuring Productivity," *Harvard Business Review*, January–February 1988, pp. 110–118.

7. Robert H. Hayes and Ramchandran Jaikumar, "Manufacturing's Crisis: New Technologies, Obsolete Organizations," *Harvard Business Review*, September–October 1988, pp. 77–85.

8. "For American Business: A New World of Workers," Business *Week*, September 19, 1988, pp. 112–120.

9. "Regulation Comes Back," *Newsweek*, September 12, 1988, pp. 44–45.

10. See Richard M. Steers and Edwin L. Miller, "Management in the 1990s: The International Challenge," *The Academy of Management Executive*, February 1988, pp. 21–23; and Richard I. Kirkland, Jr., "Entering a New Age of Boundless Competition," *Fortune*, March 14, 1988, pp. 40–48.

11. See Ian C. MacMillan, "Controlling Competitive Dynamics by Taking Strategic Initiative," *The Academy of Management Executive*, May 1988, pp. 111–118, for an interesting view of influencing competitors.

12. "National Firms Find That Selling to Local Tastes Is Costly, Complex," *The Wall Street Journal*, July 9, 1987, p. 17. See also Regis McKenna, "Marketing in an Age of Diversity," *Harvard Business Review*, September–October 1988, pp. 88–95.

13. "McDonnell, Boeing Vie for $6B Order," *USA Today*, August 19, 1988, p. 3B.

14. "Many Businesses Blame Governmental Policies for Productivity Lag," *The Wall Street Journal*, October 28, 1980, pp. 1, 22.

15. Edward E. Lawler III and Susan A. Mohrman, "Unions and the New Management," *The Academy of Management Executive*, November 1987, pp. 293–300; and John A. Fossum, "Labor Relations: Research and Practice in Transition," *Journal of Management*, Summer 1987, pp. 281–300.

16. "Needed: Human Capital," *Business Week*, September 19, 1988, pp. 100–108.

17. Benjamin M. Oviatt, "Agency and Transaction Cost Perspectives on the Manager-Shareholder Relationship: Incentives for Congruent Interests," *Academy of Management Review*, April 1987, pp. 214–225.

18. Nancy J. Perry, "Who Runs Your Company Anyway?" *Fortune*, September 12, 1988, pp. 140–146.

19. John J. Curran, "Companies That Rob the Future," *Fortune*, July 4, 1988, pp. 84–89.

20. Jeremy Main, "The Winning Organization," *Fortune*, September 26, 1988, pp. 50–60.

21. For recent studies concerning boards of directors, see Idalene F. Kesner, "Directors' Characteristics and Committee Membership: An Investigation

of Type, Occupation, Tenure, and Gender," *Academy of Management Journal*, March 1988, pp. 66–84; and Jeffrey Kerr and Richard A. Bettis, "Boards of Directors, Top Management Compensation, and Shareholder Returns," *Academy of Management Journal*, December 1987, pp. 645–664.

22. Marsha Sinetar, "Building Trust into Corporate Relationships," *Organizational Dynamics*, Winter 1988, pp. 73–79.

23. James D. Thompson, *Organizations in Action* (New York: McGraw-Hill, 1967).

24. Michael E. Porter, *Competitive Strategy: Techniques for Analyzing Industries and Competitors* (New York: Free Press, 1980).

25. Ian I. Mitroff, Paul Shrivastava, and Firdaus E. Udwadia, "Effective Crisis Management," *The Academy of Management Executive*, August 1987, pp. 283–292.

26. "Preparing for the Worst: Firms Set Up Plans to Help Deal with Corporate Crises," *The Wall Street Journal*, December 7, 1987, p. 23.

27. For recent discussions of how these processes work, see Barbara W. Keats and Michael A. Hitt, "A Causal Model of Linkages Among Environmental Dimensions, Macro Organizational Characteristics, and Performance," *Academy of Management Journal*, September 1988, pp. 570–598; and Danny Miller, "The Structural and Environmental Correlates of Business Strategy," *Strategic Management Journal*, Vol. 8, 1987, pp. 55–76.

28. "Why the Street Isn't Moved by Tenneco's Big Move," *Business Week*, September 26, 1988, pp. 130–133.

29. Tom Burns and G. M. Stalker, *The Management of Innovation* (London: Tavistock, 1961).

30. Keats and Hitt, "A Causal Model of Linkages Among Environmental Dimensions, Macro Organizational Characteristics, and Performance."

31. MacMillan, "Controlling Competitive Dynamics by Taking Strategic Initiative."

32. David B. Yoffie, "How an Industry Builds Political Advantage," *Harvard Business Review*, May–June 1988, pp. 82–89.

33. Arie Y. Lewin and John W. Minton, "Determining Organizational Effectiveness: Another Look, and an Agenda for Research," *Management Science*, May 1986, pp. 513–538; and Kim S. Cameron, "Effectiveness as Paradox: Consensus and Conflict in Conceptions of Organizational Effectiveness," *Management Science*, May 1986, pp. 539–553.

34. E. Yuchtman and S. Seashore, "A Systems Resource Approach to Organizational Effectiveness," *American Sociological Review*, Vol. 32, 1967, pp. 891–903.

35. Cameron, "Effectiveness as Paradox."

36. B. S. Georgopoules and A. S. Tannenbaum, "The Study of Organizational Effectiveness," *American Sociological Review*, Vol. 22, 1957, pp. 534–540.

37. Cameron, "Effectiveness as Paradox."

38. Fred Luthans, "Successful vs. Effective Real Managers," *The Academy of Management Executive*, May 1988, pp. 127–132; and George S. Odiorne, "Measuring the Unmeasurable: Setting Standards for Management Performance," "*Business Horizons*, July–August 1987, pp. 69–75.

CASE 3.1

American Express Manages Its Environment

In 1845 Henry Wells formed an express delivery company in Buffalo, New York, to deliver mail more cheaply than the federal government. He joined with two competitors in 1850 to form a new company, American Express. Shortly thereafter, in a dispute with the board of directors, Wells and his vice president, William Fargo, pulled out of American Express and in 1852 formed Wells Fargo & Company in San Francisco. American Express continued to prosper despite these losses in personnel.

Today, American Express (AmEx) is one of the best-known corporate names in the world. The main reasons for its high visibility and name recognition are that over 30 million people worldwide have American Express cards and travel-related services are the company's major source of revenue (about 40 percent) and profit (about 54 percent). Another reason for AmEx's visibility is the continued strong growth of this diversified financial-services corporation—from a net income of around $200 million in 1977 to over $1,100 million in 1987. AmEx's bank business accounts for about 12 percent of revenues and 10 percent of profits, and its Shearson Lehman Hutton operations account for about 32 percent of revenues and 28 percent of profits.

By 1988, American Express Travel Related Services Company (TRS) was regularly yielding an earnings increase of 15 percent per year and had a return on equity of about 28 percent. However, this spectacular level of organizational effectiveness was beginning to be challenged by other bank-card companies. Visa, MasterCard, and Sears's Discover card were beginning to make inroads into the business-travel niche, which for years had been the almost exclusive domain of AmEx's TRS. Other bank-card companies were issuing premium cards, and expanding their markets.

AmEx responded by redoing itself. It introduced a variable-rate, revolving-credit bank card, the Optima, specifically designed for people who have large monthly charges and travel abroad a great deal. It expanded its AmEx Travelers Cheques, despite grumbling from the banking industry, and by 1988 had over 50 percent of the market in travelers checks. AmEx began to wire money around the world to compete with Western Union, CitiCorp, and even the U.S. Postal Service.

In addition to these changes, TRS began to try to increase its base of cardholders from 30 million to over 60 million and its base of merchants from 2 million to over 6 million. TRS also began to sell more merchandise directly to its cardholders, including electronics gear, furniture, jewelry, luggage, mutual funds, mortgages, and insurance. The goal is to have these sales account for about 25 percent of TRS's profits by the year 2000. Travel Management Services (TMS) was introduced. TMS offers the bank card, travel and consulting services, and savings in corporate travel costs to corporations that become corporate sponsors. To ensure that all of this works efficiently, AmEx is expending over $100 million on a computer network that will tie all information about all customers together worldwide.

The computer information system promises to be a major factor in AmEx's ability to continue to be effective. The information can be made available to merchants who use their AmEx cards, and it can be sold to any merchant. The information that is available is continually being improved. An analysis of cardholder purchasing patterns could reveal preferences for food, merchandise, and entertainment so that these could be more precisely targeted by merchants.

Clearly, privacy issues, the potential for fraud, and the routine errors that normally occur could be major problems in such a system. AmEx is moving to use the latest technology, including artificial intelligence and handwriting recognition systems, in efforts to reduce such problems. Even so, a 99 percent accuracy rate for someone with 200 charges a year would still mean a problem every six months for that customer.

European banks and merchants appear to be moving toward a common payments system that will exclude American Express. That would be a major blow to AmEx and make signing up European merchants even more difficult. Further, the expansion of banking deregulation portends complicated times for AmEx. For the first time, more and more major banks will be able to offer services offered by AmEx. This increase in competition will increase the challenge facing American Express in the years ahead.

Questions

1. Describe the general environment of American Express. Cite specific examples of each dimension. How does each one impact upon the firm?
2. Identify a specific example of each dimension of the task environment of American Express. Describe the impact of each one on AmEx.
3. What do you think of AmEx's responses to its changing environment? Do you think that they will enable AmEx to continue to dominate its market? Why or why not?
4. How would each dimension of AmEx's task environment and internal environment assess AmEx's effectiveness? Can AmEx successfully respond to each of these different groups? Why or why not?

REFERENCES: "How AMEX Is Revamping Its Big, Beautiful Money Machine," *Business Week*, June 13, 1988, pp. 90–92; "Do You Know Me?" *Business Week*, January 25, 1988, pp. 72–82; Bill Powell and Carolyn Friday, "Leadership Has Its Privileges," *Newsweek*, March 14, 1988, p. 38; Barbara Kallen, "Who Cares What Eszter Balint Drinks?" *Forbes*, November 2, 1987, pp. 192–193.

CASE 3.2

Environmental Balancing Acts at Guinness

Guinness PLC, the centuries-old Anglo-Irish beer and spirits maker long known for its dark and foamy stout, faces major challenges from several components of its environment. One such challenge arose late in 1986 when executives at Guinness were implicated in illegal financial dealings by convicted inside trader Ivan F. Boesky. Another major challenge is the consumer movement away from the consumption of alcoholic beverages. That movement, which became especially pronounced during the 1980s, is slowing but nevertheless continuing.

In 1981 Ernest Saunders, an Austrian-born marketing manager at Nestlé in Switzerland, was named the chief executive at Guinness. Saunders had been an advertising executive for J. Walter Thompson Company and head of the international division at Beecham, the consumer products firm. Profits rose from $84 million in 1981 to $354 million by 1986. Saunders sold 150 marginally profitable units. He moved to redefine the firm as a consumer brands business rather than as just a brewer and liquor business. The core business was still beverages, though, and Saunders continued to acquire other firms to expand the Guinness empire so that it would be an international beverage conglomerate.

That expansion included the acquisition in 1986 of Bell's, the best-selling brand of Scotch in Britain, through the purchase of Arthur Bell & Sons. The acquisition of Distillers Company pushed Guinness into the hard-liquor market even further. When it turned out that the Distillers deal was not based on excellence in marketing but instead involved an extremely complicated pattern of financial arrangements, some of which were illegal, Saunders was quickly immersed in scandal.

That scandal grew and quickly spread to both sides of the Atlantic. It involved numerous top officials at several companies as well as the Zurich's Bank Leu. Legislation was passed in Great Britain; standards were tightened in both the United States and Britain; and a great many executives resigned or were fired, including Saunders.

By late 1987, Guinness had hired a new head, Anthony M. Tennant. Tennant came from the liquor unit of a major competitor, Grand Metropolitan PLC, and he quickly moved to clean up the mess. He set out to focus the firm as a brewing and liquor business. He sold unrelated holdings such as a chain of 7-Eleven stores and newspaper stores. He also regained control of the distribution rights for Dewar's White Label brand by buying Schenley Industries, Inc. Executives closely linked to Saunders were eased out. These changes may not only enable Guinness to respond to the scandal effectively but they may also enable Guinness to shore up its position in a declining world liquor market.

Whiskey (bourbon, Scotch, etc.) sales in the United States fell from about 225 million gallons in 1977 to 156 million gallons in 1987. Although nonwhiskey (vodka, gin, rum, etc.) sales increased from 208 million gallons in 1977 to 232 million gallons in 1987, the increase was not enough to prevent a dramatic reduction in total consumption. Total consumption of liquor in the United States fell by over 10 percent during that time.

Guinness has taken several steps to deal with this trend. Its advertising has been radically changed to try to appeal to people with youthful, active lifestyles. Some of the ads do not even show the product but merely mention the brand (albeit prominently). Marketing strategies have been overhauled so that obvious, direct, brand competition within the organization has been reduced. Thirty lesser Scotch brands that were not selling well have been eliminated, and the entire group of brands is being scrutinized to identify local market patterns that can be used to boost profits.

Distribution methods are also being reworked. In the past, each country had several local agents who did not coordinate efforts at all. Now there are distributors over whom Guinness has some control so that a better-coordinated system can be used. Some distribution joint ventures are also being formed, such as those with Jardine Matheson PLC in Japan and Moët-Hennessy in the United States and France. Advertising is also being increased because there is a clear pattern indicating that even when overall consumption is declining, the most-advertised brands hold their own or even increase sales.

Brand repositioning and distribution shifts should result in solid returns for Guinness. The firm believes that the scandal and its impact are history, and it is striving to deal with the changes in consumer tastes and increased competition. The results as of 1988 suggested that Guinness was effective, because it had operating margins of around 23.5 percent compared to 6.6 percent at Seagram, a major competitor.

Questions

1. From which environment did Guinness's challenges arise? What dimensions were involved? Cite specific examples.
2. Is Guinness effective? Why or why not? Be sure to indicate from which perspective you are making your assessment. Now, pick a different perspective and remake your assessment. Are there any changes? Why?
3. Do you think that Guinness will continue to be as effective in the future as it has been in the past? Why or why not?

REFERENCES: "Guinness: A Lesson in Dealing with Drier Times," *Business Week*, June 27, 1988, pp. 52–54; "More Trouble Brewing," *Barron's*, May 18, 1987, pp. 44–46; "Guinness' New Boss Starts Plugging the Holes," *Business Week*, October 5, 1987, p. 51; "Fearing That 'Muck Will Stick,'" *Time*, March 9, 1987, p. 61; "Guinness Is In Talks With Moet Vuitton About Future Role In The French Firm," *The Wall Street Journal*, January 11, 1989, p. A14.

ENHANCEMENT MODULE 1

Managerial Careers

Ellen Marram received her M.B.A. from Harvard in 1970 and then accepted a position as a marketing assistant at Lever Brothers. Two years later she jumped to Johnson & Johnson and then went to Standard Brands in 1977. That company was acquired by Nabisco in 1981. Marram stayed on and has since received four promotions. Today, she is president of the company's $1.2 billion-a-year grocery products' division (maker of such products as Fleischman's margarine and Nabisco Cream of Wheat). Her unit has 4,000 employees, and she earns $250,000 per year. Marram has earned a reputation as a shrewd manager and will likely be a candidate one day for the top spot at a major corporation.[1]

The work experiences of Ellen Marram are both common and unique. Most managers of today graduate from college and go on to work for an organization. They sometimes leave their original employer and work for someone else. They also get promoted occasionally. Other managers, such as Donald Peterson of Ford and Jim Treybig of Tandem Computers, have had some of the same experiences, like college and promotions, but each has had unique experiences as well. For example, Peterson has spent virtually his whole working life at Ford; Treybig, by contrast, left Hewlett-Packard to start his own company. This Enhancement Module provides some insight into managerial careers.

THE NATURE OF MANAGERIAL CAREERS

A person's career is the set of work-related experiences, behaviors, and attitudes encountered throughout his or her working life. One person may spend his entire career doing the same kind of work for the same company. Another may work for a number of different companies in a number of different jobs. Still another may open her own business and never work for someone else. Each of these patterns represents a career in its fullest sense.[2] This contrasts sharply with the notion of a job—a single work assignment performed for an organization.

Perhaps the key distinction between a job and a career is the level of psychological involvement by the employee. When employees think of their work only in terms of what they have to do between 8 and 5 everyday and how much they are paid for doing it, and they do not consider what they will be doing next year or the year after or how important the work itself is to them, they are viewing their work as simply a job. When individuals view their work in the context of a career, however, they are much more involved with what they do. They view the career with a long-term outlook and recognize that it is made up of a sequence of steps that, taken together, will engage their entire working lives. And although money is important, it is only one of many things (including promotion opportunities, recognition, personal satisfaction, etc.) that influence their behavior.

Figure EM1.1 illustrates the general stages people go through in their careers. The first stage, which generally occurs during the first few years of the individual's adult life, is called exploration. Through a long period of self-examination (based on observations of others, part-time jobs, talking to other people, and educational coursework), the person gradually decides that she or he may want to be an engineer, a doctor, a manager, or an artist and begins to prepare. The exploration stage continues even after the person finishes school and takes her or his first job. The chosen career may not live up to expectations, or the person may decide to work a few years and then return to graduate, medical, or law school.

Most people eventually settle on a career and then proceed into the establishment stage. During this phase, the individual is likely to receive occasional promotions and reassignments. Although changes may still occur, at this stage the person generally knows what she or he is interested in and starts to establish an occupational identity.[3] Even though El-

FIGURE EM1.1

Common Career Stages

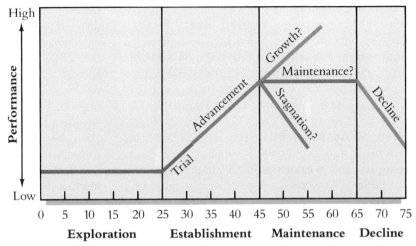

SOURCE: Adapted from *Careers in Organizations,* by Douglas T. Hall. Copyright © 1976 by Scott, Foresman and Co. Reprinted by permission.

len Marram changed jobs several times early in her career, she always worked for consumer products firms. Such job changes are common during this phase. Few people spend their whole careers with the same organization.

The next phase, which starts around the age of 45 for the average person, is called the maintenance, or midcareer, stage. During this time, several things are possible. Some people continue on an upward track toward an upper-level management position. Others reach a plateau—a position where they are likely to remain.[4] Still others begin to stagnate and decline. Managers in the first position are likely to be groomed for specific openings at the highest levels of the organization. Managers on a plateau often find themselves serving as mentors for younger managers. Those in the last group find themselves increasingly less valued by the organization and may be subject to demotion, termination, or early retirement.

The final career stage for most people is decline or disengagement. During this stage, the person can look ahead and see the end of her or his career. She or he begins to plan for retirement and gradually starts psychologically withdrawing from the organization. Many top executives stay on for a while after their formal retirement, however, to work as advisers and to help train their replacements. And more and more "retired" managers, not content to relax at home, are starting new careers late in life.

For example, when he retired at the age of 63 after thirty years as an insurance agent, Thomas S. Duck founded the Ugly Duckling Rent-a-Car company in Tucson. Today he has over 600 outlets and annual revenues of $85 million.[5]

CAREER MANAGEMENT

Given this basic understanding of how careers unfold, and given the importance of a career to the person involved, you should not be surprised to learn that managing career dynamics is important both to individuals and to organizations.

Individual Career Planning

Career planning must start with the individual. After all, only the individual can truly know what he or she wants from life and work. However, people must avoid overplanning. For example, some people set specific goals as to when they want to be promoted, and they identify specific jobs they want to have as they progress up the organizational ladder. Such rigidity promises disappointment if the promotion is delayed and may cause the person to miss an opportunity to have an exciting new job. Walter Wriston, former CEO of Citibank, held several jobs on his way to the top spot—and not one of them had even existed when he joined the bank![6] Thus, it is important to achieve a balance between knowing generally what you want and how to go about getting it and being rigidly fixed on a specific goal with an inflexible timetable and agenda. Two important tools for achieving this balance are personal assessment and mentor relationships.

Personal Assessment   Personal assessment is learning about yourself—your aspirations, strengths, and weaknesses—and about career opportunities. Many people argue that it is important that you choose a career in an area you enjoy. For example, Debbi Fields enjoyed baking cookies more than anything else. After several years of frustration while searching for a career, she decided to open a store and sell her cookies. Today, Mrs. Fields' Cookies is a multi-million-dollar business with hundreds of stores around the world. The starting point in individual career management is learning about oneself. This inner exploration can be achieved through analysis of the kinds of part-time work you have enjoyed, the courses you have enjoyed, and an honest assessment of what you want from life. University counseling centers offer tests and aptitude profiles that can provide useful insights.

Coupled with this kind of assessment is determining what kind of organization you want to be a part of. Some people want to work for a large company like Xerox or Digital Equipment because it provides security and prestige. Others want to work in a smaller organization. Others want to start their own business in order to be independent.[7] And, of course, preferences and options often change over the course of a career. It may be necessary to work for a big company at first in order to save enough money to launch your own business later.

You should try to be realistic about your options. If you are a small adult with limited athletic skills, you are not likely to succeed as a professional football player. You might be successful as a coach or trainer. If your grades are mediocre and you have no aptitude for science, you are unlikely to gain admittance to medical school, and you might as well rule out a career as a doctor. But you might succeed as a medical administrator.

Another important element of personal assessment is learning about opportunities. A field that is growing and expanding provides more opportuni-

ties than one that is shrinking. Some fields are more difficult to break into than are others. Consider, for example, the hundreds of young people who trek to Hollywood to become movie stars. Only a few succeed. Many fields, like medicine, university teaching, and law, require extra years of formal education. You must decide what is best for you, what sacrifices you are willing to make to reach your goals, and then, with realistic expectations, set out to reach them.

Mentor Relationships   Another useful tool for managing one's career is mentor relationships. A mentor is a senior manager who acts as a sponsor, advocate, and teacher for a younger and less experienced new manager, sometimes called a protégé.[8] Mentors are usually in the maintenance stage of their own careers. The mentor-protégé relationship is usually informal and can be initiated by either party. The younger manager may ask the mentor for advice or assistance, or the senior manager may recognize special traits in the younger manager and start taking special interest in his or her performance. At various times during the mentor-protégé relationship, the mentor teaches and counsels the protégé about performance-related issues, organizational politics, and other important matters. If the mentor thinks it appropriate, he or she also helps advance the protégé's career by telling others how good the protégé's work is, recommending her or him for new job assignments, and so forth.

Johnson & Johnson, Jewel Food Stores, Federal Express, AT&T Bell Laboratories, Colgate-Palmolive, and other organizations have formal mentor programs. Colgate-Palmolive CEO Reuben Marks is a firm believer in the importance of mentor relationships. Besides taking part in the formal program within his company, Marks also participates in another program where he serves as a mentor to disadvantaged minority youths.[9]

Organizational Career Planning

Mentoring can be either an individual or an organizational approach to career planning. Other techniques are more purely organizational. Table EM1.1 summarizes several career-planning programs used by American companies.[10] AT&T, Bank of Amer-

TABLE EM1.1

Organizational Career Planning Techniques

Technique	Description
Career management program	Formal and comprehensive program to help organizations and individuals understand career dynamics within the organization
Career counseling	Formal method for providing employees with counseling and advice about their careers
Career-pathing	Identification of logical and coherent progressions of jobs that individuals might choose to pursue
Career resources planning	Application of planning methods to help people and organizations understand and predict when specific jobs might be open and when specific individuals might be prepared to fill them
Career information systems	Formal information system that provides some or all of the information from the above-mentioned techniques to employees in a highly accessible manner

ica, General Electric, General Foods, and Sears all have formal career management programs for employees. Each attempts to help employees understand career options and limits within the company, identify their individual priorities and potential, and develop general strategies for achieving a good match between what the organization and the individual want and need.

Increasingly, organizations are also confronting the interrelationships of career management and the globalization of the business world. Nestlé and other organizations have a cadre of international managers who have been trained to accept work assignments anywhere in the world. Some companies are just beginning to recognize the role of international work assignments in individual careers.[11]

SPECIAL ISSUES IN CAREERS

Recent years have seen the advent of new career issues for managers to contend with. These issues include opportunities for women and minorities, dual-career couples, and career transitions.

Women and Minorities

Most people are generally aware of the dramatic changes in recent years in the number of women and minorities pursuing professional careers of all types, but especially as managers. In 1972, only 4 percent of those receiving M.B.A. degrees were women and women held only 20 percent of U.S. management and administrative positions. By 1987, those figures increased to 33 and 37 percent, respectively.[12]

Nevertheless, women still experience various forms of discrimination, often subtle; and although some have made it to the upper echelons, there are still few women in the top-management ranks of large American companies. Those companies, however, recognize the importance of women managers to organizational success and are actively working to help them attain top positions.[13]

The situation of minorities is less positive. Even though many organizations have hired large numbers of black managers, for example, few have moved into meaningful top-management positions.[14] And there are very few Hispanic managers in American business. Still, progress is being made, and the minority communities have success stories they can be proud of. Reginald F. Lewis, for example, is a successful black entrepreneur. His TLC Group is one of the largest investment companies on Wall Street. Its biggest deal to date was purchasing Beatrice International Foods for $985 million in 1987.[15]

Dual-Career Couples

The entry of more and more women into the workplace has created an issue that organizations must increasingly confront—the dual-career couple. A dual-career couple exists when both partners in a relationship are pursuing careers. The tensions and problems caused by two careers range from the mundane to the traumatic. For example, with both partners working, there are relatively simple problems of coordination like buying groceries and scheduling vacations. More significant, however, are questions about who will stay home with a sick child (especially if the illness is long-term) and what will happen if one partner is transferred to another city. Some couples decide that one partner's career will take precedence over the other's; some couples manage with a "commuter" marriage.

Some organizations are becoming sensitive to the needs and problems faced by dual-career couples. General Motors provides counseling and referral services for the spouse of a transferred employee. IBM provides childcare assistance and provides all employees with up to a year of unpaid leave for childcare at home. Merck provides childcare, flexible working hours, and work-at-home options to dual-career couples. Still, most businesses are just beginning to address the problem.[16]

Career Transitions

A final area of concern and interest involves career transitions. Most people go through a series of stages in the course of their careers. Transitions through these stages may be either planned or unplanned.

Planned Transition   A planned transition occurs when the individual or the organization knows about a change in advance and can plan for it. Candidates for top-management positions often know about new job assignments several months in advance, for example, and can carefully plan things associated with the new assignment. Even middle and lower-level managers often have some advance word about transfers or promotions. More problematic, but no less important, is an employee who has reached a career plateau. Some people in this circumstance are no longer valued by the organization and may be targeted for early retirement or termination. Many others, though, are quite valuable in their current positions, and both the manager and the organization must work together to preserve a valuable working relationship.[17]

Unplanned Transition   Unplanned transitions occur when the individual or the organization has little or no advance warning about a career change. For example, a death or unexpected resignation can prompt a promotion with no advance warning. Corporate restructurings, unexpected layoffs and terminations, mergers, acquisitions, and takeovers can create circumstances in which managers previously secure in their jobs find themselves out of work.[18] Some organizations do little to help in these circumstances, but more and more firms provide outplacement assistance to terminated employees. Outplacement assistance, usually administered by a specialized service firm, helps the employee cope with the problem and locate new employment. Such services are likely to become increasingly common.[19]

NOTES

1. Monci Jo Williams, "Women Beat the Corporate Game," *Fortune*, September 12, 1988, pp. 128–138 and "Corporate Women," *Business Week*, June 22, 1987, pp. 72–78.
2. For recent reviews of the careers literature, see Edgar H. Schein, "Individuals and Careers," in Jay W. Lorsch, ed., *Handbook of Organizational Behavior* (Englewood Cliffs, N.J.: Prentice-Hall, 1987), pp. 155–171; and Douglas T. Hall and Associates, *Career De-*

velopment in Organizations (San Francisco: Jossey-Bass, 1986).

3. Mary Pat McEnrue, "Length of Experience and the Performance of Managers in the Establishment Phase of Their Careers," *Academy of Management Journal*, March 1988, pp. 175–185.

4. Daniel C. Feldman and Barton A. Weitz, "Career Plateaus Reconsidered," *Journal of Management*, Winter 1988, pp. 69–80; and Walter Kiechel III, "High Up and Nowhere to Go," *Fortune*, August 1, 1988, pp. 229–233.

5. Faye Rice, "Lessons from Late Bloomers," *Fortune*, August 31, 1987, pp. 87–91.

6. "Expert View," *Working Woman*, October 1985, p. 154.

7. Glenn R. Carroll and Elaine Mosakowski, "The Career Dynamics of Self-Employment," *Administrative Science Quarterly*, December 1987, pp. 570–589.

8. Raymond A. Noe, "Women and Mentoring: A Review and Research Agenda," *Academy of Management Review*, January 1988, pp. 65–78; Charles D. Orth, Harry E. Wilkinson, and Robert C. Benfari, "The Manager's Role as Coach and Mentor," *Organizational Dynamics*, Spring 1987, pp. 66–74; and Kathy E. Kram, *Mentoring at Work: Developmental Relationships in Organizational Life* (Glenview, Ill.: Scott, Foresman, 1985).

9. Dan Hurley, "The Mentor Mystique," *Psychology Today*, May 1988, pp. 38–43.

10. See Cherlyn Skromme Granrose and James D. Portwood, "Matching Individual Career Plans and Organizational Career Management," *Academy of Management Journal*, December 1987, pp. 699–720; and Douglas T. Hall, "Careers and Socialization," *Journal of Management*, Summer 1987, pp. 301–321.

11. Rosalie L. Tung, "Career Issues in International Assignments," *The Academy of Management Executive*, August 1988, pp. 241–244.

12. "Corporate Women."

13. Mariann Jelinek and Nancy J. Adler, "Women: World-Class Managers for Global Competition," *The Academy of Management Executive*, February 1988, pp. 11–19; and Jan Grant, "Women as Managers: What They Can Offer to Organizations," *Organizational Dynamics*, Winter 1988, pp. 56–63.

14. "Many Hurdles, Old and New, Keep Black Managers Out of Top Jobs," *The Wall Street Journal*, July 10, 1986, p. 25.

15. "Beatrice Deal a Landmark for Black Business," *USA Today*, August 11, 1987, p. 2B.

16. "Best Employers for Women and Parents," *The Wall Street Journal*, November 30, 1987, p. 21.

17. Feldman and Weitz, "Career Plateaus Reconsidered." See also Priscilla M. Elsass and David A. Ralston, "Individual Responses to the Stress of Career Plateauing," *Journal of Management*, March 1989, pp. 35–47.

18. Diane Cole, "Fired, but Not Frantic," *Psychology Today*, May 1988, pp. 24–25; and "Stable Cycles of Executive Careers Shattered by Upheaval in Business," *The Wall Street Journal*, May 26, 1987, p. 27.

19. "The Do's and Don'ts of Outplacement," *Psychology Today*, May 1988, p. 26.

INTEGRATIVE CASE

The Martian Empire

The Martian empire isn't located on a distant planet in our solar system. The $12 billion–plus empire is centered in McLean, Virginia, the home of the Mars family's privately owned business. The company operates production facilities in several states and markets its products worldwide. In 1988, four of the ten best-selling chocolate candies in the United States were made by Mars—Snickers (number 1), M&M peanuts (3), M&M plain (4), Milky Way (8)—and others, like Twix (which is growing) and Three Musketeers (which is shrinking), are not far behind. Pet foods (Kal Kan, Pedigree, Whiskas) account for nearly as many dollars of sales as does candy—over $3 billion each. The rest of the Mars empire consists of the food products business of Uncle Ben's (rice, prepared dinners) and a small electronics business.

In 1932, Forest Mars, Sr., was told by his father (Frank Mars) that the candy company, then based in Chicago, was not big enough for both of them. The elder Mars gave his son the rights to manufacture and sell Milky Way overseas and told him to start his own business. Forest did just that.

Forest founded his new company in Britain and was very successful there with both Milky Way and Mars bars. He also entered the pet-food business and soon commanded over half of the British market. In 1964, after a bitter family quarrel, Forest wrested the original company away from his father, integrated it into his Mars organization, and built it into a unique and highly successful conglomerate. One of his new products, which proved to be tremendously successful, was an American version of Smarties, a British sugar-coated candy with a chocolate center. Dubbed M&M's (Mars & Mars), it soon joined other Mars brands as a top seller in the United States and launched the firm toward dominance of the candy industry.

During the 1960s, the Mars company developed management practices that were both innovative and controversial. To promote an egalitarian atmosphere, all employees are called associates. Pay scales about 10 percent above industry norms were established. Unusually good fringe-benefit packages were established. Special privileges for executives were eliminated: Everyone has to hunt for parking spaces, and everyone has to punch a time clock. To assure fast and effective communication, private offices were eliminated in favor of a pattern of desks in concentric circles (higher-ranking personnel toward the center). Money that might have gone into offices and executive privileges went into the best technology available for Mars plants, which are kept spotless. A strong emphasis on quality led Mars to date its products and take back unsold merchandise well before government regulation required such practices of the whole industry. These practices worked well, enabling Mars to pass Hershey as the leader in the candy market during the 1970s.

A tall organizational structure was instituted to allow for rapid promotion as an incentive to bright young managers. Over time, however, decision making became centralized and managers did not have authority commensurate with their responsibility. Recent downsizing of the organization eliminated some of the career development that had been possible through rapid promotion. The continued presence of a large number of family members in managerial positions has also tended to reduce perceived if not real career options for managers who are not family members.

Struggles between the brothers and a growing inability to effect change have caused problems within the organization, and some valuable executives have left. The head of the new-product development department left, as did several managers in the electronics unit. Most of the departures were over the planned strategies of the units involved and the inability of the managers to influence any change in those strategies.

The departure of the new-product development official was particularly damaging to Mars because of the need to introduce new confections to expand market share. As a result, Mars has had to focus its attention on developing and expanding sales of existing brands rather than on the development and introduction of new products or product lines.

In an effort to break into the frozen confectionary market, which Nestlé and Heath had already entered, in 1986 Mars acquired Dove International, a Chicago manufacturer of ice cream on a stick. It has been struggling with Dove ever since. Mars expanded production facilities but was unable to expand sales sufficiently. It has been making Three Musketeers and Snickers ice cream bars to utilize the extra capacity of the plant. Despite its long-established image as a maker of wholesome snacks, Mars's entry into granola snacks with Kudos was three years behind Hershey's entry with New Trail.

The managers who left had felt that the environment faced by the firm was changing and that strategies should be changed to respond to those environmental changes. In particular, candy sales had flattened during the mid-1950s, leveling at a per capita amount of around 19 pounds per year. Moreover, competition in the candy business is increasing in the United States and abroad.

The competitive environment is also changing in pet foods. Quaker Oats purchased Gaines Pet Foods in 1987 to become the number 2 firm in that industry behind Ralston Purina. ALPO was acquired by the British conglomerate Grand Metropolitan in 1980, and Carnation was acquired by Nestlé shortly thereafter. Thus the composition of the industry altered to heighten the competitive battle in pet foods. Mars has used its knowledge and skill in the international market to respond to these changes, moving strongly throughout Europe and Japan.

Mars did exceedingly well in the past. It grew from a local organization into an international one that totally dominated its domestic market. The question is can Mars continue to grow? A tightly held organization filled with family members striving to make it to the top and plagued with a battle between brothers may have a bleak future, especially in increasingly competitive markets.

Questions

1. Identify each of the different parts of the management process at Mars. Cite specific examples. What managerial skills can you identify?
2. How does knowledge about the beginnings of Mars help you to understand the company's present position and problems? Which management perspective(s) is (are) most obvious in the operation of Mars? Cite specific examples.
3. From which environment did challenges to Mars arise? What dimensions were involved? Cite specific examples. Describe the several environments surrounding Mars. Which, in your judgment, is most important and why?
4. Is Mars effective? Would Mars be considered equally effective from several perspectives? Is Mars likely to be as effective in the future? Why or why not?
5. Is Mars the type of organization for which you would like to work? Is it the type of organization in which you would like to invest your money?

REFERENCES: Bill Saporito, "Uncovering Mars' Unknown Empire," *Fortune*, September 26, 1988, pp. 98–104; Jaclyn Fierman, "The Americans," *Fortune*, September 22, 1988, pp. 49–58; Janet Myers, "Mars Shuffles Shops, but Maintains Strategy," *Advertising Age*, February 1, 1988, p. 73; Wayne Walley, "Disney Enlists Time, Inc., Mars to Honor Mickey," *Advertising Age*, June 6, 1988, pp. 3, 78; Bill Saporito, "Cashing In on Food and Drink," *Fortune*, October 12, 1987, pp. 152–153; "Candy May Be Dandy, but Confectioners Want a Sweeter Bottom Line," *Business Week*, October 6, 1986, pp. 66–70; Steve Lawrence, "Bar Wars: Hershey Bites Mars," *Fortune*, July 8, 1985, pp. 52–57; "Mars Struggles To Reclaim Candy Crown," *The Wall Street Journal*, March 29, 1989, p. B1.

II DECISION MAKING AND PLANNING

OUTLINE

The Nature of Decision Making
Decision Making Defined · Types of Decisions · Decision-making Conditions

Models of the Decision-making Process
The Classical Model · The Administrative Model

Steps in Rational Decision Making
Recognizing and Defining the Decision Situation · Identifying Alternatives · Evaluating Alternatives · Selecting an Alternative · Implementing the Chosen Alternative · Following Up and Evaluating the Results

The Behavioral Nature of Decision Making
Political Forces in Decision Making · Intuition and Escalation of Commitment

Group Decision Making
Forms of Group Decision Making · Advantages of Group Decision Making · Disadvantages of Group Decision Making Managing Group Decision-making Processes

Quantitative Tools for Decision Making
Payoff Matrices · Decision Trees · Other Techniques

4

Managerial Decision Making

OBJECTIVES

After studying this chapter, you should be able to:

- Discuss the nature of decision making.
- Summarize the basic models of decision making.
- Identify and discuss the steps in decision making.
- Describe the behavioral nature of decision making.
- Discuss group decision making.
- Discuss quantitative tools for decision making.

OPENING INCIDENT

Compaq Computer is one of America's fastest-growing large companies. The company was founded a few years ago by a group of former Texas Instruments executives. Its initial strategy, making high-quality computers compatible with IBM machines and working closely with retailers to market them, propelled the young company into the *Fortune* 500 in only four years. Compaq's sales increased from a little over $100 million in 1983 to $1.25 billion in 1987.

One of the key factors that Compaq executives cite in describing their amazing success is their approach to decision making. They work hard to deal with every situation rationally and objectively. Their goal is to make no mistakes. They scrutinize every problem and opportunity until they have all the information they feel they need to make a decision. Then they discuss every alternative, focusing on assumptions and facts. Finally, they eliminate assumptions that are inaccurate or ungrounded, concentrating on the facts themselves. The end result is usually consensus about what needs to be done. And the consensus is usually right.[1]

*E*xecutives at Compaq Computer exemplify the way many managers think about decision making—rationally, logically, and precisely. Some experts feel that decision making is the most basic and fundamental of all managerial activities. Thus, we begin our in-depth treatment of the first managerial function, planning, with a discussion of this critical activity. Keep in mind, however, that although decision making is perhaps most closely linked to the planning function, it is also part of the organizing, leading, and controlling functions. Remember too that although managers at Compaq and other companies pursue rationality, many decisions are affected by such nonrational factors as emotion, attitudes, and individual preferences and needs.

We begin our discussion by exploring the nature of decision making. We then describe two models of decision making, the classical and administrative models. After summarizing the steps in the decision-making process, we describe the behavioral nature of decision making. We then discuss group decision making and conclude by identifying some other useful tools for making decisions.

THE NATURE OF DECISION MAKING

Managers at Chrysler recently made the decision to buy American Motors for $2 billion-plus. At about the same time, the manager at the Chrysler dealership in Bryan, Texas, made a decision to sponsor a local Little League team for $100. Each of these examples includes a decision, but the decisions differ in many ways. Thus, as a starting point in understanding decision making, we must first explore its meaning, as well as the types of decisions and conditions under which decisions are made.

Decision Making Defined

decision making   The act of choosing one alternative from among a set of alternatives

decision-making process Recognizing and defining the nature of a decision situation, identifying alternatives, choosing the "best" one, and putting it into practice

Decision making is the act of choosing one alternative from among a set of alternatives. The decision-making process, however, is much more than this. For example, the person making the decision must have somehow recognized that a decision was necessary and identified the set of feasible alternatives before selecting one. Hence, the **decision-making process** includes recognizing and defining the nature of a decision situation, identifying alternatives, choosing the "best" alternative, and putting it into practice.[2]

The word "best" implies effectiveness. Effective decision making requires an understanding of the situation driving the decision. Most people would consider an effective decision to be one that optimizes some set of factors such as profits, sales, employee welfare, and market share. In some situations, though, an effective decision may be one that minimizes loss, expenses, or employee turnover. It may even mean selecting the best method for going out of business or terminating a contract.

It may take an extended period of time before a manager can know if the right decision was made. For example, Jack Welch, CEO of General Electric, took an enormous gamble by trading his company's consumer-electronics business to Thompson S.A., a French company, for its medical-equipment business. At the time of the exchange, GE held 23 percent of the U.S. color-television market and 17 percent of the U.S. VCR market. Moreover, it was the only serious consumer-electronics business left in the United States and was generating enormous profits. Welch, however, believed the medical-equipment business held even more promise for growth and profits. Analysts believe that the "winner" of the exchange will not be known until at least the turn of the century.[3]

Types of Decisions

programmed decision   One that is fairly structured and/or recurs with some frequency

Managers must make many different types of decisions. In general, however, most decisions fall into one of two categories: programmed and nonprogrammed.[4] A **programmed decision** is one that is fairly structured or recurs with some frequency. For example, suppose a manager of a distribution center knows from experience that he needs to keep a 30-day supply of a particular item on hand. He can then establish a system whereby a reorder is automatically entered for the appropriate quantity whenever the inventory drops below the 30-day requirement. Likewise, the Bryan Chrysler dealer made a decision that

The decision to build Joe Robbie Stadium was a nonprogrammed decision. Nonprogrammed decisions are relatively unstructured, and require managers to explore the situation and to use all available resources before making a final decision.

Joe Robbie, the owner of the Miami Dolphins professional football team, felt that the City of Miami was taking advantage of his team's leasing arrangements for the Orange Bowl. After considerable deliberation, Robbie made the decision to build his own stadium. Joe Robbie Stadium was built outside of Miami, and showcased internationally as the site of the Superbowl in January 1989.

nonprogrammed decision
Relatively unstructured and may occur much less often than a programmed decision

state of certainty When managers know with reasonable certainty what their alternatives are and what conditions are associated with each

he will sponsor a Little League team each year. Thus, when the league president calls, the dealer already knows what he will do. Many decisions regarding basic operating systems and procedures and standard organizational transactions are of this variety and can therefore be programmed.

Nonprogrammed decisions, on the other hand, are relatively unstructured and may occur much less often. GE's decision to exchange businesses with Thompson and Chrysler's decision to buy American Motors were nonprogrammed. No business makes multi-billion-dollar decisions like those on a regular basis. Managers faced with such options must treat each one as unique, investing enormous blocks of time, energy, and resources into exploring the situation from all perspectives. Intuition and experience also play large roles in the making of nonprogrammed decisions. Most of the decisions made by top managers involving strategy (including mergers, acquisitions, and takeovers) and organization design are nonprogrammed. So are decisions about new facilities, new products, labor contracts, and legal issues.

Decision-making Conditions

Just as there are different kinds of decisions, there are also different conditions in which decisions must be made. For example, Jack Welch at GE has no guarantees that his new medical-equipment business will be successful, whereas he had a pretty clear picture of how his electronics business was doing. Managers sometimes have an almost perfect understanding of conditions surrounding a decision, but at other times they have few clues about those conditions. In general, the circumstances that exist for the decision maker are conditions of certainty, risk, or uncertainty.[5] These conditions are represented in Figure 4.1.

Decision Making Under Certainty When managers know with reasonable certainty what their alternatives are and what conditions are associated with each alternative, a **state of certainty** exists. Suppose, for example, that American Airlines needs to buy ten new jumbo jets. The decision becomes who to buy them from. There are only four real choices: Boeing, McDonnell Douglas, Lockheed, and Airbus. Each manufacturer has a proven product and will quote prices and delivery dates. American, then, knows the alternatives and can determine the conditions associated with each. Thus, there is a low level of ambiguity facing the manager and relatively low chance of making a bad decision.

In organizational settings, few decisions are made under conditions of true certainty.[6] The complexity and turbulence of the contemporary business world make such situations rare. Even the airplane purchase decision we just considered is not completely realistic. The aircraft companies may not be able to guarantee delivery dates, and contractors typically write cost-increase or inflation clauses into contracts. Thus, the airline manager may not be 100 percent certain of the conditions surrounding each alternative.

FIGURE 4.1

Decision Making Conditions

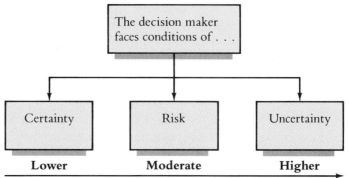

Level of ambiguity and chances of making bad decision

Decision Making Under Risk   A more common decision-making condition is a state of risk. Under a **state of risk**, the availability of each
alternative and its potential payoffs and costs are all associated with
probability estimates.[7] Suppose, for example, a labor contract negotiator for a company receives a "final" offer from the union right before
a strike deadline. The negotiator has two alternatives: to accept the
offer or to reject it. The risk centers on whether the union representatives really mean it when they say their offer is final or whether they
are bluffing. If the company negotiator accepts the offer, she avoids a
strike but also commits to a costly labor contract. If she rejects the
contract, she may get a more favorable contract if the union negotiators
are bluffing, or she may provoke a costly strike if they are not.

   On the basis of past experiences, relevant information, the advice of
others, and her own intuition, she may feel there is a 75 percent chance
that the union is bluffing and a 25 percent chance that they'll back up
their threats. Thus, she can base a calculated decision on the two
alternatives (accept or reject the contract demands) and the probable
consequences of each. The key element in decision making under a
state of risk is accurately determining the probabilities associated with
each alternative. For example, if the union negotiators are absolutely
committed to a strike if their demands are not met, and the company
negotiator rejects their demands because she guesses they will not strike,
her miscalculation will prove costly. "The Global View" describes a
risky situation faced by the French company Schlumberger. One alternative was to continue with its brand name and current management
team; the other was to use its corporate name and a new management team. As indicated in Figure 4.1, decision making under conditions of risk is accompanied by moderate ambiguity and chances of a
bad decision.

Decision Making Under Uncertainty   Most of the significant decision
making in contemporary organizations is done under a **state of uncertainty**. The decision maker does not know all the alternatives, the
risks associated with each, or the consequences each alternative is likely
to have.[8] This uncertainty stems from the complexity and dynamism

of contemporary organizations and their environments. Consider, for example, a recent decision made by several U.S. computer companies, including Compaq. For years, the standard operating software for computers was the one used by IBM machines. Plagued by clones and aging technology, IBM introduced a new generation of machines using a new kind of operating system. The other companies were faced with a number of alternatives. Should they follow IBM's lead? Should they wait and gauge consumer reactions? Should they introduce their own operating systems? After much deliberation, several of them forged a loose alliance and announced plans to use a new system that was compatible with most existing ones. Even then, however, they continued to face uncertainty about consumer reaction, the marketplace, and IBM's response.[9]

Many of the decisions referred to earlier—Chrysler's decision to buy American Motors and GE's decision to get out of consumer electronics, for example—were made under conditions of uncertainty. The key to effective decision making in these circumstances is to acquire as much relevant information as possible and to approach the situation from a logical and rational perspective. Intuition, judgment, and experience always play major roles in the decision-making process under conditions of uncertainty. Even so, this condition is the most ambiguous for managers and the one most prone to error.

MODELS OF THE DECISION-MAKING PROCESS

Over the years, the process of managerial decision making has been described from a variety of perspectives. Two of the most intriguing and illuminating views are the classical model and the administrative model.[10] Their differences are highlighted in Figure 4.2.

The Classical Model

classical decision model
A prescriptive approach that tells managers how they should make decisions. It assumes managers are logical and rational and that their decisions will be in the best interests of the organization

The **classical decision model** is a prescriptive approach that tells managers how they should make decisions. It is grounded in the assumptions that managers are logical and rational and that they always make decisions that are in the best interests of the organization. Managers at Compaq work hard to follow this model. Figure 4.2 shows how this view presumes decisions are made: (1) Decision makers have complete information about the decision situation and possible alternatives. (2) They can effectively eliminate uncertainty so as to achieve a decision condition of certainty. (3) They evaluate all aspects of the decision situation logically and rationally.

Managerial thinking during the heyday of the classical model was heavily influenced by economic concepts and quantitative methods, including the belief that human behavior is unerringly rational. Even today, many managers assume that they and others will be rational when decisions must be made. But it has been shown in many cases

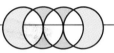

THE GLOBAL VIEW

SCHLUMBERGER CONFRONTS RISK

Schlumberger (pronounced Schloombear-shay) Ltd., the French industrial giant, essentially invented and has always dominated the oil-field service business. During the 1970s as oil boomed, so did Schlumberger. Large sums of money made at that time enabled the company to diversify in an effort to spread its risks rather than continue to be so dependent upon only one industry—especially an industry noted for large swings in prices and activity. Much of that diversification was risky, for it moved Schlumberger into the electronics field, in which it had little experience. Suddenly, electric meters, electric and electronic sensing devices, microprocessors, and related products became part of Schlumberger's business.

Fairchild Camera, which manufactured semiconductors, was acquired by Schlumberger in 1979 when Fairchild was in trouble. Schlumberger assumed the risk of trying to turn it around. Schlumberger changed its name to the Fairchild Semiconductor Corporation and pumped billions into it. The effort was to no avail, however. In 1987, after two years of substantial losses, Schlumberger realized that it could not make Fairchild profitable and sold Fairchild to National Semiconductor Corporation for $122 million.

Another firm acquired by Schlumberger was Applicon. Applicon was one of several CAD/CAM (computer-aided design/computer-aided manufacturing) companies that Schlumberger bought and merged to move into that field of business. Moving into an unfamiliar area is always risky, and Schlumberger intensified the risk by dropping the established Applicon name and management team the instant performance dropped.

In 1986 Applicon earned a profit and was moving to become one of the top five firms in the industry. However, when increasing competition led to a fall in profits during 1987, Schlumberger changed the company's name from Applicon to Schlumberger and replaced the experienced management team with a new one from outside the CAD/CAM industry. The head of the new team, Bruce McCann, formerly headed a Schlumberger unit that made controls for electric motors. Although the goal is still to make the former Applicon unit one of the top five CAD/CAM producers, the effort is now under the Schlumberger name.

REFERENCES: Charles R. Day, Jr., "Industry's Gutsiest Decisions of 1987," *Industry Week*, February 15, 1988, pp. 33–39; "Why National Came to the Fairchild Fire Sale," *Business Week*, September 14, 1987, pp. 38–39; "From Reds to Riches—and Now Red Ink," *U.S. News & World Report*, March 9, 1987, pp. 44–45; "What's Behind the Shakeup at Schlumberger," *Business Week*, October 13, 1986, pp. 62–63.

that personal preferences, attitudes, emotions, and motives influence decision-making behavior. A view of decision making that better reflects these subjective considerations is the administrative model.

The Administrative Model

One of the first people to recognize that rationality and logic do not invariably characterize decision-making processes was Herbert A. Simon.[11] (Simon was subsequently awarded the Nobel Prize in economics for his contributions.) His view of decision making has come to be called the **administrative model**. Rather than prescribe how decisions should be made, the administrative model describes how decisions often actually are made. As illustrated in Figure 4.2, the model holds

■ **administrative model of decision making**   Argues that decision makers are not always logical and rational

FIGURE 4.2

Two Models of How
Managers Make Decisions

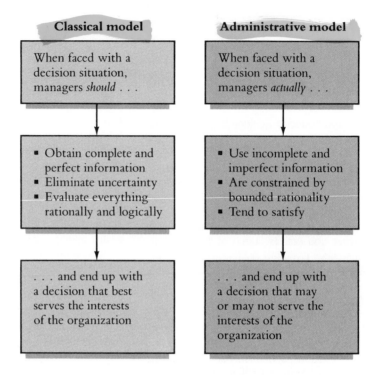

that managers (1) have incomplete and imperfect information, (2) are constrained by bounded rationality, and (3) tend to satisfice when making decisions.

bounded rationality Suggests that decision makers are limited by their values and unconscious reflexes, skills, and habits

Bounded rationality suggests that decision makers are limited by their values and unconscious reflexes, skills, and habits. They are also limited by information and knowledge that are less than complete. This partially explains how U.S. auto executives allowed Japanese car makers to become so strong in the United States. For years, executives at GM, Ford, and Chrysler compared their companies' performance only to one another and ignored foreign imports. The foreign "threat" wasn't recognized until the domestic auto market had been changed forever. If managers had seen things more clearly from the beginning, they might have been better able to thwart foreign competitors.[12] Essentially, then, the concept of bounded rationality suggests that although people try to be rational decision makers, their rationality has limits.

satisficing The tendency to search for alternatives only until one is found that meets some minimum standard of sufficiency

Another important part of the administrative model is **satisficing**. This concept suggests that rather than conducting an exhaustive search for the best possible alternative, decision makers tend to search only until they identify an alternative that meets some minimum standard of sufficiency. Consider, for example, a manager looking for a site for a new plant. There is reasonable chance that he will select the first site he finds that meets basic requirements for transportation, utilities, and price, even though further search might yield a better location.

People tend to satisfice for a variety of reasons. Managers may simply be unwilling to ignore their own motives and therefore not be able to continue searching after a minimally acceptable alternative is identified. The decision maker may be unable to weigh and evaluate large numbers of alternatives and criteria. Also, subjective and personal considerations often intervene in decision situations. For all these reasons, satisficing plays a major role in decision making.

Because of the inherent imperfection of information, bounded rationality, and satisficing, the decisions made by a manager may or may not actually be in the best interests of the organization. A manager may choose a particular location for the new plant because it offers the lowest price and best availability of utilities and transportation. Or the location may be chosen because it's in a community the manager subconsciously would prefer to live in.

In summary, then, the classical and administrative models paint quite different pictures of decision making. Which is more correct? Actually, each can be used to better understand how managers make decisions. The classical model is prescriptive: It explains how managers can at least attempt to be more rational and logical in their approach to decisions. The administrative model can be used by managers to develop a better understanding of their inherent biases and limitations. In the following section, we describe more fully how decisions can be approached from a classical point of view. We then discuss additional behavioral forces that can influence decisions.

STEPS IN RATIONAL DECISION MAKING

■ **steps in decision making**
Recognize and define the decision situation; identify appropriate alternatives; evaluate each alternative in terms of its feasibility, satisfactoriness, and consequences; select the best alternative; implement the chosen alternative; follow-up and evaluate the results of the chosen alternative

A manager who really wants to approach a decision rationally and logically should try to follow the steps listed in Table 4.1. Those steps help keep the decision maker focused on facts and logic and help guard against inappropriate assumptions and pitfalls.

Recognizing and Defining the Decision Situation

The first step in making a decision is recognizing that a decision is necessary—that is, there must be some stimulus or spark to initiate the process.[13] For many decisions, the stimulus may occur without any prior warning. When a piece of equipment breaks, the manager must decide whether to repair or replace it. Or when a major crisis erupts, as described in Chapter 3, the manager must spontaneously decide how to deal with it. The stimulus for a decision may be positive as well as negative for the organization. A manager who must decide how to invest unexpected surplus funds, for example, faces a positive decision situation. A negative financial stimulus could involve having to trim budgets because of cost overruns.

Inherent in problem recognition is the need to define precisely what the problem is. This is important because the definition plays a major role in subsequent steps. A manager who sees a problem of declining

Step	Detail	Example
1. Recognizing and defining the situation	Some stimulus indicates that a decision must be made. The stimulus may be positive or negative.	A plant manager sees that employee turnover has increased by 5 percent.
2. Identifying alternatives	Both obvious and creative alternatives are desired. In general, the more significant the decision, the more alternatives should be generated.	The plant manager can increase wages, increase benefits, or change hiring standards.
3. Evaluating alternatives	Each alternative is evaluated to determine its feasibility, its satisfactoriness, and its consequences.	Increasing benefits may not be feasible. Increasing wages and changing hiring standards may satisfy all conditions.
4. Selecting the best alternative	Consider all situational factors, and choose the alternative that best fits the manager's situation.	Changing hiring standards will take an extended period of time to cut turnover, so increase wages.
5. Implementing the chosen alternative	The chosen alternative is implemented into the organizational system.	The plant manager may need permission of corporate headquarters. The human resource department establishes a new wage structure.
6. Follow-up and evaluation	At some time in the future, the manager should ascertain the extent to which the alternative chosen in step 4 and implemented in step 5 has worked.	The plant manager notes that, six months later, turnover has dropped to its previous level.

TABLE 4.1

Steps in the Decision-making Process

sales as an indication of product obsolescence will define the problem in terms of finding new products. But if the problem is seen in terms of poor marketing, problem definition will center on how to improve marketing. Thus, it is critical that the manager develop a complete understanding of the problem, its causes, and its relationship to other factors. This understanding comes from careful analysis and thoughtful consideration of the situation.

Consider the recent situation faced by Rorer Group, Inc., makers of Maalox and other pharmaceuticals. Its CEO, Robert Cawthorn, recognized that other firms in the industry were dramatically increasing their product lines and, consequently, their market shares. Cawthorn reasoned that if Rorer was to keep pace, it, too, needed to expand its product lines. He further reasoned that the best route for expansion was to buy an existing firm.[14] Thus, the stimulus that

Glen Taylor, CEO of Taylor Corp., made a major decision a few years ago that has started paying real dividends. In 1979, his company was growing at a rapid clip, but was having a difficult time finding and keeping qualified employees. A major obstacle was that so many single parents lacked access to acceptable child care. Taylor's solution to the problem was to provide on-site child care. Taylor opened the facility and has subsequently found that recruiting, retaining, and promoting employees has become much easier.

prompted the decision was rapid expansion by competitors, and the problem was subsequently defined as the need to buy another pharmaceutical company.

Identifying Alternatives

Once the decision situation has been recognized and appropriately defined, the second step is to identify alternative courses of action that might be effective. It is generally useful to develop both obvious, standard alternatives and creative, innovative alternatives.[15] In general, the more important the decision, the more attention is directed to developing alternatives. If the decision involves where to build a multi-million-dollar office building, a great deal of time and expertise will be devoted to identifying the best locations—Union Carbide spent two years searching before selecting Danbury, Connecticut, for its new corporate headquarters. If the problem is to choose a color for the company softball-team uniforms, less time and expertise will be brought to bear.

Although managers should encourage creative solutions, they should also recognize that various constraints often limit their alternatives. Common constraints include legal restrictions, moral and ethical norms, authority constraints, or constraints imposed by the power and authority of the manager, available technology, economic considerations, and unofficial social norms. After Robert Cawthorn of Rorer decided to acquire a new pharmaceutical company, he identified four possible candidates. He might have identified more, but he chose to limit his search to American firms that might be obtained for a reasonable price.

Evaluating Alternatives

The third step in the decision-making process is evaluating each of the alternatives generated in the previous step. Figure 4.3 is a decision tree that can be used to judge different alternatives. The figure suggests that each alternative be evaluated in terms of its feasibility, its satisfactoriness, and its consequences.

The first question to ask is whether an alternative is feasible. Is it within the realm of probability and practicality? For a small, struggling firm, an alternative requiring a huge financial outlay would probably be out of the question. Even larger firms have financial limits that would rule out various alternatives. Other alternatives may not be feasible because of legal barriers such as legislation and zoning ordinances. And limited human, material, and information resources may make other alternatives impracticable.

When an alternative has passed the test of feasibility, it must next be examined to see how satisfactory it would be. Satisfactoriness refers to the extent to which the alternative will satisfy the conditions of the decision situation. For example, a manager may be searching for ways to expand production capacity by 50 percent. One alternative is to purchase an existing plant from another company. If closer examination reveals that the new plant would increase production capacity by only 35 percent, it may not be satisfactory. Depending on the circumstances,

FIGURE 4.3

Evaluating Alternatives in the Decision Making Process

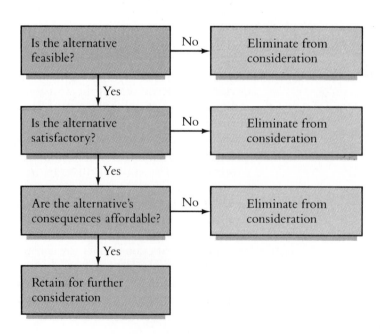

the manager may decide to buy the plant anyway and search for other ways to achieve the remaining 15 percent expansion. Or the manager may simply drop the proposed purchase of that plant from consideration.

Finally, when an alternative has proved both feasible and satisfactory, its probable consequences must still be assessed. To what extent will a particular alternative influence other parts of the organization? What costs (both financial and nonfinancial) will be associated with such influences? For example, a plan to boost sales by cutting prices may disrupt cash flows, require a new advertising program, and alter the behavior of sales representatives because it requires a different commission structure. (This bears out what we learned from systems theory in Chapter 2—that changes in one subsystem are likely to affect other subsystems as well.) The manager, then, must put "price tags" on the consequences of each alternative. Even an alternative that is both feasible and satisfactory must be eliminated if its consequences are too expensive for the total system.

Managers at Rorer eliminated one acquisition target because it would cost too much (not feasible) and another because it competed too directly with existing Rorer products (consequences not affordable). This left them with two remaining targets for acquisition.

Selecting an Alternative

Even though many alternatives may fail to pass the triple test of feasibility, satisfactoriness, and affordable consequences, it is likely that two or more alternatives will remain. Choosing the best of these is the real crux of decision making. Several points should be considered when selecting an alternative from those that remain. One approach is to choose the alternative with the highest combined level of feasibility, satisfactoriness, and affordable consequences. Even though most situations do not lend themselves to objective, mathematical analysis, the manager can often develop subjective estimates and weights for choosing an alternative.

Closely related is the issue of optimization. Because any decision is likely to affect several individuals or subunits, any feasible alternative will probably not maximize, or completely achieve, all of the relevant goals. Suppose the manager of the Kansas City Royals needs to select a starting center fielder for the next baseball season. Bill might hit .350 but not be able to catch a fly ball; Joe might hit only .175 but be perfect in the field; and Sam might hit .290 and be a solid but not perfect fielder. Most managers would select Sam because of the optimal balance of hitting and fielding.

Managers charged with making the decision should remember that it may be possible to find multiple acceptable alternatives—it may not be necessary to select just one alternative and reject all the others. For example, the Royals' manager might decide that Sam will start each game, Bill will be retained as a pinch hitter, and Joe will be retained as a defensive substitute. In many hiring decisions, the candidates remaining after evaluation are ranked. If the top candidate rejects the offer, it may be automatically extended to the number 2 candidate, and so on. Rorer managers chose to go after A. H. Robins Co., Inc. Robins makes numerous well-known products such as Chap Stick and Robitussin.

Implementing the Chosen Alternative

After an alternative has been selected, the manager must put it into effect. In some decision situations, implementation may be fairly easy; in others, it will be more difficult. Take the case of an acquisition. Managers must decide how to integrate all the activities of the new business, ranging from purchasing to personnel practices to distribution, into an ongoing organizational framework. When Texas Air acquired People Express, it took months to consolidate People's operations into existing systems. Operational plans, discussed in Chapter 7, are very useful in implementing alternatives.

Another issue to consider when implementing decisions is people's resistance to change. The reasons for such resistance include insecurity, inconvenience, and fear of the unknown. When Electronic Data Systems (EDS) was acquired by General Motors, many EDS employees balked at the transition, which took much longer than originally planned to make final.[16] Hence, managers should anticipate potential resistance at various stages of the implementation process. (Resistance to change is covered in Chapter 12.)

Managers should also recognize that, even when all alternatives have been evaluated as precisely as possible and the consequences of each alternative weighed, unanticipated consequences are still likely. Unexpected cost increases, a less-than-perfect fit with existing organizational subsystems, unpredicted effects on cash flow or operating expenses, and any number of other situations could develop after the implementation process has begun. When Rorer announced its intentions to buy A. H. Robins, other companies took note. Several decided that Robins would indeed be an attractive acquisition and also made offers. The bidding reached fever pitch, and Rorer eventually lost out to American Home Products Corp.

Following Up and Evaluating the Results

As the final step in the decision-making process, managers should evaluate the effectiveness of their decision—that is, they should make sure that the alternative chosen has served its original purpose. If the initial problem was an increase in absenteeism and turnover, the alternative chosen to deal with this situation may have been an incentive system designed to reward attendance. If attendance does in fact improve to the desired level, the manager can assume that the optimal alternative was chosen and the problem has been corrected. On the other hand, if attendance does not improve, the manager should recognize that the chosen alternative is not working and take other action.

If an implemented alternative appears not to be working, the manager has several potential responses. Another previously identified alternative (the second or third choice) could be adopted. Or the manager might recognize that the situation was not correctly defined to start with and begin the decision-making process all over again. Finally, the manager might decide that the alternative originally chosen is in fact appropriate but has not yet had time to work or should be implemented in a different way.

Failure to evaluate decision effectiveness may have serious consequences. The Pentagon spent $1.8 billion and eight years developing the Sergeant York anti-aircraft gun. From the beginning, tests revealed major problems with the weapon system, but not until it was in its final stages, when it was demonstrated to be completely ineffective, was the project scrapped.[17] In a classic case of poor decision making, managers at Coca-Cola decided to change the formula for the venerable soft drink. Consumer response was extremely negative. In contrast to the Pentagon, however, Coca-Cola moved rapidly to reintroduce the old formula as Coca-Cola Classic within three months. Had managers stubbornly stuck with their decision and failed to evaluate its effectiveness, the results would have been disastrous. And when Rorer lost its bid for A. H. Robins, Cawthorn decided to step back and explore other opportunities for expansion.

THE BEHAVIORAL NATURE OF DECISION MAKING

If all decision situations were approached as logically as described in the previous section, more decisions would prove to be successful. Yet, decisions are often made with little consideration for logic and rationality. Kepner-Tregoe, a Princeton-based consulting firm, estimates that American companies use good decision-making techniques less than 20 percent of the time.[18] And even when organizations try to be logical, they sometimes fail. For example, managers at Coca-Cola decided to change Coke's formula after four years of extensive marketing research, taste tests, and rational deliberation—but the decision was still wrong. On the other hand, sometimes when a decision is made with little regard for logic, it can still turn out to be correct. A key ingredient in how these forces work is the behavioral nature of decision making.[19] "Management in Practice" explains how one company, Sun Microsystems, recognizes and capitalizes on this behavioral orientation.

Political Forces in Decision Making

Political forces are one major element in the behavioral nature of decision making. Organizational politics is covered in Chapter 13, but

coalition An informal alliance of individuals or groups formed to achieve a common goal

one major element of politics, coalitions, is especially relevant to decision making. A **coalition** is an informal alliance of individuals or groups formed to achieve a common goal. This common goal is often a preferred decision alternative. In Chapter 3 we noted how the Coniston partners forced the board of directors of Allegis to fire the company's CEO, sell Westin, Hertz, and other companies, and change the corporation's name back to United. Exactly how did they bring this off? They created a coalition of several large institutional investors and threatened to replace the board if it did not adopt their preferred strategy.

In similar fashion, coalitions led to the formation of Unisys, a large computer firm. Sperry was once one of America's computer giants, but bad management and a series of poor decisions put the company behind the eight ball. Two key executives waged battle for three years over what to do. One wanted to get out of the computer business altogether, and the other wanted to stay in. Finally, the manager who wanted to remain in computers, Joseph Kroger, garnered enough support to earn promotion to the corporation's presidency. The other manager, Vincent McLean, took early retirement. Shortly thereafter, Sperry agreed to be acquired by Burroughs Corporation. The resultant combined company is called Unisys.[20]

The impact of coalitions can be either positive or negative. They can help astute managers get the organization on a path toward effectiveness and profitability, or they can strangle well-conceived strategies and decisions. A key, then, is for managers to recognize when to use coalitions, how to assess whether coalitions are acting in the best interests of the organization, and how to constrain their dysfunctional effects.

Intuition and Escalation of Commitment

Two other important decision processes that go beyond logic and rationality are intuition and escalation of commitment to a chosen course of action.

intuition An innate belief about something without conscious consideration

Intuition **Intuition** is an innate belief about something without conscious consideration. Managers sometimes decide to do something because it "feels right" or they have a hunch. In most cases, this feeling is not arbitrary. Rather, it is based on years of experience and practice in making decisions in similar situations. Some inner sense comes into play, helping managers make an occasional decision without going through a full-blown rational sequence of steps.

Consider, for example, the case of Liz Claiborne. Claiborne and three other people founded Liz Claiborne Inc. to design and sell clothes for working women. Conventional wisdom at the time suggested that they needed to build plants to make the clothing and develop a traveling sales force to market it. Pure intuition, however, told them to not follow this "wisdom." Thus, they subcontracted production to other

MANAGEMENT IN PRACTICE

SUN STRUCTURES SPONTANEITY

Sun Microsystems prides itself on an emotional, creative approach. The success of that approach is unquestioned. By 1988, Sun and Apollo Computer jointly controlled over 50 percent of the work-station market. That market is the fastest-growing segment of the computer industry and by 1992 is expected to amount to three-fourths of total sales in the industry. Sun became a billion-dollar company in just six years and one of Wall Street's hottest prospects among computer stocks.

Sun tries to create an environment where its over 7,000 people can enjoy working and will work hard. The environment is emotional, people get fired up, adrenaline gets going, and things happen. There are weekly dress-down days and monthly beer parties. On April Fool's Day outlandish stunts prevail. Those stunts may involve the CEO, Scott McNealy, who one year came to work to find that his office had been replaced with a one-hole golf course overnight.

McNealy's approach to management involves extensive participation and consensus if at all possible. That participation involves obtaining both agreements and disagreements prior to making a decision, but strong commitment from all parties once the decision has been made.

Sun's growth is across relatively broad lines. Sun is trying to ensure that growth continues by keeping business units small and flexible so that they can respond to their environments and take advantage of opportunities when they arise. In some cases, unusual action is taken to preserve the entrepreneurial spirit of growth. When one project got bogged down, for example, McNealy ordered the team to finish the task at another location.

Sun tries to have business discipline without hierarchical structures to slow it down. Establishing order without dampening the excitement is the managerial challenge at Sun. All employees are encouraged to share their ideas about products, procedures, management, and all aspects of the organization. Meetings are frequent and noisy but quickly reach decisions. The decisions are usually made by consensus, but the more important characteristic is that they are made fast. Product strategies come from autonomous divisions rather than from a central executive or planning committee.

REFERENCES: Stuart Gannes, "IBM and DEC Take on the Little Guys," *Fortune*, October 10, 1988, pp. 108–114; "Sun Microsystems Turns on the Afterburners," *Business Week*, July 18, 1988, pp. 114–118; Michael Rogers, "Silicon Valley's Rising Sun," *Newsweek*, March 21, 1988, p. 62; Stuart Gannes, "America's Fastest-growing Companies," *Fortune*, May 23, 1988, pp. 28–40; "Sun Microsystems' Efforts to Attract Clone Makers Finally Get Results," *The Wall Street Journal*, January 16, 1989, p. B3.

makers instead of building plants, and they sold their clothes only to large department and specialty store buyers willing to travel to New York. The result? Very low overhead and sales of over $1 billion in 1987.[21]

Of course, all managers, but most especially inexperienced ones, should be careful not to rely on intuition too heavily. If rationality and logic are continually flaunted for what "feels right," the odds are that disaster will strike one day.

escalation of commitment
When a manager stays with a decision even when it appears to be wrong

Escalation of Commitment   Another important behavioral process that influences decision making is **escalation of commitment** to a chosen course of action. In particular, managers sometimes make decisions and then become so committed to the course of action suggested by that decision that they stay with it even when it appears to have been wrong.[22] For example, when people buy stock in a company, they sometimes refuse to sell it even after repeated drops in price. They chose a course of action—buying the stock in anticipation of making a profit—and then stay with it even in the face of increasing losses.

Consider the case of Pan American World Airways. When the airline industry was deregulated, Pan Am expanded too rapidly and was soon financially strapped. One course of action would have been to get out of the airline business and into more profitable businesses. Instead, the company started selling off assets to pay the bills, hoping things would get better. First it sold its headquarters building in New York, then its profitable Intercontinental Hotel chain, and finally its lucrative Pacific routes. What was left? An airline, albeit one with little chance of success. Management never seriously considered selling or closing the airline, because that was the business they had decided to be in. And even today, the airline is struggling to turn a profit.[23]

Thus, decision makers must walk a fine line. On the one hand, they must guard against sticking with an incorrect decision too long. To do so can bring about financial decline. On the other hand, they should not bail out of a seemingly incorrect decision too soon. For example, Adidas once dominated the market for professional athletic shoes. It subsequently entered the market for amateur sports shoes and did well there also. Managers then interpreted a sales slowdown as a sign that the boom in athletic shoes was over. They thought they had made the wrong decision and ordered drastic cutbacks. The market took off again with Reebok and Nike at the head of the pack, and Adidas has never recovered.[24]

How does a manager walk this fine line? Using the steps in the classical model and relying on intuition can sometimes help. So, too, can getting as much information and help as possible. Using groups to help make certain decisions is a common method for doing just this.

GROUP DECISION MAKING

In more and more organizations today, important decisions are made by groups rather than individuals. Examples range from the executive committee of Rockwell International to product design teams at Texas Instruments to marketing planning groups at General Foods. Managers can typically choose whether to have individuals or groups make a particular decision. Thus, it's important to know about forms of group decision making and their advantages and disadvantages.[25]

Forms of Group Decision Making

Group decision making can take place in a variety of forms. The most common methods are interacting groups, nominal groups, and Delphi groups.

■ **interacting group**   A decision making group in which members openly discuss, argue about, and/or agree on the best alternative

Interacting Groups   An **interacting group** is the most common form of group decision making. The format is simple—either an existing or a newly designated group is asked to make a decision about something. Existing groups might be functional departments, regular work groups, or standing committees. Newly designated groups can be ad hoc committees, task forces, or teams. The group members talk among themselves, argue, agree, argue some more, form internal coalitions, and so forth. Finally, after some period of deliberation, a decision is made. An advantage of this method is that the interaction between people often sparks new ideas and promotes understanding. A significant disadvantage, though, is that political processes can play too big a role.

■ **Delphi group**   Used to achieve a consensus of expert opinion

Delphi Groups   A **Delphi group** is sometimes used for developing a consensus of expert opinion. Developed by the Rand Corporation, the Delphi procedure solicits input from a panel of experts who contribute individually. Their opinions are combined and, in effect, averaged. Assume, for example, that the problem is to establish an expected date for a major technological breakthrough in converting coal into usable energy. The first step in using the Delphi procedure is to obtain the cooperation of a panel of experts. For this situation, experts might include various research scientists, university researchers, and executives in a relevant energy industry. At first, the experts are asked to predict anonymously a time frame for the expected breakthrough. The persons coordinating the Delphi group collect the responses, average them, and ask the experts for another prediction. In this round, the experts who provided unusual or extreme predictions are often asked to justify them. These explanations may then be relayed to the other experts. When the predictions stabilize, the average prediction is taken to represent the decision of the "group" of experts. The time, expense, and logistics of the Delphi technique rule out its use for routine, everyday decisions, but it has been successfully used for forecasting technological breakthroughs at Boeing, market potential for new products at General Motors, research and development patterns at Eli Lilly, and future economic conditions by the U.S. government.[26]

■ **nominal group**   A structured technique used to generate creative and innovative alternatives or ideas

Nominal Groups   Another useful group decision-making technique occasionally used is the **nominal group**. Unlike the Delphi method, where group members do not see one another, nominal group members are together. However, the members represent a group in name only— they do not talk to one another freely like the members of interacting groups. Nominal groups are used most often to generate creative and innovative alternatives or ideas. To begin, the manager assembles a group of knowledgeable people and outlines the problem to them. The group members are then asked to individually write down as many alternatives as they can think of. The members then take turns stating their ideas, which are recorded on a flip chart or blackboard at the front of the room. Discussion is limited to simple clarification. After all alternatives have been listed, more open discussion takes place. Group members then vote, usually by rank-ordering the various alternatives. The highest-ranking alternative represents the decision of the group. Of course, the manager in charge may retain the authority to accept or reject the group decision.

Advantages of Group Decision Making

The advantages and disadvantages of group decision making relative to individual decision making are summarized in Table 4.2.[27] One advantage of group decision making is that there is simply more information available in a group setting—as suggested by the old axiom "Two heads are better than one." When a group is assembled, a variety of education, experience, and perspective is represented. Partly as a result of this increased information, groups typically can identify and evaluate more alternatives than can an individual who makes the decision and imposes it. The people involved in a group decision understand the logic and rationale behind it and are equipped to communicate the decision to their work groups or departments. Finally, research evidence suggests that groups may make better decisions than individuals.[28] As noted at the beginning of this chapter, Compaq Computer frequently uses group decision making to capitalize on these advantages.

Disadvantages of Group Decision Making

Perhaps the biggest drawback of group decision making is the additional time and (hence) the greater expense entailed. The increased time stems from interaction and discussion among group members. If a manager's time is worth $50 an hour, and if the manager spends two hours making

TABLE 4.2

Advantages and Disadvantages of Group Decision Making

Advantages	Disadvantages
1. More information and knowledge are available.	1. The process takes longer, so it is costlier.
2. More alternatives are likely to be generated.	2. Compromise decisions resulting from indecisiveness may emerge.
3. More acceptance of the final decision is likely.	3. One person may dominate the group.
4. Enhanced communication of the decision may result.	4. Groupthink may occur.
5. More accurate decisions generally emerge.	

Henry Henderson, CEO of Henderson Industries, has made good use of group decision making during his career. HI is a leading manufacturer of industrial scales and microprocessor control panels. Henderson was recently faced with a major decision about a reorganization of the company. He convened his top management group for a two-day strategy session and spent the time identifying and evaluating alternative modes of organization. Henderson came away from the meeting feeling that the group had done an outstanding job of working together toward finding solutions to the company's problems.

a decision, the cost of the decision activity to the organization is $100. For the same decision, a group of five managers might require three hours of time. At the same $50-an-hour rate, the organization is paying $750 for the decision. If the group decision is somehow better, the additional expense may be justified, but group decision making is more costly and should be used only when the results are likely to justify the expense.

Group decisions may also represent undesirable compromises. For example, hiring a compromise top manager may be a bad decision in the long run because he or she may not be able to respond adequately to any of the various special subunits in the organization. Sometimes one individual dominates the group process to the point where others cannot make a full contribution. This dominance may stem from a desire for power or from a naturally dominant personality. The problem is that what appears to emerge as a group decision may actually be the decision of one person. For example, George Sella, CEO of American Cyanamid, has been criticized for asking for and then ignoring advice from others.[29]

Finally, a group may succumb to a phenomenon known as groupthink. **Groupthink** occurs when the group's desire for consensus and cohesiveness overwhelms its desire to reach the best possible decisions.[30] Under the influence of groupthink, the group may arrive at decisions that are not in the best interest of either the group or the organization but rather avoid conflict among group members. One of the clearest examples of groupthink that has been documented arose among President John F. Kennedy and his advisers as they came to their decision to support the Bay of Pigs invasion of Cuba in the early 1960s. The

groupthink   When a group's desire for consensus and cohesiveness overwhelms its desire to reach the best possible decision

Bay of Pigs invasion, intended to undermine Fidel Castro's government, turned out to be one of America's greatest military fiascoes. Yet Kennedy and all of his key advisers had given the invasion their whole-hearted support because they felt that the United States' involvement would be kept secret, that the Cuban military was not effective, that the invasion would spark the Cuban underground into action, and that retreat would be possible if the invasion failed. When all of these assumptions proved wrong, the tragedy that ensued was inevitable.

Managing Group Decision-making Processes

Managers can do several things to help promote the effectiveness of group decision making. One is simply being aware of the pros and cons of having a group make a decision. Time and cost can be managed by setting a deadline by which the decision must be made final. Dominance can be at least partially avoided if a special group is formed just to make the decision. An astute manager, for example, should know who in the organization may try to dominate a group and either can avoid putting that person in the group or can put several strong-willed people together.

There are also a few things a group can do to avoid groupthink. Each member of the group should critically evaluate all alternatives. So that divergent viewpoints can be presented, the leader should not make his or her own position known too early. At least one member of the group should be assigned the role of devil's advocate. And, after reading a preliminary decision, the group should hold a follow-up meeting wherein divergent viewpoints can be raised again if any group members wish to do so.[31] Gould Company used these methods by assigning managers to two different teams. The teams then spent an entire day in a structured debate presenting the pros and cons of each side of an issue in order to ensure the best possible decision.

QUANTITATIVE TOOLS FOR DECISION MAKING

Still another way managers can improve their decision making is by using a selection of quantitative tools for evaluating alternatives. Two commonly used procedures are the payoff matrix and the decision tree. Other techniques are also available.

Payoff Matrices

payoff matrix Specifies the probable value of different alternatives depending on different possible outcomes associated with each

A **payoff matrix** specifies the probable value of different alternatives, depending on different possible outcomes associated with each.[32] The use of a payoff matrix requires that several alternatives be available, that several different events could occur, and that the consequences depend on which alternative is selected and on which event or set of events occurs. An important concept in understanding the payoff matrix, then, is probability.

probability The likelihood that a particular event will or will not occur

A **probability** is the likelihood, expressed as a percentage, that a particular event will or will not occur. If we believe that a particular event will occur 75 times out of 100, we can say that the probability of its occurring is 75 percent, or .75. Probabilities range in value from 0 (no chance of occurrence) to 1.00 (certain occurrence—also referred to as 100 percent). In the business world, there are few probabilities of either 0 or 1.00. Most probabilities that managers use are based on subjective judgment, intuition, and historical data.

expected value The sum of all possible values of outcomes due to that action multiplied by their respective probabilities

The **expected value** of an alternative course of action is the sum of all possible values of outcomes due to that action multiplied by their respective probabilities. Suppose, for example, that a venture capitalist is considering investing in a new company. If he believes there is a .40 probability of making $100,000, a .30 probability of making $30,000, and a .30 probability of losing $20,000, the expected value (EV) of this alternative is

$$EV = .40(100,000) + .30(30,000) + .30(-20,000)$$

$$= 40,000 + 9,000 - 6,000$$

$$= \$43,000$$

The investor can then weigh the expected value of this investment against the expected values of other available alternatives. The highest EV signals the investment that should be selected.

For example, suppose another venture capitalist is looking to invest $20,000 in a new business. He has identified three possible alternatives: a leisure products company, an energy enhancement company, and a food-producing company. Because the expected value of each alternative depends on short-run changes in the economy, especially inflation, he decides to develop a payoff matrix. He estimates that the probability of high inflation is .30 and the probability of low inflation is .70. He then estimates the probable returns to him for each investment in the event of both high and low inflation. Figure 4.4 shows what the payoff matrix might look like (a minus sign indicates a loss). The expected value of investing in the leisure products company is

$$EV = .30(-10,000) + .70(50,000)$$

$$= -3,000 + 35,000$$

$$= \$32,000$$

Similarly, the expected value of investing in the energy enhancement company is

$$EV = .30(90,000) + .70(-15,000)$$

$$= 27,000 + (-10,500)$$

$$= \$16,500$$

FIGURE 4.4

An Example of a Payoff
Matrix

		High inflation *(Probability of .30)*	Low inflation *(Probability of .70)*
Investment alternative 1	Leisure products company	− $10,000	+ $50,000
Investment alternative 2	Energy enhancement company	+ $90,000	− $15,000
Investment alternative 3	Food processing company	+ $30,000	+ $25,000

And the expected value of investing in the food-processing company is

$$EV = .30(30,000) + .70(25,000)$$
$$= 9,000 + 17,500$$
$$= \$26,500$$

Investing in the leisure products company, then, has the highest expected value.

Other potential uses for payoff matrices include determining order quantities, deciding whether to repair or replace broken machinery, and deciding which of several new products to introduce. Of course, the real key to effectively using payoff matrices is making accurate estimates of the relevant probabilities.

Decision Trees

decision tree   Extends the
concept of a payoff matrix
through a sequence of decisions

Decision trees are like payoff matrices in that they enhance a manager's ability to evaluate alternatives by making use of expected values. However, they are most appropriate when there are a number of decisions to be made in sequence.[33]

Figure 4.5 illustrates a hypothetical decision tree. The firm represented wants to begin exporting its products to a foreign market, but limited capacity restricts it to only one market at first. Managers feel that either France or China would be the best alternative to start with. Whichever alternative is selected, sales for the product in that country may turn out to be high or low. In France, there is a .80 chance of high sales and a .20 chance of low sales. The anticipated payoffs in these situations are predicted to be $20 million and $3 million, respectively. In China, the probabilities of high versus low sales are .60 and .40 respectively, and the associated payoffs are presumed to be $25 million and $6 million. As shown in the figure, the expected value of shipping

FIGURE 4.5

A Hypothetical Example of a
Decision Tree

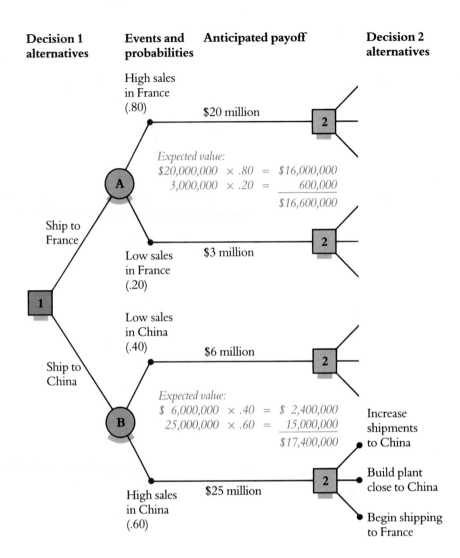

Decision 1
alternatives

Events and
probabilities

Anticipated payoff

Decision 2
alternatives

High sales
in France
(.80)

$20 million

Expected value:
$20,000,000 × .80 = $16,000,000
3,000,000 × .20 = 600,000
$16,600,000

Ship to
France

Low sales
in France
(.20)

$3 million

Ship to
China

Low sales
in China
(.40)

$6 million

Expected value:
$ 6,000,000 × .40 = $ 2,400,000
25,000,000 × .60 = 15,000,000
$17,400,000

High sales
in China
(.60)

$25 million

Increase
shipments
to China

Build plant
close to China

Begin shipping
to France

to France is $16,600,000, whereas the expected value of shipping to
China is $17,400,000.

The astute reader will note that this part of the decision could have
been set up as a payoff matrix. However, the value of decision trees is
that we can extend the model to include subsequent decisions. Assume,
for example, that the company begins shipping to China. If high sales
do in fact materialize, the company will soon reach another decision
situation. It might use the extra revenues to (1) increase shipments to
China, (2) build a plant close to China in order to cut shipping costs,
or (3) begin shipping to France. Various outcomes are possible for each
decision, and each outcome will also have both a probability and an
anticipated payoff. It is therefore possible to compute expected values
back through several tiers of decisions all the way to the initial one. As
it is with payoff matrices, determining probabilities accurately is the

crucial element in the process. Properly used, however, decision trees can provide managers with a useful road map through complex decision situations.

Other Techniques

In addition to payoff matrices and decision trees, a number of other quantitative methods are also available to facilitate decision making.[34]

Inventory Models   Inventory models are techniques that help the manager decide how much inventory to maintain. Inventory consists of both raw materials (inputs) and finished goods (outputs). Polaroid, for example, maintains a supply of the chemicals it uses to make film, the cartons it packs film in, and packaged film ready to be shipped. For finished goods, both extremes are bad: Excess inventory ties up capital, whereas a small inventory may result in shortages and customer dissatisfaction. The same holds for raw materials: Too much inventory ties up capital, but if a company runs out of resources, work stoppages may occur. Finally, because the process of placing an order for raw materials and supplies has associated costs (such as clerical time, shipping expenses, and higher unit costs for small quantities), it is important to minimize the frequency of ordering. Inventory models help the manager make decisions in such a way as to optimize the size of inventory. Because inventory models are most often used as a method of control, we discuss them in detail in Chapter 17.

Queuing Models   Queuing models are intended to help organizations manage waiting lines. We are all familiar with such situations: shoppers waiting to pay for groceries at Kroger, drivers waiting to buy gas at an Exxon station, travelers calling American Airlines for reservations, and customers waiting for a teller at Citibank. Take the Kroger example. If a store manager has only one checkout stand in operation, the store's cost for checkout personnel is very low; however, many customers are upset by the long line that frequently develops. To solve the problem, the store manager could decide to keep twenty checkout stands open at all times. Customers would like the short waiting period, but personnel costs would be very high. A queuing model would be appropriate in this case to help the manager determine the optimal number of checkout stands: the number that would balance personnel costs and customer waiting time.

Distribution Models   A decision facing many marketing managers relates to the distribution of the organization's products. Specifically, the manager must decide where the products should go and how to transport them. Railroads, trucking, air freight—each has associated shipping costs. The problem is to identify the combination of routes that optimizes distribution effectiveness and distribution costs.

Game Theory   Game theory was originally developed to predict the effect of one company's decisions on competitors. Models developed from game theory are intended to predict how a competitor will react to various activities that an organization might undertake, such as price changes, promotional changes, and the introduction of new products. If Bank of America were considering raising its prime lending rate by 1 percent, it might use a game theory model to predict whether Citicorp would follow suit. If the model revealed that Citicorp would, Bank of America would probably proceed; otherwise, it would probably maintain the current interest rates. Unfortunately, game theory has not yet proved as useful as it was originally expected to be. The complexities of the real world combined with the limitation of the technique itself restrict its applicability. Game theory, however, does provide a useful conceptual framework for analyzing competitive behavior, and its usefulness may be improved in the future.

expert system   A computer program that tries to duplicate the thought processes of experienced decision makers

Artificial Intelligence   A fairly new addition to the manager's quantitative tool kit is artificial intelligence (AI). The most useful form of AI is the expert system.[35] An **expert system** is essentially a computer program that tries to duplicate the thought processes of experienced decision makers. For example, Digital Equipment has developed an expert system that checks sales orders for new computer systems and then designs preliminary layouts for those new systems. Digital can now ship the computer to a customer in components for final assembly on site. This has enabled the company to cut back on its own final assembly facilities.

Singapore's container cargo port is the busiest of its kind in the world. It handles 63 containers per ship per hour, far more than any port of comparable size. Much of the scheduling for the port is handled through an elaborate expert system. The system, capable of handling a new ship every 15 minutes, directs new ships to the appropriate wharf for loading or unloading and then schedules how the cargo is to be loaded or unloaded, accounting for weight distribution, stacking priorities, and so forth.

SUMMARY OF KEY POINTS

Decisions are an integral part of all managerial activities, but they are perhaps most central to the planning process. Decision making is the act of choosing one alternative from among a set of rational alternatives. Two common types of decisions are programmed and nonprogrammed. Decisions may be made under states of certainty, risk, or uncertainty.

The classical model of decision making assumes that managers have complete information and that they will behave rationally. The more realistic administrative model recognizes that managers will have incomplete information and that they will not always behave rationally. The administrative model also recognizes the concepts of bounded rationality and satisficing.

The primary steps in an ideal decision-making process are (1) recognizing and defining the situation, (2) identifying alternatives, (3) evaluating each alternative, (4) selecting the best alternative, (5) implementing the chosen alternative, and (6) following up and evaluating the effectiveness of the alternative after it is implemented.

Behavioral processes also affect decision making. Political activities by coalitions, managerial intuition, and the tendency to become increasingly committed to a chosen course of action are all important.

To help enhance decision-making effectiveness, managers often use interacting, Delphi, or nominal groups. Group decision making in general has several advantages as well as disadvantages relative to individual decision making. Managers can do a number of things to help groups make better decisions.

Finally, managers can also draw on a number of useful quantitative techniques to assist them in making decisions. Payoff matrices and decision trees are the most common techniques.

DISCUSSION QUESTIONS

Questions for Review

1. Describe the nature of decision making.
2. What are the main features of the classical model of the decision-making process? What are those of the administrative model?
3. What are the steps in rational decision making? Which step is the most difficult to carry out? Why?
4. Describe the behavioral nature of decision making. Be certain to provide some detail about political forces and commitment in your description.

Questions for Analysis

5. Was your decision about what college or university to attend a rational decision? Did you go through each step in rational decision making? If not, why not?

6. Can any decision be purely rational, or are all decisions at least partially behavioral in nature? Defend your answer against alternatives.
7. Under what conditions would you expect group decision making to be preferable to individual decision making, and vice versa? Why?

Questions for Application

8. Interview a local business manager about a major decision that he or she made recently. Try to determine if each of the steps in rational decision making were used. If not, which were omitted? Why might the omissions have occurred?
9. Interview a local business manager about a major decision that he or she made recently. Try to determine if aspects of the behavioral nature of decision making were involved. If so, which were involved? Why might this have occurred?
10. Interview a department head at your college or university to determine if group decision making is used at all. If it is, for what types of decisions is it used?

NOTES

1. Stuart Gannes, "America's Fastest-growing Companies," *Fortune*, May 23, 1988, pp. 28–40; "Compaq Growth Records Keep Coming," *USA Today*, February 2, 1989, p. 3B.
2. For recent reviews of decision making, see E. Frank Harrison, *The Managerial Decision Making Process*, 3rd ed. (Boston: Houghton Mifflin, 1987); and David J. Hickson, Richard J. Butler, David Cray, Geoffrey R. Mallory, and David C. Wilson, *Top Decisions* (San Francisco: Jossey-Bass, 1986).
3. Charles R. Day, Jr., "Industry's Gutsiest Decisions of 1987," *Industry Week*, February 15, 1988, pp. 33–39; Stratford P. Sherman, "Inside the Mind of Jack Welsh," *Fortune*, March 27, 1989, pp. 38–50.
4. George P. Huber, *Managerial Decision Making* (Glenview, Ill.: Scott, Foresman, 1980).
5. Huber, *Managerial Decision Making*. See also David W. Miller and Martin K. Starr, *The Structure of Human Decisions* (Englewood Cliffs, N.J.: Prentice-Hall, 1976); and Alvar Elbing, *Behavioral Decisions in Organizations*, 2nd ed. (Glenview, Ill: Scott, Foresman, 1978).
6. Huber, *Managerial Decision Making*.
7. See Avi Fiegenbaum and Howard Thomas, "Attitudes Toward Risk and the Risk-Return Paradox: Prospect Theory Explanations," *Academy of Management Journal,* March 1988, pp. 85–106; Jitendra V. Singh, "Performance, Slack, and Risk Taking in Organizational Decision Making," *Academy of Management Journal*, September 1986, pp. 562–585; and James G. March and Zur Shapira, "Managerial Perspectives on Risk and Risk Taking," *Management Science*, November 1987, pp. 1404–1418.
8. See Richard M. Cyert and Morris H. DeGroot, "The Maximization Process Under Uncertainty," in Patrick D. Larkey and Lee S. Sproull, eds.,

Information Processing in Organizations (Greenwich, Conn.: JAI Press, 1984), pp. 47–61.

9. "Will Computers Take a Dive?" *Business Week*, October 17, 1988, pp. 26–27.

10. For recent reviews, see Paul C. Nutt, "Types of Organizational Decision Processes," *Administrative Science Quarterly*, September 1984, pp. 414–450; and Lawrence T. Penfield, "A Field Evaluation of Perspectives on Organizational Decision Making," *Administrative Science Quarterly*, September 1986, pp. 365–388.

11. Herbert A. Simon, *Administrative Behavior* (New York: Free Press, 1945). Simon's ideas have been recently refined and updated in Herbert A. Simon, *Administrative Behavior*, 3rd ed. (New York: Free Press, 1976), and Herbert A. Simon, "Making Management Decisions: The Role of Intuition and Emotion," *The Academy of Management Executive*, February 1987, pp. 57–63.

12. "The Wisdom of Solomon," *Newsweek*, August 17, 1987, pp. 62–63.

13. See R. T. Lenz and Jack L. Engledow, "Environmental Analysis Units and Strategic Decision-making: A Field Study of Selected 'Leading-Edge' Corporations," *Strategic Management Journal*, Vol. 7, 1986, pp. 69–89, for a recent analysis of how decision situations are recognized.

14. Day, "Industry's Gutsiest Decisions of 1987."

15. See Charles A. O'Reilly III, "The Use of Information in Organizational Decision Making: A Model and Some Propositions," in Larry L. Cummings and Barry M. Staw, eds., *Research in Organizational Behavior*, Vol. 5 (Greenwich, Conn.: JAI Press, 1983), pp. 103–139.

16. Brian O'Reilly, "EDS After Perot: How Tough Is It?" *Fortune*, October 24, 1988, pp. 72–76.

17. Kenneth Labich, "Coups and Catastrophes," *Fortune*, December 23, 1985, p. 125.

18. "The Wisdom of Solomon."

19. Elbing, *Behavioral Decisions in Organizations*.

20. "Unisys: So Far, So Good—But the Real Test Is Yet to Come," *Business Week*, March 2, 1987, pp. 84–86; "So Far, Married Life Seems to Agree With Unisys," *Business Week*, October 3, 1988, pp. 122–126.

21. Gannes, "America's Fastest-growing Companies." See also "Can Ms. Fashion Bounce Back?" *Business Week*, January 16, 1989, pp. 64–70.

22. Barry M. Staw and Jerry Ross, "Good Money After Bad," *Psychology Today*, February 1988, pp. 30–33. See also Michael G. Bowen, "The Escalation Phenomenon Reconsidered: Decision Dilemmas or Decision Errors?" *Academy of Management Review*, January 1987, pp. 52–66; and Ed Bukszar and Terry Connolly, "Hindsight Bias and Strategic Choice: Some Problems in Learning from Experience," *Academy of Management Journal*, September 1988, pp. 628–641.

23. "Airline's Chief Seeks a Miracle," *USA Today*, August 2, 1988, pp. 1B, 2B; "Pan Am Turns Situation To Its Benefit," *The Wall Street Journal*, March 17, 1989, p. B1.

24. Gannes, "America's Fastest-growing Companies."

25. Marvin E. Shaw, *Group Dynamics—The Psychology of Small Group Behavior*, 3rd ed. (New York: McGraw-Hill, 1981); and Edwin A. Locke, David M. Schweiger, and Gary P. Latham, "Participation in Decision Making: When Should It Be Used?" *Organizational Dynamics*, Winter 1986, pp. 65–79; and Nicholas Baloff and Elizabeth M. Doherty, "Potential Pitfalls in Employee Participation," *Organizational Dynamics*, Winter 1989, pp. 51–62.

26. Andre L. Delbecq, Andrew H. Van de Ven, and David H. Gustafson, *Group Techniques for Program Planning* (Glenview, Ill.: Scott, Foresman, 1975) and Michael J. Prietula and Herbert A. Simon, "The Experts in Your Midst," *Harvard Business Review*, January–February 1989, pp. 120–124.

27. Norman P. R. Maier, "Assets and Liabilities in Group Problem Solving: The Need for an Integrative Function," in J. Richard Hackman, Edward E. Lawler III, and Lyman W. Porter, eds., *Perspectives on Business in Organizations*, 2nd ed. (New York: McGraw-Hill, 1983), pp. 385–392.

28. James H. Davis, *Group Performance* (Reading, Mass.: Addison-Wesley, 1969).

29. "American Cyanamid: An Overhaul That's More like a Tune-up," *Business Week*, February 8, 1988, pp. 70–71.

30. Irving L. Janis, *Groupthink*, 2nd ed. (Boston: Houghton Mifflin, 1982).

31. Janis, *Groupthink*.

32. See Robert E. Markland, *Topics in Management Science*, 3rd ed. (New York: Wiley, 1989).

33. Markland, *Topics in Management Science*.

34. Everett Adam, Jr. and Ronald J. Ebert, *Production and Operations Management*, 4th ed. (Englewood Cliffs, N.J.: Prentice-Hall, 1989).

35. Beau Sheil, "Thinking About Artificial Intelligence," *Harvard Business Review*, July–August 1987, pp. 91–97; and Dorothy Leonard-Barton and John J. Sviokla, "Putting Expert Systems to Work," *Harvard Business Review*, March–April 1988, pp. 91–98.

CASE 4.1

Kellogg: Champion of Breakfast Cereals

While trying to make foods healthier and more appetizing for his sanitarium patients, Dr. J. H. Kellogg accidentally discovered how to make wheat flakes. The discovery radically changed the breakfast-eating habits of Americans. His brother, W. K. Kellogg, purchased the commercial rights to wheat flakes, expanded the offering to include corn and rice flakes, and began operations in 1906. Using shrewd coupon advertising, the company was soon dominating the market; by 1909 the company was selling over a million cases of cereal a year. In the 1920s and 1930s, Kellogg expanded to include overseas operations.

The health-food origins of the Kellogg company are enabling it to be immensely successful in growth and market share in an industry often described as having peaked or as having become saturated. In the early 1980s, Kellogg had about a third of the market in ready-to-eat cereal. By the late 1980s, Kellogg's portion had risen to over 40 percent, and the target was to control 50 percent or more. Kellogg's nearest rivals are trailing far behind and have little or no prospect of catching up. As of 1987, when Kellogg had nearly 42 percent of the market, General Mills had just over 20 percent, General Foods under 15 percent, Quaker Oats less than 10 percent, and Nabisco and Ralston Purina about 5.5 percent each.

During the 1970s, Kellogg was so successful that it began to take things for granted and its market share slipped. At about that time, growth in the breakfast-cereal market began to slow down. Competitors began to take away market share through effective advertising and new-product introductions, and they began to diversify to offset the slowdown in market growth. Kellogg acquired Mrs. Smith's pies and Eggo Nutri-Grain waffles but resisted pressure to diversify further, except in limited areas closely related to its main line (Whitney's Yogurt and Salada caffeine-reduced tea, for instance). Instead, Kellogg decided to take advantage of its strengths as a leader in the field and of its reputation for making healthy products in order to concentrate on the cereal business instead of becoming a conglomerate as some of its competitors appeared to be doing.

The birthrate may have fallen and the amount of cereal children can eat may have peaked, but the baby-boom generation represented a substantial potential adult market. Baby-boomers may have given up the sugar-coated cereals of their youth, but they could be interested in the convenience and nutritional value of breakfast cereals. That idea was the basis of Kellogg's strategy during the 1980s, and it worked. Consumers in the 25 to 49 age bracket were eating 26 percent more cereal by the late 1980s than they had been eating in the early 1980s, and total retail sales rose to $5.4 billion in 1988 from $3.7 billion in 1983.

The effort has been not merely to use advertising to inform the baby-boomers about existing market, but also to continually introduce new products designed specifically to appeal to those adults rather than to children. Raisin Squares, for instance, consists of a nugget of toasted wheat surrounding a small amount of raisin puree. That and similar products have enabled Kellogg to move into the shredded-wheat market long controlled by Nabisco. Likewise, Crispix let Kellogg move into the spoon-sized cereal segment of the market long dominated by Ralston Purina's Chex group of products.

Kellogg has moved into a superpremium, upscale market, too. Müeslix, which combines fruits, nuts, and grains into a nutritional cereal, was developed from European traditions and so was able to win customers both in the United States and abroad. The European *muesli* was a mushy, oat-based porridge. When the idea of bringing it to America was brought up, Kellogg's researchers, marketing specialists, and even its advertising agency were opposed. However, the idea appealed to Kellogg's CEO, William E. LaMothe. He authorized development work. Working closely with researchers, Horst W. Schroeder, the executive in charge, developed Müeslix. Müeslix is a toasted flake product that looks very little like its European predecessor but has had enormous appeal to consumers.

Kellogg's new plant in Memphis, Tennessee, will increase its production capacity in the United States by over a third and will be the most expensive food-processing plant ever built. The technology is so automated that human operators are virtually nonexistent. Operations are continuous, monitored by computer, and controlled all the way from mixing the basic ingredients to packing the boxes in cartons for shipment. Evidence from experimental installations suggests that the quality of products produced in automated facilities is approximately 25 percent more consistent than the quality of products produced in other facilities.

Questions

1. Describe the nature of decision making at Kellogg. Be sure to mention both types of decisions and conditions of decision making.
2. Which model of the decision-making process seems to best describe Kellogg? Why? Cite specific examples to support your position.
3. Identify both rational and behavioral aspects of decision making at Kellogg. Cite specific examples.
4. Do you feel that Kellogg's decision to focus so heavily on the cereal market was a good decision? Why or why not?

REFERENCES: Patricia Sellers, "How King Kellogg Beat the Blahs," *Fortune*, August 29, 1988, pp. 54–64; "The Health Craze Has Kellogg Feeling G-R-R-Reat," *Business Week*, March 30, 1987, pp. 52–53; "Sour Grapes from Sweet Raisins," *Advertising Age*, September 7, 1987, p. 16; Beth Austin, "Kellogg Opens Superpremium Niche for Cereal," *Advertising Age*, September 7, 1987, pp. 3–4.

CASE 4.2

Critical Decisions at Porsche

Ferdinand Porsche left Daimler-Benz in 1929 to design luxury and racing cars. He added a mass-market vehicle, eventually known as the Volkswagen, and during World War II also produced military vehicles. In 1948, his son started Porsche AG in Stuttgart to produce sports cars bearing the family name. Porsche AG soon began to sell most of its output to the United States (about two-thirds during the 1950s and about half until the late 1980s). So strong were its U.S. sales, that they almost led to the company's downfall when they and profits collapsed in 1987.

Porsche father and son both stressed competence and performance, not flashiness and show. Because the Porsche car was made to be enjoyed as much as it was to be used, the racing-car heritage was maintained. The car was fast and prestigious. Production was kept to modest levels to ensure the exclusiveness that helped maintain its prestige. The low production levels also kept costs and prices relatively high, which also contributed to the prestigious reputation of the car.

In 1981, Porsche AG went outside the family and outside of Germany for a new CEO. Peter W. Schutz, a German-born American whose family had fled religious persecution in Germany, was selected. Under Schutz's leadership, six key decisions were made: (1) to increase sales in the United States; (2) to produce Porsche models that were more affordable in an attempt to move into a lower and larger market segment; (3) to develop an airplane engine; (4) to invest heavily in capital in order to upgrade and modernize all of Porsche's plants; (5) to alter the way in which Porsches were distributed in the United States; (6) to return to the support of racing as a way to protect Porsche's image.

For a time, the wisdom of those decisions seemed clear. Under Schutz's leadership, growth was steady and substantial.

By the mid-1980s, many of the cars being sold were two new four-cylinder, less expensive models. By the end of 1982 an airplane engine was being produced for Mooney aircraft of Texas. The modernization of facilities was well underway, although the completion of that effort would not occur for some time. The move to change the U.S. distribution system from Audi to Porsche, after some expected problems from existing dealers, was starting to take hold. Finally, the racing effort was underway, although it was having problems because Porsche's Indianapolis car program was not successful.

The problems encountered in the reworking of the distribution system and the racing setback might have been a foreshadowing of things to come. Corporate performance began to slip almost as quickly as it had risen. Overreliance on the U.S. market backfired for Porsche. It made Porsche particularly sensitive to changes in exchange rates. When the Deutsche mark strengthened and the U.S. dollar weakened, Porsches became extremely expensive to purchase in America. This meant that the new four-cylinder models, instead of fitting the lower end of the American market as planned, suddenly were in the middle of the market in terms of price but at the lower end in terms of performance and features. The implication of this was that Porsche had a luxury-priced car but a middle-of-the-road image.

Then came the Black Monday stock-market crash in October 1987. Demand for luxury goods in general and for small sports cars in particular plummeted. The new Porsche models, those with four cylinders, saw their sales figures drastically reduced. Coupled with the changing exchange rates, image problems, and increased competition, the impact of the stock-market crash on Porsche was rapid and dramatic.

Porsche's response was equally rapid and dramatic. Hard decisions were quickly made. Despite the fact that most of the key decisions made under Schutz had been successful, after the drop in performance Schutz was forced to resign as CEO. One thousand workers were laid off. Production was slashed by more than a third, from just over 50,000 cars in 1987 to about 31,000 in 1988. Porsche also decided to beef up design and marketing to regain its former image.

Recovery will not be easy for Porsche. During the latter part of 1988 many market observers felt that the only way in which Porsche would be able to recover was through a merger with a larger automobile manufacturer. Porsche is expanding its design facility, which does work for other car companies, is moving to upgrade all of its models, and has changed the head of its distribution organization in the United States. Whether or not these changes coupled with cost reduction techniques will enable Porsche to recover and remain independent remains to be seen.

Questions

1. Describe the nature of decision making at Porsche. Be sure to mention both types of decisions and conditions of decision making.
2. Which model of the decision-making process seems to best describe Porsche? Why? Cite specific examples to support your position.
3. Identify both rational and behavioral aspects of decision making at Porsche. Cite specific examples.
4. What similarities and differences can you note between the decision making at Porsche and that of Kellogg described in Case 4.1?

REFERENCES: "British Ad Man Takes Wheel at Porsche Unit," *USA Today*, October 4, 1988, p. 2B; "Porsche's Detour," *Fortune*, October 24, 1988, pp. 8–9; "Porsche's U.S. Backfire," *International Management*, April 1988, pp. 42–45; "Stalled Porsche But Is There a U-Turn in Its Future?" *Barron's*, June 27, 1988, pp. 14–15, 37; "Jaguar and Porsche Try to Pull Out of the Slow Lane," *Business Week*, December 12, 1988, pp. 84–85.

OUTLINE

The Planning Process

The Nature of Organizational Goals
Purposes of Goals · Kinds of Goals · Responsibilities for
Setting Goals

Managing the Goal-setting Process
Managing Multiple Goals · Barriers to Effective Goal Setting ·
Making Goal Setting Effective

Goals and Organizational Planning
Kinds of Organizational Plans · Time Frames for Planning ·
Responsibilities for Planning

CHAPTER 5

Organizational Goals and Planning

OBJECTIVES

After studying this chapter, you should be able to:

- Describe the planning process.
- Discuss the nature of organizational goals.
- Describe how to manage the goal-setting process.
- Relate goals to organizational planning.

OPENING INCIDENT

When Harry Hoffman assumed the presidency of Waldenbooks in 1979, he had a clear vision of where he wanted the company to go. At the time, Waldenbooks operated only 542 stores and sold about 20 million books each year. This put the chain far back of industry leader B. Dalton. Hoffman wanted to change things. He set a goal of making Waldenbooks the largest bookstore chain in the United States by 1990. And when K mart bought Waldenbooks in 1984, this goal was heartily endorsed.

Of course, wishing for something and making it happen are two different things. To accomplish his ambitious goal, Hoffman outlined two sets of plans geared toward growth. First, the company began an aggressive campaign of opening new stores, and by the end of 1988, there were 1,319 Waldenbooks outlets. Second, he sought to increase sales volume for each store by heavily promoting and discounting popular titles. Bestsellers with discount stickers are piled by the door, and customers who place orders for new bestsellers before they are released get even bigger discounts. Waldenbooks also gets additional revenue from sales of audio cassettes, videotapes, calendars, and so forth.

Did Waldenbooks achieve Hoffman's goal? In 1988, the chain sold in excess of 100 million books and was tied with B. Dalton for industry leadership. Not content to stay there, Hoffman announced a series of ambitious sales-increase targets for each of the next five years. Waldenbooks was also expanding into other markets—upscale books with Brentano's, books and giftshop combinations with Waldenbooks & More, children's merchandise with Waldenkids, and software with Waldensoftware stores. The chain even started publishing a few of its own books.[1]

A number of factors contribute to the success Waldenbooks has enjoyed over the last decade. One key factor has been having a CEO with a clear vision of where the company should go. Another has been his ability to transform that vision into well-conceived plans of how to get there. Of course, having a vision is no guarantee of success. The vision has to be suitable for the company and the company's unique situation. Without the vision and some sense of how to achieve it, though, the organization is almost certainly doomed to wander and drift.

Where does vision come from, and how is it transformed into action? In the most general sense, management develops and articulates the organization's vision through its goals and describes how to achieve the goals through its planning function. This chapter begins an examination of this critical function. We develop a framework of the overall planning function to guide our discussion through this and the next two chapters.

We then explore the nature of organizational goals more closely. Next we discuss how the goal-setting process can be most effectively managed. Finally, we relate goals to planning and provide an overview of several important aspects of planning.

THE PLANNING PROCESS

Planning is a generic activity. All organizations do it, but no two organizations do it in exactly the same fashion. Figure 5.1 is a general representation of how planning is done.[2] Most firms follow this general framework, but each also has its own nuances and variations. A **goal** is a target state or condition that the organization wants to achieve. Thus, Waldenbooks' target of becoming the largest bookstore chain was a goal. A **plan** is the means by which goals are pursued. The dual activities of adding stores and increasing sales volume at each Waldenbooks store were plans. Finally, **planning** itself is a comprehensive process that includes setting goals, developing plans, and related activities. Setting the initial goal, outlining the plans, putting them into place, and refining them as time passed were all part of the planning process at Waldenbooks.

As shown in Figure 5.1, the starting point for planning is the organization's mission. The mission outlines the organization's purpose, premises, values, and directions (the mission and other concepts introduced here are discussed more fully later). Flowing from the mission are parallel streams of goals and plans. Directly following the mission are strategic goals. These goals and the mission help determine strategic

goal A target state or condition the organization wants to achieve

plan The means by which goals are pursued

planning A comprehensive process that includes setting goals, developing plans, and related activities

FIGURE 5.1

The Organizational Planning Process

plans. Strategic goals and plans are primary inputs for developing tactical goals. Tactical goals and the original strategic plans help shape tactical plans. Tactical plans, in turn, combine with the tactical goals to shape operational goals. These goals and the appropriate tactical plans determine operational plans. Finally, goals and plans at each level can also be used as input for future activities at all levels.

Texas Instruments, for example, uses a planning system that follows this basic framework. It calls the system OST (objectives, strategies, tactics). Top management has established a series of broad, general strategic goals regarding Texas Instruments' defense, microelectronics, and artificial intelligence businesses. Those goals are then translated into strategic plans. Middle managers and engineers develop tactical goals and plans to reach the strategic goals. First-line managers and engineers carry out a variety of operational goals and plans derived from these tactics.[3]

THE NATURE OF ORGANIZATIONAL GOALS

Goals are critical to organizational effectiveness; they serve a number of important purposes. Organizations can have several different kinds of goals. And a number of different kinds of managers must be involved in setting goals. Each of these points is explored in the sections that follow.

Purposes of Goals

Goals serve four important purposes.[4] First, they provide guidance and a unified direction for people in the organization. Goals can help everyone understand where the organization is going and why getting there is important. General Electric's goal of being either number 1 or number 2 in every industry it enters helps set the tone for each decision made by GE managers. And the goal set for Waldenbooks let everyone know that the chain was no longer content to languish behind industry leaders.

Second, as an outgrowth of guidance, planning is facilitated. As indicated in Figure 5.1, goals and planning are highly interrelated. Thus, effective goal-setting practices enhance good planning—effective goal setting promotes good planning, and good planning facilitates future goal setting. The success of Waldenbooks demonstrates how setting goals and developing plans to reach them are complementary activities. Without goals, expansion plans would not have been developed. Moreover, the successful implementation of those plans has made future goal setting easier.

Third, goals can serve as a source of motivation and inspiration to employees of the organization.[5] Goals that are specific and moderately difficult can motivate people to work harder, especially if attaining the goal is likely to result in rewards. When Stanley Gault became CEO

Steven Jobs, co-founder and former CEO of Apple Computer, recently unveiled his newest company and its star product—the NeXT computer. The processes by which he created his new company illustrate the inspirational appeal of organizational goals. For example, when he hired engineers and designers, he refused to tell them about the computer until they had signed on. He wanted them to join the team based solely on their belief in him. He used his goals to push his employees to create a remarkable new computer priced at a level far below what others thought would be possible for a machine of NeXT's capabilities.

of Rubbermaid in 1980, he set a sales-increase goal of 15 percent annually. He also promised to give employees more say in how the company was run and bigger rewards for success. Workers in the company were galvanized into actions aimed at surpassing Gault's goal, and to date they have succeeded each year since the original goal was set.[6]

Finally, goals provide an effective mechanism for evaluation and control. This means that performance can be assessed in the future in terms of how successfully today's goals are accomplished. For example, suppose officials of the United Way set a goal of collecting $250,000 from a particular community. If midway through the campaign they have raised only $50,000, this will suggest they need to change or intensify their efforts. If they end up only raising $100,000 by the end of their drive, they will need to carefully study why they did not reach their goal and what they need to do differently next year. On the other hand, if they succeed in raising $265,000, evaluations of their efforts will take on an entirely different character. The board of directors at Waldenbooks applauded the ambitious growth goals set for the company years ago. They also expected to see annual progress made toward reaching the goal within the framework initially established.

Kinds of Goals

Organizations establish many different kinds of goals. In general, these goals vary by level, by area, and by time frame. Figure 5.2 provides examples of each type of goal for a hypothetical fast-food chain.

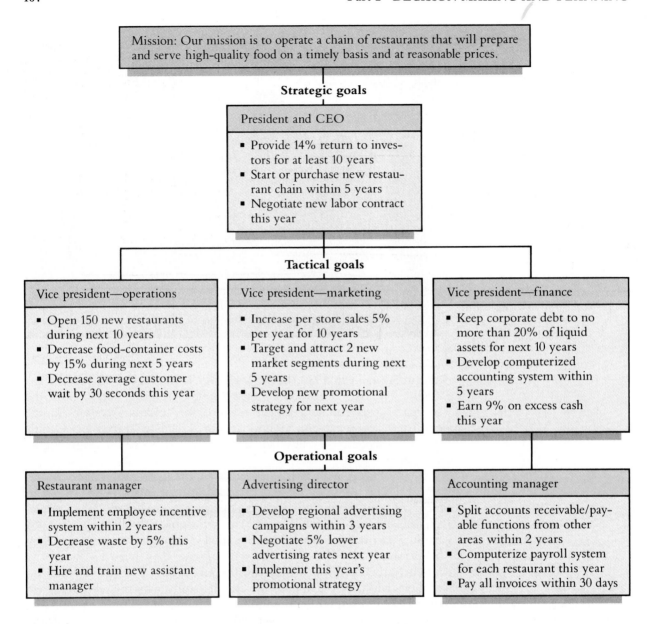

FIGURE 5.2

Kinds of Organizational Goals for a Regional Fast Food Chain

Level   Goals are set for and by different levels within an organization. As noted earlier, the four basic levels of goals are the mission and strategic, tactical, and operational goals. An organization's **mission** is a statement of its "fundamental, unique purpose that sets a business apart from other firms of its type and identifies the scope of the business's operations in product and market terms."[7] Table 5.1 identifies the basic components of a typical corporate mission statement and provides an example of each component taken from actual mission statements. Of course, not every mission statement includes all eight of these components, but most statements include several of them.

mission   A statement of an organization's fundamental purpose

TABLE 5.1

Components of Corporate
Mission Statements

Target Customers and Markets
Example: "We believe our first responsibility is to the doctors, nurses, and patients, to mothers and all others who use our products." (Johnson & Johnson)

Principal Products or Services
Example: "AMAX's principal products are molybdenum, coal, iron ore, copper, lead, zinc, petroleum and natural gas, potash, phosphates, nickel, tungsten, silver, gold, and magnesium."

Geographic Domain
Example: "We are dedicated to the total success of Corning Glass Works as a worldwide competitor."

Core Technologies
Example: "Control Data is in the business of applying microelectronics and computer technology in two general areas: computer-related hardware; and computing-enhancing services, which include computation, information, education, and finance."

Concern for Survival, Growth, and Profitability
Example: "In this respect, the company will conduct its operations prudently, and will provide the profits and growth which will assure Hoover's ultimate success." (Hoover Universal)

Company Philosophy
Example: "It's all part of the Mary Kay philosophy—a philosophy based on the golden rule. A spirit of sharing and caring where people give cheerfully of their time, knowledge, and experience." (Mary Kay Cosmetics)

Company Self-Concept
Example: "Hoover Universal is a diversified, multi-industry corporation with strong manufacturing capabilities, entrepreneurial policies, and individual business unit autonomy."

Desired Public Image
Example: "To share the world's obligation for the protection of the environment." (Dow Chemical)

John A. Pearce II and Fred David, "Corporate Mission Statements: The Bottom Line," The Academy of Management Executive, May 1987, pp. 109–115. Reprinted with permission.

■ **organizational goals**
Strategic, tactical, and operational goals set for and by top, middle, and first-line managers, respectively

Strategic goals are goals set by and for top management of the organization. Their focus is usually on broad, general issues. For example, Sony recently set a strategic goal of reducing its reliance on the consumer-electronics market. Managers felt that the volatile nature of the market made continued reliance on it too risky.[8]

Tactical goals, in contrast, are set by and for middle managers. Their focus is on how to operationalize actions necessary to achieve the strategic goals. One tactical goal at Sony to help achieve Sony's strategic goal was to buy at least one new business in 1987; the goal was realized when the company bought CBS Records.

Operational goals are set by and for lower-level managers. Their concern is with shorter-term issues associated with the tactical goals. At Sony, this means things like boosting sales at the company's existing security systems business. (Some people use the words "objectives" and "goals" interchangeably. When they are differentiated, however, the term "objectives" is usually used instead of "operational goals.")

Area Organizations set goals for different areas. The restaurant chain represented in Figure 5.2 has goals for operations, marketing, and finance. Manufacturing firms like Dresser Industries also set production goals for quality, productivity, and so forth. Human resource goals might be set for management development, employee turnover, and absenteeism. Companies with a strong research and development thrust like 3M and Rubbermaid set goals for product innovations and breakthroughs. Beyond purely functional areas like those, organizations also set goals across a number of general areas. Peter Drucker, for example, suggests that well-managed businesses set goals across eight general areas. The areas are summarized in Table 5.2. Nonbusiness organizations would need to consider a different mix of goals.

Time Frame Organizations also set goals across different time frames. In Figure 5.2, three goals are listed in each of the boxes at the strategic, tactical, and operational levels. The first is a long-term goal, the second an intermediate-term goal, and the third a short-term goal. There tend to be more long-term than short-term strategic goals, and more short-

TABLE 5.2

Goals for Well-managed Businesses

1. **Market standing.** An indication of the percentage market share desired by the firm or the specification of a competitive niche.
2. **Innovation.** Recognition of the need to develop new services or products.
3. **Productivity.** An efficiency measure that relates resources used to output generated.
4. **Physical and financial resources.** The acquisition and efficient use of physical and financial resources.
5. **Profitability.** An indication of the firm's profitability as measured by one or more financial indexes, such as return on investment.
6. **Manager performance and development.** Effective conduct of the managerial roles and development of potential in the individual.
7. **Worker performance and attitude.** Effective conduct of the operational roles and maintenance of positive attitudes on the part of employees.
8. **Public responsibility.** A consideration for the firm's impact on society.

Chart from The Practice of Management by Peter F. Drucker. Copyright © 1954 by Peter F. Drucker. Reprinted by permission of Harper & Row, Publishers, Inc., and the author.

term than long-term operational goals. And there tends to be a balanced mix of all three time frames at the tactical level. Some goals have an explicit time frame (i.e., open 150 new restaurants during the next ten years) and others have an open-ended time horizon (i.e., maintain 10 percent annual growth). Finally, we should also note that the meaning of different time frames varies by level. For example, at the strategic level, long-term often means ten years or longer, intermediate term around five years or so, and short-term around one year. In contrast, only two or three years may be long-term at the operational level, and short-term may mean a matter of weeks or even days.

Other Kinds of Goals   There are also other kinds of goals. One useful perspective is between official goals and operative goals.[9] **Official goals** are the goals the organization espouses publicly to its stockholders, the local community, and so forth. **Operative goals** are goals the organization will not publicly disclose or admit to pursuing. A state university may be publicly asking for a 10 percent budget increase from the state legislature (its official goal) while privately planning to receive and manage with less than 10 percent (its operative goal). Likewise, when automobile companies say their goal is to build the best cars in the world (official goal), they really mean that they want to optimize acceptable quality and costs to achieve maximum profits (operative goal). Finally, makers of alcoholic beverages argue publicly for restraint and moderation (official goal) but no doubt still want to maximize total sales (operative goal).

official goals   Those goals espoused publicly to stockholders, the local community, and so forth

operative goals   Those goals the organization will not publicly disclose or admit to pursuing

Responsibilities for Setting Goals

Who sets goals? The answer is actually quite simple: All managers should be involved in the goal-setting process. However, each manager generally has responsibilities for setting goals that correspond to his or her level in the organization. The mission and strategic goals are generally determined by the board of directors and top managers. Top and middle managers then work together to establish tactical goals. Finally, middle and lower-level managers are jointly responsible for operational goals. Many managers also set individual goals for themselves. These goals may involve career paths, informal work-related goals outside the normal array of official goals, or just about anything of interest or concern to the manager.

MANAGING THE GOAL-SETTING PROCESS

Given the importance of organizational goals, it follows that managers are especially concerned about how to manage the goal-setting process. Areas of most concern are managing multiple goals, barriers to effective goal setting, and making the goal-setting process effective.

Robert Maxwell's goal is to create a global media empire. His base of operations is Maxwell Communication in London. In recent years he has added to that several U.S. printing companies and Macmillan publishing company. Maxwell expects to achieve considerable synergy from the various media businesses he is amassing.

Managing Multiple Goals

Organizations set many different kinds of goals, and if the process is not closely managed, there may be significant conflicts or contradictions among goals. Nike suffered major problems with inconsistent goals a few years ago. Manufacturing was producing high-quality shoes that should have had wide appeal, but design was not concerned with making the shoes look stylish. Marketing was interested more in absolute sales than in market share. As a result, the company fell far behind Reebok. When the inconsistencies were recognized and corrected, Nike soon caught up with Reebok.[10] "Management in Practice" illustrates what can happen when owners and managers have different goals.

The starting point in managing multiple goals is simply to recognize that they exist. This recognition is facilitated by the preparation of a formal statement of organizational goals. A formal goal statement fosters understanding and communication and hence helps everyone in the organization know what's going on. Formal goal statements are a part of most corporate annual reports and should always be a part of strategic planning documents.

optimizing Balancing and reconciling possible conflicts among goals

The manager should also understand the importance and necessity of optimizing. **Optimizing** involves balancing and reconciling possible conflicts between goals. Because goals may conflict with one another, the manager must look for inconsistencies and decide whether to pursue one goal to the exclusion of another or whether to find a midrange target to aim for.

American Express, for example, has long had a goal of maintaining good relations with the banks that sell its travelers checks. However, the company recently began offering its own customers products and services previously available only from banks. An example is the Optima credit card, with terms and uses similar to Visa's and MasterCard's but a lower interest rate. Not surprisingly, this has changed American Express's relationship with banks. A few have stopped carrying American Express travelers checks. Officials at American Express hope that the extra profits earned by Optima will offset the lost business from the banks that begin to push competitors' travelers checks.[11]

Barriers to Effective Goal Setting

Another key to managing the goal-setting process is to recognize the many barriers that can disrupt things. Four significant barriers are inappropriate goals, unattainable goals, overemphasis on quantitative or qualitative goals, and improper reward systems.[12]

Inappropriate Goals Inappropriate goals come in many forms. Paying a large dividend to stockholders may be inappropriate if it comes at the expense of necessary research and development. Driving a competitor out of business, paying off local officials to obtain a favorable zoning

MANAGEMENT IN PRACTICE

REVCO'S CONFLICTING GOALS

Revco began as Regal Drugs in Detroit, Michigan, in 1947. It adopted the discount, self-service model of operations in 1956 when there were only two stores. At that time the chain began to grow. By 1961 there were 20 stores in the Detroit area and 40 more were added in Cleveland, Ohio. After Revco went public in 1964, growth became even more pronounced. Sidney Dworkin, who joined the company in 1963, became its president in 1966. By the early 1980s, Revco was operating over 1,700 stores and was marketing vitamins, drugs, and drug supplies under its own name. Just a couple of years later, Revco was the nation's largest drugstore chain with over 2,000 stores.

It may have been the largest, but it was not the most successful. Revco was in serious trouble. The reason for the trouble was that there was conflict between the goals of the managers and the owners.

In 1983 vitamins made by Carter-Glogau for Revco were implicated in the deaths of thirty-eight infants. The price of Revco's stock plunged and provided an opportunity for someone to buy a controlling interest in the firm. The CEO, Sidney Dworkin, had been with Revco so long that he regarded it as a family business despite the fact that he and his family held only about 3 percent of the stock. Dworkin moved to keep control. In 1984, he persuaded two friends to buy 12 percent of Revco's stock through their company to assure his continued position with Revco.

The company was getting into trouble because the CEO wanted to keep his position and let that desire drive his decision making. In fact, in 1986 Dworkin arranged for a leveraged buyout (LBO) whereby a group of investors would purchase control of Revco for a price above the going market rate. He succeeded in swinging the deal, but the firm's financial situation was a disaster. When profits turned to losses in 1987, the board voted to buy out Dworkin and replace him as CEO with another outsider.

The conflict between the goals of owners and managers was joined by bondholders concerned about repayment of debts to them. The final result was that Revco went bankrupt and filed for Chapter 11 reorganization. Chapter 11 provides protection from creditors while the firm reorganizes its financial affairs to satisfy those creditors. Many companies emerge from Chapter 11 as healthy corporations and are able to begin operations anew. It seems likely that Revco will be one of those companies.

REFERENCES: "Revco: Anatomy of an LBO That Failed," *Business Week*, October 3, 1988, pp. 58–62; John J. Curran, "Companies That Rob the Future," *Fortune*, July 4, 1988, pp. 84–89; "Revco's Leveraged Buyout Comes Apart," *The Wall Street Journal*, June 14, 1988, p. 6; "Two Banks Agree on Loans to Revco," *The New York Times*, August 5, 1988, p. D3.

---

means-end inversion   The means selected to obtain an end can inadvertently become the end itself

decision, and evading anti-pollution regulations are illegal as well as inappropriate. Inappropriate goals may also arise from what is called a **means-end inversion**—that is, the means selected to obtain an end (or goal) can inadvertently become the end itself. American Home Products is a good example of a company that was guilty of this error. The company originally had a goal of maintaining a high stock price. One way managers decided to help hold the stock price up was by paying out a large percentage of profits in dividends. Sometimes this was done even when the money might have been better spent on other areas. Recently, managers at American Home Products indicated that their goal is to pay out 57 percent of their profits as dividends. Thus, the means (high dividends) to a goal (high stock price) was transformed into a new goal. Some experts speculate that the company's stock price will suffer in the long run because the company has neglected research and development to support its dividend policy.[13]

Other inappropriate goals are those that are inconsistent with the organization's mission. Imagine a business violating its basic purpose by giving all its profits to charity, or imagine a church attempting to earn a profit! Coleco Industries, Inc., a toy company most noted for its phenomenally successful Cabbage Patch dolls, has made several blunders with its corporate goals. One clearly inappropriate goal a few years ago was to enter the home-computer market. It was a market where the company lacked expertise, where sales were already slowing down, and where several large competitors like Texas Instruments had already bowed out. Sales of the Adam computer were abysmal, and Coleco ended up losing almost $120 million.[14]

Unattainable Goals   Another obstacle to the goal-setting process is setting unattainable goals—goals so extreme that accomplishing them is virtually impossible. Of course, goals should not be so easily attainable that employees see them as a joke or an insult. Goals must be challenging but within reach.[15] If Chrysler were to set a goal of selling more cars than General Motors next year, people at the company would probably be embarrassed because achieving such a goal would be impossible. However, setting a goal of selling 250,000 more cars next year than last year might be within the realm of possibility.

Setting an unattainable goal is destructive for one simple reason: No matter how well an individual, unit, or organization performs, if goals are not met, many people assume that someone has failed. Consider the case of Sun Microsystems, a company highlighted in Chapter 4. One of Sun's goals is continued growth. However, managers recognize that there are limits to how fast the company can actually grow. A goal of maintaining the current rate of growth, for example, would most likely be unattainable. If Sun were to continue to grow as fast as it did during its first five years of existence, the company would be bigger than Du Pont by 1993 and half the size of the entire U.S. economy by 1998! Consequently, Sun has a goal of growth, albeit growth at an increasingly modest pace.[16]

Overemphasis on Quantitative or Qualitative Goals   Another barrier to goal setting is placing too much emphasis on either quantitative or qualitative goals. In some settings, quantitative goals are necessarily emphasized. Making a certain profit margin, increasing productivity to a designated level, publishing a certain number of articles, and winning a specific number of games are all worthwhile objectives. Because they are quantitative, they are convenient benchmarks against which to measure actual performance. But because of this convenience, managers sometimes tend to overemphasize quantitative goals as an indicator of performance. For example, a sales representative may have two basic goals for this year: increase sales by 10 percent and improve customer relations. At the end of the year, the representative's sales manager is likely to place more weight on the sales increase, simply because it can be more objectively assessed than can an improvement in customer relations. This may result in shortsighted and unfair slighting of the less tangible aspect of the employee's performance.

Equally significant problems may arise if only qualitative goals are developed. If a manager's objectives for the year are to revitalize her or his unit, develop the unit's human resources, and make a greater social contribution, assessing the manager's performance at the end of the year will be quite difficult. How do we decide whether "a greater social contribution" has been made?

Some goals, especially those relating to financial considerations, are by nature quantifiable, objective, and verifiable. Other goals, such as employee satisfaction and development and many aspects of environmental relations, are difficult if not impossible to quantify. Both kinds of goals should be considered in developing goals and in evaluating the results.[17]

Improper Reward Systems   In some settings, an improper reward system acts as a barrier to the goal-setting process. For example, people may inadvertently be rewarded for poor goal-setting behavior or go unrewarded or even punished for proper goal-setting behavior. Suppose a manager sets a goal of decreasing turnover next year. If turnover is decreased by even a fraction, the manager can claim success and perhaps be rewarded for the accomplishment. In contrast, a manager who attempts to decrease turnover by 5 percent but actually achieves a decrease of only 3 percent may receive a smaller reward because of her or his failure to reach the "letter" of the established goal.

In some situations people may even be rewarded for achieving goals that are counterproductive to the organization's intent. United Way's solicitors, for example, may be rewarded (in the form of compliments and congratulations) for dollars pledged rather than for actual dollars collected. Such solicitors have an incentive to accept pledges from people who are not likely to pay, and these unfulfilled pledges distort United Way's expectations of donations that are forthcoming. Similarly, a bank that rewards solicitors for signing up new credit-card holders may suffer long-term losses if the solicitors give cards to poor credit-risk individuals as a way to meet their quotas.[18]

Making Goal Setting Effective

Fortunately, there are several guidelines for making goal setting effective. Some of the guidelines are listed in Table 5.3.

Understanding the Purposes of Goals   One of the best ways to facilitate the goal-setting process is to make sure that managers understand the four main purposes of goals: as a (1) source of guidance and direction, (2) catalyst for planning, (3) stimulus for motivation and inspiration, and (4) mechanism for evaluation and control. Goal setting and implementation should be undertaken with those purposes in mind. When

TABLE 5.3

Making Goal Setting Effective

1. Managers should understand the purposes of goals.
2. Goals should be properly stated.
a. They should be specific.
b. They should be concise.
c. They should be time-related.
3. Goals should be horizontally and vertically consistent.
4. Managers must accept and be committed to the goals.
5. The goal-setting process shoud be integrated with the reward system, but it should also have a diagnostic component.

Steven Jobs announced the development of a new computer called NeXT, his stated goals were to have the machine on the market in 1988 at a price of no more than $3,000. As the product was refined, however, it became apparent that neither target would be met. The technological sophistication of the machine meant longer time for development and a much higher price tag. The computer was unveiled in late 1988 but was not available for sale until mid-1989—and at a price of $6,500. Although neither of the original two goals was met, they nevertheless served their intended purpose. They pointed out what the company wanted to do, directed effort toward doing it, and generally helped to keep things on track.[19]

Stating Goals Properly   Making sure that goals are properly stated is another way to improve the goal-setting process. To the extent possible, goals should be specific, concise, and time-related.[20] For example, when James R. Houghton became CEO of Corning Glass Works, he set four major financial goals to be achieved within eight years: a return on equity of at least 17 percent, annual revenue growth of over 5 percent (adjusted for inflation), a debt-to-capital ratio below 25 percent, and an average dividend payout of 33 percent.[21] These goals clearly meet the three criteria noted above. They are specific in terms of what outcomes are being sought. They are concise. And they specify a clear window of time over which they are to be pursued.

Goal Consistency   A third way to improve the goal-setting process is to make sure that goals are consistent both horizontally and vertically.[22] By horizontal consistency, we mean that goals should be consistent across the organization. Vertical consistency means that goals should be consistent up and down the organization—strategic, tactical, and operational goals must agree with one another. Citicorp, for example, recently announced goals of trimming its total work force by 3,000, cleaning up its loan portfolio, and building a mergers and acquisition finance group. The first two goals are consistent in that they both aim at reducing costs. The third, however, calls for additional employees. Thus, in developing plans to achieve these goals, managers at Citicorp

Goal consistency has become the hallmark of a major new program at Whistler Radar. The firm's top management had to face the fact that the quality of the company's radar detectors was far below what it should be. Indeed, 100 of the firm's 250 employees were spending all their time fixing defective units. So Whistler adopted a new goal directed at high quality products and made quality a responsibility of all the employees. Company President Charles Stott, shown here, and other top executives now spend at least one day each quarter working on the line as a symbol of their dedication to quality.

will need to recognize that they can either transfer some of the 3,000 excess employees to the new group or else will need to eliminate more than 3,000 existing employees to make way for the new ones.[23] (One method for facilitating goal consistency, called management by objectives, is discussed in Chapter 7).

Goal Acceptance and Commitment   People in the organization also need a high level of acceptance and commitment to work toward organizational goals. To encourage goal acceptance and commitment by those who work for them, managers should demonstrate their vision for the organization in everything they do. Ray Kroc, founder of McDonald's, coined the company motto "Quality, service, cleanliness, and value" when the company had only a few restaurants. He repeated it, however, throughout his career. Thus, people who came to work for him knew his values, his vision, and his goals—and they accepted them as their own.

Managers should also allow broad-based participation in the goal-setting process whenever appropriate, and they should make sure that goals are properly communicated. People are much more likely to accept and become committed to goals if they helped set them, or at least know how and why they were established. Steven Chen, the top research scientist at Cray Research, left that company because managers changed their goal of building the world's most powerful supercomputer. Chen believed very strongly that the computer should be built and was unhappy that the company ignored his advice and dropped it as a priority.[24]

Effective Reward Systems   Goal setting can also be improved if it is integrated with the reward system of the organization. People should be rewarded first for effective goal setting and then for successful goal attainment. However, since failure sometimes results from factors outside the manager's control, people should also be assured that failure to reach a goal will not necessarily bring punitive consequences. Frederick Smith, founder and CEO of Federal Express, has a stated goal of encouraging risk. Thus, when Federal Express lost $233 million on an unsuccessful new service called ZapMail, no one was punished. Smith believed the original idea had been a good one but was unsuccessful for reasons beyond the company's control.[25] Changing economic conditions, changing government regulations, and activities in the marketplace may all make goal attainment unlikely. Accordingly, the goal-setting process should have a diagnostic as well as an evaluative component.

Consider the case of a sales manager reviewing performance with three sales representatives. One representative may have established inappropriate goals to begin with. His evaluation should perhaps focus on how to do a better job of setting goals in the future. The second sales representative may have set appropriate goals but failed to meet them because of unexpected circumstances. For this person, the evaluation can focus on diagnosing whether the unexpected circumstances could have been foreseen, how they could be avoided in the future, and so forth. The third sales representative, who set proper goals and then met them, should be rewarded.

GOALS AND ORGANIZATIONAL PLANNING

We earlier established a clear link between organizational goals and planning. With our increased understanding of goals as a foundation, we can now consider broader issues associated with the planning function. First, we identify kinds of plans. Next, we consider time frames for planning. Finally, we discuss responsibilities for planning.

Kinds of Organizational Plans

Just as organizations establish many different kinds of goals, so too do they develop many kinds of plans. At a general level, and as noted in Figure 5.1, organizations develop strategic, tactical, and operational plans.

strategic plan   A general plan outlining decisions of resource allocation, priorities, and action steps necessary to reach strategic goals

Strategic Plans   Strategic plans are the plans developed to achieve strategic goals. More precisely, a **strategic plan** is a general plan outlining decisions of resource allocation, priorities, and action steps necessary to reach strategic goals.[26] These plans are set by the board of directors and top management, generally have an extended time hori-

Organizations must develop strategic, tactical, and operational plans that require time, coordination, expertise, and objectivity.

Marina v.N. Whitman, a vice president of General Motors, oversees staff functions in the areas of public relations, economics, environmental activities, and industry-government relations. Whitman is responsible for making sure the corporate chiefs at GM understand the immediate and ultimate effects of monetary policy.

tactical plan   Aimed at achieving tactical goals and is developed to implement parts of a strategic plan

operational plan   Focuses on carrying out tactical plans and on achieving operational goals

zon, and address questions of scope, resource deployment, competitive advantage, and synergy.

For example, recall our example of Corning Glass Works' goals. To reach the ambitious goals he set for the company, James Houghton developed a strategy centered on improved quality. His belief is that enhanced employee motivation directed at improving product quality will reduce costs and increase sales, thereby achieving the financial goals he set for the company. Also recall our opening incident about Waldenbooks. To achieve the strategic goal of becoming the number 1 bookseller, Waldenbooks developed strategic plans to increase the number of stores in its chain as well as to increase the sales for each individual store. (We discuss strategic planning further in Chapter 6.)

Tactical Plans   **Tactical plans**, aimed at achieving tactical goals, are developed to implement specific parts of a strategic plan. They typically involve upper and middle management, have a somewhat shorter time horizon than strategic plans, and have a more specific and concrete focus. Thus, tactical plans are concerned more with actually getting things done than with deciding what to do. Within Waldenbooks' strategic plan, there were several tactical plans. One focused on how to most effectively train large numbers of managers to operate all the new stores being opened. Another was concerned with the timetable for opening new stores—how many per year, how close together, what size markets to enter, and so forth. Another focused on exactly what merchandise mix to carry within the stores. (Tactical planning is covered in detail in Chapter 7.)

Operational Plans   **Operational plans** focus on carrying out tactical plans in order to achieve operational goals. Developed by middle and lower-level managers, operational plans have a short-term focus and are relatively narrow in scope. Each one deals with a fairly small set of activities. For example, Waldenbooks has an operational plan to help manage inventory. The home office monitors buying patterns across the nation and sends individual stores computer printouts telling them when to pull various books from their shelves, to mark them down, and so forth. This approach was conceived by middle managers but is carried out by the individual store managers. (Chapter 7 provides more information about operational plans.)

Time Frames for Planning

We noted above that strategic plans tend to have a long-term focus, tactical plans an intermediate-term focus, and operational plans a short-term focus. "The Global View" describes a variety of planning issues, including the time frames for planning, at Canadian Pacific. The sections that follow describe more fully the time frames that organizations plan for.

Long-Range Planning   Long-range planning covers many years, perhaps even decades. Large firms like General Motors and Exxon routinely develop plans for ten- to twenty-year intervals. Waldenbooks' plan for reaching its strategic goal of market leadership covered a period of ten years. Assume that K mart has developed a strategy calling for a major expansion over a ten-year period. The vice president of human resources, therefore, must deal with an increased need for human resources. He or she will most likely develop a long-range plan describing how many potential managers must be identified each year, whether they should come from inside or outside the organization, and how they are to be groomed for the job.

The time span for long-range planning varies from one organization to another. For our purposes, we will regard any plan that extends beyond five years as being long-range in character. Managers of organizations in complex, volatile environments face a special dilemma. These organizations probably need a longer time horizon than do organizations in less dynamic environments, yet the complexity of their environment makes long-range planning more difficult. Thus, managers at these companies develop long-range plans but also must constantly monitor their environment for possible changes.[27]

Typical areas of long-range planning include major expansions, development of top managers, large issues of new stocks and bonds, new-product or new-service development, and new-plant construction. In recent years, J. C. Penney moved its corporate headquarters from Manhattan to Plano, Texas; Sears entered the financial services industry with its Discover card; Disney began construction of a European Disney World; and Hilton issued $75 million in ten-year bonds. Each of these activities no doubt resulted from long-range planning undertaken in the past, and each is expected to play a major role in corporate operations for a long time to come.

All managers face a complex problem when attempting long-range planning. On the one hand, there are increasing concerns that many managers are neglecting the long run because of short-term pressure from investors for high returns. For example, short-run concerns for high profits were forcing Carnation to cut back on promotion. As a result, the firm was losing market share for its successful Contadina tomato paste and Carnation milk. When the company was purchased by Nestlé, however, a long-run outlook was adopted, promotion was increased, and market share was recaptured.[28] On the other hand, Deere and Company recently ran into problems by worrying too much about the long run. The company was so concerned with building an automated factory of the future that it failed to recognize that pressure from organized labor and decreased demand for tractors would make the plant unprofitable.[29] Thus, managers need to take a balanced perspective when planning across different time frames.

Intermediate Planning   Intermediate plans are somewhat less tentative and subject to change than are long-range plans. They usually cover periods from one to five years. Whereas long-range plans serve as

THE GLOBAL VIEW

CANADIAN PACIFIC EYES THE LONG TERM

Canadian Pacific Ltd. has long been regarded as a barometer of the Canadian economy. That barometer began to forecast weakening conditions during the late 1970s and early 1980s as consistent growth in profits eluded it. Canadian Pacific had expanded over the years into virtually every aspect of the Canadian economy and was beginning to suffer from an inability to manage highly diverse holdings. Having them function smoothly together was one problem; another was that the managerial skills and knowledge necessary to effectively manage one unit were different from those required for the management of other units.

In 1985, William Stinson was named CEO and given the authority to improve Canadian Pacific's performance. His short-term goals were to focus the company more tightly and to improve its immediate profit position. To accomplish those goals, Canadian Pacific divested itself of nine units.

As of 1988, Canadian Pacific assets were in rail transportation (about 36%), forest products (16%), energy (18%), manufacturing (12%), and real estate (18%). Early in 1988, Canadian Pacific bought Canadian National's hotel chain as a link to its real estate operations. Canadian Pacific will have to carefully monitor operations in each of these areas to assure the attainment of both short- and long-term goals.

Canadian Pacific plans steps to ensure the accomplishment of its longer-term goals. One is to sell units that are not very profitable or do not have strong growth potential (or both). One such unit is the Minneapolis railway, Soo Line Corporation. Another step is to increase Canadian Pacific holdings in CNCP Telecommunications. Canadian Pacific also plans to expand the operations of its oil and gas group, PanCanadian Petroleum Ltd., and its forest product unit, Canadian Pacific Forest Products Ltd. The forest product group is already becoming larger as a result of the combining of all forest product aspects of the company in one organizational unit. Finally, Canadian Pacific is going to be far more aggressive in the handling of its real estate holdings through Marathon Realty Company, its real estate unit. Apparently, the huge landholdings will be developed or sold to obtain cash for other acquisitions. Attempts at development, however, may meet opposition, as is one being considered for the waterfront at Vancouver, British Columbia.

REFERENCES: "Canadian Pacific Overhaul Boosts Profits," *The Wall Street Journal*, October 12, 1988, p. A12; Allan Fotheringham, "Trouble on the Waterfront," *MacLean's*, June 13, 1988, p. 60; "Canadian Pacific Planning to Merge 2 Pulp, Paper Units," *The Wall Street Journal*, April 20, 1988, p. 26; "You, Too, Can Land a Boeing 747! Just Fly a Lot of Miles with CP," *Canadian Business*, May 1987, p. 12.

general guidelines derived from an organization's strategy, intermediate plans are more relevant on a day-to-day basis for middle and first-line managers. Thus, they generally parallel tactical plans. Waldenbooks' long-range plan calling for sales leadership in ten years may have had an accompanying intermediate plan for getting the company to target levels in two and four years, for example.

Long-range planning is plagued by the uncertainties associated with long time horizons, so for many organizations intermediate planning has become the central focus of planning activities. Philip Morris developed a long-range plan that called for diversifying away from the tobacco industry, even though identifying specific possible mergers and acquisitions several years ahead is difficult. Philip Morris bought General Foods in 1985 after only two years of planning, and the company's recent move to buy Kraft Foods for over $10 billion grew from an intermediate plan developed about a year earlier. Thus, there was a long-range plan guiding the firm's actions, but intermediate plans actually defined those actions.[30]

Short-Range Planning   Managers also develop sets of plans dealing with a time frame of one year or less. These short-range plans have more impact on the manager's day-to-day activities than do long-range or intermediate plans. At Waldenbooks, for example, opening a specific new store is essentially a short-range issue. So, too, are most instances of product repackaging, changes in advertising campaigns, promoting lower-level managers, and so forth.

In general, there are two general kinds of short-range plans—action plans and reaction plans. An **action plan** serves to operationalize any other kind of plan. For example, Hamish Maxwell, CEO of Philip Morris, made the actual decision to buy Kraft on Friday, October 14, 1988. Lawyers and top managers then worked through the weekend on the proposal so that it could be delivered to Kraft's CEO the following Monday.[31] Their actions and accomplishments were action plans that flowed logically from a decision made by their CEO.

Reaction plans, in turn, are plans designed to allow the company to react to an unforeseen circumstance. The circumstance may or may not be a pleasant one for the organization, and the reaction itself may or may not result in favorable consequences. For example, when Kraft received the takeover bid from Philip Morris, its managers had to decide whether to accept the terms, fight the offer, seek another takeover candidate (a "white knight"), or some other alternative. Any of these constitutes a reaction plan—the firm is reacting to a condition created by its environment. In fact, reacting to any form of environmental turbulence, as described in Chapter 3, is a form of reaction planning.

Integrating Time Frames   A potential problem that managers face when planning across different time horizons is balancing and integrating plans. Short-range plans calling for personnel cuts may be inconsistent with a long-range plan for increasing productivity. But a series of short-range and intermediate plans for increasing promotion are probably congruent with a long-range plan that calls for increasing sales. In this instance, the short- and long-range plans support each other. The challenge, then, is to achieve and maintain consistency and congruency across planning time horizons.

Figure 5.3 shows how plans might be formally integrated. Beginning in 1990, suppose a growing manufacturing firm develops a long-range plan extending over several years, an intermediate plan extending over three years, and a one-year short-range plan. A year later, in 1991, the short-range plan has, by definition, been completed—but not necessarily with 100 percent success. The organization then develops a new short-range plan for the coming year. Using additional information now available, the company might also revise and extend its intermediate and long-range plans from their original three- and seven-year lengths.

action plan   One that is used to operationalize any other kind of plan

reaction plan   Developed to deal with unforeseen circumstances

FIGURE 5.3

Integrating Planning Time
Frames

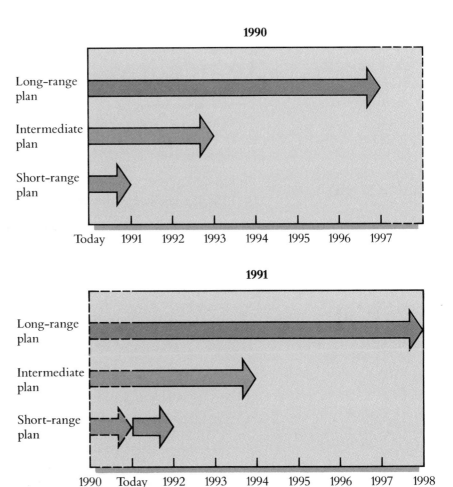

Responsibilities for Planning

We earlier noted briefly who is responsible for setting goals. We can
now expand that initial perspective a bit and examine more fully how
different parts of the organization participate in the overall planning
process. All managers engage in planning to some degree. Marketing
sales managers develop plans for target markets, market penetration,
and sales increases. Operations managers plan cost-cutting programs
and better inventory control methods. As a general rule, however, the
larger an organization becomes, the more the primary planning activities become associated with groups of managers rather than with individual managers.[32] This section explores parts of the organization that
are especially important to planning.

The Planning Staff   Many large organizations develop a professional
planning staff. Tenneco, General Motors, General Electric, Caterpillar,
Raytheon, NCR, Ford, and Boeing all have a planning staff.[33] And
although the planning staff was an American invention, foreign firms

like Nippon Telegraph & Telephone have also started establishing a corporate planning staff.[34] Organizations make the decision to use a planning staff for one or more of the following reasons:

1. Planning takes time. A planning staff can reduce the workload of individual managers.
2. Planning takes coordination. A planning staff can help integrate and coordinate the planning activities of individual managers.
3. Planning takes expertise. A planning staff can bring to a particular problem more tools and techniques than any single individual can bring.
4. Planning takes objectivity. A planning staff can take a broader view than individual managers and go beyond pet projects and particular departments.

There are many possible approaches to organizing the planning staff. Two extreme approaches are illustrated in Figure 5.4. In some cases, there may be a single corporate planning staff under the direct supervision of the CEO. This staff is responsible for most of the major planning activities of the firm. In other cases, each division of a large company may have its own planning staff. In this decentralized arrange-

FIGURE 5.4

Structural Alternatives for the Planning Staff

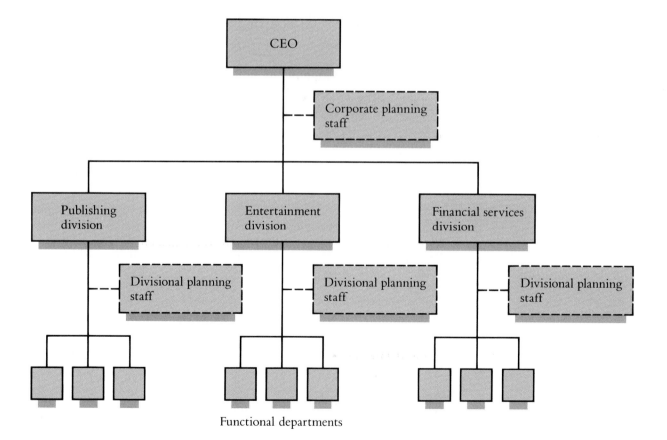

Functional departments

ment, the divisional planning staffs report to the division head, usually a corporate vice president. When this structure is used, there is still often a small corporate-level staff to coordinate the activities of the various divisions. General Motors has a planning group for each of its automobile divisions, as well as a corporate planning staff.

Top management must decide how the planning staff is to be organized. Factors that influence this decision include:

1. Degree of centralization: In highly centralized organizations, top managers are likely to keep the planning staff under their own control. In decentralized organizations the planning staff may be given more power. Decentralized firms often have divisional planning staffs.
2. Nature of the environment: The more dynamic and complex an organization's environment, the more likely the planning staff is to enjoy more resources, responsibility, and power. Texas Instruments recently recognized that its mechanistic, centralized planning system caused the company to react too slowly to environmental shifts. As a result, the company is moving to give corporate planners more authority.[35]
3. The personality of top managers: Some managers simply prefer to retain more control than others over planning activities, so a planning staff reporting to this kind of manager is likely to have little power or responsibility. Jack Welch at General Electric froze the budget of the company's planning staff in an effort to reduce the numbers and power of the corporate planners.[36]

Planning Task Force   Organizations sometimes use a planning task force to help develop plans. Such a task force is often comprised of line managers with a special interest or involvement in the relevant area of planning. The task force may also have members from the formal planning staff if the organization has one. Such a task force is most often created when there is a special circumstance the organization wants to address, as opposed to normal and ongoing planning activities. For example, when Electronic Data Systems decided to expand its services to Europe, managers knew that the firm's normal planning approach would not suffice, and top management created a special planning task force. The task force had representatives from each of the major units within the company, the corporate planning staff, and the management team that would run the European operation. Once the plan for entering the European market was formulated and implemented, the task force was eliminated.[37]

Board of Directors   As we discussed in Chapter 3, the board of directors is a group of people elected by the company's stockholders to represent their own interests. Among other responsibilities, the board of directors has the duty to establish the corporate mission and strategy. In some companies the board takes an active role in the planning process. At CBS, for example, the board of directors has traditionally played a major role in planning. In other companies the board selects a competent chief executive and delegates planning to that individual. Jim Treybig, chairman of Tandem Computers' board of directors, delegates much of the company's planning activities to a senior vice president.

The Chief Executive Officer The chief executive officer (CEO) is usually the president or the chairman of the board of directors. In any case the CEO is probably the single most important individual in any organization's planning process. Even when the board takes the lead in developing strategy, the CEO plays a major role in the complete planning process and is responsible for implementing the strategy. The board and CEO, then, assume directive roles in planning. The other organizational components involved in the planning process have more of an advisory or consulting role.

The Executive Committee Another group that plays a major role in the planning process of many organizations is some form of executive committee. The executive committee is usually composed of the top executives in the organization working together as a group. Committee members usually meet on a regular basis to provide input to the CEO on the proposals that affect their own units and to review the various strategic plans that develop from this input. The number of individuals on an executive committee varies considerably from one organization to another; in a very large organization, the executive committee might have several dozen members. Members of the executive committee are frequently assigned to various staff committees, subcommittees, and task forces to concentrate on specific projects or problems that might confront the entire organization at some time in the future.

Line Management The final component of most organizations' planning activities is line management. Line managers are those individuals with formal authority and responsibility for the management of the organization. They play an important role in an organization's planning process for two reasons. First, they are a valuable source of inside information for other managers as plans are formulated and implemented. Second, it is usually the line managers at the middle and lower levels of the organization who must execute the plans developed by top management. Line management identifies, analyzes, and recommends program alternatives, develops budgets and submits them for approval, and finally sets the plans in motion.

The Individual Planner Even when organizations have large, sophisticated planning staffs and well-developed planning cycles, individual managers are the key to successful planning. They must be willing and able to make appropriate contributions to any overall planning framework. But they must also be willing to take the initiative in planning for their units of responsibility and their own individual activities. Individual managers (occasionally acting alone but more often working within the context of a larger group) are the core of the planning process in organizations.

SUMMARY OF KEY POINTS

Planning is a vital component in organizational effectiveness. The planning process involves the determination of the organization's mission and a hierarchy of strategic, tactical, and operational goals and plans.

Goals serve four basic purposes: to provide guidance and direction, to facilitate planning, to inspire motivation and commitment, and to promote evaluation and control. Kinds of goals can be differentiated by level, area, and time frame. All managers within an organization need to be involved in the goal-setting process.

Managers need to pay special attention to the importance of managing multiple goals through optimization and other approaches. Major barriers to goal setting include setting goals that are inappropriate or unattainable, putting too much emphasis on either quantitative or qualitative goals, and an improper reward system. Methods for overcoming these barriers include understanding the purposes of goals, stating goals properly, maintaining goal consistency, promoting goal acceptance and commitment, and maintaining an effective reward system.

Goals are closely related to planning. The major types of planning are strategic, tactical, and operational plans. Plans are developed across a variety of time horizons, including long-range, intermediate, and short-range time frames. Key people in an organization responsible for effective planning are the planning staff, planning task forces, the board of directors, the CEO, the executive committee, and line management.

DISCUSSION QUESTIONS

Questions for Review

1. What is meant by the planning process?
2. Describe the nature of organizational goals. Be certain to include both the purposes and kinds of goals.
3. What are the barriers to effective goal setting? How might they be overcome?
4. Which time frame for planning is most likely to be overlooked by most managers? Why? How might this problem be alleviated?

Questions for Analysis

5. Are there differences between goals, aims, missions, purposes, objectives, targets, and standards? If so, what are they? If not, why do all of these different terms exist?

6. Can an organization accomplish all of the various multiple goals that it has? Why or why not?

7. Does the existence of goals imply planning? Does planning imply the existence of goals? Why or why not?

Questions for Application

8. Interview the head of the department in which you are majoring. What kinds of goals exist for the department and for the members of the department? Share your findings with the rest of the class.

9. Go to the library and look up the history of a major business firm. What role did planning have in the development of that firm?

10. Interview a local small-business manager about the time frames for planning that he or she uses. How do your results compare with what you might have expected from the presentation in the textbook?

NOTES

1. "Waldenbooks Peddles Books a Bit like Soap, Transforming Market," *The Wall Street Journal*, October 10, 1988, pp. A1, A4.

2. This framework is inspired by numerous sources: George Steiner, *Top Management Planning* (New York: Macmillan, 1969); John E. Dittrich, *The General Manager and Strategy Formulation* (New York: Wiley, 1988); Henry Mintzberg, "Crafting Strategy," *Harvard Business Review*, July–August 1987, pp. 66–75; Michael E. Porter, *Competitive Advantage* (New York: Free Press, 1985); Charles W. L. Hill and Gareth R. Jones, *Strategic Management: An Analytical Approach* (Boston: Houghton Mifflin, 1989); Thomas L. Wheelen and J. David Hunger, *Strategic Management and Business Policy*, 3rd ed. (Reading, Mass.: Addison-Wesley, 1989).

3. "Texas Instruments: Casting a Long Technological Shadow," *Texas Business*, July 1986, p. 30; "What's Behind the Texas Instruments–Hitachi Deal," *Business Week*, January 16, 1989, pp. 93–96.

4. Max D. Richards, *Setting Strategic Goals and Objectives*, 2nd ed. (St. Paul, Minn.: West, 1986).

5. See Robert D. Pritchard, Philip L. Roth, Steven D. Jones, Patricia J. Galgay, and Margaret D. Watson, "Designing a Goal-setting System to Enhance Performance: A Practical Guide," *Organizational Dynamics*, Summer 1988, pp. 69–78, for a discussion of how goals affect motivation.

6. Carol Davenport, "America's Most Admired Corporations," *Fortune*, January 30, 1989, pp. 68–94.

7. John A. Pearce II and Fred David, "Corporate Mission Statements: The Bottom Line," *The Academy of Management Executive*, May 1987, p. 109.

8. "Sony Deal Cashes In on Dollar Woes," *USA Today*, November 27, 1987, p. 3B; "Sony Isn't Mourning the 'Death' of Betamax," *Business Week*, January 25, 1989, p. 37.

9. Charles Perrow, *Complex Organizations—A Critical Essay*, 3rd ed. (New York: Random House, 1986).

10. "Nike Catches Up with the Trendy Frontrunner," *Business Week*, October 24, 1988, p. 88.

11. "Optima Moves Quickly into Ranks of Top Credit Cards," *The Wall Street Journal*, October 4, 1988, p. B1.
12. Richards, *Setting Strategic Goals and Objectives*.
13. John J. Curran, "Companies That Rob the Future," *Fortune*, July 4, 1988, pp. 84–89.
14. "Coleco Industries Plans to Broaden Its Product Base," *The Wall Street Journal*, October 28, 1986, p. 6.
15. Craig Pinder, *Work Motivation* (Glenview, Ill.: Scott, Foresman, 1984).
16. Stuart Gannes, "America's Fastest-growing Companies," *Fortune*, May 23, 1988, pp. 28–40.
17. Edwin A. Locke, "The Ubiquity of the Technique of Goal Setting," *Academy of Management Review*, July 1978, pp. 594–602.
18. Edward E. Lawler III, *Pay and Organization Development* (Reading, Mass.: Addison-Wesley, 1981); Douglas B. Gehrman, "Beyond Today's Compensation and Performance Appraisal Systems," *Personnel Administrator*, March 1984, pp. 21–33.
19. "Steve Jobs Comes Back," *Newsweek*, October 24, 1988, pp. 46–51.
20. Locke, "The Ubiquity of the Technique of Goal Setting."
21. "At Corning, A Vision of Quality," *Fortune*, October 24, 1988, p. 64.
22. William Ouchi, "Markets, Bureaucracies, and Clans," *Administrative Science Quarterly*, March 1980, pp. 129–141.
23. "John Reed's Citicorp," *Business Week*, December 8, 1986, pp. 90–96.
24. Kenneth Labich, "The Seven Keys to Business Leadership," *Fortune*, October 24, 1988, pp. 58–66.
25. Labich, "The Seven Keys to Business Leadership."
26. See Hill and Jones, *Strategic Management*.
27. H. Donald Hopkins, "Long-Term Acquisition Strategies in the U.S. Economy," *Journal of Management*, Vol. 13, No. 3, 1987, pp. 557–572.
28. Curran, "Companies That Rob the Future."
29. "Thinking Ahead Got Deere in Big Trouble," *Business Week*, December 8, 1986, p. 69.
30. "Hamish Maxwell's Big Hunger," *Business Week*, October 31, 1988, pp. 24–26; Ronald Henkoff, "Deals of the Year," *Fortune*, January 30, 1989, pp. 162–170.
31. "Hamish Maxwell's Big Hunger."
32. Wheelen and Hunger, *Strategic Management and Business Policy*.
33. Peter Lorange and Balaji S. Chakravarthy, *Strategic Planning Systems*, 2nd ed. (Englewood Cliffs, N.J.: Prentice-Hall, 1989).
34. Carla Rapoport, "The World's Most Valuable Company," *Fortune*, October 10, 1988, pp. 92–104.
35. "New Chief Is Hustling at Texas Instruments," *The Wall Street Journal*, June 14, 1985, p. 6.
36. "Why Jack Welch Is Changing G.E.," *The New York Times*, May 5, 1985, Section 3, pp. 1, 8.
37. Richard I. Kirkland, Jr., "Outsider's Guide to Europe in 1992," *Fortune*, October 24, 1988, pp. 121–127.

CASE 5.1

Borden's Plan for Growth

Gail Borden founded the New York Condensed Milk Company in 1857. At first it grew relatively slowly. But then, because of government orders arising out of the need to supply the military during the Civil War, the company underwent a period of rapid expansion. By the beginning of the twentieth century, Borden was operating in seventeen cities in the United States and in one city in Canada. It continued to grow and soon was the largest dairy business in the United States. Borden remained basically a dairy business until after the 1950s, when a plan to reduce its dependency on the dairy industry was made.

For over a quarter of a century, Borden has maintained a consistent long-term plan not to be overly dependent upon any one business or product line. Indeed, Borden has at times seemed to be more of a trader of companies than a company itself. Consider its recent purchases and sales. In 1988 it bought Illinois-based Crane Brand potato chips, several snack-food firms in Britain and West Germany, and a wall-covering organization in Britain. It also got rid of several lines, including women's sportswear, cosmetics, fertilizers, and bulk cheese and sugar.

Borden is consolidating and diversifying at the same time; it is restructuring and repositioning continually. The results of these efforts are clear. Sales and earnings are up. From 1986 to 1987, sales rose 30 percent to well over $6 billion, and earnings rose 20 percent to over $250 million. The results of these efforts are noteworthy when viewed from a market perspective, too. Borden has become the world's largest dairy company, the world leader in pasta, and second only to PepsiCo's Frito-Lay in snack foods. The plan is working.

Borden also has a goal of keeping costs down and profit margins up. To achieve that goal, it has developed a plan that tends to focus on regions rather than on the nation as a whole. As Borden expands its operations and acquires new companies, production is centralized on a regional basis to utilize the most efficient facility available. This regional plan also enables Borden to introduce new products quickly, since it can do so on a regional level rather than on a national level like some of its competitors. In a sense, all Borden has to do is add a few cases of a product to a truck that is already delivering to a retail outlet. The local distributor then provides a bit of shelf space, and Borden lets the public know about the availability of the product through local advertising. Thus, with virtually no major effort or expenditure of funds, Borden is able to introduce a product into a region where its sales serve as a gauge of consumer reaction to the product.

If a product works well in a region, Borden can then move it to the national level. Doing that, however, is not always easy and, in some cases, may be impossible. When Borden finds that a regional brand is not very movable, it frequently simply seeks another regional brand to sell in the other regions. This practice assures Borden a presence in all regions even though brands may vary from one region to another. In other cases, Borden adopts a slower approach to national introduction, one that is coupled with already existing successful regional brands. Another aspect of the regional plan is that the regions can create new products, too. Further, a new product that is a success in one region can be borrowed by another region and may be successful there as well. Both product innovation and marketing strategy are hard for Borden's competitors to predict and imitate.

The regional plan means that Borden is a conglomerate of small brands rather than a distributor of a small number of well-known national brands. That, too, has its advantages. Small brands tend to be less vulnerable to the introduction of other new products, and they tend to require less advertising. Again, the regional plan leads to lower costs and higher profits as well as to operations that are less susceptible to competitive pressures.

But, even though brands may be regional, the purchasing of supplies can be done nationally to obtain huge volume with the resulting ability to bargain for good prices. The huge volume also permits some plants to operate 24 hours a day, seven days a week—a schedule that greatly reduces production costs as well. In pasta, for instance, Borden keeps fourteen U.S. plants running around the clock and buys over 800 million pounds of wheat each year to manufacture seventeen different brands of pasta. Accommodating regional tastes, especially in brand names and advertising, while still taking advantage of economies of scale that are available with national volumes, enables Borden to maintain high sales revenues and high profits. Thus, Borden has the best of two worlds.

Questions

1. What kinds of goals can you identify at Borden? What purpose do they serve?
2. What kinds of plans can you identify at Borden? What time frames for planning are involved for each of the plans you have identified? Are those different kinds of plans integrated with one another?
3. What is likely to be the relationship between the various brands of the same product in an organization like Borden? Why?
4. What do you see as the long-term consequences of Borden's plan on corporate performance?

REFERENCES: "Borden Feasts on Acquisitions," *USA Today*, April 20, 1988, pp. 1B–2B; Walter Guzzardi, "Big Can Still Be Beautiful," *Fortune*, April 25, 1988, pp. 50–64; Bill Saporito, "How Borden Milks Packaged Goods," *Fortune*, December 21, 1987, pp. 139–141; "There Could Be a Delicious Play in Borden," *Business Week*, November 10, 1986, p. 112; "Borden Officials Link Jobs in New Anti-Takeover Plan," *The Wall Street Journal*, January 5, 1989, p. B1.

CASE 5.2

Fiat Plans For The Long Haul

Fiat (Fabbrica Italiana Automoboli Torino) was founded by Giovanni Agnelli in 1899 in Turin, Italy. His grandson, who bears his name (although the grandson is called Gianni), joined the company at the end of World War II after having fought during that war first for the Fascists and then on the side of the Allies. Some twenty years later, Giovanni Agnelli became chairman and CEO of Fiat. The Agnelli family still owns over a third of the stock in Fiat and will no doubt control the executive suite well into the next century. When Agnelli took over in 1966, the Italian economy was booming, and prosperous Italians were moving up—trading in their motor scooters for Fiat's small, inexpensive cars. Fiat prospered and grew along with the economy.

The 1970s were a different matter. The OPEC oil cartel generated an oil crisis that severely disrupted the Italian economy. That economic disruption led to serious and prolonged social and labor unrest. Labor unions demanded job protection and wage increases despite extremely high absenteeism and declining productivity throughout the country but especially in the automobile industry. Fiat's product line was aging and quality was poor.

One of Fiat's short-term plans is to expand its nontransportation businesses. Those businesses accounted for about one-fourth of Fiat's total revenues during the latter 1980s but hold great promise for growth during the 1990s.

A longer-term plan involves the development of strategic ventures with other organizations. Fiat had a robotics joint venture with General Motors; a factory and office automation joint venture with IBM; a joint venture with Ford's British truck unit; and a series of alliances in the automobile components area. These all worked well, and Fiat saw the opportunity to benefit from more such alliances. It began discussions with the state-controlled IRI group to swap Fiat's rail-car business for IRI's jet-engine business and is exploring a venture between its telecommunications operations and Spain's national telephone company.

The important time frame for Fiat, however, is 1992. In 1992 all customs barriers within the European Economic Community will be eliminated. Fiat's domination of the Italian market will not be protected; hence, competition will become fierce on its home territory. Of course, that also means that Fiat can move into France, Spain, Germany, and Britain more readily. Planning for that event dominated all European companies during the 1980s. Fiat is no exception.

Fiat has international operations not only in its automobile business but also in numerous other areas, including financial services, biotechnology, and robotics. Fiat makes cars, trucks, buses, tractors, harvesters, bulldozers, airplane and helicopter components, and artificial hearts. It is active in marine and civil engineering as well as in telecommunications, defense, and aviation. It sees the reduction in trade barriers as more of an opportunity to expand its markets than a threat of increased competition. Although Fiat is the largest private organization in Italy and one of the largest in Europe, it is planning for substantial growth by 1992. Fiat hopes to increase revenues by over 25 percent with corresponding improvements in its profit picture. Fiat will continue to be dominated by its automotive operations, although nonautomotive businesses are expected to account for about half of its future revenues.

New car models are clearly one part of Fiat's plan for increasing its revenues. Uno, a subcompact introduced in 1983, has sales volume in excess of 3 million units thus far. Tipo, a midsize model introduced in 1988, has been selling well in Italy and gaining some recognition in other European countries as well. At the upper end of the market, Fiat hopes that Lancia's Thema and Alfa's 164 will join with its Ferrari in competing with BMW, Volvo, and other luxury automobiles, especially in the U.S. market, in which Alfa has been a disaster but Ferrari has done reasonably well. Other new models are being developed to continually improve Fiat's image and ability to compete outside of Italy.

Competition in Europe will be one thing; competition with the Japanese will be another. As trade barriers go down within Europe, they may still block both American and Japanese manufacturers, or the barriers may be dropped for them as well. In any event, American and Japanese competitors are a potential threat, and Fiat will need to be prepared to meet them.

Questions

1. What goals can you identify for Fiat? Are there any apparent conflicts in multiple goals? Why or why not?
2. What kinds of plans can you identify at Fiat? What time frames for planning are involved? Do the different kinds of plans appear to be integrated with one another?
3. What are the pros and cons of the kinds of alliances that Fiat is developing? Are they likely to continue to work well for Fiat after 1992? Why or why not?
4. Is Fiat likely to achieve its 1992 goals? Why or why not? After you have answered this question, you may wish to go to the library and determine what Fiat's most recent performance has actually been.

REFERENCES: "Its Turnaround Was Brilliant—But Can Fiat Stay the Course?" *Business Week*, August 15, 1988, pp. 66–70; "Fiat Is Setting Ambitious Goals for 1992 and Beyond," *The Wall Street Journal*, June 17, 1988, p. 22; Tatiana Pouschine, "We Were Trapped," *Forbes*, March 21, 1988, pp. 37–38; "Giovanni Agnelli," *Forbes*, October 5, 1987, pp. 141–142.

OUTLINE

The Nature of Strategic Management
The Components of Strategy · The Levels of Strategy ·
Strategy Formulation and Implementation

Strategy Formulation
Strategic Goals · Environmental Analysis · Organizational
Analysis · Matching Organizations and Environments

Corporate-Level Strategy
Grand Strategy · The Business Portfolio

Business-Level Strategy
The Adaptation Model · Porter's Competitive Strategies ·
Product Life Cycles

Functional Strategies
Marketing Strategy · Financial Strategy · Production Strategy ·
Human Resource Strategy · Research and Development
Strategy

Strategy Implementation
Structure · Leadership · Information and Control Systems ·
Human Resources · Technology

CHAPTER 6

Strategy and Strategic Management

OBJECTIVES

After studying this chapter, you should be able to:

- Describe the nature of strategic management.
- Describe how strategy is formulated.
- Discuss the meaning of and major approaches to corporate-level strategy.
- Discuss the meaning of and major approaches to business-level strategy.
- Identify and discuss the major functional strategies.
- Describe the major ways strategy is implemented.

OPENING INCIDENT

Managers at Hershey Foods faced a dilemma. The company had battled Mars Inc. for years for the number 1 spot in the U.S. candy industry. Hershey was holding its own but could not gain any market share on its arch rival, and the company was vulnerable to a possible takeover: It had a lot of extra cash and undervalued stock.

In the past, Hershey had tried to diversify into such areas as hotels and restaurants. Its Friendly Ice Cream chain, however, was doing poorly and managers saw little opportunity for growth in the hotel business. So managers decided to continue to do what they did best—make confectionery products.

First Hershey bought Dietrich Corporation, makers of such products as Luden's cough drops and Fifth Avenue candy bars. Then it bought Nabisco's Canadian business. In its biggest move to date, Hershey announced in 1988 that it was buying Cadbury, which makes Peter Paul Mounds and Almond Joy, York Peppermint Patties, and numerous other products.

This series of moves accomplished several goals for Hershey. It firmly entrenched the company ahead of Mars in the U.S. market. It used up excess cash and brought about an increase in the price of Hershey stock. And it solidified Hershey's image as a marketing firm that is concentrating on doing what it does best.[1]

*M*anagers at Hershey faced a classic dilemma—what to do about "tomorrow." What they did was a classic solution. They assessed their strengths and weaknesses (surplus cash and candy-making skills), evaluated environmental opportunities and threats (competition and possible takeover), formulated a strategic response to those conditions (growth), and then implemented that response (acquisition of other companies). In short, they engaged in effective strategic management.

This chapter explores strategic management in depth. We examine the general nature of strategic management. We then discuss how strategy is formulated. Next we describe the three basic levels of strategic management—corporate, business, and functional strategy. Finally, we conclude with a discussion of how strategy is actually implemented.

THE NATURE OF STRATEGIC MANAGEMENT

In Chapter 5 we described a strategic plan as a general plan outlining decisions of resource allocation, priorities, and action steps necessary to reach strategic goals. Strategic management, however, is much more than this. It is a way of thinking about management—and a way of

■ **strategic management**   A comprehensive and on-going management process aimed at formulating and implementing effective strategies that promote a superior alignment between the organization and its environment and the achievement of strategic goals

approaching business opportunities and challenges. **Strategic management** is a comprehensive and ongoing management process aimed at formulating and implementing effective strategies that promote a superior alignment between the organization and its environment and the achievement of strategic goals.[2] To fully understand how strategic management is practiced, it is first necessary to understand the components of strategy, the different levels of strategy, and the distinction between strategy formulation and strategy implementation.

The Components of Strategy

■ **strategy**   A well-conceived strategy consists of four basic areas—scope, resource deployment, distinctive competence, and synergy

What exactly does a strategy address? What questions does it try to answer? In general, a well-conceived **strategy** deals with four basic areas of concern: scope, resource deployment, distinctive competence, and synergy.[3]

scope   Specifies the range of markets in which the organization will compete

Scope   The **scope** of a strategy specifies the range of markets in which the organization will compete. Hershey has essentially restricted its scope to the confectionery business, with a few related activities in other food-processing areas. In contrast, its biggest competitor, Mars, has adopted a broader scope by competing in the pet-food business, the electronics industry, and so forth. Some organizations, called conglomerates, compete in dozens or even hundreds of markets.

resource deployment   How the organization will distribute its resources across various areas

Resource Deployment   A strategy should include an outline of the organization's projected **resource deployment**—how it will distribute its resources across various areas. For example, Raytheon has used profits from its large defense businesses to support growth in its publishing (D. C. Heath) and appliance (Amana, Speed Queen, and Caloric) businesses. The company could have chosen to reinvest those profits in its defense businesses and let the other units stand alone. Instead, it chose a different deployment.[4]

distinctive competence   Something the organization does especially well

Distinctive Competence   A strategy should specify the distinctive competence the organization has relative to its competitors. A **distinctive competence** is something the organization does exceptionally well. The Limited, a large clothing chain, stresses the distinctive competence of speed. It tracks consumer preferences daily with point-of-sale computers, uses facsimile machines to transmit orders to suppliers in Hong Kong, charters 747s to fly products to the United States, and has products in stores forty-eight hours later. Other retailers take weeks or sometimes months to accomplish the same things. Thus, The Limited uses its distinctive competence to stay ahead of the competition.[5]

synergy   How the different areas of the business are expected to complement or enhance one another

Synergy   A strategy should specify the synergy expected to result from decisions about scope, resource deployment, and distinctive competence. In this sense, **synergy** refers to how different areas of the business complement or enhance other areas. Disney, for example, uses synergy

Disney is an excellent example of an organization that benefits from synergy. For example, its film, television, and theme park operations all complement one another. And the company is currently capitalizing on still another level of synergy in Europe. For a long time its animated films have been popular abroad, and both home video products and fashion clothing using a Disney motif have been very successful. So Disney is taking the next logical step—opening a theme park there. Shown here in its early design stages, Euro Disneyland is now scheduled to open on a site 20 miles east of Paris in 1992.

among all of its businesses. Its movies make money at the box office and then spur sales of videotapes; its network television program results in vacations to Disneyland and Disney World; the vacations lead to purchases of licensed souvenirs and greater interest in movies; and the Disney Channel cable network helps promote the whole empire.[6]

The Levels of Strategy

It is necessary to draw a distinction between three basic levels of strategy. Businesses today often establish corporate, business, and functional strategies.

■ **corporate strategy** The course charted for the total organization that specifies what areas the organization will compete in

Corporate Strategy **Corporate strategy** is the course charted for the total organization. It answers the question "In what markets will we compete?" Hence, corporate strategy is primarily concerned with the scope and resource deployment components of strategy. To illustrate corporate strategy, consider again the case of Mars. As detailed in the Integrative Case for Part 1, Mars has chosen to compete in four basic areas: candy, food, pet food, and electronics. Mars could have chosen to compete in a single business like Hershey, or in dozens of other businesses. Instead, its managers chose those four areas.[7]

■ **business strategy** Focuses on how the organization will compete in each of its chosen areas

Business Strategy **Business strategy** is focused less on scope and resource deployment than on competitive advantage and synergy. It attempts to answer the question "How should we compete in each of the markets we have chosen to enter?" Thus, Mars has a business strategy for its candy business, a business strategy for its pet-food business, and so forth.

■ **functional strategy** A
strategy developed for a single
functional area

Functional Strategy Organizations also establish **functional strategies** for each of the major areas they engage in. The most common functions are marketing, finance, production, human resources, and research and development. For example, Mars' candy business has had a marketing strategy of expanding sales of existing products rather than developing new ones. And it has a production strategy centered on high-quality state-of-the-art manufacturing.

Strategy Formulation and Implementation

strategy formulation The
set of processes involved in
creating or determining the
strategies of the organization

strategy implementation
The methods by which strategies are operationalized or executed within the organization

It is instructive to draw a distinction between strategy formulation and strategy implementation.[8] Simply stated, **strategy formulation** is the set of processes involved in creating or determining the strategies of the organization, and **strategy implementation** is the methods by which strategies are operationalized or executed within the organization. Hence, the primary distinction is along the lines of content versus process: The formulation stage determines *what* the strategy is, and the implementation stage focuses on *how* the strategy will be achieved.

Figure 6.1 illustrates the relationship between formulation and implementation across the three levels of strategy. At a general level, the formulation-implementation cycle starts at the corporate level, then

FIGURE 6.1

Strategy Formulation and
Implementation Across Three
Levels

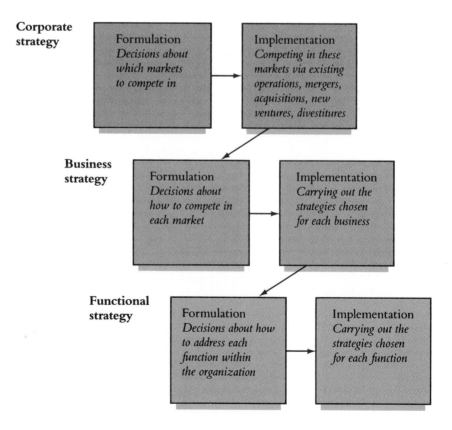

follows systematically across the business and functional levels. Of course, the process is considerably more complex and dynamic than this simple example, but the example does represent the general nature of the strategic-planning process. Most of our attention in this chapter is on formulating strategy. Chapter 7 addresses implementation issues more fully.

STRATEGY FORMULATION

Although every organization has its own unique approach to formulating strategy, most use a general framework consisting of four general steps: setting strategic goals, analyzing the environment, analyzing the organization, and attempting to match the organization with the environment.

Strategic Goals

The starting point in formulating strategy is to establish strategic goals. The processes and issues associated with strategic goal setting were thoroughly explored in Chapter 5. In particular, recall that strategic goals are set by top management, focus on broad, general issues, and generally have a long-range time horizon.

Environmental Analysis

Next, the organization conducts an environmental analysis. This analysis involves looking carefully at the environment to determine the primary opportunities and threats confronting the organization.[9] As detailed in the opening incident, Hershey's biggest threats were Mars Inc. and being taken over by another company.

There are many ways in which organizations can gather the information they need for this analysis. One source is published articles in outlets like *Business Week*, *The Wall Street Journal*, and *Fortune*. Personal contacts with managers in other firms are also a valuable source of information. Government reports, bankers, lawyers, suppliers, customers, consultants, and professional associations can also be useful. Finally, managers can learn a great deal about a competitor by reading its annual report.

In some cases, organizations can learn valuable information directly or indirectly from their competitors. Marriott, in preparation for launching Fairfield Inn, its economy motel chain, sent managers all around the country to stay in competing motels. They asked questions, recorded information about the kinds of soap provided, the number of towels in the rooms, general cleanliness, and so forth, and then used this information in setting up their new business, which has been a big success. Hewlett-Packard recently wanted to rent hotel conference

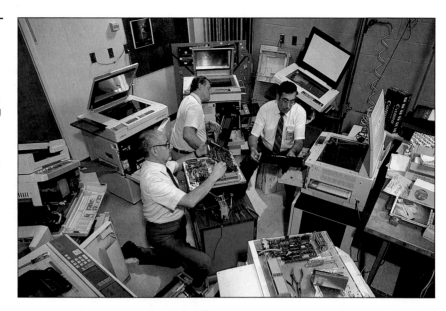

One especially useful form of environmental analysis is benchmarking. Benchmarking involves buying a competitor's product and then taking it apart piece by piece to see exactly how it works. The ultimate aim of benchmarking is to identify how to improve on the quality and/or price of each component. After it lost a large share of its market for office copiers to Canon, Xerox engineers like the ones shown here successfully benchmarked competitive machines and stopped the company's sales declines.

rooms around the country to unveil a new product. Learning that a rival had already reserved the rooms for the same day, managers at Hewlett-Packard deduced that the rival was planning its own new-product announcement, so they moved their schedule up and beat the rival to the punch.[10]

Organizational Analysis

The organizational analysis phase of strategy formulation involves a detailed diagnosis of the strengths and weaknesses of the organization.[11] The analysis should be as detailed and thorough as possible. It generally includes, but is not limited to, the following areas:

1. The organization's human resources (quality and quantity of appropriate managerial personnel, etc.)
2. The organization's physical resources (plant and equipment, office space, etc.)
3. The organization's financial resources (cash, assets, lines of credit, debt, etc.)
4. The organization's information resources (quality and quantity of available information about competition, etc.)
5. Market position (market share, strength of product line, etc.)
6. Research and development efforts (quality and quantity of breakthroughs expected from R&D efforts, etc.)

Some of this information is readily available from normal information systems within the organization; other information must be obtained specifically for the strategy formulation process. In general, however, the efforts needed to gather the necessary data are a good investment.

Matching Organizations and Environments

Once the strategic goals have been established and environmental and organizational analyses completed, the final step is to match the strengths and weaknesses of the organization with the corresponding opportunities and threats in the environment.[12] In general, the purpose of this exercise is to align the organization with its environment in such a way as to take advantage of opportunities in the environment and avoid threats through the recognition of internal strengths and weaknesses. Marriott used this approach recently to formulate a new strategy.[13] A simplified version of this analysis is shown in Figure 6.2. At the time, in addition to its successful hotel and food services businesses, Marriott owned cruise ship, travel agency, and theme park businesses. Because these three businesses were performing poorly, however, they represented a weakness. So, too, did a poor cash position. And in the environment, there was low growth in the market for upscale lodging of the type currently offered by Marriott. Managers also saw an interesting opportunity, though—high growth in the market for low-cost lodging. And they realized that their distinctive competence was in hotels and food services, not in the other businesses currently being operated. So Marriott sold its low-performing businesses and used the cash to launch Fairfield Inns.

The framework suggests several specific relationships of interest. First, organizational strengths and weaknesses and environmental opportunities and threats are usually interrelated. For example, a firm might have a surplus of cash (a strength) because it has not spent much on R&D (a weakness). Similarly, a growing market for a firm's products (an opportunity) has the potential to attract new entrants (a threat). Second, organizational strengths should generally be targeted toward environmental opportunities. For example, Kodak's dominance in the

FIGURE 6.2

Strategy Formulation at Marriott

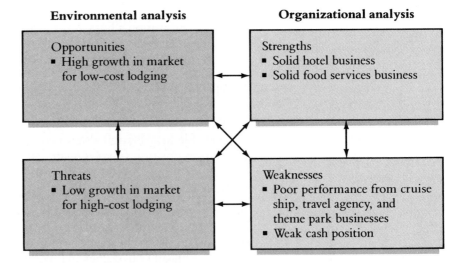

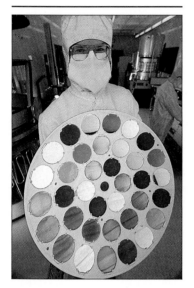

A growth strategy is often achieved through joint ventures. These semiconductor devices are the result of a joint venture between IBM and Rockwell International.

photography industry (a strength) made entry into the growing market for videotape products (an opportunity) a logical decision.

Third, the organization should recognize that its weaknesses are particularly vulnerable to environmental threats. For example, if the organization is dependent on a single supplier (organizational weakness), then the power of that supplier relative to the organization is extremely strong (environmental threat). Finally, to the extent possible, the firm might consider using its strengths to offset environmental threats. For example, Du Pont was dependent on petroleum companies for oil needed in its chemical business. However, during the energy crisis, supplies ran short and prices increased dramatically (environmental threat). So Du Pont used surplus cash (organizational strength) to buy Conoco (environmental opportunity) and assure itself of a dependable source of petroleum. "The Global View" illustrates how one successful Japanese firm, Matsushita, has done an excellent job of environmental alignment.

CORPORATE-LEVEL STRATEGY

There are three basic levels at which strategy formulation activities occur: the corporate level, the business level, and the functional level. This section focuses on the two dominant approaches to corporate strategy—grand strategy and the business portfolio.

Grand Strategy

grand strategy An overall framework for action developed at the corporate level

Grand strategy is an overall framework for action developed at the corporate level. It is most commonly used when a corporation competes in a single market or in a few highly related markets.[14] There are three basic grand strategies that corporations choose to pursue: growth, stability, and retrenchment.

growth strategy Calls for overall corporate growth on one or more dimensions

Just as the term implies, a **growth strategy** calls for overall corporate growth—in sales, market share, total assets, and other dimensions. Growth can be generated internally by introducing new products, opening new outlets, and increasing market share. It can be induced externally through acquisitions of other businesses, mergers, and joint ventures. Growth is most often appropriate when the corporation has ample resources to support it and when there is reasonable likelihood that growth is possible. For example, Western Sizzlin' is the third-largest steak-house chain in the United States with nearly 600 restaurants. The company recently announced a goal of doubling its number of restaurants within five years. This growth is to be accomplished primarily by expanding into parts of the country not currently served.[15]

retrenchment strategy Involves shrinking current operations, cutting back in a variety of areas, or eliminating unprofitable operations altogether

A **retrenchment strategy** (also called a turnaround strategy) calls for shrinking current operations, cutting back in a variety of areas, or eliminating unprofitable operations altogether. Such downsizing has been quite popular in recent years. It is most likely to be employed when a firm is unprofitable, has excessive operating costs, has excess capacity, or has diversified into markets it should never have entered.[16] It may also be necessary after a bitter price war with a competitor or when the firm takes extreme measures to protect itself. For example, Brunswick had to sell its most profitable unit to American Home Products in order to prevent a complete takeover by Whittaker (Whittaker planned to buy the entire corporation just to get the one unit Brunswick sold). As a result, the company remained independent but was weakened financially. In response, it worked hard to expand its remaining businesses, cut costs, and increase productivity. Only recently has it begun to regain its corporate health.[17]

stability strategy Calls for maintaining the status quo

A **stability strategy** calls for maintaining the status quo. A company adopting such a strategy plans to stay in the businesses it's currently in, manage them as they've been managed, and try to protect itself from environmental threats. This approach is most often adopted by companies that lack the resources to grow or are in markets where little growth is feasible or whose managers simply aren't interested in growth. Stability is also a useful strategy to adopt after a period of rapid growth or a period of retrenchment. Firestone, for example, recently went through a period of retrenchment during which it cut its work force from 107,000 to 55,000, closed eight plants, and sold several businesses unrelated to its tire business. Now the company has entered a period of stability. Management is working to settle into a new way of doing business and recover from the trauma induced by the cutbacks.[18]

The Business Portfolio

An overall grand strategy is useful when the corporation has only a few related businesses. When it has many different businesses, and especially when those businesses are unrelated, a different approach is needed. A common tool used to manage multiple businesses is the business portfolio. The business portfolio involves viewing the corporation as a collection of businesses, each of which can have its own competitive business strategy.[19]

strategic business unit (SBU) A separate division within the company that has its own mission, its own competitors, and its own unique strategy

Strategic Business Units   The starting point in using the portfolio approach is to identify within the corporation **strategic business units**, or **SBUs**. The concept of strategic business units (SBUs) was developed by managers at General Electric who realized that they needed a framework for evaluating their very large and diverse organization. They decided to conceptualize the firm as a portfolio of businesses. One business was defined as the set of all food preparation appliance producers (toaster ovens, ranges, and so on). A total of forty-three SBUs were identified within the company. In short order, several other firms, including Union Carbide and General Foods, also began to view themselves as a set of SBUs. Usually, each SBU is a separate division within the company. It has its own mission, its own competitors, and its own

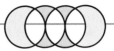

THE GLOBAL VIEW

MATSUSHITA ELECTRIC INDUSTRIAL COMPANY

In 1918, Konosuke Matsushita started an electric-plug factory in Osaka, Japan. In 1922, he began to diversify the company by adding bicycle lights. In the same year, he began selling directly to the retail network. In 1930, he added radios and began to build the conglomerate of electrical and electronic companies that make up the Matsushita group today.

At first, many of the group companies did not work very well together because they were in different markets, but in 1956 Matsushita introduced a five-year business plan to begin to achieve better interconnectedness. Every employee was encouraged to feel responsible for each task and for the success of the plan. Good labor relations became the foundation upon which the Matsushita empire was built; and now the numerous companies mesh well.

Since the initiation of that first five-year plan, Matsushita has always operated with a long-term strategic plan. That plan involves letting others develop basic technology and then advancing its product design and using its manufacturing and distribution efficiencies to obtain a large share of the already developed market. This strategy enables management to take a long-term view of product markets so that Matsushita enters only those that seem likely to have a long life.

The VCR market provides an example of this strat-

egy. Ampex invented the technology in 1956. Sony introduced the Betamax format to the consumer market in 1975. JVC entered the market in 1976, and Matsushita entered with its own brand in 1977. By 1986, VCRs accounted for nearly one-fourth of Matsushita's revenues and Matsushita and JVC controlled about 40 percent of Japan's VCR market.

Looking ahead, Akio Tanii, Matsushita's president, believes the consumer markets are largely saturated. For that reason, Matsushita is expanding its industrial electronics operations, which accounted for just over 10 percent of revenues during 1987. Four areas have been targeted: semiconductors, factory automation, office automation, and audiovisual products. The distribution network that has been fundamental to Matsushita's past success, however, is not likely to be much help in this expansion because it is a consumer and not an industrial network. Hence, this expansion will not be so easy as others have been, although the possibility of converting some industrial products into consumer products is not being overlooked.

References: Andrew Tanzer, "We Do Not Take a Short-Term View," *Forbes*, July 13, 1987, pp. 372–374; "A Half-baked Idea," *Fortune*, October 26, 1987, p. 14; "An Optical Memory That Can Be Wiped Clean," *Business Week*, June 15, 1987, pp. 56–58; "Matsushita Electric Industrial Co.," *The Wall Street Journal*, June 29, 1988, pp. 18–19; "Matsushita Plans Workstation Entry," *Electronic News*, September 5, 1988, pp. 12–13.

unique strategy apart from that of other SBUs in the organization.[20] "Management in Practice" identifies the dominant SBUs within Sante Fe. After a corporation's SBUs have been appropriately defined, the next step is to classify them. The most frequently used method of categorization is the BCG matrix.

BCG matrix Classifies SBUs into four categories defined by market growth rate and market share

The BCG Matrix   The **BCG matrix** was the framework originally developed for General Electric by the Boston Consulting Group.[21] Figure 6.3 illustrates the BCG matrix. Each SBU is evaluated in terms of the growth rate of its market (high or low) and its relative share (high or low) of that market.

stars Large share of high-growth market

Stars are SBUs that have a relatively large share of a high-growth market. Typically, stars require a large amount of short-run cash to support their rapid growth, and managers try to invest in the future by

FIGURE 6.3

The BCG Matrix

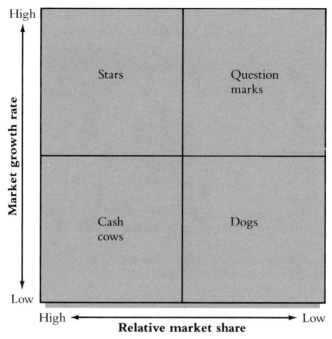

SOURCE: Adapted from: The Product Portfolio Matrix, © 1970,
The Boston Consulting Group, Inc.

cash cows Large share of
low-growth market

question marks Low share
of high-growth market

dogs Low share of low-
growth market

maximizing long-term potential. As markets mature, many stars become cash cows for the organization. A **cash cow** is an SBU that has
a large share of a low-growth market. It requires little money for
growth and expansion, thereby generating surplus revenue that the
company can use in other areas (to promote stars, for example). **Question marks** are SBUs with a relatively low share of a high-growth
market. Managers must decide whether to commit the financial resources necessary to transform the SBU into a star or else get rid of it.
Finally, a **dog** is an SBU that has a small share of a market with little
growth. Dogs are often unable to support themselves and are frequently
a cash drain on other SBUs within the organization.

In general, most organizations that use the BCG matrix like to have
cash cows in their portfolio to generate cash and stars that can become
cash cows in the future. They are willing to keep a few question marks
because of their potential, but they often sell or liquidate dogs.[22] Greyhound Corporation uses the BCG matrix in managing its businesses.
Long considered just a bus company, Greyhound now has six basic
SBUs: consumer products; financial services; transportation services;
bus manufacturing; meat and poultry products; and airport, travel, and
food services. The transportation services and bus-manufacturing businesses are cash cows; the financial services business is a clear star; and
the other three are question marks. Greyhound recently disposed of its
bus line, considered a dog (no pun intended!).[23]

MANAGEMENT IN PRACTICE

SANTA FE'S PORTFOLIO STRATEGY

Santa Fe Southern Pacific Corporation has adopted a portfolio approach to its corporate strategy. At present, Santa Fe has three large strategic business units in its portfolio. The largest SBU, and the one for which the company is best known, is its railroad business. The railroad business operates the Santa Fe line, the Southern Pacific line, and several other smaller rail companies.

A second important SBU at Santa Fe is the company's mining division. This SBU owns large oil and gas reserves, as well as several coal mining operations. Geologists also recently struck gold in one of the company's Nevada mines. The mining division also owns a significant stake in a large pipeline company.

Finally, the third SBU is Santa Fe's real estate division. At one point, the company thought about selling the real estate to outside interests. However, a member of the board of directors persuaded top management to hold on to the land and start developing it instead. All told, the firm controls almost 3 million acres of land, including a large parcel in downtown San Francisco.

Taken together, the three businesses put Santa Fe in a solid financial position. The rail business is in a slow decline as business is lost to trucking companies. However, it still generates large profits and should continue to do so for many years. The mining business is also quite profitable, although its future revenues are less predictable due to oil price fluctuations and similar uncertainties. Meanwhile, the profits generated by these two businesses are providing the capital needed to develop the land in the real estate business.

Not surprisingly, Santa Fe's success has not escaped the notice of others. There has been recent speculation, for example, that Sante Fe might be more valuable if broken up into three different companies. That is, a takeover artist might reap huge profits by buying the company and then reselling it as three distinct entities. Management at Santa Fe has also recognized this possibility and is taking steps to put the company in a position of strength to bargain with such suitors.

REFERENCES: "Almost Everybody Wants to Break Up Santa Fe," *Business Week*, March 6, 1989, p. 67; "Is Santa Fe Home Free? Henley Sells its Stake—Sort of," *Business Week*, August 8, 1988, p. 25; "Santa Fe Keeps Throwing the Raiders Off Track," *Business Week*, February 15, 1988, pp. 20–21; "You Can Hear That Whistle. . . ." *Financial World*, November 28, 1988, pp. 24–25.

GE business screen   A sophisticated matrix that classifies SBUs in terms of industry attractiveness and business strength

The GE Business Screen   The BCG matrix is useful, but it is quite simplistic. Thus, General Electric recently pioneered a more sophisticated form of matrix called the **business screen**.[24] One axis of the business screen matrix is industry attractiveness, based on things like growth rate, profit margins, seasonality, and technology. The other is business strength, measured by market share, competitive strengths and weaknesses, quality of management, and similar factors. Industry attractiveness and business strengths are each categorized as high, medium, or low. Thus, the matrix has nine cells, rather than four. Businesses that are high on both dimensions or high on one and medium on the other are top performers. Businesses that are low on both dimensions or low on one and medium on the other are poor performers and are likely candidates for divestment or liquidation. Businesses that are medium on both dimensions or high on one and low on the other are marginal. They may be kept or eliminated but should always be carefully monitored. The business screen is fairly new and has not been studied very much. It does seem, however, to be a potentially useful framework for managing corporate-level strategy.

BUSINESS-LEVEL STRATEGY

Managers and researchers have worked extensively to develop effective approaches to business-level strategy.[25] A business-level strategy is concerned with how a single business unit within a corporation should compete. If a business competes in only one market and is essentially a self-contained SBU, these approaches might also be useful. The three most common approaches to business-level strategy are the adaptation model, Porter's competitive strategies, and the product life cycle.

The Adaptation Model

adaptation model Managers should attempt to match business strategy with environmental conditions

The **adaptation model** of business strategy argues that managers of a business should attempt to match the business's strategy with basic conditions in its environment.[26] In particular, this model suggests that different levels of environmental complexity and change call for different forms of strategy. Three suggested forms of strategy, matched with different environmental conditions, are shown in Figure 6.4. Also shown is a fourth approach, the reactor, which is not recommended.

FIGURE 6.4

The Adaptation Model

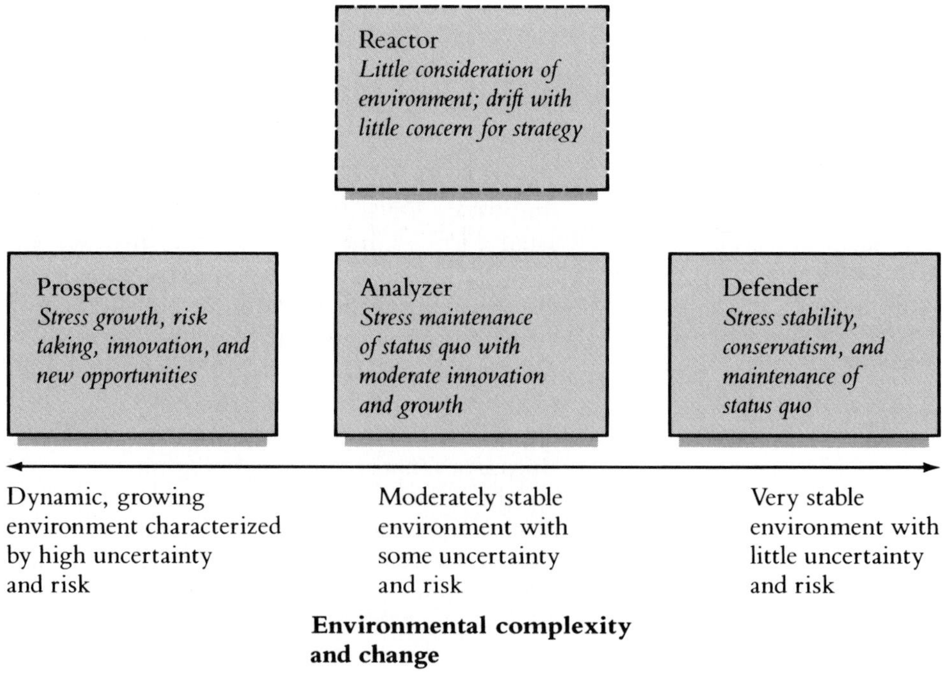

Reactor
Little consideration of environment; drift with little concern for strategy

Prospector	Analyzer	Defender
Stress growth, risk taking, innovation, and new opportunities	*Stress maintenance of status quo with moderate innovation and growth*	*Stress stability, conservatism, and maintenance of status quo*

| Dynamic, growing environment characterized by high uncertainty and risk | Moderately stable environment with some uncertainty and risk | Very stable environment with little uncertainty and risk |

Environmental complexity and change

defender strategy Suggested when the business operates in an environment with stability and little uncertainty or risk

Defenders   A **defender strategy** is called for when the business operates in an environment characterized by stability and little uncertainty or risk. The defender attempts to carve out for itself a relatively narrow niche in the market and to direct a limited set of products or services at that niche. Although defenders may employ competitive pricing or high-quality production standards to guard their positions, they are likely to ignore trends and developments outside their chosen domains. Defenders also tend to concentrate on the most efficient production and distribution techniques, with little concern for long-term effectiveness. They also tend to maintain a rigid, bureaucratic form of organization to facilitate control and efficiency. McDonald's and Firestone might be classified as defenders. Each has chosen a certain position in the environment and has as a major goal maintenance of that position.

prospector strategy Advocated when the environment is dynamic, growing, and characterized by uncertainty and risk

Prospectors   The **prospector strategy** is almost the exact opposite of the defender. The prospector approach usually works best when the environment is dynamic, growing, and characterized by uncertainty and risk. Prospectors develop a knack for discovering and capitalizing on new-product and new-market opportunities. They often have an exceptional ability to locate and then systematically develop such opportunities. Because prospectors focus on new products and markets, they try to avoid a long-term commitment to any single type of technology, instead using several technologies, each with little routine and mechanization. This allows the organization to shift from one product or market to another without having to scrap existing technology and invest in new plants and equipment. Prospectors usually adopt flexible forms of organization, relying on decentralization and rewarding creativity, innovation, and risk taking. Reebok International is a good example of a prospector. The fast-growing shoe company continues to look for new opportunities for growth and recently entered both the walking-shoe and the apparel businesses.[27]

analyzer strategy Recommended when the environment is moderately stable but there's some degree of uncertainty and risk

Analyzer   The **analyzer strategy** is a midrange approach appropriate when the environment is moderately stable but still offers some degree of uncertainty and risk. It attempts to identify and take advantage of new products and markets while maintaining a nucleus of traditional products and customers. The analyzer works to achieve a balance between the conflicting demands for flexibility and stability in its technology. Analyzers are usually structured in such a way as to support the forces for stability associated with the nucleus of existing products and technologies while still accommodating the forces for dynamism stimulated by the desire for new products and new technologies. The organization must have some units and groups maintaining the traditional products and other units exploring and developing new products and markets. A prime example of an analyzer is Procter & Gamble. The firm has a core of traditional products, such as Crest toothpaste and Head and Shoulders shampoo, but continues to search for new products to add to its list.

reactors strategy Strategic failures that respond to their environments in inappropriate ways

Reactors A strategy occasionally adopted by some firms is the **reactor strategy.** Essentially, reactors are strategic failures. They respond to their environment in inappropriate ways, which result in poor performance. Poor performance causes reactors to become less aggressive in the future. Several factors might cause organizations to become reactors. First, top management may not have clearly articulated the organization's strategy. Second, management may not have shaped the organization's structure to fit its chosen strategy. Or management may try to maintain the organization's strategy-structure relationship despite major changes in environmental conditions. An excellent illustration of an organization employing the reactor mode of operation was W. T. Grant, one of the largest retailers in the United States before its bankruptcy in 1976. In response to the success of K mart in the discounting area, Grant adopted the ill-conceived strategy of expanding rapidly without the necessary resources. Further, the company had inadequate training programs for its managers and too few controls over day-to-day operations. The company simply tried to do too many things too fast, and then it refused to step back and retrench.[28]

Porter's Competitive Strategies

Another approach to business-level strategy, developed by Michael Porter, describes three so-called generic strategies.[29] The generic label is used because a strategy may be appropriate to a wide variety of organizations across diverse industries. Porter suggests that businesses should thoroughly analyze their industry and then define a competitive niche by adopting one of the three generic strategies. The goal is to develop a competitive advantage that can best serve the business.[30]

differentiation strategy Involves developing an image of the business's products or services that customers perceive as being different from others

Differentiation The **differentiation strategy** involves developing an image of the business's product or service such that customers perceive it as being different. The product or service might be differentiated by quality, design, service, or other attributes. The rationale behind differentiation is that the organization can charge higher prices (and therefore make more profit per unit) for a unique product. Examples of businesses that have successfully used a differentiation strategy include Rolex and Honda (on the basis of high quality) and Ralph Lauren (on the basis of image).

cost leadership strategy An attempt to maximize sales by minimizing costs (and hence price) per unit

Cost Leadership Businesses that adopt the **cost leadership strategy** attempt to maximize sales by minimizing cost (and hence price) per unit. The business tries to increase its total sales volume by charging low prices, or exercising cost leadership. Low costs may be achieved through efficiencies in production, product design, distribution channels, and similar means. Volume retailers like K mart make a low profit per unit but compensate by selling more units. Examples of other businesses that have successfully used this approach include Timex, Bic, Motel 6, and Emerson Electronics.

Katha Diddèl saw the perfect market opportunity. Aided by Chinese artisans, she formed Twin Panda, Inc. in 1980, a manufacturer of fine quality embroidery, needlepoint, and linen goods. As her success grew, however, competitors began to undermine her business with lower quality copies of her work. So Ms. Diddèl decided to fight back with a differentiation strategy. To distinguish her product from competitors, she increased the quality of her products, concentrated on top-of-the-line products, and added a greater variety of designs. And so far, her new strategy has worked—her market share and profits have continued to climb.

focus strategy   Involves targeting products or services at certain geographic markets, customer groups, and so on

product life cycle   A useful framework managers can use to better understand how demand for a product changes over time

Focus   In the **focus strategy** products or services are targeted at certain geographic locations, certain customer groups, and so on. Campbell's has recently started focusing on specific consumer groups like students. Another very successful company adopting this strategy has been Fiesta Mart, a Houston-based grocery chain. Its managers noted that the Houston population has large segments of immigrants, especially Hispanics. So the stores sell Mexican soft drinks, corn husks for wrapping tamales, and thousands of other products in demand by the various nationalities represented in the city.[31]

Of course, a business can adopt more than one generic strategy. For example, Fort Howard Paper Company simultaneously stresses cost leadership by using recycled pulp products while also focusing on commercial customers like hotels and restaurants for sales of its tissue products. The key message underlying Porter's framework is that a business needs some form of competitive advantage. It might be one of the three Porter describes, some combination of the three, or perhaps something else altogether. Without some advantage, though, a business is likely to take on characteristics of a reactor from the adaptation model and drift toward eventual failure.

Product Life Cycles

A final business-level strategy is the product life cycle. The **product life cycle** itself is not a true strategy, however. It is a useful framework for managers to use as they plot strategy over time. The basic idea underlying the product life cycle notion is illustrated in Figure 6.5.

When a new product is first introduced, some period of time must pass before it becomes accepted. It may then go through a period of rapid growth. Eventually, however, demand slows and the market for the product matures. Finally, the product may enter into a decline stage. Consider the pocket calculator. After its initial introduction, prices started to drop and demand increased dramatically. Now, the market for pocket calculators is a mature one, and decline may eventually set in. The calculator replaced the slide rule, forcing it into decline, and other innovations may someday do the same to the calculator.

The duration of the life cycle varies dramatically for different kinds of products. Fad items like Pet Rocks may go through the entire cycle in a matter of months or even weeks. Products like automobiles have been around for decades and are still in the maturity stage.

Note also that the stages can be viewed in a context similar to that of the other approaches we've discussed. During the introduction stage, a product may be viewed as a question mark. If growth sets in, it becomes a star. When maturity is reached, it serves as a cash cow. When decline starts, it may become a dog. Similarly, different adaptation or competitive strategies may be appropriate at different stages of the cycle. During the introduction stage, the business may want to differentiate itself from other products. And it may adopt an analyzer stance

FIGURE 6.5

The Product Life Cycle

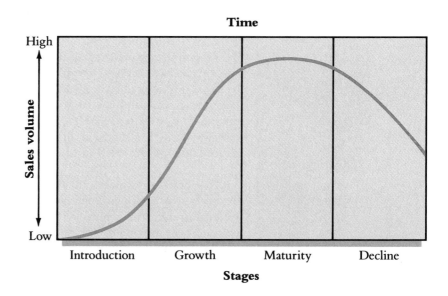

FUNCTIONAL STRATEGIES

to avoid becoming too dependent on an unknown new product. As growth takes off, the business may choose a prospector approach as it seeks to find new opportunities for the product while simultaneously continuing to stress differentiation. When the product enters the maturity stage, the business may deem it appropriate to shift to a defender position to hold on to its market share. Cost leadership or focus might be useful as a means to increase profits and sales even more. Finally, as decline sets in, the business might revert back to an analyzer position to cautiously search for new opportunities, or it might go through a period of retrenchment.

FUNCTIONAL STRATEGIES

functional strategies Commonly developed for marketing, financial, production, human resource, and research and development

The third basic level of strategic planning involves the development of functional strategies. These **functional strategies** focus on how the organization will approach its basic functional activities. Many organizations develop marketing, financial, production, research and development, and human resource strategies. Issues that these strategies typically address are summarized in Table 6.1, Functional Strategies and Their Major Concerns.

marketing strategy Addresses issues such as promotion techniques to be used, pricing, product mix, and overall image

Marketing Strategy

For many organizations, the **marketing strategy** is the most important functional strategy. Some companies (like McDonald's and Coca-Cola)

TABLE 6.1

Functional Strategies And
Their Major Concerns

Functional Area	Major Concerns
Marketing	Product mix
	Market position
	Distribution channels
	Sales promotions
	Pricing issues
	Public policy
Finance	Debt policies
	Dividend policies
	Assets management
	Capitalization structure
Production	Productivity improvement
	Production planning
	Plant location
	Government regulation
Research and development	Product development
	Technological forecasting
	Patents and licenses
Human resource	Personnel policies
	Labor relations
	Executive development
	Government regulation

promote their products heavily. Their goal is to establish customer loyalty and make sure customers always remember their products. Toys 'R' Us has achieved phenomenal success by promoting itself as a warehouse of playthings where you can find any toy a child wants for a reasonable price. And Kellogg has increased its sales in a stable cereal market by promoting the health benefits of some of its cereals. Companies need a marketing strategy, whether they want one or not. Managers at Coors, for example, would prefer to not advertise—they think they make the best beer in the market and people should just buy it for that reason. However, heavy marketing has been necessary to grow into a national brewing company.[32]

The marketing strategy deals with a number of major issues confronting the organization. One of these is the product mix. For General Motors' Chevrolet Division, the product mix includes the various lines, such as Camero, Corsica, and Berreta, and different versions of each model. Other major issues in marketing strategy include the desired market position (K mart and Sears compete for first place in retailing), distribution channels (a major reason for the initial success of Timex was its decision to sell watches in drugstores), sales promotion (such as advertising budget and the size of the sales force), pricing policies (such as an initially high price to skim off the "cream," followed by planned price cuts), and public policy (dealing with legal, cultural, and regulatory constraints).

Financial Strategy

financial strategy Must specify the capital structure of the organization, debt policy, assets management procedures, and dividend policy

Developing the right **financial strategy** is essential to an organization.[33] An important part of this strategy is deciding on the most appropriate capital structure: What combination of common stock, preferred stock, and long-term debt (such as bonds) will provide the firm with the capital it needs at the lowest possible costs? Another element in financial strategy is debt policy: How much borrowing will be allowed and in what forms? Assets management focuses on the handling of current and long-term assets: How should the firm invest a cash surplus to optimize both return and availability? Dividend policy determines what proportion of earnings is distributed to stockholders and what proportion is retained for growth and development. Disney has adopted a financial strategy of low debt. Even though Epcot Center in Florida cost nearly $1 billion, it was financed almost entirely by operating funds. And the new European Disneyland outside Paris is being paid for the same way. In contrast, Texas Air has borrowed heavily to buy the various airlines it owns and is one of the most heavily leveraged companies in America today.

Production Strategy

production strategy Concerned with issues of quality, productivity, and technology

In some ways, an organization's **production strategy** stems from its marketing strategy.[34] If the marketing strategy calls for promoting high-quality, high-priced products, production should naturally focus on quality, with cost only a secondary consideration. Several major issues still remain, however. For example, methods for improving productivity need to be developed. Production planning (when to produce, how much to produce, and how to produce) is especially important for manufacturers. Finally, production strategy must take into account the regulations of government bodies such as the Environmental Protection Agency (EPA) and the Occupational Safety and Health Administration (OSHA).

Areas of great significance for the production strategies of many companies are automation, robotics, and flexible manufacturing systems. Some companies (such as General Electric, Nissan, and Toyota) are investing large sums of money in automated technology; other manufacturers (such as Du Pont and Exxon) are proceeding more slowly. Nevertheless, continuing breakthroughs in production technologies will keep these issues of major concern for managers.

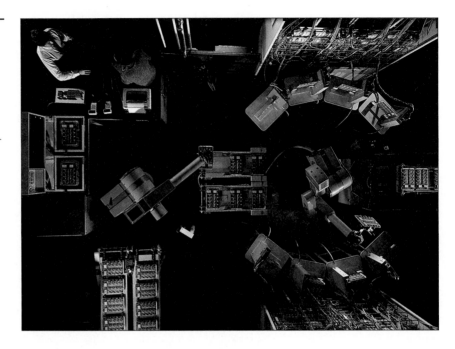

GTE Communication Systems is using this computer-integrated manufacturing (CIM) system to expedite the manufacturing process. This robotics operation computer-tests printed circuit boards. The adoption of a computer-integrated manufacturing system is a part of GTE's production strategy.

Human Resource Strategy

Many organizations find it useful to develop a human resource strategy.[35] Human resource policies are required on such matters as compensation, selection, and performance appraisal. Another aspect of human resource strategy is labor relations, especially negotiations with organized labor. Government regulations, such as the Civil Rights Act of 1964, also need to be taken into account. And executive development usually warrants strategic attention. For example, if an organization anticipates opening eight new plants in six years, it must start now to locate and develop potential managers for those plants. We mentioned in Chapter 1 that some companies (such as Procter & Gamble, General Foods, and General Mills) have developed training programs that are so good they are thought of by some recruiters as second M.B.A.s. Strong emphasis on management development, then, is also an element of some firms' human resource strategy.

Research and Development Strategy

Most large organizations, and many smaller ones as well, find it important to have a research and development strategy.[36] A primary area of concern here is making decisions about product development. Should the firm concentrate on new products or on the modification of existing products? What use should be made of technological forecasting—predictions of technical trends, new discoveries and breakthroughs, and so on? R&D strategies might also include a policy on patents and licenses. If a firm develops a new product or procedure and patents it, other firms cannot use it. However, it may be profitable to license the use of the patent—that is, to sacrifice some degree of competitive advantage in return for fees gained by allowing other firms to use the product or procedure. Merck & Company is one of the United States' most-admired companies. One reason for its success has been a long history of new-product breakthroughs and technological innovation. This innovation is brought about by a strong and consistent commitment to research and development.[37]

STRATEGY IMPLEMENTATION

■ **strategy implementation**
Strategies are implemented through organization structure, leadership, information and control systems, human resources, and technology

After strategy is formulated, it must be implemented. Although it is not possible to draw a precise line of demarcation between formulation and implementation, they are nevertheless conceptually distinct parts of strategic management.[38] Figure 6.6 provides a general framework of what is involved in implementing strategy.

Structure

Organization structure is one key element in strategy implementation.[39] Structure both affects and is affected by strategy. For example, in a highly decentralized firm, lower-level managers will have a much greater impact on strategic management than they would have in a centralized firm. The adoption of certain kinds of strategies will, in turn, dictate appropriate levels of future decentralization. The Franklin Mint recently developed a new strategy aimed at increasing its sales and profits. As part of the implementation process, the organization cut the number of levels of management from six to four and doubled the number of people reporting directly to the CEO.[40] These and related issues are explored again in Chapter 9.

Leadership

Effective leadership is also necessary to successfully implement strategy.[41] The leader must promote communication and motivation and help establish the culture necessary to get things done. When John Sculley joined Apple Computer, he was mistrusted because he knew little about computers. He learned the business from the bottom up, however, and became a personal computer expert. When the board of directors had to choose between Sculley and founder Steven Jobs, they supported Sculley, and he has had little trouble selling his strategic ideas to the company ever since. (Leadership is discussed more fully in Chapter 13.)

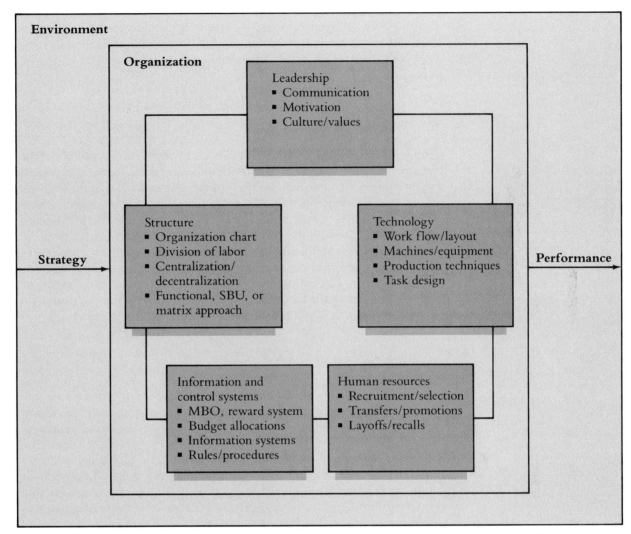

FIGURE 6.6

Strategy Implementation

Information and Control Systems

Successful strategy implementation also depends on effective information and control systems.[42] Managers formulating strategy need access to information. Information systems are also necessary to communicate strategic goals and decisions to others in the organization. And control is important in monitoring ongoing efforts to reach those goals. Suppose that as part of a company's strategic plans the decision is made to open a new manufacturing facility. A key ingredient in implementing the decision is establishing a budget for constructing and operating the facility. And adherence to the budget will provide feedback to management about how well the strategy is being implemented. Information and control systems issues are explored in several chapters, including 15, 16, and 19.

Human Resources

Appropriate human resources are needed to implement strategies. The organization needs to have the right kinds of people trained in the right ways in order to carry out strategic plans. For example, S. C. Johnson Wax recently adopted a new strategic plan calling for increased market share for its insect control products. For several years, Beth Pritchard had been groomed by the company to take over the division. After she was given her assignment, she changed product formulas, had packaging redesigned, and developed regional products for different regions of the country. Her employees responded with enthusiasm and dedication. Ms. Pritchard maintains, "My philosophy is that you can't do anything yourself. Your people have to do it."[43]

Technology

An organization must ensure that it has the proper technology to implement its strategies effectively. Proper technology includes plant and equipment and work-flow design. A key strategic issue facing managers today is speed—getting new products from the design stage to the customer as soon as possible. Thus, Deere and Company recently generated a new product in two years, whereas it had taken five to seven years before. As rapidly as technology is changing today, its role in strategy implementation is likely to become even more important in the future.

SUMMARY OF KEY POINTS

Strategic management is a comprehensive and ongoing management process aimed at formulating and implementing effective strategies that promote a superior alignment between the organization and its environment and the achievement of strategic goals. Its components include scope, resource deployment, distinctive competence, and synergy. Strategy is implemented at the corporate, business, and functional levels. Strategies must first be formulated and then implemented.

Strategy formulation consists of four general steps. First, strategic goals are developed. Next, an analysis of the environment is conducted. Similarly, an analysis of the organization itself is needed. Finally, environmental opportunities and threats are matched with organizational strengths and weaknesses to develop a strategy.

Corporate strategy addresses the question of what businesses to be in. Grand strategies include growth, stability, and retrenchment. Portfolio management involves defining strategic business units (SBUs) and then classifying them using the BCG matrix or the GE business screen.

Business-level strategy is concerned with how to compete in a particular business. The adaptation model suggests aligning strategy with environmental conditions. Porter's competitive strategies are differentiation, overall cost leadership, and focus. The product life cycle perspective can help managers plot business strategy for different situations.

The five basic functional strategies are marketing, financial, production, research and development, and human resource strategies. These are usually developed for each business within a corporation.

Successful strategy implementation is dependent upon the organization's structure, leadership, information and control systems, human resources, and technology.

DISCUSSION QUESTIONS

Questions for Review

1. Discuss the nature of strategic management. Be certain to include both the components and levels of strategy in your discussion.
2. What is meant by strategy formulation? Describe strategy implementation. Differentiate strategy formulation from strategy implementation.
3. Differentiate corporate, business, and functional strategies. Does an organization need all three? Why or why not?
4. Briefly describe each of the following: the business portfolio, the adaptation model, Porter's competitive strategies, product life cycles, and any two functional strategies.

Questions for Analysis

5. How would an organization ensure that high-quality strategic planning is taking place? Would an organization want to engage in strategic planning in all circumstances? Why or why not?
6. How would an organization ensure that all strategies developed at different levels within the organization are consistent with one another?
7. What impact would an organization's strategy have on the structure of that organization? Why? What impact would an organization's strategy have on the type of leadership exercised by the executives of that organization? Why?

Questions for Application

8. Read a history of a major corporation and determine what strategies seem to have been used by that corporation. Did the strategies

impact on the structure, leadership, or other aspects of the firm?

9. Interview the manager of a local small business to determine how (or if) he or she formulates strategy. How does what you found compare with what you expected after having read this chapter? Share your findings with the class.

10. Interview an executive of a business firm large enough to have multiple functions about how strategy is formulated in that organization. How does what you found compare with what you expected after having read this chapter? Share your findings with the class.

NOTES

1. "Hershey to Buy U.S. Business from Cadbury," *The Wall Street Journal*, July 25, 1988, p. 2; "A Trimmer Hershey Craves More Brands for Its Food Business," *The Philadelphia Inquirer*, January 8, 1989, pp. 1–G, 2–G.

2. For recent or classic discussions of the meaning of strategic management, see Kenneth R. Andrews, *The Concept of Corporate Strategy*, rev. ed. (Homewood, Ill., 1980); Paul Shrivastava, "Is Strategic Management Ideological?" *Journal of Management*, Vol. 12, No. 3, 1986, pp. 363–377; H. Igor Ansoff, "The Emerging Paradigm of Strategic Behavior," *Strategic Management Journal*, Vol. 8, 1987, pp. 501–515; James Brian Quinn, Henry Mintzberg, and Robert M. James, *The Strategy Process* (Englewood Cliffs, N.J.: Prentice-Hall, 1988); and Henry Mintzberg, "Crafting Strategy," *Harvard Business Review*, July–August 1987, pp. 66–75.

3. Andrews, *The Concept of Corporate Strategy*.

4. "Forecasters Expect Raytheon to Shed Some of Its Units," *The Wall Street Journal*, September 13, 1988, p. 6.

5. Jeremy Main, "The Winning Organization," *Fortune*, September 26, 1988, pp. 50–60.

6. "Do You Believe in Magic?" *Time*, April 25, 1988, pp. 66–73.

7. Bill Saporito, "Uncovering Mars' Unknown Empire," *Fortune*, September 26, 1988, pp. 98–104.

8. See Andrews, *The Concept of Corporate Strategy*. See also Charles W. Hofer and Dan Schendel, *Strategy Formulation: Analytical Concepts* (St. Paul, Minn.: West, 1978); Gregory G. Dess, "Environment, Structure, and Consensus in Strategy Formulation: A Conceptual Integration," *Academy of Management Review*, April 1987, pp. 313–330; Gregory G. Dess, "Consensus on Strategy Formulation and Organizational Performance: Competitors in a Fragmented Industry," *Strategic Management Journal*, Vol. 8, 1987, pp. 259–277; and William D. Guth and Ian C. MacMillan, "Strategy Implementation Versus Middle Management Self-Interest," *Strategic Management Journal*, Vol. 7, 1986, pp. 313–327.

9. Cornelius H. Sullivan, Jr., and John R. Smart, "Planning for Information Networks," *Sloan Management Review*, Winter 1987, pp. 39–44; Robert J. Mockler, "Computer Information Systems and Strategic Corporate Planning," *Business Horizons*, May–June 1987, pp. 32–37.

10. Brian Dumaine, "Corporate Spies Snoop to Conquer," *Fortune*, November 7, 1988, pp. 68–76.

11. R. T. Lenz, "Managing the Evolution of the Strategic Planning Process," *Business Horizons*, January–February 1987, pp. 34–39; R. Duane Ireland, Michael A. Hitt, Richard A. Bettis, and Deborah Auld De Porras, "Strategy Formulation Processes: Differences in Perceptions of Strength and Weaknesses Indicators and Environmental Uncertainty by Managerial Level," *Strategic Management Journal*, Vol. 8, 1987, pp. 469–485; Rohit Deshpande and A. Parasuraman, "Linking Corporate Culture to Strategic Planning," *Business Horizons*, May–June 1986, pp. 28–37.

12. Balaji S. Chakravarthy, "On Tailoring a Strategic Planning System to Its Context: Some Empirical Evidence," *Strategic Management Journal*, Vol. 8, 1987, pp. 517–534.

13. Walter Kiechel III, "Corporate Strategy for the 1990s," *Fortune*, February 29, 1988, pp. 34–42.

14. See John A. Pearce III, D. Keith Robbins, and Richard B. Robinson, Jr., "The Impact of Grand Strategy and Planning Formality on Financial Performance," *Strategic Management Journal*, Vol. 8, 1987, pp. 125–134.

15. "Western Sizzlin': Cooking Up a Cash Cow," *Business Week*, September 5, 1988, p. 63.

16. Anthony Di Primio, "When Turnaround Management Works," *The Journal of Business Strategy*, January–February 1988, pp. 61–64.

17. "Brunswick's Dramatic Turnaround," *The Journal of Business Strategy*, January–February 1988, pp. 4–7.

18. "John Nevin Rescued Firestone—His Way," *Business Week*, May 11, 1987, pp. 96–104.

19. For recent discussions of this approach, see Charles W. L. Hill and Gareth R. Jones, *Strategic Management: An Analytical Approach* (Boston: Houghton Mifflin, 1989); and Robert E. Hoskisson, "Multidivisional Structure and Performance: The Contingency of Diversification Strategy," *Academy of Management Journal*, December 1987, pp. 625–644.

20. Anil K. Gupta, "SBU Strategies, Corporate-SBU Relations, and SBU Effectiveness in Strategy Implementation," *Academy of Management Journal*, September 1987, pp. 477–500; Richard B. Robinson, Jr., and John A. Pearce II, "Planned Patterns of Strategic Behavior and Their Relationship to Business-Unit Performance," *Strategic Management Journal*, Vol. 9, 1988, pp. 43–60; and Mark Kroll and Stephen Caples, "Managing Acquisitions of Strategic Business Units with the Aid of the Arbitage Pricing Model," *Academy of Management Review*, October 1987, pp. 676–685.

21. See Hill and Jones, *Strategic Management*, for a complete review.

22. Irene M. Duhaime and Inga S. Baird, "Divestment Decision-making: The Role of Business Unit Size," *Journal of Management*, Vol. 13, 1987, pp. 483–498.

23. "Can Greyhound Leave the Dog Days Behind?" *Business Week*, June 8, 1987, pp. 72–74; "Under the Gun," *Forbes*, June 13, 1988, pp. 90–92.

24. James H. Higgins and Julian W. Vincze, *Strategic Management and Organizational Policy*, 3rd ed. (Hinsdale, Ill.: Dryden Press, 1986).

25. Danny Miller, "The Structural and Environmental Correlates of Business Strategy," *Strategic Management Journal*, Vol. 8, 1987, pp. 55–76; James J. Chrisman, Charles W. Hofer, and William R. Boulton, "Toward a System for Classifying Business Strategies," *Academy of Management Review*, July 1988, pp. 413–428.

26. Raymond E. Miles and Charles C. Snow, *Organizational Strategy, Structure, and Process* (New York: McGraw-Hill, 1978).

27. Stuart Gannes, "America's Fastest-growing Companies," *Fortune*, May 23, 1988, pp. 28–40.
28. John Clark, *Business Today: Success and Failures* (New York: Random House, 1979).
29. Michael Porter, *Competitive Strategy* (New York: Free Press, 1980). See also Vance H. Fried and Benjamin M. Oviatt, "Michael Porter's Missing Chapter: The Rise of Antitrust Violations," *The Academy of Management Executive*, February 1989, pp. 49–56.
30. For recent discussions of this approach, see Gareth R. Jones and John E. Butler, "Costs, Revenue, and Business-Level Strategy," *Academy of Management Review*, April 1988, pp. 202–213; Charles W. L. Hill, "Differentiation Versus Low Cost or Differentiation and Low Cost: A Contingency Framework," *Academy of Management Review*, July 1988, pp. 401–412, Alan I. Murray, "A Contingency View of Porter's 'Generic Strategies,'" *Academy of Management Review*, July 1988, pp. 390–400; and Theodore T. Herbert and Helen Deresky, "Generic Strategies: An Empirical Investigation of Typology Validity and Strategic Content," *Strategic Management Journal*, Vol. 8, 1987, pp. 135–147.
31. "Attention to Area's Demographic Change Makes Houston's Fiesta Stores a Success," *The Wall Street Journal*, October 23, 1986, p. 39.
32. Gannes, "America's Fastest-growing Companies"; "The Health Craze Has Kellogg Feeling G-R-R-Reat," *Business Week*, March 30, 1987, pp. 52–53; "New Guard Brews Beer's New Image," *USA Today*, August 21, 1987, pp. B1, B2.
33. Douglas E. Castle, "Financing Options for the Corporate Strategist," *The Journal of Business Strategy*, January–February 1988, pp. 12–16.
34. Patricia L. Nemetz and Louis W. Fry, "Flexible Manufacturing Organizations: Implications for Strategy Formulation and Organization Design," *Academy of Management Review*, October 1988, pp. 627–638; Robert J. Mayer, "Winning Strategies for Manufacturers in Mature Industries," *The Journal of Business Strategy*, March–April 1987, pp. 23–30; Jack Meredith, "The Strategic Advantages of New Manufacturing Technologies for Small Firms," *Strategic Management Journal*, Vol. 8, 1987, pp. 249–258.
35. Jeffrey A. Sonnenfeld and Maury A. Peiperl, "Staffing Policy as a Strategic Response: A Typology of Career Systems," *Academy of Management Review*, October 1988, pp. 588–600; Cynthia A. Lengnick-Hall and Mark L. Lengnick-Hall, "Strategic Human Resources Management: A Review of the Literature and a Proposed Typology," *Academy of Management Review*, October 1988, pp. 454–470; Randall S. Schuler and Susan E. Jackson, "Linking Competitive Strategies with Human Resource Management Practices," *The Academy of Management Executive*, August 1987, pp. 207–219; Lloyd Baird and Ilan Meshoulam, "Managing Two Fits of Strategic Human Resource Management," *Academy of Management Review*, January 1988, pp. 116–128.
36. Jack R. Meredith, "Strategic Control of Factory Automation," *Long Range Planning*, Vol. 20, 1987, pp. 106–112; Lex A. van Gunsteren, "Planning for Technology as a Corporate Resource: A Strategic Classification," *Long Range Planning*, Vol. 20, 1987, pp. 51–60; Judith B. Kramm, "The Portfolio Approach to Divisional Innovation Strategy," *The Journal of Business Strategy*, January–February 1987, pp. 25–36; William K. Foster and Austin K. Pryor, "The Strategic Management of Innovation," *The Journal of Business Strategy*, January–February 1986, pp. 38–42.

37. Carol Davenport, "America's Most Admired Corporations," *Fortune*, January 30, 1989, pp. 68–94.
38. Hofer and Schendel, *Strategy Formulation*; Ari Ginsberg, "Operationalizing Organizational Strategy: Toward an Integrative Framework," *Academy of Management Review*, July 1984, pp. 548–557. See also Jay R. Galbraith and Robert K. Kazanjian, *Strategy Implementation: Structure, Systems and Process*, 2nd ed. (St. Paul, Minn.: West, 1986).
39. Danny Miller, "Strategy Making and Structure: Analysis and Implications for Performance," *Academy of Management Journal*, March 1987, pp. 7–32; Danny Miller, "Configurations of Strategy and Structure: Towards a Synthesis," *Strategic Management Journal*, Vol. 7, 1986, pp. 233–249; William G. Egelhoff, "Strategy and Structure in Multinational Corporations: A Revision of the Stopford and Wells Model," *Strategic Management Journal*, Vol. 9, 1988, pp. 1–14.
40. Jeremy Main, "The Winning Organization," *Fortune*, September 26, 1988, pp. 50–60.
41. Kenneth Labich, "The Seven Keys to Business Leadership," *Fortune*, October 24, 1988, pp. 58–66.
42. Peter Lorange, Michael F. Scott Morton, and Sumantra Ghoshal, *Strategic Control* (St. Paul, Minn.: West, 1986).
43. Labich, "The Seven Keys to Business Leadership," p. 59.

CASE 6.1

Alcoa: In or Out of Aluminum?

Alcoa was the name adopted by the Pittsburgh Reduction Company (founded in 1888) in 1907 to signify its role in the aluminum market. It was not only the Aluminum Company of America, it was essentially the *only* aluminum company in America. Alcoa controlled the major known sources of bauxite (aluminum ore) and had a tight patent on the process whereby aluminum could be economically extracted from that ore. In 1912, however, shortly after the patent expired, the federal government charged Alcoa with anti-trust violations. For years Alcoa and the federal government battled over this issue. In 1946 Alcoa was forced to yield to competition and Alcan, its Canadian unit, was split off from the parent company. But Alcoa continued to be a strong force in the aluminum industry.

In 1919 Alcoa instituted a research bureau that gradually grew into the Research Laboratories of Alcoa. The mandate of that group was to develop aluminum as a substitute for other materials when it offered structural advantages. In particular, products and materials in the building, construction, electrification, automobile, and aircraft industries were studied and aluminum was developed as a commercial substitute. The extensive use of aluminum in buildings, automobiles, aircraft, boats, kitchen utensils, surgical instruments, and the like attests to the success of those efforts.

By the mid-1980s, however, that research effort had altered. The idea of material substitution had replaced aluminum as the focus. This meant that, although the building, construction, electrification, automobile, and aircraft industries were still seen as the main areas for growth, aluminum was not seen as the material to be used in that growth. New materials were being sought to replace aluminum just as aluminum had displaced other materials in the past. Aluminum was no longer the "given" in the research equation.

Alcoa's CEO at that time, Charles W. Parry, espoused this notion and provided the funds and executive backing for that research effort. In 1987 approximately 85 percent of Alcoa's sales revenues came from aluminum, and Parry predicted that by 1995 about half of its revenues would be derived from nonaluminum businesses—some, brand-new ventures; others, acquisitions. Furthermore, the aluminum side of Alcoa's operations would be quite different from what they had been in the past. There would be a strong focus on custom-made and fabricated products and less of a focus on industrial materials and products.

Parry's long-term strategy was to keep the same markets but change the products being produced and sold. The new products would be based on novel aluminum hybrids, ceramics, plastics, composites, and powders. Developing the materials, forming the strategic business units necessary to produce and market the materials, and educating and expanding the markets themselves would take years, but Parry felt that Alcoa's future depended upon movement in that direction.

A new unit, the Materials Science Division, was created to assist in moving ideas from the laboratory into commercial ventures. Other existing plants were to be modernized at considerable expense. These efforts were going to put a severe financial strain on Alcoa. Nevertheless, the strategy seemed to be both clear and needed.

In April 1987, Parry retired as CEO and Paul H. O'Neill, not C. Fred Fetterolf, was named as his replacement. The annual report for 1987 stated that Alcoa's future was in the core aluminum business and not in any major diversification and acquisition moves. Alcoa's long-term strategy had been changed. The change seemed sudden but was quietly done. There was, however, considerable behind-the-scenes activity.

Alcoa is a century-old corporation with a strongly entrenched culture, which is not that of a wheeling-dealing, risk-taking, entrepreneurial organization. Parry's strategy had run counter to the established culture. Numerous executives and, more importantly, the board of directors, had had trouble envisioning how the results of that strategy were going to fit in with Alcoa's established way of operating.

Soon it became apparent that O'Neill, who was a member of the existing board and president of the International Paper Company, was the sort of person the board was seeking. O'Neill agreed to take the position, if Parry would take early retirement. A year later, not a single top-level executive had resigned, not even Fetterolf, whom both O'Neill and Parry begged to stay on in the best interests of the company.

Alcoa's short-term strategy is to concentrate on aluminum. In the long term, some change still seems necessary. O'Neill may be in a better position to deal with that than was Parry because the board that caused Parry so much trouble will be largely gone through mandatory retirement in a few years. O'Neill may eventually return to the diversification and acquisition strategy, but, if he does, it will be with a board likely to understand and back such a strategy.

Questions

1. How would you describe the nature of strategic management at Alcoa?
2. In terms of strategy formulation, did Alcoa analyze both its environment and its organization equally well? Why or why not?
3. How well did Alcoa implement its diversification and acquisition strategy? Try to provide specific examples to support your view.
4. What do you feel the long-term strategy of Alcoa should be? Why is the strategy that you recommend superior to possible alternatives?

REFERENCES: "The Quiet Coup at Alcoa," *Business Week*, June 27, 1988, pp. 58–65; "Alcoa: Recycling Itself to Become a Pioneer in New Materials," *Business Week*, February 9, 1987, pp. 56–58; G. D. Smith and B. H. Pruitt, "The Rise of Alcoa Laboratories," *Research Management*, Vol. 30, March–April 1987, pp. 24–33; "The Basics Come Back," *Fortune*, August 31, 1987, p. 8.

CASE 6.2

Nissan Motor Company's Strategic Maneuver

During the mid-1970s, Nissan Motor Company decided that it could not effectively compete one on one with Toyota Motor Corporation in the Japanese market. (Toyota had traditionally been number 1 in that market and held a commanding lead over Nissan, which was number 2.) Nissan thus inaugurated an aggressive internationalization strategy. It built plants in Mexico, the United States, and nineteen other countries and started several joint ventures. The international program seemed to work quite well. Nissan's Datsun cars and trucks earned a reputation for sporty engineering and high performance that enabled them to almost surpass Toyota's share of the U.S. market and to earn substantial profits for the firm. As those profits accrued, they were plowed back into the company for further international expansion.

In the mid-1980s, Nissan began to concentrate on vehicles that were less sporty, that were cheaper and boxier but seemed to have the potential to increase Nissan's market share. In addition, Nissan slowed its introduction of new models. These changes began to have a negative impact on Nissan's performance.

By 1986, it was clear that the shift in emphasis to cheaper vehicles coupled with the other changes was not working. Nissan was experiencing difficult times both at home and in the U.S. market, although sales in Europe continued to be a bright spot. The increased value of the yen was the single most important factor underlying those difficulties, but the new, stodgy designs and the expensive expansion efforts were contributing factors. Nissan had used its cash reserves for expansion at a time when they were needed for product design and to counteract the changing value of the yen. Nissan began a series of strategic moves to alleviate these problems.

One move was to reduce costs in order to strengthen profits. Nissan engaged in a variety of cost-cutting efforts. It lowered the pay of its executive director, cut salaries and bonuses throughout the organization, reduced part-time employment, cut back substantially on the use of overtime, and slowed the hiring of new employees.

A second strategic move was to look toward the future in terms of research and development. Nissan increased its research efforts in areas such as the development of ceramic parts for automobile engines. Because ceramic parts are much lighter than metal parts, cars with ceramic engine parts can accelerate more quickly and have better fuel economy than cars with metal parts.

Another strategic move was to try to improve the demand for Nissan products in order to increase sales. Nissan launched an all-out price war in Japan to try to gain market share from Toyota. Simultaneously, it tried to gradually increase prices of cars being marketed in the United States. Nissan stepped up design changes and began to introduce higher-priced models to the United States.

The new products to be introduced in the United States were announced in 1988 to begin to change the public's perception of Nissan vehicles, even though many of them would not be available for several years. Nissan announced that in 1990 it would release a new minivan or multipurpose vehicle called Axxess and the 300ZX sports car, which is described as having bold styling. Its 1989 models included an updated sports car, the 240SX, which went on sale in late 1988, and a redesigned top-of-the-line four-door sedan version of the Maxima.

The most significant part of this strategy, however, is the introduction of Infiniti, the luxury Nissan. Following the pattern set by Honda's Acura Division, Nissan created for Infiniti a whole separate unit with its own marketing network. There will be separate, posh showrooms and displays and separate advertising. Nissan hopes that the aura of Infiniti will touch its other products as well. Infiniti started with a luxury sedan and a sports coupe in order to penetrate two segments of the upper end of the market. Nissan expects that it will take several years to establish itself in that market but feels that the investment and the wait will be worthwhile.

To spearhead these efforts, Nissan hired a Ford Motor Company executive, Thomas D. Mignanelli, as executive vice president of U.S. marketing. Mignanelli instituted tight inventory control procedures to reduce inventory carrying costs. He began working with dealers to improve working relations, obtain suggestions for improving U.S. sales, and pep up enthusiasm for the new models. Whether or not Mignanelli can transfer his success from Ford to Nissan remains an open question.

Questions

1. How would you describe the nature of strategic management at Nissan?
2. What different kinds or levels of strategy can you identify at Nissan? Cite specific examples.
3. In terms of strategy formulation, did Nissan match its organization with its environment effectively? Why or why not?
4. What do you feel the long-term strategy of Nissan should be? Why is the strategy that you recommend superior to possible alternatives?

REFERENCES: "Nissan Is Counting on New Models to Turn Around Falling U.S. Sales," *The Wall Street Journal*, October 6, 1988, p. B6; James R. Healey, "'89 Models Designed to Restore Pizzazz," *USA Today*, September 28, 1988, pp. 1B–2B; "How Nissan Plans to Shift Out of Reverse," *Business Week*, July 18, 1988, pp. 120–121; Edwin Whenmouth, "Japan's Price for a Weaker Dollar," *Industry Week*, January 18, 1988, pp. 44–45; "Nissan Hurt by Yen Rise, Lowers Pay of Its Executive Director," *The Wall Street Journal*, March 14, 1986, p. 31; Louis Kraar, "Japan's Gung-Ho U.S. Car Plants," *Fortune*, January 30, 1989, pp. 98–108; "Zen and the Art of Auto Sales," *The Wall Street Journal*, March 13, 1989, p. B1.

OUTLINE

The Nature of Tactical and Operational Planning

Tactical Planning
Developing Tactical Plans · Implementing Tactical Plans

Operational Planning
Single-Use Plans · Standing Plans

Contingency Planning

Managing the Planning Process
Barriers to Effective Planning · Overcoming the Barriers

Using MBO to Implement Plans
The Nature and Purpose of MBO · The MBO Process · The Effectiveness of MBO

CHAPTER 7

Tactical and Operational Planning

OBJECTIVES

After studying this chapter, you should be able to:

- Describe the nature of tactical and operational planning.
- Discuss how to develop and implement tactical plans.
- Identify and discuss different kinds of operational plans.
- Discuss the role of contingency planning.
- Identify the major barriers to effective planning and discuss how managers can overcome them.
- Describe how MBO can be used to implement plans.

OPENING INCIDENT

Andrew Grove, CEO of Intel, has become something of a management guru. He has written several popular books on management, including *High-Output Management* and *One-on-One with Andy Grove*. Since assuming the position of CEO in 1987, he has rapidly developed a reputation for being very detail oriented and hard driving in his approach to getting things done. His resentment of the restrictions placed on individual freedom in his home country of Hungary have led him to become extremely direct and outspoken in his dealings with others.

When Grove took over, Intel was getting itself into a bad spot. Though still the dominant firm in the microprocessor industry, the company was bleeding red ink and rapidly losing market share. Almost overnight, Grove turned things around by closing eight plants, cutting the work force by 30 percent, and boosting productivity, innovation, and quality.

One of Grove's hallmarks as a manager is zeal for planning. Each quarter he leads several different groups of managers through a comprehensive planning meeting, focusing on both the long and the short run. He also stresses the importance of contingency planning. In particular, he strives to predict every possible outcome of a particular course of action and then decides ahead of time how each can be addressed.[1]

*A*ndrew Grove is widely recognized as a consummate manager. Even Intel's biggest competitors will miss him when he retires in a few years. A major factor in his success has been his ability to conceptualize problems and opportunities and then translate them into action plans that others in the firm can address. This process involves the successful implementation of strategic plans.

This chapter is primarily concerned with the implementation of organizational plans, especially through tactical and operational planning. It completes a three-chapter sequence devoted to the planning function of management. Chapter 5 introduced organizational goals and planning, and Chapter 6 addressed strategy and strategic management. The final piece of the planning puzzle is translating plans into reality.

We first develop more fully the nature of tactical and operational planning and describe each in detail. Contingency planning and the importance of alternative courses of action are discussed. We then describe ways to manage the planning process, focusing on barriers to effective planning and ways managers can overcome those barriers. We conclude by exploring a widely used system of implementing plans called management by objectives, or MBO.

THE NATURE OF TACTICAL AND OPERATIONAL PLANNING

We noted in Chapter 5 that organizations establish three kinds of plans: strategic, tactical, and operational. These three types of organizational plans differ in important ways but are highly interdependent. The general interrelationships among them are shown in Figure 7.1.[2]

Note that a strategic plan is at the top of the organization. It has an extended time horizon and is broad in scope. Organizations can have more than one strategic plan, but they usually don't have large numbers of them. In contrast, tactical plans are generally located in the middle of the organization, have an intermediate time horizon, and are less broad in scope. Several tactical plans are likely to be developed during the course of carrying out a strategic plan. Finally, operational plans are located at the lower levels of the organization, have a short time horizon, and are relatively narrow in scope. There are many of them.[3]

Note also that the various plans are interrelated. (The arrows in Figure 7.1 indicate hypothetical or potential relationships, rather than standard or normal ones.) Tactical plans tend to be derived from strategic plans. They also affect one another and may provide feedback into the original strategy. Operational plans derive primarily from tactical plans and, to a lesser degree, from strategic plans. Operational plans, too, are interrelated and provide feedback to higher-level plans.[4]

FIGURE 7.1

Relationships Among Strategic, Tactical, and Operational Plans

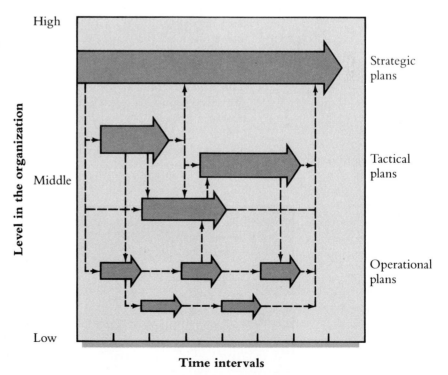

TACTICAL PLANNING

■ **tactical plan** Developed to implement specific parts of a strategic plan

As introduced in Chapter 5, a **tactical plan** is developed to implement specific parts of a strategic plan. You have probably heard the saying about "winning the battle but losing the war." Tactical plans are to battles what strategy is to a war: an organized sequence of steps designed to execute strategic plans and achieve strategic goals. Strategy focuses on resources, environment, and mission, whereas tactics deal primarily with people and action.[5] Figure 7.2 identifies the major elements in developing and executing tactical plans.

Developing Tactical Plans

Effective tactical planning depends on many factors that vary from one situation to another, but there are some guidelines. First, the manager needs to recognize that tactical planning must address a number of tactical goals derived from a broader strategic goal.[6] An occasional situation may call for a stand-alone tactical plan, but most of the time tactical plans flow from and must be consistent with a strategic plan.

For example, when Roberto Goizueta became CEO of Coca-Cola, he developed a strategic plan for carrying the firm into the twenty-first century. As part of developing the plan, Goizueta identified a critical environmental threat—considerable unrest and uncertainty among the independent bottlers who packaged and distributed Coca-Cola's products. To simultaneously counter this threat and strengthen the company's position, Coca-Cola bought several large independent bottlers and combined them into one new organization called Coca-Cola Enterprises. Selling half of the new company's stock reaped millions in profits while still effectively keeping control of the enterprise in Coca-Cola's hands. Thus, the creation of the new business was a tactical plan developed to contribute to the achievement of an overarching strategic goal.[7]

Second, although strategies are often stated in general terms, tactics must deal more with specific resource and time issues. A strategy can

FIGURE 7.2

Developing and Executing Tactical Plans

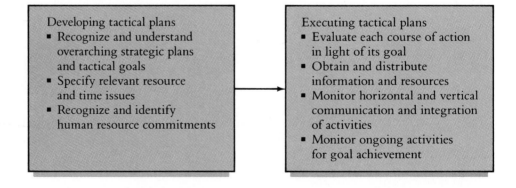

Developing tactical plans
- Recognize and understand overarching strategic plans and tactical goals
- Specify relevant resource and time issues
- Recognize and identify human resource commitments

Executing tactical plans
- Evaluate each course of action in light of its goal
- Obtain and distribute information and resources
- Monitor horizontal and vertical communication and integration of activities
- Monitor ongoing activities for goal achievement

As a part of its human resource strategy in the United States, Honda of America has worked hard to implement several Japanese business practices in its facilities here. For example, requiring that everyone wear company uniforms and eat in the same cafeteria is part of a tactical plan to promote team spirit and group unity. Everyone is expected to participate in making decisions and help keep quality at the highest levels possible.

call for being number 1 in a particular market or industry, but a tactical plan must specify precisely what activities will be undertaken to achieve that goal.[8] Consider the Coca-Cola example again. Another element of its strategic plan involves increased worldwide market share. To facilitate additional sales in Europe, managers developed tactical plans for building a new plant in the south of France to make soft-drink concentrate and for building another canning plant in Dunkirk. Building these plants represents a concrete action involving measurable resources (i.e., funds to build the plants) and a clear time horizon (i.e., a target date for completion).

Finally, tactical planning requires the use of human resources. Managers involved in tactical planning spend a great deal of time working with other people. They must be in a position to receive information from others in and outside the organization, process that information in the most effective way, and then pass it on to others who might make use of it. Coca-Cola executives have been intensively involved in planning the new plants mentioned above, setting up the new bottling venture noted earlier, and exploring a joint venture with Cadbury Schweppes in the United Kingdom. Each activity has required considerable time, effort, and energy from dozens of different managers. One manager, for example, crossed the Atlantic twelve times while negotiating the Cadbury deal.

Implementing Tactical Plans

Regardless of how well a tactical plan may be formulated, its ultimate success depends on the way it is carried out. Successful implementation, in turn, depends on the astute use of resources, effective decision making, and insightful steps to ensure that the right things are done at the right time and in the right ways. A manager can have an absolutely brilliant idea, but it can fail if not properly executed.

Proper execution depends on a number of important factors. First the manager needs to evaluate every possible course of action in light of the goal it is intended to reach. Next he or she needs to make sure each decision maker has the information and resources necessary to get the job done. There also need to be vertical and horizontal communication and integration of activities in order to minimize conflict or inconsistent activities. And finally, the manager must monitor ongoing activities derived from the plan to make sure they are achieving the desired results. This monitoring typically takes place within the context of the organization's ongoing control systems.

For example, managers at Disney recently developed a strategic plan aimed at spurring growth and profits. One tactical plan developed to stimulate growth was to increase attendance at Walt Disney World in Florida. To boost attendance, the resort needed new attractions and activities. Thus, planners designed a new water park, film studio, and studio tour. In order for the tactical plan to succeed, the new facilities had to be implemented effectively. The new water park had to have the right mix of attractions, be situated in the right place, be managed and maintained correctly, have an acceptable admissions price, and be properly promoted. Because all those things were done right, Typhoon Lagoon has been a big success. If things hadn't been done right, it could have been a flop.[9]

OPERATIONAL PLANNING

operational plan Derived from a tactical plan and aimed at achieving one or more operational goals

Another critical element in effective organizational planning is the development and implementation of appropriate operational plans. As noted in Chapter 5, an **operational plan** is derived from a tactical plan and is aimed at achieving one or more operational goals. Thus, operational plans tend to be narrowly focused, have relatively short time horizons, and involve lower-level managers. "The Global View" provides numerous examples of how Nippon Telegraph & Telephone uses operational plans. The two most basic forms of operational plans are single-use and standing plans.

Single-Use Plans

single-use plans Developed to carry out a course of action that is not likely to be repeated in the future

Single-use plans are developed to carry out a course of action that is not likely to be repeated in the future. Most organizations find it necessary to develop single-use plans on a regular basis for a wide range of activities. The activities being planned may be fairly unimportant or extremely important to the organization. For example, Sears recently

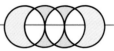

THE GLOBAL VIEW

PLANNING AT NTT

Nippon Telegraph & Telephone (NTT) is arguably the largest and most valuable company in the world. Its profits rank it as number 1 in Japan, where it is also the largest employer. Its assets are nearly three times those of AT&T. NTT's market value is nearly ten times that of AT&T; indeed, its stock-market valuation is greater than that of AT&T, IBM, and General Motors combined—all of this from a company formed in 1952 as a government monopoly to provide telephone service.

Initially, NTT was supplied chiefly by a former subsidiary of AT&T's Western Electric Company, the Nippon Electronic Company (NEC). Now, however, NTT uses numerous suppliers and is no longer a government monopoly but is a private telephone company. Although NTT was still deriving 80 percent of its revenues from the provision of Japanese telephone service as late as 1988, NTT's operational plans had led to the establishment of an international subsidiary to expand its operations throughout the globe.

NTT uses a form of operational planning—project planning—for much of its work. One project that NTT expects to be a major success worldwide is the Integrated Systems Digital Network, or ISDN. The project involves the use of digital communications in a network employing fiber-optic technology. The intent is to bring voice, picture, and data capabilities into offices and homes by means of special telephone outlets. Planning for the project has been extensive because NTT is developing the hardware and software to make it all possible. The products developed so far are expensive, but NTT expects costs to fall as production is increased to meet expected demand.

NTT expects ISDN to be the company's fastest-growing project during the 1990s. To ensure that strong growth, NTT executives are trying to develop better relations with foreign firms.

In addition to trying to develop foreign suppliers to support the ISDN project, NTT is seeking to establish other overseas projects. It is soliciting joint-venture research projects with firms from other countries. Such joint research projects would enable foreign companies to participate in the beginnings of technological developments in the telephone and communications industry. Progress has been slow because many foreign companies are fearful that the exchange of technology may be too one-sided in NTT's favor. Nevertheless, over time, such joint ventures are expected to prove beneficial to companies from all countries involved and are likely to be expanded.

REFERENCES: Carla Rapoport, "The World's Most Valuable Company," *Fortune*, October 10, 1988, pp. 92–104; "Data General Gets the Call," *Business Week*, October 19, 1987, p. 96; "Researchers on Trail of Fluoride Fiber," *Photonics Spectra*, July 1988, p. 8.

---

announced plans to sell its headquarters building, the Sears Tower in Chicago, for as much as $1 billion.[10] Deciding to sell the building, determining the price, negotiating with prospective buyers, and closing the deal constitute a single-use plan, since this type of activity is not likely to be repeated soon. The two most common forms of single-use plans are programs and projects.

program   A single-use plan for a large set of activities

Programs   A **program** is a single-use plan for a large set of activities. It could consist of identifying procedures for introducing a new product line, opening a new facility, or changing the organization's mission. Guidelines for effective program development include the following:

1. Divide the total set of activities into meaningful steps.
2. Study the relationships among steps, taking special note of any required sequence of steps.

Dunkin' Donuts has recently pioneered a new approach to distribution—Regional Distribution Centers owned and operated by franchise owners. This self-distribution concept was developed by Dunkin' Donuts and its franchise owners to service member shops. This arrangement allows franchise owners to control costs, quality, and delivery.

project A single-use plan of less scope and complexity than a program

standing plans Developed for activities that recur regularly over a period of time

3. Assign responsibility for each step to appropriate managers or units, or both.
4. Determine and allocate the resources needed for each step.
5. Estimate the starting and completion dates for each step.
6. Assign target dates for the completion of each step.

For example, a few years ago Black & Decker bought General Electric's small-appliance business. The deal involved the largest brand-name switch in history, with a total of 150 products being converted from GE to the Black & Decker label. Each product was carefully studied, redesigned, and reintroduced with an extended warranty. A total of 140 steps were used for each product. It took three years to convert all 150 products over to Black & Decker. The total conversion of the product line was a program. It was large in scope, was broken down into manageable steps, had specified timetables, and so forth.[11]

Projects A **project** is similar to a program but is generally of less scope and complexity. A project may be a part of a broader program, or it may be a self-contained single-use plan. Thus, for Black & Decker, the conversion of each of the 150 products was a separate project in its own right. Each product had its own manager, its own schedule, and so forth. Projects are also used to introduce a new product within an existing product line or to add a new benefit option to an existing salary package.

Most programs and projects are developed in conjunction with a budget. A budget is a statement of the resources allocated for a particular set of activities (such as a program or a project) and a description of how the resources are to be divided among the activities. Suppose that Xerox initiates a program for developing a new product and establishes a $5 million start-up budget for it. One million dollars might be designated for research and development and marketing research, $2.5 million for modifications to an existing production facility and initial production costs, and the remainder for promotion and advertising. In addition to being part of many plans, a budget is also a control device to ensure that resources are used in the proper manner.[12] We discuss budgets in detail in Part 5.

Standing Plans

Whereas single-use plans (programs and projects) are used for nonrecurring situations, **standing plans** are used for activities that recur regularly over a period of time. As long as they are not overdone, standing plans are great contributors to efficiency. They routinize decision making and keep managers from having to "reinvent the wheel" every time a routine and recurring problem or situation arises. Policies, standard operating procedures, and rules and regulations are three kinds of standing plans.[13]

policy A standing plan that specifies the organization's general response to a designated problem or situation

Policies As a general guide for action, a policy is the most general form of standing plan. A **policy** specifies the organization's general response to a designated problem or situation. For example, McDonald's has a policy that it will not grant a franchise to an individual who already owns another fast-food restaurant. Likewise, a university admissions office might establish a policy that admission will be granted only to applicants with a minimum SAT score of 1,000 and a ranking in the top quarter of their high-school classes. Admissions officers may routinely deny admission to applicants who fail to reach these minimums. A policy is also likely to describe how exceptions are to be handled. The university's policy statement, for example, might create an admissions appeals committee to evaluate applicants who do not meet minimum requirements but may warrant special consideration.

standard operating procedure (SOP) A standing plan that outlines the steps to be followed in a particular circumstance

Standard Operating Procedures Another type of standing plan is the **standard operating procedure,** or **SOP**. An SOP is more specific than a policy in that it outlines the steps to be followed in particular circumstances. The admissions clerk at the university, for example, might be told that when an application is received, he or she should (1) set up a file for the applicant; (2) add test-score records, transcripts, and letters of reference to the file as they are received; and (3) give the file to the appropriate admissions director when it is complete. The E. & J. Gallo Winery in California has a 300-page manual of standard operating procedures. This planning manual is credited for making Gallo one of the most efficient wine operations in the United States.[14] McDonald's has SOPs explaining exactly how Big Macs are to be cooked, how long they can stay in the warming rack, and so forth. Indeed, virtually all organizations have SOPs for directing routine activities.

rules and regulations Describe exactly how specific activities are to be carried out

Rules and Regulations The narrowest of the standing plans, **rules and regulations**, describe exactly how specific activities are to be carried out. Rather than guiding decision making, rules and regulations actually take the place of decision making in various situations. Each McDonald's restaurant has a rule prohibiting customers from using its telephones, for example. The university admissions office might have a rule stipulating that if an applicant's file is not complete two months prior to the beginning of a semester, the student cannot be admitted until the next semester. Of course, in most organizations a manager at a higher level can suspend or bend the rules. If the high-school transcript of the daughter of a prominent university alumnus and donor arrives a few days late, the director of admissions would probably waive the two-month rule. Rules and regulations can become a problem if they become excessive or if they are enforced too rigidly.

Rules and regulations and SOPs are similar in many ways. They are both relatively narrow in scope, and each can serve as a substitute for decision making. However, an SOP typically describes a sequence of activities, whereas rules and regulations focus on one activity. Recall our examples: The admissions-desk SOP consisted of three activities, whereas the two-month rule related to one activity only. In an industrial setting, the SOP for orienting a new employee could involve enrolling the person in various benefit options, introducing him or her to co-workers and supervisors, and providing a tour of the facilities. A pertinent rule for the new employee might involve when to come to work each day.

In summary, there are two basic categories of operational plans: single-use and standing plans. Table 7.1 summarizes the various forms of each. These and other kinds of operational plans are necessary to implement both strategic plans and tactical plans, and they help managers focus quite specifically on day-to-day activities and events. It is important, however, that managers not allow their organizations to become so bogged down with operational plans that they become rigid and inflexible.

CONTINGENCY PLANNING

■ **contingency planning**
The determination of alternative courses of action to be taken if an intended plan is unexpectedly disrupted or rendered inappropriate

Another important element of an effective planning system is the development of contingency plans. **Contingency planning** is the determination of alternative courses of action to be taken if an intended plan of action is unexpectedly disrupted or rendered inappropriate.[15] Suppose that a rapidly expanding franchised food company has made plans to build 100 new units during each of the next four years. Its top managers realize, however, that a shift in the economy might call for a different rate of expansion. Therefore, the firm develops two contingency plans based on extreme positive or negative economic shifts. First, the company decides that if the economy begins to expand beyond some specific

TABLE 7.1
Types of Operational Plans

Single-use plans. Plans developed to carry out a course of action not likely to be carried out in the future

    Program: Single-use plan for a large set of activities

    Project: Single-use plan of less scope and complexity than a program

Standing plans. Plans developed for activities that recur regularly over a period of time

    Policy: Standing plan specifying the organization's general response to a designated problem or situation

    Standard Operating Procedure: Standing plan outlining steps to be followed in particular circumstances

    Rules and Regulations: Standing plans describing exactly how specific activities are to be carried out

level (contingency event), then (contingency plan) the rate of the company's growth will increase from 100 to 150 new stores per year. Second, the company also decides that if inflation increases substantially, the expansion rate will drop from 100 to 75 new stores per year. The organization has now specified two crucial contingencies (expansion or inflation in the economy outside the tolerable range) and two alternative plans (increased or decreased growth).

The mechanics of contingency planning are shown in Figure 7.3. In relation to an organization's ongoing planning process, contingency planning comes into play at and between what we will call four "action points." At action point 1, the basic plans of the organization are developed. These may include strategic, tactical, and operational plans. As part of this development process, managers usually consider various contingency events. Certain management groups even assign someone the role of devil's advocate to ask "But what if . . ." about each course of action.[16] Moreover, most managers consider probabilities from the beginning and base their plans on the extent to which various assumptions are likely to be realized. If a plan is based on a market increase of 10 percent, and if this 10 percent increase has a 98 percent chance of happening, we are probably on sound footing. If the 10 percent increase

FIGURE 7.3

Contingency Planning

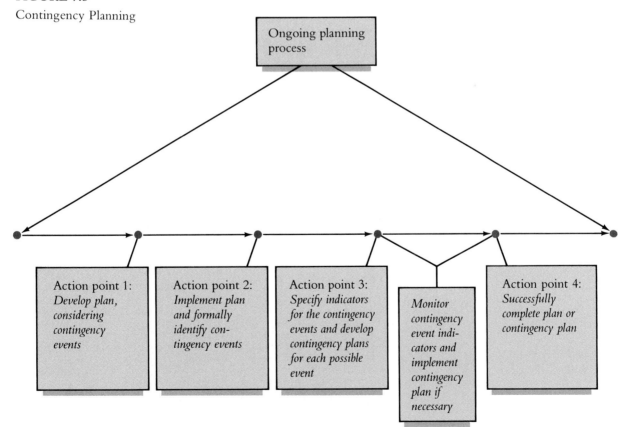

has only a 15 percent chance of occurring, however, we should not depend too heavily on its happening. Various other contingencies (such as a market increase greater than or less than 10 percent) should also be considered.

At action point 2, the plan that has been chosen is put into effect. The most important contingency events are also identified in a more formal manner. Because there could theoretically be an almost infinite array of contingency events, it is important to pinpoint those that have the greatest probability of happening. Only the events that are likely to occur and whose effects would have a substantial impact on the organization are used in the contingency-planning process.

Next, at action point 3, the company specifies certain indicators or signs that might suggest that a contingency event is about to take place. A company might decide that an annual inflation rate of more than 9 percent should be considered a contingency event. In that case, a good early indicator might be a monthly inflation rate of 1 percent or greater for three consecutive months. As indicators of contingency events are being defined, the contingency plans themselves should also be developed. Possible contingency plans for various situations might include delaying plant construction, developing a new manufacturing process, and cutting prices.

After this stage, the managers of the organization monitor the indicators identified at action point 3. If the situation dictates, a contingency plan may be implemented. Otherwise the primary plan of action continues in force. Finally, action point 4 marks the successful completion of either the original plan or the contingency plan.

To illustrate again, recall the opening incident suggesting that Intel uses contingency planning extensively. As one component of its strategy, Intel is hard at work developing a new microprocessor that it hopes will become the standard for the next generation of personal computers, and the company has a number of planned activities predicated on achieving this goal. Yet, managers at Intel are aware that Sun Microsystems and Hewlett-Packard, among others, are also furiously working toward the same goal. Thus, they have developed a series of contingency plans that will provide guidance if one or more of the other companies win the race for the new technology.[17]

Contingency planning is becoming more and more important for most organizations and especially for those operating in particularly complex or dynamic environments. Few managers have such an accurate view of the future that they can anticipate and plan for everything. Contingency planning is a useful technique for helping cope with uncertainty and change.[18]

MANAGING THE PLANNING PROCESS

Obviously, all of the elements of planning discussed to this point involve managing the planning process in some way or another. There are, however, other useful perspectives that the manager needs to understand when dealing with the planning process. It is helpful to recognize and understand that significant barriers sometimes impede effective planning. Likewise, it is important to know how to at least partially overcome some of the barriers.

Barriers to Effective Planning

■ **major barriers to effective planning** Dynamic and complex environments, a reluctance to establish goals, resistance to change, various kinds of constraints, and time and expense

Very few plans unfold as smoothly or systematically as managers might like. Indeed, five major hurdles can hamper an organization's efforts at planning. These barriers, along with methods for overcoming them, are illustrated in Figure 7.4 and discussed in the following paragraphs.

Dynamic and Complex Environments   The nature of an organization's environment is often a major barrier to effective planning. Rapid change, technological innovation, intense competition, and similar factors can each make it difficult for an organization to accurately assess future opportunities and threats. For example, when an electronics firm like Intel develops a long-range plan, it tries to take into account how much technological innovation is likely to occur during that interval. But forecasting such uncontrollable external events is very difficult. During the early boom years of personal computers, data were stored

FIGURE 7.4

Managing the Planning Process

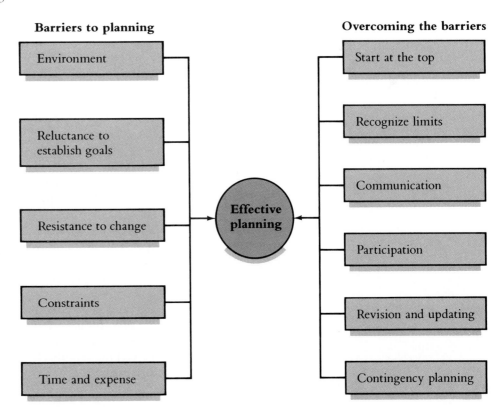

primarily on floppy disks. Because these disks had a limited storage capacity, hard disks were developed. Whereas the typical floppy disk can hold about 250 typed pages of information, the hard disk can store thousands of pages. Today even more complex and sophisticated forms of storage devices are being developed. The NeXT computer recently introduced by Steve Jobs has an erasable optical-disk drive capable of holding enough information to fill several hundred books.[19] The manager attempting to plan in this rapidly changing environment faces a truly formidable task.

Reluctance to Establish Goals   Another barrier to effective planning is the reluctance of some managers to establish goals for themselves and their units of responsibility. The reason for this reluctance may be lack of confidence or fear of failure. If a manager sets a goal that is specific, concise, and time related, then whether he or she attains it is obvious. Managers who consciously or unconsciously try to avoid this degree of accountability are likely to hinder the organization's planning efforts. Pfizer, a large pharmaceutical company, recently ran into problems because its managers did not set goals for research and development. Consequently, the organization fell farther and farther behind because the managers had no way of knowing how effective their R&D efforts actually were.[20] Other factors contributing to management's reluctance to establish goals may include a lack of ability, a lack of information, and a poor reward system.

Resistance to Change   A third major barrier to the planning process is resistance to change. Almost by definition, planning involves changing one or more aspects of the organization's current situation. Managers resist change for any number of reasons, including fear of the unknown, a preference for familiar goals and plans, and economic insecurity. Avon Products almost drove itself into bankruptcy because it insisted on continuing a policy calling for large dividend payments to its stock-holders. When profits started to fall, managers resisted cutting the dividends and started borrowing to pay them. The company's debt grew from $3 million to $1.1 billion in eight years. Eventually, managers were forced to confront the problem and decided to cut dividends.[21] We discuss resistance to change more fully in Chapter 11.

Constraints   Constraints that limit what an organization can do are another major obstacle in the planning process. Common constraints include a lack of human resources, a lack of financial resources, a lack of physical resources, government restrictions, strong competition, and a lack of information. For example, Owens-Corning Fiberglass recently took on an enormous debt burden as part of its fight to avoid being taken over by Wickes Cos. The company now has such a large debt to service that it has been forced to cut back on capital expenditures and research and development. And those cutbacks have greatly constrained what the firm can plan for the future.[22]

Time and Expense   Some managers also fail to plan effectively because good planning is both time consuming and expensive. It's easy to say, "I'm too busy to plan today; I'll do it tomorrow," or to put off good planning for lack of funds. Effective planning takes hours and hours of time, enormous energy, and an unwavering belief in its importance. And planning may involve substantial financial outlays. For example, developing a particular plan may require technical expertise or a data-base that is not available within the organization. Thus, the manager must purchase the needed expertise and information.

Overcoming the Barriers

■ **overcoming barriers to planning**   Start at the top of the organization, recognize the limits to planning, enhance communication, promote participation, revise and update plans as necessary, and develop contingency plans

Fortunately, there are techniques and guidelines that managers can use to overcome some of the planning barriers. The most common methods are shown in Figure 7.4.[23]

Start at the Top   Perhaps the most critical factor in overcoming barriers to planning is starting at the top. Top management must take the lead in establishing the importance of planning in determining the mission and strategy that the organization is to follow. Such action sets the stage for subsequent planning at lower levels and also reinforces the importance of planning to everyone in the organization. CEO Andrew Grove leads each of Intel's major planning groups and in that way emphasizes the importance of planning to the future of the company. And because planning starts at the top, everyone recognizes that it is important.

Recognize the Limits to Planning   Although it may sound paradoxical, another guideline for effective planning is to recognize that planning has its limits. Planning is not a panacea that will solve all of an organization's problems, nor is it an iron-clad set of procedures to be followed at any cost. Managers should recognize that good planning does not necessarily ensure success and that adjustments and exceptions are to be expected as the plan unfolds. For example, one facet of the comprehensive Coca-Cola strategy discussed earlier was introducing a new formula for the soft drink to combat inroads being made by Pepsi. Managers at Coke quickly reversed the decision—now recognized as one of the biggest business blunders in history—and reintroduced the old formula as Coca-Cola Classic. And it has a larger market share than before. Thus, even though careful planning resulted in a big mistake, the company came out ahead in the long run.[24]

Communication   Not only must planning be initiated at the top, but it must also be communicated to others in the organization. Everyone involved in the planning process should know what the overriding organizational strategy is, what the various functional strategies are, and how they are all to be integrated and coordinated. Andrew Grove, for example, works hard to ensure that each manager at Intel likely to be affected by a decision or plan is fully informed about what is going on and why. And Ford has established a company conference center where executives from around the world can learn about the company's plans for the future.[25]

Participation   It is important that people responsible for implementing plans have a voice in developing them from the outset. These individuals almost always have valuable information to contribute, and because they will be implementing the plans, their involvement is critical: People are usually more committed to plans that they have helped to shape. Even when an organization is somewhat centralized or uses a planning staff, managers from a variety of levels in the organization should be involved in the planning process. Ford has demonstrated leadership in this area. Managers from all levels of the organization, and even operating employees, are given a large voice in how things are done.

Revision and Updating   The manager should recognize that planning is a dynamic process in which long-range and intermediate plans are frequently revised and updated in response to new information and the completion of short-range plans. Many organizations are seeing the need to revise and update on an increasingly frequent basis. Citicorp, for example, used to use a three-year planning horizon for developing and providing new financial services. That cycle has been cut to two years, and the bank hopes to get it to one very soon.[26]

Contingency Planning   Contingency planning is especially useful when environmental turbulence is likely. Proper contingency planning enables

The USAir Group recently bought Piedmont Airlines. Successful integration of the two airlines into one large carrier depended on employee participation. It also required the development of numerous tactical and operational plans in order for the consolidation to go off smoothly. As a result of the merger, USAir is now one of the largest airlines in the United States.

the organization to avoid crisis management. When a contingency event occurs, the prepared organization is able to make a smooth transition to the appropriate contingency plan rather than having to react hastily by throwing a new plan together on short notice.

In this section, we have discussed five barriers to effective planning and six methods for at least partially overcoming them. One generalization we can draw from this discussion is that planning is most effective when managers at all levels of the organization recognize the purposes, values, and limitations of planning. Another is that planning is most effective when managers understand the importance of treating planning as a critical priority and devoting the requisite care, attention, time, and resources to doing it right.

USING MBO TO IMPLEMENT PLANS

A well-developed and widely used method for implementing organizational plans is called management by objectives, or MBO. Although some experts view MBO as merely a technique for systematizing the goal-setting process, it actually serves to communicate and implement a wide range of organizational plans across a number of different organizational levels. We discuss first the nature and purpose of MBO, then the steps in the MBO process, and finally MBO's effectiveness as a planning technique.

The Nature and Purpose of MBO

■ **management by objectives (MBO)** The process of collaborative goal setting by a manager and subordinate. The extent to which goals are accomplished is a major factor in evaluating and rewarding the subordinate's performance

Although it's hard to pinpoint the actual origins of MBO, most people credit General Motors with being the first company to use it and Peter Drucker with being the first to describe it.[27] In **management by objectives**, or **MBO**, a manager and a subordinate collaborate in setting goals and developing plans for the subordinate, with the understanding that the extent to which these goals are attained will be a major factor in evaluating and rewarding the subordinate's performance.

MBO, then, is concerned with goal setting and planning for individual managers and their units or work groups, as opposed to the overall organization. However, goal setting and planning in an MBO system should start at the top of the organization, and the goals of top management should reflect the organization's overall goals.

The purpose of MBO is to give subordinates a voice in the goal-setting and planning process and to clarify for them exactly what they are expected to accomplish in a given time span. We will describe MBO in its "pure" form, although each organization that adopts MBO is likely to make at least minor adjustments to accommodate its own unique needs and perspectives.[28] Indeed, many firms have even come up with their own names for MBO. Some of the most popular include "management for (or by) results," "management by goals," and "objectives management." The basic mechanics of the MBO process, summarized in the next section, are shown in Figure 7.5.[29]

The MBO Process

It's important to keep in mind that the MBO process is being described here from an ideal perspective. In a real organization, the various steps and components of the process are likely to vary in importance and

FIGURE 7.5

The MBO Process

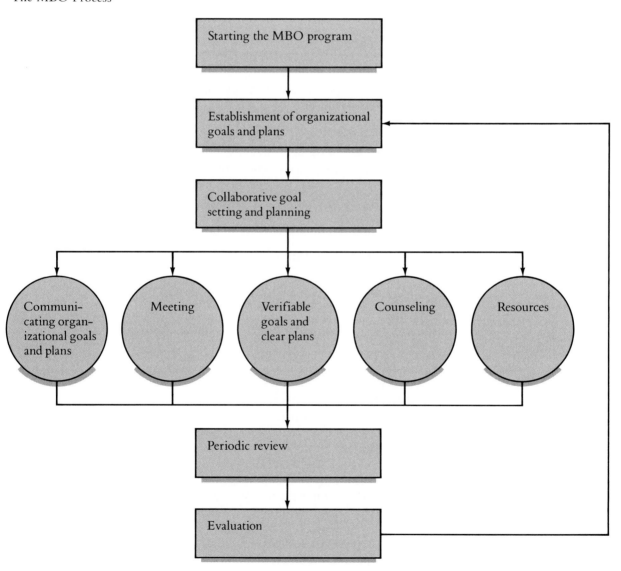

may even take a different sequence. For purposes of this presentation, however, we assume we are dealing with a fairly large organization that has just decided to adopt MBO.

Starting an MBO Program   For an MBO program to be successful, it must start at the top of the organization. Top managers must communicate why they have adopted MBO, what they think it will do, and the fact that they have accepted and are committed to MBO. Employees must also be educated about what MBO is and what their role in it will be.

Establishment of Organizational Goals and Plans   Having adopted the MBO philosophy, managers must develop overall organizational goals and plans. (This is probably already being done as a part of the organization's normal planning process.) Goals and plans are developed by top management and flow from the organization's basic mission and strategy. Some of the goals and plans will coincide with the organization's budgeting cycle; others will involve a longer time. The idea is that goals set at the top will cascade down throughout the organization in a systematic way.

Collaborative Goal Setting and Planning   Although establishing the organization's basic goals and plans is extremely important, collaborative goal setting and planning are the essence of MBO. The collaboration involves a series of distinct steps:

1. Superiors tell their subordinates what organizational and unit goals and plans have been established. Subordinates are asked to think about how they can help achieve these goals.
2. Superiors meet with their subordinates on a one-to-one basis. The purpose of these meetings is to arrive at a set of goals and plans for each subordinate that both the subordinate and the superior have helped develop and to which both are committed.
3. Each goal should be as verifiable (quantitative) as possible and should specify a time frame for its accomplishment. In general, the goals should meet the three criteria of specificity, conciseness, and time-relatedness, and they should be expressed in writing. Further, the plans developed to achieve the goals need to be as clearly stated as possible and relate to each goal in a direct way.
4. Superiors must play the role of counselors in the goal-setting and planning meeting. For example, they must ensure that the subordinates' goals and plans are attainable and workable and that they will facilitate both the unit's and the organization's goals and plans.
5. Finally, the meeting should spell out the resources that the subordinate will need in order to implement his or her plans and work effectively toward goal attainment. For example, if a sales manager's goals and plans for increasing sales are predicated on the assumption that his or her district will receive four new sales representatives and

Danskin's new president Rose Peabody Lynch accepted a goal from Danskin's owners, Esmark Corporation, of boosting its marketshare for exercise clothing from 35 percent to 50 percent. And she has subsequently convinced others in the company to accept similar or compatible goals for their areas of responsibility as well.

a 15 percent travel budget increase, those assumptions need to be agreed on. Similarly, if a production manager needs another quality control inspector to achieve a certain quality goal, some indication of whether the new inspector's position will be approved is required before the goal is accepted.

Periodic Reviews During the course of time specified for goal attainment, it is usually advisable to conduct periodic reviews. If the goals and plans are established for a one-year period, it may be a good idea for subordinate and supervisor to meet quarterly to discuss progress to date. Additions to, deletions from, and notes regarding the goals and plans of a particular employee may be appropriate, especially if organizational goals and plans have changed or if necessary resources are unavailable.

Evaluation At the end of the MBO cycle, the manager meets with each subordinate again to review the degree of goal attainment. They discuss which goals the employee was able to meet and which were not met in the context of the original plans. The reasons for both success and failure are explored. (This is the diagnostic phase.) Finally, the employee is rewarded (praise, a pay increase, or promotion) on the basis of his or her goal attainment. In an ongoing MBO program, the evaluation meeting may also serve as the collaborative goal-setting and planning meeting for the next time period.

The Effectiveness of MBO

A fairly large number of organizations use some form of MBO. "Management in Practice" illustrates how Cypress Semiconductor, a fast-growing California firm, uses MBO. Other MBO users include Alcoa, Tenneco, Du Pont, General Motors, Boeing, Caterpillar, Westinghouse, and Black & Decker.[30] In fact, approximately 40 percent of the companies on *Fortune*'s list of the 500 largest industrial firms in the United States use some form of MBO. As might be expected, MBO has both strengths and weaknesses.

Strengths A primary benefit of MBO is improved employee motivation. By clarifying exactly what is expected, by allowing the employee a voice in determining expectations, and by basing rewards on the achievement of those expectations, organizations create a powerful motivational system for their employees.

Communication is also enhanced through the process of goal and plan discussion and collaboration. And performance appraisals may be done more objectively, with less reliance on arbitrary or subjective assessment. MBO also focuses attention on appropriate goals and plans, helps identify superior managerial talent for future promotion, and

MANAGEMENT IN PRACTICE

MBO AT CYPRUS SEMICONDUCTOR

Cyprus Semiconductor Corporation has consistently remained profitable in an industry characterized by horrendous ups and downs. It has done so because of the technological developments it has wrought and the precision of its production and management.

Sales revenues at Cypress rose from just over $3 million in 1984 to well over $80 million by 1988. Net income rose along with sales, and profit margins at Cypress are now running at about 18 percent, which is very good in that industry. Needless to say, the book value per share of stock also has risen—by a multiple of 8 in that same time period. The technological developments that led to this financial success were made possible by precision in management, especially careful and detailed goal setting and planning.

The key to goal setting and planning at Cypress is known as a "turbo MBO." This is an elaborate, computerized management-by-objectives (MBO) system developed by T. J. Rogers, the president and CEO of Cypress. With this system, thousands of goals for each of the several hundred employees are set each and every week and then monitored to assure their successful and timely completion. The system does not stop mistakes, but it can identify them so early that they can be rectified before they become serious.

Every Monday, project groups map out everything that has to be done during the week, enter that information into the computer system, and get to work. On Tuesday, managers sit down at their computers, review the goals for their subordinates, and adjust them so that no one is over- or underworked. On Wednesday, the president and vice presidents review the status of all goals (in 1987 there were 3,543 goals in the system). If a manager is behind in several goals, a vice president will work with him or her to get them in line; if a vice president cannot get his or her managers operating at acceptable levels, the president investigates the problem to seek a more permanent solution such as assigning more personnel to the tasks in the affected area. Although this process occurs each week, it involves only about six hours of any given manager's or vice president's time.

The system cuts in half the time it used to take for new products to be developed and delivered to market. Thus it enables Cypress to start obtaining revenues faster than most other firms in the industry. Interestingly, the system does not involve highly complex software or equipment. The managers and executives all have microcomputers and the company has a minicomputer, all of which are linked together.

REFERENCES: "A Start-up's New 'Engine' Could Lead the 32-Bit Derby," *Business Week*, July 4, 1988, p. 112; William M. Alpert, "Speed Freaks: Two Newcomers Cash In on Fast Chips," *Barron's*, May 23, 1988, pp. 15, 42–43; Steven B. Kaufman, "The Goal System That Drives Cypress," *Business Month*, July 1987, pp. 30–32.

---

provides a systematic management philosophy that can have a positive effect on the overall organization.

MBO facilitates control—the process of monitoring progress toward goal attainment. The periodic development and subsequent evaluation of individual goals and plans helps keep the organization on course toward its own long-run goals and plans.

Criticisms MBO has been criticized for certain shortcomings. Perhaps the major problem that can derail an MBO program is lack of top-management support. Some organizations decide to use MBO, but then its implementation is delegated to lower management. This limits the program's effectiveness, because the goals and plans cascading throughout the organization may not actually be the goals and plans of top management and because others in the organization are not motivated to accept and become committed to them.

Another problem with MBO is that some firms overemphasize quantitative goals and plans and burden their systems with too much paperwork and record keeping. Some managers will not or cannot sit down and work out goals and plans with their subordinates. Rather, they "suggest" or even "assign" goals and plans to people. The result is resentment and a lack of commitment to the MBO program.[31]

SUMMARY OF KEY POINTS

After plans have been developed, the manager must address how they will be achieved. This often involves tactical and operational plans. Tactical plans are at the middle of the organization and have an intermediate time horizon and moderate scope. Operational plans are at the lower levels of the organization, have a shorter time horizon, and are narrower in scope.

Tactical plans are developed to implement specific parts of a strategic plan. They must flow from strategy, deal with specific resource and time issues, and commit human resources. It is also important that tactical plans be effectively executed.

Operational plans are derived from a tactical plan and are aimed at achieving one or more operational goals. Two major types of operational plans are single-use and standing plans. Single-use plans are designed to carry out a course of action that is not likely to be repeated in the future. Programs and projects are examples of single-use plans. Standing plans are designed to carry out a course of action that is likely to be repeated several times. Policies, standard operating procedures, and rules and regulations are all standing plans.

Contingency planning is the determination of alternative courses of action to be taken if an intended plan of action is unexpectedly disrupted or rendered inappropriate. Contingency planning is an increasingly important part of the planning process in many organizations.

Barriers to the planning process include dynamic and complex environments, a reluctance to establish goals, resistance to change, various constraints, and the time and expense involved. Methods for overcoming these barriers include starting at the top, recognizing the limits of planning, careful communication, a broad base of participation, effective integration of time frames, and contingency planning.

One particularly useful technique for implementing plans is management by objectives, or MBO. MBO is a process of collaborative goal setting and planning. Superiors and subordinates jointly establish and record for the subordinate goals and plans that are consistent with the goals of the superior. At the end of a designated period of time, the subordinate's performance is evaluated, and the degree of goal attainment becomes the basis for rewards.

DISCUSSION QUESTIONS

Questions for Review

1. What is tactical planning? What is operational planning? What are the similarities and differences between them?
2. What is contingency planning? Is being flexible about your plans the same as contingency planning? Why or why not?
3. What are the barriers to planning? How can they be overcome? Can you think of any ways to overcome any of the barriers other than the ways identified in the text?
4. Describe the MBO process and indicate how to assess its effectiveness.

Questions for Analysis

5. Which kind of plan, tactical or operational, should an organization develop first? Why? Does the order of development really make a difference as long as plans of both types are made?
6. Can you think of a time when an organization to which you belong avoided one or more roadblocks to planning? Describe what happened and why.
7. Can operational plans be developed for each level of strategy (refer to Chapter 6) for an organization? Why or why not?

Questions for Application

8. Interview a college or university official to determine the use of single-use and standing plans at your institution. How were these plans developed?
9. Interview a local government official to determine the nature of contingency planning being done by that level of government. What is the official's assessment of its effectiveness?
10. Survey local small businesses to determine the extent of use and effectiveness of MBO. Share your findings with the class and discuss them in terms of why the usage rate is what it is.

NOTES

1. "Intel—The Next Revolution," *Business Week*, September 26, 1988, pp. 74–80; "Intel Is Developing a New Type of Chip," *The Wall Street Journal*, January 12, 1989, p. B4; Carrie Gottlieb, "Intel's Plan for Staying on Top," *Fortune*, March 27, 1989, pp. 98–100.
2. See Charles W. L. Hill and Gareth R. Jones, *Strategic Management: An Analytical Approach* (Boston: Houghton Mifflin, 1989), for an overview of planning.
3. Arie P. De Geus, "Planning as Learning," *Harvard Business Review*, March–April 1988, pp. 70–74.

4. Dennis P. Slevin and Jeffrey K. Pinto, "Balancing Strategy and Tactics in Project Implementation," *Sloan Management Review*, Fall 1987, pp. 33–41.

5. James Brian Quinn, Henry Mintzberg, and Robert M. James, *The Strategy Process* (Englewood Cliffs, N.J.: Prentice-Hall, 1988).

6. Vasudevan Ramanujam and N. Venkatraman, "Planning System Characteristics and Planning Effectiveness," *Strategic Management Journal*, Vol. 8, 1987, pp. 453–468.

7. Gary Hector, "Yes, You *Can* Manage Long Term," *Fortune*, November 21, 1988, pp. 64–76; "Coca Cola Starts Drive to Pull Diet Coke Ahead of Pepsi," *The Wall Street Journal*, January 24, 1989, p. B1.

8. Henry Mintzberg, "Crafting Strategy," *Harvard Business Review*, July–August 1987, pp. 66–75.

9. Hector, "Yes, You *Can* Manage Long Term." See also "How Disney Does It," *Newsweek*, April 3, 1989, pp. 48–54.

10. "Sears to Sell Unit and Tower, Buy Back Stock," *The Wall Street Journal*, November 1, 1988, p. A3; "Will the Big Markdown Get the Big Store Moving Again?" *Business Week*, March 13, 1989, pp. 110–114.

11. Bill Saporito, "Ganging Up on Black & Decker," *Fortune*, December 23, 1985, pp. 63–72; John Huey, "The New Power in Black & Decker," *Fortune*, January 2, 1989, pp. 89–94.

12. Neil C. Churchill, "Budget Choice: Planning vs. Control," *Harvard Business Review*, July–August 1984, pp. 150–164.

13. Thomas L. Wheelon and J. David Hunger, *Strategic Management and Business Policy*, 3rd ed. (Reading, Mass.: Addison-Wesley, 1989).

14. Jaclyn Fierman, "How Gallo Crushes the Competition," *Fortune*, September 1, 1986, pp. 23–31.

15. Robert D. Gilbreath, "Planning for the Unexpected," *The Journal of Business Strategy*, Vol. 8, 1987, pp. 44–49.

16. David M. Schweiger, William R. Sandberg, and James W. Ragan, "Group Approaches for Improving Strategic Decision Making: A Comparative Analysis of Dialectical Inquiry, Devil's Advocacy, and Consensus," *Academy of Management Journal*, March 1986, pp. 51–71.

17. "Intel—The Next Revolution."

18. Gilbreath, "Planning for the Unexpected." See also Donald C. Hambrick and David Lei, "Toward an Empirical Prioritization of Contingency Variables for Business Strategy," *Academy of Management Journal*, December 1985, pp. 763–788.

19. "Steve Jobs Comes Back," *Newsweek*, October 24, 1988, pp. 46–51.

20. John J. Curran, "Companies That Rob the Future," *Fortune*, July 4, 1988, pp. 84–89.

21. Curran, "Companies That Rob the Future."

22. Curran, "Companies That Rob the Future."

23. See William Bridges, "Managing Organizational Transitions," *Organizational Dynamics*, Summer 1986, pp. 24–33.

24. Hector, "Yes, You *Can* Manage Long Term."

25. Kenneth Labich, "The Seven Keys to Business Leadership," *Fortune*, October 24, 1988, pp. 58–66; Alex Taylor III, "Fords for the Future," *Fortune*, January 16, 1989, pp. 36–49.

26. Jeremy Main, "The Winning Organization," *Fortune*, September 26, 1988, pp. 50–60.

27. Peter F. Drucker, *The Practice of Management* (New York: Harper & Brothers, 1954).

28. See John M. Ivancevich, J. Timothy McMahon, J. William Streidl, and Andrew D. Szilagyi, "Goal Setting: The Tenneco Approach to Personnel Development and Management Effectiveness," *Organizational Dynamics*, Winter 1978, pp. 48–80, for a discussion of one variation of MBO.
29. Stephen J. Carroll and Henry L. Tosi, *Management by Objectives* (New York: Macmillan, 1973); A. P. Raia, *Managing by Objectives* (Glenview, Ill.: Scott, Foresman, 1974).
30. For descriptions of MBO at Tenneco and Black & Decker, respectively, see Ivancevich et al., "Goal Setting"; and Carroll and Tosi, *Management by Objectives*.
31. See Jack N. Kondrasuk, "Studies in MBO Effectiveness," *Academy of Management Review*, July 1981, pp. 419–430, for a review of the strengths and weaknesses of MBO.

CASE 7.1

Campbell's Plans for Soups and More

Campbell's was founded in 1869 by Joseph Campbell and Abram Anderson. Like other soup companies, it struggled at first because it was constrained by shipping problems—high costs and cans that were heavy because the soups were water based. Not until around the turn of the century, when a Campbell's chemist overcame those problems by inventing condensed soup, did the firm become market leader. In 1911, Campbell's became one of the first American companies to sell a brand-name food product throughout the United States. Campbell's invention of condensed soup enabled it to take over the canned-soup business. Campbell's has never lost that dominance in the soup industry, and it has been somewhat successful in transferring that dominance to other areas as well.

During the late 1960s, Campbell's dominance was challenged directly. H. J. Heinz decided to use its reputation for quality and its expertise in marketing, which it derived from its number 1 position in the ketchup market, to take on Campbell's in the soup market. Heinz held over half of the British soup market and felt confident that it could take market share from Campbell's in the United States. Heinz introduced new products, advertised heavily, and did everything it could, but Campbell's market position was unassailable. In the period just following that direct challenge, in the early 1970s, Campbell's market share was in excess of 80 percent, and its continued dominance seemed assured. Nevertheless, by the late 1980s, Campbell's market share had dropped to around 60 percent.

If the powerful onslaught of Heinz could not take share from Campbell's, who was able to do so? Campbell's lost market share to an interesting mixture of companies: Progresso of St. Louis, Missouri; Thomas J. Lipton, the Anglo-Dutch tea and soup company; and Japanese noodle manufacturers Maruchan and Nissin Foods.

Campbell's countered these market-share losses with advertising, promotion, and new products. In 1987 Campbell's spent five times more on advertising than did its nearest competitor. That effort seemed to have far less impact than was expected or hoped for. One reason is that commercial television advertising is losing its impact as more and more households turn to cable networks and use VCRs to view movies. Another reason is that smaller, entrepreneurial businesses were being more innovative and aggressive than was Campbell's. Further, Campbell's was introducing a wealth of new products of its own, and some of those ended up substituting for its already existing products rather than staving off competition.

Campbell's quickly began to develop plans to offset the lackluster performance of its usual approaches. One of the most ambitious of those plans involved a major switch in concept—from national to regional marketing.

In the past, Campbell's had always used a nationwide marketing approach. If it were going to discount a particular soup flavor, the discount would apply nationwide despite the fact that discounting would be unnecessary in some areas and might need to be even greater in other areas. However, as part of its effort to stave off competition, Campbell's moved to establish programs that could be used to counter the regional efforts of competitors and in some areas even agreed to honor competitors' coupons.

Another of Campbell's plans was to introduce new products that are, in fact, new and not merely extensions of existing products. Many of the new products have a regional or ethnic orientation. The Prego brand was designed to directly counter the Progresso brand. Casera was developed as a Caribbean-Hispanic oriented brand to counter Goya Foods. Pepperidge Farm, a Campbell's subsidiary, came out with its own pricy soups to move into the high-priced end of the market. These brands are so different from Campbell's usual red and white brand that many consumers are not even aware that they are manufactured by Campbell's.

Campbell's biggest plan continues under development, however. It involves moving away from cans toward other forms of packaging. There is mounting evidence that cans are no longer the dominant form of packaging even for food products containing significant amounts of moisture. Plastic and coated-paper containers, many of which are microwavable, are increasing in numbers, quality, and consumer acceptance every year. Campbell's must develop an effective plan to move away from cans and to utilize those forms of packaging.

As a corporation, Campbell's is also moving to become less reliant on soups. It brought out over 500 new products in the late 1980s and strengthened lines such as Pepperidge Farms and Mrs. Paul's to enable them to more solidly contribute to the profit picture of the corporation. In addition, Campbell's is shoring up offerings in vegetables, sauces, and the like to ensure that it is a more broadly based food corporation in the future.

Questions

1. What kinds of tactical and operational plans can you identify at Campbell's? Cite specific examples.
2. In what areas do you think Campbell's could and should use contingency planning? Why?
3. Can you identify any possible barriers to effective operational planning at Campbell's? How has or can Campbell's overcome those barriers?
4. How could Campbell's use MBO to improve its tactical and operational planning processes?

REFERENCES: Bill Saporito, "The Fly in Campbell's Soup," *Fortune*, May 9, 1988, pp. 67–70; "America's Champion Corporations," *Management Today*, July 1986, pp. 53–57; Judann Dagnoli and Gary Levin, "Pasta Sauce Rivals Stirring," *Advertising Age*, March 21, 1988, p. 2.

CASE 7.2

France's Thomson Plans Big

In 1987, France's Thomson S.A. bought 80 percent of General Electric's consumer-electronics business, including the RCA brand. In addition, Thomson bought the Ferguson television and VCR operations of Thorn EMI PLC. Those two major acquisitions enabled Paris-based Thomson to become one of the world's largest consumer-electronics corporations. Thomson had long been France's leading electronics manufacturer as well as Europe's biggest defense electronic contractor; now it was a worldwide electronics corporation with real clout. On the basis of 1986 data, Thomson would be the second-largest producer of color television sets in the world, behind Netherlands' Philips but ahead of Japan's Matsushita. By contrast, it would also be nearly triple the size of the largest U.S. producer, Zenith.

The Thomson purchases also meant that although the Japanese had six of the top ten producers of color televisions in the world and manufactured just over 18 million sets in 1986, Europe had the world's two largest producers and manufactured 15 million sets. Thomson's plan was to emerge with a corporation large enough to compete directly with Japan's major manufacturers. After the GE purchase, Thomson became the number 1 seller of color television sets in the United States, with approximately 23 percent of the market. It was about even with Matsushita in selling VCRs in the United States. The Japanese, who were initially caught off guard by the GE and Thomson deal, quickly responded in order to keep international competition in this market extremely high and active.

Thomson planned to capitalize not only on its size, which enabled it to take advantage of economies of scale, but on the advantages of its and GE/RCA's experience in marketing and distribution. Further, Thomson planned to become a leader in technology. The feeling was that only very large companies could come up with the funds for the technological research and development necessary to be a market leader. The purchase was intended to provide funding so that Thomson could develop its own new products, such as high-resolution digital televisions and stereos.

However, as late as the latter part of 1987, Thomson had not yet developed a specific plan for the combination and integration of the research and development units from Thomson and General Electric. That plan was obviously soon to come, however, since Thomson had reorganized its operations, creating Thomson Consumer Electronics as an over $3 billion unit of Thomson S.A. That reorganization was done to separate consumer electronics from defense and other aspects of the parent firm. The separation was especially important because Thomson was also moving to acquire other businesses to add to its strength in defense electronics. Those acquisitions would need to be absorbed smoothly, too.

Part of Thomson's long-term plan for success, especially in consumer electronics, depends on its being a state-owned corporation. That has two very important implications for Thomson. First, the nation of France will help provide the financial backing and leverage necessary to ensure supplier cooperation and government purchases, particularly in defense. These are important to Thomson to keep its cash flow steady as it absorbs its new acquisitions and organizes its operations, marketing, and distribution in consumer electronics. Second, as a state-owned venture Thomson does not have to achieve the same high, 15 percent return on assets for its products and divisions that General Electric always sought. Thomson is also planning on the European Economic Community's anti-dumping campaign to help it compete with Asian, particularly Japanese, competitors for a few years. During that time, Thomson plans to develop Far Eastern connections so as to be in a better position in the long term.

Thomson had not planned for all of the changes that its new acquisitions entailed. One unplanned problem was executive retention. RCA had recently been purchased by General Electric. So when GE sold its consumer-electronics business to Thomson, it was the second major reorganization in just a few years for many former RCA executives. One key executive left for that reason, and Thomson had to replace him on relatively short notice. A second unplanned problem was that a new advertising agency had to be selected to work with the newly organized consumer-electronics division. Each of these matters was dealt with expeditiously and effectively, but each consumed time and energy that had not been planned for.

Questions

1. What kinds of tactical and operational plans can you identify at Thomson? Cite specific examples.
2. Contingency planning should be useful to Thomson. In what specific areas could Thomson use contingency planning? Why?
3. What barriers to effective operational planning can you identify at Thomson? How could Thomson overcome those barriers? In what way do the barriers suggest why Thomson did not plan for a couple of the major problems resulting from its acquisitions?
4. If you were a planning consultant to Thomson, what suggestions would you make and why would you make them?

REFERENCES: "Thomson Folds RCA-GE into European Operation," *Television Digest*, June 13, 1988, p. 12; "New Thomson Alignment," *Television Digest*, June 13, 1988, p. 14; "Thomson's Miller to Join Partnership, Giving Up Life of Corporate Vagabond," *The Wall Street Journal*, April 11, 1988, p. 34; "Thomson S.A. Unit Picks Johnson Fogliano for Two Top Positions," *The Wall Street Journal*, April 13, 1988, p. 36; "Overnight, Thomson Has the Stuff to Take on the Titans," *Business Week*, August 10, 1987, pp. 36–37.

ENHANCEMENT MODULE 2

Planning Tools

Managers and engineers at Northern Research & Engineering Corporation, a consulting subsidiary of Ingersoll-Rand Co., were recently planning and designing a new factory for a customer. Their initial projections indicated that the plant would need 77 machine tools performing at least sixteen different processes. However, after plugging all their data into a computer and creating a sophisticated simulated model of the plant, they learned that they could eliminate four of the machines and save their customer $750,000.[1]

Just a few years ago, Northern Research & Engineering would have had to rely solely on their first projections. As a result, their client would have spent more money than necessary in opening its new plant. New technology and sophisticated planning techniques enabled the company to save a considerable sum of money. This module summarizes a number of planning tools and techniques that managers can use to enhance their efficiency and effectiveness. We first describe forecasting, an extremely important tool, and then discuss several other planning techniques. We conclude by assessing their strengths and weaknesses.

FORECASTING

To plan, managers must make assumptions about future events. But unlike wizards of old, planners cannot simply look into a crystal ball. Instead, they must develop forecasts of probable future circumstances. **Forecasting** is the process of developing assumptions or premises about the future that managers can use in planning or decision making.[2]

Sales and Revenue Forecasting

As the term implies, sales forecasting is concerned with predicting future sales. Because monetary resources (derived mainly from sales) are necessary to finance both current and future operations, knowledge of future sales is of vital importance. Sales forecasting is something that every business, from Exxon to a neighborhood pizza parlor, must do. Consider, for example, the following questions that a manager might need to answer:

1. How much of each of our products should we produce next week, next month, and next year?
2. How much money will we have available to spend on research and development and on new-product test marketing?
3. When and to what degree will we need to expand our existing production facilities?
4. How should we respond to union demands for a 15 percent pay increase?
5. If we borrow money for expansion, can we pay it back?

None of these questions can be adequately answered without some notion of what future revenues are likely to be. Thus sales forecasting is generally one of the first steps in planning.

Unfortunately, the term sales forecasting suggests that this form of forecasting is appropriate only for organizations that have something to sell. But other kinds of organizations also depend on financial resources, and so they also must forecast. The University of South Carolina, for example, must forecast future state aid before planning course offerings, staff size, and so on. Hospitals must forecast their future income from patient fees, insurance payments, and other sources to assess their ability to expand. Although we will continue to use the conventional term, keep in mind that what is really at issue is **revenue forecasting**.

Several sources are used to develop a sales forecast. Previous sales figures and any obvious trends, such as the company's growth or stability, usually serve as the base. General economic indicators, technological improvements, new marketing strategies, and the competition's behavior all may be added together to ensure an accurate forecast. Once projected, the sales (or revenues) forecast becomes a guiding framework for a variety of other activities. Raw-material expenditures, advertising budgets, sales-commission structures, and similar operating costs are all based on projected sales figures.

Chapter 5 explains how firms integrate short-range, intermediate, and long-range planning horizons by means of systematic updating and refining. In like fashion, organizations often forecast sales across several time horizons. The longer-run forecasts may then be updated and refined as various shorter-run cycles are completed. For obvious reasons, a forecast should be as accurate as possible, and the accuracy of sales forecasting tends to increase as organizations learn from their previous forecasting experience.[3] But the more uncertain and complex future conditions are likely to be, the more difficult it is to develop accurate forecasts. To partially offset these problems, forecasts are more useful to managers if they are expressed as a range rather than as an absolute index or number. If projected sales increases are expected to be in the range of 10 to 12 percent, a manager can consider all the implications for the entire range. A 10 percent increase could dictate one set of activities; a 12 percent increase could call for a different set of activities.

Other Types of Forecasting

Technological forecasting is another type of forecasting used by many organizations. It focuses on predicting what future technologies are likely to emerge and when they are likely to be economically feasible.[4] In an era when technological breakthrough and innovation have become the rule rather than the exception, it is important that managers be able to anticipate new developments. If a manager invests heavily in existing technology (such as production processes, equipment, and computer systems) and the technology becomes obsolete in the near future, the company has wasted its resources. This was the mistake that Gulf made a few years ago. Gulf developed a strategy to become the number 2 company in the low-density polyethylene film market over a five-year period. An explicit assumption made in

building a new plant was that no new technological breakthroughs were likely. Thus, when Union Carbide developed a new process that cut production costs by 20 percent, Gulf's plant was obsolete before it was even finished.

The most striking technological innovations in recent years have been in electronics, especially semiconductors. Home computers, electronic games, and sophisticated communications equipment are all evidence of the electronics explosion. In contrast to Gulf, Steven Jobs did an excellent job of technological forecasting during the development of the NeXT computer. At three different stages, he committed to future actions based on technologies that did not exist at the time. In each instance, he gambled that breakthroughs would be achieved before he needed them—and he was right in each instance.[5] Given the increasing importance of technology and the rapid pace of technological innovation, it follows that managers will grow increasingly concerned with technological forecasting in the years to come.

Other types of forecasting are also important to many organizations. Resource forecasting projects the organization's future needs for and the availability of human resources, raw materials, and other resources. General economic conditions are the subject of economic forecasts. For example, some organizations undertake population or market-size forecasting. And government fiscal policy and various government regulations affect most firms. Virtually any component in an organization's environment may be an appropriate area for forecasting.

Quantitative Forecasting Techniques

To carry out the various kinds of forecasting we have identified, managers use several different techniques. Time-series analysis and causal modeling are two common quantitative techniques.

Time-Series Analysis   The underlying assumption of time-series analysis is that the past is a good predictor of the future. This technique is most useful when the manager has quite a lot of historical data available and when stable trends and patterns are apparent. In a time-series analysis, the variable under consideration (such as sales or enrollment) is plotted across time, and a "best-fit" line is identified.[6] Figure EM2.1 shows how a time-series analysis might look. The dots represent the number of units sold for each year from 1982 through 1990. The "best-fit" line has also been drawn in. This is the line around which the dots cluster with the least amount of variability. A manager who wants to know what sales to expect in 1991 simply extends the line. In this case, the projection would be around 8,200 units.

It is important to add that real time-series analysis involves much more than simply plotting sales data and then using a ruler and a pencil to draw and extend the line. Sophisticated mathematical procedures, among other things, are necessary to account for seasonal and cyclical fluctuations and to identify

the true "best-fit" line. In real situations, data seldom follow the neat pattern found in Figure EM2.1. Indeed, the data points may be so widely dispersed that they mask meaningful trends from all but painstaking, computer-assisted inspection.

Causal Modeling   Another useful forecasting technique is causal modeling. Actually, the term causal modeling represents a group of several different techniques.[7] Table EM2.1 summarizes three of the most useful approaches. Regression models are equations created to predict a variable (such as sales volume) that depends on a number of other variables (such as price and advertising). The variable being predicted is called the dependent variable; the variables used to make the prediction are called independent variables. The following is a typical regression equation:

FIGURE EM2.1

An Example of Time-Series Analysis

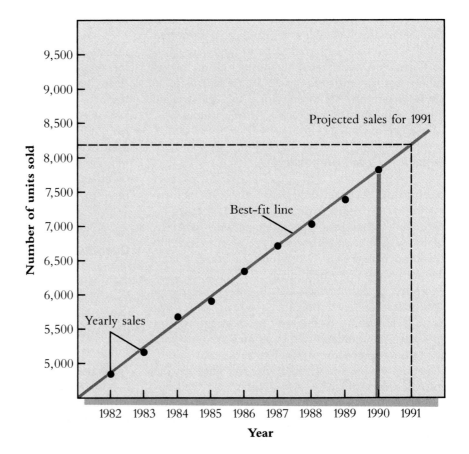

TABLE EM2.1

Summary of Causal Modeling Forecasting Techniques

Regression models	Used to predict one variable (called the dependent variable) on the basis of known or assumed other variables (called independent variables). For example, we might predict future sales based on the values of price, advertising, and economic levels.
Econometric models	Make use of several multiple-regression equations to consider the impact of major economic shifts. For example, we might want to predict what impact the migration toward the Sun Belt might have on our organization.
Economic indicators	Various population statistics, indexes, or parameters that predict organizationally relevant variables such as discretionary income. Examples include cost-of-living index, inflation rate, and level of unemployment.

$$y = ax_1 + bx_2 + cx_3 + d$$

where

$y =$ the dependent variable (sales, in this case)

$x_1, x_2,$ and $x_3 =$ independent variables (advertising budget, price, and commissions)

$a, b,$ and $c =$ weights for the independent variables calculated during development of the regression model

$d =$ a constant

To use the model, a manager could plug in various alternatives for advertising budget, price, and commissions and then compute y. The resultant value of y represents the forecast.[8]

Econometric models employ regression techniques at a much more complex level. Econometric models attempt to predict major economic shifts and the potential impact of those shifts on the organization. They might be used to predict various age, ethnic, and economic groups that will characterize different regions of the United States in the year 2000 and to further predict the kinds of products and services these groups may want. A complete econometric model may consist of hundreds or even thousands of equations. Computers are almost always necessary to apply them. Given the complexities involved in developing econometric models, many firms that decide to use them rely on outside consultants specializing in this approach.

Economic indicators, another form of causal model, are population statistics or indexes that reflect the economic well-being of a population. Examples of widely used economic indicators include the current rates of inflation and unemployment. In using such indicators, the manager draws on past experiences that have revealed a relationship between a particular indicator and one or more facets of the company's operations. Pitney Bowes's Data Documents Division, for example, has found that it can predict future sales of its business forms largely on the basis of current GNP estimates and other economic growth indexes.

Qualitative Forecasting Techniques

There are several qualitative techniques that organizations use to develop forecasts. A qualitative technique is one that relies more on individual or group judgment or opinion rather than on sophisticated mathematical analyses. The Delphi procedure, described in Chapter 4 as a mechanism for managing group decision-making activities, can also be used to develop forecasts. A variation of it—the jury-of-expert-opinion approach—involves using the basic Delphi process with members of top management. In this instance, top management serves as a collection of experts asked to make a prediction about something—competitive behavior, trends in product demand, and so forth. Either a pure Delphi or a jury-of-expert-opinion approach might be useful in technological forecasting.

The sales-force-composition method of sales forecasting is a pooling of the predictions and opinions of experienced sales personnel. Because of their experience, these individuals are often able to forecast quite accurately what various customers will do. Management takes these forecasts and combines and interprets the data in order to create plans.

The customer evaluation technique goes beyond an organization's sales force and collects data from customers of the organization. The customers provide estimates of their own future needs for the goods and services that the organization supplies. Managers must combine, interpret, and act on this information. It is important to recognize that there are two major limitations to this approach. Customers may be less interested in taking time to develop accurate predictions than are members of the organization itself, and the method makes no provision for including any new customers that the organization may acquire.

Selecting an appropriate forecasting technique can be as important as applying it correctly. Some techniques are appropriate only for specific circumstances. For example, the sales-force-composition technique is good only for sales forecasting. Other techniques, like the Delphi method, are useful in a variety of situations. Some techniques, like the econometric models, require extensive use of computers, whereas others, like customer evaluation models, can be used with little mathematical expertise. For the most part, selection of a particular technique depends on the nature of the problem, the experience and preferences of the manager, and available resources.[9]

OTHER PLANNING TECHNIQUES

Of course, planning involves more than just forecasting. Other quantitative techniques that are of help for a variety of planning purposes include linear programming, breakeven analysis, and simulations.

Linear Programming

Linear programming is one of the most widely used quantitative tools for planning.[10] Linear programming is a procedure for calculating the optimal combination of resources and activities.[11] It is appropriate when there is some objective to be met (such as a sales quota or a certain production level) within a set of constraints (such as a limited advertising budget or limited production capabilities).

Assume that a small electronics company produces two basic products—a high-quality cable television tuner and a high-quality receiver for picking up television audio and playing it through a stereo amplifier. Both products go through the same two departments: production, and inspection and testing. Each product has a known profit margin and a high level of demand. The production manager's job is to produce the optimal combination of tuners (T) and receivers (R) in order to maximize profits and use the time in production (PR) and in inspection and testing (IT) most efficiently. Table EM2.2 gives the information needed for the use of linear programming to solve this problem.

The objective function is an equation that represents what we want to achieve. In technical terms, it is a mathematical representation of the desirability of the consequences of a particular decision. In our example, the objective function can be represented as follows:

$$\text{Maximize profit} = \$30X_T + \$20X_R$$

where

TABLE EM2.2

Production Data for Tuners
and Receivers

	Number of Hours Required per Unit		Production Capacity for Day (in Hours)
Department	**Tuners (T)**	**Receivers (R)**	
Production (PR)	10	6	150
Inspection and testing (IT)	4	4	80
Profit margin	$30	$20	

T = the number of tuners to be produced

R = the number of receivers to be produced

The $30 and $20 figures are the respective profit margins of the tuner and receiver, as noted in Table EM2.2. The objective, then, is to maximize profits.

However, this objective must be accomplished within a set of constraints. In our example, the constraints are the time required to produce each product in each department and the total amount of time available. These data are also found in Table EM2.2, and can be used to construct the relevant constraint equations:

$$10T + 6R \leq 150$$

$$4T + 4R \leq 80$$

(that is, we cannot use more capacity than is available), and, of course,

$$T \geq 0$$

$$R \geq 0$$

The set of equations consisting of the objective function and constraints can be solved graphically. We first assume that production of each product is maximized when production of the other is at zero. The resultant solutions are then plotted on a coordinate axis. In the PR department, if $T = 0$, then

$$10T + 6R \leq 150$$

$$10(0) + 6R \leq 150$$

$$R \leq 25$$

In the same department, if $R = 0$, then

$$10T + 6R \leq 150$$

$$10T + 6(0) \leq 150$$

$$T \leq 15$$

Similarly, in the IT department, if no tuners are produced,

$$4T + 4R \leq 80$$

$$4(0) + 4R \leq 80$$

$$R \leq 20$$

and, if no receivers are produced,

$$4T + 4R \leq 80$$

$$4T + 4(0) \leq 80$$

$$T \leq 20$$

The four resulting inequalities are graphed in Figure EM2.2. The shaded region represents the feasibility space, or production combinations that do not exceed the capacity of either department. The optimal number of products will be defined at one of the four corners of the shaded area—that is, the firm should produce 20 receivers only (point C), 15 tuners only (point B), 13 receivers and 7 tuners (point E), or no products at all. With the constraint that production of both tuners and receivers must be greater than zero, it follows that point E is the optimal solution. That combination requires 148 hours in PR and 80 hours in IT and yields $470 in

FIGURE EM2.2

The Graphical Solution of a
Linear Programming Problem

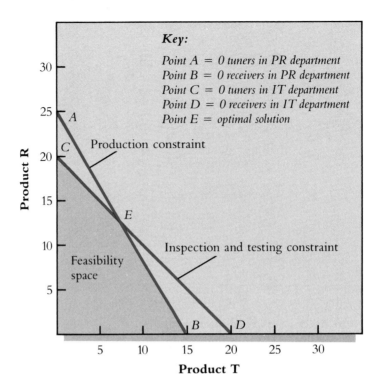

Key:

Point A = 0 tuners in PR department
Point B = 0 receivers in PR department
Point C = 0 tuners in IT department
Point D = 0 receivers in IT department
Point E = optimal solution

Breakeven Analysis

Linear programming is called a normative procedure because it prescribes the optimal solution to a problem. Breakeven analysis is a descriptive procedure because it simply describes relationships among var-

profit. (Note that if only receivers were produced, the profit would be $400; producing only tuners would mean $450 in profit.)

Unfortunately, only two alternatives can be handled by the graphical method, and our example was extremely simple. When there are other alternatives, a complex algebraic method must be employed. Many real-world problems may require several hundred equations and variables. Clearly, computers are necessary to execute such sophisticated analyses. Linear programming is a powerful technique, playing a key role in both planning and decision making. It can be used to schedule production, select an optimal portfolio of investments, allocate sales representatives to territories, or produce an item at some minimum cost.[12]

iables; then it is up to the manager to make decisions. We can define breakeven analysis as a procedure for identifying the point at which revenues start covering their associated costs. It might be used to analyze the effects on profits of different price and output combinations or various levels of output.[13]

Figure EM2.3 represents the key cost variables in breakeven analysis. Creating most products or services includes three types of costs: fixed costs, variable costs, and total costs. Fixed costs are costs that are incurred regardless of what volume of output is being generated. They include rent or mortgage payments on the building, managerial salaries, and depreciation of plant and equipment. Variable costs are those that vary with the number of units produced, such as the cost of raw materials and direct labor used to make each unit. Total costs are simply fixed costs plus variable costs. Note that because of the fixed costs, the line for total costs never begins at zero.

Other important factors in breakeven analysis are revenue and profit. Revenue, the total dollar amount of sales, is computed by multiplying the number of

FIGURE EM2.3

An Example of Cost Factors for Breakeven Analysis

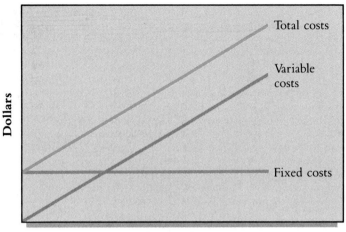

Total costs

Variable costs

Fixed costs

Dollars

Volume of output

units sold by the sales price of each unit. Profit is then determined by subtracting total costs from total revenues. When revenues and total costs are plotted on the same axes, the breakeven graph shown in Figure EM2.4 emerges. The point at which the lines representing total costs and total revenues cross is the breakeven point. If the company represented in Figure EM2.4 sells more units than are represented by point A, it will realize a profit; selling below that level will result in a loss.

Mathematically, the breakeven point (expressed as units of production or volume) is shown by the formula

$$BP = \frac{TFC}{P - VC}$$

where

$$BP = \text{breakeven point}$$

$$TFC = \text{total fixed costs}$$

$$P = \text{price per unit}$$

$$VC = \text{variable cost per unit}$$

Assume that you are considering the production of a new garden hoe with a curved handle. You have determined that an acceptable selling price will be $20. You have also determined that the variable costs per hoe will be $15, and you have total fixed costs of $400,000 per year. The question is how many hoes must you sell each year to break even.

Using the breakeven model, you find that

$$BP = \frac{TFC}{P - VC}$$

$$= \frac{400,000}{20 - 15}$$

$$= 80,000 \text{ units}$$

You must sell 80,000 hoes to break even. Further analysis would also show that if you could raise your price to $25 per hoe, you would need to sell only 40,000 to break even, and so on.

The state of New York used a breakeven analysis to evaluate seven different variations of prior approvals for its Medicaid service. Comparisons were conducted of the costs involved in each variation against savings gained from efficiency and improved quality of service. The state found that only three of the variations were cost effective.[14]

Breakeven analysis is a popular and important planning technique, but we should note its major weaknesses.[15] It considers revenues only up to the breakeven point, and it makes no allowance for the time value of money. For example, because the funds used to cover fixed and variable costs could be used for other purposes (such as investment), the organization is losing interest income by tying up its money prior to reaching the breakeven point. Thus, managers often used breakeven analysis as only the first step in planning. After the preliminary

FIGURE EM2.4

Breakeven Analysis

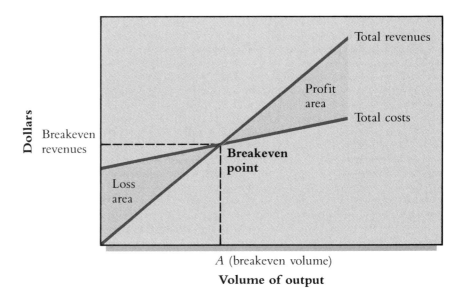

analysis has been completed, more sophisticated techniques (such as rate-of-return analysis or discounted-present-value analysis) are used. Those techniques can help the manager decide whether to proceed or to divert resources into other areas.

Simulations

Another useful planning device is simulation. The word "simulate" means to copy or to represent. An organizational simulation is a model of a real-world situation that can be manipulated to discover how it "behaves." Simulation is a descriptive rather than a prescriptive technique. A computer simulation of a new plant was the technique used by Northern Research & Engineering, as described at the beginning of this module.

Suppose the city of Denver was going to build a new airport. Issues to be addressed might include the number of runways, the direction of those runways, the number of terminals and gates, the allocation of various carriers among the terminals and gates, and the technology and human resources needed to achieve a target frequency of takeoffs and landings. (Of course, actually planning such an airport would involve many more variables than these.) A model could be constructed to simulate

these factors, as well as their interrelationships. The planner could then plug in several different values for each factor and observe the probable results.

Simulation problems are in some ways similar to those addressed by linear programming, but simulation is more useful in very complex situations characterized by diverse constraints and opportunities. The development of sophisticated simulation models may require the expertise of outside specialists or consultants, and the complexity of simulation almost always necessitates the use of a computer. For these reasons, simulation is most likely to be used as a technique for planning in large organizations that have the required resources.[16]

STRENGTHS AND WEAKNESSES OF PLANNING TOOLS

Like all issues confronting management, planning tools of the type described here have a number of strengths and weaknesses.

Weaknesses and Problems

One weakness of the planning tools discussed in this module is that they may not always adequately reflect reality. Even with the most sophisticated and powerful computer-assisted technique, reality must often be simplified. Many problems are also not amenable to quantitative analysis because important elements of them are intangible or nonquantifiable. Employee morale or satisfaction, for example, is often a major factor in managerial decisions.

The use of planning aids may also be quite costly. Few companies can afford to develop their own econometric models. Even though the computer explosion will increase the availability of quantitative aids, there is still some expense involved, and it will take time for many of these techniques to become widely used. Resistance to change also limits the use of planning tools in some settings. If a manager for a retail chain has always based decisions for new locations on personal visits, observations, and intuition, she or he may be less than eager to begin using a computer-based model for evaluating and selecting sites. Finally, problems may arise when managers have to rely on technical specialists to use sophisticated models. Experts trained in the use of complex mathematical procedures may not understand or appreciate other aspects of management.

Strengths and Advantages

On the plus side, planning tools offer many advantages. For situations that are amenable to quantification, they can bring sophisticated mathematical processes to bear on planning and decision making. Properly designed models and formulas also help decision makers "see reason." For example, a manager might not be inclined to introduce a new product line simply because she or he doesn't think it will be profitable. After seeing a forecast predicting first-year sales of 100,000 units coupled with a breakeven analysis showing profitability after only 20,000, however, the manager will probably change her or his mind. Thus, rational planning tools and techniques force the manager to look beyond personal prejudices and predispositions. Finally, the computer explosion is rapidly making sophisticated planning techniques available in a wider range of settings than ever.

The crucial point to remember is that planning tools and techniques are a means to an end, not an end in themselves. Just as a carpenter uses a handsaw in some situations and an electric saw in others, a manager must recognize that a particular model may be useful in some situations but not in others that may call for a different approach. Knowing the difference is one mark of a good manager.

NOTES

1. "This Video 'Game' Is Saving Manufacturers Millions," *Business Week*, August 17, 1987, pp. 82–84.
2. See Wayne W. Daniel, *Essentials of Business Statistics*, 2nd ed. (Boston: Houghton Mifflin, 1988), for an overview of basic forecasting methods.
3. See Robert Carbone and Wilpen Gorr, "Accuracy of Judgmental Forecasting of Time Series," *Decision Sciences*, Summer 1985, pp. 237–247, for a detailed discussion of how companies attempt to improve their forecasts.
4. R. Balachandra, "Technological Forecasting: Who Does It and How Useful Is It?" *Technological Forecasting and Social Change*, January 1980, pp. 75–85.
5. "Steve Jobs Comes Back," *Newsweek*, October 24, 1988, pp. 46–51.
6. Charles Ostrom, *Time-Series Analysis: Regression Techniques* (Beverly Hills, Calif.: Sage Publications, 1980).
7. John C. Chambers, S. K. Mullick, and D. Smith, "How to Choose the Right Forecasting Technique," *Harvard Business Review*, July–August 1971, pp. 45–74.
8. Fred Kerlinger and Elazar Pedhazur, *Multiple Regression in Behavioral Research* (New York: Holt, 1973).
9. Chambers, Mullick, and Smith, "How to Choose the Right Forecasting Technique"; see also J. Scott Armstrong, *Long-Range Forecasting: From Crystal Ball to Computers* (New York: Wiley, 1978).
10. Edward Markowski and Carol Markowski, "Some Difficulties and Improvements in Applying Linear Programming Formulations to the Discriminant Problem," *Decision Sciences*, Summer 1985, pp. 237–247, provides a comprehensive explanation of the technique.
11. Robert E. Markland, *Topics in Management Science*, 3rd ed. (New York: Wiley, 1989).
12. Markland, *Topics in Management Science*.
13. Markland, *Topics in Management Science*.
14. Edward Hannan, Linda Ryan, and Richard Van Orden, "A Cost-Benefit Analysis of Prior Approvals for Medicaid Services in New York State," *Socio-Economic Planning Sciences*, Vol. 18, 1984, pp. 1–14.
15. Markland, *Topics in Management Science*.
16. Markland, *Topics in Management Science*.

ENHANCEMENT MODULE 3

Computers and the Manager

In the grocery business twenty-five years ago, one of the major daily tasks facing a store manager was handling piles of papers in order to make crucial decisions. Today, however, at stores like Super Shop 'n Save, computers do everything from figuring invoices to setting up work schedules for checkout clerks. Hannaford Brothers, owners of Super Shop 'n Save, have been able to use computers to outperform industry averages and become one of the most profitable supermarket chains in the United States. A manager can retrieve the direct profit contribution of a particular brand of a product at a particular store during a given time period. That information can be used to precisely target-market products and increase profits for the organization.[1]

Most supermarkets now use bar-code scanners to read product codes and prices at checkout counters.[2] Well over a fourth also use computers to help make major decisions such as when to place orders, how much merchandise of each type to display, and what schedule for rotating produce to follow. Changes and innovations in other industries have been just as significant. Computers in manufacturing firms assist with the scheduling of production. Indeed, the use of computers in management is increasing so fast that keeping pace with it is difficult. Those changes are profoundly influencing managers' jobs. This module traces the evolution of computers and then describes the use of computers by managers.

THE EVOLUTION OF COMPUTERS

People have always tried to make counting and calculating easy and fast through the use of machines and other devices.[3] The earliest such device was probably the abacus. After John Napier devised logarithms in the early 1600s, William Oughtred developed sliding scales or rules to aid in computation.

The true ancestor of modern computers, however, was the analytical engine designed around 1864 but never completed by Charles Babbage. The machine was to use punched cards which had earlier been developed for looms in the textile industry. The use of punched cards was carried out by Herman Hollerith in special counting machines in the later 1800s. In 1944 the first electronic machine, the ASCC (Automatic Sequence Controlled Calculator, or Mark I) was developed by Howard Aiken in conjunction with IBM. Two years later, John Mauchly and J. Presper Eckert built ENIAC (Electronic Numerical Integrator and Calculator), which could do in an hour what it took the Mark I a week to do. Eckert and Mauchly then developed the UNIVAC (Universal Automatic Computer) for Remington Rand for use by the U.S. Census Bureau in 1952. In 1959, Jack Kilby of Texas Instruments invented the integrated circuit, and the size and speed of computers developed by leaps and bounds from that point on. Indeed, as shown in Figure EM3.1, the memory capacity of a microchip has increased from 64 kilobytes (1,000 bytes of memory; a byte is 8 bits or **bi**nary dig**it**s) in 1980 to 1,024 kilobytes in 1987 and is expected to reach 16,384 kilobytes during the early 1990s. At the same time, the speed of computers has also increased dramatically, but at an even slower rate.[4]

Computers are extremely accurate and fast; thus, they can analyze and process extremely large amounts of information in a short period of time. This capability presents managers with a powerful tool to help them do their jobs. Whereas complex paper-based systems tend to bog down under the volume of work being moved about, stored, read, and reread, properly designed computer systems reduce the volume by condensing data, storing it electronically, and presenting it in a variety of usable formats.

Types of Computers

Computers come in several types and sizes. The two basic types are analog and digital.[5] **Analog com-**

FIGURE EM3.1

Microchip Memory

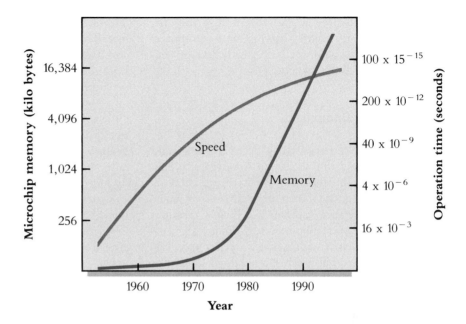

puters are direct extensions of slide rules and other mechanical devices whereby matching physical scales or electrical signals are used to represent the data—a low physical value representing a low number, a high value representing a high number. Analog computers are usually large. **Digital computers** represent data electronically by digits, usually using the binary system. Most computers with which you are familiar are digital computers. Digital computers come in a wide variety of sizes.

COMPUTERS AND THE MANAGER'S JOB

The information used on the job by a manager does not have to be computerized. Much of the information in organizations is not computerized and is available in manuals, file folders, and typewritten lists. As of the 1970s, only 15 percent of the data of most corporations was automated.[6] Although there is nothing wrong with paper systems, they can be cumbersome and costly to use and maintain.

Organizations generate and retain large amounts of data concerning many different things. Their key concern is how to manage and provide access to that data. Computers provide selectivity and accessibility by storing data electronically. Once stored, data may be retrieved in an infinite number of combinations.

In fact, not only does the computer store the data electronically, it can also retrieve, sort, analyze, process, and report the information faster than a human operator, and then it can store the information again for use in the future.

Uses of Computers

Computers are used for business information systems in a variety of ways. Business information systems transform data into usable information for the organization. The availability of new technology has greatly increased the organization's capability to acquire, store, and process large amounts of data. Over the last decade, improvements in information technology have been astronomical.

Numerous uses that a manager can make of computers have been identified. Major areas include accounting, reporting, and calculating data; writing; searching for and retrieving information; communications; graphics presentations; planning, scheduling, and monitoring; analysis; memory; processing organizational records; learning; developing new programs; and decision making.[7]

Given the pace of computer development, managers will have to stay abreast of advances if their organizations are to remain productive. However, it is easy to fall prey to the fallacy that only the latest models are useful. Buying new computers each year or so would not be cost-effective or necessary in most circumstances.

Limitations of Computers

Computers, of course, cannot do everything, and they are certainly not a cure-all for organizations. Computers are most valuable for repetitive tasks that involve frequent interaction with stored data.[8] They cannot replace humans for many creative, complex types of problem solving. There are compatibility problems with today's technology, although they are rapidly being overcome. Unless an organization has an emergency-power back-up capability, it may be unable to conduct business during a power shortage or blackout. "Viruses" can invade a computer system despite precautions taken against them. Very real privacy concerns surround computer information that is available about members of organizations. Security is also a concern.

THE FUTURE ROLE OF COMPUTERS

Most current managers are not "computer literate," because they did not grow up with computers. Further, the rapid change in computer technology makes some managers reluctant to invest much money in systems that might become obsolete in just a few years. Nevertheless, use of the computer as a tool for modern managers is growing.

Office automation holds out the hope of increasing the productivity of the largest information-processing unit within all organizations—the office. The major information-processing centers in any organization are the many offices that exist within the organization. Office personnel create, capture, process, store (file), retrieve, and disseminate information.[9] Computers can automate these tasks to make them faster, easier, and more accurate.[10]

Electronic decision support systems have been designed to reduce the cognitive overload experienced by managers.[11] A decision support system, or DSS, is an interactive computer-based system that helps decision makers solve poorly structured problems.

It does this through the use of a human–machine interface called a dialog, decision aids called models, and data provided by the manager called a database. If you have used a software package such as LOTUS or SuperCalc, then you already are familiar with one type of DSS tool. Boeing, Chase Manhattan, Gillette, Whirlpool, and many other companies are investing large sums of money to develop decision support systems to give them a competitive advantage, and increasing numbers of companies are expected to follow suit.

Generally speaking, many of the problems that a manager faces on a daily basis cannot be represented in quantitative terms, and decision support systems are often not very useful in those cases. Often the manager must use comments and thoughts of other managers to make a decision. This type of information is difficult, if not impossible, to quantify. Expert systems, however, allow a manager to manipulate this type of data and information and use it in making decisions.[12] An expert system is an intelligent computer program that uses knowledge and inference procedures to solve problems that are difficult enough to require significant human expertise for their solutions.[13] Expert systems are an attempt to share expertise among individuals through the use of computerized systems. An expert system distills the knowledge of many human experts.

Until recently, research on expert systems was confined to a few university research laboratories. In the next decade, however, expert-system technology will revolutionize what we do with computers, and it will change the world of business.[14] Expert-system technology will help business solve productivity problems. It will assist managers in solving poorly structured and complex problems more quickly and efficiently than they can solve those problems today. For these reasons managers must know about expert systems and stay abreast of this new and powerful technology.

Another recent development in computing is the growth of end-user computing. End-user computing is computing done directly by individuals at their work stations rather than by programmers at a central location. In the early years of data processing, computing hardware and software were typically under the control of a centralized data-processing staff. Application development was done by professional programmers and systems analysts on mainframe computers. End users received reports generated by the application programs. Eventually, online applications that allowed end users to enter and retrieve data using computer terminals became more common. However, the programs were still developed and controlled by the data-processing professionals. Now, however, end-user computing is moving the development and control to end users through the use of user-friendly software packages and tools.[15]

The demand for computing resources occurred so quickly that many organizations had no plans for controlling the growth of end-user computing.[16] The result was an uncontrolled proliferation of hardware and software within organizations. Users sometimes purchased computer tools without knowing if they would really serve the intended purpose.

It is now possible for users to transfer data from a mainframe computer to microcomputers (download) and from a microcomputer to a mainframe (upload). The technology exists that enables users to extract data from the corporate databases and then to perform ad hoc queries and "what if" modeling. In the past, some users felt that this type of data manipulation was not worth the delay or the cost of having these systems developed by the data-processing group, but that is now changing.

The use of centralized mainframes for computing involved the computer as a tactical tool of management; the use of microcomputers for end-user computing by individual managers involves the computer as a strategic tool. As individual managers have access to all information and are able to use the power of expert systems to make more complex decisions than before, job distinctions will blur. In 1985 there was about one microcomputer for every five white-collar employees; by 1990 there will be about one for every three. That pace is expected to continue as the number of microcomputers in offices quadruples by the year 2000.[17]

Soon, daily coordination tasks will also be eased through the use of computers. The software to do that is known as groupware. It coordinates calendars and mail for many separate groups across several levels of an organization. It can be used to track projects, remind users of deadlines, help arrange meetings, facilitate communications through the use of electronic mail, and keep track of all interactions between groups using the software.[18]

NOTES

1. "At Today's Supermarket, the Computer Is Doing It All," *Business Week*, August 11, 1986, pp. 64–65.
2. "At Today's Supermarket."
3. The following section is based largely on W. A. Atherton, *From Compass to Computers* (San Francisco: San Francisco Press, 1984).
4. T. Athey and R. Zmud, *Introduction to Computers and Information Systems* (Glenview, Ill.: Scott, Foresman, and Company, 1986).
5. J. D. Perrolle, *Computers and Social Change* (Belmont, Calif.: Wadsworth, 1987).
6. H. Gellman, "Knowledge Workers: It's Your Choice," *Business Quarterly*, Fall 1985, pp. 48–50.
7. "What's Happening with DSS?" *EDP Analyzer*, July 1984, pp. 1–16.
8. L. Long and N. Long, *Computers* (Englewood Cliffs, N.J.: Prentice-Hall, 1986).
9. R. J. Golfield, "Aiming OA Towards the Top," *Modern Office Technology*, February 1985, p. 55.
10. K. Kobayashi, *Computers and Communication* (Cambridge, Mass.: MIT Press, 1986).
11. P. G. Keen and G. R. Wagner, "DSS: An Executive Mind-Support System," *Datamation*, November 1979, pp. 117–122.
12. R. W. Blanning, "A Survey of Issues in Expert Systems for Management," in B. G. Silverman, ed., *Expert Systems for Business* (Reading, Mass.: Addison-Wesley, 1987), pp. 24–39.
13. C. W. Holsapple and A. B. Whinston, *Business Expert Systems* (Homewood, Ill.: Irwin, 1987).
14. J. Deardon, "Will the Computer Change the Job of Top Management?" *Sloan Management Review*, Fall 1983, pp. 57–60.
15. D. Flaherty, *Humanizing the Computer* (Belmont, Calif.: Wadsworth, 1986).
16. L. E. Raho and J. A. Belohlav, "Integrating Personal Computers into Organizations: Problems, Benefits, and Training Issues," *Journal of Systems Management*, March 1985, pp. 16–19.
17. J. Dreyfus, "Catching the Computer Wave," *Fortune*, September 26, 1988, pp. 78–82.
18. "Catching the Computer Wave."

INTEGRATIVE CASE

Pepsi Aims to Top Pop Market

Pepsi-Cola was founded in 1896 and flourished until World War I. At the end of the war, however, managers at Pepsi-Cola made several mistakes and plunged the company into bankruptcy. Several ownership changes had little effect until the company was finally bought by Loft, a New York candy-store chain. Loft achieved considerable success with Pepsi-Cola by increasing the size of its bottles and promoting it with a catchy new jingle.

These changes helped keep Pepsi successful up to and throughout World War II, but Coca-Cola soon established complete domination of the cola market. During the war, General Eisenhower had arranged for Coca-Cola bottling plants to be built all over the world so that American soldiers could always get a nickel bottle of Coke as a reminder of home and of better times. After World War II, Coke was so entrenched in the minds and hearts of those consumers that it seemed unlikely that any other brand would ever be able to compete effectively with Coke.

However, a top executive left Coca-Cola, joined the Pepsi-Cola organization, and brought several other top managers with him. Their objective was to remake the Pepsi organization. Pepsi's image was changed from that of an inexpensive beverage to that of a chic beverage attuned to the younger generation—the Pepsi Generation. Using songs and well-known personalities in its advertising, Pepsi quickly became the clear challenger to Coke in the cola market.

Pepsi then initiated a strategy that had a profound impact on the organization. Pepsi became PepsiCo and began to acquire numerous other firms. PepsiCo expanded its vision from that of a soft-drink company to that of a large conglomerate. Its holdings included soft drinks, snack foods, restaurants, transportation companies, and sporting-goods businesses. PepsiCo became a multi-billion-dollar corporation with operations all over the world.

PepsiCo acquired North American Van Lines, Lee Way Motor Freight, and the Wilson Sporting Goods chain. These unrelated acquisitions proved to be more burdens than blessings. PepsiCo had trouble integrating them into any coherent strategic plan and had trouble developing effective tactical and operational plans for them. Thus, during the early 1980s, PepsiCo began divesting itself of those companies and focusing on more closely related operations—beverages, salty snacks, and restaurants. The money from the divestitures was used for acquisitions, but the acquisitions were narrowly focused.

The Frito-Lay acquisition, made in 1965, proved to be a tremendously effective strategic move. Frito-Lay quickly became the dominant firm in its field, capturing and maintaining over half of the salty-snack market. Frito-Lay expanded its market share through aggressive marketing and the introduction of new products, such as its highly successful cheese-flavored O'Grady potato chips and Doritos tortilla chips. PepsiCo has become the undisputed leader in this market and has used that position to develop expertise to enhance its marketing and management in the other two areas.

In its restaurant operations, PepsiCo has three strong entries—Pizza Hut, acquired in 1977; Taco Bell, acquired in 1979; and Kentucky Fried Chicken, acquired in 1986. These operations all use cola syrup, the major part of any cola company's sales, and, hence, are strategically linked to PepsiCo's beverage operations. Fast-food chains usually sign long-term contracts with soft-drink companies to serve only that company's drinks. Obviously, owning major fast-food chains enhances the sales of PepsiCo's beverages. (Kentucky Fried Chicken had been one of Coca-Cola's two largest customers in the fast-food market).

PepsiCo has not ignored its beverage operations, however. Pepsi introduced the highly successful new brand, Slice, to compete against Sprite and then quickly came out with other flavored versions to expand upon that success. It also continued to aggressively promote both Pepsi and Diet Pepsi through the endorsements of such stars as Michael Jackson and Madonna. Pepsi has also worked hard to develop a strong bottling network. For example, the company recently bought MEI Corporation, a major soft-drink bottling firm.

The purchase of MEI and other, smaller bottlers has enabled Pepsi to control its distribution more effectively than it had done in the past. Coca-Cola created Coca-Cola Enterprises as its bottling arm to obtain similar control. That control, the battle for shelf space, general economic conditions that lowered the cost of some ingredients, and corporate egos all became involved late in 1988 when price wars erupted between the two cola giants. With national market shares very close for the two colas, attention focused on regions and individual city markets, and prices were slashed to as low as 10 cents a can at times. The price war did not always seem entirely rational because the price drop in many cases reduced earnings more than a gain in market share would raise them. Nevertheless, the prospect of gaining market share that might be held after the price war kept the battle going.

In Brazil, the competition late in 1988 in many ways resembled combat, as employees wore combat fatigues, put war paint on their faces, and played recordings of howitzers to psych themselves up for their jobs. Coke still outsells Pepsi in that market by about four to one, but Pepsi has more than doubled its market share and continues to aggressively introduce new products and tactics. When Pepsi introduced screw-on caps, Coke ran ads stating that the caps would not keep the fizz in, though it quickly introduced its own screw-on caps to hold its market share. When Pepsi launched a publicity campaign featuring Tina Turner, Coke responded with Sting and a Brazilian idol, Xuxa. Plastic bottles are being introduced—each company offers a different size and argues that its bottle fits Brazilian refrigerators better. Diet drinks are not popular in Brazil. They are believed to be a health hazard because of their artificial sweeteners. However, Brazil has a natural sugar substitute that it would gladly sell to the cola companies for use in a diet version. Initially reluctant, both companies have been experimenting with the product. There is no sign of a reduction in hostilities in this war.

Questions

1. Identify different decisions made at Pepsi. Cite specific examples. Which model of the decision-making process seems to best describe Pepsi's approach to decision making? Why? Use the steps in the rational decision-making process to describe how one of the decisions you identified might have been made.
2. What goals or objectives can you identify at Pepsi? Cite specific examples. What time frame is involved for each of those goals? Be as specific as you can in describing how Pepsi is planning to achieve each of those goals.
3. How does knowledge about the beginnings of Pepsi help you to understand its present position, problems, and opportunities? Which levels of strategic planning are most obvious in this discussion of Pepsi? Cite specific examples.
4. What tactical and operational plans can you identify at Pepsi? What barriers to effective planning seem to be involved? Cite specific examples.

REFERENCES: "Pepsi Aims to Liberate Big Market in Brazil from Coke's Domination," *The Wall Street Journal*, November 30, 1988, p. B6; "Coke and Pepsi Step Up Bitter Price War," *The Wall Street Journal*, October 10, 1988, p. B1; "Pepsi Machine Fine-Tunes Formula," *USA Today*, February 11, 1988, p. 3B; "Flat Pepsi Aims to Regain Its Fizz," *USA Today*, November 26, 1986, p. 3B; Carol Davenport, "America's Most Admired Corporations," *Fortune*, January 30, 1989, pp. 68–94.

III THE ORGANIZING
PROCESS

OUTLINE

Building Blocks of Organizations

Designing Jobs
Job Specialization · Benefits and Limitations of Specialization
Alternatives to Specialization

Group Jobs
Rationale for Departmentalization · Common Bases for
Departmentalization

Establishing Reporting Relationships
The Chain of Command · Narrow Versus Wide Spans · Tall
Versus Flat Organizations · Determining the Appropriate
Span

Distributing Authority
The Delegation Process · Decentralization and Centralization

Coordinating Activities
The Need for Coordination · Structural Coordination
Techniques

Differentiating Between Positions
Differences Between Line and Staff · Administrative Intensity

CHAPTER *8*

Components of Organization Structure

OBJECTIVES

After studying this chapter, you should be able to:

- Identify the basic building blocks of organizations.
- Describe alternative approaches to designing jobs.
- Discuss the rationale and the most common bases for grouping jobs into departments.
- Describe the basic elements involved in establishing reporting relationships.
- Discuss how authority is distributed in organizations.
- Discuss the basic coordinating activities undertaken by organizations.
- Describe basic ways in which positions within an organization can be differentiated.

OPENING INCIDENT

George J. Sella likes to do things his own way, and it shows in how he runs American Cyanamid. Sella became CEO of Cyanamid in 1983. At the time, the company was a troubled conglomerate with little focus or strategic identity. After careful study, Sella developed a two-pronged strategy: sell the company's cyclical businesses and expand in specialty areas like medical products.

Cyanamid regained its financial health and started developing its own unique corporate identity. Some analysts give Sella credit for turning the company around; others feel he has stifled innovation and creativity. Sella practices extreme centralization—he insists on final approval of all major decisions. And not everyone likes it.

One of his strategic moves was selling Cyanamid's Formica Corporation to its own managers, who believed they could do a better job if they had a greater say in decision making. The results suggest they were right. During the first four years of their ownership, they doubled both sales and profits. Even Sella agrees that they might have been too tightly controlled as part of Cyanamid. Still, he insists that his approach is best for the company and, at least for now, has no plans to relinquish any of his power.[1]

G*eorge Sella made a decision* that all CEOs must make—how much decision-making power to keep for himself and how much to give to others. Sella decided to retain much for himself; many other American managers are making different choices. However the choice is made, it is just one of many that managers must make in deciding how to structure an organization.

This chapter discusses many of the critical elements of organization structure that managers can control, and it is the first of four devoted to organizing, the second basic managerial function identified in Chapter 1. In Part 2, we described managerial planning—deciding what to do. Organizing, the subject of Part 3, focuses on how to do it. We first elaborate on the meaning of organization structure. Subsequent sections explore the basic building blocks that managers use to create an organization.

BUILDING BLOCKS OF ORGANIZATIONS

Imagine a child playing with a set of building blocks. He wants to build a castle, so he selects a few small blocks and more larger ones. He uses some square ones, some round ones, and some triangular ones. Some are red; others are blue. When he finishes, he has his own castle, unlike any other. Any other child, presented with the same set of blocks, will choose to construct a castle in a different way or to build something else. The child's activities—choosing a certain combination of blocks and then putting them together in his own unique way—are analogous to the manager's job of organizing.

organizing Deciding how best to group organizational activities and resources

At its simplest, **organizing** is deciding how best to group organizational activities and resources. Just as the child selects different kinds of building blocks, the manager can choose a variety of structural possibilities. And just as the child can assemble the blocks in any number of ways, so too can the manager put the organization together in many different ways. In this chapter, our focus is on the building blocks themselves—**organization structure**. In Chapter 9 we focus on how the blocks can be put together—organization design.

organization structure The set of building blocks that can be used to configure an organization

There are six basic building blocks that managers must address: designing jobs, grouping jobs, establishing reporting relationships between jobs, distributing authority among jobs, coordinating activities between jobs, and differentiating among jobs. The logical starting point is the first building block—designing jobs for people within the organization.

DESIGNING JOBS

job design The determination of an individual's work-related responsibilities

The first building block of organization structure is job design. **Job design** is the determination of an individual's work-related responsibilities.[2] For a machinist at Caterpillar, job design would involve specifying exactly what machines are to be operated, how they are to be operated, what decisions the machinist can make, what decisions are to be made by others, and what performance standards are expected. For a manager at Caterpillar, job design would involve defining areas of decision-making responsibility, identifying goals and expectations, and establishing appropriate indicators of success. The natural starting point for designing jobs is determining the level of desired specialization.

Job Specialization

job specialization The degree to which the overall task of the organization is broken down and divided into smaller component parts

Job specialization is the degree to which the overall task of the organization is broken down and divided into smaller component parts. Job specialization evolved from the concept of division of labor, first described by Adam Smith.[3] Smith, an eighteenth century economist, described how division of labor was used in a pin factory to improve productivity. One man drew the wire; another straightened it; a third cut it; a fourth ground the point, and so on. In this fashion, Smith claimed, ten men were able to produce 48,000 pins in a day, whereas each man would have been able to produce only 20 pins per day working alone.

In the twentieth century, the best example of the impact of specialization is the automobile assembly line pioneered by Henry Ford and his contemporaries. Mass-production capabilities stemming from job specialization techniques have had a profound impact in the United States and the rest of the world. High levels of low-cost production transformed American society during the first several decades of this century into one of the strongest economies in the history of the world.

Job specialization is a normal extension of organizational growth. For example, when an entrepreneur first starts her own business, she probably does every job herself. As the business grows, however, she will almost certainly need to hire others to help. Thus, she may hire an accountant, a sales representative, and some production workers. Each does something the entrepreneur previously did herself. As the organization gets even bigger, the need to break it down into more and more specialized tasks grows. A large corporation like General Motors has thousands of different specialized jobs. Clearly, no one person could perform them all.

Benefits and Limitations of Specialization

In general, job specialization is believed to provide four benefits to organizations.[4] First, individual dexterity is presumed to increase. If a worker has to learn only a small, simple task, he or she will probably become very proficient at that task. Second, transfer time between tasks is expected to decrease. If an employee is performing several different tasks, it stands to reason that some time will be lost as the worker stops doing the first task and starts doing the next. Third, the more narrowly defined a particular task is, the easier it may be to develop specialized machinery and equipment to assist with that task. Fourth, job specialization reduces training costs. When an employee who performs a highly specialized task is absent or resigns, the manager should be able to train someone new at relatively low cost. Although specialization is generally thought of in terms of operating jobs, many organizations have extended the basic elements of specialization to managerial and professional levels as well.[5]

On the other side of the coin, job specialization can have negative consequences. The foremost criticism is that workers who perform highly specialized jobs are likely to become bored and dissatisfied. The job may be so specialized that it offers no challenge or stimulation. Boredom and monotony set in; absenteeism rises; and the quality of the work may suffer. Furthermore, the anticipated benefits of specialization do not always occur. For example, a study conducted at Maytag found that the time spent moving work-in-process from one worker to another was greater than the time needed for the same individual to change from job to job.[6]

Thus, although some degree of job specialization is necessary, it should not be carried to extremes because of the negative consequences that could result. Managers should be sensitive to situations where extreme specialization should be avoided. And indeed, there are several alternative approaches to designing jobs that have been developed in recent years.

Some companies have started using a form of job rotation to improve flexibility. Brad Davis, shown here, is an employee of the Lechmere department store in Sarasota, Florida. He has been trained to serve as a forklift operator, a cashier, and a salesman. He received a pay increase for learning each of the new jobs. And people like Brad Davis get enjoyment not only from the additional pay but also from knowing that their workday will have variety. The company also benefits. Its other stores are staffed with only 30 percent full-time workers. But the Sarasota store has 60 percent full-timers.

job rotation   An alternative to job specialization that involves systematically moving employees from one job to another

job enlargement   An alternative to job specialization that involves giving the employee more tasks to perform

Alternatives to Specialization

To counter the problems associated with specialization, managers have sought other approaches to job design that achieve a better balance between organizational demands for efficiency and productivity and individual needs for creativity and autonomy. Five alternative approaches to designing jobs are job rotation, job enlargement, job enrichment, the job characteristics approach, and autonomous work groups.[7]

Job Rotation   **Job rotation** involves systematically moving employees from one job to another. A worker in a warehouse might unload trucks on Monday, carry incoming inventory to storage on Tuesday, verify invoices on Wednesday, pull outgoing inventory from storage on Thursday, and load trucks on Friday. Under this arrangement, the jobs do not change. Rather, the worker moves from job to job. Unfortunately, for this very reason, job rotation has not been very successful in enhancing employee motivation or satisfaction. Jobs that are amenable to rotation tend to be relatively standard and routine. A worker who is rotated to a "new" job may show increased interest at first, but this interest soon wanes. Although many companies (among them American Cyanamid, Baker International, Bethlehem Steel, Ford Motor Company, Prudential Insurance, TRW, and Western Electric) have tried job rotation, it is most often used today as a training device to improve worker skills and flexibility.

Job Enlargement   On the assumption that doing the same basic task over and over is the primary cause of worker dissatisfaction, **job enlargement** was developed to increase the total number of tasks each worker performs. Enlargement gives each worker more activities to perform in the production process. As a result, all workers perform a wide variety of tasks, hence reducing the level of job dissatisfaction. Many organizations have adopted job enlargement, including IBM, Detroit Edison, American Telephone & Telegraph, the Colonial Life

Insurance Company, the U.S. Civil Service, the Social Security Administration, and Maytag. At Maytag, for example, the assembly line for producing washing-machine water pumps was systematically changed so that work that had originally been performed by six workers, who passed the work sequentially from one person to another, was performed by four workers, each of whom assembled a complete pump.[8] Unfortunately, although some benefits are associated with job enlargement, they are often offset by several disadvantages: (1) Training costs usually rise. (2) Unions have argued that pay should increase because the worker is doing more things. (3) In many cases the work remains boring and routine even after job enlargement.

job enrichment   An alternative to job specialization that involves giving the employee more tasks to perform while also giving him or her more control over how they are done

Job Enrichment   A more comprehensive approach to designing jobs is **job enrichment**. Job enrichment is based on Frederick Herzberg's two-factor theory of motivation, which is described in detail in Chapter 12.[9] Herzberg argued that because job rotation and job enlargement do not provide workers with any additional responsibility or control over their jobs, they do not really enhance employee motivation. Increasing the range and variety of tasks is not sufficient by itself to improve employee motivation. What is needed instead is a means for providing the worker with actual control over the task. Job enrichment purports to increase both the number of tasks a worker does and the control the worker has over the job.

To accomplish this, a number of job changes are made. The manager removes some controls from the job, delegates more authority to employees, and structures the work in complete, natural units. These changes increase the subordinates' sense of responsibility. Another change suggested by Herzberg is to continually assign new and challenging tasks, thereby increasing the employees' opportunity for growth and advancement. AT&T was one of the first companies to try job enrichment. In one experiment, eight typists in a service unit prepared customer service orders. Faced with low output and high turnover, management determined that the typists felt little responsibility to clients and received little feedback. The unit was changed to create a typing team. Typists were matched with designated service representatives; the task was changed from ten specific steps to three more general steps; and job titles were upgraded. As a result, the frequency of order processing increased from 27 percent to 90 percent, the need for messenger service was eliminated, accuracy improved, and turnover became practically nil.[10] Other organizations that have tried job enrichment include Texas Instruments, IBM, and General Foods. Problems have also been found with this approach, however. For example, analysis of work systems before enrichment is needed but seldom performed, and managers rarely deal with employee preferences when enriching jobs.

job characteristics approach   An alternative to job specialization that accounts for the work system and employee preferences

Job Characteristics Approach   The **job characteristics approach** is an alternative to job specialization that does take into account the work system and employee preferences. This approach, illustrated in Figure

8.1, was developed by J. Richard Hackman and Greg Oldham.[11] As indicated in the figure, the job characteristics approach suggests that jobs should be diagnosed and improved along five core dimensions:

1. *Skill variety:* the number of things a person does in a job
2. *Task identity:* the extent to which the worker does a complete or identifiable portion of the total job
3. *Task significance:* the perceived importance of the task
4. *Autonomy:* the degree of control the worker has over how the work is performed
5. *Feedback:* the extent to which the worker knows how well the job is being performed.

The higher a job rates on those dimensions, the more employees will experience various desirable psychological states. Experiencing these states is expected to lead to high motivation, high-quality performance, high satisfaction, and low absenteeism and turnover. Finally, an individual variable called growth-need strength is presumed to affect how the model works for different people. People with a strong desire to grow, develop, and expand their capabilities (indicative of high growth-need strength) are expected to respond strongly to the presence or

FIGURE 8.1

The Job Characteristics Approach

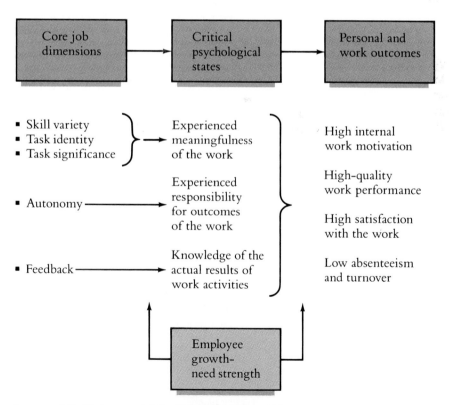

SOURCE: J. R. Hackman and G.R. Oldham, "Motivation Through the Design of Work: Test of a Theory," *Organizational Behavior and Human Performance,* Vol. 16 (1976), pp. 250–279. Copyright © Academic Press, Inc. Reprinted by permission of Academic Press, and the authors.

absence of the basic job characteristics; individuals with low growth-need strength are expected not to respond as strongly or consistently.

A large number of studies have been conducted to test the usefulness of the job characteristics approach. The Southwestern Division of Prudential Insurance, for example, used this approach in its claims division. Results included moderate declines in turnover and a small but measurable improvement in work quality. Other research findings have not supported this approach as strongly. Thus, although the job characteristics approach is one of the most promising alternatives to job specialization, it is probably not the final answer.[12]

autonomous work groups
An alternative to job specialization that allows an entire group to design the work system it will use to perform an interrelated set of tasks

Autonomous Work Groups Another alternative to job specialization is **autonomous work groups**. Under this arrangement, a group is given responsibility for designing the work system to be used in performing an interrelated set of jobs. The group assigns specific tasks to members, monitors and controls its own performance, and has considerable autonomy over work scheduling. In the typical assembly-line system, the work flows from one worker to the next, and each worker has a specified job to perform. In the autonomous work-group arrangement, however, workers are combined into a group. The group itself then decides how jobs will be allocated. The effect is much like working in a small team rather than a large manufacturing plan.

Volvo, the Swedish automobile manufacturer, has successfully used autonomous work groups in one of its plants. The groups in the plant range in size from fifteen to twenty-five members. Each group has a complete set of tasks, such as wiring or upholstering. The group members themselves determine who will perform each task. They can speed up or slow down the flow of work somewhat without disrupting the work of other groups. The group receives frequent feedback on its productivity on computer display screens. Although the plant cost more to build than Volvo's conventional facilities, the company has witnessed an improvement in quality and decreased turnover and absenteeism.[13]

GROUPING JOBS

The second building block of organization structure is the grouping of jobs according to some logical arrangement. This process is called **departmentalization**. After establishing the basic rationale for departmentalization, we identify some common bases along which departments are created.

departmentalization The
grouping of jobs according to
some logical arrangement

Rationale for Departmentalization

When organizations are small, the owner-manager can personally oversee everyone who works there. However, as an organization grows, it becomes more and more difficult for the owner-manager to personally supervise all the employees. Consequently, new managerial positions are created to supervise the work of others. The assignment of employees to particular managers is not done randomly. Rather, jobs are grouped according to some plan. The logic embodied in such a plan is the basis for all departmentalization.[14]

Common Bases for Departmentalization

Figure 8.2 presents a partial organizational chart for Apex Computers, a hypothetical firm that manufactures and sells computers and software. The chart shows that Apex uses each of the four most common bases for departmentalization: product, function, customer, and location.

FIGURE 8.2

Bases for Departmentalization:
Apex Computers

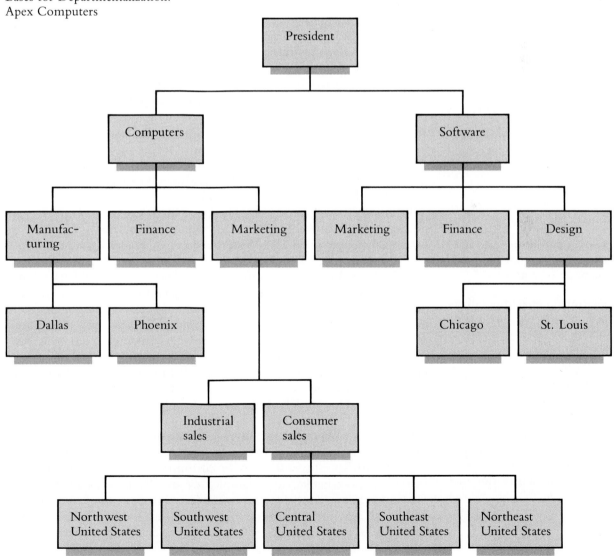

U.S. Shoe company is one of the largest footwear manufacturers in the world. Its divisions include Red Cross, Selby, Joyce, Pappagallo, Calvin Klein, Garolini, and Texas Boot. The company finds that departmentalizing by product allows it to concentrate on different department store and specialty shop chains. U.S. Shoe has thousands of retail accounts, with no single one accounting for more than 5 percent of its sales. Thus, the company is not dependent on any single customer.

product departmentalization Groups activities around products or product groups

functional departmentalization Groups together jobs involving the same or similar activities

customer departmentalization Groups activities so as to respond to and interact with specific customers or customer groups

Product Departmentalization **Product departmentalization** is the grouping and arranging of activities around products or product groups. Apex Computers has two product-based departments at the highest level of the firm. One is responsible for all activities associated with Apex's personal computer business, and the other handles the software business. Most larger businesses adopt this form of departmentalization. There are three major advantages to product departmentalization. First, all activities associated with one product or product group can be easily integrated and coordinated. Second, the speed and effectiveness of decision making are enhanced. Third, the performance of individual products or product groups can be assessed more easily and objectively, thereby improving the accountability of departments for the results of their activities. There are also two major disadvantages of product departmentalization. For one thing, managers in each department tend to focus on their own product or product group to the exclusion of the rest of the organization. For another, administrative costs rise because each department must have its own functional specialists for things like marketing research and financial analysis.

Functional Departmentalization Another common base for departmentalization is by function.[15] **Functional departmentalization** involves grouping together those jobs involving the same or similar activities. (The word "function" is used here to mean organizational functions such as finance and production, rather than the basic managerial functions such as planning or controlling.) The computer department at Apex, for example, has manufacturing, finance, and marketing departments. Functional departmentalization is most common in smaller organizations. There are three primary advantages of functional departmentalization. Each department can be staffed by experts in that functional area. Supervision is facilitated because an individual manager needs to be familiar with only a relatively narrow set of skills. It is also easier to coordinate activities inside each department. On the other hand, as an organization begins to grow in size, several disadvantages of functional departmentalization may emerge. Decision making tends to become slower and more bureaucratic. Employees may also begin to concentrate too narrowly on their own units and lose sight of the total organizational system. Finally, accountability and performance become increasingly difficult to monitor. For example, it may not be possible to determine whether the failure of a new product is due to production deficiencies or to a poor marketing campaign.

Customer Departmentalization Under **customer departmentalization**, the organization structures its activities so as to respond to and interact with specific customers or customer groups. The lending activities in most banks, for example, are usually tailored to meet the needs of different kinds of customers (i.e., business, consumer, mortgage, and agricultural loans). Figure 8.2 shows that the marketing branch of Apex's computer business has two distinct departments—

industrial sales and consumer sales. The industrial sales department handles marketing activities aimed at business customers, whereas the consumer sales department is responsible for wholesaling computers to retail stores catering to individual purchasers. The basic advantage of customer departmentalization is that it allows the organization to use skilled specialists to deal with unique customers or customer groups. It takes one set of skills to evaluate a balance sheet and lend a business $50,000 for operating capital and a different set of skills to evaluate an individual's creditworthiness and lend $10,000 for a new car. However, customer departmentalization also requires a fairly large administrative staff to integrate the activities of the various departments. In banks, for example, coordination is necessary to make sure the organization does not overcommit itself in any one area and to handle collections on delinquent accounts from a diverse set of customers.

location departmentalization   Involves grouping jobs on the basis of defined geographic sites or areas

Location Departmentalization   **Location departmentalization** involves grouping jobs on the basis of defined geographic sites or areas. The defined sites or areas may range in size from a hemisphere to only a few blocks of a large city. The manufacturing branch of Apex's computer business has two location-based plants—one in Dallas and another in Phoenix. Similarly, the design division of its software design unit has two labs, one in Chicago and the other in St. Louis. Apex's consumer sales group has five sales territories corresponding to different regions of the United States. Transportation companies, police departments (precincts represent geographic areas of a city), and the Federal Reserve Bank all use location departmentalization. The primary advantage of location departmentalization is that it enables the organization to respond easily to unique customer and environmental characteristics in the various regions. A larger administrative staff may be required if the organization is to keep track of units in scattered locations.

Other Forms of Departmentalization   Most organizations are departmentalized by function, product, location, or customer. However, other forms are occasionally used as well. Some organizations find it useful to group certain activities by time. One of the machine shops of Baker-Hughes in Houston, for example, operates on three shifts. Each shift has a superintendent who reports to the plant manager, and each shift has its own functional departments. Time (8:00 A.M.–4:00 P.M., 4:00 P.M.–12:00 midnight, and 12:00 midnight–8:00 A.M.) is thus the framework for many organizational activities. Other organizations that use time as a basis for grouping jobs include some hospitals and many airlines. In other situations, departmentalization by sequence is appropriate. By sequence we mean some differentiating factor such as a number or letter. Many college students must register in sequence: last names starting with A through E in line 1, F through L in line 2, and so on, or student numbers less than 200000 at 8:00 A.M. and those between 200001 and 400000 at 10:00 A.M. Other areas that may be organized in sequence include credit departments (specific employees run credit checks according to customer name), insurance claims divisions (by policy number), and prisons (inmates eat according to serial number or cell block).

Other Considerations   Two final points about departmentalization remain to be made. First, departments are often called something entirely different—divisions, units, sections, and bureaus are all common synonyms. The higher we look in an organization, the more likely we are to find departments referred to as divisions. The underlying logic behind all the labels is the same, however: They represent groups of jobs that have been yoked together according to some unifying principle. Second, almost any organization is likely to employ multiple bases of departmentalization, depending on level. Although Apex Computer is a hypothetical firm we created to explain departmentalization, it is quite similar to many real organizations in that it uses a variety of bases of departmentalization for different levels and different sets of activities.

ESTABLISHING REPORTING RELATIONSHIPS

The third basic building block of organizations is the establishment of reporting relationships among positions. Suppose, for example, that the owner-manager of a small business has just hired two new employees, one to handle marketing and one to handle production. Will the marketing manager report to the production manager; will the production manager report to the marketing manager; or will each report directly to the owner-manager? These questions reflect the basic issues involved in establishing reporting relationships. Specifically, the purpose of this activity is to clarify the chain of command and the span of management.

The Chain of Command

■ **chain of command** A clear and distinct line of authority among the positions in an organization

The chain of command concept is an old one, first popularized in the early years of this century. Essentially, the notion of **chain of command** argues that clear and distinct lines of authority need to be established among all positions in the organization. There are actually two components of the chain of command. The first, called unity of command, suggests that each person within an organization should have a clear reporting relationship to one and only one boss (as we will see in Chapter 9, newer models of organization design successfully violate this premise). The second, called the scalar principle, suggests that there should be a clear and unbroken line of authority that extends from the lowest to the highest position in the organization. The popular saying "The buck stops here" is derived from this idea—someone in the organization must ultimately be responsible for every decision.

Narrow Versus Wide Spans

span of management The number of people who report to a particular manager

Another part of establishing reporting relationships involves determining how many people will report to each particular manager. This defines the **span of management**, sometimes called the span of control. One of the earliest examples of attention to the span of management is found in the Old Testament. Moses is advised by his father-in-law, Jethro, to designate "rulers of thousands, and rulers of hundreds, rulers of fifties, and rulers of tens" (Exodus 18:13–26).

The optimal span of management was a primary concern of managers and researchers for many years. Should it be relatively narrow (with few subordinates per manager) or relatively wide (many subordinates)? What is the optimal number of subordinates that a manager can deal with? As shown in "The Global View," the question is still of concern to managers in China.

One early writer, A. V. Graicunas, attempted to quantify problems with the span of management.[16] Graicunas noted that a manager must deal with three kinds of interactions with and among subordinates: direct (the manager's one-to-one relationship with each subordinate), cross (among the subordinates themselves), and group (between groups of subordinates). The number of possible interactions of all types between a manager and subordinates can be determined by the following formula:

$$I = N \left(\frac{2^N}{2} + N - 1 \right)$$

where I is the total number of interactions with and among subordinates and N is the number of subordinates.

If a manager has only two subordinates, six potential interactions exist. If the number of subordinates increases to three, the possible interactions total eighteen. With five subordinates there are one hundred possible interactions. Although Graicunas's formula offers no prescription for what N should be, it does demonstrate how complex the relationships can become when more subordinates are added. The key point is that, as the span of management increases, each additional subordinate adds more complexity than the previous one did. Going from nine to ten subordinates is very different from going from three to four.

Another early writer, Ralph C. Davis, described two kinds of spans: an operative span for lower-level managers and an executive span for middle and top managers. He argued that operative spans could approach thirty subordinates, whereas executive spans should be limited to three to nine (depending on the nature of the managers' jobs, the growth rate of the company, and similar factors). Lyndall F. Urwick suggested that an executive span should never exceed six subordinates, and General Ian Hamilton reached the same conclusion.[17] Today, we recognize that the span of management is a crucial factor in structuring organizations but that there are no universal, cut-and-dried prescriptions for an ideal or optimal span.[18] Later we summarize some important variables that influence the appropriate span of management in a particular situation. First, however, we describe how the span of management affects the overall structure of an organization.

Tall Versus Flat Organizations

Imagine an organization with thirty-one managers and a narrow span of management. As shown in Figure 8.3, the result is a relatively tall

FIGURE 8.3

Tall Versus Flat Organizations

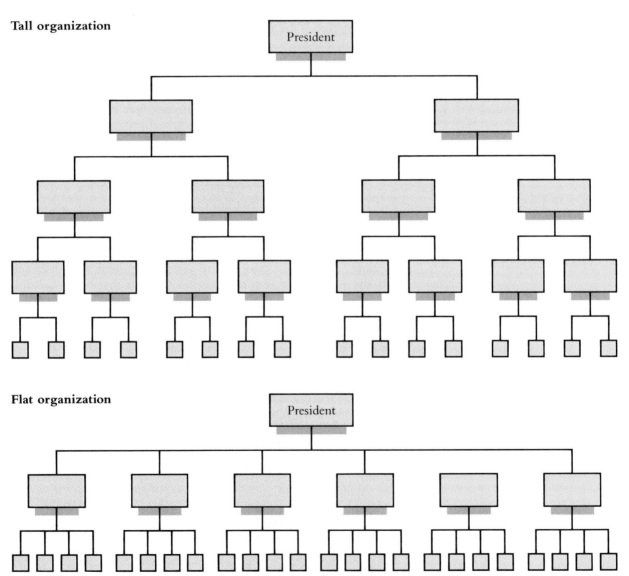

Tall organization

Flat organization

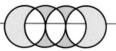

THE GLOBAL VIEW

CHINA'S ORGANIZATIONAL CONCERNS

In recent years, the People's Republic of China has opened its doors to the exchange of information and interaction with the people of the Western world. As China attempts to modernize its industry and develop trade relations with the rest of the world, it has sought scientific Western management techniques that could be applied to organizations in China. China appears to be most interested in traditional, scientific management approaches that seem to suggest pat answers, rather than in contemporary, contingency approaches that suggest experimentation to obtain workable solutions for differing situations.

The best-selling book *In Search of Excellence* has become extremely popular in China (at least six bootleg translations have become available). One of its authors, Tom Peters, toured China to lecture on the approach to management described in the book. To his surprise, his ideas met with a cool reception; his audiences did not seem particularly interested in what he had to say. Peters kept talking about the importance of people in organizations, saying that there are no absolute rules for managing organizations and that flexibility is what counts in today's world. His listeners were unconcerned with these ideas. Instead, he found that the question that kept recurring was how to determine the correct span of management. "What is the optimal ratio of managers to workers?" seemed to be

the prime concern of the Chinese managers whom he addressed.

Structural questions like that are most appropriate in stable organizational environments where management has the luxury of determining the optimum and then sticking with it long enough to recover the costs incurred in making the determination. In dynamic organizational environments, quality and flexibility are important to overall organizational effectiveness, and the question of the appropriate span of management is less relevant. In the United States, where almost all organizational environments are highly dynamic, the span-of-management question has been of little concern for twenty years. But in China, where the state controls the mix, quality, and delivery of products, organizational environments are more stable and the span-of-management question is relevant. Traditional managerial models are likely to be more relevant to China and other emerging industrial countries than are contemporary, contingency and systems models of management and organization.

REFERENCES: "The Inscrutable West," *Newsweek*, April 18, 1988, p. 52; D. D. Van Fleet and A. G. Bedeian, "A History of the Span of Management," *Academy of Management Review*, July 1977, pp. 356–372; "China Throws Open Its Seaboard," *The Economist*, March 21, 1988, pp. 61–62; Noel Fletcher, "China Will Dump Failing State Firms," *Journal of Commerce and Commercial*, August 4, 1988, pp. 1A, 10A.

organization with five layers of management. With a somewhat wider span of control, however, the flat organization shown in Figure 8.3 emerges. This configuration has only three layers of management.

What difference does it make whether the organization is tall or flat? In an early study at Sears, James Worthy found that a relatively flat structure led to higher levels of employee morale and productivity.[19] It has also been argued that a tall structure is more expensive (due to the larger number of managers involved) and that it fosters more communication problems (due to the increased number of people through whom vertical information must pass).[20] On the other hand, a wide span of management in a flat organization may result in a manager having more administrative responsibility (because there are fewer managers) and more supervisory responsibility (because there are more subordinates reporting to each manager). If these additional responsibilities become excessive, the flat organization may suffer.[21]

Many experts agree that businesses can function effectively with fewer layers of organization than they currently have. The Franklin Mint, for example, recently reduced its number of management layers from six to four. At the same time, CEO Stewart Resnick increased his span of management from six to twelve. In similar fashion, IBM has recently eliminated one layer of management. One reason for this trend is that improved organizational communication networks allow managers to stay in touch with a larger number of subordinates than was possible even just a few years ago.[22]

Determining the Appropriate Span

Of course, the big question remains: How does a manager determine the appropriate span for her or his unique situation? Although there is no perfect formula, researchers have identified a set of factors that influence the span for a particular circumstance.[23] Some of these factors are listed in Table 8.1. One factor is competence. If a manager is competent and well trained, he or she can supervise more subordinates. Similarly, if the subordinates are also competent and well trained, they usually require less supervision. The more competent the manager and the subordinates, the wider the span of management can be.

Physical dispersion is also important. The more widely subordinates are scattered, the narrower the span should be. If an organization uses location departmentalization, sales managers may be scattered across a large part of the country. A regional sales manager could spend all of her or his time traveling if the span were wide. A narrower span solves this problem. On the other hand, if all the subordinates are in one location, the span can be somewhat wider. The amount of nonsupervisory work expected of the manager is also important. Some managers, especially at the lower levels of an organization, spend most or all of their time supervising subordinates. Other managers spend a lot of time doing paperwork, planning, and engaging in other managerial activities; thus, these managers may need a narrower span.

TABLE 8.1

Factors Influencing the Span of Management

1. Competence of supervisor and subordinates
2. Physical dispersion of subordinates
3. Extent of nonsupervisory work in manager's job
4. Degree of required interaction
5. Extent of standardized procedures
6. Similarity of tasks being supervised
7. Frequency of new problems
8. Preferences of supervisors and subordinates

Some job situations also require a great deal of interaction between supervisor and subordinates; other jobs require less. In general, the more interaction that is required, the narrower the span of management should be. Similarly, if there is a fairly comprehensive set of standard procedures, a relatively wide span is possible because most difficulties can be handled by following a standard procedure. If only a few standard procedures exist, however, the supervisor usually has to play a larger role in overseeing day-to-day activities and may find a narrower span more efficient.

Task similarity is also important. If most of the jobs being supervised are similar, a supervisor can handle a wider span. When each employee is performing a different task, more of the supervisor's time is spent on individual supervision. Likewise, if new problems that require supervisory assistance arise frequently, a narrower span may be called for. If new problems are relatively rare, though, a wider span can be established. Finally, the preferences of both supervisor and subordinates may affect the optimal span. If the supervisor prefers to monitor her or his subordinates closely or the subordinates themselves prefer close supervision, a narrower span may be appropriate. Some managers prefer to spend less time actively supervising their employees, and many employees prefer to be more self-directed in their jobs. A wider span may be possible in these situations.[24]

In some organizational settings, other factors may influence the optimal span of management. The relative importance of each factor also varies in different settings. It is unlikely that all eight factors will suggest the same span; some may suggest a wider span, and others may indicate a need for a narrow span. Hence, the manager must assess the relative weight of each factor or set of factors when deciding what the optimal span of management is for his or her unique situation.

DISTRIBUTING AUTHORITY

■ **authority** Power that has been legitimized by the organization

Another important building block in structuring organizations is the determination of how authority is to be distributed among positions. **Authority** is power that has been legitimized by the organization.[25] Distributing authority is another normal outgrowth of increasing organizational size. For example, when an owner-manager hires a sales representative to market his products, he needs to give the new employee appropriate authority to make decisions about delivery dates, discounts, and so forth. If every decision to be made requires the approval of the owner-manager, he is no better off than he was before he hired the sales representative. The power given to the sales representative to make certain kinds of decisions, then, represents the establishment of a pattern of authority: There are some decisions that the sales representative can make alone, some that are to be made in consultation with others, and some on which the sales representative must defer to the boss. Two specific issues that managers must address when distributing authority are delegation and decentralization.

The Delegation Process

delegation The process by
which a manager assigns a portion of his or her total work
load to others

Delegation is the establishment of a pattern of authority between a
superior and one or more subordinates. Specifically, **delegation** is the
process by which the manager assigns a portion of his or her total
workload to others.[26]

Reasons for Delegation The primary reason for delegation is to enable
the manager to get more work done. Subordinates help ease the manager's burden by doing major portions of the organization's work. In
some instances, a subordinate may have more expertise in addressing a
particular problem than the manager does. For example, the subordinate
may have had special training in developing computer information
systems or may be more familiar with a particular product line or
geographic area. Delegation also helps develop the subordinate for
future promotion. By participating in decision making and problem
solving, subordinates learn more about overall operations and improve
their managerial skills.

Parts of the Delegation Process In theory, as shown in Figure 8.4, the
delegation process involves three steps. First, the manager assigns responsibility, or gives the subordinate a job to do. The assignment of
responsibility might range from telling a subordinate to prepare a report
to placing the person in charge of a six-month task force. Along with
the assignment, the individual is also given the authority to do the job.
The manager may give the subordinate the power to requisition needed
information from confidential files or to direct a group of other workers. Finally, the manager establishes accountability by the subordinate—
that is, the subordinate accepts an obligation to carry out the task
assigned by the manager.

FIGURE 8.4

Parts of the Delegation
Process

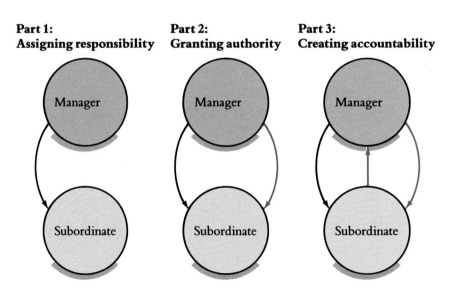

These three steps do not occur in rigid 1-2-3 sequence. Indeed, when a manager and a subordinate have developed a good working relationship, the major parts of the process may be implied rather than stated. The manager may simply mention that a particular job must be done. A perceptive subordinate may realize that the manager is actually assigning the job to her. From past experience with the boss, she may also know, without being told, that she has the necessary authority to do the job and that she is accountable to the boss for finishing the job as "agreed."

Problems in Delegation   Unfortunately, problems often arise in the delegation process. For a variety of reasons, a manager may be reluctant to delegate. For one thing, the manager may be so disorganized that he or she is unable to plan work in advance and, as a result, is unable to delegate appropriately. For another, the manager may worry that the subordinate will do too well and pose a threat to her or his own advancement. And finally, the manager may not trust the subordinate to do the job well. Similarly, some subordinates are reluctant to accept delegation. They may be afraid that failure will result in a reprimand or disciplinary action. They may perceive that there are no rewards for accepting additional responsibility. Or they may simply prefer to avoid risk and, therefore, want their boss to take all responsibility.

There are no quick fixes for these problems. The basic issue is communication. Subordinates must understand their own responsibility, authority, and accountability, and the manager must come to recognize the value of effective delegation. With the passage of time, subordinates should develop to the point where they can make substantial contributions to the organization. At the same time, the manager should recognize that a subordinate's satisfactory performance is not a threat to his or her own career but an accomplishment by both the subordinate who did the job and the manager who trained the subordinate and was astute enough to entrust the subordinate with the project. Ultimate responsibility for the outcome, however, continues to reside with the manager, who is, in turn, accountable to a higher-level manager.

Decentralization and Centralization

decentralization The process of systematically delegating power and authority throughout the organization to middle and lower-level managers

centralization The process of systematically retaining power and authority in the hands of higher-level managers

Just as authority can be delegated from one individual to another, organizations also develop patterns of authority across a wide variety of positions and departments. **Decentralization** is the process of systematically delegating power and authority throughout the organization to middle and lower-level managers. It is important to remember that decentralization is actually one end of a continuum anchored at the other end by **centralization**, the process of systematically retaining power and authority in the hands of higher-level managers. Hence, a decentralized organization is one in which decision-making power and authority are delegated as far down the chain of command as possible. Conversely, in a centralized organization, decision-making power and

Aptus is a joint venture formed by Westinghouse and National Electric, Inc., of Lakeville, Minnesota. Aptus collects, treats, and disposes of hazardous waste products. Westinghouse has imbued the company with its own heritage of decentralized management. Managers at this Aptus facility in Coffeyville, Kansas, have considerable autonomy over how they run their operation.

authority are retained at the higher levels of management. George Sella at American Cyanamid practices extreme centralization. No organization is ever completely decentralized or completely centralized; some firms position themselves toward one end of the continuum; some lean the other way.[27]

What factors determine an organization's position on the decentralization-centralization continuum? One common determinant is the organization's external environment. Usually, the greater the complexity and uncertainty of the environment, the greater is the tendency to decentralize. Another crucial factor is the history of the organization. Firms have a tendency to do what they have done in the past, so there is likely to be some relationship between what an organization did in its early history and what it chooses to do today in terms of centralization or decentralization. The nature of the decisions being made is also considered. The costlier and riskier the decision, the more pressure there is to centralize. Organizations also consider the abilities of lower-level managers. If lower-level managers do not have the ability to make high-quality decisions, there is likely to be a high level of centralization. If lower-level managers are well qualified, top management can take advantage of their talents by decentralizing; in fact, if top management doesn't, talented lower-level managers may leave the organization.

There is no set of clear-cut guidelines for a manager to use in determining whether to centralize or decentralize. Many successful organizations such as Sears and General Electric are quite decentralized. Equally successful firms such as McDonald's and K mart have tended to remain centralized. IBM has recently undergone a transformation from using a highly centralized approach to a much more decentralized approach to managing its operations. A great deal of decision-making

MANAGEMENT IN PRACTICE

DECENTRALIZATION AT KEMPER

The Kemper Corporation consists of nineteen different although loosely related companies. Those companies overlap and compete with one another to some extent as they sell everything from stocks to life insurance to financial services. Because they are members of the same parent corporation, the companies benefit from shared expertise and experience at the corporate level. They also benefit from being part of a highly decentralized organization, one in which they are permitted to run as autonomous or independent business firms. Some of the companies (Kemper Financial Services, Inc., for instance) are clearly identified with Kemper Corporation. Others, especially the regional brokerage houses (Blunt, Ellis & Loewi in Milwaukee; Bateman Eichler, Hill Richards in Los Angeles; Boettcher in Denver; Prescott, Ball & Turben in Cleveland), do not even use the Kemper name. A decentralized approach has worked well for Kemper. Its operating earnings and revenues were skyrocketing during the late 1980s, and its stock performance was quite strong, leading to a stock split in 1986.

A major reason for the success of this decentralized organization is that the individual companies, because of their local autonomy, can take advantage of changes and opportunities in their individual markets. Kemper, for instance, was one of the first insurance companies to note customers' movement away from traditional whole-life insurance policies.

Effectively managing such a decentralized organization requires skill at reconciling differences among middle managers who do not want interference from a corporate hierarchy. This ability is vital in a business in which managers have such close ties with clients that if the managers became sufficiently upset, they could leave and take the clients with them. Decentralization requires a willingness to tolerate differences, uncertainty, and diversity among the members of the organization and especially among the managers.

There are, of course, problems inherent in such a system. The regional brokerage houses may compete with other organizations that sell Kemper products, and as Kemper expands the former it may upset some of the latter. However, if all of the regional houses were combined into a single Kemper superbrokerage house, other Wall Street firms might drop Kemper products altogether. For Kemper, the decentralized approach seems preferable to a centralized one. Kemper is treading a fine line and so far is being highly successful in doing so.

REFERENCES: "The Loose-Reins Approach Pays Off for Kemper," *Business Week*, September 8, 1986, pp. 78–79; Rick Reiff, "Broker Blues," *Forbes*, September 5, 1988, pp. 39–40.

---

authority was passed from the hands of a select group of top executives down to six product and marketing groups. The reason for the move was to speed the company's ability to make decisions, introduce new products, and respond to customers.[28] "Management in Practice" illustrates how the Kemper Group practices decentralization. And even the Japanese are getting in on the act. For years, most Japanese firms have been highly centralized. Recently, though, many leading Japanese firms have adopted a more decentralized structure.[29]

COORDINATING ACTIVITIES

A fifth major building block of organization structure is coordination. As discussed earlier, job specialization and departmentalization involve breaking jobs down into small units and then combining those jobs

■ coordination The process of linking the activities of the various departments of the organization

into departments. Once this has been accomplished, the activities of the departments must be linked—systems must be put into place to keep the activities of each department focused on the attainment of organizational goals. This is accomplished by **coordination**—the process of linking the activities of the various departments of the organization.

The Need for Coordination

The primary reason for coordination is that departments and work groups are interdependent; they depend on each other for information and resources to perform their respective activities. For example, the sales and production departments of a manufacturing firm are interdependent because sales provides production with information about how much to produce to satisfy customer needs. The greater the interdependence between departments, the more coordination the organization requires if departments are to be able to perform effectively. James Thompson has identified three major forms of interdependence: pooled, sequential, and reciprocal.[30]

Pooled Interdependence　Pooled interdependence represents the lowest level of interdependence. Units with this level of interdependence operate with relatively little interaction—the output of the units is pooled at the organizational level. Banana Republic clothing stores operate with pooled interdependence. Each is considered a department by the parent corporation. Each has its own operating budget, staff, and so forth. The profits (or losses) from each store are "added together" at the organizational level. The stores are interdependent to the extent that the final success or failure of one store affects the others, but they do not generally interact on a day-to-day basis.

Sequential Interdependence　In sequential interdependence, the output of one unit becomes the input for another in a sequential fashion. This represents a moderate level of interdependence. At Nissan, for example, one plant assembles engines and then ships them to a final assembly site at another plant where the cars are completed. The plants are interdependent in that the final assembly plant must have the engines from engine assembly before it can perform its primary function of producing finished automobiles. But the level of interdependence is generally one-way—the engine plant is not necessarily dependent on the final assembly plant.

Reciprocal Interdependence　Reciprocal interdependence exists when activities flow both ways between units. This form is clearly the most complex. In a hospital, each ward or unit (such as intensive care and pediatrics) provides inputs to surgery. After surgery, patients are sent back to their respective wards. There is a two-way flow between units. Similarly, American Airlines is dependent on Marriott Food Services to deliver food and drinks to each of its aircraft prior to departure. And

Sarah Kelly, a vice president of Metropolitan Life, recognizes both the importance and the complexity of achieving coordination among different groups. After her promotion to her current job, Kelly saw a great deal of intergroup conflict among the various units handling Met Life's 25 million claims each year. She restructured workflow arrangements and facilitated teamwork and cooperation between the various groups. Today she is well along in her quest to streamline and speed up processing time for claims.

Marriott is dependent on American to keep it informed as to flight schedules, meal requirements, and so forth.

Structural Coordination Techniques

Given the obvious coordination requirements that characterize most organizations, it follows that many techniques for achieving coordination have been developed. Some of the most useful devices for maintaining coordination among interdependent units are the managerial hierarchy, rules and procedures, liaison roles, task forces, and integrating departments.[31]

The Managerial Hierarchy   Using the hierarchy to achieve coordination involves placing one manager in charge of interdependent departments or units. In K mart distribution centers, major activities include receiving and unloading bulk shipments from railroad cars and loading other shipments onto trucks for distribution to retail outlets. The two groups (receiving and shipping) are interdependent in that they share the loading docks and some equipment. To ensure coordination and to minimize conflict, one manager is in charge of the whole operation.

Rules and Procedures   Routine coordination activities can often be handled by means of rules and standard procedures. In the K mart distribution center, an outgoing truck shipment has priority over an incoming rail shipment. Thus, when trucks are to be loaded, the shipping unit is given access to all of the center's auxiliary forklifts. This priority is specifically stated in a rule. But, as useful as rules and procedures often are in routine situations, they are not particularly effective when coordination problems are complex or unusual.

Liaison Roles   The liaison role of management was introduced in Chapter 1. As a device for coordination, a manager in a liaison role is called upon to coordinate two or more interdependent units by acting as a common point of contact. This individual may not have any formal authority over the groups but instead simply facilitates the flow of information between units. Two engineering groups working on component systems for a large project might interact through a liaison. The liaison maintains familiarity with each group as well as with the overall project. She or he can answer questions and otherwise serve to integrate the activities of all the groups.[32]

Task Forces   A task force may be created when the need for coordination is acute. When interdependence is complex and several units are involved, a single liaison person may not be sufficient. Instead, a task force might be assembled by drawing one representative from each group. The coordination function is thus spread across several individuals, each of whom has special information about one of the groups involved. When the project is completed, task force members return to their original positions. For example, a college overhauling its degree requirements might establish a task force made up of representatives from each department affected by the change. Each person retains her or his regular departmental affiliation and duties but also serves on the special task force. After the new requirements are agreed upon, the task force is dissolved.

Integrating Departments   Integrating departments are occasionally used for coordination. These are somewhat similar to task forces but are established on a more permanent basis. An integrating department generally has some permanent members, as well as members who are assigned temporarily from units that are particularly in need of coordination. One study found that successful firms in the plastics industry, which is characterized by complex and dynamic environments, used integrating departments to maintain internal integration and coordination.[33] An integrating department usually has more authority than a task force and may even be given some budgetary control by the organization.

In general, the greater the degree of interdependence, the more attention the organization must devote to coordination. When interdependence is of a pooled or simple sequential nature, the managerial hierarchy or rules and procedures are often sufficient. When more complex forms of sequential or simpler forms of reciprocal interdependence exist, liaisons, or task forces may be more useful. When reciprocal interdependence is complex, task forces or integrating departments are needed. Of course, the manager must also rely on her or his own experience and insights when choosing coordination techniques for the organization.

DIFFERENTIATING BETWEEN POSITIONS

■ **line positions**   Positions in the direct chain of command that are responsible for the achievement of an organization's goals

■ **staff positions**   Intended to provide expertise, advice, and support for line positions

The last building block of organization structure is differentiating between line and staff positions in the organization. A **line position** is a position in the direct chain of command that is responsible for the achievement of an organization's goals. A **staff position** is intended to provide expertise, advice, and support for line positions. These distinctions are illustrated in Figure 8.5. The president and the vice presidents for production, finance, and marketing are considered line managers—they occupy a position in the direct chain of command and contribute directly to the firm's goals. The assistant to the president and the assistant to the vice president of production hold professional staff positions—they assist the individual manager in a variety of activities. The legal adviser and the vice presidents of research and development (R&D) and human resources are also called professional staff, because they have special skills and because they work with many departments rather than with just one individual. The vice president of human

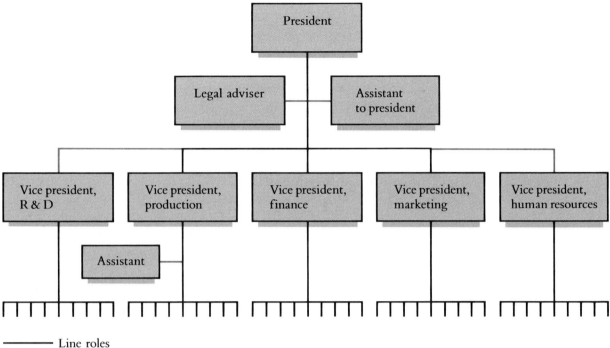

——————— Line roles

——————— Staff roles

FIGURE 8.5
Line and Staff Roles

resources, for example, would work with all of the other job managers to hire and train employees for their units.

Differences Between Line and Staff

The most obvious difference between line and staff is purpose. The purpose of line is to work directly toward organizational goals, whereas staff advises and assists. But other distinctions exist as well. One very important difference is authority. Line authority is generally thought of as the formal or legitimate authority created by the organizational hierarchy. Staff authority is less concrete and may take a variety of forms. One form is the authority to advise. In this instance, the line manager can choose whether to seek or to avoid input from the staff; and even when advice is sought, the manager might still choose to ignore it.

Another form of staff authority is called compulsory advice. In this case the line manager must listen to the advice but can choose to heed it or ignore it. For example, the pope is expected to listen to the advice of the Sacred College when dealing with church doctrine, but he may follow his own beliefs when making decisions. Perhaps the most important form of staff authority is called functional authority—formal or legitimate authority over activities related to the staff member's specialty. In Figure 8.5 the vice president of human resources is a member of the professional staff. This individual is likely to have expertise in such special areas as Equal Employment Opportunity. When a legal question arises that pertains to hiring, this expert is likely to be given authority to make appropriate decisions. Conferring functional authority is probably the most effective way to use staff positions, because it allows the organization to take advantage of specialized expertise while also maintaining a chain of command.

Administrative Intensity

administrative intensity
The degree to which managerial positions are concentrated in staff positions

Organizations sometimes attempt to balance their emphasis on line versus staff positions in terms of administrative intensity. **Administrative intensity** is the degree to which managerial positions are concentrated in staff positions. An organization with a high administrative intensity is one with many staff positions relative to the number of line positions; low administrative intensity reflects relatively more line positions. Although staff positions are important in many different areas, there is a tendency for them to proliferate unnecessarily. All else equal, organizations would like to be spending most of their human resource dollars on line managers, since by definition they are contributing to the organization's basic goals. A surplus of staff positions represents a drain on an organization's cash and an inefficient use of resources.

Many organizations have taken steps over the past few years to reduce their administrative intensity by eliminating staff positions. CBS recently cut 400 staff positions at its New York headquarters, and IBM has cut its corporate staff work force from 7,000 to 2,700. Burlington Northern generates almost $7 billion in annual sales and manages a work force of 43,000 with a corporate staff of only 77 managers![34]

SUMMARY OF KEY POINTS

Organizations are made up of a series of building blocks. The most common of these involve designing jobs, grouping jobs, establishing reporting relationships, distributing authority, coordinating activities, and differentiating between positions.

Job design is the determination of an individual's work-related responsibilities. The most common form is job specialization. Because of various drawbacks to job specialization, managers have experimented with job rotation, job enlargement, job enrichment, the job characteristics approach, and autonomous work groups as alternatives.

After jobs are designed, they are grouped into departments. The most common bases for departmentalization are product, function, customer, and location.

Establishing reporting relationships starts with the chain of command. The span of management partially dictates whether the organization is relatively tall or flat. Several situational factors influence the ideal span.

Distributing authority starts with delegation. Delegation is the process by which the manager assigns a portion of his or her total workload to others. Systematic delegation throughout the organization is decentralization. Several factors influence the appropriate degree of decentralization.

Coordination is the process of linking the activities of the various departments of the organization. Interdependence among departments is a primary reason for coordination. Managers can draw upon several techniques to help achieve coordination.

A line position is a position in the direct chain of command that is responsible for the achievement of an organization's goals. In contrast, a staff position provides expertise, advice, and support for line positions. Administrative intensity is the degree to which managerial positions are concentrated in staff positions.

DISCUSSION QUESTIONS

Questions for Review

1. What is job specialization? What are its advantages and disadvantages?
2. What is meant by departmentalization? Why and how is departmentalization carried out?
3. In what general ways may organizations be shaped? What implications does each of these ways have with regard to the distribution of authority within the organization?
4. How are positions differentiated in organizations? What are the advantages and disadvantages of such differentiation?

Questions for Analysis

5. It is easy to see how specialization can be utilized in manufacturing organizations. How can it be used by other types of organizations such as hospitals, churches, schools, and restaurants? Should those organizations use specialization? Why or why not?
6. Try to develop a different way to departmentalize your college or university, a local fast-food restaurant, a manufacturing firm, or some other organization. What might be the advantages of your form of organization?
7. Which type of position (line, staff, administrative) is most important to an organization? Why? Could an organization function without any of them? Why or why not?

Questions for Application

8. Go to the library and locate organization charts for ten different organizations. Look for similarities and differences among them and try to account for what you find.

9. Contact two very different local organizations (retailing firm, manufacturing firm, church, civic club, etc.) and interview top managers to develop organizational charts for each organization. How do you account for the similarities and differences that you find?

10. How many people does the head of your academic department supervise? The dean of your college? The president of your university or college? Why do different spans of management exist among these officials? How might you find out if the spans are appropriate in size?

NOTES

1. "American Cyanamid: An Overhaul That's More like a Tune-up," *Business Week*, February 8, 1988, pp. 70–71; Saul W. Gellerman and William G. Hodgson, "Cyanamid's New Take on Performance Appraisal," *Harvard Business Review*, May–June 1988, pp. 36–40; "Cyanamid: Getting Eyed from Afar?" *Business Week*, May 9, 1988, p. 134.

2. Ricky W. Griffin, *Task Design—An Integrative Approach* (Glenview, Ill.: Scott, Foresman, 1982).

3. Adam Smith, *Wealth of Nations* (New York: Modern Library, 1937; originally published in 1776).

4. Griffin, *Task Design*.

5. Anne S. Miner, "Idiosyncratic Jobs in Formal Organizations," *Administrative Science Quarterly*, September 1987, pp. 327–351.

6. M. D. Kilbridge, "Reduced Costs Through Job Enlargement: A Case," *Journal of Business*, Vol. 33, 1960, pp. 357–362.

7. Griffin, *Task Design*.

8. Kilbridge, "Reduced Costs Through Job Enrichment: A Case."

9. Frederick Herzberg, *Work and the Nature of Man* (Cleveland: World Press, 1966).

10. Robert Ford, "Job Enrichment Lessons from AT&T," *Harvard Business Review*, January–February 1973, pp. 96–106.

11. J. Richard Hackman and Greg R. Oldham, *Work Redesign* (Reading, Mass.: Addison-Wesley, 1980).

12. For recent analyses of job design issues, see Donald J. Campbell, "Task Complexity: A Review and Analysis," *Academy of Management Review*, January 1988, pp. 40–52; Michael A. Campion, "Interdisciplinary Approaches to Job Design: A Constructive Replication with Extensions," *Journal of Applied Psychology*, August 1988, pp. 467–481; and Roger L. Anderson and James R. Terborg, "Employee Beliefs and Support for a Work Redesign Intervention," *Journal of Management*, September 1988, pp. 493–500; Norm Alster, "What Flexible Workers Can Do," *Fortune*, February 13, 1989, pp. 62–66.

13. Griffin, *Task Design*.

14. Richard L. Daft, *Organization Theory & Design*, 3rd ed. (St. Paul, Minn.: West, 1989).

15. Daniel Twomey, Frederick C. Scherr, and Walter S. Hunt, "Configuration of a Functional Department: A Study of Contextual and Structural Variables," *Journal of Organizational Behavior*, Vol. 9, 1988, pp. 61–75.

16. A. V. Graicunas, "Relationships in Organizations," *Bulletin of the International Management Institute*, March 7, 1933, pp. 39–42.

17. Ralph C. Davis, *Fundamentals of Top Management* (New York: Harper & Row, 1951); Lyndall F. Urwick, *Scientific Principles and Organization* (New York: American Management Association, 1938), p. 8; Ian Hamilton, *The Soul and Body of an Army* (London: Edward Arnold, 1921), pp. 229–230.

18. David D. Van Fleet and Arthur G. Bedeian, "A History of the Span of Management," *Academy of Management Review*, 1977, pp. 356–372.

19. James C. Worthy, "Factors Influencing Employee Morale," *Harvard Business Review*, January 1950, pp. 61–73.

20. Rocco Carzo, Jr., and John N. Yanouzas, "Effects of Flat and Tall Organization Structures," *Administrative Science Quarterly*, June 1969, pp. 178–191.

21. Dan R. Dalton, William D. Todor, Michael J. Spendolini, Gordon J. Fielding, and Lyman W. Porter, "Organization Structure and Performance: A Critical Review," *Academy of Management Review*, January 1980, pp. 49–64.

22. Jeremy Main, "The Winning Organization," *Fortune*, September 26, 1988, pp. 50–60; and "Vaunted IBM Culture Yields to New Values: Openness, Efficiency," *The Wall Street Journal*, November 11, 1988, pp. A1, A4.

23. David Van Fleet, "Span of Management Research and Issues," *Academy of Management Journal*, September 1983, pp. 546–552.

24. See Edward E. Lawler III, "Substitutes for Hierarchy," *Organizational Dynamics*, Summer 1988, pp. 4–15, for a recent analysis of these and other factors that can influence the appropriate span of management.

25. See Daft, *Organization Theory & Design*.

26. Carrie R. Leana, "Predictors and Consequences of Delegation," *Academy of Management Journal*, December 1986, pp. 754–774.

27. Daft, *Organization Theory & Design*. See also John Meyer, W. Richard Scott, and David Strang, "Centralization, Fragmentation, and School District Complexity," *Administrative Science Quarterly*, June 1987, pp. 186–201.

28. "IBM Unveils a Sweeping Restructuring in Bid to Decentralize Decision-making," *The Wall Street Journal*, January 29, 1988, p. 3.

29. "Maverick Managers," *The Wall Street Journal*, November 14, 1988, p. R14.

30. James Thompson, *Organizations in Action* (New York: McGraw-Hill, 1967). For a recent discussion, see Bart Victor and Richard S. Blackburn, "Interdependence: An Alternative Conceptualization," *Academy of Management Review*, July 1987, pp. 486–498.

31. Jay R. Galbraith, *Designing Complex Organizations* (Reading, Mass.: Addison-Wesley, 1973); and Jay R. Galbraith, *Organizational Design* (Reading, Mass.: Addison-Wesley, 1977).

32. Elizabeth V. Reynolds and J. David Johnson, "Liaison Emergence: Relating Theoretical Perspectives," *Academy of Management Review*, October 1982, pp. 551–559.

33. Paul R. Lawrence and Jay W. Lorsch, "Differentiation and Integration in Complex Organizations," *Administrative Science Quarterly*, March 1967, pp. 1–47.

34. "Vaunted IBM Culture Yields to New Values: Openness, Efficiency," *The Wall Street Journal*, November 11, 1988, pp. A1, A4; Thomas Moore, "Goodbye, Corporate Staff," *Fortune*, December 21, 1987, pp. 65–76; and "CBS Frantically Woos Hollywood To Help It Win Back Viewers," *The Wall Street Journal*, February 9, 1989, pp. A1, A12.

CASE 8.1

Apple Slices

Apple Computer has organized and reorganized several times during its existence. Steven Jobs and Steve Wozniak first organized the company in the late 1970s, starting operations out of a garage. This simple organization grew rapidly and soon became a multi-million-dollar corporation. Naturally, the organization changed as it grew. Wozniak was uninterested in management and left Apple in 1985. Jobs, in contrast, was very interested in management and reorganized the company. Jobs put a team of vice presidents over operations, and, despite maintaining some technical involvement, he became chairman of the board and vice president. In addition, he had a president and chief executive officer (CEO). Teams were used to develop new products and ideas, and vertical integration was begun in software and product distribution.

As Apple grew, so did its operating and marketing problems. Jobs insisted on developing machines that were not compatible with those of IBM despite the growth to dominance of IBM equipment in the marketplace. New Apple products were late coming to market and many turned out to be failures. Finally, Jobs became convinced of the need for top-level, professional managerial experience in the Apple organization. In May 1983, he hired John Sculley to be president and CEO of Apple. Jobs remained chairman of the board.

Sculley immediately moved to reorganize Apple. He changed the structure from nine product divisions to three divisions that were not parallel in terms of departmentalization. One division was a functional division, and it was to handle all marketing and sales. Another division was a product division in charge of the entire Apple II product line. The third division was a product division headed by Jobs and charged with developing, producing, and marketing the Macintosh line of computer products.

The two product divisions soon began to compete internally for resources: time, money, and talent. The Apple II was a cash cow that generated funds for the corporation, and the Macintosh was a cash drain that soaked up those funds. Because Jobs headed the Macintosh unit, it became the elite place in the organization to work. The Macintosh division fell behind schedule and sales goals. In 1984, the Apple division accounted for nearly $1 billion in revenues compared to around $500 million for the Macintosh division

Members of the board began to pressure Sculley to obtain better performance from the Macintosh division. Board members began to talk of putting someone else in charge of the Macintosh division in order to turn it around. A battle erupted between Jobs and Sculley. Sculley won; Jobs was out. Late in 1985, Sculley advanced to chairman to replace Jobs. A unit was created to handle product development; six factories were closed and 1,200 employees were laid off; and a new head for Macintosh was named. Since that time, there have been numerous small reorganization activities going on with Apple, especially in sales and marketing.

The 1985 reorganization paid off. Sales, which had leveled off at around $2 billion in 1985, nearly doubled after the reorganization, reaching almost $4 billion by the end of 1988. Net income went from about $50 million in 1985 to just under $400 million in 1988. The company was doing so well that Sculley took advantage of a corporate perk by taking a six-week sabbatical and three weeks of vacation to rest, recuperate, and revitalize himself in mid-1988.

Just as Sculley returned, Apple announced the completion and implementation of major reorganization plans that had been under way for over a year. In that reorganization, Sculley remained as chairman of the board and CEO, and the duties associated with the presidency were divided among four other executives. Thus, Apple, which had gone from nine divisions to three, became a four-division structure.

A new division combined Apple sales and educational marketing efforts to the Pacific region. This division accounted for about 40 percent of sales revenues in 1988. The Apple Europe division was created to focus on European sales and marketing. The third new division, Apple Products, combines new-product development, manufacturing, and marketing. The fourth new division, Apple USA, deals with internal information systems and technology operations, including U.S. sales and business marketing, service, and support.

Questions

1. Construct organization charts for Apple Computer showing its initial organization under Jobs and Wozniak, its organization right after Sculley was hired, the 1985 reorganization, and the 1988 reorganization. What can you learn from this exercise?
2. What forms of job specialization are evident at Apple? Why?
3. What forms of departmentalization are evident at Apple? Why?
4. Do you think the 1988 reorganization is likely to solve problems of coordination and authority distribution that might exist for Apple? Why or why not? Can you suggest any potential improvements in the organization structure at Apple?

REFERENCES: "Sculley Slices Apple Computer into 4 Divisions," *USA Today*, August 23, 1988, p. 3B; "Apple Sets Plan to Reorganize into 4 Divisions," *The Wall Street Journal*, August 23, 1988, p. 2; "Celebrity Chief," *The Wall Street Journal*, August 18, 1988, pp. 1, 14; "Sabbaticals at Core of Apple Perks," *USA Today*, June 10, 1988, pp. 1B–2B; "Apple: The No-Nonsense Era of John Sculley," *Business Week,* January 7, 1986, pp. 96–98; John Sculley, "John Sculley on Sabbatical," *Fortune*, March 27, 1989, pp. 79–80.

CASE 8.2

IBM in Europe

In 1986 IBM reorganized its European operations. Those operations had been growing fast, and it had become clear that some form of reorganization was necessary. In particular, local managers in each country felt that they needed more authority to respond to local conditions, market demands, and customer preferences. IBM's relatively centralized structure had high administrative costs and seemed to be too slow in providing the sort of customer service necessary for continued growth and development. To cut costs and improve service, decentralization was in order. IBM delivered on that order.

The European reorganization involved two important steps. In the first step, major parts of the IBM-Europe function were delegated to local subsidiaries in each nation. Those parts included primarily marketing activities. The second step involved splitting the local subsidiaries into two groups, each of which would report to IBM-Europe's Paris headquarters. One group consisted of the three largest and fastest-growing customer countries: France, Italy, and West Germany. The second group consisted of all the other countries. The presidents of each country's local subsidiary reported to a contact executive for the group. The contact executive, in turn, reported to and was a part of a five-member executive operating committee, which was responsible for the performance of IBM-Europe. Sales and marketing were largely decentralized at this time, but product decisions continued to be made at IBM's home office in Armonk, New York.

European sales for IBM continued their upward trend, going from just over $10 billion in 1982 to over $15 billion in 1986 to around $20 billion by the latter part of 1987. However, much of the increase from early 1986 through late 1987 was due to the declining value of the dollar and not to real increases in business activity. Indeed, when a country-by-country examination was made in terms of local currency, IBM learned that sales had fallen over that two-year period in most major countries except Italy, where moderate growth continued. Sales in smaller countries were a bit better and helped boost overall results just enough so that IBM-Europe sales grew slightly in 1988, even when adjusted for the falling dollar. However, IBM felt that it could do better—after all, despite the slump IBM was still the top-selling computer in every European market.

IBM moved C. Michael Armstrong to Paris in 1987 to strengthen the company's position abroad. Armstrong was in charge of the $20-plus billion IBM World Trade Europe/Middle East/Africa Corporation. The activities of that corporation encompass eighty-five countries spread over three continents. Armstrong's real responsibility, however, was Europe because sales in that region account for about 95 percent of the total sales of IBM World Trade.

Armstrong has continued the decentralization process begun in 1986. His efforts have led to a reduction in the headquarters staff by about 40 percent and a significant drop in administrative costs. Armstrong has also worked to change the perception that IBM's European strategy came completely from New York with no consideration for local European conditions. He has brought together groups of large European customers to meet with top development executives from America to hear about and question long-term product developments and activities. The sales force is being increased to assure excellent customer service. Each country is being pressured to decentralize its operations.

In mainframe sales, Armstrong also demonstrated his independence. Rather than following the price book from New York, he ordered all European mainframe sales to be negotiated individually and secretly. Extra technical service and advice are frequently provided at no extra charge and discounts are not unheard of. This new flexibility and responsiveness are boosting IBM's image and sales in the mainframe market. One impressive result was the signing of the Amadeus airline-reservation system with Air France, Lufthansa, Iberia, and SAS. This contract was important because it was worth over $100 million and established a long-term partnership between those airline companies and IBM. That partnership involves everything from training operators to assisting in the design of facilities.

Questions

1. Describe the organization of IBM-Europe in terms of departmentalization and reporting relationships. Does that organization seem effective? Why or why not?
2. Does the organization of IBM-Europe seem effective in terms of coordinating activities and achieving its objectives? Why or why not? Can you suggest any ways in which it might improve its organization? If so, what are they?
3. Has the reorganization solved problems for IBM? Why or why not? Can you suggest any potential improvements in the organization structure at IBM-Europe or the IBM World Trade Europe/Middle East/Africa Corporation?
4. Compare and contrast the organizational arrangements described in Case 8.1 for Apple Computer with those in this case for IBM. What similarities and differences can you note? In view of the fact that Apple and IBM are both computer companies, how do you account for the differences in their organizations?

REFERENCES: "Mike Armstrong Is Improving IBM's Game in Europe," *Business Week*, June 20, 1988, pp. 96–101; "IBM Says Europe Now Is Best Market for Its PS/2 Line," *The Wall Street Journal*, June 7, 1988, p. 19; "IBM Is Planning Another Staff Redeployment," *The Wall Street Journal*, June 27, 1988, p. 3; "IBM Proposes to Reorganize European Units," *The Wall Street Journal*, August 1, 1986, p. 4.

OUTLINE

The Nature of Organization Design

Universal Perspectives on Organization Design
The Bureaucratic Model · The Behavioral Model

Situational Influences on Organization Design
Technology · Environment · Size and Organizational Life
Cycle

Common Forms of Organization Design
The Functional (U-Form) Design · The Conglomerate
(H-Form) Design · The Divisional (M-Form) Design · The
Matrix Design · Hybrid Designs

Emerging Issues in Organization Design
Information-processing Requirements · The Global
Organization

Linking Strategy and Organization Design
The Simple Structure · The Machine Bureaucracy · The
Professional Bureaucracy · The Divisionalized Form · The
Adhocracy

Organizational Culture
The Importance of Organizational Culture · Determinants of
Culture · Managing Organizational Culture

CHAPTER 9

Organization Design
and Culture

OBJECTIVES

After studying this chapter, you should be able to:

- Describe the basic nature of organization design.

- Identify and explain universal perspectives on organization design.

- Identify and explain the effects of situational influences on organization design.

- Describe common forms of organization design.

- Describe emerging issues in organization design.

- Discuss how an organization's strategy and design are interrelated.

- Describe the nature of organizational culture.

OPENING INCIDENT

For the past several years, Limited Inc. has been one of the fastest-growing women's specialty apparel chains in the United States. The keys to its success have been staying in touch with consumer trends and tastes, manufacturing and getting new products into stores quickly, and maintaining tight controls over inventory. Limited's total sales approached $250 million in 1988.

The retail giant is organized around four large divisions. Its cornerstone is The Limited chain, which accounts for almost one-third of the company's total sales. The Limited Express is a chain of smaller stores catering to younger women. The Lerner division focuses on less expensive fashions geared to low-to-middle-income shoppers. Victoria's Secret specializes in lingerie. In addition, Limited Inc. owns a number of smaller chains, like Abercrombie & Fitch and Henri Bendel, scattered around the country.

Each of the company's divisions acts as an autonomous entity, planning its own stores, developing its own marketing campaigns, and so forth. Each has its own management team, its own buyers, and its own identity. Not surprisingly, this arrangement is occasionally the source of internal conflict and competition. It is not uncommon, for example, for a Limited and Limited Express store in the same shopping mall to carry some of the same products for different prices. Although other chains, such as The Gap, have started making inroads on Limited Inc.'s market share, executives still believe their formula for success works and have no plans to change it.[1]

*M*anagers at Limited Inc. have been quite successful in creating a large, national retail chain. One of the key ingredients in managing any business is the arrangement of its various pieces into an effective overall design. Limited Inc.'s managers have chosen a divisional approach. The divisional design, however, is but one of several different designs they could have chosen to structure the company.

In Chapter 8, we identified the building blocks that go into creating an organization. In this chapter, we explore how the building blocks can be put together to create an overall design for the organization. We discuss the nature of organization design. We then describe early approaches aimed at identifying universal models of organization design. Situational factors, such as technology and environment, that have been found to influence design are discussed. We next focus on common and emerging approaches to organization design. After describing the linkage between an organization's strategy and its design, we conclude with a discussion of organizational culture.

THE NATURE OF ORGANIZATION DESIGN

What is organization design? In Chapter 8, we noted that job specialization and span of management are among the common building blocks of organization structure. We also described how the appropriate degree of specialization could vary, as could the appropriate span of management. Not really addressed, however, were questions of how specialization and span might be related to one another. For example, should a high level of specialization be matched with a certain span? And will different combinations of each work best with different bases of departmentalization? These and related issues are associated with questions of organization design.[2]

■ **organization design** The overall pattern of structural components and arrangements used to manage the total organization

Organization design is the overall pattern of structural components and arrangements used to manage the total organization. Thus, organization design is a means used to implement strategies and plans to achieve organizational goals. As we discuss organization design, there are two important points to keep in mind. First, remember that organizations are seldom, if ever, designed and then left intact. Indeed, most organizations change constantly as a result of situations, people, and other factors. (The processes of organization change are discussed in Chapter 11.) Second, recognize that organization design for large organizations is complex and has so many associated nuances and variations that descriptions of them must be considerably simplified in order to be described in basic terms.

UNIVERSAL PERSPECTIVES ON ORGANIZATION DESIGN

In Chapter 2, we noted the distinction between contingency and universal approaches to solving management problems. The foundation of what we know today about organization design comes from two early universal perspectives: the bureaucratic model and the behavioral model.

The Bureaucratic Model   •

In Chapter 2 we noted that Max Weber, an influential German sociologist, was a pioneer of classical organization theory. Weber stimulated much research on organization structure and design. At the core of Weber's writings was the bureaucratic model of organization design.[3] The Weberian perspective suggests that a **bureaucracy** is an organization based on a legitimate and formal system of authority. Many people associate bureaucracy with red tape, rigidity, and buck-passing. For example, how many times have you heard people refer disparagingly to "the federal bureaucracy"?

■ **bureaucracy** An organization design based on a legitimate and formal system of authority

NASA is a classic example of a bureaucratic form of organization design. It uses a tall hierarchical structure, narrow spans of control, and standardized rules and procedures to get things done. This shuttle launch was successful because each of these NASA employees used their expertise to accomplish a single goal.

Weber viewed the bureaucratic form of organization design as logical, rational, and efficient. He offered the bureaucratic model as the framework to which all organizations should aspire, the "one best way" of doing things. According to Weber, the ideal bureaucracy exhibits five basic characteristics. First, the organization should adopt a distinct division of labor, and each position should be filled by an expert. Second, the organization should develop a consistent set of rules to ensure that task performance is uniform. Third, the organization should establish a hierarchy of positions or offices so that a chain of command from the top of the organization to the bottom is created. Fourth, managers should conduct business in an impersonal way. They should especially maintain an appropriate social distance between themselves and their subordinates. Fifth, employment and advancement in the organization should be based on technical expertise. As a corollary, employees should be protected from arbitrary dismissal. As a consequence, employees should develop a high level of loyalty to the organization.

Perhaps the best examples of contemporary bureaucracies are government agencies and universities. Consider, for example, the steps you must go through and the forms you must fill out to apply for admission to college, request housing, register each semester, change majors, submit a degree plan, substitute a course, and file for graduation. The reason these procedures are necessary is that universities deal with large numbers of people who must be treated equally and fairly. Hence, rules, regulations, and standard operating procedures are needed. The U.S. Postal Service and other bureaucracies are working to change their image—to portray themselves as less mechanistic and impersonal. The strategy of the Postal Service is to become more service-oriented as a way to fight back against competitors like Federal Express and UPS.[4]

The bureaucratic model of organization has two primary strengths. First, several of its elements (such as division of labor, reliance on rules, a hierarchy of authority, and employment based on expertise) do, in fact, often improve efficiency. And second, as noted earlier, because the bureaucratic model was the starting point for much of our current thinking about organizations, it played a foundational role in understanding organization design. Unfortunately, the pursuit of an ideal bureaucracy results in several disadvantages. For one thing, bureaucracies tend to be inflexible and rigid. For another, human and social processes within the bureaucracy are neglected. And finally, Weber's assumptions about loyalty and impersonal relations are unrealistic.[5]

The Behavioral Model

behavioral model Organization design that paralleled the emergence of the human relations school of management thought

Another important universal model of organization design was Rensis Likert's System 4 approach, more generally known as the **behavioral model** because it paralleled the emergence of the human relations school of management thought. Like the bureaucratic model, the behavioral model was universal in its orientation. Working at the University of Michigan, Likert studied several large organizations to determine what made some of them effective and others less so.[6] He found that the organizations in his sample that used the bureaucratic model tended to be less effective than those that paid more attention to developing work groups and were more concerned about behavioral and social processes.

Likert developed a framework that characterized organizations in terms of eight key elements: leadership processes, motivational processes, communication processes, interaction processes, decision processes, goal-setting processes, control processes, and performance goals. Likert believed all organizations could be placed on a set of dimensions describing each of these eight elements. He argued that the basic bureaucratic form of organization, which he called a **System 1** design, anchored one end of each dimension. The characteristics of the System 1 organization in Likert's framework are summarized in Table 9.1.

System 1 A form of organization design based on legitimate and formal authority. It was developed as part of the behavioral model of organization design

System 4 A form of organization design that uses a wide array of motivational processes and promotes open and extensive interaction processes

Also summarized in this table are characteristics of Likert's other extreme form of organization design, called **System 4**. A System 4 organization uses a wide array of motivational processes and that its interaction processes are open and extensive. People communicate with each other in an unguarded way, everybody talks to everybody else, and so on. Other distinctions between System 1 and System 4 organizations are equally obvious. In between the System 1 and System 4 extremes lie the System 2 and System 3 organizations.

Likert argued that System 4 should be adopted by all organizations. He suggested that managers should emphasize supportive relationships, establish high performance goals, and practice group decision making to achieve the System 4 state. Many organizations attempted to adopt the System 4 design during its period of peak popularity. In 1969, a General Motors plant in the Atlanta area was converted from a System

System 1 Organization	System 4 Organization
1. **Leadership process** includes no perceived confidence and trust. Subordinates do not feel free to discuss job problems with their superiors, who in turn do not solicit their ideas and opinions.	1. **Leadership process** includes perceived confidence and trust between superiors and subordinates in all matters. Subordinates feel free to discuss job problems with their superiors, who in turn solicit their ideas and opinions.
2. **Motivational process** taps only physical, security, and economic motives through the use of fear and sanctions. Unfavorable attitudes toward the organization prevail among employees.	2. **Motivational process** taps a full range of motives through participatory methods. Attitudes are favorable toward the organization and its goals.
3. **Communication process** is such that information flows downward and tends to be distorted, inaccurate, and viewed with suspicion by subordinates.	3. **Communication process** is such that information flows freely throughout the organization—upward, downward, and laterally. The information is accurate and undistorted.
4. **Interaction process** is closed and restricted; subordinates have little effect on departmental goals, methods, and activities.	4. **Interaction process** is open and extensive; both superiors and subordinates are able to affect departmental goals, methods, and activities.
5. **Decision process** occurs only at the top of the organization; it is relatively centralized.	5. **Decision process** occurs at all levels through group processes; it is relatively decentralized.
6. **Goal-setting process** is located at the top of the organization; discourages group participation.	6. **Goal-setting process** encourages group participation in setting high, realistic objectives.
7. **Control process** is centralized and emphasizes fixing of blame for mistakes.	7. **Control process** is dispersed throughout the organization and emphasizes self-control and problem solving.
8. **Performance goals** are low and passively sought by managers who make no commitment to developing the human resources of the organization.	8. **Performance goals** are high and actively sought by superiors who recognize the necessity for making a full commitment to developing, through training, the human resources of the organization.

Source: Adapted from Rensis Likert, *The Human Organization* (New York: McGraw-Hill, 1967), pp. 197–211. Used with permission.

TABLE 9.1

System 1 and System 4 Organizations

2 to a System 4 status. Over a period of three years, direct and indirect labor efficiency improved, as did tool-breakage rates, scrap costs, and quality.[7]

Like the bureaucratic model, the behavioral approach to organization design has both strengths and weaknesses. The major strength is its emphasis on behavioral processes in organizations. Whereas the classical perspective treated people like components of a large machine and minimized the importance of any one person, the behavioral model recognized the individual value of an organization's employees. Likert and his associates thus paved the way for a more humanistic perspective. The behavioral approach, however, was based on the premise that there is only one best way to design organizations, but there is clear evidence that there is no one best way to design organizations.[8] What works for one organization may not work for another, and what works for one organization may change as that organization's situation changes. Hence, universal models like bureaucracy and System 4 have been largely supplanted by newer models that take contingency factors into account. In the next section, we identify a number of factors that help determine the best organization design for a particular situation.

SITUATIONAL INFLUENCES ON ORGANIZATION DESIGN

situational view of organization design Based on the assumption that the optimal design for any given organization depends on a set of relevant situational factors

The **situational view of organization design** is based on the assumption that the optimal design for any given organization depends on a set of relevant situational factors.[9] Three such factors—technology, environment, and size and organizational life cycle—are discussed here. Another, organizational strategy, is described later in this chapter.

Technology

■ **technology** The set of conversion processes used by an organization in transforming inputs into outputs

One situational factor that has an impact on organization design is technology. **Technology** is the conversion processes used by an organization to transform inputs (such as materials or information) into outputs (such as products or services). Although most people visualize assembly lines and machinery when they think of technology, the term can also be applied to service organizations. For example, a brokerage firm like Dean Witter uses technology to transform investment dollars into income in much the same way that Union Carbide uses natural resources to manufacture chemical products.

Much of what we know about the link between technology and organization design we owe to the pioneering work of Joan Woodward.[10] In the early 1960s she led a team of researchers studying 100 manufacturing firms in southern England. They collected information about such things as the history of each organization, its manufacturing processes, its forms and procedures, and financial data. Woodward expected to find a relationship between the size of an organization and its structure, but no such relationship emerged. So she began to seek other explanations for differences in organization design.

This follow-up analysis led Woodward to classify the organizations according to their technology. Three basic forms of technology were identified by Woodward:

1. *Unit or small-batch technology*. The product is custom-made to customer specifications, or else it is produced in small quantities. Examples of organizations using this form of technology include a

tailor shop like Brooks Brothers (custom suits) and a printing shop like Kinko's (business cards, company stationery).

2. *Large-batch or mass-production technology.* The product is manufactured in assembly-line fashion by combining component parts into another part or finished product. Examples include automobile manufacturers like Subaru and washing-machine companies like Whirlpool.

3. *Continuous-process technology.* The product is transformed from raw materials to a finished good by a series of machine or process transformations. The composition of the materials themselves is changed. Examples include petroleum refineries like Exxon and chemical refineries like Dow.

These forms of technology are listed in order of their predicted levels of complexity—unit or small-batch technology is presumed to be the least complex, continuous-process technology the most complex. Woodward found that different configurations of organization design were associated with each technology.

Table 9.2 summarizes the differences in structural components for each kind of technology. For example, as technology becomes more complex, the number of levels of management increases (that is, the organization becomes taller). The executive span of management also increases, and the relative size of the staff component grows. (In the small-batch organizations, Woodward and her associates found one staff member for every eight line workers; in the continuous-process organizations, they found one staff member for every two line workers.) However, the supervisory span of management first increases and then decreases as technology becomes more complex. This is attributable to the fact that much of the work in continuous-process technologies is automated. Fewer workers are needed, but the skills necessary to do the job increase. These findings are consistent with the discussion of

TABLE 9.2

Woodward's Findings on Technology and Organization Design

| Technology Type | Structural Component[a] | | | |
	Number of Levels of Management	Supervisory Span of Control	Executive Span of Control	Ratio of Industrial Workers (Line) to Staff Workers
Unit or small batch	3	23	4	8:1
Large batch or mass production	4	48	7	5:1
Continuous process	6	15	10	2:1

[a]The numbers in the table are medians for the organizations in each group.

the span of management in Chapter 8—the more complex the job, the narrower the span should probably be.

At a more general level of analysis, Woodward found that the two extremes (unit or small batch, and continuous process) tended to be very similar to Likert's System 4 organization, whereas the middle-range organizations (large batch or mass production) were much more like bureaucracies or System 1. There was also a higher level of specialization in the large-batch and mass-production organizations.[11] Finally, she found that organizational success was related to the extent to which organizations followed the typical pattern. For example, note in Table 9.2 that the median executive span of control in large-batch or mass-production organizations was 7. Successful organizations employing that technology tended to have an executive span very close to 7. Less successful large-batch or mass-production organizations tended to have an executive span considerably smaller or larger than 7.

Thus, technology clearly appears to play an important role in determining organization design. As future technologies become even more diverse and complex, managers will have to be even more aware of their impact on the design of organizations.[12] But technology is not the only variable that can influence organization design. Another important element is the environment of the organization.

Environment

Chapter 3 devotes considerable attention to organizational environments. In addition to the various relationships described in that discussion, there are a number of specific linkages among environmental elements and organization design. The first widely recognized contemporary analysis of potential environment–organization design linkages was provided by Tom Burns and G. M. Stalker.[13] Burns and Stalker worked in England. Their first step was identifying two extreme forms of organizational environment—stable (one that remains relatively constant over time) and unstable (subject to uncertainty and rapid change). Next, they studied the designs of a variety of organizations functioning in each type of environment. Not surprisingly, they found that organizations operating in stable environments tended to have a different kind of design from organizations operating in unstable environments. The two kinds of organization design that emerged, summarized in Table 9.3, were called mechanistic and organic.

A **mechanistic organization**, quite similar to the bureaucratic or System 1 model, was most frequently found in stable environments. Free from uncertainty, organizations could structure their activities in rather predictable ways by means of rules, specialized jobs, and centralized authority. Although no environment is completely stable, Wendy's and K mart each use a mechanistic design. An **organic organization**, on the other hand, was most often found in unstable and unpredictable environments. The constant change and uncertainty of

■ **mechanistic organization**
A rigid and bureaucratic form of design most appropriate for stable environments

■ **organic organization**   A fluid and flexible design most appropriate for unstable and unpredictable environments

Mechanistic	Organic
1. Tasks are highly fractionated and specialized; little regard paid to clarifying relationship between tasks and organizational objectives.	1. Tasks are more interdependent; emphasis on relevance of tasks and organizational objectives.
2. Tasks tend to remain rigidly defined unless altered formally by top management.	2. Tasks are continually adjusted and redefined through interaction of organizational members.
3. Specific role definition (rights, obligations, and technical methods prescribed for each member).	3. Generalized role definition (members accept general responsibility for task accomplishment beyond individual role definition).
4. Hierarchic structure of control, authority, and communication. Sanctions derive from employment contract between employee and organization.	4. Network structure of control, authority, and communication. Sanctions derive more from community of interest than from contractual relationship.
5. Information relevant to situation and operations of the organization formally assumed to rest with chief executive.	5. Leader not assumed to be omniscient; knowledge centers identified where located throughout organization.
6. Communication is primarily vertical between superior and subordinate.	6. Communication is both vertical and horizontal, depending upon where needed information resides.
7. Communications primarily take form of instructions and decisions issued by superiors, of information and requests for decisions supplied by inferiors.	7. Communications primarily take form of information and advice.
8. Insistence on loyalty to organization and obedience to superiors.	8. Commitment to organization's tasks and goals more highly valued than loyalty or obedience.
9. Importance and prestige attached to identification with organization and its members.	9. Importance and prestige attached to affiliations and expertise in external environment.

SOURCE: Adapted from Tom Burns and G. M. Stalker, *The Management of Innovation* (London: Tavistock, 1961), pp. 119–122. Used with permission.

TABLE 9.3

Mechanistic and Organic Organizations

such environments usually dictates a much higher level of fluidity and flexibility. Motorola (with rapid technological change) and Limited Inc. (with constant change in consumer tastes) each use a design that is basically organic.

The ideas of Burns and Stalker were extended in the United States by Paul R. Lawrence and Jay W. Lorsch, two Harvard professors.[14] They agreed that environmental factors influence organization design but believed that this influence varies between different units or departments of the same organization. In fact, they predicted that each organizational unit has its own unique environment and responds by developing unique attributes. Lawrence and Lorsch suggested that organizations could be characterized along two primary dimensions. One

differentiation The extent to which the organization is broken down into subunits

integration The extent to which the subunits of an organization must work together in a coordinated fashion

of these dimensions, **differentiation**, is the extent to which the organization is broken down into subunits. A firm with many departments is highly differentiated; one with few departments has a low level of differentiation. The second dimension, **integration**, is the degree to which the various units must work together in a coordinated fashion. If each unit competes in a different market and has its own production facilities, little integration may be needed; if the units share resources and have a common sales staff, more integration will be required. Lawrence and Lorsch reasoned that the degree of differentiation and integration needed by an organization would depend on the stability of the environments that its subunits faced.[15]

Size and Organizational Life Cycle

■ **organizational size** The number of full-time or full-time equivalent employees

Size is another factor that affects organization design. Recall, for example, that Woodward initially studied size. Although several definitions of size exist, we will view **organizational size** in terms of the total number of full-time or full-time-equivalent employees. Interesting research on organization size and design was conducted by a team of researchers at the University of Aston in Birmingham, England.[16] These researchers felt that Woodward had failed to find a size-structure relationship because almost all the organizations she studied were relatively small (three-fourths of them had fewer than 500 employees). Thus, they decided to study a wider array of organizations to determine how size and technology both individually and jointly affect the design of an organization. None of the organizations in their sample had fewer than 250 employees, and 60 percent had over 500 employees.

The primary finding of the Aston studies was that technology did in fact influence structural variables in smaller firms, probably because all their activities tended to be centered around technology. In larger firms, however, the strong technology-design link broke down, most likely because technology is not as central to ongoing activities in such organizations. The Aston studies yielded a number of basic generalizations: When compared to small organizations, large organizations tend to be characterized by higher levels of job specialization, more standard operating procedures, more rules, more regulations, and a greater degree of decentralization. "The Global View" illustrates how one firm, Saab-Scania, has attempted to retain many of the desirable attributes of smaller organizations for its Combitech subsidiary.

■ **organizational life cycle** A natural sequence of stages most organizations pass through as they grow and mature

Of course, size is not constant. Some small businesses are formed but soon disappear. Others remain as small, independently operated enterprises as long as their owner-manager lives. A few, like Compaq, Liz Claiborne, and Reebok, skyrocket to become organizational giants. And occasionally large organizations reduce their size through layoffs or divestitures. Although there is no clear pattern for explaining changes in size, many organizations progress through a four-stage **organizational life cycle**.[17]

In 1980, John Mackey founded his first natural food grocery store, the Whole Foods Market, in Austin, Texas. At the time, he found that he could communicate his operating philosophy and methods to all his employees on a face-to-face basis. When he started opening other stores, however, he realized that his current approach was no longer working. So he wrote everything down in a handbook designed to help all his employees understand the company's culture better. Today Whole Foods has eight stores in its chain, with more in the planning stages. Mackey's handbook, and indeed his guiding management philosophies, have changed and evolved as the organization grows and expands.

The first stage is the birth of the organization. At Compaq, this occurred in 1984 when a handful of Texas Instruments engineers resigned, raised some venture capital, and set up shop. The second stage, youth, is characterized by growth and the expansion of all organizational resources. Compaq passed through the youth stage in 1985 and entered the third stage, midlife, around the beginning of 1986. The company remains in midlife today, with sales in excess of $1 billion annually. The final stage of an organization's life cycle, maturity, has been achieved by one of Compaq's competitors—IBM.[18]

As the organization progresses through these stages, a number of organization design issues must be confronted. In general, as an organization passes from one stage to the next, it becomes bigger, more mechanistic, and more decentralized. It also becomes more specialized, devotes more attention to planning, and takes on an increasingly large staff component. Finally, coordination demands increase, formalization increases, organizational units become geographically more dispersed, and control systems become more extensive. Thus, there is a clear link between an organization's size and design—and this link is dynamic because of the organizational life cycle.[19]

COMMON FORMS OF ORGANIZATION DESIGN

Given that technology, environment, and size and life cycle can all influence organization design, it should come as no surprise that there are many different kinds of designs that organizations can adopt. Most designs, however, fall into one of four basic categories. Others are hybrids based on two or more of the basic forms.

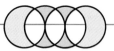

THE GLOBAL VIEW

SAAB THINKS SMALL

Saab-Scania, the Swedish car, truck, and airplane company, thinks small. Saab thinks that it can be most effective if it organizes in such a way that its units operate like small firms early in the organizational life cycle rather than like divisions of a big firm later in the life cycle. Smaller firms, Saab seems to argue, can move more quickly to take advantage of changes in consumer tastes and preferences, can operate with lower administrative costs, and can more quickly take advantage of new developments in technology.

In the early 1980s, Saab pieced together a new subsidiary from a mixture of high-tech ventures in which it had been engaged but none of which seemed to be catching on. The new subsidiary, termed Combitech, quickly doubled revenues and tripled profits. Combitech succeeded because it was run as a series of little entrepreneurial companies; its heads had 25 to 30 percent of their compensation tied directly to the performance of their units. Small units, entrepreneurial managers, and compensation linked to performance appeared to be the key features of successful performance.

Saab-Valmet is another example of the small size and entrepreneurial spirit that Saab is attempting to foster. Located in Uusikaupunki, Finland, it manufac-

tures about one-third of Saab's cars. However, it has also become an independent specialty engineering and production branch. The Valmet group is the sole producer of the 900 convertible. It developed the car on its own and then convinced the car management group in Sweden to produce the car. Saab-Valmet does not have a marketing organization, so it must sell the cars through Saab's usual channels. Nevertheless, it has outsold Peugeot and Alfa Romeo in North America. The Valmet group continues to develop the 900 and has other models under study.

Saab-Scania is attempting to create "youthful" characteristics in all of its operating units. It has created a small, independent automotive finance unit for the United States. It has separate units for buses, trucks, and airplanes, and regional units as well. Each unit is kept somewhat small (the actual size varies with technology and the history of the unit), and each tries to maintain the entrepreneurial excitement and culture of the first two stages of the organizational life cycle.

REFERENCES: Peter J. Mullins, "Scania Preps for the '90s," *Truck & Off-Highway Industries*, February 1988, pp. T-10, T-11; "Playing the Niche to Win," *Automotive Industries*, August 1988, pp. 58–60; "For Lord Einstein, Breaking Away Was the Easy Part," *Business Week*, May 9, 1988, pp. 72–76; Richard I. Kirkland, Jr., "Europe's New Managers," *Fortune*, September 29, 1986, pp. 56–60.

The Functional (U-Form) Design

functional organization design   An arrangement based on the functional approach to departmentalization, also called the U-form

The **functional design** is an arrangement based in large part on the functional approach to departmentalization as detailed in Chapter 8. This design was recently termed the **U-form** (for unitary) by noted economist Oliver E. Williamson.[20] Under this arrangement, the members of the organization are grouped into functional departments like marketing and production. Thus, for the organization to operate efficiently, there must be considerable coordination across departments. This integration and coordination are most commonly the responsibility of the chief executive. Figure 9.1 shows the U-form design as applied to a small manufacturing company.

At the corporate level, the company clearly employs a functional base of departmentalization. In a U-form organization, none of the functional areas can survive without the others. Marketing, for example, needs products from operations to sell and funds from finance to pay

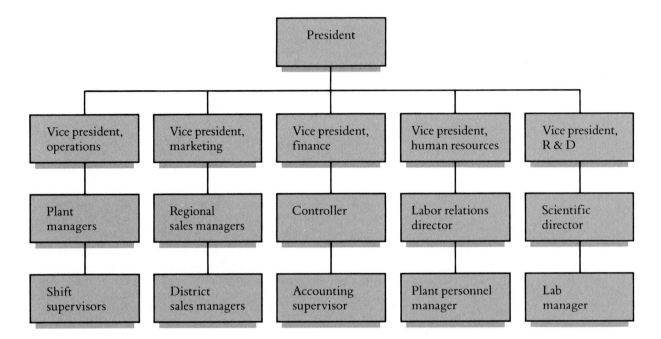

FIGURE 9.1

Functional (U-Form) Design for a Small Manufacturing Company

for advertising. In general, this approach shares the basic advantages and disadvantages of functional departmentalization as detailed in Chapter 8. And as also noted in Chapter 8, U-form design is most commonly used in small organizations, because in such organizations it is fairly easy for an individual CEO to oversee and coordinate the entire organization. As an organization grows, the CEO finds it increasingly difficult to stay on top of everything.

The Conglomerate (H-Form) Design

conglomerate organization design Used by an organization comprised of a set of smaller unrelated businesses, also called the H-form

Another fairly common form of organization design is the conglomerate, or H-form, approach.[21] A **conglomerate** is an organization made up of a set of unrelated businesses. Thus, the **H-form** design is essentially a holding company. In many ways, this approach is based loosely on the product form of departmentalization. Each business ("department") is operated by a general manager who is responsible for its profits or losses, and each general manager functions independently of the others. Until its recent breakup, Beatrice was a classic example of the H-form organization.[22] As illustrated in Figure 9.2, Beatrice once owned Avis, Playtex, Samsonite, and Tropicana, among other companies—each about as unrelated to the others as imaginable. (In 1986, Beatrice was bought and is currently being dismantled.)

In the H-form arrangement, a corporate staff usually evaluates the performance of each business, allocates corporate resources across companies, and shapes decisions about buying and selling businesses. Thus,

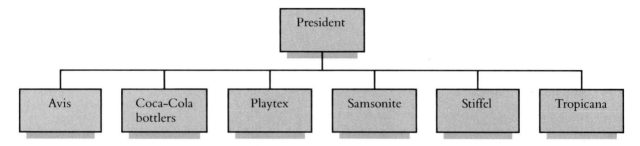

FIGURE 9.2

Classical Conglomerate
(H–Form) Design at Beatrice
Prior to 1986

the H-form is consistent with the business portfolio approach to corporate strategy as discussed in Chapter 6. The basic shortcoming of the H-form model is the complexity associated with diverse and unrelated businesses. Managers usually find it difficult to compare and integrate activities across a large number of diverse operations. Research by Michael Porter suggests that many organizations that follow this approach reflect only average-to-weak financial performance.[23] Thus, although many American firms are still using the H-form design, many are also abandoning it for other approaches.

The Divisional (M-Form) Design

A third approach to organization design, and one becoming increasingly popular, is the divisional design. In this arrangement, a product form of organization is also used; but, in contrast to the H-form, the divisions are related. Thus, the **divisional design**, or **M-form**, is based on multiple businesses in related areas operating within a larger organizational framework. Some activities are extremely decentralized down to the divisional level; others are centralized at the corporate level.[24] For example, as shown in Figure 9.3, Limited Inc. uses this approach. Each of its divisions is headed by a general manager and operates with reasonable autonomy, but the divisions also coordinate their activities as appropriate.

divisional organization design An arrangement based on the product approach to departmentalization, also called the M-form

FIGURE 9.3

Multidivisional (M–Form)
Design at Limited Inc.

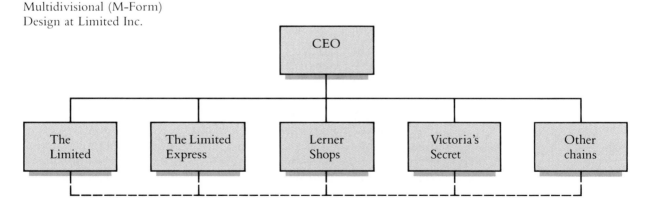

The Washington Post Company uses a divisional, or M-form, design where multiple businesses in related areas operate within a larger organizational framework. Headed up by Katherine Graham, shown here, the Post Company owns and publishes *The Washington Post* newspaper, *Newsweek* magazine, and numerous broadcast and cable television operations.

matrix organization design
An arrangement wherein a product-based form of departmentalization is superimposed onto an existing functional arrangement

multiple-command structure   When any given individual reports to a functional superior and one or more project managers simultaneously

Indeed, the opportunities for coordination and shared resources represent one of the biggest advantages of the M-form design. Limited Inc. uses a centralized marketing research department and centralized purchasing department. Thus, a buyer can inspect a manufacturer's entire product line, buy some designs for The Limited chain, others for The Limited Express, and still others for Lerner. Similarly, Disney has three fairly autonomous film divisions—Walt Disney Pictures, Touchstone Pictures, and Hollywood Pictures—but distributes all its films through the same centralized distribution company, Buena Vista Pictures Distribution Company.[25] In a comparable situation, a buyer for an H-form organization would be hard-pressed to purchase luggage for one division, lamps for another, and juice concentrate for a third.

The basic objective for the M-form organization is to strike a balance between internal competition and cooperation. Healthy competition between divisions for resources can enhance effectiveness, but cooperation should also be promoted. Research suggests that the M-form organization that can achieve and maintain this balance will outperform large U-form and all H-form organizations.[26]

The Matrix Design

The matrix design is another common approach to organization design.[27] Essentially, a **matrix design** is based upon two overlapping bases of departmentalization. The foundation of a matrix is an arrangement of functional departments. A set of product groups, or temporary departments, is then superimposed across the functional departments. Employees in a matrix are simultaneously members of a functional department (e.g., engineering) and of a project team. Figure 9.4 shows a basic matrix design.

At the top of the organizational chart are functional units headed by vice presidents of engineering, production, finance, and marketing. Each of these managers has several subordinates. Along the side of the organizational chart are a number of positions termed project manager. Each project manager heads a project group composed of representatives or workers from the functional departments. Note from the figure that a matrix reflects a **multiple-command structure**—any given individual may report both to a functional superior and to one or more project managers.

The project groups, or teams, are assigned to designated projects or programs. For example, the company might want to develop a new product. Representatives are chosen from each functional area to work as a team on the new product. They also retain membership in the original functional group. At any given time, a person may be a member of several teams as well as a member of a functional group. This is exactly what Ford did in creating its popular Taurus automobile. It formed a group called "Team Taurus" made up of designers, engineers, production specialists, marketing specialists, and other experts from different areas of the company. This group facilitated getting a very

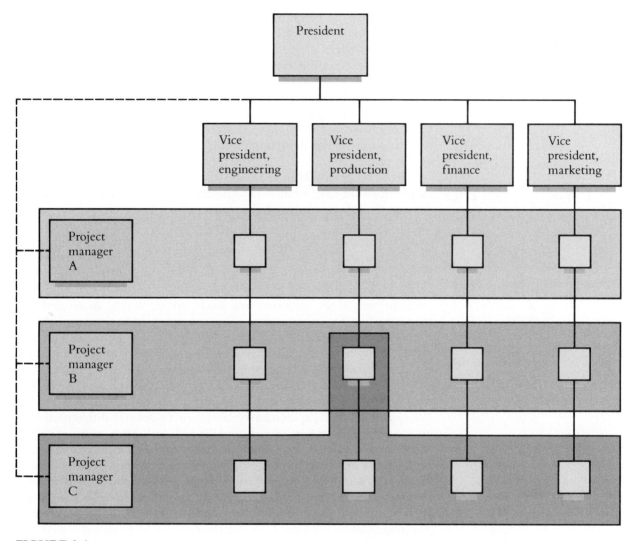

FIGURE 9.4

A Matrix Organization

successful product to the market at least a year earlier than would have been possible under previous approaches.[28]

Many major organizations have adopted the matrix form of organization design. Notable among them are American Cyanamid, Monsanto, NCR Corporation (formerly National Cash Register), Chase Manhattan Bank, Prudential Insurance, General Motors, and several state and federal government agencies. Some organizations, however, such as Citibank and the Dutch firm, Philips, adopted and then dropped the matrix design.

It is important to recognize that a matrix design is not always appropriate. The matrix form of organization design is most often used in one of three situations.[29] The first situation occurs when there is strong pressure from the environment. For example, intense external competition may dictate the sort of strong marketing thrust that is best spearheaded by a functional department, but the diversity of a company's products may argue for product departments. The second situation occurs when large amounts of information need to be processed. For example, creating lateral relations by means of a matrix is one effective way to increase the organization's capacity to process information. The third situation occurs when there is pressure for shared resources. For example, a company with ten product departments may have resources for only three marketing specialists. A matrix design would allow all the departments to share the company's scarce marketing resource.

There are both advantages and disadvantages associated with the matrix form of organization design. Six primary advantages of matrix designs have been observed. First, one of the truly significant advantages of a matrix is its flexibility. Teams can be created, redefined, and dissolved almost continuously, allowing the organization to cope readily with uncertainty, instability, and change. Second, because the teams in a matrix organization consist of specialists from different functional areas, each member assumes a major role in decision making. As a consequence, team members are likely to be highly motivated and committed to the organization. Third, employees in a matrix organization have considerable opportunity to learn new skills. This opportunity stems from their involvement in a variety of projects and from their interaction on teams containing experts from other areas.

A fourth advantage of a matrix design is that it provides an efficient way for the organization to take full advantage of its human resources. Because the same expert can be assigned to several different teams, unnecessary duplication of personnel is reduced. Fifth, team members retain membership in their functional unit, so they can serve as a bridge between the functional unit and the team, enhancing cooperation. Sixth, the matrix design gives top management a useful vehicle for decentralization. Once the day-to-day operations have been delegated, top management can devote more attention to such areas as long-range planning.

On the other hand, there are also some significant disadvantages to the matrix design. Employees may be uncertain about whom they are supposed to report to, especially if they are simultaneously assigned to a functional manager and to several project managers. What happens when their several bosses make conflicting demands on them? To complicate matters, some managers may see the matrix as a form of anarchy in which they are free to do anything they want. These problems can be minimized by explicitly defining all authority relationships. Another set of problems is associated with the dynamics of group behavior. Groups take longer than individuals to make decisions, may be dominated by a strong individual, and may compromise unnecessarily. They may also get bogged down in discussion and not focus on their primary objectives. Finally, a matrix design is expensive because more managers and staff may be needed. More time may also be required for coordinating task-related activities.[30]

MANAGEMENT IN PRACTICE

HYBRID DESIGNS AT MERCK

Merck & Company, the American descendant of the German Merck chemical and pharmaceutical company, has been in business in the United States for over a century. Merck generally ranks number 1 in sales of prescription drugs as well as in some specific categories of drugs. Merck's R&D program is often mentioned as the key to the company's success.

Merck's research and development organization has a very informal structure, avoiding explicit lines of authority, chains of command, and detailed job descriptions. The organization gives scientists extraordinary freedom to select an approach and then to carry through with that approach.

Research activity is organized around twelve classes of therapeutic drugs. Research activity in each of the twelve areas is ongoing at all times. Thus, in the functional area of research and development, the company uses what might be thought of as product-line organization.

However, there are also projects that are organized around what appear to be major product hopefuls. Mevacor, an anti-cholesterol drug, was developed through such an approach. Each project has a leader, or product champion. The task of the leader is to keep the laboratories excited about the possibilities for potential new products and to see that new ideas are constantly being generated.

Uniquely, however, projects have no separate budgets. They are not official organizational units with separate authority. Everything needed to carry them out must be obtained by persuading the twelve discipline units to relinquish funds and personnel. The task of persuasion falls most heavily on the project leader, but every member of a project team works to educate and persuade the scientists in his or her discipline that a project is worth spending money on and participating in.

The idea is to develop unity of purpose through collegiality. The exchange of information and the excitement that is generated by potential breakthroughs bring the staff close together.

Merck, then, has a hybrid form of organization, one that does not exactly match any traditional design. Traditional functional arrangements exist at Merck, as do elements of the matrix form of design. However, there are also unique arrangements tailored to fit Merck's particular strategy and environment and to bring about the effective use of its resources.

REFERENCES: "A Healthy Payoff from Nonstop Research," *Business Week*, January 11, 1988, p. 119; Ellen Schultz, "America's Most Admired Corporations," *Fortune*, January 18, 1988, pp. 32–37; Bro Uttal, "Companies That Serve You Best," *Fortune*, December 7, 1987, pp. 98–116; "The Miracle Company," *Business Week*, October 19, 1987, pp. 84–90.

Hybrid Designs

Some organizations use a form of design that represents a hybrid of two or more of the common forms. For example, an organization may have five related divisions and one unrelated division, making it a cross between an M-form and an H-form design. "Management in Practice" describes how the highly successful pharmaceutical giant Merck uses a product-based design but also employs temporary project groups that span other departments or groups.

Indeed, a great many companies follow this or similar approaches. The basic notion is to have one basic organization design as a foundation to managing the business but to maintain sufficient flexibility so that temporary or permanent modifications can be made for strategic purposes. Even the Ford example used earlier to illustrate the matrix is in reality a hybrid. Ford used the matrix approach to design the Taurus, but the company is still basically a U-form organization showing signs of moving to an M-form design. As noted earlier, any combination of environmental, technological, or life-cycle variables may dictate the appropriate form of organization design for any particular company.

EMERGING ISSUES IN ORGANIZATION DESIGN

In addition to the well-known contingency factors of environment, technology, and size, other situational determinants of organization design are emerging. Two that are becoming increasingly important are information-processing requirements and global imperatives.

Information-processing Requirements

As we noted in Chapter 3, organizational environments are becoming increasingly turbulent, complex, and uncertain. As uncertainty increases, the amount of information that the organization has to process increases. At the same time, breakthroughs in information technology allow managers to process larger quantities of information more and more efficiently. Managers are becoming increasingly aware that these information-processing requirements and capabilities influence organization design.

One clear implication relates to the span of management and the number of levels of an organization. Innovations in information technology enable a manager to stay in touch with an increasingly large number of managers and subordinates. Thus, spans of management are likely to widen and organizational levels decrease. Organizations are increasingly using their information-processing capabilities to network with other companies. Pacific Intermountain Express, a large Western trucking company, gives its customers access to Pacific's own computer network so they can check on the status of their shipments.[31]

Managers can draw on a number of organization design elements to help cope with information-processing requirements.[32] Two of these methods focus on reducing the need for information processing; two involve increasing the organization's capacity to process information. One way to decrease information-processing needs is to create **slack resources**. Consider a wholesaler who ships merchandise to retailers across the United States. The information that affects an optimal inventory level includes forecasted demand for the products, existing retail inventories, shipping time, and frequency of reorders. The wholesaler has a great deal of information to handle. If the wholesaler does not carry an inventory large enough to fill all the orders, it runs the risk of permanently losing retail customers to another wholesaler. The wholesaler could deal with this problem by increasing the size of the inventory until it is large enough to cover all orders at all times. This amount of inventory is more than enough for ordinary demands,

slack resources   Excess resources used to help an organization decrease its information processing requirements

so the excess inventory becomes a slack resource, allowing the organization to be less concerned with forecasts, shipping times, and so on. Slack resources need not be physical in nature. Slack time can be built into a schedule and contingency (slack) funds into a budget. Of course, additional costs are associated with this technique. For organization design, the effect of having slack resources depends on the nature of the resources. The wholesaler just described will need additional employees and managers to handle the new storage facilities. Such changes may also affect the planning staff and the budget department.

Another way to reduce information-processing requirements is to create **self-contained tasks**. When an organization moves from functional departments to product departments, each new department becomes self-contained, with its own engineers, marketing staff, and so on. Self-containment works to reduce the need for information processing by reducing the number of demands on each specialist. Whenever a particular product group needs the expertise of a given staff specialist, it does not have to compete with another unit for that specialist's time. Of course, the organization loses the advantages of functional departmentalization.

Whereas the preceding two techniques decrease the need to process information, **vertical information systems** allow the organization to process more information—that is, the organization can create systems to transmit information more efficiently up and down the chain of command. These systems might range from sophisticated computer networks to clerical assistants who organize and summarize information. A system could be established whereby all information about the changes in the price of raw materials would be entered automatically into a computer. A product manager who needed to calculate current production costs for his or her products could obtain the information easily without going through the finance or purchasing department.

Another way to increase an organization's capacity to process information is to create **lateral relationships**. Basically, this involves using any of the coordination techniques described in Chapter 8 (liaison roles, task forces, teams, integrating departments). Then, when two interdependent units need to coordinate their activities by sharing information, the existence of a task force facilitates the process. The matrix design also clearly depends on lateral relationships.[33]

self-contained tasks   Independent units used to help an organization decrease its information processing requirements

vertical information systems   Communication linkages between managers and their subordinates created to help the organization process more information

lateral relationships   Coordination linkages used to help the organization process more information

The Global Organization

Another situational factor increasingly affecting organization design is the trend toward the internationalization of business. Few businesses today are untouched by suppliers, customers, or competitors from other countries. The relevant issues for organization design include how to design the firm so as to most effectively deal with international forces. For example, consider a moderate-size company that has just decided to "go international." Should it set up an international division, should it retain its current structure and establish an international operating group, or should it make its international operations an auto-nomous subunit?[34]

The effects of globalization are growing. Half of the labor force in the American chemical industry works for foreign owners. IBM gets more than 50 percent of its total sales from foreign markets. LTV and U.S. Steel (now USX) chose to ignore foreign competition and have been greatly wounded as a result. The fortieth-largest industrial cor-poration in the world, excluding the United States, is General Motors of Canada. Ford Motor of Canada is forty-third, Ford-Werke (West Germany) is fifty-seventh, and Ford Motor of Britain is sixty-fifth.[35]

The effects of globalization are not confined to large businesses. Many small firms have started exporting their products to foreign markets, and many others have been quite successful in importing foreign prod-ucts for resell in America. Clearly, international forces will continue to affect organizations in many different ways. Organization design is one useful method that managers can use to help manage these opportunities and threats. We discuss different forms of organization design used for different levels of international involvement in Chapter 21.

LINKING STRATEGY AND ORGANIZATION DESIGN

Another set of factors that affect and are affected by organization design is the strategy adopted by the organization. This linkage was first recognized by Alfred D. Chandler in the early 1960s.[36] Chandler studied several large American organizations such as Du Pont, Sears, and Gen-eral Motors over a period of several years. The primary conclusion he reached was that an organization's strategy determines its technology and environment. And since these influence the design of the organi-zation, it follows that strategy ultimately affects organization design.

More recently, Henry Mintzberg has provided additional insight into the relationship between strategy and organization design.[37] In addition to the basic relationships identified by Chandler, Mintzberg goes on to suggest that an organization's growth rate and distribution of power, other factors determined by strategy, also affect the design the organi-zation adopts. Mintzberg argues that organizations can be differentiated along three basic dimensions: (1) their primary coordinating mechanism (the major approach used to coordinate organizational activities), (2) the key part of the organization (the part that plays the major role in determining the organization's success or failure), and (3) the type of decentralization employed.[38] Each of these dimensions has several dif-ferent aspects.

Mintzberg identifies five basic coordinating mechanisms that flow from different strategies. The first is direct supervision. In this ap-proach, one individual is responsible for the work of others. The second is standardization of work processes. Here the content of the work is specified or programmed. Next is standardization of skills. This approach explicitly specifies the kind of training necessary to do the work. Fourth is standardization of output. This method specifies the results, or output, of the work. Finally, mutual adjustment coordinates activities through informal communication.

There are also five key parts of an organization. One is the strategic apex, consisting of top management and its support staff. Another is the operative core, composed of workers who actually carry out the organization's tasks. The middle line is made up of middle and lower-level management. Analysts such as industrial engineers, accountants, planners, and human resource managers make up the technostructure. Finally, the support staff consists of units that provide support to the organization outside the operating work flow (for example, legal counsel, executive dining room staff, and consultants).

Mintzberg suggests that there are three types of decentralization. Under vertical decentralization, there is a well-defined distribution of power down the chain of command, or shared authority between superiors and their subordinates. Horizontal decentralization is the extent to which nonmanagers (including staff) make decisions, or share authority between line and staff. Selective decentralization is the extent to which power over different kinds of decisions rests with different units within the organization. Using the relevant forms of coordinating mechanism, key parts, and types of decentralization, Mintzberg proposes that the strategy that an organization adopts and how far the organization has moved to fulfill that strategy result in five different forms of organization design. These forms are summarized in Table 9.4.

TABLE 9.4

Mintzberg's Five Designs

Structural Configuration	Prime Coordinating Mechanism	Key Part of Organization	Type of Decentralization
Simple structure	Direct supervision	Strategic apex	Vertical and horizontal centralization
Machine bureaucracy	Standardization of work processes	Technostructure	Limited horizontal decentralization
Professional bureaucracy	Standardization of skills	Operating core	Vertical and horizontal decentralization
Divisionalized form	Standardization of outputs	Middle line	Limited vertical decentralization
Adhocracy	Mutual adjustment	Support staff	Selective decentralization

SOURCE: Henry Mintzberg, *The Structuring of Organizations: A Synthesis of the Research*, © 1979, p. 301. Reprinted by permission of Prentice-Hall, Inc., Englewood Cliffs, N.J.

The Simple Structure

■ **simple structure** A form of organization design that uses direct supervision as its primary coordinating mechanism, has as its most important part its strategic apex, and employs vertical and horizontal centralization

The **simple structure** uses direct supervision as its primary coordinating mechanism, has as its most important part its strategic apex, and employs vertical and horizontal centralization. Relatively small corporations controlled by aggressive entrepreneurs, new government departments, and medium-size retail stores are all likely to exhibit a simple structure. These organizations tend to be relatively young. The CEO (often the owner) retains much of the decision-making power. The organization is relatively flat and does not emphasize specialization. Many smaller U-form organizations are structured in this fashion.

The Machine Bureaucracy

■ **machine bureaucracy** Uses standardization of work processes as its prime coordinating mechanism, the technostructure as its most important part, and establishes limited horizontal decentralization

The **machine bureaucracy** uses standardization of work processes as its prime coordinating mechanism; the technostructure is its most important part; and limited horizontal decentralization is established. The machine bureaucracy is quite similar to Burns and Stalker's mechanistic design discussed earlier. Examples include McDonald's and most large branches of the U.S. government. This kind of organization is generally mature in age, and its environment is usually stable and predictable. A high level of task specialization and a rigid pattern of authority are also typical. Spans of management are likely to be narrow, and the organization is usually tall. Large U-form organizations are also likely to fall into this category.

The Professional Bureaucracy

■ **professional bureaucracy** Uses standardization of skills as its prime coordinating mechanism, has the operating core as its most important part, and practices both vertical and horizontal decentralization

The third form of organization design suggested by Mintzberg is the **professional bureaucracy**. Examples of this form of organization include universities, general hospitals, and public accounting firms. The professional bureaucracy uses standardization of skills as its prime coordinating mechanism, has the operating core as its most important part, and practices both vertical and horizontal decentralization. It has relatively few middle managers. Further, like some staff managers, its members tend to identify more with their professions than with the organization. Coordination problems are common.

The Divisionalized Form

■ **divisionalized form of organization design** Exhibits standardization of output as its prime coordinating mechanism, the middle line as its most important part, and practices limited vertical decentralization

The **divisionalized form**, Mintzberg's fourth design, exhibits standardization of output as its prime coordinating mechanism, the middle line as its most important part, and limited vertical decentralization.

Bombardier, Inc., a large Canadian corporation, is an example of a firm using the divisional (M-form) design. Its various products and divisions include aerospace (planes), mass transit (buses and subways), rail and diesel (locomotives), and recreational and utility vehicles (snowmobiles). Each business is clearly related to the others—they all involve transportation. But each is also operated independently with a corporate staff of only 36 (including the CEO and secretaries).

This design is the same as both the H-form and the M-form described earlier. Limited Inc. and Disney are illustrative of this approach. Power is generally decentralized down to middle management—but not any further. Hence each division itself is relatively centralized and tends to structure itself as a machine bureaucracy. As might be expected, the primary reason for an organization to adopt this kind of design is market diversity.

The Adhocracy

■ **adhocracy** Uses mutual adjustment as a means of coordination, has as its most important part the support staff, and maintains selective patterns of decentralization

The **adhocracy** uses mutual adjustment as a means of coordination, has as its most important part the support staff, and maintains selective patterns of decentralization. Most organizations that use a fully developed matrix design are adhocracies. An adhocracy avoids specialization, formality, and unit of command. Even the term itself, derived from "ad hoc," suggests a lack of formality. Sun Microsystems is an excellent example of an adhocracy.

Clearly, our understanding of the relationship between an organization's strategy and its design is still in its infancy. However, the work begun by Chandler and continued by Mintzberg has laid a reasonable foundation for arguing that such a relationship exists. In the future, managers and researchers will no doubt develop better and stronger insights into how organization strategy and design are interrelated.[39]

ORGANIZATIONAL CULTURE

■ **culture** The set of values of an organization that helps its members understand what the organization stands for, how it does things, and what it considers important

A final element of organization design that warrants our attention is organizational culture. We will define **culture** as the set of values of an organization that help its members understand what the organization stands for, how it does things, and what it considers important.[40] We can draw a picture to illustrate bases of departmentalization or span of management, but culture is an amorphous concept that defies objective measurement or observation. Nevertheless, its importance is being increasingly recognized by managers and researchers alike.

The Importance of Organizational Culture

To illustrate the effects culture can have on an organization, consider what happened to Levi Strauss & Company. Several years ago, Strauss executives felt that the company had outgrown its 68-year-old building. Even though everyone enjoyed the casual atmosphere, more space was needed. So Levi Strauss moved into a modern office building in downtown San Francisco, where its new headquarters spread over twelve floors in a skyscraper. It quickly became apparent that the change was affecting the corporate culture—and that people did not like it. Executives felt isolated and other managers missed the informal chance meetings in the halls. Within just a few years, Strauss moved out of the skyscraper and back into a building that fosters informality. For example, there is an adjacent park area where employees frequently converge for lunchtime conversation. Clearly, Levi Strauss has a culture that is important to everyone who works there.[41]

Culture determines the "feel" of the organization. The stereotypic image of the IBM executive is someone wearing a white shirt and dark suit. In contrast, Texas Instruments likes to talk about its shirt-sleeve culture, in which ties are avoided and few managers ever wear jackets. In all probability, the design of the organization and its culture are highly interrelated. A highly specialized, centralized organization with an overall design that is bureaucratic, System 1, mechanistic, or a machine bureaucracy is likely to be perceived as impersonal and formal. Alternatively, if tasks are not specialized and authority is decentralized, and if overall design is closer to System 4, organic, or an adhocracy, the organization's culture will probably have a more positive effect on its members.

The same culture is not necessarily found throughout an entire organization. For example, the sales and marketing department may have a culture quite different from that of the operations and manufacturing department. Within a divisionalized organization, cultures can vary

Sun Microsystems has a unique corporate culture. Its managers want the workplace to be fun and as different from other organizations as possible. It holds weekly dress-down days where all employees wear casual clothes and it throws a monthly beer bash. On Halloween, everyone wears gorilla suits to work. One night recently, a group of engineers tore out the wall behind the CEO's office, moved all his furniture, and turned the office into a tricky par-4 one-hole golf course. The CEO, Scott McNealy, bogeyed the hole on his first try. McNealy credits Sun's unique culture with transforming it into a major player in the computer industry in only a few years.

dramatically from one division to another. Regardless of an organization's form, culture is a powerful force in organizations, one that can shape the firm's overall effectiveness and long-term success. Companies that can develop and maintain a strong culture, such as Hewlett-Packard and Procter & Gamble, tend to be more effective than companies that have trouble developing and maintaining a strong culture.[42]

Determinants of Culture

Where does a culture come from? Typically, it develops and blossoms over a long period of time. Its starting point is often the organization's founder. For example, James Cash Penney believed in treating employees and customers with respect and dignity. Employees at J. C. Penney are still called associates rather than employees (to reflect partnership), and customer satisfaction is of paramount importance.

As an organization grows, its culture is modified, shaped, and refined by symbols, stories, heroes, slogans, and ceremonies. For example, a key value at Hewlett-Packard is the avoidance of bank debt. A popular story still told at the company involves a new project being considered for several years. All objective criteria indicated that HP should incur bank debt to finance it, yet Bill Hewlett and David Packard rejected it out of hand simply because "HP avoids bank debt."[43] This story, involving two corporate heroes and based on a slogan, dictates corporate culture today.

Corporate success and shared experiences also shape culture. For example, Hallmark Cards has a strong culture derived from its years of success in the greeting cards industry. Employees speak of the Hallmark family and care deeply about the company; many of them have worked at the company for years. At Atari, in contrast, the culture is quite weak, the management team changes rapidly, and few people sense any direction or purpose in the company. The differences in culture at Hallmark and Atari are in part attributable to past successes and shared experiences.[44]

Managing Organizational Culture

How can managers deal with culture, given its clear importance but intangible nature? The key is for the manager to understand the current culture and then decide if it should be maintained or changed. By understanding the organization's current culture, managers can take appropriate actions. At Hewlett-Packard, the values represented by "the HP way" still exist. Moreover, they guide and direct most significant activities undertaken by the firm. Culture can also be maintained by rewarding and promoting people whose behaviors are consistent with the existing culture and by articulating the culture through slogans, ceremonies, and so forth.

To change culture, managers must have a clear idea of what it is they want to create. Many organizations today are attempting to adopt a form of culture like that espoused by Ouchi in his Theory Z or Peters and Waterman in their excellence framework.[45] As described more fully in Chapter 2, each of those approaches represents a form of organizational culture. Another way to shape culture is by bringing outsiders into important managerial positions. The choice of a new CEO from outside the organization is often a clear signal that things will be changing. Adopting new slogans, telling new stories, staging new ceremonies, and breaking with tradition can also alter culture.[46] Culture can also be changed by means of a number of other techniques and methods discussed in Chapter 11.

SUMMARY OF KEY POINTS

Organization design is the overall pattern of structural components and arrangements used to manage the total organization. Two early universal models of organization design were the bureaucratic model and the behavioral model.

The situational approach to organization design is based on the premise that appropriate organization design is a function of situational factors. Three important situational factors are technology, environment, and size and organizational life cycle.

Many organizations today adopt one of four basic forms of organization design: functional (U-form), conglomerate (H-form), divisional (M-form), or matrix. Others use a hybrid design derived from two or more of these basic designs. Information-processing requirements and the internationalization of business are also being recognized as forces that shape organization design.

Another contemporary view of organization design focuses on the link between strategy and design. On the basis of differences in three dimensions, five forms of organization design have been identified that result from differences in strategy. These forms of design are the simple structure, the machine bureaucracy, the professional bureaucracy, the divisionalized form, and the adhocracy.

Culture is also an important part of an organization's design. Culture is the set of values of an organization that help its members understand what the organization stands for, how it does things, and what it considers important. A strong culture can be a contributor to organizational effectiveness. Managers should understand how culture is determined and how it can be changed.

DISCUSSION QUESTIONS

Questions for Review

1. Compare and contrast the bureaucratic and behavioral models of organization design. What are the advantages and disadvantages of each?
2. Describe the common forms of organization design. Outline the advantages and disadvantages of each.
3. Identify emerging issues in organization design and discuss their impacts on existing forms of organization.
4. What is organizational culture? Why is it important to managers considering the design of organizations?

Questions for Analysis

5. Can bureaucratic organizations avoid the problems usually associated with bureaucracies? If so, how? If not, why not? Do you think bureaucracies are still relevant? Why or why not? Would it be possible to retain the desirable aspects of bureaucracy and eliminate the undesirable ones? Why or why not?
6. The matrix organization design is complex and difficult to implement successfully. Why, then, do organizations continue to try to use it?
7. Identify aspects of organizational culture in organizations with which you are familiar (education, family, government, religion, etc.). Have any of those aspects changed over time? If so, why? If not, why not?

Questions for Application

8. What form of organization does your university or college use? What form does your city or town government use? What form is used by other organizations with which you are familiar? What similarities and differences do you see? Why?

9. In Chapter 6 you interviewed the manager of a local small business to determine how (or if) he or she formulates strategy. Interview that same manager again to obtain a description of his or her organization design. Can you identify any links between the manager's strategy and the structure of his or her organization? Share your findings with the class.

10. Interview members of a local organization (fast-food chain, department store, book store, bank, church, home and school association, etc.) to ascertain the culture in the organization. Share your results with the class.

NOTES

1. "Limited Inc. Struggles to Improve Its Growth in Sales," *The Wall Street Journal*, October 13, 1988, p. B6; Steven B. Weiner, "The Unlimited?" *Forbes*, April 6, 1987, pp. 74–80; Benjamin J. Stein, "A Saga of Shareholder Neglect," *Barron's*, May 4, 1987, pp. 8–9, 70–75; "Limited Inc., on New Tack Pulls Ahead of Retail Gang," *The Wall Street Journal*, February 24, 1989, pp. B1, B4.

2. See Jay R. Galbraith, "Organization Design," in Jay W. Lorsch, ed., *Handbook of Organizational Behavior* (Englewood Cliffs, N.J.: Prentice-Hall, 1987), pp. 343–357. See also Richard L. Daft, *Organization Theory & Design*, 3rd ed. (St. Paul, Minn.: West, 1989).

3. Max Weber, *Theory of Social and Economic Organizations,* translated by T. Parsons (New York: Free Press, 1947).

4. "Postal Service Moves to Dispel Its Bureaucratic Image," *The Wall Street Journal*, May 27, 1988, p. 6.

5. For recent discussions of the strengths and weaknesses of the bureaucratic model, see James L. Perry and Hal G. Rainey, "The Public-Private Distinction in Organization Theory: A Critique and Research Strategy," *Academy of Management Review*, April 1988, pp. 182–201; and Thomas A. Leitko and David Szczerbacki, "Why Traditional OD Strategies Fail in Professional Bureaucracies," *Organizational Dynamics*, Winter 1987, pp. 52–65.

6. Rensis Likert, *New Patterns in Management* (New York: McGraw-Hill, 1961); Rensis Likert, *The Human Organization* (New York: McGraw-Hill, 1967).

7. William F. Dowling, "At General Motors: System 4 Builds Performance and Profits," *Organizational Dynamics*, Winter 1975, pp. 23–28.

8. Daft, *Organization Theory & Design*.

9. For recent descriptions of situational factors, see Robert K. Kazanjian and Robert Drazin, "Implementing Internal Diversification: Contingency Factors for Organization Design Choices," *Academy of Management Review*, April 1987, pp. 342–354; and Danny Miller, "The Genesis of Configuration," *Academy of Management Review*, October 1987, pp. 686–701.

10. Joan Woodward, *Industrial Organization: Theory and Practice* (London: Oxford University Press, 1965).

11. Joan Woodward, *Management and Technology, Problems of Progress Industry*, No. 3 (London: Her Majesty's Stationery Office, 1958).

12. For recent discussions of the impact of technology on organization design, see Judith W. Alexander and W. Alan Randolph, "The Fit Between Technology and Structure as a Predictor of Performance in Nursing Sub-Units," *Academy of Management Journal*, December 1985, pp. 844–859; and Frank M. Hull and Paul D. Collins, "High-Technology Batch Production Systems: Woodward's Missing Type," *Academy of Management Journal*, December 1987, pp. 786–797.

13. Tom Burns and G. M. Stalker, *The Management of Innovation* (London: Tavistock, 1961).

14. Paul R. Lawrence and Jay W. Lorsch, *Organization and Environment* (Homewood, Ill.: Irwin, 1967).

15. For recent discussions of the environment–organization design relationship, see Masoud Yasai-Ardekani, "Structural Adaptations to Environments," *Academy of Management Review*, January 1986, pp. 9–21; Christine S. Koberg and Geraldo R. Ungson, "The Effects of Environmental Uncertainty and Dependence on Organizational Performance: A Comparative Study," *Journal of Management*, Winter 1987, pp. 725–737; and Barbara W. Keats and Michael A. Hitt, "A Causal Model of Linkages Among Environmental Dimensions, Macro Organizational Characteristics, and Performance," *Academy of Management Journal*, September 1988, pp. 570–598.

16. Derek S. Pugh and David J. Hickson, *Organization Structure in Its Context: The Aston Program I* (Lexington, Mass.: D. C. Heath, 1976).

17. Robert H. Miles and Associates, *The Organizational Life Cycle* (San Francisco: Jossey-Bass, 1980). See also "Is Your Company Too Big?" *Business Week*, March 27, 1989, pp. 84–94.

18. Stuart Gannes, "America's Fastest-growing Companies," *Fortune*, May 23, 1988, pp. 28–40; and "Compaq vs IBM: Peace Comes to Shore," *Business Week*, March 13, 1989, p. 132.

19. See Jerome Katz and William B. Gartner, "Properties of Emerging Organizations," *Academy of Management Review*, July 1988, pp. 429–441; and Robert K. Kazanjian, "Relation of Dominant Problems to Stages of Growth in Technology-based New Ventures," *Academy of Management Journal*, June 1988, pp. 257–279.

20. Oliver E. Williamson, *Markets and Hierarchies* (New York: Free Press, 1975).

21. Williamson, *Markets and Hierarchies*.

22. "Tarnished Trophy: Beatrice, Once Hailed Deal of the Century, Proves Disappointing," *The Wall Street Journal*, November 21, 1988, pp. A1, A8.

23. Michael E. Porter, "From Competitive Advantage to Corporate Strategy," *Harvard Business Review*, May–June 1987, pp. 43–59.

24. Williamson, *Markets and Hierarchies*.

25. "Disney Sets Third Film-Production Firm, Buoyed by Touchstone Division's Success," *The Wall Street Journal*, December 2, 1988, p. B4.

26. Jay B. Barney and William G. Ouchi, eds., *Organizational Economics* (San Francisco: Jossey-Bass, 1986); Robert E. Hoskisson, "Multidivisional Structure and Performance: The Contingency of Diversification Strategy," *Academy of Management Journal*, December 1987, pp. 625–644.

27. Stanley M. Davis and Paul R. Lawrence, *Matrix* (Reading, Mass.: Addison-Wesley, 1977).

28. Alex Taylor III, "Why Fords Sell like Big Macs," *Fortune,* November 21, 1988, pp. 122–125.

29. Harvey F. Koloday, "Managing in a Matrix," *Business Horizons*, March–April 1981, pp. 17–24.

30. For recent discussions of the matrix design, see William F. Joyce, "Matrix Organization: A Social Experiment," *Academy of Management Journal*, September 1986, pp. 536–561; and Erik W. Larson and David H. Gobeli, "Matrix Management: Contradictions and Insights," *California Management Review*, Summer 1987, pp. 126–138.

31. Jeremy Main, "The Winning Organization," *Fortune*, September 26, 1988, pp. 50–60.

32. Jay Galbraith, *Designing Complex Organizations* (Reading, Mass.: Addison-Wesley, 1973); Jay Galbraith, *Organization Design* (Reading, Mass.: Addison-Wesley, 1977).

33. Gareth R. Jones, "Organization-Client Transactions and Organizational Governance Structures," *Academy of Management Journal*, June 1987, pp. 197–218; and Lynda M. Applegate, James I. Cash, Jr., and D. Quinn Mills, "Information Technology and Tomorrow's Manager," *Harvard Business Review*, November–December 1988, pp. 128–136.

34. See William G. Egelhoff, "Strategy and Structure in Multinational Corporations: A Revision of the Stopford and Wells Model," *Strategic Management Journal*, Vol. 9, 1988, pp. 1–14, for a recent discussion of these issues.

35. Richard I. Kirkland, Jr., "Entering a New Age of Boundless Competition," *Fortune*, March 14, 1988, pp. 40–48; "The International 500," *Fortune*, August 1, 1988, p. D7.

36. Alfred D. Chandler, Jr., *Strategy and Structure* (Cambridge, Mass.: MIT Press, 1962); Alfred D. Chandler, Jr., *The Visible Hand: The Managerial Revolution in America* (Cambridge, Mass.: Belknap Press, 1977).

37. Henry Mintzberg, *The Structuring of Organizations: A Synthesis of the Research* (Englewood Cliffs, N.J.: Prentice-Hall, 1979).

38. This material follows Henry Mintzberg, *The Structuring of Organizations: A Synthesis of the Research*, copyright 1979. Adapted by permission of Prentice-Hall, Inc., Englewood Cliffs, N.J.

39. For recent studies, see Danny Miller, "Relating Porter's Business Strategies to Environment and Structure: Analysis and Performance Implications," *Academy of Management Journal*, June 1988, pp. 280–308; and Danny Miller, Cornelia Droge, and Jean-Marie Toulouse, "Strategic Process and Content as Mediators Between Organizational Context and Structure," *Academy of Management Journal*, September 1988, pp. 544–569.

40. Gregory Moorhead and Ricky W. Griffin, *Organizational Behavior*, 2nd ed. (Boston: Houghton Mifflin, 1989), Chapter 16. See also Terrence E. Deal and Allan A. Kennedy, *Corporate Cultures: The Rights and Rituals of Corporate Life* (Reading, Mass.: Addison-Wesley, 1982).

41. Gurney Breckenfield, "The Odyssey of Levi Strauss," *Fortune*, March 22, 1982, pp. 110–124. See also "Levi Strauss . . . at $3 Billion Plus," *Daily News Record*, October 10, 1988, p. 44.

42. Jay B. Barney, "Organizational Culture: Can It Be a Source of Sustained Competitive Advantage?" *Academy of Management Review*, July 1986, pp. 656–665.

43. Moorhead and Griffin, *Organizational Behavior*. See also "Hewlitt-Packard's Whip-Crackers," *Fortune*, February 13, 1989, pp. 58–59.

44. See Yoash Wiener, "Forms of Value Systems: A Focus on Organizational Effectiveness and Cultural Change and Maintenance," *Academy of Management Review*, October 1988, pp. 534–545.

45. William Ouchi, *Theory Z—How American Business Can Meet the Japanese Challenge* (Reading, Mass.: Addison-Wesley, 1981); and Thomas J. Peters and Robert H. Waterman, Jr., *In Search of Excellence* (New York: Harper & Row, 1982).

46. John J. Sherwood, "Creating Work Cultures with Competitive Advantage," *Organizational Dynamics*, Winter 1988, pp. 4–27.

CASE 9.1

Organization Design At Philip Morris

As smoking declines, Philip Morris steps up its attack on anti-smoking efforts. Those efforts have enabled Philip Morris to keep its tobacco sales and profits rising while those of the tobacco industry as a whole grow more slowly every year. There is no question that Philip Morris is succeeding. Its net income was up 25 percent in 1987 and continued to rise through 1988. Philip Morris derived 53 percent of its sales revenues from tobacco and 81 percent of its profits.

Despite that success, Philip Morris needs to guard against overreliance on what almost all observers feel is a dying industry, and after being a tobacco company for nearly 150 years, Philip Morris seems to be getting the message. It diversified through acquisitions into beer, soft drinks, and foods. Those acquistions, however, have not faired very well.

Seven-Up was a money loser for Philip Morris from the start. Philip Morris tried unsuccessfully to impose cigarette strategies on soft drinks; it was slow to introduce new products; and it could not effectively distribute the new cola, Like, because bottlers were already committed to either Coke or Pepsi. After eight years, Philip Morris gave up and sold Seven-Up.

The General Foods Corporation had a massive bureaucracy in place when Philip Morris acquired it in 1985, and Philip Morris has not succeeded in reducing that bureaucracy very much or in making it more responsive to its markets. As a result, operating margins at General Foods lag behind those of the rest of the industry. Even such well-known brands as Maxwell House, Sanka, Birds Eye frozen foods, Kool-Aid, Jell-O, Tang, Oscar Mayer, and Post cereals have not enabled General Foods to rebound. Indeed, General Foods has not introduced new products on a timely basis, and it has not had the ability to identify and develop market opportunities. The chairman of General Foods resigned in 1988 to accept the top job at Pillsbury. Although he had been instrumental in trying to bring about changes at General Foods, he had also been criticized as having been at least part of the problem there. Nevertheless, his departure left a severe gap in the top-executive team charged with effecting improvements at General Foods.

Philip Morris may have given up on Seven-Up, but it has not given up on General Foods or Miller Beer. Nor has it given up on acquisition as a way to develop the organization it needs to protect itself against the oncoming decline in tobacco products. Philip Morris's chairman, Hamish Maxwell, is determined to improve the internal operations of the company. In an effort to do so, he has gotten involved in day-to-day operations and decisions. He pushed General Foods to invest in a new decaffeination process that has enabled Sanka brand to improve its market share. He sent

Miller officials to Japan to study how the Japanese make and market bottled draft beer. That initiative led to Miller Genuine Draft, which seems to be gaining market share.

Late in 1987, General Foods Corporation was reorganized into three operating units. General Foods Coffee & International is the largest unit; Oscar Mayer Foods handles all of that brand's products; and General Foods USA handles all other brands and products. The reorganization cut about 2,000 jobs and saved over $75 million annually. In addition, the position of chief executive officer at General Foods was divided among the three units in order to decentralize operations somewhat.

Late in 1988, Philip Morris acquired Kraft Inc. As of late October 1988, that merger was the second-largest takeover in history (its earlier merger with General Foods was the ninth largest). The acquisition of Kraft made Philip Morris the world's largest consumer products company with 1987 sales of about $38 billion, compared to $27 billion for Unilever, $24 billion for Nestlé, $17 billion for Procter & Gamble, and $16 billion for RJR Nabisco (another tobacco and food combination).

In addition to the mix of top-brand products that Philip Morris obtained through the merger with Kraft, it got a highly experienced food-business executive who could be invaluable to Philip Morris's efforts to improve the picture at General Foods. It is expected that the two food units will eventually be combined under a single chairman. Kraft is noted for its marketing success, and Philip Morris hopes to transfer that expertise to its other nontobacco operations.

Questions

1. Does the bureaucratic or behavioral model best describe the organization design of Philip Morris? Why?
2. Which forms of organization design can you identify at Philip Morris (either the corporation or any of its subsidiary units)? Give specific examples to illustrate your choices.
3. What strategies seem to exist at Philip Morris? Can you see any links between those strategies and the organization designs you identified in the first two questions? If so, what links do you think seem to exist?
4. Describe the organizational culture at Philip Morris. What have been the major determinants of that culture? Does that culture serve the organization well or would a changed culture enable the company to be more effective? If you feel that changes would be beneficial, suggest some of those changes and explain why you think they would be beneficial.

REFERENCES: "Beyond Marlboro Country," *Business Week*, August 8, 1988, pp. 54–58; "Kraft Accepts $13.1B Bid by Philip Morris," *USA Today*, October 31, 1988, p. 1B; "Kraft Accepts a Sweetened Offer of $13.1 Billion from Philip Morris," *The Wall Street Journal*, October 31, 1988. pp. A3–A4; "Hamish Maxwell's Big Hunger," *Business Week*, October 31, 1988, pp. 24–26; "Philip Morris Rehires a Top Gun to Coordinate Sales, Marketing," *The Wall Street Journal*, October 11, 1988, p. B6; "Upstart Miller Brew May Start Beer War," *The Wall Street Journal*, October 5, 1988, p. B1.

CASE 9.2

ICI's Life Cycle

Imperial Chemical Industries (ICI) is not yet a household name in America, although it has long been one in Great Britain. Formed by a four-company merger in 1926, ICI came through the two world wars with a long list of product and process innovations and a superior reputation—a true blue-chip corporation. ICI had never declared a loss since its founding—until 1980, when it seemed to be in serious trouble. Massive organization change, however, has brought it back. ICI posted pretax profits of over £1 billion in both 1984 and 1986 on sales exceeding £10 billion. The organization changes included closing plants, withdrawing from whole areas of manu-facturing, and laying off one-third of ICI's domestic work force.

ICI's structure at the time of its troubles was an organization design with strong divisional management. The heads of the divisions focused more on the need to operate plants at maximum efficiency than on developing markets for the future. There were from eight to ten UK divisional boards of directors, and each board reported to the main board through a group director. Each divisional director looked after a staff function, a geographic area, and a business sector. Thus, if a major proposal were put forth, it inevitably involved several directors. Directors frequently became com-petitors with one another, each pulling for his or her own division or business. There was a strong bureaucratic style of management, and the focus of attention seemed to be domestic performance. Although "policy groups" or "councils" were frequently set up to study such things as expansion plans, once a group or council arrived at a plan, action seemed either to grind to a halt or to proceed so slowly as to be ineffectual.

In the new organizational arrangement, each divisional chairperson was made individually accountable for the performance of his or her group. The main Commonwealth markets of Australia, Canada, India, and Africa were served by mini-ICIs—subsidiaries with separate manufacturing facil-ities operating relatively independently in a decentralized manner. The function-territory-business matrix for directors still exists, but it has been modified so that all directors take first and foremost a global view. This change assures that they no longer serve as advocates for the big UK divisions but rather do what is best for ICI as an international corporation.

Below the director level, layers of staff have been eliminated to flatten the organization and get top management closer to operations. The head of each international business, who is a principal executive officer, works with a business director but makes his or her own presentations to the executive team for any necessary top-level approval.

Subsidiaries were few prior to the reorganization. The most notable subsidiary was Atlas, a medium-size producer of specialty chemicals and pharmaceuticals, which had been purchased in 1971. The Atlas merger seemed quite beneficial. It enabled ICI to establish Tenormin as a major cardiovascular drug and ICI as a strong contender in that field. Even though that acquisition was very successful, ICI did not make any other substantial moves in that direction until after the reorganization. ICI then became far more aggressive in acquisitions.

ICI acquired Beatrice Foods' chemical and specialty plastics division for $750 million in late 1984. That acquisition established ICI's presence in America. Hansen Industries' Glidden paint unit was acquired in 1986. That acquisition made ICI the largest paint maker in the world and the third largest in the United States after Sherwin-Williams and PPG. About a billion dollars was spent to acquire numerous other small American companies in areas as diverse as seeds and dental products.

Acquisition was not the only method of expansion used by ICI. ICI expanded through growth into new markets for existing units. Cellmark Diagnostics, an ICI subsidiary, opened a laboratory in Maryland in 1987. Cellmark has developed DNA matching for use in forensic work for paternity suits, immigration cases, and criminal investigations.

What has happened at ICI is a pattern repeated frequently as organizations go through the organizational life cycle. A successful company becomes complacent with its success—becomes fat and lazy, does not monitor environmental change or its competitors very well, and gets into serious trouble because of internal inefficiencies or external competition or both. Retrenchment is used to save the company. Then, after severe cutbacks and reorganization, a careful analysis is made to establish a new and more viable strategy for the company, which begins to grow again. In ICI's case, most of the new growth has been through acquisitions, although some has come internally as well.

Questions

1. Which model, the bureaucratic or the behavioral, best describes the organization design of ICI? Why?
2. Which forms of organization design can you identify at ICI (either the corporation or any of its subsidiary units)? Give specific examples to illustrate your choices.
3. What does ICI's strategy seem to be? Can you see any links between its strategy and its organization design? If so, what links do you think exist?
4. What is the organizational culture at ICI and what have been the major determinants of that culture? Does that enable the company to be effective or should changes be made? If you feel that changes should be made, indicate what they should be.

REFERENCES: "The Legacy of Harvey-Jones," *Management Today*, January 1987, pp. 35–88; Richard I. Kirkland, Jr., "A Busy Body Bent on Doing Better," *Fortune*, August 3, 1987, p. 60; "Leaving Holmes in the Dust," *Newsweek*, October 26, 1987, p. 81; "ICI Wants to Be a Household Name in the U.S.," *Business Week*, September 1, 1986, p. 40.

OUTLINE

The Strategic Importance of Human Resource Management

The Legal Environment of Human Resource Management
Equal Employment Opportunity · Compensation and Benefits · Labor Relations · Health and Safety · Emerging Legal Issues

Job Analysis and Human Resource Planning
Job Analysis · Forecasting Human Resource Demand and Supply · Matching Human Resource Supply and Demand

Recruiting and Selection
Sources for Recruiting · Common Selection Techniques

Training and Development
Assessing Training Needs · Common Training Methods · Evaluation of Training

Performance Appraisal and Feedback
Reasons for Appraising Performance · Common Appraisal Methods · Providing Feedback

Compensation and Benefits
The Role of Compensation · Determining Compensation · Determining Benefits

Labor Relations
How Employees Form Unions · Collective Bargaining · Grievances and Discipline · Future Trends

CHAPTER 10

Managing Human Resources

OBJECTIVES

After studying this chapter, you should be able to:

- Describe the strategic importance of human resource management.

- Characterize the legal environment of human resource management.

- Discuss job analysis and human resource planning.

- Describe the role of recruiting and selection in human resource management.

- Discuss the importance of training in human resource management.

- Discuss performance appraisal and the importance of feedback.

- Describe the role of compensation and benefits in human resource management.

- Discuss labor relations.

OPENING INCIDENT

Mazda cares about the people it hires. Its managers believe that the company's future success is dependent upon its employees, and they also feel that picking the right employee is a difficult task. That's why Mazda spent $40 million ($13,000 per employee) in hiring and training workers for its assembly plant in Flat Rock, Michigan. And the company is just as particular about whom it hires today.

Mazda stresses interpersonal skills, motivation, an aptitude for learning, and an interest in teamwork and participation. Applicants perform tasks that mimic jobs in the plant. They are subjected to an array of personality and psychological tests and must go through a battery of interviews with several other workers and managers.

Once hired, recruits aren't put to work immediately. First they go through three weeks of skill-building training programs with a group of other new hires. These programs help them develop their abilities to work as part of a team, better understand interpersonal relations, and be more creative. Assembly-line workers then go through five to seven weeks of technical training and then practice three to four more weeks under direct supervision. Then, and only then, are they a part of the Mazda team.[1]

*M*anagers at Mazda clearly recognize the importance of human resources, and Mazda goes to great lengths to get the best human resources possible. Without people, no organization could function. Some managers might argue that Mazda's system goes too far, but most would also agree that it's better to pay too much attention to human resources than to pay too little attention to them.

human resource management The set of organizational activities directed at attracting, developing, and maintaining an effective workforce

This chapter is about **human resource management**—the activities directed at attracting, developing, and maintaining an effective work force for the organization. Chapters 8 and 9 were essentially concerned with drawing the boxes and lines that configure an organization. This chapter addresses putting names and faces in those boxes. We describe the strategic importance of human resource management and characterize its legal context and the laws that regulate various aspects of employer-employee relations are discussed. We then focus sequentially on the five basic components of ongoing human resource management: job analysis and human resource planning, recruiting and selection, training and development, performance appraisal and feedback, and compensation and benefits. We conclude with a discussion of another critical dimension of human resource management, labor relations. The discussion covers collective bargaining, grievances and discipline, and the future trends of unions.

THE STRATEGIC IMPORTANCE OF HUMAN RESOURCE MANAGEMENT

Human resources are critical for effective organizational functioning. Human resource management (or personnel, as it is sometimes called) was once relegated to second-class status in many organizations. However, its importance has grown dramatically in the last two decades. This increase in importance stems from increased legal complexities, the recognition that human resources are a valuable means for improving productivity, and the increased awareness of the costs associated with poor human resource management.[2]

Indeed, managers today are coming to realize that the effectiveness of their human resource function has a substantial impact on the bottom-line performance of the firm. Poor human resource planning can result in spurts of hiring followed by layoffs—costly in terms of unemployment compensation payments, training expenses, and morale. Haphazard compensation systems do not attract, keep, and motivate good employees, and outmoded recruitment practices can lay the firm open to expensive and embarrassing discrimination lawsuits.[3] Consequently, the chief human resource executive of most large businesses is a vice president directly accountable to the CEO, and more and more firms are developing strategic human resource plans and are integrating those plans with other strategic planning activities.[4]

Even organizations with as few as 200 employees usually have a human resource manager and a human resource department charged with overseeing these activities. However, responsibility for human resource activities is invariably shared between the human resource department and line managers. The human resource department may recruit and do the initial screening of candidates, but the final selection is usually made by managers in the department where the new employee will work. Similarly, although the human resource department may establish performance appraisal policies and procedures, the actual evaluating and coaching of employees is done by their immediate superiors.

THE LEGAL ENVIRONMENT OF HUMAN RESOURCE MANAGEMENT

A number of laws regulate various aspects of employee-employer relations, especially in the areas of Equal Employment Opportunity, compensation and benefits, labor relations, and occupational safety and health.

Title VII of the Civil Rights Act of 1964   Forbids discrimination on the basis of sex, race, color, religion, or national origin in all areas of the employment relationship

Equal Employment Opportunity

Title VII   Several laws forbid unfair discrimination by employers, but the most important is **Title VII of the Civil Rights Act of 1964**.

Title VII forbids discrimination on the basis of sex, race, color, religion, or national origin in all areas of the employment relationship, including hiring, layoff, discharge, discipline, compensation, access to training, and promotion. Title VII applies to all private employers with fifteen or more employees, to state and local governments, and to educational institutions, labor unions, and employment agencies. The intent of Title VII is to ensure that employment decisions are made on the basis of an individual's qualifications for a particular job, rather than personal biases. The law has reduced such practices as refusing to promote blacks into management, failing to hire men as telephone operators and flight attendants, and refusing to hire women as construction workers.

adverse impact When minority group members pass a selection standard at a rate less than 80 percent of the pass rate of majority group members

Less overt forms of discrimination have also been curbed. For instance, the use of employment tests that whites pass at a higher rate than blacks is forbidden unless the employer can document that the test is a valid predictor of job performance. Similarly, many height and weight standards for police officers and firefighters have been eliminated because they excluded a disproportionate number of female, Hispanic, and Asian applicants and could seldom be proved necessary for success as a police officer or firefighter. Such requirements have an **adverse impact** on minorities and women when such individuals pass the selection standard at a rate less than 80 percent of the pass rate for majority group members. Tests or other standards that have an adverse impact on protected groups can be used only when there is solid evidence that they are valid—that they effectively identify individuals who are better able than others to do the job.[5] The Equal Employment Opportunity Commission is charged with ensuring that Title VII is enforced.[6]

Age Discrimination in Employment Act Outlaws discrimination against people aged 40 through 69 years

Age Discrimination in Employment Act The **Age Discrimination in Employment Act** was passed in 1967 and amended in 1978. It applies to the same types of employers and situations as Title VII but outlaws discrimination against people aged 40 through 69. Individuals cannot be forced to retire before age 70 except for documented health- or performance-related reasons. People under the age of 40 who are discriminated against because they are too young have no protection under this federal law. Some states, however, have broader age discrimination acts that may provide relief.

Both the Age Discrimination Act and Title VII require passive nondiscrimination, or Equal Employment Opportunity. Employers are not required to seek out and hire large numbers of older employees or minority group members, but they must treat fairly all who apply. Some regulations do require employers to go one step further—to actively seek, hire, and advance particular classes of individuals. We discuss these next.

Affirmative Action Intentionally seeking and hiring qualified or qualifiable employees from racial, sexual, and ethnic groups that are underutilized or underrepresented in the organization

Executive Orders A series of executive orders issued in the last twenty-five years requires employers holding government contracts to engage in **Affirmative Action**—intentionally seeking and hiring qualified or qualifiable employees from racial, sexual, and ethnic groups that are

Avon has a very aggressive affirmative action plan. The company has never had any trouble hiring women and minorities. But it did have a history of losing them before they advanced very far up the corporate hierarchy. To cope with the problem, Avon sent all its managers to training seminars to help them understand their own prejudices and assumptions about different groups. Today, Avon has 22 minorities at the director level and has dramatically improved its performance in promoting women and minorities to high-level positions throughout the company.

"underutilized" or underrepresented in the organization. Ideally, an employer's work force should reflect the racial, sexual, and ethnic makeup of the relevant labor market. If 15 percent of the carpenters in the area where a company is located are black, then approximately 15 percent of the carpenters whom the firm employs should also be black. Employers with federal contracts over $100,000 per year must have a written Affirmative Action Plan that spells out employment goals for each underutilized group and the company's plans for meeting those goals. The latter might include recruiting at largely minority schools or making special efforts to attract women into apprenticeship programs.[7] Employers with government contracts are also required to act affirmatively in hiring Vietnam-era veterans and qualified handicapped individuals.

Compensation and Benefits

A number of important state and federal laws regulate the payment of wages and the provision of benefits to employees.

Fair Labor Standards Act
Sets a minimum wage and requires overtime pay for work in excess of forty hours per week

Fair Labor Standards Act   The wage law with the widest impact is the **Fair Labor Standards Act**, passed in 1938 and amended frequently since then. Among many other provisions, this law sets the so-called minimum wage and requires the payment of overtime rates for work in excess of 40 hours per week. Not all employees are covered. Salaried professional, executive, and administrative employees are "exempt" from the minimum hourly wage and overtime provisions.

Equal Pay Act of 1963   Requires that men and women be paid the same amount for doing the same jobs

Equal Pay Act   The **Equal Pay Act of 1963** requires that men and women be paid the same amount for doing the same jobs (assuming the jobs demand equal skill, effort, and responsibility and are performed under the same working conditions). For instance, it is illegal to pay male chemistry teachers more than female chemistry teachers merely because of sex or assumed head-of-household status. Attempts to circumvent the law by having different job titles and pay rates for males and females who perform essentially the same work (she is the "head secretary," he the "office manager") are also illegal. However, it is perfectly reasonable to base an individual's pay on her or his seniority, performance, or qualifications, even if doing so results in a particular man and woman being paid different amounts for doing the same job. The Equal Pay Act is important, but it overlaps with Title VII in that both cover pay discrimination on the basis of sex.

Employee Retirement Income Security Act of 1974
Sets standards for pension plan management and provides federal insurance if pension funds go bankrupt

Laws About Benefits   The provision of benefits is also regulated in some ways by state and federal laws. Certain benefits are mandatory—unemployment compensation for employees who are laid off and worker's compensation insurance for employees who are injured on the job. Employers who provide a pension plan for their employees are subject to the **Employee Retirement Income Security Act of 1974 (ERISA).** This law sets standards for pension plans and provides federal insurance if pension funds go bankrupt. The primary goals of ERISA are to ensure that employees get the pension benefits due them when they retire and that they do not lose accrued benefits if they change employers.

Labor Relations

Union activities and management behavior toward unions constitute another heavily regulated area. Before the 1930s, federal laws generally inhibited unionization, and unions were often prosecuted as "conspiracies in restraint of trade."[*] However, during the New Deal era, new laws affirmed the right of unions to exist and the obligation of management to bargain collectively with them.

National Labor Relations Act (Wagner Act)   Set up procedures for employees to vote whether to have a union

National Labor Relations Act   The **National Labor Relations Act** (Wagner Act), passed in 1935, set up a procedure for employees of a firm to vote whether to have a union. If they vote for a union, management is required to bargain collectively with the union. The Wagner Act lists certain "unfair labor practices"—firing or otherwise punishing employees known to be pro-union, threatening or bribing employees to vote against the union, attempting to dominate the union, and sending spies to union meetings. The **National Labor Relations Board** was established by the Wagner Act to enforce its provisions.

National Labor Relations Board   Established by the Wagner Act to enforce its provisions

Labor-Management Relations Act   Passed to limit union power

Labor-Management Relations Act   Following a series of severe strikes in 1946, the **Labor-Management Relations Act** (Taft-Hartley Act) was passed in 1947 to limit union power. The law lists unfair labor practices by unions, such as refusing to bargain in good faith, harassing both union members and nonmembers, and charging excessive dues and fees. It gives management more rights to speak out against the union during an organizing campaign, though management must still be careful not to threaten employees. Finally, the Taft-Hartley Act contains the National Emergency Strike provision, which allows the president of the United States to obtain a court injunction to prevent or end a strike that endangers the national health and safety. The injunction has a duration of up to eighty days—in hopes that the strike can be settled during this cooling-off period.

Taken together, those laws balance the power of unions and management. Employees are entitled to be represented by a properly constituted union, and management retains the right to make nonemployee-related business decisions without interference.

Health and Safety

Occupational Safety and Health Act of 1970 (OSHA)
Mandates the provision of safe working conditions

Occupational Safety and Health Act   The **Occupational Safety and Health Act of 1970 (OSHA)** directly mandates the provision of safe working conditions. OSHA is undoubtedly the most influential occupational safety law. It requires that employers (1) provide a place of employment that is free from recognized hazards that may cause death or serious physical harm and (2) obey the safety and health standards established by the Occupational Safety and Health Administration. Safety standards are intended to prevent accidents (such as being injured by a moving piece of machinery); occupational health standards are concerned with preventing occupational disease (due to long-term exposure to hazards such as excessive noise, carcinogenic chemicals, or other contaminants). For example, there are standards that limit the concentration of cotton dust in the air, because this contaminant has been associated with lung disease in textile workers. The standards are enforced by OSHA inspections, which are conducted when an employee files a complaint of unsafe conditions or when a serious accident occurs. Spot inspections of plants in especially hazardous industries are also made. Employers who fail to meet OSHA standards may be fined.[8]

Emerging Legal Issues

Several other areas of legal concern have emerged during the past few years. One is sexual harassment. Although sexual harassment is covered under Title VII, it has received additional attention in the courts recently as more and more victims have decided to publicly confront the problem. Another issue revolves around alcohol and drug abuse. Both alcoholism and drug dependence are seen as major problems today. Recent court rulings have tended to define alcoholics and drug addicts as handicapped, protecting them under the same laws that protect other handicapped people. Finally, AIDS has emerged as a significant legal issue for organizations to confront. AIDS victims too are most often protected under various laws protecting the handicapped.

JOB ANALYSIS AND HUMAN RESOURCE PLANNING

With our new understanding of the legal environment of human resource management as a foundation, we are now ready to address its first substantive concern—determining the types and number of people the organization needs to be effective. The first step in this process is job analysis.

Job Analysis

■ **job analysis** A systematized procedure for collecting and recording information about jobs

job descriptions List the duties of a job, its working conditions, and the tools, materials, and equipment used to perform it

job specification Lists the skills, abilities, and other credentials needed to do a job

Job analysis is a systematized procedure for collecting and recording information about jobs. A job analysis is usually made up of two parts. The **job description** lists the duties of a job, its working conditions, and the tools, materials, and equipment used to perform it. The **job specification** lists the skills (such as typing), abilities (such as manual dexterity), and other credentials (a college degree, a chauffeur's license) needed to do the job. There are many methods of collecting and presenting job analysis data, from simple homemade forms to standardized and computer-scored questionnaires.[9] Job analysis information is used in many human resource activities. For instance, it is necessary to know about job content and job requirements to develop appropriate selection methods and job-relevant performance appraisal systems and to set equitable compensation rates across jobs. Job analysis information is used in the development of training programs and also in human resource planning.

■ **human resource planning** Forecasting future needs for employees in different jobs, forecasting the availability of such employees, and then taking steps to match supply and demand

Human resource planning consists of forecasting future needs for employees in different jobs, forecasting the availability of such employees, and then taking steps to match supply and demand. Figure 10.1 shows this process. Short-range planning (one to two years) to guide immediate recruiting needs is most common, but mid- and long-range planning (up to ten years) can also be helpful. More and more organizations are increasing their human resource planning activities. Systematic planning of this type results in improved efficiency and effectiveness throughout the organization.[10]

Forecasting Human Resource Demand and Supply

Managers need a great deal of information to accurately forecast the organization's demand for employees.[11] The manager needs to know trends in past human resource usage, future organizational plans, and general economic trends. A good sales forecast is often a good begin-

FIGURE 10.1

Human Resource Planning

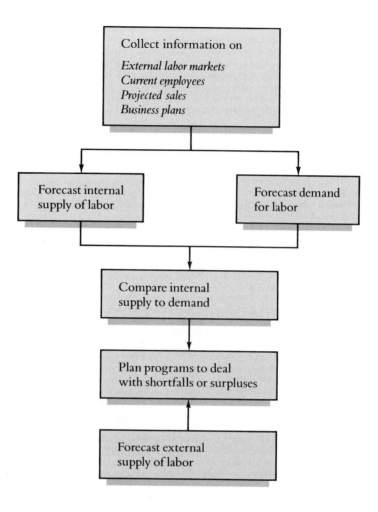

ning, especially for smaller organizations. The first part of Table 10.1 shows how to calculate the number of assembly workers needed for an air-conditioner plant. Historical ratios can then be used to predict demand for staff workers, sales representatives, and so forth. Of course, large organizations use much more complicated models to predict their future human resource needs. However, most models rely on basic assumptions about the future, much like this simple example.

Forecasting the supply of labor is really two tasks—forecasting the internal supply (the number and type of employees who will be in the firm at some future date) and forecasting the external supply (the number and type of people who will be available for hiring in the labor market at large). The simplest approach merely adjusts present staffing levels for anticipated turnover and promotions. On the basis of past data, for example, one might make the predictions shown in the lower portion of Table 10.1 about the number of air-conditioner assemblers who will still be employed in that job next year. More sophisticated models apply this kind of procedure simultaneously to all jobs in the

TABLE 10.1

Forecasting the Demand for
and Internal Supply of Air-
Conditioner Assemblers

Predicted Demand for Air-Conditioner Assemblers

Predicted sales of air-conditioner units	150,000 units
Times direct labor hours to assemble one unit (based on past data)	20 hours
Equals total direct labor hours	3,000,000
Divided by hours worked per year per assembler (48[a] weeks/year × 40 hours/week)	1,920
Equals number of full-time assemblers needed	1,562

[a]Assume 4 weeks per year lost due to vacation, holidays, and sick leave.

Predicted Internal Supply of Air-Conditioner Assemblers

Present number of assemblers	1244
Minus average number lost per year to voluntary turnover (10%)[a]	−124
Minus average number lost per year to firing (1.5%)[a]	−19
Minus average number expected to retire (3%)[a]	−37
Minus average number promoted or transferred per year (6%)[a]	−75
Equals predicted internal supply	989

[a]Percentages based on past several years of data for this job.

---

organization and can predict conditions more than one year in advance. Union Oil Company, for example, has a complex forecasting system for keeping tabs on the present and future distributions of professionals and managers. The Union Oil system can spot areas where there will eventually be too many qualified professionals competing for too few promotions or, conversely, too few good people available to fill important positions.

Thus far we have talked about forecasting the supply of human resources in the aggregate. For instance, we have predicted that we will have 989 assemblers left next year. Exactly who the 989 are is of no real concern. However, at the higher levels of the organization, we need to plan for specific people and positions. The technique most commonly used is the **replacement chart**, which lists each important managerial position, who occupies it now, how long he or she will probably stay in it before moving on, and who (by name) is now qualified or soon will be qualified to move into the position. This allows ample time to plan developmental experiences for individuals identified as potential successors to critical managerial jobs.

To facilitate both planning and the identification of individuals for

replacement charts List each managerial position in the organization, who occupies it now, how long he or she will probably remain in the position, and who is or will be qualified to replace them

Matching the supply and demand for labor is always a tricky process. Hire too many people and costs get out of hand; hire too few and crucial work may not get done. Continental Corporation uses part-time and temporary workers to help keep things in balance. Ed Bonk, center, is a project manager at Continental. His group consists largely of computer science students from Drexel University and the University of Pennsylvania. Bonk's group writes programs for various special projects undertaken by the company. By using students, Bonk has tremendous flexibility to add workers when demand is high and cut back when things are slow. Five percent of Continental's workforce fits this pattern.

employee information system or **skills inventory**
Contains information on each employee's education, skills, experience, and career aspirations

■ **recruiting**   The process of attracting individuals to apply for jobs that are open

current transfer or promotion, some organizations also have an **employee information system**, or **skills inventory**. Such systems are often computerized, containing information on each employee's education, skills, work experience, and career aspirations. Such a system could quickly locate all the employees in a large organization who are ostensibly qualified to fill a position requiring, for instance, a degree in chemical engineering, three years of experience in an oil refinery, and fluency in Spanish.

Forecasting the external supply of labor is a different problem altogether. How does a manager, for example, predict how many electrical engineers will be seeking work in Georgia three years from now? To get an idea of the future availability of labor, planners must rely on information from outside sources such as state employment commissions, government reports, and figures supplied by colleges on the number of students in major fields.

Matching Human Resource Supply and Demand

After comparing future demand and future internal supply, managers charged with human resource planning can make plans to deal with predicted shortfalls or overstaffing. If a shortfall is predicted, new employees can be hired from outside, present employees can be retrained and transferred into the understaffed area, individuals approaching retirement can be tempted by additional benefits to stay on, or labor-saving or productivity-enhancing systems can be installed. If hiring will be needed, the forecast of the external supply of labor helps managers plan how extensively to recruit, based on whether the type of person needed is readily available or scarce in the labor market. If overstaffing is expected to be a problem, the main options are transferring the extra employees, not replacing individuals who quit, encouraging early retirement, and laying people off.[12] As "Management in Practice" illustrates, many businesses today are relying on temporary workers to help smooth fluctuations in the demand for and supply of human resources.

RECRUITING AND SELECTION

Once an organization has an idea of its future human resource needs, the next phase is usually recruiting and selecting new employees. **Recruiting** is the process of attracting individuals to apply for the jobs that are open. The goal is to attract qualified candidates. Attracting too few candidates is a problem, because those who are hiring either will not be able to be very selective or will have to leave openings unfilled. On the other hand, attracting far too many candidates is also undesirable, because evaluating candidates is costly and time consuming, particularly when individual testing or interviews are used.

IBM Japan has enjoyed considerable success in recent years recruiting female employees in Japan. Women in Japan are only now beginning to enjoy widespread career opportunities. For those that choose to pursue a career, IBM is a popular choice. While most Japanese people prefer to work for Japanese companies, IBM Japan was recently ranked second by women science majors. While many companies in Japan still pressure women to quit if they marry, IBM not only encourages them to stay but also provides extended maternity leaves and helps arrange child-care when a mother returns to work.

internal recruiting Getting current employees to apply for higher level jobs in the organization

external recruiting Getting people from outside the organization to apply for openings

Sources for Recruiting

Where do recruits come from? Some recruits are found internally; others come from the outside.

Internal Recruiting   **Internal recruiting** means considering present employees as candidates for openings. Such a policy of promotion from within can help build morale and keep high-quality employees from leaving the firm. In unionized companies, the procedures for notifying employees of internal job change opportunities are usually spelled out in the union contract. They are often called job posting and bidding. For higher-level positions, a skills inventory system may be used to identify internal candidates, or superiors may be asked to recommend individuals who should be considered. One disadvantage of internal recruiting is its "ripple effect." When a current employee moves to a different post, someone else must be found to take her or his old job. If this replacement was already an employee, then her or his now-vacant job must also be filled. In one organization, 454 job movements were necessary as a result of filling 195 initial openings![13] Although internal recruiting gives many employees a chance to move up, it also increases training costs and other problems associated with inexperienced incumbents.

External Recruiting   **External recruiting** involves attracting individuals outside the organization to apply for jobs. A number of methods and sources are available, including advertising, campus recruiting, public or private employment agencies or executive search firms, union hiring halls, referrals by present employees, and hiring "walk-ins" or "gate-hires" (people who show up without being solicited). It is important to select the most appropriate methods. For instance, one would probably not go to the local state employment service office to find a nuclear physicist, but the state office could be used to find blue-collar workers. Private employment agencies can be a good source of clerical and technical employees, and executive search firms specialize in locating top-management talent. Newspaper ads are often used because they reach a wide audience and thus allow minorities "equal opportunity" to find out about and apply for job openings.

In selecting a recruiting method, both costs and results must be considered. Newspaper ads are quite inexpensive compared with executive search firms or campus recruiting. Different methods also differ in terms of the quality or quantity of applicants generated. A bank in New York City, for example, studied the quality of tellers hired through each of seven recruiting methods. Managers found that three of the methods they had been using (newspaper advertising, major private employment agency, and other agencies) produced tellers who were more likely to quit than those hired by the other recruiting methods (rehiring former employees, acting on referrals from high schools or present employees, and hiring walk-ins). Analyses showed that the bank could save over $50,000 per year in hiring and training costs by using only the four most effective recruiting methods.[14]

MANAGEMENT IN PRACTICE

TEMPS AT TEKTRONIX

Temporary, part-time, and contract workers, better known as temps, currently make up approximately one-third of the U.S. work force and number in the tens of millions. Companies hire such "outside" workers to assist in the reduction of a temporary overload, handle special projects, cover for workers on vacation or leave, and do jobs when it is not economically feasible to hire permanent employees. Saving money is usually not a major reason for the use of temps because temps may not be worth the cost of using them.

As the U.S. work force changes, more and more temps are going to be used. As this practice becomes more common, temps will gain more bargaining power and will demand and receive better wages and benefits. Some labor economists predict that by the end of the 1990s there will be such a shortage of labor that wages and benefits will be driven to very high levels in order to lure temps out of the house and as moonlighters from other jobs. Thus it is crucial for managers to learn how to manage and motivate temps.

Tektronix of Beaverton, Oregon, is a manufacturer of electronic test and measurement equipment for which demand changes rapidly. It has begun to use temps to deal with fluctuations in its work force. It used five times as many temps in 1988 as it had used in 1986. Tektronix uses a firm to provide its temps.

This is expensive because the firm can be aggressive in negotiating wage rates, but it is also convenient because Tektronix has to deal with only one firm rather than with hundreds of individual workers.

Tektronix managers try to maintain a careful distance between themselves and those workers. If the distance is too great, the workers are unmotivated and uncaring and their on-the-job performance declines. If the distance is too close, the temps think that they should be treated the same as permanent employees and their elevated expectations easily lead to problems when they must be terminated or their contracts are not renewed.

At some firms, managers arrange for temps to have nameplates, restroom keys, and other perquisites often reserved for full-time employees. In many companies, temps are given special consideration when job openings occur, including openings for positions that would be considered promotions. In such companies, the opportunity for advancement is seen as a very powerful motivator for temps as well as for other employees. In contrast, some companies have policies that prohibit temps from applying for full-time jobs.

REFERENCES: "Managers Face Dilemma with 'Temps,' *The Wall Street Journal*, April 5, 1988, p. 27; David Kirkpatrick, "Smart New Ways to Use Temps," *Fortune*, February 15, 1988, pp. 110–116; "Union Militancy—and Beyond," *Barron's*, June 8, 1987, p. 11.

---

realistic job preview (RJP)
Providing the applicant with a real picture of what it would be like to perform the job the organization is trying to fill

The organization must also keep in mind that recruiting and selection decisions often go both ways—the organization is selecting an employee, but the prospective employee is also selecting a job. Thus, the organization wants to put its best foot forward, treat all applicants with dignity, and strive for a good person-job fit. Recent estimates suggest that hiring the "wrong" operating employee—one who flops and either quits or must be fired—generally costs the organization $5,000 in lost productivity and training. For a manager, the costs skyrocket to as much as $75,000.[15] One generally successful method for facilitating a good person-job fit is through the so-called **realistic job preview**, or **RJP**.[16] As the term suggests, the RJP involves providing the applicant with a real picture of what it would be like to perform the job that the organization is trying to fill.

Common Selection Techniques

Once the recruiting process has attracted a pool of applicants, the next step is to select whom to hire. The intent of the selection process is to gather from applicants information that will predict their job success and then to hire the candidates predicted to be most successful. Information about candidates can be collected in many ways, including application blanks, tests, interviews, and reference checks. As noted in the opening incident, Mazda uses a variety of selection techniques. Each device used, however, must deal only with factors that are predictive of future performance. The process of proving that any selection device is really predictive of future job performance is called **validation**. Recall that any selection device that has an adverse impact on members of certain groups must be validated. In practice, all selection devices should be validated. It's a waste of time and money to use a selection device without being certain that it helps pinpoint the best candidates.

validation Determining the extent to which a selection device is really predictive of future job performance

Validation   There are two basic approaches to validation. The first is **predictive validation**. This involves collecting the scores of employees or applicants on the device to be validated and correlating their scores with actual job performance. A statistically significant correlation means that the selection device is a valid predictor of job performance. For instance, certain SAT test scores are used as admissions criteria by many colleges because the scores are correlated with later academic performance.

predictive validation Collecting the scores of employees or applicants on a selection device and correlating them with subsequent performance

The second major validation method is called **content validation**. To apply this method, one uses logic and thorough study of the job to establish that the selection device (usually a work-sample test) measures the exact skills needed for successful job performance. For example, if a job requires a great deal of typing of tables and figures, a typing test involving this kind of material is content-valid for the job. The most critical part of content validation is a careful job analysis showing exactly what duties are to be performed. The test is then developed to measure the applicant's ability to perform those duties.

content validation Using logic and a thorough study of the job to establish that the selection device measures the exact skills necessary for job performance

Application Blanks   The first step in selection is usually asking the candidate to fill out an application blank. Application blanks are an efficient method for gathering information about the applicant's previous work history, educational background, and other job-related demographic data. They should not contain questions about sex, religion, national origin, or other areas not related to the job. Application blank data are generally used informally to decide whether a candidate merits further evaluation, and interviewers use application blanks to familiarize themselves with candidates before interviewing them.

Tests   Tests are also used to select employees. Tests of ability, skill, aptitude, or knowledge that is relevant to the particular job are usually the best predictors, although tests of general intelligence or personality are occasionally useful as well. If tests are used, they should be validated and should be administered and scored in a very consistent fashion. All candidates should be given the same directions, should be allowed the same amount of time, and should experience the same testing environment (temperature, lighting, distractions). If properly used, tests can be very helpful in selection.[17]

Interviews   The interview is a very popular selection device. Besides evaluating the applicant, the interviewer can tell the applicant about the company. Unfortunately, interviews are sometimes poor predictors of job success.[18] There are many reasons for this, most of them stemming from biases inherent in the way people perceive and judge others on first meeting.[19] Interview validity can be improved by training interviewers to be aware of potential biases and by increasing the structure of the interview. In a structured interview, questions are written down in advance, and all interviewers follow the same question list with each candidate they interview. This procedure is helpful for two reasons. It introduces consistency into the interview procedure, and the questions can be carefully screened and refined so that they are all relevant to job ability and are not discriminatory.[20] Table 10.2 gives an outline of what format a structured interview might take. For interviewing managerial or professional candidates, a somewhat less structured approach can be used. Question areas and information-gathering objectives are still planned by the interviewer in advance, but the specific questions that are asked vary with the candidates' backgrounds. Trammell Crow Co. uses a novel interviewing approach in hiring managers. Each applicant is interviewed not only by two or three other managers but also by a secretary or young leasing agent. This provides information about how the prospective manager relates to nonmanagers.[21]

Assessment Centers   Assessment centers are rapidly gaining in popularity as a selection tool. They are used primarily to select managers and are particularly good for selecting present employees for promotion into management. The assessment center is a content-valid simulation of key parts of the managerial job. A typical center lasts two to three days, with groups of six to twelve assessees participating in a variety of managerial exercises. Most assessment centers include an "in-basket test" of individual decision-making and group exercises to assess interpersonal skills. Centers may also include an interview, public speaking, and standardized ability tests. Candidates are assessed by several trained observers, usually managers several levels above the job for which the candidates are being considered. Assessment centers are quite valid if properly designed and are fair to members of minority groups and women.[22] AT&T pioneered the assessment center concept.

Other Techniques   In certain circumstances, organizations also use other selection techniques. Polygraph tests, once very popular, are used less often today than in earlier years. On the other hand, more and

TABLE 10.2

Format for a Structured
Interview

1. Greet the applicant, state the purpose of the interview, and mention that you will be taking notes during the interview.

2. Ask yes-no questions about unchangeable aspects of the job. For instance:

   Are you willing to work nights? Overtime?
   Do you have a Red Cross life-saving certificate?
   Do you have or can you get a chauffeur's license?

   Ask only about *absolute* prerequisites here. If the employee cannot meet these requirements, tactfully terminate the interview.

3. If you have an application blank, you should already have read through it to avoid asking redundant questions. At this point, ask questions designed to fill in any gaps left in the application blank. For example, "I notice that you didn't list a reason for leaving your last job. Can you tell me the reason?"

4. Tell the candidate about the job and the organization. Candidates will not be able to assess their interest in the job or to answer your questions about why they are qualified unless they know something about the job.

5. Ask structured oral questions. This is the heart of the interview. Lay out many questions ahead of time in the areas of work history, education and training, career goals, performance on earlier jobs, absenteeism and tardiness record, expected salary and benefits, and so on. Avoid any questions that are not relevant to job ability. Take notes on the answers, or you may forget half of what the candidate tells you!

6. Give the applicant a chance to ask questions or tell you about any qualifications you might have missed.

7. Tell the applicant what happens next and when he or she can expect to hear from you. Say goodbye.

8. Review your notes and rate the applicant on scales prepared ahead of time, being careful to avoid biases.

SOURCE: Adapted from E. L. Levine *The Joy of Interviewing* (Tempe, Ariz.: Personnel Services Organization, 1976). Used with permission.

more organizations are requiring applicants that they are very interested in to take physical exams. Drug tests are also being increasingly used, especially in situations where drug-related performance problems could create serious safety hazards.[23]

TRAINING AND DEVELOPMENT

After an individual is chosen for hiring or promotion, the next step is often some form of training. In human resource management, **training**

■ **training** Teaching operational or technical employees how to do the job for which they were hired

development   Teaching managers and professionals the skills needed for both present and future jobs

usually refers to teaching operational or technical employees how to do the job for which they were hired. As we noted previously, Mazda relies heavily on training, especially for its new employees. **Development** refers to teaching managers and professionals the skills needed for both present and future jobs. Most organizations provide regular training and development programs for managers and employees.[24] For example, IBM spends $750 million annually on programs and has a vice president in charge of employee education. All told, American business spends $30 billion each year on formal training and development programs away from the office or shop floor. This figure doesn't include wages and benefits paid to employees while they are participating in such programs.[25]

Assessing Training Needs

The first step in developing a training plan is to determine what needs exist. For instance, if employees do not know how to operate machinery required to do their jobs, a training program on how to operate the machinery is clearly needed. On the other hand, when a group of office workers is performing poorly, training may or may not be the answer. The problem could be motivation, aging equipment, poor supervision, inefficient work design, or a deficiency of skills and knowledge. Only the last could be remedied by training.

If, after careful investigation, the problem does seem to require training, the manager should thoroughly assess the present level of skill and

American Airlines has one of the airline industry's best training programs. Flight attendants, for example, learn a variety of safety procedures and service techniques. And they practice in full-size cabin mockups like the one shown here at the company's Dallas/Fort Worth Learning Center. American's commitment to quality has helped keep it at the top of the industry for the last several years.

knowledge and then define the desired level of skill and knowledge in concrete, measurable form. For example, a manager might set the following objective for a training program in word processing: "Trainees will be able to type from handwritten copy at 60 words per minute with no more than one error per page." After the training is completed, trainee performance can be assessed against the objectives that were set prior to training. Training programs should always be evaluated; they are costly and should be modified or discontinued if they are not effective. The training process from start to finish is diagrammed in Figure 10.2.

FIGURE 10.2

The Training Process

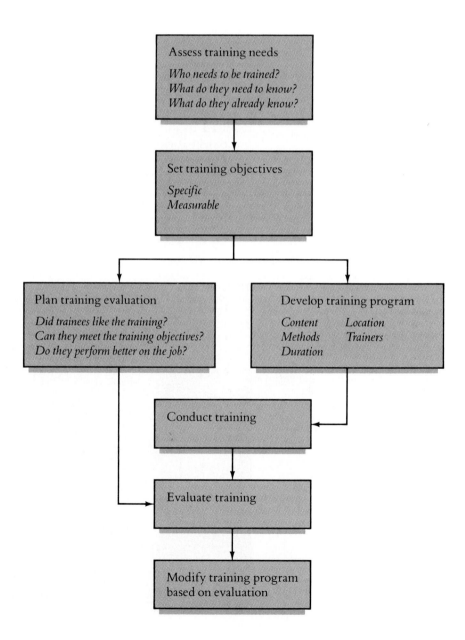

Method	Comments
Assigned readings	Readings may or may not be specially prepared for training purposes.
Behavior modeling training	Use of a videotaped model displaying the correct behavior, then trainee role playing and discussion of the correct behavior. Used extensively for supervisor training in human relations.
Business simulation	Both paper simulations (such as in-basket exercises) and computer-based business "games" are used to teach management skills.
Case discussion	Real or fictitious cases or incidents are discussed in small groups.
Conference	Small-group discussion of selected topics, usually with the trainer as leader.
Lecture	Oral presentation of material by the trainer, with limited or no audience participation.
On the job	Ranges from no instruction, to casual coaching by more experienced employees, to carefully structured explanation, demonstration, and supervised practice by a qualified trainer.
Programmed instruction	Self-paced method using text or computer followed by questions and answers. Expensive to develop.
Role playing	Trainees act out roles with other trainees, such as "boss giving performance appraisal" and "subordinate reacting to appraisal" to gain experience in human relations.
Sensitivity training	Also called T-group and laboratory training, this is an intensive experience in a small group, wherein individuals give each other feedback and try out new behaviors. It is said to promote trust, open communication, and understanding of group dynamics.
Vestibule training	Supervised practice on manual tasks in a separate work area where the emphasis is on safety, learning, and feedback rather than productivity.
Interactive video	Newly emerging technique using computers and video technology.

TABLE 10.3

Training and Development Methods

Common Training Methods

As shown in Table 10.3, a wide variety of training methods is available. Selection of a particular method or methods depends on many considerations, but perhaps the most important is training content. When the training content is factual material (such as company rules or explanations of how to fill out forms), then assigned reading, programmed learning, and lecture methods work well. However, when the content is human relations or group decision making, firms must use a method that allows interpersonal contact, such as role playing or case discussion groups. When a physical skill is to be learned, methods allowing practice and the actual use of tools and material are needed, as in on-the-job training or vestibule training. Interactive video is also becoming popular. This approach, relying on a computer-video hookup, is a promising method for combining several of the others. Xerox, Massachusetts Mutual, and Ford have all reported tremendous success with this method.[26] Other considerations in selecting a training method are cost, time, number of trainees, and whether the training is to be done by in-house talent or contracted to an outside training firm.[27]

Evaluation of Training

Training or development programs should always be evaluated. There are two basic kinds of evaluation measures: those collected in or at the end of training and actual performance measures collected when the trainee is on the job. The former are easier to get but the latter are more important. Trainees may say they enjoyed the training and learned a lot, but the true test is whether their job performance is better after their training than before.

PERFORMANCE APPRAISAL AND FEEDBACK

■ **performance appraisal** A formal assessment of how well an employee is doing his or her job

When employees are trained and settled into their jobs, one of the next concerns is performance appraisal. **Performance appraisal** is a formal assessment of how well an employee is doing his or her job.

Reasons for Appraising Performance

There are many reasons to evaluate employee performance regularly. One reason is that performance appraisal may be necessary for human resource research efforts, such as validating selection devices or assessing the impact of training programs. A second reason is administrative—to aid in making decisions about pay raises, promotions, and training. Still another reason is to provide feedback to employees to help them improve their present performance and plan future careers. Because performance evaluations often help determine wages and promotions, they must be fair and nondiscriminatory—that is, valid. In the case of appraisals, content validation is used to show that the appraisal system accurately measures performance on important job elements and does not measure traits or behavior that are irrelevant to job performance.[28]

Common Appraisal Methods

Several appraisal methods are commonly used in organizations. Three basic categories are objective methods, judgmental methods, and management by objectives.

Objective Methods   Objective measures of performance include actual output (i.e., number of units produced), scrappage rate, dollar volume of sales, and number of claims processed. Objective performance measures may be contaminated by "opportunity bias" if some individuals have a better chance to perform than others. Suppose a company manufacturing snow blowers sends one sales representative to Michigan and another to Florida. The former clearly has a greater opportunity than does the latter. Fortunately, it is often possible to adjust raw performance figures for the effect of opportunity bias and thereby arrive at figures that accurately represent each individual's performance.

Another type of objective measure is the special performance test— a method in which each employee is assessed under standardized conditions. This kind of appraisal also eliminates opportunity bias. For example, General Telephone Company has a series of prerecorded calls that operators in a test booth answer. The operators are graded on speed, accuracy, and courtesy in handling the calls. Performance tests measure ability but do not measure the extent to which one is motivated to use that ability on a daily basis. (A high-ability person may be a lazy performer except when being tested.) Therefore, special performance tests must be supplemented by other appraisal methods to provide a complete picture of performance.

Judgmental Methods   By far the most common way to measure performance is through judgmental methods, including ranking and rating techniques. Ranking compares employees directly with each other and orders them from best to worst, usually on the basis of "overall performance." Ranking has a number of drawbacks. First, it is difficult to do for large groups, because the persons in the middle of the distribution may be hard to distinguish from one another accurately. Second, intervals are unequal between ranks. Number 1 is better than number 2, but by a lot or a little? This kind of information is not conveyed by ranks. Third, comparison of people in different work groups is impossible. Each group has a person ranked first, but which first is best? The final criticism of ranking is that it is a global technique. The whole employee is being assessed at once as to overall goodness or badness compared with others. This is a bit simple-minded in that each employee certainly has both good and bad points. In addition, an employee never knows what subjective criteria each evaluator used in arriving at a global judgment. One evaluator may consider quantity of performance above all else, whereas another may attend more to quality or cooperativeness. Furthermore, rankings (and global rating) do not provide useful information for feedback. To be told that one is ranked third is not nearly so helpful as to be told that the quality of one's work is outstanding, its quantity is satisfactory, one's punctuality could use improvement, and one's paperwork is seriously deficient.

Rating differs from ranking in that it compares each employee with a fixed standard rather than with other employees. A rating scale provides the standard. Figure 10.3 gives examples of three graphic rating

FIGURE 10.3

Graphic Rating Scales for a
Bank Teller

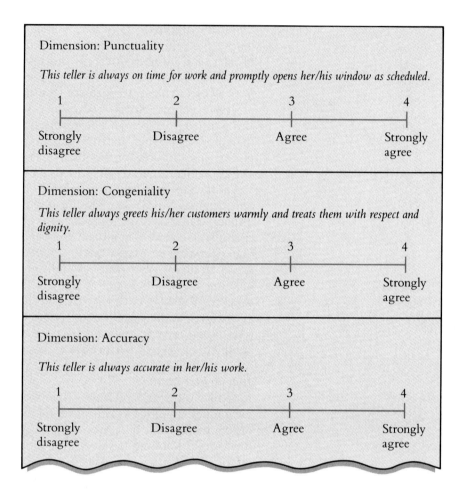

scales for a bank teller. Such scales are very common. They consist of a performance dimension to be rated (such as punctuality, congeniality, and accuracy) followed by a scale on which to make the rating. In constructing graphic rating scales, it is important to select performance dimensions that are relevant to job performance. In particular, they should be focused on job behaviors and results rather than on personality traits or attitudes.

The Behaviorally Anchored Rating Scale (BARS) is a very sophisticated and useful rating method that has been well researched but not yet widely adopted. Supervisors construct rating scales with associated behavioral anchors. They first identify relevant performance dimensions and then generate anchors—specific, observable behaviors typical of each performance level. An example of a behaviorally anchored rating scale for the dimension "inventory control" is given in Figure 10.4. The other scales in this set, which was developed for the job of department manager in a chain of specialty stores, include "handling customer complaints," "planning special promotions," "following

FIGURE 10.4

Behaviorally Anchored Rating
Scale

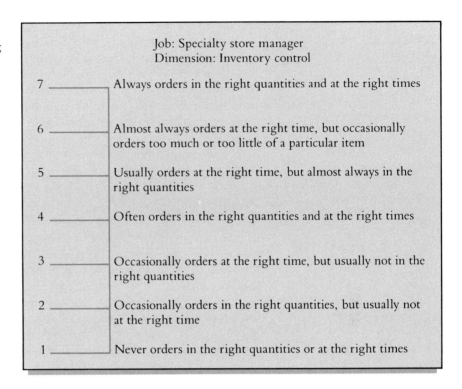

Job: Specialty store manager
Dimension: Inventory control

7 _____ Always orders in the right quantities and at the right times

6 _____ Almost always orders at the right time, but occasionally
orders too much or too little of a particular item

5 _____ Usually orders at the right time, but almost always in the
right quantities

4 _____ Often orders in the right quantities and at the right times

3 _____ Occasionally orders at the right time, but usually not in the
right quantities

2 _____ Occasionally orders in the right quantities, but usually not
at the right time

1 _____ Never orders in the right quantities or at the right times

company procedures," "supervising sales personnel," and "diagnosing
and solving special problems." BARS can be an effective method because it requires that proper care be taken in constructing the scales and
it provides useful anchors for supervisors to use in evaluating people.
It is costly, however, because outside expertise is usually needed and
because scales must be developed for each unique job within the
organization.

Management by Objectives   Management by objectives (MBO), introduced in Chapter 7, can be used for performance appraisal. In MBO,
the superior and subordinate agree on performance objectives for the
subordinate. At the end of the planning period, the superior and subordinate meet to assess the extent to which the objectives were met. In
an MBO system, the objectives provide individualized performance
standards, just as rating scales provide generalized performance standards for all who are assessed.

Judgmental Errors   In any kind of rating or ranking system, judgmental errors or biases can occur. One common problem is recency error—
the tendency to base judgments on the subordinate's most recent performance because it is most easily recalled. Often a rating or ranking
is intended to evaluate performance over an entire time period, such as

six months or a year, so the recency error does introduce error into the judgment. Other errors include overuse of one part of the scale—being either too lenient or too severe or giving everyone a rating of "average." Halo error is allowing the assessment of an employee on one dimension to "spread" to ratings of that employee on other dimensions. For instance, if an employee is outstanding on quality of output, a rater might tend to give her or him higher marks than deserved on other dimensions. Additional errors can occur owing to race, sex, or age discrimination, either intentional or unintentional.[29]

Providing Feedback

The last step in most performance appraisal systems is giving feedback to subordinates about their performance. This is usually done in a private meeting between superior and subordinate. The discussion should generally be focused on the facts—the assessed level of performance, how and why that assessment was made, and how it can be improved in the future. Feedback interviews are not easy to conduct. Many managers are uncomfortable with the task, especially if feedback is negative and subordinates are disappointed by what they hear. Proper training of managers, however, can help them conduct more effective feedback interviews.[30]

COMPENSATION AND BENEFITS

compensation The financial remuneration given by the organization to its employees in exchange for their work

benefits Things of value besides compensation that an organization provides to its workers

Another critical part of human resource management is compensation and benefits. **Compensation** is the financial remuneration given by the organization to its employees in exchange for their work. **Benefits** are other things of value provided by the organization to its workers.

The Role of Compensation

Compensation is an important and complex part of the organization-employee relationship. Basic levels of compensation are necessary to provide employees with the means to maintain a reasonable standard of living. Beyond this, however, compensation also provides a tangible measure of the value of the individual to the organization. If employees do not earn enough to meet their basic economic goals, they will seek employment elsewhere. Likewise, if they feel their contributions are undervalued by the organization, they may leave or exhibit poor work habits, low morale, and little commitment to the organization. Thus, it is clearly in the organization's best interests to design an effective compensation system.[31] The motivational aspects of rewards are considered in Chapter 12.

Determining Compensation

A good compensation system can help attract qualified applicants, retain present employees, and stimulate high performance at a cost that is reasonable for one's industry and geographic area. To set up a successful system, decisions must be made about wage levels, the wage structure, and the individual wage determination system.

Wage-Level Decision   The wage-level decision is a management policy decision about whether the firm wants to pay above, at, or below the going rate for labor in the industry or the geographic area. Most firms choose to pay near the average. Those that cannot afford more pay below average. Large, successful firms may like to cultivate the image of being "wage leaders" by intentionally paying more than average and thus attracting and keeping high-quality employees. IBM, for example, pays top dollar to get the new employees it wants. The level of unemployment in the labor force also affects wage levels. Pay declines when labor is plentiful (high unemployment) and increases when labor is scarce (low unemployment).

Once the wage-level decision is made, outside information is needed to help set actual wage rates. Pay administrators need to know what the maximum, minimum, and average wages are for particular jobs in the appropriate labor market. This information is collected by means of a wage survey. Area wage surveys can be conducted by individual firms or by local human resources or business associations. Professional and industry associations often conduct regional or nationwide surveys and make the results available to employers.

Survey data, however, do not provide enough information for making all wage decisions. First, it is unlikely that survey data will be available for every single job in an organization. Second, paying average or above-average rates based on survey data creates external equity (employees feel fairly paid relative to others in the community, industry, or profession doing the same work) but does not address the issue of internal equity (the perception that different jobs within the firm are fairly paid relative to each other). A common situation creating internal inequity arises when production workers earn as much as or more than their supervisors. This can happen when the former are on incentive plans or put in a lot of overtime and the latter on fixed salaries are "exempt" from the overtime pay requirement of the Fair Labor Standards Act. The setting of pay differentials among different jobs within an organization is called the wage structure.

Wage-Structure Decision   Wage structures are usually set up through a procedure called job evaluation—an attempt to assess the worth of each job relative to other jobs. Job evaluation is usually done by a committee made up of several managers and a few nonmanagerial employees. The simplest method is to rank jobs from those that should be paid the most (for example, the president) to those that should be paid the least (for example, a mail clerk or a janitor). In a small firm with few jobs, this method is quick and practical, but medium-size and large firms with many job titles require a more sophisticated approach. The most popular is known as the point method. To use this method, the committee first selects "compensable factors," or aspects of jobs that should affect how much pay each job warrants, and then sets up scales like those in the top portion of Table 10.4. Examples of compensable factors might include the amount of formal education required, physical demands, working conditions and hazards, amount of responsibility, and degree of skill. Jobs requiring more education would be assigned more points on the education factor than jobs requiring less

TABLE 10.4

The Point System

A Simple Point System for Job Evaluation

Points Associated with Degrees of the Factors

Compensable Factors	Very Little	Low	Moderate	High	Very High[a]
Education	20	40	60	80	100
Responsibility	20	40	70	110	160
Skill	20	40	60	80	100
Physical demand	10	20	30	45	60

[a]The job evaluation committee that constructed the system believed that responsibility should be the most heavily weighted factor and physical demand the least. That is why the maximum points for these factors are different.

Applying the Point System to Three Jobs

Job

Compensable Factors	Secretary II	Office Manager	Janitor
Education	Moderate = 60	High = 80	Very low = 20
Responsibility	Low = 40	Moderate = 70	Low = 40
Skill	High = 80	Moderate = 60	Low = 40
Physical demand	Low = 20	Low = 20	High = 45
Total points	200	230	145

NOTE: The job analysis committee carefully reviews the content of each job and decides what degree of each factor best describes the job.

education. Jobs performed under unpleasant or dangerous working conditions would be assigned more points on this factor than safe, comfortable jobs. Each job is carefully studied and evaluated on each factor, and then all the points assigned to each job are added up. The bottom portion of Table 10.4 illustrates how points might be allocated across three jobs. A job assigned 230 points would be paid more than a job assigned 200 points. Such a system makes it easier for managers to explain to employees why one job is paid more than another and thus enhances perceptions of internal equity.[32]

The next step is setting actual wage rates on the basis of a combination of survey data and the wage structure that results from job evaluation. Often jobs with similar numbers of points are grouped together into wage grades for ease of administration. For instance, if there are nine jobs with point totals between 375 and 400, it makes sense to group them in a single wage grade with the same pay rate.

Individual Wage Decision   After those decisions have been made, there is only one more issue to address—the individual wage decision. This concerns how much to pay each employee in a particular job. The easiest decision is to pay a single rate for each wage grade—for example, $6.10 per hour for the grade including jobs with 375 to 400 points. All individuals holding jobs in this grade would be paid this rate. More typically, however, a range of pay rates is associated with each wage grade. The range for the example grade might be $5.85 to $6.39 per hour, with different employees earning different rates within the range. Then a system is needed for setting individual rates. This may be done on the basis of seniority (enter the job at $5.85, for example, and increase 5 cents per hour every six months on the job), on the basis of initial qualifications (inexperienced people start at $5.85, more experienced at a higher rate), or on the basis of merit (raises above the entering rate are given for good performance). Combinations of these bases may also be used.

Determining Benefits

The average company spends an amount equal to over one-third of its cash payroll on employee benefits. Thus, an average individual who is paid $18,000 per year would get about $6,588 more per year in benefits. (Little wonder, then, that they are no longer called fringe benefits.) Benefits come in several forms, including pay for time not worked, insurance benefits, retirement benefits, and employee services. Pay for time not worked includes sick leave, vacation, holidays, and unemployment compensation. Insurance benefits often include life and health insurance for employees and their dependents. Some organizations pay the entire cost of insurance, others share the cost with employees, and still others negotiate group rates but let employees pay the full cost.

Many companies are experimenting with new kinds of benefits in
order to attract and retain qualified workers. Perkins Geddis
Eastman of New York recognized
that its architects, designers, and
professional staff wanted more
opportunities to be with their children. So it offers both female and
male employees parental leaves.
The company also allows employees like this architect to work one
or two days a week at home to
help smooth the transition back to
work.

Workers' compensation is a legally required insurance benefit that provides medical care and disability income for employees injured on the
job. Social Security is a government pension plan to which both employers and employees contribute. Many employers also provide a
private pension plan to which they and their employees contribute.
Employee service benefits include such things as credit unions, tuition
reimbursement, and recreational opportunities.

A good benefits plan may help encourage people to join and stay
with an organization, but it seldom stimulates high performance because benefits are tied to mere membership in the organization rather
than to performance. To get a good return on their benefit dollars,
companies should shop carefully, avoid redundant coverage, and provide only those benefits that their employees want. Benefit programs
should also be explained to employees in plain English so that they can
use the benefits appropriately and appreciate what the company is
providing.

Some organizations have instituted "cafeteria benefit plans," whereby
some basic coverage is provided for all employees but employees are
then allowed to choose which additional benefits they want (up to a
cost limit based on salary). An employee with five children might
choose medical and dental coverage for dependents; a single employee
might prefer more vacation time; and an older employee might elect
increased pension benefits. Such a flexible system would be expected
to encourage people to stay in the organization and perhaps to help the
company attract new employees.[33]

In recent years, companies have also started offering even more innovative benefits as a way of accommodating different needs. On-site childcare, mortgage assistance, and generous paid leave programs are becoming popular.[34] At the same time, however, J. C. Penney, Chrysler, Allied-Signal, Genentech, and other companies have started eliminating some benefits because of the escalating cost of insurance.[35]

LABOR RELATIONS

■ **labor relations** The process of dealing with employees when they are represented by an employee association (union)

Labor relations is a term used to refer to dealing with employees who are represented by an employee association (union). As we noted earlier, nonmanagement employees have the legal right to organize and bargain collectively with management. In this section we discuss how unions are formed, the process of collective bargaining, and how collective-bargaining contracts are enforced through the grievance procedure.

How Employees Form Unions

For a new local union to be formed, several things must occur. First, employees must become interested in having a union. Nonemployees who are professional organizers employed by a national union (such as the Teamsters or United Auto Workers) may generate interest by making speeches and distributing literature outside the workplace. Inside, employees who want a union try to convince other workers of the benefits of a union.

The second step is to collect signatures of employees on authorization cards. These cards state that the signer wishes to have a vote to determine if the union will represent him or her. Thirty percent of the employees in the potential bargaining unit must sign these cards to show the National Labor Relations Board (NLRB) that there is sufficient interest to justify holding an election. Before an election can be held, however, the bargaining unit must be defined. The bargaining unit consists of all employees who will be eligible to vote in the election and to join and be represented by the union if one is formed. The bargaining unit must be a logical grouping of employees, such as "all nonmanagement employees at the Acme plant in Cleveland" or "all clerical employees at State University."

The election is supervised by an NLRB representative (or, if both parties agree, the American Arbitration Association) and is conducted by secret ballot. If a simple majority of those voting (not of all those eligible to vote) votes for the union, then the decision is for certification of the union as the official representative of the bargaining unit.[36] The new union then organizes itself by officially signing up members and electing officers and will soon be ready to negotiate the first contract. This process is diagrammed in Figure 10.5. (We should also note that

FIGURE 10.5

The Union-Organizing Process

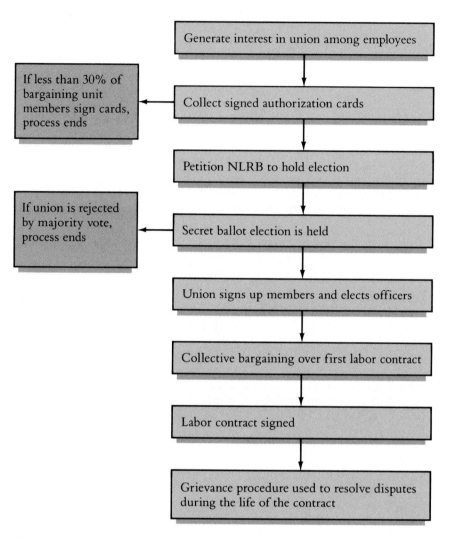

if workers become disgruntled with their union, or if management presents strong evidence that the union is not representing workers appropriately, the NLRB can arrange a decertification election. The results of such an election determine whether or not the union remains certified.)

Management usually prefers that employees not be unionized, because unions limit management's freedom in many areas. So management may wage its own campaign to convince employees to vote against the union. It is at this point that "unfair labor practices" are often committed. For instance, it is an unfair labor practice for management to interrogate employees about their feelings toward unions and to discriminate in hiring, firing, or layoffs on the basis of participation in union activities. It is also an unfair labor practice to promise

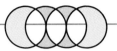

THE GLOBAL VIEW

LABOR PROBLEMS AT BASF

BASF is one of Europe's largest chemical companies. BASF has had a very traditional management process, concentrating on doing a few things very well rather than trying to be a highly diversified company. BASF's management has always taken pride in its extensive knowledge of both its people and its operations.

That traditional, conservative approach to management has also been reflected in BASF's operations. It stuck to the manufacture of basic chemicals for almost all of its existence, but in recent years, BASF has begun to move slowly into the production of specialty products and has begun innovative projects, too.

The price of such developments has been that BASF's management has started to become more removed from workers. That separation has caused labor problems for BASF. For instance, a BASF plant in Geismer, Louisiana, began using contract workers as a major component of its work force to ease the fluctuations in demand that the industry was experiencing for the products produced at the Louisiana plant. Although the use of temporary workers was a common practice among chemical plants in the area BASF's management became the focus of an attack by the Industrial Union Department of the AFL-CIO.

The IUD charged that BASF's use of contract workers meant that a major chemical plant was being run by relatively untrained workers and the result could be a tremendous disaster like the one at Union Carbide's Bhopal, India, plant in December 1984.

The type of union protest activity directed at BASF is called a corporate campaign. Such efforts are said to be "corporate" because they involve a coordinated, far-flung effort to prevail against management not through collective bargaining but through a public relations (or anti-public relations) campaign based on vilification, harassment, and the use of negative media tactics. Media events such as boycotts, marching demonstrations, and sit-down strikes outside plants are used to obtain free local and network television and radio coverage that casts a bad light on the corporation. The intent is to cause the firm so much embarrassment or economic hardship that it gives in to the demands of the union.

BASF has condemned the union's approach as irresponsible. BASF feels that the union is desperate and resorted to the corporate campaign when it saw that it could not achieve its ends through normal collective-bargaining processes. The contract workers hired by BASF average over ten years of experience, and BASF provides them with training to do their jobs safely and productively. The fact that the Occupational Safety and Health Administration received no formal complaints against BASF seems to indicate that the union's charges were not well founded.

REFERENCES: "Union Militancy—and Beyond," *Barron's*, June 8, 1987, p. 11; "Clean Desk on the Rhine," *Fortune*, August 3, 1987, pp. 50–51; Joani Nelson-Horchler, "A Bhopal in Louisiana?" *Industry Week*, February 3, 1986, pp. 17–18.

to give employees a raise (or any other benefit) if the union is defeated.

Experts agree that the best way to avoid unionization is to practice good employee relations all the time—not just when threatened by a union election. Providing absolutely fair treatment with clear standards in the areas of pay, promotion, layoff, and discipline; having a complaint or appeal system for individuals who feel unfairly treated; and avoiding any kind of favoritism will help make employees feel that a union is unnecessary. As detailed in "The Global View," labor-management problems are not unique to American firms. There has also been increased labor strife in Europe and South Korea.[37]

Collective Bargaining

collective bargaining The process of agreeing on a labor contract between management and a union

The intent of **collective bargaining** is to write and agree on a labor contract between management and the union that is satisfactory to both parties. The contract contains agreements about wages, hours, and other conditions of employment, including promotion, layoff, discipline, benefits, methods of allocating overtime, vacations, rest periods, and the grievance procedure. Unions typically want a "union security clause" that helps ensure the union's continued existence by requiring new employees to join the union or at least contribute to its support or perhaps by requiring present members to remain members. Management will likewise want a "management rights clause" in the contract that says that management retains the right to make unilateral decisions in all areas except those specified in the contract. A "no strike clause" is also usually included, stating that the union will not strike during the term of the contract (usually three years). The union (unless it is a union of federal, state, or municipal workers) is still free to strike before the contract is approved or after it expires if a new contract has not been agreed on.

The process of bargaining may go on for weeks, months, or longer, with representatives of management and the union meeting to make proposals and counterproposals. The resulting agreement must be ratified by the union membership. If it is not approved, the union may strike to put pressure on management, or it may choose not to strike and simply continue negotiating until a more acceptable agreement is reached.

Grievances and Discipline

grievance procedures The means by which a labor contract is enforced

The **grievance procedure** is the means by which the contract is enforced. Most of what is in a contract concerns how management will treat employees; so when employees feel that they have not been treated fairly under the contract, they file a grievance to correct the problem. If the contract says that the most senior person will be given the first chance to work overtime, but a supervisor offers the overtime to a less senior employee first, the more senior employee can file a grievance. If an employee feels that he or she was unfairly bypassed for a promotion, the employee can file a grievance. The first step in a grievance procedure is for the aggrieved employee to discuss the alleged contract violation with her or his immediate superior. Often the grievance is resolved at this stage. However, if the employee still believes that she or he is being mistreated, the grievance can be appealed to the next higher level, perhaps the foreman. A union official may help an aggrieved employee present her or his case. If the foreman's decision is also unsatisfactory to the employee, additional appeals to successively higher management are made, until finally all in-company steps are exhausted. The final step is to submit the grievance to binding arbitration. An arbitrator is a labor-law expert who is paid jointly by the union and management. The arbitrator studies the contract, hears both sides of the case, and renders a decision that must be obeyed by both parties. The grievance system for resolving disputes about contract enforcement prevents any need to strike during the term of the contract.[38]

In recent years, some companies have begun to experiment with new methods for resolving grievances. One interesting strategy is to allow workers a voice in resolving their own grievances. This approach typically involves establishing a grievance committee with members drawn from both management and operating employees. The aggrieved employee presents her or his case to the committee, which then rules on the validity of the grievance. Prominent companies using this system include General Electric, Control Data Corp., and Honda of America. At Honda, for example, an employee who is discharged can appeal the firing to a committee of operating employees and one manager. Although there are some problems with this strategy, it is likely to become more prevalent.[39]

Many grievances arise from disciplinary actions. The labor contract usually says that management may discipline an employee for "just cause." However, perceptions of what constitutes "just cause" and what is fair punishment may differ between management and employees. For instance, an employee in a meat-packing plant was given a three-day suspension without pay for throwing a piece of bologna at another worker. He filed a grievance stating that the punishment was excessive for such minor horseplay and that he was really aiming the bologna at a trash can. The company replied that there were closer trash cans and that the employee he threw the bologna at was working at an operating slicing machine. Thus, the horseplay had been potentially dangerous. Further, employees had recently been warned that they would be punished for throwing meat. The arbitrator ruled in favor of the company, concluding that the suspension was justified.[40]

To avoid this kind of problem, rules should be clearly spelled out and communicated to employees. Penalties should also be made known and should "fit the crime." Most discipline systems use "progressive penalties"—the more often the violation is repeated, the more serious the penalty. For instance, a first incident of tardiness might occasion only a reminder, the second a stern warning, the third a written warning in the employee's file, and the fourth a short suspension. Some violations, such as fighting, stealing from the employer, and sabotage, would call for a much more severe initial penalty. An Amoco Chemicals Corporation plant has a rule whereby the punishment for a first offense of playing a radio on the job is immediate discharge. At first glance, this penalty does not seem to fit the crime. However, employees in this plant are monitoring a very expensive continuous-process chemical unit on which many of the warning signals are auditory and could be drowned out by a radio. Therefore, the rule is reasonable if it has been clearly communicated to all employees.

Patricia M. Carrigan is the plant manager of General Motors' Bay City plant in upstate Michigan. The relationship she has forged with the United Auto Workers is indicative of how more and more employers are dealing with their unions. The plant is actually managed jointly by Carrigan's GM management team and officials of the UAW. The two groups make all important decisions together and share information about what each is doing. Training efforts concentrate on communication, teamwork, and cooperation. Quality circles help identify and solve problems. And participative management has been institutionalized throughout the plant.

Future Trends

Unions will likely always be a part of the American business scene. Their roles, however, will continue to change and evolve. For one thing, unions are becoming more and more willing to work as partners with business, rather than as adversaries. This partnership is exemplified by such agreements as wage concessions and changes in work rules. Another change is that unions are becoming increasingly decentralized. Rather than being tightly controlled by a powerful national organization, some unions are becoming loosely organized federations of local unions, with the national organization playing more of a coordinating role. Finally, more unions are being formed for professionals such as teachers, engineers, and even managers.[41]

SUMMARY OF KEY POINTS

Human resource management is concerned with acquiring and maintaining the human resources needed by an organization. It is being increasingly recognized for its strategic importance. Human resource management itself includes a number of specific activities, many of which are now regulated by law. Key areas of legislation relate to Equal Employment Opportunity, compensation and benefits, labor relations, and health and safety.

Job analyses typically include both job descriptions and job specifications. Human resource planning consists of forecasting the organization's future need for employees, forecasting the availability of employees both within and outside the organization, and planning programs to ensure that the proper number and type of employees will be available when needed.

Recruitment and selection are the processes by which job applicants are attracted, assessed, and hired. Methods for assessing applicants include application blanks, tests, interviews, and assessment centers. Any method used for selection should be properly validated.

Training and development are necessary to enable employees to perform their present jobs well and to prepare for future jobs. Steps in training include assessing training needs, planning and conducting the training program by means of an appropriate training method, and then evaluating the effectiveness of the training program.

Performance appraisals are important for determining training needs, deciding pay raises and promotions, and providing helpful feedback to employees. Both objective and judgmental methods of appraisal can be applied, and a good system usually includes several methods. The validity of appraisal information is always a concern, because it is difficult to evaluate accurately the many aspects of a person's job performance.

Compensation and benefit administration is also an important human resources management task. Compensation rates must be fair compared both with rates for other jobs within the organization and with rates for the same or similar jobs in other organizations in the labor market. Properly designed incentive or merit pay systems can encourage high performance, and a good benefit program can help attract and retain employees.

If a majority of a company's nonmanagement employees so desire, they have the right to be represented by a union. Management must engage in collective bargaining with the union in an effort to agree on a contract. While the contract is in effect, employees do not strike but use the grievance system to settle disputes with management.

DISCUSSION QUESTIONS

Questions for Review

1. What is job analysis and why is it central to so many human resource activities? How is it related to human resource planning?
2. Describe recruiting and selection. What are the major sources for recruits? What are the common selection techniques?
3. What training methods would you use to teach a group of 16-year-olds to drive? Why would you use those methods? How would you evaluate the effectiveness of your training program?
4. What is the role of compensation and benefits in organizations? How should the amount of compensation and benefits be determined?

Questions for Analysis

5. What are the advantages and disadvantages of internal and external recruiting? Which do you feel is best in the long term? Why? Be sure to think about this issue from the standpoint of the organization and the standpoint of individuals (whether inside or outside of the organization) who might be considered for positions.

6. How do you know if a selection device is valid? What are the possible consequences of using invalid selection methods? How can an organization ensure that its selection methods are valid?

7. Are benefits more important than compensation to an organization? To an individual? Why?

Questions for Application

8. Write a description and specifications for a job that you have held (office worker, checkout clerk, salesperson, lifeguard). Then contact a company with such a job and obtain an actual description and specification from that firm. In what ways are your description and specification like theirs? In what ways are they different?

9. Contact a local organization to determine how that organization evaluates the performance of complex jobs, such as middle or higher-level manager, scientist, lawyer, or market researcher. What problems with performance appraisal can you note?

10. Interview someone who is or has been a member of a union to determine his or her reasons for joining. Would you join a union? Why or why not?

NOTES

1. "How Does Japan Inc. Pick Its American Workers?" *Business Week*, October 3, 1988, pp. 84–88; Marc Beauchamp, "A Third Miracle?" *Forbes*, December 15, 1986, pp. 108–110; Richard I. Kirkland, Jr., "Entering a New Age of Boundless Competition," *Fortune*, March 14, 1988, pp. 40–48; Louis Kraar, "Japan's Gung-Ho U.S. Car Plants," *Fortune*, January 30, 1989, pp. 98–108.

2. Thomas A. Mahoney and John R. Deckop, "Evolution of Concept and Practice in Personnel Administration/Human Resource Management (PA/HRM)," *Journal of Management*, Summer 1986, pp. 223–241.

3. Brian D. Steffy and Steven D. Maurer, "Conceptualizing and Measuring the Economic Effectiveness of Human Resource Activities," *Academy of Management Review*, April 1988, pp. 271–286.

4. For recent reviews, see Lloyd Baird and Ilan Meshoulam, "Managing Two Fits of Strategic Human Resource Management," *Academy of Management Review*, January 1988, pp. 116–128; and Cynthia A. Lengnick-Hall and Mark L. Lengnick-Hall, "Strategic Human Resources Management: A Review of the Literature and a Proposed Typology," *Academy of Management Review*, July 1988, pp. 454–470.

5. David P. Twomey, *A Concise Guide to Employment Law* (Dallas: Southwestern Publishing, 1986).

6. Equal Employment Opportunity Commission, "Uniform Guidelines on Employee Selection Procedures," *Federal Register*, August 25, 1978, pp. 38290–38315.

7. Robert Calvert, Jr., *Affirmative Action: A Comprehensive Recruitment Manual* (Garrett Park, Md.: Garrett Park Press, 1979). For recent perspectives on Affirmative Action, see "Affirmative Action Faces Likely Setback," *The Wall Street Journal*, November 30, 1988, p. B1.

8. "OSHA Awakens from Its Six-Year Slumber," *Business Week*, August 10, 1987, p. 27.

9. For more information on job analysis methods, see Ernest J. McCormick, *Job Analysis: Methods and Applications* (New York: AMACOM, 1979).

10. Lee Dyer, "Strategic Human Resources Management and Planning," in Kendrith M. Rowland and Gerald R. Ferris, eds., *Research in Personnel and Human Resources Management* (Greenwich, Conn.: JAI Press, 1985).

11. Thomas H. Stone and Jack Fiorito, "A Perceived Uncertainty Model of Human Resource Forecasting Technique Use," *Academy of Management Review*, July 1986, pp. 635–642.

12. Leonard Greenhalgh, Anne T. Lawrence, and Robert I. Sutton, "Determinants of Work Force Reduction Strategies in Declining Organizations," *Academy of Management Review*, April 1988, pp. 241–254.

13. Michael R. Carrell and Frank E. Kuzmits, *Personnel: Human Resource Management*, 3rd ed. (New York: Merrill, 1989).

14. Martin F. Gannon, "Sources of Referral and Employee Turnover," *Journal of Applied Psychology*, June 1971, pp. 226–228.

15. Brian Dumaine, "The New Art of Hiring Smart," *Fortune*, August 17, 1987, pp. 78–81.

16. Mary K. Suszko and James A. Breaugh, "The Effects of Realistic Job Previews on Applicant Self-Selection and Employee Turnover, Satisfaction, and Coping Ability," *Journal of Management*, Fall 1986, pp. 513–523.

17. Frank L. Schmidt and John E. Hunter, "Employment Testing: Old Theories and New Research Findings," *American Psychologist*, October 1981, 1128–1137.

18. John F. Binning, Mel A. Goldstein, Mario F. Garcia, and Julie H. Scattaregia, "Effects of Preinterview Impressions on Questioning Strategies in Same- and Opposite-Sex Employment Interviews," *Journal of Applied Psychology*, February 1988, pp. 30–37.

19. Neal Schmitt, "Social and Situational Determinants of Interview Decisions: Implications for the Employment Interview," *Personnel Psychology*, Spring 1976, pp. 79–102. For an opposing view, see M. Ronald Buckley and Robert W. Eder, "B. M. Springbett and the Notion of the 'Snap Decision' in the Interview," *Journal of Management*, March 1988, pp. 59–67.

20. Tom Janz, Lowell Hellervik, and David C. Gilmore, *Behavior Description Interviewing* (Boston: Allyn and Bacon, 1986).

21. Dumaine, "The New Art of Hiring Smart."

22. Paul R. Sackett, "Assessment Centers and Content Validity: Some Neglected Issues," *Personnel Psychology*, Vol. 40, 1987, pp. 13–25.

23. Abby Brown, "To Test or Not to Test," *Personnel Administrator*, March 1987, pp. 67–70.

24. See Bernard Keys and Joseph Wolfe, "Management Education and Development: Current Issues and Emerging Trends," *Journal of Management*, June 1988, pp. 205–229, for a recent review.

25. Michael Brody, "Helping Workers to Work Smarter," *Fortune*, June 8, 1987, pp. 86–88.

26. "Videos Are Starring in More and More Training Programs," *Business Week*, September 7, 1987, pp. 108–110.

27. Kenneth N. Wexley and Gary P. Latham, *Developing and Training Human Resources in Organizations* (Glenview, Ill.: Scott, Foresman, 1981).

28. For recent discussions of why performance appraisal is important, see Walter Kiechel III, "How to Appraise Performance," *Fortune*, October 12, 1987, pp. 239–240; and Donald J. Campbell and Cynthia Lee, "Self-Appraisal in Performance Evaluation: Development Versus Evaluation," *Academy of Management Review*, April 1988, pp. 302–314.

29. Jerry W. Hedge and Michael J. Kavanagh, "Improving the Accuracy of Performance Evaluations: Comparison of Three Methods of Performance Appraiser Training," *Journal of Applied Psychology*, February 1988, pp. 68–73; Gregory H. Dobbins, Robert L. Cardy, and Donald M. Truxillo, "The Effects of Purpose of Appraisal and Individual Differences in Stereotypes of Women on Sex Differences in Performance Ratings: A Laboratory and Field Study," *Journal of Applied Psychology*, August 1988, pp. 551–558; and Clinton O. Longnecker, Dennis A. Gioia, and Henry P. Sims, Jr., "Behind the Mask: The Politics of Employee Appraisal," *The Academy of Management Executive*, August 1987, pp. 183–194.

30. James S. Russell and Dorothy L. Goode, "An Analysis of Managers' Reactions to Their Own Performance Appraisal Feedback," *Journal of Applied Psychology*, February 1988, pp. 63–67.

31. Edward E. Lawler III, "The Design of Effective Reward Systems," in Jay W. Lorsch, ed., *Handbook of Organizational Behavior* (Englewood Cliffs, N.J.: Prentice-Hall, 1987), pp. 255–271; and Robert J. Greene, "Effective Compensation: The How and Why," *Personnel Administrator*, February 1987, pp. 112–116.

32. Robert M. Madigan and David J. Hoover, "Effects of Alternative Job Evaluation Methods on Decisions Involving Pay Equity," *Academy of Management Journal*, March 1986, pp. 84–100.

33. "To Each According to His Needs: Flexible Benefits Plans Gain Favor," *The Wall Street Journal*, September 16, 1986, p. 29.

34. "The Future Look of Employee Benefits," *The Wall Street Journal*, September 7, 1988, p. 21.

35. "Firms Forced to Cut Back on Benefits," *USA Today*, November 29, 1988, pp. 1B, 2B.

36. John A. Fossum, "Labor Relations: Research and Practice in Transition," *Journal of Management*, Summer 1987, pp. 281–300.

37. "Korean Labor's New Voice Is Saying: 'More,'" *Business Week*, May 2, 1988, pp. 45–46; and "The Militant of the Mine Shafts," *Newsweek*, September 26, 1988, p. 35.

38. For recent research on collective bargaining, see Wallace N. Davidson III, Dan L. Worrell, and Sharon H. Garrison, "Effect of Strike Activity on Firm Value," *Academy of Management Journal*, June 1988, pp. 387–394; John M. Magenau, James E. Martin, and Melanie M. Peterson, "Dual and Unilateral Commitment Among Stewards and Rank-and-File Union Members," *Academy of Management Journal*, June 1988, pp. 359–376; and Brian E. Becker, "Concession Bargaining: The Meaning of Union Gains," *Academy of Management Journal*, June 1988, pp. 377–387.

39. "Letting Workers Help Handle Workers' Gripes," *Business Week*, September 15, 1986, pp. 82–86.

40. "Working with People," from Bureau of National Affairs, *Bulletin to Management*, as reprinted in Mary Green Miner and John B. Miner, *Policy Issues*

in Contemporary Personnel and Industrial Relations (New York: Macmillan, 1977), pp. 421–435.

41. Kirkland Ropp, "State of the Unions," *Personnel Administrator*, July 1987, pp. 36–40; Donald F. Ephlin, "Revolution by Evolution: The Changing Relationship Between GM and the UAW," *The Academy of Management Executive*, February 1988, pp. 63–66; Edward E. Lawler III and Susan A. Mohrman, "Unions and the New Management," *The Academy of Management Executive*, November 1987, pp. 293–300; J. H. Foegen, "Labor Unions: Don't Count Them Out Yet!" *The Academy of Management Executive*, February, 1989, pp. 67–69.

CASE 10.1

Coors and the Unions

The Adolph Coors Company was begun by Adolph Herman Joseph Coors in 1873. The firm grew slowly until the early 1970s, when it skyrocketed up to the point where its sales were one-third as much as those of Anheuser-Busch, the world's largest brewer. That growth was especially remarkable because it occurred during a period of extreme labor and social problems for Coors. Indeed, those problems caused a drop in Coors's performance. By the mid-1980s, Coors had dropped to the number 5 position among domestic brewers; by the late 1980s, however, it had risen to number 4 with about an 8 percent market share.

Coors's labor and social problems began in 1966, when Mexican-American union members organized a strike against the company. Mexican-Americans were practically nonexistent in the Coors work force, although they made up a very large proportion of the local Colorado population. Mexican-Americans felt that staffing practices at Coors were unfair and discriminatory and thus called the strike. That strike and sub-sequent boycotts continued for twelve years. At issue were several griev-ances in addition to hiring. One was Coors's requiring lie-detector tests of all job applicants. The tests focused on drug use, subversive or revolution-ary leanings, and criminal activity whether successfully prosecuted or not. The minority issues seemed settled in the late 1970s, but union troubles lingered on.

In 1977, 1,472 brewery workers struck Coors. Because the Coors family was so passionately anti-union, the AFL-CIO, in 1978 after losing a bitterly fought decertification election, called for a boycott against Coors. Because of the anti-union posture of the family and firm, the boycott became widespread and stunted the company's growth.

The boycott was successful. Coors not only lost market share but also saw its profits drop substantially. From 1977 to 1984, Coors had expanded its sales and distribution from its original base in eleven Western states to reach practically every state in the country. Despite that tremendous growth in its sales area, profits fell from just under $70 million to less than $45 million. The company was distributing to a wider area but was selling less and incurring high costs to do so.

One factor for the success of the boycott was intense competition from other brewers. Highly competitive advertising had succeeded in breaking long-held brand loyalties among beer drinkers. Anheuser-Busch, Miller, and Stroh were getting beer drinkers to switch from one brand to another and to try different brands; thus it was relatively easy to get them to switch from Coors altogether. However, the AFL-CIO expended an enormous amount of time, money, and energy to make the boycott work.

Coors eventually saw the writing on the wall and quietly contacted the National Education Association to see if it would serve as an intermediary to negotiate an end to the boycott. The negotiations lasted three years. In mid-1987, in exchange for a promise from Coors's management not to fight a union election, the AFL-CIO called off the boycott. The union believed that a notable victory had been achieved and that the Coors family had been forced to back down from its fierce opposition to unions. Coors's management believed that the end to the boycott had opened up the heavily unionized market in the East because new accounts were rolling in every day. Then along came another union—the Teamsters.

When the agreement to end the boycott was negotiated, the International Association of Machinists was the union chosen by the AFL-CIO to run the campaign for the union certification election. The election was to be supervised by the American Arbitration Association to avoid the cumbersome election process used by the National Labor Relations Board (NLRB).

The Teamsters rejoined the AFL-CIO in October of 1987 and suddenly became the union spearheading the election campaign. Unfortunately, the Teamsters did not like all aspects of the previously signed agreement, and in mid-1988 they asked the NLRB to intervene and oversee the election. That request delayed action for months and sparked another round of controversy between Coors and the unions.

Because the Teamsters had involved the NLRB, the NLRB could rule in favor of the company. If that happened, then the union was likely to lose the election, which it most certainly would have won if the NLRB had not become involved. And if the union lost the election and another boycott resulted, Coors could be in far worse shape than it would have been in if the union had won. Coors, therefore, found itself in an extremely uncomfortable position. The family and company had a history of anti-unionism, yet the situation was such that the company would be better off with a union than without one.

Questions

1. Describe the legal environment surrounding staffing at Coors. You may wish to go to the library to obtain more information on unions and the NLRB.
2. Why was the boycott of Coors successful? Have other union boycott efforts been equally successful? Why or why not? You will need to do some library research to answer this question.
3. In what way did the union seem to be better able to address those concerns than management?

REFERENCES: "A Silver Bullet for the Union Drive at Coors," *Business Week*, July 11, 1988, pp. 61–62; Jonathan Tasini, "The Beer and the Boycott," *The New York Times Magazine*, January 31, 1988, pp. 19–21, 28–29; "In a World of Millers and Buds, Coors Beer Has to Play Catch-up," *The Wall Street Journal*, November 3, 1988, pp. A1 A8; Marian Sutta, "Rocky Mountain High," *Barron's*, April 14, 1986, pp. 30–31.

CASE 10.2

Selection at Toyota

Toyota Motor Corporation was founded in 1937 by Kiichiro Toyoda. The current president is Shoichiro Toyoda, son of the founder. The younger Toyoda wanted to become a scientist or an entrepreneur, but instead he was trained as an engineer to work in his father's firm. When his father died suddenly in 1952, the company was struggling to recover from a bitter labor dispute. In a surprise move, senior executives asked the young engineer to take over despite the fact that he was still in his twenties. Working with Eiji Toyoda, the chairman of the board, Shoichiro Toyoda established a corporate structure that relies on consensus decision making. Consensus decision making is a slow process; however, once a decision has been made, the action necessary to implement it is almost unbelievably quick because all of the parties concerned are already informed and ready to move.

Because of Toyota's slow decision-making process, employee selection at the new Toyota facilities takes far more time than it would at a similar facility run by a U.S.-based firm. A quality control manager at Toyota's Georgetown plant, for instance, underwent 25 hours of paper-and-pencil tests, workplace simulations, and a probing interview before finally landing the job. Because those 25 hours were spread out over 25 days, the applicant had to work on another job while awaiting the results from Toyota. The applicant felt that procedure was worthwhile, however, and his willingness to submit to it demonstrated his commitment to working for Toyota.

Every person who applies for a job at Toyota's Georgetown plant undergoes a battery of tests lasting at least 14 hours. Literacy is important because Toyota expects employees to be able to read material and instructions and to constantly learn on the job. Each applicant's level of technical knowledge is assessed because neither certificates and diplomas nor years of experience are reliable indicators of what an applicant really knows about a job. Interpersonal skills are also evaluated because everyone must get along with everyone else in order to create the work culture valued by Toyota.

The tests begin with coverage of reading, mathematics, manual dexterity, "job fitness," and, where appropriate, technical knowledge. One of the most important parts of the initial tests is the job fitness part, which deals with the potential employee's attitude. There are 100 items with which respondents must agree or disagree.

After the initial tests, Toyota uses workplace simulations developed for Toyota by a private consulting firm. Groups of applicants deal with different problems such as ranking automobile features in terms of potential market acceptance. Multiple evaluators observe the groups and take notes on who says what.

Toyota hires carefully. It is careful because it wants to preserve its corporate culture. Toyota wants to maintain a culture that emphasizes teamwork, corporate loyalty, and versatility. Members of the organization must be able to cooperate to accomplish the organization's goals. Toyota promises long-term employment and loyalty to the worker and expects loyalty from the worker in return.

Toyota can afford to be choosy. The initial number of applicants for the 2,700 production jobs at Georgetown was 90,000 from every county in Kentucky. After the first round of screening, there were still about 40,000 applicants. There were also thousands of applicants for 300 office jobs. No labor agreements in any way restricted the number of applicants, and economic conditions in Kentucky were poor, creating a large pool of available workers. However, Toyota's reputation as a good place to work and the good reputation of Japanese firms in general also stirred interest in and enthusiasm for working for Toyota.

In Japan, a company like Toyota would recruit nearly all of its employees from high schools. Indeed, the initial group of workers hired at Georgetown was very well educated. All had at least high-school diplomas; many had college degrees; and a very few had M.B.A. degrees (they were hired for leadership rather than production positions). Toyota tends to emphasize education rather than experience because experience is so frequently inappropriate and the company must spend time and money for retraining. It is less costly and easier to train workers, especially if their educational background indicates that they can learn well and fast.

Questions

1. Compare and contrast the selection process at Toyota with that at Mazda (described in the opening incident of the chapter). Both firms are automobile companies competing on an international scale, yet there are differences. Why?
2. Do you feel that the intense selection process at Toyota is worthwhile? Why or why not? Would you be willing to undergo such a process to obtain a job? Why or why not?
3. If the labor market were to suddenly change so that very few people were applying for jobs at Toyota, would Toyota continue its rigorous selection process? Why or why not?
4. What impact is Toyota's selection process likely to have on labor relations in its U.S. plants? Why?

REFERENCES: "Toyota Takes Pains, and Time, Filling Jobs at Its Kentucky Plant," *The Wall Street Journal*, December 1, 1987, pp. 1, 29; Richard Rescigno, "Invasion of the Body Shops," *Barron's*, December 7, 1987, pp. 13–14, 36, 38, 40, 42, 46–47; "Slow Decision, Quick Action," *Fortune*, August 3, 1987, p. 35; "Toyota to Build Plants in U.S. and in Canada," *The Wall Street Journal*, July 24, 1985, p. 25; Louis Kraar, "Japan's Gung-Ho U.S. Car Plants," *Fortune*, January 30, 1989, pp. 98–108; "Zen and the Art of Auto Sales," *The Wall Street Journal*, March 13, 1989, p. B1; "Japanese Carmakers Flash Their Cash At the EC," *Business Week*, February 13, 1989, pp. 43–46.

OUTLINE

The Nature of Organization Change
Forces for Change · Planned Versus Reactive Change

Managing Organization Change
Steps in the Change Process · Managing Resistance to Change

Areas of Organization Change
Changing Strategy · Changing Structure and Design ·
Changing Technology · Changing People

Organization Development
OD Assumptions · OD Techniques · The Effectiveness of OD

Organization Revitalization
The Need for Revitalization · Approaches to Revitalization

CHAPTER 11

Organization Change, Development, and Revitalization

OBJECTIVES

After studying this chapter, you should be able to:

- Describe the nature of organization change.
- Discuss the management of organization change.
- Identify and describe major areas of organization change.
- Discuss the assumptions, techniques, and effectiveness of organization development.
- Discuss the need for and approaches to organization revitalization.

OPENING INCIDENT

For fifty consecutive years, Caterpillar posted solid profits and returns to stockholders. Then came 1982. A worldwide recession in the construction industry dramatically curtailed demand for Caterpillar equipment. At the same time, plunging oil prices cut demand for mining, logging, and pipe-laying equipment, and Japanese companies like Komatsu started attacking. Following record profits of $579 million in 1981, Caterpillar lost $953 million over the next three years.

Top management saw that changes were needed if Caterpillar was to regain its industry leadership and over the next several years, therefore, undertook a number of initiatives. The organization became more decentralized in order to put decision-making power in the hands of the managers who most needed it. The company revamped its plants to capitalize on new technology. And it changed the way it treated employees. Rather than being considered mere cogs in a machine, employees are now seen as valuable contributors. Today, innovative ideas and suggestions are encouraged and rewarded.

The results? Caterpillar has bounced back sharply. The threat from Komatsu has been deflected, at least for now. Sales and profits are back up, and some new ventures are performing even better than expected. Management, however, is determined not to rest on its laurels. Cost-cutting programs are still underway, and Caterpillar is pushing forcefully into several new markets.[1]

M*anagers at Caterpillar* were forced to grapple with something all managers must eventually confront: the need for change. Environmental circumstances changed, and the company was forced to change with them. Some might argue that managers at Caterpillar should have anticipated the need for change earlier, but few can question their effectiveness once they did choose to act.

Understanding when and how to implement change is a vital part of management. This chapter explores change from a variety of perspectives. We examine the nature of organization change and describe how change can be managed. Major areas of change are identified and described, and two distinct but related areas of managerial concern—organization development and organization revitalization—are examined.

THE NATURE OF ORGANIZATION CHANGE

organization change Any substantive modification to some part of the organization

Organization change is any substantive modification to some part of the organization.[2] In actual practice, change can involve virtually any aspect of an organization: work schedules, bases for departmentalization, span of management, machinery, overall organization design, people themselves, and so on. It is important to keep in mind that any change in an organization may have effects extending beyond the actual arena in which the change takes place. For example, when Westinghouse installed a new computerized production system at one of its plants, employees had to be trained to operate new equipment, the compensation system was adjusted to reflect new skill levels, the span of management of several supervisors was altered, and a number of related jobs had to be redesigned. Moreover, selection criteria for new employees were changed, and a new quality control system was installed.[3]

Forces for Change

Why do organizations find it necessary to change? The most general reason is that something relevant to the organization either has changed or is going to change. The organization consequently has little choice but to change as well. Indeed, a primary reason for the problems that organizations often face is failure to anticipate or respond properly to changing circumstances. As shown in Figure 11.1, the forces for change may be external or internal to the organization.

External Forces   External forces for change derive from the organization's general and task environments. For example, two energy crises, a maturing Japanese automobile industry, floating currency exchange rates, and floating international interest rates, all manifestations of the international dimension of the general environment, profoundly influenced Ford Motor Company. New rules of production and competition forced the company to dramatically alter the way it does business.[4] In the political area, new laws, court decisions, and regulations affect organizations. The technological dimension may yield new production techniques that the organization needs to explore. The economic dimension is affected by inflation, the cost of living, and money supplies. The sociocultural dimension, reflecting societal values, determines what kinds of products or services will find a ready market.

Because of its proximity to the organization, the task environment is usually an even more powerful force for change. Competitors influence an organization through their price structures and product lines. When General Motors offers a rebate on new cars, Ford has little choice but to follow suit. Customers determine what products can be sold at what prices. Thus, the organization must constantly be concerned with consumer tastes and preferences. Suppliers affect organizations by raising or lowering prices, changing product lines, or even severing trade relations with a company. Regulators can have dramatic effects on an organization. For example, if OSHA rules that a particular production process is dangerous to workers, it can force the plant to close until

FIGURE 11.1

Forces for Organization
Change

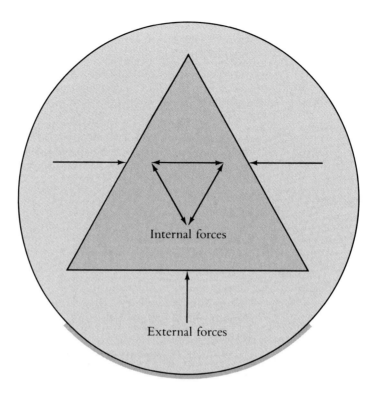

higher safety standards are met. Unions are a force for change when
they negotiate for higher wages, win a certification election, or go out
on strike. Owners can be a force for change by threatening actions
against the board of directors. Partners can attempt to modify or even
cancel working relationships.

Internal Forces   A variety of forces inside the organization may cause
change. If top management revises the organization's strategy, organization change is likely to result. A decision by an electronics company
to enter the home computer market or a decision to increase a ten-year
product sales goal by 3 percent would occasion many organization
changes. John F. McGillicuddy, the CEO of Manufacturers Hanover
and a powerful internal force, recently decided that the organization
needed a major overhaul to face the banking environment of tomorrow.
Thus, he restructured the organization, changed its basic control systems, altered the compensation system for managers, and modified the
company's strategy.[5] Other internal forces for change may be reflections
of external forces. As sociocultural values shift, for example, workers'
attitudes toward their jobs may also shift—and workers may demand
a change in working hours or working conditions. In such a case, even
though the force is rooted in the external environment, the organization
must respond directly to the internal pressure it generates.

Planned Versus Reactive Change

planned change Change that is designed and implemented in an orderly and timely fashion in anticipation of future events

reactive change A piecemeal response to circumstances as they develop

Some organization change is planned well in advance; other change comes about as a reaction to unexpected events. **Planned change** is change that is designed and implemented in an orderly and timely fashion in anticipation of future events. **Reactive change** is a piecemeal response to circumstances as they develop. Because reactive change may have to be hurried, the potential for poorly conceived and poorly executed change is increased. Planned change is almost always preferable to reactive change.

Southwestern Bell is a good example of an organization recently faced with the need for planned change. As a result of the deregulation of the telephone industry and the subsequent breakup of AT&T, Southwestern had to adapt itself in order to function as an independent corporation. Top managers developed a comprehensive change plan consisting of 2,000 major activities that needed to be modified or replaced, and the change went off remarkably well, with only a few slip-ups along the way.[6]

Caterpillar is a good example of a firm guilty of reactive change. It was caught flat-footed by the catastrophic events of 1982. The firm is back on solid footing today, but it needed several years to get there. Had managers at Caterpillar anticipated the need for change earlier, they might have been able to respond more quickly.

These points become especially telling in view of the frequency of organization change. Most companies or divisions of large companies must implement some form of moderate change at least every year and one or more major changes every four to five years.[7] Managers who sit back and respond only when they have to are likely to spend a lot of time hastily changing and rechanging things. A more effective approach is to anticipate forces urging change and plan ahead to deal with them. "The Global View" provides a good illustration of how the English firm Beecham recently addressed planned change.

MANAGING ORGANIZATION CHANGE

Organization change is a complex phenomenon. A manager cannot simply wave a magic wand and have an intended change magically occur. Instead, change must be approached in a systematic and logical fashion for it to have a meaningful opportunity to succeed. To carry this off, the manager needs to understand the steps needed for effective change and how to deal with employee resistance to change.[8]

Steps in the Change Process

A number of models or frameworks outlining steps for change have been developed over the years. The Lewin model was one of the first, although a more comprehensive approach is usually more useful.

The Lewin Model   Kurt Lewin, a noted organizational theorist, suggested that every change requires three steps.[9] The first step is unfreezing—individuals who will be affected by the impending change must be led to recognize why the change is necessary. Next the change itself is implemented. Finally, refreezing involves reinforcing and supporting the change so that it becomes a part of the system. For example, one of the changes at Caterpillar involved a massive work-force reduction. The first step (unfreezing) was convincing the United Auto Workers to support the reduction because of its importance to long-term effectiveness. After this unfreezing was accomplished, 30,000 jobs were eliminated (implementation). Then Caterpillar worked to improve its damaged relationship with its workers (refreezing) by guaranteeing future pay hikes and promising no more cutbacks. As valuable as Lewin's model is in pointing out the importance of planning the change, communicating its value, and reinforcing it after it has been made, the model lacks operational specificity. Thus, a more comprehensive perspective is often needed.

A Comprehensive Approach to Change   A comprehensive approach to change takes a broad view and carefully outlines a series of steps that

FIGURE 11.2

Steps in the Change Process

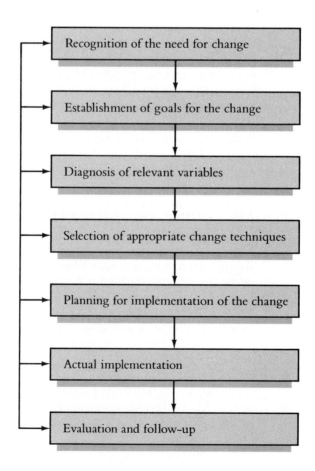

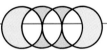

THE GLOBAL VIEW

CALCULATED CHANGE AT BEECHAM

The Beecham Group PLC had several well-known brands among its products, but it lacked a plan for development and continued success. Beecham wanted a plan so that it could overcome its lethargic corporate style and match the performance of its major competitors. Beecham directors decided to change the way in which the corporation functioned. In a careful and deliberate move, they hired a highly successful American executive, Robert P. Bauman. Bauman's charge was to impart the American corporate culture to their organization, develop plans, and revitalize Beecham.

Bauman oversaw the development of Beecham's first corporate plan and has succeeded in shaking up the organization. He forced fifteen senior executives to leave the firm and created fifteen more executive jobs, eleven of which he filled with individuals from outside the Beecham organization. Bauman stated that he wanted Beecham to be a leader, not a follower. To carry out that vision, he pushed the development of new products. He stressed the need for more aggressive marketing and established a bigger advertising budget. Other changes introduced by Bauman include the hiring of the company's first pharmaceutical licensing director in spite of strong internal opposition. Extensions of existing products were to be stressed, too. Indeed, the first of those, a liquid version of Tums, met with solid market success.

Bauman has modified some of his planned changes, however. Reaction to the idea of having an American consulting firm review the whole organization was so negative that he dropped that plan. He has tempered his use of incentive pay and performance bonuses because they are so radically different from what both employees and managers had grown used to.

Despite such limited modifications, Bauman has generally plunged ahead with change. That practice has not always been popular. He tends to make overly optimistic predictions about where Beecham will be in the future, and there is some feeling that financial analysts will be turned off by them. His push to have a majority of the board of directors come from outside the company is also meeting with opposition. Some people believe that as the drug and pharmaceutical industry becomes increasingly competitive, Bauman's lack of drug-industry knowledge and experience will prove to be his downfall.

REFERENCES: "Beecham's Chief Imports American Ways," *The Wall Street Journal*, October 27, 1988, p. B9; "Beecham Recruits Upjohn to Help Sell Its New Heart-Attack Medicine in U.S.," *The Wall Street Journal*, May 18, 1988, p. 36; "Management Group to Buy U.S. Unit for $91.5 Million," *The Wall Street Journal*, July 12, 1988, p. 53.

often lead to more successful change. This expanded model is illustrated in Figure 11.2. The first step is recognizing the need for change. Recognition of the need for reactive change might stem from employee complaints, declines in performance indicators like productivity or turnover, court injunctions, sales slumps, labor strikes, and so forth. In the case of planned change, recognition may simply be the manager's awareness that change in a certain area is inevitable. For example, the manager may be aware of the general frequency of organizational change undertaken by most organizations and recognize that his or her organization should probably follow the same pattern. The immediate stimulus might be the result of a forecast indicating new market potential, the accumulation of cash surplus for possible investment, or an opportunity to achieve and capitalize on a key technological breakthrough. The manager might also initiate change today because forecasts indicate that it will be necessary in the near future anyway.

The manager must then set goals for the proposed change. To maintain or increase market standing, to enter new markets, to restore employee morale, to reduce turnover, to settle a strike, to identify good investment opportunities—all are examples of possible goals for change. Third, the manager must determine what has brought on the need for change. Turnover, for example, might be caused by low pay, inferior working conditions, poor supervisors, better alternatives in the job market, or employee dissatisfaction about a variety of things. Thus, although turnover may be the immediate stimulus for change, the manager must understand its causes in order to make the right changes.

The next step is to select a change technique that will accomplish the intended goals. If turnover is being caused by low pay, a new reward system may be needed. If the cause is poor supervision, interpersonal skills training for supervisors may be called for. (Various change techniques are summarized later in this chapter.) After the most appropriate technique has been chosen, its implementation must be planned. Issues to consider include the costs of the change, the effect of the change on other areas of the organization, and the degree of employee participation that is appropriate for the situation. If the change is implemented as planned, the manager should then evaluate and follow up on the results of the change. If the change was intended to reduce turnover, the manager must check turnover after the change has been in effect for a while. If turnover is still too high, other changes may be necessary.

Managing Resistance to Change

Another important element in the effective management of change in organizations is the resistance that often greets change. The manager needs to know why people often resist change and what can be done about their resistance. When Westinghouse recently replaced all its typewriters with computer terminals and personal computers, most people responded favorably, but one manager resisted the change to the point where he began leaving work every day at noon. It was some time before he began staying in the office all day again. "Management in Practice" describes problems at Winnebago associated with resistance to change. Such resistance is common for a variety of reasons.

Uncertainty   Perhaps the biggest cause of employee resistance to change is uncertainty. In the face of impending change, employees are likely to become anxious and nervous. They may worry about their ability to meet the new job demands; they may think their job security is threatened; or they may simply dislike ambiguity. During the last few months of 1988, RJR Nabisco Inc. was the target of an extended, bitter, and confusing takeover battle, and during the entire time, employees were nervous about the impending change. *The Wall Street Journal* described them this way: "Many are angry at their leaders and fearful for their jobs. They are swapping rumors and spinning scenarios for the ultimate outcome of the battle for the tobacco and food giant.

MANAGEMENT IN PRACTICE

WINNEBAGO WASN'T READY

Since the mid-1970s, Winnebago Industries Inc. has had seven different CEOs as its fortunes have ebbed and flowed. Some of that turnover in the executive suite has been the result of changes in the product line or production processes. For instance, in 1983 Winnebago introduced two snazzy new motor homes and a van, all based on diesel engines. But the diesel engines and the transmissions designed to accompany them turned out to be disasters.

In 1986, Gerald Gilbert became Winnebago's CEO. He had been vice president in charge of operations support services at Control Data Corporation, where he worked in an environment characterized by high technology and rapid change. When Gilbert arrived at Winnebago, he was struck by the slow pace and the antiquated production practices. To help him bring about change, he quickly hired another Control Data vice president, and together they set about to transform Winnebago into a modern production and marketing corporation and to restore its highly successful record.

Gilbert discovered that Winnebago's production system was designed so that each vehicle was essentially assembled by hand. Because all appliances had to go through narrow doors and windows, their installation often caused minor damage to the appliances and to the doors and windows. Gilbert and his associate wanted to redesign the production system to eliminate that problem.

When an economic downturn decreased demand, Gilbert took the opportunity to change the production lines because the decreased productivity during the learning period would not hurt the firm. When the economy recovered, however, Winnebago was still in the process of conversion because workers and lower-level managers were unconvinced of the necessity for and the value of the changes. Production was down though demand had increased, shipments were delayed, and the firm was in trouble again.

John Hansen, the founder, was the largest single stockholder and the domineering and demanding chairman of the board. When Gilbert got in trouble, Hanson quickly pressured him to resign. Gilbert and his associate from Control Data left Winnebago after less than three years. Once again, Winnebago had stymied any change in its operations by changing its executives.

REFERENCES: "Winnebago's Breakdown-prone Diesels Assailed by Owners and Consumer Groups," *The Wall Street Journal*, November 3, 1988, p. B1; "Maybe Winnebago Just Wasn't Ready for Big-City Bosses," *The Wall Street Journal*, October 17, 1988, pp. A1, A5; "Winnebago's Gilbert Quits Top Post in Wake of Rumors on Output Problems," *The Wall Street Journal*, September 30, 1988, p. 31; "Some Top Products Are a Tight Squeeze in Crowded Japan," *The Wall Street Journal*, September 29, 1988, p. 26.

Headquarters staffers in Atlanta know so little about what's happening in New York that some call their office 'the mushroom complex,' where they are kept in the dark."[10]

Threatened Self-Interests   Many impending changes threaten the self-interests of some managers within the organization. A change might potentially diminish their power or influence within the company, so they fight it. A few years ago, managers at Sears developed a plan calling for a new type of Sears store. The new stores would be somewhat smaller than typical Sears stores and would not be located in large shopping malls. Instead, they would be located in smaller strip centers. They would carry clothes and other "soft goods" but not hardware, appliances, furniture, or automotive products. When executives in charge of the excluded product lines heard about the plan, they raised such strong objections that the entire idea was dropped.[11]

Different Perceptions   People resist change because they perceive circumstances in a different way from one another. A manager may make a decision and recommend a plan for change on the basis of her own assessment of a situation. Others in the organization may resist the change because they do not agree with the manager's assessment or perceive the situation differently. Texas Air had major problems with Eastern Airlines for over two years because of different perceptions. When Frank Lorenzo bought Eastern, he thought its labor leaders would agree with his belief that labor costs were too high and would submit to contract concessions. Labor, however, perceived the problems to be the result of mismanagement and so refused to give in.[12]

Feelings of Loss   Some people resist change because of feelings of loss. Many changes involve altering work arrangements in ways that disrupt existing social networks. Because social relationships are important, most people resist any change that might adversely affect those relationships. Other intangibles that are threatened by change include power, status, security, familiarity with existing procedures, and self-confidence. For example, Steven Jobs recruited John Sculley to bring professional management to Apple. He later found that he did not like Sculley's changes and longed for the way things were before. His own status and self-confidence were being threatened. Jobs subsequently tried to oust Sculley, lost a bitter power struggle with the board of directors, and then left himself.[13]

Of course, a manager should not give up in the face of resistance to change. Although there are no sure-fire cures, there are several techniques that at least have the potential to overcome resistance.[14]

Participation   Participation is generally considered the most effective technique for overcoming resistance to change. Employees who participate in planning and implementing a change are better able to understand the reasons for the change. Uncertainty is reduced and self-interests and social relationships may be less threatened. Having had an opportunity to express their ideas and to assume the perspectives of others, employees are more likely to accept the change gracefully.

The value of participation was shown in a classic study by Coch and French, who monitored the introduction of a change in production methods among four groups in a Virginia pajama factory.[15] One group was not given any voice in the change. Its members responded with no change in performance and a high level of turnover and hostility; 17 percent of its members quit within forty days. Another group was allowed to send representatives to help plan the change. The efficiency of that group increased somewhat and there was no turnover. Two other groups were allowed to participate fully in planning and implementing the change. The results for these two groups were significant improvements in productivity and a high level of morale and cooperation. Recently, 3M Company attributed $10 million in cost savings to employee participation in several organization change activities.[16]

Avis has changed its organization structure by adding a number of employee participation groups to it. Representatives from each job category meet at least once a month at each of the company's locations to discuss new ideas and problems faced by the company. These meetings often result in dividends to the company. For example, members of the Avis sales force used to use corporate American Express cards whenever they rented an Avis car to work an account. One employee group suggested that Avis provide its own internal credit card for the sales representatives to use. Since Avis now has to pay no service charge to either American Express or the airport where the rental is based, cost savings have been estimated at between $30,000 to $40,000 per year.

Education and Communication   Educating employees about the need for and the expected results of an impending change should reduce their resistance. If open channels of communication are established and maintained during the change process, uncertainty can be minimized. Caterpillar used these methods during many of its changes in order to reduce resistance. First, UAW representatives were educated about the need for and potential value of the planned changes. Then all employees were told what was happening, when it would happen, and how it would affect them individually.

Facilitation   Introducing a change gradually can work wonders. Making only necessary changes, announcing those changes well in advance, and allowing time for people to adjust to new ways of doing things can help reduce resistance to change. One manager at a Prudential regional office spent several months systematically planning a change in work procedures and job design. He then got in too big a hurry, coming in over the weekend with a work crew and rearranging the office layout. When employees walked in on Monday morning, they were hostile, anxious, and resentful. What was a promising change became a disaster and the manager had to scrap the entire plan. Managers must recognize that employees are likely to resist change, and mangers must do as many things as possible to help employees cope with uncertainty and feelings of loss.

Force-Field Analysis   Although force-field analysis may sound like something out of a Star Trek movie, it can help overcome resistance to change. In almost any change situation, there are forces acting for and forces acting against the change. To facilitate the change, the manager should start by listing each set of forces and then try to tip the balance so that the forces facilitating the change outweigh those hindering the change. It is especially important to try to remove or at least minimize some of the forces acting against the change.

Suppose, for example, the change being contemplated was a plant closing during Caterpillar's retrenchment period. As shown in Figure 11.3, there were three factors reinforcing the change: Caterpillar needed to cut costs; it had excess capacity; and the plant had outmoded production facilities. At the same time, there was resistance from the UAW, concern for workers being put out of their jobs, and a feeling that the plant might be needed again in the future. Thus, Caterpillar first convinced the UAW that the closing was necessary by presenting profit and loss figures. It then offered relocation and retraining to many displaced workers. And it didn't sell the plant. Caterpillar just shut down the plant and put it in "moth balls" so that it could be renovated and reopened. The three major factors hindering the change were eliminated or reduced in importance, and the subsequent closing went off as planned.

AREAS OF ORGANIZATION CHANGE

We noted earlier that organization change can involve virtually any part of an organization. In general, however, most change interventions involve organizational strategy, organization structure and design, technology and operations, or people.[17] The most common areas of change within each of these broad categories are listed in Table 11.1.

Changing Strategy

FIGURE 11.3

Force-Field Analysis for Plant Closing at Caterpillar

A change in organizational strategy is a planned attempt to alter the organization's alignment with its environment. As noted in Table 11.1, the change might be focused on any area of strategy. For example, an

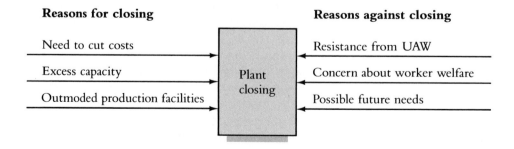

Reasons for closing		Reasons against closing
Need to cut costs	Plant closing	Resistance from UAW
Excess capacity		Concern about worker welfare
Outmoded production facilities		Possible future needs

Strategy	Organization Design	Technology/ Operations	People
Strategic goals	Job design	Equipment	Abilities/skills
Grand strategy	Departmentalization	Work processes	Performance
Business portfolio	Reporting relationships	Work sequences	Perceptions
Business strategy	Authority distribution	Information systems	Expectations
Functional strategy	Coordination mechanisms	Control systems	Attitudes
Partnerships	Line/staff structure		Values
Internationalization	Overall design		
	Culture		
	Human resource management		

TABLE 11.1

Areas of Organization Change

organization might change its strategic goals. It might also change its grand strategy—moving from a growth into a retrenchment mode, for example. A multidivisional corporation might change its portfolio of businesses by buying or selling a business. Or it might alter the strategy for a particular business—for example, dropping a differentiation strategy and adopting a cost leadership strategy. Similarly, a business might choose to change any functional strategy. For example, it might change its posture regarding debt or spending on research and development. Or the organization might decide to enter into a joint venture by means of a partnership or move into international markets. Any of these decisions would reflect a change in the organization's strategy and would be subject to the same considerations as any other change.

Changing Structure and Design

Organization change might also be focused on any of the basic components of organization structure or on the organization's overall design. Thus, the organization might change the way it designs its jobs or its bases of departmentalization. Likewise, it might change reporting relationships or the distribution of authority. For example we noted in Chapter 8 the trend toward flatter organizations. Coordination mechanisms and line/staff configurations are also subject to change. On a larger scale, the organization might change its overall design. For example, a growing business could decide to drop its functional design and adopt a divisional design. Or it might transform itself into a matrix. Many organizations also try to change their culture, at least occasionally. Finally, the organization might change any part of its human resource management system, such as its selection criteria, its performance appraisal methods, or its compensation package.[18]

Apple Computer has achieved notable success from a change in its strategy. In its early days, Apple disdained the business world. It thought its only customers were individuals and schools. When John Sculley came on board, however, he soon realized that while that strategy had served Apple well in its earlier days, changes were needed. So he began to pursue the corporate customer. Led by the versatile and easy-to-use Macintosh, Apple has become a major player in the market for business computers.

Changing Technology

Technology is the conversion process used by an organization to transform inputs into outputs. Caterpillar's plants have undergone dramatic technological and operations change. Because of the rapid rate of all technological innovation in our society, technological and operations changes are becoming increasingly important to many organizations.[19] Several areas where technological change is likely to be experienced are listed in Table 11.1. One key area of change involves equipment. To keep pace with competitors, firms periodically find it necessary to replace existing machinery and equipment with newer models.

A change in work processes or work activities may be necessary if new equipment is introduced or new products are manufactured. In manufacturing industries, the major reason for changing a work process is to accommodate a change in the materials used to produce a finished product. Consider a firm that manufactures battery-operated flashlights. For many years flashlights were made of metal, but now most are made of plastic. A firm might decide to move from metal to plastic flashlights because of consumer preferences, raw materials costs, or other reasons. Whatever the reason, there are major differences in the technology necessary to make flashlights from plastic instead of metal.

Work process changes may occur in service organizations as well as in manufacturing firms. As traditional male barber shops and female beauty parlors are replaced by hair salons catering to both sexes, for example, the hybrid organizations have to develop new methods for handling appointments and setting prices.

A change in work sequence may or may not accompany a change in equipment or a change in work processes. Essentially, making a change in work sequence means altering the order or sequence of the work stations involved in a particular manufacturing process. For example, a manufacturer might have two parallel assembly lines producing two similar sets of machine parts. The lines might converge at one central quality control unit where tolerances are verified by inspectors. The manager, however, might decide to change to periodic rather than final inspection. Under this arrangement, one or more inspections are established farther up the line. Work sequence changes can also be made in settings that don't use traditional production methods. The processing of insurance claims, for example, could be changed. The sequence of logging claims, verifying claims, requesting checks, getting counter-signatures, and mailing checks could be altered in several ways, such as combining the first two steps or routing the claims through one person while another handles checks.

One form of technological change that has been especially important in recent years is change in information systems. It is hard to find a major popular magazine that has not run an article on the computer invasion. Simultaneous advances in large mainframe computers, personal computers, and network tie-in systems have created vast potential for change in most workplaces. The basic goal behind the adoption of

Changing technology is a major concern and interest for all organizations. One new innovation with considerable promise is the fiber optic cable. The cables can handle far more telephone calls and do it much more efficiently than the old copper cable. Telephone companies are eager for the day when they can wire your house with fiber optic cable. They believe it will greatly enhance their marketing opportunities, because the new cable can also handle video and other computer transmissions. Cable television operators, however, are fighting the move, because they fear it will make them obsolete. The Home Shopping Network, shown here, uses fiber optic lines to allow home shoppers to order merchandise they see on their television screens. The same lines connect everything through the company's computer network.

computers in offices is the creation of an information-processing station for each employee. The person at each work station may manipulate ideas and drafts that are still in preliminary form, create, store, and retrieve documents, and distribute final copies. We focus on information systems in Chapter 18.

Another technological/operations change that has been pervasive in recent years has affected control systems. A new inventory control system at Caterpillar, for example, has greatly reduced the time it takes to move components through its plants. In one instance, the time necessary to assemble a clutch used to stretch over twenty days, but it has now been reduced to just four hours. The entire change grew from a new approach to inventory management.[20]

Changing People

Another area of organization change has to do with human resources. An organization might decide to change the abilities or skills of its work force. This change might be prompted by changes in technology or by a general desire to upgrade the quality of the work force. Thus, training programs and new selection criteria might be needed. The organization might also decide to improve the level of performance being demonstrated by its workers. In this instance, a new incentive system or performance-based training might be in order.

Perceptions and expectations are also a common focus of organizational change. Workers in an organization might feel that their wages and benefits are not as high as they should be. Management, however, might have evidence that shows the firm is paying a competitive wage and providing a superior benefit package. The change, then, would be centered on informing and educating the work force about the comparative value of its compensation package. A common way to do this is to publish a statement that places an actual dollar value on each benefit provided and compares that amount to what other local organizations are providing their workers.

The change might also be directed at employee attitudes and values. In the "old days" at Caterpillar, labor and management worked together grudgingly. Workers were told what to do and were basically expected to do just that. Today, labor and management work together as partners. Each employee is expected to offer insights into how to be more effective, and management listens. In many ways, changing attitudes and values is perhaps the hardest thing to do. Indeed, a separate body of thinking—organization development—relates just to those areas.

ORGANIZATION DEVELOPMENT

Organization change and organization development are related, but organization development activities are principally directed at improving the process or interpersonal side of organization life. Moreover, organization development, or OD, reflects a broader, comprehensive approach to individual-organization relationships.[21] In this section, we explore the assumptions, techniques, and effectiveness of organization development.

OD Assumptions

■ organization development
An effort that is planned, organization wide, and managed from the top, intended to increase organization effectiveness and health, through planned interventions in the organization's process, using behavioral science knowledge

Organization development is concerned with changing attitudes, perceptions, behaviors, and expectations. More precisely, **organization development** can be defined as "an effort (1) *planned*, (2) *organization wide*, and (3) *managed* from the *top*, to (4) increase *organization effectiveness* and *health* through (5) *planned interventions* in the organization's 'process,' using *behavioral science* knowledge."[22] Any attempt to use OD in an organization needs to be systematic, must be supported by top management, and should be broad in its application.

The theory and practice of OD are based on several very important assumptions. The first is that employees have a desire to grow and develop. Another is that employees have a strong need to be accepted by others within the organization. Still another critical assumption of OD is that the total organization and the way it is designed will influence the way individuals and groups within the organization behave. Thus, some form of collaboration between managers and their employees is necessary to (1) take advantage of the skills and abilities of the employees and (2) eliminate aspects of the organization that retard employee growth, development, and group acceptance. Because of the intense personal nature of many OD activities, many large organizations rely on one or more OD consultants (either full-time employees assigned to this function or outside experts hired specifically for OD purposes) to implement and manage their OD program.

OD Techniques

Wendell L. French and Cecil H. Bell, Jr., have identified several kinds of interventions or activities that are generally considered to be part of organization development.[23] Some OD programs may use only one or a few of these; other programs use several of them at once.

Diagnostic Activities   Just as a medical doctor examines a patient to diagnose her or his current condition, diagnostic OD activities analyze the current condition or welfare of an organization. Diagnostic activities rely on such techniques as questionnaires, opinion or attitude surveys, interviews, archival data, and meetings. The results from this diagnosis may generate profiles of the organization's operating procedures and growth patterns, which can then be used to identify problem areas in need of correction.

Team Building   Team-building activities are intended to enhance the effectiveness and satisfaction of individuals who work in groups or teams and to promote overall group effectiveness. Project teams in a matrix organization are good candidates for these activities. An OD consultant might interview team members to determine how they feel about the group; then an off-site meeting could be held to discuss the issues that surfaced and to iron out any problem areas or member concerns. Caterpillar used team building as one method for changing the working relationships between workers and supervisors from confrontational to cooperative.[24]

Survey Feedback   In survey feedback, each employee responds to a questionnaire intended to measure perceptions and attitudes (for example, satisfaction and supervisory style). The results of the survey are provided to everyone involved, including the supervisor. Often, the aim of this approach is to change the behavior of supervisors by showing them how they are viewed by their subordinates. After the feedback has been provided, workshops may be conducted to evaluate results and suggest constructive changes.

Education   Educational activities focus on classroom training. Although such activities can be used for technical or skill-related purposes, an OD educational activity typically focuses on "sensitivity skills"—that is, it teaches people to be more considerate and understanding of the people they work with. Participants often go through a series of experiential or role-playing exercises to learn better how others in the organization feel.

Intergroup Activities   The focus of intergroup activities is on improving the relationships between two or more groups. We noted in Chapter 8 that, as group interdependence increases, so do coordination difficulties. Intergroup OD activities are designed to promote cooperation or resolve conflict that may have arisen as a result of interdependence. Experiential or role-playing activities are often used to bring this about.

Third-Party Peacemaking   Another approach to OD is through third-party peacemaking. It is most often used when substantial conflict exists within the organization. Thus, third-party peacemaking can be appropriate on the individual, group, or organization level. The third party, usually an OD consultant, uses a variety of mediation or negotiation techniques to resolve any problems or conflicts between individuals or groups.

Technostructural Activities   Technostructural activities are concerned with the design of the organization, the technology of the organization, and the interrelationship of design and technology with people on the job. A structural change such as an increase in decentralization, a job design change such as an increase in the use of automation, and a technological change involving a modification in work flow would all qualify as technostructural OD activities if their objective is to improve group and interpersonal relationships within the organization.

Process Consultation   In process consultation, an OD consultant observes groups in the organization to develop an understanding of their communication patterns, decision-making and leadership processes, and methods of cooperation and conflict resolution. The consultant then provides feedback to the involved parties about the processes he or she has observed. The goal of this form of intervention is to improve the observed processes. A leader who is presented with feedback outlining deficiencies in his or her leadership style, for example, might be expected to change in order to overcome them.

Life and Career Planning   Life and career planning helps employees formulate their personal goals and evaluate strategies for integrating their goals with the goals of the organization. Such activities could include specification of training needs and plotting a career map. General Electric is recognized as an organization that does an outstanding job in this area.

Coaching and Counseling   Coaching and counseling provide nonevaluative feedback to individuals. The purpose is to help people develop a better sense of how others see them and to help people learn behaviors that will assist others in achieving their work-related goals. The focus is not on how the individual is performing today; instead, it is on how the person can perform better in the future.

General Electric provides life and career planning to its employees as a part of its on-going management development programs. For example, all newly-hired professionals at GE go through its Management Development Institute. While there, they participate in a series of discussions and debates with senior GE executives about the company's guiding philosophy and culture. They also develop a better understanding of themselves and of their career options and opportunities at General Electric.

Planning and Goal Setting   More pragmatically oriented than many other interventions are activities designed to help managers improve their planning and goal setting. Emphasis still falls on the individual, however, because the intent is to help individuals and groups integrate themselves into the overall planning process. The OD consultant might use the same approach as in process consultation, but the focus is more technically oriented on the mechanics of planning and goal setting.

Grid® OD   The grid approach to OD is based on the Managerial Grid®, developed by Robert Blake and Jane Mouton.[25] The Managerial Grid provides a means for evaluating leadership styles and then training managers to move toward an ideal style of behavior. The Managerial Grid is shown in Figure 11.4. The horizontal axis represents concern for production, and the vertical axis represents concern for people. Note the five extremes of managerial behavior: the 1,1 manager (impoverished management) who exhibits minimal concern for both production and people; the 9,1 manager (authority-obedience) who is highly concerned about production but exhibits little concern for people; the 1,9 manager (country club management) who has the exact opposite concerns from the 9,1 manager; the 5,5 manager (organization management) who maintains adequate concern for both people and production; and the 9,9 manager (team management) who exhibits maximum concern for both people and production.

According to Blake and Mouton, the ideal style of managerial behavior is 9,9. Thus, they have developed a six-phase program (seminar training, team building, intergroup interventions, organizational goal setting, goal attainment, and stabilization) to assist managers in achieving this style of behavior. A. G. Edwards, Westinghouse, FAA, Equicor, and many other companies have used the Managerial Grid® with reasonable success. However, there is little published scientific evidence regarding its true effectiveness.

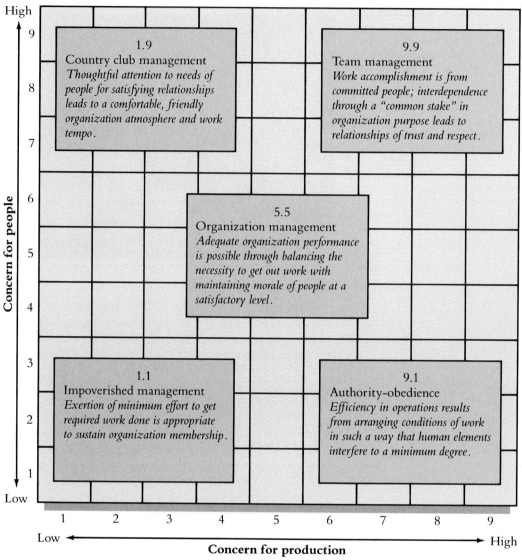

SOURCE: From *The Managerial Grid III: The Key to Leadership Excellence,* by Robert R. Blake and Jane Srygley Mouton (Houston: Gulf Publishing Company, Copyright © 1985, page 12. Reproduced by permission.

FIGURE 11.4

The Managerial Grid®

The Effectiveness of OD

Given the diversity of activities encompassed by organization development, it is not surprising that managers report mixed results from various OD interventions. Organizations that actively practice OD include American Airlines, Texas Instruments, Federated Department Stores, Procter & Gamble, ITT, Polaroid, and B. F. Goodrich. B. F. Goodrich, for example, has trained sixty individuals in OD processes and techniques. These trained experts have subsequently become internal OD consultants to assist other managers in applying the techniques.[26] Many other managers, in contrast, report that they have tried OD but discarded it.[27]

OD will probably remain an important part of management theory and practice. Of course, there are no sure things when dealing with social systems such as organizations, and the effectiveness of many OD techniques is difficult to evaluate. Because all organizations are open systems interacting with their environments, an improvement in an organization after an OD intervention may be attributable to the intervention, but it may also be attributable to changes in economic conditions, luck, or other factors.[28]

ORGANIZATION REVITALIZATION

■ **revitalization** The infusion of new energy, vitality, and strength into an organization

A final area for discussion in this chapter, also related to but distinct from organization change, is organization revitalization. **Revitalization** can be defined as the infusion of new energy, vitality, and strength into the organization.[29]

The Need for Revitalization

Why do organizations find it necessary to revitalize themselves? We noted in Chapter 2 that all systems, including organizations, are subject to entropy—a normal process leading to system decline. An organization is behaving most typically when it sits still, doesn't change in time with its environment, and starts consuming its own resources in order to survive. In a sense, that is what Caterpillar did. The firm's managers grew complacent and assumed that Caterpillar's historic prosperity would continue and that they need not worry about environmental shifts, foreign competition, and so forth—and entropy set in.

Only truly exceptional companies are able to avoid this problem. Even such well-managed firms as IBM and Disney have gone through periods of decline. The key is to recognize when the decline is starting and to immediately move toward revitalization. The major problems occur when managers either don't recognize the onset of entropy until it is well advanced or else are complacent in taking steps to correct it.

Approaches to Revitalization

The general stages of revitalization are shown in Figure 11.5. The first stage is contraction. Contraction involves cutting back—on expenses, on the work force, on facilities, and so forth. At Caterpillar, contraction involved work-force reductions, closing some facilities, and developing new methods for cost control. The next stage is consolidation. In this

FIGURE 11.5

Stages in Revitalization

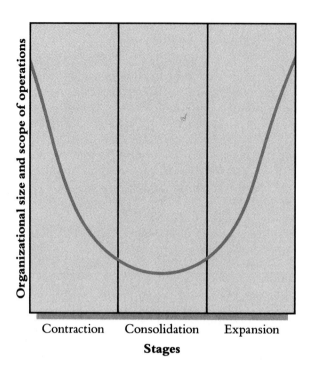

phase the organization essentially learns to live with a leaner, tighter way of doing things. Caterpillar's managers learned the real value of cost control and adopted a new management philosophy aimed at maintaining the company's regained cost leadership. The third stage, expansion, is where the true revitalization occurs. The firm starts building on its new base for operations, perhaps entering new markets, gradually expanding production again, adding to its work force as the need arises, and so forth. Caterpillar cautiously started raising prices to increase its profit margins and started making products like backhoes and excavators for small-scale contractors.

Whereas Caterpillar's revitalization was moderate in scope, Disney's recent revitalization was fairly small. Its movie division had declined and everything else was standing still. Things were turned around, however, and the company began a rapid growth spurt. In contrast, Greyhound went through a major revitalization effort. Its entire set of core businesses was changed. Gone is the bus business, for example, replaced by financial service operations.

Beyond these general guidelines, managers must usually rely on their own experiences and unique situations when planning efforts to revitalize their organizations. Any organization change or development activity could be the basis for revitalization. A new strategy, a new technology, a new organization design, a new set of values, or a company-wide organization development program might all fill this important need.

SUMMARY OF KEY POINTS

Organization change is any substantive modification to some part of the organization. Change may be prompted by forces internal or external to the organization. In general, planned change is preferable to reactive change.

Managing the change process is very important. The Lewin model provides a general perspective on the steps in change, although a more comprehensive model is usually more effective. People tend to resist change because of uncertainty, threatened self-interests, different perceptions, and feelings of loss. Participation, education and communication, facilitation, and force-field analysis are methods for overcoming this resistance.

Many different change techniques or interventions are used. The most common ones involve changing strategy, structure and design, technology, and people.

Organization development is concerned with changing attitudes, perceptions, behaviors, and expectations. Its effective use relies on an important set of assumptions. There are conflicting opinions about the effectiveness of several OD techniques.

Revitalization is the infusion of new energy, vitality, and strength into the organization. It is occasionally needed to offset entropy. The basic steps in revitalization are contraction, consolidation, and expansion. Any organization change or development activity could be the basis for revitalization.

DISCUSSION QUESTIONS

Questions for Review

1. What forces or kinds of events lead to organization change? Identify each force or event as planned or reactive change.
2. How is each step in the process of organization change implemented? Are some of the steps likely to meet with more resistance than others? Why or why not?
3. What are the various areas of organization change? In what ways are they similar and in what ways do they differ?
4. Define organization development. How could a manager assess the effectiveness of an OD effort?

Questions for Analysis

5. Could reactive change of the type identified in question 1 have been planned for ahead of time? Why or why not? Should all organization change be planned? Why or why not?
6. A company has recently purchased equipment that, when installed, will do the work of 100 employees. The work force of the company is very concerned and is threatening to take some kind of action.

If you were the human resource manager, what would you try to do to satisfy all parties concerned? Why?

7. "All organizations need constant revitalization." Can you present a logical counterargument to this statement?

Questions for Application

8. Some people seem to resist change while others seem to welcome change enthusiastically. To deal with the first group, one needs to overcome resistance to change; to deal with the second, one needs to overcome resistance to stability. What advice can you give a manager facing the latter situation?

9. Can a change made in one area of an organization—in technology, for instance—not lead to change in other areas? Why or why not?

10. Find out more about one of the techniques for organization development presented in this chapter. What are the advantages and disadvantages of that technique relative to other techniques?

NOTES

1. Ronald Henkoff, "This Cat Is Acting like a Tiger," *Fortune*, December 19, 1988, pp. 69–76.

2. For recent reviews of this area, see Roy McLennan, *Managing Organizational Change* (Englewood Cliffs, N.J.: Prentice-Hall, 1989); and Richard Beckhard and Reuben T. Harris, *Organizational Transitions*, 2nd ed. (Reading, Mass.: Addison-Wesley, 1987).

3. For additional insights into how technological change affects other parts of the organization, see Robert H. Hayes and Ramchandran Jaikumar, "Manufacturing's Crisis: New Technologies, Obsolete Organizations," *Harvard Business Review*, September–October 1988, pp. 77–85.

4. Allan D. Gilmour, "Changing Times in the Automotive Industry," *The Academy of Management Executive*, February 1988, pp. 23–28.

5. "The Turnaround Trauma at Manufacturers Hanover," *Business Week*, August 24, 1987, pp. 68–69.

6. Kenneth Labich, "Was Breaking Up AT&T a Good Idea?" *Fortune*, January 2, 1989, pp. 82–87; and Zane E. Barnes, "Change in the Bell System," *The Academy of Management Executive*, February 1987, pp. 43–46.

7. John P. Kotter and Leonard A. Schlesinger, "Choosing Strategies for Change," *Harvard Business Review*, March–April 1979, p. 106.

8. See Gloria Barczak, Charles Smith, and David Wilemon, "Managing Large-Scale Organizational Change," *Organizational Dynamics*, Autumn 1987, pp. 22–35; and Thomas H. Fitzgerald, "Can Change in Organizational Culture Really Be Managed?" *Organizational Dynamics*, Autumn 1988, pp. 4–15.

9. Kurt Lewin, "Frontiers in Group Dynamics: Concept, Method, and Reality in Social Science," *Human Relations*, June 1947, pp. 5–41.

10. "RJR Employees Fight Distraction Amid Buy-out Talks," *The Wall Street Journal*, November 1, 1988, p. A8.

11. Patricia Sellers, "Why Bigger is Badder at Sears," *Fortune*, December 5, 1988, pp. 79–84. See also "Sears Will Reorganize Its Bureaucracy As Part

of Drive to be More Competitive," *The Wall Street Journal*, March 30, 1989, p. B7.

12. "Is Eastern Frank Lorenzo's Vietnam?" *Business Week*, December 26, 1988, pp. 62–63.

13. "Steve Jobs Comes Back," *Newsweek*, October 24, 1988, pp. 46–51.

14. See Paul R. Lawrence, "How to Deal with Resistance to Change," *Harvard Business Review*, January–February 1969, pp. 4–12, 166–176, for a classic discussion.

15. Lester Coch and John R. P. French, Jr., "Overcoming Resistance to Change," *Human Relations*, August 1948, pp. 512–532.

16. Charles K. Day, Jr., "Management's Mindless Mistakes," *Industry Week*, May 29, 1987, p. 42. See also "Inspection from the Plant Floor," *Business Week*, April 10, 1989, pp. 60–61.

17. Harold J. Leavitt, "Applied Organization Change in Industry: Structural, Technical, and Human Approaches," in W. W. Cooper, H. J. Leavitt, and M. W. Shelly II, eds., *New Perspectives in Organization Research* (New York: Wiley, 1964), pp. 55–71.

18. David A. Nadler, "The Effective Management of Organizational Change," in Jay W. Lorsch, ed., *Handbook of Organizational Behavior* (Englewood Cliffs, N.J.: Prentice-Hall, 1987), pp. 358–369.

19. Paul D. Collins, Jerald Hage, and Frank M. Hull, "Organizational and Technological Predictors of Change in Automaticity," *Academy of Management Journal*, September 1988, pp. 512–543.

20. Henkoff, "This Cat Is Acting like a Tiger."

21. For a recent review, see Marshall Sashkin and W. Warner Burke, "Organization Development in the 1980s," *Journal of Management*, Summer 1987, pp. 393–417.

22. Richard Beckhard, *Organization Development: Strategies and Models* (Reading, Mass.: Addison-Wesley, 1969), p. 9. (Italics in original.)

23. Wendell L. French and Cecil H. Bell, Jr., *Organization Development: Behavioral Science Interventions for Organization Improvement*, 2nd ed. (Englewood Cliffs, N.J.: Prentice-Hall, 1978). See also McLennan, *Managing Organizational Change*.

24. William G. Dyer, *Team Building Issues and Alternatives* (Reading, Mass.: Addison-Wesley, 1980).

25. Robert R. Blake and Jane S. Mouton, *The Managerial Grid* (Houston: Gulf Publishing, 1964); Robert R. Blake and Jane S. Mouton, *The New Managerial Grid* (Houston: Gulf Publishing, 1978).

26. Roger J. Hower, Mark G. Mindell, and Donna L. Simmons, "Introducing Innovation Through OD," *Management Review*, February 1978, pp. 52–56.

27. "Is Organization Development Catching On? A Personnel Symposium," *Personnel*, November–December 1977, pp. 10–22.

28. For a recent discussion on the effectiveness of various OD techniques in different organizations, see John M. Nicholas, "The Comparative Impact of Organization Development Interventions on Hard Criteria Measures," *Academy of Management Review*, October 1982, pp. 531–542; and Richard W. Woodman and Sandy J. Wayne, "An Investigation of Positive-Findings Bias in Evaluation of Organization Development Interventions," *Academy of Management Journal*, December 1985, pp. 889–913.

29. Michael Beer, "Revitalizing Organizations: Change Process and Emergent Model," *The Academy of Management Executive*, February 1987, pp. 51–55; and Willem Mastenbroek, "A Dynamic Concept of Revitalization," *Organizational Dynamics*, Spring 1988, pp. 52–61.

CASE 11.1

Shakeup at Exxon

John D. Rockefeller formed Standard Oil in 1870 to control the emerging oil industry in the United States. He was so successful that the federal government accused his firm of being a trust operating in restraint of trade. In 1911, the Supreme Court ordered Standard Oil broken up into thirty-four separate companies. Many of the companies retained the name "Standard Oil" or "Standard." If they expanded operations outside their original areas, however, they had to use different names to avoid conflicts.

The Standard Oil Company of New Jersey wanted to establish itself as a nationally known organization but was blocked by the other Standard Oil firms against which it would be competing. So in 1972, Standard Oil of New Jersey dropped its Esso brand and changed its corporate name and the names of all its brands to Exxon. Doing so enabled it to expand into territory dominated by Standard Oil companies because it no longer used any "Standard Oil" identification. Exxon used the same brand and corporate name for all its products and quickly became nationally known. Expansion enabled Exxon to emerge as the number 1 oil, gas, and retail gasoline company in America by the late 1970s. Worldwide, Exxon is also the largest oil company.

The most recent changes at Exxon have not shaken the company so much that customers, suppliers, or financial analysts are concerned. Indeed, the general public probably is completely unaware of them, because Exxon so skillfully maintains its public image as a large, dependable, secure, slow-to-change organization. The reality, however, is quite different.

Recent changes are primarily the result of one executive, Lawrence G. Rawl, and his response to the oil industry environment. In the early 1980s he became a junior member of Exxon's powerful management committee. It was immediately apparent that he was different. He was blunt, sometimes seemed arrogant, and frequently dissented with superiors. At first, it was assumed that his differences stemmed from his youth, but those differences have persisted throughout his career. He became chairman and CEO of Exxon in 1987 and continues to be different.

Employment was reduced by about 30 percent during 1987 and 1988. Businesses were sold. Employees were reassigned. Jobs were redefined. Layers of bureaucracy were eliminated. Numerous regional subsidiaries were merged into strategic business units. Worldwide operations were consolidated. Exxon's office automation endeavor was scrapped. Exxon's main office building in New York's Rockefeller Center was sold to the Japanese. Exxon sold the Reliance Electric Company (its electric motor business) and its nuclear and solar businesses. Exxon's oil-refining capacity was reduced by 1.5 million barrels a day.

The immediate result was that Exxon experienced negative growth, but this was not surprising because many of the changes involved downsizing the organization. Revenues dropped, although Exxon remained number 1 in sales. Profitability increased, and it increased so dramatically that Exxon was the most profitable major oil company in the world as well as the largest. With the increase in profitability came an increase in the price of Exxon stock. Oil industry stocks in general rose during the late 1980s, but Exxon's stock price rose far more than did the stock prices of other firms in the industry.

Besides bringing about all of those changes in structure and design, Rawl also changed the corporate culture of Exxon. An internal executive concerned with performance in a highly competitive international market, Rawl focuses almost exclusively on Exxon and gets involved with seeing that the company accomplishes its objectives through a strategy of doing what it knows best—energy and chemicals. He holds few press conferences and does little to involve himself in public affairs or as a public spokesman for Exxon. Public service grants have been reduced by about 20 percent since he became CEO.

Many people support the changes that have taken place at Exxon, but there are those both within and without the organization who do not. Some say that too much has been changed too quickly. Others argue that Rawl's single-mindedness will hurt Exxon's opportunities to diversify and spread its risks over a wider base. In many parts of the organization, morale has been lowered as both managers and workers worry about their jobs. And many observers criticized Exxon in general and Rawl in particular for the company's handling of the 1989 oil spill off the coast of Alaska. Nevertheless, almost everyone agrees that Exxon is now in a better position to survive tough times than it was just a few years ago.

Questions

1. What forces for change have been at work over the years at Exxon? Give specific examples.
2. What areas of the organization have been involved in the recent changes at Exxon? How have these different parts of the organization interacted?
3. Have the recent changes at Exxon been effective? Why or why not? Do you expect the effectiveness of those changes to increase, decrease, or stay about the same over the next ten years? Why?
4. To what extent has Rawl revitalized Exxon? Was there a need for revitalization? Why or why not?

REFERENCES: "The Rebel Shaking Up Exxon," *Business Week*, July 18, 1988, pp. 104–111; "Lean Exxon Tiger, Still a Giant, Has a Smaller Appetite," *The Wall Street Journal*, March 17, 1987, p. 6; Toni Mack, "Oil," *Forbes*, January 12, 1987, pp. 198–200; David Landis, "Exxon Sells Reliance Unit for $1.35B," *USA Today*, December 12, 1986, p. B1; "Critics Fault Chief Executive of Exxon on Handling of Oil Spills," *The Wall Street Journal*, March 31, 1989, p. B1.

CASE 11.2

Transformation at Daimler-Benz

In 1982, Daimler-Benz unveiled a compact version of its famous luxury Mercedes-Benz automobile. That series was designed to compete in the lower end of the luxury market long dominated by BMW. Daimler's move was highly successful and its sales and profits skyrocketed.

In 1987, Daimler-Benz was hurting because of three major forces. The first was the falling value of the dollar, which made it difficult to sell expensive foreign cars in the United States. The second was increased competition, especially from BMW and Jaguar. The third was Daimler's own internal problems in assimilating recent acquisitions.

Thanks largely to the profits from the success of its 190 series, Daimler made three major acquisitions from 1985 through 1987. Those acquisitions transformed Daimler-Benz into West Germany's largest conglomerate, with sales of over $30 billion a year and hundreds of products including vacuum cleaners, toasters, computers, and airplanes. Daimler acquired the engine maker MTU in 1985, and then in 1986 it acquired AEG, the German electronics and appliance manufacturer. Shortly thereafter, amid a family feud and under considerable pressure, Daimler obtained Dornier, a major aerospace concern.

In mid-1987, Daimler was still integrating those businesses into its organization. Preoccupation with that process, coupled with the falling dollar and increased competition in its major markets, made Daimler vulnerable to aggressive competition in automobile and truck sales. Although it remained a strong company, many analysts felt that its stock was in trouble and would remain so until competitive pressures stabilized or the company's long-term strategy was clarified.

In the middle of 1987 Daimler changed CEOs in order to unify the company with respect to its strategy. The new CEO was the architect of the diversification strategy. The Daimler organization is still dominated by cars and trucks (they account for about three-fourths of all sales), but other areas are growing more quickly and are expected to receive more attention under the new CEO.

Meanwhile, Daimler was being pressured by the West German government to take over state-controlled and financially troubled Messerschmitt-Bolkow-Blohm G.m.b.H. (MBB), the German aircraft and aerospace giant. If it did assume a major stake in MBB, Daimler would become West Germany's largest defense contractor and could account for nearly 4 percent of West Germany's gross national product by itself! However, there were so many problems with MBB operations that Daimler was extremely cautious about getting involved. Management felt that it needed to iron out other acquisition problems before accepting any new ones. Further, there were several political issues involved in a merger that would make Daimler so large and powerful.

By late 1988, it appeared that Daimler would acquire a 30 percent stake in MBB. Because MBB holds almost a 40 percent share in Europe's Airbus consortium, Daimler would also control those operations at a distance. The acquisition agreement called for the West German government to provide up to $2.4 billion a year through the year 2000 to protect Daimler from anticipated Airbus losses. Daimler would then control 60 percent of the West German defense budget—a situation that caused considerable controversy because it put so much power in so few hands.

To assure the smooth assimilation of MBB, Daimler was reorganized into three major subsidiaries late in 1988. The first, Mercedes-Benz, handles automobiles and trucks. It is still the dominant part of Daimler's business and will continue to be so for many years to come, although it is expected to decrease as a percent of total sales. The second, AEG, deals with all of Daimler's electronics, automation, and communications products and operations. The third, Deutsche Aerospace, includes MTU and Dornier as well as AEG's aerospace operations and would also include MBB operations. Having the organizational structure for the MBB acquisition in place before it occurred was a tremendous improvement over the past.

Throughout these changes, Daimler has been very successful at balancing its many constituencies. Shareholders have been promised that the firm will have earnings in excess of $1 billion. Bankers have been persuaded that Daimler-Benz is a far better investment risk as a conglomerate than it was as just an automobile and truck company. Managers and employees are being assured that the transformed corporation offers far greater potential for growth and, hence, promotion. Whether or not Daimler lives up to all those promises remains to be seen.

Questions

1. Have the changes at Daimler-Benz been planned or reactive? Explain the reasons for your answer.
2. Was there resistance to change at Daimler? If so, what was the nature of that resistance and how was it managed?
3. What areas of organization change were impacted at Daimler?
4. Do you feel that the changes at Daimler were well managed? Why or why not?
5. Compare and contrast the change processes at Exxon and Daimler. What reasons can you advance for the similarities and differences that you note?

REFERENCES: "Daimler: The Giant May Turn into a Behemoth," *Business Week*, November 14, 1988, pp. 80–82; "The Banker Behind the Shakeup at Daimler-Benz," *Business Week*, July 27, 1987, pp. 36–37; "Daimler-Benz Resists Bonn's New Lures to Take Over State-run Aerospace Firm," *The Wall Street Journal*, June 20, 1988, p. 8; Michael Parrott, "Will BMW Overtake Daimler?" *Barron's*, October 5, 1987, p. 28.

ENHANCEMENT MODULE 4

Participative Management

In some ways, Munich, West Germany, is like California's famed Silicon Valley: It is populated with large numbers of young professionals who are anxious to advance their careers and who have abundant job opportunities. Thus, when two former Siemens engineers decided to form their own software company, they felt they needed to do something a little bit different to attract the right people. After careful consideration, they decided to establish their whole company, called Softlab, around the principle of employee participation. They chose not to establish any form of hierarchy or management structure. The people they hired have almost total autonomy over what they do and how they do it. The results? Softlab had sales of $51 million and pretax profits of $14 million in 1987, and BMW recently paid $18 million for a mere 10 percent stake in the company.[1]

Managers at Softlab recognized what some managers have known for years and what increasingly large numbers of other managers are learning: Employee participation often enhances motivation, commitment, and overall organizational effectiveness. This module explores participative management by describing its nature and discussing common methods for implementing it.

THE NATURE OF PARTICIPATIVE MANAGEMENT

Participative management is not just a management tool to get greater output from workers. For it to work properly, it must be institutionalized by an organization as a basic and guiding philosophy. Participative management is a planned approach to involve lower-level employees in one or more areas of operation previously reserved for management. Such participation is related to but different from decentralization. Whereas decentralization focuses on giving middle and lower-level managers more decision-making power, participation is more concerned with involving lower-level managers and op-

erating employees. After a brief discussion of the history of participation, we will explain current perspectives and areas of participation, as well as potential problems that organizations sometimes confront.[2]

Historical Perspectives on Participation

The human relations movement in vogue from the 1930s through the 1950s (discussed in Chapter 2) assumed that employees who are happy and satisfied will work harder than those who are not happy and dissatisfied. The movement stimulated general interest in worker participation in various aspects of organizational activities. The hope was that if employees participated in decision making about their work environment, they would be satisfied and their satisfaction would result in improved performance. At first, managers tended to regard employee participation merely as a means to enhance satisfaction, not as a source of potentially valuable input and expertise. Eventually, however, managers began to recognize that employee input itself was useful, independent of its presumed effect on satisfaction, and employees came to be seen as valued human resources capable of making substantive contributions to organizational effectiveness.

Current Perspectives on Participation

Participative management has become especially popular in recent years. The catalyst has been foreign competition, especially from the Japanese. As firms like Honda, Sony, and Samsung became increasingly competitive in the United States, American managers turned to those firms to learn more about their success. An answer that often appeared was participation. Japanese firms encouraged widespread employee participation and cited it as a basic reason for their effectiveness. Thus, some American firms began to emulate the Japanese in order to regain a competitive edge.

Not surprisingly, the firms that adopted token participation achieved the same results as their human relations predecessors—little if any improvement in any area of operation. However, the firms that institutionalized participation and embraced it as a worthwhile and guiding management philosophy often realized significant improvements and enhanced effectiveness. Ford, Westinghouse, Delta, Motorola, and General Electric have all reported successful outcomes from enhanced participation. A former Ford executive proclaimed, "We stopped shipping products if an employee on the floor said they weren't right, and we stopped penalizing people if they didn't make their quotas because of worries about quality. That was a radical departure for Ford."[3] One survey found that in a sample of 101 firms, the more participative firms outperformed the less participative firms on thirteen of fourteen financial measures.[4]

There is a clear trend in the United States toward a more participative approach to management. The research evidence to date looks fairly promising regarding the benefits of participation, although there have been some failures with participation. For example, General Electric dropped participative management in eleven of twelve plants in one of its divisions.[5] And scientific research suggests that a number of organizational and individual contingency factors influence the success of participation.[6]

Participation is also becoming more widespread in other countries. West Germany even has laws that mandate a certain degree of employee participation. As a result of a 1976 law, major West German firms must give labor representatives half of the votes on their supervisory boards (similar to the board of directors of an American corporation). Volkswagen, for example, has twenty members on its board— five blue-collar workers, three union representatives, two white-collar representatives, and ten management representatives.[7]

Areas of Participation

Employee participation may be appropriate in many areas.[8] Employees can participate in questions and decisions about their own individual jobs. Instead of being told how to do their jobs, employees can make their own decisions about how to do them. Workers might be in a good position to enhance their productivity if they are allowed to base procedures on their own expertise and experience with their tasks. In many situations, they might also be allowed to make decisions about what materials to use, what tools to use, and so forth.

Workers can also make administrative decisions about work schedules and the like. For example, if jobs are relatively independent of one another, workers might be able to decide when to take breaks and when to go to lunch. They might also be able to schedule their own vacations and days off. Increasingly, employees are also being given opportunities to participate in broader issues of product quality. Such participation is a hallmark of successful Japanese firms, and American companies have followed suit.

Figure EM4.1 presents a useful framework that identifies four areas of employee participation and indicates how participative managment may affect performance and productivity. Employees who participate in problem solving, change, goal setting, and decision making are able to complete meaningful tasks and have more control over their work. These outcomes, in turn, produce feelings of satisfaction, challenge, security, and acceptance and commitment. Finally, these feelings, with innovation an important by-product, enhance performance and productivity.[9]

Problems with Participation

Participative management does not always work smoothly. Indeed, any number of things can sidetrack a participative management program. Perhaps the major stumbling block is top-management support. As noted earlier, participative management is not necessarily a technique that can be taken off the shelf and installed into a work system in one day. Nevertheless, some companies attempt to use participation in just this way, and when they do, it usually fails.

Another barrier is middle and lower-level managers. In order for participative management to work, people in these positions must usually give

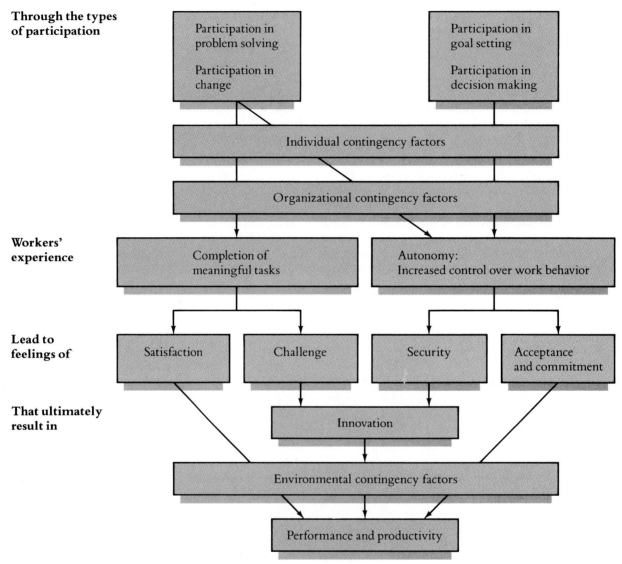

FIGURE EM4.1

Areas of Participative
Management

up some of their power. Employees are given control over decisions previously reserved for managers. Consequently, the managers may resist the new approach because they fear losing power and perhaps their jobs. The failures at General Electric mentioned earlier were attributed to problems caused by middle managers.

Unions also hamper some efforts at participative management. At one GE plant, the union repeatedly thwarted efforts to adopt participative management—first because the union wasn't consulted and later because it thought some of the rules governing participation were unwarranted. GE, for example, tried to prohibit employee discussion of grievances and reprimands.[10] Finally, there are concerns being voiced that some aspects of participative management may be illegal. It has been argued that participative management may violate several sections of the National Labor Relations Act regarding collective bargaining and unionization agreements.[11]

APPROACHES TO PARTICIPATIVE MANAGEMENT

When an organization decides to adopt a participative style, there are a number of approaches it can use: structural approaches, quality circles, and system-based integrative approaches.

Structural Approaches

Structural approaches to participative management involve changing or adding an organization design element to provide a specific avenue for participation. The two most frequently used design elements are autonomous work groups and work teams. The concept of autonomous work groups was introduced in Chapter 8 as a job design alternative to specialization. The use of such groups involves letting the work group design its own system for performing a set of interrelated tasks. By definition, then, an organization that starts to use autonomous work groups is adopting a participative management approach.[12]

Work teams are also a popular structural method for increasing employee participation. This approach is introduced in Chapter 14 in the opening incident about AAL. Autonomous work groups and work teams are similar, but they differ in a few respects. A work team tends to be more structured than an autonomous work group. The team has a set of prescribed tasks that must be performed in certain ways. The members of a work team learn more than one set of tasks and have some flexibility in performing different tasks assigned to the team. In an autonomous work group, group members have even more freedom to define tasks for themselves and to determine how tasks are to be performed. Both have been shown to be viable and useful for increasing employee participation in the workplace. Another increasingly popular method is the quality circle.

Quality Circles

Quality circles became popular in the United States in the early 1980s. They were actually an American invention but were not widely adopted in the United States until the Japanese had demonstrated their usefulness. **Quality circles** are small groups of volunteers who meet regularly to identify, analyze, and solve quality and related problems that pertain to their work.

The operation of quality circles is summarized in Table EM4.1. The first step is to seek volunteers through avenues such as newsletters and bulletin boards. Recruitment usually stresses the circle's potential for helping the organization by influencing its future. Members of a quality circle usually receive

TABLE EM4.1

Steps in Forming Quality Circles

1. Organization solicits volunteers through company newsletter, bulletin boards, etc.

2. Circles are formed, usually by work area or area of responsibility.

3. Members are provided with appropriate training in problem solving, quality control, etc.

4. Circles hold regular meetings to identify and suggest solutions to problems.

5. Problem definitions and solution suggestions are forwarded to management for review and approval or disapproval.

no extrinsic reward for their participation; instead, their reward is the opportunity to contribute to the organization and do something meaningful.

It is crucial that the participants be true volunteers—participation through coercion would probably have more negative than positive consequences. Thus, organizations usually provide several orientation meetings to answer questions and explain how the quality circle program will work. If there is sufficient interest among the employees who attend the meetings, the organization must decide whether to go ahead with the program.

Quality circles usually have eight to ten members drawn from the same work area or from related areas so that the members have a common frame of reference. The membership of a circle is ordinarily fixed, although people may be added or dropped as appropriate. After it has been formed, the circle usually receives problem-solving training to help members deal with work problems, as well as training in quality control methods and procedures. Training may be provided at the outset or as an ongoing process.

Quality circle meetings are almost always held on company premises and on company time. A one-hour meeting per week is standard. During meetings, the circle identifies, analyzes, and develops solutions for quality problems in its areas of responsibility. Problems may range from vandalism to the need to enhance the quality of the organization's products or services.

After problems have been defined and solutions formulated, management reviews the recommended solutions. Ideally, management is able to accept a high percentage of the recommended solutions and thus reinforces and demonstrates support for the circle's efforts. If few suggestions are accepted, the circle is likely to become discouraged and disband. Westinghouse, Hewlett-Packard, Texas Instruments, Eastman Kodak, and Procter & Gamble are some of many firms that report positive results from quality circles. Texas Instruments reported savings of over $100,000 per year from suggestions made by its quality circles, and Westinghouse saved over $50,000 from suggestions made by a single circle.

Research has suggested that quality circles have a fairly predictable life cycle. If they are left to operate as originally established, they tend to start losing effectiveness after around three years. To offset this decline, the organization may need to disband groups and start new ones, adopt an even more participative approach to management, or drop the program altogether.[13]

System-based Integrative Approaches

System-based integrative approaches are broad, comprehensive efforts to change the entire organizational culture to one that encourages and values participation and collaboration. Type Z organizations, discussed in Chapter 2, represent one fairly common integrative approach.[14] Firms that choose to adopt the Type Z approach must do more than just add quality circles or work teams. They must alter their entire organization in order to institutionalize participation. Westinghouse took the participative management message to heart in this fashion. The company widened its spans of management, became more decentralized, adopted an M-form design, created a number of quality circles and work teams, trained supervisors and managers to work together as collaborators, abolished numerous rules, regulations, and standard operating systems, and increased participation in all areas of decision making, goal setting, and problem solving.[15]

Although Ford does not call itself a Type Z organization, it too has integrated participation throughout its operating systems. Donald Peterson, an advocate of management by walking around, uses the information he gets from operating employees to plan changes at all levels of the firm. Neither Westinghouse or Ford is as participative as Softlab, but they and numerous other American firms are increasingly realizing that participative work systems can be an effective means for enhancing overall organizational performance.

NOTES

1. "Hot Startups from Hong Kong to Hamburg," *Business Week*, May 23, 1988, pp. 134–138.
2. See Dean Tjosvold, "Participation: A Close Look at Its Dynamics," *Journal of Management*, Autumn 1987, pp. 739–750.
3. "A Humble Hero Drives Ford to the Top," *Fortune*, January 4, 1988, p. 24.

4. Bill Saporito, "The Revolt Against 'Working Smarter,'" *Fortune*, July 21, 1986, pp. 58–65.

5. Saporito, "The Revolt Against 'Working Smarter.'"

6. See Katherine I. Miller, "Participation, Satisfaction, and Productivity: A Meta-Analytic Review," *Academy of Management Journal*, December 1986, pp. 727–753; and John A. Wagner III and Richard Z. Gooding, "Shared Influence and Organizational Behavior: A Meta-Analysis of Situational Variables Expected to Moderate Participation-Outcome Relationships," *Academy of Management Journal*, September 1987, pp. 524–541.

7. Dennis Phillips, "How VW Builds Worker Loyalty Worldwide," *Management Review*, June 1987, pp. 38–39.

8. John L. Cotton, David A. Vollrath, Kirk L. Froggatt, Mark L. Lengnick-Hall, and Kenneth R. Jennings, "Employee Participation: Diverse Forms and Different Outcomes," *Academy of Management Review*, January 1988, pp. 8–22.

9. Marshall Sashkin, "Participative Management Is an Ethical Imperative," *Organizational Dynamics*, Spring 1984, pp. 2–21.

10. Saporito, "The Revolt Against 'Working Smarter.'"

11. Jane Hass Philbrick and Marsha E. Hass, "The New Management: Is It Legal?" *The Academy of Management Executive*, November 1988, pp. 325–329.

12. Toby D. Wall, Nigel J. Kemp, Paul R. Jackson, and Chris W. Clegg, "Outcomes of Autonomous Workgroups: A Long-Term Field Experiment," *Academy of Management Journal*, June 1986, pp. 280–304.

13. Ricky W. Griffin, "Consequences of Quality Circles in an Industrial Setting: A Longitudinal Assessment," *Academy of Management Journal*, June 1988, pp. 338–358. See also Dwight R. Norris and James F. Cox, "Quality Circle Programmes: Volunteering for Participation," *Journal of Occupational Behaviour*, Vol. 8, 1987, pp. 209–217, for other recent research.

14. William Ouchi, *Theory Z—How American Business Can Meet the Japanese Challenge* (Reading, Mass.: Addison-Wesley, 1981).

15. Jeremy Main, "Westinghouse's Cultural Revolution," *Fortune*, June 15, 1981, pp. 74–93.

ENHANCEMENT MODULE 5

Managing Creativity and Innovation

Minnesota Mining & Manufacturing, better known as 3M, is an international hotbed of creativity and innovation. The company has a stated goal of generating 25 percent of its annual sales from products less than five years old. Recent successes include Post-it Notes, removable Scotch magic tape, and new, high-quality VHS tape. The company employs 6,000 scientists and engineers and encourages them to spend 15 percent of their time working on projects outside their normal duties. 3M even finds some of its new ideas by accident. A few years ago, a researcher dropped a beaker of industrial compound and noticed a few days later that the spots it had made on her sneakers were cleaner than the rest of the shoes. This led to the development of ScotchGard, a highly successful fabric protector.[1]

3M is an excellent example of what American business does better than businesses in any other country in the world—develop new and innovative products and services. Although innovation can be part of all managerial activities, managers usually attempt to manage it through the organizing function. Thus, this module explores how organizations try to harness individual creativity and spur innovation. We first explore the nature of creativity and innovation. We then summarize some traditional approaches used by managers to promote innovation. Finally, we discuss several new methods for enhancing innovation.

THE NATURE OF CREATIVITY AND INNOVATION

Creativity and innovation are related but different phenomena. Creativity is an individual's innate ability to generate new ideas or conceive new perspectives on existing ideas. Innovation is a managed effort to create new products or services or new uses for existing products or services. Thus, creativity is an individual process that may or may not occur in an organizational setting, and innovation is an or-

ganizational activity aimed at stimulating and managing the creativity of employees.

The Importance of Creativity and Innovation

Creativity and innovation are essential for organizational survival in today's complex environment. Companies are constantly facing changing competitors, technologies, and government influences, and these new situations require new ideas. Overreliance on past successes will cause the organization to fall behind. Both Polaroid and Xerox were guilty of resting on their laurels after the big breakthroughs that propelled them to the top of their respective industries, and for years a complacent Volkswagen controlled the foreign-car market in the United States. Eventually, however, more aggressive and innovative firms leapfrogged over them, and it took several lean years for each to get back into the game.[2]

An emphasis on innovation serves several functions. For one thing, it attracts bright people to the organization. For another, it injects a sense of excitement and fun into the workplace. People enjoy coming to work when they realize they may get to participate in an exciting breakthrough of some sort. An emphasis on innovation also helps keep an organization competitive. 3M makes over 60,000 products. Some of them are marginally profitable; others are reasonably profitable; and still others are highly profitable—and in any given year, many of them did not exist the year before.

Individual Creativity

How do people become creative? How does the creative process work? Although the answers to these questions have not yet been discovered, there are a few general insights that can be gleaned.

The Process of Creativity Most creative accomplishments involve four general phases: preparation, incubation, insight, and verification.[3] These are illustrated in Figure EM5.1. The first phase, preparation, usually involves education and formal training. For example, David Morse, a research scientist at Corning , received a doctorate in chemistry from MIT. Preparation can also involve a much shorter and narrower perspective. An artist creating a new advertising campaign may prepare by researching the product and the promotional campaigns used for competing products. This may take only a few days or weeks.

The second phase, incubation, is usually a period of less intense concentration in which the brain can relax and assimilate information. The phrase "let's sleep on it" refers to the incubation period. The mind gathers and sorts data, and then needs time to let things jell and fall into place. Incubation may occur when one is sleeping, visiting with friends, driving, chopping wood, painting, or doing whatever the individual finds relaxing. David Morse enjoys rowing and reflecting on ancient theories about the physical properties of glass and ceramics.

The third phase of creativity, insight, is characterized by the individual's becoming aware of a new idea or solution. Insight may occur rapidly or develop gradually. It may be triggered by a new fact, or it may represent a synthesis of all the information gathered during the preparation phase. One day while David Morse was rowing, he hit upon a new formula for making an extremely porous glass, and he immediately realized that it would provide a way for adhering a nonstick Teflon coating to Corning's popular Visions glass cookware.

Finally, the person must verify the validity and usefulness of the idea. If a new product would cost more to build than consumers would be willing to pay, building the product would obviously not be a good idea. David Morse first sold his idea to top

FIGURE EM 5.1

Phases in Individual Creativity

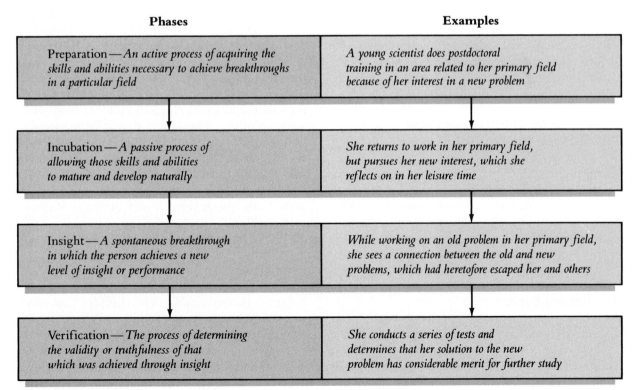

management at Corning and then spent years testing and refining his idea in the lab. The line of Visions cookware is due out soon.[4]

Characteristics of Creative People

Just as everyone wants to be considered intelligent and hardworking, people like to feel that they are creative. Unfortunately, however, not everyone is. Researchers, with varying degrees of success, have investigated relationships between creativity and a variety of individual characteristics. There appears to be little overlap between intelligence and creativity, and there appears to be no difference in creativity between males and females.[5]

On the other hand, there does seem to be an age effect. The typical period of greatest creativity for most people seems to be between the ages of 30 and 40. Creative people also tend to be less susceptible to social influence than less creative people. And there are cross-cultural differences. For example, even though experts agree that Japanese schools provide their children with more pure accumulated knowledge than do American schools, Japanese children feel such strong pressure to conform and meet high learning standards that they often lack creativity. In contrast, American children sometimes don't learn as much in school as their Japanese counterparts, but the freedom of expression and exploration that they experience tends to provide more opportunities for creativity.[6]

TRADITIONAL APPROACHES FOR PROMOTING INNOVATION

Managers have long recognized the importance of creativity. Consequently, they have sought ways to harness it in order to encourage innovation within their organizations. The reward system is one general approach; two more specific approaches are brainstorming and synectics.

The Reward System

Using the reward system to promote creativity and innovation is a fairly mechanical but nevertheless effective technique.[7] The idea is to provide rewards to people and groups that develop innovative ideas.

Monsanto gives a $50,000 award each year to the scientist or group of scientists that develops the biggest commercial breakthrough. Just as important as rewarding success, is making sure that failures are not too punishing. At 3M, 60 percent of all new ideas do not ever make it to the marketplace. 3M scientists are not afraid to propose a new idea because they know they will not be punished for failing.

Organizations also shape career paths to promote innovation. Most technical companies provide employees with two career paths—a scientific path and a managerial path. In well-developed systems, such as Texas Instruments, 3M, and Monsanto, appropriate numbers of people choose each path. Thus, there are always enough people working in the labs and heading up product development teams.

Brainstorming

Brainstorming is a technique for stimulating novel and imaginative ideas and alternatives. Its purpose is to foster free thinking while sparing participants the inhibiting threat of ridicule. Typically, six to twelve individuals from a variety of backgrounds are brought together to develop ideas or solutions to a problem, which is analyzed from a variety of perspectives. There are six ground rules for a brainstorming session.[8] First, participants should be encouraged to suggest wild and extreme ideas. Second, they should be encouraged to build on suggestions made by others. Third, they should be forbidden to criticize the ideas of others. Fourth, a record of the meeting should be maintained to aid in recalling the ideas put forth. Fifth, meetings should last between forty minutes and one hour for maximum effectiveness. Sixth, the problem under discussion must be manageable.

Synectics

Synectics is considerably more complex than brainstorming and often requires the assistance of outside experts or consultants.[9] The starting point is the formation of a group of individuals who have the skills needed to solve organizational problems. Whereas brainstorming focuses on generating a large number of alternatives, synectics attempts to identify one radically different new idea or solution. To discourage obvious or easy solutions, the group leader does not initially explain the exact nature of the situation. Instead, the leader directs the discussion toward the general topic of interest.

As the discussion progresses, four mechanisms are used to view the problem from different angles. The first tool is personal analogy; group members attempt to identify (metaphorically) with the problem. The second tool is direct analogy; comparisons are made with parallel concepts. The third tool is symbolic analogy; impersonal images are used to describe the problem. The fourth tool is fantasy analogy; members suspend reality to develop an innovative solution.

For example, some managers were recently brought together in New York to develop a new approach to running Laundromats. The leader began by asking the group to discuss the kinds of people most likely to use self-service clothes washing facilities. One large market segment identified was young single people with limited incomes. The leader then raised the question of what other activities were in vogue among young singles. Answers included drinking beer and watching television. Thus, the idea emerged for a new type of laundry facility—a brightly decorated establishment close to apartments occupied by young singles and equipped with washers and dryers, a bar, and a television and game room. Suds 'N Duds has gone on to become a successful business.[10]

NEW APPROACHES FOR PROMOTING INNOVATION

In recent years, organizations have been exploring new and better ways to stimulate innovation.[11] In this section, we examine some of the most promising approaches.

Organizational Culture

We noted the effect that organizational culture can have on a number of factors, ranging from organizational effectiveness to participative management. It can also influence creativity and innovation.[12] A strong and appropriately focused culture can serve numerous innovational purposes. It can help everyone in the organization recognize that innovation is valued and will be rewarded. It can also let everyone know that occasional failure in the pursuit of new ideas is acceptable. In addition to 3M, Corning, and Monsanto, Procter & Gamble, General Electric, Texas Instruments, Johnson & Johnson, and Merck all are known to have strong, innovation-oriented cultures.[13]

Such a culture doesn't just happen. Organizations decide that they want this strong thrust for innovation and then work to create and maintain it. 3M, for example, studies itself continuously to learn how its innovations were achieved, and it has a surprisingly rigid budgeting formula: 10 to 15 percent of R&D is earmarked for back-up work on existing products; 10 to 15 percent is dedicated to work aimed at achieving production efficiencies; 50 to 60 percent is for the pursuit of new products, and the rest is for long-term basic research projects. Thus, the company understands its culture, takes great care to nurture and sustain it, and is able to achieve its goal of having 25 percent of revenues come from new products.

Intrapreneurs

The use of intrapreneurs is another increasingly popular way to foster innovation. Just as an entrepreneur is someone who develops an idea and then starts his or her own business, an **intrapreneur** is someone who develops an idea within the context of a larger organization.[14] Such people serve many of the same purposes and achieve many of the same outcomes as entrepreneurs but do so within a large organization.

There are three different forms of the intrapreneur role in organizations. The inventor is the person who actually has the new idea or develops the new product or service. Often, this person may lack the expertise or motivation to get the product or service transformed into a marketable entity. The champion may then enter the picture. The champion is usually a middle manager who learns about the project and becomes committed to it. He or she helps overcome obstacles and gets others in the organization to take the product or service seriously. The sponsor is a top-level manager who approves of and supports the project. This person may fight for the budget needed to develop the idea, overcome arguments from others, and so forth. The three roles may not necessarily be played by three different people, although they usually are.

Several firms have embraced the concept of intrapreneurs and tried to manage it to encourage innovation. Each of the firms noted earlier for its innovative culture uses intrapreneurs. Other examples are given in Table EM5.1. Another firm that relies on intrapreneurs is Hewlett-Packard. HP actually encourages its employees to defy existing rules and procedures if they think that doing so will result in a new breakthrough. Each year the company gives an award called the Hewlett-Packard Medal of Defiance to the individual achieving the greatest breakthrough in the face of resistance from others.[15]

Other Methods

Recent programs aimed at increasing innovation tend to have four basic components.[16] The first component is usually a set of procedures involving the idea-generation process. A major aid to innovation is the creation of a fund earmarked specifically for use in developing creative ideas. Noninnovative firms tend to require proposals for funding to go through "line" channels. Truly innovative firms often have a special committee, made up of nonoperations personnel, to review all proposals. Each project is reviewed on its merits and each decision is based on its perceived strategic implications. Approval is not automatically given to the pet project of an organizational prima donna. Projects are never taken away from their original advocates. Instead, the goal is to give creative individuals the assistance they require to develop their ideas. The whole process is kept as informal as possible.

The second component of planned innovation is often a preliminary analysis. A feasibility study is done to determine whether the innovation is desirable, achievable, and advantageous for the organization. In noninnovative firms these studies usually are conducted by the idea advocate and consist of simple speculation rather than rigorous research. When the results are presented to the organization, only favorable data are given. The result may be overestimation of potential and inadequate consideration. In contrast, highly innovative firms encourage lengthy investigations conducted by teams that try to determine exactly what the market is for the innovation as well as the potential difficulties of the project.

Next comes the actual decision to commit resources to the project, making it a formal part of the organization. At this stage, the noninnovative

TABLE EM5.1

Examples of Firms Using Intrapreneurs

Colgate-Palmolive Co.: Created a separate unit called Colgate Venture Co. Staffs it with creative, risk-oriented people who want to develop new ideas.

General Foods: Created a separate unit called Culinova Group Inc. Transfers to it regular employees who want to work on a promising idea.

Scott Paper: Uses the Scott's Do-It-Yourself unit as a home for intrapreneurs.

Texas Instruments: Refuses to approve a new project unless it has an intrapreneur/champion/sponsor.

S. C. Johnson & Son: Established a $250,000 seed fund to support new ideas.

SOURCE: Adapted from "Consumer-Product Giants Relying on 'Intrapreneurs' in New Ventures," *The Wall Street Journal*, April 22, 1988, p. B1.

organization stresses power and politics. Frequently, the decision is based on a one-on-one negotiation between the idea advocate and a single superior. Often there is no formal commitment from the organization, or approval is given with little, if any, allocation of resources. In contrast, innovative firms usually follow a very formal decision-making process. The first part of this process involves allowing for time to modify the project to make it more acceptable. Reviewers are assigned to help the advocates alter the project, and the results of the preliminary study are taken into consideration. The actual decision is made through a vote. No single person possesses absolute veto power. Finally, upon adoption, the organization agrees to commit adequate resources to the project; there are no starvation diets designed to kill unpopular projects.

Implementation of the project is the final stage of planned innovation. There are two often-cited reasons for the failure of an innovation: (1) underresourcing, or starving the project, and (2) attempting an immediate, large-scale implementation. The difficulty of the second approach is that when hitches occur there is a tendency to commit more money to the project, thereby possibly compounding a mistake instead of correcting it. Highly innovative firms usually begin the implementation process with a pilot study, such as marketing a new product in a test area. This permits the organization to determine what further alterations are required or to drop the project altogether. If the project must be abandoned, no fault is placed on any individual. The decision to implement was made by a group, after going through a rigorous developmental process. Many people had responsibility for the project, and therefore the originator is not used as a scapegoat.

NOTES

1. "Keeping the Fires Lit Under the Innovators," *Fortune*, March 28, 1988, p. 45; Kenneth Labich, "The Innovators," *Fortune*, June 6, 1988, pp. 50–64; Joel Dreyfuss, "What Do You Do for an Encore?" *Fortune*, December 19, 1988, pp. 111–119; "Masters of Innovation," *Business Week*, April 10, 1989, pp. 58–63.

2. Dreyfuss, "What Do You Do for an Encore?"

3. See Thomas V. Busse and Richard S. Mansfield, "Theories of the Creative Process: A Review and a Perspective," *Journal of Creative Behavior*, Vol. 4, No. 2, 1980, pp. 91–103, 132, for other perspectives on the process of creativity.

4. Labich, "The Innovators."

5. Anne Anastasi and C. E. Schaefer, "Note on the Concepts of Creativity and Intelligence," *Journal of Creative Behavior*, Vol. 5, 1971, pp. 113–116.

6. "Conformity Vs. Creativity," *The Wall Street Journal*, November 14, 1988, p. R45.

7. Fariborz Damanpour, "The Adoption of Technological, Administrative, and Ancillary Innovations: Impact of Organizational Factors," *Journal of Management*, Autumn 1987, pp. 675–688.

8. Linda Jewell and H. Joseph Reitz, *Group Effectiveness in Organization* (Glenview, Ill.: Scott, Foresman, 1981).

9. William J. Gordon, *Synectics* (New York: Collier Books, 1968).

10. Robert Kuhn, *Creativity and Strategy in Mid-sized Firms* (Englewood Cliffs, N.J.: Prentice-Hall, 1989).

11. Alfred A. Marcus, "Implementing Externally Induced Innovations: A Comparison of Rule-bound and Autonomous Approaches," *Academy of Management Journal*, June 1988, pp. 235–256; and Alan D. Meyer and James B. Goes, "Organizational Assimilation of Innovation: A Multilevel Contextual Analysis," *Academy of Management Journal*, December 1988, pp. 897–923.

12. Steven P. Feldman, "How Organizational Culture Can Affect Innovation," *Organizational Dynamics*, Summer 1988, pp. 57–68.

13. Labich, "The Innovators." See also "Can P&G Commandeer More Shelves in the Medicine Chest?" *Business Week*, April 10, 1989, pp. 64–67.

14. Gifford Pinchot III, *Intrapreneuring* (New York: Harper & Row, 1985).

15. "Consumer-Product Giants Relying on 'Intrapreneurs' in New Ventures," *The Wall Street Journal*, April 22, 1988, p. B1.

16. Andre Delbecq and Peter Mills, "Managerial Practices That Enhance Innovation," *Organizational Dynamics*, Summer 1985, pp. 24–34.

INTEGRATIVE CASE

Johnson & Johnson

In 1885, three brothers—Robert Wood, James Wood, and Edward Mead Johnson—formed a company to make individually wrapped, antiseptic surgical dressings. Their dressings became widely used in hospitals throughout the country as they established their expertise by publishing a major text on the treatment of wounds. One of the brothers, Edward Mead, was more interested in drugs than in dressings, however. He left the organization in 1897 to form his own drug company, Mead Johnson. At that time, the company headed by Robert Wood and James Wood became Johnson & Johnson.

Over the years, Johnson & Johnson has taken risks and branched out into numerous areas. It has done so with two policies to guide it. One is to reward top executives well for their efforts, linking their compensation to the performance of their companies. The other is to decentralize the organization's structure and processes so that its subsidiary companies operate virtually autonomously. Johnson & Johnson sees its corporate culture of innovation and its organization design of decentralization as completely consistent with one another. Decentralization facilitates innovation and innovation involves risk taking. Risk taking is so much a part of Johnson & Johnson's culture that making a mistake has almost become a badge of honor; having made a mistake means that a person was innovative.

Those policies have enabled Johnson & Johnson to become a top producer of adhesive bandages, headache remedies, contraceptives, disposable diapers, and shampoo. Indeed, the decentralized structure now consists of 166 individual companies, each contributing to the success of Johnson & Johnson in its own unique way. This design makes Johnson & Johnson the most broadly based company in the healthcare field, with products ranging from Band-Aids to baby oil to Orthoclone OKT3, a monoclonal antibody used to keep a body from rejecting a kidney transplant. However, although there may be 166 separate companies in the Johnson & Johnson organization, they fall basically into three types of products and are organized into divisions following those groupings: consumer goods, pharmaceuticals, and professional products. Thus, the 166 companies are not completely unrelated. Furthermore, the companies cooperate and share ideas and innovations. This enables them to perform better and to contribute to overall corporate success.

Johnson & Johnson, however, has had its failures. Perhaps one of the most notable ones was in mouthwashes. Its Micrin brand rose to second place behind Warner-Lambert's Listerine only to be knocked completely out of the market by Procter & Gamble's Scope. Technicare, Johnson & Johnson's diagnostic imaging company, was another clear failure. Johnson & Johnson saw the purchase of Technicare as an easy way to enter a business in which it had no experience. That lack of experience may have been a critical factor, however. Despite the millions poured into it, Technicare was never very successful and Johnson & Johnson sold it in 1986 along with an ultrasound diagnostic business.

The scare over cyanide-laced Tylenol, which hit the company in 1982 and was repeated in 1986, though not a failure, nonetheless slowed Johnson & Johnson's continued growth and performance in the headache-remedy market. However, the forthright explanations of what had happened and the rapid recall of all Tylenol capsule products are still seen as a highly effective response to a crisis. Indeed, the management of that crisis is clearly responsible for Tylenol's continued success. Tylenol remains the best-selling painkilling remedy on the market.

Nevertheless, product innovation has characterized Johnson & Johnson throughout its history. In the late 1980s, Johnson & Johnson had several highly innovative and promising products just coming on the market. Retin-A, or tretinoin, a vitamin A derivative, had been developed by Johnson & Johnson during the 1960s as an acne medicine. In the late 1980s, Retin-A moved from being just an acne medication to become a drug that promises to be able to rejuvenate wrinkled, sun-aged skin. The Food and Drug Administration approval for marketing Retin-A as a product for aged skin is still pending, but sales continue strong despite studies showing that it can produce a rash on some users.

Johnson & Johnson companies are also involved in biotechnology. Ethicon Inc., which makes sutures, is working with an independent California company, Chiron Corporation, to develop sutures that will actually speed the healing process. Johnson & Johnson also developed erythropoietin (EPO) in a partnership with Amgen Inc. EPO is a hormone that stimulates the production of red blood cells. EPO could thus be useful for patients on kidney-dialysis machines or in treating the anemia of patients undergoing chemotherapy.

Johnson & Johnson expects to achieve expansion not only from domestic operations but also from overseas. Overseas markets are growth areas for existing products and outlets for new products. In the consumer products area, Johnson & Johnson was experiencing almost 2 percent per year growth in its overseas operations during the late 1980s. In some cases, the overseas market provides Johnson & Johnson a chance to correct mistakes made domestically. In Brazil, for instance, Johnson & Johnson is number 1 in disposable diapers, having benefited from being beaten out in that market domestically by Procter & Gamble and Kimberly Clark.

Despite a corporate culture promoting innovative risk taking and a highly decentralized structure, any company the size of Johnson & Johnson develops some parts that do not conform to the norm. There are some operations that are being run by risk-averse managers who prefer to use tightly controlled procedures and careful accounting practices that punish rather than reward mistakes. Such managers prefer placid and predictable organizations rather than the unpredictability that goes along with creativity. The irony is that those managers can exist because the organization is decentralized and they can control their own units. This dilemma of decentralization was at least partly the reason for a recent bonus program designed to reward entrepreneurial achievements with direct cash payments. Nevertheless, the real answer to the dilemma has to lie in the people and the corporate culture; hiring and advancing people who believe in the culture will keep it alive and may be the biggest challenge that Johnson & Johnson will face.

Questions

1. Describe the organizational design and structure of Johnson & Johnson. How is authority distributed and how are activities coordinated?
2. What are the major determinants of the organization design and culture at Johnson & Johnson? In what ways and why are they likely to change over the next ten years?
3. What problems might Johnson & Johnson encounter in staffing its organization? Why?
4. How does Johnson & Johnson manage creativity and innovation? What suggestions can you make for improving that management?

REFERENCES: "At Johnson & Johnson, a Mistake Can Be a Badge of Honor," *Business Week*, September 26, 1988, pp. 126–128; "Johnson & Johnson's Larsen Named Chief," *The Wall Street Journal*, October 25, 1988, p. 5; "Wall Street Says 'Yes' to Johnson & Johnson Drugs," *Business Week*, February 8, 1988, pp. 71–72; "Bausch & Lomb Aims at a New Market as It Prepares to Test Disposable Lens," *The Wall Street Journal*, June 20, 1988, p. 18E; Benjamin Mindell, "Interest in Retin-A Brings Healthy Sales Figures," *American Medical News*, April 8, 1988, pp. 13–14.

IV THE LEADING PROCESS

OUTLINE

The Nature of Motivation
The Importance of Employee Motivation · Historical
Perspectives on Motivation

Content Perspectives on Motivation
The Need Hierarchy · The Two-Factor Theory · Other
Important Human Needs

Process Perspectives on Motivation
Expectancy Theory · Equity Theory · Attribution Theory

Reinforcement Perspectives on Motivation
Kinds of Reinforcement · Schedules of Reinforcement

Emerging Perspectives on Motivation
Goal-setting Theory · The Japanese Approach

Motivational Programs
Behavior Modification · Modified Workweek · Work
Redesign

Organizational Reward Systems
The Effects of Organizational Rewards · Designing Effective
Reward Systems · New Approaches to Rewarding Employees

CHAPTER 12

Motivating Employee Performance

OBJECTIVES

After studying this chapter, you should be able to:

- Characterize the nature of motivation.
- Identify and describe the major content perspectives on motivation.
- Identify and describe the major process perspectives on motivation.
- Describe the reinforcement perspective on motivation.
- Identify and describe emerging perspectives on motivation.
- Discuss four popular motivational programs that organizations use to enhance employee motivation.
- Describe the role of organizational reward systems in motivation.

OPENING INCIDENT

Lincoln Electric in Cleveland, Ohio, has perhaps the most highly motivated workers of any corporation in America today—and not because of any new fad or approach. Indeed, Lincoln has gone fifty-four years without losing money and has not had to lay anyone off in forty years, and its workers are three times more productive than similar workers in other companies.

Lincoln makes industrial electric motors and welding equipment. Back in 1934, its top managers decided to install an incentive pay system to enhance employee motivation. The approach was simple—provide ample opportunity for employees to earn more money by working harder. The harder they work, the more they make.

How does the system work? First, base compensation is tied directly to individual productivity. Workers are paid a specified dollar amount for each acceptable unit they produce. Second, special rewards are available in the form of a year-end bonus. At the end of the year, each worker is evaluated in terms of his or her dependability, ideas, quantity of output, and quality of output. Recent bonuses have averaged 97.6 percent of workers' regular earnings. Lincoln's success has not gone unnoticed. In the last five years alone, 3,000 managers from other companies have visited the Lincoln's Cleveland facilities to learn more about how to motivate employee job performance.[1]

*I*t's fairly easy to understand how Lincoln's incentive system works. More difficult, however, is understanding why it works. The answer is rooted in employee motivation. Virtually any organization is capable of having the kind of work force employed by Lincoln. The trick is figuring how to make a plan like Lincoln's work somewhere else. Lincoln's plan was installed in simpler times, and managers have had decades to fine-tune it. Today's manager must start with a much more complex view of what makes people tick in order to motivate them toward higher levels of job performance.

In Chapter 1, we defined the third management function, leading, as the set of processes used to get organizational members to work together to advance the interests of the organization. This chapter is the first of four devoted to those processes. Its major emphasis is on motivating employee job performance. We examine the nature of employee motivation and explore the three major perspectives on motivation—content, process, and reinforcement. Newly emerging approaches are then discussed. After discussing popular motivational programs used by many organizations, we conclude with a description of organizational reward systems and their role in motivation.

The other three chapters in Part 4 discuss other processes involved in the leading function—leadership and influence processes (Chapter 13), interpersonal processes, groups, and conflict (Chapter 14), and communication (Chapter 15). Two Enhancement Modules at the end of Part 4 explore two other behavioral challenges that managers must address—managing the individual and coping with stress.

THE NATURE OF MOTIVATION

■ **motivation** The set of forces that cause people to behave in certain ways

Motivation is the set of forces that cause people to behave in certain ways.[2] On any given day, an employee may choose to work as hard as possible at a job, to work just hard enough to avoid a reprimand, or to do as little as possible. The goal for the manager is to maximize the occurrence of the first incident and minimize the occurrence of the last one. This goal becomes all the more important when we understand how important motivation is in the workplace.

The Importance of Employee Motivation

In most instances, employee performance is determined by three things: motivation (the desire to do the job), ability (the capability to do the job), and the work environment (the tools, materials, and information needed to do the job). If an employee lacks ability, the manager knows what to do—either provide training or replace the worker. If there is an environmental problem, the manager again knows what to do—alter the environment to promote higher performance. If motivation is the problem, the task for the manager is more challenging. Individual behavior is a complex phenomenon, and the manager may be hard-pressed to figure out the precise nature of the problem and how to solve it. Thus, motivation is important because of its significance as a determinant of performance and because of its intangible character.[3]

The motivation framework in Figure 12.1 is a good starting point for understanding how motivated behavior occurs. The motivation process begins with needs that reflect a deficiency within the individual. For example, a worker may feel that she is underpaid, and this deficiency results in a need. In response to this need, the worker searches for ways to satisfy it. She may ask for a raise, work harder to try to earn a raise, or seek a new job. Next, she chooses an option to pursue (of course, a person may pursue multiple options at the same time—working harder while simultaneously looking for a new job, for example). After carrying out the chosen option—working harder and putting in more hours for a reasonable period of time, for example—she then evaluates her success. If her hard work resulted in a pay raise, she probably feels good about things and will continue to work hard. If no raise has been provided, she is likely to try another option.

FIGURE 12.1

The Motivation Framework

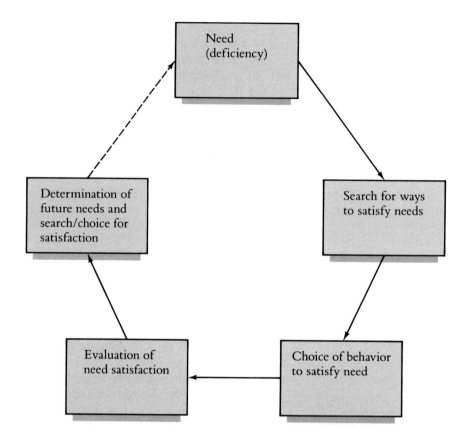

Historical Perspectives on Motivation

To appreciate what we know about employee motivation, it is helpful to review earlier approaches. In general, motivation theory has evolved through three different eras: the traditional approach, the human relations approach, and the human resource approach.

The Traditional Approach   The traditional approach to understanding employee motivation is best represented by the work of Frederick W. Taylor.[4] As we noted in Chapter 2, Taylor suggested the use of an incentive pay system. He believed that management knew more about the jobs being performed than the workers did, and he assumed that economic gain was the primary thing that motivated everyone. Other assumptions of the traditional approach were that work is inherently unpleasant for most people and that the money they earn is more important to employees than the nature of the job they are performing. Hence, people could be expected to perform any kind of job if they were paid enough. Although the role of money as a motivating factor cannot be dismissed, proponents of the traditional approach took too narrow a view of the role of monetary compensation and also failed to consider other motivational factors.

The Human Relations Approach   The human relations approach (also summarized in Chapter 2) grew out of the work at Western Electric of Elton Mayo and his associates.[5] The human relationists emphasized the role of social processes in the workplace. Their basic assumptions were that employees want to feel useful and important, that employees want to belong to a social group, and that these needs are more important than money in motivating employees. Advocates of the human relations approach advised managers to make workers feel important, keep them informed, and allow them a modicum of self-direction and self-control in carrying out routine activities. The illusion of involvement and importance were expected to satisfy workers' basic social needs and result in higher motivation to perform. For example, a manager might allow a work group to participate in making a decision, even though he or she had already determined what the decision would be. The symbolic gesture of seeming to allow participation was expected to enhance motivation, even though no real participation took place.

The Human Resource Approach   The human resource approach to motivation carries the concepts of human needs and motivation one step farther. Whereas the human relationists believed that the illusion of contribution and participation would enhance motivation, the human resource view assumes that the contributions themselves are valuable to both individuals and organizations. It assumes that people want to contribute and are able to make genuine contributions. Management's task, then, is to encourage participation and to create a work environment that makes full use of the human resources available. This philosophy guides most contemporary thinking about employee motivation. At Ford, Westinghouse, Texas Instruments, and Hewlett-Packard, for example, work teams are being called upon to solve a variety of problems and to make substantive contributions to organizational effectiveness.[6] Lincoln Electric's philosophy has passed through all three eras as well.

CONTENT PERSPECTIVES ON MOTIVATION

■ **content perspectives** Approaches to motivation that try to answer the question "what factor or factors motivate people?"

Content perspectives on motivation deal with the first part of the motivation process—needs and need deficiencies. More specially, **content perspectives** try to answer the question "What factor or factors motivate people?" Labor leaders often argue that workers can be motivated by more pay, shorter working hours, and improved working conditions. Meanwhile, some behavioral scientists suggest that motivation can be enhanced by providing employees with more autonomy and greater responsibility. Both of these views represent content views of motivation. The former asserts that motivation is a function of pay, working hours, and working conditions; the latter suggests that autonomy and responsibility are the causes of motivation.[7] Two widely known content perspectives on motivation are the need hierarchy and the two-factor theory.

The Need Hierarchy

The concept of a need hierarchy has been advanced by many theorists, but the version most popular in the management field is the one developed by Abraham Maslow in the 1940s.[8] Maslow assumed that people are motivated to satisfy various needs and that these needs can be arranged in a hierarchy of importance. As shown in Figure 12.2, **Maslow's hierarchy of needs** assumes there are five need levels.

Maslow's hierarchy of needs
Suggests that people must satisfy five groups of needs in order—physiological, security, belongingness, esteem, and self-actualization

The *physiological needs* for such things as food, sex, and air represent basic issues of survival and biological function. In organizational settings, physiological needs are generally satisfied by adequate wages and the work environment itself, which provides restrooms, adequate lighting, comfortable temperatures, and ventilation.

Next are the *security needs*—the needs for a secure physical and emotional environment. Examples include the desire for adequate housing and clothing and the need to be free from worry about money and job security. Security needs are satisfied for many people in the workplace by job continuity (no layoffs), a grievance system (to protect against arbitrary supervisory actions), and an adequate insurance and retirement benefit package (for security against illness and provision of income in later life). Even today, however, depressed industries and general economic decline can put people out of work and restore the primacy of security needs.

Belongingness needs are related to social processes. They include the need for love and affection and the need to be accepted by one's peers. These needs are satisfied for most people by a combination of family and community relationships outside of work and friendships on the job. A manager can help the satisfaction of these needs by allowing social interaction and by making employees feel like part of a team or

FIGURE 12.2

Maslow's Hierarchy of Needs

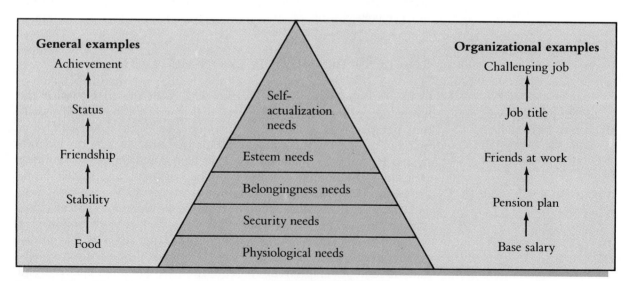

SOURCE: Adapted from Abraham H. Maslow, "A Theory of Human Motivation," *Psychological Review,* Vol. 50, 1943, pp. 370–396.

work group. The manager can also be sensitive to the probable effects (such as absenteeism or low performance) when an employee has family problems.

Esteem needs actually comprise two different sets of needs: the need for a positive self-image and self-respect and the need for recognition and respect from others. A manager can help address esteem needs by providing a variety of extrinsic symbols of accomplishment such as job titles, spacious offices, and similar rewards as appropriate. At a more intrinsic level, the manager can provide challenging job assignments and opportunities for the employee to feel a sense of accomplishment.

At the top of the hierarchy are what Maslow calls the *self-actualization needs*. These involve realizing one's potential for continued growth and individual development. The self-actualization needs are perhaps the most difficult for a manager to address. In fact, it can be argued that these needs must be met entirely from within the individual. But a manager can help by promoting a climate wherein self-actualization is possible. For instance, a manager could give employees a chance to participate in making decisions about their work and the opportunity to learn new things about their jobs and the organization.

Maslow suggests that the five need categories constitute a hierarchy. At the foundation of the hierarchy are physiological needs. An individual is motivated first and foremost to satisfy physiological needs. As long as they remain unsatisfied, the individual is motivated only to fulfill them. When satisfaction of physiological needs is achieved they cease to act as primary motivational factors and the individual moves "up" the hierarchy and becomes concerned with security needs. This process continues until the individual reaches the self-actualization level.

Maslow's concept of the need hierarchy has a certain intuitive logic and has been accepted by many managers. But research has revealed certain shortcomings and defects in the theory. Some research has found that five levels of need are not always present and that the order of the levels is not always the same as postulated by Maslow.[9]

ERG theory of motivation
Suggests that people's needs are grouped into three possibly overlapping categories—existence, relatedness, and growth

In response to these and similar criticisms, Clayton Alderfer has proposed an alternative hierarchy of needs called the **ERG theory of motivation**.[10] The letters E, R, and G stand for existence, relatedness, and growth. The ERG theory collapses the need hierarchy developed by Maslow into three levels. *Existence needs* correspond to the physiological and security needs of Maslow's hierarchy. *Relatedness needs* focus on how people relate to their social environment. In Maslow's hierarchy, they would encompass both the need to belong and the need to earn the esteem of others. *Growth needs*, the highest level in Alderfer's schema, include the needs for self-esteem and self-actualization.

Although the ERG theory assumes that motivated behavior follows a hierarchy in somewhat the same fashion as suggested by Maslow, there are two important differences. First, the ERG theory suggests that more than one level of need can cause motivation at the same time. For example, it allows for the possibility that people can be motivated by a desire for money (existence), friendship (relatedness), and the opportunity to learn new skills (growth) all at once.

Maslow's hierarchy suggests that self-actualization needs are the ultimate set of needs that people can be motivated to satisfy. Self-actualization needs involve realizing one's potential for growth and individual development. The picketers in this photograph, members of the Writers Guild of America, went on strike because of their perceived deficiencies in opportunities for self-actualization as represented by creative rights. Their salaries are quite high (averaging $43,000) and they enjoy reasonable job security. But they have no control over what changes are made in a television or movie script once it leaves their hands. Thus, they felt that they had limited opportunity to achieve self-actualization since someone else was given the opportunity to change and modify their work without their input or permission.

Second, the ERG theory has what has been called a frustration-regression element that is missing from Maslow's need hierarchy. Maslow maintained that one need must be satisfied before an individual can progress to a higher need level (from security to belongingness, for instance). The individual, then, is motivated by higher-level needs until they are satisfied. In contrast, ERG theory suggests that if needs remain unsatisfied at this higher level, the individual will become frustrated, regress to the lower level, and begin to pursue those things again. For example, a worker previously motivated by money (existence needs) may have just been awarded a pay raise sufficient to satisfy those needs. Suppose that he or she then attempts to establish more friendships to satisfy relatedness needs. If for some reason the employee finds that it is impossible to become better friends with others in the workplace, the employee eventually gets frustrated and regresses to being motivated to earn even more money.

The ERG theory is relatively new compared with Maslow's need hierarchy, but research suggests that it may be a more valid account of motivation in organizations.[11] Managers should not, of course, rely too heavily on any one particular perspective to guide their thinking about employee motivation. Perhaps the key insights to be gleaned from the need hierarchy view are that some needs may be more important than others and that people may change their behavior after any particular set of needs has been satisfied.

two-factor theory of motivation Suggests that people's satisfaction and dissatisfaction are influenced by two independent sets of factors—motivation factors and hygiene factors

The Two-Factor Theory

Another popular content perspective on motivation is the **two-factor theory** developed by Frederick Herzberg.[12] Herzberg developed his theory after interviewing 200 accountants and engineers in Pittsburgh. He asked them to recall occasions when they had been especially satisfied with their work and highly motivated and occasions when they had been dissatisfied and unmotivated. Surprisingly, he found that entirely different sets of factors were associated with satisfaction and with dissatisfaction—that is, an individual might identify "low pay" as causing dissatisfaction but would not necessarily mention "high pay" as a cause of satisfaction. Instead, different factors—such as recognition or accomplishment—were cited as causing satisfaction.

This finding led Herzberg to conclude that the traditional model of job satisfaction was incomplete. As shown in Figure 12.3, that view holds that satisfaction and dissatisfaction are at opposite ends of a single continuum. Employees might be satisfied, dissatisfied, or somewhere in between. But Herzberg's interviews had identified two different sets of factors: one ranging from satisfaction to no satisfaction and the other ranging from dissatisfaction to no dissatisfaction.

Table 12.1 lists the two sets of factors identified by Herzberg as causing either satisfaction or dissatisfaction. Note that the factors influencing the satisfaction continuum—called motivation factors—are related specifically to the work content. The factors presumed to cause dissatisfaction—called hygiene factors—are related to the work environment.

Herzberg then argued that there are two stages in the process of motivating employees. First, the manager must ensure that the hygiene factors are not deficient. Pay and security must be appropriate, working conditions must be safe, technical supervision must be acceptable, and

FIGURE 12.3

Two Views of Job Satisfaction

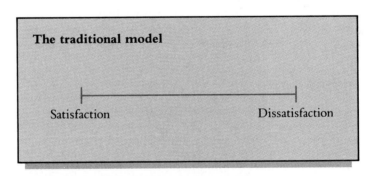

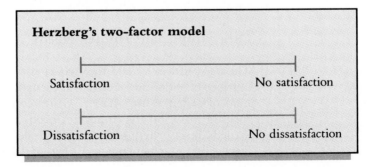

TABLE 12.1

Motivation and Hygiene
Factors in the Workplace

Motivation Factors	Hygiene Factors
Achievement	Supervisors
Recognition	Working conditions
The work itself	Interpersonal relationships
Responsibility	Pay and security
Advancement and growth	Company policy and administration

SOURCE: Reprinted by permission of the *Harvard Business Review*. An exhibit from "One More Time: How Do You Motivate Employees?" by Frederick Herzberg, *Harvard Business Review* (January–February, 1968). Copyright © 1968 by the President and Fellows of Harvard College; all rights reserved.

so on. By providing hygiene factors at an appropriate level, the manager does not stimulate motivation but merely ensures that employees are "not dissatisfied." Employees whom managers attempt to "satisfy" through hygiene factors alone will usually do just enough to get by.

Thus, managers should proceed to stage two—giving employees the opportunity to experience motivation factors such as achievement and recognition. The result is predicted to be a high level of satisfaction and motivation. Herzberg also goes a step farther than most theorists and describes exactly how to use the two-factor theory in the workplace. Specifically, he recommends job enrichment, as discussed in Chapter 8. He argues that jobs should be redesigned to provide higher levels of the motivation factors.

Although widely accepted by many managers, Herzberg's two-factor theory is not without its critics. One criticism is that the findings in Herzberg's initial interviews are subject to different explanations. Another charge is that his sample was not representative of the general population and that subsequent research often failed to uphold the theory.[13] At the present time, Herzberg's theory is not held in high esteem by researchers in the field. The theory has had a major impact on managers, however, and has played a key role in increasing their awareness of motivation and its importance in the workplace.

Other Important Human Needs

The need hierarchy and the two-factor theory of motivation identify a number of individual needs and then attempt to arrange them in some kind of order of importance. Other content views of motivation have focused more on the important needs themselves without being concerned about ordering them. The three needs most often discussed are the needs for achievement, affiliation, and power.[14]

need for achievement   The desire to accomplish a goal or task more effectively than in the past

The **need for achievement**, the best known of the three, reflects the desire to accomplish a goal or task more effectively than in the past. People with a high need for achievement are assumed to have a desire to assume personal responsibility, a tendency to set moderately difficult goals, a need for specific and immediate feedback, and a preoccupation with their task. David C. McClelland, the psychologist who first identified this need, argues that only about 10 percent of the U.S. population has a high need for achievement. Because such a need is assumed to be important for managerial success, he has devised a training program for increasing one's need for achievement. Studies have found that people who complete this achievement training tend to make more money and receive promotions faster than other managers.[15]

need for affiliation   The desire for human companionship and acceptance

The **need for affiliation** is less well understood. Like Maslow's belongingness need, the need for affiliation is a desire for human companionship and acceptance. People with a strong need for affiliation are likely to prefer (and perform better in) a job that entails a lot of social interaction and offers opportunities to make friends. The **need for power** has recently received considerable attention as an important ingredient in managerial success.[16] The need for power might be defined as the desire to be influential in a group and to control one's environment. Research has shown that people with a strong need for power are likely to be superior performers, have good attendance records, and occupy supervisory positions. One study found that managers as a group tend to have a stronger power motive than the general population and that successful managers tend to have stronger power motives than less successful managers.[17]

need for power   The desire to be influential in a group and to control one's environment

In summary, the major content perspectives on motivation focus on individual needs. Maslow's need hierarchy, the ERG theory, the two-factor theory, and the needs for achievement, affiliation, and power all provide useful insights into factors that cause motivation. What they do not do is shed much light on the process of motivation. They do not explain why people might be motivated by one factor rather than by another at a given level or how people might go about trying to satisfy the different needs. These questions involve behaviors or actions, goals, and feelings of satisfaction—concepts that are addressed by various process perspectives on motivation.

PROCESS PERSPECTIVES ON MOTIVATION

process perspectives   Approaches to motivation that focus on why people choose certain behavioral options to fulfill their needs and how they evaluate their satisfaction after they have attained these goals

Process perspectives on motivation are concerned with how motivation occurs. Rather than attempting to identify or list motivational stimuli, **process perspectives** focus on why people choose certain behavioral options to fulfill their needs and how they evaluate their satisfaction after they have attained these goals. Two of the most useful process perspectives on motivation are expectancy theory and equity theory. Attribution theory is an emerging process theory that is gaining recognition and is worth examining.

Expectancy theory suggests that motivation is determined by how much we want something and how likely we think we are to get it. Children from lower economic backgrounds may not be motivated in school because they see little chance of being able to go to college. Gerald Greenwood, Chairman of Chrysler Motors and Lee Iacocca's heir apparent, is working to change that. He has set up a foundation in his hometown (a St. Louis suburb called University City) to pay the college expenses of 50 children now in the 5th grade. Thus, his efforts are aimed at improving their performance-to-outcome expectancy. If all 50 make it through college, it could end up costing him $775,000. But Greenwood hopes he gets to spend every penny of it.

expectancy theory Suggests that motivation depends on two things—how much we want something and how likely we think we are to get it

effort-to-performance expectancy The individual's perception of the probability that his or her effort will lead to high performance

Expectancy Theory

The expectancy theory of motivation has many different forms and labels. We will describe it from a general perspective. Basically, **expectancy theory** suggests that motivation depends on two things—how much we want something and how likely we think we are to get it. Assume for a moment that you are approaching graduation and are therefore looking for a job. You see in the want ads that Exxon is seeking a new vice president with a starting salary of $250,000 per year. Even though you might want the job, you probably do not apply because you realize that you have little chance of getting it. The next ad you see is for someone to scrape bubble gum from underneath theater seats for a starting salary of $4 an hour. Even though you realize that you could probably get the job, you do not apply because you do not want it. Then you see an ad for a management trainee for a big company with a starting salary of $25,000. You apply for this job because you want it and because you think you have a reasonable chance of getting it. "Management in Practice" illustrates expectancy theory at work; it describes how a new incentive system at Du Pont provides employees with an opportunity to achieve their desired rewards.

The formal expectancy framework as we now recognize it was developed by Victor Vroom.[18] Expectancy theory rests on four basic assumptions. First, the theory assumes that behavior is determined by a combination of forces in the individual and in the environment. Second, it assumes that people make decisions about their own behavior in organizations. Third, it assumes that different people have different types of needs, desires, and goals. Fourth, expectancy theory assumes that people make choices from among alternative plans of behavior based on their perceptions of the extent to which a given behavior will lead to desired outcomes.[19]

Figure 12.4 summarizes the basic expectancy model of employee motivation. The model suggests that motivation leads to effort and that effort, when combined with employee ability and environmental factors, results in performance. Performance, in turn, leads to various outcomes, each of which has an associated value called its valence. The most important parts of the expectancy model cannot be shown in the figure, however. These are the individual's expectation that effort will lead to high performance, that performance will lead to outcomes, and that each outcome will have some kind of value.

Effort-to-Performance Expectancy

The **effort-to-performance expectancy** is the individual's perception of the probability that his or her effort will lead to high performance. When the individual believes that effort will lead directly to high performance, expectancy will be quite strong (close to 1.00). When the individual believes that effort and performance are unrelated, the effort-to-performance expectancy is very weak (close to 0). The belief that effort is somewhat but not strongly related to performance carries with it a moderate expectancy (somewhere between 0 and 1).

MANAGEMENT IN PRACTICE

EXPECTATIONS AT DU PONT

In October 1988, Du Pont announced a new incentive plan for the fibers division. The plan began in January 1989 and involves every member of the division—management and labor alike. It links pay to the attainment of divisional profit goals.

Some companies, when installing profit-sharing plans, require employees to take pay cuts in order to provide the funds necessary to finance the early part of the plan. Du Pont, however, has designated a five-year introductory period during which employee pay raises will be less than those of competitors in order to launch the plan. After that, if profits are below 80 percent of the goal, nothing happens. If profits are from 80 to 99 percent of the goal, a 3 percent bonus is earned; from 100 to 149 percent of the goal, a 6 percent bonus; above 149 percent of the goal, a 12 percent bonus. These bonuses are all in terms of other Du Pont employees, that is, an employee who receives a 3 percent bonus gets 3 percent more than that received by other Du Pont employees.

Early response among Du Pont employees was favorable to the plan. By late 1988, over 30 percent of the 7,000 unionized employees had voted in favor of the plan and only about 22 percent had voted against it; others were to vote during 1989. Of 13,000 nonunion employees, about 60 percent had elected to adopt an accelerated version of the plan. The accelerated version required employees to start with a slight pay cut but to receive bonuses more quickly if the overall profit goal was achieved. Employees with high expectations about the plan were the ones who opted for the accelerated version.

As a result of the plan, Du Pont employees are starting to view their jobs differently. They look for ways to cut costs, and they review budget items three or four times instead of only once or twice. Whereas in the past things were done merely because they had "always been done that way," the cost and impact of procedures and processes are now being scrutinized.

There are, of course, problems with any incentive plan, and Du Pont's is no exception. Many employees feel that they have little impact on profits. They contend that managers' actions and accounting practices, such as taking write-offs on bad debts or poor investments, have a far greater impact on profits than does hard work by those at the lower levels of the organization.

REFERENCES: "All Eyes on Du Pont's Incentive-Pay Plan," *The Wall Street Journal*, December 5, 1988, p. B1; "Du Pont Raises Dust by Ending Venture," *The Wall Street Journal*, September 1, 1988, p. 6; "Du Pont's Difficulties in Selling Kevlar Show Hurdles of Innovation," *The Wall Street Journal*, September 9, 1987, pp. 1, 20; "Du Pont's Version of a Maverick," *Business Week*, April 3, 1989, pp. 80–81.

---

performance-to-outcome expectancy The individual's perception that her or his performance will lead to a specific outcome

Performance-to-Outcome Expectancy The **performance-to-outcome expectancy** is the individual's perception that her or his performance will lead to a specific outcome. For example, the individual may believe that high performance will result in a pay raise, and the performance-to-outcome expectancy is high (approaching 1.00). The individual who believes that high performance may lead to a pay raise has a moderate expectancy (between 1.00 and 0). The individual who believes that performance has no relationship with rewards has a low performance-to-outcome expectancy (close to 0).

outcomes Results of the motivation process in an organizational setting, usually rewards

Outcomes and Valences Expectancy theory recognizes that an individual may experience a variety of **outcomes**, or rewards, in an organizational setting. A high performer, for example, may get bigger pay raises, faster promotions, and more praise from the boss. On the other hand, she may also be subject to more stress and incur resentment from

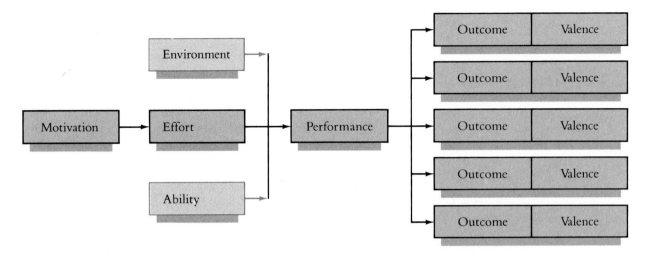

FIGURE 12.4

The Expectancy Model of
Motivation

valence An index of how
much an individual desires a
particular outcome; it is the attractiveness of the outcome to
the individual

co-workers. Each of these outcomes has an associated value, or **valence**—an index of how much an individual desires a particular outcome. If the individual wants the outcome, its valence is positive; if the
individual does not want the outcome, its valence is negative; and if
the individual is indifferent to the outcome, its valence is zero.

It is this part of expectancy theory that goes beyond the content
perspectives on motivation. Different people have different needs, and
they will try to satisfy these needs in different ways. For an employee
who has a high need for achievement and a low need for affiliation, the
pay raise and promotions cited above as outcomes of high performance
might have positive valences, the praise and resentment zero valences,
and the stress a negative valence. For a different employee with a low
need for achievement and a high need for affiliation, the pay raise,
promotions, and praise might all have positive valences, whereas both
resentment and stress could have negative valences.

For motivated behavior to occur, three conditions must be met. First,
the effort-to-performance must be greater than zero (the individual
must believe that if effort is expended, high performance will result).
The performance-to-outcome expectancy must also be greater than zero
(the individual must believe that if high performance is achieved, certain
outcomes will follow). And the sum of the valences for all relevant
outcomes must be greater than zero. (One or more outcomes may have
negative valences if they are more than offset by the positive valences
of other outcomes. For example, the attractiveness of a pay raise, a
promotion, and praise from the boss may outweigh the unattractiveness
of more stress and resentment from co-workers.) Expectancy theory
maintains that when all of these conditions are met, the individual is
motivated to expend effort.

The Porter-Lawler Extension   An interesting extension of expectancy
theory has been proposed by Porter and Lawler.[20] Recall from Chapter
2 that the human relationists assumed that employee satisfaction causes

good performance, but we noted that research has not supported such a relationship. Porter and Lawler suggest that there may indeed be a relationship between satisfaction and performance but that it goes in the opposite direction—that is, high performance may lead to high satisfaction.

Figure 12.5 summarizes Porter and Lawler's logic. Performance results in various rewards for an individual. Some of these are extrinsic (such as pay and promotions); others are intrinsic (such as self-esteem and a feeling of accomplishment). The individual evaluates the equity, or fairness, of the various rewards relative to the effort expended and the level of performance attained. If the rewards are felt to be equitable, the individual is satisfied.

Implications for Managers   Expectancy theory can be useful for managers who are trying to improve the motivation of their subordinates. Nadler and Lawler suggest a series of steps in using the basic ideas of the theory. First, figure out the outcomes each employee is likely to want. Second, decide what kinds and levels of performance are needed to meet organizational goals. Then make sure that the desired levels of performance are attainable. Also make sure that desired outcomes and desired performance are linked. Next, analyze the complete situation for conflicting expectancies, and ensure that the rewards are large enough. Finally, make sure the total system is equitable (fair to all).[21] These issues will be explored in more detail later in this chapter when we discuss organizational reward systems.

Besides the Du Pont example mentioned earlier, another firm that has had considerable success with expectancy theory is A&P. At its Philadelphia stores, A&P workers took a 25 percent pay cut, but they

FIGURE 12.5

The Porter-Lawler Extension of Expectancy Theory

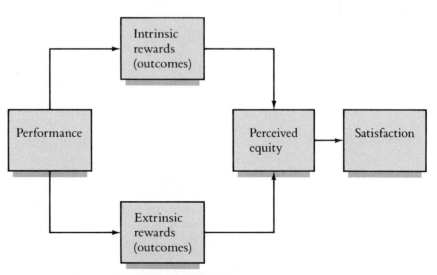

Source: Edward E. Lawler III, and Lyman W. Porter, "The Effect of Performance on Job Satisfaction," *Industrial Relations,* October 1967, p. 23. Used with permission of the University of California.

can now earn large bonuses by working more efficiently. Even though the final verdict is not in on this experiment, results so far look promising. Employees are earning more money than before, yet the stores are also achieving higher levels of profitability.[22] Lincoln Electric's incentive system is also clearly consistent with expectancy theory.

Of course, expectancy theory has its limitations. Although the theory makes sense and has been generally supported by empirical research, it is quite difficult to apply.[23] To really use the complete theory in the workplace, for example, it would be necessary to identify all the potential outcomes for each employee, to determine all relevant expectancies, and then to balance everything somehow to maximize employee motivation.

Equity Theory

equity theory Suggests that people are motivated to seek social equity in the rewards they receive for performance

After needs have stimulated the motivation process and the individual has chosen an action that is expected to satisfy those needs, the individual assesses the fairness, or equity, of the resultant outcome. Much of our current thinking on equity has been shaped by the **equity theory** of motivation developed by J. Stacy Adams. Adams contends that people are motivated to seek social equity in the rewards they receive for performance.[24] Equity can be defined as an individual's belief that the treatment he or she is receiving is fair relative to the treatment received by others.

According to equity theory, outcomes from a job include pay, recognition, promotions, social relationships, and intrinsic rewards. To get these rewards, the individual makes inputs to the job, such as time, experience, effort, education, and loyalty. The theory suggests that people view their outcomes and inputs as a ratio and then compare it to the ratio of someone else. This other "person" may be someone in the work group or some sort of group average or composite. The process of comparison looks like this:

$$\frac{\text{outcomes (self)}}{\text{inputs (self)}} \stackrel{?}{=} \frac{\text{outcomes (other)}}{\text{inputs (other)}}$$

The ratios are arrived at in a nonquantitative and subjective way. Comparison of the two ratios is likewise imprecise but still affects the individual's attitudes. Three alternatives are possible: the individual may feel equitably rewarded, under-rewarded, or over-rewarded. The individual will experience a feeling of equity when the two ratios are equal. This may occur even though the other person's outcomes are greater than the individual's own outcomes—provided that the other's inputs are also proportionately greater. Suppose that Mark has a high school education and earns only $15,000. He may still feel equitably treated relative to Susan, who earns $20,000, because she has a college degree.

People who feel under-rewarded try to reduce the inequity. Such an individual might decrease her inputs by exerting less effort, increase her outcomes by asking for a raise, distort the original ratios by rationalizing, try to get the other person to change her or his outcomes or inputs, leave the situation, or change the object of comparison. An individual may also feel over-rewarded relative to another person. This is not likely to be terribly disturbing to most people, but research suggests that some people who experience inequity under these conditions are somewhat motivated to reduce it.[25] Under such a circumstance, the person might increase his inputs by exerting more effort, reduce his outcomes by producing fewer units (if paid on a per unit basis), distort the original ratios by rationalizing, or try to reduce the inputs or increase the outcomes of the other person.

Implications for Managers   The single most important idea for managers to remember from equity theory is that if rewards are to motivate employees, they must be perceived as being equitable and fair. If the individual achieves various intrinsic and extrinsic rewards as a result of performance and regards these rewards as equitable, satisfaction will result. A second implication of equity theory is that managers need to consider the nature of the "other" to whom the employee is comparing herself or himself. In recent years, for example, the number of dual-career couples has increased dramatically, and husband-and-wife equity comparisons have ruined both marriages and careers.[26] On balance, the research support for equity theory is mixed.[27] The concepts of equity and social comparisons are certainly important for the manager to consider, but it is also apparent that managers should not rely only on this framework in attempting to manage employee motivation.

Attribution Theory

attribution theory   Suggests that individuals observe behavior, including their own, and then attribute cause and meaning to it

Another process theory gaining recognition is attribution theory. **Attribution theory** suggests that individuals observe behavior, including their own, and then attribute cause and meaning to it.[28] As indicated in Figure 12.6, this means that individuals observe their own behavior (with potential major problems related to self-perception) and decide whether it is primarily motivated by internal or external factors. That decision subsequently shapes the individual's responses to future motivational factors.

An individual who has decided that she is intrinsically motivated (by the challenging nature of the task, for instance) will seek more internal motivational factors in the future. Likewise, an individual who has decided that he is motivated more by extrinsic factors, such as pay, will seek more of those in the future. Individuals will not only seek more of the factors that they feel "fit" themselves, but they will also value them more and so respond more strongly to them.

Attribution theory suggests that individuals can alter their perceptions. Managers need to be aware of these effects because they may lead to unexpected and even unwanted change. An intrinsically motivated person assigned to a job that is extrinsically rewarded might

FIGURE 12.6

An Attributional Model of Motivation

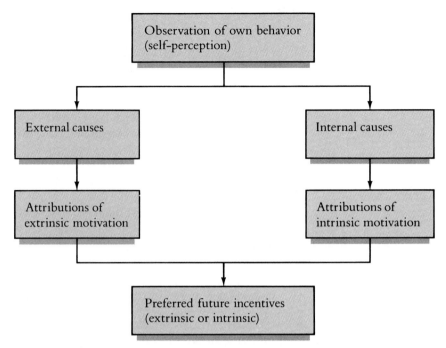

SOURCE: Gregory Moorhead and Ricky W. Griffin, *Organizational Behavior, 2nd ed.* (Boston: Houghton Mifflin, 1989), p. 152.

become more extrinsically and less intrinsically motivated. An over-emphasis on extrinsic factors for professional employees, for instance, could cause them to be less concerned with the nature of their assignments and more concerned with "doing well." Paying people who volunteer to do a task because they enjoy it might cause them to like it less in the future and decrease their likelihood of volunteering, especially if the pay was later withheld. Attributional processes can play an important role in the motivation process, and the impact may lead to unanticipated and dysfunctional consequences. Unfortunately, little research has been conducted on attribution theory, but the concept and the work that has been done present interesting implications. Thus, attribution theory is a promising new perspective on motivation.

REINFORCEMENT PERSPECTIVES ON MOTIVATION

A final element of the motivational process focuses on why some behaviors are maintained over time and why other behaviors change. As we have seen, content perspectives relate to the needs that stimulate behavior. Process perspectives explain why people choose various behaviors to satisfy needs and how they evaluate the equity of the rewards

■ **reinforcement perspective**
Approach to motivation that
explains the role of rewards as
they cause behavior to change
or remain the same over time

they get for those behaviors. The **reinforcement perspective** explains
the role of those rewards as they cause behavior to change or remain
the same over time. Specifically, reinforcement theory is based on the
fairly simple assumption that behavior that results in rewarding consequences is likely to be repeated, whereas behavior that results in
punishing consequences is less likely to be repeated. This approach to
explaining behavior was originally tested on animals, but B. F. Skinner
and others have been instrumental in demonstrating how it also applies
to human behavior.[29]

Figure 12.7 illustrates the basic premises of reinforcement theory.
The starting point is a stimulus. Because an employee's rent has gone
up, he sees that he needs a pay raise. Thus, he chooses the response at
the end of path 1. For example, he decides to work harder in hopes of
getting a raise. As a result of this response, the individual experiences
various consequences. Perhaps he gets the raise he needs. The value of
the consequences affects future responses, as shown in path 3. If the
consequences were pleasant or desirable, the individual will probably
choose the same response (path 4) the next time he encounters the same
stimulus. But if the original consequences were unpleasant or undesirable, a different response (path 5) is more likely. Thus, if the employee's
efforts led to a raise, the next time his rent increases he will probably
work even harder to get another raise. On the other hand, if his efforts
were futile, the next rent increase may cause him to engage in political
behavior, look for a new job, or try some other alternative. (The astute
reader will note that there are similarities between expectancy theory
and reinforcement theory. However, the former focuses more on behavior choices, and the latter is more concerned with the consequences
of those choices.[30])

FIGURE 12.7

The Reinforcement Theory of
Motivation

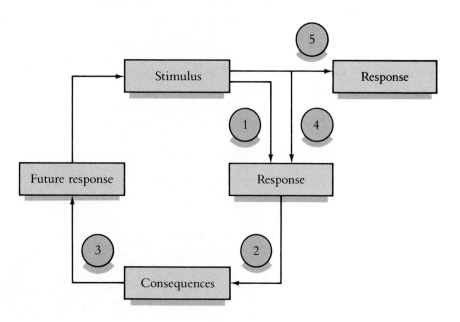

Kinds of Reinforcement

In organizational settings, there are four basic kinds of reinforcement that can result from behavior—positive reinforcement, avoidance, punishment, and extinction.[31] These are summarized in Table 12.2.

Two kinds of reinforcement strengthen or maintain behavior, whereas the other two weaken or decrease behavior. **Positive reinforcement**, a method of strengthening behavior, is a reward or a positive outcome after a desired behavior is performed. When a manager observes an employee doing an especially good job and offers praise, the praise serves to positively reinforce the behavior of good work. Other positive reinforcers in organizations include pay raises, promotions, and awards. Employees who work at General Electric's customer service center receive clothing, sporting goods, and even trips to Disney World as rewards for outstanding performance.[32] The other method of strengthening desired behavior is through **avoidance**. An employee may come to work on time to avoid a reprimand. In this instance, the employee is motivated to perform the behavior of punctuality to avoid an unpleasant consequence that is likely to follow tardiness.

Punishment is used by some managers to weaken undesired behaviors. When an employee is loafing, coming to work late, doing poor

positive reinforcement A method of strengthening behavior with rewards or positive outcomes after a desired behavior is performed

avoidance Used to strengthen behavior by avoiding unpleasant consequences which would result if the behavior were not performed

punishment Used to weaken undesired behaviors by using negative outcomes or unpleasant consequences when the behavior is performed

TABLE 12.2

Elements of Reinforcement Theory

Arrangement of the Reinforcement Contingencies	Schedules for Applying Reinforcement
1. **Positive reinforcement.** Strengthens behavior by providing a desirable consequence.	1. **Fixed interval.** Reinforcement applied at fixed time intervals, regardless of behavior.
2. **Avoidance.** Strengthens behavior by allowing escape from an undesirable consequence.	2. **Variable interval.** Reinforcement applied at variable time intervals, regardless of behavior.
3. **Punishment.** Weakens behavior by providing an undesirable consequence.	3. **Fixed ratio.** Reinforcement applied after a fixed number of behaviors, regardless of time.
4. **Extinction.** Weakens behavior by not providing a desirable consequence.	4. **Variable ratio.** Reinforcement applied after a variable number of behaviors, regardless of time.

work, or interfering with the work of others, the manager might resort to reprimands, discipline, or fines. The logic is that the unpleasant consequence will reduce the likelihood that the employee will choose that particular behavior again. Given the counterproductive side effects of punishment (such as resentment and hostility), it is often advisable to use the other kinds of reinforcement if at all possible.[33] **Extinction** can also be used to weaken behavior, especially behavior that has previously been rewarded. When an employee tells an off-color joke and the boss laughs, the laughter reinforces the behavior and the employee may continue to tell off-color jokes. By simply ignoring this behavior and not reinforcing it, the boss can cause the behavior to subside and eventually become "extinct."

extinction   Used to weaken undesired behaviors by simply ignoring or not reinforcing that behavior

Schedules of Reinforcement

Not only is the kind of reinforcement important, but so is when or how often it occurs. Various strategies are possible for the scheduling or timing of reinforcement. These are also listed in Table 12.2. The **fixed-interval schedule** provides reinforcement at fixed intervals of time, regardless of behavior. A good example of a fixed-interval schedule of reinforcement is the weekly or monthly paycheck. This method provides the least incentive for good work, because employees know they will be paid regularly regardless of their effort or lack of it. A **variable-interval schedule** also uses time as the basis for reinforcement, but the time interval varies from one reinforcement to the next. This schedule is appropriate for praise or other rewards based on visits or inspections. When employees do not know when the boss is going to drop by, they tend to maintain a reasonably high level of effort all the time.

A **fixed-ratio schedule** gives reinforcement after a fixed number of behaviors, regardless of the time that elapses between behaviors. This results in an even higher level of effort. For example, when Sears is recruiting new credit-card customers, salespersons get a small bonus for every fifth application returned from their department. Under this arrangement, motivation will be high because each application gets the person closer to the next bonus. The **variable-ratio schedule**, the most powerful schedule in terms of maintaining desired behaviors, varies the number of behaviors needed for each reinforcement. A supervisor who praises an employee for her second order, the seventh order after that, the ninth after that, then the fifth, and then the third is using a variable-ratio schedule. The employee is motivated to increase the frequency of the desired behavior because each performance increases the probability of receiving a reward. Of course, a variable-ratio schedule is difficult (if not impossible) to use for formal rewards such as pay because it would be too complicated to keep track of who was rewarded when.

fixed-interval schedules   Provide reinforcement at fixed intervals of time, such as regular weekly pay checks

variable-interval schedules   Provide reinforcement at varying intervals of time, such as occasional visits by the supervisor

fixed-ratio schedules   Provide reinforcement after a fixed number of behaviors regardless of the time interval involved, such as a bonus for every fifth sale

variable-ratio schedules   Provide reinforcement after varying numbers of behaviors are performed, such as the use of complements by a supervisor on an irregular basis

EMERGING PERSPECTIVES ON MOTIVATION

In addition to the established models and theories of motivation, there are also others that are emerging. Two of the most promising are goal-setting theory and the Japanese approach.

Goal-setting Theory

Organizational goal setting was explored fully in Chapter 5. From a motivation perspective, Edwin Locke and his associates have formulated similar concepts and ideas into a theory of goal setting for individuals.[34] Goal-setting theory suggests that managers and subordinates should set goals for the individual on a regular basis. These goals should be moderately difficult and very specific. Moreover, they should be of a type that the employee will accept and commit to accomplishing. Rewards should also be tied directly to reaching the goals. Goal-setting theory helps the manager tailor rewards to individual needs, clarify expectancies, maintain equity, and provide reinforcement on a systematic basis. Thus, it provides a comprehensive framework for integrating the other approaches. In all likelihood, goal-setting theory will become increasingly popular in organizations.[35]

The Japanese Approach

Another approach to motivation that has earned increasing popularity is the so-called Japanese approach. This is not really a theory or model but a philosophy of management. In many ways, it extends from the

More and more American companies are exploring the Japanese approach to employee motivation—bringing managers and workers together as partners working toward the same goals. A prime example of this approach is NUMMI (New United Motor Manufacturing, Inc.), a joint venture of Toyota and General Motors in California. The plant turns out some of the highest quality cars in America and union members and managers are helping one another rather than arguing and bickering. At the NUMMI annual picnic, shown in this photo, American and Japanese workers enjoy getting better acquainted.

human resource perspective. It is also related to participative management, described in an Enhancement Module at the end of Part 3.

The basic idea underlying the Japanese approach is to bring management and workers together as partners. Historically, in the United States the management–worker relationship has ranged from antagonistic to merely indifferent. In Japan, however, managers and workers see themselves as one group, and the result is that everyone is highly committed and motivated.

A good example of the Japanese approach in the United States is Domino's Pizza. No one at Domino's is called an employee; instead, employees are said to be team members, team leaders, or coaches. A large percentage of the company's profits is distributed back to workers; all employees own stock; and all employees work together toward Domino's best interests.[36] Like goal-setting theory, the Japanese approach is likely to become more common in American business.

MOTIVATIONAL PROGRAMS

Managers trying to enhance the motivation of their employees can draw on any of the theories described in this chapter. They also frequently adopt specific motivational programs derived more generally from one or more theories. Most of the theories have already been introduced, so we will only summarize them briefly in the context of their motivational impact.

Behavior Modification

behavior modification (OB Mod; organizational behavior modification) A technique for applying the concepts of reinforcement theory in organizational settings

Behavior modification, or **OB Mod** (for organizational behavior modification), is a technique for applying the concepts of reinforcement theory in organizational settings.[37] An OB Mod program typically proceeds through five stages. First, the manager specifies behaviors that are to be increased (such as producing more units) or decreased (such as coming to work late). Next, these target behaviors are measured to establish a baseline against which the effectiveness of OB Mod will be assessed. Then the manager analyzes the situation to ascertain what rewards subordinates value most and how best to tie these rewards to the target behaviors. Now action plans and strategies revolving around positive reinforcement, avoidance, punishment, or extinction are implemented so that desired behaviors have pleasant consequences and undesirable behaviors have unpleasant consequences. Finally, the target behaviors are measured again to determine the value of the program.

Although many organizations (such as Procter & Gamble, Warner-Lambert, and Ford) have used OB Mod, the best-known application has been at Emery Air Freight. Management felt that the containers used to consolidate small shipments into fewer, larger shipments were not being packed efficiently. Through a system of self-recorded feed-back and rewards, Emery increased container usage from 45 percent to 95 percent and saved over $3 million during the first three years of the program.[38]

Modified Workweek

Many organizations use a **modified workweek** for employees as a strategy for increasing motivation. The modified workweek helps individuals satisfy higher-level needs and provides an opportunity to fulfill several needs simultaneously. One alternative is the compressed workweek, whereby people work 40 hours in less than the traditional five full workdays. The most common plan has people work 10 hours a day for four days. Another popular plan is the flexible work schedule. In this approach, employees are required to work during a certain period called core time and can choose what other hours to work. Thus, an individual can come in early and leave early, come in late and leave late, or come in early, take a long lunch, and leave late. Allowing employees to work at home or to share jobs with others is also becoming popular. Working at home is especially useful for writers and others using computers. Job sharing allows two people to work part-time while the organization still gets the benefit of a full-time "worker."[39]

Many companies, including John Hancock, ARCO, General Dynamics, Metropolitan Life, Control Data Corporation, and IBM have experimented successfully with one or more of these modifications. By allowing employees some independence in terms of when they come to work and when they leave, managers acknowledge and show "esteem" for the employees' ability to exercise self-control. The hope is that employees will respond with increased levels of motivation.

Work Redesign

Changing the nature of the task-related activities of work is also being used more and more as a motivational technique. The idea is that managers can use any of the alternatives to job specialization described in Chapter 8 as a motivational tool. More precisely, job rotation, job enlargement, job enrichment, the job characteristics approach, and autonomous work groups can all be used as part of a motivational program. Expectancy theory helps explain the role of job design in motivation.[40] The basic premise is that employees will improve their performance if they believe that improvement will lead to intrinsic rewards. A number of studies have shown that improvements in the design of work do often result in higher levels of motivation. One study at Texas Instruments, for example, found that job design resulted in decreased turnover and improved employee motivation.[41]

ORGANIZATIONAL REWARD SYSTEMS

An organization's reward system is its most basic tool for managing employee motivation. An organizational **reward system** consists of the formal and informal mechanisms by which employee performance is defined, evaluated, and rewarded. The primary rewards in most organizations are pay, promotions, benefits, and status.

■ **reward systems** The formal and informal mechanisms by which employee performance is defined, evaluated, and rewarded

The Effects of Organizational Rewards

Organizational rewards can affect attitudes, behaviors, and motivation. Thus, it is important for managers to clearly understand and appreciate their importance.

Effect of Rewards on Attitudes Although employee attitudes such as satisfaction are generally not a major determinant of job performance, they are nonetheless important. They contribute to (or discourage) absenteeism and affect turnover, and they help establish the climate, or internal environment, of the organization. Edward Lawler has advanced four major generalizations about employee attitudes toward rewards.[42] First, employee satisfaction is influenced by how much is received and how much the individual thinks should be received. Employee expectations thus play a key role. Second, employee satisfaction is affected by comparisons with what happens to others. This argument is closely related to equity theory. Third, employees often misperceive the rewards of others. This suggestion also has implications from equity theory. When an employee believes that someone else is making more money than that person really makes, the potential for dissatisfaction increases. Fourth, overall job satisfaction is affected by how satisfied employees are with both the extrinsic and the intrinsic rewards they derive from their jobs. Drawing from the content theories and expectancy theory, this conclusion suggests that a variety of needs may cause behavior and that behavior may be channeled toward a variety of goals.

Effect of Rewards on Behaviors An organization's primary purpose in giving rewards is to influence employee behavior. Research has shown that extrinsic rewards affect employee satisfaction, which, in turn, plays a major role in determining whether an employee will remain on the job or seek a new job. Reward systems also influence patterns of attendance and absenteeism; and, if rewards are based on actual performance, employees tend to work harder to earn those rewards.

Effect of Rewards on Motivation Reward systems are clearly related to the expectancy theory of motivation. The effort-to-performance expectancy is strongly influenced by the performance appraisal that is

People work for an organization for many different reasons. Thus, an organizational reward system must be able to provide a number of different rewards. A group of new Disney cast members (they're never called employees) is shown here learning more about how the company works. Disney seeks to hire a certain kind of person—enthusiasm, friendliness, and helpfulness are key traits. The company uses the employment interview to better assess these characteristics in its job applicants. It rewards current employees $100 for bringing in new workers. Disney also rewards its employees for helping train others—the lecturer shown here, for example, is an hourly worker who does this one day a week. While starting wages may be a little on the low side ($4.85 an hour), Disney also has a liberal promotion-from-within policy. Officials believe this provides the best incentive to those wanting to better themselves.

often a part of the reward system. An employee is likely to put forth extra effort if he or she knows that performance will be measured, evaluated, and rewarded. The performance-to-outcome expectancy is affected by the extent to which the employee believes that performance will be followed by rewards. Finally, as expectancy theory predicts, each reward or potential reward has a somewhat different value for each individual. One person may want a promotion more than benefits; someone else may want just the opposite.

Designing Effective Reward Systems

Organizations around the world are concerned with designing effective reward systems. Several American examples have been presented, and more are described later. "The Global View" describes how Bertelsmann, the European publishing giant, uses participation and profit sharing. What are the elements of an effective reward system? Lawler has identified four major characteristics.[43] First, the reward system must meet the needs of the individual for food, shelter, and other basic necessities. These needs include the physiological and security needs identified by Maslow and Alderfer and the hygiene factors identified by Herzberg.

Next, the rewards should compare favorably with those offered by other organizations. Unfavorable comparisons with people in other settings could result in feelings of inequity. Third, the distribution of

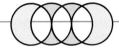

THE GLOBAL VIEW

MOTIVATION THROUGH PARTICIPATION AT BERTELSMANN

During World War II, Reinhard Mohn, a German soldier, was captured by Americans and held in a prison camp in Concordia, Kansas, where he read about Alfred P. Sloan and his philosophy of decentralization at General Motors. When Mohn returned to Germany after the war, he learned that the family business, Bertelsmann publishing, was devastated by bombing. Bertelsmann had been founded in Gütersloh, Germany, in 1825 by Mohn's grandfather, Carl Bertelsmann, to produce hymnals and Bibles.

Mohn gave up his engineering career, set out to rebuild Bertelsmann, and succeeded beyond most people's dreams. He remembered Sloan's ideas and, instead of using the traditional, hierarchical structure found in virtually all German companies, decentralized operations. Each operating group was relatively autonomous and able to retain entrepreneurial motivation and aggressiveness. Mohn used participation to motivate managers and employees and to integrate and coordinate the independent units. He also developed a generous benefits package for employees.

The twofold strategy of a tight focus and motivation through decentralization and participation has helped make Bertelsmann the publishing giant it is today. Bertelsmann's book and record clubs, which were started in the 1950s, now have over 16 million members in nineteen countries. Bertelsmann has sales of well over $5 billion and is a strong competitor in books, music, magazines, and television.

During the late 1970s, Bertelsmann bought a couple of U.S. firms (Bantam Books and Brown Printing). In the late 1980s, Bertelsmann began to expand its presence in the United States because it had largely saturated its domestic market. It purchased RCA Records in September 1986 and two weeks later acquired Doubleday, a publishing company. Its U.S. operations now include RCA Records and RCA's affiliate, Arista; Bantam Books, Doubleday, and Doubleday's subsidiary, Dell Publishing; Delta Lithograph, Offset Paperback Manufacturers, and Brown Printing; Literary Guild and several other small book clubs; and *Parents* and *Young Miss* magazines.

Mohn retired in 1981, but he owns 89.9 percent of the firm and controls its destiny (there is only one other owner, Gerd Bucerius, who publishes the newspaper *Der Zeit*). Because the motivation-through-participation concept was Mohn's, there is little likelihood that it will be discontinued as long as he is alive. Indeed, his first successor resisted the idea of expanding overseas and lasted less than two years on the job. The current CEO, is expanding internationally into the United States, Latin America, Australia, and Israel and throughout Europe. Those operations will soon account for two-thirds of Bertelsmann's revenues worldwide.

REFERENCES: "The Press Barons Duke It Out Across Europe," *Business Week*, October 3, 1988, pp. 48–49; "Bertelsmann's U.S. Invasion May Be Just Beginning," *Business Week*, August 10, 1987, pp. 72–73; "Reinhard Mohn, the Alfred P. Sloan of Publishing," *Forbes*, October 5, 1987, p. 124.

rewards within the organization must be equitable. When some employees feel underpaid compared with others in the organization, the probable results are low morale and poor performance. (People are more likely to compare their situation with that of others in their own organization than with that of outsiders.) Fourth, the reward system must recognize that different people have different needs and choose different paths to satisfy those needs. Both content theories and expectancy theory contribute to this conclusion. Insofar as possible, a variety of rewards and a variety of methods for achieving them should be made available to employees.

New Approaches to Rewarding Employees

Organizational reward systems have traditionally been one of two kinds: a fixed hourly or monthly rate or an incentive system. Fixed-rate systems are familiar to most people. Hourly employees are paid a specific wage (based on job demands, experience, or other factors) for each hour they work. Salaried employees receive a fixed sum of money on a weekly or monthly basis. Although some reductions may be made for absences, the amount is usually the same regardless of whether the individual works less than or more than a normal amount of time.[44]

From a motivational perspective, such rewards can be tied more directly to performance through merit pay raises. A **merit system** is one whereby people get different pay raises at the end of the year, depending on their overall job performance.[45] When the organization's performance appraisal system is appropriately designed, merit pay is a good system for maintaining long-term performance.

Increasingly, however, organizations are experimenting with various kinds of incentive systems. **Incentive systems** attempt to reward employees in proportion to what they do. A piece-rate pay plan is a good example of an incentive system. In a factory manufacturing luggage, for example, each worker may be paid 50 cents for each handle and set of locks installed on a piece of luggage. Hence, there is incentive for the employee to work hard: the more units produced, the higher the pay. Four increasingly popular incentive systems are profit sharing, gain sharing, lump-sum bonuses, and pay for knowledge.[46]

Profit sharing provides a varying annual bonus to employees based on corporate profits. This system unites workers and management toward the same goal—higher profits. However, there can be equity problems in deciding how to allocate the profits. Ford, USX, and Alcoa all have profit-sharing plans.[47] Gain sharing is a group-based incentive system in which group members all get bonuses when predetermined performance levels are exceeded. This system facilitates teamwork and trust. Or it may focus workers too narrowly on attaining the specific goals needed for the bonus while neglecting other parts of their jobs.

Another innovative method for rewarding employees is the lump-sum bonus. This method gives each employee a one-time cash bonus, rather than a base salary increase. The organization can control its fixed costs by not increasing base salaries; however, employees sometimes feel resentful that their increase is contingent on future performance. Aetna Life and Casualty, Timex, and B. F. Goodrich have successfully used this approach. Finally, pay-for-knowledge systems focus on paying the individual rather than the job. Under a traditional arrangement two workers doing the same job are paid the same rate, regardless of their skills. Under the new arrangement, people are advanced in pay grade for each new skill or set of skills they learn. This approach increases training costs but also results in a more highly skilled work force. Schoolteachers often receive higher pay for increased training. General Foods and Texas Instruments have also experimented with this method and have had favorable results.

merit system A reward system whereby people get different pay raises at the end of the year depending on their overall job performance

incentive system A reward system whereby people get different pay amounts at each pay period in proportion to what they do

SUMMARY OF KEY POINTS

Motivation is the set of forces that cause people to behave in certain ways. Motivation is an important consideration of managers because it, along with ability and environmental factors, determines individual performance. Thinking about motivation has evolved from the traditional view through the human relations approach to the human resource view.

Content perspectives on motivation are concerned with what factor or factors cause motivation. Popular content theories include Maslow's need hierarchy, the ERG theory, and Herzberg's two-factor theory. Other important needs are the needs for achievement, affiliation, and power.

Process perspectives on motivation deal with how motivation occurs. Expectancy theory suggests that people are motivated to perform if they believe that their effort will result in high performance, that this performance will lead to rewards, and that the positive aspects of the outcomes outweigh the negative aspects. Equity theory is based on the premise that people are motivated to achieve and maintain social equity. Attribution theory is a new process theory.

The reinforcement perspective focuses on how motivation is maintained. Its basic assumption is that behavior that results in rewarding consequences is likely to be repeated, whereas behavior resulting in negative consequences is less likely to be repeated. Reinforcement contingencies can be arranged in the form of positive reinforcement, avoidance, punishment, and extinction, and they can be provided on fixed-interval, variable-interval, fixed-ratio, or variable-ratio schedules.

Two newly emerging approaches to employee motivation are goal-setting theory and the Japanese approach. Managers often adopt behavior modification, modified workweeks, and work redesign programs to enhance motivation.

Organizational reward systems are the primary mechanisms managers have for managing motivation. Properly designed systems can improve attitudes, motivation, and behaviors. Effective reward systems must provide sufficient rewards on an equitable basis at the individual level. Contemporary reward systems include merit systems and various kinds of incentive systems.

DISCUSSION QUESTIONS

Questions for Review

1. What were the basic historical perspectives on motivation?
2. Compare and contrast content, process, and reinforcement perspectives on motivation.
3. In what ways are the emerging perspectives on motivation like the content, process, and reinforcement perspectives? In what ways are they different?

4. What are the similarities and differences between the motivational programs described in this chapter?

Questions for Analysis

5. Compare and contrast the different content theories. Can you think of any ways in which the theories are contradictory?
6. Expectancy theory seems to make a great deal of sense, but it is complicated. Some people argue that its complexity reduces its value to practicing managers. Do you agree or disagree?
7. Offer examples other than those from this chapter to illustrate positive reinforcement, avoidance, punishment, and extinction.

Questions for Application

8. Think about the worst job you have held. What approach to motivation was used in that organization? Now think about the best job you have held. What approach to motivation was used there? Can you base any conclusions on this limited information? If so, what?
9. Interview both managers and workers (or administrators and faculty) from a local organization. What views of or approaches to motivation seem to be in use in that organization?
10. Can you locate any local organizations that have implemented or are implementing any of the motivational programs discussed in this chapter? If so, interview a manager and a worker to obtain their views on the program.

NOTES

1. Nancy J. Perry, "Here Come Richer, Riskier Pay Plans," *Fortune*, December 19, 1988, pp. 50–58.
2. Richard M. Steers and Lyman W. Porter, *Motivation and Work Behavior*, 4th ed. (New York: McGraw-Hill, 1987).
3. Jeremiah J. Sullivan, "Three Roles of Language in Motivation Theory," *Academy of Management Review*, January 1988, pp. 104–115.
4. Frederick W. Taylor, *Principles of Scientific Management* (New York: Harper and Brothers, 1911).
5. Elton Mayo, *The Social Problems of an Industrial Civilization* (Boston: Harvard University Press, 1945); Fritz J. Rothlisberger and W. J. Dickson, *Management and the Worker* (Boston: Harvard University Press, 1939).
6. "A Humble Hero Drives Ford to the Top," *Fortune*, January 4, 1988, pp. 22–24.
7. See Kenneth A. Kovach, "What Motivates Employees? Workers and Supervisors Give Different Answers," *Business Horizons*, September–October 1987, pp. 58–65. See also Ann Landi, "When Having Everything Isn't Enough," *Psychology Today*, April 1989, pp. 27–30.

8. Abraham H. Maslow, "A Theory of Human Motivation," *Psychological Review*, Vol. 50, 1943, pp. 370–396; Abraham H. Maslow, *Motivation and Personality* (New York: Harper & Row, 1954).

9. For a review, see Craig Pinder, *Work Motivation* (Glenview, Ill.: Scott, Foresman, 1984). See also Steers and Porter, *Motivation and Work Behavior*.

10. Clayton P. Alderfer, *Existence, Relatedness, and Growth* (New York: Free Press, 1972).

11. For an example, see Clayton P. Alderfer, "An Empirical Test of a New Theory of Human Needs," *Organizational Behavior and Human Performance*, April 1969, pp. 142–175. See also Pinder, *Work Motivation*.

12. Frederick Herzberg, Bernard Mausner, and Barbara Snyderman, *The Motivation to Work* (New York: Wiley, 1959); Frederick Herzberg, "One More Time: How Do You Motivate Employees?" *Harvard Business Review*, January–February 1987, pp. 109–120.

13. Robert J. House and Lawrence A. Wigdor, "Herzberg's Dual-Factor Theory of Job Satisfaction and Motivation: A Review of the Evidence and a Criticism," *Personnel Psychology*, Winter 1967, pp. 369–389; Victor H. Vroom, *Work and Motivation* (New York: Wiley, 1964). See also Pinder, *Work Motivation*.

14. David C. McClelland, *The Achieving Society* (Princeton, N.J.: Van Nostrand, 1961); David C. McClelland, *Power: The Inner Experience* (New York: Irvington, 1975).

15. David McClelland, "That Urge to Achieve," *Think*, November–December 1966, p. 22; John G. Nicholls, "Achievement Motivation: Conceptions of Authority, Subjective Experience, Task Choice, and Performance," *Psychological Review*, July 1984, pp. 328–346. See also Walter Kiechel III, "The Workaholic Generation," *Fortune*, April 10, 1989, pp. 50–62.

16. E. Cornelius and F. Lane, "The Power Motive and Managerial Success in a Professionally Oriented Service Company," *Journal of Applied Psychology*, January 1984, pp. 32–40.

17. David McClelland and David H. Burnham, "Power Is the Great Motivator," *Harvard Business Review*, March–April 1976, pp. 100–110.

18. Victor H. Vroom, *Work and Motivation* (New York: Wiley, 1964).

19. David A. Nadler and Edward E. Lawler III, "Motivation: A Diagnostic Approach," in J. Richard Hackman, Edward E. Lawler, and Lyman W. Porter, eds., *Perspectives on Behavior in Organizations*, 2nd ed. (New York: McGraw-Hill, 1983), pp. 67–78.

20. Lyman W. Porter and Edward E. Lawler III, *Managerial Attitudes and Performance* (Homewood, Ill.: Dorsey Press, 1968).

21. Nadler and Lawler, "Motivation: A Diagnostic Approach."

22. "How A&P Fattens Profits by Sharing Them," *Business Week*, December 22, 1986, p. 44.

23. Terrence Mitchell, "Expectancy Models of Job Satisfaction, Occupation Preference, and Effort: A Theoretical, Methodological, and Empirical Appraisal," *Psychological Bulletin*, December 1974, pp. 1053–1077; John P. Wanous, Thomas L. Keon, and Jania C. Latack, "Expectancy Theory and Occupational/Organizational Choices: A Review and Test," *Organizational Behavior and Human Performance*, August 1983, pp. 66–86. For recent findings, see also Lynn E. Miller and Joseph E. Grush, "Improving Predictions in Expectancy Theory Research: Effects of Personality, Expectancies, and Norms," *Academy of Management Journal*, March 1988, pp. 107–122.

24. J. Stacy Adams, "Towards an Understanding of Inequity," *Journal of Ab-*

normal and Social Psychology, November 1963, pp. 422–436; Richard T. Mowday, "Equity Theory Predictions of Behavior in Organizations," in Steers and Porter, *Motivation and Work Behavior*, pp. 91–113.

25. For a review, see Paul S. Goodman and Abraham Fiedman, "An Examination of Adam's Theory of Inequity," *Administrative Science Quarterly*, September 1971, pp. 271–288.

26. "Pay Problems: How Couples React When Wives Out-Earn Husbands," *The Wall Street Journal*, June 19, 1987, p. 19.

27. Richard A. Cosier and Dan R. Dalton, "Equity Theory and Time: A Reformulation," *Academy of Management Review*, April 1983, pp. 311–319; and Richard C. Huseman, John D. Hatfield, and Edward W. Miles, "A New Perspective on Equity Theory: The Equity Sensitivity Construct," *Academy of Management Review*, April 1987, pp. 222–234.

28. H. H. Kelly, *Attribution in Social Interaction* (Morristown, N.J.: General Learning Press, 1971).

29. B. F. Skinner, *Beyond Freedom and Dignity* (New York: Knopf, 1971).

30. See E. Leroy Plumlee and Kenneth S. Keleman, "A Proposal for the Convergence of the Behavior Modification and the Expectancy Theories of Work Motivation," *Business Review*, Winter 1987, pp. 13–17.

31. Fred Luthans and Robert Kreitner, *Organizational Behavior Modification and Beyond: An Operant and Social Learning Approach* (Glenview, Ill.: Scott, Foresman, 1985).

32. Patricia Sellers, "How to Handle Customers' Gripes," *Fortune*, October 24, 1988, pp. 88–100.

33. Mel E. Schnake, "Vicarious Punishment in a Work Setting," *Journal of Applied Psychology*, May 1986, pp. 343–345.

34. Edwin Locke, "Toward a Theory of Task Performance and Incentives," *Organizational Behavior and Human Performance*, Vol. 3, 1968, pp. 157–189.

35. For recent developments, see Dov Eden, "Pygmalion, Goal Setting, and Expectancy: Compatible Ways to Boost Productivity," *Academy of Management Review*, October 1988, pp. 639–652; and Gary P. Latham, Miriam Erez, and Edwin A. Locke, "Resolving Scientific Disputes by the Joint Design of Crucial Experiments by the Antagonists: An Application to the Erez-Latham Dispute Regarding Participation in Goal Setting," *Journal of Applied Psychology*, November 1988, pp. 753–772.

36. "When Are Employees Not Employees? When They're Associates, Stakeholders . . . ," *The Wall Street Journal*, November 9, 1988, p. B1.

37. Luthans and Kreitner, *Organizational Behavior Modification and Beyond*; W. Clay Hamner and Ellen P. Hamner, "Behavior Modification on the Bottom Line," *Organizational Dynamics*, Spring 1976, pp. 2–21.

38. "At Emery Air Freight: Positive Reinforcement Boosts Performance," *Organizational Dynamics*, Winter 1973, pp. 41–50.

39. Allan R. Cohen and Herman Gadon, *Alternative Work Schedules: Integrating Individual and Organizational Needs* (Reading, Mass.: Addison-Wesley, 1978).

40. Ricky W. Griffin, *Task Design—An Integrative Approach* (Glenview, Ill.: Scott, Foresman, 1982).

41. Earl D. Weed, "Job Environment 'Cleans Up' at Texas Instruments," in J. R. Maher, ed., *New Perspectives in Job Enrichment* (New York: Van Nostrand, 1971), pp. 55–77.

42. Edward E. Lawler III, *Pay and Organizational Development* (Reading, Mass.: Addison-Wesley, 1981). See also Edward E. Lawler III, *Pay and Organi-*

zational *Effectiveness: A Psychological View* (New York: McGraw-Hill, 1971).

43. Lawler, *Pay and Organizational Development*.
44. Robert J. Greene, "Effective Compensation: The How and Why," *Personnel Administrator*, February 1987, pp. 112–116.
45. "Grading 'Merit Pay,'" *Newsweek*, November 14, 1988, pp. 45–46; Frederick S. Hills, K. Dow Scott, Steven E. Markham, and Michael J. Vest, "Merit Pay: Just or Unjust Desserts," *Personnel Administrator*, September 1987, pp. 53–59.
46. Perry, "Here Come Richer, Riskier Pay Plans," pp. 50–58.
47. "Watching the Bottom Line Instead of the Clock," *Business Week*, November 7, 1988, pp. 134–136.

CASE 12.1

Flexible Steelcase

Steelcase, a manufacturer of office furniture based in Grand Rapids, Michigan, has sponsored extensive surveys on motivation and productivity by the Lou Harris polling organization. A finding from one survey was that nearly half of all workers feel that they are doing as much as they can, working as hard as they can. The same survey reported that only about a fourth of workers feel that they could probably do more than they were currently doing. In contrast, very few managers seem to feel that workers are producing as much as they could; managers seem to feel that workers could do more. This extreme difference in perceptions is likely to have a negative impact on relations between workers who feel that they are doing their best and managers who want more productivity.

In 1987, a Steelcase survey found that only about half of office workers felt that the quality of their work life was improving, compared to nearly three-fourths who felt that it was improving in 1978. Managers in most American companies pay a lot of lip service to the idea that employees are important assets, but workers seem not to see any real or lasting attention being paid to them or their working environments. Here, too, the disparity between what workers want and what is being provided by their organizations is large enough to suggest that many workers are not highly motivated by their organizations.

Steelcase decided to do something about these discrepancies. Since individuals vary considerably, Steelcase instituted a flexible approach to dealing with employees. The firm hopes that this approach will produce a more productive and loyal work force. Steelcase has instituted a series of "flex" policies: flexible benefits, flexible pay, flexible hours, and flexible managerial attitudes toward the implementation of the policies.

Flexible benefits are available under what is known as a cafeteria-style plan. Like customers in a cafeteria who spend their money on their own individual choices, workers are allotted credits that they can allocate to obtain benefits from a menu of options. At Steelcase, there are eight medical plans, three dental options (including receiving no coverage at all), various forms of long- and short-term disability insurance, and life insurance. Credits not used for medical benefits can be taken home in cash, used for retirement benefits, or used to cover out-of-pocket costs for healthcare or childcare. By giving employees control over their own benefits, Steelcase has been able to cut costs and improve morale at the same time. Employees feel that they are exercising at least some control over their own work, and they can tailor their benefits to more nearly fit their age, career plans, and immediate needs.

Steelcase uses a combination of profit sharing and piecework incentive pay to provide flexibility in direct pay. In a piecework plan, workers are paid a bonus for each piece of work they do above some minimum standard. Some workers are concerned about the piecework plan because management controls the standard; they worry that, if incentive pay gets too high, management will simply raise the standard. Other workers, however, don't share that apprehension and push to make as much as they can. Profit sharing is used because it tends to make jobs "recession resistant" and ties the interests of workers to those of the firm and also because it creates peer pressure to produce. Slow workers are called bonus-busters and are pressured by other workers to work harder so that everyone can earn a greater bonus at year's end.

Flexible hours are achieved through the use of flextime and job sharing. These options seem primarily to benefit working mothers, but all employees can take advantage of them. Steelcase feels that reductions in absenteeism resulting from these options have been beneficial. The flextime program permits workers to set their own starting and stopping times as long as they put in a 40-hour week. Job sharing permits two individuals to share one job. In some cases sharing means two and a half days of work each week for each person; in other cases, two workers alternate weeks. In any event, job sharing is difficult and requires great care and close communication between the sharers. Steelcase has had several job-sharing disasters. Thus, although the company still supports the concept, each situation is individually evaluated and approved to try to ward off bad experiences. Steelcase has found that most successful job sharers eventually become full-time employees who then can assume their duties quickly because they need no additional training. Job sharing worked so well with office workers that Steelcase began a pilot program for factory workers.

Questions

1. Upon what perspectives are the motivational programs at Steelcase primarily based? Cite specific examples and link them to particular theories to support your views.
2. Describe the motivation programs at Steelcase in terms of the programs discussed in the chapter. Which program discussed in the chapter seems to be most like those used at Steelcase? Why?
3. Is the system of organizational rewards used at Steelcase effective? Why or why not? How might it be made more effective?
4. What other things might Steelcase do to try to improve the motivation of its employees? Why?

REFERENCES: Bob Cohn, "A Glimpse of the 'Flex' Future," *Newsweek*, August 1, 1988, pp. 38–39; "Home Is Where the Heart Is," *Time*, October 3, 1988, pp. 46–48, 53; "How's Your Quality of Work Life?" *Industry Week*, June 15, 1987, p. 7; "Are You Really Running as Fast as You Can?" *Inc.*, October 1987, p. 10.

CASE 12.2

Hitachi Is a Hit with Workers

Hitachi Ltd., the Japanese electrical and electronic equipment manufacturer, prizes technical knowledge. In describing its corporate culture, the firm refers to itself as dedicated to technology. Dedication to technology is now being redirected to dedication to loyal employee teams as a way of keeping productivity high. One area in which dedication to employees is noticeable is in the Hitachi operations located in the United States. Hitachi's American operations are highly successful, and Hitachi continues to expand into the U.S. market.

Hitachi Consumer Products established a plant in the Los Angeles area in 1979 to make color television sets. Hitachi was concerned that the U.S. government was going to impose import quotas on televisions and established the production facility in the United States to get around such restrictions. The Japanese plant manager, however, was interested in developing an American plant with a happy, family-like atmosphere that would lead to a more productive work force than most American manufacturing facilities had at that time. He wanted American workers to learn the Japanese way of doing things and to be able to quickly move upward through the organization.

The Japanese way tends to minimize waste and maximize quality and has earned Hitachi huge increases in profits. Loyalty is also a key: loyalty from customers for high-quality products marketed at fair prices; loyalty to employees through personnel policies that reduce the need for terminations in recessions and that train workers to constantly develop and improve; loyalty from employees, which reduces turnover and the need to go outside the firm for promotions. Japanese firms stress the team concept as a way to foster loyalty. The team concept suggests that everyone is critical to success and that cooperation rather than internal competition fosters success. The team concept also suggests that everyone is equal and that it is inappropriate for managerial elites to order subordinate workers around. The team concept is supported through the use of group incentive pay plans, which reward groups of workers rather than individual workers for good performance. Group incentive plans also bring about peer pressure to deal with individuals who are not producing as much as they could.

The president of Hitachi Consumer Products tries to listen to his employees and act upon what he hears. Employees who have problems with their personal finances or other family problems come to him for advice. Those who have problems in the plant also come to him.

In 1986, a group of workers met with the president and suggested that a four-day week with longer working days was more desirable than the conventional five-day, 8-hour-day workweek. They felt that a four-day week would enable them to spend more "quality" time with their families and that their productivity would be unaffected. Managers throughout the plant were asked about the pros and cons of such a system and then met with all of the employees in a series of small group meetings to discuss the idea. Finally, a vote was taken to determine which system would be used. The five-day week won the vote.

Nevertheless, because some workers were not satisfied with the outcome, the president did not let the issue drop. He worked with the managerial personnel in the plant to come up with an option that might satisfy the losing side. They came up with the idea of a four-day weekly schedule for a new assembly line that would assemble video-cassette recorders. Workers who were interested were given the opportunity to transfer to that line to take advantage of the different work schedule. This creative use of democratic voting coupled with a dedication to the maintenance of loyal employee teams led to a unique solution that made everyone happy.

In addition to being highly successful, Hitachi's approach seems to be a hit with its employees. One employee at Hitachi Consumer Products, for instance, began work as an electronics technician after a Navy career. As he learned the Japanese way of doing things, his performance improved and he was given managerial responsibility. He moved to lead technician, group leader, supervisor, and then to assistant manager. He is so grateful for the opportunities he has had at Hitachi that he claims the only way in which he would leave would be for the plant to close.

Questions

1. Is the motivational program at Hitachi primarily content, process, or reinforcement based? Cite specific examples and link them to particular theories to support your views.
2. Which motivational programs discussed in the chapter seem to be most like those used at Hitachi? Why?
3. Is the system of organizational rewards used at Hitachi effective? Why or why not? How might it be made more effective?
4. What might Hitachi do to try to further improve the motivation of its employees? Why?
5. In what ways are the motivational effects of Hitachi similar to and different from those of Steelcase described in Case 12.1? What might explain these results?

REFERENCES: "Hitachi Reports 39% Rise in Group Profit for Year," *The Wall Street Journal*, June 6, 1988, p. 16; "Japanese Computer Firms See a Market in Domestic Customers' U.S. Operations," *The Wall Street Journal*, May 4, 1988, p. 19; Henry Eason, "The Corporate Immigrants," *Nation's Business*, April 1987, pp. 12–19; "The Mountain Priest," *Fortune*, August 3, 1987, p. 42; "Hitachi Will Offer Trade Concessions to Its U.S. Rivals," *The Wall Street Journal*, July 31, 1985, p. 23; "Hitachi; GM Unit Team Up to Buy National Semiconductor Subsidiary," *The Wall Street Journal*, February 28, 1989, p. B4.

OUTLINE

The Nature of Leadership
The Meaning of Leadership · Leadership Versus
Management · Power and Leadership

The Search for Leadership Traits

Leadership Behaviors
The Michigan Studies · The Ohio State Studies · The
Managerial Grid

Situational Approaches to Leadership
Fiedler's Contingency Theory · The Path-Goal Theory · The
Vroom–Yetton–Jago Model · Other Situational Approaches

New Perspectives on Leadership
Substitutes for Leadership · Transformational Leadership

Political Behavior in Organizations
Common Political Behaviors · Managing Political Behavior

CHAPTER 13

Leadership and Influence Processes

OBJECTIVES

After studying this chapter, you should be able to:

- Describe the nature of leadership.
- Discuss the trait approach to leadership.
- Discuss models of leadership focusing on behaviors.
- Identify and describe situational approaches to leadership.
- Identify and describe new perspectives on leadership.
- Discuss political behavior in organizations.

OPENING INCIDENT

How much difference can a leader make? Consider the case of Polaroid. Polaroid had been run by its founder, Edwin Land, until his retirement in 1982. At that time, Polaroid was entering a critical era. Its market share was plummeting; it had few new products under development; and morale was low. The man called upon to turn things around was Israel MacAllister Booth—a quiet, unassuming person who described himself as dull and colorless.

Although this description might have been apt at the time, Booth knew he would have to change if he was to succeed. In his old job in operations, he had remained isolated from most others in the organization. In his new job, he consciously adopted a more outgoing nature, roaming the hallways, explaining his ideas, and listening to the ideas of others. He maintained his folksy mannerisms, though, and to this day drives his beat-up old jeep to work.

Booth's new management style seems to have blended well with his old-fashioned values and decision-making acumen. He trimmed the work force from a bloated 20,000 to a lean 13,000, reorganized Polaroid's organization from a functional to a multidivisional design, eliminated bureaucratic red tape, and restored morale. He also got the highly successful Spectra camera on the market and has a steady stream of innovations in the pipeline. How does this success add up? It adds up so well that Polaroid has become the target of takeover speculation on Wall Street.[1]

*I*srael *MacAllister Booth* apparently has a rare combination of skills that sets him apart from many others: He is both an astute leader and a fine manager, and he recognizes many of the challenges necessary to play both roles. He knew he had to tailor his behavior to fit his new situation; he knew he had to make tough decisions; and he knew it was necessary to focus on a wide range of issues and problems. Thus far, he has done an excellent job.

This chapter examines people like Booth more carefully—by focusing on leadership and its role in management. We characterize the nature of leadership and trace through the three major approaches to studying leadership—traits, behaviors, and situations. After examining newly emerging perspectives on leadership, we conclude by describing another approach to influencing others—political behavior in organizations.

THE NATURE OF LEADERSHIP

In Chapter 12, we described employee motivation. From the manager's standpoint, trying to motivate people is an attempt to influence their

Leadership is a quality found in individuals who are capable of inspiring and motivating individuals or groups. The lead climber in this photo has the trust and confidence of the people climbing with him.

behavior. In many ways, leadership is the opposite side of the same coin—that is, it too is an attempt to influence the behavior of others. In this section, we first define leadership, then differentiate it from management, and conclude by relating it to power.

The Meaning of Leadership

■ **leadership** The use of noncoercive influence to shape the group's or organization's goals, motivate behavior toward the achievement of those goals, and help define group or organization culture; the set of characteristics attributed to individuals who are perceived to be leaders

Leadership can be defined as either a process or a property.[2] As a process, **leadership** is the use of noncoercive influence to shape the group's or organization's goals, motivate behavior toward the achievement of those goals, and help define group or organization culture.[3] As a property, leadership is the set of characteristics attributed to individuals who are perceived to be leaders. Thus, **leaders** are people who can influence the behaviors of others without having to rely on force, and leaders are people whom others accept as leaders.

leaders People who can influence the behaviors of others without having to rely on force; those accepted by others as leaders

Leadership Versus Management

From these definitions, it should be clear that leadership and management are related, but it should be equally clear that they are also different. Thus, a person can be a manager, a leader, both, or neither. This view is illustrated in Figure 13.1. Steven Jobs had charisma and could inspire motivation and loyalty, but he eventually failed as a manager at Apple because he lacked managerial ability. Similarly, Billy Martin can inspire baseball players to new heights, but he eventually fails because he too lacks managerial ability.

James Dutt, former CEO of Beatrice, and Harold Geneen, former CEO of ITT, were very good managers. They made effective decisions,

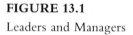

FIGURE 13.1

Leaders and Managers

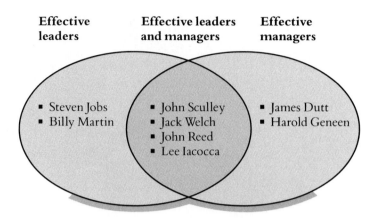

guided the fortunes of their respective companies admirably, and achieved financial success. They also alienated their subordinates and lost their positions prematurely because of a lack of leadership.

Shown in the intersection of Figure 13.1 are John Sculley (Apple), Jack Welch (GE), John Reed (Citicorp), and Lee Iacocca (Chrysler). These individuals possess an abundant supply of what it takes to be a manager and to be a leader. Sculley, for example, knew nothing about the computer business when he took over at Apple, but he worked hard to learn it and is today a fine technical manager. He is also able to inspire his followers and seldom has to rely on formal authority to get things done.[4] "Management in Practice" provides additional insights into the importance of John Reed to Citicorp.

Organizations around the world are putting a premium on the importance of leadership. CEOs like Welch and Iacocca make millions of dollars each year, and companies like General Foods, General Electric, Johnson & Johnson, and Apple spend millions more each year trying to identify potential leaders and hone their skills.[5] On the other hand, many critics argue that leadership cannot be developed in people in a systematic fashion. Their position is that leaders are born or that they emerge through some random series of events. The truth probably lies somewhere in between. There are no magical formulas that transform nonleaders into leaders, but it is possible, as demonstrated by Polaroid's Booth, for a person to change his or her approach to things and assume the leadership mantle. It is also possible for leadership skills and abilities to be improved with education and practice.[6]

Power and Leadership

power   The ability to affect the behavior of others

In order to fully understand leadership, it is necessary to understand power. **Power** is the ability to affect the behavior of others. One can have power without actually using it. For example, a football coach has the power to bench a player who is not performing up to par. The

---

MANAGEMENT IN PRACTICE

JOHN REED LEADS CITICORP

When John S. Reed took over as chairman of Citicorp in 1984, it appeared that his style was quite different from that of his predecessor, Walter B. Wriston. Reed seemed to be more of a manager. He was accommodative, seemed concerned with the details of execution and cost control, and tended to avoid publicity and meetings with business analysts.

Citicorp faced intense Japanese competition as Reed became chairman. For that reason, he moved to alter its direction somewhat. He improved communication among offices and trading rooms around the globe. He trimmed the work force and cleaned up Citicorp's loan portfolio. He encouraged the growth of Citicorp overseas and the development of new products. The initial impact of these changes was to reduce profitability and thereby worry analysts. Reed's low profile did not help. He rarely met with analysts to explain his strategy, and when he did meet with them, they typically raised short-term issues while he discussed long-term prospects.

Then, after three years on the job, Reed clearly became a leader in the banking community. He became more visible, and new labels were attached to his style. He was called bold and brash when he announced that Citicorp was setting up a $3 billion reserve to cushion itself against bad loans, particularly loans to Third World countries. This action was dictated by sound management practices, according to Reed, and was necessary to bolster Citicorp's ability to withstand Japanese competition in the future. Everyone in the industry knew that many of the loans were bad, but no one had been sufficiently strong to take such decisive action.

Although it took a few years for Reed's leadership style to be recognized by those outside of Citicorp, insiders had been aware of it for a while. Reed's immediate subordinates have clear goals and are committed to accomplishing them. Reed has developed a highly motivated executive work group. So vigorous are the group's efforts that it has been referred to as Reed's "A-Team." The executive work group is dedicated to making Citicorp the best financial institution in the world and, under Reed's leadership and management, may do just that.

REFERENCES: "Citicorp Is Negotiating with Regulators to Buy Connecticut Thrift, Sources Say," *The Wall Street Journal*, June 6, 1988, p. 4; "Citicorp to Pare 400 Jobs as Part of Cost Cutting," *The Wall Street Journal*, January 7, 1988, p. 4; "Citicorp's Reed Takes Firm Stand on Third World Debt," *The Wall Street Journal*, February 4, 1987, p. 6; Jaclyn Fierman, "John Reed's Bold Stroke," *Fortune*, June 22, 1987, pp. 26–32; "John Reed's Citicorp," *Business Week*, December 8, 1986, pp. 90–96; Edward Boyer, "Citicorp: What the New Boss Is Up To," *Fortune*, February 17, 1986, pp. 40–44.

---

coach seldom has to use this power, because players recognize that the power exists and work hard to keep their starting positions. In organizational settings, there are usually five kinds of power: legitimate, reward, coercive, referent, and expert power.[7]

legitimate power   Power granted through the organizational hierarchy; power defined by the organization that is to be accorded people occupying particular positions

Legitimate Power   **Legitimate power** is power granted through the organizational hierarchy; it is the power defined by the organization that is to be accorded people occupying a particular position. A boss can tell a subordinate to do something, and a subordinate who refuses can be reprimanded or even fired. Such outcomes stem from the boss's legitimate power as defined and vested in her or him by the organization. Legitimate power, then, is the same as authority. All managers have legitimate power over their subordinates. The mere possession of legitimate power, however, does not by itself make someone a leader.

In many cases, subordinates follow only orders that are strictly within the letter of organizational rules and policies. If asked to do something outside their defined domain, they refuse or do a slipshod job. In such cases, their manager is exercising authority but not leadership.

reward power   The power to give or withhold rewards, such as salary increases, promotions, praise, recognition, and interesting job assignments

Reward Power   **Reward power** is the power to give or withhold rewards. Rewards that may be under the control of an individual manager include salary increases, bonuses, promotion recommendations, praise, recognition, and interesting job assignments. In general, the greater the number of rewards controlled by a manager and the more important the rewards are to subordinates, the greater is the manager's reward power. If the subordinate sees as valuable only the formal organizational rewards provided by the manager, then there is no leadership. However, if the subordinate also wants and appreciates informal rewards like praise, gratitude, and recognition from the manager, then the manager is also exercising leadership.

coercive power   The power to force compliance via psychological, emotional, or physical threat

Coercive Power   **Coercive power** is the power to force compliance by means of psychological, emotional, or physical threat. In some isolated settings, coercion can take the form of physical punishment. Examples include the military and prisons, where first-line supervisors occasionally strike or beat subordinates until they comply or as punishment for breaking rules and regulations. In most organizations, however, the available means of coercion are limited to verbal reprimands, written reprimands, disciplinary layoffs, fines, demotion, and termination. Some managers occasionally go so far as to use verbal abuse, humiliation, and psychological coercion in an attempt to manipulate subordinates. James Dutt, former CEO of Beatrice, once told a subordinate that if his wife and family got in the way of his working a 24-hour-day, 7-day-week job, he should get rid of them.[8] The more punitive the elements under a manager's control and the more important they are to subordinates, the more coercive power the manager possesses. On the other hand, the more a manager uses coercive power, the more likely he or she is to provoke resentment and hostility—and the less likely he or she is to be seen as a leader.

referent power   The personal power that accrues to someone based on identification, imitation, or charisma

Referent Power   Compared with legitimate, reward, and coercive power, which are relatively concrete and grounded in objective facets of organizational life, **referent power** is more abstract. It is based on identification, imitation, or charisma. Followers may react favorably because they identify in some way with a leader, who may be like them in personality, background, or attitudes. In other situations, followers might choose to imitate a leader with referent power by wearing the same kinds of clothes, working the same hours, or espousing the same management philosophy. Referent power may also take the form of charisma, an intangible attribute in the leader's personality that inspires loyalty and enthusiasm. Thus, while a manager might have referent power, it is more likely to be associated with leadership.

expert power   The personal power that accrues to someone based on the information or expertise that they possess

Expert Power   **Expert power** is derived from information or expertise. A manager who knows how to deal with an eccentric but important customer, a scientist who is capable of achieving an important technical breakthrough that no other company has dreamed of, and a secretary who knows how to unravel bureaucratic red tape—all have expert power over anyone who needs that information. The more important the information and the fewer the people who have access to it, the greater is the degree of expert power possessed by any one individual. In general, people who are both leaders and managers tend to have a lot of expert power.

Using Power   How does a manager/leader use power? Several methods have been identified. One method is the legitimate request—a request based on legitimate power. It involves the manager requesting that the subordinate comply because the subordinate recognizes that the organization has given the manager the right to make the request. Most day-to-day interactions between manager and subordinate are of this type.

Another use of power is instrumental compliance. This form of exchange is based primarily on reward power, and it bears out the reinforcement theory of motivation. Suppose that a manager asks a subordinate to do something outside the range of the subordinate's normal duties, such as working extra hours on the weekend, terminating a relationship with a long-standing buyer, or delivering bad news. The subordinate complies and, as a direct result, reaps praise and a bonus from the manager. The next time the subordinate is asked to perform a similar activity, that subordinate will recognize that compliance will be instrumental in her or his getting more rewards. Hence the basis of instrumental compliance is clarifying important performance-reward contingencies.

Another method for using power is coercion—using coercive power. When the manager suggests or implies that the subordinate will be punished, fired, or reprimanded if he or she does not do something, coercion is being practiced. Rational persuasion occurs when the manager can convince the subordinate that compliance is in the subordinate's best interest. For example, a manager might argue that the subordinate should (or should not) accept a transfer because it would (or would not) be good for the subordinate's career. In some ways, rational persuasion is similar to reward power, except that the manager does not really control the reward. Elements of expert power are also present in that the manager may be seen as a knowledgeable person.

Still another way to use power is through personal identification. A manager who recognizes that he or she has referent power over a subordinate can shape the behavior of that subordinate by engaging in desired behaviors—that is, the manager consciously becomes a model for the subordinate and exploits personal identification. Sometimes a manager can induce someone to do something through inspirational appeal because it is consistent with a set of higher ideals or values. For example, a plea for loyalty represents an inspirational appeal. Referent power plays a role in determining the extent to which an inspirational appeal is successful, because its effectiveness depends at least in part on the persuasive abilities of the leader.

A dubious method of using power is through information distortion. The manager withholds or distorts information to influence subordinates' behavior. For example, if a manager has agreed to allow everyone to participate in choosing a new group member but subsequently finds one individual whom she really prefers, she might withhold some of the credentials of other qualified applicants so that the desired member is selected. This use of power is dangerous. It may be unethical, and if subordinates find out the manager has deliberately misled them, they will lose their confidence and trust in that manager's leadership.[9]

THE SEARCH FOR LEADERSHIP TRAITS

The first organized approach to studying leadership was to analyze the personal, psychological, and physical traits of strong leaders. The underlying assumption of the trait approach was that there existed some basic trait or set of traits that differentiated leaders from nonleaders. If those traits could be defined, potential leaders could be identified. It was thought that leadership traits might include intelligence, assertiveness, above-average height, good vocabulary, attractiveness, self-confidence, and similar attributes.[10]

During the first several decades of this century, literally hundreds of studies were conducted in an attempt to identify important leadership traits. For the most part, the results of the studies were disappointing. For every set of leaders who possessed a common trait, a long list of exceptions was also found, and the list of suggested traits soon grew so long that it had little practical value. Alternative explanations usually existed even for relations between traits and leadership that initially appeared valid. For example, it was observed that many leaders have good communication skills and are assertive. Rather than those traits being the cause of leadership, however, it might be that successful leaders begin to display those traits after they have achieved leadership positions.

As it was determined that such traits vary with the situation, many researchers gave up trying to identify traits as predictors of leadership ability. However, many people still explicitly or implicitly adopt a trait orientation. For example, politicians are all too often elected on the basis of personal appearance, speaking ability, or an aura of self-confidence.[11]

LEADERSHIP BEHAVIORS

Spurred on by their lack of success in identifying useful leadership traits, researchers soon began to investigate other variables, especially the behaviors or actions of leaders. The new hypothesis was that the

The search for leader behaviors generally identified two basic styles of leadership, one focused on tasks and one focused on people. Keith Dunn provides an excellent example of a leader who has changed his style of behavior—twice. Dunn began his restaurant chain, McGuffey's, because he thought other restaurants had forgotten how to treat their employees. His plan for McGuffey's was to be employee-centered and avoid the kinds of mistreatment he himself had experienced at other chains. At first, he was wildly successful—so successful, that he launched an ambitious expansion plan. During this period, however, he got so wrapped up in his own success and in getting the job done that he forgot his founding principles—strong concern for employee well-being. Soon, as he was forced to confront declining revenues, poor morale, and high turnover, he realized his error and reaffirmed his concern for his employees. Consequently, things have turned around. The employees of McGuffey's in Charlotte, North Carolina (shown here) now have a turnover rate that is one-quarter of the industry average—only 60 percent.

behaviors of effective leaders were somehow different from the behaviors of less effective leaders. Thus, the goal was to develop a fuller understanding of leadership behaviors.

The Michigan Studies

Researchers at the University of Michigan, led by Rensis Likert, began studying leadership in the late 1940s.[12] Based on extensive interviews with both leaders and followers (that is, with managers and subordinates), the Michigan studies identified two basic forms of leader behavior. The first was called **job-centered leader behavior**. When using this behavior, the leader pays close attention to subordinates' work, explains work procedures, and is keenly interested in performance. The second behavior identified in this research was **employee-centered leader behavior**. In this case, the leader is interested in developing a cohesive work group and ensuring that employees are satisfied with their jobs. Thus, the leader's primary concern is the welfare of subordinates.

The two styles of leader behavior were presumed to be at the ends of a single continuum. Although this suggests that leaders may be extremely job-centered, extremely employee-centered, or somewhere in between, Likert studied only the two end styles for contrast. He found that employee-centered leader behavior generally tended to be more effective. We should also note the similarities between Likert's leadership research and his Systems 1 through 4 organization design

■ **job-centered leader behavior**   Involves paying close attention to the job and work procedures involved with that job

■ **employee-centered leader behavior**   Involves developing cohesive work groups and ensuring employee satisfaction

(discussed in Chapter 9). Job-centered leader behavior is associated with the System 1 design, whereas employee-centered leader behavior is more consistent with the System 4 design. When Likert talks about moving organizations from System 1 to System 4, he is also advocating a transition from job-centered to employee-centered leader behavior.

The Ohio State Studies

At about the same time that Likert was beginning his leadership work at Michigan, a group of researchers at Ohio State also began studying leadership.[13] The extensive questionnaire surveys conducted during the Ohio State studies again suggested that there are two basic leader behaviors or styles. The first was called **initiating-structure behavior**. When using this behavior, the leader clearly defines the leader-subordinate role so that everyone knows what is expected, establishes formal lines of communication, and determines how tasks will be performed. The second leadership style identified is **consideration behavior**. In this instance, the leader shows concern for subordinates and attempts to establish a friendly and supportive climate.

The job-centered and employee-centered behaviors identified at Michigan are similar to the initiating-structure and consideration behaviors recognized at Ohio State, but there are significant differences. The most obvious difference is that the forms of leader behavior are not seen by the Ohio State researchers as being at opposite ends of a single continuum. Rather, they are assumed to be independent variables. A leader can exhibit varying levels of initiating structure and at the same time varying levels of consideration. Figure 13.2 shows the Ohio State view of leader behavior.

At first, the Ohio State researchers thought that leaders who exhibit high levels of both behaviors would tend to be more effective than other leaders. A study at International Harvester (now Navistar), however, suggested a more complicated pattern.[14] The researchers found that employees of supervisors who ranked high on initiating structure were higher performers but expressed lower levels of satisfaction. Conversely, employees of supervisors who ranked high on consideration had lower performance ratings but had fewer absences from work.

■ **initiating-structure behavior** Involves defining the leader-subordinate role so that everyone knows what is expected, establishing formal lines of communication, and determining how tasks will be performed

■ **consideration behavior** Involves showing concern for subordinates and attempting to establish a warm, friendly, and supportive climate

FIGURE 13.2

The Ohio State View of Leader Behaviors

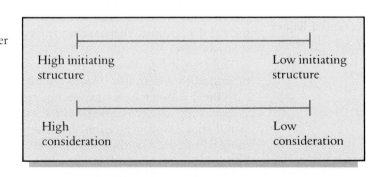

Later research isolated other variables that make consistent prediction difficult and determined that situational influences also occurred.

The Managerial Grid

concern for people That part of the Managerial Grid that deals with the human aspects of leader behavior

concern for production That part of the Managerial Grid that deals with the job and task aspects of leader behavior

In Chapter 11 we discussed an organization development technique called the Managerial Grid.[15] The Managerial Grid can also be seen as a model of leadership based on two forms of leader behavior: **concern for people** (similar to employee-centered and consideration behavior) and **concern for production** (similar to job-centered and initiating-structure behaviors). By combining the two forms of behavior, the Managerial Grid offers a way to analyze leader behavior in ongoing organizations. Note that the Managerial Grid, like the Michigan and Ohio State frameworks, implies that there is one generally appropriate combination of leader behaviors—the 9,9 coordinates, or maximum concern for both people and production.

The leader-behavior theories have played an important role in the development of contemporary thinking about leadership. In particular, they urge us not to be preoccupied with what leaders are (the trait approach) but to concentrate on what leaders do (their behaviors). Unfortunately, they also fall prey to the trap of making universal prescriptions about what constitutes effective leadership. When we are dealing with complex social systems composed of complex individuals, there are few if any consistently predictable relationships, and certainly there are no infallible formulas for success. Yet the behavior theorists tried to identify consistent relationships between leader behaviors and employee responses, in the hope of finding a dependable prescription for effective leadership. As we might expect, they often failed. Thus, other approaches to understanding leadership were needed. The catalyst for these new approaches was the realization that, although interpersonal and task-oriented dimensions might be useful to describe the behavior of leaders, they were not useful for predicting or prescribing it. The next step in the evolution of leadership theory was the creation of situational models.[16]

SITUATIONAL APPROACHES TO LEADERSHIP

The basic assumption of situational models is that appropriate leader behavior varies from one situation to another. The goal of a situational theory, then, is to identify key situational factors and to specify how they interact to determine appropriate leader behavior. Recall the opening incident about Israel Booth. When he ran operations at Polaroid, he was low-key, unassuming, and a loner. As Polaroid's CEO, however, he retained the first two attributes but changed his social behaviors completely. And he has been remarkably successful doing both jobs using different approaches.

Before discussing the three major situational theories, we should first note an important early model that laid the foundation for subsequent developments. In 1958 Robert Tannenbaum and Warren H. Schmidt proposed a continuum of leadership behavior in the decision-making process. Their model is much like the original Michigan framework.[17] However, besides purely job-centered behavior (or "boss-centered" behavior, as they termed it) and employee-centered (which they termed "subordinate-centered") behavior, they identified several intermediate possibilities that a manager might consider. These are shown on the leadership continuum in Figure 13.3.

This continuum of behavior moves from the one extreme of having the manager make the decision alone to the other extreme of having the employees make the decision with minimal guidance. Each point on the continuum is influenced by factors relating manager, subordinates, and situation. Managerial factors include the manager's value system, confidence in subordinates, personal inclinations, and feelings of security. Subordinate factors include the subordinates' need for independence, readiness to assume responsibility, tolerance for ambiguity, interest in the problem, understanding of goals, knowledge, experience, and expectations. Situational factors that affect the decision making include the type of organization, group effectiveness, the problem itself, and time pressures.

Although the Tannenbaum and Schmidt framework pointed out the importance of situational factors, it was only speculative. It remained for others to develop more comprehensive and integrated theories. In the following sections, we describe the three most important and most widely accepted situational theories of leadership: Fiedler's contingency theory, the path-goal theory, and the Vroom-Yetton-Jago model.

Situational approaches to leadership suggest that leaders need to employ different behaviors in different situations. Fred Smith, CEO of Federal Express, provides a good example of how managers must tailor their behaviors to different situations. He played the part of a hard-nosed negotiator, for example, when buying Flying Tiger. But he had to be more conciliatory as he convinced the Japanese government to transfer Tiger's landing rights in that country to Federal. And still different behaviors will be called for as he tries to integrate Tiger's unionized workforce with Federal's non-unionized employees.

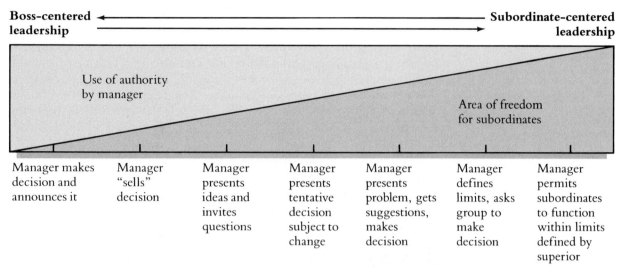

Boss-centered leadership ←——————————————————————————————————→ Subordinate-centered leadership						
Use of authority by manager					Area of freedom for subordinates	
Manager makes decision and announces it	Manager "sells" decision	Manager presents ideas and invites questions	Manager presents tentative decision subject to change	Manager presents problem, gets suggestions, makes decision	Manager defines limits, asks group to make decision	Manager permits subordinates to function within limits defined by superior

FIGURE 13.3

Tannenbaum and Schmidt's Leadership Continuum

■ **contingency theory of leadership** Suggests that the appropriate style of leadership varies with situational favorableness

least preferred co-worker (LPC) The measuring scale that asks leaders to describe the person with whom he or she is able to work least well

Fiedler's Contingency Theory

Fiedler's **contingency theory of leadership** was the first true situational theory of leadership.[18] Beginning with a combined trait and behavior approach, Fiedler identifies two styles of leadership—task-oriented (analogous to job-centered and initiating-structure behavior) and relationship-oriented (similar to employee-centered and consideration behavior). However, he goes beyond the leadership-behavior approaches by arguing that the style of leader behavior is a reflection of the leader's personality (hence, rooted in traits) and is basically constant for any person—that is, a leader is presumed to be task-oriented or relationship-oriented all of the time.

Fiedler measures leader style by means of a controversial questionnaire called the **least preferred co-worker** (**LPC**) measure. To use the measure, a manager or leader is asked to describe the person with whom he or she is able to work least well—the LPC—by filling a set of sixteen scales anchored at each end by a positive or negative adjective. For example:

Helpful	__ __ __ __ __ __ __ __	Frustrating
	8 7 6 5 4 3 2 1	
Tense	__ __ __ __ __ __ __ __	Relaxed
	1 2 3 4 5 6 7 8	
Boring	__ __ __ __ __ __ __ __	Interesting
	1 2 3 4 5 6 7 8	

The leader's LPC score is then calculated by adding up the numbers below the line checked on each scale. Note in these three examples that the higher numbers are associated with the "good" words (helpful, relaxed, and interesting), whereas the "bad" words (frustrating, tense, and boring) have low point values. A high total score is assumed to reflect a relationship orientation and a low score a task orientation on the part of the leader. The LPC measure is controversial because researchers disagree about its validity. Some question exactly what an LPC measure reflects and whether the score is an index of behavior, personality, or some other factor.[19]

Favorableness of the Situation   The underlying assumption of situational models of leadership is that appropriate leader behavior varies from one situation to another. According to Fiedler, the key situational factor is the favorableness of the situation from the leader's point of view. This factor is determined by three things: leader-member relations, task structure, and position power.

Leader-member relations refer to the nature of the relationship between the leader and the work group. If the leader and the group have a high degree of mutual trust, respect, and confidence, and if they like one another, relations are assumed to be good. If there is little trust, respect, or confidence, and if they do not like one another, relations are assumed to be poor. Good relations are assumed to be favorable and poor relations unfavorable.

Task structure is the degree to which the group's task is well defined. When the task is routine, easily understood, and unambiguous, and when the group has standard procedures and precedents to rely on, the task is considered to be structured. An unstructured task is the opposite: nonroutine, ambiguous, complex, with no standard procedures or precedents. High structure results in a more favorable position for the leader; low structure is more unfavorable. For example, if the task is unstructured, the group will not know what to do and the leader will have to play a major role in guiding and directing its activities. If the task is structured, the leader will not have to get so involved and can devote time to other activities.

Position power is the power vested in the leader's position. If the leader has the power to assign work, reward and punish employees, and recommend employees for promotion or demotion, position power is assumed to be strong. If the leader must get job assignments approved by someone else, does not administer rewards and punishment, and has no voice in promotions or demotions, position power is weak. From the leader's point of view, strong position power is clearly favorable and weak position power is unfavorable.

Favorableness and Leader Style   Fiedler and his associates have conducted numerous studies linking the favorableness of various situations to leader style and group effectiveness.[20] The results of these studies—and the overall framework of the theory—are shown in Figure 13.4.

To interpret the model, look first at the situational factors at the bottom of the figure. Note that good or poor leader-member relations, structured or unstructured task, and strong or weak leader-position

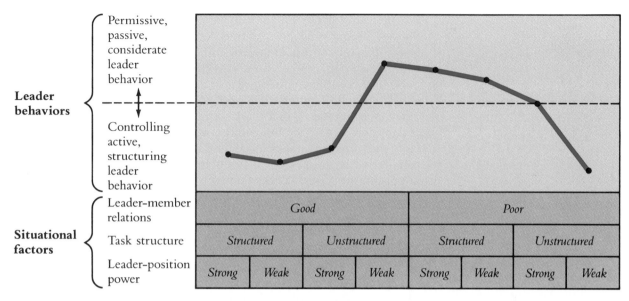

SOURCE: Fred E. Fiedler, "The Effects of Leadership Training and Experience: A Contingency Model Interpretation," *Administrative Science Quarterly,* December 1972, p. 455. Used with permission of *Administrative Science Quarterly.*

FIGURE 13.4

Fiedler's Contingency Theory of Leadership

power can be combined to yield eight unique situations. For example, good leader-member relations, structured task, and strong leader-position power (at the far left) are presumed to define the most favorable situation; poor leader-member relations, unstructured task, and weak leader-power (at the far right) are the least favorable. The other combinations reflect intermediate levels of favorableness.

Above each situation is shown the form of leader behavior found to be most strongly associated with effective group performance in that situation. When the situation includes good relations, structured task, and strong power, Fiedler has found that a task-oriented leader is most effective. However, when relations are good but the task is unstructured and position power is weak, a relationship-oriented leader is predicted to be most effective. Note that a task-oriented leader is supposedly effective when the situation is very favorable and when the situation is very unfavorable. The relationship-oriented style is most effective under the intermediate conditions.

Flexibility of Leader Style   Fiedler argues that leader style is essentially fixed and cannot be changed, that a leader cannot change her or his behavior to fit a particular situation. According to Fiedler, leaders are either task oriented or relationship-oriented. When a leader's style and the situation do not match, Fiedler argues that the situation should be changed to fit the leader's style. When leader-member relations are good, task structure low, and position power weak, the leader style most likely to be effective is relationship-oriented. If the leader is task-oriented, a mismatch exists. According to Fiedler, the leader can make the elements of the situation more congruent by structuring the task (by developing guidelines and procedures, for instance) and increasing power (by requesting additional authority or by other means).

Fiedler's contingency theory has been attacked on the grounds that it is not always supported by research, that his findings are subject to other interpretations, that the LPC measure lacks validity, and that his assumptions about the inflexibility of leader behavior are unrealistic.[21] However, Fiedler's theory was one of the first to adopt a situational perspective on leadership. It has helped many managers recognize the important situational factors they must contend with, and it has fostered additional thinking about the situational nature of leadership.

The Path-Goal Theory

path-goal theory of leadership   Suggests that the primary functions of a leader are to make valued or desired rewards available and to clarify the kinds of behavior that will lead to those rewards

The **path-goal theory of leadership**—associated most closely with Martin Evans and Robert House—is a direct extension of the expectancy theory of motivation discussed in Chapter 12.[22] Recall that the primary components of expectancy theory included the likelihood of attaining various outcomes and the value associated with those outcomes. The path-goal theory of leadership suggests that the primary functions of a leader are to make valued or desired rewards available in the workplace and to clarify for the subordinate the kinds of behavior that will lead to goal accomplishment and valued rewards—that is, the leader should clarify the paths to goal attainment.

Leader Behavior   The most fully developed version of path-goal theory identifies four kinds of leader behavior. First is directive leader behavior—letting subordinates know what is expected of them, giving guidance and direction, and scheduling work. Second is supportive leader behavior—being friendly and approachable, showing concern for subordinate welfare, and treating members as equals. Third is participative leader behavior—consulting subordinates, soliciting suggestions, and allowing participation in decision making. Fourth is achievement-oriented leader behavior—setting challenging goals, expecting subordinates to perform at high levels, encouraging subordinates and showing confidence in subordinates' abilities.

In contrast to Fiedler's theory, path-goal theory assumes that leaders can change their style or behavior to meet the demands of a particular situation. For example, when encountering a new group of subordinates and a new project, the leader may be directive in establishing work procedures and in outlining what needs to be done. Next, the leader may adopt supportive behavior in an effort to foster group cohesiveness and a positive climate. As the group becomes more familiar with the task and as new problems are encountered, the leader may exhibit participative behavior to enhance group members' motivation. Finally, achievement-oriented behavior may be used to encourage continued

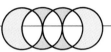

THE GLOBAL VIEW

WANG'S PATH TO IMPROVEMENT

Dr. An Wang came to America from Shanghai, China, founded Wang Laboratories, and for several years maintained tight control over the organization. He was able to persuade employees to produce at high levels and convince customers that Wang products were among the best available.

In the early 1980s, the firm's performance began to slip. Commitments to customers were not being met; the accounting and billing systems became nightmares; and new-product development failed to keep pace with the rest of the industry. Dr. Wang moved to correct the problems. His approach was to centralize decision making and to take personal charge of operations. At first, that approach seemed to work, but between 1985 and 1987, growth in revenues slowed and losses began to occur in some quarters. Wang Labs' directors persuaded Dr. Wang to share his power with a new president. There was only one candidate—Dr. Wang's son, Frederick A. Wang.

Some of the firm's problems may have been the result of a series of executive departures around 1985, when top managers realized that young Wang would be promoted over them sometime in the future. Those departures indicated that family control, which frequently brings stability to an organization, may lead to instability and turnover if managers feel that their career paths are blocked by family members.

Fred Wang presents a more polished appearance than did his father. He is soft-spoken and speaks with no trace of an accent; in addition, he listens more than he speaks. Although he has never worked anywhere else, his positions at Wang Labs amount to fifteen years of experience in the computer industry.

The biggest difference in the leadership styles of the two Wangs seems to lie in their approach to management. Dr. Wang relied on his expertise and his charismatic personality to get things done in a centralized, almost autocratic manner. Fred Wang delegates extensively and uses participation to motivate subordinates.

Fred imposed financial controls on the firm and is given credit for seeing to it that products are delivered on time. He has also been broadening the firm's product line. In 1987, Wang Labs introduced two IBM-compatible machines and a very powerful VS minicomputer. It has plans to expand beyond its traditional office market with a work station for factory use. Fred Wang keeps the goals of the firm clearly in the minds of his subordinates and tries to help them achieve those goals.

REFERENCES: "How the Doctor's Son Is Getting Wang Back on Its Feet," *Business Week*, January 25, 1988, pp. 84–87; "Wang Sees a Ray of Hope in Son's Rise," *The Wall Street Journal*, July 13, 1987, p. 6; Arthur M. Louis, "Doctor Wang's Toughest Case," *Fortune*, February 3, 1986, pp. 106–109.

high performance. "The Global View" provides an illustration of how a change in leader behavior helped Wang Labs get back on track.

Situational Factors   Like other situational theories of leadership, path-goal theory suggests that appropriate leader style depends on situational factors. Two general categories of situational factors that receive special attention in path-goal theory are the personal characteristics of subordinates and the environmental characteristics of the workplace.

Two important personal characteristics are the subordinates' perception of their own ability and their locus of control. If people perceive that they are lacking in ability, they may prefer directive leadership to help them understand path-goal relationships better. If they perceive themselves to have a lot of ability, however, employees may resent directive leadership. Locus of control is a personality trait. People who have an internal locus of control believe that what happens to them is a function of their own efforts and behavior. Those who have an external locus of control assume that fate or luck or "the system" determines what happens to them. A person with an internal locus of control may prefer participative leadership, whereas a person with an external locus of control may prefer directive leadership. Managers can do little or nothing to influence the personal characteristics of subordinates, but they can shape the environment to take advantage of these personal characteristics.

Environmental characteristics include factors outside the subordinate's control. Task structure is one such factor. When structure is high, directive leadership is less effective than when structure is low. Subordinates do not usually need their boss to continually tell them how to do an extremely routine job. The formal authority system is another important environmental characteristic. Again, the higher the degree of formality, the less directive is the leader behavior that will be accepted by subordinates. The nature of the work group also affects appropriate leader behavior. When the work group provides the individual with social support and satisfaction, supportive leader behavior is less critical. When social support and satisfaction cannot be derived from the group, the individual may look to the leader for this support.

The basic path-goal framework as illustrated in Figure 13.5 shows that different leader behaviors affect subordinate motivation to perform. Personal and environmental characteristics are seen as defining which behaviors lead to which outcomes. The path-goal theory of leadership is a dynamic and incomplete model. The original intent was to state the theory in general terms so that a variety of interrelationships could be explored and the theory modified as a result of future research findings. Research that has been done suggests that the path-goal theory is a reasonably good description of the leadership process and that future investigations along these lines should enable us to discover more about the link between leadership and motivation.[23]

The Vroom-Yetton-Jago Model

■ **Vroom-Yetton-Jago model (VYJ model)** Predicts what kinds of situations call for what degrees of group participation

The third major situational theory of leadership that we discuss is the **Vroom-Yetton-Jago model**, or **VYJ model**. This model was first proposed by Victor Vroom and Philip Yetton in 1973 and was revised and expanded in 1988 by Vroom and Arthur G. Jago.[24] The VYJ model is somewhat narrower than the other situational theories in that it focuses on only one part of the leadership process—how much decision-making participation to allow subordinates. Drawing from the Tannenbaum and Schmidt continuum of leadership behaviors, the model predicts what kinds of situations call for what degrees of group participation. The VYJ model, then, sets norms or standards for including subordinates in decision making.

Basic Premises   The VYJ model argues that decision effectiveness is best gauged by the quality of the decision and by employee acceptance

FIGURE 13.5

The Path-Goal Framework

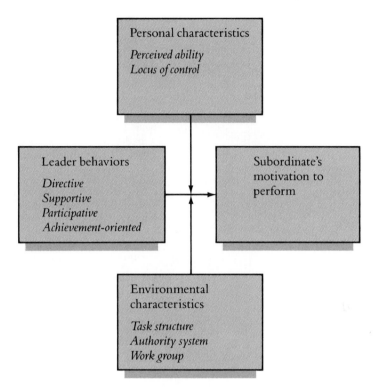

of the decision. Decision quality is the objective effect of the decision on performance. Decision acceptance is the extent to which employees accept and are committed to the decision. To maximize decision effectiveness, the VYJ model suggests that managers adopt one of five decision-making styles. The appropriate style depends on the situation. As summarized in Table 13.1, there are two autocratic styles (AI and AII), two consultative styles (CI and CII), and one group style (GII).

The situation that is presumed to dictate an appropriate decision-making style is defined by a series of questions about the characteristics or attributes of the problem under consideration. To address the questions, the manager uses one of four decision trees. Two of the trees are for use when the problem affects the entire group, and the other two are appropriate when the problem relates to an individual. One of each is to be used when the time necessary to reach a decision is important, and the others are to be used when time is less important but the manager wants to develop subordinates' decision-making abilities.

The tree for time-driven group problems is shown in Figure 13.6. The problem attributes defining the situation are arranged along the top of the tree and are expressed as questions. To use the tree, the manager starts at the left side of it and asks the first question. Thus, the manager first decides whether the problem involves a quality requirement—that is, whether there are quality differences in the alternatives and if there are do they matter. The answer determines the path

TABLE 13.1

Decision Styles in the VYJ
Model

Decision Style	Definition
AI	Manager makes the decision alone.
AII	Manager asks for information from subordinates but makes the decision alone. Subordinates may or may not be informed about what the situation is.
CI	Manager shares the situation with individual subordinates and asks for information and evaluation. Subordinates do not meet as a group, and the manager alone makes the decision.
CII	Manager and subordinates meet as a group to discuss the situation, but the manager makes the decision.
GII	Manager and subordinates meet as a group to discuss the situation, and the group makes the decision.

A = autocratic; C = consultative; G = group

SOURCE: Reprinted from *Leadership and Decision-making* by Victor H. Vroom and Philip W. Yetton by permission of the University of Pittsburgh Press. © 1973 by the University of Pittsburgh Press.

to the second node, where another question is asked. The manager continues in this fashion until a terminal node is reached and an appropriate decision style is indicated. Each prescribed decision style is designed to protect the original goals of the process (decision quality and subordinate acceptance) within the context of the group versus individual and time versus development framework.

Evaluation　The original version of the VYJ model has been widely tested. Indeed, one recent review concluded that it had received more scientific support than any other leadership theory.[25] However, even the original version was criticized because of its complexity, and the revised VYJ model is far more complex than the original. To aid managers, computer software has been developed to facilitate their ability to define their situation, answer the questions about problem attributes, and develop a strategy for decision-making participation.[26] Still, the inherent complexity of the model presents a problem for many managers.

Other Situational Approaches

In addition to those three major theories, other situational models have been developed in recent years. Two of the best known are the vertical-dyad linkage model and the life cycle model.

QR Quality Requirement: *How important is the technical quality of this decision?*

CR Commitment Requirement: *How important is subordinate commitment to the decision?*

LI Leader's Information: *Do you have sufficient information to make a high-quality decision?*

ST Problem Structure: *Is the problem well structured?*

CP Commitment Probability: *If you were to make the decision by yourself, is it reasonably certain that your subordinate(s) would be committed to the decision?*

GC Goal Congruence: *Do subordinates share the organizational goals to be attained in solving this problem?*

CO Subordinate Conflict: *Is conflict among subordinates over preferred solutions likely?*

SI Subordinate Information: *Do subordinates have sufficient information to make a high-quality decision?*

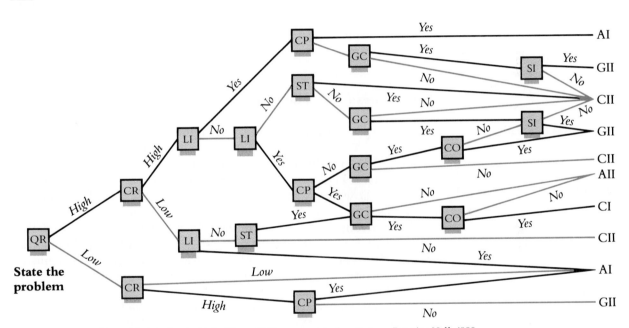

SOURCE: Reprinted from *The New Leadership* by Victor H. Vroom and Arthur G. Jago. Prentice-Hall, 1988. Used by permission of the authors.

FIGURE 13.6

Time-Driven Group Problem Decision Tree for VYJ Model

vertical-dyad linkage model (VDL model) Stresses that leaders have different kinds of relationships with different subordinates

The Vertical-Dyad Linkage Model The **vertical-dyad linkage model**, or **VDL**, stresses the fact that leaders have different kinds of relationships with different subordinates.[27] Each manager-subordinate relationship represents one vertical dyad. The model suggests that leaders establish special working relationships with a handful of subordinates called the in-group. Other subordinates remain in the out-group. Those in the in-group receive more of the manager's time and attention and also tend to be better performers. Early research on this model is quite promising.

The Life Cycle Theory   Another well-known situational theory is the life cycle theory.[28] This model suggests that appropriate leader behavior depends on the maturity of the followers. In this context, maturity includes motivation, competence, and experience. The theory suggests that as followers become more mature, the leader needs to gradually move from a high level of task orientation to a low level. Simultaneously, employee-oriented behavior should start low, increase at a moderate rate, and then decline again. This theory is well-known among practicing managers, but it has received little scientific support from researchers.[29]

NEW PERSPECTIVES ON LEADERSHIP

Because of its importance to organizational effectiveness, leadership continues to be the focus of a great deal of research and theory building. Two new approaches that have attracted much attention are the concepts of substitutes for leadership and transformational leadership.

Substitutes for Leadership

substitutes for leadership
Factors in the situation that neutralize or replace leader behaviors; include characteristics of subordinates, the task, and the organization

The concept of **substitutes for leadership** was developed in response to the fact that existing leadership models and theories do not account for situations in which leadership is not needed.[30] They simply try to specify what kind of leader behavior is appropriate. The substitute concepts, however, identify situations in which leader behaviors are neutralized or replaced by characteristics of the subordinate, the task, and the organization. For example, when a patient is delivered to a hospital emergency room, the professionals on duty there do not wait to be told what to do by a leader. Nurses, doctors, and attendants all go into action without waiting for directive or supportive leader behavior from the emergency-room supervisor.

Characteristics of the subordinate that may serve to neutralize leader behavior include ability, experience, need for independence, professional orientation, and indifference toward organizational rewards. For example, employees with a high level of ability and experience may not need to be told what to do. Similarly, a strong need for independence by the subordinate may render leader behavior ineffective. Characteristics of the task that may substitute for leadership include routineness, the availability of feedback, and intrinsic satisfaction. When the job is routine and simple, the subordinate may not need direction. When the task is challenging and otherwise intrinsically satisfying, the subordinate may not need or want social support from a leader.

Organizational characteristics that may serve as substitutes include formalization, group cohesion, inflexibility, and a rigid reward structure. When policies and practices are formal and inflexible, for example, leadership may not be needed. Similarly, a rigid reward system may

In certain circumstances, organizations can employ substitutes for leadership—factors that can replace the need for a formal leader. One such substitute is professional orientation of the employees. Such is the case for this team of Kodak employees. This team of highly skilled mathematicians is working on applying super computer power to a variety of research programs for Kodak. And they don't need a supervisor looking over their shoulders every day to see how they're doing.

rob the leader's role of reward power, thereby decreasing the importance of the role. Preliminary research has provided support for this concept of substitutes for leadership.[31]

Transformational Leadership

Another new perspective on leadership has been called by a number of labels: charismatic leadership, inspirational leadership, symbolic leadership, and transformational leadership. We will use the term **transformational leadership** and define it as leadership that goes beyond ordinary expectations by transmitting a sense of mission, stimulating learning experiences, and inspiring new ways of thinking.[32] Transformational leaders are increasingly being seen as vital to the success of business.

For example, a recent popular-press article identified seven keys to successful leadership: trusting subordinates, developing a vision, keeping cool, encouraging risk, being an expert, inviting dissent, and simplifying things.[33] Although this list was based on a simplistic reading of the leadership literature, it is nevertheless consistent with the premises underlying transformational leadership. So, too, are recent examples cited as effective leadership. Take, for example, the case of Gerald Tsai, Jr. Tsai took over American Can in the early 1980s and set about transforming it into an entirely different company. He sold twenty-six businesses, including the canning business, and bought almost as many

transformational leadership
Leadership that goes beyond ordinary expectations by transmitting a sense of mission, stimulating learning experiences, and inspiring new ways of thinking

more, mostly in the financial services industry. Today, the company is known as Primerica and is a Wall Street powerhouse. Transformational leadership was needed to pull off the transformation.[34] Given both its theoretical appeal and its practical significance, the notion of transformational leadership is destined to become even more popular.

POLITICAL BEHAVIOR IN ORGANIZATIONS

■ **political behavior** The activities carried out for the specific purpose of acquiring, developing, and using power and other resources to obtain one's preferred outcomes

Another common influence on behavior, albeit one that is often less appealing than leadership, is politics and political behavior. **Political behavior** is activities carried out for the specific purpose of acquiring, developing, and using power and other resources to obtain one's preferred outcomes.[35] Decisions ranging from where to locate a manufacturing plant to where to put the company coffeepot are subject to political action. In any situation, individuals may engage in political behavior to further their own ends, to protect themselves from others, to further goals they sincerely believe to be in the organization's best interest, or simply to acquire and exercise power. And power may be sought by individuals, by groups of individuals, or by groups of groups.

A recent survey provides some interesting insights into how political behavior is perceived in organizations.[36] Some 33 percent of the respondents (428 managers) felt that politics influenced salary decisions in their firms, and 28 percent felt that politics influenced hiring decisions. The respondents also felt that the incidence of political behavior was greater at the upper levels of their organizations and less at the lower levels. Well over half of the respondents felt that organizational politics was bad, unfair, unhealthy, and irrational; but most suggested that successful executives have to be good politicians and that one has to be political to "get ahead."

Common Political Behaviors

Research has identified four basic forms of political behavior widely practiced in organizations.[37] One form is inducement. Inducement occurs when a manager offers to give something to someone else in return for that individual's support. For example, a product manager might suggest to another product manager that she will put in a good word with his boss if he supports a new marketing plan that she has developed. A second tactic is persuasion. Persuasion relies on emotion and logic. For example, an operations manager wanting to construct a new plant on a certain site might persuade others to support his goal on grounds that seem objective and logical but that may really be subjective and personal.

A third political behavior involves the creation of an obligation. For example, one manager might support a recommendation made by another manager for a new advertising campaign. Although he may really have no opinion on the new campaign or may even be secretly opposed to it, he may think that by going along he is incurring a debt from the other manager and will be able to "call in" that debt when he wants to get something done and needs additional support. Finally, coercion is the use of force to get one's way. For example, a manager may threaten to withhold support, rewards, or other resources as a way to influence someone else.

Managing Political Behavior

How can managers handle political behavior so that it does not do excessive damage? By its very nature, political behavior is tricky to approach in a rational and systematic way. As practical guidelines, several actions have been suggested. First, managers should be aware that even if their actions are not politically motivated, others may assume that they are. Second, by providing subordinates with autonomy, responsibility, challenge, and feedback, managers reduce the likelihood of political behavior by subordinates. Third, managers should avoid using power if they want to avoid charges of political motivation. Fourth, managers should get disagreements out in the open so that subordinates will have less opportunity for political behavior, using conflict for their own purposes. Finally, managers should avoid covert activities. Behind-the-scene activities give the impression of political intent even if none really exists.[38] Other guidelines include clearly communicating the bases and processes for performance evaluation, tying rewards directly to performance, and minimizing competition among managers for resources.[39]

Of course, those guidelines are a lot easier to list than they are to implement. The point is that the well-informed manager should not assume that political behavior does not exist or, worse yet, attempt to eliminate it by issuing orders or commands. Instead, the manager should recognize that political behavior exists in virtually all organizations and that it cannot be ignored or stamped out. It can, however, be managed in such a way that it will seldom inflict serious damage on the organization. It may even play a useful role in some situations.

SUMMARY OF KEY POINTS

As a process, leadership is the use of noncoercive influence to shape the group's or organization's goals, motivate behavior toward the achievement of those goals, and help define group or organization culture. As a property, leadership is the set of characteristics attributed to those who are perceived to be leaders. Leadership and management are often related but are also different. Managers and leaders use legitimate, reward, coercive, referent, and expert power.

The trait approach to leadership assumed that some basic trait or set of traits differentiated leaders from nonleaders. The leadership-behavior approach to leadership assumed that the behavior of effective leaders was somehow different from the behavior of nonleaders. Research at Michigan and Ohio State identified two basic forms of leadership behavior—one concentrating on work and performance and the other concentrating on employee welfare and support. The Managerial Grid attempts to train managers to exhibit high levels of both forms of behavior.

Situational approaches to leadership recognize that appropriate forms of leadership behavior are not universally applicable and attempt to specify situations in which various behaviors are appropriate. Fiedler's contingency theory suggests that a leader's behaviors should be either task-oriented or relationship-oriented, depending on the favorableness of the situation. The path-goal theory suggests that directive, supportive, participative, or achievement-oriented leader behaviors may be appropriate, depending on the personal characteristics of subordinates and the environment. The Vroom-Yetton-Jago model maintains that leaders should vary the extent to which they allow subordinates to participate in making decisions as a function of problem attributes. The vertical-dyad linkage model and the life cycle theory are two new situational theories.

Several new leadership perspectives are emerging. Two of them are the concept of substitutes for leadership and the role of transformational leadership in organizations.

Political behavior is another influence process frequently used in organizations. There are four basic forms of political behavior, but there are also things managers can do to limit their effects.

DISCUSSION QUESTIONS

Questions for Review

1. Could someone be a manager but not a leader? A leader but not a manager? Both a leader and a manager? Explain.
2. What were the major findings of the Michigan and Ohio State studies of leadership behaviors? Briefly describe each group of studies and compare and contrast their findings.
3. What are the situational approaches to leadership? Briefly describe each and compare and contrast their findings.
4. What new perspectives on leadership are discussed in this chapter? How can they be integrated with existing approaches to leadership?

Questions for Analysis

5. How is it possible for a leader to be both task-oriented and employee-oriented at the same time? Can you think of other forms of leader behavior that would be important to a manager? If so, share your thoughts with your class.
6. When all or most of the leadership substitutes are present, does the follower no longer need a leader? Why or why not?

7. Why should members of an organization be aware that political behavior may be going on within the organization? What might occur if they were not aware?

Questions for Application

8. What traits seem best to describe student leaders? Military leaders? Business leaders? Political leaders? Religious leaders? What might account for the similarities and differences in your lists of traits?

9. Think about a decision that would affect you as a student. Use the Vroom-Yetton-Jago model to decide whether the administrator making that decision should involve students in the decision. Which parts of the model seem most important in making that decision? Why?

10. How do you know if transformational leadership is present in a group or organization? Could transformational leadership ever lead to dysfunctional outcomes for individuals or organizations? If so, why; if not, why not?

NOTES

1. "Why Polaroid Must Remake Itself—Instantly," *Business Week*, September 19, 1988, pp. 66–72; and Brian Dumaine, "How Polaroid Flashed Back," *Fortune*, February 16, 1987, pp. 72–76.

2. Arthur G. Jago, "Leadership: Perspectives in Theory and Research," *Management Science*, March 1982, pp. 315–336.

3. Gary A. Yukl, *Leadership in Organizations*, 2nd ed. (Englewood Cliffs, N.J.: Prentice-Hall, 1989), p. 5.

4. Examples are drawn from Kenneth Labich, "The Seven Keys to Business Leadership," *Fortune*, October 24, 1988, pp. 58–66; Walter Kiechel III, "The Case Against Leaders," *Fortune*, November 21, 1988, pp. 217–220; and Jeremy Main, "Wanted: Leaders Who Make a Difference," *Fortune*, September 28, 1987, pp. 92–102; John Sculley, "John Sculley on Sabbatical," *Fortune*, March 27, 1989, pp. 79–80.

5. Main, "Wanted: Leaders Who Make a Difference."

6. David V. Day and Robert G. Lord, "Executive Leadership and Organizational Performance: Suggestions for a New Theory and Methodology," *Journal of Management*, September 1988, pp. 453–465.

7. John R. P. French and Bertram Raven, "The Bases of Social Power," in Dorwin Cartwright, ed., *Studies in Social Power* (Ann Arbor, Mich.: University of Michigan Press, 1959), pp. 150–167.

8. Hugh D. Menzies, "The Ten Toughest Bosses," *Fortune*, April 21, 1980, pp. 62–73.

9. For more information on the bases and uses of power, see Philip M. Podsakoff and Chester A. Schriesheim, "Field Studies of French and Raven's Bases of Power: Critique, Reanalysis, and Suggestions for Future Research," *Psychological Bulletin*, Vol. 97, 1985, pp. 387–411; Robert C. Benfari, Harry E. Wilkinson, and Charles D. Orth, "The Effective Use of Power," *Business Horizons*, May–June 1986, pp. 12–16; and Yukl, *Leadership in Organizations*.

10. Bernard M. Bass, *Stogdill's Handbook of Leadership*, rev. ed. (Riverside, N.J.: Free Press, 1981).

11. Robert G. Lord, Christy L. De Vader, and George M. Alliger, "A Meta-Analysis of the Relation Between Personality Traits and Leadership Perceptions: An Application of Validity Generalization Procedures," *Journal of Applied Psychology*, August 1986, pp. 402–410.

12. Rensis Likert, *New Patterns of Management* (New York: McGraw-Hill, 1961); Rensis Likert, *The Human Organization* (New York: McGraw-Hill, 1967).

13. The Ohio State studies stimulated many articles, monographs, and books. A good overall reference is Ralph M. Stogdill and A. E. Coons, eds., *Leader Behavior: Its Description and Measurement* (Columbus, Ohio: Bureau of Business Research, Ohio State University, 1957).

14. Edwin A. Fleishman, E. F. Harris, and H. E. Burt, *Leadership and Supervision in Industry* (Columbus, Ohio: Bureau of Business Research, Ohio State University, 1955).

15. Robert R. Blake and Jane S. Mouton, *The Managerial Grid* (Houston: Gulf Publishing, 1964); Robert R. Blake and Jane S. Mouton, *The Versatile Manager: A Grid Profile* (Homewood, Ill.: Dow Jones–Irwin, 1981).

16. See Jan P. Muczyk and Bernard C. Reimann, "The Case for Directive Leadership," *The Academy of Management Executive*, November 1987, pp. 301–309, for a recent update.

17. Robert Tannenbaum and Warren H. Schmidt, "How to Choose a Leadership Pattern," *Harvard Business Review*, March–April 1958, pp. 95–101.

18. Fred E. Fiedler, *A Theory of Leadership Effectiveness* (New York: McGraw-Hill, 1967).

19. Recent critiques include Ramadhar Singh, "Leadership Style and Reward Allocation: Does Least Preferred Co-Worker Scale Measure Task and Relation Orientation?" *Organizational Behavior and Human Performance*, October 1983, pp. 178–197; D. Hosking, "A Critical Evaluation of Fiedler's Contingency Hypothesis," *Progress in Applied Psychology*, Vol. 1, 1981, pp. 103–154; and Chester A. Schriesheim, B. D. Bannister, and W. H. Money, "Psychometric Properties of the LPC Scale: An Extension of Rice's Review," *Academy of Management Review*, April 1979, pp. 287–294.

20. Fiedler, *A Theory of Leadership Effectiveness*; Fred E. Fiedler and M. M. Chemers, *Leadership and Effective Management* (Glenview, Ill.: Scott, Foresman, 1974).

21. For recent reviews and updates, see Lawrence H. Peters, Darrell D. Hartke, and John T. Pohlmann, "Fiedler's Contingency Theory of Leadership: An Application of the Meta-Analysis Procedures of Schmidt and Hunter," *Psychological Bulletin*, Vol. 97, pp. 274–285; and Fred E. Fiedler, "When to Lead, When to Stand Back," *Psychology Today*, September 1987, pp. 26–27.

22. Martin G. Evans, "The Effects of Supervisory Behavior on the Path-Goal Relationship," *Organizational Behavior and Human Performance*, May 1970, pp. 277–298; Robert J. House and Terence R. Mitchell, "Path-Goal Theory of Leadership," *Journal of Contemporary Business*, Autumn 1974, pp. 81–98. See also Yukl, *Leadership in Organizations*.

23. For a thorough review, see Yukl, *Leadership in Organizations*.

24. Victor H. Vroom and Philip H. Yetton, *Leadership and Decision-making* (Pittsburgh: University of Pittsburgh Press, 1973); and Victor H. Vroom and Arthur G. Jago, *The New Leadership* (Englewood Cliffs, N.J.: Prentice-Hall, 1988).

25. Yukl, *Leadership in Organizations.*

26. Vroom and Jago, *The New Leadership.*

27. Fred Dansereau, George Graen, and W. J. Haga, "A Vertical-Dyad Linkage Approach to Leadership Within Formal Organizations: A Longitudinal Investigation of the Role-Make Process," *Organizational Behavior and Human Performance*, Vol. 15, 1975, pp. 46–78; Richard M. Dienesch and Robert C. Liden, "Leader-Member Exchange Model of Leadership: A Critique and Further Development," *Academy of Management Review*, July 1986, pp. 618–634.

28. Paul Hersey and Kenneth H. Blanchard, *Management of Organizational Behavior*, 3rd ed. (Englewood Cliffs, N.J.: Prentice-Hall, 1977).

29. Yukl, *Leadership in Organizations.*

30. Steven Kerr and John M. Jermier, "Substitutes for Leadership: Their Meaning and Measurement," *Organizational Behavior and Human Performance*, December 1978, pp. 375–403.

31. See Charles C. Manz and Henry P. Sims, Jr., "Leading Workers to Lead Themselves: The External Leadership of Self-managing Work Teams," *Administrative Science Quarterly*, March 1987, pp. 106–129.

32. James MacGregor Burns, *Leadership* (New York: Harper & Row, 1978). See also John J. Hater and Bernard M. Bass, "Superiors' Evaluations and Subordinates' Perceptions of Transformational and Transactional Leadership," *Journal of Applied Psychology*, November 1988, pp. 695–702; Karl W. Kuhnert and Philip Lewis, "Transactional and Transformational Leadership: A Constructive/Developmental Analysis," *Academy of Management Review*, October 1987, pp. 648–657.

33. Labich, "The Seven Keys to Business Leadership."

34. "No Cans, But New Chief Is Can-Do Type," *USA Today*, January 29, 1987, pp. 1B, 2B.

35. Jeffrey Pfeffer, *Power in Organizations* (Marshfield, Mass.: Pitman Publishing, 1981), p. 7.

36. Victor Murray and Jeffrey Gandz, "Games Executives Play: Politics at Work," *Business Horizons*, December 1980, pp. 11–23; Jeffrey Gandz and Victor Murray, "The Experience of Workplace Politics," *Academy of Management Journal*, June 1980, pp. 237–251.

37. Don R. Beeman and Thomas W. Sharkey, "The Use and Abuse of Corporate Power," *Business Horizons*, March-April 1987, pp. 26–30.

38. Murray and Gandz, "Games Executives Play."

39. Beeman and Sharkey, "The Use and Abuse of Corporate Power."

CASE 13.1

Armand Hammer, Leader for All Seasons

Armand Hammer was born on May 21, 1898, in New York City. His father struggled as a pharmacist and eventually became a doctor. Armand entered medical school in 1917, but in that same year he was forced to take charge of the drug and pharmaceutical business for his ailing father. The firm had a product that contained alcohol and thus, in this period just before the enactment of national Prohibition, sold extremely well. Hammer moved quickly to cement a near-monopoly on the product. As a result, in 1919, while he was still a medical student, his income reached $1 million.

Hammer retired from the drug and pharmaceutical business when he graduated from medical school in 1921 and immediately became involved in another venture. He put together a field hospital and went to the Soviet Union to help famine victims. His organizing skills as well as his dedication and compassion led to a meeting with Lenin. Lenin asked Hammer to help with the rebuilding of the Soviet economy. Hammer set up an asbestos concession and became an agent for other American businesses throughout the Soviet Union. As a result of these activities, he once again became a millionaire.

In 1956, Hammer moved to Los Angeles to retire. He was looking around for a tax shelter, a business that was losing money that he could use as a deduction to reduce his income taxes. The Occidental Petroleum Corporation (Oxy) seemed to be just the thing. It had not paid dividends to its stockholders in years and had few assets. However, much to his surprise, Oxy struck oil south of Los Angeles and Hammer had to come out of retirement to run his new oil firm. When oil was found in Libya in 1959, Hammer flew to that country and convinced the king that the major oil companies would all come and try to take over his country. Because of his conversations with Hammer and his experiences with the major oil companies, the king of Libya granted oil concessions to Oxy in 1961. Occidental Petroleum struck a billion-barrel oil field in 1966 and soon became a major oil company in its own right. Hammer was once again a millionaire.

Hammer pursued his business interests around the globe so successfully that he became highly regarded for his ability to get along with heads of state all over the world. Because of his skills, he has been repeatedly tapped by American presidents to assist in overseas assignments, especially those involving the Soviets. He helped Franklin Roosevelt develop the Lend Lease program. He negotiated trade agreements with the Soviets for presidents ranging from Kennedy to Reagan.

As head of Oxy, Hammer continued to wheel and deal. There have been a lot of downs as well as ups, but the overall result has been positive. In

1955, Oxy's market value was just over $100,000; as of late 1988, it was nearly $7 billion. Oxy is the tenth-largest oil company in the world and has interests in energy, chemicals, and beef and pork processing. Many analysts argue that without the sales of assets that have frequently occurred, Oxy would have reported losses in many years. Indeed, from 1978 through 1987, its stock did not do nearly as well as the stock of the other oil giants, despite the fact that in some years Oxy performed spectacularly well. Nevertheless, Oxy has enormous assets, stable sources of supply, some very profitable divisions, a couple of new acquisitions (Cain Chemical and Cities Service), and a new pattern of leadership at the top.

Armand Hammer has become a traveling spokesman and a figurehead for the company. He is a hands-off, but watchful, chairman of the board. In May 1988, he celebrated his ninetieth birthday. He is still at the office from about 10 A.M. until 7 or 8 P.M., although a short nap breaks the afternoon. He is concentrating less on day-to-day operations and more on strategic developments and social movements. He has been working hard on two projects: raising money for cancer research and improving U.S.-Soviet relations. He is able to do this and not worry about Oxy because the company is in the capable hands of its president, Ray Irani.

Irani came to Oxy in 1983 from the presidency of Olin Corporation. A native of Lebanon, Irani holds a Ph.D. in physical chemistry from the University of Southern California. His initial position was as head of Oxy's chemical division. He rarely socializes with colleagues and is usually blunt in dealing with subordinates. Irani and his team run Oxy while Hammer basks in the limelight. That self-affacing behavior may be why Irani, unlike five of his predecessors, has succeeded in the presidency under Hammer.

Questions

1. What traits and behaviors can you identify as being characteristic of Armand Hammer? Cite specific examples.
2. Take one of the situational approaches to or new perspectives on leadership discussed in this chapter and use it to discuss Hammer's leadership. Has he been an effective leader? Why or why not?
3. In what ways has Hammer demonstrated political behavior and what impact has that behavior had on his leadership?
4. Despite the fact that Oxy's stock does not do as well as the stock of other oil companies, it has sold well. What role has Hammer's leadership played in that success?

REFERENCES: Anthony Ramirez, "Hammer Hits 90! Oxy Grows Up Too," *Fortune*, November 7, 1988, pp. 59–64; "Doctor Hammer Is 90—and the Road Show Keeps Rolling On," *Business Week*, May 30, 1988, pp. 48–52; "New Name Is Taking Hold at Occidental," *The Oil Daily*, April 5, 1988, p. 2; Armand Hammer and Neil Lyndon, *Hammer* (New York: Putnam, 1987).

CASE 13.2

Samsung on the March

The Samsung Group is Korea's largest *chaebol*, or family-run conglomerate. It ranks ahead of other Korean firms such as Hyundai, Daewoo, and Lucky-Goldstar. The Samsung Group includes consumer electronics, semiconductors, hotels, shipbuilding, textiles, refined sugar, food processing, genetic engineering, insurance, aerospace, robots, and paper among its major product areas. It was founded by Lee Byung-Chull in 1938 as a general trading store to export fruit and dried fish to Japanese-occupied Manchuria. Lee soon built Samsung into a large, diverse group of companies. A member of a wealthy Korean family, Lee had studied at Tokyo's Waseda University. In building Samsung, he kept his Japanese ties and frequently consulted his colleagues in Japan on strategic decisions.

Lee studied the way in which the Japanese trained and treated employees, and he brought those practices back to his organization in Korea. To indicate his interest in people, he participated in every final interview for managerial positions in Samsung. Lee established an open system of examination and recruitment to lure the best university graduates to Samsung organizations. He worked hard to make unions unnecessary in the Samsung Group by having the firm offer high wages, good benefits, and good working conditions. In addition, he set up the Samsung Education and Training Center to both indoctrinate and train employees. Every employee must pass a 24-day course that stresses teamwork and the Samsung business philosophy.

Lee Byung-Chull's approach certainly seemed to work. Samsung Electronics Company, the largest manufacturing company in the Samsung Group, was founded in 1969. By 1984 it had surpassed Goldstar to become the number 1 electronics manufacturing firm in Korea. It is vertically integrated so that it is not at the mercy of independent suppliers. Located in Suwon, a suburb of Seoul, it consists of dozens of buildings connected by a series of underground conveyor belts. This arrangement makes Samsung Electronics highly efficient and makes possible the centralization of shipping, which is important because nearly three-fourths of the company's output is exported.

Despite the apparent ease of its success, Samsung has had to survive numerous environmental threats and upheavals. The Korean War devastated the organization, reducing it to one operation, a brewery. Lee brought Samsung back, however, quickly diversifying and expanding the group into a giant conglomerate. During the early 1960s, the government of Park Chung Hee grabbed much of the firm, charging that businessmen such as Lee were amassing disgraceful fortunes. Lee rebuilt again. In 1980, President Chun Doo Hwan seized the television and radio stations of the Group, but Lee simply replaced them with a semiconductor operation and once again directed expansion of the Group. Lee accomplished all of this with a mixture of centralization and decentralization. Each company is given full authority to run itself, but extremely tight standards are set by the central administrative group, known as the secretariat. Lee set an example with his strong belief in flawless planning and strong action.

Lee brought these characteristics to the issue of succession. In recent years, thirteen Samsung companies have gone public to raise capital; thus, the Lee family's direct ownership has been weakened. To keep Samsung in the family, Lee had to ensure that a family member would assume the chief executive position after him. He turned to his sons and apparently decided that his oldest sons were not well suited to take over the Group. He turned then to his youngest son, Lee Kun-Hee. The youngest Lee was young and inexperienced, so his father developed a careful plan to help him. In 1987, he hired two senior government officials to assist in the change-over, in effect enabling Lee Kun-Hee to operate through the senior officials until his leadership was established and accepted within the firm.

The basis of Korea's initial success, the availability of inexpensive labor, is disappearing. Labor rates are increasing in Korea, so reliance on cheap labor to compete is no longer possible. In addition, Lee recognizes that in the past Samsung placed more emphasis on growth and size than on quality, and he sees changing that emphasis as one of his biggest challenges. He is determined to plan for rising export prices by focusing on the manufacture of high-quality, high-value-added products. He also plans to invest profits in research and development as well as in education to provide for the long-term success of the Samsung Group.

Questions

1. Describe Lee Byung-Chull's leadership. What were his personal characteristics, his behavior, and the environment in which he was a leader?
2. Take one of the situational approaches to or new perspectives on leadership discussed in this chapter and use it to discuss the elder Lee's leadership. Has he been an effective leader? Why or why not?
3. Use the Vroom-Yetton-Jago model to analyze the succession decision faced by the elder Lee. Should he have involved others in that decision? Why or why not?

REFERENCES: Andrew Tanzer, "Samsung: South Korea Marches to Its Own Drummer," *Forbes*, May 16, 1988, pp. 84–89; John McBeth and Mark Clifford, "Rivals—and Partners; the Participants in Seoul's Aerospace Venture," *Far Eastern Economic Review*, June 9, 1988, pp. 104–105; "Samsung's Succession," *The Economist*, November 28, 1987, p. 89; "Korea's New Corporate Bosses: Made in America," *Business Week*, February 23, 1987, pp. 58–59; Laurie Baum, "Korea's Newest Export: Management Style," *Business Week*, January 19, 1987, p. 66.

OUTLINE

The Interpersonal Nature of Organizations
Interpersonal Dynamics · Outcomes of Interpersonal
Behaviors

Groups in Organizations
Definition of a Group · Types of Groups

Group Formation Processes
Why People Join Groups · Stages of Group Development

Characteristics of Mature Groups
Role Structures · Behavioral Norms · Cohesiveness · Informal
Leadership

Managing Groups in Organizations
Committees · Work Groups · The Japanese Approach

Interpersonal and Intergroup Conflict
The Nature of Conflict · Causes of Conflict · Managing
Conflict

CHAPTER *14*

Interpersonal Processes, Groups, and Conflict

OBJECTIVES

After studying this chapter, you should be able to:

- Describe the interpersonal nature of organizations.
- Define and identify types of groups in organizations.
- Discuss reasons people join groups and the stages of group development.
- Identify and discuss characteristics of mature groups.
- Explain how various kinds of groups can be managed.
- Discuss interpersonal and intergroup conflict in organizations.

OPENING INCIDENT

Though not as well known as other huge insurers like Prudential and State Farm, the Aid Association for Lutherans (AAL) is nevertheless a big company. Although it is operated on a nonprofit basis as a fraternal society, AAL has over $6 billion in assets and is ranked among the largest 2 percent of U.S. insurance companies.

In 1986, managers at AAL realized that the association had grown so fast that it had taken on all the trappings of a bureaucracy—red tape, formalized work procedures, functional departmentalization, and so forth. Like most similar organizations, AAL was slowly but surely increasing its operating costs, alienating its employees, and becoming more and more sluggish.

After long and careful study, managers decided that the entire organization would operate more smoothly if a team approach was adopted. Thus, AAL decided to structure itself around several groups of operating employees. Each group would have a great deal of input into how it did its job and how its performance was assessed. Rules and red tape were eliminated, and each team can now operate with virtually no supervision. The result? So far, things look good—a 20 percent increase in productivity and a 75 percent reduction in the time needed to process claims.[1]

*M*anagers at AAL recognized and took advantage of what many experts are increasingly seeing as a tremendous resource for all organizations—the power of groups. Rather than operate as individual performers reporting to a supervisor, employees at AAL now function as members of a group. Group members schedule their own work hours, assign themselves to jobs, and rotate across jobs as a way to learn new skills. They also develop a high level of loyalty and commitment to the other members of their group.

This chapter is about processes that lead to and follow from activities like those at AAL. We begin by characterizing the interpersonal nature of organizations. We then introduce basic concepts of group dynamics. Subsequent sections explain group formation processes, the characteristics of mature groups, and the managing of groups. We conclude with a discussion of interpersonal and intergroup conflict.

THE INTERPERSONAL NATURE
OF ORGANIZATIONS

In Chapter 1, we defined an organization as two or more people working together in a structured fashion to attain a set of goals. Note how this definition relies on interpersonal relations—"people working together." We also noted in Chapter 1 how much of a manager's job involves scheduled and unscheduled meetings, telephone calls, and related activities. Indeed, a great deal of what all managers do involves interacting with other people, both inside and outside the organization. The schedule that follows is a typical day for the president of a Houston-based company, part of a larger firm headquartered in California. He kept a log of his activities for several different days so you could better appreciate the nature of managerial work.

8:00–8:15 A.M.   Arrive at work, review mail sorted by secretary.

8:15–8:30 A.M.   Read *The Wall Street Journal*.

8:30–9:15 A.M.   Meet with labor officials and plant manager to resolve minor labor disputes.

9:15–9:30 A.M.   Review internal report and dictate correspondence for secretary to type.

9:30–10:00 A.M.   Meet with two marketing executives to review advertising campaign.

10:00–noon   Meet with company executive committee to discuss strategy, budgetary issues, and the competition (this committee meets weekly).

12:00–1:15 P.M.   Lunch with the financial vice president and two executives from another subsidiary of the parent corporation. Primary topic of discussion is the Houston Oilers football team.

1:15–2:00 P.M.   Meet with human resource director and assistant about a recent OSHA inspection; establish a task force to investigate the problems identified and to suggest solutions.

2:00–2:30 P.M.   Conference call with four other company presidents.

2:30–3:00 P.M.   Meet with financial vice president about a confidential issue that came up at lunch (unscheduled).

3:00–3:30 P.M.   Work alone in office.

3:30–4:15 P.M.   Meet with a group of sales representatives and the company purchasing agent.

4:15–5:30 P.M.   Work alone in office.

5:30–7:00 P.M.   Play racquetball at nearby athletic club with marketing vice president.

How did this manager spend his time? He spent most of it working and interacting with other people. And this compressed daily schedule does not include several brief telephone calls, brief conversations with his secretary, and brief conversations with other managers. Clearly, interpersonal relations are a pervasive part of all organizations and a vital part of all managerial activities.[2]

Interpersonal Dynamics

What kinds of interpersonal relations exist in organizations? There is no definitive taxonomy of such behaviors, but it is safe to say that a range of potential relationships can exist. These are shown in Figure 14.1. At one extreme, interpersonal relations can be personal and positive. This occurs when the two parties know each other, have mutual respect and affection, and enjoy interacting with one another. For example, two managers who have known each other for years, play golf

FIGURE 14.1

Interpersonal Dynamics

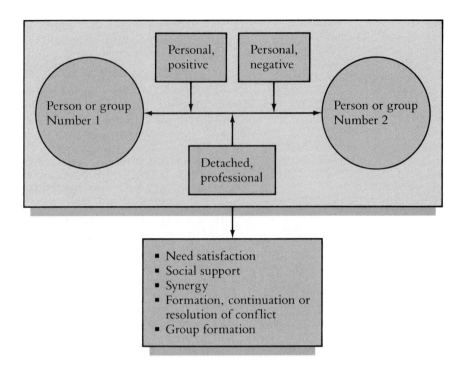

together on weekends, and are close personal friends will likely interact at work in a positive fashion.

At the other extreme, interpersonal dynamics can be personal but negative. This is most likely when the parties dislike one another, do not have mutual respect, and do not enjoy interacting with one another. For example, suppose a manager has fought openly for years to block the advancement of another manager within the organization. Over the objections of the first manager, however, the other manager eventually gets promoted to the same rank. When the two of them must interact, it will most likely be in a negative manner.

In between those extremes, the parties may interact in a detached and professional way focused almost exclusively on goal accomplishment. The interaction focuses on the job at hand, is relatively formal and structured, and is task-directed. For example, two managers may respect each other's work and recognize the professional competence that each brings to the job. However, they may also have few common interests and little to talk about besides the job they are doing. Hence, they are likely to interact in a detached manner.

These different types of interaction may occur between individuals, between groups, or between individuals and groups; and they can change over time. The two managers in the second scenario, for example, might decide to bury the hatchet and adopt a detached, professional manner. The two managers in the third example could find more common ground than they anticipated and evolve to a personal and positive interaction.

Much of a manager's activities are interpersonal in nature. That is, the manager spends much of his or her time interacting with others both inside and outside the organization. Hermann R. Werner, a Vice President and General Manager at Mobay (a dye manufacturer) is shown here (on the right) discussing a process with Norvin A. Clontz, an executive with Milliken & Company, one of Mobay's customers. Top managers like Werner and Clontz spend a great deal of their time working with other people. Thus, they clearly need to understand interpersonal dynamics.

Outcomes of Interpersonal Behaviors

A variety of things can happen as a result of interpersonal behaviors. These are also shown in Figure 14.1. Recall from Chapter 12, for example, that numerous perspectives on motivation suggest that people have belongingness or affiliation needs. Interpersonal relations in organizations can be a primary source of need satisfaction for people who have those needs. For people with a strong need for affiliation, high-quality interpersonal relations can be an important positive element in the workplace. However, when this same person is confronted with poor-quality working relationships, the effect can be just as great in the other direction.

Interpersonal relations also serve as a solid basis for social support in an organization. Suppose that an employee receives a poor performance evaluation or is denied a promotion. Others in the organization can lend support because they share a common frame of reference—the organization's culture, an understanding of the causes and consequences of what happened, and so forth.[3]

Good interpersonal relations throughout an organization can also be a tremendous source of synergy. People who support one another and who work well together can accomplish much more than people who do not support one another and who do not work well together. At AAL, one factor cited for the success of the group-based method of organization was that everyone was committed to cooperation and to making the new approach work. Another outcome, implied earlier, is conflict—people may leave an interpersonal exchange feeling angry or hostile. Conflict is discussed later in the chapter. Still another outcome is the formation of groups, discussed next.

GROUPS IN ORGANIZATIONS

Groups are a ubiquitous part of organizational life. They are the basis for much of the work that gets done, and they evolve both inside and outside the normal structural boundaries of the organization.

Definition of a Group

group Consists of two or more people who interact regularly to accomplish a common purpose or goal

Groups have been defined in terms of perceptions, needs, motives, composition, and a variety of other characteristics. For our purposes, we will define a **group** as two or more people who interact regularly to accomplish a common purpose or goal.[4] First of all, note the similarity between this definition and the definition of an organization. The basic differences are that an organization has a formal structure and its basic activities are work. A group may have a less formal structure and its activities may or may not include work. Three additional elements of the definition of a group warrant special attention. First, at least two people must be involved for a group to exist. A single individual cannot constitute a group. On the other hand, when the size of a group increases to a certain point, usually around twenty members, the group often ceases to be a group in its own right and formally or informally breaks up into subgroups.

Second, the individuals must interact regularly if they are really a group. This interaction need not always follow the same pattern, but it must occur. The necessity for interaction is a primary reason for the upper limit on group size. When a group gets too large, it is difficult for members to interact with all other members. It is more comfortable to interact with only a few of the other members, facilitating the formation of a new, smaller group. Third, group members must have a common goal or purpose. The goal or purpose may range from preparing a new advertising campaign to informally sharing information to making important decisions to fulfilling social needs. A collection of five people riding an elevator is not a group. Even though five people are involved, and even though they share the same goal (moving from one floor to another), they do not interact regularly. By the same token, labor and management officials may interact regularly, but they probably do not have a common purpose. The goal or purpose of the group is a primary factor in distinguishing among different types of groups in organizations.[5]

Types of Groups

In general, three basic kinds of groups are found in organizations—functional groups, task groups, and informal or interest groups.[6] These are illustrated in Figure 14.2.

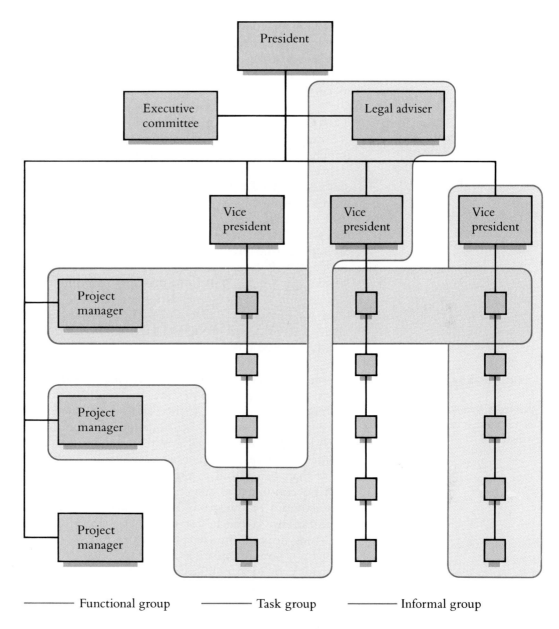

——— Functional group   ——— Task group   ——— Informal group

FIGURE 14.2

Types of Groups in
Organizations

■ **functional group** A group
created by the organization to
accomplish a number of organizational purposes with an indefinite time horizon

Functional Groups   A **functional group** is a group created by the
organization to accomplish a number of organizational purposes with
an indefinite time horizon. The marketing department of K mart, the
management department of Memphis State University, and the nursing
staff of the Mayo Clinic are functional groups. Operative work groups,
autonomous work groups, and standing committees are also functional
groups. The new work teams at AAL are also functional groups. Each
is created by the organization to serve a number of purposes specified

by the organization. The marketing department at K mart, for example, seeks to plan effective advertising campaigns, increase sales, run in-store promotions, and develop a unique identity for the company. It is assumed that the functional group will remain in existence after it attains its current objectives.[7]

■ **task group** A group created by the organization to accomplish a relatively narrow range of purposes within a stated or implied time horizon

Task Groups A **task group** is a group created by the organization to accomplish a relatively narrow range of purposes within a stated or implied time horizon. Ad hoc committees, task forces, teams, and your class are all task groups. The organization specifies group membership and assigns a relatively narrow set of goals, such as developing a new product, evaluating a proposed grievance procedure, or studying the field of management. The time horizon for accomplishing these purposes is either specified (your class ceases to exist at the end of the term) or implied (the project team will disband when the new product is developed). For example, the changes at AAL were based on recommendations from a task force that spent six months studying various options. Once its recommendations were made and accepted, the task force was dissolved. "The Global View" describes how Texas Instruments is using a task group to facilitate its evolution toward becoming an international business.

■ **informal or interest group** Created by its members for purposes that may or may not be relevant to those of the organization

Informal or Interest Groups An **informal** or **interest group** is created by its members for purposes that may or may not be relevant to the goals of the organization. It also has an unspecified time horizon. Recall the company president's schedule provided earlier. The president's lunch group is an informal group. He and his racquetball partner are an interest group. The members of these groups choose to participate rather than being told to do so. An informal group is spontaneous, with no continued existence; an interest group continues over time. The activities of the group may or may not match the goals of the organization. At lunch, for example, a group of employees may be discussing how to improve productivity (relevant to and desired by the company), how to embezzle money (relevant to but not desired by the company), or local politics and sports (not relevant to the company). Time considerations are usually not discussed. As long as the company president enjoys playing racquetball with his friend, he will probably continue to do so. When the game ceases to be pleasant, he will seek other company or a different activity. Further, even though the racquetball schedule is relatively structured, the two partners probably did not initially discuss whether they would or would not play every Wednesday for the rest of their lives.

Informal groups can be a powerful organizational force that managers cannot ignore. One writer recently described how a group of employees at a furniture factory worked to subvert their boss's efforts to increase production. They all tacitly agreed to produce a reasonable amount of work but not to work too hard. One man kept a stockpile of completed work hidden as a back-up in case he ever got too far behind. In another example, workers in an automobile plant described how they engaged

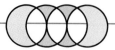

THE GLOBAL VIEW

TEXAS INSTRUMENTS—INTERNATIONAL

Texas Instruments (TI) began in 1930 as Geophysical Services, Inc., to map underground strata and provide other oil-field services. After World War II it was renamed Texas Instruments and continued to develop and produce a wide variety of electronic instruments. In 1958 TI began to emerge as an international organization as it became one of the largest electronics firms in the United States and the largest manufacturer of semiconductors in the world.

TI's early success prompted its move overseas to find customers and suppliers. Until the late 1980s, TI's approach was to encourage managers to develop their expertise in very narrow product or market areas. Little attention was paid to developing corporate viewpoints. This approach worked until the competitive difficulties of expanding international competition increased and conflict became more of a problem.

To become a truly international organization, TI needed to develop a new breed of managers. The jobs of many local managers were redesigned so that the managers had global rather than just local responsibility. TI then moved to require all managers with global responsibilities to meet with one another at least once each quarter to establish a worldwide strategy.

The global managers meet in small groups to de-velop strategy. Managers must hammer out conflicts and produce a detailed agreement specifying how much will be spent on what and where. Conflict resolution requires a lot of interaction and an appeal to the corporate, international viewpoint. When an agreement is finally reached, each participant signs his or her name on a blackboard and an instant photograph is made of each to memorialize his or her commitment to the agreement.

On a day-to-day basis, managers keep in touch with one another through a computerized communications network of over 40,000 terminals in 50 countries. In this way, potential conflicts can be reduced. Now, a plant manager facing overcapacity can locate in the TI organization other units that might be in need of his or her output. More stable production results.

This new level of international cooperation is enabling TI to continue to be profitable despite tremendous downward cost pressures resulting from intensive global competition.

REFERENCES: "What's Behind the Texas Instruments-Hitachi Deal," *Business Week*, January 16, 1989, pp. 93, 96; "Chip Maker to Build Plant Costing $250 Million in Italy," *The Wall Street Journal*, January 11, 1989, p. B3; "The Long Arm of Jerry Junkins," *Fortune*, March 14, 1988, p. 48; "Texas Instruments: Casting a Long Technological Shadow," *Texas Business*, July 1986, p. 30; Brian O'Reilly, "Texas Instruments: New Boss, Big Job," *Fortune*, July 8, 1985, pp. 60–64.

in planned sabotage, such as not welding critical spots, leaving out gaskets and seals, not tightening bolts, and putting soft-drink bottles inside doors.[8] Of course, informal groups can also be a positive force, as demonstrated several years ago when Delta's employees worked together to buy a new plane for the company to demonstrate their commitment. We pay special attention to informal groups throughout this chapter.

GROUP FORMATION PROCESSES

We noted earlier that groups may form as a result of interactions between people. In fact, people may join a group for a number of reasons. Once a group has been formed, it usually evolves through a number of distinct stages.

Organizations use groups in a variety of ways, and people join groups for a variety of reasons. Three groups are shown here meeting together—the Black Officers Council, the Black Agents Council, and the Black Business Resource Group of the Equitable Company. Equitable established the groups as one way to ensure that it stays on track in its Equal Employment Opportunity efforts. Company employees are eager to join because they support the groups' goals of promoting minority interests. Equitable has a workforce of almost 18,000 workers, around 2,000 of whom are black. And 319 of its 5,760 managers are black.

Why People Join Groups

People join groups for a variety of reasons. They join functional groups simply by virtue of joining organizations. People accept employment to earn money or to practice their chosen profession. Once inside the organization, they are assigned to jobs and roles and thus become members of functional groups. Usually, but not always, membership in functional groups precedes membership in task groups. People in existing functional groups are told, are asked, or volunteer to serve on ad hoc committees, task forces, and teams. At AAL, the task group that planned the new organization was made up of volunteers from existing functional groups. People join informal or interest groups for a variety of reasons, most of them quite complex.[9]

Interpersonal Attraction   Perhaps the most obvious and logical reason that people choose to form informal or interest groups is that they are attracted to each other. Many different factors contribute to interpersonal attraction.[10] When people see a lot of each other, pure proximity increases the likelihood that interpersonal attraction will develop. Physical features, especially as perceived by members of the opposite sex, can play a major role in interpersonal attraction. Attraction is also facilitated by similarity of attitudes, personality, or economic standing. Finally, the perceived abilities and usefulness of others affects interpersonal attraction. All of these factors lead in varying degrees to the interpersonal attraction that can result in the formation of an informal or interest group.

Group Activities   Individuals may also be motivated to join an informal or interest group because the activities of the group appeal to them. Jogging, playing bridge, bowling, discussing poetry, playing war games, and flying model airplanes are all activities that some people enjoy. Many of them are more enjoyable to participate in as a member of a group, and most actually require more than one person. Many large firms like Exxon and Apple have a league of football, softball, or bowling teams. A person may join a bowling team not because of any noticeable attraction to other group members but simply because being a member of the group allows that person to participate in a pleasant activity. Of course, if the level of interpersonal attraction of the group is very low, a person may choose to forgo the activity rather than join the group.

Group Goals   The goals of a group may also motivate people to join. The Sierra Club, which is dedicated to environmental conservation, is a good example of this kind of interest group. As another illustration, consider the groups that form to collect money for various charities. Members may or may not be personally attracted to the other fund raisers, and they probably do not enjoy the activity of knocking on doors asking for money, but they join the group because they subscribe to its goal. Workers join unions like the United Auto Workers because they support its goals.

Need Satisfaction   Still another reason for joining a group is to satisfy the need for affiliation. New residents in a community may join the Newcomers Club partially as a way to meet new people and partially just to be around other people. Likewise, newly divorced individuals often join support groups as a way to have companionship.

Instrumental Benefits   A final reason people join groups is that membership is sometimes seen as instrumental in providing other benefits to the individual. For example, it is fairly common for college students entering their senior year to join several professional clubs or associations because listing such memberships on a résumé is thought to enhance the chances of getting a good job. Similarly, a manager might join a certain racquet club not because she is attracted to its members (although she might be) and not because of the opportunity to play tennis (although she may enjoy it). The club's goals are not relevant and her affiliation needs may be satisfied in other ways. However, she may feel that being a member of this club will lead to important and useful business contacts. The racquet club membership is instrumental in establishing those contacts. Membership in civic groups such as Kiwanis and Rotary may be solicited for similar reasons.

Stages of Group Development

Imagine the differences between a collection of five people who have just been brought together to form a group and another group that has functioned like a well-oiled machine for years. Members of a new group are unfamiliar with how they will function together and are tentative in their interactions. In a group with considerable experience, members are familiar with one another's strengths and weaknesses and are more secure in their role in the group. The former group is generally considered to be immature; the latter, mature. To progress from the immature phase to the mature phase, a group must go through certain stages of development. The basic stages of group development are presented in Figure 14.3.

Note first the four basic stages of development—forming, storming, norming, and performing. Passage through these stages represents a general evolution from immaturity to maturity. The evolution varies from group to group, but it is generally a function of time or frequency of interaction. Note also that at any given stage, the group may skip a stage or regress to a previous stage. It is also possible that the group may dissolve at any stage.[11]

■ **forming** The first stage of group development; a period of testing and dependence

Forming The first stage of development is a period of testing and dependence, or **forming**. The members of the group get acquainted and begin to test which interpersonal behaviors are acceptable and

FIGURE 14.3

Stages of Group Development

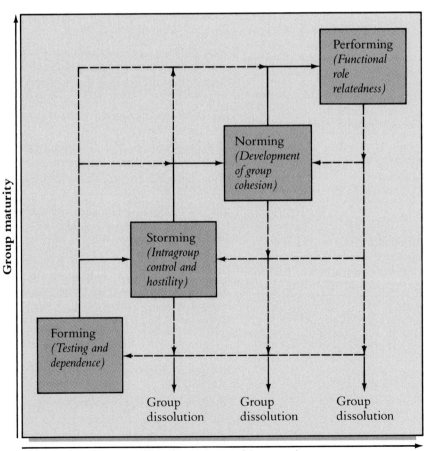

which are unacceptable to the other members. The members are very dependent on others at this point to provide cues about what is acceptable. The basic ground rules for the group are established and a tentative group structure may emerge. At Reebok, for example, a merchandising group was created to handle its new sportswear business. The group leader and his team members were barely acquainted and therefore had to spend a few weeks getting to know one another.

storming The second stage of group development; a period of intragroup conflict and hostility

Storming   Intragroup conflict and hostility, or **storming**, is the second stage of group development. Often members of the group resist the structure that has begun to emerge. Each member wants to retain her or his individuality. There may be a general lack of unity, and patterns of interaction are uneven. At the same time, some members of the group may begin to exert themselves to become recognized as the group leader or at least to play a major role in shaping the group's agenda. In Reebok's group, some members advocated a rapid expansion into the marketplace; others argued for a slower entry. The first faction won, with disastrous results. Because of the rush, product quality was poor and deliveries were late. As a result, the group leader was fired and a new manager placed in charge.

norming The third stage of group development; a period of group cohesion when each person begins to recognize and accept her or his role and to understand the roles of others

Norming   The third stage is the development of group cohesion, or **norming** (both cohesion and norms are discussed in detail later). During this stage each person begins to recognize and accept her or his role and to understand the roles of others. Members also begin to accept one another and to develop a sense of unity. There may also be temporary regressions to the storming stage. For example, the norming group might begin to accept one particular member as the leader. If this person later violates important norms and otherwise jeopardizes his or her claim to leadership, conflict (storming) might re-emerge as the group rejects this leader and searches for another. Reebok's new leader transferred several people away from the group and set up a new system and structure for managing things. The remaining employees accepted his new approach and settled into doing their jobs.

performing The fourth and final stage of group development; a period when the group begins to focus on the problem at hand

Performing   **Performing** is the final stage of group development. The group really begins to focus on the problem at hand. The members enact the roles they have accepted; interaction occurs; and the efforts of the group are directed toward goal attainment. The basic structure of the group is no longer an issue but has become a mechanism for accomplishing the purpose of the group. Reebok's sportswear business is now growing consistently and has successfully avoided the problems that plagued it at first.[12]

CHARACTERISTICS OF MATURE GROUPS

As groups mature and pass through the four basic stages of development, they begin to take on four important characteristics—a role structure, norms, cohesiveness, and informal leadership. These characteristics of mature groups are all important to managers.

Role Structures

roles The parts individuals play in groups in helping the group reach its goals

The word role is commonly used in a theatrical sense. Harrison Ford, for example, plays the role of Indiana Jones in the movies. **Roles** in a group are quite similar. Each individual in a group has a part to play, or role, in helping the group reach its goals. Some people are leaders, some do the work, some interface with other groups, and so on. Indeed, a person may take on a task-specialist role (concentrating on getting the group's task accomplished) or a socioemotional role (providing social and emotional support to others in the group). A few people, usually the leaders, perform both roles; a few others may do neither. Each of us belongs to many groups and therefore plays multiple roles—in work groups, classes, families, and social organizations.[13]

Perhaps the easiest way to introduce the concept of role structures is to describe the development of a role (see Figure 14.4). The process begins with the expected role—what other members of the group expect the individual to do. The expected role gets translated into the sent role—the messages and cues that group members use to communicate the expected role to the individual. The perceived role is what the individual perceives the sent role to mean. Finally, the enacted role is what the individual actually does in the role. The enacted role, in turn, influences future expectations of the group.

Consider the case of a new employee joining a mature work group in a factory. Over the years, the group members have probably set norms for how much each member will produce. Producing too much makes the boss think everyone else is underproducing; producing too little also gets the boss's attention (we discuss norms later). The existing members want the newcomer to accept their norms for production (expected role), and they provide cues like glaring or making comments when the newcomer is working too hard (sent role). The newcomer, however, may interpret the cues as a show of hostility to an outsider (perceived role) and work even harder to become accepted (enacted role). Finally, a group member might openly explain the situation (thus clarifying the sent role), causing the newcomer to better accept the group's norms (perceived and enacted roles).

At each step of the process, of course, distortions may creep in. The group members may choose the wrong messages or cues to commu-

FIGURE 14.4

The Development of a Role

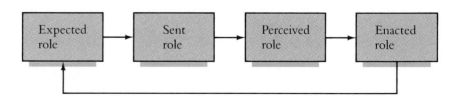

nicate their expectations. The individual may not perceive the messages and cues correctly because of differing frames of reference and experiences (as was the case above). Or the enacted role may deviate from the expected role because the individual does not have the ability to carry out the role or chooses not to do so. The results of these various breakdowns in role development may include role ambiguity, role conflict, and role overload.

role ambiguity   Arises when the sent role is unclear and the individual does not know what is expected of him or her

Role Ambiguity   **Role ambiguity** arises when the sent role is unclear. If your instructor tells you to write a term paper but refuses to provide more information, you will probably experience role ambiguity. You do not know what the topic is, how long the paper should be, what format to use, or when the paper is due. In work settings, role ambiguity can stem from poor job descriptions, vague instructions from a supervisor, or unclear cues from co-workers. The result is likely to be a subordinate who does not know what to do. Role ambiguity can be a significant problem for both the individual who must contend with it and the organization that expects the employee to perform.

role conflict   Occurs when the messages and cues comprising the sent role are clear but contradictory or mutually exclusive

Role Conflict   **Role conflict** occurs when the messages and cues composing the sent role are clear but contradictory or mutually exclusive. A number of different forms of role conflict can occur.[14] One common form is interrole conflict—conflict between roles. For example, if a person's boss says that to get ahead one must work overtime and on weekends, and the same person's spouse says that more time is needed at home with the family, conflict may result.[15] In a matrix organization, interrole conflict often arises between the roles one plays in different task groups as well as between task group roles and one's permanent role in a functional group.

Another form of role conflict is intrarole conflict—the person gets conflicting demands from different sources within the context of the same role. A manager's boss may tell her that she needs to put more pressure on subordinates to follow new work rules. At the same time, her subordinates may indicate that they expect her to get the rules changed. Thus, the cues are in conflict, and the manager may be unsure about which course to follow.

Intrasender conflict occurs when a single source sends clear but contradictory messages. If the boss says one morning that there can be no more overtime for the next month but after lunch tells someone to work late that same evening, intrasender conflict is evident. Person-role conflict results from a discrepancy between the role requirements and the individual's personal values, attitudes, and needs. If a person is told to do something unethical or illegal, or if the work is distasteful (for example, firing a close friend), person-role conflict is likely. This sort of role conflict may also arise for employees with families. Role conflict of all varieties is of particular concern to managers. Research has shown that conflict may occur in a variety of situations and lead to a variety of adverse consequences, including stress, poor performance, and rapid turnover.[16]

role overload Occurs when expectations for the role exceed the individual's capabilities to perform

Role Overload A final consequence of a weak role structure is **role overload**, which occurs when expectations for the role exceed the individual's capabilities. When a manager gives an employee several major assignments at once while increasing the person's regular workload, the employee will probably experience role overload. Role overload may also result when an individual takes on too many roles at one time. For example, a person trying to work extra hard at his job, run for election to the school board, serve on a committee in church, coach Little League baseball, maintain an active exercise program, and be a contributing member to his family will probably encounter role overload.

Implications In a functional or task group, the manager can take steps to avoid role ambiguity, role conflict, and role overload. Having clear and reasonable expectations and sending clear and straightforward cues go a long way toward eliminating role ambiguity. Consistent expectations that take into account the employee's other roles and personal value system may minimize role conflict. Role overload can be avoided simply by recognizing the individual's capabilities and limits. In friendship and interest groups, role structures are likely to be less formal; hence, the possibility of role ambiguity, conflict, or overload may not be so great. However, if one or more of these problems do occur, they may be difficult for the individual to handle. Because roles in friendship and interest groups are less likely to be partially defined by a formal authority structure or written job descriptions, the individual cannot turn to these sources to clarify a role.

Behavioral Norms

■ **norms** Standards of behavior that the group accepts and expects of its members

A second major characteristic of groups is their norms. **Norms** are standards of behavior that the group accepts for its members. Most committees, for example, develop norms governing their discussions. A person who talks too much is perceived as doing so to make a good impression or to get his or her own way. Other members may not talk so much to this person, may not sit nearby, may glare at the person, and may otherwise "punish" the individual for violating the norm. Norms, then, define the boundaries between acceptable and unacceptable behavior.[17] Some groups develop norms that limit the upper bounds of behavior to "make life easier" for the group. In general, these norms are counterproductive: Don't make more than two comments in a committee discussion. Don't produce any more than you have to. Don't hurry to greet customers. Other groups may develop norms that limit the lower bounds of behavior. These norms tend to reflect motivation, commitment, and high performance: Don't come to committee meetings unless you've read the reports to be discussed. Produce as much as you can. Greet every customer with a smile.

Norm Generalization   The norms of one group cannot also be generalized to another group. Some academic departments, for example, have a dress norm that suggests that male faculty members wear a coat and tie on teaching days. People who fail to observe this norm are "punished" by sarcastic remarks or even formal reprimands. In other departments the norm may be jeans and casual shirts, and the person unfortunate enough to wear a tie may be punished just as vehemently. Even within the same work area, similar groups can develop different norms. One work group may strive always to produce above its assigned quota; another may maintain productivity just below its quota. The norm of one group may be to be friendly and cordial to its supervisor; that of another group may be to remain aloof and distant. Some differences are due primarily to the composition of the groups.

Norm Variation   Norms may sometimes dictate role structures in that the norms prescribe different roles for different group members. A very common norm is that the least senior member of a group is expected to perform unpleasant or trivial tasks for the rest of the group. These tasks might be to wait on customers who are known to be small tippers (in a restaurant), to deal with complaining customers (in a department store), or to handle the low commission line of merchandise (in a sales department). Another example of norm variation is that certain individuals, especially informal leaders, may violate the norms with impunity in certain situations. If the group is going to meet at 8 o'clock, anyone arriving late will be chastised for holding things up. Occasionally, however, the informal leader may arrive a few minutes late. As long as this does not happen too often, and as long as the leader is not too late, the group will probably not do anything. People with expert power may also be allowed to violate norms. If a member of a student study group happens to be a friend of the instructor, he or she may be accorded special privileges by the group.

Norm Conformity   Norms have the power to force a certain degree of conformity among group members. The power of norm conformity was first demonstrated in a classic experiment by Solomon Asch.[18] Asch set up a situation in which groups of people were asked to indicate which of three lines was the same length as another line. All the group members except one were actually Asch's confederates—they only pretended to be subjects. When all the confederates agreed on an answer that was obviously incorrect, the real subject went along with the rest of the group more than one-third of the time, even when he or she had already decided to give the correct answer!

Four sets of factors contribute to norm conformity. First, factors associated with the group itself affect conformity. For example, some groups may exert more pressure for conformity than others. Second, the initial stimulus that prompts behavior can affect conformity. The more ambiguous the stimulus (for example, news that the group is going to be transferred to a new unit), the more pressure there is to conform. Third, individual traits such as intelligence determine the individual's propensity to conform (for example, more intelligent people are often less susceptible to pressure to conform). Finally, situational factors such as group size and unanimity influence conformity.

As an individual begins to recognize the group's norms, he or she can do several different things. The most obvious is to accept the norms and subsequently obey them. For example, the new male professor who notices that all the other men in the department dress up to teach can also start wearing a suit. A variation is to try to obey the "spirit" of the norm while retaining individuality. The professor may recognize that the norm is actually to wear a tie; thus, he might succeed by wearing a tie with his sport shirt, jeans, and sneakers.

The individual may choose to ignore the norm. When a person does not conform, several things can happen. At first the group may increase its communication with the deviant individual to try to bring him or her back in line. If this does not work, communication may decline. Over time, the group may begin to exclude the individual from its activities and, in effect, ostracize the person. If the norm is especially powerful and fraught with emotional overtones, physical coercion may even be used. Thus, people who cross union picket lines are occasionally subjected to physical abuse.

Finally, we need to briefly consider another aspect of norm conformity—socialization. **Socialization** is generalized norm conformity that occurs as a person makes the transition from being an outsider to being an insider. A newcomer to an organization, for example, gradually begins to learn the organizational norms about such things as appropriate dress, working hours, and interpersonal relations. As the newcomer adopts these norms, he or she is being socialized into the organizational culture. Some organizations, like Texas Instruments, work to actively manage the socialization process; others leave it to happenstance.[19]

socialization Generalized norm conformity that occurs as a person makes the transition from being an outsider to being an insider in the organization

Cohesiveness

A third group characteristic that is important to managers is group cohesiveness. **Cohesiveness** is the extent to which members are loyal and committed to the group. In a highly cohesive group, the members work well together, support and trust one another, and are generally effective at achieving their chosen goal. In contrast, a group that lacks cohesiveness is not very coordinated, and its members do not necessarily support one another fully and may have a difficult time reaching goals. Of particular interest are the factors that increase and reduce cohesiveness and the consequences of group cohesiveness. These are listed in Table 14.1.

■ **cohesiveness** The extent to which members are loyal and committed to the group; the degree of mutual attractiveness within the group

Factors That Increase Cohesiveness   Five factors apparently increase the level of cohesiveness in a group. One of the strongest is intergroup competition. When two or more groups are in direct competition (for

TABLE 14.1

Factors That Influence Group Cohesiveness

Factors That Increase Cohesiveness	Factors That Reduce Cohesiveness
Intergroup competition	Group size
Personal attraction	Disagreement on goals
Favorable evaluation	Intragroup competition
Agreement on goals	Domination
Interaction	Unpleasant experiences

example, three sales groups competing for top sales honors or two football teams competing for a conference championship), each group is likely to become more cohesive. Second, just as personal attraction plays a role in causing a group to form, so too does attraction seem to enhance cohesiveness. Third, favorable evaluation of the entire group by outsiders can increase cohesiveness. Thus, a group's winning a sales contest or a conference title or receiving recognition and praise from a superior will tend to increase cohesiveness. Similarly, if all the members of the group agree on their goals, cohesiveness is likely to increase. And the more frequently members of the group interact with each other, the more likely the group is to become cohesive. A manager who wants to foster a high level of cohesiveness in a group might do well to establish some form of intergroup competition, assign members to the group who are likely to be attracted to one another, provide opportunities for success, establish goals that all members are likely to accept, and allow ample opportunity for interaction.

Factors That Reduce Cohesiveness   There are also five factors that are known to reduce group cohesiveness. We noted earlier in this chapter that size is an important element in groups and that when size reaches a certain point (perhaps around twenty members), subgroups tend to emerge. In a similar fashion, cohesiveness tends to decline as group size increases beyond a certain point. Second, when members of a group disagree on what the goals of the group should be, cohesiveness may decrease. For example, when some members believe the group should maximize output and others think output should be restricted, cohesiveness declines. Third, intragroup competition reduces cohesiveness. When members are competing among themselves, they focus more on their own actions and behaviors than on those of the group. Fourth, domination by one or more persons in the group may cause overall cohesiveness to decline. Other members may feel that they are not being given an opportunity to interact and contribute, and they may become less attracted to the group as a consequence. Finally, unpleasant

Socialization is generalized norm conformity that occurs as a person makes the transition from being an outsider to being an insider. Genetics Institute, a fast-growing Cambridge firm, works hard to manage the socialization of its new-hires. The new bio-tech firm adds about 100 new employees each year. To help them get better acquainted with others in the company, Genetics Institute holds a party like the one shown here every week.

experiences that result from group membership may reduce cohesiveness. A sales group that comes in last in a sales contest, an athletic team that sustains a long losing streak, and a work group reprimanded for poor-quality work may all become less cohesive as a result of their unpleasant experience.

Consequences of Cohesiveness   In general, as groups become more cohesive their members tend to interact more frequently, conform more to group norms, and become more satisfied with the group. Cohesiveness may also influence group performance. However, performance is also influenced by the group's performance norms. Figure 14.5 shows how cohesiveness and performance norms interact to help shape group performance.

When both cohesiveness and performance norms are high, high performance should result because the group wants to perform at a high level (norms) and its members are committed to working together toward that end (cohesiveness). When performance norms are high and cohesiveness is low, performance will be moderate. Although the group wants to perform at a high level, its members are not necessarily working well together. When performance norms are low, performance will be low, regardless of whether group cohesiveness is high or low. The least desirable situation occurs when low performance norms are combined with high cohesiveness. In this case all group members enthusiastically embrace the standard of restricting performance (owing to the low performance norm), and the group is united in its efforts to maintain that standard (owing to the high cohesiveness). If cohesiveness were low, the manager might be able to raise performance norms by

FIGURE 14.5

The Interaction Between Cohesiveness and Performance Norms

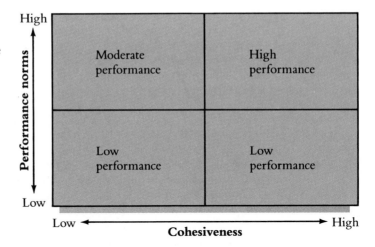

establishing high goals and rewarding goal attainment or by bringing in new group members who were high performers. But a highly cohesive group is likely to resist these interventions.[20]

Informal Leadership

Most functional and task groups have a formal leader—that is, one appointed by the organization. Because friendship and interest groups are formed by the members themselves, however, any formal leader must be elected or designated by the members. Although some groups do designate such a leader (a softball team may elect a captain, for example), many do not. Moreover, even when a formal leader is designated, the group may also look to others for leadership.

A formal leader is one appointed by the organization or officially chosen by the group itself. An **informal leader** is a person who engages in leadership activities but whose right to do so has not been formally recognized. The formal and the informal leader in any group may be the same person, or they may be different people. We noted earlier the distinction between the task-specialist and socioemotional roles within groups. An informal leader is likely to be a person capable of carrying out both roles effectively. If the formal leader can fulfill one role but not the other, an informal leader often emerges to supplement the formal leader's functions. If the formal leader cannot fill either role, one or more informal leaders may emerge to carry out both sets of functions.

Is informal leadership desirable? In many cases informal leaders are quite powerful because they draw from referent or expert power. When they are working in the best interest of the organization, they can be a tremendous asset. Notable athletes such as Larry Bird, Roger Staubach, and Nolan Ryan are classic examples of informal leaders. However,

■ **informal leader**   A person who engages in leadership activities but whose right to do so has not been formally recognized by the organization or group

when informal leaders work counter to the goals of the organization, they can cause significant difficulties. Such leaders may lower performance norms, instigate walkouts or wildcat strikes, or otherwise disrupt the organization.

MANAGING GROUPS IN ORGANIZATIONS

In addition to the general kinds of groups identified and discussed earlier, it is useful to note special-purpose groups occasionally used by organizations. Committees and work groups are two common types. The Japanese approach is also becoming more and more popular.

Committees

■ **committee** A group assembled to make a decision, submit a recommendation, conduct an investigation, or solve a problem

Almost everyone has heard the quip about the camel being a horse designed by a committee. In fact, committees are very common in most organizations, and they offer an effective means for managing group decision making. In general, a **committee** can be defined as a group assembled to make a decision, submit a recommendation, conduct an investigation, or solve a problem. Ad hoc committees, standing committees, task forces, and boards are the most frequently used forms of committee.

Ad Hoc Committees   An ad hoc committee is a committee created for a relatively narrow and short-run purpose, although that purpose may be extremely important to the organization. For example, an ad hoc committee might be appointed by a chief executive officer to evaluate a proposal to merge with another company. An ad hoc committee might also be created to deal with routine problems such as listing new-equipment needs or reviewing employee benefit packages. When its purpose has been fulfilled, the ad hoc committee is normally dissolved.

Standing Committees   A standing committee, as the name implies, is a relatively permanent committee. The membership of a standing committee is relatively long-term and stable. Some standing committees, such as budget review committees, deal with the same set of issues on a continuous basis. Others deal with a variety of problems. One special kind of standing committee is the executive committee, composed of top managers and primarily concerned with strategy and policy. General Motors makes effective use of its executive committee to explore how and why the company has or has not been successful at various activities. The committee reviews all of the company's top managers annually for possible promotion and, if necessary, replacement.

Task Forces   In many ways, a task force is similar to an ad hoc committee. It usually has a relatively narrow purpose and a limited time horizon, but it also has some unique characteristics. First, a task force is generally associated with the integration or coordination of activities between units. Task forces often function to integrate units that are highly interdependent. Second, the membership of a task force may change regularly as new skills and abilities are needed. For example, in its early stages, a new-product-development task force may need production and engineering people to develop technical specifications or cost estimates. Marketing people will become more important later, as promotion and advertising campaigns are planned.

Boards   Boards are a type of committee found in many organizations, especially public ones. Members of public boards may be elected, as are the members of school boards and hospital boards. Government boards, often called commissions, include the Federal Trade Commission and the Equal Employment Opportunity Commission. Most private corporations have a board of directors elected by the stockholders to oversee and guide top management. Some experts have noted that a major factor in Japan's economic success is a high degree of cooperation between management and boards of directors. This view argues that such cooperation is often missing in American industry.[21]

Advantages and Disadvantages of Committees   The advantages and disadvantages of committees closely parallel those of group decision making discussed in detail in Chapter 4, so we will only summarize them here. The advantages of committee decisions over individual decisions include the availability of more information; increased acceptance of the committee's decision, solution, or recommendation; better communication; and (perhaps) improved accuracy of the decision. Major disadvantages are that the deliberations of a committee can be quite lengthy and, therefore, costly; too much compromising may occur; one person may dominate the process; and there is some possibility of the members' succumbing to groupthink.[22]

Work Groups

A great deal of work in organizations is done by various kinds of work groups: operative work groups, autonomous work groups, teams, and quality circles.

Operative Work Groups   The operative work group is used when a group can do a particular job more efficiently than a set of individuals can. For example, the maintenance of a Boeing 747 for Delta Air Lines is best carried out by an operative work group. Each group member has individual responsibilities, and coordination is achieved by means of a common supervisor.

Autonomous Work Groups   As noted in Chapter 8, the autonomous work group generally works more independently than an operative work group. The members may rotate jobs among themselves and are

Work groups are a ubiquitous part of most organizations. The people shown here are a part of an engineering team at Apple Computer. Groups like this one work to identify new products and/or new uses and applications for existing products. Because of these efforts, Apple has remained a major force in the computer industry. And products like the Apple II continue to sell very well, even when they are several years old—a lifetime in the computer industry.

often rewarded for group rather than individual performance. The group leader is seen more as a facilitator than as a supervisor. Organizations that have successfully used autonomous work groups include Volvo and General Foods. The group-based approach to organization design adopted by AAL uses groups that are similar to autonomous work groups.

Teams   Teams bring together functional expertise from several areas to work on a single project. Basically, creating a team involves selecting representatives from appropriate departments (such as finance, marketing, and production) and assigning them to a particular project such as introducing a new product. Teams are the bases of the matrix form of organization design discussed in Chapter 9. They can also be used by nonmatrix organizations for special projects.

Quality Circles   Quality circles are another form of work group being increasingly used in American organizations. Quality circles are discussed in the Enhancement Module "Participative Management" at the end of Part 3.

The Japanese Approach

Most American businesses have adopted quality circles because of their success in Japan, but the Japanese actually go far beyond the use of quality circles to capitalize on the strengths offered by groups. Indeed, the Japanese approach involves using groups structurally in interaction with a well-defined culture based on cooperation and trust between labor and management. In many ways, the methods adopted by AAL are the beginning of this approach. The Japanese, however, carry it further, creating a work environment in which everyone works together in small groups and the small groups working together constitute a large group.

A good example of the effectiveness of the Japanese approach is the Toyota–General Motors' joint venture in California, New United Motor Manufacturing, Inc. (NUMMI). The facility was originally opened and operated by GM but was shut down in 1982 because of quality problems and bad labor relations. Then Toyota entered the picture. The new management came in and trained each of the plant's 2,500 workers in group harmony, trust, and cooperation. A team-based approach to work was developed in conjunction with a new culture. The result? The plant now makes higher-quality Chevrolets and Toyotas than any other GM plant—even better than some Toyota plants in Japan.[23]

INTERPERSONAL AND INTERGROUP CONFLICT

Throughout this chapter, we have addressed a variety of interpersonal relationships that transpire in organizations. Another important type of relationship is conflict. **Conflict** is a disagreement between two or more individuals or groups. Organizational conflict results from disagreement between individual employees, work groups, or departments. The management of conflict is of considerable importance to all organizations. Union Carbide, for example, once sent 200 of its managers to a three-day workshop on conflict management. The managers engaged in a variety of exercises and discussions to learn whom they were most likely to have conflict with and how they should try to resolve it.[24]

■ **conflict** A disagreement between two or more individuals or groups

The Nature of Conflict

Most people assume that conflict is something to be avoided because it connotes antagonism, hostility, unpleasantness, and dissension. Indeed, managers and management theorists have traditionally viewed conflict as a problem to be avoided.[25] In recent years, however, we have come to recognize that although conflict can be a major problem, certain kinds of conflict may be beneficial. Consider the example of two hospitals that disagree over how best to provide healthcare or two manufacturing plants that disagree over how to improve efficiency. As each hospital strives to demonstrate the value of its own approach, the community may realize an overall increase in the quality of healthcare. Or the manufacturer may discover numerous techniques for improving efficiency.

A general relationship between conflict and performance is suggested in Figure 14.6. If there is no conflict, complacency and stagnation may

FIGURE 14.6

The Nature of Organizational
Conflict

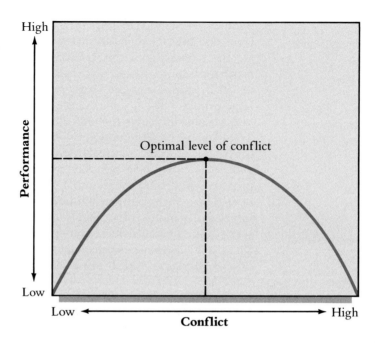

set in, and performance may suffer as a result. A moderate level of
conflict can spark motivation, creativity, innovation, and initiative. Too
much conflict can produce such undesirable results as hostility and lack
of cooperation. The key is to find and maintain the optimal level of
conflict that fosters the highest level of performance. Thus, managers
need to be concerned with the management of conflict within their
organizations. The starting point for management is an understanding
of the causes of conflict.

Causes of Conflict

Many factors cause conflict in organizations. Some of these factors are
the result of organizational design; others are individual or social in
nature.

Group Interdependence   In Chapter 8, we described three forms of
group interdependence: pooled, sequential, and reciprocal. Just as increased interdependence increases coordination problems, it also increases the potential for conflict. For example, recall that in sequential
interdependence work is passed from one unit another. Conflict may
arise if the first group is turning out too much work (the second group
will get behind), too little work (the second group cannot meet its
goals), or work of poor quality. At a Penney's department store, conflict
arose because stockroom employees were slow in delivering merchandise to the sales floor so that it could be priced and shelved.

Differences in Goals   Just like different people, different departments have different goals, and these goals may be incompatible. A marketing goal of maximizing sales, achieved partially by offering a wide variety of sizes, shapes, colors, and models, may conflict with a production goal of minimizing costs, achieved partially by long production runs of a limited number of items. We noted earlier the problems at Reebok when some people wanted to introduce the new sportswear line as quickly as possible, while others wanted to be more deliberate.

Resource Competition   Most organizations—especially universities, hospitals, government agencies, and businesses in depressed industries—do not have unlimited resources. Hence conflict may arise from competition for limited resources. In one New England town, the public works department and the library recently battled over funds from a federal construction grant.

Interpersonal Dynamics   Conflict may arise from interpersonal dynamics. The most general situation is the so-called personality clash—when two people distrust each other's motives, dislike one another, or for some other reason simply can't get along. New management trainees may resent having to learn routine administrative duties, whereas senior managers may believe it is necessary for them to learn the business from the ground up. Some people are extremely competitive, so conflict may arise when two managers are vying for a promotion. There is an ongoing high level of conflict between H. Ross Perot and his old friends at EDS. After Perot sold EDS to General Motors, he eventually resigned and started a new company to compete with his old firm. When he left EDS, he signed a contract agreeing not to compete for a specified time and in specified areas. Perot contends that his new company lives up to that agreement; EDS maintains otherwise. The result has been name calling, insults, lawsuits, and countersuits—with the end nowhere in sight. The strong personalities of the participants have played a major role in their battles.[26]

Managing Conflict

How does a manager best cope with conflict? There are ways to stimulate it in constructive ways, to avoid it before it arises, and to resolve it if it does happen. "Management in Practice" provides a good example of conflict management at Community Benefits Corporation.

Encouraging Conflict   Conflict can often be stimulated by placing individuals or groups in competitive situations. Recall, for example, the number of "disagreements" you have observed between two football, baseball, basketball, or hockey teams. Managers can establish sales contests, bonuses, or other competitive stimuli to spark competition.

Another useful method for stimulating conflict is to bring in outsiders. Such outsiders can shake things up and stimulate a certain level of

One way managers can stimulate positive forms of conflict is through competition. Robert Tasca, owner of a very successful Lincoln-Mercury dealership in New England, divided his service department into six color-coded teams, which compete with one another for monthly bonuses. The bonuses are based on quality of service provided, accuracy of work performed, and customer satisfaction. The Yellow Team, shown here, won almost $6,000 in one year from customer satisfaction bonuses.

conflict. "The Global View" in Chapter 11 describes how the Beecham Group, a British company, hired an American for its CEO position expressly to change how the company did business.[27]

Finally, a manager can stimulate conflict by changing established procedures, especially procedures that have outlived their usefulness. For example, a university president announced that all vacant staff positions could be filled only after written justification had received his approval. Most requests were okayed, but department heads had to think through their staffing needs and a few positions were eliminated.

Reducing Conflict   There are also several methods for reducing or avoiding conflict. One is to expand the resource base. Suppose that a top manager receives two budget requests for $100,000 each. If she has only $180,000 to distribute, the stage is set for conflict. If both proposals are worthwhile, it may be possible for the manager to come up with the extra $20,000 from some other source and thereby avoid difficulty.

Pooled, sequential, and reciprocal interdependencies can all result in conflict, so the manager should use an appropriate technique for enhancing coordination and reducing the probability that conflict will arise. Techniques for coordination (in Chapter 8) include making use of the managerial hierarchy; relying on rules and procedures; and enlisting liaison persons, task forces, and integrating departments. At the Penney store mentioned earlier, the conflict was addressed by providing salespeople with clearer forms on which to specify what merchandise they needed and in what sequence.

Differences in goals can also be a potential source of conflict. Managers can sometimes focus the employees' attention on higher-level, or supraordinate, goals as a way of eliminating lower-level conflict. When labor unions such as the United Auto Workers recognize that they must make wage concessions to ensure survival of the industry, industry

MANAGEMENT IN PRACTICE

COUNSELING IMPROVES COMMUNITY BENEFITS CORPORATION

For much of this century, psychologists have consulted with business organizations on problems with the organization's human resources. Recently, such consultation has often been akin more to family or marriage counseling than to traditional problem-solving approaches. Therapists are increasingly being used by organizations to help resolve conflicts.

The president of Community Benefits Corporation of Richmond, Virginia, and his top branch manager were having problems. They were avoiding each other and harboring secret resentments about one another. When they were forced to interact because of the nature of their work, the interaction was strained and distorted. As a result, the branch manager eventually resigned. The president, however, knew that the organization needed him and so called in a psychiatrist to deal with them both in an effort to uncover their problems and resolve their differences.

The president did not want to lose the valuable experience and talent of his top branch manager, but he was also sure that the manager was not pursuing customers as aggressively as he should have been. The branch manager felt that he was not getting credit for the business he did bring in and was constantly being pressured to do more.

Each man agreed to meet individually with the therapist and then to meet together to see if their differences could be resolved. The individual meetings lasted about five hours each, and the joint meetings were at the therapist's office around a circular table so that no one would occupy a prominent "head of the table" position. The joint meetings began with the therapist summarizing what each had indicated in the private meetings. The therapist then got the two managers talking about their concerns and asked probing questions designed to force them to face the issues.

In this way, each of the executives came to understand better the other's point of view. The president came to realize that he was not reinforcing desired behavior but only attempting to punish undesired behavior and was constantly raising standards. The branch manager recognized that he constantly resisted authority and even ignored or played games with those over him as a way of rebelling. The president and branch manager also began to reach agreements on business issues.

REFERENCES: "Battling Executives Seek Out Therapists," *The Wall Street Journal*, November 7, 1988, p. B1; "The GM System Is like a Blanket of Fog," *Fortune*, Feburary 15, 1988, pp. 48–49; Monika Henderson and Michael Argyle, "The Informal Rules of Working Relationships," *Journal of Occupational Behaviour*, Vol. 7, 1986, pp. 259–275.

survival is considered a supraordinate goal. The immediate goal may be higher wages for union members, but the members realize that without the automobile industry they would not even have jobs.

Another way to avoid conflict is through the management of interpersonal dynamics. A manager who has two valuable subordinates, one a chain smoker and the other a vehement anti-smoker, should avoid requiring them to work together in a confined space. In general, managers should try to match the personalities and work habits of employees in order to avoid conflict between individuals.

Resolving Conflict   Despite everyone's best intentions, conflict is still inevitable in any organization. If it is harming the firm, attempts must be made to resolve it. The avoidance approach is simply to ignore the conflict and hope it will go away. Some managers adopt avoidance because they are uncomfortable when dealing with conflict. Avoidance is sometimes effective in the short run, but it does little to resolve long-run or acute conflict. Smoothing is minimizing the conflict and telling everyone that things will "get better." In many cases, though, the conflict gets worse as people continue to think about it. Smoothing is generally not advisable.

Compromise can work if it is used with care, but in most compromise situations someone wins and someone loses. Budget problems may be amenable to compromise because of their objective nature. Assume, for example, that additional resources are not available, there is $180,000 to divide, and each of two groups claims to need $100,000. If the manager believes that both projects warrant funding, she can allocate $90,000 to each, and the fact that the two groups have at least been treated equally may still the conflict.

The confrontation approach to conflict resolution—also called interpersonal problem solving—involves bringing the parties together to confront the conflict. The parties discuss the nature of their conflict and attempt to reach an agreement or a solution. Confrontation requires a reasonable degree of maturity on the part of the participants, and the manager must structure the situation carefully. If handled well, this approach can be an effective means of resolving conflict.

Some techniques for avoiding conflict may be used to resolve conflict. If conflict arises from incompatible personalities, the manager might transfer one or both parties to other units. If conflict stems from group interdependence, the manager might realize that he is using an inappropriate coordination technique and shift to another.

SUMMARY OF KEY POINTS

Interpersonal dynamics occur throughout an organization. They may be positive and personal, detached and professional, or negative and personal. Several outcomes result from interactions with other people, including need satisfaction, social support, synergy, conflict, and group formation.

A group is two or more people who interact regularly to accomplish a common purpose or goal. General kinds of groups in organizations are functional groups, task groups, and informal or interest groups.

People join functional or task groups to pursue a career. Their reasons for joining informal or interest groups include interpersonal attraction, group activities, group goals, need satisfaction, and potential instrumental benefits. The stages of group development include testing and dependence (forming), intragroup conflict and hostility (storming), development of group cohesion (norming), and focusing on the problem at hand (performing).

Four important characteristics of mature groups are role structures, group norms, group cohesiveness, and informal leadership. Role structures define task and socioemotional specialists and may be victimized by role ambiguity, role conflict, or role overload. Group norms are standards of behavior for group members. Group cohesiveness is the extent to which members are loyal and committed to the group and to one another. Several factors can increase or reduce group cohesiveness. The relationship between performance norms and cohesiveness is especially important. Informal leaders are those leaders whom the group members themselves choose to follow.

Managers can choose to use a variety of specific types of groups to get work done. Several types of committees and work groups each have their own advantages and disadvantages. The Japanese approach is also becoming increasingly popular.

Conflict can be either a constructive or a destructive force in organizations. Conflict can arise from several different circumstances. Managers can stimulate constructive forms of conflict in certain situations. It is also possible to avoid or resolve conflict through the use of several techniques.

DISCUSSION QUESTIONS

Questions for Review

1. What is a group? Describe the several different types of groups and indicate the similarities and differences between them.
2. Why do people join groups? Do all groups develop through all of the stages discussed in this chapter? Why or why not?
3. Describe the characteristics of mature groups. How might the management of a mature group differ from the management of groups that are not yet mature?
4. Describe the nature and causes of conflict in organizations. Is conflict always bad? Why or why not?

Questions for Analysis

5. Is it possible for a group to be of more than one type at the same time? If so, under what circumstances? If not, why not?
6. Think of several groups of which you have been a member. Why did you join each? Did each group progress through the stages of development discussed in this chapter? If not, why not?
7. Can you think of additional guidelines that might be useful in managing groups? Can you think of times or circumstances when the approaches to managing groups presented in this chapter might not be effective?

Questions for Application

8. See if you can locate local organizations that regularly use groups in their operations. What kinds of groups are being used? How are they being used? Is that use effective? Why or why not?
9. Most colleges and universities use committees for many tasks.

Identify several committees at your institution. For what tasks is each committee being used? Is the use of a committee appropriate for all of these tasks? Why or why not?

10. Would a manager ever want to stimulate conflict in his or her organization? Why or why not? Interview several managers of local business organizations to obtain their views on the use of conflict and compare them to your answer to this question.

NOTES

1. "Work Teams Can Rev Up Paper-Pushers, Too," *Business Week*, November 28, 1988, pp. 64–72.

2. See John J. Gabarro, "The Development of Working Relationships," in Jay W. Lorsch, ed., *Handbook of Organizational Behavior* (Englewood Cliffs, N.J.: Prentice-Hall, 1987), pp. 172–189.

3. See Marcelline R. Fisilier, Daniel C. Ganster, and Bronston T. Mayes, "Effects of Social Support, Role Stress, and Locus of Control on Health," *Journal of Management*, Fall 1987, pp. 517–528.

4. See Gregory Moorhead and Ricky W. Griffin, *Organizational Behavior*, 2nd ed. (Boston: Houghton Mifflin, 1989), for a review of definitions of groups.

5. Marilyn E. Gist, Edwin A. Locke, and M. Susan Taylor, "Organizational Behavior: Group Structure, Process, and Effectiveness," *Journal of Management*, Summer 1987, pp. 237–257.

6. Dorwin Cartwright and Alvin Zander, eds., *Group Dynamics: Research and Theory*, 3rd ed. (New York: Harper & Row, 1968).

7. See Gregory P. Shea and Richard A. Guzzo, "Group Effectiveness: What Really Matters?" *Sloan Management Review*, Spring 1987, pp. 25–31, for a discussion of performance in functional groups.

8. Robert Schrank, *Ten Thousand Working Days* (Cambridge, Mass.: MIT Press, 1978); Bill Watson, "Counter Planning on the Shop Floor," in Peter Frost, Vance Mitchell, and Walter Nord, eds., *Organizational Reality*, 2nd ed. (Glenview, Ill.: Scott, Foresman, 1982), pp. 286–294.

9. Marvin E. Shaw, *Group Dynamics—The Psychology of Small Group Behavior*, 4th ed. (New York: McGraw-Hill, 1985).

10. Rupert Brown and Jennifer Williams, "Group Identification: The Same Thing to All People?" *Human Relations*, July 1984, pp. 547–560.

11. For other perspectives, see Connie J. G. Gersick, "Time and Transition in Work Teams: Toward a New Model of Group Development," *Academy of Management Journal*, March 1988, pp. 9–41.

12. Stuart Gannes, "America's Fastest-growing Companies," *Fortune*, May 23, 1988, pp. 28–40.

13. David Katz and Robert L. Kahn, *The Social Psychology of Organizations*, 2nd ed. (New York: Wiley, 1978), pp. 187–221.

14. Robert L. Kahn, D. M. Wolfe, R. P. Quinn, J. D. Snoek, and R. A. Rosenthal, *Organizational Stress: Studies in Role Conflict and Role Ambiguity* (New York: Wiley, 1964).

15. For recent research in this area, see Donna L. Wiley, "The Relationship Between Work/Nonwork Role Conflict and Job-related Outcomes: Some Unanticipated Findings," *Journal of Management*, Winter 1987, pp. 467–472; and Arthur G. Bedeian, Beverly G. Burke, and Richard G. Moffett, "Out-

comes of Work-Family Conflict Among Married Male and Female Professionals," *Journal of Management*, September 1988, pp. 475–485.

16. See Donna M. Randall, "Multiple Roles and Organizational Commitment," *Journal of Organizational Behavior*, Vol. 9, 1988, pp. 309–317.

17. Daniel C. Feldman, "The Development and Enforcement of Group Norms," *Academy of Management Review*, January 1984, pp. 47–53. See also Monika Henderson and Michael Argyle, "The Informal Rules of Working Relationships," *Journal of Organizational Behavior*, Vol. 7, 1986, pp. 259–275.

18. Solomon E. Asch, "Effects of Group Pressure upon the Modification and Distortion of Judgment," in H. Guetzkow, ed., *Group, Leadership, and Men* (Pittsburgh: Carnegie Press, 1951), pp. 177–190.

19. Walter Kiechel III, "Love, Don't Lose, the Newly Hired," *Fortune*, June 6, 1988, pp. 271–274.

20. For an example of how to increase cohesiveness, see Paul F. Buller and Cecil H. Bell, Jr., "Effects of Team Building and Goal Setting on Productivity: A Field Experiment," *Academy of Management Journal*, June 1986, pp. 305–328.

21. P. Bruce Buchan, "Boards of Directors: Adversaries or Advisers," *California Management Review*, Winter 1981, pp. 31–39.

22. Paul D. Lovett, "Meetings That Work: Plans Bosses Can Approve," *Harvard Business Review*, November–December 1988, pp. 38–44.

23. "Hands Across the Workplace," *Time*, December 26, 1988, pp. 14–17.

24. "Teaching How to Cope with Workplace Conflicts," *Business Week*, February 18, 1980, pp. 136, 139.

25. Clayton P. Alderfer, "An Intergroup Perspective on Group Dynamics," in Lorsch, ed., *Handbook of Organizational Behavior*, pp. 190–222. See also Eugene Owens and E. Leroy Plumlee, "Intraorganizational Competition and Interorganizational Conflict: More Than a Matter of Semantics," *Business Review*, Winter 1988, pp. 28–32.

26. "Perot War with EDS Pits Former Friends in High-Stakes Affair," *The Wall Street Journal*, October 6, 1988, pp. A1, A12.

27. Joann S. Lublin, "Beecham's Chief Imports His American Ways," *The Wall Street Journal*, October 27, 1988, p. B9; "Smith Kline Merger Terms Give Control of New Concern to Beecham Chairman," *The Wall Street Journal*, April 13, 1989, p. A4.

CASE 14.1

Groups and Conflicts at the U.S. Olympic Committee

In August 1987, George D. Miller, the executive director of the U.S. Olympic Committee (USOC) stepped down after a bitter two-and-a-half-year battle with the USOC leadership and a series of disagreements with Robert H. Helmick, president of the USOC. Miller had tried to run the organization from Colorado Springs while Helmick had seemed to be trying to run it from Iowa. That duality led to conflict, which eventually ended in Miller's ouster.

Because funding is a major problem for the USOC, Miller had concentrated on raising funds. This effort seemed particularly important because the U.S. Congress does not back the USOC the way other countries' governments back their counterpart organizations. Miller tried to organize a joint marketing-licensing program, but many of the sports groups rejected the idea. He wanted to convert the annual Olympic Festival Games from a small regional event into a major national event to raise funds, but many of the sports groups refused to send their athletes. When Miller warned the sports groups that their participation in Ted Turner's Goodwill Games would make it difficult to get sponsorship for the Olympics later, many ignored his warning and participated anyway. It seemed that all of Miller's efforts were stymied by lack of cooperation, petty bickering, and diverse interests.

After Miller's forced resignation, a search for a replacement was begun in the fall of 1987, and a new executive director was soon named. On January 15, 1988, at the Omni Hotel in Atlanta, Georgia, the USOC was present to hear the introductory speech of that new executive director, Harvey W. Schiller. Schiller spoke with enthusiasm about the importance of the Olympic movement and the role of the USOC, and the crowd of over 150 gave him a standing ovation. He resigned three days later, having served only 19 days on the job.

Schiller's resignation came as a complete surprise. He had seemed perfectly fitted to the executive director's role. The job paid well—$150,000 a year. He had been active in the Olympics—he had been director of boxing competition in the 1984 Summer Games. Schiller's resignation was seen as a silent statement about the almost hopeless mess the USOC was in. It was clear that internal squabbling led to his departure.

The USOC has an amazing structure. It is an organization of organizations. It consists of a large federation of individuals and groups consisting predominantly of volunteers who represent their own organizations. The volunteer portion has 6 officers, a 20-person administrative committee, an executive board of about 90 people, and a house of delegates of 400 or so members. There is also a small group of paid professionals—an executive director and staff.

One of the problems leading to conflict is that these various parts do not communicate on a day-to-day basis or share any common goal. In addition, the house of delegates is basically a majority-rule organization with a wide diversity of interests. It has representatives from state committees from all 50 states as well as the District of Columbia; 40 Olympic/Pan Am sport federations (such as archery, badminton, baseball, basketball, and biathlon); 6 non-Olympic/Pan Am sport federations (curling, karate, orienteering, racquetball, sports acrobatics, and waterskiing); 14 multiple-sport bodies (such as the Amateur Athletic Union, the National Federation of State High School Associations, and the YWCA); and 7 organizations for the disabled (such as the American Athletic Association for the Deaf, the National Wheelchair Athletic Association, and the Special Olympics). These groups all see themselves as representing their own members, not as being members of a unified organization.

All of these groups and the International Olympic Committee (IOC) must be balanced in some way. Needless to say, conflict is almost continuous, and many of the individuals involved are so provincial that appeals to patriotism or to some other lofty motive to resolve conflict is often fruitless. The USOC is a $150-million (or more) business being run by volunteers who have little or no business experience.

Questions

1. What types of groups exist in the USOC? Why did people join those groups? What does this information suggest about the potential effectiveness of a federation of representatives responsible for running the Olympic effort?
2. Have the different groups in the USOC been managed effectively? Why or why not?
3. What is the nature of the conflict in the USOC? What caused the conflict? Cite specific examples to describe the conflict and to indicate its causes.
4. Are the task force recommendations likely to be accepted? Why or why not?
5. Would a new organization resolve the conflicts? If so, what would that organization need to be? If not, why not?

REFERENCES: "If There Were a Gold Medal for Bickering, the U.S. Would Win," *Business Week*, March 21, 1988, pp. 106–108; "Bruised U.S. Olympic Committee Looks Beyond This Year to 1992," *The Wall Street Journal*, February 12, 1988, p. 17; E. M. Swift and Robert Sullivan, "An Olympian Quagmire," *Sports Illustrated*, September 12, 1988, pp. 38–42; Craig Neff, "Not-So-Silent Statement," *Sports Illustrated*, February 1, 1988, p. 7; Gillian MacKay, "Keeper of the Flame," *Maclean's*, February 1988, p. 88.

CASE 14.2

International Conflict at First Boston

Conflict and change are nothing new at First Boston. In the late 1970s, it was an old-fashioned, slow-moving company that was almost failing. Then in 1978 Peter T. Buchanan took over as president. Buchanan transformed First Boston into a major investment banking power. Needless to say, a great many internal conflicts developed as the transformation took place.

In the 1970s, First Boston's CEO, George Shinn, had a vision of the firm becoming an international force in banking. To enact that vision, he started a European affiliate with Crédit Suisse, a large Swiss bank. Shinn promoted Buchanan and brought in a couple of other key executives to emphasize a mergers and acquisition practice so that First Boston would be a full-service investment bank. Buchanan, in turn, named John M. Hennessy, who was a strong contender for a top slot in competition with Buchanan and who was a very different personality type from Buchanan, to head Crédit Suisse First Boston (CSFB) in London to move him out of the way. Both domestic and international operations were highly successful during the early 1980s, but by 1986 things began to change.

In the United States, rapid increases in interest rates brought about more than $100 million of losses in the mortgage-backed securities business in 1986 alone. Profit margins in both stock and bond trading were beginning to narrow, and underwriting competition sliced fees so finely that underwriting almost became a losing business. Fixed-income trading led to several losses, too. Clearly, First Boston was in trouble.

That trouble led to more internal conflict as old-line managers and employees began to clash with the new breed of entrepreneurial managers running the parts of First Boston that were succeeding. Managers on the same level began to try to undermine the performance of one another. Executives and their managerial subordinates began to feud openly. Members of the bond group began to do battle with members of the stock group. When bond trading lost another $100 million in 1987, conflict boiled over into the executive committee. Two groups emerged. One wanted to maintain the firm as a full-service investment bank; the other wanted to make First Boston a more narrowly focused, merchant bank. Buchanan squelched that conflict and insisted on awaiting a strategic review of the firm.

Meanwhile, at CSFB everything was running far more smoothly despite fierce Japanese competition. Hennessy's response to narrowing margins was to search for mergers and new products in global underwriting. As CSFB expanded into those areas, it found that First Boston itself was also expanding in the same way. Conflict between the two international affiliates emerged. The two organizations argued over who would have access to what international clients and who would handle foreign-currency trading and interest-rate swaps.

In 1986 Buchanan began talking about a possible divorce of CSFB and First Boston. Because a breakup would weaken both firms, it was not likely to happen. Further, it would have been extremely difficult to bring about because CSFB owned 40 percent of First Boston. Finally, a divorce might have been disastrous for First Boston because it could have put CSFB's stock in unfriendly hands. By mid-1987, it appeared that the way to resolve the conflict was to merge the two firms.

In January 1988, the strategic review was completed and stated that no major changes were necessary. A number of executives were incredulous, and in February executives and managers who felt that strong change was necessary and who had endorsed the idea of changing First Boston into a merchant bank began to leave. The two top executives under Buchanan resigned and took about a dozen key personnel with them to start their own firm. After that, numerous others also moved to other firms, retired, or went into other kinds of business. As a result, a merger with CSFB seemed even more important as a way to strengthen the firm.

Late in 1988 the merger took place. Despite the fact that merger talks had been going on for some time, the final moves surprised a great many people. The biggest surprise was that the smaller organization, CSFB, became the controlling firm. The Zurich-based bank held 44.5 percent of the equity of the new firm. A management group from First Boston would own only 25 percent, and the remaining 30.5 percent would be owned by a Saudi Arabian businessman, who was to retain that stock until a consortium of Asian investors or a Japanese life-insurance company could be brought into the deal. The new firm would be truly international, solidly based in terms of owners, managers, and customers in the three biggest financial centers of the world—the United States, Europe, and Japan.

Questions

1. What types of groups have existed in First Boston? Why did people join those groups?
2. Were the different groups in First Boston managed effectively? Why or why not?
3. What was the nature of the conflict in First Boston? What caused the conflict? Cite specific examples to describe the conflict and to indicate its causes.
4. Is the new organization likely to resolve the conflicts or will they merely emerge with new twists? Why?

REFERENCES: "First Boston's Slide into Swiss Hands Is Laid to Poor Management," *The Wall Street Journal*, October 14, 1988, pp. 1, 6; "The Merger That Will Make First Boston a Trinity," *Business Week*, October 24, 1988, p. 28; James R. Kraus, "Shake-up at First Boston Corp. Applauded by Analysts," *American Banker*, October 18, 1988, p. 22; "First Boston Sticks to Its Guns and Loses Its Stars," *Business Week*, February 15, 1988, p. 90; "The Assets Walk Out," *The Economist*, February 6, 1988, p. 76.

OUTLINE

Communication and the Manager's Job
A Definition of Communication · The Role of
Communication in Management · The Communication
Process

Forms of Interpersonal Communication
Oral Communication · Written Communication · Choosing
the Right Form

Forms of Group and Organizational Communication
Vertical Communication · Horizontal Communication ·
Communication Networks · The Grapevine · Other Forms of
Communication

Behavioral Elements of Communication
Perception · Nonverbal Communication

Managing Organizational Communication
Barriers to Communication · Improving Communication
Effectiveness · Formal Information Systems

Electronic Communication

CHAPTER *15*

Communication in Organizations

OBJECTIVES

After studying this chapter, you should be able to:

- Describe the role and importance of communication in the manager's job.

- Identify forms of interpersonal communication and cite advantages and disadvantages of each.

- Identify forms of group and organizational communication and cite characteristics of each.

- Discuss behavioral elements of communication.

- Describe how the communication process can be managed.

- Note trends in electronic communication.

OPENING INCIDENT

It was a pleasant summer afternoon in Kansas City. Hundreds of people had gathered in the atrium of the Hyatt Regency hotel for an afternoon tea dance. Suddenly, two bridge-like walkways where people were dancing collapsed on top of other dancers below. The accident claimed the lives of 114 people and injured 216 others. It was one of the great tragedies in the history of the American hotel industry, and many of its causes can be traced to breakdowns in communication.

Because of the tight schedule under which the building was constructed, many design decisions were made at the site by subcontractors. During construction of the walkways two subcontractors made a crucial design change during a telephone conversation. Neither bothered to run a routine stress calculation for the new design. Each one assumed that doing so was the other's responsibility.

Ironically, the project manager had devised plans to keep just such a thing from occurring. He had developed a 27-page guide outlining procedures for making design changes and decisions. The subcontractors, however, failed to follow the written procedures, and the consequences were disastrous.[1]

*A*lthough a number of factors contributed to the Hyatt Regency tragedy, communication problems rank high on the list. Everyone involved in the project was committed to top-quality work, yet several breakdowns occurred. This example underscores both the importance and the fragility of organizational communication.

This chapter explores both managerial and organizational communication. We begin by relating communication to the manager's job. We then identify and discuss forms of interpersonal, group, and organizational communication. After discussing behavioral elements of communication, we describe how organizational communication can be effectively managed and conclude with a brief note on electronic communication.

COMMUNICATION AND THE MANAGER'S JOB

A typical day for a manager includes doing desk work, attending scheduled meetings, placing and receiving telephone calls, reading correspondence, answering correspondence, attending unscheduled meetings, and tours.[2] Most of these activities involve communication. In fact, managers usually spend over half of their time on some form of communication. Communication always involves two or more people, so behavioral processes such as motivation, leadership, and group dynamics all come into play.

A Definition of Communication

Imagine three managers working in an office building. The first is all alone but is nevertheless yelling for a subordinate to come help. No one appears, but he continues to yell. The second is talking on the telephone to a subordinate, but static on the line causes the subordinate to misunderstand some important numbers being provided by the manager. As a result, the subordinate sends 1,500 crates of eggs to 150 Fifth Street, when he should have sent 150 crates of eggs to 1500 Fifteenth Steet. The third manager is talking in her office with a subordinate who clearly hears and understands what is being said. What do these three managers have in common? Each is in a building and has at least one subordinate. How do these three managers differ? Each is attempting to communicate but is achieving different levels of success.

■ **communication** The process of transmitting information from one person to another

Communication is the process of transmitting information from one person to another.[3] Did any of our three managers communicate? The last did and the first did not. How about the second? In fact, she did communicate. She transmitted information and information was received. The problem was that the message transmitted and the message received were not the same. The words spoken by the manager were distorted by static and noise. **Effective communication**, then, is the process of sending a message in such a way that the message received is as close in meaning as possible to the message intended. Although the second manager engaged in communication, she did not engage in effective communication.

effective communication The process of sending a message in such a way that the message received is as close in meaning as possible to the message intended

Three conditions are necessary for communication to take place. First, at least two people must be involved. However, the relationship between these two people can vary significantly in terms of proximity, intensity, and time. Two managers having a discussion in an office engage in communication. So do a student reading a book written 500 years ago and the Renaissance philosopher who wrote it. Of course, many more than two people can also be involved in communication. Second, there must be information to be communicated. And third, some attempt must be made to transmit this information.

Our definition of effective communication incorporates the ideas of meaning and consistency of meaning. Meaning is the idea that the individual who initiates the communication exchange wishes to convey. In effective communication, the meaning is transmitted in such a way that the receiving person understands it. For example, consider the following messages:

1. The high today will be only 40 degrees.
2. It will be cold today.
3. Ceteris paribus
4. Xn1gp bo5cz4ik ab19

You probably understand the meaning of the first statement. The second statement may seem clear at first, but it is somewhat less clear than the first statement because cold is a relative condition and the word can mean different things to different people. Fewer still understand the

Product managers and developers at Kemper Financial Services rely on information provided by David D. Hale (third from left). The economic updates and forecasts provided by Hale, Kemper's first vice president and chief economist, allow managers to plan their investment strategies successfully.

third statement, because it is written in Latin. None of you understands the last statement, because it is written in a secret code that your author developed as a child.

The Role of Communication in Management

We noted earlier the variety of activities that fill a manager's day. Meetings, telephone calls, and correspondence are all a necessary part of every manager's job—and all clearly involve communication. On a typical Monday, Nolan Archibald, CEO of Black & Decker, attended five scheduled meetings and two unscheduled meetings, had fifteen telephone conversations, received 29 letters, memos, and reports, and dictated ten letters.[4] The opening incident provides a sober reminder of how important such communication can be.

As a starting point for understanding the importance of communication in management, recall the variety of roles that managers must fill. Each of the ten basic managerial roles discussed in Chapter 1 (see Table 1.2) would be impossible to fill without communication.[5] Interpersonal roles involve interacting with supervisors, subordinates, peers, and others outside the organization. Decisional roles require managers to seek out information to use in making decisions and then communicate those decisions to others. Informational roles focus specifically on the acquiring and disseminating of information.

Communication also relates directly to the basic management functions of planning, organizing, leading, and controlling. Environmental scanning, integrating planning-time horizons, and decision making, for example, all necessitate communication. Delegation, coordination, and organization change and development also entail communication. Developing reward systems and interacting with subordinates as a part of the leading function would be impossible without some form of communication. And communication is essential to establishing standards, monitoring performance, and taking corrective actions as a part of control. Clearly, communication is a pervasive part of virtually all managerial activities. "Management in Practice" provides another important perspective on the importance of communication and how AT&T is working to cope with it.

The Communication Process

Figure 15.1 illustrates how communication generally takes place between people. The process of communication begins when one person (the sender) wants to transmit a fact, idea, opinion, or other information to someone else (the receiver). This fact, idea, or opinion has meaning to the sender, whether it be simple and concrete or complex and abstract. For example, Linda Porter, a marketing representative at Xerox, recently landed a new account and wanted to tell her boss about it. This fact and her motivation to tell her boss represented meaning.

The next step is to encode the meaning into a form appropriate to the situation. The encoding might take the form of words, facial expressions, gestures, or even artistic expressions and physical actions. For example, the Xerox representative might have said, "I just landed the Acme account," "We just got some good news from Acme," "I just spoiled Canon's day," "Acme just made the right decision," or any

FIGURE 15.1

The Communication Process

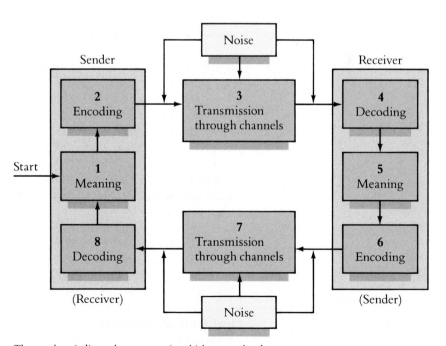

The numbers indicate the sequence in which steps take place.

number of other things. She actually chose the second message. Clearly, the encoding process is influenced by the content of the message, the familiarity of sender and receiver, and other situational factors.

After the message has been encoded, it is transmitted through the appropriate channel or medium. The channel by which the present encoded message is being transmitted to you is the printed page. Common channels or media in organizations include meetings, memos, letters, reports, and telephone calls. Linda Porter might have written her boss a note, called him on the telephone, or dropped by his office to convey the news. Because both she and her boss were out of the office when she got the news, she called and left a message for him.

After the message is received, it is decoded back into a form that has meaning for the receiver. As noted earlier, this meaning may be the same as, almost the same as, or quite different from the meaning intended by the sender. Upon hearing about the Acme deal, the sales manager at Xerox might have thought, "This'll mean a big promotion for both of us," "This is great news for the company," "She's blowing her own horn too much again," or something else altogether different. His actual feelings were closest to the second statement.

In many cases, the meaning prompts a response, and the cycle is continued when a new message is sent by the same steps back to the original sender (steps 6, 7, and 8 in Figure 15.1). The manager might have called the sales representative to offer congratulations, written her a personal note of praise, or sent a formal letter of acknowledgment. Linda's boss chose to write her a personal note.

"Noise" may disrupt communication anywhere along the way. Noise can be the sound of someone coughing, a truck driving by, or two people talking close at hand. It can also include disruptions such as a letter being lost in the mail, a telephone line going dead, or one of the participants in a conversation being called away before the communication process is completed. If the note written by Linda's boss had gotten lost, she might have felt unappreciated. As it was, his actions positively reinforced not only her efforts at Acme but also her effort to keep him informed.

FORMS OF INTERPERSONAL COMMUNICATION

Managers need to understand several kinds of communication. Two forms, oral and written, are primarily interpersonal in nature; thus, we discuss them together here. Other forms of organizational communication are addressed in the next section.

Oral Communication

oral communication
Face-to-face conversation, group discussions, telephone calls, and other circumstances in which the spoken word is used to transmit meaning

Oral communication takes place in face-to-face conversation, group discussions, telephone calls, and other circumstances in which the

MANAGEMENT IN PRACTICE

INFORMATION OVERLOAD AND AT&T

The emphasis on communication in organizations has led to an information explosion. Interestingly, although many experts predicted that computers would reduce the amount of paper used in organizational communication, the reverse seems to have occurred. There is so much information from so many different sources that some organizations are experiencing information overload. Information overload, in turn, is causing information anxiety.

At AT&T, efforts are being made to reduce information overload and the accompanying anxiety. Victor A. Pelson, president of AT&T's General Markets Group, has banned fancy slide-show presentations from the board room and thick, bound reports from offices. Pelson noted that he receives several inches of material every day. Most of that material is of little or no value. Because people can absorb only so much information, Pelson wanted to make sure that the information that employees are exposed to is relevant to the performance of their jobs. One way to reduce paperwork, he said, is to go directly to the source rather than relying on committees and middle managers to obtain, process, and present information to executives.

AT&T has found that the direct approach also works well in communicating with customers. Early in 1989, AT&T announced plans to reorganize to achieve that end. It split into five business groups, which will coordinate the operations of from 12 to 25 business units. Each business unit will have sole responsibility for a product or service; as a result, managers will have a small customer base with which to stay in touch. The idea is to get managers to focus on customers and costs by giving them sole responsibility for profits (and losses) on their products or services.

Experts have suggested ways for managers to reduce information anxiety, too. One is to simply admit that they cannot keep up with everything and accept that fact. Another is to carefully analyze the materials that routinely cross their desks and stop the flow of those that are of no value because they are incomprehensible or irrelevant. Whether one or all of these approaches are used, organizations must somehow cope with the problems of information overload and information anxiety.

REFERENCES: "AT&T to Break Main Businesses into Small Units," *The Wall Street Journal*, February 17, 1989, p. A3; "Information Overload Is Here," *USA Today*, February 20, 1989, pp. B1–B2; "AT&T Says One Vice Chairman to Retire Soon," *The Wall Street Journal*, February 1, 1989, p. B8; Kenneth Labich, "Was Breaking Up AT&T a Good Idea?" *Fortune*, January 2, 1989, pp. 82–87; Richard Saul Wurman, *Information Anxiety* (New York: Doubleday, 1988); "AT&T's Bob Allen Is Pushing All the Right Buttons," *Business Week*, November 28, 1988, pp. 133, 136; "A Future in Information," *USA Today*, April 25, 1989, pp. 1B, 2B.

spoken word is used to express meaning. Henry Mintzberg demonstrated the importance of oral communication when he found that most managers spend between 50 and 90 percent of their time talking to people.[6] Oral communication is so prevalent for several reasons. As summarized in Table 15.1, the primary advantage of oral communication is that it promotes prompt feedback and interchange in the form of verbal questions or agreement, facial expressions, and gestures (we discuss nonverbal communication later). Oral communication is also easy (all the sender needs to do is talk), and it can be done with little preparation (though careful preparation is advisable in certain situations). The sender does not need pencil and paper, typewriter, or other equipment. In one survey, 55 percent of the executives sampled felt that their own written communication skills were fair or poor, so they chose oral communication to avoid embarrassment![7]

TABLE 15.1

Interpersonal Communication

Form	Advantages	Disadvantages
Oral	1. Promotes feedback and interchange 2. Is easy to use	1. May suffer from inaccuracies 2. Leaves no permanent record
Written	1. Tends to be more accurate 2. Provides a record of the communication	1. Inhibits feedback and interchange 2. Is more difficult and time consuming

However, oral communication also has drawbacks. It may suffer from problems of inaccuracy if the speaker chooses the wrong words to convey meaning or leaves out pertinent details, if noise disrupts the process, or if the receiver forgets part or all of the message. In a two-way discussion, there is seldom time for a thoughtful, considered response or for introducing many new facts, and there is no permanent record of what has been said. For example, investigators of the Hyatt tragedy had a difficult time determining what actually occurred, in part because so much interaction had taken place by telephone. After the fact, participants disagreed on what was said, when, and by whom.

Written Communication

"Putting it in writing" can solve many of the problems inherent in oral communication. Nevertheless, and perhaps surprisingly, **written communication** is not as common as one might imagine, nor is it a mode of communication much respected by managers. One sample of managers indicated that only 13 percent of the mail they received was of immediate use to them.[8] Over 80 percent of the managers who responded to another survey indicated that the written communication they received was of fair or poor quality.[9]

The biggest single drawback of written communication is that it inhibits feedback and interchange (see Table 15.1). When one manager sends another manager a letter, it must be written or dictated, typed, mailed, received, routed, opened, and read. If there is a misunderstanding, it may take several days for it to be recognized, let alone rectified. A phone call could settle the whole matter in just a few minutes. Thus, written communication often inhibits feedback and interchange and is usually more difficult and time consuming than oral communication.

Of course, written communication offers some advantages. It is often quite accurate and provides a permanent record of the exchange. The sender can take the time to collect and assimilate the information and

■ **written communication** Memos, letters, reports, notes, and other circumstances in which the written word is used to transmit meaning

Oral communication is a necessary part of many managerial jobs. It is easy, fast, and allows quick feedback. Marci Maniker, vice president, organization development for Great Western, must have good verbal skills. Ms. Maniker conducts employee seminars and answers questions employees may have about company changes.

can draft and revise it before it is transmitted. The receiver can take the time to read it carefully and can refer to it repeatedly, as needed. For these reasons, written communication is generally preferable when important details are involved. At times it is important to one or both parties to have a written record available as evidence of exactly what took place. Julie Regan, founder of Toucan-Do, an importing company based in Honolulu, relies heavily on formal business letters in establishing contacts and buying merchandise from vendors in Southeast Asia. She believes that such letters give her an opportunity to carefully think through what she wants to say, to tailor her message to each individual, and to avoid misunderstandings later.[10]

Choosing the Right Form

Which form of interpersonal communication should the manager use? The best medium will be determined by the situation. Oral communication is often preferred when the message is personal, nonroutine, and brief. Written communication is usually best when the message is more impersonal, routine, and longer.[11] The manager can also combine media to capitalize on the advantages of each. For example, a quick telephone call to set up a meeting is easy and gets an immediate response. Following the call up with a reminder note helps ensure that the recipient will remember the meeting, and it provides a record of the meeting having been called. Recent breakthroughs in electronic communication have facilitated just such actions. As we discuss more fully later, mobile telephones, facsimile machines, and computer networks blur the differences between oral and written communication and help each be more effective.

FORMS OF GROUP AND ORGANIZATIONAL COMMUNICATION

In addition to the two pure forms of interpersonal communication described above, there are other varieties of organizational communication of concern to managers. Each of these involves oral or written communication, but each also extends to broad patterns of communication across the organization. As shown in Figure 15.2, these four forms of communication are vertical and horizontal communication, communication networks, and the grapevine.

Vertical Communication

■ **vertical communication**
Communication that flows up and down the organization usually along formal reporting lines; it takes place between managers and their subordinates and may involve several different levels of the organization

Vertical communication is communication that flows both up and down the organization, usually along formal reporting lines—that is, it is the communication that takes place between managers and their

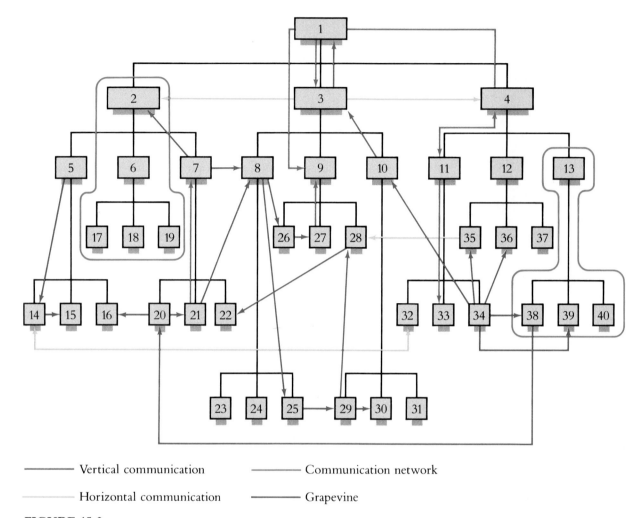

—— Vertical communication   —— Communication network

—— Horizontal communication   —— Grapevine

FIGURE 15.2

Group and Organizational
Communication

superiors and subordinates. Vertical communication may involve only
two people, or it may flow through several different levels in the
organization.

Upward Communication   Upward communication consists of messages from subordinates to superiors. This flow is usually from a subordinate to his or her direct superior, then to that person's direct
superior, and so on up the hierarchy. Occasionally, a message might
by-pass a particular superior. In Figure 15.2, the exchange between
manager 27 and manager 9, manager 4 and manager 1, and manager
21 and manager 7 is of this type. The typical content of upward communication is requests, information that the lower-level manager thinks
is of importance to the higher-level manager, responses to requests
from the higher-level manager, suggestions, complaints, and financial

information. Research has shown that upward communication is more subject to distortion than is downward communication. Subordinates are likely to withhold or distort information that makes them look bad. The greater the degree of difference in status between superior and subordinate and the greater the degree of distrust, the more likely the subordinate is to suppress or distort information.[12] For example, when Harold Geneen was CEO of ITT, subordinates routinely withheld information about problems from him if they thought the news would make him angry and if they thought they could solve the problem themselves without his ever knowing about it.[13]

Downward Communication   Downward communication occurs when information flows down the hierarchy from superiors to subordinates. In Figure 15.2, the communication taking place between managers 1 and 3, 1 and 9, and 11 and 33 is downward communication. The typical content of these messages is directives on how something is to be done, the assignment of new responsibilities, performance feedback, and general information that the higher-level manager thinks will be of value to the lower-level manager. Vertical communication can, and usually should, be two-way in nature. For example, in Figure 15.2, managers 4 and 11 are engaged in a dialogue about something.

Horizontal Communication

■ **horizontal communication** Communication that flows laterally within the organization; it involves colleagues and peers at the same level of the organization and may involve individuals from several different organizational units

Whereas vertical communication involves a superior and a subordinate, **horizontal communication** involves colleagues and peers at the same level of the organization. For example, the production manager might communicate to the marketing manager that inventory levels are running low and that projected delivery dates should be extended by two weeks. Horizontal communication probably occurs more among managers than among nonmanagers. In Figure 15.2, horizontal communication is taking place between managers 2, 3, and 4, managers 28 and 35, and managers 14 and 32.

This type of communication serves a number of purposes. It facilitates coordination among interdependent units. For example, a manager at Motorola was recently researching the strategies and activities of Japanese semiconductor firms in Europe. He found a great deal of information that was relevant to his assignment. He also uncovered some additional information that was potentially important to another department; so he passed it along to a colleague in that department, who used it to improve his own operations.[14] Horizontal communication can also be used for joint problem solving, as when two plant managers at Westinghouse got together to work out a new method to improve productivity. Finally, horizontal communication plays a major role in matrix designs and in committees with representatives drawn from several departments.

Horizontal communication is communication between colleagues and peers at the same levels of the organization. It is most often used for coordination and general information sharing. The men in this photo are the executive committee of Datacraft, a large Australian firm. They meet regularly to discuss how operations in each of their functional areas are going, to solicit ideas for problem solving, and to coordinate various interdependent activities, projects, and programs.

Communication Networks

■ **communication network**
The pattern through which the members of a group communicate

A **communication network** is the pattern through which the members of a group communicate. In Figure 15.2, managers 2, 6, 17, 18, and 19 constitute a communication network and so do managers 13, 38, 39, and 40. Researchers studying group dynamics have discovered several typical networks in groups consisting of three, four, and five members.[15]

Representative networks among members of five-member groups are shown in Figure 15.3. In the wheel pattern, all communication flows through one central person who is probably the group's formal or informal leader. In a sense the wheel is the most centralized network, because one person receives and disseminates all information. The Y pattern is slightly less centralized—two persons are close to the center. The chain offers a more even flow of information among members, although two people (the ones at each end) interact with only one other person. This path is closed in the circle pattern. Finally, the all-channel network allows a free flow of information among all group members.

FIGURE 15.3

Types of Communication Networks

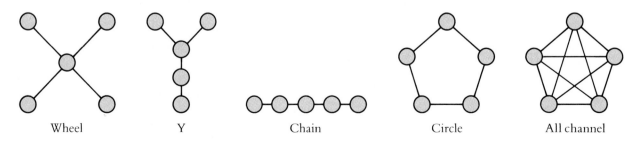

Wheel   Y   Chain   Circle   All channel

It is the most decentralized. Everyone participates equally, and the group's leader, if there is one, is not likely to have excessive power.

Research conducted on networks suggests some interesting connections between the type of network and group performance. For example, when the group's task is relatively simple and routine, centralized networks tend to perform with greatest efficiency and accuracy. The dominant leader facilitates performance by coordinating the flow of information. When a group of accounting clerks is logging incoming invoices and distributing them for payment, for example, one centralized leader can coordinate things efficiently. When the task is complex and nonroutine, such as making a major decision about organizational strategy, decentralized networks tend to be most effective because open channels of communication permit more interaction and a more efficient sharing of relevant information. Managers should recognize the effects of communication networks on group and organizational performance and should try to structure networks appropriately.

The Grapevine

■ **grapevine** An informal communication network among people in an organization

The **grapevine** is an informal communication network. Grapevines are found in all organizations except the very smallest, but they do not always follow the same patterns as, nor do they necessarily coincide with, formal channels of authority and communication. Figure 15.2 illustrates three grapevines. One starts with manager 7, who passes information on to managers 2 and 8. Manager 2 tells no one else, but manager 8 passes the information on to 26, who subsequently tells 27. The second grapevine is short, running from manager 5 to 14 to 15. The third grapevine, starting with manager 34, is considerably longer and more complex.

Research has identified several kinds of grapevines.[16] The two most common are illustrated in Figure 15.4. The gossip chain occurs when one person spreads the message to as many others as possible. Each of

FIGURE 15.4

Common Grapevine Chains Found in Organizations

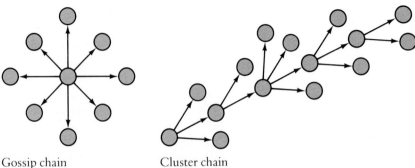

Gossip chain
(One person tells many)

Cluster chain
(Many people tell a few)

Source: Based on Keith Davis and John W. Newstrom, *Human Behavior at Work: Organizational Behavior,* 8th ed. (New York: McGraw-Hill, 1989). Reproduced with permission.

these people, in turn, may either keep the information confidential or pass it on to others. The gossip chain is likely to carry personal information. The other common grapevine is the cluster chain, in which one person passes the information to a selected few individuals. Some of the receivers pass the information to a few other individuals; the rest keep it to themselves.

There is some disagreement about how accurate the information carried by the grapevine is, but research is increasingly finding it to be fairly accurate, especially when the information is based on fact rather than speculation. One recent study found that the grapevine may be between 75 percent and 95 percent accurate.[17] That same study also found that informal communication is increasing in many organizations for two basic reasons. One contributing factor is the recent increase in merger, acquisition, and takeover activity. Because such activity can greatly affect the people within an organization, it follows that they may spend more time talking about it. The second contributing factor is that as more and more corporations move facilities from inner cities to suburbs, employees tend to talk less and less to others outside the organization and more and more to each other.

Attempts to eliminate the grapevine are fruitless, but fortunately the manager does have some control over it. By maintaining open channels of communication and responding vigorously to inaccurate information, the manager can minimize the damage the grapevine can do. The grapevine can actually be an asset. By learning who the key people in the grapevine are, for example, the manager can partially control the information they receive and use the grapevine to sound out employee reactions to new ideas such as a change in human resource policies or benefit packages. The manager can also get valuable information from the grapevine and use it to improve decision making.

Other Forms of Communication

A few other kinds of group and organizational communication warrant note. One that has become especially popular of late is called "management by wandering around."[18] The basic idea is that some managers keep in touch with what's going on by wandering around and talking with people—immediate subordinates, subordinates far down the organizational hierarchy, delivery people, customers, or anyone else who is involved with the company in some way. Bill Marriott, for example (featured in Case 1.1), frequently visits the kitchens, loading docks, and custodial work areas whenever he tours a Marriott hotel. He claims that by talking with employees throughout the hotel, he gets new ideas and has a better feel for the entire company.

Another form of organizational communication is the informal interchange that takes place outside the normal work setting. Employees attending the company picnic, playing on the company softball team, or taking fishing trips together will almost always spend part of their

Some managers have started practicing "management by wandering around"—keeping in touch with people throughout the organization by occasionally walking around and talking to them without a set agenda or schedule. Nolan Archibald, CEO of Black & Decker, is a strong believer in management by wandering around. He is shown here talking informally with a group of Black & Decker assembly line workers packaging the firm's new Air Station compressor. He credits the employees with identifying new ideas for both product design and packaging.

time talking about work. For example, Texas Instruments engineers at TI's Lewisville, Texas, facility often frequent a local bar in town after work. On any given evening, they talk about the Dallas Cowboys, the newest government contract received by the company, the weather, their boss, the company's stock price, local politics, and problems at work. There is no set agenda, and the key topics of discussion vary from group to group and from day to day. Still, the social gatherings serve an important role. They promote a strong culture and enhance understanding of how the organization works.

BEHAVIORAL ELEMENTS OF COMMUNICATION

To a certain extent, the grapevine, management by wandering around, and informal communication are behavioral in nature. In addition to these, however, there are two other important behavioral elements that can be a part of all organizational communication—perception and nonverbal communication.

Perception

perception The set of processes people use to receive and interpret information from their environment

Perception is the set of processes that people use to receive and interpret information from their environment. Perception starts with the five senses of hearing, seeing, feeling, tasting, and smelling, but it also involves awareness, meaning, and interpretation. Perception plays a major role in receiving and decoding the message transmitted by the sender.

Each of us is constantly bombarded with information from the environment. Everywhere we turn we encounter information—so much information that we cannot handle it all. To illustrate, answer the following questions:

1. What color shirt was worn by the last person you saw?
2. What was the last song you heard on the radio?
3. Exactly how much did you pay for the tank of gas you most recently purchased?
4. When you were last watching television, how many commercials did you see?

For managers, the daily barrage of information takes the form of sales forecasts, economic indexes, memos, letters, reports, phone calls, and conversations. As shown in Figure 15.5, perception acts as a filter. It screens out information that is trivial or that we do not want to know. Perception helps us select and organize information in ways that may or may not reflect reality.

selective perception The process of screening out information we are uncomfortable with or do not want to bother about

Selective Perception   **Selective perception** is the process of screening out information we are uncomfortable with or do not want to bother about. In one classic study of selective perception, a group of executives read a case study about a steel company and then were asked to identify the major problem facing the company. Almost all of them identified a problem associated with their own areas of expertise. Five out of six sales managers said the company's major problem was in sales, and four out of five production managers identified production problems. These executives had filtered out information that dealt with other areas and had focused almost exclusively on the information most relevant to their own jobs.[19] Executives at Black & Decker historically "saw" the company as a product-driven manufacturing concern. The new

FIGURE 15.5

Basic Perceptual Processes

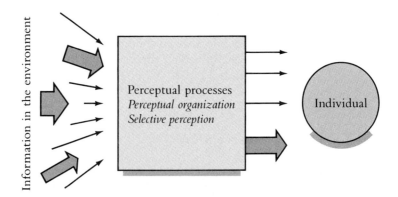

team, however, shifted this perception so that managers now "see" that the company needs to be a customer-driven marketing concern. During construction of the ill-fated Kansas City Hyatt, construction managers probably chose to "not see" guidelines that would add requirements to their already tight schedules.

perceptual organization
The process of categorizing, grouping, and filling in information in a systematic fashion

stereotyping A form of perceptual organization in which the primary means of categorization is based on one attribute of the group like race, sex, or alma mater

Perceptual Organization   As we select and filter information from our environment, we also tend to organize information in some way. **Perceptual organization** is the process of categorizing, grouping, and filling in information in a systematic fashion. The primary means of categorizing information is **stereotyping**—sorting people into groups based on one attribute like race, sex, or alma mater. Whereas stereotyping by race or sex is not a good idea, other forms of stereotyping can be helpful. If we are looking for a person with good public relations skills for an assignment, we may be able to categorize potential candidates into acceptable or unacceptable groups with relative ease. Of course, we also must be sure not to exclude qualified people through such a simplistic approach. We also organize information by grouping it into categories. There is also a tendency to fill in gaps in order to make information more meaningful. Suppose that a manager has started to form the opinion that a particular subordinate is lazy and tries to avoid work whenever possible. One day, the manager observes the subordinate placing three telephone calls and then sitting idly at his desk. The manager may tend to assume that the subordinate is making personal telephone calls and then daydreaming. This assumption may be true, but another possibility is that all the calls were work-related and that the apparent daydreaming was really intense concentration about a job assignment.

There are several important implications that managers can draw about perception. Perception can distort communication at any stage of the communication process. It can add noise to the basic communication cycle and alter meaning and interpretation by the sender, the receiver, or both. It is a crucial variable that can mean the difference between simple communication and effective communication. Later we provide some specific guidelines for avoiding this distortion, but first we need to address another important behavioral element of communication—nonverbal communication.

Nonverbal Communication

■ **nonverbal communication**
Any communication exchange that does not use words or that uses words to carry more meaning than the strict definition of the words themselves

Nonverbal communication is any communication exchange that does not use words or that uses words to carry more meaning than the strict definition of the words themselves. Nonverbal communication is a powerful but little-understood form of communication in organizations. It often relies on facial expression, body movements, physical contact, and gestures. One study found that as much as 55 percent of the content of a message is transmitted by facial expression and body

Nonverbal communication is a powerful force in organizations. Much of what we communicate to others is done through facial expression, body language, and so forth. The man shown here, for example, is having a conversation with another manager. Beyond the words that are being spoken, however, other information is being transmitted through his facial expression, his posture, and other nonverbal signals.

posture and that another 38 percent derives from inflection and tone. Words themselves account for only 7 percent of the content of the message.[20]

Research has identified three important kinds of nonverbal communication practiced by managers—images, settings, and body language.[21] In this context, images are the kinds of words people elect to use. "Damn the torpedoes, full speed ahead" and "Even though there are some potential hazards, we should proceed with this course of action" may convey the same meaning. Yet the person who uses the first expression may be perceived as a maverick, a courageous hero, an individualist, or a reckless and foolhardy adventurer. The person who uses the second expression might be described as aggressive, forceful, diligent, or narrow-minded and resistant to change. In short, our choice of words conveys much more than just the strict meaning of the words we choose.

The setting for communication also plays a major role in nonverbal communication. Boundaries, familiarity, the home turf, and other elements of the setting are all important. Much has been written about the symbols of power in organizations. The size and location of one's office, the kinds of furniture in the office, and the accessibility of the person in the office all communicate useful information. For example, H. Ross Perot positions his desk so that it is always between him and a visitor. This keeps him in charge. When he wants a less formal dialogue, he moves around to the front of the desk and sits beside his visitor. Jim Treybig of Tandem Computers has his desk facing a side window so that when he turns around to greet a visitor there is never anything between them.[22]

A third form of nonverbal communication is body language.[23] The distance we stand from someone as we speak has meaning. In the United States, standing very close to someone you are talking to generally signals either familiarity or aggression. The English and Germans stand farther apart than Americans when talking, whereas the Arabs, Japanese, and Mexicans stand closer together.[24] (Consider the confusion that can result when individuals who are unaware of the different customs regarding distance during conversation try to communicate with each other!) Eye contact is another effective means of nonverbal communication. Depending on the situation, prolonged eye contact might suggest either hostility or romantic interest. Other kinds of body language include body and arm movement, pauses in speech, and mode of dress.

The manager is best advised to be aware of the importance of nonverbal communication and to recognize its potential impact. Giving an employee good news about a reward with the wrong nonverbal cues can destroy the reinforcement value of the reward. Likewise, reprimanding an employee but providing inconsistent nonverbal cues can limit the effectiveness of the sanctions. The tone of the message, where and how the message is delivered, facial expressions, and gestures can all amplify or weaken the message or change the message altogether.

THE GLOBAL VIEW

COMMUNICATION IN THE NEW EUROPE

Europe is changing. The changes began in the 1960s when the European Common Market started people dreaming about a United States of Europe. Finally, in 1992, a great many barriers to communication within Europe will come down, greatly facilitating trade and the movement of people. Most business firms are preparing now for 1992. If events unfold as planned, additional moves to facilitate communication and travel in Europe will take place in the year 2000.

The New Europe, as it is called by Europeans, is the product of a continent-wide economic deregulatory movement. In 1988, about one-third of the regulations that restricted trade within the European Economic Community were lifted. The impact of those changes has been dramatic. In the past, truck drivers crossing four borders and passing through five countries on their way from Holland to Portugal needed hundreds of documents. Because of the new rules, a single piece of paper is all that is necessary. Indeed, the long-term plan is to have a single driver's license and a European passport that will be valid in all European Community countries.

Merging two companies in the same country can be an enormously difficult task because of the possible involvement of different corporate cultures and different communication processes. Mergers across national boundaries that involve different languages are an even greater challenge. Because of the added communication problems, it takes years for such mergers to be finalized, and that is why so many are under way well in advance of 1992. The long-term consequences, however, will be the simplification of communication, perhaps through the adoption of one or two languages for business purposes.

Bringing about the New Europe has not been easy, and extending it further is likely to be difficult. Two political blocs are forming within the European Community. One is a free market group led by West Germany and Great Britain in the north. The other group is led by France and consists mostly of socialist nations along the Mediterranean who favor an *économie mixte*. Bringing about a unified tax structure and a common currency, both of which are essential to a strong economic community, will be difficult unless political problems can be resolved.

REFERENCES: Richard I. Kirkland, Jr., "Merger Mania Is Sweeping Europe," *Fortune*, December 19, 1988, pp. 157–166; "Reshaping Europe: 1992 and Beyond," *Business Week*, December 12, 1988, pp. 48–51; "Will the New Europe Cut U.S. Giants Down to Size?" *Business Week*, December 12, 1988, pp. 54–58; Richard I. Kirkland, Jr., "Outsider's Guide to Europe in 1992," *Fortune*, October 24, 1988, pp. 121–127.

MANAGING ORGANIZATIONAL COMMUNICATION

In view of the importance and pervasiveness of communication in organizations, it is vital for managers to understand how to manage the communication process.[25] Managers should understand how to maximize the potential benefits of communication and minimize the potential problems. "The Global View" provides numerous examples of how political barriers in Europe have long hindered communication and how major changes scheduled to occur in 1992 will eliminate or reduce them. We begin our discussion of communication management by considering the factors that might disrupt effective communication, and then we describe how to deal with them. We conclude with a brief description about formal information systems.

Barriers to Communication

Several factors may disrupt the communication process or serve as barriers to effective communication.[26] As shown in Table 15.2, these may be divided into four classes: characteristics of the sender, characteristics of the receiver, interpersonal dynamics occurring between the sender and the receiver, and environmental factors.

Characteristics of the Sender   Several characteristics of the sender may disrupt effective communication. One common problem is conflicting or inconsistent signals. Another is lack of credibility. A manager is sending conflicting signals when she says on Monday that things should be done one way but then prescribes an entirely different procedure on Wednesday. Inconsistent signals are being sent by a manager who says that he has an "open door" policy and wants his subordinates to drop by but keeps his door closed and becomes irritated whenever someone stops in.

Credibility problems arise when the sender is not considered a reliable source of information. He or she may not be trusted or may not be perceived as knowledgeable about the subject at hand. When a politician is caught withholding information or when a manager makes a series of bad decisions, the extent to which they will be listened to and believed thereafter diminishes. In extreme cases, people may talk about something they obviously know little or nothing about.

Some people are simply reluctant to initiate a communication exchange. This reluctance may occur for a variety of reasons. A manager may be reluctant to tell subordinates about an impending budget cut because he knows they will be unhappy about it. Likewise, a subordi-

TABLE 15.2

Barriers to Effective Communication

Characteristics of the sender
- Conflicting or inconsistent signals
- Credibility about the subject
- Reluctance to communicate

Characteristics of the receiver
- Poor listening habits
- Predispositions about the subject

Interpersonal dynamics between sender and receiver
- Semantics
- Status/power differences
- Different perceptions

Environmental factors
- Noise
- Overload

nate may be reluctant to transmit information upward for fear of reprisal or because it is felt that such an effort would be futile.[27]

Characteristics of the Receiver   Characteristics of the receiver that may impede effective communication include poor listening habits and predispositions about the subject at hand. Some people are poor listeners. When someone is talking to them, they may be daydreaming, looking around, reading, or listening to another conversation. Because they are not concentrating on what is being said, they may not comprehend part or all of the message. They may even think that they really are paying attention, only to realize later that they cannot remember parts of the conversation.

Receivers may also bring certain predispositions to the communication process. They may already have their minds made up, firmly set in a certain way. Consider the recent labor problems between Frank Lorenzo of Texas Air and labor leaders at Eastern. When Lorenzo bought Eastern, the unions assumed they were in for a battle because of Lorenzo's previous anti-union activities at Continental, and Lorenzo no doubt expected problems with the unions because of their earlier firm stands on different issues. Thus, each approached the bargaining table with a predisposition that the other side would be hard to deal with, and each was right.

Interpersonal Dynamics   Sometimes problems develop because the characteristics of a particular sender conflict with those of a particular receiver. Three primary problems of this type are semantics, status/power differences, and different perceptions. Semantics problems arise when words have different meanings for different people. Words and phrases such as "profit," "increased productivity," "retained earnings," and "return on investment" may have positive meanings for managers but less positive (or even negative) meanings for labor.

Communication problems may arise when people of different status or power try to communicate with each other. The company president may not pay much attention to a suggestion from an operating employee, thinking, "How can someone at that level help me run my business?" Or, when the president goes out to inspect a new plant, workers may be reluctant to offer suggestions because of their lower status. Even when two people are of the same status in the organization, power differences can disrupt communication. The marketing vice president may have more power than the human resource vice president, for example, and consequently may not pay much attention to a staffing report submitted by the human resource department.

If people perceive a situation differently, they may have difficulty communicating with one another. When two managers observe that a third manager has not spent much time in her office lately, one may believe that she has been to several important meetings while the other may think she is "hiding out." If they need to talk about her in some official capacity, problems may arise because one has a positive impression and the other a negative impression.

Environmental Factors   Environmental factors may also disrupt effective communication. As mentioned earlier, noise may affect communication in many ways. Similarly, overload may be a problem when the receiver is being sent more information than he or she can effectively handle. When the manager gives a subordinate many jobs on which to work and at the same time the subordinate is being told by family and friends to do other things, overload may result and communication effectiveness diminish.

Improving Communication Effectiveness

Considering how many factors can disrupt communication, it is fortunate that managers can resort to several techniques for improving communication effectiveness.[28] As shown in Table 15.3, these techniques may be used by the sender, the receiver, or both.

Techniques for the Sender   As much as possible, the sender should bear in mind four elements that can improve communication effectiveness—feedback, awareness, credibility, and sensitivity. Feedback, perhaps the most important of these, is facilitated by two-way communication. Two-way communication allows the receiver to ask questions, request clarification, and express opinions that let the sender know whether he or she has been understood. In general, the more complicated the message, the more useful two-way communication is.

Second, the sender should be aware of the meanings that different receivers might attach to various words. For example, when addressing stockholders, a manager might use the word "profits" often. When addressing labor leaders, however, she may choose to use "profits" less

TABLE 15.3

Improving Communication
Effectiveness

Techniques for the sender
- Encourage two-way communication
- Be aware of language and meaning
- Maintain credibility
- Be sensitive to the receiver's perspective

Techniques for the receiver
- Develop listening skills
- Be sensitive to the sender's perspective

Techniques for both sender and receiver
- Follow up
- Regulate information flow
- Understand the richness of media

often. Third, the sender should try to maintain credibility. This can be accomplished by not pretending to be an expert when one is not, by "doing one's homework" and checking facts, and by otherwise being as accurate and honest as possible.

Finally, the sender should try to be sensitive to the receiver's perspective. A manager who must tell a subordinate that she has not been recommended for a promotion should recognize that the subordinate will be frustrated and unhappy. The content of the message and its method of delivery should be chosen accordingly. The manager should be primed to accept a reasonable degree of hostility and bitterness without getting angry in return.[29]

Techniques for the Receiver There are two especially good techniques that managers can use to develop their effectiveness as receivers—being a good listener and being sensitive to the sender's perspective. Being a good listener requires that the individual be prepared to listen, not interrupt the speaker, concentrate on both the words and the meaning being conveyed, be patient, and ask questions as appropriate.[30] So important are good listening skills that companies like Delta, IBM, and Unisys conduct programs to train their managers to be better listeners.

Another technique for the receiver is to be sensitive to the sender's point of view. Suppose that a manager has just received some bad news—for example, that his position is being eliminated next year. Others should understand that he may be disappointed, angry, or even depressed for a while. Thus, they might make a special effort not to take too much offense if he snaps at them, and they might look for signals that he needs someone to talk to.

Techniques for Both Sender and Receiver Three useful ideas can enhance communication effectiveness for both the sender and the receiver—following up, regulating information flow, and understanding the richness of different media. Following up simply involves checking at a later time to be sure that a message has been received and understood. After a manager mails a report to a colleague, she might call a few days later to make sure the report has arrived. If it has, the manager might ask whether the colleague has any questions about it. Of course, carrying this practice to an extreme can become a problem in itself.

Regulating information flow means that the sender or receiver takes steps to ensure that overload does not occur. For the sender, this could mean not passing too much information through the system at one time. For the receiver, it might mean calling attention to the fact that he is being asked to do too many things at once. Many managers limit the influx of information by periodically weeding out the list of journals and routine reports they receive, or they train a secretary to screen phone calls and visitors.

Both parties should also understand the richness associated with different media. When a manager is going to lay off a subordinate temporarily, the message should be delivered in person. A face-to-face channel of communication gives the manager an opportunity to explain the situation and answer questions. When the purpose of the message is to grant a pay increase, written communication may be appropriate because it can be more objective and precise. The manager could then follow up the written notice with personal congratulations.

Formal Information Systems

Another increasingly important method for managing organizational communication is through the use of formal information systems. This is accomplished by a managerial approach or an operational approach. The managerial approach involves the creation of a position usually called the chief information officer, or CIO.[31] Unisys, General Mills, and Burlington Industries are firms that have created such a position. The CIO is responsible for developing a keen understanding of the information-processing needs and requirements of the organization and then putting in place systems that facilitate smooth and efficient organizational communication.

The operational approach, often a part of the CIO's efforts, involves the creation of one or more formal information systems linking all relevant managers, departments, and facilities in the organization. In the absence of such a system, a marketing manager, for example, may need to call a warehouse manager to find out how much of a particular product is in stock before promising shipping dates to a customer. An effective formal information system allows the marketing manager to get the information more quickly, and probably more accurately, by plugging directly into a computerized information system. Because of the increased emphasis and importance of these kinds of information systems, we cover them in detail in Chapter 18.

ELECTRONIC COMMUNICATION

In recent years, the nature of managerial and organizational communication has changed dramatically, mainly because of breakthroughs in electronic communication capabilities, and the future promises even more change. Electronic typewriters and photocopying machines were early breakthroughs. The photocopier, for example, makes it possible for a manager to have a typed report distributed to large numbers of other people in an extremely short time. Computers have accelerated the process even more.

It is now possible to have teleconferences in which managers stay at their own locations (such as offices in different cities) but are seen on television monitors as they "meet."[32] A manager in New York can type a letter or memorandum into a terminal, push a few buttons, and have it printed out in San Francisco. Highly detailed information can be retrieved with ease from large electronic databanks. This has given rise to a new version of an old work arrangement—telecommuting is the

Electronic communication is becoming more and more a part of the contemporary management landscape. A. L. Williams insurance company, for example, uses a private television network to help its managers keep in touch throughout its 1,000 branches. The control room for "Monday Morning Management" is similar to the ones used for other big productions. Until just recently, Williams used videotaped messages to transmit information to workers. Although still a new technology, videotapes are already becoming obsolete in some quarters. Thus Williams turned to live television to keep his messages even more current and enjoyable. How is it working? Williams currently has the largest annual sales in the life-insurance industry.

label given to a new electronic cottage industry. In a cottage industry, people work at home (in their cottages) and periodically bring the product of their labor in to the company. In telecommuting, people work at home on their computers and transmit their work to the company by means of telephone modems. For example, David L. Hoffman, a partner in a Chicago law firm, lives in Telluride, Colorado. He consults with clients over the phone, sends them reports through the telephone lines with his modem or by Federal Express, and has calls to his Chicago office electronically routed to Telluride. Recent estimates suggest that as many as 7 million Americans use telephones, computers, and couriers to work outside their conventional offices.[33]

Cellular telephones and facsimile machines have made it even easier for managers to communicate with one another. Many now use cellular phones to make calls while commuting to and from work and carry them in briefcases so they can receive calls while at lunch. Facsimile machines make it easy for people to use written communication media and get rapid feedback.

Psychologists, however, are beginning to associate some problems with these communication advances. For one thing, managers who, like David Hoffman, are seldom in their "real" offices are likely to fall behind in their fields and to be victimized by organizational politics because they are not present to keep in touch with what's going on and to protect themselves. They drop out of the organizational grapevine and miss out on much of the informal communication that takes place. Moreover, the use of electronic communication at the expense of face-to-face meetings and conversations makes it hard to build a strong culture, develop solid working relationships, and create a mutually supportive atmosphere of trust and cooperativeness.[34]

SUMMARY OF KEY POINTS

Communication is the process of transmitting information from one person to another. Effective communication is the process of sending a message in such a way that the message received is as close in meaning as possible to the message intended. Communication is a pervasive and important part of the manager's world. The communication process consists of a sender encoding meaning and transmitting it to one or more receivers, who receive the message and decode it into meaning. In two-way communication the process continues with the roles reversed. Noise can disrupt any part of the overall process.

Interpersonal communication focuses on communication among a small number of people. Two important forms of interpersonal communication, oral and written, both offer unique advantages and disadvantages. Thus, the manager should weigh the pros and cons of each when choosing a medium for communication.

There are a variety of forms of organizational communication. Vertical communication between superiors and subordinates may flow upward or downward, although two-way communication is generally preferable. Horizontal communication involves peers and colleagues at the same level in the organization. Communication networks are recurring patterns of communication among members of a group. The grapevine is the informal communication network among people in an organization.

Two behavioral elements of communication are perception and nonverbal communication. Perception consists of the processes that individuals use to receive and interpret information from the environment. Selective perception and perceptual organization are important elements of perception. Nonverbal communication includes facial expressions, body movement, physical contact, gestures, and inflection and tone.

Managing the communication process necessitates recognizing the barriers to effective communication and understanding how to overcome them. It is possible for both sender and receiver to learn and practice effective techniques for improving communication. Organizations also use both managerial and operational approaches to managing communication.

Electronic communications, represented by computer networks, word-processing systems, cellular telephones, facsimile machines, and the like, are likely to have a profound effect on managerial and organizational communication in the years to come.

DISCUSSION QUESTIONS

Questions for Review

1. Define communication. What are the components of the communication process?
2. Which form of interpersonal communication is best for long-term

retention? Why? Which form is best for getting across subtle nuances of meaning? Why?

3. Describe three different communication networks. Which type of network seems to most accurately describe the grapevine? Why?

4. What are the behavioral elements of communication? Identify five examples of nonverbal communication that you have recently observed.

Questions for Analysis

5. Is it possible for an organization to function without communication? Why or why not?

6. At what points in the communication process can problems occur? Give examples of communication problems and indicate how they might be prevented or alleviated.

7. In terms of the barriers most likely to be encountered, what are the differences between horizontal and vertical communication in an organization? How might a formal information system be designed to reduce such barriers?

Questions for Application

8. What forms of communication have you experienced today? What form of communication is involved in a face-to-face conversation with a friend? A telephone call from a customer? A traffic light or crossing signal? A picture of a cigarette in a circle with a slash across it? An area around machinery defined by a yellow line painted on the floor?

9. Interview a local manager to determine what forms of communication are used in his or her organization. Arrange to observe that manager for a couple of hours. What forms of communication did you observe?

10. How are electronic communication devices likely to affect the communication process in the future? Why? Interview someone from a local organization who uses electronic communications to see if she or he feels as you do.

NOTES

1. Mary Scoviak, "After 30 Years, Risk-taking Remains a Hyatt Trademark," *Hotels and Restaurants International*, May 1987, pp. 54–60; and Courtland L. Bovée and John V. Thill, *Business Communication Today* (New York: Random House, 1986).

2. Henry Mintzberg, *The Nature of Managerial Work* (New York: Harper & Row, 1973).

3. See Karl E. Weick and Larry D. Browning, "Argument and Narration in Organizational Communication," *Journal of Management*, Summer 1986, pp. 243–259.

4. John Huey, "The New Power in Black & Decker," *Fortune*, January 2, 1989, pp. 89–94.

5. Mintzberg, *The Nature of Managerial Work*.

6. Mintzberg, *The Nature of Managerial Work*.

7. Walter Kiechel III, "The Big Presentation," *Fortune*, July 26, 1982, pp. 98–100.

8. Mintzberg, *The Nature of Managerial Work*.

9. Kiechel, "The Big Presentation."

10. Bovée and Thill, *Business Communication Today*, p. 147.

11. Robert H. Lengel and Richard L. Daft, "The Selection of Communication Media as an Executive Skill," *The Academy of Management Executive*, August 1988, pp. 225–232.

12. Michael J. Glauser, "Upward Information Flow in Organizations: Review and Conceptual Analysis," *Human Relations*, August 1984, pp. 613–644.

13. Myron Magnet, "Is ITT Fighting Shadows—Or Raiders?" *Fortune*, November 11, 1985, pp. 25–28.

14. Brian Dumaine, "Corporate Spies Snoop to Conquer," *Fortune*, November 7, 1988, pp. 68–76.

15. A. Vavelas, "Communication Patterns in Task-oriented Groups," *Journal of the Accoustical Society of America*, Vol. 22, 1950, pp. 725–730; Jerry Wofford, Edwin Gerloff, and Robert Cummins, *Organizational Communication* (New York: McGraw-Hill, 1977).

16. Keith Davis, "Management Communication and the Grapevine," *Harvard Business Review*, September–October 1953, pp. 43–49.

17. "Spread the Word: Gossip Is Good," *The Wall Street Journal*, October 4, 1988, p. B1.

18. See Tom Peters and Nancy Austin, *A Passion for Excellence* (New York: Random House, 1985).

19. D. C. Dearborn and H. A. Simon, "Selective Perception: A Note on the Departmental Identification of Executives," *Sociometry*, Vol. 21, 1958, pp. 140–144.

20. Albert Mehrabian, *Non-verbal Communication* (Chicago: Aldine, 1972).

21. Michael B. McCaskey, "The Hidden Messages Managers Send," *Harvard Business Review*, November–December 1979, pp. 135–148.

22. Thomas Moore, "Make-or-Break Time for General Motors," *Fortune*, February 15, 1988, pp. 32–42; Brian O'Reilly, "How Jimmy Treybig Turned Tough," *Fortune*, May 25, 1987, pp. 102–104.

23. David Givens, "What Body Language Can Tell You That Words Cannot," *U.S. News & World Report*, November 19, 1984, p. 100.

24. Edward J. Hall, *The Hidden Dimension* (New York: Doubleday, 1966).

25. For a detailed discussion of improving communication effectiveness, see Courtland L. Bovée and John V. Thill, *Business Communication Today*, 2nd ed. (New York: Random House, 1989).

26. See Otis W. Baskin and Craig E. Aronoff, *Interpersonal Communication in Organizations* (Glenview, Ill.: Scott, Foresman, 1980).

27. M. P. Rowe and M. Baker, "Are You Hearing Enough Employee Concerns?" *Harvard Business Review*, November–December, 1984, pp. 127–133.

28. Joseph Allen and Bennett P. Lientz, *Effective Business Communication* (Santa Monica, Calif.: Goodyear, 1979).

29. For a recent discussion of these and related issues, see Eric M. Eisenberg and Marsha G. Witten, "Reconsidering Openness in Organizational Communication," *Academy of Management Review*, July 1987, pp. 418–426.

30. Walter Kiechel III, "Learn How to Listen," *Fortune*, August 17, 1987, pp. 107–108.

31. John J. Donovan, "Beyond Chief Information Officer to Network Manager," *Harvard Business Review*, September–October 1988, pp. 134–140.

32. Robert Johansen and Christine Bullen, "What to Expect from Teleconferencing," *Harvard Business Review*, March–April 1984, pp. 164–174. See also Richard C. Huseman and Edward W. Miles, "Organizational Communication in the Information Age: Implications of Computer-Based Systems," *Journal of Management*, June 1988, pp. 181–204.

33. "These Top Executives Work Where They Play," *Business Week*, October 27, 1986, pp. 132–134. See also "Escape from the Office," *Newsweek*, April 24, 1989, pp. 58–60.

34. Walter Kiechel III, "Hold for the Communicaholic Manager," *Fortune*, January 2, 1989, pp. 107–108.

CASE 15.1

Top-Level Communication Problems at Texaco

Communication between shareholders and the top executives of a firm is generally casual and infrequent at best. There are times, however, when relations between these two groups sour. At such times, communication usually deteriorates, although that is exactly the time when communication should be increased and improved. The late 1980s was just such a time for Texaco.

Texaco was founded in 1902 by Joseph Cullinan, a former employee of Standard Oil. When Standard Oil of California (Socal) found more oil in Saudi Arabia than it knew what to do with, Cullinan formed a joint venture with Socal. Called Caltex, it soon became a major force in marketing oil throughout the world.

During the late 1980s, corporate raider Carl Icahn charged that Texaco was acting in a way that was not in the best interests of its shareholders. He set out to gain sufficient control of the company to correct what he saw as major problems within the organization. The battle between Icahn and Texaco began with events in the mid-1980s.

As oil production began to decline during the 1970s, the major oil companies began to seek additional reserves. Texaco was not very successful in adding to its reserves through drilling. Instead, Texaco bought the Getty Petroleum Corporation for just over $10 billion and immediately doubled its reserves. However, Pennzoil believed that it had a prior agreement to buy part of Getty and sued to block the sale. A jury in Houston, Texas, agreed with Pennzoil and awarded it an $11 billion settlement. Rather than pay, Texaco elected to appeal in court.

In order to avoid a multi-billion-dollar bond, Texaco had to file for bankruptcy. Bankruptcy protection came at a high price, however. The judge who became the final authority over Texaco decided that a committee of shareholders should be put in charge of Texaco's dealings because it was Texaco's shareholders who were at risk in the proceedings. Texaco's CEO, James W. Kinnear, rejected several settlement schemes with Pennzoil; so the bankruptcy judge had the shareholders committee negotiate with Pennzoil. The committee reached a settlement for $3 billion.

Carl Icahn, chairman of TWA and a major Texaco shareholder, suddenly had the perfect opportunity to push for change—and push he did. He suggested that Texaco sell about $10 billion worth of its assets in a major restructuring of the company and distribute most of the cash to the shareholders. Kinnear tried for a long time to negotiate with Icahn, but they could not agree. To increase pressure on Kinnear, Icahn launched a proxy fight to obtain more voting shares of the company. As Texaco emerged from bankruptcy protection, Icahn offered to buy the company at $60 a share in cash when its going market price was only $46 a share. The board of directors voted against Icahn's offer without consulting the shareholders.

Suddenly, shareholders were virtually shouting for attention, and Kinnear woke up to the fact that management's relations with the shareholders had changed. He began to actively work at communicating with them. In the past, Texaco's shareholders were a small, disorganized group of individuals interested in dividends, not stock prices. By the 1980s, 40 percent of Texaco's shareholders were institutions and investors interested almost exclusively in stock prices. Kinnear began to talk with those institutional investors to see what they wanted and to build a coalition to keep Icahn at bay. Kinnear had to promise to distribute nearly $2 billion to shareholders, change Texaco's strategies for dealing with raiders, and eventually to put a representative of the institutional investors on Texaco's board of directors.

To ensure that shareholders' interests are well served, Kinnear is trying to change Texaco's corporate culture. He is giving speeches to employees about the importance of providing high returns to owners. Managers are being held accountable for profit performance, and their pay will be directly linked to that performance. He is telling workers to "just say no" when their bosses require make-work of them (although few report doing so). Kinnear has changed most of the top executives in the company and reduced the number of organizational levels by half in a move to decentralize decision making and push responsibility to lower levels of the organization.

Questions

1. Use the model of the communication process presented in Figure 15.1 to describe communication between Texaco and its shareholders both before and after the bankruptcy. In which situation was communication more effective? Why?
2. What role did perception play in the communication described in this case?
3. What were some of the barriers to effective communication at Texaco? How could they have been overcome?
4. Think about the long-term impact of Kinnear's actions. Would you invest money in Texaco? Why or why not?

REFERENCES: Stratford P. Sherman, "Who's in Charge at Texaco Now?" *Fortune*, January 16, 1989, pp. 69–72; "Please, Carl, We'd Rather Do It Ourselves," *Business Week*, January 25, 1988, pp. 54–55; "Texaco and Icahn Hurl Last Gibes and Prepare to Meet Their Holders," *The Wall Street Journal*, June 13, 1988, pp. 1, 6; "Wild Days for Texaco's Market Maker," *The Wall Street Journal*, May 31, 1988, p. 26; "Texaco's Chiefs Battle to Revitalize the Firm and Repulse Raiders," *The Wall Street Journal*, June 13, 1988, pp. 1, 6; Milton Moskowitz, Michael Katz, and Robert Levering, eds., *Everybody's Business* (San Francisco: Harper & Row, 1982), pp. 539–541; "Jim Kinnear is Pumping New Life Into Texaco," *Business Week*, April 17, 1989, pp. 50–52.

CASE 15.2

Communication Key to Unilever's Success

Unilever is the largest consumer products, or packaged-goods, company in the world. Its sales are about double those of Procter & Gamble and nearly five times those of Colgate-Palmolive. Lever Brothers, its American subsidiary, has not performed as well as many of the other subsidiaries in the organization, although recent efforts have strengthened its performance. Because Unilever is based jointly in London and Rotterdam, Unilever has two chairmen, two headquarters, and two sets of shareholders. International law defines the two units as separate businesses, but they operate as one and have demonstrated an almost amazing ability to communicate effectively with each other.

Effective communication starts at the top with the two chairmen—Floris Maljers and Michael Angus. They communicate and reach joint decisions by what Angus terms "a sitting together." They are well aware that this arrangement could slow decision making or paralyze it if a major disagreement occurred. Because of their awareness, they work hard to communicate well. As a result, the process works smoothly and swiftly. So well does it work that in 1987 Unilever was able to act as a white knight for Chesebrough-Pond's, fighting off American Brands in an acquisition battle.

During the 1970s, Unilever's sales had grown at a slow rate and earnings had begun to weaken. Some subsidiary businesses that were too far afield from its main packaged-goods business were sold. Lever Brothers in the United States was particularly sluggish, and Michael Angus took charge in an effort to shape it up. He revitalized existing products such as Lifebuoy and Wisk with major advertising campaigns. He introduced several successful new products such as Sunlight dishwashing detergent and Snuggle fabric softener. He also strengthened the margarine business by subcontracting production to Beatrice Foods—an arrangement that enabled Lever Brothers to cut costs and boost advertising to become the second-largest producer of margarine in the United States. Those moves greatly improved the earnings of Lever Brothers and, because a Briton was in charge, improved communication between the U.S. operations and Unilever's main offices in London. This change was particularly important because no expatriate manager of any importance had worked with Lever Brothers for many years, and the lack of effective communication between Lever Brothers and the London office had become at least part of its problem.

The complete Unilever organization consists of 200 individually defined subsidiaries doing business in 75 countries. Managers in the subsidiaries have high levels of authority to run their own businesses as autonomous companies. Unilever maintains appropriate levels of communication and contact between the corporate headquarters and foreign affiliates. It regularly rotates corporate-level managers through its various units around the globe to maintain communication among the various units and between the units and corporate headquarters. This procedure ensures that subsidiary managers maintain an identity with and appreciation for the parent corporation.

Unilever's successful acquisition of Chesebrough-Pond's helped make up for its unsuccessful attempt to take over Richardson-Vicks in 1985. Building on the momentum of that successful acquisition, late in 1988 Unilever bought Durkee Industrial Foods Corporation from Hanson Industries Inc., the American branch of Hanson PLC, a British conglomerate. Durkee, based in Cleveland, Ohio, makes vegetable and specialty oils, frozen bakery products, and confectionery coatings that are sold to the food service and processing industries. That acquisition gave Unilever a strong presence in consumer and industrial markets.

In addition to making those acquisitions, Unilever continued to sell parts of its business that were weak or did not fit with its other subsidiaries, in order to improve its earnings picture. In 1986, for example, it sold a soybean-processing plant in the port of Rotterdam along with other facilities in West Germany to Archer-Daniels-Midland, the largest processor of grains and other agricultural products in the United States. The result of these moves has been that Unilever's managers can communicate better because their businesses have more in common with one another. Improved communication, in turn, has favorably impacted earnings. Earnings in 1988 were about 10 percent higher than they had been in 1987.

Questions

1. Use the model of the communication process presented in Figure 15.1 to describe communication between Unilever's corporate headquarters and its foreign affiliates. Does that communication seem to be effective? Why or why not?
2. What form of communication is used by the two Unilever chairmen to reach joint decisions? Does it seem to work effectively? Why or why not?
3. Think about the long-term prospects for Unilever, including changes in European economic competition and the continued strength of Procter & Gamble. What would you suggest as ways for Unilever to improve its organizational communication? Why?
4. How might a formal information system, perhaps using electronic media, benefit Unilever?

REFERENCES: David Dreman, "Armageddon It Wasn't," *Forbes*, July 25, 1988, p. 264; "Unilever Says Pretax Profit Rose 4.7% in First Quarter," *The Wall Street Journal*, May 17, 1988, p. 35; "Pulling Together a Two-Part Company," *Fortune*, August 3, 1987, p. 40; "Unilever's U.S. Invasion," *Fortune*, January 5, 1987, p. 12; Andrew Tank, "Billionaires!" *Marketing*, May 7, 1987, pp. 28–29; Andrew C. Brown, "Unilever Fights Back in the U.S.," *Fortune*, May 26, 1986, pp. 32–38; "Unilever Will Buy Bulk of Fabergé, Bolstering Personal-Products Sales," *The Wall Street Journal*, February 13, 1989, p. A 10.

ENHANCEMENT MODULE 6

Managing the Individual

Sam Walton drives a ten-year-old pickup truck with dog cages in the back. He insists that people call him Sam and maintains the old-fashioned values he grew up with. He is also one of the richest men in the world. His company, Wal-Mart, is the fastest-growing retailer in the United States and is almost certain to become the largest within a very few years. One of the keys to his success is the way he treats people. For example, he calls his employees associates and works hard to make sure they believe in the company and espouse positive attitudes toward it. He treats them fairly, inspiring top performance, and rewards that performance.[1]

Sam Walton learned something long ago that many managers today need to better understand—the nature and importance of the individual in an organization. Walton himself is different from other managers in the retailing industry, and he recognizes the individuality of his employees. Various concepts explored in the preceding four chapters (motivation, leadership, groups, and communication) are related to the individual. This Enhancement Module explores two others—individual differences and employee attitudes.

BASIC PERSPECTIVES ON INDIVIDUAL DIFFERENCES

In 1988, General Motors employed 813,400 people—making it the size of a small nation.[2] Yet not one of those employees was exactly the same as any other. Each had his or her own unique set of personality traits and characteristics. Some were gregarious; some were quiet. Some were aggressive; some were reserved. Some respected authority; some didn't. Some understood their importance to the organization; some didn't. Moreover, each one came to work every day with different emotions and different attitudes. Individual differences are the characteristics that differentiate one person from another.[3]

The Nature of Individual Differences

Managers need to acknowledge that individual differences exist and try to take them into account as they attempt to train employees and motivate, evaluate, and reward job performance. Managers must not discriminate against anyone on the basis of sex, race, religion, and so forth. But managers do need to recognize that individual differences are important determinants of how people perceive, evaluate, and respond to the workplace.

When people enter organizations, they bring with them previous experiences, knowledge, needs, aspirations, opinions, personality traits, and attitudes. Once a person is a member of an organization, those characteristics influence how that person perceives and is perceived by others. Those experiences, in turn, become still another part of the individual's uniqueness.

The Uniqueness of People   People are like jigsaw puzzles. Just as a puzzle is an image assembled by putting pieces together in a certain way, people are made up of various attributes fitted together in a certain way. Just as puzzles have pieces that fit together to form a whole, each of us has a unique set of attributes that together represent the essence of what we are. Furthermore, although an individual may resemble some people, no two persons are exactly the same.

People and Situations   People do not function independently of the situation in which they find themselves. Situational differences can impact how people respond in numerous ways. Consider an average manager working for a big company. His attitudes and behaviors have always been what most people would consider normal. One day, however, his life changes significantly. Perhaps he gets a big promotion, or he gets terminated because of a major cutback, or he and his wife decide to divorce. Any of these events will place him in a dramatically changed situation, and as a result of it his attitudes and behavior may change. He may become happier, more upbeat, and work even harder than in the past; or he may become moody, depressed, and withdrawn.

Personality and Work

One critical component of individual differences is personality. Personality is the set of distinctive traits and characteristics that can be used to characterize a person. Although a full discussion of personality is beyond the scope of this book, there are a number of important personality traits that have been studied in the workplace.[4]

Locus of Control   Locus of control is the extent to which a person believes that her or his behavior has a direct impact on the consequences of that behavior.[5] Some people believe they can control what happens to them—that if they work hard, for instance, they will be successful. Sam Walton has always held this view of himself. Such people are said to have an internal locus of control. In contrast, people who have an external locus of control tend to think that what happens to them is a function of fate or luck. They see little or no connection between their own behavior and subsequent events. Understanding employees' locus of control can often help managers understand their subordinates. "Internals" are likely to want a voice in how they perform their jobs because they believe that they control their environment. "Externals" may be less inclined to want to participate in decision making.

Authoritarianism   Authoritarianism is the extent to which a person believes in and accepts power and status differences within a social system like an organization. The stronger the belief, the more the individual is said to be authoritarian. Authoritarianism has several helpful implications for managers. Subordinates who are highly authoritarian may be more willing to accept a directive style of supervision. They are also less likely to raise arguments against the manager's suggestions or resist following instructions. Subordinates who are highly authoritarian can make a manager's life easier, although the

manager may lose the advantage of having multiple viewpoints and opinions to consider when making decisions.

Other Traits   Self-esteem has been recognized as an important personality trait.[6] Self-esteem is the extent to which a person believes that he or she is a worthwhile and deserving individual. Recent studies have linked self-esteem to job performance, job satisfaction, and the job search process.[7] For example, a person with high self-esteem may be likely to seek a higher-status job, whereas a person with low self-esteem may be satisfied with the status quo. Besides self-esteem, other traits that may be important for managers to recognize include the extent to which a person is willing to make risky decisions (called risk propensity) and the tendencies for a person to be withdrawn, outgoing, open-minded, or intolerant.

EMPLOYEE ATTITUDES

Another important characteristic of individuals in organizations is attitude. An attitude is a person's feelings about something—job, boss, salary, co-workers. Managers need to understand the determinants and consequences of attitudes, as well as several important work-related attitudes.

Determinants of Attitudes

How are attitudes formed? Two different views have been described—the dispositional view and the situational view. Attitudes are also influenced by cognitive dissonance.

The Dispositional View   Historically, attitudes were viewed as stable dispositions that predict behavior toward something or somebody. For example, a manager might decide that she did not like a certain employee or some other manager (a disposition). That manager would then be expected to express consistently negative opinions about the other person and to behave in ways consistent with that negative view (not socializing with the person, not recommending him or her for promotion). As shown in Figure EM6.1, this view suggests that

FIGURE EM6.1

The Dispositional View of
Employee Attitudes

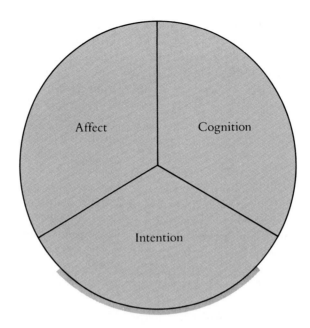

attitudes are composed of three components: affect, cognition, and intention.

Affect refers to the individual's emotional reactions toward something. Suppose that a manager is in charge of identifying the site for a new plant. When he says he does not like a possible site in Chicago, he is expressing the affective part of his attitude toward that site. The cognitive part of the attitude is the knowledge the person presumes to have about something. Cognitions are based on perceptions of truth and reality. If the manager says he doesn't like the Chicago site because it is too far from warehouse and transportation facilities, he is expressing the cognitive part of the attitude. Finally, the third part of the attitude is the intention. The intention serves as an indicator of how the person might be expected to behave. The manager might indicate his intentions by stating a preference for another site.

The Situational View   An alternative view of attitudes is the situational view.[8] This view suggests that attitudes are not a reflection of an individual's own evaluation; instead, they are presumed to be a function of social information in the workplace. Suppose that a newcomer joins an existing work group. Its members quickly tell the newcomer that

the boss is okay, the pay is lousy, but the work pace is excellent. This set of cues plays a significant role in how the newcomer forms her attitude toward her new job. In particular, she may decide that the most important things about her job are the boss, the pay, and the work pace, because her attitudes are at least partially defined by others in the organization.

Cognitive Dissonance   Attitudes are also influenced by cognitive dissonance. Cognitive dissonance is the mental anxiety that a person experiences when two sets of information or perceptions are contradictory or incongruent.[9] It can also occur when a person behaves in a fashion that is inconsistent with his or her attitudes. Suppose that a person realizes that smoking and overeating are dangerous yet continues to do both. Because the attitudes and behaviors are not consistent, the individual will probably experience tension and discomfort and may engage in dissonance reduction—seeking ways to reduce the dissonance and the tension it presumably causes. The dissonance associated with smoking might be resolved by rationalizing, "My health won't be affected," or "I can quit when I have to." With regard to overeating, the person might decide to go on a diet "next week." In general, the person attempts to change the attitude, change the behavior, or perceptually distort the circumstances in order to reduce his or her tension and discomfort.

Cognitive dissonance affects people in a variety of ways. We frequently encounter situations in which we have conflicting attitudes or conflicting attitudes and behaviors. Dissonance reduction is the way we deal with these feelings of discomfort and tension. In organizational settings, people contemplating leaving the organization may wonder why they continue to stay and work hard. As a result of this dissonance, they may conclude that the company is not so bad after all, that they have no immediate options elsewhere, or that they will leave "soon."

Consequences of Attitudes

What happens as a result of a person's attitudes? Surprisingly, not as much as might be expected. For example, a common-sense argument is that the more satisfied someone is, the harder he or she will work. Research seldom finds such a relationship, however. Indeed, as described in Chapter 12, performance—accompanied by equitable rewards—is more likely to affect future levels of satisfaction.

Still, satisfaction and dissatisfaction can influence a variety of other behaviors in organizational settings. Table EM6.1 summarizes some of the most frequent results of satisfaction and dissatisfaction. Satisfied employees are likely to remain with the organization (exhibit low turnover), come to work regularly (exhibit high attendance), and contribute to a strong culture. Dissatisfied employees are more likely to look for alternative job opportunities (exhibit high turnover), miss work regularly (exhibit low attendance), and inhibit the building of a strong culture.

In some ways, Sam Walton's success started when his employees became dissatisfied and started to form a union. His lawyer convinced him that his best bet would be to develop a cadre of satisfied employees by working together to identify the sources of their dissatisfaction and then eliminating as many of those problems as possible. Walton took his lawyer's advice and has not had to worry about unions.[10]

Key Work-related Attitudes

Attitudes are clearly an important consideration for managers. In general, employees develop consistent

TABLE EM6.1

Outcomes of Employee Satisfaction and Dissatisfaction in Organizations

People who are satisfied are more likely to . . .
- Remain with the organization
- Come to work regularly
- Contribute to high performance norms
- Contribute to organizational goals and effectiveness
- Be a positive force within the organization
- Help build a strong culture
- Be uninterested in union activities

People who are dissatisfied are more likely to . . .
- Look for alternative job opportunities
- Miss work often
- Contribute to low performance norms
- Detract from organizational goals and effectiveness
- Be a negative force within the organization
- Inhibit the building of a strong culture
- Form or join unions

and identifiable sets of attitudes toward a wide variety of organizational attributes. One crucial attitude is job satisfaction.

Job Satisfaction   Job satisfaction—an individual's attitude toward his or her job—is one of the most widely studied variables in the entire field of organizational behavior. Literally thousands of studies dealing with some aspect of job satisfaction have been published. In general, this research suggests that people develop attitudes about five basic dimensions of a job: pay, opportunities for promotion, the nature of the work itself, policies and procedures of the organization, and working conditions.[11] A person may feel differential satisfaction toward each factor. For example, an employee may feel underpaid (dissatisfied with pay) but simultaneously feel very positive about other organizational factors.

The job satisfaction of people within a work group may also be influenced by their co-workers and by their supervisor or manager. Although the supervisor could be regarded as an organizational factor, because the position is described and defined by the organization, it is often the supervisor's individual characteristics (warmth, understanding, integrity) that most influence employee attitudes. An individual's needs and aspirations can also affect satisfaction. If a person wants to be in a high-status position, gaining such a position will probably enhance his or her level of job satisfaction. The same person will be less satisfied with a job of lesser status. Also important are the instrumental benefits of the job, or the extent to which the job enables the employee to achieve other ends. A person finishing a college degree might take a particular job on a temporary basis because it allows scheduling flexibility and pays enough money to cover tuition. The person may be quite satisfied with the job if it provides the desired flexibility and wage rate. In this case, the job is serving an instrumental purpose. On the other hand, the person might be considerably less satisfied with the same job on a permanent basis.

Other Kinds of Satisfaction   Many other attitudes also exist in the workplace, some far more central and significant than others. A worker who feels drastically underpaid is likely to do something about it—quit or ask for a pay raise, for example. But employees are much less likely to quit because they feel the prices in the employee cafeteria are too high or they do not like the color of the company softball team uniforms.

Commitment and Involvement   Commitment and involvement are two related employee attitudes that are also important.[12] Commitment is the individual's feelings of identification with and attachment to the organization. Involvement is the person's willingness to go beyond the standard demands of his or her job as an organizational "citizen." Sam Walton does a masterful job of instilling commitment and involvement in his Wal-Mart employees.

Several factors have been found to lead to commitment and involvement. Both are enhanced by personal factors such as age and years of tenure in the organization and by organizational characteristics such as the degree of participation allowed in decision making and the level of perceived security. Thus, managers can help develop commitment and involvement by allowing participation whenever possible and providing reasonable levels of job security for employees.

Commitment and involvement can also lead to several positive outcomes. The more committed and involved employees are, the better is their attendance, the stronger their intention to stay with the organization, and the greater their job-related effort. These are clearly attitudes that managers should nurture and sustain.

Unfortunately, for many organizations general levels of commitment and involvement seem to have declined in recent years. The decline has been most often attributed to organizational cutbacks in human resources during the massive retrenchments that took place in the United States during the early 1980s. One recent survey found that among the 279 firms studied, 79 percent had reduced the size of their work force during the last five years, and each of those firms also reported a corresponding decline in commitment among its employees.[13] Thus, managers at those companies will need to work hard over the next several years to restore this important attitude among their employees.

NOTES

1. John Huey, "Wal-Mart—Will It Take over the World?" *Fortune*, January 30, 1989, pp. 52–61.

2. "The Fortune 500," *Fortune*, April 25, 1988, p. D49.

3. See Gregory Moorhead and Ricky W. Griffin, *Organizational Behavior*, 2nd ed. (Boston: Houghton Mifflin, 1989), for a review of individual differences.

4. See Walter Mischel, *Introduction to Personality* (New York: Holt, 1971), for a classic discussion of personality theory.

5. J. B. Rotter, "Generalized Expectancies for Internal vs. External Control of Reinforcement," *Psychological Monographs*, Vol. 80, 1966, pp. 1–28.

6. John R. Hollenbeck and Ellen M. Whitener, "Reclaiming Personality Traits for Personnel Selection: Self-Esteem as an Illustrative Case," *Journal of Management*, March 1988, pp. 81–91.

7. Moorhead and Griffin, *Organizational Behavior*.

8. Gerald Salancik and Jeffrey Pfeffer, "A Social Information Processing Approach to Job Attitudes and Task Design," *Administrative Science Quarterly*, March 1978, pp. 224–253.

9. Leon Festinger, *A Theory of Cognitive Dissonance* (Palo Alto, Calif.: Stanford University Press, 1957).

10. Huey, "Wal-Mart—Will It Take over the World?"

11. Ricky W. Griffin and Thomas S. Bateman, "Job Satisfaction and Organizational Commitment," in Cary L. Cooper and Ivan T. Robertson, eds., *International Review of Industrial and Organizational Psychology* (London: Wiley, 1986), pp. 157–188.

12. See Donna M. Randall, "Commitment and the Organization: The Organization Man Revisited," *Academy of Management Review*, July 1987, pp. 460–471, for a recent review.

13. Mitchell Lee Marks, "The Disappearing Company Man," *Psychology Today*, September 1988, pp. 34–39.

ENHANCEMENT MODULE 7

Coping with Stress

After deregulation of the telephone industry, many thought that AT&T would emerge as a lean, formidable competitor in both the communications and the computer industries. Things haven't gone as smoothly as planned, however. Numerous setbacks and actions by competitors have slowed AT&T's transformation. In response, the company has continued to cut the size of its work force, and the employees who remain often fear for their own jobs. Many report high levels of stress caused by job pressures, heavy workloads, and concerns for future job security. As a result, they continue to perform below their capabilities, and many are looking for employment with other companies.[1]

AT&T is confronting a problem that many businesses are just beginning to recognize—stress in the workplace. More than at any other time in the history of business, workers and the companies they work for are facing enormous pressures on dozens of fronts, and the resultant stress is taking a toll on both the person and the organization. This Enhancement Module explores workplace stress. We identify several key aspects of stress in the workplace. We discuss Type A and Type B behavior profiles. Finally, we discuss ways that people and organizations can better manage stress.

STRESS IN THE WORKPLACE

Stress is a complex process—and one that is often misunderstood. We will define stress as an individual's adaptive response to a stimulus that places excessive psychological or physical demands on that person.[2] The stimulus that induces stress is usually called a stressor. Stressors can be either psychological or physical.

The Nature of Stress

Stress generally follows a cycle referred to as the General Adaptation Syndrome, or GAS.[3] This cycle is shown in Figure EM7.1. According to this view,

FIGURE EM7.1

The General Adaptation Syndrome

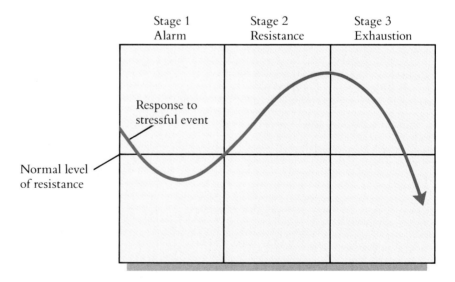

Stage 1
Alarm

Stage 2
Resistance

Stage 3
Exhaustion

Response to
stressful event

Normal level
of resistance

each of us has a normal level of resistance to stressful events. Some of us can tolerate a great deal of stress; others can handle much less. When a person first encounters a stressor, the GAS is initiated and the first stage, alarm, is activated. The person may feel panic, may wonder how to cope, and may feel helpless. Suppose that a manager is told to prepare a detailed report on a proposed acquisition within 24 hours. The manager's first reaction may be, "How will I ever get this done by tomorrow?"

If a stressor is too intense, the person may feel that she simply cannot cope with it and never really try. In most cases, however, after a short period of alarm, the individual gathers her strength (physical or emotional) and starts resisting the negative effects of the stressor. For example, the manager with the long report to write may calm down, call home to say he's working late, roll up his sleeves, order out for coffee, and set to work to get the job done. Thus, at stage 2 of the GAS, the person is resisting the effects of the stressor.

In many cases, the resistance phase may end the GAS. If, for example, the manager is able to complete the report earlier than expected, he may drop it in his briefcase, smile to himself, and head home tired but happy. On the other hand, prolonged exposure to a stressor without resolution may bring on phase 3 of the GAS—exhaustion. At this stage, the person literally gives up and can no longer fight the stressor. The manager, for example, might fall asleep at his desk at 3 A.M. and not get the report finished.

Stress need not be bad.[4] For example, receiving a bonus and then having to decide what to do with the money can be stressful. So, too, can getting a promotion, gaining recognition, getting married, and similar "good" things. This type of stress is called eustress. Of course, there is also negative stress. This kind of stress, called distress, is what most people think of when they hear the word "stress." Excessive pressure, unreasonable demands on our time, and bad news all fall into this category. The point to remember is that stress can be good or bad. Too little stress can lead to lethargy, indifference, and stagnation. An optimal level of stress can result in motivation, excitement, and innovation. Too much stress, however, can have very negative consequences.

Causes of Stress

In general, there are five categories of things that can result in stress.[5] These include task demands, physical demands, role demands, interpersonal demands, and life stressors.

Task Demands   Task demands are stressors associated with the specific job the person is performing. Some occupations are simply more stressful than others. The jobs of surgeon, airline pilot, and stock broker are relatively more stressful than are the jobs of general practitioner, airplane baggage loader, and office receptionist. Beyond task-related pressures, physical threats to health can also result in stress. Such conditions are found in jobs like coal mining, toxic-waste handling, and law enforcement.[6] Security is also an important task demand that can cause stress. This is one of the problems faced by AT&T. Finally, overload can also cause stress. Overload occurs when a person simply has more work to do than he or she can handle.

Physical Demands   Physical demands relate to the setting of the job. Working outdoors in extreme temperatures, for example, can result in stress. Even an improperly heated or cooled office can be a problem. Office design can also lead to stress. A poorly designed office can make it difficult for people to have privacy or can promote too much or too little social interaction. Poor lighting, inadequate work surfaces, and similar factors can also lead to stress.[7]

Role Demands   Another source of stress is role demands.[8] As discussed in Chapter 14, a role is a set of expected behaviors associated with a particular position in a group or organization. Stress can result from either role ambiguity or role conflict.

Interpersonal Demands   Still another set of organizational stressors includes interpersonal demands that may confront people in organizations. Group pressures regarding such things as restriction of output and norm conformity can lead to stress. Leadership style may also cause stress. For example, an employee may feel a strong need to participate in decision making and want to be actively involved in a variety of areas. His boss, however, may be very autocratic, refusing to allow any participation and limiting involvement only to what pertains directly to the job. Such a difference in style can lead to stress. Individual differences can also cause stress. A person with an internal locus of control, always wanting to be proactive in getting things done, might be frustrated when working with an external person, who prefers to wait and just let things happen. Likewise, a smoker and nonsmoker assigned to share an office are both likely candidates for stress.

Life Stressors   Stress in organizational settings can be influenced by events that take place outside the organization. Life change is any meaningful change in a person's personal or work situation.[9] Such changes can lead to stress. For example, when many people finish college, they start a career, assume more responsibility, have more money, get married, and so forth. Each of these events represents a significant life change.

Stress can also be induced by a trauma from outside the workplace. Such a trauma could be any upheaval that disrupts a person's attitudes, emotions, or behaviors—marital problems, family problems, other personal problems, and health problems initially unrelated to stress. Suppose that a person learns that she has a congenital disease that will limit her future participation in a favorite activity such as skiing. Her disappointment over the news may translate into stress at work.

Consequences of Stress

When stress occurs, a number of consequences can result. If the stress is positive, the results may be increased energy, enthusiasm, and motivation. Of more critical concern, of course, are the negative consequences of stress. There are three sets of consequences that can result from stress: individual consequences, organizational consequences, and burnout.[10]

Individual Consequences   Individual consequences of stress are outcomes that primarily affect the individual. The organization may also suffer, but it is the individual who pays the real price. Three categories of individual consequences of stress are

behavioral, psychological, and medical. Behavioral consequences are detrimental or harmful behaviors by the person involved. Common examples are smoking, alcoholism, and drug abuse. Other examples are accident proneness, violence, and appetite disorders.

Psychological consequences are things that relate to the individual's mental health and well-being. They include sleep disturbances, depression, family problems, and sexual dysfunctions. Finally, stress can also lead to medical disorders for the individual. Medical consequences affect the person's physiological well-being. Heart disease and stroke, for example, have been linked to stress, as have headaches, backaches, ulcers and related stomach and intestinal disorders, and skin conditions like acne and hives.[11]

Organizational Consequences   Obviously, any of the individual consequences of stress discussed above can impact the organization. There are still other consequences of stress, however, that have an even more direct impact on the organization. For example, too much stress can lead to a decline in an individual's performance. For an operating worker, this can translate into poor-quality work or lower productivity. For a manager, it can mean faulty decision making or disruptions in working relationships as the manager becomes irritable and hard to get along with.

Withdrawal behaviors such as absenteeism and quitting can also result from stress. People who are having difficulties coping with stress in their jobs are more likely to call in sick or consider leaving the organization for alternative opportunities. Other, more subtle forms of withdrawal can result from stress. A manager may start missing deadlines or taking long lunch breaks. An employee may withdraw psychologically by developing feelings of indifference.[12] A final direct organizational consequence of employee stress relates to attitudes. Job satisfaction, morale, and organizational commitment can all suffer. So, too, can motivation to perform at high levels.

Burnout   A final consequence of stress with implications for both people and organizations is burnout. Burnout is a general feeling of exhaustion that may develop when an individual simultaneously experiences too much pressure and has too few sources of satisfaction.[13] The most likely effects of burnout are constant fatigue and feelings of frustration and helplessness. Increased rigidity of thinking and feeling follows, as does a loss of self-confidence and psychological withdrawal. When this happens, the individual starts dreading going to work in the morning, often puts in longer hours but gets less accomplished than before, and generally exhibits mental and physical exhaustion.

TYPE A AND TYPE B BEHAVIOR PROFILES

Not everyone responds to stress in the same way. In fact, virtually every aspect of stress, including its causes and its consequences, can vary from person to person. One line of thinking about systematic differences between people focuses on Type A and Type B personality profiles.[14] The Type A individual is extremely competitive and very devoted to work and has a strong sense of time urgency. This individual is likely to be aggressive, impatient, and very work-oriented. He or she has a lot of drive and wants to accomplish as much as possible in as short a period of time as possible.

The Type B person, in contrast, is less competitive and less devoted to work and has a weaker sense of time urgency. This person feels less conflict with people or time and has a more balanced, relaxed approach to life. He or she has more confidence and is able to work at a constant pace. A Type B person is not necessarily any more or less successful than is a Type A person.

Research suggests that few people are purely Type A or Type B. Instead, most people generally have tendencies toward one or the other. An individual might exhibit marked Type A characteristics much of the time but still be able to relax occasionally and even not worry about time in a few situations. Likewise, a person leaning toward the Type B profile might occasionally get caught up in a task or become especially concerned with time in some situations. Early research on the Type A and B profile differences yielded some alarming findings. For example, it was argued that Type A's were much more likely to experience coronary heart disease than were Type B's.[15] In recent years, however, follow-up research suggested that the relationship between Type A behavior and the risk of coronary heart disease is not all that straightforward.[16]

MANAGING STRESS

Given the pervasiveness and potential consequences of stress in organizations, it follows that people and organizations should be concerned about how to limit the most damaging effects of stress. Numerous ideas and approaches have been developed to help manage stress. Some are strategies for individuals; others are strategies for organizations.[17]

Individual Approaches to Managing Stress

Numerous approaches have been suggested as ways an individual can manage his or her own experienced stress. One method is through exercise. People who exercise regularly are less likely to have heart attacks than are inactive people. It has also been suggested that people who exercise regularly feel less tension and stress, are more self-confident, and are more optimistic. People who don't exercise regularly, in contrast, feel more stress and are more likely to be depressed.[18]

A related method that people can use to manage stress is relaxation. Proper relaxation allows the individual to adapt to, and therefore deal with, the stress being experienced. Relaxation comes in many forms. One approach is to take regular vacations. A recent study found that people's attitudes toward a variety of workplace characteristics improved significantly following a vacation.[19] People can also relax while on the job. It has been recommended that people take regular rest breaks during the normal workday. Sitting quietly with eyes closed for ten minutes every afternoon is one popular method.

Time management is another method for controlling stress. The idea is that many daily pressures can be reduced or eliminated if the individual does a better job of managing time. One popular approach to time management is to make a list every morning of the things to be done that day. The items on the list are then grouped into three categories: critical activities that must be performed, important activities that should be performed, and optional or trivial things that can be delegated or postponed. The person then does the things on the list in the order of their importance.

A related approach is role management. In role management the individual actively works to avoid overload, ambiguity, and conflict. For example, a person who doesn't know what is expected of him should not sit and worry. An effective strategy might be to ask for clarification from his boss. Another aspect of role management is learning to say no. A lot of people create problems for themselves by always saying yes. In addition to performing their regular job, they agree to serve on committees, volunteer for extra duties, and accept extra assignments. Sometimes, of course, there is no way to avoid an extra obligation. For example, if the boss tells a subordinate to complete a new project, the subordinate most likely will need to comply. In many cases, however, saying no is a viable option.[20]

A final method that people can use to manage stress is to develop and maintain support groups. A support group is a group of family members or friends that a person can spend time with. Going out after work with a couple of co-workers to a basketball game, for example, can help relieve the stress that built up during the day. Thus, family and friends can help deal with normal stress on an ongoing basis. Support groups can be particularly useful during times of crisis. Suppose that an employee has just learned that she did not get the promotion she has been working toward for months. It may help her tremendously if she has a good friend to lean on, to talk to, or to yell at.[21]

Organizational Approaches to Managing Stress

Organizations are beginning to realize that they should be involved in helping their employees cope with stress. There are two different arguments for this view. One is that because the organization is at least partially responsible for creating the stress, it should help relieve it. The other is that workers experiencing low levels of detrimental stress will be able to function more effectively. AT&T has initiated a series of seminars and workshops to help its employees cope with job-related stress.

Institutional Programs   Institutional efforts to manage stress are based on established organizational mechanisms.[22] For example, poorly designed jobs and work schedules can cause stress. Shiftwork, in particular, can be a major problem. Thus, one possibility is for organizations to change the design of especially stressful jobs or rearrange work schedules in a less stressful manner.[23] The organization's culture can also be used to help manage stress. In some organizations there is a strong norm against ever taking time off or going on vacation. In the long run, such practices can be a major stress-inducing problem. Thus, the organization should strive to foster a culture that reinforces a healthy mix of work and nonwork activities. Finally, supervision can also play an important institutional role in managing stress. A potentially major source of overload is too frequent assignments of work by one's supervisor. Thus, if supervisors are aware of their potential role in the creation of stress, they can act to limit it.

Collateral Programs   In addition to institutional efforts aimed at stress reduction, many organizations are increasingly turning to collateral programs. A collateral stress program is one that is a new or special part of the organization specifically created to help deal with stress. Organizations have adopted stress management programs, health promotion programs, and other kinds of programs for this purpose. B. F. Goodrich has a nine-hour training program to help employees better cope with stress. More and more companies are developing their own programs or using existing programs of this type.[24] Johns-Manville has a gym at its corporate headquarters. These kinds of programs attack stress indirectly by facilitating employee exercise. The exercise is presumed to reduce stress. On the negative side, such programs involve considerable costs, because the firm must invest in physical facilities. Nevertheless, more and more companies are developing fitness-based programs for their employees.[25] Organizations also help address employee stress through other kinds of programs. Existing career development programs at companies like General Electric are used for this purpose. Other companies use programs promoting everything from humor to massage as an antidote for stress.[26] Of course, there is little or no research to support some of the claims made by advocates of these programs. Hence, the manager must be careful to balance the costs against the benefits when developing any form of stress management program.

NOTES

1. "Stress: The Test Americans Are Failing," *Business Week*, April 18, 1988, pp. 74–76; "Stress on the Job," *Newsweek*, April 25, 1988, pp. 40–45; Brian Dumaine, "Cool Cures for Burnout," *Fortune*, June 20, 1988, pp. 78–84.
2. James L. Gibson, John M. Ivancevich, and James H. Donnelly, Jr., *Organizations—Behavior, Structure, Processes*, 6th ed. (Plano, Texas: BPI, 1988), p. 230.
3. Hans Selye, *The Stress of Life* (New York: McGraw-Hill, 1976).
4. Selye, *The Stress of Life.*
5. Selye, *The Stress of Life.* See also Stephan J. Motowidlo, John S. Packard, and Michael R. Manning, "Occupational Stress: Its Causes and Consequences for Job Performance," *Journal of Applied Psychology*, August 1986, pp. 618–629; and James C. Quick and Jonathan D. Quick, *Organizational Stress and Preventive Management* (New York: McGraw-Hill, 1984).
6. John M. Jermier, Jeannie Gaines, and Nancy J. McIntosh, "Reactions to Physically Dangerous Work: A Conceptual and Empirical Analysis," *Journal of Organizational Behavior*, January 1989, pp. 15–33.
7. Robert I. Sutton and Anat Rafaeli, "Characteristics of Work Stations as Potential Occupational Stressors," *Academy of Management Journal*, June 1987, pp. 260–276.
8. John Schaubroeck, John L. Cotton, and Kenneth R. Jennings, "Antecedents and Consequences of Role Stress: A Covariance Structure Analysis," *Journal of Organizational Behavior*, January 1989, pp. 35–58.
9. T. H. Holmes and R. H. Rahe, "Social Readjustment Rating Scale," *Journal of Psychosomatic Research*, Vol. 29, 1967, pp. 213–218.
10. Quick and Quick, *Organizational Stress and Preventive Management.* See also John M. Ivancevich and Michael T. Matteson, *Stress and Work: A Managerial Perspective* (Glenview, Ill.: Scott, Foresman, 1980); Paul E. Spector, Daniel J. Dwyer, and Steve M. Jex, "Relation of Job Stressors to Affective, Health, and Performance Outcomes: A Comparison of Multiple Data Sources," *Journal of Applied Psychology*, February 1988, pp. 11–19.
11. Quick and Quick, *Organizational Stress and Preventive Management.* See also Brian D. Steffy and John W. Jones, "Workplace Stress and Indicators of Coronary-Disease Risk," *Academy of Management Journal*, September 1988, pp. 686–698.
12. Quick and Quick, *Organizational Stress and Preventive Management.*
13. Leonard Moss, *Management Stress* (Reading, Mass.: Addison-Wesley, 1981).
14. M. Friedman and R. H. Rosenman, *Type A Behavior and Your Heart* (New York: Knopf, 1974).
15. Friedman and Rosenman, *Type A Behavior and Your Heart.*
16. Joshua Fischman, "Type A on Trial," *Psychology Today*, February 1987, pp. 42–50.
17. Quick and Quick, *Organizational Stress and Preventive Management.*
18. C. Folkins, "Effects of Physical Training on Mood," *Journal of Clinical Psychology*, April 1976, pp. 385–390. See also James M. Rippe, "CEO Fitness: The Performance Plus," *Psychology Today*, May 1989, pp. 50–53.
19. John W. Lounsbury and Linda L. Hoopes, "A Vacation from Work: Changes in Work and Nonwork Outcomes," *Journal of Applied Psychology*, May 1986, pp. 392–401.
20. "Eight Ways to Help You Reduce the Stress in Your Life," *Business Week Careers*, November 1986, p. 78.
21. Daniel C. Ganster, Marcelline R. Fusilier, and Bronston T. Mayes, "Role of Social Support in the Experiences of Stress at Work," *Journal of Applied Psychology*, February 1986, pp. 102–110.
22. Randall S. Schuler and Susan E. Jackson, "Managing Stress Through PHRM Practices: An Uncertainty Interpretation," in K. Rowland and G. Ferris, eds., *Research in Personnel and Human Resources Management*, Vol. 4 (Greenwich, Conn.: JAI Press, 1986), pp. 183–224.
23. Quick and Quick, *Organizational Stress and Preventive Management.*
24. Quick and Quick, *Organizational Stress and Preventive Management.*
25. Richard A. Wolfe, David O. Ulrich, and Donald F. Parker, "Employee Health Management Programs: Review, Critique, and Research Agenda," *Journal of Management*, Winter 1987, pp. 603–615. See also Marjory Roberts and T. George Harris, "Wellness at Work," *Psychology Today*, May 1989, pp. 54–58.
26. "A Cure for Stress?" *Newsweek*, October 12, 1987, pp. 64–65.

INTEGRATIVE CASE

The Magic of Disney

In 1923, after failing in the cartoon business in Kansas City, Walt Disney went to Hollywood and joined his brother Roy, who was making silent comedies in his garage. In 1928, working with a small group of animators, Walt made *Steamboat Willie*, the first Mickey Mouse cartoon. Although he was not good at drawing, he was good at coming up with ideas and stories for animation. He followed *Steamboat Willie* with a series of short cartoons that were fairly successful. They included *The Three Little Pigs*, which contained the first hit song from a cartoon ("Who's Afraid of the Big Bad Wolf"). In 1937, the Disney company made the first full-length animated feature, *Snow White*, and was finally able to earn a profit on a regular basis.

Walt Disney's genius was as an idea person, a story editor, and a decision maker. He was an amazing strategic planner, able to envision and take advantage of environmental trends missed by others. During the 1950s, he foresaw the impact that television would have on films and quickly moved into that medium with two highly successful programs, "The Mickey Mouse Club" and "The Wonderful World of Disney." Disney's vision of a theme park, as opposed to the carnival-like concept of an amusement park, was almost ridiculed. He had a hard time selling it to investors and had to come up with almost all of the initial funds himself by cashing in his insurance and selling television shows.

Following Walt's death in 1966, the Disney company seemed to be at a standstill. Unable to communicate with its audiences, the company disappeared from television and its movies generated little revenue.

Roy E. Disney, Walt's nephew, grew angry over the company's inactivity, lack of success, and possible dismemberment by raiders. He resigned his position on the board of directors and launched a revolt to dislodge the company's entrenched officers. In 1984, Roy was successful. The Disney company brought in Frank G. Wells, a former vice chairman of Warner Bros., as a legal and financial expert, and Michael D. Eisner, then president of Paramount Pictures, as the new president and chief operating officer, and named Roy vice chairman. The turnaround was remarkable, and as a result of it Eisner soon became chairman and Wells president.

Monitoring costs became important. Every effort was made to ensure that films did not go over budget. As a result, Disney became second in gross revenues in films in 1987, capturing 14 percent of the over $4 billion market. Even more striking is that in an industry where only 3 of 10 films on average return a profit, 22 of 23 films released by Eisner's management team made a profit. Concern about costs also shows up in Disney's financial strategy. That strategy calls for maintaining a very low debt. In fact, Epcot Center, part of Disney World in Florida, was built with almost $1 billion from operating funds without incurring any debt.

Disney is rapidly becoming a powerhouse in the video market, thanks in part to six decades of material in its film library. It is also expanding production and increasing the number of outlets for its video products. In addition, the Disney Channel on cable television is being expanded.

The Disney company is becoming more aggressive in licensing and selling products. It plans to expand its own chain of stores into a 100-shop operation within five years and be in numerous shopping malls. It has a catalog that is currently mailed to more than 8 million households to sell Disney products. The licensing division of the organization has grown because of these activities. Its profits were over $97 million in 1987, an increase of more than one-third from the profits of the previous year.

Theme parks have been expanded and improved, and a new one was opened in Japan near Tokyo. They continue to be highly successful. At the end of 1987, theme parks accounted for over 60 percent of sales and 70 percent of operating earnings at Disney. In 1992, a new park, Euro Disneyland, will open near Paris.

Late in 1988, the Disney company established its third motion-picture production company, Hollywood Pictures. Marketing and distribution are centralized in the Buena Vista Pictures Marketing and Distribution divisions of the Disney company. Production is handled by the original Walt Disney Pictures, which does children's films; Touchstone Pictures, which was created in 1984 to do films for the teen and adult market; and Hollywood Pictures, which will do films similar to those done at Touchstone. With the creation of the new film group, the production of films by the Disney company is expected to double in about three years. One reason for establishing the new film group was to encourage creative executives to stay with Disney instead of going to some other studio in search of greater independence. Eisner provided them that independence within the Disney organization.

Building and expanding are not the only things Eisner has done at Disney. In a move perhaps designed to mark a symbolic break with the former managers, Eisner sold Disney's real estate unit, Arvida, to JMB Realty Trust for about $400 million. The sale not only moved the company out of the real estate business but also provided funds earmarked for a major entertainment acquisition when one becomes available or for the continuing development of current parks and hotels.

The success of Eisner and his team is clear. Disney's net income, which had risen from $98 million in 1978 to $135 million in 1980 only to fall back to $98 million in 1984, rose to nearly $250 million by 1986 and $445 million by 1987. Disney's stock, which had been hovering between $10 and $15 a share from 1978 through 1984, skyrocketed, going to around $60 a share early in 1988. There are some concerns that increased competition in films, videos,

and cable television as well as in theme parks may make it difficult for Disney to extend this recent pattern of success. However, it seems clear that under the leadership of Eisner the company is quite likely to withstand such competition.

Questions

1. What seem to be the primary motivational processes at work in the Disney company? Which perspectives on motivation seem to be most useful in understanding the energy and enthusiasm felt by Disney personnel? Why?
2. What might account for the Disney company's sluggishness after Walt's death? What might account for the conflict between Walt's nephew, Roy, and the older executives in the Disney company?
3. Communication in the Disney company seemed to improve under Eisner. What might account for that improvement?
4. Is the Disney company likely to be as effective in the future as it has been in the past? Why or why not? How might it change in order to improve its future possibilities?
5. Would you like to be a manager in the Disney company? Why or why not? Would you invest your money in it? Why or why not?

REFERENCES: "Disney Sets Third Film-Production Firm, Buoyed by Touchstone Division's Success," *The Wall Street Journal*, December 2, 1988, p. B4; "A Sweet Deal for Disney Is Souring Its Neighbors," *Business Week*, August 8, 1988, pp. 48–49; "People Magazine, Walt Disney Plan New Ad Approach," *The Wall Street Journal*, June 2, 1988, p. 24; "Do You Believe in Magic?" *Time*, April 25, 1988, pp. 66–73; "Michael Eisner's Hit Parade," *Business Week*, February 1, 1988, p. 27; "Disney's Magic: A Turnaround Proves Wishes Can Come True," *Business Week*, March 9, 1987, pp. 62–69; "How Disney Does It," *Newsweek*, April 3, 1989, pp. 48–54.

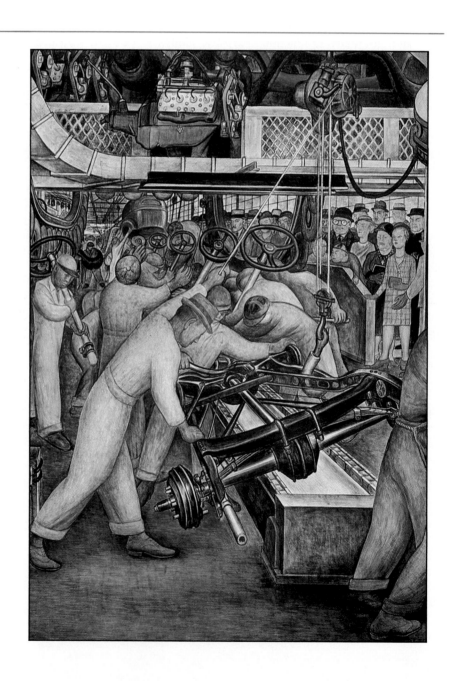

V THE CONTROLLING
PROCESS

OUTLINE

Control in Organizations
The Purpose of Control · The Importance of Control · Areas of Control · Responsibilities for Control · The Planning-Control Link

Steps in the Control Process
Establishing Standards · Measuring Performance · Comparing Performance Against Standards · Evaluation and Action

Forms of Operations Control
Preliminary Control · Screening Control · Postaction Control · Multiple Control Systems

Forms of Organizational Control
Bureaucratic Control · Clan Control

Strategic Control

Managing the Control Process
Developing Effective Control Systems · Understanding Resistance to Control · Overcoming Resistance to Control

Choosing a Style of Control

CHAPTER 16

The Nature of Control

OBJECTIVES

After studying this chapter, you should be able to:

- Describe the nature of control in organizations.
- Identify and explain the steps in the control process.
- Identify and explain major forms of operations control.
- Discuss approaches to organizational control.
- Describe strategic control.
- Discuss how managers can effectively manage the control process.
- Describe major issues in choosing a style of control.

OPENING INCIDENT

When most people think of greeting cards, they think of Hallmark. But although Hallmark controls 40 percent of the market, the number 2 firm in the industry, American Greetings, has a respectable 35 percent market share. The primary difference in image and visibility is that most Hallmark cards are sold in Hallmark Card Shops. In contrast, American Greetings' products are sold primarily through outlets like department- and grocery-store card departments. Another notable difference is that although Hallmark has almost always been profitable and successful, American has had its share of ups and downs.

After floundering for several years recently, American Greetings has taken major steps toward regaining its past levels of profitability. One major program has focused on inventory and distribution. In years gone by, American did a poor job of distributing seasonal cards. Large numbers of cards arrived in stores too early, resulting in soilage, or too late, resulting in weak sales. A new inventory system has greatly reduced these problems.

The company has cut its operating costs significantly, trimmed its work force, and boosted productivity by investing in computerized printing and production equipment. A new advertising campaign has increased sales. The jury is still out, but the results of these actions are promising. Costs have dropped sharply; sales and profits have increased; and the company seems poised for a bright future.[1]

*M*anagers at American Greetings realized that their organization was not operating as efficiently or as effectively as it had in the past. They also diagnosed the key reasons—high costs and slipshod management of operations. To confront these problems, they undertook a number of major programs that had one thing in common: They were all concerned with control.

We noted in Chapter 1 that control focuses on monitoring and evaluating the activities of an organization. This chapter is the first of four devoted to the control function of management. We begin by exploring the nature of control and discuss the purpose, importance, and areas of control, as well as who is responsible for control. We then discuss the general steps in the control process—establishing standards, measuring performance, comparing performance against standards, and evaluation and action—and the major forms of operations control. Subsequent sections address forms of organizational control, strategic control, how managers can make control systems effective, and key issues to consider when choosing a method of control. The other chapters in Part 5 cover operations management and productivity, the managing of information systems, and control techniques and methods.

CONTROL IN ORGANIZATIONS

■ **control** The regulation of one or more organizational activity in such a way as to facilitate goal attainment

We will define **control** as the regulation of one or more organizational activity in order to facilitate goal attainment. Managers at American Greetings took steps to improve the regulation of their distribution, production, and inventory functions. As a result, organizational effectiveness improved.

The Purpose of Control

In many ways, the purpose of control should be obvious. Without control, organizations would have no indication of how well they were performing in relation to their goals. The purpose of control is to provide managers with an assessment of where the organization is in comparison to where it is supposed to be at a certain point in time and in terms of one or more indicators of performance. For example, Federal Express has a performance goal of delivering 99 percent of its packages on time. If on-time deliveries fall to 96 percent, management knows that there is a problem. On the other hand, an on-time rate of 99.5 percent would indicate that the company is operating more effectively than expected.

The Importance of Control

Given the basic purpose of control, it follows that control is important. An organization without effective control is not likely to achieve its goals. Control helps an organization adapt to changing conditions, limits the compounding of errors, helps an organization cope with complexity, and helps minimize costs.

Changing Conditions In today's complex and turbulent environment, all organizations must contend with change.[2] If managers could establish goals and achieve them instantaneously, control would not be needed. But between the time a goal is established and the time it is reached, many things can happen in the organization and its environment to disrupt movement toward the goal or even to change the goal itself. A properly designed control system can help managers anticipate, monitor, and respond to changing circumstances. For example, Metalloy, a 43-year-old family-run metal-casting company, recently signed a contract to make engine-seal castings for NOK, a Japanese parts maker. Metalloy was satisfied when its first 5,000-unit production run yielded 4,985 acceptable castings and only 15 defective ones. NOK, however, was quite unhappy and insisted that Metalloy raise its standards. Managers at Metalloy had not realized that quality standards had increased so much in recent years.[3]

Control is important to all organizations. It helps the organization respond to changing conditions, prevent the compounding of errors, cope with organizational complexity, and minimize costs. Rosemarie B. Greco is President of Fidelity Bank, a 124-branch Philadelphia institution. She focuses a great deal of her attention on quality control. For example, she reads all letters the bank receives from customers, as well as summaries of all complaints and inquiries. Greco feels that this helps her control the quality of customer service.

Compounding of Errors   Small mistakes and errors do not often seriously damage the health of an organization. With the passage of time, however, small errors may accumulate and become very serious. For example, Whistler Corporation, a large radar-detector manufacturer, was faced with such rapidly escalating demand that it essentially stopped worrying about quality. Its defect rate rose from 4 percent to 9 percent to 15 percent and eventually reached 25 percent. One day, a manager realized that 100 of the firm's 250 employees were spending all their time fixing defective units, and $2 million worth of radar detectors was awaiting repair. If the company had had an adequate control system, the problem would have never reached such proportions.[4]

Organizational Complexity   When a firm purchases only one raw material, produces but one product, has a simple structure, and enjoys constant demand for its product, its manager can probably maintain control with a note pad and pencil. But in an organization that produces many products from myriad raw materials, has a large market area and a complicated organization structure, and operates in a competitive environment, it is difficult (if not impossible) to maintain adequate control without an elaborate control system. Emery Air Freight was quite effective until it bought Purolator Courier Corporation in 1987. The "new" Emery that resulted from the acquisition was much more complex than the "old" one, but no new controls were added. Consequently, Emery began to lose money and market share, costs increased, and service deteriorated until the company was on the verge of bankruptcy, and it's still fighting for its life.[5]

Minimizing Costs   When control is practiced effectively, it can help reduce costs and boost output. For example, managers at Georgia-Pacific Corporation recently replaced the blades in their sawmills. What does this have to do with control? The new blades are much thinner than the old ones and take a smaller "bite" out of logs. The wood that is saved by the new blades each year can fill 800 railcars.[6] Effective control systems can eliminate waste, lower labor costs, and improve output per unit of input.

Areas of Control

Organizational control can focus on any area of an organization. Two useful ways of identifying areas of control are in terms of resource focus and level.

Resource Focus   The resource view of control, as shown in Figure 16.1, deals with financial, physical, human, and information resources. The management process itself involves efficiently and effectively combining these resources into appropriate outputs. Control of physical resources includes inventory management (stocking neither too few nor too many units in inventory), quality control (maintaining appropriate levels of output quality), and equipment control (having the proper kinds of buildings, office equipment, and so on). Control of human

FIGURE 16.1

The Resource Focus of
Organizational Control

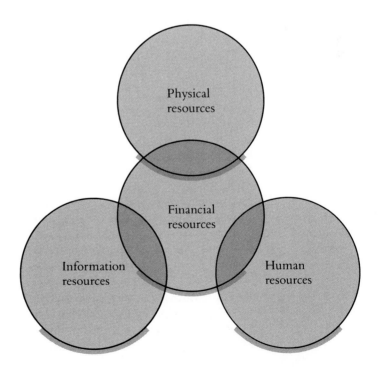

Control can be focused on each of the basic types of resources used by organizations—financial, physical, human, and informational. Union Pacific has recently entered the business of toxic waste disposal. It is clearly important that the equipment, storage tanks, and other resources used to carry out this task are of vital importance. A single leak, for example, could be disastrous to both the surrounding environment and to the company's reputation. Thus, Union Pacific has set extremely high technical and quality standards for the materials it buys from suppliers.

resources includes selection and placement activities, training and development, performance appraisal, and compensation levels. Control of information resources involves sales and marketing forecasting, environmental analysis, public relations, production scheduling, and economic forecasting.

Financial resources are at the center of Figure 16.1 because they, in addition to being organizational resources in their own right, are related to the control of all the other resources. Pure financial control does exist. (An example is ensuring that the organization always has enough cash on hand to meet its obligations and does not have excess cash lying around in a checking account.) But financial control extends to the other three kinds of resources as well: Too much inventory is bad because it leads to storage costs; poor selection of personnel is bad because it leads to termination and rehiring expenses; inaccurate sales forecasts are bad because they lead to disruptions in cash flows and other financial effects. Financial issues, then, tend to pervade most control-related activities. Indeed, this was the basic problem faced by Emery Air Freight. Various inefficiencies and operating blunders put the company into a position where it lacked the money to service its debt, had little working capital, and was too heavily leveraged to borrow more money.

Level Control can also be classified by level. This view is shown in Figure 16.2. Operations control is control focused on one or more operation systems within an organization. Quality control is one type of operations control. Organizational control is concerned with the overall functioning of the organization. Strategic control is concerned

FIGURE 16.2

Levels of Control

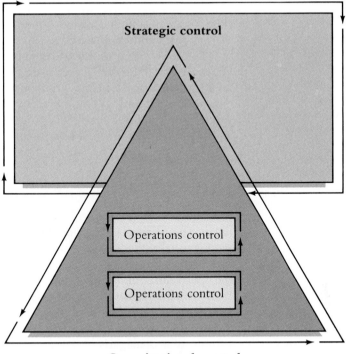

with how effectively the organization understands and aligns itself with its environment.[7] We discuss these levels of control more fully later in this chapter.

Responsibilities for Control

Given the wide array of control systems and concerns in organizations, who exactly is responsible for managing control? The traditional answer has always been managers. It is they who decide on the kinds of control that will be used. It is they who actually implement control systems and take appropriate actions based on the information provided by those control systems.

Most large organizations also have one or more specialized managerial positions called controller. The controller is responsible for helping line managers with their control activities, coordinating the organization's overall control system, and gathering and assimilating relevant information. Many businesses that use a divisional form of organization design have several controllers: one for the corporation and one for each division.[8] The increased importance of the controller is reflected in the large number of controllers who climb farther up the managerial ranks. Recent chief executive officers of Cooper Industries, Singer, FMC Corporation, CPC International, General Motors, Pfizer, and Fruehauf were all former controllers.[9]

More and more organizations are involving operating employees in their control systems. As described in Enhancement Module 4, employee participation is often used as a vehicle for allowing operating employees an opportunity to become more involved in organizational effectiveness. Whistler Corporation increased employee involvement in an effort to turn its quality problems around. The quality-control unit was abolished, and all employees were subsequently made responsible for product quality. As a result, Whistler eliminated its quality problems and is now highly profitable once again.

The Planning-Controlling Link

Managers need to recognize the importance of establishing a tight linkage between planning and control. As indicated in Chapter 1, planning is usually the first part of the management process. The organizing and leading functions get the actual work of the organization done, and the controlling function is directly tied back into planning. For example, management plans to increase market share by 2 percent in each of the next seven years. At the end of year 1, as expected, market share has increased 2 percent. This performance, as measured by the control system, tells management that it should continue with the existing plan. At the end of year 2, market share has increased only 1 percent. This performance tells management that some adjustment is needed to steer the firm back toward its desired rate of growth. At the end of year 3, the control system reveals that the firm is exceeding its projected 2 percent growth rate by so much that a new plan is called for.

The organization continuously cycles back and forth between planning and controlling. The manager makes plans and then uses the control system to monitor progress toward fulfillment of those plans. The control system, in turn, tells the manager that things are going as they should (the current plan should be maintained), that things are not going as they should (the current plan should be modified), or that the situation has changed (a new plan should be developed). American Greetings has done a good job of establishing a link between its planning and control processes. Certain managers are now expected to do a good job of planning for seasonal card printing and distribution, and the control system keeps them and their bosses informed about how well they're doing. On the other hand, "Management in Practice" describes how Worlds of Wonder did a poor job of relating planning to control— with sobering results.

STEPS IN THE CONTROL PROCESS

Regardless of the type or number of control systems needed by an organization, there are four general steps in any control process.[10] They are illustrated in Figure 16.3.[11]

MANAGEMENT IN PRACTICE

POOR PLANNING—CONTROL LINK DOOMS WOW

Worlds of Wonder Inc. (WOW) was begun in Fremont, California, in 1985. WOW planned to manufacture and sell Teddy Ruxpin, an electronic talking toy bear. However, the toy was very costly to manufacture, so WOW set about finding ways to reduce those costs. A variety of options enabled WOW to get the market price below $100, and it was in business.

Sales were so strong that the company went public in 1986 with an initial stock offering. WOW stock sold extremely well despite a warning by some investors that it was overpriced.

WOW soon began to offer other talking dolls and toys along with an assortment of accessories. The company became one of the fastest-growing new manufacturing firms in history, racking up profits of nearly $20 million on sales of over $300 million in 1986. Early in 1987, WOW began to expand its product line from toys into school products such as binders and communication devices for children. WOW was a whiz at wooing customers; but it did not plan its growth well, nor did it provide for the quality and cost controls necessary to keep itself profitable.

Even priced at less than $100, Teddy Ruxpin was still expensive. By early 1987 numerous problems began to occur; its quality became an issue with consumers. Similar products were quickly introduced by other companies, and WOW maintained sales only by

slashing prices, which cut profit margins drastically. Sales of Lazer Tag sagged.

WOW's CEO, Donald D. Kingsborough, began to get a reputation for telling people what they wanted to hear and making promises that were never kept. Creditors began to push for their money, uncertain about the future of the firm. Retailers began to reduce their orders out of a fear that WOW would not be able to deliver the quantities ordered at the prices promised or on a timely basis. WOW began to lose its luster. Cost-cutting programs were introduced along with a flurry of new and less expensive products.

The end was at hand. In the third quarter of 1987, WOW lost over $180 million, owed over $250 million to creditors, and defaulted on nearly $4 million in interest payments to bondholders. Sales were not generating enough money to cover promotion costs. Lack of proper planning and control caught up with WOW, which filed for protection under Chapter 11 of the bankruptcy laws and spent 1988 trying to reorganize and restructure.

REFERENCES: "Worlds of Wonder: From Wall Street Charmer to Chapter 11." *Business Week*, March 21, 1988, pp. 74–78; Eugene Linden, "The Big Money in Busted Bonds," *Fortune*, February 15, 1988, pp. 100–106; "Chapter 11 for Teddy Ruxpin," *Time*, January 4, 1988, p. 59; Howard Rudnitsky, "Teddy Ruxpin Stumbles," *Forbes*, August 24, 1987, p. 35.

Establishing Standards

■ **standard** A target against which subsequent performance is to be compared

The first step in the control process is the establishment of standards. A **standard** is a target against which subsequent performance is to be compared. Standards for a fast-food restaurant like McDonald's might include the following:

1. A minimum of 95 percent of all customers will be greeted within three minutes of their arrival.
2. Precooked hamburgers will not sit in the warmer more than five minutes before they are served to customers.
3. All empty tables will be cleaned within five minutes after they have been vacated.

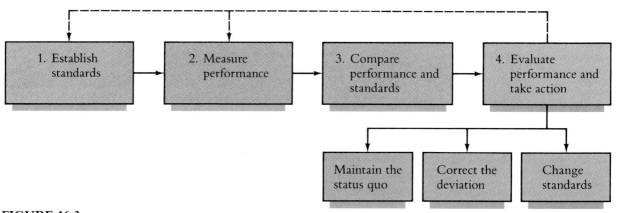

FIGURE 16.3

Steps in the Control Process

As much as possible, standards established for control purposes should be derived from the organization's goals. Like objectives, they should be expressed in measurable terms. Note that standard 1 for a fast-food restaurant has a time limit of three minutes and an objective target of 95 percent of all customers. In standard 2, the objective target is implied: "all" precooked hamburgers.

On a broader level, control standards also reflect organizational strategy. A control standard for a retailer might be the goal of increasing annual sales volume by 25 percent within five years. A hospital might aim to increase its patient recovery rate to 98 percent within six years. A university might adopt a standard, or goal, of graduating 80 percent of its student athletes within five years of their initial enrollment by the year 1993. In short, control standards can be as narrow or as broad as the level of activity to which they apply. Further, they must also follow logically from organizational goals and objectives.

A final aspect of establishing standards is to decide which performance indicators are relevant. When a new product is introduced, its manufacturer should have some idea in advance whether the first month's sales will accurately indicate long-term growth or whether sales will take a while to gather momentum. Similarly, when a retailer adopts a standard of increasing sales by 12 percent next year, management should have some idea whether to expect even growth of 1 percent per month or growth of 2 percent for the first ten months and 10 percent during the Christmas season. If the former, a 1 percent increase during the first six months is cause for alarm; if the latter, a 1 percent increase by July is probably acceptable.

Sharper Image, an upscale specialty shop, recently set two performance standards for yearly sales. One was that same-store sales (i.e., sales from stores already in operation) should increase by 5 percent from the previous year, while overall sales, including revenues from new stores, should increase by 25 percent. Those sales-increase levels represent both a goal and a standard, and each was also viewed as a relevant indicator of performance.[12]

Measuring Performance

■ **performance**   In a control context, that which one is attempting to control

The second step in the control process is measuring performance. In this context, **performance** refers to that which we are attempting to control. The measurement of performance is a constant, ongoing activity for most organizations, and for control to be effective, relevant performance measures must be valid. When a manager is concerned with controlling sales, daily, weekly, or monthly sales figures represent actual performance. For a production manager, performance may be expressed in terms of unit cost, quality, or volume. For employees, performance may be measured in terms of quality or quantity of output.

For many jobs, measuring performance is not easy. A research and development scientist at Merck, for example, may spend years working on a single project before achieving a major breakthrough. A manager who takes over a business that is on the brink of failure may need months or even years to turn things around. Nevertheless, some performance indicators can usually be developed. The scientist's progress can be partially assessed by peer review. The crucial point to recognize is that valid performance measurement, however difficult to obtain, is necessary to maintain effective control. At the end of its fiscal year, Sharper Image measured its total sales and sales for each individual store. The results indicated that although overall sales did indeed reach the desired 25 percent level of increase, same-store sales actually declined by 7 percent.

Comparing Performance Against Standards

The third step in the control process is to compare measured performance against the standards developed in step 1. Performance may be higher than, lower than, or the same as the standard. The issue is how much leeway is permissible before remedial action is taken. In some cases comparison is easy. Each product manager at General Electric has a goal of being either number 1 or number 2 in her or his market. It is relatively simple to determine whether this standard has been met. At Sharper Image, comparisons were also fairly easy to make—one standard was met and the other was not.

In other settings, however, comparisons are less clear-cut. Assume that each of three sales managers has a goal of increasing sales by 10 percent during the year. At the end of the year, one manager has increased sales by 9.9 percent, another by 9.3 percent, and the third by 8.7 percent. How do we decide whether each has met the standard? For the most part, this is a management decision that must be based on many relevant factors, including the absolute dollar amounts involved and any mitigating circumstances. Although none of the three sales managers attained the precise goal of 10 percent, one was very close. Another may have met with unexpected competition from a new company. These and other relevant factors must be considered.

It is also important that comparisons be made as often as necessary. For long-run and high-level standards, comparisons may be appropriate on an annual basis. In other circumstances, however, more frequent comparisons are called for. For example, a business with a cash shortage may need to monitor its on-hand cash reserves on a daily basis. We noted earlier that Emery Air Freight faced this dilemma, and managers there did indeed check their cash reserves often.

Evaluation and Action

The final step in the control process is to evaluate performance (by means of the comparisons made in step 3) and then take appropriate action. This evaluation draws heavily on a manager's analytic and diagnostic skills, which are discussed in Chapter 1. After evaluation, one of three actions is usually appropriate.

Maintain the Status Quo One response is to do nothing, or maintain the status quo. This action is generally appropriate when performance more or less measures up to the standard. If the standard for cost reductions this year is 4 percent and we have achieved a reduction of 3.99 percent, we are clearly on the right track. At Sharper Image, new-store sales were doing even better than expected, so no action was deemed necessary regarding their performance.

Correct the Deviation It is more likely that some action will be needed to correct a deviation from the standard. If the cost-reduction standard is 4 percent and we have thus far managed only a 1 percent reduction, something must be done to get us back on track. We may need to motivate our employees to work harder or supply them with new machinery. Managers at Sharper Image saw a clear problem with their same-store sales and took corrective action immediately. They increased advertising, brought in new products, and started paying more attention to their product mix.

In some situations, companies may be doing better than anticipated but still need to correct the deviation. For example, Ford has experienced such strong demand for its cars in recent years that there are waiting lists for some models. Critics have complained that pressure to make cars faster and faster has led to quality problems. Ford is reluctant to build new plants for fear of increasing costs too much, so the company has leased production facilities from other manufacturers and added extra shifts in existing plants in order to boost output.

Change Standards A final response to the outcome of comparing performance to standards is to change the standards. The standard may have been too high or too low to begin with. This is apparent if large numbers of employees exceed the standard by a wide margin or if no one ever meets the standard. In other situations, a standard that was perfectly good when it was set may need to be adjusted because circumstances have changed. A sales-increase standard of 10 percent may have to be modified when a new competitor comes on the scene. Given new market conditions, the old standard of 10 percent may no longer be realistic. One cause cited for Sharper Image's problems is increased competition from other specialty chains as well as department stores. Thus, the company may need to reassess its standard and adopt a lower one to better reflect the realities of its marketplace.

FORMS OF OPERATIONS CONTROL

We now turn our attention to the three levels of control practiced by most organizations. This section describes operations control systems. The next two sections address organizational and strategic control. (Chapter 19 discusses specific control techniques that may be used in these types of control.) As shown in Figure 16.4, operations control can take one of three forms—preliminary, screening, and postaction. The three forms vary primarily in terms of where they occur in relation to the transformation processes used by the organization.[13]

Preliminary Control

■ **preliminary control (steering or feedforward control)**   Attempts to monitor the quality or quantity of financial, physical, human, and information resources before they actually become part of the system

Preliminary control (also called **steering control or feedforward control**) concentrates on inputs to the system early in the overall process. Preliminary control attempts to monitor the quality or quantity of financial, physical, human, and information resources before they become part of the system.[14] Firms like Procter & Gamble and General

FIGURE 16.4

Forms of Operations Control

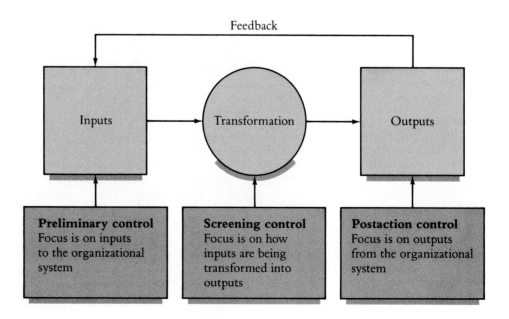

Mills hire only college graduates for their management training program—and only after several interviewers and other selection criteria have been satisfied. Thus, they control the quality of the human resource entering the organization. When Sears orders merchandise to be manufactured under its own brand name, it specifies rigid standards of quality, thereby controlling material inputs. Similarly, organizations often take steps to control financial and information resources as they enter the system. For example, privately held companies like UPS and Mars limit the extent to which outsiders can buy stock. Television networks like ABC and CBS refuse to accept certain kinds of advertising. And the Associated Press verifies the accuracy of its news stories before they are released.

Screening Control

■ **screening control (yes/no or concurrent control)** Relies heavily on feedback processes during the transformation process

Screening control (also called **yes/no control or concurrent control**) takes place during the transformation process. Screening control relies heavily on feedback processes. Suppose that a manager of a manufacturing plant establishes a number of checkpoints along the assembly line. As the product moves along the line, it is periodically checked to make sure that all of the components assembled so far are working properly. This is screening control, because the product is being controlled during the transformation process itself. Because screening controls are widely applicable and useful in identifying the cause of problems, they tend to be used more often than other forms of control.

More and more companies are adopting a screening control philosophy. Such control systems are an effective way to promote employee

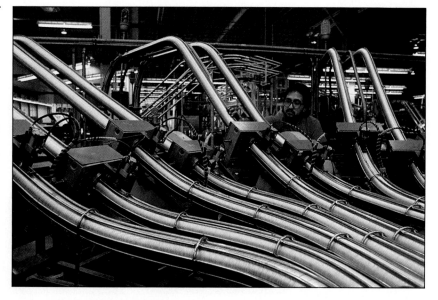

Forms of control include preliminary, screening, and postaction. Ball Corporation has made extensive use of screening control to reduce labor and material costs. One system called FastTrack, illustrated here, uses machines to visually inspect the ends of beer and soft drink cans. The company can inspect 100 percent of its products as they are being manufactured, faster and with less expense than if it relied on human inspectors.

participation and catch problems early in the transformation process. For example, Corning Glass Works recently adopted such a system for use in manufacturing television glass. Under its old system, finished television screens were casually inspected only after they were finished, and over 4 percent of them were later returned by customers because of tiny defects. Under Corning's new system, the glass screens are inspected at each step in the production process, and the return rate from customers has dropped to .03 percent.[15]

Postaction Control

postaction control   Monitors the outputs or results of the organization after the transformation process is complete

Postaction control focuses on the outputs of the organization after the transformation process is complete. Corning's old system was postaction control—final inspection only after everything is done. Even though Corning abandoned postaction control, it is useful and effective in certain situations, such as when a product or service is fairly simple and routine. If a product can be manufactured in only two or three steps, postaction control may be the most effective method. Although postaction control is generally not so useful as preliminary or screening control, it can be effective in two important ways. It provides management with information for future planning. For example, when a quality check of finished goods indicates an unacceptably high defective rate, the manager knows that he or she must ferret out the causes and take steps to correct them. Postaction control also provides a basis for rewarding employees. Recognizing that an employee has exceeded her or his sales goals (planned outputs) by a wide margin, for example, may alert the manager that a bonus or promotion is in order.[16]

Multiple Control Systems

Most organizations cannot survive by using only one form of operational control; thus, most firms adopt multiple controls. For example, Ford Motor Company uses preliminary control by hiring only qualified employees and specifying required quality standards when ordering parts from other manufacturers. It also uses numerous screening controls by checking the quality of various components of its cars as they are being assembled. A final inspection and test drive as each car rolls off the assembly line is part of the company's postaction control system. Figure 16.5 shows how multiple controls might be used by a small manufacturing firm, and "The Global View" describes how a large international company, British Airways, used multiple controls to regain its competitive advantage in the airline industry.

FORMS OF ORGANIZATIONAL CONTROL

We noted earlier that organizations practice various kinds of control over their overall design and operating systems. Two dominant forms

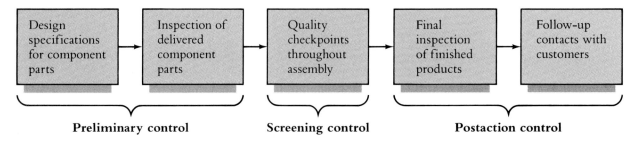

FIGURE 16.5

Multiple Control Systems

of organizational control are bureaucratic control and clan control.[17] These two forms anchor opposite ends of a series of dimensions, as shown in Figure 16.6. A few organizations may fall at one extreme or the other, but most have tendencies toward one form but characteristics of both.

Bureaucratic Control

■ **bureaucratic control**   A form of organizational control characterized by formal and mechanistic structural arrangements

Bureaucratic control is a form of organizational control characterized by formal and mechanistic structural arrangements. As shown in Figure 16.6, the goal of bureaucratic control is to extract employee compliance. Organizations that use it rely on strict rules and a rigid hierarchy, concentrate on ensuring that people meet minimally acceptable levels of performance, and have a tall structure. Moreover, they focus their rewards on individual performance and allow only limited and formal employee participation.

NBC television approaches organizational control in ways that reflect many elements of bureaucratic control. Numerous rules have been established to regulate employee travel, expense accounts, and so forth. A new performance appraisal system goes to great lengths to specify minimally acceptable levels of performance. The organization's structure is considerably taller than those of the other major networks. Rewards are based on individual contributions. And finally, many employees have argued that they have too small a voice in how the organization is managed.[18]

Clan Control

■ **clan control**   An approach to organizational control based on informal and organic structural arrangements

Clan control is an approach to organizational control based on informal and organic structural arrangements. As indicated in Figure 16.6, its goal is employee commitment. Accordingly, it relies heavily on group norms, a strong corporate culture, and self-control of behavior. The focus of performance is not so much on minimally acceptable levels, but rather on how people can enhance their levels of performance

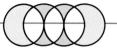

THE GLOBAL VIEW

BRITISH AIRWAYS CONTROLS EFFECTIVENESS

British Airways, or BA as it is popularly known, was in trouble throughout the 1970s. It had an inattentive management group and a huge, unproductive work force. Service was so poor that people began to say that BA stood for "Bloody Awful." In fact, BA had losses of nearly $1 billion by 1981. Then a new management team was brought in and instituted a program of multiple controls that restored the company to success and enabled it to compete effectively in a highly competitive international market.

The first effort of the new management team was to get control of costs through the sale of surplus aircraft and the reduction of the work force from nearly 60,000 to around 36,000. Next came changing the habits and patterns of business, which was accomplished by switching banks and advertising agencies to signal that BA was changing and improving.

In other control efforts, BA concentrated on its customers. Paying attention to their needs and wants greatly improved service. New uniforms conveyed a sense of change. Business-class lounges lured managers to BA flights. Food service was improved. "Hunters" were located in London's Heathrow Airport to locate and help bewildered passengers. At several airports BA passengers can videotape comments or criticisms to be viewed later by the company.

BA has implemented the use of advanced technology in operations to ensure the achievement of flight schedules, proper maintenance of all aircraft, efficient baggage handling, and proper delivery of meals to aircraft. Marketing programs are utilizing sophisticated techniques with splashy graphics and targeted appeals.

BA has used acquisitions and joint ventures to make its massive global route structure more capable of closely matching the travel patterns of its clientele. It developed a unique arrangement with United Airlines in the United States to share ground facilities and various customer services to better link BA with cities within the borders of the continental United States. Because United is the largest U.S. carrier, this arrangement substantially increased BA travel loads. Further, BA and United are jointly marketing vacation travel packages that utilize both carriers.

The impact of these control efforts has been to turn the company around in a relatively short period of time. BA's profits at the end of its fiscal year early in 1988 were the highest in the industry—$284 million from sales of about $7 billion. To achieve these results, BA expanded its routes so that it now serves 166 cities in 80 countries. BA is now the largest international airline, with over 23 million passengers logging over 30 billion passenger-miles.

REFERENCES: Kenneth Labich, "The Big Comeback at British Airways," *Fortune*, December 5, 1988, pp. 163–174; John R. Stodden, "Investors Endorse British Airways' Strategies for Growth, Profits," *Aviation Week & Space Technology*, July 10, 1988, pp. 99–100; Amy Dermar, "Airline Cargo Tracking Plan Promises One Stop Shipping," *PC Week*, May 31, 1988, p. 815; "British Airways PLC," *The Wall Street Journal*, October 19, 1988, p. 11.

beyond minimum levels. Organizations using this approach are usually relatively flat and encourage shared influence. Rewards are often directed at group performance, and participation is widespread.

Levi Strauss practices clan control. Much of the work of the company is accomplished by groups and teams. Thus, group norms help facilitate high performance, and rewards are subsequently provided to the best-performing groups and teams. The company's culture reinforces contributions to the overall team effort, and employees are very loyal to the organization. Levi's has a flat structure and power is widely shared. Participation is also encouraged in all areas of operation.[19]

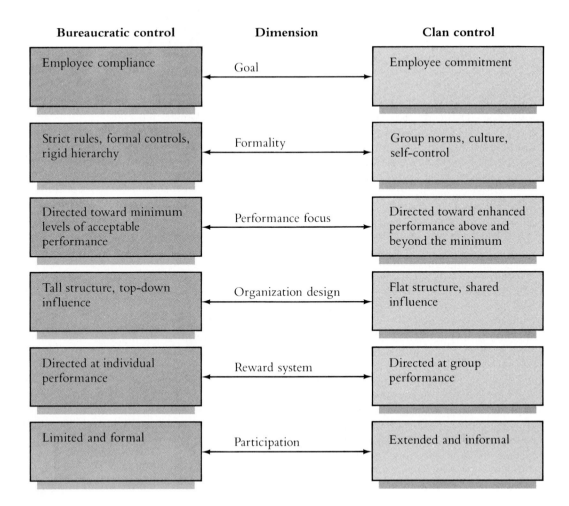

Bureaucratic control	Dimension	Clan control
Employee compliance	Goal	Employee commitment
Strict rules, formal controls, rigid hierarchy	Formality	Group norms, culture, self-control
Directed toward minimum levels of acceptable performance	Performance focus	Directed toward enhanced performance above and beyond the minimum
Tall structure, top-down influence	Organization design	Flat structure, shared influence
Directed at individual performance	Reward system	Directed at group performance
Limited and formal	Participation	Extended and informal

FIGURE 16.6

Bureaucratic Versus Clan Control

■ **strategic control** Control aimed at insuring that the organization is maintaining an effective alignment with its environment and moving toward achieving its strategic goals

STRATEGIC CONTROL

Strategic control—the third level of control practiced by organizations—is aimed at ensuring that the organization is maintaining an effective alignment with its environment and moving toward achieving its strategic goals.[20] Because the study of strategic control is still in its infancy, there are no generally accepted models or theories. In general, however, as we noted in Chapter 6, the implementation of strategy generally involves five basic areas: structure, leadership, technology, human resources, and information and control systems. Thus, it follows that strategic control should focus on these five areas in order to ensure that strategy has been and is being effectively implemented.

For example, the organization should periodically examine its structure to determine whether it is facilitating the strategic goals being sought. Suppose that a firm using a functional (U-form) design has a goal of growing at a rate of 20 percent per year but is currently growing at a rate of 10 percent per year. Close examination might reveal that

One vitally important area of strategic control is technology. Organizations that fail to keep pace with technological breakthroughs and innovations may suffer competitive disadvantages. General Electric attempts to be at the forefront of technological developments. These satellite dishes at the GE American station in California receive and transmit signals to orbiting communications satellites. GE satellites carry over 14,000 hours of radio and television programming every week.

the firm's current structure is inhibiting growth in some way (for example, by slowing decision making and inhibiting innovation). This examination could also suggest that the adoption of a divisional (M-form) design is more likely to facilitate the desired growth (for example, by speeding decision making and promoting innovation).

Strategic control should be focused on the extent to which the five areas of strategy implementation are facilitating the accomplishment of the organization's strategic goals. If they are, the organization should respond in the same way as with other forms of control—maintain the status quo. If, on the other hand, one or more of the methods of implementation are inhibiting the attainment of goals, it should be changed. Consequently, the firm might find it necessary to alter its structure, replace key leaders, adopt new technology, modify its human resources, or change its information and operational control systems.[21]

For example, the board of directors at Borden's realized that the company was not meeting its strategic goals and was not providing its stockholders with an adequate return on their investment. The board's starting point in correcting things was to bring in a new CEO (change in leadership). The new CEO, Romeo Ventres, then changed the company's structure (from an H-form to an M-form), implemented a variety of new manufacturing techniques to enhance productivity (change in technology), brought in several new managers (change in human resources), installed a new management information system to help him keep track of all areas of the organization's operations (change in information systems), and mandated new levels of product quality (change in operational control). As a result, Borden became much more effective.[22]

MANAGING THE CONTROL PROCESS

Understanding the steps and levels of control is necessary if a manager truly wants to have effective control. There are also other aspects of effective control, however. And managers need to understand how to overcome the occasional resistance to control.

Developing Effective Control Systems

What constitutes an effective control system? Control systems tend to be most effective when they are integrated with planning and are flexible, accurate, timely, and objective.

Integrated with Planning   We noted earlier that control should be linked with planning. In general, the more explicit and precise this linkage is, the more effective the control system will be. The most important factor in effectively integrating planning and control is to account for control as plans are developed. For example, as goals are set as part of the planning process, allowances should be made at the

Joe Avery, V.P. of operations for Adept Technology, Inc., keeps a careful eye on Adept's newest robot—the AdeptThree. Avery realizes that control systems are important to the success of the company, so he appreciates the company's policy of integrating inventory control, manufacturing performance, and quality control.

Adept's goal is to be a world-class robot manufacturer and they are moving closer to that goal because of their successful control process.

same time for converting goals into standards to reflect how well the plan is being realized. For example, managers at Champion Spark Plug Company recently decided to broaden their product line to include a full range of automotive accessories—a total of 21 new products altogether. As a part of this plan, managers decided in advance what level of sales they wanted to realize from each product for each of the next five years, and they established those sales goals as standards against which actual sales would be compared. Thus, by accounting for their control system as they developed their plan, managers at Champion did an excellent job of tying planning and control together.[23]

Flexible Another characteristic of an effective control system is flexibility—that is, the control system itself must be flexible enough to accommodate change. Consider an organization whose diverse product line requires 75 different raw materials. The company's inventory control system must be able to manage and monitor current levels of inventory for all 75 materials. When a change in product line changes the number of raw materials needed, or when the required quantities of any of the existing materials change, the control system should be able to accommodate the revised requirements. Designing and implementing a new control system would be an unnecessary expense. Champion had to revise one of its standards when one of its biggest customers, Montgomery Ward, decided to not stock the full line of Champion products.

Accurate Control systems must also be accurate. This seems obvious enough, but it is surprising how many managers base decisions on inaccurate information. Sales representatives in the field may hedge their sales estimates to make themselves look good. Production managers may hide costs to meet their targets. Human resource managers may overestimate their minority recruiting prospects to meet Affirmative Action goals. In each case the information received by upper management is inaccurate.

Denied accurate measurement and reporting of performance, managers may take inappropriate action, and the results of inaccurate information can be quite dramatic. If sales estimates are artificially high, a manager might either cut advertising (thinking it is no longer needed) or increase advertising (to further build momentum). In either case the action may not be appropriate. Similarly, having been fed artificially low production costs, a manager who is unaware of the hidden costs may quote a sales price much lower than desirable. Or a human resource executive may speak out publicly on the effectiveness of the company's minority recruiting, only to find out later that the number of prospects has been overestimated.

Timely   Another characteristic of an effective control system is that it provides performance information in a timely way. Timeliness does not necessarily mean fast; it simply means that information is provided as often as is suitable for that which is being controlled. Champion has a wealth of historical data on its spark-plug sales and so needs new information on a regular but not necessarily constant basis. For its new products, however, managers took steps to get sales feedback on a more frequent basis. In a retail store, sales results are usually needed daily so that cash flow can be managed, advertising and promotion adjusted, and so on. Physical inventory counts, however, may be taken only quarterly or even annually. When a new product comes on the market, managers may need frequent sales reports to gauge public acceptance. For older, more established products, sales reports are needed less often. In general, the more uncertain and unstable the situation, the more frequently measurement is needed; the more predictable and stable the situation, the less often it is needed.

Objective   To the extent possible, the information provided by the control system should be objective. Consider a human resource manager who is responsible for the control of an organization's human resources. He asks two plant managers to submit reports summarizing their respective plants' human resource situations. One manager notes that morale at his plant is "okay," that grievances are "about where they should be," and that turnover is "under control." The other reports that absenteeism at her plant is running at 4 percent, that sixteen grievances have been filed this year (compared with twenty-four last year), and that turnover is 12 percent. Which manager's report is more useful?

Of course, objectivity is not everything, and managers need to look beyond the numbers when making decisions. When a sales representative is posting impressive sales increases every month, or when a production manager is cutting costs consistently, upper-level managers should be pleased. However, one way to increase sales is to offer unauthorized discounts, make unrealistic guarantees about product performance, or promise early delivery dates. Costs can be cut by decreasing quality or putting unreasonable pressure on employees. For obvious reasons, those techniques may not be in the best interests of the organization. The control system should therefore provide objective information to the manager for evaluation and action, but the manager must take appropriate precautions in interpreting it.

Understanding Resistance to Control

As useful and effective as properly designed control systems can be, many people still resist control. Some common reasons for resistance are overcontrol, inappropriate focus, rewards for inefficiency, and accountability.

Overcontrol   Occasionally, organizations make the mistake of overcontrol—they try to control too many things. This becomes especially problematic when the control relates directly to employee behavior. If an organization tells its employees when to come to work, where to park, when to have morning coffee, and when to leave for the day, it is exerting considerable control over their daily activities. Yet many organizations find it necessary to impose these rules. Troubles arise when additional, gratuitous controls are added. If a company also tells its employees how to dress, what they can and cannot put on their desks, and how to wear their hair, employees are likely to feel overcontrolled. Employees at Chrysler used to complain because if they drove a non-Chrysler vehicle they were forced to park in a distant parking lot. Drivers of Chrysler products, however, were allowed to park close to the building. Thus, the point to remember is that if controls are perceived as excessive, employees resist them.

Inappropriate Focus   Another reason for resistance is that the focus of the control system may be inappropriate. The control system may be too narrow, or it may focus too much on quantifiable variables and leave no room for analysis or interpretation. A sales standard that encourages high-pressure tactics to maximize short-run sales may do so at the expense of goodwill from long-term customers. Such a standard is too narrow. A university reward system that encourages faculty members to publish large numbers of articles but fails to consider the quality of the work is also inappropriately focused.

Rewards for Inefficiency   Imagine two operating departments that are approaching the end of the fiscal year. One department expects to have $5,000 of its budget left over; the second is already $3,000 in the red. As a result, department 1 is likely to have its budget cut for the next year ("They had money left, so they obviously got too much to begin with"), and department 2 is likely to get a budget increase ("They obviously haven't been getting enough money"). Thus, department 1 is punished for being efficient and department 2 is rewarded for being inefficient. (No wonder departments commonly hasten to deplete their budgets as the end of the year approaches!) People naturally resist this kind of control, because the rewards and punishments associated with spending and conserving are unfair. Budgeting processes are examined in detail in Chapter 19.

Accountability   Another reason some people resist control is that effective control systems create accountability. When people have the responsibility to do something, effective controls allow managers to determine whether they successfully discharge that responsibility. If standards are properly set and performance is accurately measured, managers not only know when problems arise but also which departments and even which individuals are responsible. Some people, especially those who are not doing a good job, do not want to be answerable for their mistakes and therefore resist control. The issue of accountability is becoming even more sensitive today. For example, American Express has a computer system that provides daily information on how many calls each of its operators handles. And not surprisingly, some of the operators are unhappy with the system.

Overcoming Resistance to Control

Several techniques can help managers overcome resistance to control. The most common ones are ensuring the effectiveness of controls, encouraging participation, using MBO, and developing a good blend of checks and balances.

Create Effective Controls   Perhaps the best way to overcome resistance to control is to create effective control to begin with. If control systems are properly integrated with an organization's planning system and if the controls are flexible, accurate, timely, and objective, the organization should not fall victim to the problems of overcontrol, incorrect focus, or rewarding inefficiency. Those employees who fear accountability most will perhaps be held even more accountable for their poor performance.

Encourage Participation   Chapter 11 notes that participation can help overcome resistance to change. By the same token, when employees are involved with planning and implementing the control system, they are less likely to resist it. For instance, employee participation in planning, decision making, and quality control at the Chevrolet Gear Axle plant in Detroit has resulted in increased employee concern for quality and a greater commitment to meeting standards.[24]

Use MBO   Management by objectives, or MBO (discussed in Chapter 7), can also overcome employee resistance to control. When MBO is used properly, employees help establish their own goals. These goals, in turn, become standards against which their performance will be measured. Employees also know in advance that their rewards will be based on the extent to which they achieve and maintain those goals and standards. MBO, then, is a vehicle for facilitating the integration of planning and control.

Use Checks and Balances   Another way to overcome employee resistance to control is to maintain a system of checks and balances. Suppose that a production manager argues that he or she failed to meet a certain cost standard because of the increased prices of raw materials. If the inventory control system is properly designed, it should either clearly support or clearly refute the production manager's explanation. Or suppose that an employee who has been fired for excessive absences argues that she or he has not been absent "for a long time." The human resource control system should have records on the matter. Multiple standards and information systems provide checks and balances for control. Resistance declines because the system of checks and balances serves to protect employees as well as management. For example, if the production manager's argument about the rising cost of raw materials is supported by the inventory control records, he or she will not be held solely accountable for failing to meet the cost standard. Instead, action should be taken to correct the problems of raw materials cost.

CHOOSING A STYLE OF CONTROL

How should a manager develop a style of control? One approach to selecting a style of control bases the decision on four factors: management style, organizational style, performance measures, and employee desire to participate.[25] Table 16.1 suggests four questions about these factors that managers can ask themselves. Management styles are presumed to be either participative (consulting with subordinates) or directive (telling others what to do). Organizational style, which is a composite of culture, structure, and reward systems, can be participative (participative decision making throughout the organization) or nonparticipative (centralized, with few people participating in the decision-making process). Performance measures are classified as accurate (reliable, valid, and truly reflective of performance) or relatively inaccurate (unreliable, ambiguous, and not totally reflective of performance). Finally, employees are assumed to have either considerable desire to participate in decision making or little desire to participate.

The answers to the questions posed in Table 16.1 indicate the form of organizational control a manager should adopt. The decision tree shown in Figure 16.7 illustrates how different answers lead to different types of control. The manager answers each of the questions in Table 16.1 and follows the appropriate path along the decision tree. For example, if the manager's leadership style is participative, the organization has a participative culture, and the employees want to participate

1. **In general, what kind of managerial style do I have?**

   Participative: I frequently consult my subordinates on decisions, encourage them to disagree with my opinion, share information with them, and let them make decisions whenever possible.

   Directive: I usually take most of the responsibility for and make most of the major decisions, pass on only the most necessary job-relevant information, and provide detailed and close direction for my subordinates.

2. **In general, what kind of culture, structure, and reward system does my organization have?**

   Participative: Employees at all levels of the organization are used to participate in decisions and influence the course of events. Managers are clearly rewarded for developing employees' skills and decision-making capacity.

   Nonparticipative: Most important decisions are made by a few people at the top of the organization. Managers are not rewarded for developing employee competence or encouraging employees to participate in decision making.

3. **How accurate and reliable are the measures of key areas of subordinate performance?**

   Accurate: Measures are reliable, all major aspects of performance can be adequately measured, changes in measures accurately reflect changes in performance, measures cannot be easily sabotaged or faked by subordinates.

   Inaccurate: Not all important aspects of performance can be measured, measures often do not pick up on important changes in performance, good performance cannot be adequately defined in terms of the measures, measures can be easily sabotaged.

4. **Do my subordinates desire to participate and respond well to opportunities to take responsibility for decision making and performance?**

   High desire to participate: Employees are eager to participate in decisions, can make a contribution to decision making, and want to take more responsibility.

   Low desire to participate: Employees do not want to be involved in many decisions, do not want additional responsibility, and have little to contribute to decisions being made.

SOURCE: Reprinted by permission of the *Harvard Business Review*. An exhibit from "Fit Control Systems to Your Management Style" by Cortlandt Cammann and David A. Nadler (January–February 1976). Copyright © 1976 by the President and Fellows of Harvard College; all rights reserved.

TABLE 16.1

Useful Questions to Ask When Choosing a Control Strategy

(the top path through the diagram), clan control will probably work best. Note that not all paths (including the one we just traced) involve all four questions. This stems from the fact that if managers and organizations are participative and employees desire to participate, clan control is probably appropriate regardless of the accuracy of performance measures.

Viewed in this context, clan control would provide employees with intrinsic rewards such as feelings of accomplishment, well-being, responsibility, growth, and achievement. Hence, the organization might also adopt job enrichment or modified workweeks. On the other hand, a bureaucratic control system might be compatible with an external motivation strategy offering extrinsic rewards such as pay status symbols. Most organizations need multiple control systems and require not only organizational control but also operational and strategic control.

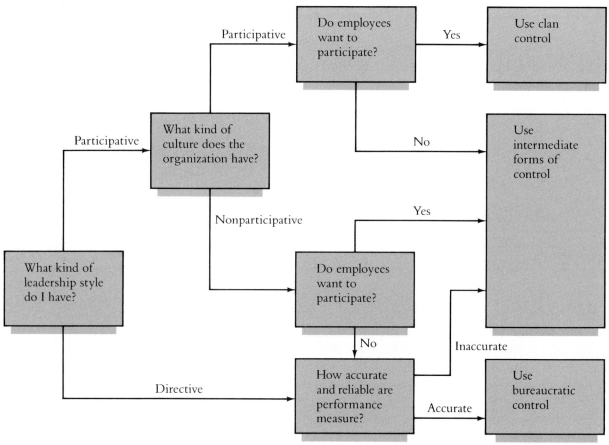

SOURCE: Adapted from Cortlandt Cammann and David A. Nadler, "Fit Control Systems to Your Management Style," *Harvard Business Review*, January–February 1976, pp. 65–72.

FIGURE 16.7

Selecting a Control Strategy

Thus, this framework should be seen as only a general guide to help managers understand more about how they should approach control in their organization.

SUMMARY OF KEY POINTS

Control is the regulation of one or more organizational activities in such a way as to facilitate goal attainment. The purpose of control is to guide the organization toward its goals; thus, control is very important. In general, it is directed toward financial, physical, information, and human resources. Control is the responsibility of managers, the controller, and, increasingly, operating employees. Planning and controlling are intimately related.

Four basic steps are involved in the control process. Standards of expected performance must be established, actual performance measured, comparisons made between performance and the standards, and appropriate action taken.

There are three basic forms of operations control. Preliminary control focuses on inputs to the system. Screening control, perhaps the most effective kind, concentrates on the transformation process itself. Post-action control focuses on outputs; it provides information for future planning and for rewarding employees. Most organizations need multiple control systems.

There are two basic forms of organizational control, bureaucratic and clan. Each represents one extreme, but most organizations use a form of organizational control somewhere in between.

Strategic control is undertaken to ensure that strategic goals are achieved. Most strategic control efforts are directed at one or more of the methods used to implement strategy.

One way to increase the effectiveness of control is to ensure that planning and control are fully integrated. The control system should also be flexible, accurate, timely, and as objective as possible. Many employees resist organizational control because of overcontrol, inappropriate focus on control, rewards for inefficiency, and fear of accountability. Managers can help overcome their resistance by concentrating on the things that improve the effectiveness of control. In addition, they can allow employee participation, use MBO, and establish a system of checks and balances.

Four situational factors that help determine the appropriate control strategy are management style, organizational style, the accuracy of performance measures, and employee desire to participate. Managers may adopt a bureaucratic, a clan, or a combined approach to control based on those four factors.

DISCUSSION QUESTIONS

Questions for Review

1. What is the purpose of organizational control? Why is it important?
2. What are the steps in the control process? Which step is likely to be the most difficult to perform? Why?
3. What are the similarities and differences between the various forms of operations control? What are the costs and benefits of each form?
4. How can a manager understand and overcome resistance and make control effective?

Questions for Analysis

5. How is the controlling process related to the functions of planning, organizing, and leading?
6. Are the differences in bureaucratic control and clan control related to differences in organization structure? If so, how? If not, why

not (the terms do sound similar to those used to discuss the organizing process)?

7. How does one go about choosing a style of control?

Questions for Application

8. Does your college or university have a controller? If so, find out how the position fits into the organization's design. If not, why do you think such a position has not been created?

9. Interview several local managers to determine which form of operations control is most frequently used by them—preliminary, screening, postaction, or multiple. How might you account for what you found?

10. Ask managers from different parts of the same organization or from different organizations what makes controls effective. How do their views compare with those presented in this chapter? Why might differences exist?

NOTES

1. "American Greetings Is Carding Gains," *USA Today*, August 24, 1988, p. 3B; "Flounder," *Forbes*, April 25, 1988, p. 352; Sara E. Stern, "Card Rivals Deal Ads," *Advertising Age*, July 27, 1987, p. 28.

2. Peter F. Drucker, *Managing in Turbulent Times* (New York: Harper & Row, 1980).

3. Joel Dreyfuss, "Victories in the Quality Crusade," *Fortune*, October 10, 1988, pp. 80–88.

4. Dreyfuss, "Victories in the Quality Crusade."

5. "Why Emery Is Biting Its Nails," *Business Week*, August 29, 1988, p. 34.

6. "America's Leanest and Meanest," *Business Week*, October 5, 1987, pp. 78–84.

7. Charles W. L. Hill, "Differentiation Versus Low Cost or Differentiation and Low Cost: A Contingency Framework," *Academy of Management Review*, July 1988, pp. 401–412.

8. Vijay Sathe, "Who Should Control Division Controllers?" *Harvard Business Review*, September–October 1978, pp. 99–104.

9. "The Controller—Inflation Gives Him More Clout with Management," *Business Week*, August 15, 1977, pp. 85–87, 90, 95.

10. Edward E. Lawler III and John G. Rhode, *Information and Control in Organizations* (Pacific Palisades, Calif.: Goodyear, 1976).

11. Robert N. Anthony, *The Management Control Function* (Boston: Harvard Business School Press, 1988).

12. "The Sharper Image May Need to Refocus," *Business Week*, November 21, 1988, p. 84.

13. See Stephen G. Green and M. Ann Welsh, "Cybernetics and Dependence: Reframing the Control Concept," *Academy of Management Review*, April 1988, pp. 287–301.

14. Harold Koontz and Robert W. Bradspies, "Managing Through Feedforward Control," *Business Horizons*, June 1972, pp. 25–36.

15. Dreyfuss, "Victories in the Quality Crusade."

16. Anthony, *The Management Control Function*.

17. William G. Ouchi, "The Transmission of Control Through Organizational Hierarchy," *Academy of Management Journal*, June 1978, pp. 173–192; Richard E. Walton, "From Control to Commitment in the Workplace," *Harvard Business Review*, March–April 1985, pp. 76–84.

18. "As NBC News Cuts Costs Will It Clobber Quality?" *Business Week*, December 5, 1988, pp. 137–138.

19. "The Push for Quality," *Business Week*, June 8, 1987, pp. 130–135.

20. Peter Lorange, Michael F. Scott Morton, and Sumantra Ghoshal, *Strategic Control* (St. Paul, Minn.: West, 1986).

21. For other perspectives, see Georg Schreyogg and Horst Steinmann, "Strategic Control: A New Perspective," *Academy of Management Review*, January 1987, pp. 91–103.

22. Walter Guzzard, "Big Can Still Be Beautiful," *Fortune*, April 25, 1988, pp. 50–64.

23. "Champion Is Starting to Show a Little Spark," *Business Week*, March 21, 1988, p. 87; "Champion Spark Plug Agrees to Merge with Dana Corp. for $17.50 a Share," *The Wall Street Journal*, January 26, 1989, p. A4.

24. Charles G. Burck, "What Happens When Workers Manage Themselves," *Fortune*, July 27, 1981, pp. 62–69.

25. Cortlandt Cammann and David A. Nadler, "Fit Control Systems to Your Management Style," *Harvard Business Review*, January–February 1976, pp. 65–72.

CASE 16.1

Pan Am's Struggles

Juan Trippe and a group of financial backers put together several air service organizations in the early 1920s. One was particularly successful because of U.S. mail contracts, but a split among the owners led Trippe to form yet another aviation company. To bid successfully for a Key West to Havana mail route, Trippe had to merge his company with two other far less successful outfits, one of which was named Pan American Airways. Trippe kept that name and slowly expanded the operations of Pan Am. By 1930, it was the world's largest air transport company. At the end of World War II, Trippe tried to sell 49 percent of Pan Am to the federal government so that the United States would have only a single carrier with which to compete internationally. That did not happen.

What did happen was not just a tremendous increase in international competition from the flag carriers of other countries, but an increase in domestic competition as well. Trans World Airlines began to compete with Pan Am along its Atlantic routes and United along its Pacific ones. Pan Am began to lose market share but continued to operate as if it were still almost a monopoly—buying the latest equipment whether it was necessary or not, trying to fly into every airport in the world whether or not there were enough passengers to make flights worthwhile, and showing such disdain for passengers that Pan Am became known as one of the most unfriendly airlines in the world. Pan Am had no effective control systems to deal with its finances or its operations.

When Pan Am actually lost money in 1969, Trippe left the organization. The company's losses continued to mount, and Trippe's successor seemed even worse than he had been. The board of directors asked for his resignation after he had been on the job only 27 months. Then, in 1972, William Seawell took over. Seawell shrank the route system in order to make Pan Am more profitable, negotiated a substantial wage cut from Pan Am's employees on the promise to make it back up to them later when the firm was again profitable, and lobbied arduously with the government over fares and routes in a further effort to provide enough profitable routes to keep the company alive. Finally, in 1977, Pan Am was profitable for the first time since 1968 and seemed to have turned around.

The turnaround was short-lived, however, because the federal government began to deregulate the airlines industry. Pan Am was unprepared for deregulation because it had never been allowed to operate domestic flights and had never learned by experience the lessons of competition. By 1981, the company was again in the red. After several years of losses, Pan Am sold its Pacific routes to United and was able to show a profit in 1985. The year 1986, however, showed huge losses again, and a dissident group of shareholders confronted the CEO to try to bring about changes in the company. The result was another change at the top. In January 1988, Thomas G. Plaskett, a former American Airlines marketing executive who also had experience with Continental, was named president, chairman, and CEO of Pan Am. Although he had all three titles, it was clear that if he failed to perform he would be replaced.

Plaskett immediately began to implement control systems designed to correct Pan Am's situation. To gain control over costs, he followed through on negotiations that had already begun with Pan Am's unions for concessions on wages, salaries, and benefits. He was relatively successful, obtaining contracts from two unions quickly and from a third soon after that and not getting a strike from the others even though contract negotiations became protracted and eventually had to be settled through arbitration. Throughout these negotiations, care was taken so that employee morale would not be further eroded. Discouraged or ambivalent employees could damage service, driving passengers away and worsening the company's problems. To gain control over finances, the company installed a new computerized system to balance the mix of discount and higher fares on flights. These moves, it was hoped, would enable the company to become profitable again. Profitability, in turn, would induce investors to support the company so that it would have money to upgrade other aspects of its operations, such as renovating the interiors of its jets. Plaskett also stressed the importance of flights arriving on time and proper maintenance.

Plaskett moved to improve communication. He holds regular meetings with subordinate managers, drafts letters to employees on his personal computer, and has made a videotape to answer many common questions raised by employees. These moves have met with favorable reactions, and morale within the organization has improved.

Questions

1. What happened to the planning-control link at Pan Am? Why might that have occurred?
2. Which forms of control can you identify at Pan Am? Which forms seem clearly absent?
3. How might controls at Pan Am be made more effective? What would you recommend with regard to Pan Am's control systems? Why?
4. Go to the library and find out how Pan Am is faring today. Has its situation improved? Why or why not? Is it likely to improve? Why or why not?

REFERENCES: "Airline's Chief Seeks a Miracle," *USA Today*, August 2, 1988, pp. 1B–2B; "Pan Am and TWA, Battered by Rivals, Struggle to Survive," *The Wall Street Journal*, October 18, 1988, pp. A1, A20; "Pan Am May Get Labor Cost Concessions; Changes in Senior Management Planned," *The Wall Street Journal*, January 6, 1988, p. 3; "Pan Am's New Chief: In the Cockpit—But Not Yet in Control," *Business Week*, February 8, 1988, pp. 30–31; "Pan Am Needs a Patron, But Does Anybody Need Pan Am?" *Business Week*, April 10, 1989, pp. 92–94.

CASE 16.2

Benetton Busting at Its Seams

Benetton, the Italian sportswear company, came into being in 1955 in Treviso near Venice, Italy, when Luciano Benetton persuaded his sister to let him sell to stores the sweaters that she knit. By the early 1960s, the company was becoming successful, and Luciano decided to market the sweaters only through specialized knitwear outlets rather than through department stores. In 1965, the Benetton company was formally organized, and its first factory was built in Ponzano just outside of Treviso. In 1967, the first Benetton store opened.

Benetton controlled the early stores carefully. Store managers were taught by area representatives how to dress windows and develop advertisements. The success of such careful control was clear, and more and more stores began to open. By 1975, there were about 200 stores in Italy. In an interesting and novel move, Benetton developed different small shops to appeal to different segments of the market.

Benetton computerized its information flow and modified operations to make it responsive to the market. Benetton manufactures and keeps a certain portion of products uncolored. As reports from stores start arriving about which colors are most popular, products are quickly colored and rushed to the stores to meet demand. Though expensive, this way of operating keeps inventories low and, by meeting demand precisely, attracts customers.

America was the market into which Benetton wanted to move for the greatest possible impact and success. Luciano felt that the company could eventually support 4,000 shops in the United States. Thus, in the early 1980s, Benetton began to open its American stores and adapted its product offerings to meet local tastes. For the U.S. market, it added T-shirts because they are a fashion staple in America.

The marketing organization for the United States is carefully controlled. The country is organized into 14 regions, each of which is controlled by an agent. The agents show new collections to store owners, take orders for the retail outlets, select shopkeepers and store managers, and convey market information to Benetton headquarters. The agents earn a 4 percent commission on the orders they place. The shops and stores are not franchises but rather are licensed. The retailers pay no royalties and receive no investment backing from Benetton. They do sign an agreement to conform to a strict set of standards and to buy exclusively from Benetton.

The standards encompass everything from window displays to merchandising. The sweaters on display, for example, must be folded in a very precise way so that they are stacked neatly and beautifully. The folding has been likened to origami, Japanese paper folding, in its precision. Managers are trained in folding by Benetton personnel; those managers, in turn, train their employees. Argyles are folded on the diamond; cardigans have a button showing on the shelf edge, and so on. Folding is so important that some employees get upset when customers mess up the carefully folded stacks of sweaters. However, those employees must also be trained not to react negatively to customers for fear that they will lose sales.

To ensure that orders are processed swiftly for the U.S. market, Benetton opened a factory in Rocky Mount, North Carolina, in 1986. This facility enables the company to utilize domestic cotton and protects it against the falling value of the dollar, which would drive up the cost of goods shipped from Italy.

Benetton's approach to the North American market seems to be working. Beginning with just a couple of stores in 1980, Benetton had expanded to about 250 stores in the United States, Canada, and the Caribbean by 1983. That number more than tripled by 1988 and was continuing to grow during 1989. Some store owners, however, were beginning to complain about Benetton's tactics. The complaints were that Benetton puts too many stores too close together, that its U.S. operations are poorly organized, and that reordering products during a selling season is difficult.

Because the licensees are so important to the continued success of Benetton, the company has been working to improve relations with them and to foster better communication between them and the parent company. Convinced that it could not run its U.S. operations from Italy, Benetton brought in a former consultant to head a newly organized Benetton USA unit, which operates autonomously from New York. The mission of that unit is to consolidate operations and stress service to licensees as well as to customers.

Questions

1. What role do standards play in organizational control at Benetton? How important are such controls to the company? Why?
2. Is organizational control at Benetton bureaucratic or clan? Why? Explain your response.
3. How effective is the control system at Benetton? What changes can you suggest that might make control more effective than it is?
4. Do you think Benetton will be able to sustain its growth and success, or will it saturate the market and discover that its name loses its appeal over time? Defend your response.

REFERENCES: "Why Some Benetton Shopkeepers Are Losing Their Shirts," *Business Week*, March 14, 1988, pp. 78–79; "Benetton Is Accused of Dubious Tactics by Some Store Owners," *The Wall Street Journal*, October 24, 1988, pp. A1, A9; Alan Zakon and Richard W. Winger, "Consumer Draw: From Mass Markets to Variety," *Management Review*, April 1987, p. 27; "Benetton Is Betting on More of Everything," *Business Week*, March 23, 1987, p. 93; "Benetton Targets a New Customer—Wall Street," *Business Week*, May 29, 1989, pp. 32–33.

OUTLINE

The Nature of Operations Management
The Importance of Operations · Manufacturing and Production · Service Operations · The Role of Operations in Organizational Strategy

Designing Operations Systems
Products and Services · Capacity · Facilities · Technology

Using Operations Systems
Operations Management as Control · Purchasing Management · Inventory Management · Quality Control

Managing Productivity
The Meaning of Productivity · The Importance of Productivity · Productivity Trends · Improving Productivity

Managing Quality
The Meaning of Quality · The Importance of Quality · Approaches to Managing Quality

CHAPTER *17*

Operations Management, Productivity, and Quality

OBJECTIVES

After studying this chapter, you should be able to:

- Explain the nature of operations management.
- Identify and discuss the components involved in designing operations systems.
- Identify and discuss the components involved in using operations systems.
- Explain the importance of managing productivity.
- Explain the importance of managing quality.

OPENING INCIDENT

Not long ago, General Electric needed three weeks from the time an order was placed to deliver a custom-made industrial circuit-breaker box. Now delivery can be done in three days. Even more incredible is the fact that during the three-week era, GE had six plants making the boxes. Now they're made at a single facility.

The key to GE's success has been a new approach to design and manufacturing. In the old days (circa 1985), each box was custom designed from 28,000 unique parts that were assembled by hand. There are now only 1,275 parts, and the design of each box is created by a computer using specifications supplied by the customer.

To avoid delays, supervisory and quality-control positions were eliminated. All decisions are made on the shop floor by the 129 workers in the plant, and they make them faster and better than their managers did before the change. Productivity has increased by 20 percent. The plant used to have a two-month backlog of orders; the backlog now hovers around two days.[1]

*M*anagers at General Electric have reaped huge payoffs from an area that many organizations used to take for granted—operations. Manufacturing and production were of primary importance during the early decades of this century as mass-production and assembly-line techniques greatly enhanced an organization's ability to produce large quantities of goods and services. After a while, however, managers turned their attention to finance, marketing, and human resource issues and pushed operations to the wings. In recent years, things have come full circle and operations is once again on center stage.

This chapter explores the nature of operations management. We describe two critical areas of operations management—designing operations systems and using operations systems. We then discuss in detail two other related areas—productivity and quality.

THE NATURE OF OPERATIONS MANAGEMENT

■ **operations management**
The total set of managerial activities used by an organization to transform resource inputs into products and/or services

Operations management is the total set of managerial activities used by an organization to transform resource inputs into products and services.[2] When NCR buys electronic components, assembles them into computers, and then ships them to customers, it is using operations management. When a Pizza Hut employee orders new food products and paper napkins and then combines dough, cheese, and tomato paste to create a pizza, he or she is using operations management.

The Importance of Operations

Operations is an important functional concern for any organization. Efficient and effective management of operations goes a long way toward ensuring organizational success. Inefficient or ineffective operations management can undermine almost any strategy, no matter how well conceived it might have been.

In an economic sense, operations management provides utility of one type or another, depending on the nature of the firm's products or services. If the product is a physical good, such as a Yamaha motorcycle, operations provides form utility by combining many dissimilar inputs (sheet metal, rubber, paint, combustion engines, and human craftsmanship) to produce the desired output. The inputs are converted from their incoming forms into a new physical form. This conversion is typical of operations in manufacturing organizations.

By contrast, the operations activities of American Airlines create a service providing time and place utility. The airline transports passengers and freight according to agreed-on departure and arrival places and times. Other service operations, such as a Coors Beer distributorship or The Gap retail chain, provide place and possession utility by bringing together products made by others and the customer. Although the organizations in these examples produce different kinds of products or services, their operations processes share many important features.[3]

Manufacturing and Production

Because much of American industry used to be concentrated in manufacturing, the entire area of operations management used to be called production management. Manufacturing is a form of business that combines and transforms resource inputs and other resources into tangible outcomes that are then sold to others. Hence, Goodyear is a manufacturer because it combines rubber and chemical compounds, uses blending equipment and molding machines, and creates tires. Broyhill is a manufacturer because it buys prefabricated wood and metal components, pads, and fabric and then combines them into tables, sofas, and chairs.[4]

During the 1970s, manufacturing entered a long period of decline in the United States. The major cause of the decline was foreign competition. American firms had grown lax and sluggish. New foreign competitors came onto the scene with new equipment and much higher levels of efficiency. For example, steel companies in the Far East were able to produce high-quality steel for much lower prices than were American companies like Bethlehem Steel and U.S. Steel (now USX). Similar effects were felt in other areas such as the electronics and automobile industries.

Faced with a battle for survival, many American companies underwent a long and difficult period of change—eliminating waste and

While many people equate operations management with manufacturing, it is just as applicable to service organizations. For example, MCI field engineers are shown here servicing a digital microwave transmission tower near Reno, Nevada during a snow storm. They relied on numerous concepts and techniques from operations management in determining the best way to get the job done.

transforming themselves into leaner, more efficient and responsive entities. They reduced their work forces dramatically, closed antiquated or unnecessary plants, and modernized their remaining plants. In recent years, their efforts have started to pay dividends. Steel companies, for example, are now using over 80 percent of their production capacity, whereas just a few years ago they were mired at less than 50 percent. In everything from copper to paper to textiles to rubber, American industry has regained its competitive position in the world marketplace. Although manufacturers from other parts of the world are still formidable competitors and American firms may never again be competitive in some markets, the overall picture is much better than it was just a few years ago. And prospects continue to look bright.[5]

Service Operations

During the initial decline of the manufacturing sector, one of the things that kept the American economy from declining at the same rate was a tremendous growth in the service sector.[6] A service organization is one that transforms resources into services. For example, Merrill Lynch handles stock transactions for its customers, National Car Rental leases cars to its customers for short periods of time, and your local hairdresser cuts your hair. None of these businesses produces tangible products; instead, they provide intangible services to customers for a fee.

In 1947, the service sector was responsible for less than half of America's gross national product. By 1975, however, this figure reached 65 percent, and by 1985 it exceeded 70 percent. The service sector was responsible for almost 90 percent of all new jobs created in the United States during the 1970s. Today, even though manufacturing is once again on the upswing, the service sector is also continuing its strong growth.[7]

Managers have come to see that many of the tools, techniques, and methods that are used in a factory are also useful to a service firm. For example, managers of auto plants and hair salons each have to decide how to design their facility, identify the best location for it, determine their optimal capacity, make decisions about inventory storage, set procedures for purchasing raw materials, and set standards for productivity and quality.

The Role of Operations in Organizational Strategy

It should be clear by this point that operations management is very important to organizations. Indeed, it is of sufficient importance that it needs to be addressed at every level of the organization, starting at the top. Managers face a myriad of decisions that must be integrated with the organization's strategy. For example, the deceivingly simple strategic decision of whether to stress high quality regardless of cost, lowest possible cost regardless of quality, or some intermediate combination of the two has numerous important implications. The first decision will dictate state-of-the-art technology, rigorous control of product design and materials specifications, and thorough quality checks throughout the production process. The last decision might call for lower-grade technology, less concern about product design and materials specifications, and fewer quality checks.

Just as strategy affects operations management, so too does operations management affect strategy. Suppose that a firm makes the decision to upgrade the quality of its products or services. The ability of the organization to implement the decision is dependent in part on current production capabilities and other resources. If existing technology will not permit higher-quality work and if the organization lacks the resources to replace its technology, increasing quality to the desired new standards will be difficult.

A recent strategic development affecting operations management involves speed—the time needed by the organization to get something accomplished. One recent survey identified speed as the number 1 strategic issue confronting managers in the 1990s.[8] The emphasis on speed can be directed at any area, including developing, making, and distributing products or services. The opening incident provides an example of the kinds of breakthroughs being achieved by organizations like General Electric.

Table 17.1 identifies a number of basic suggestions that have helped some companies increase the speed of their operations. For example, General Electric found it better to start from scratch with a totally remodeled plant. GE also wiped out the need for approvals by eliminating most managerial positions. Teams are used at GE as a basis for

TABLE 17.1

Guidelines for Increasing the Speed of Operations

1. Start from scratch (it's usually easier than trying to do what the organization does now but in a faster way).
2. Minimize the number of approvals needed to do something (the fewer people who have to approve something, the faster it will get done).
3. Use work teams as a basis for organization (teamwork and cooperation work better than individual effort and conflict).
4. Develop and adhere to a schedule (a properly designed schedule can greatly increase speed).
5. Don't ignore distribution (making something faster is only part of the battle).
6. Integrate speed into the organization's culture (if everyone understands the importance of speed, things will naturally get done quicker).

SOURCE: Adapted from Brian Dumaine, "How Managers Can Succeed Through Speed," *Fortune*, February 13, 1989, pp. 54–59. The Time Inc. Magazine Company. All rights reserved.

organizing work. Attaching significance to the schedule helped Motorola build a new plant and start production of a new product in only 18 months.

Distribution is equally important. Benetton, for example, has only one warehouse to serve 5,000 stores in 60 countries. But the state-of-the-art facility, which cost $30 million to build, ships 230,000 pieces of clothing daily—and employs only eight people! And, finally, organizations must instill an appreciation for speed in their corporate culture. Honda, for example, started supporting Formula One car racing only a few years ago. But since new engineers have been rotating through the Formula One team, the entire organization has placed a higher value on the whole notion of speed.

DESIGNING OPERATIONS SYSTEMS

The problems faced by operations managers generally revolve around the acquisition and utilization of resources for conversion. Their goals include both efficiency and effectiveness. In any organization, a number of issues and decisions must be addressed as operations systems are designed.[9] Periodic adjustments and changes are also necessary as circumstances and strategies change. Figure 17.1 shows four basic issues in designing operations systems. "Management in Practice" describes how Black & Decker has faced some of them.

Products and Services

■ **product/service mix**
How many and what kinds of products and/or services to offer

A natural starting point in designing operations systems is determining the mix and kinds of products and services to be offered. This decision flows from corporate, business, and marketing strategies. Managers

FIGURE 17.1
Designing Operations Systems

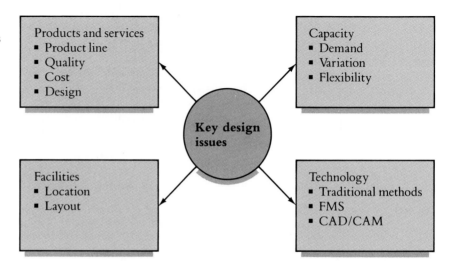

MANAGEMENT IN PRACTICE

BLACK & DECKER PRESSES ON

Since its founding in 1910, Black & Decker has pursued effectiveness through innovation, product design, and management and marketing expertise. Black & Decker has been selling its products in the international market for nearly three-quarters of a century; its name recognition and reputation extend far beyond the United States.

In the early 1980s, that reputation began to suffer. The company was losing market share and money. Customers were grumbling and the company was in trouble. A new CEO arrived in 1985. He gambled by immediately taking a write-off of over $200 million to restructure the organization. The restructuring included closing five plants, putting 2,000 workers out of jobs, and rolling back wages. The gamble worked. Black & Decker has improved every year since that time. By early 1989, Black & Decker was the fastest-growing power-tool company in the world.

Production equipment at Black & Decker plants has been modernized; factory automation has been increased; and there is greater emphasis on efficient ordering and shipping. Product design and marketing staffs have been strengthened. Every product was carefully examined and redesigned to reduce the number of parts per product. Fewer parts per product

decreases production time and costs and increases product quality and dependability. Reducing parts has been accomplished in part by standardizing the motors used in Black & Decker products. Just-in-time continuous-flow production methods were instituted to reduce inventories of parts and materials.

In the power-tool side of the business, Black & Decker introduced over 60 new or redesigned products during the late 1980s. Most of them were in the cordless-tool market, the fastest-growing segment of the power-tool market. As a result of these efforts, cordless tools are expected to account for about half of Black & Decker's power-tool sales by 1991.

The household-products side of the business has also been active. Redesign has invigorated some very mature products—adding automatic shutoff features to irons, making blenders cordless, making hand-held vacuum cleaners more powerful. Black & Decker irons now are the leading sellers.

REFERENCES: John Huey, "The New Power in Black & Decker," *Fortune*, January 2, 1989, pp. 89–94; "Black & Decker Goes to Full-Court Press," *The Wall Street Journal*, November 10, 1988, p. A8; "Black & Decker Lifts American Standard Offer," *The Wall Street Journal*, February 24, 1988, p. 5; "How Black & Decker Got Back in the Black," *Business Week*, July 13, 1987, pp. 86, 90.

have to make a number of decisions about their products and services, starting with how many and what kinds to offer. Procter & Gamble, for example, makes regular, tartar-control, and gel formulas of Crest toothpaste and packages them in several different sizes of tubes and pumps. Decisions also have to be made regarding the level of quality desired, the optimal cost of each product or service, and exactly how each is to be designed. General Electric, for example, reduced the number of parts in its industrial circuit breakers from 28,000 to 1,275. A key element of this breakthrough was making many of the parts interchangeable, and the whole process involved product design.

Capacity

The capacity decision involves choosing the amount of conversion capacity appropriate for the organization.[10] Determining whether to build a factory capable of making 5,000 or 8,000 units per day is a capacity decision. So, too, is deciding whether to build a restaurant with 100 or 150 seats or a bank with 5 or 10 teller stations. The capacity decision is truly a high-risk one, because of the uncertainties of future product demand and the large monetary stakes involved. An organization can build capacity that exceeds its needs and requires resource commitments (capital investment) that may never be recovered. This was the mistake made by many American firms during the 1960s and 1970s. Or an organization can build a facility with a smaller capacity than expected demand. Doing so may result in lost market opportunities, but it may also free capital resources for use elsewhere in the organization.

■ **capacity** The amount of products and/or services that can be produced by an organization

A key consideration in determining **capacity** is demand. For example, a company operating in a stable environment with fairly constant monthly demand might build a plant capable of producing an amount each month roughly equivalent to its demand. But if its market is characterized by seasonal fluctuations, it might be better advised to build a smaller plant to meet normal demand and then add extra shifts during peak periods. Likewise, a restaurant that needs 150 seats for Saturday night dinner but never needs more than 100 at any other time during the week would probably be foolish to expand to 150 seats. During the rest of the week, it must still pay to light, heat, cool, and clean the excess capacity. Of course, 150 seats might be a good idea if the manager has good reason to believe that demand will or can be increased in the near future.

Facilities

■ **facilities** The physical locations where products or services are created, stored, and distributed

Facilities are the physical locations where products or services are created, stored, and distributed. Key decisions pertain to location and layout.

location The physical positioning or geographic site of facilities

Location   **Location** must be determined by the needs and requirements of the organization. A company that relies heavily on railroads to transport raw materials or finished goods needs to be located close to rail facilities. General Electric decided that it did not need six plants to make circuit breakers, so it invested heavily in automating one plant and closed the other five. Different organizations in the same industry may have different facilities requirements. Benetton uses only one distribution center for the entire world. K mart, in contrast, has several distribution centers in the United States alone. A retail business must choose its location very carefully so as to be convenient for consumers.

layout The physical configuration of facilities and/or the arrangement of equipment within facilities

Layout   The choice of physical configuration, or the **layout**, of facilities is closely related to decisions on product or service line, capacity, and location. The three entirely different layout alternatives shown in

All organizations need to carefully consider where they locate their facilities. To some organizations, however, facilities location decisions are especially important. For example, Luz International operates solar electric generator stations around the world. To be most effective, the stations need to be in locations where there are few clouds and where there are many hours of bright sunshine most days. This station is located in the Mojave Desert.

product layout A physical configuration of facilities arranged around the product

process layout A physical configuration of facilities arranged around the process

fixed-position layout A physical configuration of facilities arranged around a single work area

Figure 17.2 help demonstrate the importance of the layout decision. A **product layout** is appropriate when large quantities of a single product are needed. It makes sense to custom design a straight-line flow of work for a product when a specific task is performed at each work station as each unit flows past. Most large-scale assembly lines use this format. For example, IBM PC factories use a product layout.

Process layouts are used in operations settings that create a variety of products. Auto repair shops and healthcare clinics are good examples. Each automobile and each individual is a separate "product." Only the general nature of each job is known in advance. Detailed product specifications cannot be known until the customer's arrival. The needs of each incoming job are diagnosed as it enters the operations system, and the job is routed through the unique sequence of work stations needed to create the desired finished product. In a process layout, each type of conversion task is centralized in a single work station or department. All welding is done in one designated shop location, and any auto that requires welding is moved to that area. This is in contrast to the product layout, in which several different work stations may perform welding operations if the conversion task sequence so dictates.

The **fixed-position layout** is used when the organization is creating a few very large and complex products. Aircraft manufacturers like Boeing and shipbuilders like Newport News (subsidiary of Tenneco) use this method. An assembly line capable of moving a 747 would require an enormous plant; so instead the airplane itself remains stationary, and people and machines move around it as it is assembled.

FIGURE 17.2

The Approaches to Facilities
Layout

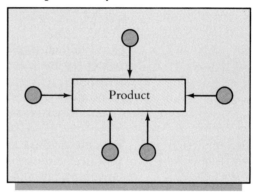

 Work station

Technology

The organization must make decisions about the technology it will employ in creating products or services. The operations technology used can vary along a continuum from highly labor-intensive to highly capital-intensive. A home-cleaning service and a football team are highly labor-intensive—people do the work. An automated plant is very capital-intensive—expensive machinery does the work. The degree of mechanization and automation chosen by an organization has a significant impact on output quality, production costs, labor and management skills required, and operations flexibility.

Although the technologies of most service organizations continue to be highly labor-intensive, relatively more capital-intensive options have evolved. Especially with increasing applications of computers, such traditionally labor-intensive professional services as medicine, law, and education and other service industries such as commercial banking have adopted new, capital-intensive technologies for creating and delivering their products.

New technologies have also had a significant impact on organizations over the last few years.[11] One approach, called **flexible manufacturing systems (FMS)** relies on computers to coordinate and integrate automated facilities.[12] This approach is also called **computer-integrated manufacturing (CIM)**. At Allen-Bradley in Milwaukee, an IBM mainframe computer controls a manufacturing system that produces 600 units per hour—with only four technicians in the whole plant.

flexible manufacturing systems (FMS) or **computer-integrated manufacturing (CIM)**   Relies on computers to coordinate and integrate automated machines in manufacturing

computer-aided design (CAD)   Involves the use of computers in the design of new products and services

computer-aided manufacturing (CAM)   Uses computers in the actual manufacturing process

Another new technology involves **computer-aided design (CAD)**, usually used in conjunction with **computer-aided manufacturing (CAM)**. CAD involves the use of computers to design new products and services. General Electric used CAD in changing the design of its circuit breakers. Benetton uses CAD in designing new styles and product specifications. A properly designed CAD system can tie directly into a CAM system. Suppose that a Benetton store needs to order some new blue sweaters. The order is transmitted to a Benetton mainframe computer in Italy. The system already knows all the product specifications, because it designed the product. Thus, the reorder is relayed to a knitting machine that actually makes the new sweaters. Meanwhile, another machine is printing out an address label and a copy of the original order. Only when everything is finished does a human being get involved—and only then to provide a final check for quality and accuracy.[13] More information about these and other technologies is discussed in Enhancement Module 8 at the end of Part 5.

USING OPERATIONS SYSTEMS

After operations systems have been properly designed, they must then be put into use by the organization. Their basic functional purpose is to control the transformation processes within the organization so as to ensure relevant goals of quality, costs, and so forth. Within this control framework, there are a number of special purposes, including purchasing management, inventory management, and quality control. "The Global View" illustrates how one company, Scott Paper, has made effective use of its operations management systems as a means for competing in international markets.

Operations Management as Control

One way of using operations management as control is to coordinate it with the other functions. Monsanto, for example, established a consumer products division that mass produces and distributes a line of fertilizers and lawn chemicals. The operations function was set up organizationally as an autonomous profit center for purposes of organizational control. The division is responsible for attaining profitability. Monsanto finds this useful and effective because its manufacturing division is given the authority to determine not only the costs of creating the product but also the product price and the marketing programs.

In terms of overall organizational control, a division like the one established by Monsanto should be accountable only for the activities over which it has decision-making authority. In an organization using bureaucratic control, this accountability will be spelled out in rules and regulations. In a clan system, it is likely to be simply understood and accepted by everyone. It would be inappropriate, of course, to make operations accountable for profitability in an organization with a marketing-dominated competitive strategy. Misplaced accountability results in ineffective organizational control, to say nothing of hostility and conflict. Depending on the strategic role of operations, then, operations managers are accountable for different kinds of results.

Within operations, managerial control ensures that resources and activities achieve primary goals such as a high percentage of on-time deliveries, low unit-production cost, or high product reliability. A key question is which of the many system subcomponents should be emphasized. The answer is that the control system should focus on the elements that are most crucial to goal attainment. For example, if product quality is a key concern (as it is at Rolex), the firm might adopt a screening control system to continually monitor the product as it is being created. If quantity is a pressing issue (as it is at Timex), a postaction system might be used to identify defects at the end of the system without disrupting the manufacturing process itself. The particular conversion technology used will have a major effect on the design of the control system.

In capital-intensive operations such as oil refining and steel manufacturing, a substantial amount of control is achieved through design and engineering. Intricate, special-purpose facilities and equipment are engineered to perform precisely specified activities repetitively. The technology is geared intensively to a narrow, relatively stable product line. The reliability and quality of the products that are produced reflect the precision of the equipment that is designed to monitor critical stages of the process. Accordingly, highly technical staffs are maintained to provide control expertise.

Labor-intensive operations introduce entirely different types of control complexities. Many control problems and variations in processes cannot be anticipated, nor can management economically design its way around them. Plumbing services, auto repair services, and job shop manufacturing firms exhibit very dissimilar complexities in operations control. When product specifications are unpredictable, most operations control occurs during and after resource conversion—that is, the emphasis is on screening and postaction control. Some degree of indirect control is achieved before conversion by the careful selection

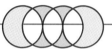

THE GLOBAL VIEW

SCOTT PAPER ON AN INTERNATIONAL ROLL

Scott Paper was begun in 1879 when two brothers bought large rolls of tissue and rerolled it onto smaller rolls for use in home bathrooms. Initially they sold numerous brands but soon settled on just a few while stressing quality and softness. That approach enabled them to dominate the toilet-tissue market for half a century. Along the way, Scott Paper introduced or branched out into paper towels, napkins, facial tissues, food wrappings, and baby products.

That willingness to branch out has made Scott Paper an international paper company. Scott began to focus on developing its European operations and sales during the mid-1980s. Scott built a paper-making machine in Belgium and plans to do the same in France, Italy, and Spain very soon. In 1992, when the 12-nation European Community eliminates trade barriers between member countries, Scott's plants will be ready to serve several countries at the same time.

Asian markets also beckon. Not only does per capita consumption of paper products in Asia lag behind that of Europe and America but there are also far more people living in Asian countries. With that in mind, in 1989 Scott began a huge project in a remote part of Indonesia. The project will take years to complete, but Scott spent years in deciding on the final site and is prepared to move cautiously. The project involves developing a plantation to grow a quarter-billion eucalyptus trees.

Scott has received approval from Indonesia's investment board but plans a 130-acre experimental plantation as well as a massive environmental study before the full project gets under way. Those efforts will take two years. The area has no infrastructure at present but is near a port and is flat and will be relatively easy to clear and plant. However, primitive tribespeople inhabit some of the land that will be involved, and the project will alter the ecology of the surrounding area.

Scott wants its international efforts, especially those in Third World countries, to go smoothly and is thus proceeding slowly. It is developing reforestation plans to ensure that the long-term impact is acceptable to all parties involved. It is also working with environmental groups to alleviate their concerns. The Scott executive in charge of the Indonesian project has stated that the company is prepared to drop the entire project if major, insurmountable difficulties arise rather than damage Scott Paper's reputation or jeopardize its future expansion plans elsewhere in the world.

REFERENCES: "Scott Paper Moves Gingerly on Project to Set Up Huge Indonesian Plantation," *The Wall Street Journal*, January 20, 1989, p. A14; "Scott Paper Bets It Can Continue on a Roll," *The Wall Street Journal*, October 4, 1988, p. A8; Steve Redmond, "Clash of the Tissue Titans," *Marketing*, May 12, 1988, p. 15; "Scott Paper: Improvements in Operations in Asia," *The New York Times*, November 4, 1988, p. 31.

of inputs such as reliable component suppliers, proven materials, and skilled employees. Still, direct product and process control is exerted by human intervention during the conversion process.

Effective control in labor-intensive systems is often a matter of managerial judgment and experience with the capabilities of the particular operations processes and employees. Even the most highly skilled employees perform variably from day to day, so operations control in labor-intensive operations requires managerial skill in interpersonal relations and motivation. The first-line manager or supervisor, who is most likely to be aware of employee capabilities and limitations, needs to consider control standards in making work assignments and designing job content.

Purchasing Management

Purchasing management is concerned with buying the materials and resources needed to produce the organization's products and services.[14] Thus, the purchasing manager for Sears is responsible for buying the merchandise the store will sell. The purchasing manager for a manufacturer buys raw materials, parts, and machines needed by the organization. Large companies like General Motors, IBM, and Westinghouse have large purchasing departments.

The manager responsible for purchasing must balance a number of constraints. Buying too much of a particular material or product ties up capital and increases storage costs. Buying too little might lead to shortages and high reordering costs. Likewise, the manager must make sure that the quality of what is being purchased meets the organization's needs, that the supplier is reliable, and that the best financial terms are negotiated.

Many firms have recently changed their approach to purchasing as a means to lower costs and improve quality and productivity. In particular, rather than relying on hundreds or even thousands of suppliers to buy only what those firms make, many companies have started reducing the number of suppliers they use and negotiating special production/delivery arrangements. For example, the Honda plant in Marysville, Ohio, found a local businessman looking for a new opportunity. They negotiated an agreement whereby he would start a new company to mount car stereo speakers into plastic moldings. He delivers finished goods to the plant three times a day, and Honda buys all he can manufacture. Thus, he has a stable sales base, Honda has a local and reliable supplier, and both companies benefit.[15] Other companies like Ford and Sears have streamlined their purchasing systems, choosing to restrict the number of suppliers they use in exchange for greater cooperation and higher quality standards.

Inventory Management

A closely related area of operations management is management of the organization's inventory. Inventory control, also called materials control, is essential for effective operations management.[16] The four basic kinds of inventories are raw materials, work-in-process, finished-goods, and in-transit inventories. As shown in Table 17.2, the sources of control over these inventories are as different as their purposes. Work-in-process inventories, for example, occur when products are partially completed and need further processing. Shop managers, by their decisions on how to sequence the jobs awaiting further build-up, determine the amounts of these inventories and hence the related costs that are incurred. By contrast, the quantities and costs of finished-goods inventories are under the control of the overall production scheduling system, which is determined by high-level planning decisions. In-transit

TABLE 17.2

Inventory Types, Purposes, and Sources of Control

Type	Purpose	Source of Control
Raw materials	Provides the materials needed to make the product	Purchasing models and systems
Work-in-process	Enables overall production to be divided into stages of manageable size	Shop-floor control systems
Finished goods	Provides ready supply of products upon customer demand and enables long, efficient production runs	High-level production scheduling systems in conjunction with marketing
In-transit (pipeline)	Distributes products to customers	Transportation and distribution control systems

just-in-time or **JIT**   An inventory system that has necessary materials arriving just-in-time so that the production process is not interrupted

inventories are controlled by the transportation and distribution system. Managers in each of these areas have goals for inventory cost and quantity, and they monitor inventories and take action to correct significant deviations from the path toward those goals.

Like most other areas of operations management, inventory management has been the scene of much change in recent years. One particularly significant breakthrough is the **just-in-time**, or **JIT** method. First popularized by the Japanese, the JIT system reduces the organization's investment in storage space for raw materials and in the materials themselves. Historically, manufacturers built large storage areas and filled them with materials, parts, and supplies that would be needed days, weeks, and even months in the future. A manager using the JIT approach orders materials and parts more often and in smaller quantities, thereby reducing investment in both storage space and actual inventory. The ideal arrangement is for materials to arrive just as they are needed—or just in time.

Recall our example about the small firm that assembles stereo speakers for Honda and delivers them three times a day, making it unnecessary for Honda to carry large quantities of the speakers in inventory. In an even more striking example, Johnson Controls makes automobile seats for Chrysler and ships them by small truckloads to a Chrysler plant 75 miles away. Each shipment is scheduled to arrive two hours before it is needed. Clearly, the JIT approach requires high levels of coordination and cooperation between the company and its suppliers.

If shipments arrive too early, Chrysler has no place to store them. If they arrive too late, the entire assembly line may have to be shut down, resulting in enormous expense. When properly designed and used, the JIT method controls inventory very effectively. (Inventory management is discussed again in Chapter 19.)

Quality Control

Another area that has been widely discussed of late is quality control. Given its importance to contemporary organizations and to their managers, we provide a detailed separate discussion of it later in this chapter. First, however, we consider another area of great importance—managing productivity.

MANAGING PRODUCTIVITY

Productivity has been a topic of considerable discussion, research, and debate over the past several years. The stimulus for this attention was a recognition by many people that the gap between productivity in the United States and productivity in other industrialized countries was narrowing. This section describes the meaning of productivity and underscores its importance. After summarizing recent productivity trends, we suggest ways organizations can increase their productivity.

The Meaning of Productivity

■ **productivity** An economic measure of efficiency indicating what is produced relative to resources used to produce it

What exactly is productivity? Actually, there are many different definitions of the term. In a general sense, **productivity** is an economic measure of efficiency that summarizes what is produced relative to the resources used to produce it.[17] But productivity can be and often is assessed at different levels of analysis and in different forms.

Levels of Productivity Levels of productivity are the units of analysis used to calculate or define productivity. For example, aggregate productivity is the total level of productivity achieved by a country. Industry productivity is the total productivity achieved by all the firms in a particular industry. Company productivity, just as the term suggests, is the level of productivity achieved by an individual company. We can also speak of unit and individual productivity—the productivity achieved by a unit or department within an organization and the level of productivity attained by a single individual.

Forms of Productivity There are many different forms of productivity.[18] Total factor productivity is defined by the following formula:

$$\text{Productivity} = \frac{\text{Outputs}}{\text{Labor + Capital + Materials + Energy Inputs}}$$

Total factor productivity is an overall indicator of how well an organization uses all of its resources to create all of its products and services.

The biggest problem with total factor productivity is that all the ingredients must be couched in the same terms—dollars (it is difficult to add hours of labor to number of units of a raw material in a meaningful way). Total factor productivity also gives little insight into how things can be changed to improve productivity. Consequently, most organizations find it more useful to calculate a partial productivity ratio. Such a ratio uses only one category of resource. For example, labor productivity could be calculated by this simple formula:

$$\text{Labor Productivity} = \frac{\text{Outputs}}{\text{Direct Labor}}$$

This method has two advantages. First, it is not necessary to transform the units of input into some other unit. Second, this method provides managers with specific insights into how changing different resource inputs affects productivity. Suppose that an organization can manufacture 100 units of a particular product with 20 hours of direct labor. The organization's labor productivity index is 5 (or 5 units per labor hour). Now suppose that worker efficiency is increased (through one of the ways to be discussed later in this chapter) so that the same 20 hours of labor results in the manufacture of 120 units of the product. The labor productivity index increases to 6 (6 units per labor hour), and the firm can see the direct results of a specific managerial action.

The Importance of Productivity

Productivity is important for a variety of reasons. Firm productivity is a primary determinant of an organization's level of profitability and, ultimately, its ability to survive. If one organization is more productive than another, it will have more products to sell, be able to sell them at lower prices, and have more profits to reinvest in other areas.

Productivity is also important because it partially determines people's standards of living within a particular country. At an economic level, businesses consume resources and produce goods and services. The goods and services created within a country can be used by that country's own citizens or exported for sale in other countries. The more goods and services the businesses within a country can produce, the more goods and services the country's citizens will have. Even goods that are exported result in financial resources flowing back into the home country. Thus, the citizens of a highly productive country are likely to have significantly higher standards of living than are the citizens of a country with low productivity.

Productivity is clearly one of the most important challenges facing today's managers. Cardinal Industries Inc., based in Columbus, Ohio, is the world's largest builder of modular housing. The company owes much of its success to productivity. For example, it can build, deliver, and install a single-family home for half the cost per square foot of a site-built house. By building the houses in a factory, multiple jobs can be done at the same time and automation can also be used more extensively than would be possible at an individual building site. Cardinal's size also allows it to negotiate lower prices from suppliers and invest in research development as a way of finding other ways to lower costs and raise quality.

Productivity Trends

The United States has the highest level of productivity in the world. In 1986, each worker in America produced goods or services worth $37,600. The second-best productivity was achieved by Canada ($35,700).[19] However, an alarming trend began in the 1960s and continued into the early 1980s. During this time, the rate of productivity growth in the United States stalled, especially in comparison to the rates in other industrialized countries. From 1966 to 1976, productivity growth in the United States averaged only 1.6 percent per year; from 1976 to 1981, only 0.7 percent per year. In the same period, productivity grew in France, West Germany, and Japan at a much faster pace.

This trend was a primary factor in the decisions made by many American businesses and industries to retrench, retool, and become more competitive in the world marketplace. Consequently, manufacturing productivity in the United States has rebounded strongly. As shown in Figure 17.3, it has continued to grow rapidly since around the end of 1982. For example, General Electric's dishwasher plant in Louisville has cut its inventory requirements by 50 percent, reduced labor costs from 15 percent to only 10 percent of total manufacturing costs, and cut product development time in half.[20] The chapter-opening incident clearly documents significant productivity gains in another GE business.

Several factors have been cited to account for the productivity slowdowns recorded during the 1960s and 1970s.[21] First of all, there have been some major changes in the composition of the American work force. After World War II more and more of the general population

FIGURE 17.3

Productivity Trends in the
United States in Manufacturing
and Services

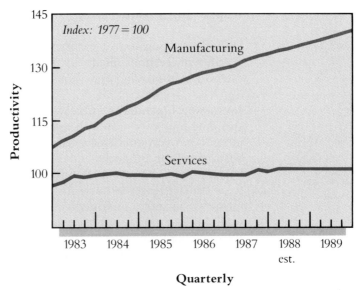

SOURCE: "Rising Factory Productivity is Giving the Expansion Room to
Run," *Fortune,* August 1, 1988, p.25. Time Inc. All rights reserved.

went to college. Thus, postwar gains in productivity were at least
partially attributable to higher levels of education. Later, as the proportion of workers with higher education leveled off, productivity gains
also tended to level off. Another factor is that the work force absorbed
many new and inexperienced employees during the last decade, as more
and more women and younger workers joined the work force.

A second contributing factor was a decline in the quality of American
production facilities relative to facilities in the rest of the world. American managers were generally content to allow existing factories to
continue operating as they had in years past. Meanwhile, companies in
other countries were investing heavily in new and highly efficient facilities. In 1980 the average American plant was almost 15 years old.
Its counterpart in Japan was less than 10 years old.

A final contributor was the tremendous growth of the service sector—growth that helped spark much of America's economic growth in
recent years. However, organizations in the service sector have generally been unable to boost the productivity of their employees. Figure
17.3 shows that the productivity of service workers has remained essentially flat since 1983. Since U.S. aggregate productivity includes both
measures, gains in manufacturing productivity have been partially offset
by little or no growth in service-sector productivity.

One part of this problem relates to measurement. For example, it is
fairly easy to calculate the number of tons of steel produced at a Bethlehem Steel mill and divide it by the number of labor hours used; it is
more difficult to determine the output of an attorney or a CPA. Still,
virtually everyone agrees that improving service-sector productivity is
the next major hurdle facing American business.

Improving Productivity

How does a business or industry improve its productivity? Numerous specific suggestions made by experts generally fall into two broad categories: improving operations and increasing employee involvement.

Improving Operations   One way firms can improve operations is by spending more on research and development. R&D spending helps identify new products, new uses for existing products, and new methods for making products; and each of these contributes to productivity. For example, Bausch & Lomb almost missed the boat on extended-wear contact lenses because the company had neglected R&D. Recognizing its mistake, management made R&D a top-priority item. As a result, the company made several scientific breakthroughs, shortened the time needed to introduce new products, and greatly enhanced both total sales and profits—and all with a smaller work force than the company used to employ.[22] Even though other countries are greatly increasing their spending on R&D, the United States continues to be the world leader in this area.[23]

Another way firms can improve operations to boost productivity is by reassessing and revamping their transformation facilities. The opening incident describes how one modernized plant at GE does a better job than six antiquated ones. Just building a new factory is no guarantee of success, but IBM, Ford, Allen-Bradley, Caterpillar, and many other American businesses have achieved dramatic productivity gains by revamping their production facilities. Facilities refinements are not limited to manufacturers. In recent years, many McDonald's restaurants have added drive-through windows, and many are moving soft-drink dispensers out to the restaurant floor so that customers can get their own drinks. Each of these moves is an attempt to increase the speed with which customers can be served—and to thus increase productivity.

Increasing Employee Involvement   The other major thrust in productivity enhancement has been toward employee involvement. Enhancement Module 4 at the end of Part 3 describes how companies are adopting participative management techniques. A key reason is that employee involvement often increases productivity. The involvement might range from an individual worker being given a bigger voice in how she does her job, to a formal agreement of cooperation between management and labor, to total involvement throughout the organization. Recall how General Electric eliminated most of the supervisors at its remaining circuit-breaker plant and put most of the control in the hands of workers. Specific programs like quality circles are also common ways to increase employee involvement.

Another method popular in the United States is increasing the flexibility of an organization's work force by training employees to perform a number of different jobs. Such cross-training allows the firm to function with fewer workers, because workers can be transferred easily to areas where they are most needed. For example, the Lechmere department store in Sarasota, Florida, encourages workers to learn numerous jobs within the store. One person in the store can operate a forklift in the stockroom, serve as a cashier, or provide customer service on the sales floor. At a Motorola plant, 397 out of 400 employees have learned at least two skills under a similar program.

A key to making employee involvement work is rewards. Firms have to reward people for learning new skills and using them proficiently. At Motorola, for example, workers who master a new skill are assigned for a five-day period to a job requiring them to use that skill. If they perform with no defects, they are moved to a higher pay grade, and then they move back and forth between jobs as they are needed. If there is a performance problem, they receive more training and practice. This approach is fairly new, but preliminary indicators suggest that it can increase productivity significantly. Many unions resist such programs because they threaten job security and reduce a person's identification with one skill or craft.[24]

MANAGING QUALITY

The importance of productivity was recognized several years ago; a parallel interest in quality is more recent in origin. The catalyst for its emergence as a mainstream management concern was foreign business, especially Japanese; and nowhere was it more visible than in the auto industry. During the energy crisis in the late 1970s, many people bought Toyotas, Hondas, and Datsuns (now Nissans) because they were more fuel efficient than their American counterparts. Consumers soon found, however, that not only were the Japanese cars more fuel efficient, they were also of higher quality than American-made cars. Parts fit together better; the trim work was neater; and the cars were more reliable. Thus, after the energy crisis subsided, Japanese cars remained formidable competitors because of their reputations for quality.

The Meaning of Quality

quality The totality of features and characteristics of a product or service that bear on its ability to satisfy stated or implied needs

Exactly what is quality? The American Society for Quality Control has accepted the following definition: **Quality** is the totality of features and characteristics of a product or service that bear on its ability to satisfy stated or implied needs.[25] It is also useful to note that quality has several different attributes. Table 17.3 lists eight basic dimensions that determine the quality of a particular product or service. For example, a product that has durability and is reliable is of higher quality than a product with less durability and reliability.

We should also note the relative nature of quality. For example, a Lincoln Continental is a higher-grade car than a Ford Taurus, which, in turn, is a higher-grade car than a Ford Escort. The difference in quality stems from differences in design and other features. The Escort, however, is considered a high-quality car relative to its engineering

TABLE 17.3

Eight Dimensions of Quality

1. **Performance.** A product's primary operating characteristic. Examples are automobile acceleration and a television set's picture clarity.
2. **Features.** Supplements to a product's basic functioning characteristics, such as power windows on a car.
3. **Reliability.** A probability of not malfunctioning during a specified period.
4. **Conformance.** The degree to which a product's design and operating characteristics meet established standards.
5. **Durability.** A measure of product life.
6. **Serviceability.** The speed and ease of repair.
7. **Aesthetics.** How a product looks, feels, tastes, and smells.
8. **Perceived quality.** As seen by a customer.

SOURCE: Reprinted by permission of *Harvard Business Review*. An exhibit from "Competing on the Eight Dimensions of Quality," by David A. Garvin, *Harvard Business Review* (November/December 1987). Copyright © 1987 by the President and Fellows of Harvard College; all rights reserved.

specifications and price. Likewise, the Taurus and Continental may also be high-quality cars, given their standards and prices. Thus, quality is both an absolute and a relative construct.

The Importance of Quality

Quality is an important concern for management for three basic reasons: competition, productivity, and costs.[26]

Competition   Quality has become one of the most competitive points in business today. Ford, Chrysler, and General Motors each argues, for example, that its cars are higher in quality than the cars of the others. IBM, Apple, and DEC stress the quality of their products as well. Indeed, it seems that virtually every American business has adopted quality as a major point of competition. Thus, a business that fails to keep pace may find itself falling behind not only foreign competition but also other American firms.

Productivity   Managers have come to recognize that quality and productivity are related. In days gone by, many thought that productivity and quality were inversely related—that is, management could increase output (productivity) only by decreasing quality. Managers today have learned the hard way that such an assumption is virtually always wrong. If a firm installs a meaningful quality enhancement program, three things are likely to result. First, the number of defects is likely to decrease, causing fewer returns from customers. Second, because the number of defects goes down, resources (materials and people) dedicated to reworking flawed output will be decreased. Third, because making operative employees responsible for quality reduces the need

Quality is a critical variable in today's business world. Consumers are demanding higher levels of quality than ever before. Rosemount, an Australian vintner and winery, has used the highest possible quality standards in the production of its wines. For example, its managers carefully study every aspect of the wine-making process always on the alert for ways to do things better. As a result of their concern for quality, Rosemount is starting to gain a strong following in the United States.

■ **total quality control**   A strategic commitment by top management to change its whole approach to business so as to make quality a guiding factor in everything it does

for quality inspectors, the organization is able to produce more units with fewer resources—with a positive effect on productivity.

Costs   Improved quality lowers costs. Poor quality results in higher returns from customers, high warranty costs, and lawsuits from customers injured by faulty products. Future sales are lost because of disgruntled customers. An organization with quality problems often has to increase inspection expenses just to catch defective products. We noted in Chapter 16 how Whistler Corporation was using 100 of its 250 employees just to fix poorly assembled radar detectors.[27]

Approaches to Managing Quality

Once an organization makes a decision to enhance the quality of its products and services, there are a number of areas to be addressed. Figure 17.4 highlights the major factors that can be used to improve quality.

Strategic Commitment   The starting point for quality is a strategic commitment by top management. This general commitment is often referred to as **total quality control**—a real and meaningful effort by an organization to change its whole approach to business to make quality a guiding factor in everything the organization does. Such commitment is important for several reasons. First, the organizational culture must change to recognize that quality is not just an ideal but is instead an objective goal that must be pursued. Second, a decision to pursue the goal of quality carries with it some real costs—for new equipment, facilities, and so forth. Thus, without a commitment from top management, quality improvement will prove to be just a slogan or gimmick, with little or no real change.

FIGURE 17.4

Managing Quality

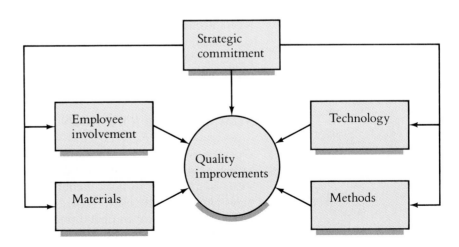

Employee Involvement   We noted earlier the importance of employee involvement in enhancing productivity. It is no less important here. Virtually all successful quality enhancement programs involve making the person responsible for doing the job responsible for making sure it is done right.[28] By definition, then, employee involvement is a critical component in improving quality. A common method for focusing involvement directly on quality is the use of quality circles, discussed in Enhancement Module 4.

Technology   New forms of technology are also useful in improving quality. Automation and robots, for example, can often make products with higher precision and better consistency than can people. CAD/CAM systems in particular have been shown to enhance quality. Individual machines used by workers are also a frequent source of quality improvements. Investing in higher-grade machines capable of doing jobs more precisely and reliably often improves quality. For example, AT&T has achieved significant improvements in product quality by replacing many of its machines with new equipment.[29]

Materials   Another effective way organizations can improve quality is to improve the quality of the materials they use. Suppose that a company that assembles stereos buys chips and circuits from another company. If the chips have a high failure rate, consumers will be returning defective stereos to the company whose nameplate appears on them, not to the company that made the chips. Thus, many firms have increased the quality requirements they impose on their suppliers as a way of improving the quality of their own products and services.

Methods   Improved methods can improve product and service quality. Methods are operating systems used by the organization during the actual transformation process. Shearson Lehman Hutton, a large brokerage firm owned by American Express, recently found that its offices were late in redeeming customers' bonds 80 percent of the time and that the amount of the redemption was wrong 20 percent of the time. Basic operating methods were studied and improved. The results have been impressive: The time needed to redeem customers' bonds has been cut in half, and the accuracy of the redemptions has increased to 98 percent.[30] Statistical quality control, another way to improve methods, is discussed in Chapter 19.

SUMMARY OF KEY POINTS

Operations management is the set of managerial activities that organizations use in creating their products and services. Operations management is important to both manufacturing and service organizations. It plays an important role in an organization's strategy.

The starting point in operations management is designing operations systems. Key areas of concern are product and service design, capacity, facilities, and technology.

After an operations system has been designed and put into place, it serves a critical role in control. Major areas of interest during the use of operations systems are purchasing, inventory management, and quality control.

Productivity has recently become a major concern to managers. Productivity is a measure of how efficiently an organization is using its resources to create products or services. The United States still leads the world in individual productivity, but other industrialized nations are catching up.

Quality is an even more recent concern to managers. Quality affects competition, productivity, and costs. Several different things are necessary to improve quality, although everything must start with top-management commitment.

DISCUSSION QUESTIONS

Questions for Review

1. What is the relationship of operations management to overall organizational strategy? Where do productivity and quality fit into that relationship?
2. What are the major components of operations systems? How are they designed?
3. How are operations systems used in purchasing and inventory management and quality control?
4. What is meant by productivity and quality? What are the key elements to managing each of them?

Questions for Analysis

5. How might each of the other basic management functions (planning, organizing, and leading) relate to operations management?
6. Is operations management most closely linked to corporate-level, business-level, or functional strategies (refer to Chapter 6)? Why or in what way?
7. Some people argue that quality and productivity are inversely related; as one goes up, the other goes down. How can that argument be refuted?

Questions for Application

8. Interview local managers in different kinds of organizations (business, service, religious) to determine which operations systems are used in their organizations. How are those systems used?
9. Consider students as material upon which an operations transformation is worked. How would the college or university manage

students as "inventory"? How would it manage the quality of its products?

10. Go to the library and locate information on several different organizations' uses of operations management. What similarities and differences do you find? Why do you think those similarities and differences exist?

NOTES

1. Brian Dumaine, "How Managers Can Succeed Through Speed," *Fortune*, February 13, 1989, pp. 54–59; Bro Uttal, "Speeding New Ideas to Market," *Fortune*, March 2, 1987, pp. 62–66.
2. For a review, see Everett E. Adam, Jr., and Ronald J. Ebert, *Production and Operations Management*, 4th ed. (Englewood Cliffs, N.J.: Prentice-Hall, 1989).
3. Richard B. Chase and Eric L. Prentis, "Operations Management: A Field Rediscovered," *Journal of Management*, Summer 1987, pp. 351–366.
4. Robert J. Mayer, "Winning Strategies for Manufacturers in Mature Industries," *The Journal of Business Strategy*, Vol. 8, 1987, pp. 23–29.
5. Sylvia Nasar, "America's Competitive Revival," *Fortune*, January 4, 1988, pp. 44–52.
6. Richard B. Chase and Warren J. Erikson, "The Service Factory," *The Academy of Management Executive*, August 1988, pp. 191–196.
7. James Brian Quinn and Christopher E. Gagnon, "Will Service Follow Manufacturing into Decline?" *Harvard Business Review*, November–December 1986, pp. 95–103.
8. Dumaine, "How Managers Can Succeed Through Speed."
9. For a full discussion, see Everett Adam, "Towards a Typology of Production and Operations Management Systems," *Academy of Management Review*, July 1983, pp. 365–375. See also Byron J. Finch and James F. Cox, "Process-oriented Production Planning and Control: Factors that Influence System Design," *Academy of Management Journal*, March 1988, pp. 123–153.
10. Adam and Ebert, *Production and Operations Management*.
11. Jack R. Meredith, "Strategic Control of Factory Automation," *Long Range Planning*, Vol. 20, 1987, pp. 106–112.
12. Patricia L. Nemetz and Louis W. Fry, "Flexible Manufacturing Organizations: Implications for Strategy Formulation and Organization Design," *Academy of Management Review*, October 1988, pp. 627–638.
13. Dumaine, "How Managers Can Succeed Through Speed."
14. Adam and Ebert, *Production and Operations Management*.
15. Louis Kraar, "Japan's Gung-Ho U.S. Car Plants," *Fortune*, January 30, 1989, pp. 98–108.
16. See Chan K. Hahn, Daniel J. Bragg, and Dongwook Shin, "Impact of the Setup Variable on Capacity and Inventory Decisions," *Academy of Management Review*, January 1988, pp. 91–103.
17. John W. Kendrick, *Understanding Productivity: An Introduction to the Dynamics of Productivity Change* (Baltimore: Johns Hopkins, 1977).
18. Adam and Ebert, *Production and Operations Management*.
19. "Faster May Soon Mean Foreign," *Industry Week*, November 30, 1987, p. 15.

20. "Factories Get More Competitive," *USA Today*, August 3, 1987, pp. B1, B2.

21. "The Productivity Paradox," *Business Week*, June 6, 1988, pp. 100–113; "Productivity: Why It's the No. 1 Underachiever," *Business Week*, April 20, 1987, pp. 54–60.

22. "Bausch & Lomb Is Correcting Its Vision of Research," *Business Week*, March 30, 1987, p. 91.

23. Stuart Gannes, "The Good News About U.S. R&D," *Fortune*, February 1, 1988, pp. 48–56.

24. Norm Alster, "What Flexible Workers Can Do," *Fortune*, February 13, 1989, pp. 62–66.

25. Ross Johnson and William O. Winchell, *Management and Quality* (Milwaukee: American Society for Quality Control, 1989).

26. W. Edwards Deming, *Out of the Crisis* (Cambridge, Mass.: MIT Press, 1986).

27. Joel Dreyfuss, "Victories in the Quality Crusade," *Fortune*, October 10, 1988, pp. 80–88.

28. "The Push for Quality," *Business Week*, June 8, 1987, pp. 130–135.

29. "How to Make It Right the First Time," *Business Week*, June 8, 1987, pp. 142–143.

30. Dreyfuss, "Victories in the Quality Crusade."

CASE 17.1

Operations Critical to John Deere's Success

John Deere went from Vermont to Grand Detour, Illinois, as a blacksmith. In Illinois he invented the self-cleaning plow and formed his company in 1837. The Deere company continued to be innovative over the years, introducing a wide range of farming equipment. Deere's innovation, however, was not limited to products but also included the way in which the company dealt with its customers. During the depression, Deere extended credit to customers even though it knew that they might take years to repay. The loyalty inspired by that practice assured John Deere customers for decades.

To increase its knowledge of its customers and potential customers, Deere developed an extensive computerized information system. The information that it generated enabled the firm to carefully target its marketing efforts, thus better serving its customers and at the same time expanding its customer base, especially into the upper end of the market.

Deere decentralized operations so that each factory would be responsible for one category of machines from design and testing through manufacturing. There are advantages to such an approach, but there are also disadvantages. Deere achieves singleness of purpose and economies of scale, but the decentralized plants typically have relatively high breakeven volumes. Thus, when the farm economy slumps, it is hard to reduce production and cut back on costs when there is only a single plant producing each product line.

During the 1970s there was a boom in the farm economy. Sales were brisk and every manufacturer was busy. Deere could not make machinery fast enough to keep up with demand. In response, Deere expanded substantially. That expansion, of course, simply made the company even more vulnerable to a slump. Just such a slump hit the firm in the early 1980s, with disastrous results.

Deere suddenly found itself losing money for the first time in its history. It had excess capacity and an organization that was too big. Deere could and did reduce employment, sell off excess inventory, and engage in other cost reduction activities, but it could not shut down its factories. Instead, it chose to redesign and modernize its plants.

For instance, Deere's riding mower and garden tractor plant in Horicon, Wisconsin, ran on a batch system. Under that system, one model would be manufactured for several weeks and stored as inventory. Then the plant would switch over and manufacture another model. That method of production was scrapped for a highly automated but more flexible one. An automated guided vehicle (AGV) now picks up tote boxes containing kits of parts needed to assemble a tractor or mower. Workers then assemble the product directly on the AGV as it moves through the plant. Welding is done by robots. Computers synchronize the product flow, plant arrangement, the number of AGVs, and similar factors to ensure that work proceeds smoothly with proper attention to quality. One reason this system works so smoothly is that Deere had tried a "factory of the future" at its Waterloo, Iowa, tractor plant. The effort there did not work nearly so well as had been planned, but Deere learned from the experience.

Flexible manufacturing systems (FMS) were used in the Waterloo plant to achieve the same economies with low-volume production that automobile makers get with high volume. FMS was flexible so that manual or automatic transmissions could be put in different tractors coming through the line one after another. But the system was too complex and difficult to fix when anything went wrong. In addition, workers at the Waterloo plant were unionized and went on strike to safeguard their jobs. The plant was shut down for a long time during contract negotiations.

What Deere learned from the Waterloo experience was that when it designed new production systems, the first step was to simplify the production process itself. In some cases, simplification achieved sufficient improvements and no further steps were needed. In other cases, automation or other changes were used to achieve even more benefits for the organization. At Deere's Horicon plant and at its harvester works, a new system does in only one step what used to be done in seven steps.

Deere is well positioned for the future. The company has simplified its production processes, modernized its plants, tightened its product lines, reduced inventories, strengthened its dealer network, and reduced employment by almost half compared to 1980. Throughout these changes, sales of lawn-care equipment have grown to more than double their level in the early 1980s. Sales are expected to continue to rise, and that is further good news because Deere is the largest maker of that equipment. Deere's industrial equipment division has also been making modest but steady profits as has its machinery parts business.

Questions

1. Did the Deere company design its operations systems to be effective under all normal conditions? Why or why not?
2. How does Deere use its operating systems? Are those uses effective? Why or why not?
3. How could Deere develop better means for matching its productivity to market demand? Why has that not been done?
4. What might Deere do to improve the quality of its products in the future? What impact would the changes you suggest have on other operating areas? Why?

REFERENCES: "An Assembly Line on Wheels," *Industry Week*, March 21, 1988, pp. 64, 66; "Four Ways to Play the Farm Revival," *Fortune*, March 28, 1988, pp. 158, 162; "As John Deere Sowed, So Shall It Reap," *Business Week*, June 6, 1988, pp. 84–86; Harlan S. Byrne, "Out of the Storm Cellar," *Barron's*, February 16, 1987, pp. 15, 24–26.

CASE 17.2

Siemens Stresses Productivity and Quality

Siemens AG, founded in 1847, is Europe's largest electrical products company and is succeeding through the use of modern operations management technology. Siemens's home office is now in Munich. Siemens built an electric railway in 1879, an X-ray tube in 1896, and the first telex in 1933. It has long been known for developing technologically advanced products in the electric and electronic industries. Indeed, it spends about 12 percent of its sales on research and development, a figure noticeably higher than that of many other firms.

Late in 1988, Siemens made two moves to develop its presence in the telecommunications field. It combined in a 50-50 joint venture with Britain's General Electric Company to take over Plessey Company. If that acquisition actually takes place, Siemens will become the second-largest European supplier of central telephone exchanges and equipment. While the takeover was being resisted by Plessey, Siemens entered into a joint venture with IBM to purchase much of IBM's Rolm telecommunications unit and to cooperate with IBM on marketing the rest of Rolm's business. When the IBM agreement is completed, Siemens will be the world's largest supplier of PBX's and it will have all of Rolm's sales outlets in the United States. That will add greatly to Siemens's presence in the United States, which is already substantial since it acquired some American firms.

Siemens's electronic product lines emphasize factory and office automation, computerized medical equipment, telecommunications gear, and research in computer memory chips. To hedge against exchange-rate fluctuations, Siemens must keep costs down and productivity up. To accomplish both simultaneously takes a top-notch operations management system. Siemens seems to be developing one.

In the manufacture of semiconductors, Siemens has been moving to try to catch up with the Japanese, who are currently the world leaders. Siemens's effort, dubbed the Mega Project, will cost around $1 billion but will be well worthwhile if Siemens can eventually match the Japanese. The Mega Project involves completely changing Siemens's semiconductor plant located in Regensburg, West Germany.

That plant produces 1-megabit dynamic random access memory (DRAM) chips. Each DRAM chip can store a million bits of information. Siemens bought technology from Japan's Toshiba Corporation to get this project started and began a joint venture with N. V. Philips, the Dutch electronics firm, on the next generation of chips, which will be capable of storing four megabits of information.

The Regensburg plant was constructed specifically for this product. Circuit lines on DRAMs are 1 micron wide (a micron is about 1 percent of the width of a human hair). The smaller the circuit line, the more information can be placed on the chip. The microscopic etching necessary to put those lines on the silicon wafers requires the very strictest of production standards. The plant thus rests on a special foundation designed to minimize vibration that could cause problems in the fabrication rooms. Workers wear white suits with hoods to keep contamination low. In special "clean rooms," the air is filtered and recirculated so that dust and other particles are eliminated and the air is about 1,000 times cleaner than the air in a typical hospital operating room.

Production rates at the Regensburg plant are about twice those of most Japanese chip manufacturers although about the same as those of Toshiba (from whom Siemens obtained the technology). However, the experience of building and operating this plant will eventually enable Siemens to produce the new four-megabit chips faster than anyone else in the world.

Siemens is moving to market DRAMs just as carefully and aggressively as it produces them. Departments were organized to direct the marketing effort in numerous specific areas such as automotive applications, data processing, entertainment and games, industrial controls, and telecommunications. In the United States alone, Siemens has 70 sales representatives and has increased its presence with dealers and distributors. There is no shortage of demand at present, but the computer and electronics fields have a tendency to go flat periodically. The question for Siemens is whether it will be able to cope with a downturn. If management prepares for that eventuality as well as they prepared for their efforts in DRAMs, Siemens is likely to be one of the four or five international companies dominating the market by the year 2000.

Questions

1. What is the role of operations management in Siemens's strategy? How closely are operations and strategy related? Why?
2. How are operations systems at Siemens related to other aspects of the organization?
3. What is the relation of productivity and quality in a highly technologically based field like semiconductors? Why?
4. Is Siemens likely to be able to catch up with the Japanese in the semiconductor field? Why or why not? After answering this question, go to the library and determine the correctness of your response.

REFERENCES: "Siemens Gears Up for Comeback in Chips," *The Wall Street Journal*, October 11, 1988, p. B4; "Siemens's Giant Expansion Programme," *Economic Review*, Vol. 10, April 1988, p. 20; "Siemens: Awakening Giant Still Yawning," *The Wall Street Journal*, August 8, 1988, p. 24; Richard C. Morais, "Siemens über Alles," *Forbes*, July 13, 1987, pp. 366–368; John Cosch, "How Siemens Triples Switching Speeds," *Electronics*, January 7, 1988, pp. 30–31; "Siemens Hurls Itself Into Telecom Fray," *The Wall Street Journal*, March 22, 1989, p. A10.

OUTLINE

Information and the Manager
The Role of Information in the Manager's Job ·
Characteristics of Useful Information · Information
Management as Control

Building Blocks of Information Systems

Determinants of Information System Needs
General Determinants · Specific Determinants

Basic Kinds of Information Systems
Transaction-processing Systems · Basic Management
Information Systems · Decision Support Systems

Managing Information Systems
Establishing Information Systems · Integrating Information
Systems · Using Information Systems

The Impact of Information Systems on Organizations
Performance Effects · Organizational Effects · Behavioral
Effects · Information System Limitations

Recent Advances in Information Management
Telecommunications · Networks and Expert Systems

CHAPTER 18

Managing Information Systems

OBJECTIVES

After studying this chapter, you should be able to:

- Describe the role and importance of information in the manager's job.

- Identify the basic building blocks of information systems.

- Discuss the basic factors that determine an organization's information system needs.

- Describe the basic kinds of information systems used by organizations.

- Discuss how information systems can be managed.

- Describe how information systems affect organizations.

- Identify recent advances in information management.

OPENING INCIDENT

The Pentagon has been involved in many battles over the years, but few were as formidable as the war it recently declared—a war on paper. Pentagon officials have come to realize that so much paperwork is associated with the organization's various operations that the paperwork itself is becoming a major problem. For example, a typical large naval cruiser routinely carries 26 tons of manuals on how to maintain and operate the vessel and its various weapons systems, and operations and support of an average weapons system cost seven times the system's original purchase price.

To fight back, the Pentagon recently announced the establishment of a billion-dollar program called Computer-aided Acquisitions & Logistics Support (CALS). Its goal? To create a paperless Defense Department. Most experts applaud the program, but everyone agrees that it's a tremendous undertaking. The Navy alone has over 300 million technical drawings, all stored manually.

The idea is for the Pentagon to become as efficient as many of its primary contractors. For example, Northrop Corporation recently created a paperless factory to manufacture fuselages for the F/A-18 jet. In days past, 400,000 pieces of paper would have been associated in some way with the assembly of each unit. Now the same information is stored on a single laser disk. Employees consult computers for instructions, and supervisors can check inventory levels by pressing a single key.[1]

The Pentagon is addressing a need that more and more organizations have had to confront—the need to manage information. Information comes in a variety of forms and in large quantities. If organizations aren't careful, they can lose control of how they manage the information they need to conduct business efficiently and effectively. Most people would agree, for example, that 26 tons of paper is a lot of information to carry around on a ship. Consequently, in recent years businesses like Northrop and other large organizations like the Pentagon have recognized that they need better ways to manage their information.

This chapter is about advances made by organizations in doing this. We describe the role and importance of information to managers, the characteristics of useful information, and information management as control, and identify the basic building blocks of information systems. We discuss the general and specific determinants of information system needs. We then discuss the primary kinds of information systems used in organizations and describe how these information systems are managed. Finally, we highlight recent advances in information management.

INFORMATION AND THE MANAGER

Information has always been an integral part of every manager's job. Its importance, however, and therefore the need to manage it continue to grow at a rapid clip. To appreciate this trend, we need to understand the role of information in the manager's job, characteristics of useful information, and the nature of information management as control.

The Role of Information in the Manager's Job

In Chapters 1 and 15 we highlighted the role of communication in the manager's job. Given that information is a vital part of communication, it follows that management and information are closely related. Indeed, it is possible to conceptualize management itself as a series of steps involving the reception, processing, and dissemination of information. As illustrated in Figure 18.1, the manager is constantly bombarded with data and information (the difference between the two is noted later).

Suppose that Bob Henderson is an operations manager for a large manufacturing firm. During the course of a normal day, Bob receives a great many pieces of information from both formal and informal conversations and meetings, telephone calls, personal observation, letters, reports, memos, and trade publications. He gets a report from a subordinate that explains exactly how to solve a pressing problem, so he calls the subordinate and tells him to put the solution into effect immediately. He scans a copy of a report prepared for another manager, sees that it has no relevance to him, and discards it. He sees a *Wall Street Journal* article that he knows Sara Ferris in marketing should see,

FIGURE 18.1

Managers as Information Processors

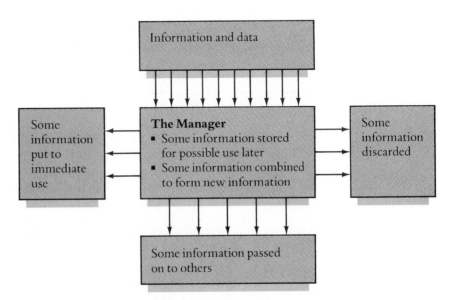

so he passes it on to her. He sees yesterday's production report, but since he knows he won't need to analyze it for another week, he stores it. He observes a worker doing a job incorrectly and realizes that the incorrect method is associated with a mysterious quality problem that someone told him about last week.

A key part of information-processing activity is differentiating between data and information. **Data** are raw figures and facts reflecting a single aspect of reality. The facts that a plant has 35 machines, that each machine is capable of producing 1,000 units of output per day, that current and projected future demand for the units is 30,000 per day, and that workers sufficiently skilled to run the machines make $15 an hour are data. **Information** is data presented in a way or form that has meaning. Thus, summarizing the four pieces of data given above provides information—the plant has excess capacity and is therefore incurring unnecessary costs. Information has meaning to a manager and provides a basis for action. The plant manager might use the information and decide to sell four machines (keeping one as a back-up) and transfer five operators to other jobs.[2]

The grocery industry has made good use of this distinction in its drive to automate inventory and checkout facilities. The average Kroger store, for example, carries 21,000 items in each of its stores. Computerized scanning machines at the checkout counters can provide daily sales figures for any product. These figures alone are data and have little meaning in their pure form. Information is compiled from this data by another computerized system. Using this system, managers can identify how any given product or product line is selling in any number of stores over any meaningful period of time.[3]

data Raw figures and facts reflecting a single aspect of reality

information Data presented in a way or form that has meaning

Characteristics of Useful Information

What factors differentiate between good and bad information? Information is good if it is accurate, timely, complete, and relevant.[4]

accurate information Provides a valid and reliable reflection of reality

Accurate   For information to be of real value to a manager, it must be accurate. Accuracy means that the information must provide a valid and reliable reflection of reality. A Japanese construction company recently bought information from a consulting firm about a possible building site in London. The Japanese were told that the land, which would be sold in a sealed bid auction, would attract bids of close to $250 million. They were also told that the land currently held an old building that could be demolished very easily. Thus, the Japanese bid $255 million—which ended up being $90 million more than the next-highest bid. A few days later, the British government declared the building historic, preempting any thought of demolition. Clearly, the Japanese acted on information that was less than accurate.[5]

timely information Available in time for appropriate managerial action

Timely   Information needs to be timely. Timeliness does not necessarily mean speediness; it means only that information needs to be available in time for appropriate managerial action. What constitutes timeliness is a function of the situation facing the manager. When Marriott was gathering information for its proposed Fairfield Inn project, managers projected a six-month window for data collection. They felt this would give them an opportunity to do a good job of getting the information they needed while not delaying things too much. In contrast, Marriott's computerized reservation and accounting system can provide a manager today with last night's occupancy level at any Marriott facility.[6]

■ **complete information** Provides the manager with all of the information he or she needs

Complete   Information must tell a complete story for it to be useful to a manager. If it is less than complete, the manager is likely to get an inaccurate or distorted picture of reality. For example, managers at Kroger used to think that house-brand products were more profitable than national brands because they yielded higher unit profits. On the basis of this information, they gave house brands a lot of shelf space and centered a lot of promotional activities around them. As Kroger's managers became more sophisticated in understanding their information, however, they realized that national brands were actually more profitable over time because they sold many more units than house brands during any given period of time. Hence, while a store might sell 10 cans of Kroger coffee in a day with a profit of 25 cents per can (total profit of $2.50), it would also sell 15 cans of Maxwell House with a profit of 20 cents per can (total profit of $3.00).

■ **relevant information**   Assures managers that the information is useful to them in their particular circumstances for their particular needs

Relevance   Information must be relevant if it is to be of use to a manager. Relevance, like timeliness, is defined according to the needs and circumstances of a particular manager. Operations managers need information on costs and productivity; human resource managers need information on hiring needs and turnover rates; and marketing managers need information on sales projections and advertising rates. As Wal-Mart begins its expansion into the western United States, it needs site information for possible stores in South Dakota, Nevada, Utah, and California in the near future. Although site information for Washington and Oregon might be valuable in a few more years, it is less relevant now.[7]

Information Management as Control

The manager needs to appreciate the role of information in control—indeed, to see information management as a vital part of the control process in the organization.[8] As already noted, managers receive much more data and information than they need or can use. Accordingly, deciding how to handle each piece of data and information involves a form of control.

The control perspective on information management is illustrated in Figure 18.2. Information enters, is used by, and leaves the organization. For example, Marriott took great pains to make sure it got all the

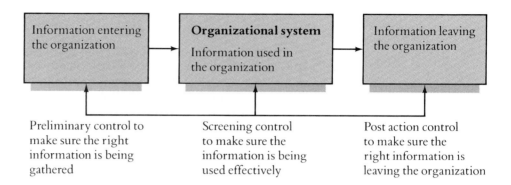

Information entering the organization	→	**Organizational system** Information used in the organization	→	Information leaving the organization

Preliminary control to make sure the right information is being gathered   Screening control to make sure the information is being used effectively   Post action control to make sure the right information is leaving the organization

FIGURE 18.2

Information Management as Control

information it needed to plan for and enter the economy lodging business. Once this preliminary information was gathered, it was necessary to make sure that the information was made available in the proper form to everyone who needed it. In general, the effort to ensure that information is accurate, timely, complete, and relevant is a form of screening control. Finally, Marriott wanted to make sure that its competitors did not learn about its plans until the last possible minute. It also wanted to time and orchestrate news releases, public announcements, and advertising for maximum benefit. These efforts thus served a postaction control function.

Clearly, information management and control processes are highly interrelated. "Management in Practice" describes how Firestone realized that it had a control problem with managing its information and how it handled its information management needs. Firestone, like many companies, developed an information management system. In the next section, we identify the basic building blocks that are used to construct and use such systems.

BUILDING BLOCKS OF INFORMATION SYSTEMS

One important building block in an information system is storage—facilities and equipment for storing data and information that managers may need for future decisions. Norstar Services' Data Center in Albany manages 2.5 million accounts daily. And every month there are over 10 million inquiries made to customer data files. Norstar uses these data tapes to store the information it uses in its daily operations.

Information systems are generally of two types—manual or computer-based. All information systems have five basic parts. Figure 18.3 diagrams these parts for a computer-based system. The *input medium* is the device that is used to add data and information into the system. For example, the optical scanner at Kroger enters point-of-sale information. Likewise, someone can also enter data through a keyboard.

The data that are entered into the system typically flow first to a processor. The *processor* is the part of the system that is capable of organizing, manipulating, sorting, or performing calculations with the data. Most systems also have one or more *storage* devices—a place where data can be stored for later use. Floppy disks, hard disks, magnetic tapes, and optical disks are common forms of storage devices. As data are transformed into useable information, the resultant information must be communicated to the appropriate person by means of an *output*

MANAGEMENT IN PRACTICE

FIRESTONE'S CIO

Firestone Tire & Rubber Company has tire plants in over 20 countries spread over five continents. It has over 2,000 Firestone stores and also sells through independent dealers like Montgomery Ward. Its products include tires for cars, trucks, buses, tractors, and airplanes. An organization of its size and complexity has sizable information management needs. To meet them, Firestone has a chief information officer (CIO), although the title used is vice president for information services. The CIO is a top executive who reports to the board of directors or to the CEO.

In 1982, Firestone conducted an internal study of its manufacturing processes. The study concluded that those processes were in deplorable condition, woefully out of date, and seriously lacking integrated control. Plant managers frequently guessed how much rubber they would need to complete an order, because they had no good information to use. If they guessed wrong, time and money were wasted, sometimes in sizable amounts. Firestone's CIO at that time, Laurance T. Burden, felt that this lack of effective organizational control was unacceptable. Working with the vice president for U.S. tire operations, Burden had a computer system developed to correct the problem and enhance organizational control.

The new computer system tracks every step in the manufacture of a tire. The system begins by ensuring that the production process has the right amount of rubber on hand and ends by checking the treads to be sure that they have the correct shape and depth. By late 1986, the system was running at two plants. The immediate impact was to help increase productivity by over 15 percent and save millions of dollars. The system was introduced into all other Firestone plants by 1988 and became an example of the benefits to the organization of applications of management information systems.

Early in 1988, Firestone was purchased by the Bridgestone Tire Company of America, an independent subsidiary of a Japanese-controlled company. Bridgestone kept the Firestone name and operates the two organizations as separate but equal entities. Products bearing the brand names of both firms are sold through outlets such as the Firestone stores in the United States. Information management has become even more critical for the new organization because it must manage manufacturing and sales operations in several countries as well as under different brands.

REFERENCES: "Management's Newest Star," *Business Week*, October 13, 1988, pp. 160–172; "Firestone Peels Out of Tires," *Business Week*, February 29, 1988, p. 29; K. F. Sarver, "CAD-CAE: A Look at Tire Design Engineering," *Rubber World*, June 1987, pp. 26–28; "Bridgestone Firestone to Operate as 'Equals,'" *Modern Tire Dealer*, April 1988, p. 9.

medium. Common ways to display output are video displays, printers that actually put the information onto paper, and other computers.

Finally, the entire information system is operated by a *control system*—most often software of one form or another. Small systems can use off-the-shelf software. MicroSoft Word, WordPerfect, and Word Star are popular systems for word processing. Lotus 1–2–3 is a popular spreadsheet program, and dBASE III is frequently used for database management. Of course, elaborate systems of the type used by large businesses require a special customized operating system. When organizations start to link computers together into a network, the operating system must be even more complex.

As we noted earlier, information systems need not be computerized. Many small organizations still function quite well with a manual system using paper documents, routing slips, file folders, file cabinets, and

FIGURE 18.3

Building Blocks of a
Computer-based Information
System

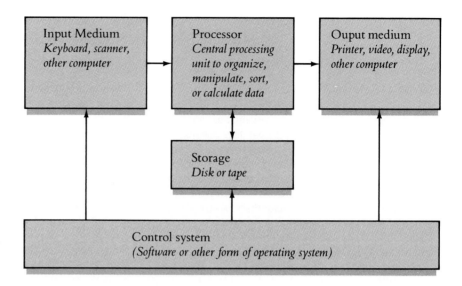

typewriters. Increasingly, however, even small businesses are abandoning their manual systems for computerized ones. As hardware prices continue to drop and software becomes more and more powerful, computerized information systems will likely be within the reach of any business that wants to have one.

DETERMINANTS OF INFORMATION SYSTEM NEEDS

What determines whether an organization needs an information system, and how do these factors help define the organization's information management needs? In general, the key factors that determine these needs fall into two categories: general determinants and specific determinants.[9] These are illustrated in Figure 18.4.

General Determinants

Two general factors help define an organization's information management needs. These factors are the environment and the size of the organization.

Environment In Chapters 3 and 9 we noted that the environment of an organization affects that organization in many different ways. Still another way that the environment affects an organization is as a determinant of its information management needs. In general, the more uncertain and complex the environment, the greater is the need to formally manage information. Given that virtually all organizations face

FIGURE 18.4

Determinants of an
Organization's Information-
Processing Needs

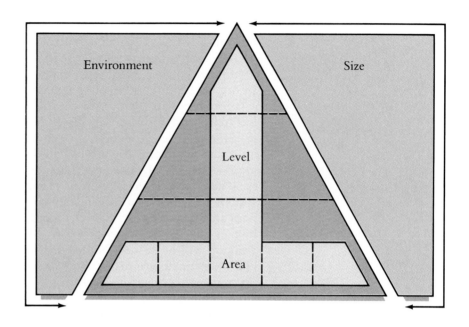

at least some degree of uncertainty, it can be argued that all organizations need to worry about managing their information. However, an
organization like Hewlett-Packard or IBM that operates in an extremely
uncertain environment has very strong needs for elaborate information
management. "The Global View" describes how the complex environment faced by Airbus, a European consortium of aircraft manufacturers,
has influenced its needs to better manage information.

Size   Size is another general determinant of an organization's information management needs. All else equal, the larger an organization
is, the greater are its needs to manage its information systematically.
Thus, General Motors has greater information management needs than
does its Cadillac division alone, and each has greater needs than does a
single Cadillac dealership. The effects of organizational size can also be
either slightly constrained or greatly accentuated by the diversity of the
organization. A large organization that is essentially a single division,
for example, has less pressure for information management than does
a firm of the same size that comprises several different divisions.

Specific Determinants

Two factors serve to define the information management needs of an
organization. These factors are the area and level of the organization.

Area   By area, we mean basic functional areas like finance, marketing,
or human resources. Each of these areas has its own unique set of
information management needs. Human resources, for example, needs

complete demographic data on all current employees, job-grade information, Affirmative Action statistics, and so forth. Marketing needs data on current prices, market share, and advertising expenditures.

Another key ingredient is the extent to which the various areas within an organization work in an integrated and coordinated fashion. If each acts totally on its own, with coordination handled by the managerial hierarchy, each area can survive with its own information system. But if different areas are expected to coordinate their activities, then their information systems need to be coordinated. For example, the marketing system may be updated to include a projection for 10 percent more sales next year than previously expected. An integrated information system could use that information to provide the operations manager with an indication that additional output will be needed, to provide the human resource manager with an indication of how many additional workers will be needed, and to provide the financial manager with an indication of how much additional working capital will be needed to support higher wage and materials costs.

Level Organizational level also helps determine the information management requirements of the organization. Managers at the top of the organization need broad, general kinds of information across a variety of time frames to help them with strategic planning. Middle managers need information of somewhat more specificity and with a shorter time frame. Lower-level managers need highly specific information with a very short time frame. For example, the vice president of marketing at General Mills might want to know projected demand for eight different cereal products over the next five years. A divisional sales manager might need to know projected demand for two of those cereal products for the next one-year period. A district sales manager might need to know how much of one cereal is likely to be sold next month.

In designing information systems, it is important that the organization determines what its needs are. James Perkins is an executive at Federal Express. He keeps tabs on the company's 50,000 employees with an elaborate information system that tracks their work histories, performance evaluations, and career goals. Whenever a promotion opportunity arises, Perkins can go directly to the database, as he is doing here, and quickly access all the information he needs to identify likely candidates.

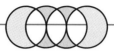

THE GLOBAL VIEW

INFORMATION CONTROL AT AIRBUS

Airbus Industrie is an unusual organization. It was formed in 1970 as a consortium backed by the governments of France, Great Britain, Spain, and West Germany. The consortium was incorporated under French law as a hybrid joint venture with more characteristics of a partnership than of a regular corporation. The basic idea was that Airbus would design and produce aircraft to compete with the American firms Boeing and McDonnell Douglas, which dominated the market at that time.

Human resource legislation varies in France, Great Britain, Spain, and West Germany. Not only does that complicate day-to-day supervision and labor relations, but it also makes rapid adjustment to market changes difficult to achieve. Because of legislation that makes reducing the work force through layoffs or termination difficult, it can take Airbus eighteen months to reduce its labor force enough to compensate for a production cut of one airplane per month.

From its beginning, Airbus has been successful at designing and delivering competitive products that exceed standards for safety and quality. Airbus products use some of the world's most sophisticated computer programs to deal with the complex information used in the intercontinental operation of jet aircraft. The production process, however, is complicated and inefficient. Most of the parts for Airbus planes are manufactured in different countries scattered across Europe. As parts are finished, they are shipped to the final-assembly plant in Toulouse, France. This geographical dispersion means that Airbus may take two or three years to deliver a plane after receiving an order. The two American companies, in contrast, can deliver a plane in about eighteen months. Nevertheless, the quality and safety of Airbus planes have enabled Airbus to improve sales almost every year.

Airbus must improve its control over operations and develop better information management systems. Operating in four countries as a joint venture, producing in those four countries and selling worldwide, manufacturing products that involve an incredible amount of information, and designing systems that must work in air-control environments throughout the world all suggest the massive nature of the information management problems facing Airbus.

REFERENCES: "A Reorganization at Airbus May Never Get Off the Ground," *Business Week*, May 16, 1988, p. 56; "In the Wild Blue Yonder," *The Economist*, January 9, 1988, p. 76; "A Better Way to Fly?" *The Economist*, April 16, 1988, p. 7; Keith Hayward, "Airbus: Twenty Years of European Cooperation," *International Affairs*, Vol. 64, Winter 1987, pp. 11–16.

BASIC KINDS OF INFORMATION SYSTEMS

Organizations that use information systems, especially large organizations, often find that they need several kinds of systems in order to manage their information effectively. The three most general kinds of information systems are transaction-processing systems, basic management information systems, and decision support systems.[10]

Transaction-processing Systems

■ **transaction-processing system** or **TPS** A system designed to handle routine and recurring transactions with a business

Transaction-processing systems were the first computerized form of information system adopted by many businesses. A **transaction-processing system**, or **TPS**, is a system designed to handle routine and recurring transactions within the business. Visa uses a TPS to record charges to individual credit accounts, credit payments made on the accounts, and send monthly bills to customers.

Transaction processing systems handle routine and recurring transactions within a business. Citizens & Southern, a large financial services company, handles millions of transactions every day. These transactions run the gamut from mortgage loan applications to credit card charges. C&S uses sophisticated cartridge storage systems to keep track of millions of transactions. Its managers can retrieve any piece of information they need in a matter of seconds.

■ **management information system** or **MIS** A system that gathers more comprehensive data, organizes and summarizes it in a form of value to managers, and provides those managers with the information they need to do their work

■ **decision support system** or **DSS** A system that automatically searches for, manipulates, and summarizes information needed by managers for use in making specific decisions

In general, a TPS is most useful when the organization has a large number of highly similar transactions to process. Thus, most forms of customer billings, bank transactions, and point-of-sale records are amenable to this form of information system. The automated scanners at Kroger that record each unit sold and its price are a form of TPS.

A TPS is especially helpful in aggregating large amounts of data into more manageable forms of information summaries. For example, a bank manager probably cares little about any given Visa transaction recorded for any single cardholder. More useful is information about the average number of purchases made by each cardholder, their average daily balances, average monthly finance charges assessed, and so forth.

In general, a TPS is most useful to lower-level managers. Even though this approach was the earliest, it is still of considerable use and relevance to many organizations. Many of these organizations, however, have also found it necessary to develop more sophisticated systems.

Basic Management Information Systems

The next step in the evolution of information management is generally called the **management information system**, or **MIS**. An MIS is a system that gathers more comprehensive data, organizes and summarizes it in a form that is of value to functional managers, and then provides those same managers with the information they need to do their work. Figure 18.5 shows how such a system might work.

An MIS for a manufacturing firm might develop a computerized inventory system that keeps track of both anticipated orders and inventory on hand. A marketing representative talking to a customer about anticipated delivery dates can "plug into the system" and get a good idea of when an order can be shipped. Likewise, the plant manager can use the system to help determine how much of each of the firm's products to manufacture next week or next month. Seminole Manufacturing Co. uses a variation on the standard MIS called an EDE—electronic data exchange. Seminole supplies Wal-Mart with men's pants. The EDE system allows Seminole to tie directly into Wal-Mart's computerized inventory system to check current sales levels and stock on hand. Wal-Mart can then transmit new orders directly into Seminole's system—and managers there are already geared up to start working on it. As a result, delivery times have been cut in half and sales are up 31 percent.[11]

Decision Support Systems

The newest, most elaborate, and most powerful form of information system is called a **decision support system**, or **DSS**. A DSS is a system that automatically searches for, manipulates, and summarizes information needed by managers for specific decisions. A DSS is much

FIGURE 18.5

A Basic Management
Information System

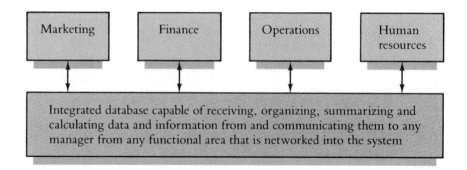

more flexible than a traditional MIS and can help cope with nonroutine problems and decisions.[12]

A manager might be interested in knowing the likely effects of a price increase for a particular product sold by the firm. Thus, she might decide to query the DSS to determine the potential outcomes for price increases of 5, 7, and 10 percent. The DSS already knows the pricing history for the product, the prices charged by competitors, their most recent price changes, the effects of price on sales, seasonal variations in demand and price, inflation rates, and virtually any other relevant piece of information that might have already been determined. The system then calculates projected sales, market share, and profit profiles for each of the potential price-increase levels and provides them to the manager.

Decision support systems are very complex. They take considerable time and resources to develop and more time and resources to maintain and to teach managers how to effectively use them. They also seem to hold considerable potential for improving the quality of information available to managers as they make important decisions.

MANAGING INFORMATION SYSTEMS

At this point, the value and importance of information systems should be apparent. There are still important questions to be answered, however. How are such systems developed, and how are they used on a day-to-day basis? This section provides insights into these issues and related areas.

Establishing Information Systems

The basic steps involved in creating an information system are outlined in Figure 18.6.[13] The first step is to determine the information needs of the organization and to establish goals for what is to be achieved with the proposed system. It is absolutely imperative that the project have full support and an appropriate financial commitment from top management if it is to be successful. Once the decision has been made to develop and install an information system, a task force is usually con-

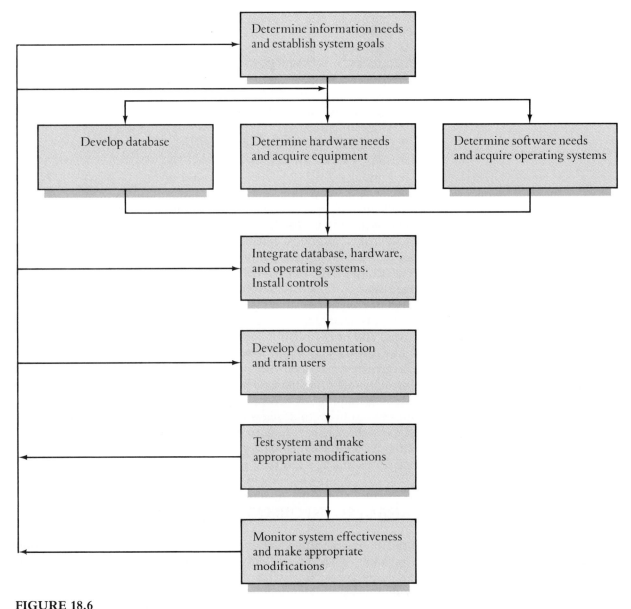

FIGURE 18.6

Establishing an Information System

stituted to oversee everything. Target users must be well represented on such a task force.

Next, three tasks can be done simultaneously. One task is to assemble a database. Most organizations already possess the information they need for an information system, but it is often not in the correct form. As noted in the opening incident, the Pentagon is spending large sums of money to transform paper records into computer records. Many other branches of the government are also working hard to computerize their data.[14]

While the database is being assembled, the organization also needs to determine its hardware needs and acquire the appropriate equipment. Some systems rely solely on one large mainframe computer; others are increasingly using personal computers. Equipment is usually obtained from large manufacturers like IBM, Wang, Unisys, and DEC. Finally, software needs must also be determined and an appropriate operating system obtained. Again, off-the-shelf packages will sometimes work, although most companies find it necessary to do some customization to suit their needs.

The actual information system is created by integrating the database, the hardware, and the software. Obviously, the mechanics of doing this are beyond the scope of this discussion. However, the company usually has to rely on the expertise of outside consulting firms along with the vendors who provided the other parts of the system to get it all put together. During this phase, the equipment is installed, cables are strung between units, the data are entered into the system, the operating system is installed and tested, and so forth. During this phase, system controls are also installed. A control is simply a characteristic of the system that limits certain forms of access or limits what a person can do with the system. For example, top managers may want to limit access to certain sensitive data to a few key people. These people may be given private codes that must be entered before the data is made available. It is important to make sure that data cannot be accidentally erased by someone who happens to press the wrong key.

The next step is to develop documentation of how the system works and train people in how to use it. Documentation refers to manuals, computerized help programs, diagrams, and instruction sheets. Essentially, it tells people how to use the system for different purposes. Beyond pure documentation, however, training sessions are also common. Such sessions allow people to practice using the system under the watchful eye of experts.

The system must then be tested and appropriate modifications made. Regardless of how well planned an information system is, there will almost certainly be glitches. For example, the system may be unable to generate a report that needs to be made available to certain managers. Or the report may not be in the appropriate format. Or certain people may be unable to access data that they need in order to get other information from the system. In most cases, the consultants or internal group that installed the system will be able to make such modifications as the need arises.

The organization must recognize that information management needs will change over time. Hence, even though the glitches get straightened out and the information system is put into normal operation, modifications may still be needed in the future. For example, after Black & Decker acquired General Electric's small-appliance business, it had to overhaul its own information system to accommodate all the new information associated with its new business. Information management is a continuous process. Even if an effective information system can be created and put into use, there is still an good chance that it will need to be occasionally modified to fit changing circumstances.

Quaker State uses its new IBM central data processing system to manage all its internal communication. Every plant and office in the Quaker State organization is connected to this system. Thus, managers can make full use of electronic mail, access information needed to make decisions, and handle all daily business transactions using a single system.

Integrating Information Systems

In very large and complex organizations, information systems must also be integrated. This integration may involve linkages between different information systems within the same organization or between different organizations altogether.[15] Within an organization, for example, it is probably necessary for the marketing system and the operations system to be able to communicate with one another.

Linking systems together is not as easy.[16] A company might install its first information system in operations using a Wang system. A couple of years later, it might put a system into marketing but decide for some reason to use IBM equipment. When a decision is made still later to integrate the two systems, differences in technology and operating systems might make such integration difficult or even impossible.

There are two ways of overcoming this problem. One is to develop everything at once. Unfortunately, doing so is expensive, and sometimes managers simply can't anticipate today exactly what their needs will be tomorrow. The other method is to adopt a standard type of system at the beginning so that subsequent additions fit properly. Even then, however, breakthroughs in information system technology may still make it necessary to change approaches in midstream.

Using Information Systems

The real test of the value of an information system is how it can be used. Ideally, an information system should be simple to use and nontechnical—that is, one should not have to be a computer expert to use the system. In theory, a manager should be able to access a modern information system by turning on a computer and pressing certain keys in response to menu prompts. The manager should also be able to enter appropriate new data or request that certain kinds of information be provided. The requested information might first be displayed on a computer screen or monitor. After the manager is satisfied, the information can then be printed out in paper form on a standard printer, or the manager can store the information back in the system for possible future use or for use by others.

The Travelers Corporation has made effective use of its information system by hiring a team of trained nurses to review health-insurance claims. The nurses tap into the company's regular information system and analyze the medical diagnoses provided with each claim. They can use this information to determine whether a second opinion is warranted before a particular surgical procedure is approved. They enter their decision directly into the system. When the claim form is printed out, it contains a provision that spells out whether the claimant must seek a second opinion before proceeding with a particular treatment.[17]

THE IMPACT OF INFORMATION SYSTEMS ON ORGANIZATIONS

Information systems are clearly an important part of most modern organizations. Their effects are felt in a variety of ways. In particular, information systems affect performance, the organization itself, and people within the organization. Information systems also have clear limits to what they can do.

Performance Effects

Organizations install information systems because they think they will make the organization more effective and efficient. Over the past ten years, almost 40 percent of all capital spending by U.S. companies has been on information systems technology—close to a trillion dollars.[18] Has the expenditure been worthwhile? Some experts say yes; others have their doubts. The problem is that although information systems can speed up an organization's ability to crunch numbers and generate documents, it is difficult to measure whether the increased speed is justified in light of the enormous costs involved. Many organizations, ranging from General Electric to K mart to American Airlines, claim that their information systems have made them enormously successful. Indeed, there seems to be a growing consensus that information systems do pay for themselves over time, although an organization needs to recognize that it may take years for the system to pay its own way.

A good example of a highly effective system is the one developed by the U.S. Forest Service. The Forest Service used to have a policy of attacking every forest fire by 10 A.M. the day after it was reported. Costs could run as high as $10 million for a major fire. The service now uses computer models as a part of its information system to determine how important containment really is. For example, rivers often provide a natural barrier that stops fires from spreading. In 1985, an Idaho blaze was determined to fit just such a pattern. Under the old plan, the Fire Service would have spent an estimated $3.7 million to extinguish the blaze. But understanding how a river would halt the fire's spread resulted in expenses of only $400,000. Information is made available to firefighters in the field through hand-held programmable computers tied back into a master information system.[19] Although not every organization will be as satisfied as the Forest Service with its information system, more and more firms are telling comparable success stories.

Organizational Effects

Information systems affect the organization's basic structure and design. These effects generally happen in two ways. First, most organizations find it useful to create a separate unit to handle the information management system; some even create a new top-management position, usually called the chief information officer, or CIO.[20] This manager and her or his staff is responsible for maintaining the information system, upgrading it as appropriate, finding new uses for it, and training people in its use.

The second way in which information affects organizations is by allowing managers to eliminate layers in the managerial hierarchy. As detailed in Chapter 8, information systems allow managers to stay in touch with large numbers of subordinates, thereby eliminating the need for hierarchical control. IBM, for example, eliminated a layer of management because of improved efficiencies achieved through its information management system. Some experts have suggested that in the future managers will be able to coordinate as many as 200 subordinates at one time.[21]

Behavioral Effects

Information systems affect the behaviors of people in organizations. Some of these effects are positive; others can be negative. On the plus side, information systems usually improve individual efficiency. Some people also enjoy their work more because they have fun using the new technology. As a result of computerized bulletin boards and electronic mail, groups can form across organizational boundaries.

On the negative side, information systems can lead to isolation as people have everything they need to do their jobs without interacting with others. Managers can work at home easily, with the possible side effects of making them unavailable to others who need them or removing them from key parts of the social system. Computerized working arrangements also tend to be much less personal than other methods. For example, a computer-transmitted "pat on the back" will likely mean less than a real one. Researchers are just beginning to determine how individual behaviors and attitudes are affected by information systems.

Information System Limitations

It is also necessary to recognize the limits of information systems.[22] Several of these are listed in Table 18.1. First of all, as already noted, information systems are expensive and difficult to develop. Thus, organizations may try to cut corners too much or install a system in such a piecemeal fashion that its effectiveness suffers.

Information systems simply are not suitable for some tasks or problems. Complex problems requiring human judgment must still be addressed by humans. Information systems are often a useful tool for managers, but they can seldom actually replace managers. Managers also may come to rely too much on information systems. As a consequence, the manager may lose touch with the real-world problems he or she needs to be concerned about.

Information may not be as accurate, timely, complete, or relevant as it appears. There is a strong tendency for people to think that because a computer performed the calculations, the answer must be correct—especially if the answer is calculated to several decimal places. But the fact of the matter is that if the initial information was flawed, all resultant computations using it are likely to be flawed as well.

Managers sometimes have unrealistic expectations about what information systems can accomplish. They may believe that the first stage of implementation will result in a full-blown Orwellian communication network that a child could use. When the manager comes to see the flaws and limits of the system, she or he may become disappointed and as a result not use the system effectively. Finally, the information system may be subject to sabotage, computer viruses, or downtime. Disgruntled employees have been known to deliberately enter false data.[23] And a company that relies too much on a computerized information system may find itself totally paralyzed in the event of a simple power outage.

TABLE 18.1

Limitations of Information Systems

1. Information systems are expensive and difficult to develop and implement.
2. Information systems are not suitable for all tasks or problems.
3. Managers sometimes rely on information systems too much.
4. Information provided to managers may not be as accurate, timely, complete, or relevant as it appears.
5. Managers may have unrealistic expectations of what the information system can do.
6. The information system may be subject to sabotage, computer viruses, or downtime.

American Information Technologies Corporation (Ameritech) recently took on a big job—it agreed to serve as the official communications company for the 1987 Pan American Games which were held in Indianapolis. The company designed a sophisticated network based on 3,000 voice, data, and video circuits which served to link 33 sites used during the competition. During the opening ceremonies for the Games, technicians like the ones shown here helped coordinate dozens of activities that had to be carefully orchestrated and sequenced.

RECENT ADVANCES IN INFORMATION MANAGEMENT

Because of the enormous promise of information systems, and despite their occasional limitations, work continues to uncover new and even more sophisticated approaches to managing information. This section highlights some of the most interesting ones.

Telecommunications

One area where great strides have been made is **telecommunications**. There are several forms of telecommunications that have been or are being developed. Videoconferencing allows people in different locations to see and talk to one another. For example, Sam Walton often uses teleconferences to talk directly with his Wal-Mart employees during their normal Saturday morning meetings.[24] Electronic mail systems allow managers to send messages to one another through computer linkups. People "post" messages on electronic bulletin boards for other interested people to read. Voice messaging allows voice messages to be stored and transferred between computers.

Networks and Expert Systems

Despite the limitations and problems noted earlier, strides continue to be made in the area of networking. Even computer systems with very different operating systems are becoming increasingly able to communicate with one another. Although there are still a variety of "standard" operating systems, as each is more finely developed it can interface with others more and more effectively.

Expert systems are also becoming more and more practical. An **expert system** is an information system created to duplicate, or at least imitate, the thought processes of a human being.[25] The starting point in developing an expert system is to identify all the "if-then" contingencies that pertain to a given situation. These contingencies form the knowledge base for the system. For example, Table 18.2 summarizes the knowledge base for a hypothetical firm's pricing policy. The facts and if-then contingencies outlined in the table determine the pricing policy. The statements in bold-type represent the current situation facing the company. Thus, a manager could query the system with the question "What is price policy?" The system would respond, "Price policy is increase price." The manager could then ask why, and the system would answer, "Price policy is increase price because margin is low and demand is strong."

Organizations have developed considerably more complex and useful expert systems. For example, Campbell's developed an expert system to recreate the thought processes of one of its key employees, a manager who was very familiar with operations of the seven-story soup kettles

■ **telecommunications** The use of electronic media to communicate over distances; includes the telephone, telegraph, electronic bulletin boards, facsimile machines

■ **expert system** An information system created to duplicate or imitate the thought processes of a human expert

TABLE 18.2

An Example Knowledge Base
for a Firm's Pricing Policy

> **Factual Knowledge**
>
> Price is $50.00.
> Cost is $45.00.
> Demand is 1,121.
> Margin is (price − cost).
>
> **Process Knowledge**
>
> 1. If margin is high and demand is weak, then price-policy is decrease-price.
> 2. If margin is normal and demand is steady, then price-policy is maintain-price.
> 3. **If margin is low and demand is strong, then price-policy is increase-price.**
> 4. If margin is greater-than 25, then margin is high.
> 5. **If margin is less-than 10, then margin is low.**
> 6. If margin is-not high and margin is-not low, then margin is normal.
> 7. **If demand is greater-than 1,100, then demand is strong.**
> 8. If demand is less-than 900, then demand is weak.
> 9. If demand is-not strong and demand is-not weak, then demand is steady.

SOURCE: David B. Paradice and James F. Courtney, Jr., "Intelligent Organizations," *Texas A&M Business Forum*, Fall 1988, pp. 18–22. Reprinted with permission.

used to cook soup. The manager, Aldo Cimino, knew so much about how the kettles worked that the company feared no one else could learn the job as well as he. So it hired Texas Instruments to study his job, interview him and observe his work, and create an expert system that could mimic his experience. The resultant system, containing over 150 if-then rules, helps operate the kettles today.[26]

SUMMARY OF KEY POINTS

Information is a vital part of every manager's job. For information to be useful, it must be accurate, timely, complete, and accurate. Information management is best conceived of as part of the control process.

Information systems, whether manual or computerized, contain five basic components. These are an input medium, a processor, storage, a control system, and an output medium.

An organization's information management requirements are determined by four factors. Two general factors are the environment and size of the organization. Two specific factors are area and level of the organization.

There are three basic kinds of information systems—transaction-processing systems, basic management information systems, and decision support systems.

Managing information systems involves three basic elements. The first is deciding how to establish information systems. The systems must then be integrated. Finally, managers must be able to use them.

Information systems impact organizations in a variety of ways. Major influences are on performance, the organization itself, and behavior within the organization. There are also limitations to the effectiveness of information systems.

Recent advances in information systems include breakthroughs in telecommunications, networks, and expert systems.

DISCUSSION QUESTIONS

Questions for Review

1. What are the characteristics of useful information? How can information management aid in organizational control?
2. What are the building blocks of information systems? How are they related to one another?
3. What is a management information system? How can such a system be used to benefit an organization?
4. What is an expert system? Do such systems have any significant potential for use by business organizations? Why or why not?

Questions for Analysis

5. In what ways is a management information system like an inventory control system or a production control system? In what ways is it different from those?
6. It has been said that the information revolution now occurring is like the industrial revolution in terms of the magnitude of its impact upon organizations and society. What leads to such a view? Why might that view be an overstatement?
7. Is it possible for the chief information officer of an organization to become too powerful? If so, how might the situation be prevented? If not, why not?

Questions for Application

8. Interview a local business manager about the use of information in his or her organization. How is information managed? Is a computer system used? How well does the information system seem to be integrated with other aspects of organizational control?
9. Your college or university library deals in information. What kind of information system is used? Is it computerized? How might the information system be redesigned to be of more value to you?
10. Go to the library and see if you can locate a reference to the use of an expert system in a business firm. If you can, share it with the class. Why might this be a difficult assignment?

NOTES

1. "A Search-and-Destroy Mission—Against Paper," *Business Week*, February 6, 1989, pp. 91–95.
2. Lynda M. Applegate, James I. Cash, Jr., and D. Quinn Mills, "Information Technology and Tomorrow's Manager," *Harvard Business Review*, November–December 1988, pp. 128–136.
3. "At Today's Supermarket, the Computer Is Doing It All," *Business Week*, August 11, 1986, pp. 64–66.
4. Charles A. O'Reilly, "Variations in Decision Makers' Use of Information Sources: The Impact of Quality and Accessibility of Information," *Academy of Management Journal*, December 1982, pp. 756–771.
5. Carla Rapoport, "Great Japanese Mistakes," *Fortune*, February 13, 1989, pp. 108–111.
6. Brian Dumaine, "Corporate Spies Snoop to Conquer," *Fortune*, November 7, 1988, pp. 68–76.
7. John Huey, "Wal-Mart—Will It Take Over the World?" *Fortune*, January 30, 1989, pp. 52–61.
8. William J. Bruns, Jr., and F. Warren McFarlin, "Information Technology Puts Power in Control Systems," *Harvard Business Review*, September–October 1987, pp. 89–94.
9. See Jesse B. Tutor, Jr., "Management and Future Technological Trends," *Texas A&M Business Forum*, Fall 1988, pp. 2–5.
10. V. Thomas Dock and James C. Wetherbe, *Computer Information Systems for Business* (St. Paul, Minn.: West, 1988).
11. "An Electronic Pipeline That's Changing the Way America Does Business," *Business Week*, August 3, 1987, pp. 80–82.
12. Applegate, Cash, and Mills, "Information Technology and Tomorrow's Manager."
13. See George W. Reynolds, *Information Systems for Managers* (St. Paul, Minn.: West, 1988), for a detailed description of developing information systems.
14. "Computerizing Uncle Sam's Data: Oh, How the Public Is Paying," *Business Week*, December 15, 1986, pp. 102–103.
15. Cornelius H. Sullivan, Jr., and John R. Smart, "Planning for Information Networks," *Sloan Management Review*, Winter 1987, pp. 39–44.
16. "Linking All the Company Data: We're Not There Yet," *Business Week*, May 11, 1987, p. 151.
17. "Office Automation: Making It Pay Off," *Business Week*, October 12, 1987, pp. 134–146.
18. "Office Automation: Making It Pay Off."
19. "Office Automation: Making It Pay Off."
20. John J. Donovan, "Beyond Chief Information Officer to Network Managers," *Harvard Business Review*, September–October 1988, pp. 134–140.
21. Jeremy Main, "The Winning Organization," *Fortune*, September 26, 1988, pp. 50–60.
22. See Reynolds, *Information Systems for Managers*.
23. "Computer Headaches," *Newsweek*, July 6, 1987, pp. 34–35.
24. Huey, "Wal-Mart—Will It Take Over the World?"
25. Dorothy Leonard-Barton and John J. Sviokla, "Putting Expert Systems to Work," *Harvard Business Review*, March–April 1988, pp. 91–98.
26. "Turning an Expert's Skills into Computer Software," *Business Week*, October 7, 1985, pp. 104–108.

CASE 18.1

Federal Express Rises to the Challenge

In 1965, when Frederick W. Smith outlined in a paper for an economics class at Yale his new idea for a package delivery service that would effectively compete with the U.S. Postal Service, he received a grade of C. In order to secure funding to launch that service, he had to commit his own funds before other investors were willing to get involved.

In 1973, Smith began Federal Express with 14 small planes and delivered only 20 packages during the first month of operations. The deregulation of the airline industry in 1977 enabled the company to really take off because it could use large planes for major cities and move its small planes into virtually any other market. Federal Express went public in 1978 with a stock price of $24 a share and with revenues of around $150 million a year. By 1983, revenues hit $1 billion, record growth for any American company at that time. By 1988, the stock price had risen to the $40 per share range and annual revenues had risen to almost $4 billion.

Federal Express dominates the overnight mail market. It has over half of that market. Federal Express handles more than 200 million documents and packages each year, and it claims that 99 percent of those are delivered on time and in good condition. It operates throughout the United States and in over 100 foreign countries. Federal Express expanded to 11 African nations in the summer of 1988, and in that same year it began to extend its operations to Japan and other Asian sites as well. Then Federal Express acquired Tiger International Inc., the parent company for Flying Tigers, the world's largest bulk air-cargo carrier. This acquisition immediately gave Federal Express access to Tiger's extensive routes and enabled it to move into the bulk package business overseas. International volume increased by about 50 percent in just one year, from 1987 to 1988, and international delivery is expected to continue as the main area of growth for the organization.

To accomplish all of this, Federal Express has had to use the latest technology and managerial techniques for handling information. It was one of the first nonfood companies to use bar-code scanning. It uses such scanning to track the movement of packages throughout its transportation network. Each driver has a hand-held computer and each truck has an electronic messaging system. When a package is picked up, the bar code on it is scanned with the hand-held computer and the information is transmitted by the truck's system to Federal Express's main computer in Memphis, Tennessee.

Federal Express wants to put tracking information directly in the hands of its customers. It installed large terminals in the facilities of about 7,000 of its largest customers so that they could monitor the location of their own shipments. In 1988 it started installing small desktop terminals in more and more customers' offices. Nicknamed "Hello Federal," these terminals, like the big ones, enable customers to keep track of their own packages as they move through the Federal Express network. The customer enters the order number for his or her shipment into the terminal, and the location is shown on the screen. Customers who ship as few as three to five packages a day will be able to have a "Hello Federal" terminal.

The future of Federal Express, however, is not as clear as its current position might suggest. Facsimile machines have dropped in price. They are becoming far more widely used and are seriously eroding the overnight-letter market. UPS has upgraded its overnight ability and now poses a clear threat to Federal Express. Internationally, a vast array of highly restrictive postal monopolies prevent Federal Express from moving into some markets as quickly as it would like.

Federal Express hopes to bolster its growth and profits by building a market for overnight packages from manufacturers and other heavy shippers moving large, heavy shipments rather than small, lightweight letters and packages. It also plans to continue to add dropoff centers in major metropolitan centers so that customers can drop off their own packages rather than waiting for a Federal Express delivery person to battle through traffic. It is also trying out drive-through kiosks and drop boxes to make it easier for customers to get their letters and packages into the Federal Express system. Federal Express is also taking charge of goods for longer periods of time with its Contract Distribution Services division. This unit manages inventories and warehouses for companies—small companies and start-ups, for instance—that prefer not to do that for themselves.

Questions

1. What is the role of information in a manager's job at Federal Express? How is that information used?
2. What kinds of information systems are used at Federal Express? Do they seem to be effective? Why or why not?
3. Do you see ways in which expert systems might be used by Federal Express? Would those uses add to the effectiveness of the organization? Why or why not?
4. Do you think that Federal Express will be able to continue to perform as successfully in the future as it has performed in the past? Why or why not?

REFERENCES: "Federal Express Faces Challenges to Its Grip on Overnight Delivery," *The Wall Street Journal*, January 8, 1988, pp. 1, 8; "Federal Express to Buy Tiger for $880 Million," *The Wall Street Journal*, December 19, 1988, p. A4; "Tiger Corners Asia for FedEx," *USA Today*, December 20, 1988, p. 3B; "It Makes Bold Push to Retain Market Share," *USA Today*, October 27, 1988, pp. 1B–2B; "Sky the Limit?" *Barron's*, February 8, 1988, p. 11; "Mr. Smith Goes Global," *Business Week*, February 13, 1989, pp. 66–72; "Federal Express to Offer Cheaper Overnight Deliveries," *The Wall Street Journal*, March 8, 1989, p. B1.

CASE 18.2

Merrill Lynch: Information International

Merrill Lynch consists of three separate businesses: the U.S. retail broker-age business, a capital market group that focuses primarily on institutional investors, and an international division that is partly a brokerage business and partly an investment bank for overseas investors and issuers. Much of Merrill Lynch's future growth will occur in the international portion of its operations.

Merrill Lynch grew to become almost a household word in America, known for "bringing Wall Street to Main Street." But despite its growth, reputation, and success, Merrill Lynch found itself in trouble in the early 1980s. Its profit margins were nearly always close to the lowest in the industry as were its profits as a percent of stockholders' equity. Assets however, were climbing and revenues grew. Merrill Lynch was growing but becoming less profitable. In time, that poor profitability showing would impact upon its growth and slow it down. In order to recover, Merrill Lynch developed a sophisticated way to manage its international information.

There are three main global stock markets—one in London, one in New York, and one in Tokyo. Merrill Lynch has effectively integrated its own internal information systems through those three markets so that it can manage international investments without huge costs and without being too late on key moves. Merrill Lynch has a group of about 40 traders in five countries who specialize in international stocks. Within that group is a specialized team that focuses solely on the stock of Japanese companies in the three major markets.

To manage effectively as an international investment firm, Merrill Lynch personnel have come to understand not just the Dow-Jones Industrial Average but also its overseas equivalents—the Nikkei average in Japan and the Financial Times–Stock Exchange 100-Share Index, or "footsie," in London. It is critically important to manage effectively across all three of the markets because the U.S. stock market, which made up 58 percent of all stock traded in the world in 1975, now makes up only about a third of the value of traded stock.

The great number of stock transactions necessitates the extensive use of computers by the markets themselves and by brokerage companies. Every Merrill Lynch transaction from all over the world is recorded in and processed by two huge computers located in New York. One is in a Lower West Side warehouse, the other in a financial district office building. A third computer is on standby in case something should happen to either of the other two; it is supposed to be able to take over within four minutes but thus far has not been called upon to do so.

Telecommunications links Merrill Lynch's international activities. Traders in London, New York, and Tokyo remain in close contact with one another during trading hours through the telephone as well as through the computer network. Indeed, the number of telephone calls can get quite large. As the market prepares to open in one location, individuals there and in the location that most recently closed may talk ten or more times in the span of just two or three hours. Those individuals also monitor news and wire services to keep track of economic, political, and financial matters that could have an impact on the markets in general or on certain company stocks in particular.

At the end of a trading session in any one market, the traders pass along information to those in the next market that will open. The New York market closes several hours before the Japanese one opens. It, in turn, closes a couple of hours before London opens. There is a fairly long period of time between the closing in London and the opening in New York, after which the cycle begins again. By exchanging information with those active in each market, Merrill Lynch is in an excellent position to forecast and take advantage of subtle market changes that can be used to improve the stock portfolios of its customers.

Despite the interconnectedness of the three global markets, domestic factors can and do continue to play an important role in what happens in a stock market. Having local traders in each country's market permits Merrill Lynch to take advantage of local knowledge of politics and domestic business affairs, and linking traders together takes advantage of information flows between markets and permits dialogues that increase each trader's market knowledge. Because of this system, Merrill Lynch is more effective as an international investment broker than it would be if it tried to handle all of its business from a centralized location in New York or in one of the other market cities.

Questions

1. What is the role of information in the international operations of Merrill Lynch? How is that information used?
2. What kinds of information systems are used in Merrill Lynch's international operations? Do they seem to be effective? Why or why not?
3. Do you see ways in which expert systems might be used by Merrill Lynch? If so, describe them. If not, why do you think they might not be useful?
4. Do you think that Merrill Lynch as an international investment firm will be able to continue to perform as successfully in the future as it has performed in the past? Why or why not?

References: Brett Duval Fromson, "Merrill Lynch," *Fortune*, June 20, 1988, pp. 44–50; Judith Graham, "Merrill Lynch Relies on 'Trust' Theme," *Advertising Age*, February 15, 1988, p. 35; "How Merrill Lynch Moves Its Stock Deals All Around the World," *The Wall Street Journal*, November 9, 1987, pp. 1, 8; "Cash, Flash, and Dash: Can This Be Merrill?" *Business Week*, May 11, 1987, pp. 124–126; "The Big Loss at Merrill Lynch: Why It Was Blindsided," *Business Week*, May 18, 1987, pp. 112–113; "Through Merrill, Main Street Met Wall Street," *The Wall Street Journal*, April 25, 1989, p. B2.

OUTLINE

An Overview of Control Techniques and Methods

Budgetary Control
Types of Budgets · Fixed and Variable Costs in Budgets ·
Developing Budgets · Zero-Base Budgets · Strengths and
Weaknesses of Budgets

Other Tools of Financial Control
Financial Statements · Ratio Analysis · Financial Audits

Using Financial Control Techniques Effectively

Operations Control
Areas of Operations Control · Operations Control Techniques

Human Resource Control
Goals of Human Resource Control · Human Resource
Control Techniques

Marketing Control
Goals of Marketing Control · Marketing Control Techniques

CHAPTER 19

Control Techniques
and Methods

OBJECTIVES

After studying this chapter, you should be able to:

- Provide an overview of control techniques and methods.
- Discuss budgetary control.
- Identify and describe other tools of financial control.
- Discuss how to use financial control effectively.
- Describe operations control.
- Describe human resource control.
- Describe marketing control.

OPENING INCIDENT

Long thought of as a company that makes metal trucks, Tonka started branching out in recent years in an effort to become a major player in the toy industry. Its shot at the big leagues came in 1987 when it acquired Kenner Parker Toys. The acquisition propelled Tonka to the number 3 spot in the industry but carried with it a heavy burden of debt. To service its debt and maintain its industry standing, Tonka needs to develop and maintain a strong line of toys that can generate demand year-round.

How bad is the debt? The total is $850 million, nearly 12 times the firm's equity. Interest payments alone exceed $90 million per year. Still, Tonka feels it made a good deal. Several of the toys it acquired with Kenner Parker—Monopoly, Play-Doh, and Nerf balls, for example—do indeed have year-round appeal. Thus, most analysts agree that if Tonka can maintain its sales and then cut its debt fairly quickly—to no more than 6 or 7 times equity—it may have gained a permanent spot in the upper echelons of the toy industry.[1]

*T*onka has made an important strategic decision—to become a major player in its industry. How analysts assess that move is determined by how well the company performs, and one set of performance indicators is how well the firm stacks up on a set of relevant financial ratios. For example, Tonka's current debt-to-equity ratio is 12 ($12 of debt for every $1 of equity), which is considered too high. A ratio of 6 or 7 is considered appropriate.

In this chapter, we examine a number of control techniques, including financial ratios like return on assets, in detail. We first provide an overview of control techniques and methods. We then discuss budgets and budgetary control and other tools of financial control. We note how such controls can be used effectively, and we describe some control techniques commonly used by managers in operations, human resources, and marketing.

AN OVERVIEW OF CONTROL TECHNIQUES AND METHODS

Control techniques and methods can be thought of as tools that help managers assess how effectively they are moving toward goals. Control techniques and methods provide performance-related information that managers can compare against standards. Managers interpret the information provided by control techniques and determine what, if any, actions are necessary. As we noted in Chapter 16, financial control is at the heart of all other areas of control. Not surprisingly, then, financial control techniques pervade most other forms of control. To illustrate their role in control, recall the chapter-opening incident. Tonka's debt-to-equity ratio currently stands at 12. If we assume that the industry average is 5 and that financial projections show that Tonka can be reasonably profitable with a ratio of 7, managers there might develop a series of goals and plans aimed at reducing the ratio to 7 within the next three years. By assessing the ratio each year, managers will know how well they are doing.

After the ratio is lowered to 7, Tonka's managers will have another decision to make. If profits are acceptable, they may decide to stop reducing debt and use surplus revenues to fuel other growth. Or they may continue to reduce debt to get closer to the industry average or perhaps even below it. This simple example indicates how control techniques provide information to managers for decision making. Ultimately, however, managers themselves must use the information to make the decision.

BUDGETARY CONTROL

■ **budgeting** The process of expressing a set of planned activities for a coming time period in numerical terms

budget A plan expressed in numerical terms

Budgeting is the process of expressing a set of planned activities for a coming time period in numerical terms. A **budget** is a plan expressed in numerical terms.[2] Organizations may establish budgets for work groups, departments, divisions, or the whole organization. The usual time period for a budget is one year, although breakdowns of budgets by the quarter or month are also common. Budgets are generally expressed in financial terms, but they may occasionally be expressed in units of output, time, or other quantifiable factors.

Budgets are the foundation of most control systems. Because of their quantitative nature, they provide yardsticks for measuring performance, and they facilitate comparisons across departments, between levels in the organization, and from one time period to another. Budgets serve four primary purposes. They help managers coordinate resources and projects (because they use a common denominator, usually dollars.) They help define the standards needed in all control systems. They provide clear and unambiguous guidelines about the organization's resources and expectations. Finally, they facilitate performance evaluations of managers and units.

Types of Budgets

Most organizations develop and make use of three different kinds of budgets—financial, operating, and nonmonetary. These are summarized in Table 19.1.[3]

Financial Budgets A financial budget summarizes where the organization expects to get its cash for the coming time period and how it

Financial budget	Focuses on incoming and outgoing cash.	**Cash-flow budget.** Focuses on short-run and current financial obligations.
		Capital expenditures budget. Focuses on major assets such as plant, equipment, and property.
		Balance sheet budget. Focuses on what the organization's balance sheet will look like if all other budgets are met.
Operating budget	Expresses planned operations in financial terms.	**Sales or revenue budget.** Focuses on anticipated income from normal operations.
		Expense budget. Focuses on anticipated expenses.
		Profit budget. Focuses on projected differences between sales or revenues and expenses.
Nonmonetary budget	Is expressed in terms that are not financial.	

TABLE 19.1

Types of Budgets

plans to use it. Usual sources of cash include sales revenue, short- and long-term loans, the sale of assets, and the issuance of new stock. For example, Sears recently modified its financial budgets to reflect an expected drop in sales revenues and special income from the sale of the Sears Tower in Chicago. Common uses of cash are to pay expenses, repay debt, purchase new assets, add to retained earnings, and pay dividends to stockholders. A company like Tonka has to commit much of its cash to repay its debt.

One special type of financial budget is the **cash-flow budget**. This budget, sometimes just called a **cash budget**, is a projection of all sources of cash income and cash expenditures in monthly, weekly, or even daily periods. Its purpose is to ensure that the organization is able to meet its current obligations. For example, the owner of a small business who has a $10,000 payroll and a $1,000 utility bill due on the last day of every month must make sure that there is sufficient cash on hand to meet those obligations.

Another type of financial budget, the **capital expenditures budget**, deals with major assets such as a new plant, machinery, or land. Companies often finance such major expenditures by borrowing significant amounts of money (through long-term loans or bonds); thus the capital expenditures budget is quite important. All organizations, even giants like Exxon and General Electric, pay close attention to these budgets because of the large investments usually reflected within them.

The **balance sheet budget** forecasts the organization's assets and liabilities in the event all other budgets are met. Hence, it serves as an overall control framework to ensure that other budgets mesh properly

cash-flow or cash budget   A projection of all sources of cash income and cash expenditures in monthly, weekly, or even daily periods

capital expenditures budget Deals with major assets such as a new plant, machinery, or land

balance sheet or master budget   Forecasts the organization's assets and liabilities in the event all other budgets are met and yield results that are in the best interests of the organization. This budget is also called the **master budget** by some organizations.

Operating Budgets   A second major category of budgets consists of operating budgets. An **operating budget** is an expression of the organization's planned operations. An operating budget outlines what quantities of products and services the organization intends to create and what resources will be used to create them.

operating budget   An expression of the organization's planned operations

A **sales** or **revenue budget** focuses on income the organization expects to receive from normal operations. First, sales are forecast for the period being budgeted. Then the selling price of each item is determined. These two amounts are combined to create the revenue budget. If a firm expects to sell 1,000 products at $10 each and 5,000 at $5 each, its sales budget is $12,500. For a government organization, the revenue budget might specify the anticipated influx of tax dollars. A nonprofit hospital would base its revenue budget on anticipated contributions, grants, and so forth. Sales or revenue budgets are important because they help the manager understand what the future financial position of the organization will be.

sales or revenue budget   Focuses on income the organization expects to receive from normal operations

An **expense budget** outlines the anticipated expenses of the organization in the coming time period. For example, a manager who has a telephone expense budget of $12,000 a year knows that the unit can spend about $1,000 a month on telephone calls. The expense budget also points out upcoming expenses so that the manager can prepare for them. A **profit budget** focuses on anticipated differences between sales or revenues and expenses. If budgeted sales are $1 million and budgeted expenses are $700,000, the manager has a budgeted profit of $300,000. If budgeted sales and expenses are too close together, the profit budget may not be acceptable because the resultant profit is too small. In that case, steps may be needed to increase the sales budget (such as cutting prices or raising sales quotas) or to cut the expense budget (such as reducing inventory costs or improving scrappage rates).

expense budget   Outlines anticipated expenses for the organization during the coming time period

profit budget   Focuses on anticipated differences between sales or revenues and expenses

Nonmonetary Budgets   A nonmonetary budget is a budget expressed in terms that are not financial, such as units of output, hours of direct labor, machine hours, or square-foot allocations. Nonmonetary budgets are generally used at the lower levels of an organization because they are especially helpful to managers at that level. For example, a plant manager can probably schedule work more effectively knowing that he or she has 8,000 labor hours to allocate in a week, rather than $76,451 in wages that can be spent.

Fixed and Variable Costs in Budgets

Regardless of their purpose, most budgets must account for three kinds of costs—fixed, variable, and semivariable.[4] **Fixed costs** are expenses that the organization incurs whether it is in operation or not. A retailer may pay for a fixed monthly rent regardless of how many days the

fixed costs   Expenses that the organization incurs whether it is in operation or not

A capital expenditures budget identifies major assets that the company is investing in. Unocal Corporation recently built this central process platform in Thailand at a cost of millions of dollars. The initial decision to build the platform and the management of its construction were each based on a capital expenditures budget.

variable costs   Costs that vary according to the scope of operations

semivariable costs   Costs that vary according to the scope of operations in a step-like fashion

store is open. Other fixed costs may include property taxes, minimum utility bills, and some salaries. For example, Kimberly-Clark must pay rent for its office space, managerial salaries, interest on its bonded indebtedness, warehouse storage costs, and various state and federal taxes whether it makes 1,000 or 100,000 boxes of Kleenex tissues today.

Variable costs are costs that vary according to the scope of operations. The best example of a variable cost is the cost of raw materials used in production. If $2 worth of material is used in making each unit, costs for ten units are $20, costs for forty units are $80, and so on. Other variable costs include travel expenses, sales taxes, and utility expenses above base rates. Kimberly-Clark's variable costs for Kleenex include the costs for the tissues themselves (paper, dye, etc.), the decorator boxes they are packaged in, and the large cases those boxes are packed in for shipping.

Semivariable costs vary as well, but in a less direct fashion. Advertising, for example, varies according to season and competition. Other major semivariable costs include direct labor, equipment and plant repairs, and maintenance. Kimberly-Clark, for example, recently boosted its television advertising efforts for its disposable diapers in response to a new campaign launched by Procter & Gamble.

When developing a budget, managers must accurately account for all three categories of costs. Fixed costs are usually the easiest to deal with. Rent, for example, is almost always governed by a lease and cannot change until the lease expires. Variable costs can often be forecast—but with less precision—from projected operations. Semivariable costs are the most difficult to predict because they are likely to vary, but not in direct relation to operations. For these costs, the manager must often rely on experience and judgment. Some forecasting techniques are also useful for estimating semivariable costs.

Finally, we should note that many American firms are reassessing the manner in which they assign costs to different products. Historically, most fixed costs were assigned on the basis of materials and labor hours needed to produce a given product. Unfortunately, such procedures introduce error into the cost estimates of particular products. For example, Continental Can makes lids for beer cans. The machines, labor, and materials used to make the lids have not changed for years; there is virtually no waste, and productivity is extremely high. New versions of the same product, however, require more expensive machines, computer-assisted design, and higher setup costs. Yet, because the actual time and materials needed to make both types of lid are the same, each is budgeted at the same unit cost. Because of these and related shortcomings, managers are looking for new ways to determine the various costs that must be accounted for in budgets.[5]

Developing Budgets

Budgets have traditionally been developed by top management and the controller and then imposed on lower-level managers. Some organizations still follow this pattern, but many contemporary organizations now allow lower-level managers to participate in the process. The typical course of a budget preparation is illustrated in Figure 19.1. As a starting point, top management generally issues a call for budget requests. The request is often accompanied by a general indication of overall patterns that the budgets may expect to take. For example, if sales are expected to drop next year, managers may be told up front to prepare for some cuts in operating budgets.

In step 1 of the actual process, the heads of each operating unit submit their budget requests to their division head. These operating-unit heads might be department managers in a manufacturing or wholesaling firm or program directors in a social service agency. The division heads might be plant managers, regional sales managers, or college deans.

The division head integrates and consolidates the various budget requests from the operating-unit heads into one overall division budget

FIGURE 19.1

Steps in the Budgeting Process

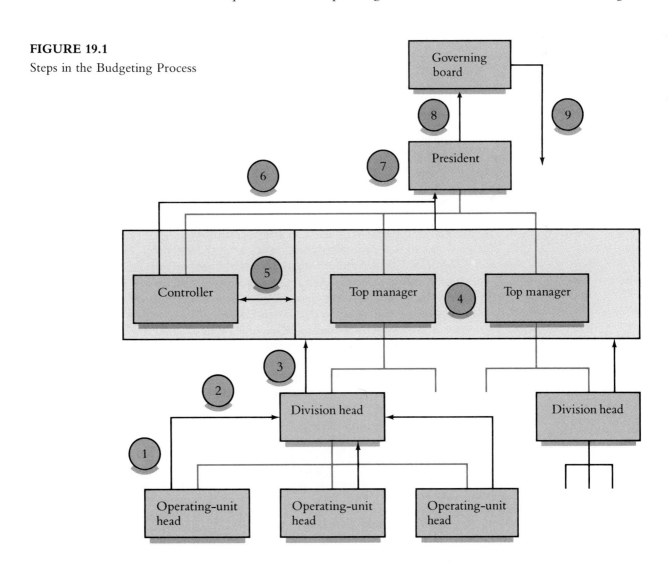

request (step 2). Overlapping or inconsistent requests are corrected at this stage. In a college budget, two department heads might each request five new word processors at a cost of $2,000 each. The dean, however, might be aware that the manufacturer grants a 10 percent discount on orders of ten or more systems, so he would forward a request of $18,000 rather than $20,000 for the ten word processors. Similarly, if a regional sales manager notices that one sales manager's budget request assumes a 15 percent increase in product price while another assumes a 12 percent increase, she would need to resolve the inconsistency. A great deal of interaction between managers usually takes place as the division head works to integrate and coordinate the budgetary needs of the various departments.

In step 3, division budget requests are forwarded to a budget committee, which is usually composed of top managers with line authority. In businesses, the committee members are likely to be vice presidents. As shown in Figure 19.1 (step 4), budget requests from several divisions are reviewed at this stage, and once again duplications and inconsistencies are corrected. A university's business college and its speech department might both request funds to develop a new course in business communication. Campus administrators would have to eliminate this duplication. Similarly, the news and the entertainment divisions of a television network might both request funds for a news-magazine show like "60 Minutes" or "Good Morning, America." The budget committee would resolve this overlap.

Step 5 of the process involves interaction between the budget committee and the controller. The interaction can take a variety of forms. All budgets could pass from the committee to the controller for further evaluation and approval. Or the controller could be a member of the budget committee. Or the controller might evaluate the budget requests before they ever go to the budget committee.

In step 6, the final budget is sent to the president or CEO for approval. After undergoing his or her scrutiny (step 7), it is then passed on to the board of directors or other governing board for review (step 8). Final budgets are then communicated back to the divisions and operating units. As budget requests pass through these various stages, it is almost certain that some changes will be made. The budget that a unit ultimately has available may be more than, less than, or the same as what it initially requested.

The budgetary process has been described here in very general terms. Endless variations are possible. Many organizations have budget departments that assist managers in preparing and evaluating budget requests. Occasionally, top management provides initial guidelines on what resources are available, so that lower-level managers will have some sense of what is realistic to ask for.

Mechanisms are needed for revising budgets during their term if necessary. For example, if demand for a firm's products were to jump unexpectedly, a plant manager should be able to request additional funds to pay for the overtime labor needed to meet this demand. This "bottom-up" approach to budgeting is often advocated because it has two primary strengths. First, individual unit managers are likely to be more familiar than anyone else with their own needs. They can call attention to special situations that top management may not be aware of and will probably include all the important elements in developing their own budgets. Second, managers are more likely to "live with" and try to meet a budget if they had a hand in developing it.

Zero-Base Budgets

zero-base budgeting or ZBB
Begins each year with a clean slate; the entire budget must be justified rather than making adjustments to the existing budget

Zero-base budgeting, or **ZBB**, was pioneered at Texas Instruments in 1970 and popularized by President Jimmy Carter when he used it in the federal government in the late 1970s.[6] The basic idea underlying ZBB is quite simple. Under a conventional budgeting system, yearly budgets start with the previous year's budget and are then adjusted up (in most cases) or down. The manager concentrates on justifying any additional funding that may be needed. The existing budget is considered a given, and debate centers on the merits of the proposed changes. Under a ZBB system, however, each budgeting unit begins with a clean slate each year. The entire budget must be justified, rather than merely the adjustments to an existing budget.

The first step in ZBB is to break down the activities of the organization into "decision packages." Each package represents an activity or set of activities and specifies the costs and benefits and the consequences if the package is not approved. Decision packages are then ranked in order of importance. Finally, funds are allocated to each decision package according to its relative rank. The higher the rank, the greater is the probability of full funding; the lower the rank, the more likely the activity is to be dropped or only partially funded.

In a relatively short period of time, ZBB has been adopted by a variety of organizations, including Xerox Corporation, Ford, Westinghouse, Playboy Enterprises, and many federal and state agencies. Ford attributes millions of dollars in savings to zero-base budgeting, and Xerox enjoyed a substantial boost in profits following a shift to ZBB.[7]

The primary advantage of ZBB is that it helps maintain vitality by constantly assessing and questioning existing programs. It also facilitates the development of new programs. However, the process of continual justification necessitates more paperwork, and managers may resort to inflating the importance of their programs to maintain funding. ZBB will probably be used even more widely in the future as a technique for organizational control.

Strengths and Weaknesses of Budgeting

Budgets offer a number of advantages, but they have potential drawbacks as well. Both are summarized in Table 19.2.

On the plus side, budgets facilitate effective control. By placing dollar values on operations, managers can monitor operations better and pin-

TABLE 19.2

Strengths and Weaknesses of
Budgeting

Strengths	Weaknesses
1. Budgets facilitate effective control.	1. Budgets may be used too rigidly.
2. Budgets facilitate coordination and communication.	2. Budgets may be time consuming.
3. Budgets facilitate record keeping.	3. Budgets may limit innovation and change.
4. Budgets are a natural complement to planning.	

point problem areas. Second, budgets facilitate coordination and communication between departments. In a sense, unit budgets are like pieces of a puzzle that fit together to yield an overall picture. By expressing diverse activities in terms of a common denominator (dollars), different units can better communicate with one another. Budgets also help maintain records of organizational performance. Finally, budgets are a natural complement to planning. The link between planning and control is examined in earlier chapters. As managers plan and then develop control systems, budgets are often a natural next step, for they provide feedback to the planners as to how accurate the predictions were.

On the other hand, some managers apply budgets too rigidly. They fail to acknowledge that changing circumstances may justify budget adjustments. Moreover, the process of developing budgets can be very time consuming. This is especially true when organizations adopt ZBB. Finally, budgets may limit innovation and change. When all available funds are allocated to specific operating budgets, it may be impossible to get additional funds to take advantage of an unexpected opportunity.[8]

OTHER TOOLS OF FINANCIAL CONTROL

Although budgets are the most common means of financial control, other tools are also used. These include financial statements, ratio analysis, and financial audits. "Management in Practice" describes some general methods of financial control used at Gould.

Financial Statements

■ **financial statement**   A profile of some aspect of an organization's financial circumstances

A **financial statement** is a profile of some aspect of an organization's financial circumstances. There are commonly accepted and required ways for preparing and presenting financial statements.[9] The two financial statements prepared and used by virtually all organizations are a balance sheet and an income statement.

MANAGEMENT IN PRACTICE

GOULD IMPROVES ITS FINANCIAL CONTROL

Gould, Inc., was losing money and was in bad shape in 1985. In an effort to transform the company from a major industrial products manufacturer into a power-house in the electronics field, top management had gotten Gould into deplorable financial condition. Its semiconductor business was in trouble, and cost overruns on a Navy radio contract forced the company to take a big write-off against earnings in 1986 and led to a loss for that year. James F. McDonald was hired from IBM to head up Gould and try to correct its problems. Gould has been restructuring itself through the sale of many of its assets in an attempt to restore the firm to financial health.

In 1986 Gould sold its medical products group for $92 million and its Palm Beach Polo and Country Club for $38 million. In 1988 it sold its industrial automation unit for $290 million, its anti-submarine-warfare tor-pedo and sonar units for approximately $100 million each and its semiconductor unit for $70 million. These selloffs shrank the size of the firm drastically. Whereas Gould used to have over $2 billion in annual sales, it now has about a third of that—around $700 million.

Not surprisingly, with a former IBM executive as CEO, Gould's primary business now is computers. They account for about 40 percent of sales. Gould sells superminicomputers for scientific research and engineering applications. It does extremely well in the flight simulation market with makers of aircraft and the military. It expanded its product line in 1987 to include a scaled-down version of the super-number-crunching machines made by Cray Research—a minisupercom-puter.

Gould's electronics units are successful and are making profits. They manufacture components such as fuses and copper foil and test and measurement devices. In addition, Gould was able to get a good price for its battery unit, which developed the proto-type for a battery that might make electric cars prac-tical. In simulated stop-and-go driving tests the battery delivered the equivalent of 200 miles of city driving without a recharge.

Gould seems in better shape now than it was in 1985. The effective use of financial controls has en-abled the company to survive and turn itself around. Management reduced overhead and restructured the organization so that the remaining units are relatively profitable. Debt has been substantially reduced and in 1988 cash flow turned positive. The turnaround, however, was not so complete that a sellout was out of the question. Late in 1988, Nippon Mining Co. of Japan bought Gould.

REFERENCES: "Nippon Mining Acquires Gould," *The Wall Street Journal*, November 2, 1988, p. 10B; "Gould Is So Thin You Can Hardly See It," *Business Week*, August 29, 1988, p. 74; "Westinghouse Buys Gould Unit," *The Wall Street Journal*, March 3, 1988, p. 8E; "A Battery That Could Make Electric Cars Practical," *Business Week*, April 6, 1987, p. 103; "Minisuper Meets Supermini," *Design News*, July 6, 1987, p. 51.

■ **balance sheet**   A listing of the assets and liabilities of the organization at a particular point in time, usually at the end of the fiscal year

Balance Sheet   The **balance sheet** is a listing of the assets and liabilities of the organization at a particular point in time, usually the end of the organization's fiscal year. An abbreviated example of the balance sheet for a small clothing store, Campus Clothing, Inc., is shown in Table 19.3. It is divided into current assets (assets that are relatively liquid, or easily convertible into cash), fixed assets (assets that are longer-term in nature and less liquid), current liabilities (debts and other obligations that must be paid in the near future), long-term liabilities (debts that are payable over an extended period of time), and stockholders' equity (the owners' claim against the assets). The sum of all current and fixed assets must equal the sum of all liabilities and equity.

Campus Clothing, Inc. Balance Sheet December 31, 1990			
Current assets		Current liabilities	
Cash	$ 10,000	Accounts payable	$ 60,000
Accounts receivable	10,000	Accrued expenses	20,000
Inventory	140,000	Long-term liabilities	150,000
	160,000		230,000
Fixed assets		Owner's equity	
Land	60,000	Common stock	200,000
Building and equipment	400,000	Retained earnings	190,000
	460,000		390,000
Total current and fixed assets	$620,000	Total liabilities and equity	$620,000

TABLE 19.3

Sample Balance Sheet for a Small Clothing Shop

■ **income statement** Captures performance over a period of time, usually one year

Income Statement   Whereas the balance sheet reflects a snapshot profile of an organization's financial position at a single point in time, the **income statement** captures performance over a period of time. The time period for income statements is usually one year and coincides with the firm's fiscal year. Table 19.4 provides a simplified income statement for Campus Clothing, Inc. In general, the income statement adds up all income to the organization and then subtracts all expenses, debts, and liabilities. The "bottom line" of the statement represents net income, or profit. Information from the balance sheet and income statement is used in computing the important financial ratios.

Ratio Analysis

The financial statements of an organization provide some useful information to managers, owners, and other interested parties. Information from financial statements is used to calculate several different ratios that provide even more insights.

liquidity ratios Indicators of how easily converted into cash an organization's assets are

Liquidity Ratios   Several **liquidity ratios** are used to learn how liquid (how easily converted into cash) an organization's assets are. The most common of these, the current ratio, is current assets divided by current liabilities. For Campus Clothing, this is 160,000 ÷ 80,000, or 2. This ratio of 2:1 is generally regarded as acceptable. It indicates how many dollars of liquid assets are available for each dollar of current liability. Creditors consider the current ratio a good index of an organization's ability to pay its bills on time.

TABLE 19.4

Sample Income Statement for a
Small Clothing Shop

Campus Clothing, Inc. Income Statement For Year Ending December 31, 1990		
Gross sales		$806,000
Less returns	6,000	
Net sales		800,000
Less expenses and cost of sales:		
Expenses	120,000	
Depreciation	40,000	
Cost of goods sold	400,000	560,000
Operating profit		240,000
Other income		20,000
Interest expense	30,000	
Taxable income		230,000
Less taxes	115,000	
Net income		115,000

debt ratios Indicators of an
organization's ability to meet
its long-term financial obligations

Debt Ratios   **Debt ratios** reflect ability to meet long-term financial
obligations. One common debt ratio is total liabilities divided by total
assets. This ratio for Campus Clothing is 230,000 ÷ 620,000, or .37.
This indicates that the company has approximately 37 cents in liabilities
for every dollar of its assets. The higher this ratio, the poorer credit
risk the organization is perceived to be. If management were to ask for
a loan of $60,000, for example, the bank would recognize that, even if
the store were to go out of business, there would still be enough money
left to repay the loan after all other debts were paid. Another common
debt ratio is the debt-to-equity ratio used earlier to describe Tonka's
financial state.

Return on Assets   A third important financial ratio is return on assets,
or ROA. The ROA is the percentage return to investors on each dollar
of assets that they own. It serves as a yardstick for investors and
managers to gauge which of several investment opportunities is most
profitable. The common formula for ROA is

$$\frac{\text{Net Income}}{\text{Total Assets}} = \text{ROA}$$

For Campus Clothing, net income is $115,000 and there are $620,000
in total assets. Hence ROA is

$$\frac{115,000}{620,000} = .19$$

Publicly-held corporations are required to report their financial performance to their stockholders on a regular basis. The major way this is done is through the publication of an annual report that contains both descriptive evaluations of what the firm has been doing and a set of basic financial statements prepared and presented in conformance with basic accounting practices. Many companies, like Archer Daniels Midland Company, prepare sophisticated and elaborate reports for their stockholders.

For each dollar invested by Campus Clothing, the company earns 19 cents, a return of 19 percent per year. This would generally be considered a good return by most investors.

Other Ratios   Liquidity ratios, debt ratios, and return on assets are widely used forms of financial analysis. Another frequently used ratio is return on investment, or ROI. ROI is determined by dividing owners' equity into net income. This ratio represents the return to the investor from each dollar of equity. For Campus Clothing, net income is $115,000 and owners' equity is $390,000. Hence ROI is

$$\frac{115,000}{390,000} = .29$$

Other ratios are also of interest to managers and investors. Coverage ratios help in estimating the organization's ability to cover interest expenses on borrowed capital. Operating ratios focus on functional areas rather than on the total organization. For example, inventory turnover (cost of goods sold divided by average daily inventory) reflects how efficiently the organization is forecasting sales and ordering merchandise. Profitability ratios reflect the relative effectiveness of an organization. For example, profits of $5 million are quite good on sales of $20 million (.25) but are poor on sales of $100 million (.05).

Financial Audits

Whereas most control techniques also have other purposes, audits are used almost exclusively for control. **Audits** are independent appraisals of an organization's accounting, financial, and operational systems. The two major types of financial audit are the external audit and the internal audit.

External Audits   **External audits** are financial audits conducted by experts who are not employees of the organization.[10] External audits are typically concerned with the extent to which the organization's accounting procedures and financial statements are compiled in an objective and verifiable fashion. Certified public accountants (CPAs) are usually engaged for this purpose. Their main objective is not to prepare financial documents and reports but to verify for stockholders, the IRS, and other interested parties the accuracy of the methods by which those documents and reports have been prepared by financial managers and accountants within the organization.

External audits are almost always extremely thorough. In some cases, auditors even count physical inventory to verify that it agrees with what is shown on the balance sheet. The reason for this precision is that auditors who make mistakes will have their reputations damaged and may even have their licenses revoked. External audits are so im-

■ **audits**   Independent appraisals of an organization's accounting, financial, and operating systems

external audits   Financial audits conducted by experts who are not employees of the organization

portant that publicly held corporations are required by law to have external audits on a regular basis, as assurance to investors that the corporations' financial reports are reliable.

internal audits Audits conducted by employees of the organization and may include much more than merely financial aspects of the organization

Internal Audits   Whereas external audits are conducted by external accountants, an **internal audit** is handled by employees of the organization. Its primary objective is the same as that of an external audit—to verify the accuracy of financial and accounting procedures used by the organization. Internal audits also focus on the efficiency and appropriateness of the financial and accounting procedures. In some cases, an accounting system may be technically correct but inefficient. Both external and internal audits verify the accuracy of reports, but only the internal audit is concerned with efficiency.

Large organizations such as Dresser Industries, Dow Chemical, and Eastman Kodak have internal auditing staffs. These staffs spend all their time conducting audits of different divisions and functional areas of the organizations. Smaller organizations may assign accountants to an internal audit group on a temporary or rotating basis. Because the staff members who conduct internal audits are permanently on the organization's payroll, internal audits tend to be expensive. However, employees may be familiar with the organization and can point out other aspects of the accounting system besides its technical correctness. For example, a simple change in accounting procedures can sometimes provide managers with more and/or better information about the financial status of the organization. External auditors may be more objective than employees and have more specialized skills. They are also generally less expensive than a full-time auditing staff.

USING FINANCIAL CONTROL TECHNIQUES EFFECTIVELY

In order to use budgets and other financial control techniques effectively, managers need to keep certain things in mind. Foremost among them is to remember that they are tools. Just as a good hammer and saw can help a carpenter construct a house, so too can a good financial control system help a manager be effective. "The Global View" describes how Daihatsu has effectively integrated its entire accounting system with its strategic planning efforts.

In addition, financial controls work most effectively if they are integrated with other information systems of the type discussed in Chapter 18. Financial information is often an important input into other information systems, and those same systems, in turn, are most effective when they can process and provide financial information back to managers. For example, a good information system can tell a manager exactly what current assets and liabilities are. This up-to-date information might then be provided to a banker from whom the firm is attempting to borrow money.

OPERATIONS CONTROL

Control techniques and methods are an essential part of operations. Whereas financial control deals with monetary resources, operations control is concerned with the processes used by the organization to transform inputs into outputs.

Areas of Operations Control

We discussed operations management in detail in Chapter 17. As noted there, there are numerous areas of control that are directly related to operations management. Key areas include quality, purchasing, inventory, and productivity. Scheduling is another important area of operations management control.

Operations Control Techniques

Numerous techniques for operations management control have also been discussed in earlier chapters. There are, however, a few other techniques that have not yet been discussed. These include materials resource planning, statistical quality control, PERT, and the economic order quantity.

Materials Resource Planning   A key part of operations management is coordination—determining what materials and services are necessary to do the work of the organization in an effective way. Consider a contractor who is about to begin construction on a new house. One of the basic materials needed will be 2 × 4-inch lumber for framing the walls. The contractor will not order lumber one piece at a time, nor is it likely that he will need several thousand pieces. Instead, the contractor determines in advance how much lumber will be required. Similarly, if the 2 × 4's are delivered too early, they may be stolen or scattered; but construction will be delayed if they are delivered too late. The process of determining how much lumber to buy and when to have it delivered is an operations coordination issue. In recent years, attention has focused on a new approach to this activity called **materials requirements planning (MRP)**.[11] An MRP system is shown in Figure 19.2. Note that all of the elements of MRP take place in the context of a computer routine or system.

■ **materials requirements planning or MRP**   A system that integrates production and inventory control

   The first step in an MRP system is to specify the materials and parts needed for production and operations. These materials and parts are generally listed in a document called a bill of materials (BOM). The BOM for a pizza parlor might include flour, tomato paste, cheese, various toppings, order pads, napkins, and soft-drink syrup. For a complex product like a computer, automobile, or airplane, the BOM would list thousands of parts. The next step is to determine existing

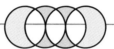

THE GLOBAL VIEW

DAIHATSU'S MANAGEMENT ACCOUNTING

Daihatsu Motor Company is a medium-size producer of automobiles in Japan. Budgetary control at Daihatsu is different from that found in most American companies. Daihatsu uses market-driven accounting practices to strengthen performance. It installed the *genka kikaku* product development system in its factories after affiliating with Toyota, which pioneered the system. The first step involves asking the functional departments to submit to a *shusa* the features and performance specifications that they believe a car should include. The *shusa* then takes over. A *shusa* is a product manager responsible for a new car from planning through sales. The *shusa* uses the information provided by the functional departments to make recommendations to senior managers, who in turn issue a development order.

The next step involves cost estimates. Daihatsu establishes a target selling price based on what it believes the market will accept. A target profit margin that reflects strategic plans and financial projections is also established. Accountants are asked to develop costs for building the car based on existing engineering standards. The difference between the target price and the accounting cost estimate is the allowable cost per car. Other cost estimates assuming innovation or no innovation are developed to obtain a fuller idea of what the new vehicle will actually cost in production.

During production, Daihatsu uses two complementary approaches to manage costs. Total plant-cost management and per unit cost management are integrated to ensure that targets are met. Executives tend to focus on total plant costs, and supervisors concentrate more on unit costs; but both must be integrated for complete financial control. Targets, however, are seen more as starting points for reductions than as ending points for production. In this way, a constant downward pressure on costs is created to keep the company competitive in the marketplace.

This market-driven approach to accounting suggests a mind-set different from that found in most American firms. In American firms, design dictates costs through engineering standards; at Daihatsu and other Japanese firms, the market dictates the target cost, which in turn causes design changes. The altered design, however, must still meet the original engineering standards for performance. This approach calls for constant innovation.

REFERENCES: Toshiro Hiromoto, "Another Hidden Edge—Japanese Management Accounting," *Harvard Business Review*, July–August 1988, pp. 22–26; Francis J. Gawronski, "Daihatsu Emphasizes Service in Field Organization," *Automotive News*, August 29, 1988, p. 14; Jesse Snyder, "Daihatsu Strategy: Big Start, All Duals," *Automotive News*, March 23, 1987, pp. 1–2; Cleveland Horton, "Daihatsu Faces Rough Road," *Advertising Age*, June 8, 1987, p. 43.

inventory on hand; the organization does not want to order more materials than it needs.

The manager using the MRP system then establishes ordering and delivery schedules for materials and parts that are needed. A fast-food restaurant like McDonald's gets daily delivery of perishables such as hamburger meat from a local supplier. Delivery time for an advanced guidance system for a fighter plane might be months or years.

One of the great assets of an MRP system is its ability to juggle different delivery schedules and lead times effectively. When hundreds of parts are needed in vastly different quantities and delivery times range from a day to several months, coordination is difficult or impossible for individual managers. An MRP system can arrange things so that parts and materials are ordered in such a way as to arrive on schedule. The ordering of parts and materials is usually initiated by a

FIGURE 19.2

Computer Routine for a
Materials Requirements
Planning System

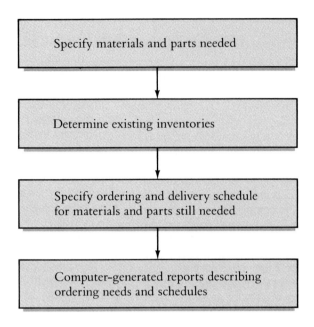

series of computer-generated reports. Suppose that a plant needs 1,000 units of a particular raw material each month, there are 3,000 units in inventory, and delivery time is two months. A computer-generated report will tell the manager when it is time to reorder. In sophisticated systems, the computer may even be programmed to place the order automatically. Many large manufacturing firms like Westinghouse, Texas Instruments, Boise-Cascade, and Lockheed have made effective use of MRP systems.

statistical quality control or SQC   A set of specific statistical techniques that can be used to monitor quality

Statistical Quality Control   Another increasingly useful operations management control technique is **statistical quality control**, or **SQC**. As the term suggests, SQC is primarily concerned with managing quality. Moreover, it is actually a set of specific statistical techniques that can be used to monitor quality.[12] Acceptance sampling involves sampling finished goods to ensure that quality standards have been met. The key to effective acceptance sampling is determining what percentage of the products should be tested (for example, 2, 5, or 25 percent). This decision is especially important when the test renders the product useless. Flash cubes, wine, and collapsible steering wheels, for example, are consumed or destroyed during testing.

Another SQC method is in-process sampling. In-process sampling involves evaluating products during production so that needed changes can be made. The painting department of a furniture company may periodically check the tint of the paint it is using. By so doing, the company can adjust the color as necessary to conform to customer standards. The advantage of in-process sampling is that it allows problems to be detected before they accumulate.

PERT, Program Evaluation and Review Technique
Used to identify the critical path within a network of activities so completion times can be controlled carefully

PERT   **PERT**, an acronym for Program Evaluation and Review Technique, was developed by the U.S. Navy to help coordinate the activities of 3,000 contractors during the development of the Polaris nuclear submarine, and it was credited with saving two years of work on the project.[13] It has subsequently been used by most large companies in a variety of ways. The purpose of PERT is to develop a network of activities and their interrelationships so as to highlight critical time intervals that affect the overall project. There are six basic steps in PERT:

1. Identify the activities to be performed and the events that will mark their completion.
2. Develop a network showing the relationships among the activities and events.
3. Calculate the time needed for each event and the time necessary to get from each event to the next.
4. Identify within the network the longest path that leads to completion of the project. This path is called the critical path.
5. Refine the network.
6. Use the network to control the project.

Suppose that a marketing manager wants to use PERT to plan the test marketing and nationwide introduction of a new product. Table 19.5 identifies the basic steps involved in carrying out this project. The

TABLE 19.5

Activities and Events for Introducing a New Product

Activities	Events
	1. Origin of project.
a. Produce limited quantity for test marketing.	2. Completion of production for test marketing.
b. Design preliminary package.	3. Completion of design for preliminary package.
c. Locate test market.	4. Test market located.
d. Obtain local merchant cooperation.	5. Local merchant cooperation obtained.
e. Ship product to selected retail outlets.	6. Product for test marketing shipped to retail outlets.
f. Monitor sales and customer reactions.	7. Sales and customer reactions monitored.
g. Survey customers in test-market area.	8. Customers in test-market area surveyed.
h. Make needed product changes.	9. Product changes made.
i. Make needed package changes.	10. Package changes made.
j. Mass produce the product.	11. Product mass produced.
k. Begin national advertising.	12. National advertising carried out.
l. Begin national distribution.	13. National distribution completed.

activities are then arranged in a network like the one shown in Figure 19.3. In the figure, each completed event is represented by a number in a circle. The activities are indicated by letters on the lines connecting the events. Notice that some activities are performed independently of one another and others must be performed in sequence. For example, test production (activity a) and test site location (activity c) can be done at the same time, but test site location has to be done before actual testing (activities f and g) can be done.

The time needed to get from one activity to another is then determined. The normal way to calculate the time between each activity is to average the most optimistic, most pessimistic, and most likely times, with the most likely time weighted by 4. Time is usually calculated with the following formula:

$$\text{Expected Time} = \frac{a + 4b + c}{6}$$

where   a = Optimistic Time

b = Most Likely Time

c = Pessimistic Time

The expected number of weeks for each activity in our example is shown in parentheses along each path in Figure 19.3.

The critical path—or the longest path through the network—is then identified. This path is considered critical because it shows the shortest time that the project can be completed in. In our example, the critical path is 1-2-3-6-7-9-10-11-12-13, totaling 57 weeks. PERT thus tells the manager that the project will take 57 weeks to complete.

The first network may be refined. If 57 weeks to completion is too long a time, the manager might decide to begin preliminary package design before the test products are finished. Or the manager might decide that 10 weeks rather than 12 is a sufficient time period to monitor sales. The idea is that if the critical path can be shortened, so too can the overall duration of the project.

The PERT network serves as an ongoing control framework

FIGURE 19.3

A PERT Network for Introducing a New Product

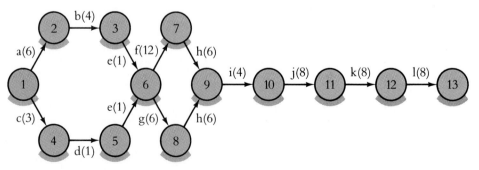

The numbers and letters correspond to the numbers and letters used in Table 19.5.

throughout the project. The manager can use it to monitor where the project is relative to where it needs to be. Thus, if an activity on the critical path takes longer than planned, the manager needs to make up the time elsewhere or live with the fact that the entire project will be late.

Economic Order Quantity   Another control technique used by many firms, especially small ones, is the economic order quantity, or EOQ. The EOQ is a mathematically determined quantity of what should be ordered to optimize the costs of carrying inventory, placing orders, and stocking out. The EOQ formula is

$$EOQ = \sqrt{\frac{2RS}{C}}$$

where   R = yearly requirement of what is being ordered

S = ordering or setup cost

C = carrying costs per unit

For example, if we use 4,500 units per year, if setup costs are $20, and if carrying costs are $.50 per unit, then

$$EOQ = \sqrt{\frac{2 \times 4500 \times 20}{.5}} = \sqrt{360,000} = 600$$

Each order, then, should be for 600 units.

HUMAN RESOURCE CONTROL

Most control efforts concentrate on budgeting, finance, or operations, but managers also try to control other areas in a systematic way. One of these areas is human resources.

Goals of Human Resource Control

Human resource control focuses on the organization's human resources. The major goal of human resource control is to ensure that the organization is acquiring, developing, and retaining the quality and quantity of human resources that it needs to achieve its strategic plans. Numerous subgoals contribute to this overriding goal, and each is reflected in one or more of the control techniques described below.

Human Resource Control Techniques

The two primary human resource control techniques are performance appraisal and the analysis of key human resource ratios.

Performance Appraisal Performance appraisal (which is also discussed in Chapter 10) is concerned with evaluating the performance of employees and managers within an organization. For control purposes, performance appraisal helps the manager monitor the performance of individuals and groups, compare observed performance levels against some standard, and correct any problems. The process of performance appraisal is shown in Figure 19.4. Each step leads logically to the next.

Assume that a manufacturer introduces a new line of machinery and therefore needs to establish a performance appraisal framework for the machine operators. First a job analysis is conducted to determine the components of the job and their relative importance. For the machine operator, the components might be adjusting machine settings, making parts, and inspecting parts for quality. Performance criteria, then,

FIGURE 19.4

The Performance Appraisal Process

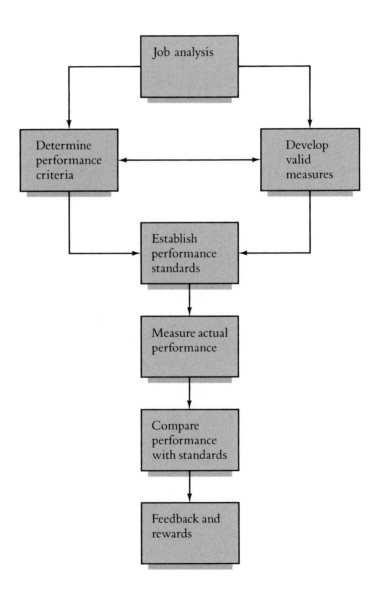

would include ability to set the machine, manufacture the parts, and inspect the finished products. Valid measures could include making spot checks of machine settings, counting the number of units produced, and conducting occasional follow-up inspections to verify quality. Establishing performance standards would involve setting the desired levels of actual performance. For the machine operator, these could be 98 percent accurate machine settings, 40 units of production per hour, and a quality acceptance rate of 93 percent. Actual performance is then measured and compared with the standard. Finally, the manager provides feedback to the individual and administers whatever rewards (or takes whatever corrective actions) are appropriate.[14]

Human Resource Ratios   Another approach to human resource control focuses on human resource ratios. One common ratio is employee turnover, which may be defined as the average percentage of an organization's work force that leaves and must be replaced over a period of time (usually one year). Some organizations, such as fast-food restaurants like McDonald's and Burger King and grocery stores like Safeway and Kroger, have turnover ratios of nearly 100 percent. Other companies like Merck, 3M, Philip Morris, and PepsiCo have ratios that are considerably lower. If a manager notes a significant increase in the turnover ratio, or if the organization's ratio is above the industry average, human resource practices may need to be changed.

Absenteeism is the percentage of an organization's work force that is absent from work over a given time period (usually one day). Ratios

Human resource managers often use turnover ratios to help keep track of how many people leave their organization each year. Fast-food restaurants typically have very high levels of turnover—often as high as 300 percent per year. Reggie Parker, a former all-pro with the Pittsburgh Steelers and owner of 11 Kentucky Fried Chicken outlets and several other businesses, now helps Kentucky Fried Chicken control its turnover. As part of his job, he visits stores on a regular basis to find out what employees are happy or unhappy about. He holds meetings with them to explain career opportunities that might eventually be available to them if they stay on as employees. This plan seems to be working—in the stores Parker works with, turnover hovers around 40 percent.

may range from 3 or 4 percent to as high as 20 or 30 percent. For some organizations, absenteeism is a special problem on Mondays and Fridays, as employees try to stretch their weekends. Managers may also monitor work-force composition ratios to guard against discrimination. For example, if a firm's surrounding labor market is composed of 45 percent female and 20 percent minority workers, the firm's own labor force should reflect approximately the same distribution. If only 20 percent of its workers are female and only 5 percent are minority workers, the firm's selection system might be ·regarded as discriminatory.

MARKETING CONTROL

A final area of control is marketing control—control directed at the marketing function of the organization.

Goals of Marketing Control

The primary goal of marketing control is to ensure that the organization is executing its marketing strategy effectively. For example, does current and planned advertising portray the company and its products in the way most desired? Are current marketing efforts contributing to the accomplishment of strategic goals? These and other goals must be satisfied if the marketing function is to be carried out properly.

Marketing Control Techniques

Two basic methods for marketing control are test marketing and the analysis of marketing ratios.

Test Marketing   When an organization introduces a new product or service, or when it begins a new advertising campaign, it runs a substantial risk if it plunges in without knowing how the public will react. Test marketing in advance is often used to control new marketing activities. Suppose that Wendy's plans to introduce a new kind of sandwich in its restaurants. It would be quite costly to buy the necessary new equipment for all Wendy's kitchens, train employees to make the sandwich, and advertise the sandwich nationally. If the public fails to accept the sandwich, Wendy's loses its entire investment and suffers embarrassment besides. The risks can be minimized by test marketing. One method would be to select a small area of the country in which to begin selling the sandwich. If it is successful there, it is introduced nationally. If it fails, it is withdrawn and the relatively low test-marketing costs are written off.[15] In other situations, consumer panels may be established to try out new products or react to commercials.

Market share is an important marketing control technique. Television networks, for example, use ratings to help them gauge how many people watch their shows in relation to other shows being aired at the same time. Hits like "Family Ties" have kept NBC the number one network for several years. Why are such ratings important? The higher the rating a particular show gets, the more the network can charge advertisers to run their commercials. Shows like "Family Ties," "Cosby," and "Who's the Boss" command premium fees.

There are many variations on test marketing, but they all have the same aim—testing new products on a relatively small scale to minimize potential loss to the organization.

Marketing Ratios   Certain marketing ratios are useful control techniques. Market share is defined as the percentage of the total market for a product (consumer demand for similar products made by all producers) that is controlled by one particular company's product. If the total demand is 1 million units per year and if one organization sells 100,000 units in that market, its market share is 10 percent. Substantial changes in market share can be of great concern to managers. Another useful ratio is profit margin on sales. This ratio, calculated by dividing net income by sales, is a measure of profitability in relation to sales. For example, sales of $1 million and net income (or profits) of $100,000 for a particular product (a ratio of 10 percent) compare unfavorably with sales of only $500,000 and profits of $100,000 (a ratio of 20 percent). This ratio helps managers identify the products that yield the highest profit margins as opposed to just the highest sales.

SUMMARY OF KEY POINTS

Budgetary control involves expressing a set of planned activities for a coming time period in objective terms. Common types of budgets include financial budgets, operating budgets, and nonmonetary budgets. Most budgets account for fixed, variable, and semivariable costs.

Many organizations allow subordinates to participate in the budgeting process. An innovative method for developing budgets called zero-base budgeting requires that each budget be developed and justified "from scratch" every year. Budgets have many advantages and are generally necessary, but there are risks associated with their use.

Other tools of financial control include financial statements, ratio analysis, and financial audits. The balance sheet and income statements are the two most common forms of financial statements. Frequently used ratios are liquidity ratios, debt ratios, return on assets, and return on investments. Financial audits, which may be external or internal, verify the accuracy and appropriateness of an organization's accounting, financial, and operations systems.

Operations control can focus on a variety of areas, including quality, purchasing, inventory, and scheduling. Common operations management control techniques include MRP, statistical quality control, PERT, and EOQ.

Human resource control centers on an organization's human resources. Techniques include performance appraisals and various ratios expressing turnover, absenteeism, and work-force composition.

Marketing control takes many forms. Test marketing and computing ratios such as market share and profit margin on sales are fairly common techniques that managers use.

DISCUSSION QUESTIONS

Questions for Review

1. List and briefly describe the steps of the budgeting process. Which step is most likely to be ignored? Why?
2. What are the tools of financial control? How can they be used effectively?
3. What is operations control? What are the primary areas of operations control? Briefly describe several techniques used in operations control.
4. What forms of control other than financial and operations control are used by organizations? Describe several of them.

Questions for Analysis

5. Marketing control is essential in order to prevent the marketing of a flop. Can you think of any companies that have marketed a flop recently? Why might those flops have occurred? How might they have been prevented?
6. All companies have some form of quality control, but the level differs between companies. Should all companies maintain the same level of quality control? Why or why not?
7. How are budgetary, financial, operations, human resource, and marketing control related?

Questions for Application

8. Examine your past expenses and create a daily budget for the next month. What type of budget did you create? How did you handle fixed and variable expenses? Do you think that you will follow your budget? Why or why not?

9. Find a copy of a corporation's annual report. Examine the financial statements in it. Calculate some of the financial analysis ratios discussed in this chapter. Do you think that they are favorable? How might they be improved?

10. Obtain permission to observe a local organization. Are any forms of operations control evident? Which ones? Can you think of any areas in which the organization has unnecessary control? Are there areas in which you would recommend more or a different form of control?

NOTES

1. "Why Tonka Needs Truckloads of Pay Dirt," *Business Week*, October 24, 1988, pp. 96–97; "Tonka Predicts Return to Profitability in '89," *The Wall Street Journal*, December 8, 1988, p. B8; "Tonka Announces Management Restructuring," *Playthings*, October 1988, p. 17.
2. See Belverd E. Needles, Jr., Henry R. Anderson, and James C. Caldwell, *Principles of Accounting*, 4th ed. (Boston: Houghton Mifflin, 1990).
3. John Dearden, "Measuring Profit Center Managers," *Harvard Business Review*, September–October 1987, pp. 84–88.
4. Needles, Anderson, and Caldwell, *Principles of Accounting*.
5. Ford S. Worthy, "Accounting Bores You? Wake Up," *Fortune*, October 12, 1987, pp. 43–50; Robert S. Kaplan, "One Cost System Isn't Enough," *Harvard Business Review*, January–February 1988, pp. 61–66; Robin Cooper, "You Need a New Cost System When . . ." *Harvard Business Review*, January–February 1989, pp. 77–82.
6. Peter Pyhrr, "Zero-Base Budgeting," *Harvard Business Review*, November–December 1970, pp. 111–121.
7. "What It Means to Build a Budget from Zero," *Business Week*, April 18, 1977, p. 160.
8. Christopher K. Bart, "Budgeting Gamesmanship," *The Academy of Management Executive*, November 1988, pp. 285–294.
9. Needles, Anderson, and Caldwell, *Principles of Accounting*.
10. Needles, Anderson, and Caldwell, *Principles of Accounting*.
11. Everett E. Adam, Jr., and Ronald J. Ebert, *Production and Operations Management*, 4th ed. (Englewood Cliffs, N.J.: Prentice-Hall, 1989).
12. Adam and Ebert, *Production and Operations Management*.
13. Adam and Ebert, *Production and Operations Management*.
14. For a good example of how a company can use performance appraisal as part of its control system, see Saul W. Gellerman and William G. Hodgson, "Cyanamid's New Take on Performance Appraisal," *Harvard Business Review*, May–June 1988, pp. 36–41.
15. Steven H. Star and Glen L. Urban, "The Case of the Test Market Toss-up," *Harvard Business Review*, September–October 1988, pp. 10–26.

CASE 19.1

Tenneco's Cooking Now

Tenneco grew out of the former Tennessee Gas and Transmission Company, which was founded in 1943 when the Chicago Corporation sold its Tennessee Division. That division had been formed to construct a pipeline from the Gulf of Mexico to the northeastern states. Tenneco's first president, Gardiner Symonds, was not content with running a pipeline company. By means of acquisitions he moved the company into an amazing variety of businesses—chemicals, petroleum, packaging, land development, automotive products, and shipbuilding. By the late 1970s Tenneco was a vast conglomerate that included over 300 different companies.

Then, in 1988, Tenneco began to move in the opposite direction. It began to sell its huge reserves of oil and natural gas. The market was glutted and prices were depressed, but Tenneco got top dollar for its properties anyway.

As it turns out, it was the reserves of natural gas that drove the deals. U.S. natural gas supplies had been decreasing steadily from 1984 through 1988; but demand, which had decreased from 1984 through 1986, turned upward and was near an all-time high. Because demand was still somewhat below supply, the price of gas was depressed. The long-term outlook, however, was quite positive. The expectation was that demand would continue to rise, capacity would stay low, and prices would gradually increase.

Shrewd budgetary and financial management enabled Tenneco to pull the deal off. Careful analysis revealed the trends, and astute managers opted to sell the properties in eight separate parts rather than try to sell them in one huge package. The timing was right for another reason, too. At 1988 prices, buying gas reserves was less expensive than trying to find them through costly exploration and drilling operations—especially if the company involved was willing to wait for its returns.

As if these changes were not enough to spur speculative buying of gas reserves, the gas market was about to get a big boost from renewed concern over the environment. The greenhouse effect is caused by carbon dioxide, much of which is released into the atmosphere during the burning of fossil fuels. Gas burns with far less carbon dioxide than any other commercially available fuel. Public pressure was mounting to get utilities and other major users of coal and oil to switch to gas. A side benefit is that gas produces less nitrous oxide and sulfuric acid, the pollutants causing acid rain. These changes led to optimistic forecasts for the gas market far into the future, much to Tenneco's delight.

All of this was significant for Tenneco because 1988 was expected to be the first year in which it had shown a profit since 1984. One reason for the company's poor performance was its unwieldy structure, the result of the diversity of its operations. In 1988, Tenneco consisted of seven major, relatively unrelated businesses plus a scattering of smaller businesses. Automotive, chemicals, farm and construction equipment, oil and gas, packaging, pipelines, and shipbuilding were the major businesses. Although there were some connections that accounted for the acquisition of those businesses, substantial differences in markets, customers, technology, and operations precluded any effective integration and made it difficult for the total organization to be very profitable. This was especially true when different businesses suffered downturns at the same time, as was happening in the oil and gas and the farm and construction equipment businesses during the mid-1980s.

Tenneco became so undervalued that it was a perfect target for an unwelcome takeover attempt. For that reason, Tenneco moved to restructure itself by selling parts of the firm. The sell-off increased the value of the whole organization, making it more expensive for any takeover specialists. One concern was how much of the company would have to be sold to stave off unfriendly takeovers.

The money generated by the sale of the different parts of the organization will be used by Tenneco for several purposes, all of which are designed to improve its financial health. Some will be used to reduce debt and cut interest payments. Some will be used to buy back stock in order to provide further protection against a possible takeover. Some will be used to expand Tenneco's packaging and automotive units, among the healthiest parts of its operation. Indeed, the automotive unit has an outstanding return on assets (about 23 percent as of the mid-1980s) and is expected to continue to perform well.

Questions

1. What control techniques and methods are used by Tenneco? Cite specific examples.
2. Take one of the control techniques or methods that you identified in question 1 and outline it in as much detail as you can. How does Tenneco's application of that technique or method compare with the discussion in this chapter?
3. What types of control techniques and methods seem to be lacking at Tenneco? Why might this be the case?
4. Do you think that Tenneco has succeeded in turning itself around? Why or why not? Do you think the future for Tenneco will be one of growth and expansion or retrenchment? Why?

References: "Why the Street Isn't Moved by Tenneco's Big Move," *Business Week*, September 26, 1988, pp. 130, 133; "Tenneco to Sell Oil Units for $7 Billion," *USA Today*, October 11, 1988, p. 1B; "Gas Is Cooking Now," *Business Week*, October 24, 1988, pp. 24–25; "Tenneco's Oil-and-Gas Asset Sales Draw Winning Bids of $7.3 Billion," *The Wall Street Journal*, October 11, 1988, p. A3.

CASE 19.2

Effective Control at Swissair

Swissair, the official flag carrier airline for Switzerland, earned a profit in every year for the past 38 consecutive years. That is the best record of any major airline in the world. Swissair is a financially sound company, but like any company it has some problems. If it needs money quickly, it can easily obtain such funds by selling portions of its fleet and then leasing them back again. Although such a move would provide quick cash, it would not have any sizable impact on Swissair's already high operating costs. It is those operating costs over which the airline must gain control.

In August 1988, Otto Loepfe took over as Swissair's CEO to tackle the cost problem of the airline. He used several different forms of control in his effort to do so. In human resource control, he shuffled management to try to get people in positions where they could more effectively work on the problems. He began to work with Swissair's unions to try to get them to accept profit sharing and merit-raise programs rather than continue to use rigid, fixed-pay scales. The unions are resisting such efforts, but the comapny's pilots did agree in 1988 to increase productivity by about 10 percent over three years by flying more hours than previously.

Loepfe also used marketing control when he established a small committee to search for alliances with other airlines in order to expand Swissair's operations. Swissair had long operated joint servicing facilities with Sweden's SAS, Netherland's KLM, and France's UTA, and wanted even more affiliations with other airlines to expand its markets and service capabilities. The committee located several possible opportunities. Swissair was able to take advantage of two. It acquired a 38 percent stake in Crossair, which is a European regional carrier based in Switzerland, and it also acquired a 3 percent stake in Austrian Airlines.

Combining this marketing control with operations control, Swissair entered into a joint venture with nine airlines to develop Galileo, an electronic reservations system valued at more than $100 million. Since most of Swissair's reservations are booked outside of Switzerland, this system was seen as a major step toward improved marketing services. The Galileo system will handle not just airline reservations but also hotel and rental-car reservations. Thus it is useful for Swissair's airline operations and for its part in Reisebüro Kuoni, Switzerland's largest tour operator.

In mid-1987 Swissair entered into an agreement to expand its access to the U.S. market. Prior to the agreement, Swissair served Atlanta, Boston, Chicago, and New York. The agreement enables Swissair to use one of those cities as a stopover point on flights to and from Mexico City. Swissair also obtained the right to use Anchorage, Alaska, as a stopover point for its Europe-to-Tokyo flights. This opening up of the U.S. market was seen as a major benefit because it will expand Swissair's revenue base. In exchange, Swissair had to agree to permit U.S. carriers to operate their own check-in facilities in Zurich and Geneva. Because Swissair used to handle all check-ins and charge a fee to other carriers, the new arrangement will reduce revenues from check-in operations. However, it was expected that increased revenues from the expanded U.S. market would more than offset this reduction. The agreement also deregulated airfares between Switzerland and the United States, including round-trip tickets on flights beginning in the United States. Further, the agreement increased security procedures to comply with the high standards set by the U.S. Federal Aviation Administration.

In 1987 Swissair began to introduce new aircraft to its fleet in an effort to bring total operating costs in line. Late in 1987 it purchased long-range jets from McDonnell Douglas for use on its international flights. In early 1988 it began to use new Fokker 100 transports for European flights originating in Basel, Geneva, and Zurich. Fokker 100s are capable of all-weather landings, have highly automated cockpits, hold 85 passengers, have two galleys, and have a rear service door. There are eight first-class seats, and the remaining seats can be separated easily into two other classes of service—business and economy. This arrangement provides an opportunity for Swissair to maximize revenues on flights using the Fokker 100s. These airplanes were expected to begin actual service in 1989. Thus training for air and ground crews was initiated in mid-1988 so that everyone would be ready when the planes were introduced.

Questions

1. What control techniques and methods are used by Swissair? Cite specific examples.
2. Take one of the control techniques or methods that you identified in question 1 and outline it in as much detail as you can. How does Swissair's application of that technique or method compare with the discussion in this chapter?
3. What types of control techniques and methods seem to be lacking at Swissair? Why might this be the case?
4. Do you think that Swissair will succeed in its efforts to reduce operating costs? Why or why not? What do you think the future holds for Swissair? Why?

REFERENCES: "Why Swissair's New Pilot Is Fixing What Ain't Broke," *Business Week*, August 29, 1988, p. 42; "Swissair Readies Air, Ground Crews for First Fokker 100s," *Aviation Week & Space Technology*, April 18, 1988, p. 95; "McDonnell Douglas Gets Swissair Order," *The Wall Street Journal*, December 21, 1987, p. 25; "Swiss, U.S. Exchange Access to Atlanta for Check-in Rights," *Aviation Week & Space Technology*, July 27, 1987, p. 34.

ENHANCEMENT MODULE 8

Automation in the Workplace

Going by a shopping mall after hours, you hear a noise and look inside. No one is around, but you see a short, fat machine running back and forth along the halls. Only 3 feet tall, it is a robot — an automatic vacuum cleaner busily cleaning the mall without human assistance of any kind. A vision of the future? Hardly. That automatic vacuuming robot is for sale now. Designed by Transitions Research Corp. to clean factories, malls, supermarkets, airports, and other facilities without human assistance, the robot sells for about $20,000. Feasibility studies indicate that any business with 35,000 or more square feet of space to be cleaned could use the machine economically. Robots like this are but one form of automation currently available on the market to managers.[1]

Most organizations use automation in some form or other. Indeed, some forms of automation have become so commonplace that we no longer even think of them as automation. Automatic telephone switching for long-distance calls, for instance, has become so routine that most people do not think of it as a form of automation; but it is. Or consider a large copying machine. The operator puts originals in one bin; pushes buttons to tell the machine the number of copies to make, whether to print front and back, collate, or staple; and hits the start button. The copier does the rest. That too is automation. Because automation is so commonplace and powerful, it is important for managers to understand and utilize it where appropriate.

THE NATURE OF AUTOMATION

Automation is the process of designing work so that it can be completely or almost completely performed by machines; hence, it is the use of machines that control their own operations with little or no human assistance. Because automated machines operate quickly and make few errors, they increase the amount of work that can be done. Thus, automation

helps to improve products and services, and it fosters innovation.

Automation is the most recent step in the development of machines and machine-controlling devices. Machine-controlling devices have been around since the 1700s. James Watt, the Scottish engineer, invented a mechanical speed control to regulate the speed of steam engines in 1787. The Jacquard loom, developed by a French inventor, was controlled by paper cards with holes punched in them. Early accounting and computing equipment was controlled by similar punched cards (see the discussion of the evolution of computers in Enhancement Module 3 at the end of Part 2).

The basic concept of automation is shown in Figure EM8.1. A thermostat has sensors that monitor air temperature and compare it to a preset low value. If the air temperature falls below the preset value, the thermostat sends an electrical signal to the furnace, turning it on. The furnace heats the air. When the sensors detect that the air temperature has reached a value higher than the low preset value, the thermostat stops the furnace. The last step (shutting off the furnace) is known as feedback; it is a critical component of any automated operation.

Automation involves feedback, information, sensors, and a control mechanism. Feedback is the flow of information from the machine back to the sensor. Sensors are the parts of the system that gather information and compare it to some preset standards. The control mechanism is the device that sends instructions to the automatic machine. Early automatic machines were primitive, and the use of automation was relatively slow to develop.

The big move to automate factories began during World War II. The shortage of skilled workers and the development of high-speed computers combined to bring about a tremendous interest in automation. Suddenly, programmable automation (the use of computers to control machines) was introduced, far outstripping conventional automation (the use of mechanical or electromechanical devices to control

FIGURE EM8.1

A Simple Automatic Control Mechanism

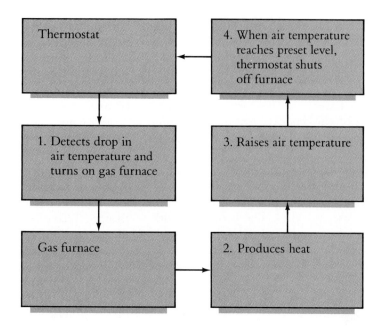

machines).[2] The automobile industry began to use automatic machines for numerous jobs. In fact, the term automation came into use in the 1950s in the automobile industry. The chemical and oil-refining industries also began to use computers to regulate their processes. It is this computerized, or programmable, automation that presents the greatest opportunities and challenges for management today.

THE IMPACT OF AUTOMATION IN THE WORKPLACE

Automation is designed to improve productivity and predictability in the workplace. People get tired and emotional and can be erratic in their performance. Machines are far less erratic, and they do not get tired or emotional. Further, automatic machines can operate around the clock, 24 hours a day, seven days a week, if they are properly maintained. It would take a large number of human operators to match their productivity.

Automation and Productivity

Automation is used by banks and credit-card companies to quickly enter transactions in customer ac-

count records and update accounts. Automobile assembly plants receive orders from customers and can use computer controllers to customize certain models. Scheduling for airlines, car rental firms, and hotels is handled by automatic computer programs. It seems that nearly everything we do involves automation in some form or other to improve productivity.

Office automation is especially extensive. There are over a million copiers and a million electronic typewriters in American offices. Over 7 million personal computers have been sold. Although many of them are used in homes and schools, a large proportion of them are used in offices. Laser printers, facsimile machines, integrated office systems, and voice messaging are also becoming extensively used.[3] Virtually all of these applications improve productivity.

Automation and People

The impact of automation on people in the workplace is complex. In the short term, people whose jobs are automated find themselves without jobs. In the long term, however, more jobs are created than are lost. Nevertheless, not all companies are able to help displaced workers find new jobs, so the human costs are sometimes high. In the coal industry, for instance, automation has been used primarily in mining. The output per miner has risen dramatically from the 1950s on. The demand for coal, however, has decreased; and productivity gains resulting from automation have lessened the need for miners. Consequently, a lot of workers have lost their jobs, and the industry has not been able to absorb them. In contrast, in the electronics industry, the rising demand for products has led to increasing employment opportunities despite the use of automation.

The introduction of computers and automation sometimes increases the stress that people at work feel. They must learn new technologies and skills when, at least in some cases, they were perfectly comfortable with the old ones. The impact of automation on people, then, may be negative in the short term but positive over the long haul.

The Problems of Automation

Automation is expensive. In addition to being expensive, it requires highly skilled personnel to design, build, program, and maintain it and sometimes to operate it. In a non-automated operation, things are more easily changed than in an automated one; thus, much more careful planning must go into an automated operation than into a non-automated one. Coordination problems can arise between the planners of the system and the users. Getting design and manufacturing together early can ward off many problems of this sort, however.[4] The introduction of automation brings about change and change frequently causes stress for many people. Thus, care must be taken during the introductory phases of automation to reduce stress and convert it to productive energy for the organization.[5]

Because no automated system can operate completely without human assistance or intervention, the importance of the human element increases rather than decreases with automation. When an operation depends heavily on a large number of relatively unskilled workers, those workers can be replaced comparatively easily and no one of them can cause much disruption to the operation. But when an operation depends heavily on automation, the few skilled workers involved cannot so easily be replaced and any one of them can have a great impact on the operation. Thus, in automated facilities good employee relations are extremely important.

Finally, automation can bring new and different safety problems. Because human operators are not usually present in many automated settings, it is easy to overlook them in designing the systems. As a result, when they are present, unexpected movements of equipment or unprotected machinery can catch them, hit them, or in other ways cause injury to them. This problem is acute in robotized work settings, where devices move throughout the work area without regard for the presence of humans. As managers have learned more about the safety issues of automation, techniques and devices have been developed to make automated workplaces safe.[6]

The major problems associated with automation, then, are high costs, the need for skilled personnel, the need for careful planning, the need for coordination between planners and users, stress, the critical need for good human relations, and the need to maintain a safe working environment. Some organizations have more difficulties surmounting these problems than do others.

CURRENT TRENDS IN AUTOMATION

Automation continues to expand in organizations of all types. The manuscript for this book was typed on a word processor that, when directed, did such things as automatically formatting pages, checking spelling, and renumbering notes. The manuscript was sent to the publisher. After copyediting, the text was transferred to printing machines that automatically reformatted the material to specifications provided by production personnel. The text was printed and bound, and the finished book was packed and shipped to bookstores. Various types of automatic equipment were used throughout the process. New uses of automation are being developed and need to be examined on an ongoing basis.

Extensions of Existing Systems

Most trends in the use of automation are extensions of existing systems or existing applications. For instance, electronic mail, which exists today in some settings, will become commonplace in the future.

Numerous computer developments now available in some settings will also be improved and more widely adopted in the future—CD-ROM (compact disks that store huge amounts of data in read-only formats), voice recognition, optical character recognition, and knowledge-based expert and decision support systems.[7]

Computer-aided design (CAD) is the use of computers to design parts and complete products and to simulate performance so that prototypes need not be constructed. McDonnell Douglas uses CAD to study hydraulic tubing in DC-10s. Japan's automotive industry uses it to speed up car design. GE used CAD to change the design of circuit breakers, and Benetton uses CAD to design new styles and products. Oneida Ltd., the table flatware firm, used CAD to design a new spoon in only two days.[8] CAD is usually combined with computer-aided manufacturing (CAM) to ensure that the design moves smoothly to production. The production computer shares the design computer's information and is able to have machines with the proper settings ready when production is needed. A CAM system is especially useful when re-orders come in because the computer can quickly produce the desired product, prepare labels and copies of orders, and send the product out to where it is wanted. Very little human involvement is necessary at all.

Closely aligned with this approach is computer-integrated manufacturing (CIM). In CIM, CAD and CAM are linked together and computers adjust machine placements and settings automatically to enhance both the complexity and the flexibility of scheduling. All manufacturing activities are controlled by computer. Because the computer can access the company's other information systems, CIM is a powerful and complex management control tool.[9]

Flexible manufacturing systems (FMS) usually have robotic work units or work stations, assembly lines, and robotic carts or some other form of computer-controlled transport system to move material as needed from one part of the system to another.[10] FMS such as the one at IBM's manufacturing facility in Lexington, Kentucky, rely on computers to coordinate and integrate automated production and materials-handling facilities.[11]

These systems are not without disadvantages.[12] They generate among employees the usual resistance to anything new and different. Additionally, CAD systems seem to break down frequently, perhaps because of their tremendous complexity. Also, because CAD systems utilize enormous computer space, they must be run in off hours or else the company must purchase extra memory for them. CIM systems are so expensive that they raise the breakeven point for firms using them.[13] This means that the firm must operate at high levels of production and sales to be able to afford the systems.

Robotics

One of the newest trends in automation is robotics. The term robot is a Czech word for worker and was first used to refer to automata in Karel Capek's 1921 play *R.U.R.* ("Rossum's Universal Robots"). Now robot refers to any artificial device that is able to perform functions ordinarily thought to be appropriate for human beings. The term robotics was first used by Isaac Asimov in his science fiction story "Runaround" in 1942. Today, robotics refers to the science and technology of the construction, maintenance, and use of robots.[14]

The first patent for an industrial robot was granted in 1954 to George C. Devol, Jr., for universal automation or unimation, the robot's control and memory system. Devol sold his patents to the Consolidated Diesel Electric Corporation in 1961, which sold them to Westinghouse in 1982. At Consolidated Diesel, under the leadership of Joseph F. Engelberger, the robotics industry slowly grew. Unimation, Inc., sold its first product in 1961 but did not return a profit until 1975.[15] As shown in Table EM8.1, however, the production of industrial robots has steadily increased since 1980 and is expected to continue to increase slowly as more companies recognize the benefits that accrue to users of industrial robots.

The words manufacture and manipulate both have their origins in the Latin word for hand, *manus*. Because many robots are substitutes for hands—manipulators—applications in manufacturing are natural for them. Welding was one of the first applications for robots, and it continues to be the area for most applications. In second place and close behind is materials handling. Other applications include machine loading and unloading, painting and

TABLE EM8.1

Estimated Production of
Industrial Robots in Selected
Countries

Country	1980*	1985	1990
Austria	50	150	na
Canada	na	280	630
Czechoslovakia	154	800	1,800
France	200	1,820	4,540
Germany	823	2,300	3,500
Italy	400	1,200	5,000
Japan	14,246	18,800	34,600
Netherlands	71	250	na
Sweden	na	750	2,400
United Kingdom	371	550	1,500
United States	3,849	4,500	24,000

na = not available
★ = estimate based on robots installed

SOURCE: Isaac Asimov and Karen A. Frenkel, *Robots: Machines in Man's Image*. Copyright © 1985 by Nightfall Inc. and Karen A. Frenkel. Reprinted by permission of Crown Publishers, a division of Random House, Inc.

finishing, assembly, casting, and machining applications such as cutting, grinding, polishing, drilling, sanding, buffing, and deburring. Chrysler, for instance, replaced about 200 welders with 50 robots on an assembly line and increased productivity about 20 percent.[16] The use of robots in inspection work is increasing. They can check for cracks and holes, and they can be equipped with vision systems to perform visual inspections.[17]

Robots are beginning to move from the factory floor to all manner of other applications. In Dallas the police used a robot to apprehend a suspect who had barricaded himself in an apartment building. The robot smashed a window and reached with its mechanical arm into the building. The suspect panicked and ran outside. At the Long Beach Memorial Hospital in California, brain surgeons are assisted by a robot arm that drills into the patient's skull with excellent precision.[18]

Some newer applications involve remote work. For example, the use of robot submersibles controlled from the surface should save the lives of divers in fields involving offshore and underwater technologies. Similarly, some tasks involving extremely hazardous conditions are readily adaptable for robot use. Surveillance robots fitted with microwave sensors can do things that a human guard cannot do such as "seeing" through nonmetallic walls and in the dark. In other applications, automated farming (agrimation) uses robot harvesters to pick fruit from a variety of trees.[19]

Robots are also used by small manufacturers. One robot slices carpeting to fit the inside of custom vans in an upholstery shop. Another stretches balloons flat so that they can be spray-painted with slogans at a novelties company. At a jewelry company, a robot holds class rings while they are engraved by a laser. These robots are lighter, faster, stronger, and more intelligent than those used in heavy manufacturing and are the types that more and more organizations will be using in the future.[20]

NOTES

1. Gene Bylinsky, "Invasion of the Service Robots," *Fortune*, September 14, 1987, pp. 81–88; "Smart Factories: America's Turn?" *Business Week*, May 8, 1989, pp. 142–148.
2. Paul D. Collins, Jerald Hage, and Frank M. Hull, "Organizational and Technological Predictors of Change in Automaticity," *Academy of Management Journal*, September 1988, pp. 512–543.

3. "The Electronic Storm," *The Wall Street Journal*, June 12, 1987, pp. 8D, 20D.

4. James W. Dean, Jr., and Gerald I. Susman, "Organizing for Manufacturable Design," *Harvard Business Review*, January–February 1989, pp. 28–36.

5. Shimon Dolan and Aharon Tziner, "Implementing Computer-based Automation in the Office: A Study of Experienced Stress," *Journal of Organizational Behavior*, Vol. 9, 1988, pp. 183–187; Ethel Roskies, Jeffrey K. Liker, and David B. Roitman, "Winners and Losers: Employee Perceptions of Their Company's Technological Transformation," *Journal of Organizational Behavior*, Vol. 9, 1988, pp. 123–137.

6. See, for example, the discussion in John V. Grimaldi and Rollin H. Simonds, *Safety Management,* 5th ed. (Homewood, Ill.: Irwin, 1989), pp. 331–332.

7. "Promises of Tomorrow," *The Wall Street Journal*, June 12, 1987, pp. 36D, 38D.

8. "Computers Speed the Design of More Workaday Products," *The Wall Street Journal*, January 18, 1985, p. 25.

9. Robert Bonsack, "Executive Checklist: Are You Ready for CIM?" *CIM Review*, Summer 1987, pp. 35–38.

10. Jack R. Meredith, "Strategic Control of Factory Automation," *Long Range Planning*, Vol. 20, 1987, pp.

106–112; and Patricia L. Nemetz and Louis W. Fry, "Flexible Manufacturing Organizations: Implications for Strategy Formulation and Organization Design," *Academy of Management Review*, October 1988, pp. 627–638.

11. M. Sepehri, "IBM's Automated Lexington Factory Focuses on Quality and Cost Effectiveness," *Industrial Engineering*, February 1987, pp. 66–74.

12. "Computers Speed the Design of More Workaday Products."

13. "How Automation Could Save the Day," *Business Week*, March 3, 1986, pp. 72–74.

14. Isaac Asimov and Karen A. Frenkel, *Robots: Machines in Man's Image* (New York: Harmony Books, 1985), p. 12.

15. Asimov and Frenkel, *Robots: Machines in Man's Image*, pp. 15, 25–48.

16. Otto Friedrich, "The Robot Revolution," *Time*, December 8, 1980, pp. 72–83.

17. "GM Bets an Arm and a Leg on a People-free Plant," *Business Week*, September 12, 1988, pp. 72–73.

18. Bylinsky, "Invasion of the Service Robots."

19. "Robots Head for the Farm," *Business Week*, September 8, 1986, pp. 66–67.

20. "Boldly Going Where No Robot Has Gone Before," *Business Week*, December 22, 1986, p. 45.

ENHANCEMENT MODULE 9

Managing Decline and Cutbacks

A few years ago, several top managers at AT&T confided in some Wall Street security analysts that the company was planning a series of large-scale job cuts. When reports of the cutbacks started appearing in the newspapers, they did nothing to keep their workers informed about what was happening. And what did happen? AT&T laid off almost 70,000 workers, a move financial experts applauded. But during the period of the layoffs, at least two managers at the company committed suicide and work essentially stopped for weeks at a time as everyone tried to sort out who would be next to go.[1]

AT&T managers faced a task that many of their counterparts in other firms have faced in recent years—the need to cut back on costs and operations. Although they did a good job of figuring out where and how to implement the cuts, they did a poor job of handling many of the associated details.

This module focuses on the management of organizational decline and cutbacks. In the first section, we explain why organizations occasionally have to make cutbacks. We then identify several common approaches to cutbacks. Finally, we describe how cutbacks can be effectively managed.

REASONS FOR ORGANIZATIONAL CUTBACKS AND DECLINE

A cutback is any planned action taken by an organization to reduce its costs or scope of operations. Laying off employees, selling a business, and closing a plant are types of cutback. In contrast, organizational decline is a gradual process during which the organization loses size and its resource base. Why do organizations sometimes find it necessary to cut back? And why does decline inadvertently set in? Figure EM9.1 illustrates the major forces that lead to cutbacks or decline.

Overexpansion

During much of the 1950s and the 1960s, American business was experiencing a boom of unprecedented

FIGURE EM9.1

Reasons for Organizational Cutbacks and Decline

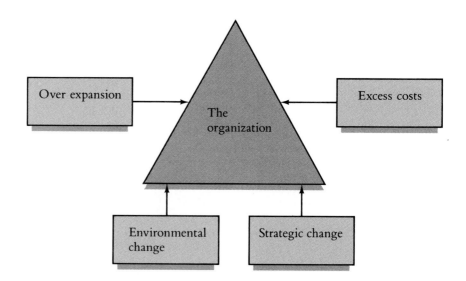

Over expansion → The organization ← Excess costs

Environmental change ↑   ↑ Strategic change

proportions. New products were being introduced left and right; income and therefore spending was increasing dramatically; and world markets were opening up. As a result, business grew rapidly.

Eventually, growth slowed. When it started to diminish in the late 1960s and early 1970s, many businesses ignored the trend and continued to grow and expand. They built new manufacturing facilities and office buildings and hired new workers. In short, they grew too big for their markets. This overexpansion eventually became a major cause of cutbacks and decline.[2]

Excess Costs

Related to the notion of overexpansion are excess costs. If an organization is growing at a rate of 15 to 20 percent per year and is making huge profits, the costs of adding new employees and building new facilities is in many ways not terribly noticeable. But when growth stops, such costs become a real drain. When the new employees were first hired, they probably started at a fairly low wage or salary level. As they built up seniority, and as new labor contracts were negotiated, the costs of compensation and benefits grew substantially. When organizational growth slowed, the impact of those costs increased significantly. Consequently, organizations realized that their costs were excessive and had eaten up too much slack in their resource base.[3]

Environmental Change

There must be some catalyst in order for overexpansion or excess costs to become an issue. One major stimulus is environmental change. As an organization's environment changes, the organization may be forced to make cutbacks. Competitors may also be a cause of decline. Declines in the American auto industry were stimulated by the entrance of fuel-efficient and high-quality products from Japan and Europe.

Economic conditions in general may hurt specific businesses. The housing industry is frequently hurt during periods of recession. Government regulation may also result in decline. Sometimes an environmental change is beyond a company's control. For example, during the product-tampering crisis a few years ago, Johnson & Johnson lost a great deal of money because sales of Tylenol plunged.

Strategic Change

Organizations may choose to cut back because of changes in strategy. In Chapter 6 we described how firms occasionally adopt a retrenchment strategy—shrinking current operations, cutting back operations, or eliminating some operations altogether. Such a strategic change might be undertaken because management believes it will help the firm in the future, or perhaps management had to take certain steps to keep the firm independent. Cutbacks are sometimes needed as a result of a merger or acquisition, most commonly because of redundant operations. For example, when Northwest Airlines merged with Republic Airways a few years ago, 800 employees, who were doing the same jobs for the airlines when they were separate entities, were laid off.[4] Regardless of the circumstances, organizational cutbacks have been an important part of many companies' strategies in recent years—and will likely remain so for the foreseeable future.[5]

COMMON APPROACHES TO CUTBACKS AND DECLINE

When organizations recognize the need to cut back, there are a number of different avenues available to them. Five common ones are summarized in Table EM9.1.

Work-Force Reductions

Work-force reductions can be accomplished through layoffs, transfers, attrition, early retirement, or the outright release of employees. Volkswagen of America once cut its work force three times within one year. IBM has a no-layoff policy but recently eased restrictions so that as many as 8,000 employees would volunteer for early retirement.[6]

TABLE EM9.1

Common Approaches to
Cutbacks and Decline

1. **Work-force reductions.** Layoffs, transfers, attrition, early
   retirement, or outright release.
2. **Facilities closures.** Plant or office shutdowns.
3. **Budget and expense restrictions.** Budget cuts or freezes,
   tightened controls.
4. **Divestiture.** Selling or closing subsidiaries, divisions, or businesses.
5. **Termination.** Going bankrupt, selling the entire business, or
   liquidation.

Facilities Closures

Facilities closures may mean closing or selling a
manufacturing plant, a warehouse, a computer center, an office building, or surplus inventory (at cost
or below). This method is commonly used when
the reason for cutbacks is overexpansion—a company built too many manufacturing plants and now
finds itself in the position of having to close some
of them. To reduce costs and raise cash, Nestlé once
sold to IBM a new U.S. headquarters facility that it
was constructing—before the building was even
completed.[7] And Sears is selling its headquarters
building in Chicago.

Budget and Expense Restrictions

Another common method for cutting back is
through budget and expense restrictions. Such efforts include reduction in operating budgets and
freezes on hiring. Firms faced with cutting back
often tell line managers that they will get no budget
increases for some specified period of time. Companies also ask managers who travel a lot to econo-
mize on their hotel bills and make only essential trips.

Divestiture

Another common approach for organizations
undergoing cutbacks is to close or sell an entire
division, subsidiary, or business. They may make
this choice from either of two perspectives. They
may sell off businesses that are not sufficiently profitable or that are losing money. Or they may have
to sell profitable operations in order to gain cash for

other needs. Diamond International had to sell its
profitable egg-carton-making business to its own
managers as a way to raise cash. But Diamond also
sold its playing-card business, because it was losing
money.[8]

Termination

In extreme cases—when the organization is unable
to meet its financial commitments through cost-
cutting measures, or when it is unable to raise funds
for current operations—termination may be the only
viable solution. There are three primary approaches
to termination. The most obvious one is to liquidate, closing down all phases of the organization,
turning all assets into cash, and using the cash to
pay creditors. Anything that remains is distributed
to stockholders. A merger involves selling all or part
of the organization to another firm. The new parent
may have the resources and ability to get things back
on track. Finally, the organization might attempt
the most difficult form of termination—a transformation.[9] A transformation is a change not just in
the organization structure but from one kind of
business to another. For example, the Mary Carter
Paint Company is now Resorts International. Paint
accounts for only a small part of the business; hotels
and resort operations account for most of it.

MANAGING CUTBACKS AND DECLINE

Regardless of why or how a firm decides to undertake a program of cutbacks, there are several things
that need to be considered. The most important ones

are setting goals, planning, understanding human costs, and evaluation.

Setting Goals

The starting point for any program of cutbacks should always be to set goals. Management needs to develop a clear understanding of how its problems arose and what its most viable options include. This analysis might lead management to any of several goals—retaining its core business, becoming a subsidiary of another business, transforming itself, and so forth. It will also help management develop a better appreciation of the severity of the company's problems. The crisis may be a short-run difficulty that can be corrected easily, or it may be a major problem threatening the future of the firm.

Planning

After goals are set, managers should undergo a systematic planning exercise to decide exactly what needs to be done, how and when to best do it, and what the results should be. Companies are increasingly bringing in outside experts to help straighten things out. These experts bring a fresh perspective and can often be more objective in deciding what areas are the best candidates for reductions.[10] For example, Jerry E. Goldress, a consultant specializing in turnarounds, has rescued 35 midsize companies.

Understanding Human Costs

It is also important for managers to acknowledge the human costs of cutbacks. Eliminating jobs and closing facilities are especially traumatic to people. Even people who stay are subject to fear of future cutbacks and concern about their former co-workers without jobs.[11] These effects are especially strong when the firm does as AT&T did—fails to communicate properly with everyone about what is and is not going to happen. To fight such negative effects, organizations should maintain open lines of communication, explain as fully as possible why cutbacks are needed, and try to fire people only as a last resort.

Evaluation

It is also important to follow up in order to assess the effectiveness of the cutback program. Suppose that the method chosen was to tighten budgets in order to cut costs by 10 percent next year. Management should determine whether the tightened budgets achieved the desired goal of a 10 percent reduction. Depending on how circumstances have unfolded, it may be necessary to tighten things even more, keep the current restrictions, or perhaps loosen up a bit. Or the organization may need to explore other cutback options.

NOTES

1. Anne B. Fisher, "The Downside of Downsizing," *Fortune*, May 23, 1988, pp. 42–52. See also Kenneth Labich, "Was Breaking Up AT&T A Good Idea?" *Fortune*, January 2, 1989, pp. 82–87.
2. Donald C. Hambrick and Richard A. D'Aveni, "Large Corporate Failures as Downward Spirals," *Administrative Science Quarterly*, March 1988, pp. 1–23.
3. See Mark P. Sharfman, Gerrit Wolf, Richard B. Chase, and David A. Tansik, "Antecedents of Organizational Slack," *Academy of Management Review*, October 1988, pp. 601–614.
4. "Signals," *Fortune*, October 13, 1986, p. 14.
5. See Charles W. L. Hill and Gareth R. Jones, *Strategic Management: An Analytical Approach* (Boston: Houghton Mifflin, 1989).
6. "A Lifetime at IBM Gets a Little Shorter for Some," *Business Week*, September 29, 1986, p. 40.
7. Robert Ball, "A 'Shopkeeper' Shakes Up Nestlé," *Fortune*, December 27, 1982, pp. 103–106.
8. Myron Magnet, "Restructuring Really Works," *Fortune*, March 2, 1987, pp. 37–46.
9. "Splitting Up," *Business Week*, July 1, 1985, pp. 50–54.
10. "The Green Berets of Corporate Management," *Business Week*, December 21, 1987, pp. 110–114.
11. Joel Brockner, Steven L. Grover, and Mauritz D. Blonder, "Predictors of Survivors' Job Involvement Following Layoffs: A Field Study," *Journal of Applied Psychology*, August 1988, pp. 436–442.
12. For a recent review, see William Weitzel and Ellen Johnson, "Decline in Organizations: A Literature Integration and Extension," *Administrative Science Quarterly*, March 1989, pp. 91–109.

INTEGRATIVE CASE

Control at Ford

Henry Ford and twelve investors founded the Ford Motor Company in 1903. Ford did not have a new product idea, but he did try a variety of models to see what the public wanted to buy. The first two models (both were Model A's) were fast and well built and sold well. Ford then produced a series of models. Some sold well; others were failures. The ones that sold best were the sturdy, inexpensive models; the failures were the large, costly models like limousines.

The Model T sold so well that Ford had a difficult time controlling operations so that production could keep up with demand. To speed up production, he changed the way the cars were produced. The chassis were pulled through the factory by a rope, and each worker did only one task as the chassis went past. This procedure reduced production time from a few hours to a few minutes, and the mass-production assembly line was born. To make sure that workers asccepted the concept, Ford stunned the industry by paying workers double what other companies were paying. Nevertheless, his autocratic methods of control, his anti-Semitism, and his blatant animosity toward unions kept Ford from being well liked and respected by his workers and made it difficult for Ford to battle the intense competition that quickly emerged in the automobile industry.

When Henry Ford retired to his estate, Fairlane, in the 1930s, his son Edsel took over the firm. General Motors was beating Ford at every turn, however, and quickly became the leading automobile company. In 1943, Edsel died and Henry II assumed the top spot in the firm. After World War II, he hired a group of systems analysts who had worked for the Air Force during the war to bring in the latest techniques in organizational control and information systems. These "Whiz Kids" proved highly capable in operating organizations.

The new techniques and methods of control were quickly successful in turning things around, but by the 1960s and 1970s growth was leveling off. By 1980 Ford was having trouble again; it began losing market share and even began to lose money. The tremendous success of Japanese car makers and the energy crunch caught American automobile companies by surprise. All of them suffered, but Ford was particularly hard hit. It had developed the reputation of an organization virtually out of control. There was a lot of internal politicking and tough infighting, which were detrimental to the operations of the company. Further, quality control seemed almost nonexistent. The company had to regain its knowledge of its environment and use that knowledge to re-establish the control that it had achieved in the past.

One way to gain control was to reduce the work force and get costs down. Ford reduced employment in both hourly and managerial jobs from over 500,000 in 1978 to around 350,000 by the end of 1988. Those reductions plus other cost-cutting efforts enabled Ford to reduce costs by over $4.5 billion during the early 1980s. Those actions lowered Ford's breakeven point, added to its profits, and enabled Ford to compete strongly again.

Working with suppliers, Ford moved to control supplies of materials and parts. Long-term contracts, typically for five years, were negotiated with many suppliers, trading assured sales for lower prices and higher quality. Single sources of supply were also frequently used to assure those sources long-term sales, again in exchange for lower prices and higher quality. This approach reduced the number of suppliers with which Ford had to negotiate from over 6,000 to around 2,300. Thus Ford had to work with fewer purchasing agents and could maintain more effective control over its suppliers.

Control of human resources was also improved. Ford began to change from autocratic approaches to more participatory ones. Its bonus and incentive plans were modified so that quality and interpersonal skills were rewarded along with the attainment of production goals. Managers were encouraged to get out on the factory floor to seek information from production workers through an Employee Involvement program. These approaches not only improved quality control but also seemed to increase workers' commitment to high performance.

By the late 1980s, Ford had some of the hottest cars on the market, and its market share and profits were up significantly. Ford's sales in 1988 were around $80 billion, and the company earned about $5 billion in profit on those sales. Some analysts felt that too many of those sales came about through the use of incentives and rebates, which tended to lessen profits. The saving grace, of course, was that all automakers, including the Japanese, were using such marketing gimmicks to boost sales. However, problems associated with that success began to mount late in 1988 and early in 1989.

Demand was so great that customers were unable to get delivery on vehicles that they had ordered. Many began to cancel orders and take their business elsewhere. Pressure to produce more and more to keep up with demand was causing defects to increase on some products and was jeopardizing Ford's new reputation for quality.

Building new plants to meet the increased demand was not necessarily the answer. A few years earlier, Ford had closed plants because of lack of demand. If it built new plants, the market might get soft again and Ford could find itself with excess capacity and the need to close the new plants. This dilemma, though not new in the automobile industry, has become especially troublesome in recent years because of the rapidly changing performance of many models in the marketplace and the apparent disappearance of brand loyalty among most customers.

To broaden its base of operations and spread its financial risk, Ford is moving toward the goal of having 30 percent of its earnings come from financial services. To achieve that end, it has been acquiring financial companies for its First Nationwide Financial Corporation. By early 1989, First Nationwide's assets had nearly doubled those of 1987, rising to about $34 billion. Ford's most recent acquisitions at that time included Mile High Federal Savings and Loan Association of Denver, Colorado; Columbia Savings in Englewood, Colorado; Pathway Financial in Chicago; and Cardinal Federal Savings Bank of Cleveland, Ohio. Because most of these acquisitions were firms that were in trouble, it will take several years before Ford can turn them around and integrate them into First Nationwide.

Questions

1. Can you identify different forms of control at Ford? Cite specific examples. How has Ford managed the control process? Has that management seemed to be effective? Why or why not?
2. How does Ford manage its operations and productivity? Cite specific examples. Have those approaches seemed to be effective? Why or why not?
3. How does knowledge about the beginnings of Ford Motor Company help you to understand its present position, problems, and opportunities? Which issues in control are apparent in this discussion of Ford? Cite specific examples.
4. How might information systems be used in control by Ford? Would recent advances be potentially valuable to Ford? If so, how? If not, why not?

REFERENCES: "The Ford Family Wants to Take the Wheel Again," *Business Week*, January 16, 1989, p. 32; "Ford's Thrift Purchases Advance Goals," *The Wall Street Journal*, January 3, 1989, p. A4; Alex Taylor III, "Fords for the Future," *Fortune*, January 16, 1989, pp. 36–49; "Ford's Strong Sales Raise Agonizing Issue of Additional Plants," *The Wall Street Journal*, October 26, 1988, pp. 1A, 6A; "What's Throwing a Wrench into Britain's Assembly Lines," *Business Week*, February 29, 1988, p. 41; "Ford's Record Earnings Dash Hopes," *USA Today*, February 19, 1988, p. 3B; "Ford Credit Is Learning To Say 'No'," *Business Week*, May 8, 1989, p. 131.

VI SPECIAL CHALLENGES OF MANAGEMENT

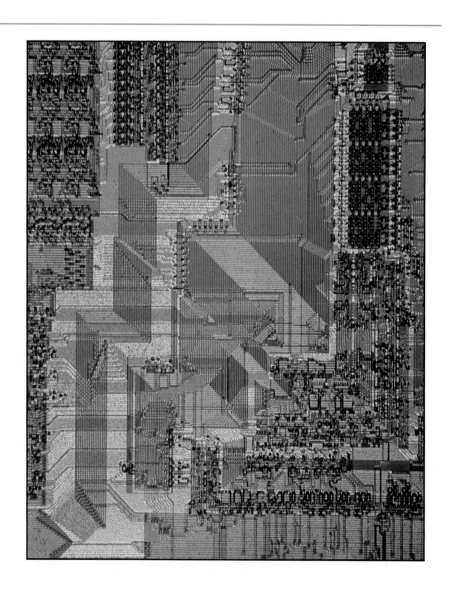

OUTLINE

The Nature of Entrepreneurship

Small Business and the U.S. Economy
The Impact of Small Business · Major Areas of Small Business

Small-Business Successes and Failures
Common Causes of Success · Common Causes of Failure

Starting a Small Business
Business Plan · Ownership and Financing · Approaches to Starting a Business

Managing the Small Business
Planning in the Small Business · Organizing in the Small Business · Leading in the Small Business · Controlling in the Small Business

Entrepreneurship in Large Businesses

CHAPTER 20

Entrepreneurship and Small-Business Management

OBJECTIVES

After studying this chapter, you should be able to:

- Characterize the nature of entrepreneurship.
- Discuss small business and its role in the U.S. economy.
- Identify the major causes of small-business success and failure.
- Describe the major issues in starting a small business.
- Discuss the major elements of managing a small business.
- Discuss entrepreneurship in large businesses.

OPENING INCIDENT

Toxic waste. The very term frightens many people. American business generates hundreds of tons of toxic waste materials every year, and toxic waste materials disposed of in years past were not properly handled. To many people, toxic waste disposal is a major problem. To others, it represents an opportunity.

In the early 1980s Alan McKim borrowed $13,000 from friends, bought a specially equipped truck, and opened a waste-cleanup company called Clean Harbors, Inc. in Massachusetts. Since then, Clean Harbors has acquired a fleet of 200 trucks and has annual revenues exceeding $100 million. There are now dozens of similar firms scattered around the United States. The largest are listed on the New York Stock Exchange and have annual profits as great as Clean Harbors's total sales. Clearly, the toxic waste disposal industry presented opportunities for a variety of entrepreneurs. And people who recognized and took advantage of those opportunities have sometimes benefited handsomely.[1]

Alan McKim did what thousands of other people in the United States do every year. He identified an opportunity and tried to capitalize on it by starting a new business. Like McKim, many of those who try, succeed in creating a new enterprise. Many others, however, fail. Some of those who fail try again, and they often succeed the second or perhaps the third time. Henry Ford, for example, went bankrupt twice before succeeding with the Ford Motor Company.

This chapter is about entrepreneurship and small-business management. We explain the nature of entrepreneurship and discuss the role of small business in the U.S. economy. We discuss major causes of small-business success and failure. We then describe how a new business is started. After discussing how small businesses are managed, we examine entrepreneurship in large businesses.

THE NATURE OF ENTREPRENEURSHIP

■ **entrepreneurship** The process of organizing, operating, and assuming the risk of a business venture

Entrepreneurship is the process of organizing, operating, and assuming the risk of a business venture.[2] An **entrepreneur** is someone who engages in entrepreneurship. A business owner who hires a professional manager to run his business and then turns his own interests to other things is not an entrepreneur. Although he is assuming the risk of the venture, he is not actively involved in organizing or operating it. Like-

entrepreneur Someone who engages in entrepreneurship; organizes, operates, and assumes the risk of his or her business venture

wise, a professional manager whose job is running someone else's business is not an entrepreneur. Although she may be organizing and operating the enterprise, she is assuming no personal risk for its success or failure.

Entrepreneurship involves starting a business and maintaining an active role in its management. The business itself may take any number of twists and turns. Figure 20.1 illustrates the most common paths of a business after it is first established. Path 1, the least common one, is an initial period of modest growth followed by a tremendous growth spurt that transforms the enterprise into a large business. This is the path taken by Sun Microsystems, Reebok International, Compaq Computer, Liz Claiborne, and Toys 'R' Us.[3] More common is path 2. Companies that follow this path reach a basic level of sales and profitability required to support their continued existence and then either stabilize at that level or perhaps continue to grow at a modest rate. Many local small businesses that have been around for several years— an automobile repair shop, a newspaper distributorship, a video rental store, for example—reflect this pattern. Many other businesses follow path 3. These businesses hang on for a while, perhaps even several years, but eventually fail.

Entrepreneurs themselves may also follow a number of paths. Some, like Rod Canion of Compaq, remain with their company as the firm grows. Others, like Steven Jobs of Apple, leave after several years and start new ventures like Jobs's NeXT Computer Company. Still others sell their business as soon as it turns profitable and start another. Some leave their business and go to work for someone else or retire.[4]

FIGURE 20.1

General Paths Taken by New Ventures

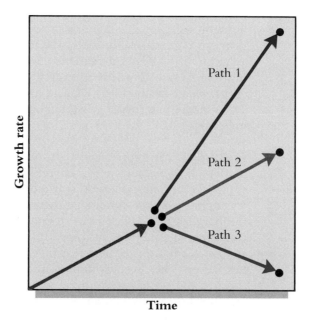

SMALL BUSINESS AND THE U.S. ECONOMY

What is a small business? There are actually many different definitions, but the most widely quoted ones are those of the U.S. Small Business Administration (SBA). Created in 1953 by the U.S. Congress, the SBA has a two fold purpose—to improve the managerial skills of entrepreneurs and to help them borrow money. For entrepreneurs seeking its help, the SBA has drafted definitions to fit virtually every industry. A partial list appears in Table 20.1. Notice that some indicators go far beyond what many people think of as small. For example, a petroleum refiner with 1,500 employees probably boasts sales of several million dollars each year. For the sake of simplicity, we will define a **small business** as one that is independently owned and operated and has relatively little influence over its environment.

The Impact of Small Business

Small business plays a major role in the U.S. economy. More than 99 percent of the nation's 16 million businesses are small. Their effects are felt in a number of areas, including financial performance, innovation, job creation, new-business formation, and contributions to big business. As described in "The Global View," small businesses are exerting an increasing influence in the international arena as well.[5]

Financial Performance   In sheer numbers alone, small business far outstrips big business. There is also evidence that suggests that small business outperforms big business financially. On average, for example, small manufacturers earn a higher return on owners' equity than do large manufacturers, for two main reasons. First, in many manufacturing industries, small business can respond more rapidly and at less cost than can big business to the quickening rate of change in products and services, processes and markets. Second, small business has become more attractive to talented, individualistic men and women.[6] In any event, small business has a positive impact on the nation's economic performance in terms of gross national product, growth rates, and other indicators.

Innovation   Entrepreneurs and small business play a major role in innovation. Small businesses or individuals working alone invented the personal computer, the transistor radio, the photocopying machine, the jet engine, and the instant photograph. Their ingenuity also gave us the pocket calculator, power steering, the automatic transmission, air conditioning, and even the nineteen-cent ballpoint pen. Clearly, we are all better off for the presence in our economy of millions of small businesses. Their resourcefulness and ingenuity have spawned new industries and contributed a great many innovative ideas and technological breakthroughs.[7] Alan McKim's business has achieved several innovative solutions to toxic waste disposal problems.

Ken Hakuta is a perfect example of an entrepreneur—someone who organizes, operates, and assumes the risk of a business venture. As Hakuta's three sons began to show more and more interest in Saturday morning television, Hakuta became alarmed at the violence and mayhem on most of the shows. So he formed his own program called "The Dr. Fad Show." Each episode features original inventions created by youngsters. The show recently achieved nationwide syndication and a product showcased in one episode has been licensed for mass production.

■ **small business** A business that is independently owned and operated and which has relatively little influence over its environment

TABLE 20.1

SBA Standards of Size for Selected Industries

Manufacturers	Fewer Employees Than
Petroleum refining	1,500
Electronic computers	1,000
Macaroni and spaghetti	500

Wholesalers	Fewer Employees Than
Sporting goods	500
Furniture	500
Paints and varnishes	500

Retailers	Annual Sales Less Than
Grocery stores	$13.5 million
Automobile agencies	11.5 million
Restaurants	10.0 million

Services	Annual Sales Less Than
Computer-related services	$12.5 million
Accounting services	4.0 million
Television repair	3.5 million

SOURCE: "U.S. Small Business Administration: Small Business Size Standards," *Federal Register*, Vol. 49, No. 28 (Washington, D.C.: U.S. Government Printing Office, February 9, 1984), pp. 5024–5048.

Job Creation   Small businesses create more new jobs than do larger businesses. One study suggested that small businesses may create as many as 66 percent of all new jobs in the United States each year.[8] In another study, the U.S. Department of Commerce found that small, young, high-technology businesses created new jobs at a much faster rate than did larger, older businesses. Such small businesses (especially those in chemistry and electronics) require employees with a high degree of scientific or engineering knowledge and thus generate additional demand for them. Clean Harbors, Inc., has created around 500 jobs in the New England area, and Reebok has created over 2,000 jobs in the last five years.

New-Business Formation   Another indicator of the importance of small business is the record number of businesses formed each year since 1960. New incorporations hit the 600,000 mark for the first time in 1983.[9] This figure is more than four times the total in 1960. Of course, some of the new corporations are mature businesses that were born as sole proprietorships or partnerships and have only recently incorporated. Nevertheless, many more small businesses are created each year than larger ones.

Contributions to Big Business   A final reason small businesses have such an enormous impact is their contributions to big business. General Motors, for example, buys from over 25,000 suppliers, most of them small businesses. Such businesses can create and deliver specialized products more efficiently than can larger businesses. Indeed, big businesses buy more of their inputs from small businesses than from other big businesses. Small businesses also play a key role in distributing and selling the products of larger businesses to consumers. Some of the reasons for these patterns are explored in the following section.

Major Areas of Small Business

Small businesses tend to do better in some industries than in others. Government statistics are confusing and classification systems contradictory; but regardless of the classification system used, small businesses tend to do well in service, retail, and wholesale businesses. They often do not perform well in manufacturing.

Wholesaling is a very popular area of small business in the United States. Jose Javier Calderon, shown on the far left of the photo, and his family have achieved considerable success in this area—and can even be considered an international business. The family buys close-out merchandise from discount stores and other retailers in El Paso. They then transport it across the border and sell it to small Mexican retailers for resale. Today, La Quemazon Wholesale is a thriving enterprise with a loyal following among Mexican retailers.

Service Businesses   Service organizations are perhaps the most common type of small business because they require a fairly small capital investment to get started. A certified accountant, for example, can go into business just by renting an office and hanging out a sign. Small businesses ranging from video rental shops to hair salons to auto repair shops have flourished in recent years.

Retail Businesses   Retail businesses are another popular area for small business. Small business is especially effective in the area of specialty retailing—retail establishments that cater to certain customer groups like golfers, college students, and people who do their own automobile repairs. Many large retail chains allow individual stores to be run by entrepreneurs who have signed franchise agreements.

Wholesale Businesses   Small businesses also dominate the wholesale industry. Wholesaling involves buying products from large manufacturers and reselling the products to retailers. Small businesses are effective in this area because they have the flexibility and can develop the personal working relationships necessary to coordinate large numbers of sellers and large numbers of buyers.

Manufacturing Businesses   Manufacturing is the one area where small businesses often perform more poorly than do larger businesses. Starting a manufacturing firm almost always requires a large initial investment in plant and equipment. Thus, few small businesses can afford to manufacture automobiles, refrigerators, or televisions. Still, in some

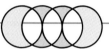

THE GLOBAL VIEW

THE INTERNATIONAL IMPACT OF SMALL BUSINESS

A company does not have to be big to be successful in the international marketplace. As of 1988, about 39,000 manufacturing firms in the United States were engaged in exporting their products. Those 39,000 firms represent only about 10 percent of the total manufacturers in the United States. Virtually all experts argue that the impetus for export sales has to come from small to mid-size manufacturing companies. Such companies must successfully enter the international market.

Bilco Tools Inc. of Houma, Louisiana, manufactures and sells custom-designed oil-field equipment. In 1983, Bilco sold about $2 million worth of those products but nevertheless thought it would have to go out of business because of the collapse of the U.S. Gulf Coast oil industry. In desperation, William E. Coyle, the firm's president, went on an around-the-world trip in search of new clients. In Abu Dhabi he discovered that the manager of a company there was a graduate of Louisiana State University and, building on that relationship, he made a sale.

Dorr-Oliver Inc. of Stamford, Connecticut, is a privately held company that has developed an international niche. It makes food-processing equipment and

gained entry to the Chinese market by repeatedly sending managers to China for months at a time and waiting for the market to develop. In 1987, Dorr-Oliver had sales of over $11 million in Asia, and over 30 percent of its total sales of about $150 million were from exports. Being patient is clearly in order for a firm interested in entering the Chinese market. Small shops proliferate and large orders are difficult to come by.

Doing business internationally presents some problems, of course. Just figuring out how to get started takes a lot of time and patience, and it may take four or five years to truly break into a foreign market. Trade barriers pose real obstacles, and a tangle of red tape may delay government permission to enter many foreign markets. Letters, brochures, advertisements, and so on must be translated into the local language or languages. Electrical equipment must meet local standards. The metric system must be used for all measurements and parts.

REFERENCES: "The Long Arm of Small Business," *Business Week*, February 29, 1988, pp. 63–66; Chris Arnold, "Small Firm Here an International Powerhouse: Atlanta Saw Up for Federal Exporters Award," *Atlanta Business Chronicle*, June 2, 1988, pp. 7A–8A; "Simplifying Global Trades," *Venture*, April 1988, p. 12; Rayna Skolnik, "Only the Brave Deserve the Fair," *Sales & Marketing Management*, June 1987, pp. 101–103.

---

instances small businesses have succeeded in manufacturing. Ron Canion and Compaq Computer, for example, have done quite well.[10]

Agriculture Agriculture is an area in transition. Small family farms were among the first small businesses, and until recently they were among the most successful. Economies of scale, high equipment prices, and increased competition from abroad, however, have forced many small farmers to sell their land. Giant agribusiness enterprises and corporate farms are gradually replacing them.

SMALL BUSINESS SUCCESSES AND FAILURES

Of all the new businesses started each year, many succeed but many also fail. In this section we discuss common reasons for small-business success and failure. They are listed in Table 20.2.

TABLE 20.2

Reasons for Small Business
Success and Failure

Reasons for success	1. Hard work, drive, and dedication
	2. Market demand for the products or services provided
	3. Managerial competence
	4. Luck
Reasons for failure	1. Managerial incompetence or inexperience
	2. Neglect
	3. Weak control systems
	4. Undercapitalization

Common Causes of Success

Many ingredients contribute to small-business success, but four of the most common ones are hard work, drive, and dedication on the part of the entrepreneur; market demand for the product or service being offered; managerial competence; and luck.[11]

Hard Work, Drive, and Dedication   A key ingredient in the success of any small business is hard work, drive, and dedication on the part of the entrepreneur. An individual must have a strong desire to work independently of others and be willing to put in long hours if she or he is to succeed.[12] Alan McKim, founder of Clean Harbors, clearly had such drive. In general, successful entrepreneurs tend to be reasonable risk-takers, self-confident, hardworking, goal setters, and innovators.[13]

Market Demand for Products or Services Provided   For any business to succeed, there must be sufficient demand for the product or service provided. If a college community of 50,000 citizens and 15,000 students has only one pizza parlor, there is probably sufficient demand for more. However, if there are already 15 pizza parlors in operation, a new one will have to serve especially good pizza or offer something unique if it is to succeed. Liz Claiborne's clothing business was successful because there was unmet demand for clothing for working women.

Managerial Competence   Regardless of the level of demand, it is necessary for the entrepreneur to possess basic managerial competence. He or she needs to understand how to select a location, what kinds of facilities are needed, how to acquire financing, and how to manage people. The manager must also understand how to manage growth, control costs, and make difficult choices and decisions. An entrepreneur who has a product for which there is tremendous demand might be able to survive for a while without managerial skills. Over time, however, and under normal circumstances, the manager who lacks basic competence is unlikely to succeed.

While hard work, market demand, and managerial competence are all necessary ingredients for small business success, a healthy dose of luck never hurts, either. Scott Wedge is chairman of E-mu Systems, a small American firm that makes electronic musical instruments. E-mu Systems was struggling until Michael Jackson chose one of its experimental synthesizers to use in his *Thriller* album. Because of the widespread exposure and popularity provided by the album, E-mu Systems achieved a measure of success that might have eluded them if Jackson hadn't heard about their products.

Luck   Some small businesses succeed because of pure luck. There was an element of luck in Alan McKim's success with Clean Harbors. He got into business just as the government committed $1.6 billion to help clean up toxic waste. Although he might have succeeded anyway, the extra revenue generated by the government's so-called Superfund no doubt contributed to his success.

Common Causes of Failure

Any number of things can contribute to organizational failure in a small business. Four most basic causes are managerial incompetence or inexperience, neglect, weak control systems, and undercapitalization.[14]

Managerial Incompetence or Inexperience   Just as competence contributes to success, so does incompetence contribute to failure. The entrepreneur may lack the basic skills or experience to recognize problems and to make hard decisions. She may have no experience in hiring and evaluating employees, dealing with bankers, or negotiating contracts. Or he may do a poor job of dealing with suppliers or customers. Regardless of one's talent, both working for a big company and working for someone else in a smaller company are quite different from running one's own business.

Neglect   Some entrepreneurs fail because they neglect some aspect of operations. They may get into business because of their impressions of its glamour and excitement. But as they experience the drudgery and sweat that go with entrepreneurship, they may be tempted to ignore key areas like inventory control and collections. Beyond operations, they may also ignore customer dissatisfaction, worker unrest, or financial difficulties—preferring to think that things will improve on their own. Over time, such neglect can lead to major problems.

Weak Control Systems   Small businesses can be ruined by weak control systems. If control systems do not provide adequate information on a timely basis, the entrepreneur may be in trouble before he or she knows it. For example, too many slow-paying customers can dramatically weaken a small business's cash flow. So, too, can excess inventory, employee theft, poor-quality products, plummeting sales, and insufficient profit margins. If the control system does not alert the entrepreneur to the problem, or alerts the entrepreneur too late, recovery may be difficult or impossible.

Undercapitalization   Another common cause of small-business failure is undercapitalization, having too few funds to survive start-up and growth. One rule of thumb is that an entrepreneur should have sufficient personal funds when starting out so as to be able to live with no business income for a year.[15] The entrepreneur needs to be able to maintain his or her personal life, cover all operating expenses, and still have an allowance for unexpected contingencies. An entrepreneur who is planning to pay next month's rent from a new business's profits may be courting disaster. An entrepreneur in College Station, Texas, recently invested $95,000 in opening a new Mexican food restaurant with plush facilities, top-of-the-line decor, and an extravagant office for himself. He closed the restaurant in less than a month because he lacked the funds to meet his payroll and pay his suppliers. If he had spent a little less on premium-quality carpet and had waited a few months before outfitting his office with oak paneling, he might have succeeded.

STARTING A SMALL BUSINESS

Whenever someone decides to start his or her own business, there are a number of critical issues to be addressed. Foremost are the needs for a well-conceived business plan and for decisions about ownership. Other important considerations involve the issues of franchising and whether to buy an existing business or start a new one.

Business Plan

business plan A document prepared by an entrepreneur in preparation for opening a new business

To bring their ideas for a product or service to fruition, entrepreneurs must do a thorough job of planning. At one time, it was possible to succeed in business simply through long hours and hard work. Although long hours and hard work may still be important, increasingly complex technology, markets, and other environmental factors necessitate paying attention to planning. A **business plan**, in this context, is a document prepared by an entrepreneur in preparation for opening a new business.[16]

The very act of preparing a business plan forces prospective entrepreneurs to crystallize their thinking about what they must do to launch their business successfully—from the moment they decide to go into business for themselves through the moment they open for business. In essence, the business plan forces them to develop their business on paper before investing time and money in it.

The idea of a business plan is not new. Big business has been engaged in planning for years. What is new is the growing use of specialized business plans by entrepreneurs, mostly because creditors and investors whom they approach for money demand such plans. These outside pressures are healthy because a business plan makes entrepreneurs aware of what it may take to succeed and because a business plan gives investors and creditors information on which to decide whether to help finance the small business.

What should a business plan cover? It should describe the match between the entrepreneur's abilities and the requirements for producing and marketing a particular product or service. It should define strategies for production and marketing, legal aspects and organization, and accounting and finance. In particular, it should answer three basic questions: (1) What does the entrepreneur want and what is he or she capable of doing? What are the entrepreneur's strengths? (2) What are the most workable ways of achieving the entrepreneur's goals? (3) What does the entrepreneur expect in the future?

Some idea of the complexity of planning a new business may be gleaned from the PERT diagram shown in Figure 20.2.[17] The diagram shows the key steps in planning to launch a new business. Notice that the development of a business plan consists of a set of specific activities having to do with such things as marketing research and marketing mix, location, and production. Of these activities, perhaps none is more pivotal than marketing research—the systematic and intensive study of all the facts, opinions, and judgments that bear on the successful marketing of a product or service. Clearly, the more entrepreneurs know about their markets, the greater are their chances of serving customers uniquely and at a profit. Often, being different is what it takes to be better than competitors in the marketplace.

Figure 20.2 also demonstrates the sequential nature of many of the decisions that must be made. For example, entrepreneurs cannot forecast sales revenues without first researching markets. In fact, the sales forecast is one of the most important elements in the business plan. Without such forecasts, it is all but impossible to estimate intelligently

FIGURE 20.2

A PERT Diagram Showing the Steps in Business Planning and How They Are Related

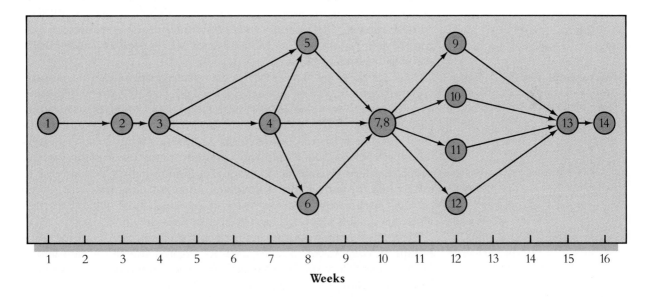

Weeks

1. Decide to go into business
2. Analyze yourself
3. Choose product or service
4. Research the market
5. Forecast sales revenues
6. Select site
7. Develop production plan
8. Develop marketing plan
9. Develop organizational plan
10. Develop legal plan
11. Develop insurance plan
12. Develop accounting plan
13. Develop financial plan
14. Write cover letter

SOURCE: Nicholas C. Siropolis, Small Business Management: A Guide to Entrepreneurship, 3rd ed. (Boston: Houghton Mifflin, 1986), p. 159. Copyright © 1986 by Houghton Mifflin Company.

the size of a plant, store, or office. Nor is it possible to determine how much inventory to carry or how many employees to hire.

Another important activity is financial planning, which translates all other activities into dollars. Generally, the financial plan is made up of a cash budget, an income statement, balance sheets, and a breakeven chart. The most important of these statements is the cash budget, because it tells entrepreneurs how much money they need before they open for business and how much money they need after they open for business.

Ownership and Financing

Entrepreneurs need to consider what form of ownership they want for their business and how the business is to be financed. There are a number of alternatives. Each alternative has strengths and weaknesses.[18]

Forms of Ownership   A popular form of legal ownership for many new businesses is the **sole proprietorship**. About 70 percent of American businesses use this form of ownership. The major advantages of a proprietorship are that the individual entrepreneur has total freedom over how he or she conducts the business; it's simple to start; start-up costs are low; and the proprietor's business profits are taxed as ordinary income. However, the proprietor has unlimited liability (his or her personal assets are at risk to cover business debts); it may be difficult to raise money; the business ends when the proprietor retires or dies; and there is no one else to rely on. Sears was started as a sole proprietorship by Richard Sears.

sole proprietorship The most popular form of legal ownership; refers to organizations that are owned by single individuals

Another form of ownership is the **partnership**. There are many varieties of partnerships, but in the basic kind two or more people agree to be partners in a business. The least popular form of ownership, partnerships are often used in accounting, legal, and architectural firms. They provide a larger pool of talent and money than do sole proprietorships, are easy to form, and offer the same tax benefits as sole proprietorships. However, they offer unlimited liability; they cease to exist when the partnership is dissolved; and conflict or tension between partners is common. Richard Sears added Alvah Roebuck as a partner when his business got too big for him to manage alone.

partnership A form of business ownership where two or more persons are joint owners of the business

Most large organizations use the **corporation** as their basis for ownership. A corporation is a legal entity created under the law and is independent of any single individual. A corporation can borrow money, enter into contracts, own property, sue, and be sued. Its owners are the people who buy its stock. On the plus side, the corporation is responsible for its own liabilities, so the owners have limited liability. There is continuity in the event of retirement or death. And corporations can often borrow money easily. However, there are higher start-up costs, more regulation, and double taxation (the corporation pays taxes on its profits, and then stockholders pay taxes on their dividends). Still, the corporation is the preferred form of ownership for most large

corporation A legal entity created under the law; independent of any single individual

businesses. As Sears, Roebuck, and Company grew into a big business, its owners chose to incorporate.

There are also a few special forms of ownership that some entrepreneurs adopt. Master limited partnerships and S-corporations are new forms of ownership that provide many of the advantages of corporations but without double taxation. Cooperatives may be used when many small entrepreneurs band together to conduct businesses on a unified basis. Ocean Spray Cranberry, for example, is a cooperative that comprises 700 cranberry growers and 100 citrus growers.

Sources of Financing   An important issue confronting all entrepreneurs is where to get the money to open and operate the business. As we noted earlier, the entrepreneur should not rely too heavily on anticipated profits. Personal resources (savings and money borrowed from friends or family) are the most common source. Personal resources are often the most important source because they underscore and reinforce the entrepreneur's personal commitment to the venture. Many entrepreneurs take advantage of various lending programs and assistance provided by lending institutions and government agencies.[19] Government programs are especially interested in helping women and minority entrepreneurs.[20] Another common source of funds is venture capitalists. A **venture capitalist** is someone who actively seeks to invest in new businesses in return for a share of ownership or profits. The advantage of this approach is access to a large resource base with fewer restrictions than might be imposed by the government or a bank. The entrepreneur, however, must give up a share of the profits or share ownership.[21]

venture capitalist   Someone who actively seeks to invest in new businesses in return for a share of the ownership and/or profits

Approaches to Starting a Business

Another set of questions to address when planning a business is whether to buy an existing business or start a new one. A related question is whether to seek a franchising agreement or remain independent.

Buying an Existing Business   Buying an existing business offers a clear set of advantages. The new entrepreneur can look at historical records for the business and see exactly how much revenue and profit has been generated, the kind of cash flow to expect, and so forth. The entrepreneur also gets existing supplier, distributor, and customer networks and has to do less guesswork about what to expect. On the negative side, the entrepreneur inherits whatever problems the business may already have and may be forced to accept contractual agreements prepared by others.

Starting a New Business   Starting a new business from scratch allows the entrepreneur to avoid the weaknesses or shortcomings of an existing business. A great deal of excitement is often associated with opening a new enterprise. The entrepreneur has the opportunity to make his or her mark and can choose suppliers, bankers, lawyers, and employees

One popular approach to starting a business is to buy a business that is already in operation. Cynthia Folino, shown here, went to work a few years ago for Soundview, a New England company that provides busy executives with summaries of popular business books. Folino soon developed an urge to run her own business, so she bought Soundview. Today, Soundview's newsletter reaches 25,000 subscribers and generates revenues of over $2 million each year.

without worrying about existing agreements or contractual arrangements. On the negative side, there is more uncertainty involved in starting a new business than in taking over an existing one. The entrepreneur will have less information about projected revenues and cash flow, will have to build a customer base from zero, and may be forced to accept unfavorable credit terms from suppliers. It is also harder for a new business to borrow money because the bank has little or no experience with it.

Franchising   An alternative that is increasingly pursued today is a franchising agreement. The entrepreneur pays a parent company (the franchiser) a flat fee or a share of the income from the business. In return, the entrepreneur (the franchisee) gets to use the company's trademarks, products, formulas, and business plan. **Franchising** may reduce the entrepreneur's risks because parent companies often provide advice and assistance. They also provide proven methods, training, financial support, and an established identity and image. Few McDonald's franchises fail.

franchising   A way to start or expand a business in which an entrepreneur pays a parent company a fee and/or a share of the income to use the name and some resources of that parent company

On the negative side, franchises may cost a lot of money. A McDonald's franchise costs several hundred thousand dollars. The franchisee is often restricted in what she or he can do. A McDonald's franchisee cannot change the formula for a milkshake or alter the preparation of Big Macs. Some franchise agreements are difficult to terminate.

Despite the drawbacks, franchising is growing by leaps and bounds. It presently accounts for one-third of the United States's retail sales, and that figure is expected to climb to one-half by the end of this

MANAGEMENT IN PRACTICE

FANTASTIC SUCCESS FOR FANTASTIC SAM'S

Fantastic Sam's was founded by Sam M. Ross in Memphis, Tennessee, in 1974. The organization began selling hair-cutting and hair salon franchises and, just two years later, subfranchises and quickly became one of the fastest-growing franchise chains in the country. In fact, it was the fifth fastest-growing franchise chain in the United States as of 1986. In 1987, because of difficulties in finding qualified, licensed cosmetologists to operate its rapidly growing numbers of franchises, Fantastic Sam's parent organization, SMR Enterprises, expanded its operations to include cosmetology schools. It opened the first one in Memphis in April 1987 and planned soon to be operating over 100 of them nationwide.

By mid-1988, Fantastic Sam's had nearly 1,300 units and was still growing. One report suggested that Sam Ross hoped to add 500 units each year for five years to get the chain to what he felt was an optimum size. The units are located in many states in the United States, although primarily in the Sunbelt and the Midwest. In addition, Fantastic Sam's has units in Australia, Bahrain, Canada, Europe, and Japan. There are numerous regional franchisees who can, in turn, sell local franchises. The Philadelphia region includes eastern Pennsylvania, southern New Jersey, Delaware, and part of Maryland. The regional office includes a central warehouse for hair-care products used in the individual, local salons.

A franchisee pays a fee to the franchiser in order to use the chain's name and offer its services. In 1987, the initial franchise fee paid to Fantastic Sam's was $20,000, and the local entrepreneur also needed between $10,000 and $75,000 of working capital depending upon the region, city, and specific site at which the unit was to be located. In addition, Fantastic Sam's charges a weekly fee rather than royalties based on sales. In 1987, the fee was $200 per week. By 1988, the licensing fee had risen to $25,000, and $30,000 worth of initial supplies also had to be purchased. At Fantastic Sam's, franchise fees are sufficiently high that during periods of rapid expansion, the parent organization derives more revenues from franchise fees than from the weekly operating fees.

REFERENCES: "Not So Fantastic Sam," *Venture*, December 1988, p. 40; "Federal Express Faces Challenges to Its Grip on Overnight Delivery," *The Wall Street Journal*, January 8, 1988, pp. 1, 8; "Fantastic Sam's Sees 50 More Stores in N.E.," *Capital District Business Review* (Albany, New York), May 4, 1987, p. 6; Paula Wade, "Fantastic Sam's Set Training Goal," *Commercial Appeal* (Memphis, Tennessee), February 14, 1987, p. B12.

century.[22] "Management in Practice" describes the success story of one franchising organization, Fantastic Sam's.

MANAGING THE SMALL BUSINESS

Until just a few years ago, the conventional wisdom among managers and researchers was that management concepts and approaches were equally applicable to business regardless of size. People believed that managing a small business was just like managing a larger one, but on a smaller scale. Now, however, there is general agreement that an entrepreneur managing a small business faces a different set of circumstances altogether, circumstances that dictate a different approach to management. Thus, planning, organizing, leading, and controlling must be approached from a special perspective when they are to be applied to a small business.

Planning in the Small Business

Planning plays a pivotal part in how well an entrepreneur does, yet perhaps no other function is ignored more than planning. Many entrepreneurs view planning as a function best done only by giant corporations such as General Motors or IBM.[23] One reason for this attitude is that entrepreneurs tend to have more technical than analytical, conceptual, or diagnostic skills. Manufacturing requires technical skills, as do selling and purchasing. Planning, however, requires conceptual, analytical, and diagnostic skills that tend to intimidate entrepreneurs. Planning is not a tangible activity, so they tend to ignore it. In doing so, they often undermine the potential success of their venture before even starting the business. Our earlier discussion of the business plan generally addresses issues to be confronted before start-up. Thus, we confine our discussion here to planning needs for the small business after start-up.

The basic planning context for the typical small business is much simpler than that faced by a larger firm. Its environment is usually much simpler. It usually has fewer regulators to contend with; its task environment is more easily identified; and its planning horizon is somewhat shorter. Moreover, its set of tactical, action, and contingency plans is likely to be smaller and more easily managed. Of course, this relative simplicity should not be overstated. For example, although a large business has a more complex planning task, it also has many more people involved in planning. The entrepreneur frequently does all planning alone, so it may be just as demanding. Moreover, the entrepreneur may be able to tolerate fewer errors in forecasts and plans than can managers employed by large organizations.

An important planning issue for the entrepreneur is the life cycles through which the organization is likely to pass. Here we apply the concept specifically to small business. Some entrepreneurs contribute to their own failure by not continuing to plan their progress—by assuming that planning takes place only before, and not after, the birth of the business. The failure to continue planning is often the reason so many small businesses grow erratically, stand still, or go under.

Many small businesses exhibit a general pattern of growth that passes through a number of stages.[24] In the acceptance stage, entrepreneurs generally struggle to break even. They are usually close enough to their business at this stage that they can spot obstacles and act quickly to remove them. For example, without some contracts in hand, an entrepreneur who leases factory space to make vinegar expects the first few months to be lean. It will probably take some time to "debug" the vinegar-making equipment and ensure it makes vinegar that meets uniformly the quality standards of prospective customers; to make vinegar with negligible waste and at low cost; and to convince prospective customers, especially food chains, to buy the vinegar, generally on a trial basis. Meanwhile, with sales limping along, the cash drain becomes severe as bills and wages must be paid. There is little relief until the marketplace begins to accept the vinegar. Then, and only then, do cash inflows begin to match and finally overtake cash outflows—perhaps months after start-up.

Next follows the breakthrough stage. Until now, the rate of growth has been slow—so slow that it often passes unnoticed. But in the breakthrough stage, growth is so fast that entrepreneurs often fail to keep up with it. Caught unprepared, they often blunder. Sales revenues continue to spiral upward as problems begin to surface that cry out for attention. For example, problems may arise with cash flow (Will we have the necessary cash when it comes time to pay our bills?), production (Are we keeping costs down in ways that are consistent with making a high-quality product?), quality (Are we making good on our guarantee of uniformly high quality?), and delivery (Are we delivering promptly on all customer orders?). At the same time, competition may become more severe.

In the face of all these pressures, entrepreneurs often react rather than respond. They apply ill-conceived solutions to problems. For example, if sales begin to level off or slip, they may add specialists such as an accountant, a quality-control analyst, or a customer services representative to relieve the problem. As a result, costs go up momentarily, squeezing profits further. Meanwhile, entrepreneurs try to regain the flexibility they lost shortly after breakthrough, and the cycle of growth begins to repeat itself as they pass through the maturity stage.

The best way to head off the problems of growth is to continue updating the business plan. For example, continuing to update the financial plan can equip entrepreneurs to head off cash-flow problems. Here the cash budget is especially useful, because it will alert them to future cash shortages.[25]

Organizing in the Small Business

Given the high level of environmental uncertainty that exists in business today, few entrepreneurs have the skills needed to succeed on their own. Until World War II, they worked in a world of few regulations, few taxes, few big competitors, few records, and no computers; but simplicity has since given way to complexity. Major corporations such as AT&T and Du Pont employ thousands of specialists. Du Pont, for example, has more than 600 marketing researchers, most of whom have at least a master's degree. Such expert help is beyond the reach of most entrepreneurs, so they often have no choice but to stand alone.

Entrepreneurs clearly need help to survive and grow. As a starting point, they must identify the kinds of help they need. To do so, they need to plan their organization before they launch their business, and they need to continue updating their plan as the business grows. Yet despite the need for it, organizing is ignored by many (if not most) entrepreneurs.[26]

Defining Skill Needs   With limited resources, entrepreneurs often have no recourse but to define their organization in terms of skills rather

Organizing is a critical mangerial function in a small business. Ballard Medical is a small company that concentrates on making and selling hospital products. Dale Ballard, the company's owner and founder has organized his business around the need to gather information and stay close to customers. In particular, Ballard trains his sales representatives not only to market his products but also to stay closely attuned to other customer needs. The sales representative shown here is demonstrating a new product to members of a hospital staff. At the same time, he pays careful attention to what they say about other things they need.

than in terms of persons. Usually they cannot afford to hire a full-time accountant or a full-time marketing researcher. Even so, they must plan their organization as though they could afford such specialists. Only by going through such a procedure can they assure themselves that needed skills have not been overlooked.

Suppose that a chemical engineer has just invented a new process to make Fiberglass-reinforced plastic for sports cars like the Corvette. This process is faster and cheaper than the present one. Ready to exploit his invention, the chemical engineer decides to go into business for himself. To start, he must define the specific skills needed to make his business a reality. A good place to begin is with a business plan. Following the plan outline shown in Figure 20.2, he might analyze the skills needed for the business by means of a skill needs assessment, as shown in Table 20.3. Notice in the table that the engineer himself is best qualified to complete six of the steps shown. For the rest, he recognizes that he must rely on outside experts. Such help may come from a variety of sources. As shown in Figure 20.3, entrepreneurs like the chemical engineer need outside professional help from accountants, bankers, lawyers, and insurance agents. We will say more later about the outside management help that is available.

Job Descriptions   The manager also needs to establish job descriptions (described in Chapter 10) that spell out who does what, who has what authority, and who reports to whom. Job descriptions spare entrepreneurs the problems associated with people not knowing exactly what their job involves, whom they report to, and so on.

Step Number	Description of Step	Skill Needed	Expert Best Suited to Meet Need	
			Entrepreneur	Other
1	Decide to go into business	Knowledge of self	√	
2	Analyze yourself		√	
3	Pick product or service		√	
4	Research the market	Knowledge of marketing research		Marketing researcher
5	Forecast sales revenues			Marketing researcher
6	Select site			Marketing researcher
7	Develop production plan	Knowledge of chemical engineering	√	
8	Develop marketing plan	Knowledge of marketing		Advertising account executive
9	Develop organizational plan	Knowledge of skill needs	√	
10	Develop legal plan	Knowledge of law		Lawyer
11	Develop insurance plan	Knowledge of insurance		Insurance agent
12	Develop accounting plan	Knowledge of accounting		Accountant
13	Develop financial plan	Knowledge of finance		Loan officer
14	Write cover letter	Knowledge of venture	√	

SOURCE: Nicholas C. Siropolis, *Small Business Management: A Guide to Entrepreneurship*, 3rd ed. (Boston: Houghton Mifflin, 1986), p. 284. Copyright © 1986 by Houghton Mifflin Company. Used with permission.

TABLE 20.3

Identifying Skill Needs

Organization Charts Many large organizations find themselves too large and complex to adequately chart all their positions and interrelationships. Such a chart can be very useful for a small business. The small-business manager should recognize, however, that such charts have their limitations. Although they symbolize how an entrepreneur plans to get out the work, they often impress more than they express. Few small businesses run precisely the way their organization charts indicate. In a growing business, a chart may soon become outdated. Or unpredictable events may change the course of an entrepreneur's plans. For these reasons and others, organization charts should be evaluated and revised at least once a year.

Perhaps the chief value of an organization chart is that the very act of putting one together forces entrepreneurs to crystallize their thinking about what work must be done to make the business profitable and how the work should be done. Without such forethought, organization charts may have little value. Organization charts are also limited in that they cannot show how all the jobs within a small business are related. To try to do so would result in a chart with solid and broken lines

FIGURE 20.3

Types of Help Available to
Entrepreneurs

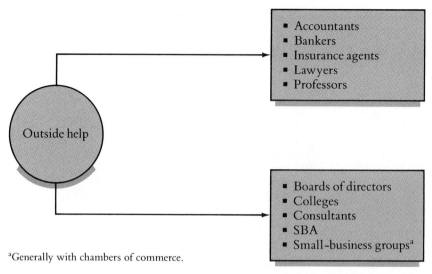

ªGenerally with chambers of commerce.

SOURCE: Nicholas C. Siropolis, Small Business Management: A Guide to Entrepreneurship,
3rd ed. (Boston: Houghton Mifflin, 1986), p. 290. Copyright © 1986 by Houghton Mifflin
Company. Used with permission.

crisscrossing the page in undecipherable confusion. A good organization
chart is a simple one that highlights only the jobs and lines of authority
that are crucial to the goals of the small business. An organization chart
must communicate if it is to be effective.

Management Help   Another aspect of organizing in the small business
is the identification of sources of assistance. Since the 1950s, the idea
that small businesses need management assistance has become increasingly widespread. Table 20.4 lists the many sources of management
help now offered at little or no cost to entrepreneurs, either before or
after they go into business for themselves. Because of the depth of
management sophistication needed to launch a high-technology business such as microcomputer manufacture, different services are available
to entrepreneurs who go into a high-technology business and to those
who go into a low-technology business.

Table 20.4 covers not only federal help but also help from such
sources as community colleges and universities, chambers of commerce,
and organizations made up of small businesses. Heading the list is the
SBA. Since it was founded in 1953, the SBA has helped hundreds of
thousands of small businesses. Most entrepreneurs have the mistaken
view that all the SBA does is lend money or guarantee repayment of
loans made by commercial banks. Even more important are the SBA's
efforts to help entrepreneurs manage better. Any entrepreneur can spend
money. The SBA's programs help them to spend wisely.

The SBA offers entrepreneurs four major management assistance
programs: SCORE (Service Corps of Retired Executives), ACE (Active
Corps of Executives), SBI (Small Business Institute), and SBDC (Small

Management Help Offered by	Where Available	Before They Go into a Business Whose Technology Is		After They Go into a Business Whose Technology Is	
		High	Low	High	Low
U.S. Small Business Administration Counseling by:					
Staff	N				✓
Service Corps of Retired Executives	N				✓
Active Corps of Executives	N				✓
Small Business Institute	N			✓	✓
Small Business Development Center	S	✓	✓	✓	✓
Prebusiness workshops	N		✓		
Nonaccredited courses and seminars	N				✓
Publications	N		✓		✓
U.S. Department of Commerce					
Seminars and workshops	N			✓	✓
Publications	N	✓	✓	✓	✓
Other federal agencies (example: IRS[a])					
Seminars and workshops	N				✓
Publications	N				✓
State, county, and local governments					
Counseling	S				✓
Seminars and workshops	S				✓
Publications	S				✓
Local development corporations and the like					
Counseling	N				✓
Seminars and workshops	N				✓

[a]U.S. Internal Revenue Service.
N = nationally; S = some parts of nation.

SOURCE: Nicholas C. Siropolis, *Small Business Management: A Guide to Entrepreneurship*, 3rd ed. (Boston: Houghton Mifflin, 1986), p. 296. Copyright © 1986 by Houghton Mifflin Company. Used with permission.

TABLE 20.4

Sources of Help for Entrepreneurs

Business Development Center). All four programs offer management help at no charge to the entrepreneur. Under the SCORE program, the SBA tries to match the expert to the need. If an entrepreneur needs a marketing plan but does not know how to put one together, the SBA pulls from its list of SCORE counselors someone with marketing knowledge and experience to help. The SBI program taps the talents available at colleges and universities. This program involves not only professors of business administration but also students working for advanced degrees. Under a professor's guidance, such students work with entrepreneurs to help solve their management problems.

Management Help Offered by	Where Available	Before They Go into a Business Whose Technology Is		After They Go into a Business Whose Technology Is	
		High	Low	High	Low
Universities					
Accredited courses	S	✓	✓	✓	✓
Nonaccredited courses and seminars	S				✓
Publications	S	✓	✓	✓	✓
Counseling	S				
Community colleges					
Accredited courses	S				✓
Nonaccredited courses and seminars	N				✓
Counseling	S				✓
Small-business groups (example: NFIB[b])					
Seminars and workshops	S				✓
Counseling	S				✓
Publications	N				✓
Large corporations (example: Bank of America)					
Publications	N		✓		✓
Counseling	S				✓
Trade associations					
Publications	N			✓	✓
Seminars and workshops	N			✓	✓

[b]National Federation of Independent Business.

TABLE 20.4

Sources of Help for Entrepreneurs *(continued)*

Leading in the Small Business

Entrepreneurs must provide effective leadership if they are to succeed. Their goal should be to help employees satisfy their own personal goals while at the same time performing organizational responsibilities effectively. Managers can do several things along these lines. First, entrepreneurs must want to help their employees become achievers. Some do not, holding fast to the idea that employees do not care about deriving satisfaction from their jobs. This attitude can cause such problems as absenteeism and high turnover, shoddy workmanship, and a decline in employees' motivation to work.

Second, just as coaches must be close to their players to be effective as leaders, so must entrepreneurs be close to their employees. Top-flight coaches generally have teams that win consistently, mostly because the coaches know their jobs and have a knack for communicating that knowledge to players. Players see their assignments clearly because the coach helps them understand what is expected of them. They know how to carry out their assignments because the coach has meticulously laid out the game plan and the plays to use against the competition. They carry out their assignments with precision because the coach has created an atmosphere of fairness, confidence, and camaraderie.

Creating such a work atmosphere is difficult. No two players—or employees—are exactly alike. What appeals to one may repel another. Because all employees are unique and complex, entrepreneurs must understand their needs in order to help them do their best.

Third, entrepreneurs, as leaders, can help employees achieve status and gain a positive opinion of themselves and their jobs. They may do so by sharing decision-making responsibilities with employees, giving employees greater responsibility as soon as they are ready for it, taking employees' ideas and suggestions to heart, and judging employees rigorously on merit and rewarding them accordingly.

Entrepreneurs who follow these suggestions are more likely to succeed than those who do not. By building up employees' self-image and improving their status, entrepreneurs are likely to grow as leaders themselves. Of all the traits that entrepreneurs must possess if they are to be effective leaders, perhaps none is so vital as the willingness to pursue excellence day in and day out. The entrepreneur must set the tone that motivates employees to excel. As noted by the famed football coach Vince Lombardi, "You don't try to win some of the time. You don't try to do things right some of the time. You do them right all of the time."[27]

Excellence usually emerges in the context of high employer expectations. Entrepreneurs who expect excellence from employees often receive it. Only highly motivated employees are likely to make and sell superior products that cause customers to develop loyalty to the business. Entrepreneurs generally want their employees to be loyal to the business, too. But some believe their employees should be blindly loyal to them. They expect employees to stick by them through good times and bad, regardless of how they treat their employees. Such unthinking loyalty means working up to one's capabilities and doing the best one can in the pursuit of excellence. In essence, true loyalty is loyalty to the job, not to the entrepreneur.

Controlling in the Small Business

Discussion of the control function brings us full circle. Without control, the other three managerial functions—planning, organizing, and leading—lose meaning, for only by practicing control can entrepreneurs tell how effective the other three functions are. It is never enough just to set goals and then organize and lead to meet those goals. Entrepreneurs must measure their progress at frequent intervals and make adjustments based on those measurements. To do that, they need information that tells them whether their goals are being met.

Despite its importance, control tends to be ignored by many entrepreneurs. One reason may be their discomfort with numbers, and many may believe that control is a function practiced only by big business. With this attitude, it is hardly surprising that so many entrepreneurs find themselves in trouble from the start. They fail to see that control is simply the process by which they may assure themselves that their actions, as well as those of their employees, conform to plans and policies.

Especially vital is accounting information, which may be useful in several ways. As a means of communication, it helps to inform employees of the actions that the entrepreneur wishes them to take. As a means of motivation, it helps to motivate employees in such a way that they will do what the entrepreneur wants them to do. As a means of getting attention, it signals the existence of problems that require investigation and possibly action. As a means of checking up, it helps the entrepreneur to assess how well employees are doing their jobs. Such an appraisal of performance can lead to salary increases, promotion, reassignment, or corrective action of various kinds.

The key element of the control process is the information that allows entrepreneurs to compare actual performance with planned performance. This information allows them to measure not only their performance but also the propriety of their goals and actions and, if need be, to adjust them. To illustrate the importance of control to the small business, consider the example of one small contracting firm. Elling Brothers Mechanical Contractors specializes in the design and installation of piping systems. After moving into the installation of custom and made-to-order systems, the company realized that tighter control was needed. On one project alone, Elling lost $250,000 on small cost overruns that escalated and snowballed over the course of a fifteen-month job. Following a set of guidelines developed by a consultant, Elling implemented a new accounting control system that saved the company from going under.[28]

Budgeting   Budgeting is perhaps the most vital control tool for a small business. The budget translates operating plans into dollar terms or other quantitative measures. To see how the budget helps entrepreneurs control their operations, consider the following extended example. An Ohio Buick dealer, Georgia Qua, expresses her new car sales in units, as shown in Table 20.5. The unit budget is used by her sales manager to control the performance of salespeople. Units and not dollars have real meaning to sales representatives; but at the sales manager's level, dollars assume importance as a control. To meet a unit goal of 2,000 new-car sales a year, the sales manager might overreact and tell his salespeople to sell at a discount or accept trade-ins, which would erode profit margins. To avoid that problem, Qua prepares another budget, one that translates units into dollars. This budget is shown in Table 20.6 But the control system is still incomplete, because the sales manager may now overspend in his efforts to reach his unit goal of 2,000 new-car sales a year. So Qua prepares a third budget, one that deals with selling expenses. This budget is shown in Table 20.7. Armed with

TABLE 20.5

New-Car Sales Budget
(in Units)

Model	First	Second	Third	Fourth	Total
			Quarter		
Small	200	300	300	200	1,000
Medium	100	150	150	100	500
Large	100	150	150	100	500
	400	600	600	400	2,000

SOURCE: Nicholas C. Siropolis, *Small Business Management: A Guide to Entrepreneurship*, 3rd ed. (Boston: Houghton Mifflin, 1986), p. 357. Copyright © 1986 by Houghton Mifflin Company. Used with permission.

these three budgets, Qua is prepared to control the performance of her new-car sales department. By providing the sales manager and his salespeople with the information they need to make sound decisions, these budgets also encourage them to do their best. These budgets enable Qua to evaluate the performance of the sales manager, and they enable the sales manager to evaluate the performance of his sales force.

Productivity   Many small businesses have begun to turn to automation and robotics to boost output per employee, especially in manufacturing. A small Connecticut die-casting plant, for example, installed seven robots and achieved a 30 percent increase in productivity.[29] Of course, given the cost of robots, now about $50,000 each, entrepreneurs should be sure of what they are doing before investing heavily in automation. But a small business that, by whatever means, achieves a reasonable level of productivity increases its chances of surviving the early, critical years and building a pattern of long-term growth.

TABLE 20.6

New-Car Sales Budget
(Net of Trade-in)

Model	First	Second	Third	Fourth	Total
			Quarter		
Small	$1,200,000	$1,800,000	$1,800,000	$1,200,000	$ 6,000,000
Medium	900,000	1,350,000	1,350,000	900,000	4,500,000
Large	1,500,000	2,250,000	2,250,000	1,500,000	7,500,000
	$3,600,000	$5,400,000	$5,400,000	$3,600,000	$18,000,000

SOURCE: Nicholas C. Siropolis, *Small Business Management: A Guide to Entrepreneurship*, 3rd ed. (Boston: Houghton Mifflin, 1986), p. 357. Copyright © 1986 by Houghton Mifflin Company. Used with permission.

Model	Quarter				
	First	Second	Third	Fourth	Total
Salaries	$300,000	$300,000	$300,000	$300,000	$1,200,000
Commissions	150,000	225,000	225,000	150,000	750,000
Advertising	30,000	60,000	90,000	60,000	240,000
Telephone	1,500	1,500	1,500	1,500	6,000
Total	$481,500	$586,500	$616,500	$511,500	$2,196,000

SOURCE: Nicholas C. Siropolis, *Small Business Management: A Guide to Entrepreneurship*, 3rd ed. (Boston: Houghton Mifflin, 1986), p. 357. Copyright © 1986 by Houghton Mifflin Company. Used with permission.

TABLE 20.7

New-Car Selling Expense Budget

ENTREPRENEURSHIP IN LARGE BUSINESSES

Strictly speaking, entrepreneurship requires the entrepreneur to run the business, but in recent years there has been a keen interest in injecting an entrepreneurial spirit into large organizations.[30] Managers have come to realize that they can't sit back and rest on their laurels. If they do, their organization becomes lethargic and susceptible to attack by competitors or takeover artists. In Enhancement Module 5 at the end of Part 3, we described the concept of the intrapreneur—someone who develops an idea within the context of a large organization. The roles of intrapreneur and entrepreneur are similar. The biggest substantive difference is that the intrapreneur works within a broader context and the entrepreneur assumes more personal risk.

Organizations often go to great lengths in their attempts to maintain an entrepreneurial spirit as they grow. For example, Toys 'R' Us has become a huge business, but the company views each store as an independent small business beneath a corporate umbrella. Store managers are held personally responsible for the performance of their stores, but they also receive large rewards if they perform well. The goal is to create a sense of hundreds of small businesses rather than one big one.[31] More and more large businesses are recognizing the value of this model. Thus, entrepreneurial zeal and spirit represent an important contribution made by small business to the nation's economy in general and to large business in particular.

SUMMARY OF KEY POINTS

Entrepreneurship is the process of organizing, operating, and assuming the risk of a business venture. An entrepreneur is someone who engages in entrepreneurship. A new enterprise established by an entrepreneur can grow rapidly, remain stable, or decline.

While entrepreneurship is most often associated with small business, it also has a place in larger businesses. Ron Shaich is president of Au Bon Pain, a Boston-based chain of around 40 bakery cafes. Until recently, the entire operation was plagued by high turnover and poor service. Shaich decided that it was because the company treated its store managers just like its other hourly employees. So Shaich revamped Au Bon Pain's compensation and reward system to make each store manager an independent entrepreneur. Managers like Gary Aronson, shown here, can run their stores any way they want and they get to keep a larger percent of the profits. The results? Dramatic increases in per-store sales and profits, lower turnover, and higher quality service across the board.

A small business is one that is independently owned and operated and has relatively little influence over its environment. Small businesses are important because of their financial performance, innovation, job creation, new-business formation levels, and contributions to big business. Many small businesses are present in the service, retailing, and wholesaling sectors; there are fewer of them in manufacturing.

Four common determinants of small-business success are hard work, drive, and dedication on the part of the entrepreneur; market demand for the product or service being offered; managerial competence; and luck. Four basic causes of failure are managerial incompetence or inexperience, neglect, weak control systems, and undercapitalization.

When starting a new business, the entrepreneur must consider a number of issues, including the need for a well-conceived business plan and decisions regarding ownership. Other important considerations involve the issues of franchising and whether to buy an existing business or start a new one. A business plan is a document prepared by a entrepreneur in preparation for opening a new business.

Entrepreneurs must plan, organize, lead, and control just like their counterparts in larger businesses. However, there are unique aspects of each managerial function relevant more to small businesses than to larger ones.

DISCUSSION QUESTIONS

Questions for Review

1. What is a small business? Why do you think definitions vary so much from agency to agency? With which definition do you agree?

2. Why has there been a boom in the creation of small businesses in recent years?
3. List some reason for the failure of small businesses. How would you sum up these reasons into one catch-all reason?
4. What is an entrepreneur? What is entrepreneurship? How do they differ?

Questions for Analysis

5. Managing a small company is different from managing a large corporation. What are some of the major differences? Can you think of any not mentioned in the text?
6. The U.S. Department of Commerce and U.S. Office of Management and Budget have stated that major inventions are just as likely to be developed in small businesses as in large companies with complete research and development divisions. Why do you think this is so?
7. A friend of yours with no college background has started a small business and has decided to take some courses in order to gain a better background in business. What courses would you recommend to your friend? Why?

Questions for Application

8. Locate and interview the owner of a small business who is also the founder of the business. Why did the interviewee establish the company? What big problems did he or she face in getting it started? What current problems is he or she facing? Would the interviewee do it again?
9. Get together with two other members of your class and try to come up with an idea for a new company with the three of you as executives. How would you go about establishing the company? How would it be organized? Who will have what responsibility? What would be your business strategy? Do you think that you could get the business to succeed? Why or why not?
10. Go to the library and locate material on three different entrepreneurs. In what ways are they similar and different? Why are they similar? Why are they different?

NOTES

1. "The Big Haul in Toxic Waste," *Newsweek*, October 3, 1988, pp. 38–39.
2. Nicholas C. Siropolis, *Small Business Management: A Guide to Entrepreneurship*, 3rd ed. (Boston: Houghton Mifflin, 1986).
3. Stuart Gannes, "America's Fastest-growing Companies," *Fortune*, May 23, 1988, pp. 28–40.
4. Murray B. Low and Ian C. MacMillan, "Entrepreneurship: Past Research and Future Challenges," *Journal of Management*, June 1988, pp. 139–159;

Barbara Bird, "Implementing Entrepreneurial Ideas: The Case for Intention," *Academy of Management Review*, July 1988, pp. 442–453.

5. Christopher Knowlton, "The New Export Entrepreneurs," *Fortune*, June 6, 1988, pp. 87–102; and "Venturing Abroad," *The Wall Street Journal*, February 24, 1989, p. R30.

6. Siropolis, *Small Business Management*.

7. "Big vs. Small," *Time*, September 5, 1988, pp. 48–50.

8. David L. Birch, *The Job Generation Process* (Cambridge, Mass.: MIT Program on Neighborhood and Regional Change, 1979), p. 8.

9. "New Incorporations," *The Wall Street Journal*, November 19, 1984, p. 1.

10. Gannes, "America's Fastest-growing Companies."

11. Arnold C. Cooper and William C. Dunkelberg, "Entrepreneurship and Paths to Business Ownership," *Strategic Management Journal*, Vol. 7, 1986, pp. 53–68.

12. Jeremy Main, "Breaking Out of the Company," *Fortune*, May 25, 1987, pp. 82–88.

13. Siropolis, *Small Business Management*.

14. "Warning Flags Up," *The Wall Street Journal*, May 15, 1987, p. 10D–11D; and "Crisis Consultant," *The Wall Street Journal*, February 24, 1989, p. R32.

15. Siropolis, *Small Business Management*.

16. Siropolis, *Small Business Management*.

17. Siropolis, *Small Business Management*.

18. Richard M. Hodgetts and Donald F. Kuratko, *Effective Small Business Management*, 3rd ed. (Chicago: Harcourt Brace Jovanovich, 1989).

19. "Persistence Pays in Search for Funds," *USA Today*, May 11, 1987, p. 3E. See also "Neighborhood Financing," *The Wall Street Journal*, February 24, 1989, pp. R13–R14.

20. "SBA Program's Toughened Rules Upset Minority Firms," *The Wall Street Journal*, January 5, 1989, p. B2.

21. Alan Deutschman, "A Case of Too Much Money," *Fortune*, November 7, 1988, pp. 95–104.

22. Faye Rice, "How to Succeed at Cloning a Small Business," *Fortune*, October 28, 1985, pp. 60–66; "Franchising Tries to Divvy Up Risk," *USA Today*, May 11, 1987, p. 5E.

23. Siropolis, *Small Business Management*.

24. Siropolis, *Small Business Management*.

25. "Small Businesses Find Electronic Banking Can Be a Useful Tool in Managing Money," *The Wall Street Journal*, July 22, 1986, p. 31.

26. Siropolis, *Small Business Management*.

27. From a film produced by the U.S. Small Business Administration, *The Habit of Winning*, 1972.

28. Matthew Berke, "Elling Bros. Got Costs Under Control," *Inc.*, January 1982, pp. 45–50.

29. Craig R. Waters, "There's a Robot in Your Future," *Inc.*, June 1982, pp. 64–74.

30. Howard H. Stevenson and Jose Carlos Jarrillo-Mossi, "Preserving Entrepreneurship as Companies Grow," *The Journal of Business Strategy*, Vol. 7, 1986, pp. 10–23. See also "Big Vs. Small," *Time*, September 5, 1988, pp. 48–50; and "Money from the Boss," *The Wall Street Journal*, February 24, 1989, pp. R10–R11.

31. Gannes, "America's Fastest-growing Companies."

CASE 20.1

Mrs. Fields Has Recipe for Success

Debra "Debbi" Sivyer earned a local reputation for herself as a teenager baking cookies in her hometown of Oakland, California. She married Randall "Randy" Fields and moved to Palo Alto, where he worked as a financial manager. While enrolled as a student at a local community college, Debbi began to want to run her own business. Her baking background seemed a natural, but everyone including her husband had doubts that it could become a viable endeavor. However, Randy finally agreed to lend her $50,000.

Mrs. Fields located used equipment and furnishings and opened Mrs. Fields' Chocolate Chippery on August 13, 1977. The location she chose was near Stanford University in an international food arcade between a delicatessen and a Tibetan restaurant. Her first morning in business she did not sell a single cookie, so in the afternoon she went up and down the street giving away samples. She sold $50 worth of cookies that afternoon. The second day she started giving away samples earlier in the day and sold $75 worth. Over time, she began to acquire a growing group of customers, and her sales increased substantially.

Excited by this success, Debbi and Randy opened another store. When it too succeeded, they opened still another. Today, there are several hundred Mrs. Fields stores in six countries with combined annual sales in excess of $50 million. Debbi's company is now a large corporation based in Park City, Utah.

When Debbi opened her first cookie store, she did everything. She bought the furnishings and equipment, negotiated a lease, baked the cookies, sold the cookies, operated the store, and kept the records. As the business grew, she began to hire others to take over parts of it for her. Debbi quickly turned baking and selling over to others in order to give herself time to develop the company and plan for expansion.

Debbi's approach to business has not changed as the company has grown. She argues that a business must be fun in order to succeed. She strongly believes that people who work in the company must be treated with kindness and respect so that they will treat customers with kindness and respect. She has refused to franchise her operations for fear that her approach to business will not be carried out by others. All Mrs. Fields stores, therefore, are company owned and controlled.

A major component of that control is the quality of the cookies that are baked and sold. Debbi insists that all Mrs. Fields' Cookies be made with fresh and high-quality ingredients. Further, because the quality of a cookie is a function of how long it has been sitting before it is sold, she insists that most unsold cookies be removed from display cases after two hours. Those cookies are donated to charity organizations.

More recently, Mrs. Fields found itself in serious trouble. After opening nearly 600 stores, Debbi had to close some and now has less than 500. The public stock offering on the London market led to the purchase of only about 16 percent of the shares. The year 1988 saw enormous losses, and the stock plummeted as investors became concerned about the firm's long-term prospects. Some say that the company's move into the international arena was premature and that the management practice of retaining company control cannot succeed in distant locations such as London and Hong Kong. Indeed, late in 1988, Mrs. Fields yielded control of its European operations to a French company, Midial S.A. However, there were other problems as well. Some of them occurred because of a move to broaden the product line and absorb La Petite Boulangerie.

La Petite Boulangerie consisted of over 100 full-service bakery stores that Mrs. Fields' private, parent company, MF Holdings, acquired from PepsiCo in 1987. The strategy is to integrate the La Petite stores into the Mrs. Field's chain by converting the chain from single-product outlets to combination stores. The combination stores are about three times the size of the older cookie outlets and sell cookies, soups, bagels, and sandwiches. But it is unclear in which direction the company really wants to go. Some of the new stores retain the name La Petite Boulangerie; some are called Mrs. Fields; and others go by the name of Mrs. Fields Bakery Cafe.

Many entrepreneurial firms have problems continuing their success as they grow, especially if growth is rapid. That seems to be the case with Mrs. Fields. Whether the company can plot a consistent strategy and develop a new, slower approach to growth that will enable the current management to continue its success remains to be seen.

Questions

1. What entrepreneurial characteristics does Debbi Fields display? Why do you think she was not content to operate only one successful store?
2. What are some of the factors that led to the success of Mrs. Fields' Chippery? What dangers did the company face as it began? How were the dangers overcome?
3. As Mrs. Fields expands into the international market, do you think that it will continue to be as successful as it has been in the past? Why or why not?
4. Would you like to be a manager in the Mrs. Fields organization? Why or why not? Would you purchase stock in the company? Why or why not?

REFERENCES: "Tough Cookies?" *Fortune*, February 13, 1989, p. 112; "How the Cookie Crumbled at Mrs. Fields," *The Wall Street Journal*, January 26, 1989, p. B1; "It Takes a Smart Cookie," *USA Today*, May 11, 1987, p. 2E; "What's in a Name? Millions If It's Licensed," *Business Week*, April 8, 1985, pp. 97–98; "The Savvy 60," *Savvy*, April 1985, pp. 50–59; Alan Furst, "The Golden Age of Goo," *Esquire*, December 1984, pp. 324–330.

CASE 20.2

Exporting at Mentor Graphics

Mentor Graphics Corp. was a small, entrepreneurial organization when it was founded in Beaverton, Oregon, in 1981. It has rapidly become a mid-size corporation with the potential to become a *Fortune* 500 corporation if it continues to be as successful in the future as it has been in the past and if it makes some well-chosen acquisitions. The growth of Mentor has come about because the company has taken over the market in its main product line—design automation equipment.

Mentor was begun by a small group of managers from the Tektronix Corporation who were interested in running their own firm. They came from various product groups within Tektronix and brought a variety of expert knowledge and experience to the new firm. The groups from which they came included design automation, information display, computer-aided engineering, and computer-aided software engineering. Their experience included production, marketing, and finance as well as design.

Mentor Graphics specializes in CAE and CASE—computer-aided engineering and computer-aided software engineering. Before it had been in business a year, Mentor had begun shipping top-quality CAE products to such firms as Delco, International Microcircuits Inc., and LSI Logic Corp. Because of the quality of its products, Mentor quickly became the leader in the CAE field, surpassing all of its competitors including Tektronix and taking over the lion's share of the market.

In 1988 Mentor had sales of over $200 million. More than half of its sales (about $110 million) were to overseas customers as a result of the firm's careful efforts to develop export markets. Its export business increased 37 percent over the previous year, and Mentor expects that in 1989 it will increase by about 20 percent over 1988. Most of Mentor's exports are currently to Europe, but the company plans to increase sales in other parts of the world, especially Japan and elsewhere in Asia, in the near future.

Mentor's vice president for Europe, Jean Claude Caraes, noted that continuing improvements in technology have enabled the company to reduce prices on most of its products by about 20 percent each year. Those price reductions, coupled with the declining value of the dollar in international trade, have enabled Mentor to grow extremely fast in the European market. To serve that market, Mentor buys U.S.-made computers, adds software that it develops, packages the machines in Amsterdam, and sells them to Europe's biggest high-tech firms—Airbus, Philips, and Siemens. The quality of the product and the ease of securing it, which results from having it packaged in Europe, have led to solid sales.

Because it was a small firm with no large marketing organization behind it, Mentor approached its move into international sales slowly and carefully. To break into the European market, it spent a full year establishing its European subsidiaries. Mentor set up wholly owned sales subsidiaries and staffed them with personnel from the countries in which they were located. Executives at Mentor felt that this approach would signal to Europeans that Mentor was not a typical American company. Further, they felt that it would enable the company to quickly establish the type of communications with customers that it deemed necessary for any long-term sales arrangements. This was felt to be particularly important in computer-aided software products, which in many cases had to be in languages other than English.

Late in 1987, Mentor moved to acquire Integrated Measurement Systems Inc., but that deal fell through as a result of a stock-market drop in early 1988. However, Mentor was cash rich and wanted an acquisition to boost its growth. After looking around, it found the opportunity close to home, indeed, in the same town. In mid-1988, Mentor Graphics bought the CAE and CASE divisions of Tektronix, where its founders had formerly worked. Thomas Bruggere, Mentor's chairman and CEO, and Cerald Langeler, president and chief operating officer, were instrumental in that purchase. Mentor obtained some top personnel and further access to international markets that Tektronix had been developing, and Mentor became a preferred supplier to the remaining businesses at Tektronix.

Questions

1. Would you describe Mentor Graphics as an entrepreneurial organization? In what ways is it entrepreneurial? Cite specific examples to support your view.
2. When Mentor started, what were some of the factors that seemed to lead to its success? What factors might have led to the opposite result? Why did they pursue them?
3. As Mentor expands into Asian markets, do you think it will continue to be as successful as it has been in the past in its international operations? Why or why not?
4. Would you like to work for Mentor? Why or why not? Would you invest your money in Mentor? Why or why not?

REFERENCES: Mark Lapedus, "How Tek Lost Bid to Enter CAE Market," *Electronic News*, April 25, 1988, pp. 1, 28, 45; Mark Lapedus, "Tek Exiting CAE Systems," *Electronic News*, April 4, 1988, pp. 1, 35; "The Long Arm of Small Business," *Business Week*, February 29, 1988, pp. 63–66; "Market Crash Fallout Foils Mentor Merger," *PC Week*, January 5, 1988, p. 115; "Apollo Computer Inc.," *The Wall Street Journal*, November 3, 1988, p. B4; Robert T. Gallagher, "Caraes's European Strategy Boosts Mentor," *Electronics*, June 9, 1986, p. 51; Fred McGrail, "Export Controls: New Rules for an Old Problem," *Electronic Business*, April 15, 1986, pp. 36–37.

OUTLINE

The Nature of International Business
The Meaning of International Business · Trends in
International Business

Special Challenges of International Management
The Economic Environment · The Political Environment ·
The Cultural Environment

The Structure of the International Economy
Industrial Market Economies · Developing Countries ·
Oil-exporting Countries · Eastern Nonmarket Economies

The Decision to Go International
Market Factors · Technological Factors · Personal Values

Levels of International Involvement
Importing and Exporting · Licensing · Joint Ventures · Direct
Investment · Global Involvement

CHAPTER 21

Managing in the International Sector

OBJECTIVES

After studying this chapter, you should be able to:

- Describe the meaning of and trends in international business.
- Identify and discuss the special challenges inherent in international management.
- Describe the structure of the international economy.
- Discuss major issues affecting the decision to go international.
- Identify and discuss levels of international involvement.

OPENING INCIDENT

For decades, Kodak had the world to itself. Ever since George Eastman founded Kodak in the late 1800s, the company has been synonymous with photography. Kodak changed every aspect of the photography industry and created the amateur market for home photography. The company dominated the market for film, paper, and processing chemicals.

But then came the Japanese. Fuji Photo, in particular, has effectively challenged Kodak's worldwide dominance over the last few decades. The Japanese have long been keenly interested in photography; indeed, most of the world's cameras are made by Japanese firms. Fuji quickly dominated the Japanese market with a 70 percent share and then started to make major inroads in the U.S. market as well.

In 1983, Colby Chandler took over as CEO at Kodak. At the time, Kodak was essentially marking time—raking in cash from its photography products and not worrying too much about the future. Chandler immediately initiated a number of programs designed to awaken the slumbering giant. One of the most significant was a plan to regain Kodak's position in the world marketplace. Increased advertising, new-product developments, and new services very quickly stopped the erosion of the company's market share in the United States. Kodak wasn't content, however; it wanted more. It started attacking Fuji on Fuji's home turf. Although Kodak had been selling film in Japan since 1889, it was never a serious player there. But all that has changed. Kodak has a large blimp that flies over Tokyo daily. The company has increased its sales force from a handful to over 4,000 and has launched a withering advertising attack. It recently announced the construction of a new research lab in Japan—Kodak's largest research investment outside the United States.[1]

*K*odak's dilemma—and its response—represent near-classic examples of the changes wrought by international business over the past several years. For decades, many American firms operated as though in a vacuum. The domestic marketplace was large enough and growing at a sufficient rate to provide sales revenue for acceptable growth and profits. When the onslaught of foreign competition came, many domestic companies were caught unprepared, and they floundered for years, trying to figure out how to fight back. In recent years, many have learned and have sparked a re-emergence of American business around the globe.[2]

Examples, boxed inserts, and international cases throughout the earlier chapters in this book have introduced you to many of the issues, challenges, and opportunities in international business. This chapter focuses on other issues even more intensively. We characterize the nature of international business and highlight special challenges of international management. We discuss the structure of the international economy. We then explore the issues to be considered by businesses deciding whether to enter the international arena and the possible levels of involvement that international businesses can adopt.

THE NATURE OF INTERNATIONAL BUSINESS

As you prepared breakfast this morning, you may have plugged in a coffee pot manufactured in Asia, perhaps ironed a shirt or blouse made in Taiwan with an iron made in Mexico, and sat in a chair designed by Italian designers. The coffee you drank was probably made from beans grown in South America. Or perhaps you chose to drink hot chocolate instead—chocolate manufactured by the Swiss firm Nestlé or its U.S. subsidiary, Carnation.

To get to school, you may have driven a German or Japanese car. But your foreign car may have been manufactured in the United States. Honda, Mazda, Toyota, and Nissan (all Japanese firms) operate manufacturing facilities in the United States. Even if you drive an American car, it probably was influenced in some way by foreign manufacturers. GM has a joint-venture arrangement with Toyota (a Japanese firm), Chrysler with Mitsubishi (a Japanese firm), and Ford with Mazda (a Japanese firm). Perhaps you didn't drive a car to school but rather rode a bus (manufactured by Damiler-Benz, a German company, or by Volvo, a Swedish company) or a motorcycle (manufactured by Honda, Kawasaki, Suzuki, or Yamaha—all Japanese firms).

The daily lives of Americans are strongly influenced by businesses from around the world. But we aren't unique in this respect. People living in other countries have much the same experience. They drive Fords in Germany, use IBM computers in Japan, eat McDonald's hamburgers in France, and snack on Mars candy bars in England. They drink Pepsi and wear Levi Strauss jeans in the Soviet Union. The Japanese buy Kodak film and use American Express credit cards. People around the world fly on United or American Airlines in planes made by Boeing. Their buildings are constructed with Caterpillar and Deere machinery; and they buy Mobil oil.

In truth, we have become part of a global village—and have a global economy where no organization is insulated from the effects of foreign markets and competition. More and more firms are increasingly viewing themselves as international businesses or multinational businesses.[3] What do these terms mean, and why has this pattern developed? These and related questions are addressed in the following sections.

The Meaning of International Business

There are many different forms and levels of international business that organizations can engage in, and it is difficult to draw sharp lines of

FIGURE 21.1

Levels of International Business Activity

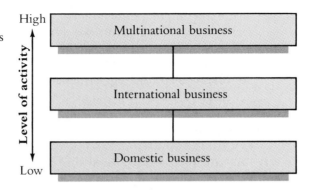

High — Multinational business

Level of activity

International business

Domestic business — Low

distinction between them. But for discussion purposes, we will identify three general forms.[4] As illustrated in Figure 21.1, a **domestic business** acquires essentially all of its resources and sells all of its products or services within a single country. An **international business** is primarily based in a single country but acquires some meaningful share of its resources or revenues from other countries. A **multinational business** transcends national boundaries—it has a worldwide marketplace from which it buys raw materials, borrows money, manufactures its products, and to which it subsequently sells its products. Ford is an excellent example of a multinational company. It has design and production facilities around the world. The new Mercury Tracer was designed and engineered in Japan, manufactured in Mexico, and sold in the United States. Ford makes and sells cars in Europe that are never seen in the United States. Ford cars are designed, produced, and sold for individual markets, wherever they are and without regard for national boundaries.[5]

More and more companies are following this path. Domestic companies are becoming international, and international companies are becoming multinational. This pattern is prompting the evolution of a worldwide phenomenon called **globalization**—the evolution of an integrated global economy that comprises interrelated markets. Globalization is likely to become even more pronounced in the future.[6] Why is this happening? To answer this question, it is necessary to examine trends in international business, beginning with forces that emerged from World War II.

domestic business   One that acquires all of its resources and sells all of its products or services within a single country

■ **international business** One that is primarily based in a single country but which acquires some meaningful share of its resources and/or revenues from other countries

multinational business   One that transcends national boundaries—it has a worldwide marketplace from which it buys raw materials, borrows money, and manufactures and sells its products

globalization   The evolution to an integrated global economy comprised of interrelated markets

Trends in International Business

Thirty-five years ago, when anyone in the world wanted to buy an automobile, an electronic instrument, or a machine tool, there was fundamentally only one place to shop—in the United States. After the Second World War, the United States was by far the dominant economic force in the world. Virtually all the countries in Europe had been devastated during the war. Asian countries, including Japan, China, and Korea, had fared no better. There were few passable roads, few standing bridges, and even fewer factories dedicated to the manufacture

Cummins Engine Company is an excellent example of an American company that has hit a home run in the international arena. Cummins makes diesel engines suitable for trucks, buses, and other heavy equipment. While many of its competitors have fallen prey to the Japanese, Cummins has held its own by keeping in touch with its customers, emphasizing quality, and promoting innovation. For example, the company's share of the United Kingdom bus market has increased steadily ever since it recently introduced its fuel-efficient L10 engine.

of peacetime products. Places not destroyed in the war—Canada, countries in South and Central America, and countries in Africa—had not yet developed the economic muscle to threaten the economic preeminence of the United States.

Businesses in war-torn countries like Germany and Japan had no choice but to rebuild from scratch. They were in the unfortunate but eventually profitable position of having to rethink every facet of their operations, from technology to production to finance to marketing. Although it took many years for these countries to recover, they eventually did so and their economic systems were poised for growth. During the same era, American companies grew complacent. Their customer base was growing rapidly. Increased population spurred by the baby boom and increased affluence resulting from the postwar economic boom greatly raised Americans' standards of living and expectations. The American public continually wanted new and better products and services. American companies profited greatly from this pattern but were perhaps guilty of taking it for granted.

Firms in the United States are no longer isolated from global competition or the global market.[7] A few simple numbers help tell the full story of international trade and industry. First of all, the volume of international trade increased 1,500 percent from 1960 to 1980 and grew at an even greater pace during the 1980s. Foreign investment in the United States rose from $27 billion in 1975 to $209 billion in 1986. U.S. foreign investments rose from $52 billion to over $260 billion during this same span. In 1960, 70 of the world's 100 largest firms were American. This figure dropped to 64 in 1970 and to 45 in 1985.[8]

American firms are finding that international operations are an increasingly important element of their sales and profits. For example, Boeing realized over 40 percent of its total income in 1987 from exports to other countries. For Caterpillar, the figure was over 25 percent. Consider General Motors. In 1986, the auto giant lost $300 million on its European operations. In 1988, however, it made $1.8 billion in profits from the same operations.[9]

It is getting increasingly difficult to measure international trade. Bayer and Siemens are two large West German companies with manufacturing facilities in the United States. In 1987, the two companies combined exported over $1 billion in goods from their U.S. facilities to other world markets. Likewise, Texas Instruments often imports microcircuits into the United States from its Japanese plant, and Honda ships back to Japan some of the cars it makes in America.[10] Some economic indices count these as exports, some as imports, some as both, and some as neither! Clearly, the international manager faces a sometimes bewildering maze of threats, opportunities, and challenges in search of the correct path for his or her business.

From any perspective, it is clear that we live in a truly global economy. The days when U.S. firms could safely ignore the rest of the world and concentrate only on their U.S. market are gone forever. Now, these firms must be concerned with the competitive situations they face in lands far from home and with how companies from distant lands are competing in the United States. "The Global View" describes how these pressures and trends affected Goodyear, one of the last major U.S. companies to confront the international arena.

SPECIAL CHALLENGES OF INTERNATIONAL MANAGEMENT

The management functions that constitute the organizing framework for this book—planning, organizing, leading, and controlling—are just as relevant to international managers as to domestic managers. International managers need to have a clear conception of where they want their firm to be in the future; they have to organize themselves to implement their plans; they have to motivate and inspire those that work for them; and they have to develop formal and informal mechanisms to control the actions of those on whom they depend.

Although much of what is management remains the same in an international context, the manager's job can be greatly complicated when a firm begins international operations. The special challenges that face managers in the international arena flow from the three broad categories shown in Figure 21.2—attributes of the economic environment, attributes of the political environment, and attributes of the cultural environment of international business.[11]

The Economic Environment

Every country is unique and creates a unique set of challenges for managers trying to do business there. However, there are four char-

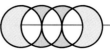

THE GLOBAL VIEW

GOODYEAR'S FOREIGN COMPETITION

Goodyear Tire & Rubber Company faces ever-increasing competition as foreign tire manufacturers continue to purchase weak U.S. rivals. To meet that competition and stave off acquisition attempts, Goodyear must make some key decisions about its international involvement. It needs to complete the construction of tire-manufacturing plants already under way in Canada and Korea and continue the aggressive marketing of its products. If it succeeds, Goodyear will maintain its share of the worldwide tire market, which was approximately 21 percent at the beginning of 1989.

In 1986, Goodyear was the target of an attempted takeover by a foreign organization. The Anglo-French financier Sir James Goldsmith, working with Merrill Lynch, made an effort to obtain Goodyear. At that time, Goodyear was the 35th-largest company in the United States, with sales in excess of $10 billion a year. Goodyear's CEO used political intervention, a commitment to restructure the company, and greenmail to stave off the takeover. Sir James sold his Goodyear stock back to Goodyear and made about $90 million on the deal. The political intervention took the form of congressional hearings launched by Ohio congressmen who were plainly hostile to Sir James. The idea was to focus on how to maintain the independence of major U.S. defense contractors.

The restructuring undertaken by Goodyear included shutting down some facilities, reducing employment, and expanding overseas operations. Goodyear sold its Celeron oil and gas holdings, its aerospace division, and some smaller parts of the company. It expanded its Servitekar tire specialty stores from Indonesia and Malaysia into Japan to compensate for the Bridgestone move. The impact of all this restructuring is clear. In 1987, sales were almost identical to those in 1983, but the number of employees was lower by about 10 percent, the operating profit margin was about double, and net income rose from barely over $300 in 1983 to nearly $800 million by 1987. Productivity in Goodyear's North American tire plants has risen about 25 percent since 1980.

Clearly, Goodyear is a more efficient organization and seems quite ready to tackle the international market with gusto.

REFERENCES: "Goodyear's New Boss Faces a Rough Road Test," *Business Week*, December 12, 1988, p. 90; "Goodyear Feels the Heat," *Business Week*, March 7, 1988, pp. 26–28; "A Hollow Victory for Bob Mercer," *Industry Week*, February 23, 1987, pp. 46, 48; Subrata N. Chakravarty, "Back to Basics," *Forbes*, September 21, 1987, pp. 40–41; "Can Goodyear Pull Out of Its Skid?" *Business Week*, March 20, 1989, p. 41.

acteristics in particular that can help managers anticipate the kinds of challenges they are likely to face in working abroad.

■ **market economy**   One in which consumers are free to make decisions about which products they prefer to purchase and firms are free to decide what products and services to provide

■ **command economy**   One in which the government decides what and at what price products and services will be provided

Resource Allocation Processes   The first of these dimensions is the way that resources are allocated among individuals and companies in an economic system. There are two pure methods of resource allocation—a market economy and a command economy. In a pure **market economy**, the key element is freedom of choice. Consumers are free to make decisions about which products they prefer to purchase, and firms are free to decide what products and services to provide. As long as both the consumer and the firm are free to decide to be in the market, then supply and demand determine which firms and which products will be available. A **command economy** operates under different principles. The government decides what is made, where it is shipped, and at what price it will be sold. The rationale is that the government

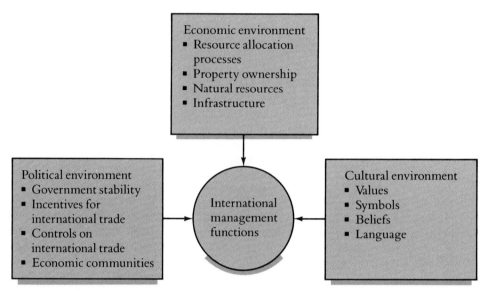

FIGURE 21.2

Special Challenges of
International Management

can take a broad view of how resources should be allocated for the good of the whole country. Individual consumers and firms would maximize their own wealth, not the overall wealth of the country.

In reality, there are few, if any, pure command or pure market economies. If we view the two at opposite ends of a continuum, most economies tend to be on one or the other side of the midpoint—that is, the economy is relatively market-like or relatively command-like. The People's Republic of China is an example of an economy that is on the command side of the midpoint. Under a five-year plan, demand in all sectors of the economy is considered, and the outputs of one sector are coordinated with the expected inputs of another sector to maximize overall production and consumption. Prior to the government upheavals in 1989 China was allowing more and more elements of free trade.[12] The United States, in contrast, is more of a market economy, but some industries still face heavy government regulation.

Property Ownership   A second important attribute of the economic system in different countries has to do with the nature of property ownership. There are two pure types—complete private ownership and complete public ownership. In systems with **private ownership**, individuals and companies—not the government—own and operate the companies that conduct business. In systems with **public ownership**, the government directly owns the companies that manufacture and sell products. Few countries have pure systems of private ownership or pure systems of public ownership. Most tend toward one extreme or the other, but usually a mix of public and private ownership exists.

One recent development of interest in the international economic environment is the trend toward **privatization**. In many countries,

■ **private ownership**   Individuals and companies own and operate the companies that conduct business

■ **public ownership**   The government owns businesses

■ **privatization**   The movement from public ownership to private ownership systems

like France and Great Britain, the government used to own many of the large businesses. In Britain, for example, the government owned British Petroleum, British Steel, Rolls-Royce, British Telecom, and Britoil. Under the direction of Prime Minister Margaret Thatcher, Britain has privatized these and many other firms. There are several reasons for this trend. In the long run, innovation, increased competition, and more efficient allocation of resources are expected. In the short term, governments receive a lump sum of funds that can be allocated elsewhere.

Natural Resources Still another important dimension for understanding the nature of the economic system in different countries is the availability of natural resources. There is a very broad range of resource availability in different countries. Some countries like Japan have virtually no natural resources of their own. Japan is thus forced to import virtually all of the oil, iron ore, and other natural resources it needs to manufacture products for its domestic and overseas markets. Countries like the United States and the Soviet Union have enormous natural resources. The United States is a major producer of oil, natural gas, coal, iron ore, copper, uranium, and other metals vital to the development of a modern economy.

One natural resource that is particularly important in the modern global economy is oil. A small set of countries in the Middle East, including Saudi Arabia, Iraq, Iran, and Kuwait, control a very large percentage of the world's total known reserves of crude oil. Access to this single natural resource has given these oil-producing countries enormous clout in the international economy.

Infrastructure A final important attribute of economic systems of particular importance to international management is infrastructure. A country's **infrastructure** comprises its schools, hospitals, power plants, railroads, highways, ports, communication systems, air fields, commercial distribution systems, and so forth. In some countries, the infrastructure is highly developed. In the United States, we have a modern educational system, roads and bridges are well developed, and most people have access to medical care. Overall, we have a relatively complete infrastructure sufficient to support most forms of economic development and activity.

Many countries lack a well-developed infrastructure. In some countries there is not enough electrical generating capacity to meet demand. Such countries often schedule periods of time during which power is turned off. These planned power failures reduce power demands but can be an enormous inconvenience to business. In the extreme, when a country's infrastructure is greatly underdeveloped, firms interested in beginning business may have to build an entire township, including housing, schools, hospitals, and perhaps even recreation facilities, to attract a sufficient overseas work force.

infrastructure The schools, hospitals, power plants, railroads, highways, ports, communication systems, air fields, and commercial distribution systems of a country

The Political Environment

A second special challenge facing the international manager is the political environment in which he or she will do business. Four important aspects of the political environment of international management are government stability, incentives for multinational trade, controls on international trade, and the influence of economic communities on international trade.

Government Stability   Stability can be viewed in two ways—as the ability of a given government to stay in power against other opposing factions in the country and as the permanence of government policies toward business. A country that is stable in both respects is preferable, since multinational managers have a higher probability of successfully predicting how government will affect their business. Civil war in countries such as Lebanon has made it virtually impossible for international managers to predict what government policies are likely to be and whether the government will be able to guarantee the safety of international workers. Without this confidence, international firms have been very reluctant to invest in Lebanon.

In many countries—the United States, Great Britain, and Japan, for example—changes in government occur with very little disruption. In other countries—Iran, Argentina, and Greece, for example—changes are likely to be chaotic. Even if a country's government remains stable, there remain risks that the policies adopted by that government might change. In some countries foreign businesses may be **nationalized** (taken over by the government) with little or no warning. For example, in 1988 the government of Peru nationalized Perulac, a local milk producer owned by Nestlé, because of a local milk shortage.

Less severe actions that can be taken by foreign governments against international business include a broad range of activities that make it more difficult for international firms to do business than for local firms. The government might force a foreign firm to charge higher prices than a local firm; it might restrict imports of vital raw materials to a foreign firm; it might restrict the flow of profits generated by a foreign firm to another country, and so forth.

Incentives for International Trade   Another facet of the political environment is incentives to attract foreign business. For example, municipal governments in Texas have offered foreign companies like Fujitsu huge tax breaks and other incentives to build facilities there.[13] In like fashion, the French government sold land to Disney far below its market value and agreed to build a connecting freeway in exchange for the company agreeing to build a theme park outside of Paris. Incentives can take a variety of forms, including reduced interest rates on loans, construction subsidies, and tax incentives. Less developed countries tend to offer different packages of incentives. In addition to

nationalized To be taken over by the government

lucrative tax breaks, for example, they can also attract investors with duty-fee entry of raw materials and equipment, market protection through limitations on other importers, and the right to take profits out of the country.

Controls on International Trade   A third element of the political environment that managers need to consider is the extent to which there are controls on international trade. In some instances, the government of a country may decide that foreign competition is hurting domestic trade. To protect domestic business, such governments may enact barriers to international trade. These barriers include tariffs, quotas, export restraint agreements, and "buy national" laws.

tariff   A tax collected on goods shipped across national boundaries

A **tariff** is a tax collected on goods shipped across national boundaries. Tariffs can be collected by the exporting country, the countries through which goods pass, and the importing country. Import tariffs, which are the most common, can be levied to protect domestic competition by increasing the cost of foreign goods. Japan charges U.S. tobacco producers a tariff on cigarettes imported into Japan as a way to keep their prices higher than the prices charged by domestic firms. Tariffs can also be levied, usually by less developed countries, as a way to raise money for the government.

quota   A limit on the number or value of goods that can be traded

Quotas are the most common form of trade restriction. A **quota** is a limit on the number or value of goods that can be traded. The quota amount is typically designed to ensure that domestic competitors will be able to maintain a certain market share. Honda is allowed to import 425,000 autos each year into the United States. This quota is one reason Honda opened manufacturing facilities here. The quota applies to cars imported into the United States, but the company can produce as many other cars within our borders as it wants.

export restraint agreements   Accords reached by governments in which countries voluntarily limit the volume or value of goods they export and import from one another

Export restraint agreements are designed to convince other governments to voluntarily limit the volume or value of goods exported to a particular country. They are, in effect, export quotas. Japanese steel producers voluntarily limit the amount of steel they send to the United States each year.

"Buy national" legislation gives preference to domestic producers through content or price restrictions. Several countries have this type of legislation. Brazil requires that Brazilian companies purchase only Brazilian-made computers. The United States requires that the Department of Defense purchase only military uniforms manufactured in the United States, even though the price of foreign uniforms would be half as much. Mexico requires that 50 percent of the parts of cars sold in Mexico be manufactured in Mexico.

Economic Communities   Just as government policies can either increase or decrease the political risk facing international managers, trade relations between countries can either help or hinder international business. If these relations are dictated by quotas, tariffs, and so forth, they can hurt international trade. However, there is currently a strong movement around the world to reduce many of these barriers. This movement takes its most obvious form in international economic communities.

An **international economic community** is a set of countries that agrees to significantly reduce or eliminate trade barriers among its member nations. The first, and in many ways still the most important, of these economic communities is the **European Economic Community** (**EEC**). The EEC was formed in 1957 with the signing of the Treaty of Rome. As shown in Figure 21.3, its current member nations include Denmark, the United Kingdom, Portugal, the Netherlands, Belgium, Spain, Ireland, Luxembourg, France, West Germany, Italy, and Greece. These countries have been committed to (1) gradually eliminating all barriers to trade among themselves, (2) developing a common tariff schedule applicable to imports from nonmember countries, (3) removing restrictions on the movement of capital and labor within the group, (4) implementing common policies relating to the regulation of industry and the production and marketing of agricultural commodities, (5) creating funding mechanisms to assist in the economic development of EEC nations, and (6) establishing a "social fund" to

international economic community A set of countries that agrees to significantly reduce or eliminate trade barriers among its member nations

European Economic Community (EEC) The first and most significant international economic community

FIGURE 21.3

The European Economic Community

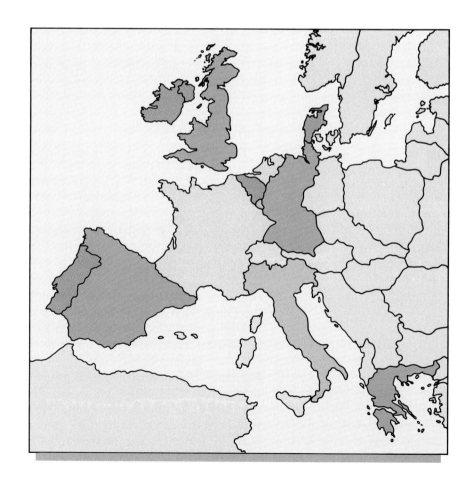

compensate workers who might experience economic injury due to the integration process.

Although the development of economic communities facilitates the movement of goods and services among firms within the community, few of these organizations have entirely done away with tariffs, quotas, and other trade barriers. However, after negotiations that required over a decade to complete, the European Economic Community agreed to drop all trade restrictions between member countries beginning in 1992. What this will mean for those European countries in their relationships with one another and in their relationships with other countries (including the United States) is not fully known at this time. It seems likely that many firms and countries in Europe will gain access to large markets previously closed to them. How this economic community evolves over the next several years will probably have a significant impact on how other economic communities evolve.[14] Other important economic communities include the Latin American Integration Association (Bolivia, Brazil, Colombia, Chili, Argentina, and other South American countries) and the Caribbean Common Market (the Bahamas, Belize, Jamaica, Antigua, Barbados, and 12 other countries).

The Cultural Environment

The final special challenge for the international manager is the cultural environment and its effects on business. A country's culture includes all the values, symbols, beliefs, and language that guide behavior.

Values, Symbols, and Beliefs   Cultural values and beliefs are often unspoken, even taken for granted by those who live in a particular country. Culture does not necessarily cause problems for international managers when the culture of the country that a firm is moving into is similar to the culture of the country in which a manager was raised. Difficulties arise when there is little overlap between the home culture of a manager and the culture of the country in which business is to be conducted. For example, most U.S.-based managers will find the culture and traditions of England familiar. After all, both countries speak the same language, they share strong historical roots, and there is a history of strong commerce between the two countries. However, when U.S. managers begin operations in Japan or the People's Republic of China, most of those commonalities disappear.[15]

Even when the cultures of two countries are similar, there is still substantial room for misunderstanding and embarrassment. For example, when someone from the United Kingdom tells you that he is going to knock you up, take a lift, and put the telly in the boot, he has told you that he will (1) wake you up in the morning, (2) take an elevator, and (3) put a television set in the trunk of your car.

Things become even more complicated when the cultures are truly different. In Japanese, for example, the word *hai* (pronounced "hi")

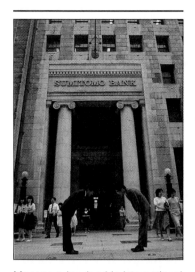

Managers involved in international business face numerous special challenges. Not the least of these challenges are the cultural differences that managers must be attuned to if they are to be accepted in those cultures. For example, even though several Japanese banks are among the world's largest and most profitable, their managers still cling to many ancient customs and practices.

means "yes." In conversation, however, this word is used much like Americans use "uh-huh," to move a conversation along, to show the person you are talking to that you are paying attention. So when does *hai* mean "yes," and when does it mean "uh-huh"? This turns out to be a relatively difficult question to answer. If an American manager asks a Japanese manager if he agrees to some trade arrangement, the Japanese manager is likely to say "hai"—which may mean "yes, I agree," or "yes, I understand," or "yes, I am listening." Many U.S. managers become very frustrated in negotiations with the Japanese, because they feel that the Japanese continue to raise issues that had already been agreed upon—after all, the Japanese managers said "yes." What many of these U.S. managers fail to recognize is that "yes" does not always mean "yes" in Japan.

Cultural differences between countries can have a very direct impact on business practice. For example, the religion of Islam teaches that people should not make a living by exploiting the misfortune of others and that making interest payments is immoral. This means that in Saudi Arabia there are no businesses that provide auto-wrecking services to tow one's car to the garage should it break down (because that would be capitalizing on misfortune), and in the Sudan banks cannot pay or charge interest. Given these cultural and religious constraints, those two businesses—auto towing and banking—don't seem to hold great promise for international managers in those particular countries.

Some cultural differences between countries can be even more subtle and yet have a major impact on business activities. For example, in the United States there is a very clear agreement among most managers about the value of time—time is money. Most U.S. managers schedule their activities very tightly and then adhere to their schedules. Other cultures don't put such a premium on time. In the Middle East, managers do not like to set appointments, and they rarely keep appointments set too far into the future. American managers interacting with managers from the Middle East might misinterpret the late arrival of a potential business partner as a negotiation ploy or an insult, when it is rather a simple reflection of different views of time and its value.

Language Language itself can be a significant factor. Table 21.1 lists several examples of language mishaps made by business. There are numerous others. Esso realized it was in trouble when it learned that its name meant "stalled car" in Japanese. Ford began to understand why its profits were lower than expected in Spain when it realized that some Spaniards read its name as "Fabrico Ordinaria Reparaciones Diaviamente," meaning "ordinarily, make repairs daily." The color green is used extensively in Moslem countries, but it signifies death in some other countries. The color associated with femininity in the United States is pink, but in many other countries yellow is the most feminine color. In Japan, the pronunciation of the word "four" sounds like the word for "death." When an American golf-ball manufacturer attempted to sell golf balls in packages of four, sales were terrible.

Source of Problem	Example
Language	One firm, trying to find a name for a new soap powder, tested the chosen name in 50 languages. In English, it meant "dainty." In other languages it meant "song" (Gaelic), "aloof" (Flemish), "horse" (African), "hazy or dimwitted" (Persian), and "crazy" (Korean). It was obscene in several Slavic languages.
	Chevy's "Nova" was spoken as "no va" in Italian, which means "doesn't go."
	Coca-Cola in Chinese became "Bite the head of a dead tadpole."
	Idioms cannot be translated literally: "to murder the King's English" becomes "to speak French like a Spanish cow" in French.
Nonverbal signs	Shaking your head up and down in Greece indicates "No"; swinging it from side to side indicates "Yes."
	In most European countries, it is considered impolite not to have both hands on the table.
	The American sign for "OK" is an obscenity in Spain.
Colors	Green: Popular in Moslem countries Disease in jungle-covered countries Cosmetics in France, Sweden, Netherlands
	Red: Blasphemous in African countries Wealth and masculinity in Great Britain
Product	Campbell Soup was unsuccessful in Britain until the firm added water to its condensed soup so it would appear to be the same amount of canned soup the British were used to purchasing.
	Long-life packaging, which is used commonly for milk in Europe, allows milk to be stored for months at room temperature if it is unopened. Americans are still wary of it.
	Coke had to alter the taste of its soft drink in China when the Chinese described it as "tasting like medicine."

SOURCE: Adapted from David A. Ricks, *Big Business Blunders: Mistakes in Multinational Marketing* (Homewood, Ill.: Dow Jones–Irwin, 1983); Nancy Bragganti and Elizabeth Devine, *The Traveler's Guide to European Customs and Manners* (St. Paul, Minn.: Meadowbrook Books, 1984); several *Wall Street Journal* articles.

TABLE 21.1

Communication Problems in
Multinational Business

THE STRUCTURE OF THE INTERNATIONAL ECONOMY

Even this brief review of the economic, political, and cultural environments facing international managers suggests the bewildering options and conflicts that managers seeking to be successful in the international arena must face. Given these challenges, it is not surprising that many U.S. firms have preferred to keep focused on their domestic market. However, while some U.S. firms have retained that relatively narrow focus, other firms have developed the skills and expertise to operate abroad. To remain competitive in the global economy, U.S. firms will have to development a stronger global vision.[16]

One thing that can be helpful to managers seeking to operate in a global environment is to recognize that although each country is different and unique, most countries in the world economy can be classified into one of the four broad categories listed in Table 21.2. Countries of each type provide their own special challenges—and opportunities—for international managers.

Industrial Market Economies

industrial market economies
Employ market forces in the allocation of resources, tend to have private ownership of property, and have highly developed infrastructures

The **industrial market economies** include countries like the United States, Japan, the United Kingdom, France, Germany, and Sweden. These countries have several things in common. First, they tend to employ market forces in the allocation of resources. They tend to be characterized by private ownership of property, although there is some variance along this dimension. France, for example, has a relatively high level of government ownership among the industrial market economies. However, compared to the other kinds of economies listed in Table 21.2, France still has a relatively high level of private ownership.[17]

The industrial market economies vary widely in terms of the natural resources they control. Some, like the United States, possess vast reserves of natural resources; others, like Japan, Belgium, and Switzerland, possess relatively few natural resources. However, they all tend to have highly developed infrastructures. This means that the populace of these counties is educated, that the transportation and communication systems are highly developed, and that the commercial distribution systems are sufficient for most business needs.

U.S. managers have relatively few problems operating in the industrial market economies, at least as compared to operating in the other types. Many of the business "rules of the game" that apply in Germany or the United Kingdom, for example, also apply in the United States. For this reason, it is not unusual for U.S. firms seeking to expand geographically to begin operations in some other industrial market economy. Although the task of managing an international business in an industrial market country is somewhat less complicated than operating in some other type of economy, it still poses some challenges, however. Perhaps foremost among them is that these kinds of countries

Economic Type	Examples	Defining Characteristics	Opportunities for International Managers	Challenges for International Managers
Industrial market economy	United States, United Kingdom, France, Japan	Mature economy; highly developed infrastructure; wealth; market resource allocation; private ownership of property	Common business "rules of the game"	Acquiring market share from established competitors
Developing countries	Brazil, South Korea	Less developed infrastructure; low level of personal wealth	Help develop infrastructure; immature economy	Lack of consumer wealth; lack of infrastructure
Oil-exporting countries	Saudi Arabia, Kuwait	Abundant supply of crude oil	Wealthy citizens; wealthy government; help develop infrastructure	Lack of infrastructure; cultural barriers
Eastern nonmarket economies	Soviet Union, Poland, East Germany	Command economies; public ownership	Moderately mature economies; underexploited business opportunities	Government regulation of trade; fluctuations in political relations

TABLE 21.2

Structure of an International Economy

are typically quite mature economically. Many of the industries in these countries are already dominated by large and successful companies. Dislodging such companies from their economic positions can be extremely difficult. Thus it is relatively difficult for U.S. firms to have a major impact in these markets.[18]

Developing Countries

developing countries Market and command mechanisms for allocating economic resources are used, private and public ownership exist, and, while most do not have well developed infrastructures, some do

In contrast to the highly developed and mature economies of industrial market countries, the economies of **developing countries** are underdeveloped and immature. These countries have adopted a whole range of market and command mechanisms for allocating economic resources. The People's Republic of China, despite recent moves toward market forms of control, is still primarily a command economy. In contrast, Chile, another developing country, has been strongly dominated by the market mechanisms of resource allocation since the government of General Pinochet came to power in the mid-1970s. Joining Chile in this emphasis are Taiwan, Singapore, South Korea, and Hong Kong. Finally, a large number of developing countries are in the middle, with some market and some command attributes. These countries include Brazil and a variety of African nations.[19]

The same kind of mixture exists for developing countries in terms of the type of property ownership they emphasize and in the availability of natural resources. For example, a developing country like Brazil has enormous natural resource potential; a country like the Sudan has considerably less. What developing countries have most in common is an undeveloped infrastructure. There is some variation, but developing countries in general have fewer educated citizens, less well developed transportation and communication systems, and less mature distribution systems than the industrial market economies. The citizens of these countries are simply not as wealthy as the citizens of more developed countries.

There is a group of developing countries, mostly in Asia and South America, that are rapidly moving toward the same level of development as that which exists in the industrial market countries. In South America, for example, Venezuela, Brazil, and Argentina, despite some serious challenges, have been able to raise their standard of living above other developing countries. In Asia, the so-called Four Tigers—South Korea, Taiwan, Hong Kong, and Singapore—have also made enormous strides economically. Indeed, in a few years, it is likely that these countries will be included in any list of developed, industrial market nations.[20]

The primary challenges presented by the developing countries to those interested in conducting international business there are the lack of wealth on the part of potential consumers and the underdeveloped infrastructure. Developing countries have enormous economic potential, but much of this potential remains untapped. Thus, international firms entering these markets often have to invest heavily in distribution systems, in training consumers how to use their products, and in providing facilities for their workers to live in.

Oil-exporting Countries

Another important economic type listed in Table 21.2 differs from the developing countries in only one important attribute—access to raw materials. The **oil-exporting countries** present mixed models of resource allocation, property ownership, and the development of infrastructure. However, these countries all have access to significant amounts of crude oil and thus are major players in the world market.

Their influence in the world has been heightened by the organization to which they all belong—OPEC. Originally founded in 1960 at the instigation of Venezuela, OPEC (the Organization of Petroleum Exporting Countries), now includes Venezuela, Iran, Iraq, Kuwait, Saudi Arabia, Algeria, Ecuador, Gabon, Indonesia, Libya, Nigeria, Qatar, and the United Arab Emirates. Through the 1970s, OPEC was able to keep the price of crude oil high by limiting production. This policy dramatically affected economies in Western Europe and Japan, which rely a great deal on oil imported from OPEC countries. For example, in 1982, Japan consumed the equivalent of 414.1 million metric tons of coal in the form of coal, oil, and other petroleum products, while

oil-exporting countries Developing countries that have access to oil, an important raw material, which greatly adds to their role in the world market

producing only 18 million metric tons of oil and coal. Of this total, only 0.4 million metric tons was crude oil. Obviously, when OPEC is successful at keeping oil prices very high, the economies of Japan and other highly dependent countries are greatly affected. This pressure, in turn, has prompted Japan to invest heavily in buying its own oil reserves from other countries.[21]

Recently, OPEC has been unsuccessful at limiting the production of crude oil by its members. As a result worldwide prices for crude oil have fallen. The impact of oil-price swings on the economies of the oil-producing nations has been dramatic. When oil prices were high, enormous amounts of wealth from all over the world flowed into these countries. Many of them invested heavily in their infrastructures. Whole new cities were built; airports were constructed; and the population was educated. As oil prices have fallen, many of the oil-producing countries have been forced to cut back on these and related activities. Nevertheless, they are among the wealthiest countries in the world. The per capita income of Kuwait ($19,610), the United Arab Emirates ($22,710), and Qatar ($27,000) is higher than the per capita incomes in the industrial market economies.

Although there is great wealth in the oil-producing nations, they provide great challenges to Western managers. These countries may be investing in their infrastructure, but it is not fully in place. This creates both an opportunity and a challenge to international firms. The opportunity is in helping build the infrastructure through the construction of roads, bridges, airports, schools, and even cities. The challenge is that many of the facilities taken for granted in the industrial economies are either underdeveloped or nonexistent in the oil-exporting countries.

Another challenge facing U.S. managers working in the oil-producing countries has to do with important cultural differences. Many members of OPEC are located in the Middle East and are dominated by Islam. Although Islam has many historical connections with the Judeo-Christian ethic that has developed in the industrial economies, these cultural systems differ in many ways.[22]

Eastern Nonmarket Economies

eastern nonmarket economies Countries in Eastern Europe which use command mechanisms and rely on public ownership

Eastern nonmarket economies include countries like Poland, Yugoslavia, and the Soviet Union. These countries have two things in common. They stress centralized government processes for allocating resources, and they stress government ownership. It is important not to underestimate the impact of these economic systems on the global economy. The Soviet Union is one of the largest economies in the world, and there are millions of people living in countries like Poland, East Germany, and Yugoslavia. These represent real opportunities for international business over the next several decades.

Although there are opportunities, there are also significant challenges. In particular, the governments in Eastern nonmarket economies are much more involved in decisions about trade than are governments in

Doing business in Eastern non-market economies is sometimes tricky. For years, starting in 1976, McDonalds tried to gain access to the vast Russian market. Finally, in 1988, McDonalds and Russian officials signed an agreement that would allow the company to open 20 restaurants in the Soviet Union. But there was more to the deal than opening restaurants. McDonalds has had to send teams of experts to Soviet farms to help farmers produce beef and other agricultural products that meet the company's standards. They are also building a large food-processing plant in Moscow.

other economic systems. Thus, instead of interacting directly with firms in these countries, U.S. and other international businesses are usually forced to interact with representatives of the government. But the government representatives are often not as interested in profits or costs as they are in meeting some government-imposed quota or objective and remaining ideologically pure.

The political climate between the industrial market economies and the Eastern nonmarket economies has an important impact on international managerial actions. During the 1960s, in the period known as the Cold War, relations between East and West were very strained and trade was very difficult. In the 1970s, a period of détente emerged and friendlier relations now exist between these sets of countries. However, conflicts still arise. In 1980 President Jimmy Carter imposed a ban on all grain shipments to the Soviet Union, and there are still restrictions on the transfer of certain kinds of technology to Eastern countries. Thus, even though relations between East and West have developed and matured over the last decade, it seems likely that tensions will remain for some time.

THE DECISION TO GO INTERNATIONAL

The decision to enter the international marketplace usually boils down to a choice between a nationally focused strategy or a global strategy. A firm that adopts a nationally focused strategy decides to develop and exploit the market in its home country and not move beyond its boundaries to other countries. A global strategy is not constrained by any country's borders. In addition to the economic, political, and cultural environment, a firm has to examine a number of other factors to determine whether a product has the characteristics that can be successfully transferred to other markets. John Welch, chairman and chief executive officer of General Electric, summarized many of the issues about going international when asked if GE is an international company:

> I don't think companies are international. Businesses are international. I think it is a mistake when businesses say, "Let's go with an international strategy." With what? Some businesses can, some can't. We could say: "General Electric, be international in appliances." That game is over. There are domestic producers in each country serving those markets very well.
>
> If you look at it business by business, you can see that in engineered materials, we're truly international—approximately a third of the business is in the United States, a third in Europe, and a third is in Japan.
>
> Let's take diagnostic imaging, our medical business. We compete very successfully in this country. We have a joint venture in Japan that's doing very well. Europe is a more nationalistic market, so we're having more difficulty there.[23]

As Welch suggested, some products, like appliances, have characteristics that do not lend themselves to multinational production or marketing. It's best for a firm not to compete in these markets or to recognize that it will have to adapt its product to fit every market in which it wants to compete. Other products are multinational in nature —people all over the world use the product in the same way. A third group of products falls in between the two extremes. In deciding whether to adopt a global or nationally focused strategy, managers need to address market factors and technological factors. These are shown in Table 21.3. In addition, the manager's personal values come into play.

TABLE 21.3

The Decision to Go International

Market factors		
1. Can the firm meet the needs of international customers?	Yes	No
2. Can the firm effectively distribute the product to the customer?	Yes	No
3. How mature is the proposed foreign market?	Immature	Mature
Technological factors		
1. Will the product need to be redesigned?	No	Yes
2. How expensive is redesign?	Inexpensive	Expensive
	↓	↓
	Consider global strategy	Consider nationally focused strategy

Market Factors

Before moving to a global strategy, managers need to ask themselves some tough questions about their products and about how well those products will travel internationally. Foremost among the questions is whether the firm can meet the needs of its potential international customers. There are many examples of successful national firms attempting to move to a global strategy only to discover that the products that meet customers' needs so well at home do not meet the needs of international customers. The lightweight, high-technology bicycle that sells so well in the United States, for example, does not meet the daily transportation needs of people in the People's Republic of China. The large, spacious refrigerator/freezer that meets the needs of U.S. consumers does not fit the much smaller homes of Japanese or European consumers. The large and luxurious Cadillac that is so attractive to many U.S. consumers does not appeal to many Europeans faced with the prospect of paying $4 per gallon for gas and driving down narrow city streets.

Suppose that a firm's product is able to meet the needs of its potential international customers. Coca-Cola, for example, can quench the thirst of someone in Japan just as well as it can the thirst of someone in the United States. Is this ability to address the consumer's needs sufficient to guarantee a successful global strategy? Not necessarily. If a firm is unable to effectively distribute its product to its foreign customers, those customers will never be able to buy it and the global strategy will be disrupted. Coca-Cola discovered this problem in Japan. There are relatively few supermarkets in Japan; instead, retail distribution in Japan is dominated by small neighborhood stores. Thus, Coca-Cola had to adjust its distribution system to take into consideration large numbers of small retail outlets. Coca-Cola discovered that the soft-drink can that is popular in Japan is considerably smaller than the can that U.S. consumers are accustomed to. To distribute soft drinks through Japanese vending machines, Coca-Cola had to change the size of the can. Fortunately, the company was able to make these adjustments and has become very successful in Japan.

Even after a firm decides that it can meet the needs of its potential foreign customers and that it can effectively distribute products to them, a third question needs to be answered: How mature is this international market? In a competitively mature market, numerous domestic firms are already meeting the needs of customers and the supply of products and services almost equals the demand for products and services. Entry by new foreign firms into competitively mature markets is difficult and very expensive. For example, as Jack Welch noted, every country in Europe and Asia has several domestic firms manufacturing appliances to meet the needs of domestic consumers. GE should not expect to be able to enter these markets with any degree of success unless it comes up with a significant design, quality, or price advantage.

If the international market is immature, a global strategy may have considerable potential. In this situation, the timing of the move to a

Deciding to go international almost always involves more than just shipping domestic products to foreign markets. In many cases it's necessary to redesign the product to meet various constraints and conditions inherent in the foreign market. While computer hardware is widely available in most developed countries, software is a rare commodity. So software companies like WordPerfect have been very successful at exporting their products to foreign markets. Even though the product is transferable, however, new packaging is still needed.

global strategy is very important. If a firm waits too long to enter the market, the market may have matured to the point where it is no longer appropriate for the firm to move forward. For example, IBM was very successful in establishing a position in the mainframe computer market in Japan in the early 1960s because no major Japanese firms were manufacturing computers. However, it is unlikely that any other company could be as successful in entering this market today because many companies are now building computers in Japan.

Technological Factors

The market determinants of whether a firm should or should not adopt a global strategy focus on the needs of customers and the actions of other firms in a foreign country. Technological determinants of this decision focus on the physical product itself. Each country in the world has its own technological standards. The coffee pot that works so well in the United States melts in Italy. The curling iron that creates a fashion statement in France causes fires in England. The computer that works so well on the east coast of Japan does not work as well on the west coast because the two regions use different electrical power standards. (Computer manufacturers who sell in Japan need to include a switch that allows users to adjust their machines to one of the two power standards that exist in that country.)

Managers must understand whether their product will need to be redesigned to meet technological standards, and, if so, how expensive the redesign will be. If redesign is necessary but involves changing only the style of plug that is used on the product, redesign can be simple and inexpensive. If redesign involves significant re-engineering, the costs may not be worth the benefits, and perhaps a nationally focused strategy would be more appropriate.

Redesign issues sometimes go beyond technological requirements and are affected by consumer tastes. Consumers in Britain have a strong preference for front-loading washing machines. When Hoover recently decided to expand from Britain into the French market, it discovered that consumers in France have strong preferences for top-loading machines. Thus, Hoover had to redesign the product.[24] "Management in Practice" describes how Boeing effectively balanced market and technological factors in its own international strategy.

Personal Values

The impact of market and technological factors on the decision to go international are important considerations. However, managers also need to recognize that their own personal values and tastes will also be a strong determinant of their actions. Entrepreneurial, risk-seeking managers who are always looking for new challenges and new opportunities often choose a global strategy; less entrepreneurial, risk-averse managers may opt for a nationally focused strategy. However, as the U.S. market continues to mature, more and more managers are likely to conclude that their personal needs and financial ambitions are most likely to be met if they steer their firm toward a global strategy. The growth in international business suggests that more and more managers are coming to this conclusion.[25]

LEVELS OF INTERNATIONAL INVOLVEMENT

Up to this point in our discussion, international management has been treated as an all-or-nothing situation, as though firms decide to go international all the way or decide to stick with a strictly national strategy. In reality, firms seeking to increase the international component of their business can use a range of options. The options include importing and exporting, licensing, joint ventures, and direct investment.[26]

Importing and Exporting

■ **exporting** Making a product in the firm's domestic marketplace and selling it in another country

■ **importing** When a good, service, or capital is brought into the home country from abroad

Importing or exporting (or both) is usually the first type of international business in which a firm gets involved. **Exporting** basically means making the product in the firm's domestic marketplace and selling it in another country. Both merchandise and services can be exported. **Importing** occurs when a good, service, or capital is brought into the home country from abroad. For example, automobiles (Mazda, Honda, Volkswagen, Mercedes-Benz, Ferrari), stereo equipment (Sony, Bang and Olufsen, Sanyo), and wine (Riunite, Dom Perignon, Swartzkatz)

MANAGEMENT IN PRACTICE

BOEING'S INTERNATIONAL SUCCESS

The Boeing Company of Seattle, Washington, is the world's largest commercial aircraft manufacturer. Although its market share slipped from over 70 percent in the early 1980s to about 55 percent by the late 1980s, Boeing continues to be strong in international as well as domestic markets. Indeed, one reason for Boeing's dominant market share has been its international market success. The Boeing 737 completely dominates the international market for jet aircraft.

In the late 1960s, Boeing introduced the 737 to compete with McDonnell Douglas's DC-9. However, Boeing entered the market three years behind McDonnell Douglas and the 737 was not quite as fast as the DC-9. The result was that although Boeing won a few orders from several U.S. airlines, sales of the 737 began to fall off during the late 1970s. Bob Norton, a Boeing engineer, was given the task of trying to save the plane. Save it he did.

Norton decided to pursue an international strategy. He focused on the underdeveloped areas of the world—the Mideast, Africa, and South America in particular. Runways in those areas were typically constructed of asphalt instead of concrete and were too soft for the 737. In addition, they were too short for takeoffs and landings. Boeing's engineers redesigned the 737's wings to permit shorter landings and added thrust to the engines to permit faster takeoffs. They redesigned the landing gear and installed low-pressure tires so that the 737 could land on asphalt runways. The redesign worked.

Slowly, Boeing began to sell one or two planes at a time to Third World airline companies rather than the 20 or so per order that American firms might have purchased. Those sales were sufficient to keep production rates for the plane at acceptable levels. As the Third World airlines grew, they bought more and more 737s, and by the mid-1980s the Boeing 737 was the best-selling commercial jet in aviation history. As a result, Boeing has garnered approximately 50 percent of the world market in jetliners, and its total sales are nearly $18 billion. Boeing used its international market to save a major investment and turn it into a highly successful venture.

REFERENCES: Andrew Kupfer, "How to Be a Global Manager," *Fortune*, March 14, 1988, pp. 52–54, 58; "Aloha Airline Accident Hearings Focus on Boeing Process in Constructing 737s," *The Wall Street Journal*, July 14, 1988, p. 6; "Big Orders Keep Boeing on a Roll," *USA Today*, May 17, 1988, p. 3B; "Bright Smiles, Sweaty Palms," *Business Week*, February 1, 1988, pp. 22–23; "Boeing to Get Loan of Workers From Lockheed," *The Wall Street Journal*, March 8, 1989, p. A2.

are imported into the United States. Firms in the United States routinely export grain to the Soviet Union, gas turbines to Saudi Arabia, locomotives to Indonesia, jeans to Great Britain, and diapers to Italy. In companies using this approach, domestic divisions are usually organized by function, and a special managerial position is created to oversee exports and imports, as shown in Figure 21.4.

This approach to international business has many advantages. It is the easiest way of entering a market with a small outlay of capital. Because the products are sold "as is," there is no need to adapt the product to the local conditions, and very little risk is involved. However, there are disadvantages. Importing and exporting can be very expensive because the products are subject to taxes and tariffs as well as transportation. Furthermore, because the products are not adapted to local conditions, they may miss the needs of a large segment of the market. Finally, some products may be restricted and thus can be neither imported nor exported.

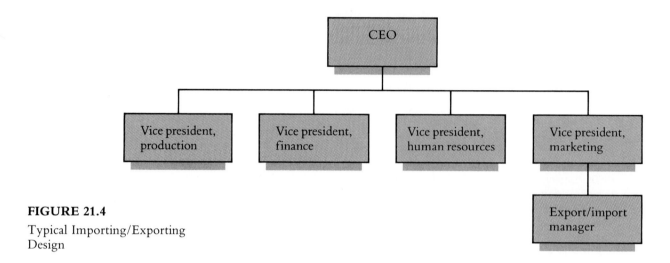

FIGURE 21.4

Typical Importing/Exporting
Design

Licensing

There are times when a company may prefer to arrange for a foreign company to manufacture or market its products under a licensing agreement. Factors that may lead to this decision include excessive transportation costs, government regulations, and home production costs. Under a licensing agreement, a firm allows another company to use its brand name, trademark, technology, patent, copyrights, or other expertise. In return, the licensee pays a royalty, usually based on sales. For example, General Instrument Corporation signed an agreement with Hyundai Electronics Industries Company in South Korea. Under terms of the agreement, Hyundai will manufacture some of General Instrument's integrated circuit products. General Instrument initiated the arrangement because it felt that the demand for its products would exceed the capacity of its Chandler, Arizona, plant. In companies using this approach, domestic divisions are usually organized by function, product, location, or some other base; and licensing arrangements are usually handled through a special international division similar to the one in Figure 21.5. The international division is organized by function, product, or location and is responsible for all licensing arrangements.

FIGURE 21.5

Typical Licensing Design

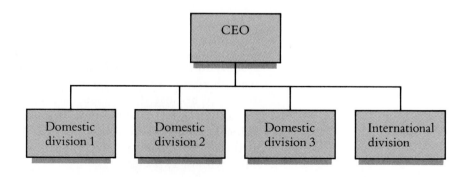

Increased profitability and extended profitability are two reasons that firms would select licensing as their international business alternative. Frequently this strategy is used for entry into less developed countries where second-generation technology may still be acceptable and, in fact, may be state of the art.

Inflexibility is one of the disadvantages of this strategy. A firm can tie up its product or expertise for a long period of time; and if the licensee does not develop the market effectively, the licensing firm can lose profits. For example, Oleg Cassini licensed Jovan, the U.S. subsidiary of Beecham from Great Britain, to market the Cassini line of beauty products. Jovan signed the agreement but then marketed Diane Von Furstenberg Cosmetics products instead. Jovan, using the licensing agreement, denied Cassini the right to license its name to anyone else. The rest of the story? Cassini sued Jovan for $78 million, but the suit tied up the Cassini line for three years. An out-of-court settlement was eventually reached, but Cassini lost considerable profit and momentum.

A second disadvantage of licensing arrangements is that licensees can take the knowledge and skill that they have been given access to for a foreign market and exploit them in the licensing firm's home market. When this happens, what used to be a business partner becomes a business competitor. As many American firms that have licensed Japanese firms have discovered, the new competitors can be formidable.

Joint Ventures

In joint ventures, two or more firms share in the ownership of an operation on an equity basis. Joint-venture arrangements have enjoyed a tremendous upsurge in the past few years. In 1988, the number of joint ventures was greater than the total number of joint ventures from 1969 to 1985. In this type of arrangement, each party provides a portion of the equity or the equivalent in physical plant, raw materials, cash, or other assets. Normally, the proportion of the investment determines the percentage of ownership in the venture. Joint ventures may take a number of organizational forms, but one common approach is to arrange them as part of existing product-based departments, as shown in Figure 21.6. Product division managers oversee both domestic and foreign activities for major products or product lines and coordinate relevant joint-venture agreements.

FIGURE 21.6

Typical Joint-Venture Design

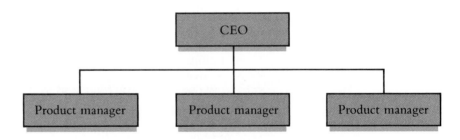

International joint ventures are becoming increasingly common. As
demands for entertainment increase around the globe, international joint ventures in the music,
television, and movie industries
have also started to increase. The
film crew shown here is working
on a film called *The Last Emperor*. The production company
shooting the movie is a joint venture between Chinese, Italian, and
British interests.

Joint-venture strategies have advantages and disadvantages. They can
allow quick entry into a market by taking advantage of the existing
strengths of participants. Japanese automobile manufacturers have used
this strategy to their advantage to enter the U.S. market by using the
already established distribution systems of U.S. automobile manufacturers. Joint ventures are also an effective way of gaining access to
technology or raw materials. The major disadvantage of this strategy
lies with the shared ownership of the operation. Although it reduces
the risk for each participant, it also limits the control and the return
that each firm can enjoy.

Direct Investment

The most common form of direct investment occurs when a company
headquartered in one country builds or purchases operating facilities,
especially manufacturing facilities, in a foreign country. The foreign
operations then become wholly owned subsidiaries of the domestic
firm. Kodak's commitment to build a new research lab in Japan represents a direct investment in that country. We noted earlier the difficulties in entering the international appliance market. To get around
that hurdle, Maytag recently spent $1 billion to acquire Chicago Pacific
Corporation. One of Chicago's subsidiaries, Hoover, has a significant
share of the appliance market in Britain, Australia, and continental
Europe.[27] Companies that are sufficiently advanced toward a multinational state often use a form of organization design similar to the one
shown in Figure 21.7. Divisions are organized by geographic region,

FIGURE 21.7

Typical Direct-Investment Design

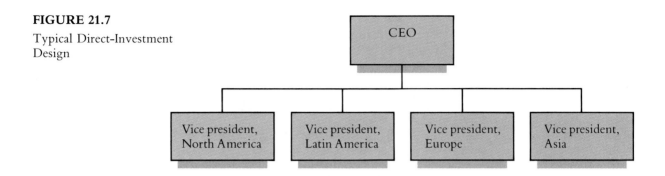

maquiladoras Light assembly plants built in northern Mexico close to the U.S. border which are given special tax breaks by the Mexican government

and each regional official is responsible for the company's investments and operations in his or her part of the world.

A fairly new approach to direct investment is the so-called maquiladoras concept. **Maquiladoras** are light assembly plants built in northern Mexico close to the U.S. border. The plants are given special tax breaks by the Mexican government, and the area is populated with workers willing to work for very low wages. There are now over a thousand plants in the region employing 300,000 workers, and more are planned. The plants are owned by major corporations, primarily from the United States, Japan, South Korea, and major European industrial countries. This concentrated form of direct investment benefits the country of Mexico, the companies themselves, and workers who might otherwise be without jobs. Some critics argue, however, that the low wages paid by the maquiladoras amount to little more than slave labor.[28]

Having wholly owned subsidiaries carries with it a number of benefits and liabilities. Managerial control is complete with direct investments, and profits do not have to be shared as they do in joint ventures. Purchasing an existing organization provides additional benefits in that the human resources, plant, and organizational infrastructure are already in place. Acquisition is also a way to purchase the brand-name identification of a product. This could be particularly important if the cost of introducing a new brand is high. Again, this is what Maytag did with its acquisition of the Hoover line. Notwithstanding these advantages, the company is now operating a part of itself entirely within the borders of a foreign country. The additional complexity in the decision making, the economic and political risks, and so forth may outweigh the advantages that can be obtained by international expansion.

Global Involvement

When a firm has engaged in numerous direct investments in foreign lands, it may be considered a fully global firm. However, global involvement reflects just as much an attitude on the part of managers.

Firms that follow this approach have a global orientation and worldwide approach to foreign markets and production. They search for opportunities all over the world and select the best strategy to serve each market. In some settings, they may use direct investment, in others licensing, in others joint ventures; in still others they might limit their involvement to exporting and importing.

There are several examples of these truly global companies. Nestlé, for example, is a Swiss firm that obtains only 3 percent of its sales from the Swiss market. CIBA-Geigy, a Swiss pharmaceutical firm, obtains only 6 percent of its sales from a domestic market. U.S. firms such as Ford, IBM, Coca-Cola, Pepsi, and McDonald's tend also to have a global character.

SUMMARY OF KEY POINTS

International business has grown to be one of the most important features of the modern worldwide economy. Learning to operate in a global economy is a significant challenge facing many managers today.

Many of the challenges of international management are unique issues associated with the international context. These difficulties reflect the economic, political, and cultural environments of international management.

The world of international business is complex, but it is possible to describe its structure through four types of countries that dominate the world economy—industrial market economies, developing nations, oil-exporting nations, and Eastern nonmarket economies.

International business is growing, but not all products or businesses should be moved in an international direction. The decision to adopt a global or nationally focused strategy depends upon both market and technological considerations. Personal values also come into play.

Even if a decision is made to enter the international arena, managers still have several options, including importing and exporting, licensing, joint ventures, and direct investment. Firms that choose among these options the best ways to enter a broad range of different countries can be thought of as truly global companies.

DISCUSSION QUESTIONS

Questions for Review

1. Define international business. What four factors have led to the rapid emergence of international business?
2. In what three areas are managers in the international arena especially challenged? List the basic factors affecting each area.
3. Identify five strategies for international marketing involvement. Briefly describe each one.

4. List four factors that influence the organizational design of international organizations. What general design alternatives are available to those organizations?

Questions for Analysis

5. An organization seeking to expand into international operations must monitor several different environments. Which aspect of each environment is likely to have the greatest impact on decisions involved in such a strategic move? Why?

6. What industries do you think will have the greatest impact on international business? Are there any industries that might not be affected by the trend toward international business? If so, which ones? If there are none, why are there none?

7. You are the CEO of an up-and-coming toy company and have plans to go international soon. What steps would you take to carry out that strategy? What areas would you stress in your decision-making process? How would you organize your company?

Questions for Application

8. Identify a local company that does business abroad. Interview an executive in that company. Why did the company go international? What major obstacles did it face? How successful has that decision been? Share your findings with the class.

9. Go to the library and find some information about the European Economic Community's move toward a relaxation of trade barriers. What will be the effect of that relaxation? What will be some of the difficulties? Do you think that it is a good idea? Why or why not?

10. Many organizations fail to allow for cultural and language differences when they do business with other countries. For example, Pepsi was introduced into Asia with the slogan "Come alive with Pepsi." The slogan, however, was translated as "Bring your ancestors back from the dead with Pepsi." Go to the library and locate mistakes made by other companies entering foreign markets. What did they do wrong? How could they have prevented their mistakes?

NOTES

1. "Photo Album: 100 Years of Snapshots," *U.S.A. Today*, June 24, 1988, pp. 1B, 2B; "Why Kodak Is Starting to Click Again," *Business Week*, February 23, 1987, pp. 134–138; "Kodak's New Research Lab in Japan Is Latest Weapon Aimed at Fuji Photo," *The Wall Street Journal*, October 17, 1988, p. B6; "New Kodak and Fuji Films Target Advanced Amateurs," *The Wall Street Journal*, March 17, 1989, p. B1.

2. "Most U.S. Companies Are Innocents Abroad," *Business Week*, November 16, 1987, pp. 168–169.

3. Richard M. Steers and Edwin L. Miller, "Management in the 1990s: The International Challenge," *The Academy of Management Executive*, February 1988, pp. 21–22; Nancy J. Adler, Robert Doktor, and S. Gordon Redding, "From the Atlantic to the Pacific Century: Cross-Cultural Management Reviewed," *Journal of Management*, June 1986, pp. 296–318.

4. For a more complete discussion of forms of international business, see Arvind Phatak, *International Dimensions of Management*, 2nd ed. (Boston: Kent, 1989).

5. "Help Wanted from the Multinationals," *Business Week*, February 29, 1988, pp. 68–70.

6. Richard I. Kirkland, Jr., "Entering a New Age of Boundless Competition," *Fortune*, March 14, 1988, pp. 40–48.

7. Raj Aggarwal, "The Strategic Challenge of the Evolving Global Economy," *Business Horizons*, July–August 1987, pp. 38–44.

8. Aggarwal, "The Strategic Challenge of the Evolving Global Economy."

9. Alex Taylor III, "The Tasks Facing General Motors," *Fortune*, March 13, 1989, pp. 52–59.

10. "U.S. Exporters That Aren't American," *Business Week*, February 29, 1988, pp. 70–71.

11. John D. Daniels and Lee H. Radebaugh, *International Business*, 5th ed. (Reading, Mass.: Addison-Wesley, 1989).

12. "Free Markets and Chapter 11—Can This Really Be China?" *Business Week*, May 9, 1988, pp. 60–62.

13. John Paul Newport, Jr., "Texas Faces Up to a Tougher Future," *Fortune*, March 13, 1989, pp. 102–112.

14. Richard I. Kirkland, Jr., "Outsider's Guide to Europe in 1992," *Fortune*, October 24, 1988, pp. 121–127; "Reshaping Europe: 1992 and Beyond," *Business Week*, December 12, 1988, pp. 48–51. See also a series of articles in a special section entitled "The Changing Map of Europe," *Harvard Business Review*, May–June 1989, pp. 77–101.

15. "Firms Address Worker's Cultural Variety," *The Wall Street Journal*, February 10, 1989, p. B1.

16. Daniels and Radebaugh, *International Business*.

17. Richard I. Kirkland, Jr., "Europe's New Entrepreneurs," *Fortune*, April 27, 1987, pp. 253–262.

18. Ben L. Kedia and Rabi S. Bhagat, "Cultural Constraints on Transfer of Technology Across Nations: Implications for Research in International and Comparative Management," *Academy of Management Review*, October 1988, pp. 559–571; Carla Rapoport, "Japan's Growing Global Reach," *Fortune*, May 22, 1989, pp. 48–56.

19. Karen Paul and Robert Barbato, "The Multinational Corporation in the Less Developed Country: The Economic Development Versus the North-South Model," *Academy of Management Review*, January 1985, pp. 8–14.

20. Louis Kraar, "The New Powers of Asia," *Fortune*, March 28, 1988, pp. 126–132.

21. Carla Rapoport, "Now Japan Is Plunging into Oil," *Fortune*, March 13, 1989, pp. 124–126.

22. Daniels and Radebaugh, *International Business*.

23. Charles F. Allison III, "A Conversation with John F. Welch, Jr., Chairman and CEO, General Electric Co.," *Outlook* (New York: Booz-Allen & Hamilton, 1985), pp. 4–12.

24. "Can Maytag Clean Up Around the World?" *Business Week*, January 30, 1989, pp. 86–87.

25. Ellen F. Jackofsky, John W. Slocum, Jr., and Sara J. McQuaid, "Cultural Values and the CEO: Alluring Companions?" *The Academy of Management Executive*, February 1988, pp. 39–49.
26. Daniels and Radebaugh, *International Business*.
27. "Can Maytag Clean Up Around the World?"
28. "The Magnet of Growth in Mexico's North," *Business Week*, June 6, 1988, pp. 48–50; "Will the New Maquiladoras Build a Better Mañana?" *Business Week*, November 14, 1988, pp. 102–106.

CASE 21.1

Cummins Overcomes International Competition

The Cummins Engine Company was founded in 1919. Clessie L. Cummins, with the backing of banker W. G. Irwin, began to try to make diesel engines that could be used for a variety of purposes. Their most spectacular success was in automobiles and trucks. It took 18 years for the firm to earn its first profit. In 1937, J. Irwin Miller, the grandnephew of the banker, took over the firm. During World War II, the value of diesel-powered trucks was apparent from their successful use by the military, and sales thereafter flourished.

In 1969, Miller saw to it that Henry B. Schacht (pronounced "Shocked") was named president of Cummins. Only 34 years old at the time, Schacht had been brought into the firm by Miller in 1964 as vice president for finance. One of Schacht's first tasks was to move to London and turn around Cummins's European division. He succeeded in just two years. Schacht went on to become CEO in 1973. In 1977, he replaced Miller as chairman, although Miller continued to serve on the board of directors and acted as a counselor and sounding board for him.

Schacht decided that rather than move Cummins into other, faster growing fields, he would keep the company in its traditional line of business and take on the international competition. During the past decade, Schacht faced and surmounted the onslaught of foreign competition.

During the late 1970s, Schacht had toured Japanese factories and realized that Cummins's plants were behind the Japanese in terms of technology. He knew that unless he could catch up, other strategic moves might not have lasting effects. So, to continue to be in a position to compete effectively with foreign rivals, Schacht decided to restructure Cummins during the early 1980s. More than $1 billion was spent to modernize plant, equipment, and engines to match the technology of the Japanese. Several plants were closed, reducing floor space use for the manufacture of engines by about 30 percent. Employment was reduced by nearly 3,500 workers.

In the mid-1980s, Japanese engine manufacturers were poised to enter the U.S. market and planned to move quickly to control it. Cummins's customers were testing engines from Komatsu Ltd. and Nissan Motor Co. and indicated to Cummins that those Japanese engines sold for 25 percent less than did comparable Cummins engines. Schacht moved swiftly. He cut prices on Cummins products by almost a third and managed to continue Cummins's position as number 1 in the industry. Indeed, the company still has over half of the North American market for heavy-duty diesel engines, and there are no Japanese engines on American built tractor-trailer trucks.

One move that Schacht feels will be of tremendous value to Cummins in the future was his effort to expand the product line and enter more markets. For years Cummins had produced a huge, 14-liter engine that is used to power dump trucks and 18-wheelers, but it did not have any of the smaller engines that were becoming more popular. In 1979 Cummins developed a 10-liter diesel that could be used in dump trucks and 18-wheelers and in many other vehicles as well. Since 1984, the company has moved into medium-duty engines for delivery trucks, pleasure boats, and power generators. Those endeavors took four years before they began to earn profits, however. Then in 1988, Cummins entered the light-truck market with a contract to supply optional diesel engines for Dodge Ram pickups. It hoped that more contracts of that sort would soon be forthcoming. Cummins is happy to be in these markets, but they are slow-growing markets, have small profit margins, and are far more competitive than the large-engine market. To expand its markets even farther, Cummins has begun work to introduce its own line of trucks and motor homes and has a division, Sytech, that is moving into the machine-tool market. Thanks at least in part to the weakening dollar, sales for Cummins's engines have increased overseas, in Britain and India.

Schacht's performance at Cummins has not gone unnoticed. In mid-1985, the Aluminum Company of America (Alcoa) was so impressed with his performance in standing up to the threat of Japanese competition that it wanted him to replace the Alcoa CEO. Alcoa directors began talking about a straight merger in which Schacht would become chairman of the combined companies. The deal, however, fell apart, although it earned Schacht a lot of favorable attention in the press. He has become one of the most highly regarded CEOs in America and has come to be called "Mr. Rust Belt" and the "Yankee Samurai."

Questions

1. What trends in international business seem most important to the Cummins Engine Company? Why?
2. How has Cummins responded to the challenge of international competition? Do you think that its response has been effective? Why or why not?
3. What levels of international involvement can you identify at Cummins Engine? Do you think that it should have more, less, or about the same level of involvement in the future? Why?
4. Do you think that Cummins will be able to maintain its market share? Why or why not?

REFERENCES: Ellen Benoit, "Cummins Engine: Hard Knocks," *Financial World*, January 12, 1988, pp. 11–12; "Mr. Rust Belt," *Business Week*, October 17, 1988, pp. 72–78, 82; "Cummins Engine Co.," *The Wall Street Journal*, October 18, 1988, p. B12; "Cummins Engine Co.," *The Wall Street Journal*, July 13, 1988, p. 30; Geoffrey N. Smith, "The Yankee Samurai," *Forbes*, July 14, 1986, pp. 82–83.

CASE 21.2

The Globalization of Sony

At the end of World War II, in 1946, Akio Morita joined with Masaru Ibuka and Tamon Maeda to form the Tokyo Tsushin Kogyo (TTK) or Tokyo Telecommunications Engineering Co. When they were unable to obtain bank financing for their venture, they turned to Akio's father, who provided them with funds through his company, Morita & Co. Morita & Co. is a 300-year-old organization that makes *sake*, the traditional Japanese rice wine, under the brand name Nenohimatsu; *miso*, a fermented soybean paste used in sauces and soups; and *shoyu*, or soy sauce. With Morita & Co.'s backing TTK became successful and gradually evolved into the consumer electronics firm of Sony.

Sony began to compete in the international market very early in its existence and has become quite effective internationally. As of 1987, approximately 70 percent of Sony's sales were derived from its international operations. Although Sony competes with such firms as RCA, GE, and Magnavox in the United States, it is a Japanese firm and must also compete with the likes of Hitachi, Toshiba, and Mitsubishi in Japan. All of these firms as well as European companies compete with one another in international markets.

Having loyal and productive personnel is not enough in the tough international market, however. Sony must keep developing new products and technologies as well. Sony learned the hard way that introducing new technologies can be tricky. In the mid-1970s, when Sony introduced the new Betamax technology, it assumed that its VCR competitors would have to follow suit or be left out in the cold. As it turned out, it was Sony that was left in the cold. Competitors banned together to support the VHS format and gradually took over the VCR market.

For that reason, Sony was very cautious as it launched yet another new VCR format, the 8-millimeter (8mm) version. Sony persuaded over 100 other companies to join with it in the research that led to its 8mm machines. The new format is so compact that Sony was able to introduce a version of its famous Walkman that could play 8mm video cassettes anywhere, including on airplanes. The problem was that virtually no commercial movies were available in the new format. So, Sony introduced camcorders, which could be used to record home movies or tape from television to provide movies in the new format.

Late in 1987, Sony bought CBS Records as a way to enter the market for digital audio tape (DAT) in the United States. CBS Records owns such titles as Bruce Springsteen's "Born in the U.S.A.," Michael Jackson's "Thriller," Benny Goodman's "Night and Day," and Frank Sinatra's "Stormy Weather." Having access to such titles and being able to produce them on DAT represented a quick way to move into this market. With this acquisition, Sony became the world's largest music producer. In 1989 Sony's CBS Records division bought Tree International of Nashville, Tennessee, a major publisher of country music. CBS Records plans to expand its operations into all forms of music publishing and serve as the foundation for further acquisitions in this area. Thus, Sony becomes a leading publisher as well as producer of music.

These moves established Sony as the world leader in several aspects of both audio and video media. Sony, however, does not believe in taking chances. It began a program to lend 8mm camcorders to schools for video yearbook productions. Sony's hope is that students will buy 8mm VCRs in order to view their yearbooks. If the plan works, Sony will have moved a long way toward introducing the new format to a new generation of video users.

To enhance its reputation in electronics, Sony has moved into computers. In 1981, Sony tried unsuccessfully to enter the U.S. computer market. Bad timing seemed to be the reason for that failure. In 1988 Sony again entered the market, and prospects appeared much better. Sony is marketing an industrial, 32-bit work station designed for high-powered business and engineering uses. Sony's machines use a second processor to speed up graphics applications and are priced about 25 percent lower than the products of some major competitors. The company hopes that these unique aspects will enable it to secure in the U.S market a toehold from which it could expand. The new work stations have been quite successful in Japan, where they have overcome the U.S. superiority mostly through aggressive price cutting and the use of Sony's established contacts and networks in the electronics industry.

Questions

1. What aspects of international business and management are most likely to be important to Sony? Why?
2. How has Sony responded to the challenge of international competition? Do you think that Sony's response has been effective? Why or why not?
3. What levels of international involvement can you identify at Sony? Do you think that Sony should have more, less, or about the same level of involvement in the future? Why?
4. Do you think that Sony will be successful with the 8mm format in video equipment? Why or why not? What impact is success or failure likely to have on Sony's future innovations and operations? Why?

REFERENCES: "Sony's CBS Records Unit Acquires Music Publisher Tree International," *The Wall Street Journal*, January 4, 1989, p. B4; "A Changing Sony Aims to Own the 'Software' That Its Products Need," *The Wall Street Journal*, December 30, 1988, pp. A1, A4; "Sony Isn't Mourning the 'Death' of Betamax," *Business Week*, January 25, 1988, p. 37; "Electronic Photographs Come into Sharper Focus," *Business Week*, March 7, 1988, p. 121; "Born in the U.S.A., Sold to Japan," *Time*, November 30, 1987, p. 66.

OUTLINE

Individual Ethics in the Workplace
How Ethics Are Formed · Managerial Ethics · The Ethical
Context of Management · Managing Ethical Behavior

Ethics, Social Responsibility, and Business
Changing Views of Social Responsibility · Organizational
Constituents · Areas of Social Responsibility

Managerial Approaches to Social Responsibility
The Social Responsibility Debate · Approaches to Social
Responsibility

The Government and Social Responsibility
Government Regulation of Business · Business Influence on
Government

Managing Social Responsibility
Formal Organizational Activities · Informal Organizational
Activities · Evaluating Social Performance

CHAPTER 22

Managing with Ethics and Social Responsibility

OBJECTIVES

After studying this chapter, you should be able to:

- Discuss individual ethics in the workplace.
- Relate ethics, social responsibility, and business.
- Identify and describe managerial approaches to social responsibility.
- Discuss the relationship between the government and social responsibility.
- Describe how organizations can manage social responsibility.

OPENING INCIDENT

Dean Witter Reynolds Inc., a subsidiary of Sears, is one of the world's largest brokerage houses. Stockbrokers at such houses receive a commission whenever their clients buy or sell securities. Thus, it is clearly in the broker's own interests to get clients to buy or sell frequently. Moreover, many brokers have ready access to the cash and securities of their clients.

Dean Witter's Boston office was recently the subject of an intensive investigation because of a number of alleged unethical and, in some cases, illegal activities by its brokers. One charge levied against them was "churning"—repeatedly buying and selling the same securities with client money to boost their own commissions.

Even more damaging, however, were criminal charges brought against one Dean Witter broker. The government charged that the broker used his professional connections to establish a good working relationship with four large investors. He then started investing their money for them outside the normal Dean Witter channels. While promising them huge returns, he was actually stealing $2.6 million of their money. Some Dean Witter officials speculated that he had bilked many other investors as well but his other victims were too embarrassed to come forward.[1]

*T*he problems faced by Dean Witter are similar in many ways to those confronted in recent years by Drexel Burnham Lambert Inc. and E. F. Hutton and Company, two other large brokerage houses.[2] They are illustrative of growing concerns throughout the American business system about issues of ethics and social responsibility. To try to overcome its newly tarnished image, Dean Witter decided to increase its advertising and give more to Boston charities. Other companies might have taken greater or lesser steps to redeem themselves.

This chapter explores the basic issues of ethics and social responsibility. We discuss individual ethics in the workplace and then expand the discussion to encompass ethics, social responsibility, and business. Next we focus on social responsibility itself by describing different perspectives and areas of concern. The role of government in social responsibility is then explored, and we conclude with an examination of how social responsibility might be effectively managed by organizations.

INDIVIDUAL ETHICS IN THE WORKPLACE

■ **ethics** An individual's personal beliefs regarding what is right and wrong or good and bad

We will define **ethics** as an individual's personal beliefs about what is right and wrong or good and bad.[3] Although this simple definition

ethical behavior Behavior that conforms to generally accepted social norms

unethical behavior Behavior that does not conform to generally accepted social norms

captures the spirit of the ethics concept, it has three specific implications that warrant discussion. First, notice that ethics are individually defined—people have ethics, organizations do not. Second, what constitutes ethical behavior can vary from one person to another. For example, one person who finds a twenty-dollar bill on the floor may feel it is all right to stick the money in his pocket; another will turn the money in to the lost-and-found department. Third, ethics are relative, not absolute. Thus, **ethical behavior** is in the eye of the beholder, but it is usually behavior that conforms to generally accepted social norms. **Unethical behavior** is behavior that does not conform to generally accepted social norms. In the sections that follow, we discuss how ethics are formed, managerial ethics, the ethical context of management, and organizations' attempts to manage ethical behavior.

How Ethics Are Formed

As illustrated in Figure 22.1, an individual's ethics are determined by five basic forces—family influences, peer influences, experiences, values and morals, and situational factors.

Family Influences Individuals start to form their ethics as children, in response to the behavior of their parents and the behaviors that their parents allow them to choose. For example, if a person's parents have

FIGURE 22.1

Determinants of Individual Ethics

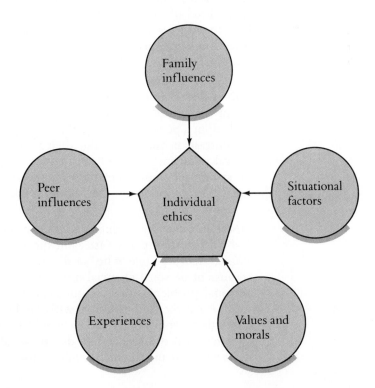

high ethical standards and adhere to those standards all the time and if they reward her for conforming and punish her for not conforming to those same standards, she is likely to adopt them for herself. If her parents engage in unethical behavior and allow her to do the same, she is likely to develop similarly low ethical standards for herself. Kenneth Harry Olsen, founder and CEO of Digital Equipment Corporation, grew up under the watchful eye of hardworking and honest parents who instilled in him their high ethical standards.[4]

Peer Influences   As people grow, mature, and enter school, they also become susceptible to influence from their peers with whom they interact everyday. If a child makes friends with a group of children who engage in shoplifting, petty theft, or drug abuse, he may come to engage in those activities. Likewise, if a person's peers have high ethical standards and reject such behaviors as drug abuse or theft, the individual is likely to adopt the same standards. In high school, Ken Olsen gravitated toward classmates who shared his interests in technology and electronics, and he had a good reputation among his neighbors as a solid citizen.

Experiences   As people go through their lives they experience literally dozens of events that shape their lives and, ultimately, their ethics. For example, if a person steals something and then feels remorse and guilt, she is not likely to steal again. But if she feels happy with her ill-gotten gain, she is likely to continue to steal. One of the events that shaped Ken Olsen's ethics was an early stint working for IBM. He was appalled at the level of insularity there and the extent to which IBM managers kept themselves away from workers. He vowed that when he had his own company, people would have more freedom and he would be more accessible to all his workers.

Values and Morals   A person's values and morals also contribute to his or her ethics.[5] A person who highly values money, for example, will adopt a personal code of ethics that promotes the pursuit of wealth. In contrast, people who value their families may have a different set of ethical guidelines. Ken Olsen's ethics have been greatly influenced by his strong religious beliefs. He has given large portions of his personal fortune to a foundation that supports Christian philanthropies.

Situational Factors   Ethics are influenced by situational factors—things that arise naturally but often unexpectedly in a person's life. For example, many people who steal money from their employers do so because of personal financial difficulties. If they had been able to avoid personal problems, they might also have avoided the temptation to steal. An early confrontation with his board of directors taught Ken Olsen that responsibility had to be widely shared. This lesson translated into the form of organization design he adopted for the company and still affects his management philosophy.

Managerial Ethics

Ethics can affect managerial work in any number of ways, but three areas are of special concern. They are summarized in Table 22.1.

Relationship of the Firm to the Employee An area of special concern regarding managerial ethics is how the firm treats its employees. Example issues include hiring and firing, wages and working conditions, and employee privacy. For example, most people would consider it unethical if a manager hired someone just because he is her cousin or fired someone because of her religion. Similarly, knowing that someone desperately needs to work and then paying abnormally low wages would be considered unethical. Finally, spreading the word that an employee has AIDS would generally be an unethical breach of privacy.

Relationship of the Employee to the Firm Numerous ethical issues surround the relationship of the employee to the firm. Examples include conflicts of interest, secrecy, and honesty and expense accounts. For example, accepting a bribe from someone would represent a conflict of interest. For this very reason, Wal-Mart does not allow its merchandise buyers to accept meals or gifts from sales representatives.[6] Divulging company secrets to someone from a competing organization would also clearly be unethical, as would stealing or padding an expense account. Some managers routinely add extra meals, service charges, and car mileage to their expense account reports to "earn" a little extra income.

Relationship of the Firm to Other Economic Agents Managerial ethics come into play in the relationship between the firm and other economic

TABLE 22.1

Special Areas of Concern For Managerial Ethics

Area of Concern	Sample Issues
Relationship of the firm to the employee	Hiring and firing Wages and Working Conditions Privacy
Relationship of the employee to the firm	Conflicts of interest Secrecy Honesty and expense accounts
Relationship of the firm to other economic agents	Customers Competitors Stockholders Suppliers Dealers Unions

SOURCE: Adapted from Thomas M. Garrett and Richard J. Klonoski, Business Ethics, 2nd ed. (Englewood Cliffs, N.J.: Prentice-Hall, 1986). Adapted by permission.

A key ingredient in managerial ethics is how the firm relates to its customers. Land's End has achieved considerable success as a mail-order retailer by stressing ethical and fair practices in all its dealings with customers. Through an astute mix of catalogs and telephones, Land's End has steadily increased its sales over the years, reaching over $336 million in 1988. The company's founder and CEO, Gary Comer, requires that all his telephone operators be thoroughly familiar with the merchandise they sell and that they treat each customer with respect and dignity.

agents, such as customers, competitors, stockholders, suppliers, dealers, and unions. Normal ethical standards suggest that products or services offered to customers should be safe, be accompanied by appropriate information on product features, uses, and limitations, and not be excessively priced.[7] Relations with competitors are also dictated by ethical standards. Unfair business practices, denigration of competitors, and price fixing, for example, would all be unethical.

Ethical standards dictate that companies be truthful and honest with their stockholders. Misleading stockholders by telling them that the company is going to report record profits next year when a manager really expects only a modest profit would generally be considered unethical, as would paying excessive compensation to the firm's management team. Similarly, organizations need to be fair and honest in their agreements and negotiations with suppliers, dealers, and unions. Convincing a supplier that a price break is needed or convincing a union that wage concessions are needed because of impending losses is unethical if the firm actually expects to make a profit.

The Ethical Context of Management

Ethical or unethical actions by particular managers do not occur in a vacuum.[8] They most often occur in an organizational context that is conducive to them. The Dean Witter scandal took place in an office where over 100 stockbrokers were supervised by a single branch manager. Each broker had ample freedom to do whatever he or she wanted with little fear of being monitored. "Management in Practice" describes how the organizational context at Anheuser-Busch has led to several questionable business practices by managers there.

The starting point for understanding the ethical context of management is the individual's own personal ethical standards. Some people are willing to risk personal embarrassment or lose their job before they would consider doing something unethical. Other people are much more easily swayed and might be willing to commit significant crimes to further their own careers or for personal gain.

Organizational practices are also an important dimension of the ethical context. Some organizations openly permit, and may even encourage, unethical business practices as long as they are in the best interests of the firm. A manager who becomes aware of an ethical dilemma and then comes down on the unethical side has added a story or legend to the organizational culture that says such activity is acceptable. For example, the CEO of Beech-Nut recently discovered that his firm was using additives in apple juice advertised as 100 percent pure. He decided to try to cover up the deception until the remaining juice could be disposed of. When the cover-up was discovered, the company had to pay several million dollars in fines, and the CEO was sentenced to a jail term.[9]

The organization's environment also contributes to its ethical context. In a highly competitive or highly regulated industry, for example, a

MANAGEMENT IN PRACTICE

ANHEUSER-BUSCH CONFRONTS QUESTIONABLE ETHICS

Anheuser-Busch was begun in 1860 by Eberhard Anheuser and his son-in-law, Adolphus Busch. Once they perfected Budweiser as a light alternative to the heavy beers that dominated the market at that time, they gradually were able to increase their market share. In terms of sales they finally overtook the market leader, Pabst, in 1901. The company struggled to survive during Prohibition but then continued to increase its market share until by 1960 it was number 1 with about 10 percent of the market.

In 1984 the Bureau of Alcohol, Tobacco and Firearms accused Anheuser of linking its purchase of advertising time on Chicago White Sox broadcasts to the stocking of Budweiser at the White Sox's Comiskey Park. That sort of linking is an illegal marketing tactic. Anheuser did not admit any wrongdoing, but the cost of settlement was over $1 million. Worse, Budweiser was advertised neither in the broadcasts nor in Comiskey Park during 1987.

In spite of increased penalties and the loss of a major outlet, Anheuser-Busch had not learned its lesson. In 1987, several key marketing executives voluntarily resigned or were forced to resign because of alleged kickbacks from suppliers. Included among them was the president, who had been with Anheuser-Busch for 35 years. Court records from bankruptcy

proceedings for a St. Louis promotions company, Hanley Worldwide Inc., indicated that Anheuser's director of promotions had a Porsche partially paid for by Hanley. A deposition taken in those proceedings indicated that Anheuser's vice president for sales and vice president for wholesale operations had together received more than $150,000 in kickbacks. Those three executives also left the company.

While all of the involved executives were denying any wrongdoing, the Federal Bureau of Investigation and a federal grand jury began to look into the charges. In 1988 the grand jury returned indictments against two of the executives. They were charged with faking invoices over a five-year period to obtain cash, racquet-club memberships, clothing, and airline tickets. To make matters worse, the Brooklyn bottler of Soho Natural Soda sued Anheuser for allegedly copying its flavors and logo.

Efforts are under way to clean up the mess left by these scandals. The scandals, however, have not hurt sales. Anheuser's market share has continued to rise while all this was going on.

REFERENCES: "How Do You Follow an Act like Bud?" *Business Week*, May 2, 1988, pp. 118–121; Alan J. Zakon, "It's Just Not Good Enough," *Management Review*, January 1988, pp. 20–21; "Anheuser-Busch: The Scandal May Be Small Beer After All," *Business Week*, May 11, 1987, pp. 72–73; "Beer Boss Bites Bullet," *Time*, April 6, 1987, p. 55.

---

manager may feel great pressure to perform at a high level—regardless of the methods she or he chooses to use. Culture is also a factor. In Japan, managerial success is often determined by the kinds of connections the manager is able to establish. One Japanese manager, Hiromasa Ezoe, CEO of the Recruit Company conglomerate, was recently found guilty of giving lucrative stock options to a variety of well-placed government officials.[10]

Managing Ethical Behavior

Spurred in part by recent scandals involving insider trading and similarly dishonorable acts and in part by a sense of enhanced corporate consciousness, many organizations have increased their emphasis on ethical behavior by employees.[11] This emphasis has taken many forms.

The starting point in any effort to enhance ethical behavior, however, has to be top management—the group that establishes the organization's culture and defines what will and will not be acceptable to the organization. Ken Olsen plays the key role in shaping ethical standards at Digital. The CEO at Beech-Nut played just as dramatic a role in setting the tone for his company as well. Some executives have even gone so far as to charge a subordinate with the responsibility of helping them maintain appropriate ethical standards by periodically questioning their motives, challenging their reasons for certain decisions, and raising other ethical issues.[12]

Some companies offer their employees training in how to cope with ethical dilemmas. For example, at Boeing, line managers lead training sessions for other employees. The company also has an ethics committee that reports directly to the board of directors. Chemical Bank, Xerox, and McDonnell Douglas have established ethics training programs for their managers.[13]

Organizations are going to greater lengths to formalize their positions regarding ethical behavior. Some, like General Mills and Johnson & Johnson, have prepared detailed guidelines describing how employees are to deal with suppliers, customers, competitors, and other constituents. Others, like Whirlpool, Hewlett-Packard, and Raytheon, have developed and publicized formal **codes of ethics**—written statements of the values and ethical standards that guide the firms' actions. The Whirlpool code is illustrated in Figure 22.2.

codes of ethics   Formal, written statements of what values and ethical standards guide a firms' actions

Of course, no code, guideline, or training program can truly replace an individual's personal judgment about what is right or wrong in any particular situation. Such devices may explain what people should do, but they often fail to help people deal with the consequences of their choices. To make ethical choices may lead to unpleasant outcomes—firing, rejection by one's colleagues, the forfeiture of potential monetary gain. The manager at Beech-Nut who blew the whistle on the apple-juice deception was eventually forced to resign because others thought he was a traitor to the organization. Thus, managers must be prepared to confront their own conscience and weigh it against the various options available when making the difficult decisions that every manager must make.[14]

ETHICS, SOCIAL RESPONSIBILITY, AND BUSINESS

We noted earlier that ethics are held and followed by individuals and that organizations do not have ethics. Organizations, however, have to relate to their environment in ways that may involve ethical dilemmas and decisions. **Social responsibility** is the obligation of an organization to protect and enhance the societal context in which the organization functions.[15] The sections that follow trace the changing views of social responsibility, identify relevant organizational constituencies, and describe basic areas of social responsibility.

■ **social responsibility**   The set of obligations an organization has to protect and enhance the societal context in which it functions

The question of ethics in business conduct has become of the most serious challenges to the business community in modern times.

At Whirlpool, we share with millions of other Americans a deep concern over recent revelations of unethical and often illegal conduct on the part of some of this nation's most prominent business people and corporations.

The purpose of this message is not to pass judgement on any of these occurrences; each must and will be judged on its own merits by those charged with that responsibility.

Rather this message is intended to place firmly on record the position of Whirlpool Corporation regarding business ethics and the conduct of every Whirlpool employee. It represents an irrevocable commitment to our customers and stockholders that our actions will be governed by the highest personal and professional standards in all activities relating to the operation of this business.

Over the years, circumstances have prompted us to develop a number of specific policies dealing with such critical elements of ethical business practice as conflicts of interest, gifts, political activities, entertainment, and substantiation of claims.

We also have a basic statement of ethics which places the ultimate responsibility for ethical behavior precisely where it belongs in any organization . . . on the shoulders of the person in charge:

"No employee of this company will ever be called upon to do anything in the line of duty that is morally, ethically or legally wrong.

Furthermore, if in the operation of this complex enterprise, an employee should come upon circumstances of which he or she cannot be personally proud, it should be that person's duty to bring it to the attention of top management if unable to correct the matter in any other way."

Every Whirlpool manager carries the dual responsibility implicit in this policy statement, including the chairman of the board.

Our written policies deal with nearly all facets of business experience. We review, revise and recommunicate them to our managers on a regular basis . . . and we see that our managers carry on the communication throughout the company.

But as a practical matter, there is no way to assure ethical behavior with written policies or policy statements.

In the final analysis, "ethical behavior" must be an integral part of the organization, a way of life that is deeply ingrained in the collective corporate body.

I believe this condition exists at Whirlpool, and that it constitutes our greatest single assurance that this company's employees will conduct the affairs of this business in a manner consistent with the highest standards of ethical behavior.

At Whirlpool we have certain ways of doing things. They are commonly accepted practices, enforced not by edict, but rather by a mutual conviction that they will, in the long term, work in the best interest of our customers, our stockholders, the company and all its employees.

In any business enterprise, ethical behavior must be a tradition, a way of conducting one's affairs that is passed on from generation to generation of employees at all levels of the organization. It is the responsibility of management, starting at the very top, to both set the example by personal conduct and create an environment that not only encourages and rewards ethical behavior, but which also makes anything less totally unacceptable.

I believe this has been achieved at Whirlpool. The men who founded this company back in 1911 were individuals possessed of great integrity and honor. They fostered a tradition of ethical conduct in their business practices, and they perpetuate that tradition through careful selection of the people who would one day fall heir to leadership of the company.

The system works. Time and time again I have witnessed its efficacy. It shows no hospitality whatsoever to those not willing to abide by its standards, and unerringly identifies and purges them.

Unfortunately, the system is not automatically self-sustaining, it must be constantly reaffirmed by each new generation of leaders. In the position I now occupy, I view this as one of my most important responsibilities.

As this company grows, and as the pressures upon it increase, maintaining our tradition of ethical conduct becomes an increasingly difficult task. But I am confident it will be maintained, because it is necessary for continued growth, profitability and success.

FIGURE 22.2

Whirlpool's Code of Ethical Conduct

SOURCE: "Ethics As a Practical Matter: A Message from David R. Whitwam, Chairman of the Board," Whirlpool Corporation. Reprinted by permission of Whirlpool Corporation.

Changing Views of Social Responsibility

Views of social responsibility held by business, the government, and the public at large have changed dramatically over the years. There have been three critical turning points in the evolution of social responsibility. They are illustrated in Figure 22.3.[16]

Entrepreneurial Era Occurred during the late 1800s when captains of industry built huge empires in various industries

Phase 1   The first turning point in the evolution of social responsibility occurred during the late 1800s and is generally associated with what many now call the **Entrepreneurial Era**. The so-called captains of industry, including John D. Rockefeller, Cornelius Vanderbilt, J. P. Morgan, and Andrew Carnegie, were amassing fortunes and building empires in industries ranging from oil to railroads to banking to steel. Prior to their day and age, virtually all businesses were small, so they were really the first executives to control power and wield influence at a national level. Unfortunately, in many instances they chose to abuse their power through such practices as labor lockouts, discriminatory pricing, kickbacks, and tax evasion. Eventually, outcries from public officials and other leaders forced Washington to take a stand. Several laws were passed that outlawed some business practices and restricted others. These laws were significant because they defined a clear pattern of interrelationships among business, the government, and society, and they indicated for the first time that business had a role to play in society beyond the pure economics of profit maximization.

Depression Era   1929 through the 1930s; the public blamed business for economic problems and sought to regulate business through government to prevent such problems in the future

Phase 2   Although there were subtle shifts and changes in views toward social responsibility, there was not another major turning point until the **Depression Era**. During the twilight of the Entrepreneurial Era, business continued to grow and expand, but in a more orderly and acceptable fashion, and big business began to dominate the American economic scene. It was natural, then, for people to blame big business for the stock-market crash of 1929. As a part of Franklin Roosevelt's New Deal, the government passed more laws to protect investors and smaller businesses. The Securities and Exchange Commission was created in 1934 to regulate the sales of securities and to curb unfair stock-market practices. As an outgrowth of these and other actions, the social responsibility of business was even more clearly delineated. In particular, government actions provided a clear message that business could no longer play a passive role in American society but instead needed to take an active role in promoting the general welfare of the American public.

FIGURE 22.3

Three Turning Points in the Evolution of Social Responsibility

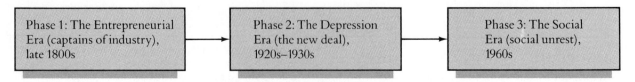

| Phase 1: The Entrepreneurial Era (captains of industry), late 1800s | → | Phase 2: The Depression Era (the new deal), 1920s–1930s | → | Phase 3: The Social Era (social unrest), 1960s |

Social Era of the 1960s   A period of great social unrest during which business was seen as responsible for social problems and called upon to help redress those problems

Phase 3   The third major turning point in views of social responsibility came during the **Social Era of the 1960s**. This period of American history was characterized by a great deal of social unrest. The civil rights movement and widespread opposition to the war in Vietnam energized many Americans to examine the nation's values, priorities, and goals and to accept greater responsibility for their own actions. Students, for example, often blamed big businesses like McDonnell Douglas and Du Pont for helping promote and extend the Vietnam War. There were general feelings of unrest among many young Americans as to what America was really like. In partial response to this unrest, the government once again increased its involvement in business. Tighter restrictions on pollution, consumer warnings on products like cigarettes and flammable clothing, and increased regulation of many other industries all grew from concerns expressed during this period. And the Social Era brought to the fore the fact that the behaviors of business were being closely watched and evaluated—rightly or wrongly—by myriad factions in American society. The unrest of the 1960s has passed, but its effects are still felt.

Organizational Constituents

To whom is business responsible? Who holds the reins of accountability? In Chapter 3 we described the task environment of organizations. Expanding on those ideas just a bit allows us to identify a broader network of **constituents**—people and organizations that are directly affected by the behaviors of an organization and that have a stake in its performance. These constituents are depicted in Figure 22.4.

constituents   People and other organizations who are directly affected by the behaviors of an organization and who have a stake in its performance

For example, the people who own and invest in an organization are affected by virtually anything the firm does. If the firm's managers commit criminal acts or breach acceptable ethical standards, organizational profits, stock prices, and so forth are all likely to decline. If the organization gives too much of its profits to social programs, the owners and investors will get a lower return on their investment. Likewise, the actions of an organization reflect on its employees, interest groups, local government, suppliers, and each of the other constituents noted in the figure.

Any firm that neglects or ignores one of its constituents is asking for trouble. For example, managers at Allegheny International invested a half-million dollars in buying a lavish Pittsburgh home in which to entertain clients. The company maintained a fleet of five corporate jets so that its managers could go anywhere at any time. The company made large loans to employees at a 2 percent interest rate. Nepotism was rampant. A close analysis of Allegheny's performance suggested that it spent too much on executive perquisites, that conflicts of interest clouded executive judgment, that improper accounting methods were used, that information was withheld from shareholders, and that the board of directors did an inadequate job of monitoring top management. Consequently, investors, the government, employees, suppliers,

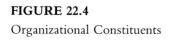

FIGURE 22.4

Organizational Constituents

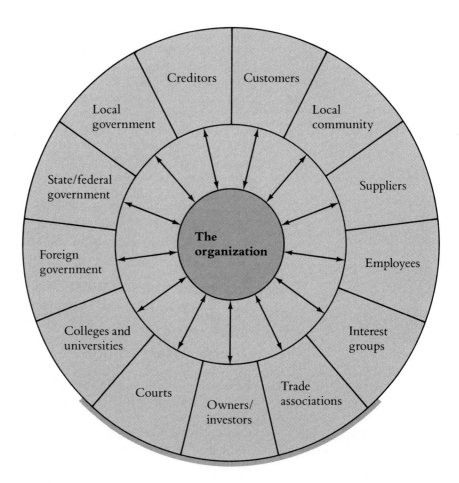

and the local community all were affected.[17] "The Global View" describes similar problems at Harrods, the London department store.

In contrast, consider the behavior of Levi Strauss. The company gives 2.4 percent of its pretax earnings to worthy causes, treats employees and suppliers with dignity and respect, plays an active role in important trade associations, has had no major ethical scandals, is respected by competitors, maintains good relations with all levels of government, and contributes annually to college and university programs. Its managers do an excellent job of maintaining good relations with the firm's constituents.[18]

Areas of Social Responsibility

Organizations that choose to exercise social responsibility have a number of areas in which to do so. We have hinted at some of them; Figure 22.5 makes the list explicit.

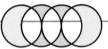

THE GLOBAL VIEW

BACK-STABBING AT HARRODS

Harrods is a huge British department store that caters to the rich. A lot of questions are being asked by the British Trade & Industry Department about the conduct of the owners of Harrods and how that conduct impacts constituencies other than the owners.

Roland W. "Tiny" Rowland is the managing director of the British conglomerate Lonrho PLC. In a career sometimes marked by charges of questionable payments to former directors and political leaders, he built an empire worth over $6 billion a year. It includes holdings in the House of Fraser, Harrods's parent company.

In 1975 Rowland met Mohamed Al-Fayed, an Egyptian-born financier, when Al-Fayed swapped his holdings in a British construction firm for a share of Lonrho. In 1981, Rowland owned almost 30 percent of the House of Fraser and moved to acquire the remainder. The Monopolies & Mergers Commission rejected his plan. It ruled that Lonrho's textile interests posed competitive complications with Harrods and that the Lonrho organization did not have enough managerial expertise to handle Harrods effectively.

In 1984, Al-Fayed offered to buy Rowland's share in the House of Fraser. Rowland turned him down; but finally agreed late in the year to accept his offer. Rowland thought that the shares would be in friendly hands and that he could buy them back from Al-Fayed if the Monopolies & Mergers Commission were to change its ruling on his plan to buy complete control of the firm. However, Rowland found that the hands that had bought his shares were not friendly. Al-Fayed and his brother became directors of the House of Fraser and moved to take complete control.

Rowland, feeling betrayed by people whom he had trusted, attacked the Al-Fayed brothers in newspapers and through the distribution of pamphlets charging that they were putting the firm too deeply in debt, had not been honest about the source of the funds for the takeover, and were disrupting operations at Harrods. The Al-Fayeds countered with libel suits, but Rowland finally persuaded the British Trade & Industry Department to investigate the takeover.

The report of the Trade & Industry Department was expected to be released early in 1989. Although no one expected it to be so damning that the Al-Fayeds need fear any specific actions against them, most financial analysts were convinced that enough problems would be uncovered to weaken their hold on the firm and weaken their ability to obtain any financing necessary to keep it functioning effectively.

REFERENCES: "Hanging Out the Dirty Laundry at Harrods," *Business Week*, September 26, 1988, pp. 116, 120; James Fallon, "Mohamed Al-Fayed Takes Personal Control of Harrods," *Daily News Record*, October 14, 1987, p. 2; Doug Carroll, "Harrods Puts Ritz on Sale," *USA Today*, July 2, 1987, p. B1; "Simple Answer Needed to Simple Question," *New Statesman*, June 13, 1986, p. 4.

The Environment   One critical area of social responsibility is the natural environment. In days gone by, many businesses indiscriminately dumped sewage, waste products, and trash into streams and rivers, the air, vacant lots, and anywhere else they could think of. Now, laws regulate such activities, and companies themselves, in many instances, have seen the error of their ways and have become more socially responsible. As a result, most forms of air and water pollution have been reduced. Nevertheless, much remains to be done. Current concerns center on business contributions to the problems of acid rain, depletion of the ozone layer, global warming, sewage disposal, ocean dumping, hazardous wastes, and the disposal of ordinary garbage.[19] To illustrate why such issues are of concern, consider the behavior of Ashland Oil. In 1988, one of its storage tanks ruptured, spilling over

FIGURE 22.5

Areas of Social Responsibility

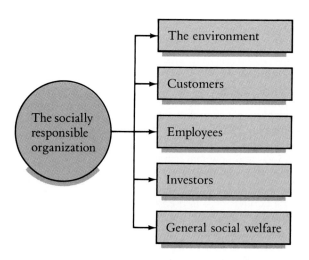

500,000 gallons of diesel fuel into the Monongahela River. The company moved quickly to clean up the spill but was indicted for violating U.S. environmental laws.[20] And the ramifications of the Exxon oil spill off the coast of Alaska in 1989 are still being felt today.

Customers   Organizations can adopt a socially responsible stance toward their customers. President John F. Kennedy outlined four basic consumer rights—the right to safe products, the right to be informed about all relevant aspects of a product, the right to be heard in the event of a complaint, and the right of consumers to choose what they buy. Land's End, a fast-growing mail-order house, is a company that has profited from good customer relations. Its operators are trained to be totally informed, to not push unwanted merchandise onto customers, to listen to complaints, and to treat customers with respect. As a result, the company's sales have been increasing 20 percent each year.[21] In contrast, Ashland Oil was found guilty of rigging bids with other contractors in order to charge inflated prices for highway work in Tennessee and North Carolina.[22]

Employees   Organizations can be socially responsible in their dealings with their employees. Treating employees fairly, making them a part of the team, and respecting their dignity and basic human needs can go a long way toward having a satisfied work force. One special case in this area involves Affirmative Action. Companies like 3M and Golden West Financial are going to great lengths to find, hire, train, and promote qualified minorities.[23] Once again, Ashland Oil provides a counterpoint. It was recently charged with wrongfully firing two employees because they refused to cover illegal payments made overseas.

Investors   Organizations need to take a socially responsible stance toward their investors. Managers should maintain proper accounting

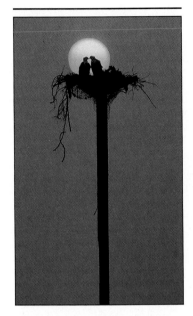

Maintaining the environment is a critical area of social responsibility. Many businesses are increasingly searching for better ways to live in harmony with nature. The Power Company is a large utility company serving a major portion of the Eastern seaboard. For years the Power Company has had problems with ospreys building nests on the top of its utility poles. Unfortunately, the electric lines posed hazards for the birds, and the birds often disrupted service to utility customers. So the Power Company has come up with a novel idea—it now builds tall nesting poles close to its other poles for the ospreys to use.

procedures, provide appropriate information to shareholders about the current and projected financial performance of the firm, and manage the organization in such a way as to protect shareholder rights and investments. Insider trading, illegal stock manipulation, and the withholding of financial data are examples of recent wrongdoings attributed to many different businesses. The former chairman of Ashland Oil was recently accused of selling important Ashland documents to Iran in order to manipulate the supply and price of oil for personal gain.[24]

General Social Welfare   Some people believe that organizations should be involved in promoting the general social welfare. Examples of such practices include making contributions to charities, philanthropic organizations, and not-for-profit foundations and associations; supporting museums, symphonies, and public radio and television; and being more involved in health and education.[25] Some people also believe that business should be taking a greater role in correcting some of the political wrongs that exist. A prominent illustration of this feeling is the argument that businesses should withdraw their operations from South Africa to protest that nation's policies of apartheid.[26] Kodak and IBM have responded to these concerns by shutting down their operations in South Africa.

MANAGERIAL APPROACHES TO SOCIAL RESPONSIBILITY

There are many different managerial views of and approaches to social responsibility. Some of the arguments for and against social responsibility border on the philosophical; others are much more pragmatic.

The Social Responsibility Debate

At first blush, there would seem to be little disagreement about the need for social responsibility. The truth of the matter, however, is that several arguments are used by those who oppose and those who advocate social responsibility.[27] Some of the most salient arguments on both sides of the issue are listed in Table 22.2.

Arguments Against Social Responsibility   On the negative side, some people, including famed economist Milton Friedman, argue that social responsibility detracts from the basic mission of business as defined by American culture—to earn profits for owners. For example, every dollar that Chevron or General Electric spend on social programs or give to charity is one less dollar that can be distributed to owners as a dividend. Another argument used in opposition to business social re-

TABLE 22.2

Arguments For and Against
Social Responsibility

Arguments For Social Responsibility	Arguments Against Social Responsibility
1. Business creates problems and should therefore help solve them.	1. The purpose of business in American society is to generate profit for owners.
2. Corporations are citizens in our society.	2. Involvement in social programs gives business too much power.
3. Business often has the resources necessary to solve problems.	3. There is potential for conflicts of interest.
4. Business is a partner in our society, along with the government and the general population.	4. Business lacks the expertise to manage social programs.

sponsibility is that corporations in America already wield enormous power. Promoting their active involvement in social programs gives them even more, and in the absence of a system of checks and balances, the chances for abuse of power increase as well.

Some arguments against social responsibility center on the idea of conflicts of interest. Suppose that a manager is in charge of deciding which charity is to receive a large grant from her business. Administrators of various charities may try to convince her that their organization is most deserving. Political leaders might get involved as well by advocating their pet causes.

A final argument against social responsibility is that business lacks the expertise to understand how to assess and make decisions about social programs. For example, a company might give its money to support the local symphony when there are much greater needs elsewhere. People who hold this position point to what they see as the alarming trend on the part of business to tie products to social causes. The trend started in 1983, when American Express said that it would donate 1 cent to the Statue of Liberty restoration project each time one of its credit cards was used. Since then, Procter & Gamble and MasterCard have jumped on the bandwagon. Critics warn that companies may start exerting too much influence over the charitable causes they become associated with and the charities may start serving as marketers to help firms sell products.[28]

Arguments for Social Responsibility   There is a set of logical arguments used by people who are in favor of social responsibility. One significant point is that since business creates many of the problems that social

Many people feel that business should work with the government and the general population in a socially responsible way toward the betterment of everyone. Xerox has taken this message to heart and made it the theme of its entire corporate culture. The ad shown here stresses the company's commitment to equal employment opportunity.

responsibility causes usually address, it should play a major role in solving them. This would especially be the case in areas like pollution and toxic waste cleanup. It is also argued that corporations are legally defined entities with most of the same obligations and privileges as private citizens. Logically, then, they should play a citizenship role.

Still another argument in favor of the social responsibility of business is that business often has the resources to help solve social problems. Government organizations may already have their budgets stretched to the limit, and private contributions may be at an upper limit as well. Many large businesses, however, often have surplus revenues that could be used for the benefit of all. Finally, some people argue that business is a partner in society in conjunction with the government and the general population; and as a partner, it should do its fair share to help the others.

Approaches to Social Responsibility

There are clear arguments on both sides of the social responsibility debate. Some advocate an even larger social role for business; others argue that business's role is already too large. Not surprisingly, business often adopts a wide range of positions on social responsibility. There are four basic stances that an organization can take vis-à-vis its environment and obligations to society. As illustrated in Figure 22.6, these four approaches fall along a continuum ranging from the lowest to the highest levels of socially responsible behavior.

FIGURE 22.6

Approaches to Social
Responsibility

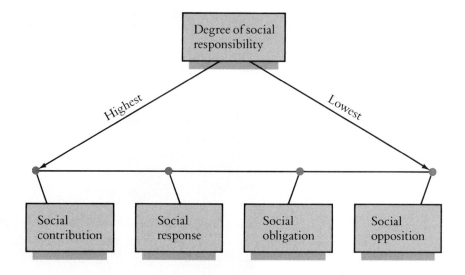

social opposition An approach to social responsibility
in which firms do as little as
possible in the social responsibility arena

social obligation A social
responsibility stance in which
an organization will do everything that is required of it
legally but nothing more

Social Opposition　A few organizations take what might be called a
social opposition approach to social responsibility. These firms usually
do as little as possible in the social responsibility arena. When they
cross the ethical or legal line that separates acceptable from unacceptable
behavior, their response is to deny or cover up what they did. We noted
Beech-Nut's problems with its apple juice. As its top managers became
aware of their problem, they in turn denied it, tried to hide it, and
eventually attempted to cover up the truth. As also noted earlier, Ashland Oil has an unfortunate history of alleged social wrongdoing followed by less-than-ideal responses.

Social Obligation　One step removed from social opposition is **social
obligation**—a stance that the organization will do everything that is
required of it legally but nothing more. This is the view most consistent
with the basic arguments used against social responsibility. Managers
in such organizations take the position that their job is to generate
profits. A firm with this position would install whatever pollution
control equipment was dictated by law but would not install higher-
quality equipment even though it might better limit pollution. They
would only do what they were required to do. Tobacco companies like
Philip Morris take this position regarding their international marketing
efforts. In the United States, tobacco companies are legally required to
include warnings to smokers on their products and to limit their advertising to prescribed media, and they follow these rules to the letter
of the law. Many other countries have no such rules, however; so the
cigarette makers use stronger methods. In many African countries,
cigarettes are heavily promoted, some cigarettes contain higher levels
of tar and nicotine than those sold in the United States, and few cigarette
packs contain health warning labels.

■ **social response** A social responsibility stance in which an organization meets its basic legal and ethical obligations and also goes beyond social obligation on a selected basis

Social Response   The next general approach to social responsibility is the social response view. A firm that adopts the **social response** position meets its basic legal and ethical obligations and will also go beyond purely social obligation on a selective basis. Such firms voluntarily agree to participate in certain limited programs, but they often have to be sold on their benefits first. For example, both Exxon and IBM will match contributions made by their employees to charitable causes, and many organizations will respond to requests for donations to Little League, Girl Scouts, and so forth. The point, however, is that someone has to knock on the door and ask.

■ **social contribution** A social responsibility stance in which an organization views itself as a citizen in a society and proactively seeks opportunities to contribute to that society

Social Contribution   The highest degree of social responsibility that a firm can exhibit is the social contribution approach. Firms that take the **social contribution** approach take to heart the arguments in favor of social responsibility. They view themselves as citizens in a society and, as a result, proactively seek opportunities to contribute to that society. An excellent example of social contribution is the Ronald McDonald House program undertaken by McDonald's Corporation. These are houses, generally located in urban areas and close to major medical centers, that families can use while their sick children are receiving medical treatment. In a similar vein, both Sears and General Electric have recently established programs to help promote artists and cultural performers. These and related activities and programs go far beyond the mere response to a request. They indicate a sincere and potent commitment to improving the general social welfare in this country.

We should also note that these categories are not necessarily pure—

The social contribution approach to social responsibility involves taking a proactive stance toward helping our general society. The Body Shop, the world's largest cosmetics retailer, clearly takes this approach. Originally based in England but with stores around the world, like the one shown here in Toronto, the Body Shop has only recently entered the United States. The company's founder and CEO, Anita Roddick, has very strong opinions about social responsibility. For example, she only grants franchises to investors who share her concern for the environment and she strongly encourages her employees to get involved in social causes ranging from AIDS relief to child abuse.

that is, organizations do not clearly fit into one approach on all dimensions. Although the McDonald's Corporation Ronald McDonald House program has been widely applauded, McDonald's came under fire a few years ago for allegedly misleading consumers about the nutritional value of its food products.[29] And even though we mentioned Beech-Nut and Ashland Oil as firms that take a social opposition stance, it is only fair to acknowledge that many individual employees and managers at both firms have no doubt made substantial contributions to society in a number of different ways.

THE GOVERNMENT AND SOCIAL RESPONSIBILITY

Another important aspect of social responsibility is the relationship that exists between business and government. We noted the government's role in shaping the role of business in contemporary society. Beyond those generalities, however, there are some specific areas in which business and the government attempt to influence one another. Several of them are shown in Figure 22.7.

FIGURE 22.7

How Business and the Government Influence Each Other

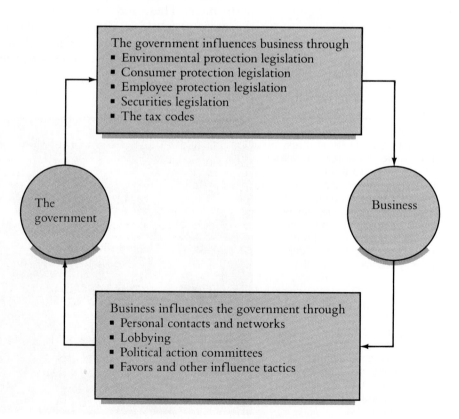

Government Regulation of Business

The government regulates business activities in many different areas. Some of this regulation is direct, while the rest is indirect.

■ **regulation** Government attempts to influence business by establishing laws and rules that dictate what businesses can and cannot do in prescribed areas

Direct Regulation   The government most often attempts to influence business through **regulation**—the establishment of laws and rules that dictate what businesses can and cannot do in prescribed areas. In terms of social responsibility, most regulation of business focuses on the environment, customers, employees, and investors. To implement legislation, the government has tended to create special agencies to monitor and control certain aspects of business activity. The Environmental Protection Agency deals with environmental issues; the Federal Trade Commission and the Food and Drug Administration work with consumer-related concerns; the Equal Employment Opportunity Commission and the Occupational Safety and Health Administration help protect employees; and the Securities and Exchange Commission deals with investor-related issues. These agencies have the power to levy fines or bring civil or even criminal charges against organizations that violate their regulations.[30] Although these are the major regulating agencies, there are also others of a more specialized nature. In addition, many state governments have their own regulatory agencies.

Indirect Regulation   Other forms of regulation are indirect. For example, the government can indirectly influence the social responsibility of business through its tax codes. In effect, the government can influence how businesses spend their social responsibility dollars by providing greater or lesser tax incentives. Suppose that the government wanted business to spend more on training the hard-core unemployed. Congress could pass laws that provided tax incentives to companies who opened new training facilities; and as a result, more businesses would do so. Mobil recently pulled out of South Africa because of a change in the IRS tax codes that make operations in that country less profitable. Some critics argue that regulation is bad and perhaps already excessive. Instead, they argue that a free market system would eventually accomplish the same goals as regulation, with lower costs to both business and the government.

Business Influence on Government

Business can influence the government. In Chapter 3 we described several ways in which organizations can influence their environment. Our concerns here focus more specifically on social responsibility.

Personal Contacts   One way that business influences government is through personal contacts and networks. Many executives and political leaders travel in the same social circles. Thus, a business executive may be able to contact a politician directly and present his or her case regarding a piece of legislation that is being considered.

lobbying The use of persons or groups to formally represent a company or group of companies before political bodies to influence legislation

Lobbying **Lobbying** is an effective way to influence the government. A lobbyist is a person or group that formally represents a company or group of companies before political bodies. For example, a few years ago Congress was close to passing the Family and Medical Leave Act, which would require business to give unpaid leave to parents. Over 150 businesses and trade associations joined forces and sent lobbyists to Washington to argue against the proposed law. As a result, passage of the bill is now unlikely.[31]

Political Action Committees (PACs) Special organizations created to solicit and distribute money to political candidates

Political Action Committees **Political action committees**, or **PACs**, are used to influence the government. Companies themselves cannot generally make direct donations to political campaigns. A PAC is a special organization created to solicit money and then distribute it to political candidates. Employees of a firm may be encouraged to make donations to a particular PAC because managers know that it will support candidates with political views similar to their own. PACs, in turn, make the contributions themselves, usually to a broad slate of state and national candidates. For example, Federal Express's PAC is called Fepac. It makes most of its donations to Democrats because that party currently has control of both the House and the Senate.[32]

Favors Organizations sometimes rely on favors and other influence tactics to gain support. For example, two key members of a House of Representatives committee were in Miami at a fund-raising function. Their assistance was needed back in Washington to finish work on a piece of legislation that Federal Express wanted passed. The law would allow the company and its competitors to give employees stand-by seats on airlines as a tax-free benefit. So Federal Express provided one of its corporate jets to fly the committee members back to Washington.[33] The company was eventually reimbursed for its expenses, and there was nothing illegal about it providing assistance.

Critics argue that such actions are dangerous—dangerous because they can easily lead to other things. Bribes, blackmail, and other unseemly tactics have been used at various times in the past as businesses have attempted to get their wishes in Washington. To combat such problems, numerous regulations have been passed in recent years governing what business can and cannot do for government officials.

MANAGING SOCIAL RESPONSIBILITY

Social responsibility is a complex issue. To deal with it adequately, managers need to approach it like any other business problem. They should view social responsibility as a basic issue of business that requires careful planning, decision making, consideration, and evaluation. There are both formal and informal methods through which social responsibility can be managed.[34]

Formal Organizational Activities

A variety of formal organizational activities can be used to help manage social responsibility. These efforts generally follow three basic thrusts—legal compliance, ethical compliance, and philanthropic giving.[35]

■ **legal compliance** The extent to which an organization complies with local, state, federal, and international laws

Legal Compliance   **Legal compliance** is the extent to which the organization complies with local, state, federal, and international laws. The management of this compliance is generally diffused to the appropriate managers. For example, the organization's top human resource executive is generally responsible for ensuring compliance with regulations concerning recruiting, selection, pay, and so forth. Likewise, the top finance executive generally oversees compliance with securities and banking regulations. The organization's legal department is likely to be involved in this area as well, providing general oversight and also answering queries from managers about the appropriate interpretation of various laws and regulations.

■ **ethical compliance** The extent to which an organization and its members follow basic ethical standards of behavior

Ethical Compliance   **Ethical compliance** is the extent to which the firm and its members follow basic ethical standards of behavior. Organizations have started doing more in this area, providing training in ethics and developing guidelines and codes of conduct. Such activities serve to enhance ethical compliance. Many organizations have established formal ethics committees, which may be asked to review proposals for new projects, help evaluate new hiring strategies, and assess a new environmental protection plan. Ethics committees might also serve as a peer review panel to help evaluate alleged ethical misconduct by an employee.

■ **philanthropic giving** Awarding funds or other gifts to charities or worthy causes

Philanthropic Giving   **Philanthropic giving** involves the awarding of funds or other gifts to charities or other worthy causes. Dayton-Hudson corporation routinely gives 5 percent of its taxable income to such causes. Unfortunately, in this age of cutbacks, many corporations have had to limit these contributions. For example, Atlantic Richfield cut its corporate giving from $37 million in 1983 to $11.4 million in 1987.[36] Firms that do engage in this form of giving usually have a committee of top executives who decide how much money can be given and how it will be allocated.

Informal Organizational Activities

In addition to those formal mechanisms for managing social responsibility, there are also informal mechanisms. Two extremely important ones are the organization's culture and the practice of whistle-blowing.

Organizational culture is often a catalyst for social responsibility. Shell Oil provides a good example of a firm that fosters a wide range of socially responsible acts by its employees. One major program organized and operated by Shell employees in Houston is designed to provide community relief to citizens in distress or need. The team shown here is helping a needy family paint and repair their house and clean up their yard.

Organization Culture   The basic culture and leadership practices of an organization can go a long way toward defining the social responsibility stance adopted by an organization and its members. For example, for years and years, Johnson & Johnson executives provided a clear and consistent message to employees. Customers, employees, communities where the company does business, and shareholders were all important, but the order of importance was as just listed. Thus, when packages of poisoned Tylenol showed up on shelves a few years ago, Johnson & Johnson employees knew exactly how to respond before they received orders from headquarters. They pulled all the packages from the shelves before other customers could buy them.[37] Such actions stand in stark contrast to the messages sent to Ashland Oil employees by the actions of their top managers.

whistle-blowing When an employee discloses illegal or unethical conduct on the part of others within the organization

Whistle-blowing   An informal organizational activity that affects social responsibility and the organization's response to it is whistle-blowing. **Whistle-blowing** occurs when an employee discloses illegal or unethical conduct by others within the organization. Whistle-blowers may have to proceed through a number of channels if they are to be heard. They may also choose to stop before going too far, or they may be fired for their efforts. Many organizations, however, welcome their contributions. The starting point is usually a report of the incident to the individual's boss. If nothing is done, the whistle-blower may go to higher-level managers or to an ethics committee (if one exists). Eventually, the person may have to go to a regulatory agency or even to the media in order to be heard.[38] The apple-juice scandal at Beech-Nut started with a whistle-blower. Jerome LiCari, manager of the firm's R&D department, began to suspect that its apple juice was not pure. His boss was unsympathetic. When LiCari went to the president, he too turned a deaf ear. LiCari then resigned and took his message to the media.

Evaluating Social Performance

Any firm that is serious about social responsibility must ensure that its efforts are producing the desired benefits. This is essentially applying the control concept to social responsibility. Several things can be and are done in this arena. Many organizations require current and new employees to read their guidelines or code of ethics and sign a statement agreeing to abide by them. The organization should also evaluate how it responds to instances of questionable legal or ethical conduct. Does it follow up immediately? Does it punish those involved? Or does it try to delay and cover things up? Answers to such questions can go a long way toward helping an organization understand how it is doing on the social responsibility front.

corporate social audit   A formal and thorough analysis of the effectiveness of a firm's social performance

On a more formal level, organizations occasionally conduct corporate social audits. A **corporate social audit** is a formal and thorough analysis of the effectiveness of the firm's social performance. Such an audit involves clearly defining all the organization's social goals, analyzing the resources being devoted to each, determining how well the various goals are being achieved, and making recommendations about which areas need additional attention. Social audits are not conducted very often because they are expensive and take a lot of time. Indeed, most organizations are probably not doing a very good job in the general area of social responsibility evaluation.

SUMMARY OF KEY POINTS

Ethics are an individual's personal beliefs about what is right and wrong or good and bad. Ethics are formed by family influences, peer influences, experiences, values and morals, and situational factors. Managerial ethics generally involve the relationship of the firm to employees, the relationship of employees to the firm, and the relationship between the firm and other organizations. The ethical context of management involves the manager's personal ethics, organizational practices, and the environment. Organizations use leadership, culture, training, codes, and guidelines to help them manage ethical behavior.

Social responsibility is the obligation of an organization to protect and enhance the societal context in which it functions. Views of social responsibility have been greatly influenced by the Entrepreneurial Era, the Depression Era, and the Social Era. Organizations are responsible to their constituents. Areas of social responsibility include the environment, customers, employees, investors, and general social welfare.

There are strong arguments both for and against social responsibility on the part of business. Organizations can adopt a variety of stances toward social responsibility. Opposition, obligation, response, and contribution are the four general alternatives.

Government influences business through regulation—the establishment of laws and rules that dictate what businesses can and cannot do in prescribed areas. Business, in turn, relies on personal contacts, lobbying, political action committees, and political favors to influence the government.

The management of social responsibility generally focuses on three formal sets of activities—legal compliance, ethical compliance, and philanthropic giving. Culture and whistle-blowing practices are informal means for managing social responsibility. Organizations should also evaluate their social responsibility effectiveness.

DISCUSSION QUESTIONS

Questions for Review

1. What are ethics? What is social responsibility? How are these two concepts related?
2. What are managerial ethics? How are they formed? How can they be managed?
3. In what ways does government (local, state, and federal) regulate business? Why does it do so?
4. How might an organization ensure that it and its members act in a socially responsible manner? Should organizations try to ensure such behavior? Why or why not?

Questions for Analysis

5. Can a manager act in a way that is legal but unethical? Illegal but ethical? Why or why not?
6. Can you think of any arguments either for or against social responsibility other than those presented in this chapter? If so, what are they?
7. What ethical dilemmas do you feel most business managers face? Why? How would you handle such dilemmas in your managerial career?

Questions for Application

8. What are some types of behavior that would be unethical for students? What are some that would be ethical? Compare your re-

sponses with those of other students, especially those from different cultures, to see how much similarity and dissimilarity exist.

9. Interview a local businessperson to obtain his or her views on managerial ethics and social responsibility. What actions, if any, has that person taken to ensure that his or her views are enacted?

10. Go to the library and locate material on an organization that has acted in a manner generally regarded as unethical or socially irresponsible. What did the organization do? Why did the organization do what it did? What lessons might be learned from the experience of that organization?

NOTES

1. "Dean Witter Braces for a Backlash in Boston," *Business Week*, March 6, 1989, p. 86; Brian Dumaine, "Beating Bolder Corporate Crooks," *Fortune*, April 25, 1988, pp. 193–202; "Drexel Faces a Stockholder Suit Claiming Injury from Wrongdoing Alleged by SEC," *The Wall Street Journal*, September 9, 1988, p. 10.

2. "SEC Accuses Drexel of a Sweeping Array of Securities Violations," *The Wall Street Journal*, September 8, 1988, pp. 1, 7; and Brian O'Reilly, "How Hutton Took a Texas-Size Bath," *Fortune*, October 13, 1986, pp. 95–96.

3. For a review of the different meanings of the word *ethics*, see Thomas M. Garrett and Richard J. Klonoski, *Business Ethics*, 2nd ed. (Englewood Cliffs, N.J.: Prentice-Hall, 1986).

4. Peter Petre, "America's Most Successful Entrepreneur," *Fortune*, October 27, 1986, pp. 24–32.

5. John Snarey, "A Question of Morality," *Psychology Today*, June 1987, pp. 6–8.

6. John Huey, "Wal-Mart—Will It Take over the World? *Fortune*, January 30, 1989, pp. 52–61.

7. Patricia Sellers, "Getting Customers to Love You," *Fortune*, March 13, 1989, pp. 38–49.

8. Linda Klebe Trevino, "Ethical Decision Making in Organizations: A Person-Situation Interactionist Model," *Academy of Management Review*, July 1986, pp. 601–617; Bart Victor and John B. Cullen, "The Organizational Bases of Ethical Work Climates," *Administrative Science Quarterly*, Vol. 33, 1988, pp. 101–125.

9. "What Led Beech-Nut down the Road to Disgrace," *Business Week*, February 22, 1988, pp. 124–128.

10. "The Dark Side of Japan Inc." *Newsweek*, January 9, 1989, p. 41; "The Recruit Scandal Bubbles to the Top," *Business Week,* March 20, 1989, p. 55.

11. Archie B. Carroll, "In Search of the Moral Manager," *Business Horizons*, March–April 1987, pp. 7–15; William D. Litzinger and Thomas E. Schaefer, "Business Ethics Bogeyman: The Perpetual Paradox," *Business Horizons*, March–April 1987, pp. 16–21.

12. Joseph A. Raelin, "The Professional as the Executive's Ethical Aide-de-Camp," *The Academy of Management Executive*, August 1987, pp. 171–182.

13. "Businesses Are Signing Up for Ethics 101," *Business Week*, February 15,

1988, pp. 56–57; "Ethics on the Job: Companies Alert Employees to Potential Dilemmas," *The Wall Street Journal*, July 14, 1986, p. 17.

14. Sir Adrian Cadbury, "Ethical Managers Make Their Own Rules," *Harvard Business Review*, September–October 1987, pp. 69–73.

15. Jerry W. Anderson, Jr., "Social Responsibility and the Corporation," *Business Horizons*, July–August 1986, pp. 22–27.

16. For a review of the evolution of social responsibility, see Archie Carroll, *Business and Society: Ethics and Stakeholder Management* (Cincinnati: Southwestern, 1989).

17. "Big Trouble at Allegheny," *Business Week*, August 11, 1986, pp. 56–61.

18. Edwin M. Epstein, "The Corporate Social Policy Process: Beyond Business Ethics, Corporate Social Responsibility, and Corporate Social Responsiveness," *California Management Review*, Spring 1987, pp. 99–114.

19. Jeremy Main, "Here Comes the Big New Cleanup," *Fortune*, November 21, 1988, pp. 102–118.

20. "Ashland Just Can't Seem to Leave Its Checkered Past Behind," *Business Week*, October 31, 1988, pp. 122–126.

21. "A Mail-Order Romance: Land's End Courts Unseen Customers," *Fortune*, March 13, 1989, pp. 44–45.

22. "Ashland Just Can't Seem to Leave Its Checkered Past Behind."

23. Alan Farnham, "Holding Firm on Affirmative Action," *Fortune*, March 13, 1989, pp. 87–88.

24. "Ashland Just Can't Seem to Leave Its Checkered Past Behind."

25. Nancy J. Perry, "The Education Crisis: What Business Can Do," *Fortune*, July 4, 1988, pp. 71–81.

26. Anthony H. Bloom, "Managing Against Apartheid," *Harvard Business Review*, November–December 1987, pp. 49–56.

27. For discussions of this debate, see Abby Brown, "Is Ethics Good Business?" *Personnel Administrator*, February 1987, pp. 67–74; Jean B. McGuire, Alison Sundgren, and Thomas Schneeweis, "Corporate Social Responsibility and Firm Financial Performance," *Academy of Management Journal*, December 1988, pp. 854–872; "Business Ethics for Sale," *Newsweek*, May 9, 1988, p. 56; Kenneth E. Aupperle, Archie B. Carroll, and John D. Hatfield, "An Empirical Examination of the Relationship Between Corporate Social Responsibility and Profitability," *Academy of Management Journal*, June 1985, pp. 446–463; and Margaret A. Stroup, Ralph L. Neubert, and Jerry W. Anderson, Jr., "Doing Good, Doing Better: Two Views of Social Responsibility," *Business Horizons*, March–April 1987, pp. 22–25.

28. "Doing Well by Doing Good," *Business Week*, December 5, 1988, pp. 53–57.

29. "Fast-Food Chains Draw Criticism for Marketing Fare as Nutritional," *The Wall Street Journal*, April 6, 1987, p. 23.

30. "Make the Punishment Fit the Corporate Crime," *Business Week*, March 13, 1989, p. 22.

31. "Should Business Be Forced to Help Bring Up Baby?" *Business Week*, April 6, 1987, p. 39.

32. "How to Win Friends and Influence Lawmakers," *Business Week*, November 7, 1988, p. 36.

33. "How to Win Friends and Influence Lawmakers."

34. Steven L. Wartick and Philip L. Cochran, "The Evolution of the Corporate Social Performance Model," *Academy of Management Review*, October 1985, pp. 758–769; Jerry W. Anderson, Jr., "Social Responsibility," *Business*

Horizons, July–August 1986, pp. 22–27; Epstein, "The Corporate Social Policy Process;" Nancy C. Roberts and Paula J. King, "The Stakeholder Audit Goes Public," *Organizational Dynamics,* Winter 1989, pp. 63–79.

35. Anderson, "Social Responsibility and the Corporation."

36. "Corporate Giving Is Flat, and Future Looks Bleaker," *The Wall Street Journal*, October 17, 1988, p. B1.

37. "Unfuzzing Ethics for Managers," *Fortune*, November 23, 1987, pp. 229–234.

38. Janelle Brinker Dozier and Marcia P. Miceli, "Potential Predictors of Whistle-blowing: A Prosocial Behavior Perspective," *Academy of Management Review*, October 1985, pp. 823–836; Janet P. Near and Marcia P. Miceli, "Retaliation Against Whistle-Blowers: Predictors and Effects," *Journal of Applied Psychology*, February 1986, pp. 137–145.

CASE 22.1

New Emphasis on Ethics at General Dynamics

John Jay Hopkins began General Dynamics in 1952. He hoped that it would become the General Motors of the weapons industry. Well known as a major producer of submarines, missiles, fighter aircraft, and tanks, General Dynamics has facilities spread from coast to coast. Its electric boat division makes submarines in Groton, Connecticut; its F-16 fighters are made in Fort Worth, Texas; and its missiles are produced in San Diego, California. These operations have made General Dynamics one of the top defense contractors as well as one of the most profitable firms in the United States.

But General Dynamics did not achieve this level of success unscathed. For years it owned one of the nation's largest shipyards at Quincy, Massachusetts, but that operation became unprofitable and had to be sold. General Dynamics got into the natural resource business with coal mines and limestone properties but was never able to make them highly profitable and so got rid of them too. It also took a $420 million writedown on its Cessna aircraft division. However, thanks to that writedown and a major reorganization in which employment was reduced and a million square feet of production area were eliminated, Cessna is now earning a profit.

General Dynamics also had problems that raised questions of ethics and improper behavior by its managers. Executives were charged with a $100 million cost overrun on a nuclear attack submarine, overbilling on the Divad anti-aircraft gun, and keeping executives' dogs in kennels at government expense. The Securities and Exchange Commission accused General Dynamics of stock-market wrongdoings. And there were numerous charges of security breaches and illegal gift giving.

To help prevent the recurrence of such problems, General Dynamics put an ethics program in place. From the top of the organization to the very bottom, details about what was proper and improper were identified. For nine months, General Dynamics ran a series of seminars on the ethical way to do defense work. Every single one of the over 100,000 employees of General Dynamics attended one of those all-day seminars.

In addition, General Dynamics created 30 ethics supervisors to monitor and assist employees to ensure that the ethics program is carried out. When a division manager, for instance, is given tickets to a play by a supplier, that manager takes the tickets to an ethics supervisor, who donates them to a local charity. There is an ethics hot line that employees can call to ask questions or report any potential or actual wrongdoing or shady practices that they have observed. The ethics supervisors were responsible for the eventual termination of 27 employees during 1987 for just such things as altering timecards.

The ethics program probably helped convince the Justice Department that General Dynamics had not engaged in unethical practices. In 1987 the Justice Department dropped all charges against the firm. Underpricing contracts initially and then overbilling or assigning costs to other programs were practices that were known and accepted by senior armed service officers. General Dynamics was exonerated on that charge. Not only was the company found guiltless but in a new scandal involving the sale of competitive bidding information by defense consultants, General Dynamics was not searched and none of its executives was subpoenaed. General Dynamics's emphasis on ethics has paid off.

Nevertheless, General Dynamics faces substantial challenges. Defense spending appears to be slowing down. In addition, the Department of Defense seems to be favoring fewer but larger programs that will have more of their developmental costs borne by the contractors. This means greater risks and more research and development as well as outright capital expenditures before a contract is awarded. General Dynamics is responding to those challenges, but its debt is beginning to move upward as it borrows to finance the expenditures.

General Dynamics is also entering into joint ventures with other countries to develop markets overseas. One joint venture involves a fighter plane in Japan, another a tank in Egypt. A third joint venture involves Belgium, Denmark, Norway, and the Netherlands in an upgrade of the F-16, converting it into a new airplane. Management at General Dynamics hopes that these international ventures will secure the firm more business as well as provide it with more funds for development activities.

Questions

1. What are the primary areas of social responsibility for General Dynamics? Are they different from those of other companies because General Dynamics is a defense contractor? Why or why not?
2. Did General Dynamics executives act unethically, or were they simply trying to ensure jobs for employees and a good rate of return for shareholders? Defend your answer against the counterargument.
3. Should the federal government do more to regulate business, especially defense contractors, to preclude any possible unethical practices by managers? Why or why not?
4. Do you think more companies should follow General Dynamics's lead and use ethics supervisors and have an ethics hot line? Why or why not?

REFERENCES: "General Dynamics: All Cleaned Up with No Place to Grow," *Business Week*, August 22, 1988, pp. 70–71; Robert Wrubel, "Gunning It," *Financial World*, March 8, 1988, pp. 22–25; "General Dynamics Explores Ada in Extensive Flight Test Program," *Aviation Week & Space Technology*, March 28, 1988, pp. 73, 75; John D. Morrocco, "General Dynamics Proposes F-16 Upgrade for 1990s," *Aviation Week & Space Technology*, August 3, 1987, pp. 22–23; "Ethics on the Job: Companies Alert Employees to Potential Dilemmas," *The Wall Street Journal*, July 14, 1986, p. 17.

CASE 22.2

Toshiba Confronts Social Responsibility

Toshiba Corp. is one of the largest Japanese multinational electronics firms. Always distinguished for the quality of its products, for many years Toshiba lacked the marketing expertise to develop an image for quality like that of Sony or distribution channels and networks as effective as those of Matsushita. During the early 1980s, however, Toshiba began to invest heavily in semiconductors, computers, and telecommunications and moved to improve its marketing function. By the mid-1980s, Toshiba was a world leader in mass-produced 1-megabit chips, accounting for about half of the world's production.

Then, in 1983 and 1984, Toshiba Machine Co., a Toshiba Corp. subsidiary, sold $17 million worth of high-technology milling-machine tools to the Soviet Union. Those tools enabled the Soviets to construct quiet submarine propellers that make detection of those craft very difficult. (With the new propellers the range of detection drops from about 200 miles to about 10 miles.) It will take the United States years and cost about $40 billion to upgrade and redeploy its antisubmarine forces to compensate. At the same time, a Norwegian arms company, Kongsberg Vaapenfabrikk, sold the Soviets a sophisticated computer control system.

In retaliation, the U.S. Senate voted 92 to 5 in 1987 to prohibit imports for two to five years from any company that violated the high-tech export regulations established by the Coordinating Committee for Multilateral Export Controls (CCMEC). The CCMEC was established by 16 nations—including Japan, Norway, and the United States—to control the access of Communist-bloc countries to high technology developed by the West. Thus, both Toshiba and Kongsberg were hit by the import ban. The president and chairman of Toshiba resigned. The new president, Joichi Aoi, moved to make changes in the company and to try to stave off the ban, which promised to cost the company $2 billion a year.

Aoi was successful in a massive lobbying effort. Toshiba was able to convince the House of Representatives not to go along with the proposed ban. Toshiba was able to convince many lawmakers that it knew nothing about the sale until after it was over. Toshiba called in a panel of U.S. lawyers and accountants to investigate the sale, and the panel's reports supported the claim of ignorance. The lobbying effort was also successful because of changes that Aoi instituted at Toshiba: hiring more export control personnel and tightening controls on high-technology sales.

One reality that influenced Congress is the complex pattern of interdependencies that exist for any multinational firm. Toshiba has ownership interests in three U.S. companies—Toshiba America, Toshiba Semiconductor USA, and Toshiba Machine Company, America. It employs over

4,000 people in plants and offices throughout the United States and is a major seller of laptop computers, VCRs, camcorders, color TVs, and data-processing products. Any substantial ban on imports from Toshiba would effect numerous consumers who own Toshiba products and need parts or technical service. But more importantly, over 40 of the U.S. high-tech companies that use Toshiba's semiconductors or other products came to its defense. Hewlett-Packard and Apple, for instance, argued that a ban on Toshiba imports would hurt American firms as much as it would hurt Toshiba.

At the government level, other issues came into play. First, the governments of Norway and Japan took action against the companies and executives involved. Toshiba Machine Co. was fined, and two of its executives were given suspended prison sentences. There were those who felt that having the Japanese and Norwegian governments control matters was preferable to United States involvement. Second, the Japanese government passed legislation that upgrades Japan's export-control system and imposes stiffer penalties for companies that violate the law. In addition, the Japanese government became far more conciliatory in trade negotiations with the United States. These results may be more valuable than sanctions. Third, Toshiba was hurt by the unfavorable publicity. Many orders were lost, including a $100 million contract with the Pentagon for laptop computers (it was awarded to Zenith) and two million-dollar contracts for heavy electrical equipment. Finally, the governments of Norway and Japan volunteered to help support research to enable the West to overcome the technological advantage that the Soviets derived from the milling-machine purchases.

Questions

1. What forces are likely to account for the sale of high-tech equipment to the Soviets by Toshiba Machine Co.?
2. How did the parent company respond to the problem once it was discovered? Why? How did the government of Japan respond? Were these responses sufficient to redress the damage done by the sale? Why or why not?
3. Do you think the U.S. government should do more to regulate companies, especially foreign ones, to prevent unethical or illegal practices by executives of those companies? Why or why not? What might the government do?
4. Do you think more companies should follow Toshiba's pattern of having the top executives resign when an illegal or unethical problem is uncovered within their firm? Why or why not?

REFERENCES: "Why Congress Is Letting Toshiba off the Hook," *Business Week*, April 4, 1988, pp. 34–35; "Toshiba Deal with Soviets Angers USA," *USA Today*, July 2, 1987, pp. B1–B2; "How Toshiba Is Beating American Sanctions," *Business Week*, September 14, 1987, p. 58; "Matter of Honor: Japanese Top Managers Quick to Resign When Trouble Hits Firm," *The Wall Street Journal*, July 10, 1987, p. 19; Edwin Whenmouth, "The Fallout from Toshiba," *Industry Week*, November 16, 1987, p. 22; "Samurais for Hire," *U.S. News & World Report*, October 5, 1987, p. 50.

ENHANCEMENT MODULE 10

Future Challenges of Management

One of the themes that has arisen in this book time and time again is the changing nature of the manager's job. The business world of today is far different from the world of Henry Ford and Andrew Carnegie, and the world of tomorrow will be far different still. This module identifies and highlights some interesting and noteworthy areas of change that are likely to confront you in your career as a manager. Most of them have been discussed in earlier chapters. They are pulled together here to provide an integrated picture of the challenges and opportunities to be faced by tomorrow's manager. As shown in Figure EM10.1, we organize them around the basic framework used for the entire book—planning, organizing, leading, and controlling. The basic functions of management are both the catalyst for change and the means through which change is facilitated.

PLANNING CHALLENGES OF TOMORROW

In Chapter 5, we defined planning as a comprehensive process that includes setting goals, developing plans, and related activities. Planning will always be a critical part of the manager's job.[1] Special chal-

lenges in the future, however, will center on environmental change, alliances, and globalization.[2]

Environmental Change

In his instant classic *Future Shock*, Alvin Toffler dramatically underscored the rate at which our lives have changed.[3] He noted that if we divide the last 50,000 years into lifetimes of 62 years each, the human race has been around for 800 lifetimes. We spent the first 650 of them in caves. Automobiles, telephones, airplanes, photography, mass production, and virtually all current medical practices have evolved only during the last two lifetimes. Pocket calculators, computers, electronic word processors, space flight, color television, and video cassette recorders have existed less than a single lifetime!

It's instructive to note that Toffler's book was written over twenty years ago. Thus, it doesn't document or consider events of the past two decades like robotics, fiber optics communication networks, personal computers, and compact disks. Indeed, some of the biggest corporations in the world today manufacture products that did not even exist as recently as twenty years ago. And change has not stopped. To the contrary, many experts argue that

FIGURE EM10.1

The Changing World of Management

	Present	Change	Future
		Planning	
		Organizing	
		Leading	
		Controlling	

change is increasing at a faster rate than at any other time in recorded history. Thus, tomorrow's manager must be capable of understanding change and working within both the constraints and the opportunities that accompany it.

Alliances

We noted in Chapters 3 and 6 that alliances and joint ventures were becoming more common. This trend is likely to continue. American auto firms continue to develop alliances with auto companies from other parts of the world. Fourteen U.S. electronics firms recently joined forces to create Sematech in Austin, Texas—a research consortium intended to help the American semiconductor industry regain its competitiveness. For years, IBM and Siemens have been battling around the world in several different high-tech markets, but the two giants recently announced a joint venture in the telecommunications field.[4]

Globalization

In numerous discussions throughout the book, and in Chapter 21 in particular, we noted the strong trends toward a global economy. Improved communication and travel capabilities, in combination with an increasingly interdependent set of world nations and markets, will facilitate this pattern. More and more businesses of all sizes will enter international markets. International assignments will increasingly become a part of the training regimens of many U.S. managers. And finally, more of the alliances noted above, like the one between IBM and Siemens, will involve companies from different countries.

ORGANIZING CHALLENGES OF TOMORROW

Organizing, the second basic managerial function, was defined as the grouping of activities and resources. It, too, will play a vital role in the job of tomorrow's manager. Two key areas are organization design and the management of the organization's human resources.

Organization Design

Organizations of tomorrow will become increasingly flat. As we noted in Chapter 8, this trend has already started. The drive for leaner organizations with lower overhead, in combination with increased technology for communicating with people, will enable the managers of tomorrow to have extremely wide spans of management. As a direct consequence, organizations will become flatter and flatter. Increased globalization effects will also spill over into the organization design area as firms seek new and more efficient ways to structure themselves for global operations.

Human Resources

The ways in which organizations manage their human resources will continue to change. Increased emphasis on flexible workers and flexible work arrangements will continue to alter and shape firms' relationships with their employees. Organizations will have to find new ways to attract and retain the best workers. In some industries, there is already a shortage of qualified workers. Business needs to figure out how to keep workers abreast of changing technology and how to tap nontraditional segments of the work force (such as the elderly and those who don't want full-time jobs) to get the workers it needs.

LEADING CHALLENGES OF TOMORROW

The third basic managerial function is leading—getting members of the organization to work together to further the interests of the organization. Both motivation and leadership patterns will continue to evolve in the years ahead.

Motivation

Motivational patterns for employees have always been dynamic—changing in harmony with cultural and social change. It should come as no surprise, then, that such change will continue. At this point, it seems most likely that tomorrow's manager will need to provide workers with increased control over and ownership of what they do. Workers want an increasingly greater say about what they do in the workplace and how they perform their jobs. Employee ownership of businesses through employee stock ownership plans will continue to grow.

Leadership

The role of leader in organizations has never remained constant, so there is no reason to expect it to do so in the future. Tomorrow's manager is likely to be less of a supervisor and more of a coach or facilitator. Leaders will be called upon to encourage risk, to invite dissent, to obtain resources—and then to stand back out of the way so that people can get on with their work. Leaders of tomorrow will also need to be prepared to deal with a work force that is increasingly heterogeneous across every imaginable dimension—color, sex, age, and nationality, to name just a few.[5]

CONTROLLING CHALLENGES OF TOMORROW

The fourth managerial function, controlling, was defined as the regulation of organizational activities in such a way as to facilitate goal attainment. This critical function is likely to change in more ways and in more areas than any of the other functions.

Costs and Measurement

Increased pressures to control costs and provide reliable measures of performance have already changed the way many organizations approach control. Indeed, it has been argued that businesses of tomorrow will have to totally revamp many of their accounting practices if they are to keep pace.[6] Leaner forms of organization design, fewer middle managers, and more decentralization are goals of organizations that are seeking to control costs.

Speed, Productivity, and Quality

In Chapter 17 we noted three important aspects of operations management—speed, productivity, and quality. Each one is likely to be of paramount importance to the manager in tomorrow's large corporation. Businesses in every industry will need to create new products and services and get them to consumers at an increasingly fast pace. And businesses will be increasingly called upon to accomplish these things with fewer resources and to meet higher quality standards than ever before.

Information

Managers of tomorrow will need to balance and juggle more information than their predecessors. More information is available than ever before; it can be used in more and more different ways; and the manager has greater technology available to help manage information. When personal computers first entered the workplace, top managers were especially wary of them. They were not raised during the computer age and lacked the technical skills to understand computers. That's all changing. Computers have gotten more powerful, but so too has the software necessary to make them useful to top managers. As a result, more executives use computers today than ever before. This pattern, too, can only increase.[7]

In summary, as you prepare to begin your managerial career, you embark on a lifelong experience that will no doubt be filled with opportunity and disappointment, with challenge and frustration, and with success and failure. There will be days when you don't want to manage anymore but many more days when you can hardly wait to begin. One aim of this text is to help you develop a foundation for your management career—a foundation based on a solid mix of research, theory, and actual practice and experience. Perhaps the text has also whetted your appetite to participate in the world of management. No text, however, can truly capture the spirit and excitement of real management in real organizations. It's up to you to make the most of the opportunities presented to you, to deal with the setbacks, and to keep the business world of tomorrow headed in all the right directions.

NOTES

1. See Peter F. Drucker, "The Coming of the New Organization," *Harvard Business Review*, January–February 1988, pp. 45–53.

2. See Jeremy Main, "The Winning Organization," *Fortune*, September 26, 1988, pp. 50–60.

3. Alvin Toffler, *Future Shock* (New York: Random House, 1970).

4. "Dealmakers Are Burning Up the Phone Lines," *Business Week*, March 13, 1989, pp. 138–146.

5. Kenneth Labich, "The Seven Keys to Business Leadership," *Fortune*, October 24, 1988, pp. 58–66.

6. Main, "The Winning Organization."

7. Jeremy Main, "At Last, Software CEOs Can Use," *Fortune*, March 13, 1989, pp. 77–83.

INTEGRATIVE CASE

Nestlé: World-Class Multinational

In 1866, two American brothers, Charles and George Page, began the Anglo-Swiss Condensed Milk Company in Cham, Switzerland. In 1867, Henri Nestlé, a German chemist, began a company in Vevey, Switzerland, to manufacture and sell a milk food for babies unable to breast-feed. Both companies grew and became fierce competitors. Eventually, however, the interests of both were seen as compatible and in 1905 they merged. Today, only the Nestlé name remains and the headquarters location is Vevey, but offices are still maintained in both cities.

The Nestlé organization is basically a confederation of about 200 separate operating units. This highly decentralized approach gives the operating companies a great deal of independence and enables them to respond to local conditions and maintain a local identity in their various host countries. The operating companies function more like smaller companies than like large ones. Many of Nestlé's 360 factories have fewer than 200 employees.

Nestlé is a multinational organization. It has had Swiss, Italian, and French chairmen, and its officers have come from those countries as well as from the United States, Germany, and Spain. It has production facilities in over 60 countries on five continents. Its major markets are Europe (43 percent of total sales) and North America (30 percent). Next come Asia (13 percent) and Latin America and the Caribbean (10 percent). Africa and Oceania account for the rest of Nestlé's sales. Nestlé has over 160,000 employees around the world. Their distribution is similar to that of sales, although not identical— North America has a somewhat smaller proportion and Asia, Latin America, and Africa have slightly larger proportions. Although Nestlé is a Swiss-based organization, only about 7,000 of its 160,000+ employees are located in Switzerland.

In any international organization, communication is frequently a problem. Nestlé has around 40,000 different products sold in many different languages, in addition to the many different languages spoken by its employees. To cope with the communication problems inherent in such a situation, Nestlé has frequent meetings among different groups of managers. Written communication tends to be in French, and oral communication tends to be in English at corporate headquarters. The use of two languages along with numerous meetings keeps communication flowing and minimizes problems.

Nestlé's planning strategy has been to focus on the special demands of the global food business. Because arrangements made with one government can be quickly canceled by a new government, Nestlé carefully balances expansion in stable countries with expansion in relatively unstable ones. That strategy helps Nestlé cope with such events as a 1988 takeover of its milk unit in Peru by the Peruvian government during a milk shortage. The government accused Nestlé of stockpiling milk to force higher prices. Nestlé denied the charge and cooperated with the government to get milk flowing to the people but warned about the impact the government's action would have on the investment climate.

For years Nestlé had a matrix form of organization but finally abandoned it and eliminated some levels of management in order to streamline its organizational structure and decentralize. In place of the 25-page monthly reports that were once the norm, managers now use one-page forms to highlight key operating results. Nestlé uses geographical departmentalization at the top levels of the organization. It staffs the operating companies with personnel from their host country as much as possible, using expatriate managers to develop locals and then move on to other assignments. The local managers meet frequently with managers from other countries and other parts of the organization.

From disciplines such as finance, economics, and engineering, Nestlé recruits young employees interested in going abroad. If recruits are to be expatriate managers, they are carefully screened for their leadership, language, and personal skills before being hired and trained for their new assignments. Indeed, Nestlé provides extensive training for all of its employees in an effort to keep their skills sharp and facilitate advancement and movement through the organization.

Although control at Nestlé is decentralized, financial performance standards worldwide are strict. Nestlé tries to finance companies with local funds wherever possible, but there are strict financial reporting procedures and regulations. Because of Switzerland's economic and political stability, Nestlé tries to maintain its liquid assets there. The mixture of decentralized control and very tight financial standards of performance keeps Nestlé so sound that it is the envy of many other companies. Nestlé's approach to its finances kept ownership in the hands of the Swiss until the late 1980s, when Nestlé removed a restriction requiring two-thirds of all shares to be held by the Swiss. That move enabled investors from around the world to share in Nestlé's success.

The Carnation Company developed Good Start, a new hypoallergenic infant formula different from other formulas because it was not based on soybeans. Good Start could be used by babies allergic to animal protein as well as by those allergic to soybeans. The market potential was substantial. Normally such products are marketed by providing free samples to hospitals and physicians and convincing them to provide new mothers with the product when they leave the hospital. New mothers, then, tend to stay with the product. Nestlé's strategy, however, was to market Good Start directly to mothers, to try to convince them to switch products. Several groups protested that this approach violated the spirit of the previous agreement. They charged that once again Nestlé was going to try to sell formula to people who were not qualified to make the best judgment. The strength of the outcry was sufficiently great that Nestlé again had to change a marketing strategy in response to adverse public reaction.

Questions

1. What is the strategy of the Nestlé organization? Has that strategy been working? What changes can you suggest that might improve upon that strategy?
2. Describe Nestlé's organization structure. How are activities coordinated? What impact does the diversity of cultures in the operating companies around the world have on Nestlé's organization design?
3. How has Nestlé managed the control process? Has that management seemed to be effective? Why or why not?
4. How does the Nestlé organization keep communication flowing? Does its communications system seem effective? How might it be improved?
5. How does the management process in an international organization such as Nestlé differ from the management process in a national organization?
6. Is Nestlé likely to be as effective in the future as it has been in the past? Why or why not? How might Nestlé change in order to improve its prospects?
7. Would you like to be a manager in the Nestlé organization? Why or why not? Does your answer depend upon which operating company and which host country you would be working in?

References: "Nestlé's Bid to Crash Baby-Formula Market in the U.S. Stirs a Row," *The Wall Street Journal*, February 16, 1989, pp. A1, A6; Shawn Tully, "Nestlé Shows How to Gobble Markets," *Fortune*, January 16, 1989, pp. 74–78; "Nestlé Is Threatened with Boycott in Distribution of Infant Formula," *The Wall Street Journal*, June 29, 1988, p. 22; "Little Tolerance for Nestlé Formula," *USA Today*, June 7, 1988, p. 3B; "Peru Government Takes Control of Nestlé Milk Unit," *The Wall Street Journal*, January 8, 1988, p. 10; "Candy Is Dandy," *U.S. News & World Report*, May 9, 1988, p. 62; Nestlé Public Affairs Department, *Nestlé: A Long Adventure* (Vevey, Switzerland: Nestlé S.A., 1986).

NAME INDEX

Acar, William, 71n
Adam, Everett E., Jr., 70n, 153n, 654n, 715n
Adams, J. Stacy, 450, 465–466
Adler, Nancy J., 117n, 800n
Aggarival, Raj, 800n
Agnelli, Giovanni, 188
Aiken, Howard, 264
Ainslie, Michael L., 32–33
Akers, John, 14
Akin, Gib, 29n
Alderfer, Clayton, 441, 460, 465n, 539n
Alexander, Judith W., 337n
Alexander the Great, 40
Alfarabi, 41
Al-Fayed, Mohamed, 819
Allen, Joseph, 572n
Alliger, George M., 500n
Allison, Charles F., III, 800n
Alpert, William M., 245
Alster, Norm, 300n, 655n
Ames, Katrine, 33
Anastasi, Anne, 429n
Anderson, Abram, 250
Anderson, Henry R., 715n
Anderson, Jerry W., Jr., 834n–835n
Anderson, Roger L., 300n
Andrews, Kenneth R., 216n
Angus, Michael, 576
Anheuser, Eberhard, 813
Ansoff, H. Igor, 216n
Anthony, Robert N., 611n
Aoi, Joichi, 4
Applegate, Lynda M., 338n, 683n
Archibald, Nolan, 548, 559
Argyle, Michael, 535, 539n
Armstrong, C. Michael, 304–305
Armstrong, J. Scott, 263n

Arnold, Chris, 741
Aronoff, Craig E., 572n
Aronson, Gary, 761
Asch, Solomon E., 523, 539n
Ashmos, Donde P., 70n
Asimov, Isaac, 723, 724, 725n
Atherton, W. A., 267n
Athey, T., 267n
Aupperle, Kenneth E., 71n, 834n
Austin, Beth, 155
Austin, Nancy, 572n

Babbage, Charles, 42–43, 69n, 264
Baird, Lloyd, 218n, 380n
Baker, M., 572n
Balachandra, R., 263n
Ball, Robert, 729n
Ballard, Dale, 752
Baloff, Nicholas, 152n
Bannister, B. D., 500n
Barbato, Robert, 800n
Barczak, Gloria, 412n
Barnard, Chester, 46, 48, 69n
Barnes, Zane E., 412n
Barney, Jay B., 106n, 337n, 338n
Bart, Christopher K., 715n
Baskin, Otis W., 572n
Bass, Bernard M., 500n, 501n
Bass, R. E., 70n
Bateman, Thomas S., 583n
Baum, Laurie, 505
Bauman, Robert P., 395
Beard, Donald W., 106
Beauchamp, Marc, 380n
Becker, Brian E., 382n
Beckhard, Richard, 412n, 413n
Bedeian, Arthur G., 287, 301n, 538n–539n
Beeman, Don R., 501n

Beer, Michael, 413n
Bell, Cecil H., Jr., 405, 413n, 539n
Belohlav, J. A., 267n
Benetton, Luciano, 626
Benfari, Robert C., 117n, 499n
Benoit, Ellen, 803
Berke, Matthew, 763n
Bertalanffy, Ludwig von, 70n
Bettis, Richard A., 107n, 217n
Bhagat, Rabi S., 800n
Bickerstaffe, G., 23
Binning, John F., 381n
Birch, David L., 763n
Bird, Barbara, 763n
Black, Cathleen, 18
Blackburn, Richard S., 301n
Blackett, P. M. S., 54
Blake, Robert R., 407, 413n, 500n
Blanchard, Kenneth H., 501n
Blanning, R. W., 267n
Blonder, Mauritz D., 729n
Bloom, Anthony H., 834n
Bluhdorn, Charles G., 203
Boesky, Ivan F., 110
Bond, Michael Harris, 41
Bonk, Ed, 355
Bonsack, Robert, 725n
Booth, David E., 71n
Booth, Israel MacAllister, 474, 483
Borden, Gail, 186
Boulton, William R., 217n
Bovée, Courtland L., 571n, 572n
Bowen, Michael G., 152n
Bowen, William, 71n
Boyer, Edward, 477
Bradspies, Robert W., 622n
Bragg, Daniel J., 654n
Bragganti, Nancy, 783

Breaugh, James A., 381n
Breckenfield, Gurney, 338n
Bridges, William, 248n
Bristow, Nigel J., 69n
Brockner, Joel, 729n
Brody, Michael, 381n
Broedling, Laurie, 29n
Brown, Abby, 381n, 834n
Brown, Andrew C., 577
Brown, Rupert, 538n
Browning, Larry D., 571n
Bruggere, Thomas, 767
Bruns, William J., Jr., 683n
Bucerius, Gerd, 461
Buchan, P. Bruce, 539n
Buchanan, Peter T., 542, 543
Buckley, M. Ronald, 381n
Bukszar, Ed, 152n
Bullen, Christine, 573n
Buller, Paul F., 539n
Burck, Charles G., 623n
Burden, Laurance T., 667
Burke, Beverly G., 538–539
Burns, James MacGregor, 501n
Burns, Tom, 107n, 315–316, 330, 337n
Burt, H. E., 500n
Busch, Adolphus, 813
Busse, Thomas V., 429n
Butler, John E., 218n
Butler, Richard J., 151n
Bylinsky, Gene, 724n, 725n
Byrne, Harlan, 657
Byung-Chull, Lee, 504

Cadbury, Adrian, Sir, 834n
Caldwell, James C., 715n
Calvert, Robert, Jr., 381n
Cameron, Kim S., 107n
Cammann, Cortlandt, 619, 623n
Campbell, Donald J., 300n, 382n
Campbell, Joseph, 250
Campion, Michael A., 300n
Canion, Rod, 737, 741
Capek, Karel, 723
Caples, Stephen, 217n
Caraes, Jean Claude, 766
Carbone, Robert, 263n
Cardy, Robert L., 382n
Carnegie, Andrew, 38, 816
Carrell, Michael R., 381n
Carrigan, Patricia M., 378
Carroll, Archie B., 833n, 834n

Carroll, Doug, 819
Carroll, Glenn R., 117n
Carroll, Stephen J., 69n, 249n
Carter, Jimmy, 697, 788
Cartwright, Dorwin, 538n
Carzo, Rocco, Jr., 301n
Casey, James E., 72
Cash, James I., Jr., 338n, 683n
Castle, Douglas E., 218n
Castro, Fidel, 144
Cawthorn, Robert, 132, 133–134
Chakravarthy, Balaji S., 185n, 217n, 775
Chambers, John C., 263n
Chandler, Alfred D., Jr., 328, 331, 338n
Chandler, Colby, 770
Chapman, Jonathan, 87
Chase, Richard B., 70n, 654n, 729n
Chemers, M. M., 500n
Chen, Steven, 173
Chew, W. Bruce, 106n
Chrisman, James J., 217n
Chun Doo Hwan, 504
Churchill, Neil C., 248n
Churchill, Winston, 38
Cimino, Aldo, 681
Claiborne, Liz, 138
Clark, John, 218n
Clegg, Chris W., 423n
Clifford, Mark, 505
Clontz, Norvin A., 511
Coch, Lester, 398, 413n
Cochran, Philip L., 834n
Cohen, Allan R., 466n
Cohn, Bob, 469
Cole, Diane, 117n
Collins, Paul D., 337n, 413n, 724n
Comer, Gary, 814
Confucius, 41
Conger, Jay A., 28n
Connolly, Terry, 152n
Conte, James, 548
Coons, A. E., 500n
Cooper, Arnold C., 763n
Cooper, Robin, 715n
Coors, Adolph Herman Joseph, 384
Cornelius, E., 465n
Cosch, John, 659
Cosier, Richard A., 466n

Cotton, John L., 423n, 589n
Courtney, James F., Jr., 681
Cox, James F., 423n, 654
Coyle, William E., 741
Cray, David, 151n
Cullen, John B., 833n
Cullinan, Joseph, 574
Cummings, Larry L., 70n
Cummins, Clessie L., 802
Cummins, Robert, 572n
Curran, John J., 106n, 185n, 106n, 169, 185n, 248n
Cyert, Richard, 151n–152n

Daft, Richard L., 300n, 301n, 336n, 572n
Dagnoli, Judann, 251
Dalton, Dan R., 301n, 466n
Daly, James, 61
Damanpour, Fariborz, 429n
Daniel, Wayne W., 263n
Daniels, John D., 800n, 801n
Dansereau, Fred, 501n
D'Aveni, Richard A., 729n
Davenport, Carol, 184n, 218n, 269a
David, Fred, 165, 184n
Davidson, Wallace N., III, 382n
Davis, Brad, 277
Davis, James H., 153n
Davis, Keith, 557
Davis, Ralph C., 285, 301n
Davis, Stanley M., 337n
Day, Charles K., Jr., 413n
Day, Charles R., Jr., 139, 151n
Day, David V., 499n
Deal, Terrence E., 338n
Dean, James W., Jr., 725n
Dearborn, D. C., 572n
Dearden, John, 715n
Deardon, J., 267n
Deckop, John R., 380n
Deere, John, 656
De Geus, Arie P., 247n
DeGroot, Morris H., 151n–152n
Delbecq, Andre L., 153n, 429n
Deming, W. Edwards, 655n
De Porras, Deborah Auld, 217n
Deresky, Helen, 218n
Dermer, Amy, 611
Deshpande, Rohit, 217n
Dess, Gregory G., 106n, 216n
Deutschman, Alan, 763n

De Vader, Christy L., 500n
Devine, Elizabeth, 783
Devol, George C., Jr., 723
Dickson, W. J., 464n
Diddèl, Katha, 207
Dienesch, Richard M., 501n
Di Primo, Anthony, 217n
Disney, Roy, 590
Disney, Roy E., 590
Disney, Walt, 590
Dittrich, John E., 184n
Dobbins, Gregory H., 382n
Dock, V. Thomas, 683n
Doherty, Elizabeth M., 152n
Doktor, Robert, 800n
Dolan, Shimon, 725n
Donnelly, James H., Jr., 589n
Donovan, John J., 573n, 683n
Dowling, William F., 336n
Dozier, Janelle Brinker, 835n
Drazin, Robert, 336n
Dreman, David, 577
Dreyfus, J., 267n
Dreyfuss, Joel, 429n, 622n, 655n
Drucker, Peter F., 166, 241, 248n,
    622n, 843
Dubashi, Jagannath, 61
Duck, Thomas S., 113
Dumaine, Brian, 31, 216n, 381n,
    572n, 589n, 633, 654n, 683,
    833n
Dunkelberg, William C., 763n
Dunn, Keith, 481
Dupin, Charles, 43
Dutt, James, 475–476, 478
Dworkin, Sidney, 169
Dwyer, Daniel J., 589n
Dyer, Lee, 381n
Dyer, William G., 413n

Eason, Henry, 471
Eastman, George, 770
Ebert, Ronald J., 70n, 153n, 654n,
    715n
Eckert, J. Presper, 264
Eden, Dov, 466n
Eder, Robert W., 381n
Egelhoff, William G., 219n, 338n
Eisenberg, Eric M., 572n
Eisenhower, Dwight, 268
Eisner, Michael D., 590–591
Elbing, Alvar, 151n, 152n
Eller, David, 10

Eller, James, 10
Elsass, Priscilla M., 117n
Emerson, Harrington, 43, 45–46
Engeberger, Joseph F., 723
Engledow, Jack L., 152n
Ephlin, Donald F., 383n
Epstein, Edwin M., 834n, 835n
Erez, Miriam, 466n
Erikson, Warren J., 654n
Evans, Martin G., 488–490, 491,
    500n

Fallon, James, 819
Fargo, William, 108
Farnham, Alan, 834n
Fayol, Henri, 46, 47, 69n
Feldman, Daniel C., 117n, 539n
Feldman, Steven P., 429n
Ferris, Richard, 91
Fetterolf, C. Fred, 221
Fiedler, Fred E., 485–488, 500n
Fiedman, Abraham, 466n
Fiegenbaum, Avi, 151n
Fielding, Gorden J., 301n
Fields, Debbie, 4, 114, 764–765
Fields, Randall "Randy", 764
Fierman, Jaclyn, 119, 248n, 477
Finch, Byron J., 654n
Fiorito, Jack, 381n
Fischman, Joshua, 589n
Fisher, Anne B., 729n
Fisher, Cynthia D., 70n
Fisilier, Marcelline R., 538n
Fitzgerald, Thomas H., 412n
Flaherty, D., 267n
Fleishman, Edwin A., 500n
Fletcher, Noel, 287
Foegen, J. H., 383n
Folino, Cynthia, 748
Folkins, C., 589n
Follett, Mary Parker, 49–50
Foote, Donna, 33
Ford, Edsel, 730
Ford, Henry, 275, 730
Ford, Henry, II, 730
Ford, Robert, 300n
Fossum, John A., 106n, 382n
Foster, William K., 218n
Fotheringham, Allan, 177
French, John R. P., 499n
French, John R. P., Jr., 398, 413n
French, Wendell L., 405, 413n

Frenkel, Karen A., 724, 725n
Friday, Carolyn, 109
Friedman, M., 589n
Friedrich, Otto, 725n
Froggatt, Kirk L., 423n
Fromson, Brett Duval, 687
Fry, Louis W., 218n, 654n, 725n
Furst, Alan, 765
Fusilier, Marcelline R., 589n

Gabarro, John J., 538n
Gadon, Herman, 466n
Gagnon, Christopher E., 654n
Gaines, Jeannie, 589n
Galbraith, Jay R., 219n, 301n,
    336n, 338n
Galgay, Patricia J., 184n
Gallagher, Robert T., 767
Gandz, Jeffrey, 501, 501n
Gannes, Stuart, 129, 151n, 152n,
    185n, 218n, 337n, 538n, 655n,
    762n, 763n
Gannon, Martin F., 381n
Ganster, Daniel C., 538n, 589n
Gantt, Henry, 43, 45
Garcia, Mario F., 381n
Garrett, Thomas M., 815, 833n
Garrison, Sharon H., 382n
Gartner, William B., 337n
Garvin, David A., 650
Gault, Stanley, 102, 162–163
Gawronski, Francis J., 705
Gehrman, Douglas B., 185n
Gellerman, Saul W., 300n, 715n
Gellman, H., 267n
Geneen, Harold, 19, 475–476, 555
Georgopoules, B. S., 107n
Gerloff, Edwin, 572n
Gersick, Connie J. G., 538n
Ghoshal, Sumantra, 219n, 623n
Gibson, James L., 589n
Gilbert, Gerald, 397
Gilbreath, Robert D., 248n
Gilbreth, Frank, 43, 44–45
Gilbreth, Lillian, 43, 44–45
Gillen, Dennis J., 69n
Gilmore, David C., 381n
Gilmour, Allan D., 412n
Gioia, Dennis A., 382n
Gist, Marilyn E., 538n
Givens, David, 572n
Glauser, Michael J., 572n
Gobeli, David H., 338n

Goes, James B., 429n
Goizueta, Roberto, 228
Goldsmith, James, Sir, 775
Goldstein, Mel A., 381n
Golfield, R. J., 267n
Goode, Dorothy L., 382n
Gooding, Richard Z., 423n
Goodman, Paul S., 466n
Gordon, William J., 429n
Gorr, Wilpen, 263n
Gottlieb, Carrie, 28n, 247n
Graen, George, 501n
Graham, Judith, 687
Graham, Katherine, 322
Graicunas, A. V., 285, 300n
Granrose, Cherlyn Skromme,
    117n
Grant, Jay, 117n
Greco, Rosemarie B., 598
Green, Stephen G., 622n
Greene, Robert J., 382n, 467n
Greenhalgh, Leonard, 381n
Greenwood, Gerald, 446
Griffin, Ricky W., 41, 70n, 300n,
    338n, 423n, 466n, 538n, 583n
Grimaldi, John V., 725n
Grove, Andrew, 38, 226, 239–240
Grover, Steven L., 729n
Grush, Joseph E., 465n
Gunsteren, Lex A. van, 218n
Gupta, Anil K., 217n
Gustafson, David H., 153n
Guth, William D., 216n
Guzzardi, Walter, 187, 623n
Guzzo, Richard A., 538n

Haas, Marsha E., 423n
Hackman, J. Richard, 279, 300n
Haga, W. J., 501n
Hage, Jerald, 413n, 724n
Hahn, Chan K., 654n
Hakuta, Ken, 738
Hall, Douglas T., 113, 116n–117n
Hall, Edward J., 572n
Hall, Richard H., 105n
Hambrick, Donald C., 248n, 729n
Hamilton, Ian, 285, 301n
Hammer, Armand, 502–503
Hannan, Edward, 263n
Hansen, John, 397
Harrington, Irene, 99
Harris, E. F., 500n
Harris, Reuben T., 412n

Harris, T. George, 589n
Harrison, E. Frank, 151n
Hart, David K., 28n
Hartke, Darrell D., 500n
Hater, John J., 501n
Hatfield, John D., 466n, 834n
Hayes, Robert H., 106n, 412n
Hayward, Keith, 676
Healey, James R., 223
Heard, Joyce, 103
Hector, Gary, 248n
Hedge, Jerry W., 382n
Hellervik, Lowell, 381n
Helmick, Robert H., 540
Hempel, C. G., 70n
Henderson, Henry, 143
Henderson, Monika, 535, 539n
Henkoff, Ronald, 185n, 412n,
    413n
Herbert, Theodore T., 218n
Hersey, Paul, 501n
Herzberg, Frederick, 278, 300n,
    442–444, 460, 465n
Hewlett, Bill, 18–19, 333
Hickson, David J., 151n, 337n
Higgins, James H., 217n
Hill, Charles W. L., 184n, 185n,
    217n, 218n, 247n, 622n, 729n
Hill, Kenneth D., 29n
Hills, Frederick S., 467n
Hiromoto, Toshiro, 705
Hitt, Michael A., 71n, 107n,
    217n, 337n
Hodgetts, Richard M., 763n
Hodgson, William G., 300n, 715n
Hofer, Charles W., 216n, 217n,
    219n
Hoffman, David L., 569
Hoffman, Harry, 160
Hofstede, Geert, 41
Hollenbeck, John R., 583n
Hollerith, Herman, 264
Holmes, Steven, 111
Holmes, T. H., 589n
Holmgren, Kathleen, 37
Holsapple, C. W., 267n
Homer, 38
Hoopes, Linda L., 589n
Hoover, David J., 382n
Hopkins, H. Donald, 185n
Hopkins, John Jay, 836
Horton, Cleveland, 705
Hosking, D., 500n

Hoskisson, Robert E., 217n
Houghton, James R., 172, 175
House, Robert J., 465n, 488–490,
    491, 500n
Hower, Roger J., 413n
Huber, George P., 70n, 151n
Huey, John, 248n, 571n, 583n,
    635, 683n, 833n
Hull, Frank M., 337n, 413n, 724n
Hunger, J. David, 184, 185n,
    248n
Hunt, Walter S., 300n
Hunter, John E., 381n
Hurley, Dan, 117n
Huseman, Richard C., 466n, 573n

Iacocca, Lee, 63, 476
Ibuka, Masaru, 804
Icahn, Carl, 7, 574
Irani, Ray, 503
Ireland, R. Duane, 71n, 217n
Irwin, W. G., 802
Ivancevich, John M., 249n, 589n

Jackofsky, Ellen F., 801n
Jackson, Michael, 269, 743
Jackson, Paul R., 423n
Jackson, Susan E., 218n, 589n
Jaffe, Thomas, 269a
Jago, Arthur G., 490–492, 499n,
    500n, 501n
Jaikumar, Ramchandran, 106n,
    412n
James, Robert M., 216n, 248n
Janis, Irving L., 153n
Janz, Tom, 381n
Jarrillo-Mossi, Jose Carlos, 763n
Jelinek, Mariann, 117n
Jennings, Kenneth R., 423n, 589n
Jermier, John M., 501n, 589n
Jethro, 285
Jewell, Linda, 429n
Jex, Steve M., 589n
Jobs, Steven, 163, 172, 212, 238,
    255, 302, 398, 475, 737
Johansen, Robert, 573n
John Paul II, Pope, 4, 8
Johnson, Edward Mead, 430
Johnson, Ellen, 729n
Johnson, J. David, 301n
Johnson, Ross, 655n
Jonas, H., 70n

Jones, Gareth R., 184n, 185, 217n, 218n, 247n, 338n, 729n
Jones, John W., 589n
Jones, Leonade D., 14
Jones, Steven D., 184n
Joyce, William F., 338n

Kahn, Robert L., 538n
Kallen, Barbara, 108
Kanter, Rosabeth Moss, 29n
Kantrow, Alan M., 69n
Kaplan, Robert S., 715n
Kapstein, Jonathan, 103
Kast, Fremont E., 70n
Katz, David, 538n
Katz, Jerome, 337n
Katz, Michael, 575
Katz, Robert L., 29n
Kaufman, Steven B., 245
Kavanagh, Michael J., 382n
Kay, William, 75, 111
Kazanjian, Robert K., 219n, 336n, 337n
Keats, Barbara W., 107n, 337n
Kedia, Richard I., Jr., 800n
Keen, P. G., 267n
Keleman, Kenneth S., 466n
Kellogg, D. H., 154
Kellogg, W. K., 154
Kelly, H. H., 466n
Kelly, Sarah, 295
Kemp, Nigel J., 423n
Kendrick, John W., 654n
Kennedy, Allan A., 338n
Kennedy, John F., 143–144, 502, 820
Keon, Thomas L., 465n
Kerlinger, Fred, 263n
Kerr, Jeffrey, 107n
Kerr, Steven, 29n, 501n
Keys, Bernard, 381n
Kiechel, Walter, III, 117n, 217n, 382n, 465n, 499n, 539n, 572n, 573n
Kilbridge, M. D., 300n
Kilby, Jack, 264
King, Paula J., 835n
Kingsborough, Donald D., 603
Kinnear, James, 4, 574, 575
Kirkland, Richard I., Jr., 71n, 106n, 185n, 319, 338n, 343, 380n, 563, 800n
Kirkpatrick, David, 357

Klein, Janice A., 29n
Klonoski, Richard J., 811, 833n
Klugt, Cornelius J. van der, 103
Knowlton, Christopher, 763n
Kobayashi, K., 267n
Koenig, Helena, 81
Koloday, Harvey F., 338n
Kondrasuk, Jack N., 249n
Koontz, Harold, 622n
Kotter, John P., 28n, 412n
Kovach, Kenneth A., 464n
Kraar, Louis, 223, 380n, 387, 654n, 800n
Kram, Kathy E., 117n
Kramm, Judith B., 218n
Kraus, James R., 543
Kreitner, Robert, 466n
Kroc, Ray, 173
Kroger, Joseph, 138
Kroll, Mark, 217n
Kuhn, Robert, 429n
Kuhnert, Karl W., 501n
Kupfer, Andrew, 29n, 793
Kuratko, Donald F., 763n
Kuzmits, Frank E., 381n

Labich, Kenneth, 73, 152n, 185n, 219n, 248n, 412n, 429n, 499n, 501n, 551, 611, 729n, 843n
Lachman, Ran, 29n
LaMothe, William E., 155
Land, Edwin, 474
Landi, Ann, 464n
Landis, David, 415
Lane, F., 465n
Langeler, Cerald, 767
Lapedus, Mark, 767
Larson, Erik W., 338n
Latack, Jania C., 465n
Latham, Gary P., 152n, 382n, 466n
Lawler, Edward E., III, 106n, 185n, 301n, 382n, 383n, 448–449, 459, 460, 465n, 466n–467n, 622n
Lawrence, Anne T., 381n
Lawrence, Paul R., 70n, 301n, 316–317, 337n, 413n
Lawrence, Steven, 119
Leana, Carrie R., 301n
Leavitt, Harold J., 413n
Lee, Byung-Chull, 504
Lee, Cynthia, 382n

Lee Kun-Hee, 505
Lei, David, 248n
Leitko, Thomas A., 336n
Lengel, Robert H., 572n
Lengnick-Hall, Cynthia A., 218n, 380n
Lengnick-Hall, Mark L., 218n, 380n, 423n
Lenin, Vladimir I., 502
Lenz, R. T., 152n, 217n
Leonard-Barton, Dorothy, 153n, 683n
Leong, Kathy Chin, 61
Levering, Robert, 575
Levin, Gary, 251
Levine, E. L., 360
Lewin, Arie Y., 107n
Lewin, Kurt, 412n
Lewis, Philip, 501n
Lewis, Reginald F., 116
LiCari, Jerome, 831
Liden, Robert C., 501n
Lientz, Bennett P., 572n
Liker, Jeffrey K., 725n
Likert, Rensis, 311–313, 336n, 481–482, 500n
Linden, Eugene, 603
Litzinger, William D., 833n
Locke, Edwin A., 69n, 152n, 185n, 465n, 466n, 538n
Loepfe, Otto, 718
Lombardi, Vince, 757
Long, L., 267n
Longnecker, Clinton O., 382n
Lorange, Peter, 185n, 219n, 623n
Lord, Robert G., 499n, 500n
Lorenzo, Frank, 398, 565
Lorsch, Jay W., 301n, 316–317, 337n
Louis, Arthur M., 489
Lounsbury, John W., 589n
Lovett, Paul D., 539n
Low, Murray B., 762n
Lubin, Joann S., 539n
Luthans, Fred, 28n, 107n, 466n
Lynch, Rose Peabody, 244
Lyndon, Neil, 503

McBeth, John, 505
McCallum, Daniel, 43
McCaskey, Michael B., 572n
McClelland, David C., 445, 465n
McCormick, Ernest J., 381n

McDonald, James F., 699
McEnrue, Mary Pat, 117n
McFarlin, F. Warren, 683n
McGillicuddy, John F., 392
McGrail, Fred, 767
McGregor, Douglas, 51, 52–53
McGuigan, Cathleen, 33
McGuire, Jean B., 834n
Machiavelli, 38
McIntosh, Nancy J., 589n
Mack, Toni, 415
MacKay, Gillian, 541
McKenna, Regis, 106n
Mackey, John, 318
McKim, Alan, 737, 738, 742, 743
McLean, Vincent, 138
McLennan, Roy, 412n
McMahon, J. Timothy, 249n
Macmillan, Ian C., 106n, 107n, 216n, 762n
McNealy, Scott, 129, 333
Macomber, John D., 38
McQuaid, Sara J., 801n
Madigan, Robert M., 382n
Madonna, 269
Magenau, John M., 382n
Magnet, Myron, 572n, 729n
Mahoney, Thomas A., 380n
Maier, Norman P. R., 153n
Main, Jeremy, 106n, 216n, 219n, 248n, 301n, 338n, 423n, 499n, 683n, 763n, 834n, 843n
Malcolm, Andrew H., 87
Maljers, Floris, 576
Mallory, Geoffrey R., 151n
Malone, Maggie, 33
Maniker, Marci, 553
Manning, Michael R., 589n
Mansfield, Richard S., 429n
Mant, Alistair, 23
Manz, Charles C., 501n
March, James G., 151n
Marcus, Alfred A., 429n
Marion, John L., 32
Markham, Steven E., 467n
Markland, Robert E., 153n, 263n
Markowski, Carol, 263n
Markowski, Edward, 263n
Marks, Mitchell Lee, 583n
Marks, Reuben, 114
Marram, Ellen, 112, 113
Marriott, Bill, 558
Marriott, J. W., Jr., 30, 31

Marriott, J. Willard, 30n
Mars, Forest, Sr., 118
Mars, Frank, 118
Martin, James E., 382n
Martin, Philip, 25
Maslow, Abraham, 51–52, 53, 70n, 440–442, 460, 465n
Mastenbrook, Willem, 413n
Matsushita, Konosuke, 201
Matteson, Michael T., 589n
Mauchly, John, 264
Maurer, Steven D., 380n
Mausner, Bernard, 465n
Maxwell, Hamish, 178, 340
Maxwell, Robert, 167
Mayer, Robert J., 218n, 654n
Mayers, Bronston T., 538
Mayes, Bronston T., 589n
Mayo, Elton, 50–51, 60, 70n, 439, 464n
Mehrabian, Albert, 572n
Menzies, Hugh D., 499n
Meredith, Jack R., 218n, 654n, 725n
Meshoulam, Ilan, 218n, 380n
Meyer, Alan D., 429n
Meyer, John, 301n
Meyer, John W., 105n–106n
Miceli, Marcia P., 835n
Mignanelli, Thomas D., 223
Miles, Edward W., 466n, 573n
Miles, Raymond E., 217n
Miller, Danny, 107n, 217n, 219n, 336n, 338n
Miller, David W., 151n
Miller, Edwin L., 106n, 800n
Miller, George D., 540
Miller, Katherine, 423n
Miller, Lynn E., 465n
Mills, D. Quinn, 338n, 683n
Mills, Peter, 429n
Mindell, Benjamin, 431
Mindell, Mark G., 413n
Miner, Anne S., 300n
Minton, John W., 107n
Mintzberg, Henry, 16–18, 19, 28n, 29n, 184n, 216n, 248n, 328–331, 338n, 551, 571n, 572n
Mischel, Walter, 583n
Mitchell, Terence R., 465n, 500n
Mitroff, Ian, 97, 107n
Mockler, Robert J., 216n
Moffett, Richard G., 538n–539n

Mohn, Reinhard, 461
Mohrman, Susan A., 106n, 383n
Monaghan, Thomas, 176
Money, W. H., 500n
Moore, Thomas, 301n, 572n
Moorhead, Gregory, 70n, 338n, 538n, 583n
Morais, Richard C., 659
Morgan, J. P., 816
Morita, Akio, 804
Morrison, Ann M., 29n
Morrocco, John D., 837
Morse, David, 425–426
Morton, Michael F. Scott, 219n, 623n
Mosakowski, Elaine, 117n
Moses, 285
Moskowitz, Milton, 575
Moss, Leonard, 589n
Motowidlo, Stephan J., 589n
Mouton, Jane S., 407, 413n, 500n
Mowday, Richard, T., 466n
Muczyk, Jan P., 500n
Mullick, S. K., 263n
Mullins, Peter J., 319
Munsterberg, Hugo, 49, 70n
Murray, Alan I., 218n
Murray, Victor, 501n
Musashi, Miyamoto, 41
Myers, Janet, 119

Nader, Ralph, 90
Nadler, David A., 413n, 449n, 465n, 619, 623n
Napier, John, 264
Nasar, Sylvia, 654n
Near, Janet P., 835n
Needles, Belverd E., Jr., 715n
Neff, Craig, 541
Nelson-Horchler, Joani, 375
Nemetz, Patricia L., 218n, 654n, 725n
Nestlé, Henri, 844
Neubert, Ralph L., 834n
Newport, John Paul, Jr., 800n
Newstrom, John W., 557
Nicholas, John M., 413n
Nicholls, John G., 465n
Nielsen, Richard P., 75
Noe, Raymond A., 117n
Norris, Dwight R., 423n
Norton, Bob, 19, 793
Nutt, Paul C., 152n

Odiorne, George S., 107n
Oglevee, Bill, 4
Oldham, Greg R., 279, 300n
Olsen, Kenneth Harry, 810, 814
Olson, James, 15
O'Neill, Paul H., 221
O'Reilly, Brian, 61, 152n, 515, 572n, 833n
O'Reilly, Charles A., III, 152n, 683n
Orth, Charles D., 117n, 499n
Ostrom, Charles, 263n
Ouchi, William, 63–65, 71n, 106n, 185n, 334, 337n, 339n, 423n, 623n
Oughtred, William, 264
Oviatt, Benjamin M., 106n
Owen, Robert, 42
Owens, Eugene, 539n

Packard, David, 18–19, 333
Packard, John S., 589n
Page, Charles and George, 844
Paradice, David B., 681
Parasuraman, A., 217n
Park Chung Hee, 504
Parker, Donald F., 589n
Parker, Reggie, 711
Parrott, Michael, 417
Parry, Charles W., 220–221
Paul, Karen, 800n
Pearce, John A., II, 165, 184n
Pearce, John A., III, 217n
Pedhazur, Elazar, 263n
Peiperl, Maury A., 218n
Penfield, Lawrence T., 152n
Penney, James Cash, 333
Perelman, Ronald, 8, 11
Perkins, James, 670
Perot, H. Ross, 533, 562
Perrolle, J. D., 267n
Perroni, Amedeo G., 69n
Perrow, Charles, 184n
Perry, James L., 29n, 336n
Perry, Nancy J., 106n, 464n, 467n, 834n
Peters, Lawrence H., 500n
Peters, Thomas J., 65, 71n, 334, 339n
Peters, Tom, 71n, 287, 572n
Petersen, Donald, 4, 7, 8, 13, 24, 112
Peterson, Melanie M., 382n

Peterson, Thane, 103
Petre, Peter, 833n
Pfeffer, Jeffrey, 69n, 501n, 583n
Phatak, Arvind, 800n
Philbrick, Jane Hass, 423n
Philips, N. V., 658
Phillips, Dennis, 423n
Pinchot, Gifford, III, 429n
Pinder, Craig, 185n, 465n
Pinochet, General, 785
Pinto, Jeffrey K., 248n
Plaskett, Thomas G., 625
Plato, 38, 40
Plumlee, E. Leroy, 466n, 539n
Podsakoff, Philip M., 499n
Pohlmann, John T., 500n
Poor, Henry, 43
Porsche, Ferdinand, 156
Porter, Lyman W., 301n, 448–449, 464n, 465n
Porter, Michael, 206, 218n, 321
Porter, Michael E., 95, 107n, 184n, 337n
Portwood, James D., 117n
Pouschine, Tatiana, 189
Powell, Bill, 108
Prentis, Eric L., 70n, 654n
Prietula, Michael J., 153n
Pritchard, Beth, 214
Pritchard, Max D., 184n
Pruitt, B. H., 221
Pryor, Austin K., 218n
Pugh, Derek S., 337n
Pyhrr, Peter, 715n

Quick, James C., 589n
Quick, Jonathan D., 589n
Quinn, James Brian, 216n, 248n, 654n
Quinn, R. P., 538n

Radebaugh, Lee H., 800n, 801n
Raelin, Joseph A., 833n
Rafaeli, Anat, 589n
Ragan, James W., 248n
Rahe, R. H., 589n
Raho, L. E., 267n
Rainey, Hal G., 29n, 336n
Ralston, David A., 117n
Ramanujam, Vasudevan, 248n
Rameriz, Anthony, 11, 503
Ramsey, D. K., 269a
Randall, Donna M., 539n, 583n

Randolph, W. Alan, 337n
Rapoport, Carla, 185, 231, 683n, 800n
Raven, Bertram, 499n
Rawl, Lawrence G., 414, 415
Reagan, Ronald, 502
Rebello, Kathy, 303
Redding, S. Gordon, 800n
Redmond, Steve, 641
Reed, John, 476, 477
Regan, Julie, 553
Reiff, Rick, 293
Reimann, Bernard C., 500n
Reitz, H. Joseph, 429n
Rescigno, Richard, 387
Resnick, Stewart, 288
Reynolds, Elizabeth V., 301n
Reynolds, George W., 683n
Rhode, John G., 622n
Rice, Faye, 117n, 763n
Richards, Max D., 184n, 185n
Ricks, David A., 783
Rippe, James M., 589n
Robbie, Joe, 126
Robbins, D. Keith, 217n
Roberts, Marjory, 589n
Roberts, Nancy C., 835n
Robinson, Richard B., Jr., 217n
Rockefeller, John D., 38, 414, 816
Roddick, Anita, 825
Roebuck, Alvah, 746
Rogers, Michael, 129
Rogers, T. J., 245
Roitman, David B., 725n
Roosevelt, Franklin, 502, 816
Ropp, Kirkland, 29n, 383n
Rosenman, R. H., 589n
Rosenthal, R. A., 538n
Rosenzweig, James E., 70n
Roskies, Ethel, 725n
Ross, Ian M., 38
Ross, Jerry, 152n
Ross, Sam M., 749
Roth, Philip L., 184n
Rothlisberger, Fritz J., 464n
Rotter, J. B., 583n
Rowe, M. P., 572n
Rowland, Roland W. "Tiny," 819
Rudnitsky, Howard, 603
Russell, James S., 382n
Ryan, Linda, 263n

Sackett, Paul R., 381n
Salancik, Gerald, 583n
Sandberg, William R., 248n
Saporito, Bill, 119, 187, 216n, 248n, 251, 423n
Sarver, K. F., 667
Sashkin, Marshall, 413n, 420, 423n
Sathe, Vijay, 622n
Saunders, Ernest, 110
Scattaregia, Julie H., 381n
Schacht, Henry B., 802–803
Schaefer, C. E., 429n
Schaefer, Thomas E., 833n
Schaubroeck, John, 589n
Schein, Edgar H., 116n
Schendel, Dan, 216n, 219n
Scherr, Frederick C., 300n
Schiller, Harvey W., 540
Schiller, Zachary, 103
Schlender, Benton R., 303
Schlesinger, Leonard A., 29n, 412n
Schmidt, Frank L., 381n
Schmidt, Warren H., 484–485, 490, 500n
Schmitt, Neal, 381n
Schnake, Mel E., 466n
Schneeweis, Thomas, 834n
Schrank, Robert, 538n
Schreisheim, Chester A., 499n, 500n
Schreyogg, Georg, 623n
Schroeder, Horst W., 155
Schuler, Randall S., 218n, 589n
Schultz, Ellen, 325
Schutz, Peter W., 156, 157
Schweiger, David M., 152n, 248n
Scott, K. Dow, 467n
Scott, William G., 28n, 69n
Scott, W. Richard, 105n–106n, 301n
Scoviak, Mary, 571n
Sculley, John, 212, 302–303, 398, 402, 476, 499n
Sears, Richard, 746
Seashore, S., 107n
Seawell, William, 624
Sella, George J., 143, 274, 292
Sellers, Patricia, 155, 412n, 466n, 833n
Selye, Hans, 589n
Sepehri, M., 725n

Shaich, Ron, 761
Shapira, Zur, 151n
Sharfman, Mark P., 729n
Sharkey, Thomas W., 501n
Sharpe, Richard, 103
Shaw, Marvin E., 152n, 538n
Shea, Gregory P., 538n
Sheil, Beau, 153n
Sherman, Stratford, P., 151n, 575
Sherwood, John J., 339n
Shin, Donkwood, 654n
Shinn, George, 542
Shoen, L. S., 78
Shrivastava, Paul, 97, 107n, 216n
Simmons, Donna L., 413n
Simon, Herbert A., 129, 152n, 153n, 572n
Simonds, Rollin H., 725n
Sims, Henry P., Jr., 382n, 501n
Sinetar, Marsha, 107n
Singh, Jitendra V., 151n
Singh, Ramadhar, 500n
Siropolis, Nicholas C., 745, 753, 754, 755–756, 759, 760, 762n, 763n
Sivyer, Debra "Debbi," 764. *See also* Fields, Debbie
Skinner, B. F., 453, 466n
Skolnik, Rayna, 741
Slevin, Dennis P., 248n
Sloan, Alfred P., 461
Sloan, Pat, 11
Slocum, John W., Jr., 801n
Smart, John R., 216n, 683n
Smith, Adam, 275, 300n
Smith, C. D., 221
Smith, Charles, 412n
Smith, D., 263n
Smith, Fred, 484
Smith, Frederick W., 174, 684
Smith, Geoffrey N., 803
Smith, Page, 28n, 69n
Smith, Roger, 14
Smucker, Jerome M., 87
Smucker, Paul, 87
Smucker, Richard, 87
Snarey, John, 833n
Snoek, J. D., 538n
Snow, Charles C., 217n
Snyder, Jesse, 705
Snyder, Richard, 203
Snyderman, Barbara, 465n
Socrates, 40

Sonnenfield, Jeffrey A., 218n
Spector, Paul E., 589n
Spendolini, Michael J., 301n
Stalker, G. M., 107n, 315–316, 330, 337n
Star, Steven H., 715n
Starr, Martin K., 151n
Staw, Barry M., 70n, 152n
Steers, Richard M., 106n, 464n, 465n, 800n
Steffy, Brian D., 380n, 589n
Stein, Benjamin J., 336n
Steiner, George, 184n
Steinmann, Horst, 623n
Stern, Sara E., 622n
Stevenson, Howard H., 763n
Stewart, Rosemary, 29n
Sting, 269
Stinson, William, 177
Stodden, John R., 611
Stogdill, Ralph M., 500n
Stoka, Ann Marie, 69n
Stone, Thomas H., 381n
Stott, Charles, 173
Strang, David, 301n
Strauss, Gary, 87
Streidl, J. William, 249n
Stroup, Margaret A., 834n
Sullivan, Cornelius H., Jr., 216n, 683n
Sullivan, Jeremiah J., 71n, 464n
Sullivan, Robert, 541
Sundgren, Alison, 834n
Susman, Gerald I., 725n
Suszko, Mary K., 381n
Sutta, Marian, 385
Sutton, Robert I., 381n, 589n
Sviokla, John J., 153n, 683n
Swift, E. M., 541
Symonds, Gardiner, 716
Szczerbacki, David, 336n
Szilagyi, Andrew D., 249n

Tanii, Akio, 201
Tank, Andrew, 577
Tannenbaum, A. S., 107n
Tannenbaum, Robert, 484–485, 490, 500n
Tansik, David A., 729n
Tanzer, Andres, 201, 505
Tasca, Robert, 534
Tasini, Jonathan, 385
Taubman, A. Alfred, 32

Taylor, Alex, III, 28n, 29n, 248n, 338n, 731, 800n
Taylor, Frederick W., 28n, 43–44, 45, 60, 69n, 438, 464n
Taylor, Glen, 133
Taylor, M. Susan, 538n
Tennant, Anthony M., 110
Terborg, James R., 300n
Thatcher, Margaret, 777
Thill, John V., 571n, 572n
Thomas, Howard, 151n
Thompson, James, 294, 301n
Thompson, James D., 93–94, 105n, 107n
Tjosvold, Dean, 422n
Todor, William D., 301n
Toffler, Alvin, 840, 843n
Tosi, Henry L., 249n
Toyoda, Eiji, 386
Toyoda, Kiichiro, 386
Toyoda, Shoichiro, 386
Trevion, Linda Klebe, 833n
Treybig, Jim, 60, 61, 112, 182, 562
Trippe, Juan, 624
Truel, Peter, 73
Truxillo, Donald M., 382n
Tsai, Gerald, Jr., 495
Tully, Shawn, 23, 103, 845
Tung, Rosalie L., 117n
Turner, Ted, 540
Turner, Tina, 269
Tutor, Jesse B., Jr., 683n
Twomey, Daniel, 300n
Twomey, David P., 380n
Tziner, Aharon, 725n

Udwadia, Firdaus E., 97, 107n
Ueberroth, Peter, 7,
Ulrich, David O., 589n
Ungson, Geraldo R., 337n
Urban, Glen L., 715n
Ure, Andrew, 43
Urwick, Lyndall F., 46, 285, 301n
Utall, Bro, 325, 654n

Vanderbilt, Cornelius, 38–39, 816
Van de Ven, Andrew, 153n
Van Fleet, David D., 23, 41, 287, 301n
Van Fleet, Ella W., 23
Van Orden, Richard, 263n
Vavelas, A., 572n

Venkatraman, N., 248n
Ventres, Romeo, 613
Vest, Michael J., 467n
Victor, Bart, 301n, 833n
Vincze, Julian W., 217n
Vollrath, David A., 423n
Vroom, Victor H., 446, 465n, 490–492, 500n, 501n

Wade, Paula, 749
Wagner, G. R., 267n
Wagner, John A., III, 423n
Wall, Toby D., 423n
Walley, Wayne, 119
Walton, Richard E., 623n
Walton, Sam, 578–579, 581, 582
Wang, An, 489
Wang, Frederick A., 489
Wanous, John P., 465n
Warhol, Andy, 32
Wartick, Steven L., 834n
Waterman, Robert H., Jr., 65, 71n, 334, 339n
Waters, Craig R., 763n
Watson, Bill, 538n
Watson, Margaret D., 184n
Watt, James, 720
Wayne, Sandy J., 413n
Weber, Max, 46, 47, 69n, 309, 310, 311, 336n
Wedge, Scott, 743
Weed, Earl D., 466n
Weick, Karl E., 571n
Weiner, Steven B., 336n
Weis, Richard M., 69n
Weitz, Barton, 117n
Weitzel, William, 729n
Welch, Jack, 8, 10, 11, 24, 102, 125, 126, 181, 476, 789, 790
Wellemeyer, Marilyn, 69n
Wells, Frank G., 590
Wells, Henry, 108
Welsh, M. Ann, 622n
Werner, Hermann R., 511
Wesner, Idalene F., 106n–107n
Wetherbe, James C., 683n
Wexley, Kenneth N., 382n
Wheelen, Thomas L., 184n, 185n
Wheelon, Thomas L., 248n
Whenmouth, Edwin, 223, 839
Whinston, A. B., 267n
Whitely, William, 28n, 29n
Whitener, Ellen M., 583n

Whitman, Marina V. N., 175
Whitsett, David A., 70n
Wiener, Yoash, 339n
Wigdor, Lawrence A., 465n
Wilemon, David, 412n
Wiley, Donna L., 538n
Wilkins, Alan L., 69n
Wilkinson, Harry E., 117n, 499n
Williams, A. L., 556, 569
Williams, Jennifer, 538n
Williams, Monci Jo, 70n, 116n, 203
Williamson, Oliver E., 319, 337n
Wilson, David C., 151n
Wilson, David, Sir, 4
Winchell, William O., 655n
Winger, Richard W., 627
Witten, Marsha G., 572n
Wofford, Jerry, 572n
Wolf, Gerrit, 729n
Wolfe, D. M., 538n
Wolfe, Joseph, 381n
Wolfe, Richard A., 589n
Wolman, Karen, 103
Wood, James, 430
Wood, Robert, 430
Woodman, Richard W., 413n
Woodward, Joan, 313–315, 337n
Worrell, Dan L., 382n
Worthy, Ford S., 29n, 715n
Worthy, James C., 287, 301n
Wozniak, Steve, 302
Wrage, Charles D., 69n
Wren, Daniel, 69n, 70n
Wright, Robert C., 24
Wriston, Walter B., 113–114, 477
Wrubel, Robert, 837
Wurman, Richard Saul, 551

Xuxa, 269

Yanouzas, John N., 301n
Yasai-Ardekani, Masoud, 337n
Yetton, Philip H., 490–492, 500n
Yoffie, David B., 107n
Yorks, Lyle, 70n
Yuchtman, E., 107n
Yukl, Gary A., 499n, 500n, 501n

Zakon, Alan, 627, 813
Zander, Alvin, 538n
Zmud, R., 267n

ORGANIZATION AND
PRODUCT INDEX

ABC, 608
Abercrombie & Fitch, 308
Adidas, 85
Adolph Coors Company, case on, 384–385
AEG, 416, 417
Aetna Life and Casualty, 462
AFL-CIO, 384, 385
Aid Association for Lutherans (AAL), 508, 511, 513, 514, 530, 531
Airbus Industrie, 126, 766
  information management at, 671
Air France, 305
Airline Passengers Association, 90
Alfa, 189
Alfa Romeo, 319
Allegheny International, 817–818
Allegis, 91
Allen-Bradley, 639, 648
Allied-Signal, 373
ALPO, 119
Aluminum Company of America (Alcoa), 803
AMAX, 165
American Airlines, 96, 126, 148, 408, 629, 631, 771
  information system of, 677
  reciprocal interdependence at, 294–295
  training programs at, 361
American Arbitration Association, 385
American Brands, 576
American Can, 495–496
American Cyanamid, 143, 277, 323
  centralization at, 292

structure of, 274
American Express, 59, 652, 771
  accountability and, 617
  Avis and, 399
  case on, 108–109
  Optima credit card, 168
  social responsibility and, 822
American Greetings, 596, 602
American Home Products Corp., 136, 169
American Information Technologies Corporation (Ameritech), 680
American Motors, 124–125
American Telephone & Telegraph, see AT&T
Amoco Chemicals Corporation, 377
Anglo-Swiss Condensed Milk Company, 844
Anheuser-Busch, 384, 813
A&P, 449–450
Apollo Computer, 129
Apple, 476, 650, 839
  Apple II, 302
  case on, 302–303
  group activities at, 517
  Jobs, 163, 172, 212, 238, 255, 302, 398, 475, 737
  Macintosh, 302, 303, 402
  organization change and, 398
  Sculley, 212, 302–303, 398, 402, 476, 499n
  work groups at, 530
Aptus, 292
Archer Daniels Midland Company, 577, 702
ARCO, 458
Arista, 461
Arvida, 591

Ashland Oil, social responsibility and, 819–820, 821, 824, 826, 830
Associated Press, 14, 608
Atari, 334
Atlantic Richfield, 829
Atlas, 342–343
AT&T, 15, 36, 91, 114, 277, 393, 751
  assessment center concept and, 359
  Bell Laboratories, 38, 114
  communication in, 551
  cutbacks at, 726, 729
  job enrichment at, 278
  stress and, 584, 585, 588
Au Bon Pain, 761
Audi, 156
Austrian Airlines, 718
Avis, 320, 399
Avon, 65, 349

Baker-Hughes, 283
Baker International, 277
Ballard Medical, 752
Ball Corporation, 94, 608
Banana Republic, 294
Bang and Olufsen, 792
Bank Leu, 110
Bank of America, 114–115, 149
Bank of New England, 55
Bantam Books, 461
BASF, 375
Bateman Eichler, Hill Richards, 293
Bausch & Lomb, 648
Bayer, 774
Beatrice Foods Company, 475, 478, 576

Beatrice Foods Company (*cont.*)
  as H-form organization, 320–
    321
  ICI and, 343
Beatrice International Foods, 116
Beecham Group PLC, 110, 795
  planned change at, 395
Beech-Nut, 826
  ethics and, 812, 814
  social responsibility and, 831
Bell, Arthur & Sons, 110
Bell's, 110
Bennetton
  CAD at, 639
  case on, 626–627
  control at, 614
  distribution at, 634, 636
Bertelsmann, 461
Bethlehem Steel, 44, 45, 277, 631
Bilco Tools Inc., 741
Bill's Garden Center, 4
Black Business Resource Group,
    516
Black & Decker, 16, 548
  communication at, 560–561
  GE and, 675
  management by wandering
    around at, 559
  operations systems at, 635
Black Officers Association, 516
Blunt, Ellis & Loewi, 293
BMW, 189, 416, 418
Bob's Big Boy, 31
Body Shop, 825
Boeing, 25, 84, 89, 96, 126, 141,
    179, 637, 671, 771
  decision support systems and,
    266
  ethics and, 814
  international operations, 773–
    774, 793
  737 of, 19–20
Boettcher, 293
Boise-Cascade, 706
Bombardier, Inc., 331
Borden, 37
  case on, 186–187
  strategic control at, 613
Bosch-Siemens, 103
Boston Celtics, 4
Brentano's, 160
Bridgestone Tire Company, 667,
    775

Bristol-Myers, 37
British Airways (BA), 611
British Museum, 4
British Petroleum, 24, 777
British Steel, 777
British Telecom, 777
Britoil, 777
Brooks Brothers, 314
Brown Printing, 461
Broyhill, 631
Burger King, 94
  employee turnover ratio, 711
Burlington Industries, 568
Burlington Northern, 298
Burroughs Corporation, 99, 138
Business Week, 88, 196

Cain Chemical, 503
Caltex, 574
Campbell Soup, 87
  communication at, 548
  expert system of, 680–681
  international business and, 783
  poisoned cans and, 97
Canadian Pacific Forest Products,
    Ltd., 177
Cardinal Federal Savings Bank,
    731
Cardinal Industries Inc., 646
  productivity at, 646
Carnation Company, 91, 119,
    176, 771, 845
Carnival Cruise Lines, 86
Carter, Mary, Paint Company,
    728
Carter-Glogau, 169
Cassini, Oleg, 795
Caterpillar Tractor, 25, 179, 648,
    771
  international operations of, 774
  job design and, 275
  organization change at, 390,
    393, 394, 399, 400, 402, 403,
    404
  revitalization at, 409, 410
  team-building at, 405
CBS Records, 25, 804–805
  administrative intensity and,
    298
  goal of, 165
  planning at, 182
  preliminary control and, 608
Celanese, 38

Celeron, 775
Cellmark Diagnostics, 343
Center for the Study of Respon-
    sive Law and Consumers
    Union, 90
Century 21, 25
Champion Spark Plug Company,
    614, 615
Chase Manhattan Bank, 24, 266,
    323
Chemical Bank, 814
Chesebrough-Pond's, 576, 577
Chevrolet, 617, 783
Chevron, 92
Chicago Pacific Corporation, 796
Chicago White Sox, 813
Chiron Corporation, 431
Choctaw Indian Tribe, 25
Christie's, 33
Chrysler Motors, 4, 58, 86, 99,
    101, 124, 130, 170, 446, 650,
    771
  American Motors and, 124–126
  benefits and, 373
  Iacocca, 63, 476
  inventory, 643–644
  overcontrol at, 616
  robots at, 724
CIBA-Geigy, 798
Circle K, 86
Citibank, 113, 148, 323
Citicorp, 24, 108, 149
  goals of, 172–173
  Reed at, 477
Cities Service, 503
Citizens and Southern, 672
Claiborne, Liz, Inc., 138–139,
    317, 737, 742
Clean Harbors, Inc., 736, 738,
    739, 742, 743
Club Med, 86
CNCP Telecommunications, 177
Coca-Cola Company, 88, 96, 798
  formula change and, 137
  in Japan, 790
  language and international busi-
    ness and, 783
  Pepsi-Cola and, 268, 269
Coca-Cola Enterprises, 269
Cohen-Hatfield, 11
Coleco Industries, 170
Colgate-Palmolive Company,
    114, 428, 576

Colonial Life Insurance Company, 277–278
Columbia Savings, 731
Combitech, 319
Community Benefits Corporation, 535
Compact Video, 11
Compaq Computer, 741
  decision making at, 124, 128, 142
  organization life cycle of, 317, 318
  starting, 737
Coniston Partners, 91, 138
Conoco, 100
Consolidated Cigar, 11
Consolidated Diesel Electric Corporation, 723
Consolidated Edison, 25, 36
Consolidated Freightways, 25, 56
Contadina, 176
Continental Airlines, 84, 99, 565
Continental Can, 694
Continental Corporation, 355
Control Data Corporation, 165, 377, 397, 458
Cooper Industries, 601
Coors Beer, 631
Corning Glass Works, 88, 425, 426
  goals of, 172
  innovation at, 427
  mission of, 165
  plans of, 173
  screening control at, 609
Council of Better Business Bureaus, 90
CPC International, 601
Crane Brand, 186
Cray Research, 173
Crédit Suisse First Boston (CSFB), 542, 543
Crossair, 718
Cummins Engine Company
  case on, 802–803
  international operations of, 773

Dae-Woo, 88, 504
Daihatsu Motor Company, 705
Daimler-Benz, 156, 771
  case on, 416–417
Dalton, B., 160

Datsun, 649. *See also* Nissan Motor Company
Dayton-Hudson, 829
Dean Witter Reynolds Inc., 313
  ethics and, 808, 812
DEC, 650
Deere, John, 176, 771
  case on, 656–657
Delco, 766
Dell Publishing, 461
Delta Air Lines, 25, 65, 90, 567
  informal groups at, 515
  operative work group at, 529
  plane crash and, 97
  suppliers, 88–89
Delta Lithograph, 461
Der Zeit, 461
Detroit Edison, 55, 277
Deutsche Aerospace, 417
Dewar's, 110
Diamond International, 728
Digital Equipment Corporation, 61, 65, 149, 810, 814
Disney Channel, 590
Disney, Walt, Pictures, 591
Disney, Walt, Productions, 65, 86, 88, 176, 778
  case on, 590–591
  divisional design at, 322, 331
  revitalization at, 409, 410
  reward system and, 460
Disney Channel, 590
Distillers Company, 110
Domino's Pizza, 176, 457
Dom Perignon, 792
Dornier, 416
Dorr-Oliver Inc., 741
Doubleday, 461
Dove International, 119
Dow Chemical, 15, 65, 165, 314, 703
Dresser Industries, 166, 703
Drexel Burnham Lambert Inc., 808
"Dr. Fad Show, The", 738
Du Pont, 14, 55, 65, 100, 328,
  expectancy theory at, 447
  social responsibility and, 817
Durkee Industrial Foods Corporation, 577

Eastern Airlines, 30, 84, 99
  labor problems at, 565
  organization change and, 398

Eastman Kodak, 64, 65, 422, 703
  Japan and, 770, 771, 796
  social responsibility and, 821
  substitutes for leadership at, 495
Eaton, 85
Edwards, A. G., 407
Eggo Nutri-Grain Waffles, 154
Electrolux, 103
Electronic Data Systems (EDS), 136, 181, 533
Eli Lily, 15, 98, 141
Elling Brothers Mechanical Contractors, 758
Elsenham Quality Foods, 87
Emery Air Freight, 457–458, 598, 600, 606
E-mu Systems, 743
Epcot Center, 590
Equicor, 407
Equitable Company, 516
Esso, 782
Ethicon Inc., 431
Euro Disneyland, 591
Exxon, 8, 84, 90, 148, 176, 314, 692
  case on, 414–415
  group activities at, 517
  oil spill and, 820
  social responsibility and, 825

FAA, 407
Fairfield Inn, 31, 665–666
Fantastic Sam's, 749
Farah Manufacturing Company, 90
Federal Express, 72, 98, 114, 310, 569
  case on, 684–685
  control and, 597
  goals of, 174
  information systems at, 670
  leadership at, 484
  legislation and, 828
  political action committee of, 828
Federal Paper Board, 94
Federal Reserve Bank, 283
Federated Department Stores, 408
Ferrari, 189, 792
Fiat, 26
  case on, 188–189
Fidelity Bank, 598

Firestone Tire & Rubber Company, 667
First Boston, case on, 542–543
First Nationwide Financial Corporation, 731
First World Cheese, 96
Fisher, 100
Flying Tiger, 484, 684
FMC Corporation, 601
Ford Motor Company, 8, 13, 14, 21, 24, 25, 58, 83, 84, 90, 91, 130, 179, 277, 439, 457, 648, 650, 771, 772, 798
  of Britain, 328
  of Canada, 328
  case on, 730–731
  Escort, 649–650
  Fiat and, 188
  general environment of, 80, 82, 83–84
  interactive video training program of, 364
  language and international business and, 782
  multiple control systems at, 609
  organization change at, 391
  participative management at, 419, 422
  Petersen of, 4, 7, 8, 13, 24, 112
  production increase at, 606
  purchasing at, 642
  task environment of, 85, 86, 91
  Taurus, 322–323, 325–326, 649–660
  -Werke, 328
  zero-base budgeting at, 697
Formica Corporation, 274
Fortune, 88, 196
Franklin Mint, 288
Frito-Lay, 268
Fruehauf, 601
Fuji Bank, 24
Fuji Photo, 770
Furstenburg, Diane Von, Cosmetics, 795

Gaines Pet Foods, 119
Gap, The, 308, 631
Garolini, 282
Genentech, 373
General Dynamics, 458
  case on, 836–837

General Electric Company, 10, 11, 16, 24, 25, 55, 103, 115, 179, 377, 427, 476, 692, 804
  Black & Decker and, 675
  in Britain, 658
  computer-aided design at, 639, 723
  decentralization at, 292
  employee involvement at, 648
  goal of, 162
  Hawthorne studies and, 50
  information system of, 677
  international operations and, 789, 790
  life and career planning at, 406, 407
  operations management at, 630, 633, 635, 636
  participative management at, 419, 420–421
  positive reinforcement at, 454
  productivity at, 646, 648
  social responsibility, 825
  standards, 605
  stress reduction at, 588
  technology and, 613
  Thompson and, 125, 126
  Welch of, 8, 10, 11, 24, 102, 125, 126, 181, 476, 789, 790
General Foods Corporation, 24, 37, 88, 115, 140, 154, 177, 278, 462, 476
  intrapreneurs at, 428
  groups at, 530
  Philip Morris and, 340
General Foods USA, 341
General Instrument Corporation, 56, 794
General Mills, 24, 154
  CIO at, 568
  ethics and, 814
  information systems at, 670
  preliminary control at, 607–608
General Motors, 4, 14, 25, 55, 58, 85, 90, 130, 136, 141, 170, 175, 176, 179, 276, 323, 461, 601, 642, 650, 750, 771
  of Canada, 328
  dual-career couples and, 116
  employees, 578
  executive committee of, 528
  Fiat and, 188
  Ford and, 730

information management at, 669
  international operations of, 774
  organization change at, 391
  planning staff of, 181
  small businesses and, 740
  System 1 to System 4 design at, 311–312
  uncertainty faced by, 95
  United Auto Workers and, 378
General Telephone Company, 365
Genetics Institute, 526
Geophysical Services, Inc., 515
Georgia-Pacific Corporation, 599
Gerber's, 87
Getty Oil, 40
Getty Petroleum Corporation, 574
Gillette, 266
Glidden paint, 343
Golden West Financial, 820
Goodrich, B. F., 408–409, 462, 588
Goodyear Tire & Rubber Company, 85, 631, 775
Gould Company, 144
Gould, Inc., 699
Granada Corporation, 10
Grand Metropolitan PLC, 110, 119
Grandtravel, 81
Grant, W. T., 59
Great Western, 553
Greyhound, 409, 410
Groupe Carnaud, 23
Guinness PLC, case on, 110–111
Gulf, 255

Hallmark Cards, 334, 596
Hancock, John, Mutual Life Insurance, 458
Hanley Worldwide Inc., 813
Hannaford Brothers, 264
Hanson Industries Inc., 343, 577
Hanson PLC, 577
Harris Corporation, 59
Harris Semiconductor Sector, 59
Harrods, 819
Harvard University, 79
Heath, 119
Henderson Industries, 143
Henri Bendel, 308
Hershey, 118, 119
Hertz Rent-A-Car, 85, 91, 138

Hewlett-Packard, 19, 61, 64, 65, 112, 422, 439, 839
  ethics and, 814
  intrapreneurs at, 428
  organizational culture of, 333, 334
Hilton International, 91, 176
Hitachi Consumer Products, 470–471
Hitachi Ltd., 91, 804
  case on, 470–471
Hollywood Pictures, 591
Home Depot, 55
Home Shopping Network, 403
Honda, 6, 101, 418, 649, 771, 792
  of America, 90, 337
  international operations of, 774
  inventory, 643
  purchasing at, 642
  quotas and, 779
  speed and, 634
Hoover Universal
  international operations, 792, 796
  mission, 165
Host International, Inc., 30
Hot Shoppes, 30, 31
House of Fraser, 819
Howard Johnson, 31
Hughes Aircraft, 55
Hutton, E. F., and Company, 808
Hyatt Regency, 546, 561
Hyundai, 504
Hyundai Electronics Industries Company, 794

Iberia, 305
IBM, 14, 61, 64, 65, 84, 91, 95, 124, 128, 277, 278, 409, 458, 567, 642, 648, 650, 750, 771, 798, 810
  administrative intensity and, 298
  Apple and, 302
  case on, 304–305
  compensation at, 369
  customers of, 88
  cutbacks and decline and, 728
  decentralization at, 292–293
  dual-career couples and, 116
  evolution of computers and, 264

Fiat and, 188
flexible manufacturing system at, 723
globalization and, 328
information system of, 676
Japan, 356, 791
organizational culture and, 332
organization life cycle at, 318
product layout used at, 637
Rolmr and, 658
Siemens and, 658, 841
social responsibility and, 821, 825
span of management at, 288
training and development programs at, 361
work-force reductions at, 727
IESE (Institute de Estudios Superiores de la Empresa), 23
IMEDE (International Management Development Institute), 23
IMI (International Management Institute), 23
Imperial Chemical Industries (ICI), case on, 342–343
Ingersoll-Rand Co., 254
INSEAD (Insitut Europeén D'Administration des Affaires), 23
Integrated Measurement Systems Inc., 767
Intel, 38, 65
Intercontinental Hotel, 140
International Association of Machinists, 385
International Harvester, 482. *See also* Navistar
International Microcircuits Inc., 766
International Telephone and Telegraph Corporation (ITT), 408, 475–476
  communication in, 555
  Geneen of, 19
IRI, 188

Jaguar, 416
Jalisco, 97
Jardine Matheson PLC, 111
Jewel Food Stores, 114
JMB Realty Trust, 591
Johns-Manville, 588

Johnson Controls, 85, 643
Johnson & Johnson, 112, 114, 427, 476
  case on, 430–431
  ethics and, 814
  mission, 165
  Retin-A and, 430–431
  Tylenol poisonings and, 96, 97, 727, 830
Johnson, S. C. & Sons, 428
Jovan, 795
Joyce, 282

Kawasaki, 771
Kay, Mary, Cosmetics, 165
Kellogg, 155
  case on, 154–155
Kelly Services, 25, 88
Kemper Corporation, 293
Kemper Financial Services, Inc., 293
Kenmore, 85
Kenner Parker Toys, 690
Kentucky Fried Chicken, 268, 269, 711
Kepnoe-Tregoe, 137
Kimberly-Clark, 37, 431, 694
Kinder Care, 25
Kinko's, 314
Kiwanis Club, 517
Klein, Calvin, 282
KLM, 96, 718
K mart, 25, 87, 90, 160, 176
  centralization at, 292
  coordination at, 295
  distribution at, 636
  information system of, 677
  marketing department of, 513, 514
  mechanistic organization at, 315
Kodak, *see* Eastman Kodak
Komatsu Ltd., 390, 802
Kongsberg Vaapenfabrikk, 838
Kraft, Inc., 87, 177–178, 341
Kroger, 85, 148
  information system at, 665, 666
  transaction processing systems at, 672

Lancia, 189
Land's End, 812, 820
La Petite Boulangerie, 765
Last Emperor, The, 796

Laundromats, 427
Lauren, Ralph, 83
LBS (London Business School), 23
League of Women Voters, 90
Lechmere department store, 277, 649
Lee, 94
Lee Way Motor Freight, 268
Lerner, 308, 322
Lever Brothers, 112, 576
Levi Strauss & Company, 24, 94, 771
  organizational culture and, 332
  clan control at, 611
  social responsibility, 818
Limited, The, 308, 322
Limited Express, The, 308, 322
Limited Inc.
  divisional design at, 331
  multidivisional design at, 321–322
  organization design of, 308, 316
Lincoln Continental, 649–650
Lincoln Electric, 436, 439
Literary Guild, 461
Little, Arthur D., Inc., 55
Little League Baseball, 26
Lloyd's of London, case on, 74–75
Lockheed, 126, 706
Loft, 268
Lonrho PLC, 819
LSI Logic Corp., 766
LTV, 328
Lucky-Goldstar, 504
Lufthansa, 305
Luz International, 637

MacAndrews & Forbes Holdings, 11
McDonald's, 94, 330, 748, 771, 798
  centralization at, 292
  employee turnover ratio of, 711
  goals of, 173
  MRP system at, 705
  productivity, 648
  Ronald McDonald House program, 825, 826
  in Soviet Union, 788
  standards of, 603

McDonnell Douglas, 83, 88–89, 126, 671, 793
  Boeing and, 793
  computer-aided design at, 723
  ethics and, 814
  social responsibility and, 817
  Swissair and, 719
McGuffey's, 481
Macmillan publishing company, 167
Magnavox, 103, 804
Manufacturers Hanover, 392
Marathon Realty Company, 177
Marriott Corporation, 558
  case on, 30–31
  Fairfield Inn of, 31, 665–666
Marriott Food Services, 294–295
Mars
  case on, 118–119
  preliminary control and, 608
Massachusetts Mutual, 364
Massey-Ferguson, 26
MasterCard, 108, 822
Matsushita Electric, 103, 838
Mattel, 58
Maxwell Communication, 167
Maxwell House, 88
Mayo Clinic, 513
Maytag, 65, 85, 796
  job enlargement at, 278
  job specialization and, 276
Mazda, 91, 346, 358, 771, 792
MCI, 632
Mead, 88
Mead Johnson, 430
MEI Corporation, 269
Memphis State University, 513
Mentor Graphics Corp., case on, 766–767
Mercedes-Benz, 792
Merck & Company, 15, 78, 427
  dual-career couples and, 116
  employee turnover ratio at, 71
  hybrid organization designs at, 325
  performance measured at, 605
Mercury Tracer, 772
Merrill Lynch, 88, 632, 775
  case on, 686–687
Messerschmitt-Bolkow-Blohm G.m.b.H. (MBB), 416
Metalloy, 597
Methodist Church, 85

Metropolitan Edison, 97
Metropolitan Life, 25, 295, 458
MF Holdings, 765
Michigan State University, 6
Midial S. A., 765
Midvale Steel Company, 43, 45
Mile High Federal Savings and Loan Association, 731
Miles, Robert H., and Associates, 337n
Miller Beer, 340, 341, 384
Milliken & Company, 511
Minnesota Mining & Manufacturing, see 3M Company
Mitsubishi, 771, 804
Mobay, 511
Mobil Corp., 6, 14, 100, 771, 827
Moët-Hennessy, 111
Monsanto, 15, 25, 84, 323, 426
  innovation at, 427
  operations management at, 639–640
Montgomery Ward, 614
Mooney, 156
Moral Majority, 100
Morgan Guaranty, 65
Morita and Co., 804
Mothers Against Drunk Drivers (MADD), 90
Motorola, 419, 634
  communication at, 555
  employee involvement at, 649
  organization design at, 316
Mrs. Fields Bakery Cafe, 765
Mrs. Fields' Chocolate Chippery, 764
Mrs. Fields' Cookies, 4, 114
  case on, 764–765
Mrs. Smith's pies, 154
MTU, 416, 417
Mutual of Omaha, 100

Nabisco, 112, 154, 155
NASA, 12, 15
  as bureaucracy, 310
  Challenger explosion and, 97
National Advertising Review Board, 90
National Car Rental, 632
National Cash Register, see NCR Corporation
National Education Association, 385

National Electric, Inc., 292
National Football League Players
    Association, 90
National Labor Relations Board
    (NLRB), 385
National Organization for
    Women (NOW), 90
National Science Foundation, 26
National Steel, 99
National Trust for Historic Pres-
    ervation, 32
Navistar, 36, 482
NBC, 24, 610, 713
NCR Corporation, 25, 179, 323,
    630
Nestlé, 23, 26, 91, 119, 771, 778,
    798
    career management and, 115
    case on, 844–845
    cutbacks and decline and, 728
New Jersey Bell Telephone, 48
Newport News, 637
Newsweek, 14
New United Motor Manufactur-
    ing, Inc., *see* NUMMI
New York Condensed Milk
    Company, 186
New York Life, 100
New York Times Company, The, 25
NeXt Computer Company, 16,
    163, 737
Nike, 85, 140, 168
Nippon Mining Co., 699
Nippon Telegraph & Telephone,
    180
Nissan Motor Co., 85, 91, 294,
    802
NOK, 597
Norelco, 103
Norstar, 666
North American Van Lines, 268
Northern Research & Engineering
    Corporation, 254
Northrop Corporation, 662
Northwest Airlines, 727
Norton, 88
NUMMI (New United Motor
    Manufacturing, Inc.), 456,
    531
Nutra-Sweet, 96

Occidental Petroleum Corpora-
    tion (Oxy), 502–503

Ocean Spray Cranberry, 747
Offset Paperback Manufacturers,
    461
Olin Corporation, 503
Oneida Ltd., 723
Oscar Mayer Foods, 341

Pacific Gas & Electric, 25
Pacific Intermountain Express,
    326
Pan American Airways, 140
    case on, 624–625
Pan American Games, 680
Pan Canadian Petroleum Ltd.,
    177
Pappagallo, 282
Paramount Pictures, 590
Parents, 461
Pathway Financial, 731
Peace Corps, 85
Penn Central Railroad, 59
Penney, J. C., 87, 176
    benefits at, 373
    conflict at, 532, 534
    organizational culture of, 333
Pennzoil, 40, 574
Pentagon, 137, 662
People Express, 60, 99, 136
PepsiCo, 96, 268, 771, 798
    case on, 268–269a
    employee turnover ratio at, 711
Perkins Geddis Eastman, 372
Perulac, 778
Peugot, 319
Pfizer, 601
Philip Morris, 15, 78
    case on, 340–341
    employee turnover ratio at, 711
    planning at, 177–178
    social responsibility and, 824
Philips, 85, 103, 323, 766
    international dimension and, 85,
    103
Pillsbury, 340
Pioneer, 100
Pitney Bowes, 257
Pittsburgh Steelers, 711
Pizza Hut, 268, 630
Playboy Enterprises, 697
Playtex, 320
Plessey Company, 658
Polaroid, 36, 148, 408, 424, 474,
    483

Porsche AG, case on, 156–157
Post Company, 322
Power Company, 821
PPG, 343
Prescott, Ball & Turben, 293
Primerica, 496
Probe automobile, 91
Procter & Gamble, 24, 64, 65,
    341, 408, 422, 427, 430, 431,
    457, 576, 635, 694
    organizational culture of, 333
    preliminary control at, 607–608
    social responsibility and, 822
Prudential Insurance, 15, 24, 100,
    277, 323
    job characteristics approach at,
    280
    organization change and, 399
Purolator Courier Corporation,
    598

Quaker Oats, 119
Quaker State, 50, 676

Ralston Purina, 102, 119, 154, 155
Rand Corporation, 141
Raychem, 88, 179, 814
RCA Records, 461, 804
Red Cross, 81, 282
Reebok International, 85, 140,
    168, 317
    groups at, 519, 533
    starting, 737
Regal Drugs, 169
Reisebüro Kuoni, 718
Reliance Electric Company, 414
Remington Rand, 264
Republic Airways, 727
Resorts International, 728
Revco, 168
Revlon, 8
Revlon Group, 11
Richardson-Vicks, 577
Riunite, 792
RJR Nabisco Inc., 341, 396–397
Robbie, Joe, Stadium, 126
Robins, A. H., Co., 136, 137
Rockwell International, 15, 140
Rolex, 640
Rolls-Royce, 777
Roman Catholic Church, 26
Ronald McDonald House, 825,
    826

Rorer Group, 132–134, 135, 136
Rosemount, 651
Rotary Club, 517
Roy Rogers, 31
Rubbermaid, 55, 166
    goal approach of, 102
    goals of, 163
Ryder System, 78

Saab-Scania, 317, 319
Saab-Valmet, 319
Safeway, 25, 711
Salada, 154
Salvation Army, 81
Samsonite, 320
Samsung Electronics Company,
    418, 504
Samsung Group, case on, 504–505
Sanyo, 792
Sara Lee, 88
SAS, 305, 718
Schenley Industries, 110
Schlumberger Ltd., 139
Schwinn, 86
Scott Paper, 428, 641
Seagram, 111
Sears, Roebuck and Company,
    25, 85, 100, 115, 328, 642,
    747
    cutbacks and decline and, 728
    Dean Witter Reynolds Inc. and,
        808
    decentralization at, 292
    Discover card, 108, 176
    flat organization at, 287
    preliminary control and, 608
    purchasing at, 642
    resistance to change at, 397
    Sears Tower sale, 692
    social responsibility and, 825
    start of, 746–747
Selby, 282
Sematech, 841
Seminole Manufacturing Co., 672
Servitekar, 775
7-Eleven, 110
Seven-Up, 340
Sharper Image, 604, 605, 606, 607
Shearson Lehman Hutton, 108,
    652
Shell Oil, 25–26, 37, 830
Sherwin-Williams, 343

Siemens AG, 418, 776
    case on, 658–659
    IBM and, 841
    international operations of,
        774
Sierra Club, 90, 517
Simonds Rolling Machine Com-
    pany, 44, 45
Singer Sewing Machine Com-
    pany, 601, 786
SMR Enterprises, 749
Smucker, J. M., Company, 87,
    88
Softlab, 418, 422
Sohio Pipe Line, 25
Soho Natural Soda, 813
Sony, 100, 418, 792
    case on, 804–805
    goal of, 165–166
Soo Line Corporation, 177
Soundview, 748
Southeby's Holdings Inc., case
    on, 32–33
Southwestern Bell, 393
Sperry Corporation, 91–92, 99,
    138
Standard Brands, 112
Standard Oil, 414
Standard Oil of California (Socal),
    574
Standard Oil Company of New
    Jersey, 414
State Farm, 24
Steelcase, case on, 468–469
Stevens, J. P., 90
Stroh, 384
Studebaker, 59
Subaru, 314
Suds 'N Duds, 427
Sun Microsystems
    as adhocracy, 331
    decision making and, 129
    goals of, 170
    management theory used by,
        37
    organizational culture of, 333
    starting, 737
Super Stop 'n Save, 264
Suzuki, 771
"Swampmaster," 92
Swartzkatz, 792
Swissair, case on, 718–719
Sylvania, 103

Taco Bell, 94, 268
Tandem Computers, 112, 562
    contingency management and,
        60, 61
    planning, 182
Taylor Corp., 133
Teamsters, 373, 385
Technicare, 430
Technicolor, 11
Tektronix Corporation, 357, 766,
    767
Tenneco, 24, 99, 179
    case on, 716–717
Tennessee Gas and Transmission
    Company, 716. *See also*
    Tenneco
Texaco, 4, 37, 40
    case on, 574–575
Texas Air, 60, 84, 99, 136, 398,
    565
Texas A&M University, 92
Texas Boot, 282
Texas Instruments, 20, 66, 124,
    140, 278, 318, 408, 427, 439,
    462
    Coleco and, 170
    communication at, 559
    groups at, 524
    innovation at, 426
    integrated circuit and, 264
    international operations of, 774
    intrapreneurs at, 428
    job design and, 458
    MRP system at, 706
    organizational culture and, 332
    planning at, 162, 181
    quality circles and, 422
    task groups at, 515
    zero-base budgeting at, 697
Thompson, J. Walter, Company,
    110
Thompson S.A., 125, 126
3M Company, 166
    employee participation at, 398
    employer turnover ratio at, 711
    innovation and, 424, 426, 427
    Post-it Note Pad, 18
    social responsibility and, 820
Tiger International Inc., 684
Timex, 462, 640
TLC Group, 116
Tokyo Tsushin Kogyo (TTK),
    804. *See also* Sony

Tonka, 690, 692
Toshiba America, 838
Toshiba Corporation, 4, 658, 804
 case on, 838–839
Toshiba Machine Company,
 America, 838, 839
Toshiba Semiconductor USA, 838
Toucan-Do, 553
Touchstone Pictures, 591
Toyota Motor Corporation, 24,
 85, 95, 649, 771
 case on, 386–387
Toys 'R' Us, 78, 737
Tramwell Crow Co., 359
Transitions Research Corp., 720
Trans World Airlines, 624
Travelers Corporation, 677
Travel Plazas, 31
Tree International, 805
Trinova, 85
Tropicana, 320
TRW, 277
TWA, 574

Ugly Duckling Rent-a-Car, 113
U-Haul, 78, 101
Ungermann-Bass, 61
Unilever, 24, 341
 case on, 576–577
Unimation, Inc., 723
Union Carbide, 17, 40, 133, 255,
 313
 Bhopal poison gas leak and, 96,
 97
 conflict management at, 531
Union Oil Company, 354
Union Pacific, 600
Unisys, 99, 138, 567, 568
United Airlines, 91, 96, 138, 771
United Auto Workers, 373, 517,
 534–535
 Caterpillar and, 393, 399, 400
 GM and, 378
United Parcel Service (UPS), 310
 case on, 72–73
 preliminary control and, 608

U.S. Olympic Committee
 (USOC), case on, 540–541
U.S. Shoe Company, 282
U.S. Steel, 328, 631
 see also USX
United Way, 163, 171
University of Iowa, 4
University of Oregon, 79
University of South Carolina, 254
University of Texas, 92
Unocal Corporation, 694
USA Today, 18
USX, 85, 328. See also U.S. Steel
UTA, 718

Vatican, 8
Victoria's Secret, 308
Visa, 108, 671, 672
Volkswagen, 85, 91, 156, 424,
 792
 of America, 727
 participative management at,
 419
Volvo, 189, 280, 771
 autonomous work groups in,
 280
 groups at, 530

Waldenbooks
 goals of, 160, 161, 162, 163
 planning at, 177, 178
 plans of, 175, 176
Waldenbooks & More, 160
Waldenkids, 160
Waldensoftware, 160
Wall Street Journal, The, 88, 196
Wal-Mart, 578, 582
 ethics and, 811
 information system at, 665
 Seminole as supplier of, 672
 telecommunications and, 680
Wang Laboratories, 489, 676
Warner Bros., 590
Warner-Lambert, 430, 457
Washington Post Company, 14,
 322

Welch Foods, Inc., 87
Wells Fargo & Company, 24, 36,
 108
Wendy's, 94, 315
Western Electric, 277
 Hawthorne studies, 50–51
 human relations approach and,
 439
Western Union, 108
Westin hotels, 91, 138
Westinghouse, 66, 407, 419, 439,
 555, 642, 697
 Aptus and, 292
 MRP system at, 706
 quality circles and, 422
 resistance to change at, 396
Weyerhaeuser, 37
Whirlpool, 85, 103, 314
 code of ethical conduct of, 814,
 815
 decision support systems and,
 266
Whistler Corporation, 598, 602,
 651
Whitney's Yogurt, 154
Whole Foods Market, 318
Wilson Sporting Goods, 268
Winn-Dixie, 86
Winnebago Industries Inc., 397
WordPerfect, 791
Worlds of Wonder Inc. (WOW),
 603
Wrangler, 94
Writers Guild of America, 442

Xerox Corporation, 24, 424
 ethics and, 814
 interactive video training program at, 364
 social responsibility and, 823
 zero-base budgeting at, 697

Yamaha, 86, 631, 771
Young Miss, 461

Zenith, 839

SUBJECT INDEX

Absenteeism, 711–712
  stress and, 586
Acceptance stage, in small businesses, 750–751
Accountability
  control systems and, 617
  in delegation process, 290–291
  for small businesses, 758
Accuracy
  of control system, 614–615
  of information, 664
ACE (Active Corps of Executives), 754, 755
Achievement, motivation and need for, 445
Achievement-oriented leader behavior, in path-goal theory of leadership, 488
Acquisitions, organizational response to environment by, 99
Action plan, 178
Adaptation model, in business strategy, 204–206
Ad hoc committees, 528
Adhocracy, as organization design, 329, 331
Administrative managers, 15
Administrative model, of decision making, 129–131
Affiliation, motivation and need for, 445
Affirmative Action, 348–349, 820
Age Discrimination in Employment Act (1967), 348
Agriculture, small business in, 741
AIDS, as legal concern, 352
Alcohol abuse, as legal concern, 351–352

Alliances, management in future and, 841
American Arbitration Association, union formation and, 373
Analog computers, 264–265
Analyzer strategy, in adaptation model, 204, 205
Application blanks, as employee selection technique, 358
Arbitrator, in grievance system, 377
Area, information systems and, 669–670
Artificial intelligence (AI), for decision making, 149
Assembly line, 37
  job specialization and, 275
Assessment centers, as employee selection technique, 359
Assets management, in financial strategy, 210
Attribution theory, of motivation, 451–452
Authoritarianism, 579
Authority, 289
  Fayol on, 47
  legitimate power as, 477–478
  line vs. staff, 297–298
Authority distribution, 289–293
  decentralization and, 291–293
  delegation and, 290–291
Automation, 266, 720–725
  people and, 721–722
  problems of, 722
  in production strategy, 210
  productivity and, 720
  robotics, 720, 723–724
  trends in, 722–723
  see also Computers

Autonomous work groups, 529–530
  participative management and, 421
Avoidance, as reinforcement, 454

Balance sheet, 699–700
  for planning small business, 746
Balance sheet budget, 692–693
BARS, see Behaviorally Anchored Rating Scale
BCG matrix, 201–202
Behavior, information systems and, 678–679
Behaviorally Anchored Rating Scale (BARS), 365–366
Behavioral management theory, 42, 48–54, 61
  contributions and limitations of, 53–54
  Follett and, 49–50
  Hawthorne studies, 50–51
  human relations movement, 51–53
  Munsterberg and, 48–49
  organizational behavior, 53
  Owen and, 42
Behavioral model, of organization design, 311–313
Behavior modeling training, as training method, 363
Behavior modification, for motivation, 457–458
Beliefs, international management and, 781–782
Belongingness needs, 440–441
Benchmarking, as environmental analysis, 197

Benefits, 368
  laws on, 350
Binding arbitration, 377
Board of directors, 92–93
  planning by, 181–182
"Bottom-up" approach, to budgeting, 696–697
Boundary spanner, for information management, 98, 99
Bounded rationality, in administrative model of decision making, 130
Breakeven analysis, for planning, 260–262
Breakeven chart, for planning small business, 746
Breakthrough stage, of small businesses, 751
Budgets and budgeting, 691–698
  balance sheet, 692–693
  capital expenditures, 692, 694
  cash-flow, 692
  cutbacks and decline and, 728
  developing, 694–697
  expense, 692, 693
  fixed costs in, 693–694
  operating, 692, 693
  profit, 692, 693
  sales or revenue, 692, 693
  for small businesses, 758–759, 760
  strengths and weaknesses of, 697–698
  variable costs in, 694
  zero-based, 697
Bureaucratic control, 610, 612
Bureaucratic design, 99
Bureaucratic model, of organization design, 309–311
Burnout, stress and, 586–587
Business, influence of on government, 827–828
Business plan, for starting small business, 744–746
Business portfolio, 200–204
  BCG matrix in, 201–202
  strategic business units in, 200–202, 203
Business simulation, as training method, 363
Business strategy, 194, 204–208
  adaptation model in, 204–206

Porter's competitive strategies in, 206–207
  product life cycle in, 207–208

CAD, *see* Computer-aided design
CAM, *see* Computer-aided manufacturing
Capital structure, in financial strategy, 210
Career counseling, as organizational career planning technique, 115
Career-pathing, as organizational career planning technique, 115
Career resources planning, as organizational career planning technique, 115
Careers, 112–117
  dual-career couples and, 116
  individual planning of, 113–114
  job versus, 112
  management of, 113–115
  mentor relationships for, 114
  minorities and, 115–116
  organizational planning of, 114–115
  stages of, 112–113
  transitions in, 116
  women and, 115
Caribbean Common Market, 781
Case discussion, as training method, 363
Cash cows, in BCG matrix, 202
Cash-flow budget, 692
  for planning small business, 746
Causal modeling, 256–257
CD-ROM, 723
Centralization
  authority distribution and, 291–293
  Fayol on, 47
CEO (chief executive officer), 13
  planning by, 182
  tasks of, 7, 18
Chain of command, 284
Charisma, referant power as, 478
Charismatic leadership, *see* Transformational leadership
Checks and balances, control and, 618
Chief executive officer, *see* CEO
Chief information officer (CIO), 567, 568, 678

CIM (computer-integrated manufacturing), *see* Flexible manufacturing systems
Civil Rights Act of 1964, 211
  Title VII of, 347–348
Clan control, 610–612
Classical decision model, 128–129, 130
Classical management theory, 43–48, 49, 60–61
  Barnard, 46, 48
  classical organization theory, 46–48
  contributions and limitations of, 48, 49
  Emerson, 43, 45–46
  Fayol, 46, 47
  Gantt, 43, 45
  Gilbreths, 43, 44–45
  scientific management, 37, 43–46
  Taylor, 43–44, 45
  Urwick, 46
  Weber, 46, 47
Classical organization theory, 46–48
Closed systems, 58
  organizations viewed as, 79
Cluster chain, 557, 558
Coalitions, decision making and, 138
Codes of ethics, 814, 815
Coercion
  as political behavior in organization, 497
  power used by, 479
Coercive power, 478, 479
Cognitive dissonance, attitudes and, 580–581
Cohesiveness, of groups, 524–527
Collateral programs, stress reduction and, 588–589
Collective bargaining, 376
Command economy
  developing countries as, 785
  international management and, 775–776
Commitment
  employee attitude and, 582
  escalation of in decision making, 139–140
Committees, 528–529
  ad hoc, 528
  boards, 529

standing, 528
task forces, 528–529
Communication, 546–577
  barriers to, 564–566
  cases on, 574–577
  definition, 547–548
  delegation and, 291
  downward, 554, 555
  effective, 547
  electronic, 556, 568–569
  environment and, 566
  formal information systems,
    568
  grapevine, 554, 557–558
  horizontal, 554, 555
  improving, 566–568
  international management and,
    782–783
  interpersonal dynamics and,
    565–566
  in management, 548–549, 551
  management by wandering
    around, 558, 559
  managing, 563–568
  network, 554, 556–557
  nonverbal, 561–562
  oral, 550–552, 553
  perception and, 559–561
  process, 549–550
  receiver characteristics and, 565,
    567–568
  sender characteristics and, 564–
    565, 566–568
  upward, 554–555
  vertical, 553–555
  written, 552–553
Communication networks, 554,
  556–557
Compensation, 349–350
  benefits and, 350
  determining, 369–371
  Equal Pay Act of 1963 and,
    349–350
  Fair Labor Standards Act and,
    349
  in human resource strategy, 211
  individual wage decision, 371
  motivation and, 438
  reward systems and, 459–462
  role of, 368
  wage-level decision, 319
  wage-structure decision, 369–
    371
  see also Benefits

Competition, quality and, 650
Competitors
  firms influencing, 100
  organization change and, 391
  in task environment, 85–87
Complexity, organizational environments and, 94, 95
Computer-aided design (CAD),
  639, 723
  quality and, 652
Computer-aided manufacturing
  (CAM), 639, 723
  quality and, 652
Computer-integrated manufacturing (CIM), see Flexible manufacturing systems
Computers, 264–267
  analog, 265
  digital, 265
  electronic communication and,
    568–569
  evolution of, 264
  future role of, 266–267
  manager's job and, 265–266
  new technology and, 639
  for organization change, 402–
    403
  types of, 264–265
  see also Automation; Informa-
    tion systems
Conceptual skills, of managers,
  19–20
Concern for people, in Managerial Grid® leadership model,
  483
Concern for production, in Managerial Grid® leadership
  model, 483
Conference, as training method,
  363
Conflict, 531–536
  causes of, 532–533
  encouraging, 533–534
  goal differences and, 533
  group interdependence and,
    532
  interpersonal dynamics and,
    533, 535
  management of, 533–536
  reducing, 534–535
  resolving, 535–536
  resource competition and, 533
  role, 521–522
  storming as, 519

Confrontation, conflict resolution
  and, 536
Conglomerate organization design, 320–321
Conglomerates, 193
Consideration behavior, 482
Consolidation, as revitalization
  stage, 409–410
Constituents, social responsibility
  and, 817–818, 819
Constraints
  in linear programming, 259
  planning process and, 238
Content perspectives, on motivation, 439–445
Content validation, as employee
  selection technique, 358
Contingency planning, 234–236
  environmental turbulence and,
    240–241
Contingency theory, 37, 53, 59–
  60, 61, 62
Continuous-process technology,
  314–315
Contraction, as revitalization
  stage, 409, 410
Control, 6, 8, 9, 10, 11, 12, 596–
  627, 690–691
  accountability and, 617
  accuracy of, 614–615
  areas of, 599–601
  automation and, 720
  bureaucratic, 610, 612
  cases on, 624–627, 716–719
  changing conditions and, 597
  checks and balances and, 618
  choice of strategy for, 618–620
  compounding of errors and,
    598
  controller and, 601
  cost minimizing and, 599
  effective, 613–616, 617
  employee involvement and,
    602, 617
  evaluation and action for, 606–
    607
  flexibility of, 614
  goals and, 163
  importance of, 597–599
  inappropriate focus of, 616
  inefficiency and, 616–617
  information management as,
    665–666, 667
  levels of, 600–601, 607–613

Control (*cont.*)
  management by objectives and, 617–618
  multiple systems for, 609, 610, 611
  operations management as, 639–641
  organizational, 600, 609–612
  organizational complexity and, 598
  overcontrol and, 616
  performance and standards compared for, 605–606
  planning and, 602, 603, 613–614
  postaction, 609
  preliminary, 607–608
  process, 602–607
  purpose of, 597
  resistance to, 616–618
  resource focus of, 599–600
  responsibilities for, 601–602
  screening, 608–609
  small businesses and, 743, 757–759
  strategic, 600–601, 612–613
  timeliness of, 615
Controller, 601
Control system(s)
  changes in, 403
  of information system, 667
  in strategy implementation, 213–214
Cooperatives, 747
Coordination, 293–296
  conflict reduction by, 534
  integrating departments for, 296
  interdependence and, 294–295
  liaison roles for, 295
  managerial hierarchy for, 295
  need for, 294–295
  rules and procedures for, 295
  task forces for, 295–296
Corporate campaign, 375
Corporate social audit, 831
Corporate strategy, 194, 199–204
  grand strategy in, 199–200
  growth strategy in, 199
  retrenchment strategy in, 199–200
  stability strategy in, 200
Corporation, 746–747

Cost(s)
  control minimizing, 599
  fixed, 693–694
  management in future and, 842
  operation systems concerned with, 635
  quality and, 651
  semivariable, 694
  variable, 694
Counseling, for organization development, 406
Coverage ratios, 702
Creativity, 424–427
  brainstorming for, 426
  characteristics of, 426
  process of, 425–426
  reward system for, 426
  synectics for, 426–427
Credibility, communication effectiveness and, 567
Crisis management, *see* Environmental turbulence
Critical path, PERT and, 708–709
Cross-training, productivity enhancement and, 648–649
Cultural environment, international management and, 781–783
Culture, of an organization, 332–334
Current ratio, 700
Customer departmentalization, 282–283
Cutbacks and decline, 726–729
  budget and expenses and, 728
  costs and, 727
  divestiture and, 728
  environmental change and, 727
  evaluation of, 729
  facilities closure and, 728
  goals for, 729
  human costs of, 729
  managing, 728–729
  overexpansion and, 726–727
  planning for, 729
  strategic change and, 727
  termination and, 728

Data, 664. *See also* Information
dBASE III, 667
Debt ratios, 701
Debt-to-equity ratio, 701

Decentralization
  authority distribution and, 291–293
  as organization design, 329
Decisional roles, of manager, 17–18
Decision making, 6, 8, 9, 124–157
  administrative model of, 129–131
  alternatives evaluated for, 132, 134–135
  artificial intelligence for, 149
  behavioral nature of, 129, 137–140
  classical model of, 128–129, 130
  computers and, 266
  conditions of, 126–128
  decision trees for, 146–148
  definition, 125
  distribution models for, 148
  following up and evaluating for, 132, 136–137
  intuition and, 138–139
  inventory models for, 148
  models of, 128–131
  nonprogrammed decision, 126
  payoff matrices for, 144–146
  programmed decision, 125–126
  quantitative methods for, 144–149
  queuing models for, 148
  recognizing need for, 131–133
  risk and, 127, 139
  steps in, 131–137
  uncertainty and, 127–128
  Vroom-Yetton-Jago model and, 490–492
  see also Group decision making; Planning
Decision support systems (DSS), 266, 672–673
Decision trees, for decision making, 146–148
Decline stage, in product life cycle, 207, 208
Defender strategy, in adaptation model, 204, 205
Delegation, authority distribution and, 290–291
Delphi group, 141
Delphi procedure, for forecasting, 258

Demand, operations systems concerned with, 636
Demand for labor, forecasting, 352–353
Departmentalization, 280–284
    common bases for, 281–284
    customer, 282–283
    functional, 282
    location, 283
    product, 282
    rationale for, 280–281
    by sequence, 283
    by time, 283
Department integration, as structural coordination technique, 296
Descriptive procedure, breakeven analysis as, 260
Design, see Organization design
Developing countries, 785–786
Development, see Organization development
Development programs, 361. See also Training
Diagnostic activities, for organization development, 405
Diagnostic and analytic skills, of manager, 20
Differential rate system, Taylor and, 45
Differentiation, organization design and, 317
Differentiation between positions, 296–298
    administrative intensity and, 298
    line position, 296–297
    staff position, 296–298
Differentiation strategy, in Porter's competitive strategies, 206, 207
Direct analogy, synthetics using, 427
Direct investment, international management and, 796–797
Directive leader behavior, in path-goal theory of leadership, 488
Direct regulation, of business, 827
Discipline
    Fayol on, 47
    in labor relations, 377
Discrimination
    Affirmative Action and, 348–349, 820

work-force composition ratio and, 712
    see also Equal Employment Opportunity
Dispositional view, of attitudes, 579–580
Dissonance reduction, attitudes and, 581
Distinctive competence, as strategy component, 193
Distribution channels, in marketing strategy, 209–210
Distribution models, for decision making, 148
Disturbance handler, as managerial role, 17, 18
Divestiture, cutbacks and decline and, 728
Dividend policy, in financial strategy, 210
Divisionalized form, as organization design, 329, 330–331
Divisional organization design, 321–322
Division of labor
    Fayol on, 47
    job specialization and, 275
Downward communication, 554, 555

Eastern nonmarket economics, 785, 787–788
Econometric models, for forecasting, 257, 258
Economic community, see International economic communities
Economic dimension, of general environment, 81
Economic forces, management and, 39–40
Economic forecasts, 255
Economic indicators, for forecasting, 257
Economic order quantity (EOQ), 709
Education
    for managers, 22–23
    for organization development, 405
    resistance to change overcome by, 399

Educational organizations, management of, 26
EEC, see European Economic Community
Effective, management as, 6–7
Effective communication, 547
Effectiveness, 101
    case on, 30–31
    see also Organizational effectiveness
Efficiency, 101
    case on, 30–31
Efficient, management as, 6. See also Efficiency
Electronic communication, 556, 568–569
Employee attitudes, 579–582
    cognitive dissonance and, 580–581
    dispositional view of, 579–580
    employee satisfaction and dissatisfaction and, 581–582
    situational view of, 580
    stress and, 586
Employee-centered leader behavior, 481
Employee information system, forecasting labor needs by, 355
Employee involvement
    control and, 602, 617
    employee attitude and, 582
    productivity enhancement and, 648–649
Employee Retirement Income Security Act of 1974 (ERISA), 350
Employee turnover ratio, 711
End-user computing, 266–267
Entrepreneur, 737
Entrepreneurial Era, social responsibility and, 816
Entrepreneurship, 736–737
    cases on, 764–767
    in large businesses, 760, 761
    as managerial role, 17, 18
    see also Small businesses
Entropy, 59
Environment, 78–111
    adaptation model and, 204–206
    cases on, 108–111
    change and complexity in, 93–95

Environment (*cont.*)
  communication and, 566
  decentralization-centralization
    and, 292
  direct influence of, 99–101
  external, 79, *see also* General en-
    vironment; Task environment
  information management and,
    97–98
  information systems and, 668–
    669, 671
  internal, 79, 92–93
  organization affected by, 93–97
  organization change and, 391
  organization design and, 315–
    317
  organization responding to, 97–
    101, *see also* Social respon-
    sibility
  planning and, 237–238
  social responsibility and, 819–
    820–821
Environmental analysis, in strat-
    egy formulation, 196–199,
    201
Environmental change
  cutbacks and decline and, 727
  management in future and,
    840–841
Environmental Protection Agency
    (EPA), 85, 89, 210, 827
Environmental scanning, for in-
    formation management, 98
EOQ, *see* Economic order
    quantity
Equal Employment Opportunity,
    347–349
  Affirmative Action, 348–349,
    820
  Age Discrimination in Employ-
    ment Act, 348
  Title VII of Civil Rights Act of
    1964 and, 347–348
  see also Discrimination
Equal Employment Opportunity
    Commission (EEOC), 89,
    348, 529, 827
Equal Pay Act of 1963, 349–350
Equipment control, 599
Equity, Fayol on, 47
Equity theory, of motivation,
    450–451
ERG theory of motivation, 441–
    442

Esteem needs, 441
Ethical behavior, 809
  managing, 813–814, 815
  see also Ethics
Ethical compliance, social respon-
    sibility and, 829
Ethics, 808–814
  codes of, 814, 815
  employee in relationship to firm
    and, 811
  experiences and, 810
  family and, 809–810
  firm in relationship to other
    economic agents and, 811–
    812
  firm in relationship to employee
    and, 811
  formation, 809–810
  management and, 812–813
  managerial, 811–812
  managing, 813–814, 815
  peers and, 810
  situational factors and, 810
  values and morals and, 810
  see also Social responsibility
European Economic Community
    (EEC), 780–781
Executive committee, 528
  planning by, 182
Executive development, in human
    resource strategy, 211
Executive order, Affirmative Ac-
    tion as, 348–349
Existence needs, 441
Expansion, as revitalization stage,
    410
Expectancy theory, 446–450
  effort-to-performance expec-
    tancy, 446
  job design and motivation and,
    458
  managers and , 449–450
  outcomes and, 447–448
  performance-to-outcome expec-
    tancy, 447
  Porter-Lawler extension of,
    448–449
  reward systems and, 459–460
  valences and, 448
Expected value, in payoff matrix,
    145–146
Expense budget, 692, 693
Expenses, cutbacks and decline
    and, 728

Experience(s)
  ethics formation and, 810
  for managers, 23–24
Expert power, 479
Expert system(s)
  in artificial intelligence, 149
  as computer program, 266
  information systems and, 680
Exporting, international manage-
    ment and, 792–794
Export restraint agreements, in-
    ternational management and,
    779
External audits, 702–703
External environment, 79. *See also*
    General environment, Task
    environment
External locus of control, 579,
    586
External recruiting, 356–357
Extinction, as reinforcement, 454,
    455

Facilitation, resistance to change
    overcome by, 399
Facilities
  cutbacks and decline and, 728
  operations systems concerned
    with, 636–638
Fair Labor Standards Act (1938),
    349, 369
Family and Medical Leave Act,
    828
Federal Communications Com-
    mission (FCC), 89
Federal Trade Commission
    (FTC), 26, 85, 529, 827
Feedback
  automation and, 720
  communication effectiveness
    and, 566
  in performance appraisal sys-
    tems, 368
  screening control and, 608
Figurehead, as managerial role,
    16, 17
Finance strategy, as functional
    strategy, 209, 210
Financial audits, 702–703, 705
  external audits, 702–703
  internal audits, 703
Financial budgets, 691–693
Financial control, 600, 698–703,
    705

balance sheet, 699–700
coverage ratios, 702
debt ratios, 701
effective use of, 703, 705
external audits, 702–703
financial audits, 702–703
financial statements, 698–700
income statement, 700, 701
internal audits, 703
liquidity ratios, 700
operating ratios, 702
profitability ratios, 702
ratio analysis, 700–702
return on assets, 701–702
return on investment, 702
see also Budgets and budgeting
Financial managers, 14
Financial planning, for planning small business, 746
Financial resources, as goal, 166
Financial statements, 698–700
balance sheet, 699–700
income statement, 700–701
Financing, of small business, 747
Finished-goods inventories, control over, 642, 643
First-line managers, 13, 14, 19
education programs for, 22
Fixed costs, in breakeven analysis, 260, 261
Fixed-internal schedules, of reinforcement, 454, 455
Fixed-position layout, 637, 638
Fixed-ratio schedules, of reinforcement, 454, 455
Flat organizations, 286–288
Flexibility, of control system, 614
Flexible manufacturing systems (FMS), 211, 639, 723
in production strategy, 210
Flexible work schedule, for motivation, 458
Focus strategy, in Porter's competitive strategies, 207
Following up, communication effectiveness and, 567
Food and Drug Administration, (FDA), 89, 827
Force-field analysis, resistance to change overcome by, 399–400
Forecasting, 254–258
causal modeling, 256–257
econometric models, 257, 258

economic, 255
economic indicators, 257
human resource demand and supply, 352–355, 357
qualitative, 258
quantitative, 255–257
regression models, 256–257
resource, 255
revenue, 254
sales, 254–255, 258
technological, 255, 258
time-series analysis, 255–256
Formal information system, 568
Forming, as group development stage, 518–519
Franchising, 748–749
Fringe benefits, *see* Benefits
Functional authority, as staff authority, 297–298
Functional departmentalization, 282
Functional groups, 513–514
Functional organization design, 319–320
Functional strategies, 195, 208–212
financial strategy, 209, 210
human resource strategy, 209, 211
marketing strategy, 208–210
production strategy, 209, 210–211
research and development strategy, 209, 211–212

Gain sharing, as reward system, 462
Game theory, for decision making, 149
Gantt chart, 45
General Adaptation Syndrome (GAS), 584–585. *See also* Stress
General Electric business screen, 203–204
General environment, 79, 80–85
economic dimension, 81
international dimension, 84–85, 103
political-legal dimension, 84
sociocultural dimension, 83–84
technological dimension, 81–83
General and Industrial Management (Fayol), 46, 47

General managers, *see* Administrative managers
Generic strategies, Porter's competitive strategies and, 206–207
Global imperative, as contemporary management perspective, 63–65
Globalization, 772
management in future and, 841
see also International business
Goal approach, to organizational effectiveness, 102
Goals, 162–174
acceptance and commitment, 173
area of, 166
conflict and differences in, 533, 534–535
consistency of, 172–173, *see also* Management by objectives
for cutbacks and decline, 729
definition, 161
level of, 164–166
MBO and, 243–244
mission, 161–162, 164–165, 167
official, 167
operational, 161, 164, 166, 167
operative, 167
organizational, 165–166
planning and, 238
purposes of, 162–163, 171–172
qualitative, 170–171
quantitative, 170–171
responsibilities for setting, 167
strategic, 161, 164, 165, 167
in strategy formulation, 196
tactical, 161, 164, 165, 167
unattainable, 170
see also Goal setting; Management by objectives; Planning
Goal setting, 167–174
barriers to, 168–171
effective, 171–174
managing multiple goals, 168, 169
optimizing and, 168
for organization development, 407
reward system for, 171, 174
Goal-setting theory, of motivation, 456
Gossip chain, 557–558
Government
business influencing, 827–838
regulation of business and, 827

Government boards, 529
Government organizations, management of, 26
Government stability, international management and, 778
Grapevine, 554, 557–558
Grid® organization development, 407
Grievance procedures, in labor relations, 376–377
Group decision making, 140–144
    advantages of, 142
    Delphi groups, 141
    disadvantages of, 142–144
    forms of, 140–142
    groupthink, 143–144
    interacting groups, 141
    managing, 144
    nominal groups, 141–142
Grouping jobs, see Departmentalization
Group interdependence, conflict and, 532
Groups, 512–531
    activities of, 516–517
    ad hoc committees as, 528
    autonomous work groups, 421, 529–530
    boards as, 529
    characteristics of nature, 519–528
    cohesiveness of, 524–527
    committees as, 528–529
    definition, 512
    developmental stages, 517–519
    formation, 515–519
    functional, 513–514
    goals of, 517
    informal (interest), 514–515
    informal leadership in, 527–528
    instrumental benefits from, 517
    interpersonal attraction of, 516
    Japanese approach to, 520–531
    need satisfaction from, 517
    norms in, 522–524, 526
    operative work groups, 529
    performing, 519
    reasons for joining, 516–517
    roles in, 520–522
    socialization in, 524, 526
    standing committees as, 528
    storming, 519
    stress and, 585
    task, 514, 515

    task forces as, 295, 528–529
    types of, 512–515
    work groups, 529–530
    see also Conflict
Groupthink, 143–144
Growth stage, in product life cycle, 207, 208
Growth strategy, 199
    joint venture as, 199

Hawthrone studies, 50–51
Health, legal aspects of, 351. See also Occupational Safety and Health Act of 1970
Healthcare facilities, management of, 26
H-form design, 320–321
"Hierarchical needs," Maslow's theory of, 52
History, 38
    of corporations, 36
    management and, 38–43
    of organizations, 292
Homogeneity, of organizational environment, 94
Horizontal communication, 554, 555
Horizontal consistency, of goals, 172
Horizontal decentralization, as organizational design, 329
Human relations approach, to motivation, 439
Human relations movement, 51–53, 418
Human resource approach, to motivation, 439
Human resource control, 599–600, 608, 709–712
    goals of, 709
    human resource ratios, 711–712
    performance appraisal, 710–711
Human resource management, 346–387
    cases on, 384–387
    future and, 841
    human resource planning for, 352–355, 357
    job analysis and, 352
    strategic importance of, 347
    supply and demand matched for, 352–355
    see also Benefits; Compensation; Labor relations; Performance

    appraisal; Recruiting; Selection; Training
Human resource planning, 352–355, 357
Human resources
    as organization change area, 401, 403–404
    organizations utilizing, 5, 6
    in strategy implementation, 214
    in tactical planning, 229
Human resources managers, 15
Human resource strategy, as functional strategy, 209, 211
Hygiene factors, in two-factor theory of motivation, 443–444

Images, as nonverbal communication, 562
Importing, international management and, 792–794
Incentive pay system
    for motivation, 438
    for organization change, 403
    as reward system, 462
Income statement, 700, 701
    for planning small business, 746
Indirect regulation, of business, 827
Individual differences, 578–579
Individual wage decision, 371
Inducement, as political behavior in organizations, 496
Industrial market economy, 784, 785
Industrial psychology, behavioral management theory and, 48–49
Inefficiency, rewards for, 616–617
Inflation, 81
Informal group, 514–515
Informal leader, of groups, 527–528
Informational roles, of management, 16–17
Information distortion, power used by, 480
Information flow regulation, communication effectiveness and, 567
Information management, organizational response to environment by, 97–98, 99. See also

Management information
  system
Information-processing requirements, organization design
  and, 326–327
Information resources, organizations utilizing, 5, 6
Information systems, 666–687
  area and, 669–670
  behavioral effects of, 678–679
  building blocks of, 666–668
  change in, for organization
    change, 402–403
  computers for, 265
  decision support systems, 672–
    673
  environment and, 668–669, 671
  establishing, 673–675
  expert systems and, 680–681
  general determinants of, 668–
    669, 671
  integrating, 676
  level and, 670
  limitations of, 679
  management information sys-
    tem, 672, 673
  managing, 673–677
  networking and, 680
  organizational effects of, 678
  performance effects of, 677–678
  size and, 669
  specific determinants of, 669–
    670
  in strategy implementation,
    213–214
  telecommunications and, 680
  transaction-processing, 671–672
  using, 676–677
  vertical, 327
Infrastructure, international management and, 777
Initiative, Fayol on, 47
Innovation, 424–428
  brainstorming for, 426
  as goal, 166
  importance of, 424
  intrapreneurs for, 427–428
  nature of, 424
  organizational culture for, 427
  planned, 428–429
  reward system for, 426
  in small businesses, 738
  synectics for, 426–427
  see also Creativity

Input medium, of information
  system, 666
In Search of Excellence (Peters), 287
Inside directors, 93
Insight, in creativity, 425
Instrumental compliance, power
  used by, 479
Insurance benefits, 371–372
Integration, organization design
  and, 317
Interacting group, 141
Interdependence, coordination
  and, 294–295
Interest groups, 514–515
  firms influencing, 100
  as regulators, 90
Intergroup activities, for organiza-
  tion development, 406
Intermediate planning, 176–178
Internal audits, 703
Internal consultants, 15
Internal environment, 79, 92–93
Internal locus of control, 579, 586
Internal processes approach, to
  organizational approach, 102
Internal recruiting, 356
International business, 771–774,
  775
International dimension, of general environment, 84–85, 103
International economic communities, international business
  and, 779–780
International economy, 784–788
  developing countries, 785–786
  eastern nonmarket economies,
    785, 787–788
  industrial market economy,
    784, 785
  oil-exporting countries, 777,
    786–787
  see also International
    management
International management, 25–26,
  774–805
  beliefs and, 781–782
  career management and, 115
  cases on, 802–805
  cultural environment and, 781–
    783
  deciding on, 788–792
  direct investment and, 796–797
  economic communities and,
    779–780

economic environment and,
  774–777
global involvement and, 797–
  798
government stability and, 778
importing and exporting and,
  792–794
infrastructure and, 777
international trade incentives
  and, 778–779
joint ventures and, 795–796
language and, 782–783
in less developed countries,
  778–779
licensing and, 794–795
maquiladoras, 797
market factors and, 789, 790–
  791
multinational firms, 84–85, 103
natural resources and, 777
organization design and, 327–
  328
political environment and, 778–
  781
property ownership and, 776–
  777
resource allocation process and,
  775–776
small businesses and, 741
symbols and, 781–782
technological factors and, 789,
  791–792, 793
values and, 781–782, 792
see also International economy
International managers, 15, 115
International trade
  controls on, 779
  incentives for, 778–779
  see also International
    management
Interpersonal demands, stress
  caused by, 585–586
Interpersonal dynamics
  in communication, 565–566
  conflict and, 533, 535
Interpersonal problem solving,
  conflict resolution and, 536
Interpersonal relations, 508–509
  dynamics of, 509–510
  outcomes of, 511
  see also Conflict; Groups
Interrole conflict, 521
Interstate Commerce Commission
  (ICC), 89

Interviews, as employee selection technique, 359, 360
In-transit inventory, 642
    control over, 643
Intrapreneurs, innovation and, 427–428
Introduction stage, in product life cycle, 207
Intuition, in decision making, 138–139
Inventor, as intrapreneur, 427
Inventory control, 642–643
Inventory management, 56, 599, 642–644
Inventory models, for decision making, 148
Investors, social responsibility and, 820–821
Involvement, *see* Employee involvement

Japan
    creativity in, 426
    decentralization in, 293
    management and boards of directors and, 41, 529
    participative management and, 418–419
    quality circles and, 421
    Type Z model and, 63–65
    workers in, 83
Japanese approach
    to groups, 530–531
    to motivation, 456–457
JIT, *see* Just-in-time
Job, 112. *See also* Careers
Job analysis, 352
Job-centered leader behavior, 481
Job characteristics approach, 278–280
Job descriptions, 352
    for small businesses, 752
Job design, 275–280
    autonomous work groups, 280
    job characteristics approach, 278–280
    job enlargement, 277–278
    job enrichment, 278
    job rotation, 277
    job specialization, 275–276
    for motivation, 458
Job enlargement, 277–278
Job enrichment, 278

Job evaluation, for wage structures, 369–371
Job posting and bidding, 356
Job rotation, 277
Job satisfaction, 582
Job specialization, 275–276
Job specification, 352
Joint ventures, 91–92
    as growth strategy, 199
    international management and, 795–796
Judgmental performance methods, 365–367
Just-in-time (JIT), 643

Labor
    employees, 93
    in task environment, 90
    see also under Human resources
Labor-Management Relations Act (1946), 350–351
Labor productivity, 645
Labor relations, 350–351, 373–379
    collective bargaining, 376
    disciplinary actions and, 317
    future and, 378
    grievances and, 376–377
    in human resource strategy, 211
Labor-Management Relations Act, 350–351
    National Labor Relations Act, 350
    union formation, 373–375
Large-batch technology, 314–315
Large business
    entrepreneurship in, 760, 761
    management in, 24–25
    small business and, 740
Lateral relationships, information-processing requirements and, 327
Layout, operations systems concerned with, 636–638
Leader, 475
    as managerial role, 16, 17
    see also Leadership
Leader-member relations, in contingency leadership theory, 486, 487
Leadership, 6, 8, 9, 10–11, 474–505
    behaviors related to, 480–483
    cases on, 502–505

consideration behavior, 482
employee-centered leader behavior, 481–482
favorableness and style of, 486–487
flexibility of style of, 487–488
informal, 527–528
initiating-structure behavior, 482
job-centered leader behavior, 481–482
management in future and, 841–842
management versus, 475–476
Michigan studies of, 481–482
Ohio State studies of, 482–483
political behavior and, 496–497
in small business, 756–757
in strategy implementation, 212
stress and, 585–586
substitutes for, 494–495
traits of, 480
transformational, 495–496
    see also Power; Situational models of leadership
Leadership Continuum, 484–485
Least preferred co-worker (LPC), 485–486
Lecture, as training method, 363
Legal compliance, social responsibility and, 829
Legitimate power, 477–478
Legitimate request, power used by, 479
Less developed countries, international management and, 778–779. *See also* Developing countries
Level, information systems and, 670
Leveraged buyout (LBO), Revco and, 169
Lewis model, of organization change, 394
Liaison roles
    as managerial, 16, 17
    as structural coordination technique, 295
Licenses
    international management and, 794–795
    in research and development strategy, 212

Life cycles, in small business, 750–751
Life cycle theory, of leadership, 494
Life stressors, 586
Linear programming, 56
for planning, 258–260
Line authority, 297
Line management, planning by, 182
Line position, 296–297
Liquidity ratios, 701
Lobbying
business influencing government by, 828
regulators influenced by, 100
Location, operations systems concerned with, 636, 637
Location departmentalization, 283
Locus of control, personality and, 579
external, 579, 586
internal, 579, 586
Long-range planning, 176, 177
LOTUS, 266
Lump-sum bonuses, as reward system, 462
Machine bureaucracy, as organization design, 329, 330
Management
communication and, 548
definition, 5–7
functions of, 8, 9, see also Control; Decision making; Leadership; Organizing; Planning
leadership versus, 475–476
as profit-seeking organizations, 24–26
by wandering around, 558, 559
Management development, in human resource strategy, 211
Management development programs (MDPs), 22
Management, future challenges of, 840–843
alliances and, 841
costs and measurement and, 842
environmental change and, 840–841
globalization and, 841
human resources and, 841
information and, 842

leadership and, 842
motivation and, 841–842
organization design and, 841
productivity and, 842
quality and, 842
speed and, 842
Management information system (MIS), 672, 673
for information management, 98
Management by objectives (MBO), 173, 241–246
control and, 617–618
effectiveness of, 244–246
evaluation of, 244
goals and plans for, 243–244
nature and purpose of, 241–242
for performance appraisal, 367
periodic reviews in, 244
process, 242–244
starting, 243
Management science, 37, 55, 61
Management science models, 37
Management theories, 37–38
cases on, 72–75
classical organization theory, 46–48
contemporary, 63–67
contingency theory, 37, 53, 59–60, 61, 62
economic forces and, 39–40
excellence movement, 65–66
integrating framework for, 60–63
pioneers of, 42–43
political forces and, 40
quality and productivity concerns, 66
social forces and, 38–39
systems theory, 37, 57–59, 60, 61–62
Type Z model, 63–65
see also Behavioral management theory; Classical management theory; Quantitative management theory
Management training programs, 23–24
Manager development, as goal, 166
Managerial approach, formal information system and, 568
Managerial careers, see Careers

Managerial ethics, 811–812
Managerial Grid®, 407–408
as leadership model, 483
Managerial hierarchy, as structural coordination technique, 295
Manager performance, as goal, 166
organizational effectiveness and, 102–103
Managers
administrative, 15
areas of, 14–15
conceptual skills of, 19–20
decisional roles of, 17–18
definition, 7
diagnostic and analytic skills of, 20
experience for, 23–24
first-line, 13, 14, 19, 22
human resources, 15
information and, 663–664
informational roles of, 16–17
internal consultants as, 15
international, 15
interpersonal roles of, 16, 17
interpersonal skills of, 19
levels of, 12–14
marketing, 14
middle, 13–14, 22
operations, 14–15
planning by, 182–183
public relations, 15
research and development, 15
roles of, 16–18
skills of, 18–24
technical skills of, 18–19
top, 13, 22
Manufacturing
operations management and, 631, 632
small businesses in, 740–741
Market control, 712–713
market share, 713
profit margin on sales, 713
test marketing, 712–713
Market economy
developing countries as, 785
international management and, 775, 776
Market factors, international management and, 789, 790–791
Marketing managers, 14

Marketing strategy, as functional strategy, 208, 210
Market position, in marketing strategy, 209
Market share, 713
Market standing, as goal, 166
Maslow's hierarchy of needs, 440–442
Mass production technology, 314–315
Master budget, *see* Balance sheet budget
Master limited partnerships, 747
Materials control, *see* Inventory control
Materials requirements planning (MRP), 704–706
Materials resource planning, 704–706
Matrix organization design, 322–324
Maturity stage, in product life cycle, 207, 208
MBO, *see* Management by objectives
Means-end inversion, goals and, 169
Mechanistic organization design, 99, 315–316
Media, communication effectiveness and, 567–568
Mergers, organizational response to environment by, 99
Merit system, as reward system, 462
M-form design, 321–322
Michigan studies, of leadership behaviors, 481–482
Middle managers, 13–14
education programs for, 22
Minimum wage, Gantt and, 45
Minorities, careers and, 115–116
MIS, *see* Management information system
Mission, of organization, 161–162, 164–165, 167
goals inconsistent with, 170
Modified workweek, for motivation, 458
Monetary resources, organizations utilizing, 5, 6
Monitor, as managerial role, 16, 17

Morals, ethics formation and, 810
Motivation, 436–471
achievement need and, 445
affiliation need and, 445
attribution theory of, 451–452
behavior modification for, 457–458
cases on, 468–471
content perspectives on, 439–445
equity theory of, 450–451
ERG theory of, 441–442
framework of, 437–438
goal-setting theory of, 456
historical perspectives on, 438–439
human relations approach to, 439
human resource approach to, 439
importance of, 437
Japanese approach to, 456–457
management in future and, 841–842
modified workweek for, 458
need hierarchy and, 440–442
power need and, 445
process perspectives on, 445–452, *see also* Expectancy theory
reward systems and, 459–462, *see also* Compensation
stress and, 586
traditional approach to, 438
two-factor theory and, 278, 442–444
work redesign for, 458
see also Reinforcement theory of motivation
Motivation factors, in two-factor theory of motivation, 443–444
MRP, *see* Materials requirements planning
Multinational business, 772. *See also* International business
Multinational firms, 84–85
Multiple-command structure, matrix design as, 322

Nationalization, international management and, 778
National Labor Relations Act of 1935, 90, 350

participative management and, 421
National Labor Relations Board (NLRB), union formation and, 373, 379
Natural resources, international management and, 777
Need hierarchy, motivation and, 440–442
Needs, in reward system, 460. *See also* Motivation
Negotiator, as managerial role, 17, 18
Networking, information systems and, 680
New Deal, social responsibility of business and, 816
New Europe, 563
Nominal groups, 141–142
Nonmonetary budget, 692, 693
Nonprogrammed decision, 126
Nonverbal communication, 561–562
Normative procedure, linear programming as, 260
Norms, of groups, 522–524, 526
Not-for-profit organizations international dimension and, 85
management in, 26–27

Objective function, in linear programming, 258–259
Objective performance measures, 365
Objectivity, of control system, 615–616
Obligation, as political behavior in organizations, 496–497
OB MOD, *see* Behavioral modification
Occupational Safety and Health Act of 1970 (OSHA), 351
Occupational Safety and Health Administration (OSHA), 89, 210, 827
organization change and, 391
Office manager, 14
Official goal, 167
Ohio State studies, of leadership behaviors, 482–483
Oil-exporting countries, 777, 786–787
On-the-job training, 363

OPEC (Organization of Petroleum Exporting Countries), 786–787
Open systems, 58
  organizations as, 79
  see also Environment
Operating budget, 692, 693
Operating ratios, 702
Operational approach, formal information system and, 568
Operational goals, 161, 164, 166, 167
Operational planning, 161, 175, 227, 230–234
  cases on, 250–253
  policies, 233, 234
  programs, 231–232, 234
  projects, 232, 234
  rules and regulations, 233–234
  single-use plans, 230–232, 234
  standard operating procedures, 233, 234
  standing plans, 232–234
Operations, change in for organization change, 401, 402–403
Operations control, 600, 607–609, 704–709
  economic order quantity, 709
  materials resource planning, 704–705
  PERT, 707–709
  statistical quality control, 706
Operations management, 55–56, 61, 630–644
  cases on, 656–659
  importance of, 631
  manufacturing and, 631, 632
  organizational strategy and, 632–634
  production and, 631–632
  service operations and, 632
  see also Operations systems
Operations manager, 13, 14–15
Operations systems, 634–644
  capacity and, 634, 635–636
  as control, 639–641
  designing, 634–639
  facilities and, 634, 636–638
  inventory management and, 642–644
  product/service mix and, 634–635

purchasing management and, 642
quality control and, 644, see also Quality
technology and, 634, 638–639
Operative goal, 167
"Opportunity bias," in objective performance measures, 365
Optimization
  in decision making, 135
  goals and, 168
Oral communication, 550–552, 553. See also Communication
Order, Fayol on, 47
Organic design, 99
Organic organization, 315–316
Organizational analysis, in strategy formulation, 197–199
Organizational behavior, 37, 53. See also Contingency theory
Organizational behavior modification, see Behavior modification
Organizational behavior theory, 37
Organizational control, 600, 609–612. See also Control
Organizational culture, 332–334
  innovation and, 427
  social responsibility and, 830
Organizational effectiveness, 101–103, 104
  goal approach to, 102
  internal processes approach to, 102
  managerial performance and, 102–103
  models of, 101–102
  strategic constituencies approach to, 102
  systems resource approach to, 101
Organizational goals, 164, 165–166
Organizational life cycle, 317–318
Organizational size, organization design and, 317–318, 319
Organizational strategy, 17
  change in for organization change, 400–401
  operations management and, 632–634
  standards and, 604
  see also Strategy

Organization change, 390–404
  cases on, 414–417
  comprehensive approach to, 394–396
  external forces for, 391–392
  forces for, 391–392
  internal forces for, 392
  Lewin model of, 394
  managing, 393–396
  organizational environment and, 93–94
  organization design and, 315–316
  organization structure and design changed for, 401
  planned, 393, 395
  reactive, 393
  technology/operations changed for, 401, 402–403
  see also Organization change, resistance to; Organization development; Organization revitalization
Organization change, resistance to, 136, 396–400
  communication and, 399
  different perceptions and, 398
  education and, 399
  facilitation and, 399
  feelings of loss and, 398
  force-field analysis and, 399–400
  overcoming, 398–400
  participation and, 398–399
  planning and, 238, 263
  threatened self-interests and, 396–397
  uncertainty and, 396–397
Organization charts, for small businesses, 753–754
Organization design, 308–343
  adhocracy, 329, 331
  bureaucratic, 99, 309–311
  cases on, 340–343
  change in for organization change, 401
  conglomerate (H-form), 320–321
  differentiation and, 317
  divisional (M-form), 321–322
  divisionalized form, 329, 330–331
  environment and, 315–317

Organization design (*cont.*)
functional (U-form), 319–320
hybrid, 325–326
information-processing requirements and, 326–327
integration and, 317
management in future and, 841
matrix, 322–324
mechanistic, 99, 315–316
operations systems concerned
with, 635
organic, 99, 315–316
organizational culture, 332–334,
427, 830
organizational response to environment by, 99
organizational size and, 317–318
participative management and,
421
professional bureaucracy, 329,
330
simple structure, 329, 330
situational view of, 313–318
size and, 317–318, 319
strategy and, 328–332
Systems 1 through 4, 481–482
technology and, 313–315
Organization development (OD),
404–405
coaching and counseling for,
406
diagnostic activities for, 405
education for, 405
effectiveness of, 408–409
grid approach to, 407–408
intergroup activities for, 406
planning and goal setting for,
407
process consultation for, 406
team building for, 405
technostructural activities for,
406
survey feedback for, 405
Organization environment, ethics
and, 812–813
Organization revitalization, 409–
410
Organizations, 8, 9
definition, 4–5
information systems and, 678
resources used by, 5, 6
systems view of, 57–58
see also Environment; Organizational effectiveness

Organization structure, 275
cases on, 302–305
change in for organization
change, 401
decentralization, 327
see also Authority distribution;
Coordination; Departmentalization; Differentiation between positions; Job design;
Reporting relationships, establishing
Organizing, 6, 8–10, 11, 275
management in future and, 841
Output medium, of information
system, 666–667
Outside directors, 93
Overexpression, cutbacks and decline and, 726–727
Owners
corporations influencing, 101
organization change and, 392
in task environment, 91
Ownership, of small business,
746–747

PACs, *see* Political action
committees
Partial productivity ratio, 645
Participation, resistance to change
overcome by, 398. *See also*
Employee involvement
Participative leader behavior, in
path-goal theory of leadership, 488
Participative management, 418–
423
areas of, 419, 420
current perspectives on, 418–
419
history of, 419
problems with, 419–421
productivity enhancement and,
648
quality circles, 421–422
structural approaches to, 421
system-based integrative approaches, 422
Partners
organization change and, 392
in task environment, 91–92
Partnership, small business as,
746
Path-goal theory, of leadership,
488–490, 491

Payoff matrix, for decision making, 144–145
Pension plans, 350
corporate, 91
private, 372
Social Security, 372
Perception
in communication, 559–561
as communication barrier, 565–
566
perceptual organization, 561
selective, 560–561
Perceptual organization, 561
Performance
information systems and, 677–
678
standards and, 604, 605–606
Performance appraisal, 364–368,
710–711
for control, 605
errors in, 367–368
feedback in, 368
in human resource strategy,
211
judgmental methods for, 365–
368
management by objectives for,
367
objective methods for, 365
reasons for, 364
Performance-to-outcome expectancy, 447
Performing, as group development stage, 519
Personal analogy, synectics using,
427
Personal assessment, in career
planning, 114
Personal contacts, business influencing government by, 827–
828
Personality, individual differences
and, 579
Personality clash, conflicts from,
533
Personnel, *see* Human resource
management
Person-role conflict, 521
Persuasion, as political behavior in
organizations, 496
PERT (Program Evaluation and
Review Technique), 707–709
for planning new business,
745

Physical resources
  as goal, 166
  organizations utilizing, 5, 6
Physiological needs, 440
Pipeline inventory, *see* In-transit
    inventory
Plan, definition, 161
Planned change, 393, 395
Planning, 6, 8, 9, 10, 11, 174–183
  action, 178
  barriers to effective, 237–239
  by board of directors, 181–182
  cases on, 186–189
  change and, 238
  by chief executive officer, 182
  communication and, 239–240
  constraints and, 238–239
  contingency planning and, 240–
    241
  control and, 602, 603, 613–614
  for cutbacks and decline, 719
  definition, 161
  environment and, 237–238
  by executive committee, 182
  goals and, 162, 238
  human resources, 352–355,
    357
  by individual managers, 182–
    183
  intermediate, 176–178
  limits to, 239
  by line management, 182
  long-range, 176, 177
  MBO and, 233–234
  operational, 161, 175, 230–234
  for organization development,
    407
  overcoming barriers to, 239–
    241
  participation and, 240
  planning staff for, 179–181
  process, 161–162
  reaction, 178
  responsibilities for, 179–183
  revision and, 240
  short-range, 178
  in small business, 750–751
  strategic, 161, 174–175, 227
  tactical, 161, 175, 227, 228–230
  task force for, 181
  time and expense and, 239
  time frames for, 175–179
  top management and, 239
  updating and, 240

  see also Decision making; Goals;
    Management by objectives
Planning staff, 179–181
Planning task force, 181
Planning tools, 254–263
  breakeven analysis, 260–262
  evaluation of, 262–263
  linear programming, 258–260
  simulations, 262
  see also Forecasting
Point method, for wage structure,
    370–371
Political action committees
    (PACs), 828
Political behavior in organiza-
    tions, 496–497. *See also*
    Leadership
Political forces, management and,
    40
Political-legal dimension, of gen-
    eral environment, 80
Politics, decision making and,
    137–138
Pooled interdependence, 294
Porter-Lawler extension, of ex-
    pectancy theory, 448–449
Porter's competitive strategies, in
    business strategy, 206–207
Position power, in contingency
    leadership theory, 486, 487
Positive reinforcement, 454
Postaction control system, 609,
    640
Power, 476–480
  coercive, 478, 479
  as communication barrier, 565
  expert, 479
  legitimate, 477–478
  motivation and need for, 445
  referent, 478, 479–480
  reward, 478
  using, 479–480
  see also Leadership
Predictive validation, as employee
    selection technique, 358
Preliminary control, 607–608
Pricing policies, in marketing
    strategy, 210
Private ownership, international
    management and, 776
Privatization, international man-
    agement and, 776–777
Probability, in payoff matrix,
    145

Procedures, as structural coordi-
    nation technique, 295
Process layout, 637, 638
Processor, of information system,
    666
Process perspectives, on motiva-
    tion, 445–452
Product departmentalization, 282
Product development, in research
    and development strategy,
    211
Production, operations manage-
    ment and, 631–632
Production management, *see* Op-
    erations management
Production planning, in produc-
    tion strategy, 210
Production strategy, as functional
    strategy, 209, 210, 211
Productivity, 644–649
  automation and, 721
  employee involvement and,
    648–649
  as goal, 166
  importance of, 645–646
  improving, 648–649
  labor, 645
  levels of, 644
  management in future and, 842
  managerial concerns for, 66
  operations improvement and,
    648
  partial ratio, 645
  quality and, 650–651
  R&D and, 83
  of small business, 759
  stress and, 586
  total factor, 644–645
  trends in, 646–647
Product layout, 637, 638
Product life cycle, in business
    strategy, 207–208
Product line, operations systems
    concerned with, 635
Product mix, in marketing strat-
    egy, 209
Products, operations systems con-
    cerned with, 634–635
Professional bureaucracy, as organ-
    ization design, 329, 330
Profit, in breakeven analysis, 261
Profitability, as goal, 166
Profitability ratios, 702
Profit budget, 692, 693

Profit margin on sales, 713

Profit-seeking organizations, management in, 24–26

Profit sharing, as reward system, 462

Program, as single-use plan, 231–232, 234

Program Evaluation and Review Technology, *see* PERT

Programmed decision, 125–126

Programmed instruction, as training method, 363

Project planning, as operational planning, 231

Property ownership, international management and, 776–777

Prospector strategy, in adaptation model, 204, 205

Psychology and Industrial Efficiency (Munsterberg), 49

Public ownership, international management and, 776

Public policy, in marketing strategy, 210

Public relations managers, 15

Public responsibility, *see* Social responsibility

Punishment, as reinforcement, 454–455

Purchasing management, 642

Qualitative forecasting techniques, 258

Quality, 649–652
  control, 644, 651
  definition, 649–650
  employee involvement and, 652
  importance of, 650–651
  management in future and, 842
  managerial concerns for, 66
  materials and, 653
  methods and, 652
  operations systems concerned with, 635
  screening control systems and, 640
  strategic commitment and, 651
  technology and, 652

Quality circles, 41, 66, 530
  participative management and, 421–422

Quality control, 599, 600, 644
  statistical, 706
  total, 651

Quality-control movement, 41

Quantitative management theory, 37, 43, 54–56, 57, 61
  contributions and limitations of, 56, 57
  management science, 37, 55, 61
  see also Operations management

Quotas, international trade and, 779

Ranking, performance measured by, 365, 367–368

Rating, performance measured by, 365–368

Ratio analysis
  coverage ratios, 702
  debt ratios, 701
  liquidity ratios, 700
  operating ratios, 702
  profitability ratios, 702
  return on assets, 701–702
  return on investment, 702

Raw materials, control over, 642

Reaction plan, 178

Reactive change, 393

Reactor strategy, in adaptation model, 204, 206

Realistic job preview (RJP), 356

Reciprocal interdependence, 294–295

Recruiting, 355–357
  external, 356–357
  internal, 356

Referent power, 478, 479–480

Refreezing, in organization change, 394

Regression models, for forecasting, 256–257

Regulation
  of business, 84, 827
  in human resource strategy, 211
  in production strategy, 210

Regulators
  firms influencing, 100
  organization change and, 391–392
  in task environment, 89–90

Regulatory agencies, as regulators, 89

Reinforcement theory of motivation, 451–455
  avoidance, 454
  extinction, 454, 455
  positive reinforcement, 454

punishment, 454–455
  schedules of, 455

Relatedness needs, 441

Relationship-oriented leader, in contingency theory of leadership, 485, 487

Relaxation, stress and, 587

Relevant information, 665

Remuneration, Fayol on, 47

Replacement chart, forecasting supply of human resources by, 354

Reporting relationships, establishing, 284–289
  chain of command and, 284
  span of management and, 285–289

Research and development (R&D)
  goals for, 238
  managers, 15
  operations improvement and, 648
  productivity and, 83

Research and development strategy, as functional strategy, 209, 211–212

Resource allocation, international management and, 775–776

Resource allocator, as managerial role, 17, 18

Resource competition, conflict and, 533

Resource deployment, as strategy component, 193

Resource focus, of organizational control, 599–600

Resource forecasting, 255

Responsibility, in delegation process, 290–291

Retail businesses, small businesses in, 740

Retrenchment strategy, 199–200, 727

Return on assets (ROA), 701–702

Return on investment (ROI), 702

Revenue, in breakeven analysis, 260–261

Revenue budget, 692, 693

Revenue forecasting, 254–255

Revitalization, *see* Organization revitalization

Reward system
  creativity and, 426

motivation and, 459–462
see also Compensation
Risk, decision making under, 127, 129
RJP, see Realistic job preview
ROA, see Return on assets
Robots/ics, 83, 722, 723–724
in production strategy, 210, 211
in small businesses, 759
ROI, see Return on investment
Role ambiguity, in groups, 521
Role conflict, in groups, 521
Role demands, stress caused by, 585
Role management, stress and, 588
Role overload, in groups, 522
Role playing, as training method, 363
Roles, in groups, 520–522
role ambiguity, 521
role conflict, 521
role overload, 522
Rules, as structural coordination technique, 295
Rules and regulations, as standing plan, 233–234

Safety, legal aspects of, 351. See also Occupational Safety and Health Act of 1970
Salary, see Compensation
Sales budget, 692, 693
Sales-force-composition method, of sales forecasting, 258
Sales forecasting, 254–255, 258
for planning new business, 745–746
Sales promotion, in marketing strategy, 210
Satisfaction, as employee attitude, 581, 582
Satisficing, in administrative model of decision making, 130–131
SBDC (Small Business Development Center), 754–755
SBI (Small Business Institute), 754, 755
SBUs, see Strategic business units
Scalar chain, Fayol on, 47
Scalar principle, 284
Scientific management, 37, 43–46
Scientific management theory, 37

Scope, as strategy component, 193
SCORE (Service Corps of Retired Executives), 754
S-corporations, 747
Screening control, 608–609
Securities and Exchange Commission (SEC), 89, 827
social responsibility of business and, 816
Security needs, 440
Selection, 358–360
application blanks for, 358
assessment centers for, 359
case on, 386–387
in human resource strategy, 211
interviews for, 359, 360
tests for, 358–359
validation for, 358
Selective decentralization, as organization design, 329
Selective perception, 560–561
Self-actualization needs, 441, 442
Self-contained tasks, information-processing requirements and, 327
Self-esteem, 579
Self-interests, resistance to change and threatened, 396–397
Semantics, as communication barrier, 565
Sensitivity, communication effectiveness and, 567
Sensitivity training, 363
Sensors, automation and, 720
Sequential interdependence, 284
Service businesses, small businesses in, 740
Service operations, operations management and, 632
Services, operations systems concerned with, 634–635
Settings, in nonverbal communication, 562
Sexual harassment, as legal concern, 351
Short-range planning, 178
Simple structure, as organization design, 329, 330
Simulations
for planning, 262
as training method, 363
Single-use plans, 230–232, 234

Situational factors, ethics formation and, 810
Situational models, of leadership, 483–494
contingency theory, 485–488
leadership continuum and, 484–485
life cycle theory, 494
path-goal theory, 488–490, 491
vertical-dyad linkage model, 493
Vroom-Yetton-Jajo model, 490–492
Situational view
of attitudes, 580
of organizational design, 313–318
Skills inventory, forecasting labor needs by, 355
Slack resources, information processing need and, 326–327
Small-batch technology, 313–315
Small Business Administration, see U.S. Small Business Administration
Small businesses, 736–767
acceptance stage, 750–751
accounting information for, 758
agriculture, 741
breakthrough stage, 751
budgeting for, 758–759, 760
business plan for starting, 744–746
buying existing, 747
controlling in, 743, 757–759
as corporation, 746–747
definition, 738, 739
failure of, 742, 743–744
financial performances, 738
financing sources, 747
franchising, 748–749
help available to, 754–756
impact of, 738–740, 741
innovation in, 738
international impact of, 741
job creation by, 739
job descriptions for, 752
large business and, 740
leading in, 756–757
life cycles of, 750–751
management in, 25
manufacturing, 740–741
number formed, 739–740
organization charts for, 753–754

Small businesses (*cont.*)
 organizing, 751–756
 ownership forms, 746–747
 as partnership, 746
 planning, 750–751
 productivity of, 759
 retail, 740
 service, 740
 skills needed by, 751–752, 753
 as sole proprietorship, 746
 starting, 744–749
 success of, 742–743
 U.S. Small Business Administration and, 738, 739, 754–755
 wholesale, 740
Social contribution, as social responsibility approach, 825
Social Era of the 1960's, social responsibility and, 817
Social forces, management and, 38–39
Socialization, norm conformity and, 524, 526
Social obligation, as social responsibility approach, 824
Social opposition, as social responsibility approach, 824
Social response, as social responsibility approach, 825
Social responsibility, 814, 816–839
 approaches to, 823–826
 arguments for and against, 823–825
 business and government and, 827–828
 cases on, 836–839
 changing views of, 816–817
 Depression Era and, 816
 direct government regulation, 827
 Entrepreneurial Era and, 816
 environment and, 819–820, 821
 ethical compliance and, 829
 evaluating, 831
 formal organizational activities and, 829
 as goal, 166
 government and, 826–828
 indirect government regulation, 827
 informal organizational activities and, 829–830
 investors and, 820–821

 legal compliance and, 829
 organizational culture and, 830
 philanthropic giving and, 829
 Social Era of the 1960s and, 817
 social obligation approach to, 824
 social opposition approach to, 824
 social response approach to, 825
 social welfare and, 821
 whistle-blowing and, 830–831
 see also Ethics
Social Security, 372
Social Security Administration, 278
Social welfare, social responsibility and, 821
Sociocultural dimension, of general environment, 83–84
Soldiering, 43
Sole proprietorship, small businesses and, 746
Span of control, *see* Span of management
Span of management, 285–289
Special performance test, as objective performance measure, 365
Speed
 management in future and, 842
 of operations, 633–634
Spokesperson, as managerial role, 17
Stability
 Fayol on, 47
 international management and, 778
Stability strategy, 200
Staff position, 296–298
Standard operating procedure (SOP), as standing plan, 233, 234
Standards
 control and, 603–604, 606–607
 performance and, 605–606
Standing committees, 528
Standing plans, 232–234
Stars, in BCG matrix, 201–202
Statistical quality control (SQC), 706
Status, as communication barrier, 565

Steering control, *see* Preliminary control
Stereotyping, 561
Storage, of information system, 666
Storming, as group development stage, 519
Strategic business units (SBUs), 200–202, 203
Strategic constituencies approach, to organizational effectiveness, 102
Strategic control, 600–601, 612–613
Strategic goals, 161, 164, 165, 167
Strategic management, 192–193. *See also under* Strategy
Strategic plans, 161, 174–175, 227
Strategic response, organizational response to environment by, 98–99
Strategy
 cases on, 220–223
 components of, 193–194
 cutbacks and decline and, 727
 distinctive competence in, 193
 levels of, *see* Business strategy; Corporate strategy; Functional strategies
 resource deployment in, 193
 retrenchment and, 727
 scope in, 193
 synergy in, 193–194
 see also Organizational strategy
Strategy formulation, 195–199
 environmental analysis in, 196–199, 201
 goal setting in, 196
 organizational analysis in, 197–199
Strategy implementation, 195–196, 212–214
 human resources in, 214
 information and control systems in, 213–214
 leadership in, 212
 structure in, 212
 technology in, 214
Stress, 584–589
 burnout and, 586–587
 causes of, 585–586
 distress, 585
 eustress, 585

merged the efforts of the few who knew its secrets. Progress was made at greatest cost to the patients. Scarcely anyone was concerned with their recovery, and it was only when their living conditions became incredibly bad that a revolution occurred and a step forward was taken.

Even when the need was evident change seems to have taken place slowly. Pinel, by the liberation of his patients from chains and dungeons, had shown in the course of a few days a new method of therapy which was effective even beyond his own hopes. "Tranquillity and harmony succeeded to tumult and disorder; and the whole discipline was marked with a regularity and kindness, which had the most favorable effect on the insane themselves; rendering even the most furious more tractable." [46]

William Tuke had amply demonstrated that mechanical restraint was seldom necessary, that kindly personal attention, outdoor exercise, and regular employment were much more conducive to rational behavior, and that the best form of restraint is self-restraint. After fifteen years of actual experience with this new method of therapy, still doubted and criticized, his son Samuel asks: "If it be true that oppression makes a *wise* man mad, is it to be supposed that stripes and insults and injuries, for which the receiver knows no cause, are calculated to make a mad man wise? Or would they not exasperate his disease and excite his resentment?" [47]

In spite of these advances, another half century slipped by before the movement in favor of nonrestraint became established. The change undoubtedly would have come in time, but it was hastened and made more effective through the efforts of two physicians.

One of these was Robert Gardiner Hill of the Lincoln Asylum in England. This asylum was opened in 1820 and in the early days of its existence the patients were confined by "strait-waistcoats, or wearing padded iron collars, heavy cumbrous leathern muffs, belts with manacles, solid iron wrist-locks, jointed iron leg-locks . . . and these cruel substitutes for a steady system of watchfulness, but a prelude to the still greater miseries of nights to be spent under the same wretched system of restraints, painfully sacrificing the freedom and ease of the

[46] Quoted by Pliny Earle in *A visit to thirteen asylums for the insane in Europe*, p. 42.

[47] Samuel Tuke: *Description of the Retreat*, York, 1813, p. 144.

patients to the leisure of mis-employment, or inadequate number of the attendants." [48]

A growing distrust of the virtue of restraint soon led Hill to experiment with nonrestraint methods. His feeling against restraint was aggravated by his attempts to treat a patient whose wrists had been made sore by handcuffs and who had "a penchant for eating his poultices." By 1837, or within two years after his appointment to the asylum, he had removed the fetters from all patients. [49]

Among those who visited the asylums and were astonished by the improvement in the condition of the patients, the greater quietness, and the few accidents attending the abolition of mechanical restraint was John Conolly, the resident physician of the asylum at Hanwell. He was so favorably impressed that he decided to try the method with his own patients. In 1844 he writes, "After five years' experience, I have no hesitation in recording my opinion that . . . there is no asylum in the world in which all mechanical restraint may not be abolished, not only with perfect safety, but with incalculable advantage." [50]

Both Hill and Conolly did their utmost to promote the general adoption of nonrestraint methods and their influence continues to be felt. Their proposals met with vigorous opposition on the part of many physicians. It was claimed by their opponents that restraint was necessary to enforce obedience, that it promoted tranquillity, prevented acts of violence, that it lessened seclusion and made it possible for violent patients to take exercise in the open air, that it was less irritating than manual restraint, and finally that there were not enough attendants or that they could not be depended upon to maintain the necessary supervision of patients.

Many of these objections were difficult to obviate, at least at this period, but the advantages of the method were such that mechanical restraint was gradually reduced to a minimum in England, and at a somewhat later period in other countries. [51]

With the gradual liberation of patients from restraint there occurred a change in the mutual attitude of patient and keeper: the patient had

[48] *Ibid.*, p. 33.
[49] *Ibid.*, Appendix by B. W. Richardson, p. 93.
[50] D. H. Tuke: *op. cit.*, p. 208.
[51] *Ibid.*, pp. 217–219.

greater opportunity for the pursuit of human interests and the keeper was required to give more personal attention to his charge. Physicians directed their attention toward other forms of treatment, and public feeling demanded more rational and humane care of the mentally sick.

As a consequence what was commonly called moral treatment came to be of first importance in institutional life. A kindly interest in the needs of individual patients took the place of wholesale confinement at the least possible expense. Attention was directed toward the classification of patients.

Efforts were made to improve the quality of attendants—the main instruments by which this grand and delicate machinery is moved. Until that time, because of the low wages and the occasional unpleasant or dangerous nature of the work, keepers had to be selected from the coarse, uneducated persons, who "possessed physical strength, and a tolerable reputation for sobriety," and who otherwise would be unemployed. Ignorant of the nature of their task and incapable of reasoning or feeling, they were permitted to rule by terror and force. Now they were instructed in methods of kindly supervision and in the solicitation of more normal interests and habits. The surroundings of patients were made as pleasant and healthful as possible. Barren "airing-courts" were replaced by gardens, shaded walks, and ample space for taking systematic exercise or for playing games. Regular employment, especially in the open air, was encouraged. In some asylums, instruction was given in reading, writing, arithmetic, music, and dancing. Convalescent patients were permitted to attend religious services, to go on excursions, and to enjoy lectures, concerts, and theatrical productions. They were urged to read and to study. "The object of such efforts was not so much to pluck from the mind its rooted sorrow, as to . . . introduce new, and pleasing, and tranquillizing matters for contemplation; to substitute external observation for self-analysis, and to bring discussions on art, or science, or literature, within the compass of amusement." [52]

A gradual transition of this kind is exemplified in the history of the development of some of the older asylums in the United States.

[52] W. A. F. Browne: "Moral treatment of the insane." *J. Ment. Sci.*, vol. X, pp. 309–337.

The marked success attending the use of moral treatment at York Retreat in England was a potent factor in determining the course of events on the other side of the Atlantic.

One of the most direct influences of this revolution in institutional care is seen in the establishment of the Friend's Asylum at Philadelphia. This institution, opened in 1817, enjoys the distinction of being the second oldest in the United States devoted to the care of the mentally sick and also the first "in which a chain was never used for the confinement of a patient." This does not mean, however, that restraint was not employed, for there was a "substitution of leather for iron."

In this institution, as in many others, there was the general tendency to substitute solitary confinement for mechanical restraint. The violent patient was "secluded in a gloomy, rather than a dark room, and when the extremity of coercion is found to be absolutely necessary, a case which seldom occurs, he is confined in a strait waistcoat, and in a recumbent posture, by means of broad leathern belts crossing his breast and legs, with straps affixed, which encircle his wrists and ankles." [53]

In the earlier years of Bloomingdale Asylum, in New York, disturbed patients were confined with chains and leather straps which were fastened to staples fixed in the floor. No special comment was made upon this form of restraint until 1815, when Thomas Eddy, one of the Asylum Committee, having perused Samuel Tuke's *The Account of the Retreat* and being impressed with the need of an asylum within a short distance from the city, presented to the governors of the asylum the advantages which might follow the introduction of "a course of moral treatment for the lunatic patients, more extensive than had hitherto been practised in this country." [54]

Six years after this communication was received from Thomas Eddy, Bloomingdale Asylum began its career as a separate institution, and, like the Friend's Asylum, has since distinguished itself in its use of moral treatment to the fullest degree. [55]

When the controversy over the abolition of mechanical restraint

[53] *Annual report of Friend's Asylum*, 1826, p. 13.
[54] W. L. Russell: *A psychiatric milestone.* 1921, pp. 205, 206. *The institutional care of the insane in the United States and Canada.* Baltimore, 1916, vol. III, p. 137.
[55] Pliny Earle: "Bloomingdale Asylum." *Am. J. Ins.*, vol. II, p. 8.

no longer focused the attention of physicians, and when moral treatment had become definitely established in the better institutions, Dorothea Lynde Dix raised her voice for the improvement of the care of the indigent insane. Miss Dix, a schoolteacher retired because of recurring attacks of tuberculosis, began in 1841 to teach in a Sunday school for female prisoners. Through this contact she soon became acquainted with conditions in institutions.

She was peculiarly gifted in being able to discern fundamental defects, in being governed by principles of action which were beyond criticism, in not being distracted by local or petty circumstances in attaining her goal. The whole history of her campaign for reform bears evidence of her profound understanding of the situation, and shows that she was not "actuated by vindictiveness or personal feelings towards the jailers and keepers . . . for she believed the horrible conditions surrounding the insane, . . . were due to an antiquated, ignorant and callous system of public policy based upon theories and practice which must be revolutionized out of respect to Christianity and advancing civilization."

The shocking conditions which she found in jails and almshouses led her to make a personal investigation of such places of confinement. It was said of her that "no place was so distant, no circumstances so repulsive, no lack of welcome so obvious, as to deter her from the thorough performance of her mission. Neither the storms of winter nor the heats of summer could diminish the ardour of her zeal, and no kind of discouragement could prevent her from gauging exactly the dimensions of this particular form of human misery." [56] Her work was at first confined to the United States where, during the forty years of her philanthropic endeavors, she was "instrumental in founding or enlarging more than thirty state institutions for the proper custody and right treatment of the insane." [57]

In a "Memorial" submitted to the Congress of the United States in 1848, she says that she had seen "more than 9000 idiots, epileptics and insane in the United States, destitute of appropriate care and protection, . . . bound with galling chains, bowed beneath fetters and heavy iron balls attached to drag-chains, lacerated with ropes, scourged with

[56] Quoted from D. H. Tuke: *The insane in the United States and Canada*, p. 37.
[57] Tiffany: *Life of Dorothea Lynde Dix*. 1890, p. 361.

rods and terrified beneath storms of execration and cruel blows; now subject to jibes and scorn and torturing tricks; now abandoned to the most outrageous violations."

The extensive and thorough campaign for the purpose of improving the care of the indigent mentally sick was directed chiefly against the abuse and neglect prevalent in jails and almshouses. At the time each small community had to meet the responsibility of caring for those who became sick. In the course of time these communities erected special buildings for the detention of those whose condition made it requisite. There was little supervision, no uniformity in structure, and no standard by which treatment might be judged adequate. As the defects of this system became increasingly evident in the latter half of the nineteenth century, the advocates of state institutions gradually obtained control, with the result that small county institutions were replaced by large state hospitals.

One of the more serious objections to the adoption of the state hospital system was the increased cost of maintenance. However, it was learned that large groups of patients could be maintained more economically and this consideration, rather than the welfare of the patients,[58] still determines the policies of legislative bodies. Under such circumstances the medical officers become absorbed in administrative duties and although expert in the best methods of managing a hospital they cease to be practicing physicians.

A growing reaction to massive state organizations has led some of the former advocates of the state hospital system to revert to the much older form of care provided by the colonization plan. This method in its purest form has been employed for over a thousand years at Gheel in Belgium. Both private and public patients live in cottages or private homes where the greatest personal liberty is granted. Medical direction of the community is obtained through a physician in charge and his assistant, who keep all patients on admission under supervision for a short period in a small asylum in the outskirts of the village before distributing them to cottages or private dwellings. Thereafter the immediate direction of their treatment is assumed by those in charge of the homes or cottages, which are subject to frequent inspection by

[58] Judson B. Andrews: "State versus county care." *Amer. J. Ins.*, vol. XLV, p. 395.

supervisors and to the occasional visits of the physician in charge, who is required to visit each patient at least twice each year.[59]

In Scotland a modification of the cottage system has been employed with unusual success. Previous to 1839 lunatics were confined in their homes or in prisons; since then royal, district, and parochial asylums have been constructed. The "pauper lunatics who are not dangerous and who do not require curative treatment" are kept in "lunatic wards of poor-houses," [60] but chronic patients, amounting to about one fifth of the total number of those mentally sick, are "boarded out" in private homes throughout the country. By means of this system patients are kept under medical observation for a longer period of time, or until the parochial medical officer from his quarterly visits to these institutions reports that they are suitable for cottage treatment.[61]

Many objections have been offered to the colony system, especially in thickly populated regions where it probably would not be possible because of the mutual detrimental influence of frequent contact of sick and well; in spite of the greater freedom afforded to patients by this system, the risk of suicides, escapes, and the immorality or cupidity of unscrupulous persons makes it impractical. Nevertheless, in the past half century there has been a tendency toward the adoption of the colony system, and in some parts of the United States and Canada a large proportion of the mentally sick has been cared for in this way.[62]

One of the most significant developments of institutional care in the past half century has been the establishment of psychopathic hospitals. Previous to a century ago no attempt was made to classify patients for therapeutic purposes, except as they were believed to be curable or incurable. The inadequacy of such a division was obvious to Jacobi, who in 1834 asserted that patients "must be divided into certain chief classes, according to the . . . degree of influence which their disease has over their moral and social behavior, and according to the degree . . . of their ability or inability to conduct themselves in a quiet, cleanly, decent, and orderly manner, to observe prescribed rules, and to

[59] John Sibbald: "Gheel and Lierneux, the asylum-colonies for the insane in Belgium." *J. Ment. Sci.*, vol. XLIII, p. 435.

[60] Burdett: *op. cit.*, vol. I, pp. 69, 235.

[61] D. H. Tuke: "On a recent visit to Gheel." *J. Ment. Sci.*, vol. XXXI, p. 494.

[62] Herman Ostrander: "The colony system," *The institutional care of the insane, etc.*, vol. I, chapter IV.

employ themselves usefully, . . . as well as according to the different kinds of medical treatment indicated by this diversity." [63]

Although the plan of making such divisions of patients was not generally adopted until almost the end of the nineteenth century, it had become evident long before that time that purely custodial care for the mentally sick was quite inadequate, and that a considerable proportion of patients recovered rather promptly if they were given intensive study and treatment. The realization of the need for a different kind of institutional care for such patients led to the development of psychiatric wards in general hospitals and also to the establishment of independent psychopathic hospitals.

Psychiatric wards in general hospitals are not an innovation by any means, for excellent treatment was given to mentally sick patients in the thirteenth century in a general hospital at Cairo; [64] at the Juliusspital in Wurzburg patients suffering from mental diseases have been treated under the same conditions as those afflicted with other diseases since its founding in 1576; [65] lunatic wards were established in Guy's Hospital in London in 1728; [66] patients were received in similar wards of the New York Hospital in 1792.[67] But the wards in more modern hospitals have tended toward providing the most intensive treatment of acute personality disorders during a rather brief period of observation.

The growing need for scientific study and treatment of early cases of mental disorder, however, led to the establishment of psychopathic hospitals. Some of these are departments of general hospitals, while others are independent institutions. Recognition of the desirability of concentrating treatment in the incipient stages of mental disorder was evident as early as 1751, when St. Luke's Hospital in England was established for the purpose of receiving patients who had been sick less than one year.[68]

[63] Maximilian Jacobi: *On the construction and management of hospitals for the insane, etc.* Translated by John Kitching. London, 1841, p. 50.
[64] F. M. Sandwith: *op. cit.*, p. 473.
[65] R. G. Rows: "A report on the conditions of the lunacy service and of the teaching of psychiatric medicine in Germany." *J. Ment. Sci.*, vol. LVIII, p. 620.
[66] Burdett: *op. cit.*, vol. I, p. 58.
[67] Edward W. Sheldon: "Historical review." In *A psychiatric milestone*, p. 10.
[68] Henri Falret: "On the construction and organization of establishments for the insane." *Amer. J. Ins.*, vol. X, p. 219.

Priority in the establishment of strictly psychopathic hospitals belongs to Germany; the first of them was opened at Heidelberg in 1878.[69] Others soon followed in other countries. Bellevue Hospital in New York City, completed in 1879,[70] has served chiefly as an observation and temporary detention hospital, and more recently the new psychopathic hospitals in Ann Arbor, Boston, and Baltimore have served the true purpose of such hospitals by their association with medical schools, whereby psychiatric instruction and research are also facilitated.[71]

Within the last quarter of a century rapid progress has been made in serving a much larger group of individuals through the establishment of psychiatric out-patient clinics in connection with hospitals for the treatment of mental disorders, and also as departments in the dispensaries of general hospitals. By means of these clinics former patients in mental hospitals may be kept under observation and may continue their treatment, many unstable individuals and those whose illness is in the incipient stage may be given sufficient aid to avoid hospitalization, and each clinic virtually constitutes a center for mental hygiene.[72]

References to the history of some of the older institutions disclose some interesting administrative developments. The most complete perspective is afforded by the records of Bethlehem Hospital. Temptation was placed in the path of Bethlehem's chief officers from the beginning. During the first few centuries of its existence Bethlehem was nominally under the direction of masters appointed by the king, but virtually its affairs were managed by keepers. After numerous scandals had been exposed, "the office of keeper became obsolete, and a dynasty of stewards succeeded." Temptation still lurked too constantly; the first steward, appointed in 1634, was suspended for having falsified his accounts and purloined from the provisions. Apparently, conditions had not improved greatly a century later; in 1752 the visiting physician John Mours made an unsuccessful effort "to suppress

[69] L. Pierce Clark: "Suggestions and plans for psychopathic wards, pavilions and hospitals for American cities." *Amer. J. Ins.*, vol. LXI, p. 1.

[70] Mathew D. Field: "Detention hospitals for the insane." *Hospitals, dispensaries and nursing.* Baltimore, 1893, p. 320.

[71] *The institutional care of the insane in the United States and Canada*, vol. I, chapters IX and X.

[72] F. St. John Bullen: "The out-patient system in asylums." *J. Ment. Sci.*, vol. XXXIX, p. 491.

some of the feasting with which the governors indulged themselves each year at the expense of the charities." This protest by a physician, nevertheless, is indicative of the changing standards and policies in such institutions. Additional evidence of this is found in the appointment in 1769 of a resident medical officer, the "apothecary," who with Mours "introduced or inspired, reforms which gave the patients more tranquillity, privacy, and medical attention." [73]

Throughout most of the nineteenth century the public institutions of France suffered from a separation of administrative and medical powers, the law of 1838 granting to the minister of the interior the right of appointing superintendents and physicians. As a result, there were frequent conflicts terminating in the removal of one or the other. In Germany, on the other hand, the happy results of having a physician as chief administrative officer were continually visible.[74]

In the United States the advent of the physician as chief officer is also comparatively recent. Bloomingdale Hospital was under the direction of a steward or warden until 1837.[75]

Closely associated with the history of institutions is the evolution of special training for attendants and nurses. Some of the mentally sick were treated very kindly by members of religious orders during the Middle Ages, but the first attempt to provide special training for this kind of work was made in 1645 by Madame Le Gras at the Petites Maisons in France; pupils were supplied by the Order of St. Vincent de Paul. In spite of the fact that the advantages of such instruction were obvious, it was not until 1801 that legal recognition was obtained.

Pinel organized the "Filles de Service" from convalescent and recovered patients, but after a few decades of trial in France, Holland, and other countries this system gradually fell into disrepute. Attendants were selected with special care at the York Retreat; after 1850 books relating to the teaching and duties of attendants began to be published; [76] and in 1854 Browne began a course of lectures to attendants at the Crichton Institute in England.[77]

[73] O'Donoghue: op. cit., pp. 75, 177, 178, 261, 283.
[74] Falret: op. cit., vol. X, pp. 422, 423.
[75] W. L. Russell: op. cit., p. 159.
[76] Burdett: op. cit., vol. I, pp. 623–626.
[77] M. E. May: "Nursing of the insane." In Hospitals, dispensaries and nursing, p. 596.

Modern training schools did not appear until 1882, when one was organized at the McLean Hospital by Edward Cowles. Their value was so quickly appreciated that ten years later there were no less than nineteen American institutions possessing "systematically organized and thoroughly equipped training schools for attendants." [78]

Certificates were given to pupils on completion of the course, and in 1886 the McLean Hospital training school took another step forward by making an affiliation with the Massachusetts General Hospital, whereby credit for a full nursing course was given on completion of the senior year at this hospital.[79] In England a certificate "for proficiency in nursing" was given by the Medico-Psychological Association and in 1897 over two thousand of these nurses had been registered.[80]

Standardization of training began in 1906 with the report of a committee of the American Medico-Psychological Association, which was appointed "to prescribe a minimum course of instruction for training schools for nurses in hospitals for the insane." [81] Since that time registered schools have been organized in practically all large institutions in the United States, many of them giving complete nursing courses in affiliated general hospitals and some providing special training in mental nursing to students and graduates of general hospitals.

[78] C. B. Burr: "What improvements have been wrought in the care of the insane by means of training schools?" *Amer. J. Ins.*, vol. L, p. 214.

[79] May: *op. cit.*, p. 599.

[80] T. Outterson Wood: "The asylum trained and certificated nurses of the Medico-Psychological Association." *J. Ment. Sci.*, vol. XLIII, p. 530.

[81] *Amer. J. Ins.*, vol. LXIV, p. 119.

INDEX

Abano, Peter of, 134, 136, 138
abaton, 559
Abelard, 133
Abraham, 94, 493
absinthe, 404
Academia Naturae Curiosi, 248
Académie des Sciences, 248, 362
Accademia del Cimento, 248
Actuarius, 116, 136
Adler, 491, 492
administration, 486-9
Aesculapiadae, 37, 42
Aesculapius, 31, 36, n. 39, 559, 560
Aetius, 92, 106, 109
Agobard, 133
Agrippa, 19, 25, 165, 201-6, 207, 217, 230, 237, 383
ahankara, 32
Ahron, 121
air pump, 249
Ajax, 37
Akiba, 97
Albertus Magnus, 128, 134, 176
alchemy, 102, 136, 142
Alcher, 129
Alcmaeon, 38, 40, 48
alcohol, alcoholism, 79, 404-5, 442, 566-7
Alcuin, 127
Alençon, Duke of, 235
Alexander of Hales, 177

Alexander of Tralles, 72, 100, 109, 113, 114
Alexander Severus, 102
Alexander the Great, 58
Alexandria, 60, 95, 97, 100, 115
Alzheimer, 442, 544; Alzheimer's Disease, 553-4
ambivalence, 193
amentia, 91
American Psychiatric Association, 410, 411
amulets, 101
analgesia, 372
anatomy, 61, 166, 177
Anaxagoras, 41, 101
Andronicus III, 115
anesthesia, 48, 110, 374, 376
anima, 180
Anima et Vita, De, 188, 190
anima impassible, 398
animal magnetism; *see* magnetism
animal soul, 90
animal spirits, 264
animal tendencies, 55
anima sensitiva, 279
anthropologia, 164
Anthropologia, 246
Anthropologie, 308
anthropology, 490, 510
Antiochus, 61
Antipalus Maleficiorum, 146

"anti-psychosis," 431, 439
Antisthenes, 59
Antoninii, 101
Antoninus the Pius, 102
aphasias, 445
Aphrodite, 53
Apollo, 53
Apollonius of Tyana, 102
Aquinas, 134
Arabs, 119, 120
archeus, 197, 250, 261, 263
archiaters, 127
Archigenes, 72, 75, 95
Archimedes, 59
Aretaeus of Cappadocia, 72-8, 83, 140, 331, 551
Aretino, 164
Aristippus, 59
Aristo, 40
Aristophanes, 41
Aristotle, 40, 50, 54-8, 101, 102, 112, 126, 134, 192, 222, 440
Armenian stone, 114, 124
Arnauld of Villanova, 74, 134, 136, 137, 142, 145, 302, n. 334
art, 364
Asclepiades, 61-4, 79, 83
association(s), 192, 307, 451, 487
Associations, 248, n. 384
asthenic states, 286
astrology, 136, 142
Aswin, 31
asylum, 288; see also hospitals, and by name
atoms, 62
atropine, 217
attendants, 588, 589
Auenbrugger, n. 335, 351
Augustine, St., 94, 111, 112, 170, 184
autistic thinking, 501
auto da fé, 156
automatisms, 368, 369
autosuggestion, 364
Avenzoar, 125
Averrhoes (Ibn Rosch), 126 ff., 134, 222, 509
Avicenna, 125, 196, 222, 326
Azam, 357

Babcock, 544
Babinski, 375
Bacchanalias, 141
Bacon, 134, 138, 165, 177, 178, 179, 182, 194, 225, 265, 273, 274, 301

Baer, von, 448
Baglivi, 264, 266, 281, 485
Baillarger, 396, 398, 404, 533, 537
Bailly, 282, 315, 344-6
Baird, 286
Bajikarana, n. 34
Baker, Mary (Eddy), 347
Bakthishua, 120
Balfour, n. 123
Ball, 405
baquet, 344
Bartels, Max, n. 28, 440
Barthez, 253, 280
Bartholinus, 262
Bartholomaeus, 138
Bartholomeus, 172
Basil, St., 108
Battie, 301, n. 334
Bayle, 271, 274, 398, 529-31, 537-8, 540, 546-7
Beard, 443
Beaumarchais, 342
Beaunis, 367
Bechterev, 360, 436, 497
Bedlam; see Bethlehem Hospital
Beers, 13, 519
behaviorism, 497
Belhomme, 321
Bell, 411
belladonna, 217
Benedict, St., 105
Beneke, 475
"benign stupors," 397
Bergmann, 440
Bergson, 49, 190, 483
Berkeley, 282, 283, 397
Berlin Akademie, 248
Bernard, 400, 401, 454, 460, 490
Bernays, n. 39
Bernheim, n. 109, 361, 367-9, 371-4, 377, 379, 433, 485, 523
Bertrand, 356, 357
Bethlehem Hospital, 313, 339, 564, 570, 587
Bianchi, 457
Bible, 28, 29, 176, 210
Bicêtre, 313, 319, 321 ff., 339-41, 385-6, 404, 513, 517, 571, 574
Bienville, 304
bile, 46, 50, 57, 255
Binz, n. 158
black choler, 297, 301, 496
Black Plague, 176
Blandford, 421

bleeding; *see* bloodletting
Bleuler, E., 76, 77, 193, 457, 458, 491, 501-3, 505
Bleuler, M., 410
blood circulation, 250; transfusion, 275, 276
bloodletting, 47, 64, 71, 114, 137, 262, 275, 277, 314, 327
Blumroeder, 435
Boccaccio, 176
Bodin, 172, 173, 234, 235-44, 259, 305, 433, 513
body-mind relation, 284-6, 290, 426
Boerhaave, 297, 298, 334, 400, 550
Boleyn, Anne, 153
Bolten, 291
Bonet, 261, n. 262, 264, 267, 268
Bonhoeffer, 442
Borden, 253
Borelli, 248, 250
Bory, de, 344
Bosquillon, 262
Boswell, 512
boudhi, 32
Bouget, 162
Boyle, 248, 250
Brahe, 164, 226
Brahman ideal, 34
Braid, 356 ff., 359, 433
brain, 44, 46, 49, 57, 89-92, 260, 263, 265, 268, 274, 300, 301, 362, 411, 412, 436, 440, 442, 466, 467; "brain mythology," 441, 495, 509
Bramwell, n. 352, 358
Brett, n. 30, 52
Breuer, 376, 486, 493, 504
Brierre de Boismont, n. 86, 537
Brigham, 411
Brill, 504-6
Brodie, 374, 377
Brosius, 446
Brothers of Mercy, 515
Broussais, 263, 389, 439
Brown, J., 286, 443
Browne, E., n. 119
Browne, W., n. 558
Bruno, 164, 179
Bucknill, n. 67, 422, 424
Buddhistic ideal, 34
Burke, 407
Burrows, 412
Burton, n. 125
Bury, n. 93
Buthavidya, 32

Butler, 202, 454
Bytord, 366
Byzantine physicians, 113

Cabanis, 283, 284
Caelius Aurelianus, 62, 63, 78, 83-6, 106, 332, 517
Cairo, 564
calentura, 395
Caliphate, Western, 120
Calmeil, 12, n. 94, 264, 398, 529, 531-2
Calvin, 166, 173
Campanella, 179
cannibalism, 55
capital punishment, 272, 284
Caracalla, 102
Cardanus, 164, 168
Casmann, 178
Cassiodorus, 105
castor oil, 282
catalepsy, 362
catatonia, 366, 396, 448, 455, 457-8, 502
cathartic, 486
Catherine of Aragon, 184 ff., 189
Cato, 95
Cauchemare, 222
Cavendish, 250
Cellini, 164
Celsius, 250
Celsus, 64, 67-72, 83, 99, 188, 286, n. 329, 331, 517
cerebral localization, 105
Cerise, n. 30, 33
Cesbron, n. 109
Charaka, n. 30, 32, 33
Charcot, 110, 347, 360, 362-8, 369-74, 376, 377, 379, 403, 404, 433, 451, 485, 486, 523, 556
Charenton, 405
Charité, 436, 466, 475
Charlemagne, 568
Charles Martel, 120
Charles V, 183
Charles IX, 162, 167
Charlesworth, 446
Chauliac, de, 134, 136
chemical element, 250
chemical therapy, 277
chemistry, 468
Cheney, 14
Chevigné, 323, 324
Cheyne, 299
Chiarugi, 80, 316, 338
China, 28

choler, 297, 301, 496
cholera, 420
choleric temperament, 74
chorea lasciva, 199
Christ, 94, 100, 231, 237
Christian Science, 294
Christian sects, 99
Cibo (Innocent VIII), 164
Cicero, 61, 64, 65, 66, 68, n. 106, 293, 416
clairvoyance, 106, 441
classification, 47, 297, 305-11, 327, 398, 420-2, 438, 449-50; *see also* nosology
Claude, 500
Claudius, 102
Clement of Alexandria, 98
Cleomenes, 38, 554
Clifford, n. 560
Clouston, 540
clysters, 71, 314
Cnidus, 42, 44
cocaine, 404
Cockayne, n. 139
Codex Theodosianus, 103, 146
Colbert, 272
collapse, 286
Colombier, 316, 321, 571
Combe, 411
compilers, 105
Conde, n. 120
condensations, 490
Condillac, 274, 282, 283, 284, 330, 397
Condorcet, 319
Conolly, 387, 414, 415, 446, 547, 580
conscientia, 177
consensus, 73, 88, 91, 92, 263
Constantine, 103
Constantinus Africanus, 128, 138
"conversion symptom," 488
convulsionnaires, 366
convulsions, 397
Copeland, 353
Copernicus, 33, 164, 246
Copho, 134
Coquemare, 222
cortical irritation, 442
Cos, 42, 44
cottage system, 584-5
Cotton, 276
Council of Nicaea, 112
Counter Reformation, 171
Couthon, 322, 323
Cox, 411, 527-8
Cramer, 445, 447

"creationists," 111
crédivité naturelle, 369
Crichton, 336
criminal insanity; *see* forensic psychiatry
Crowther, 411
Cullen, 263, 286, 307
Cumston, 73
curability, 450, 454, 455
Cusanus, 165
cyclothymia, 448
Cynic school, 59
Cynosarges, 59
Cyprian, St., 99, 107, 109
Cyrenaic school, 59

Daemonologie, 257
Dahlman, 385
Daniel, 210
Dante, 176
Danton, 418
Daquin, 317-8, 325, 400, 452, 571
Daremberg, 86, 87, 105, 113, 163
Dark Ages, 92, 93, 104
Darwin, Charles, 453, 463, 466, 508
Darwin, Erasmus, 307, 312, 419
Daul-Kulb, 124
David, 29, 157
"degeneracy," 497
degeneration, 402, 403; *dégénérescence*, 376
Delarive, 409
Delasiauve, 398, 535
Delaye, 529
Deleboë (Sylvius), 254, 256, 266, 445
Deleuze, 349
Del Greco, 5, n. 73
delirium, 53, 123, 397, 405, 406, 451; delirium tremens, 404, 554-6
Delphian oracle, 38
Delrio, 236, 246, 513
delusions, 63, 224, 441
démence précoce, 458
dementia, 91
dementia praecox, 173, 259, 396, 455-9, 486, 493, 501, 502
Democritus, 45, 46, 59, 62
demon(s), 86, 99, 567
demonology, 25, 108, 116, 140-99, 208, 280, 299, 351, 365, 382, 419; *see also* demon, devil, *incubi*, *succubi*, witch, witchcraft
Demonology, 145
démonomanie, 236
demonopathies, 254

Denis, 275
Denton, 564
depersonalization, 288
depression, 43, 123, 286, 308
dereistic thinking, 501
Descartes, 41, 249, 250, 253, 265, 274, 277, 497
Desgenettes, 349
Deslon, 343, 344, 345, 346, 347, 349
Despine, n. 142
Dessoir, n. 177
deterioration, 421, 444, 448, 456
determinism, 509, 510
Deuteronomy, n. 29
Deutsch, n. 382
devil, 24, 150-63, 212, 213
diagnosis, differential, 77, 159, 167
diaphragm, 40
Diderot, 283
Didier (Victor III), 128
Diepgen, 93
Dieu, de, 517
Diocletian, 102
Dionysius the Areopagite, 98
Dionysus, 53, 141
Discoverie of Witchcraft, 257
displacements, 490
dissections, 106
Dix, 382, 410, 428, 583, 584
Dog-Madness, 298
Dostoevski, 464, 483
dreams, 33, 49, 100, 279, 445, 489, 490
Drebbel, 249
Dreckapotheke, 113
Dreyfus, 458
drives, 180, 497
dropsy, 48
drugs, 217, 327, 520
Dubois-Reymond, 495
Dubois, E., n. 92
Dubois, J. (Sylvius), 166, 351
Duccio, 138
ducking, 299, 327; see also immersion
Durkheim, 190
Dympna, 562-3
dysentery, 48

Earle, 411, n. 579
Eastgate House, 387
Eckhart, 176
eclecticism, 86
ecstasy, 29, 33, 48, 102, 238, 254
Eddy, Mary Baker, 347
Eddy, T., 582

Edinburgh Review, 408
education, 13, 178, 187, 190
Egypt, 60
Egyptian god, 28; priesthood, 101
Einstein, 190
élan vital, 483
electricity, 249
Elizabeth, Queen, 250
Elliotson, 347, 351, 352, 354, 433
Ellis, 482
emetics, 71
Emmelot of Chaumont, 140
Emmet, 366
emotions, 32, 40, 52, 55, 180, 193, 286, 471, 496, 508
Empedocles, 33, 40, 56, 238
Encyclopédie, 342
endocrinology, 46
England, 334, 570, 571
Ent, 276
environment, 309
Epictetus, 96
Epicureanism, 62, 96
Epicureans, 60
Epicurus, 50
Epidauros, 559, 560
epidemic(s), 121, 133, 141 ff., 221
epigenesis, 253
epilepsy, epileptics, 23, 43, 46, 168, 306
Erasistratus, 51, 61, 440
Erasmus, 165, 179, 181, 183, 185, 204, 433
Erastus, 169
Eratosthenes, 59
Erb, 451, 485
Erhard, 308
Eros, 53
Erskine, 242, 243
Eschenmeyer, 469
Esdaile, 347
Esmarch, 539
Esquirol, 350, 386, 390-3, 395, 405, 415, 417, 420, 433, 447, 468, 528, 531, 552, n. 570
ether, 57, 353
ethics, 22, 23
Ettmüller, 276
Euclid, 59, 225
Euripides, 37, 41
Eustachius, 165
excitability, 286; see also irritability
exhaustion, 286, 456
exorcism, 109, 130-2
experimentation, 38

Expressionist School, 483
Eylau, 385
Ezekiel, 29

Fabiola, 561
Fabre, 537
Fahrenheit, 250
faith-healing, 364
Fallopius, 165
Falret, 374, 395-8, 401, 404, 406, 533, 537
fantasy, fantasies, 223, 224, 226-8, 291, 292, 489, 498, 508
Fantonetti, n. 398
Faria, 356
Farrar, n. 73
fasting, 209, 334, 559
fatalism, 454
Faucett, n. 335
fauni, 106
Fawcett, 302
Fechner, 453, 508
Felkin, 361
Ferenczi, 279, 493
Fernel, 167, 512
Ferrand, 267, 268, 270
Ferriar, 301, n. 334, 338
Ferrus, 384-9, 392, 406, 409
Feuchtersleben, 475, 477, 478
feudalism, 418
fever, 48, 266, 276, 285, 551
Fichte, 292, 453, 469, 473
Fiedler, 442
Finland, 575
Flaccus, 208
Flagellants, 141
Flechsig, 451
Flemming, 444
Flos Medicinae, 128
Fodéré, 392, 393, 463
folie à deux, 374; *à double forme*, 396, 444; *circulaire*, 396, 444; *lucide*, 417, 447; *raissonante*, 405, 416, 447
Forel, 360, 482
forensic psychiatry, 45, 103, 146, 172, 230-2, 233, 238-44, 243, 272, 278, 284, 347, 368, 369, 386, 389, 391, 395, 401, 413-9, 463, 521, 563
Formicarium, 145
Forschungsanstalt, 613
Fort, n. 95
Fournier, 539, n. 540
Foville, 531

Fowlen, 338
Fracastorius, 165
France, 568-71
Francis I, 171
Frank, J., 569
Frank, P., 292
Franklin, 319, 344, 345, 418
Frederick II, 135, 318
free will, 156, 231, 294, 368, 416, 509
French Revolution, 35, 292, 315, 324, 379
Freud, 40, 49, 145, 180, 190, 192, 193, 199, 227, 253, 260, 274, 279, 363, 376, 377, 433, 441, 480, 483-500, 500-10, 520, 524
Friedreich, 12, 380, 381, 435, 439, 460, 466, 467, 470
Friends Asylum, 582
Fritsch, 447
Fuchs, n. 73
furor, 66

Galen, 73, 86-92, 93, 99, 100, 106, 127, 144, 178, 188, 207, 222, 255, 264, 269, 332, 351, 443
Galileo, 33, 226, 246, 247, 248, 249, 300, 348
Gall, 375, 412
Galt, 411
Galvani, 250
gas, 250
Gaubius, 285
Gaupp, 466
Gauthier, n. 107
Gazette de Santé, 321
general paralysis, 48, 173, 198, 302, 396, 398-400, 404, 442, 444, 456, 462, 526-51
George III, 242
Georget, 350, 363, 380, n. 391, 392-4, 468, 470, 528
Gerhard of Cremona, 128
Gheel, 584
ghirlanda delle streghe, la, 146
Gibson, 243
Giddings, 190
Gilbert, 250
Gillespie, 410
Glisson, 250, 262, 263
gnosis, gnostics, 97, 98; *see also* magic, mysticism
Goethe, 292, 508
Golden Age, 27

Gomperz, n. 45
Good Superintendent, The, 428, 429, 487
grand hypnotisme, 362
grande hystérie, 107, 305
Gray, 411, 429
Greding, 335, 435
Greek medicine, thought, 36 ff., 255, 269, 559-61
Gregory I, 146
Gregory IX, 135
Gregory of Tours, St., 108
Gregory the Great, 108
Griesinger, 398, 433, 435-8, 440, 446, 447, 460, 464, 466, 495, 539, 540
Groos, 469, 473-5
Gruhle, n. 399, 437, 441, 466, 501
Gudden, 451
Guericke, 249
Guillotin, 344, 345
Guislain, 468, 537
Gymnasium of Cynosarges, 59

Haase, 259
Habakkuk, 210
Hadfield, 242
Hadrian, 102
Hagen, 444
Haindorf, 471, 472
Hale, Lord, 241, 242
Hall, Marshall, 352, 353
Hall, S., 491, 504
Haller, von, 252, 286
hallucinations, 45, 56, 63, 160, 217, 225, 391, 396, 417, 441, 445, 449
Hamilton, 194
Hamlet, n. 251
Hannah, 29
Hanwell, 414
Haram, 124
Harper, n. 334
Hartley, 192, 282, 397
Harun-al-Rashid, 120, 515
Harvey, 250, 252, 261, 276
hashish, 217
Haslam, 302, 303, 338, 398, 411
Haziyan, 124
heart, 40, 50, 92
hebephrenia, 448, 455, 458
Hebrew sects, 99
Hecker, 448, 455, 458
Heiberg, n. 55
Heinroth, 380, 435, 438, 439, 469-71
Hell, Father, 342

hellebore, 37, 45, 71, 114, 330, 331
Helmholtz, 453
Helmont, van, 250, 251, 261, 263, 270, 334
henbane, 71, 217
Henri III, 235
Henry, George, 11, 13
Henry VIII, 153, 165, 189
Heraclitus, 39, 62
Herbart, 437
Hercules, 37, 66
heredity, 403
Herodotus, 50, 554
Herophilus, 51, 61, 440
Heurnius, 333, 334
Highmore, 262
Hildegard, St., 128
Hill, 387, 446, 579, 580
Hindu medical system, 30-5
Hipparchus, 59
Hippocrates, 30, 32, 36-54, 127, 201, 219, 252, 255, 297, 299, 320, 331, 461, 550, 554; Hippocratic medicine, 59, 256, 296, 394, 443, 444; Hippocratic oath, 43
Hippolytus, St., 110
history, 11-26, 135, 175, 194, 282, 382, 479, 510, 511, 515-9
Hitler, 493
Hobbes, 192, 265, 274
Hoch, 325, 397, 506
Höfler, n. 29
Hoffbauer, 289
Hoffmann, F., 252, 278, 334; Hoffmann drops, 252
Hoffmann, Moritz, 275
Homer, 36, 281
homme machine, L', 250, 497
homosexuality, 225
Honain; *see* Johannitius
Hooke, 248, 249, 250
Horstius, 333
hospital psychiatry, 188, 253
hospitals, 187, 287, 288, 289, 291, 292, 312-8, 321-7, 339-41, 361, 382, 385-6, 391, 394, 407-11, 414-5, 429, 444, 446, 522, 558-89; Bloomingdale, 11, 12, 410, 588; Hanwell, 414; Maudsley, 410; McLean, 589; Murray, 415; Pennsylvania, 578; St. Thomas, 352
Hôtel Dieu, 341, 568
Houdard, n. 39
Houlier, 169

Hufeland, 289, 442
Hugh of St. Victor, 129
humanism, 40, 83, 84, 226, 230, 494, 499-500
humanitarianism, 272, 273; humanitarian standards, 194
Hume, 17, 282, 397
humors, humoralism, 53, 91, 264, 281, 298
Hundt, 164, 246
Hunter, 282
Huss, 442
hyocyamus, 217
hypnagogic hallucinations, 56, 396
Hypnosis Redivivus, 360
hypnotic sleep, 356, 357
hypnotism, n. 109, 347, 356, 357, 358-63, 367-9, 375, 425, 482, 485-7; *grand hypnotisme*, 362; *see also* mesmerism
hypochondria, 268
hysteria, 47, 78, 92, 110, 130, 142, 199, 260, 354, 364, 365-7, 368, 373, 375-8; *grande hystérie*, 107, 305; "hystero-epilepsy," 306, 364, 365
hysterogenous, 368

Iamblicus, 227
iatrochemist, 251; -mathematician, 251; -mechanistic, 280; -physics, -physicist, 251, 286; -sophist, 113
Ibn Rosch; *see* Averrhoes
Ibsen, 483
idées fixes, 375
Ideler, 292, 342, 466, 475-7, 481, 485, 508
"idiopathic," 403
illusions, 170, 391, 417
imagination, 179, 227, 273
imbecility, 39
Imhotep, 28
immersion, 334, 576
impotence, 219
impressions, 282
incantation, 100
incubi, 106, 137, 145, 222, 238, 270
Incubone, De, 86
Index Librorum Prohibitorum, 233
indigestion, 263
individual, 39, 60, 61, 110, 176-9, 196, 284, 452, 453, 503
inductive method, 273
ingenium, 130
Innocent IV, 135
Innocent VIII, 164

Inquisition, 135, 152, 208, 248
insania, 66
insanity, abortive, 445; artificial, 425; hereditary, 405; ideal, 302; inhibitory, 418; moral, 406, 417-8; notional, 302; puerperal, 44, 404
insomnia, 106
instincts, theory of, 253, 482, 494
intellect, 178
intellectorium commune, 421
International Congress of Medicine, 408
international relations, 190, 194
introjections, 490
introspection, 179, 225, 226, 274
involution melancholia, 173
Ireland, 576, 577
"irresistible impulse," 243, 244, 369
irritability, 250, 264, 286
Isaac, Abbot of Stella, 129-30
Isabella, Queen, 186
Isensee, n. 43
Isis, 107

Jacobi, 433, 435, 451, 585
James I, 25, 173, 236, 256
Janet, 286, n. 356, 363, 375-7, n. 445, 493
Janoon, 123
Jayne, n. 560
Jefferson, 418
Jekels, 499
Jelliffe, 504, 505
Jerome, St., 108
Jessen, 539
Joachim of Brandenburg, 146
Joffre, 517
Joffroy, 540
Johannitius (Honain), 120-1
John of Salisbury, 133
Jolly, 388, 458
Jones, 506
journals, n. 383, 384; *Journal des Savants*, 248; *Journal of Insanity*, 410; *Journal of Mental Science*, 425
Julian the Apostate, 102
Julius II, 164
Jung, 491, 493

Kahlbaum, 366, 448, 449, 453, 455, 457, 502
Kant, 41, 289, 308-10, 453
Kayssler, 289
Kepler, 180, 225, 226, 246
Kerner, 469

khasaph, 217
Kieser, 440, 472
Kirby, 325
Kirchhoff, n. 116, 288, 291, n. 291
Kirkbride, 411, 429
König, 381
Kornfeld, n. 276
Korsakov, 405, 442, 457, 556, 557
Koty, n. 28
Kraemer, 147, 148, 150, 215, 513
Kraepelin, 76, 442, 449, 450-64, 474, 476, 486, 493, 501, 502; Kraepelinian system, 75, 455, 456, 457, 459, 460, 461, 467, 473
Krafft-Ebing, 399, 445, 449, 450, 462, 482
Krankheitsbegriff, 394
Krankheitsprozess, 394
Kremers, 209-12, 267
Kretschmer, 447, 466, 501
Krüger, n. 115
Kutrib, 124

laboratory, 400, 460
Lactantius, 99
Laehr, 442
Lagides, 61
Lamarck, 54, 282, 293
Lancre, de, 259, 372
Lange, 166, 456, 545
Langermann, 291, 292, 294, 466, 475, 485
Lanternistes, 271
Laodicea, synod of, 103
Laplace, 61, 345
larvatus, 106
Lasègue, 374, 396, 401, 406, 447
laughing gas, 353
Laurens, du, 269
Lavater, 301
Lavoisier, 61, 250, 282, 344, 345
law(s); *see* forensic psychiatry
Lebenskraft, 288, 291; *see also* life force
Le Camus, 288
Le Clerc, n. 64, 204, 211
Legrain, 442
Le Gras, 568, 588
Leibnitz, 248, 253
Leiden papyrus, the, n. 109
Leidesdorf, 440
Leloyer, 169
Lélut, 12, 40, 381
Leonardo, 164
Lepois, 260, 266

Le Roi, 344
lesions, 398, 412
lethargy, 362
Leubusher, 445
Leupoldt, 435
Levinus Lemnius, 168, 177
Leviticus, 29, 165, 250
Levy, 545
Lewin, n. 471
libido theory, 492, 494, 498, 499
Liébeault, 357-9, 361, 367, 485
Liégeois, 367
Liétard, 30
Lieutard, 286
life force, 251-3, 279, 288, 291; *see also Lebenskraft*, vital energy, vital force
life processes, 280
Lincoln Asylum, 387
Lindsay, 415
Linnaeus, 250, 306
Lister, 348
Littré, 20, n. 140
liver, 92, 125, 263
Locke, 178, 265, 274, 282, 284, 330, 397, 511, 512
locomotor ataxia, 539
Loë, Catherine, 219
Lombroso, 463
Lorenzetti, 138
Lorry, 302
Lot, 94
Louis XIV, 325, 571
Louis XVI, 320
love, 40, 60, 81, 124, 193, 303, 304, 336, 499; *see also* sex
Loyola, 164
ludibria faunorum, 106
Ludwig, 291
Luke, St., 233
Luther, 164, 173, 197, 204
lycanthropes, lycanthropy, 105, 167, 169, 171, 228, 261
lypemania, 391
Lyssa, 37

Macaulay, 18
Mac Curdy, 506
Machaon, 36, 559
Machiavelli, 165
machine (man as), 283
magic, 100-3
Magnan, 393, 403-7, 415, 432, 442, 451, 461, 462
magnetic fluid, 345, 351

magnetic wand, 344
magnetism, 249, 281, 342-55, 363, 388;
  see also hypnotism, mesmerism
Mahabharata, 32
maisons de santé, 313, 321
maladie d'amour, 267
Maladies Mentales, 393
"malady of love," 270
malaria, 48, 551
Malebranche, 265, 274
Malikholia a Maraki, 124
Malleus Maleficarum, 150-63, 171, 185,
  189, 212, 215, 216, 219, 223, 235,
  259, 489, 507
Malpighi, 250
manas, 32, 33
mania, 47, 48, 66, 91, 168, 291, 335, 394,
  530; mania sine delirio, 417; manie
  avec conscience, 417
manic-depressive; see psychoses
Manu, 32
Marascos, 56
Marcé, 537
Marcellus, 105
Marcus Aurelius, 100, 102
Marshall, 411
Martin, St., 108
Mary, Princess, 213
Masardjaweih, 121
mass hysteria, psychoses, 142, 221
Matthias, n. 137
Maudsley, 421, 422, 431, 495; Maudsley
  Hospital, 410
Maupassant, de, 464, 482
Maximilian, 151
Mazdejesnan, 109
Mead, 285
mechanisms, 490
Medici, 164
megalomania, 223
Melampus, 37, 45, 71, 277
melancholia, melancholy, 43, 47, 56, 61,
  76, 91, 124, 173, 223, 269, 270, 275,
  291, 297, 298, 302, 304, 308, 394,
  458
Melancthon, 165, 166
Meletios, 115
Mellerstadt, von, 144
memory, 178, 179, 273
Mendel, 457, 461
mensis medicalis, 137
mental hygiene, 13
mercury, 548
Mesmer, mesmerism, 281, 342-57, 378,

439, 485; see also hypnotism, mag-
  netism
Mesmeric Infirmary, 347
methodism, 79
Metz, 463
Meunier, n. 121
Meyer, A., 325, 410, 502-4
Meyer, Ernst, 457
Meynert, 260, 441, 447, 451, 495
Mibda a illut dimagh, 124
Michéa, n. 39
Michelangelo, 164, 245
Michelet, 224
Mickle, 537, 547, 548
microscope, 249, 541
Milan, Edict of, 102
Miller, 545
Mirandola, della, 171
misogyny, 158, 161, 185, 186, 304, 382
Mitchell, 443
Moebius, 375, 442, 457, 462, 483, 495
Mohammed, 119
Molière, 194
molles, 106
Molyneaux, 282
monachus, 104
monasteries, 104, 566
Mondino, 134
monomania, 94, 391, 417
Monsieur, 201, 217
Montaigne, 163, 169, n. 170, 176, 320
Montanus, 169
Monte, de, 151
Montesquieu, 407
Moore, 303, 546
Moors, 561
"moral idiocy," 420; "insanity," 406,
  417, 418; "therapy," 220, 581, 582
Moray, n. 163
morbus comitialis, 69
More, 179, 181, 183, 184, 185, 186, 469,
  498, 568
Moreau, 458, 463
Morel, 393, 400-3, 406, 417, 431, 451,
  458, 461
Morgagni, 281
Morley, n. 201, 206
morphine, morphinism, 404, 442
Moses, 99
motus tonico-vitalis, 279
Müller, A., 316
Müller, J., 433
Muham mad Akbar, 123
mulieres salernitanae, 127

Murray Hospital, 415
mutism, 218
mysticism, 34, 41, 86, 97

Näcke, 482
Nafkhae Malikholia, 124; *Maraki,* 124
Najab ud din Unhammad, 123
Nancy, school of, 362, 363, 367, 369, 370-5, 482
Napoleon, 319, 407
Narrentürme, 313, 575
Nasse, 434, 441, 473
nationalism, 431 ff.
naturalism, 226, 482
natural philosophy, 453, 454; sciences, 452, 474
Necker, 315
Neisser, 448
Nemesius, 106
neoplatonism, 198
neoromanticism, 483
nervous fluid, 301
Nestorian physicians, 120
Neuburger, n. 28
Neumann, H., 438, 449
Neumann, K., 444, 508
neurasthenia, 286, 443, 461
neuroanatomist, 261
neurology, 178, 263, 288
neuropathology, 263, 264
neurophysiology, 263, 264, 265
neuroses, 25, 123, 200, 342-78, 451, 484 ff., 493, 506
Neurypnology, 357
New Thought, 294
Newton, 225, 248, 249
New York Psychiatric Institute, 325
Nicaea, Council of, 112
Nicholas Myrepsos, 116
Nicholls, 285
Nider, 145, 513
Nietzsche, 453, 464, 483
Nissl, 442
Noguchi, 303, 546
Noizet, 356
"non-insane," 349, 371
nonrestraint, 387, 388, 413-5, 428, 446, 579-82
Nordenskiöld, n. 120, n. 126, 126 ff.
nosographers, 291, 419; *nosographie,* 326; nosological age, 478; nosologists, 291, 467; nosology, 297, 327
numbers, 100, 137
Nunberg, 502

Nuremberg, 563
nurses, 588-9
nymphomania, 304

Oliva, 248
opium, 71, 123, 217
oracle, 38
Orestes, 37
Oribasius, 105
Origen, 98
Orpheus, 238
Otto, Emperor, 132
ovariotomy, 366
ovary, 366
ovum, 252

Pagel, n. 28
Paine, 418
Pak, 124
Palacios, n. 119
Paleozoic Era, 27
Pandects, 121
pantheism, 34, 35, 274
Pappenheim, 457
Paracelsus, 165, 195-200, 201, 206, 207, 216, 230, 251, 269, n. 277, 278, 285, 356, 380, 433
Paradis, Miss, 343
paranoia, 45, 47, 447, 456, 461, 498
paraphrenia, 457
"paraphrosynias," 306
Parchappe, 398, 407, 409, 532, 535, 541
Paré, 18, 165, 166, 167, 512
paresis; *see* general paralysis
Pargeter, n. 334
Pascal, 371
Passarella, 565
passion hystérique, 373
Pasteur, 347
pathology, 541-6
pathoneuroses, 279
Patin, 262, 277
Paul, St., 98
Paul of Aegina, 113-5
Pavlov, 436, 496, 497
Péan, 366
pension, 288
Pepys, 251
perception, 178
Perfect, 301, 316, 335
Pericles, 41, 101
persecutory trends, 225; delusions, 476; ideas, 447
Persia, 463

personality, 461; double, 288; total, 68, 477
perturbationes, 66
Peter of Abano, 134-6, 138
Petites Maisons, 568, 588
Petrucci, 250
pharmakos, 217
philanthropy, 187
philiatres, 105
Philo, 96, 97
Philosophical Transactions, 248, 321
Phipps Clinic, 410
phlegmatic temperament, 74
phobia, 44
phrenitis, 62, 92, 554
phrenology, 52, 411
phrenos, 40
physiognomy, 301
pietas literata, 195, 499
Pinel, C., n. 63, 328
Pinel, P., 14, 70, 80, 188, 253, 263, 267, 280, 281, 283, 284, 292, 317, 318, 319-41, 342, 346-7, 348, n. 349, 380, 385, 389, 393, 394, 400, 404, 406, 407, 408, 415, 416, 419, 423, 495, 513, 517-9, 524, n. 558, 571, 579, 588
Pinel, S., 328, 535
Pisonis, n. 168
pithiatisme, 375
Plater, 24, 165, 167, 259, 314, 333, 434, 438, 552
Platner, 285
Plato, 40, 46, 49, 50, 51-4, 56, 58, 91, 102, 237, 238
Pleas of the Crown, 241
Pliny, 96, 106, 222
Plotinus, 102
Plutarch, 64, 67, 320
pneuma, 32, 49, 61
Población, 182, 194
Podalirius, 36, 559
poisoners, 212, 237
Pomponazzi, 167, 177, 489
Ponzinibius, 168
Posidonius, 105, 240
Poution, 338
Poyen, 347
Praestigiis Daemonum, De, 223
prana, 32, 33
prepsychotic, 74
Prichard, 406, 417, 418, 552, 553
prickers, 110
Priestley, 250
primary process, 489

primitive man, 21, 27, 28, 30, 308, 309; *see also* anthropology
principe vital, 253
prison reform, 386
prognosis, 44, 75, 456; prognostic approach, 458
projections, 490
Protestantism, 469
protoplasm, 253
Psellus, 116, 145
psychasthenia, 286
psychiatry, 11, 128, 230, 511-25; American, 13, 409-11, 415, 500 ff.; Arabian, 61, 121-30; Biblical, 28-9; Byzantine, 115, 116; English, 411 ff., 419; forensic: *see* forensic psychiatry; French, 390, 392 ff., 409; French-English, 431 ff.; German, 434, 436, 438 ff., 444, 446, 447, 451, 464; Greek, 36 ff., 255, 269, 296, 559-61; Hindu, Oriental, 30-5; history, 12, 382; institutional, 431, 432; modern, 226; primitive, 27-8; Roman, 62 ff.; teaching of, 404, 405
"psychic pain," 520
psychisms, 368
psychoanalysis, 487, 488, 490, 492, 506, 507
psychologia, 178
psychological reality, 524
Psychologische Hilfsmittel, 220
psychologist, physiological, 451
psychopathology, 32, 41, 158, 471
psychoses, 44, 124, 400, 403, 451; affective, 496; Korsakov's, 405, 556, 557; manic-depressive, 74, 396, 397, 455, 456, 457, 458, 461; mass, 142; persecutory, 124; postpartum, 266; puberty, 310, 448, 480; puerperal, 266, 404; "recoverable," 456; senile, 173, 551-3
psychosomatic disorders, 279; relationship, 441
psychotherapy, 359, 361, 377, 378, 478
Ptolemy, 58
Ptolemy-Euergetes II, 61
public health, 395
purgatives, 114, 260
Pussin, 339, 340
Putnam, 504
Puységur, de, 349
Pythagoras, 38

Quimby, 347

Quinke, 543
Quintilian, 237

Rabelais, 165, 170, 179, 181, 194, 201
Ramayana, 32
Ranke, 545
Raphael, 164
rapport, 349
rationalism, 275, 469
Ravan, 544
Ray, 387, 411, 413, 415, 419, 427-9, 431, 487
Raynor, 12
reactions, total, 55
reality, psychological, 524; sense of, 392
Réamur, 250
reason, seat of, 38
receptarii, 113
"recovery with defect," 444
"re-education," 477
reflex, 436, 496; reflexology, 497
Reformation, 434
Regiomontanus, 164
Reil, 287-90, 434, 440, 463, 472, 480, 569, 570
religion, 469
Renaissance, 180, 206, 245 ff.
Renaudin, 401, 402
Renier, 127
Renouard, 105
repression, 490
Réquin, 532, 533
restraint, 69, 70, 287, 292
"rest treatment," 443
Revere, J., 380
Rhazes, 22, 121-2, 124, 222, 552
Rhodes, 42
Richer, 364
Rickman, 487
Rivière, 260, 333
Robertson, 361
Robespierre, 418
romanticism, 190, 407, 453, 454, 469, 498; romanticists, 465, 466
Rome, 101, 561, 565
Romulus, 237
Rondeletius, 177
Rousseau, B., 458
Rousseau, J. J., 207, 282, 330
Royal Academy, 251
Royal Society, 248
Royer-Collard, 405
Royle, n. 31
Rütiner, 196

Rush, 70, 262, 299, 381, 410, 548, 550

Sacred Disease, 43, 48
Saint-André, 272
St. Anne Hospital, 386, 404, 405
St. Elizabeths Hospital, 504
Saint-Just, 418
St. Thomas' Hospital, 352
Salerno, 139
Salmon, 11, 13
Salomon, 536, 542
Salpêtrière, 319, 339, 349, 363, 384, 386, 485, 513, 517, 574; school of, 362, 365, 367, 368, 369, 370-5
salvarsan, 549
Samuel, 29, 216
Sander, 447
Sandras, 374
Santayana, 511, n. 512
Santorio, 249
Saragossa, 517
Saul, 29, 157
Sauvages, de, 280, 285, 291, 305-7, 373, 400, 419
Sauze, 537
Savage, 425
Savin, 204, 205, 211
Savonarola, 164, 197
scabies, 472
Scaliger, 178
Schaefer, 544
Schaudinn, 545
Scheidemantel, 291
Schelling, 453, 469
Schenk, 169
Schilder, 500, 501
Schiller, 292
schizophrenia, 45, 158, 173, 259, 406, 501, 502
Schoenlein, 433
scholasticism, 115
schools, medical, 134
Schopenhauer, 484
Schottmüller, 556
Schreber case, 502
Schüle, 449, 461
Schumm, 556
science, 249 ff.
Scot, 25, 257
Scotland, 576, 585
Scotus, Duns, 176
Scotus, John (Erigena), 129
Scribonius, 234, 235
Scriptures, 30

self-preservation, 279
Semelaigne, A., 12, n. 44, 328
Semelaigne, R., 12, 259, 261, 317, 323, 328, 423, 513-9
Semmelweis, 226
Seneca, 96
senescence, 551 ff.
Sennert, 254, 261, 270, 333, 521
sensation, 178
sense of reality, 392
sensorium commune, 40, 55, 57, 192, 390
sensualist, 89
sensus communis, 310; *-privatus*, 310
septimana medicalis, 137
Serbski, 457, 461
Servetus, 165, 166
Seville, 517
sex, theory of, 85, 158, 160, 161, 178, 221, 270, 489, 490
shaman, 21, 28
Shaw, 243, 483
shrines, 561-3
Siberia, 28
Sigerist, n. 130
Sigibaldus, 563
Silimachus, 106
silvani, 106
Simeon Seth, 116
Simmel, 493
sin, 144 ff.
Skae, 420, 421
sleep, hypnotic, 356, 357
smallpox, 121
Société Médico-psychologique, n. 384, 386
Société des Sciences, 271
societies, 383, n. 384
sociology, 186 ff., 510
Socrates, 41, 43, 45, 46, 101, 238
soda water, 282
solidism, 287; solidists, 61
Sollier, 461
Solomon, 237
soma, 238
somatological, 521, 522; somatologist, 434, 435, 436, 437, 439-42, 465, 466, 481
Sommers, 457
somnambulism, 362, 368, 441
somniferous chemicals, 71
Sophocles, 41
Soranus, 72, 78-84
sorcerers, 237
Souda a Tabee, 123

soul, 52, 53, 56, 90, 91, 112, 277, 285, 296, 397; irascible, 92; seat of, 40; sensual, 92; transmigration of, 33, 34
Soury, n. 49, n. 89
Southard, 13
Southey, 202
Spain, 565
Spee, von, 249
spells, 101
Spinoza, 265, 274
spirit, 22, 29, 295
spirits, animal, 90; natural, 90
spiritus, 179; *-vitae*, 199
spleen, 125, 262
Sprengel, n. 62, n. 125, 382
Sprenger, 147, 148, 150, 215, 513
Spurzheim, 412
Stahl, 250, 251, 252, 277-80, 285, 291, 294, 327, 334, 399, 401, 434, 466, 473, 475, 485, 507, 508
Starch, 432
Stark, 449
stars, influence of, 198
state hospital system, 584
states, ecstatic, 29; emotional, 44, 46
statistical methods, 390
Steckel, 500
Steganographia, 206
Stella, Abbot of (Isaac), 129
stethoscope, 351
stigmata, 110, 372; "of degeneration," 402; *diaboli*, 110
Stillman, n. 196
Stoerk, 343
Stoics, Stoicism, 59, 60, 96, 106
stomach, 125, 263
Stone Age, 27
Storch, n. 501
Strachey, 18, n. 512
Strato, 57
strictum et laxum, 62
Strümpell, 375
stultitia, 91
stupors, 45, 79, 238, 254, 396, 397, 449
subacti, 106
"subcortical irritation," 441
subjectivism, 112
Subventione Pauperum, De, 187
succubi, 145, 171, 173, 238, 270
succus melancholicus, 92, 496
Sudhoff, n. 27
suffocation, 92
suggestibility, suggestion, 368, 369, 372, 374, 486, 559; "de-suggestion," 377

suicide, 25, 35, 141, 321, 335, 391, n. 395; clubs, 35; ritualistic, 35
Summa, 133
Summers, n. 150, 153, n. 257
superintendent, 409; "The Good Superintendent," 428-30
superstitions, 84, 95, 103, 106
suppuration, 550
surgery, 276
Surya, 31
Suśruta, 32, 33
Sutton, 554-6
Swift, 577
Sydenham, 254, 255, 394, 443
Sylvius; *see* Deleboë, Dubois
sympathy, 78, 88, 263, 421
"symptom complex," 448
symptoms of depressions, 42, 43
Synesius, 116
synod of Laodicea, 103
"synteresis," 177
syphilis, 48, 302, 305, 398, 399, 462, 526 ff.; syphilitic treponema, 468; *see also* general paralysis
system, theurgic, 103

tabes dorsalis, 534 ff.
tabula rasa, 59, 497
Tagliacozzi, 165
talismans, 101
tarantism, 266
Tarde, 190
Tausk, 502
telescope, 203
Telesius, 164, 179
temperament, 89; choleric, 74; melancholic, 56; phlegmatic, 74
temples, Aesculapian, 42
Tenon, 287
terminology, 220, 223, 251, 295, 296, 310, 380-1, 448, 465, 523
Terrasson, 309
terrors, night, 106
Tertullian, 102, 106, 107, 110
Tetens, 274
Thaddeus of Florence, 134, 136
thanatophobic depression, 308
Themison, 62, 79, 80, 95, 222
Theodoric, 105
theology, 33, 98, 128, 228, 229, 247, 275, 508; theological, 467; dogma, 294; theologico-juridical, 348
theomanias, 254
Theophrastus, 167

thermometer, 249
theurgic, 39; ceremonialism, 109; philosophy, 104; system, 103
Thevet, 205, n. 206
Thiers, 135
Thilly, n. 52
Thomas, St., 54, 128, 133, 176, 509
Thucydides, 41, 43
Thurnam, 423
Tibb-i-Akbari, 123
Tiberius, 101
Tiffany, n. 382
Timothy, 168
Tissot, 285
Titus, 80
Toledo, 517
topographical, 488
Toppeus, 234
Torreblanca, 259
Torricelli, 248, 249
torture, "noninjurious," 287
total personality, 477, 488
"traducionists," 111
Traité Médico-philosophique, 326, 328-41, 380, 408, 452
Trajan, 102
Tralles, Alexander of, 72
transfusion of blood, 275, 276
transmigration of the soul, 33, 34
transubstantiation, 128
transvection, 155, 216
treatment, 507; "moral," 581, 582
Trélat, 12, n. 74, n. 113, n. 125, 381, 417
trends, 288
treponema, syphilitic, 468
"Trippa (Herr)," 202
Trithemius, 146, 147, 206, 207
Trois-Echelles, 162
trophoneuroses, 293
Trotula, 127
tuberculosis, 27
Tuke, D. H., n. 67, n. 69, 80, n. 139, 317, 360, 381, 408, 409, 411, 413, 418, 421, 422-31, 433, 439, 487, 513, 519
Tuke, Samuel, 513, 572, 579
Tuke, William, 292, 315, 317, 407, 411, 423, 513, 572, 579
twirling stool, 299
typhoid, 48

Ulysses, 37
unconscious, 130, 192, 279, 284, 376, 377, 486, 488, 489, 495, 508, 512; fantasies, 489; unconsciously, 200

understanding, 179, 273
Unzer, 291
"uterine furor," 260, 304, 366
uterus, 78, 92, 131, 132, 260, 354
Utopia, 186

vaccines, 48
Valentinian II, 104
Valenzi, de, 307
Valhalla, 25
Valladolid, 517
vapors, 57
vasomotor theory, 441
Vedas, 32
venesection, 507; *see also* bloodletting
verbigeration, 448
vernacular, 380
Vesalius, 165, 166, 178, 250, 351
"vesania," 307
Vespasian, 102
Vetter, 304
Victor, St., 107
Victor III (Didier), 128
Vieussens, 265
Villanova, Arnauld of; *see* Arnauld
violence, 80
Virchow, 400, 430, 431, 433, 443, 460
Virgil, 106, 220
vis, 180
visum, 63, 66
vital energy, force, spirits, 33, 49, 277,
   279, 285, 508; see also *élan vital*, life
   force
vitalism, 253, 293
Vives, 165, 179, 180-95, 197, 199, 206,
   207, 225, 273, 278, 295, 315, 370,
   383, 433, 498, 499, 519
Voisin, A., 361, 542
Voisin, F., n. 481, n. 558
volition, 312
Voltaire, 275, 282, 288, 342, 407, 439

Wachsmuth, 399, 473
Wagner-Jauregg, 276, 551
Wagnitz, 289, 569
Wallis, n. 108
warmth, 57
Wassermann, 399, 545
Watson, n. 181, 184
Webb, n. 96
Weickart, n. 335
Weihofen, n. 241
Wellington, 407
Wells, 366

Wenzel, 343
Wernicke, 445, 449, 501
Werwolf (werewolf), 29, 167, 228; *see
   also* lycanthropy
Western Caliphate, 120
Westphal, 445, 537
Weyer (*Wierus*), 19, 24, 163, 206, 207-
   35, 236, 243, 245, 246, 247, 254, 269,
   272, 278, 292, 317, 324, 348, 382,
   413, 433, 434, 461, 519, 524
White, 504, 505, 506
Whitehead, 505
Widal, 544
Wilks, 542
will, 305; *see also* free will
William, Duke of Jülich, Berg, and
   Cleves, 207, 213, 234
William of Conches, 129
William of Ockham, 176
Williams, 13
Williamsburg Asylum, 578
Willis, 254, 261, 262, 263-5, 270, 276,
   277, 411, 460, 521, 527
Wilson, n. 31
Winslow, n. 53
witchcraft, witches, 155, 159, 166-7, 185,
   212-24, 236-8, 243, 257, 270, 272,
   348, 372, 493, 524; last witch, 174;
   Witch of Endor, 216; *see also* demon-
   ology
"wit-sick," 139
Wolff, 253
Woodward, 411
Wren, 248
Wright, n. 119
Wundt, 451, 453, 455
Wycliffe, 176

Xavier, 164
Xenophon, 50

Yajur-Veda, 32, n. 34, 49
York Asylum, 572-3
York Retreat, 317, 407-8, 409, 411,
   422-3, 433

Zacchias, 145, 240
Zeno, 50, 59
Zephyrinus, 107
Zilboorg, n. 153, n. 155
Zimmermann, n. 335
Zoist, The, 347
Zola, 482
Zoroaster, 238
Zückert, 291

Books That Live

THE NORTON IMPRINT ON A BOOK
MEANS THAT IN THE PUBLISHER'S
ESTIMATION IT IS A BOOK NOT FOR A
SINGLE SEASON BUT FOR THE YEARS

W · W · NORTON & COMPANY · INC ·

exercise and, 587
General Adaptation Syndrome and, 584–585
individual consequences of, 580
life stressors and, 586
managing by individual, 587–588
managing by organization, 588
physical demands and, 585
relaxation and, 587
role demands and, 585
role management and, 588
support groups and, 588
task demands and, 585
time management and, 587–588
Type A and Type B behavior and, 587
Stressor, 584. *See also* Stress
Structural approaches, to participative management, 421
Structure
strategic control and, 612–613
in strategy implementation, 212
see also Organization structure
Structured interview, as employee selection technique, 359, 360
Subordination, Fayol on, 47
Substitute products, threat of, 96
Substitutes for leadership, 494–495
Subsystem, 58–59
SuperCalc, 266
Supervisor, 14
stress from, 588
Suppliers
firms influencing, 99–100
organization change and, 391
power of, 96
in task environment, 88–89
Supply of labor, forecasting, 353–355
Support groups, stress and, 588
Supportive leader behavior, in path-goal theory of leadership, 488
Survey data, for wage decisions, 369
Survey feedback, for organization development, 405
Symbolic analogy, synectics using, 427
Symbolic leadership, *see* Transformational leadership

Symbols, international management and, 781–782
Synectics, creativity and, 426–427
Synergy, 58
as strategy component, 193–194
System-based integrative approaches, to participative management, 422
System 4 approach, 311–313
System I design, 311, 312
Systems 1 through 4 organization design, leadership research and, 481–482
Systems resource approach, to organizational effectiveness, 101
Systems theory, 5, 37, 57–59, 60, 61–62

Tactical goals, 161, 164, 165, 167
Tactical planning, 161, 175, 227, 228–230
cases on, 250–253
developing, 228–229
implementing, 229–230
Taft-Hartley Act, *see* Labor-Management Relations Act
Takeovers, organizational response to environment by, 99
Tall organization, 286–288
Tariff, international trade and, 779
Task demands, stress caused by, 585
Task environment, 79, 85–92
competitors, 85–87
customers, 87–88
labor, 90
organization change and, 391
owners, 91
partners, 91–92
regulators, 89–90
suppliers, 88–89
Task forces 528–529
as structural coordination technique, 295
Task group, 514, 515
Task-oriented leader, in contingency theory of leadership, 385, 487
Task structure, in contingency leadership theory, 486, 487
Team building, for organization development, 405

Technical skills, of managers, 18–19
Technological forecasting, 255, 258
in research and development strategy, 211
Technology
case on, 72–73
change in for organization change, 401, 402–403
in general environment, 81–83
international management and, 789, 791–792, 793
operations systems concerned with, 638–639
organization design and, 313–315
strategic control and, 613
in strategy implementation, 214
Technostructural activities, for organization development, 406
Telecommunications, 680
Telecommuting, 568–569
Teleconferences, 568
Termination, cutbacks and decline and, 728
Test marketing, 712–713
Tests, as employee selection technique, 358–359
Theory, 37. *See also* Management theories
Theory X, 52
Theory Y, 52–53
Timeliness
of control system, 615
of information, 664–665
Time management, stress and, 587–588
Time-series analysis, 255–256
Title VII, of the Civil Rights Act of 1964, 347–348
Total costs, in breakeven analysis, 260, 261
Total factor productivity, 644–645
Total quality control, 651
Training, 360–364
evaluation of, 364
experience through, 23–24
job rotation for, 277
methods of, 363–364
needs assessment, 361–362
process of, 362

Transaction-processing systems (TPS), 671–672

Transformational leadership, 495–496

Turbulence, see Environmental turbulence

Turnaround strategy, see Retrenchment strategy

Two-factor theory of motivation, 278, 442–444

Type A behavior, 587

Type A companies, 63, 64

Type B behavior, 587

Type J companies, 63, 64

Type Z model, 63–65

Type Z organizations, participative management and, 422

U-form design, 319–320

Uncertainty
decision making under, 127
organization facing, 94–95
resistance to change and, 396–397

Undercapitalization, small businesses and, 743–744

Unemployment, 81

Unethical behavior, 809. See also Ethics

Unions
case on, 384–385
management bargaining with, 100–101
organization change and, 392
participative management and, 420–421
role of, 90
see also Labor relations

United Auto Workers, Honda and, 101

U.S. Chamber of Commerce, 100

U.S. Civil Service, 278

U.S. Department of Commerce, small businesses and, 755

U.S. Forest Service, information system of, 677–678

U.S. Postal Service, 108, 684
as bureaucracy, 310

U.S. Small Business Administration (SBA), 738, 739, 754–755

Unit technology, 313–315

Unity of command, 284
Fayol on, 47

Unity of direction, Fayol on, 47

UNIVAC (Universal Automatic Computer), 264

Universal approach, 60

Universal automation, 723

Upward communication, 554–555

Valences, in expectancy theory, 448

Validation, as employee selection technique, 358

Values
ethics formation and, 810
international management and, 781–782, 792

Variable costs, in breakeven analysis, 260, 261

Variable-interval schedules, of reinforcement, 454, 455

Variable-ratio schedules, of reinforcement, 454, 455

VDL model, see Vertical-dyad linkage model

Venture capitalist, 747

Verification, in creativity, 425–426

Vertical communication, 553–555

Vertical consistency, of goals, 172

Vertical decentralization, as organization design, 329

Vertical-dyad linkage model (VDL model), of leadership, 493

Vertical information systems, 327

Vietnam War, social responsibility and, 817

Vroom-Yetton-Jago model (VYJ model), of leadership, 490–492

Wage-level decision, of compensation, 369

Wages, see Compensation

Wage structure, 369–371. See also Compensation

Wage-structure decision, on compensation, 369–371

Wage surveys, 369

Wagner Act, see National Labor Relations Act

Whistle-blowing, social responsibility and, 830–831

Wholesale businesses, small businesses in, 740

Women, careers and, 115

Worker attitude, as goal, 166

Worker performance, as goal, 166

Workers' compensation, 372

Work-force composition ratio, 712

Work-force reductions, cutbacks and decline and, 728

Work groups, 529–530
autonomous, 421, 529–530
operative, 529
quality circles, 41, 66, 530, 421–422
teams, 530

Work-in-process inventories, control over, 642, 643

Work process, change in for organization change, 402

Work redesign, for motivation, 458

Work sequence, change in for organization change, 402

Work teams, participative management and, 421

Written communication, 552–553. See also Communication

Zero-base budgets/ing (ZBB), 697